DATE DUE

DEMCO 38-296

Business
Plans
Handbook

Highlights

Business Plans Handbook, Volume 4 (BPH-4) is a collection of actual business plans compiled by entrepreneurs seeking funding for small businesses throughout North America. For those looking for examples of how to approach, structure, and compose their own business plans, *BPH-4* presents 25 sample plans, including plans for the following businesses:

- Audio Production Service
- Automotive Dealer Group
- Bed & Breakfast
- Bottled Water Manufacturer
- Child Transportation Service
- Coffee House
- Coffee Roaster

- Emu Ranch
- Men's Clothing Retailer
- Online Government Contract Service
- Online Hospitality Industry Service
- Outdoor Adventure Travel Company
- Record Company
- Travel Information Service

FEATURES AND BENEFITS

BPH-4 offers many features not provided by other business planning references including:

○ Twenty-five business plans, with a focus on the uses and effects of the Internet and various online services within the small business sector. Each of these real business plans represents an owner's successful attempt at clarifying (for themselves and others) the reasons that the business should exist or expand and why a lender should fund the enter-prise.

○ Two fictional plans that are used by business counselors at a prominent small business development organization as examples for their clients. (You will find these in the Business Plan Template Appendix.)

○ An expanded directory section that includes: listings for venture capital and finance companies, which specialize in funding start-up and second-stage small business ventures, and a comprehensive listing of Service Corps of Retired Executives (SCORE) offices. In addition, the Appendix also contains updated listings of all Small Business Develop-ment Centers (SBDCs); associations of interest to entrepreneurs; Small Business Administration (SBA) Regional Offices; and consultants specializing in small business planning and advice. It is strongly advised that you consult supporting organizations while planning your business, as they can provide a wealth of useful information.

○ A Small Business Term Glossary to help you decipher the sometimes confusing terminology used by lenders and others in the financial and small business communities.

○ An expanded bibliography, arranged by subject, containing citations from over 1,500 small business reference public-ations and trade periodicals.

○ A Business Plan Template which serves as a model to help you construct your own business plan. This generic outline lists all the essential elements of a complete business plan and their components, including the Summary, Business History and Industry Outlook, Market Examination, Competition, Marketing, Administration and Management, Financial Information, and other key sections. Use this guide as a starting point for compiling your plan.

○ Extensive financial documentation required to solicit funding from small business lenders. *BPH-4* contains the most comprehensive financial data within the series to date. You will find examples of: Cash Flows, Balance Sheets, Income Projections, and other financial information included with the textual portions of the plan.

R

Business Plans Handbook

A COMPILATION OF ACTUAL BUSINESS PLANS DEVELOPED BY SMALL BUSINESSES THROUGHOUT NORTH AMERICA

VOLUME

4

Angela Shupe,
Associate Editor

GALE

DETROIT · NEW YORK · TORONTO · LONDON

Associate Editor: Angela Shupe

Contributing Senior Editor: Karin E. Koek
Contributing Editors: Eva M. Davis, Jennifer Arnold Mast, Amy Lynn Park, Deborah J. Untener
Assistant Editors: Becca Kelly

Managing Editor: Deborah M. Burek

Production Director: Mary Beth Trimper
Assistant Production Manager: Evi Seoud
Production Assistant: Deborah Milliken

Product Design Manager: Cynthia Baldwin
MacIntosh Artist: Mikal Ansari

Data Entry Supervisor: Gwendolyn S. Tucker

ISBN 0-7876-1124-7
ISSN 1084-4473

The paper used in this publication meets the minimum requirements of American National Standard for Information Sciences—Permanence Paper for Printed Library Materials, ANSI Z39.48-1984.

Printed in the United States of America

10 9 8 7 6 5 4 3 2 1

Contents

Appendixes

Introduction

METHODS OF COMPILATION

In order to provide our readers with the most timely business plan information, we corresponded with over 2,000 small business consultants and monitored small business bulletin boards on the Internet. The explosion of online and electronic mediums has unleashed a plethora of small business opportunities and entrepreneurial ventures. By utilizing these resources while compiling the fourth volume of *Business Plans Handbook (BPH-4)*, we believe that we have captured the current trends, identified the fastest growing industries, and witnessed the future possibilities available to visionary entrepreneurs.

This fourth volume, like each volume of the series, offers genuine business plans used by real people. *BPH-4* provides 25 business plans used by actual entrepreneurs to gain funding support for their new businesses. Only the business and personal names and addresses have been changed to protect the privacy of the plan authors.

NEW BUSINESS OPPORTUNITIES

There are 25 genuine business plans in the fourth volume of *BPH,* including several examples of business plans for new and growing business opportunities. Examples of such business opportunities can be found within the evolving world of Internet/Online services, health food, environmental coatings manufacturers and the coffee industry. We have included numerous plans detailing the exploitation of the Internet and various online services to develop and expand fledgling businesses. Entrepreneurs have identified new markets, creating global avenues for marketing and selling products/ services; gained accessibility to customers by utilizing e-mail and electronic surveys; and created support networks with fellow entrepreneurs to obtain essential industry statistics, resources, and advice. We have also included two plans for businesses that were developed as a result of the introduction of the Internet into the mainstream business and consumer communities. These plans are for an Online Government Contract Service and an Online Hospitality Industry Service. The business plans include detailed descriptions of the growing demand for online services within each industry, marketing strategies; competition; and financial data, including Projected Income Statements and Balance Sheets.

The business plans in *BPH-4* contain the most extensive financial data in the series. Comprehensive financial documentation has become increasingly important as today's entrepreneurs compete for the finite resources of business lenders. Our plans illustrate the financial data generally required of loan applicants, including Income Statements, Financial Projections, Cash Flows, and Balance Sheets.

ENHANCED APPENDIXES

In an effort to provide the most relevant and valuable information for our readers, we have further expanded the coverage of small business resources. For instance, you will find: an enlarged directory section, which includes listings of all of the Service Corps of Retired Executives (SCORE) offices; an informative glossary, which includes small business terms; and an expanded bibliography, which includes reference titles essential to starting and operating a business venture in all 50 states. In addition we have updated the list of Small Business Development Centers (SBDCs); Small Business Administration Regional Offices; venture capital and finance companies, which specialize in funding start-up and second-stage small business enterprises; associations of interest to entrepreneurs; and consultants, specializing in small business advice and planning. For your reference, we have also reprinted the business plan template, which provides a comprehensive overview of the essential components of a business plan and two fictional plans used by small business counselors.

SERIES INFORMATION

If you already have the first three volumes of *BPH*, with this fourth volume, you will now have a collection of 106 real business plans (not including the one plan reprinted in the second volume from the first, or the two fictional plans in the Business Plan Template Appendix section of the second, third and fourth volumes); contact information for hundreds of organizations and agencies offering business expertise; a helpful business plan template; a foreword providing advice and instruction to entrepreneurs on how to begin their research; more than 1,500 citations to valuable small business development material; and a comprehensive glossary of terms to help the business planner navigate the sometimes confusing language of entrepreneurship.

ACKNOWLEDGEMENTS

The Associate Editor wishes to thank all of the members of the Small Business Resources and Technology team, especially Becca Kelly, Debbie Burek, Deborah J. Untener, Eva M. Davis, Amy Lynn Park, Karin Koek & Jennifer Arnold Mast all of whom contributed to this project in unique and valuable ways.

Thanks are also in order for the many contributors to *BPH-4*, a number of whom have very good timing and whose business plans will serve as examples to future generations of entrepreneurs, as well as the users of the title who called with their helpful suggestions. Your help was greatly appreciated.

COMMENTS WELCOME

Your comments on *BPH-4* are appreciated. Please direct all correspondence, suggestions for future volumes of *BPH*, and other recommendations to the following:

Business Plans Handbook, Volume 4
Gale Research
835 Penobscot Bldg.
Detroit MI 48226-4094
Phone: (313)961-2242
Fax: 800-339-3374
Toll-Free: 800-347-GALE
Telex: 810 221 7087
E-mail: Shupe@gale.com@galesmtp

Business
Plans

Audio Production Service

BUSINESS PLAN

JACK CORNWALL PRODUCTIONS

58305 South 20th St.
Kellogg, ID 83837

March 31, 1995

Jack Cornwall Productions is a business founded and run using the latest high-tech sound and recording equipment. By taking advantage of the latest equipment, Cornwall can maximize quality and profits, while decreasing the amount of time spent per project. Cornwall's business plan describes how the business will take advantage of the latest and greatest in technology to grow the business and become a leader, both regionally and nationally.

- EXECUTIVE SUMMARY

- HISTORY

- PRODUCT & SERVICE DESCRIPTIONS

- OBJECTIVES

- MARKETING PLAN

- OPERATIONS PLAN

- COMPETITORS

- COMPETITIVE ADVANTAGES

- FINANCIAL DATA

- EFFECTS OF LOAN

- TARGETING NEW MARKETS

EXECUTIVE SUMMARY

Jack Cornwall has been doing freelance audio production in the Northwest since the mid-1970s, usually while involved with specific broadcast stations. Jack has also had a high interest in consumer and professional electronics since the early '60s. The two areas have interwoven well over the years...and now it's time to take that interaction to a higher level.

Area One: Productions & Narrations

- Radio & television commercial audio
- Sales, training & industrial narrations

Area Two: Business Holding Message Services

- Custom production of message-on-hold messages, with possible expansion into message system hardware

Area Three: Audio Archiving

- Transfer of irreplaceable audio from analog media
  (cassette and open-reel) to compact disc (CD).

HISTORY

Jack Cornwall Productions is an audio production service business, providing audio for radio and television commercials with both industrial and sales narrations, audio and/or video training tapes and telephone holding message services.

Jack Cornwall Productions operated as an in-home, part-time venture for just under a year. Beginning with a minimum investment in selected new and used studio equipment (financed through personal credit), the operation recouped start-up costs within 9 months. Since February, 1995, Jack Cornwall Productions has become more formal, with the filing of an Assumed Business Name, acquisition of a Federal Employer Identification Number, a business banking account and Merchant Services Agreement with Bank of America to accept VISA and MasterCard for telephone/mail orders. Jack Cornwall Productions has also been granted a Home Occupation Certificate by the city of Kellogg. The business is operated as a sole proprietorship.

PRODUCT & SERVICE DESCRIPTIONS

There are three basic areas Jack Cornwall Productions intends to expand upon and/or venture into:

Productions and Narrations

Although radio & television stations, advertising agencies, video production houses and individual businesses have contacted Jack Cornwall Productions to provide voice-overs and narrations, so far Jack Cornwall Productions has never committed time or funds to promote these services to others. If word-of-mouth is good ($3000-$4000 per year in gross income), an active promotional effort, targeted to specific users in underserved markets, should be great ($15,000-$18,000 per year).

Growth opportunities exist in providing quality voice-over services to small and medium market producers. This is simply an expansion of present operations, combined with identifying and contacting new users of produced audio and selling them on the idea of major-market quality with fast turnaround and efficient delivery.

Prior experience indicates a typical radio or television voice-over production job requires about two hours work and bills $75.00 in total charges at present rates.

Normal radio-television production experiences some seasonal swings. They are mostly oriented toward holidays and are not a major factor here.

A sample of the Jack Cornwall Productions brochure and demo cassette are available upon request.

Holding Message Service

Study shows there is very little organized marketing to the small businesses around the country that have the capability of using Holding Messages. Jack Cornwall Productions has already begun reaching into that market.

A reader of Message or Techno-Speak magazines can order the Holding Messages Kit for $7.95. The kit is shipped Priority Mail, and includes an audio cassette with music and voice samples, a self-help page detailing How to Develop a Message Script, a sample script and an order form. The $7.95 is refundable on the first order and the charge for the message is $50.00, plus shipping. VISA and MasterCard are accepted.

A typical Holding Message order will total $65.00 and require about an hour to complete. The Holding Message kit offers the customer a choice of three other voices. Message announcers are paid talent fees as needed.

It is expected that most Holding Message customers will want to seasonalize their messages. Because of this, after-sale marketing will focus on the April-May and October-November time frames. The Fall promotions will push new year images, while the Summer copy changes will remind customers about upcoming Fall holidays.

If sufficient demand is realized, Jack Cornwall Productions may offer Holding Message hardware. Distributorships are available. Samples of the Holding Message Kit are also available upon request.

Audio Archiving

Thousands of people have made family history recordings. In the '50s they were recorded on bulky tube-type open-reel tape recorders. In the '60s, many people switched to the smaller machines with the 3-inch reels. We sent tapes to loved ones in Vietnam, Korea and Europe, and they sent back their living letters. In the '70s and into the '90s, people are still recording their family history on audio cassette. While the cassette player is everywhere, most of those old open reel decks, if they still exist in the back corner of the basement, probably don't work anymore.

Today's emphasis is on digital and permanent recordings. The technology is available to transfer from the orphan format of analog open-reel and cassette tape to compact disc (CD).

Jack Cornwall Productions has access to machines that will still play many of the old orphan tape formats, as well as, the technical expertise to keep them running. Through using modern equalization software and a compact disc recorder Jack Cornwall Productions can transfer these recordings from tape to CD, and clean up the background hiss in the process.

Jack Cornwall Productions Audio Archive Service would:

- Market using 800 number advertisements in selected magazines.
- Charge a per-hour fee plus media costs.
- Return originals and new discs Mailspeed Next Day Service.

It's anticipated that there will be very little seasonality to this endeavor, except for the desire for holiday gifts. That, coupled with the natural seasonality of radio & TV production and Holding Message will make November and December very busy months at Jack Cornwall Productions.

Since this is a new endeavor, there is no definition of a "typical" job, but it is anticipated that an order for 4 hours of audio transfer, plus target media and shipping, should be approximately $100.00 and would take about 5 hours.

To accomplish these three goals, Jack Cornwall Productions needs $15,000.00, which will be used to finance working capital, equipment purchases, and the time and effort to fully market all three areas.

OBJECTIVES

Long Term

- Keep up-to-date on advances in audio and video production techniques in order to provide the best service to existing customers.
- Discover new uses for new and existing technologies.
- Expand facilities and staff as volume dictates.

Short Term

- Update studio tools to streamline production and decrease turnaround.
- Expand services offered - Real Estate/Travelers' Radio systems, etc.
- Expand marketing area.
- Use CD recorder for telephone Holding Messages to eliminate expensive hardware at end-user location.

MARKETING PLAN

Productions & Narrations

Jack Cornwall's ability to create straightforward audio production is well known to just a handful of advertising agencies, broadcast and cable operators, and businesses in the inland Northwest. Active marketing of Cornwall's capabilities and services throughout the region has been hampered by the need to work full time elsewhere.

A cursory check of the Phone Pages for Sand Point, Priest River, Wallace, St. Maries and Kellogg shows:

- 42 advertising agencies
- 49 video and cable production facilities
- 32 telephone system resellers

Dozens more in other small to medium Northwest markets.

An infusion of capital would allow Jack Cornwall Productions to:

- Actively contact these facilities to determine their audio needs.
- Produce and ship demo tapes to the decision-makers for presentation to their clients.

Holding Message Services

The marketing of this service has already begun. Depending on the results achieved with Phone Center and Connect, other areas may be explored. These may include other magazines, direct mail, participation in a card deck mailing, or other areas. Serious re-marketing to Holding Message customers for seasonal repeats is also planned.

Audio Archiving

This a brand new service. Sharing the concept with others has brought a favorable reaction. It's expected the first few months' jobs would be turned locally. Increasing to a regional or possibly national customer base would be accomplished by:

Placing classified ads in publications like *Parks in the NW, Outdoor Today, Modern Mankind* and *Trailer Expo*.

Evaluating the demographic and sociographic background of those leads and targeting the advertising appropriately.

Productions and Narrations

Modern high-quality, high-tech systems give Jack Cornwall Productions the capabilities to:

- receive a script by fax
- consult on the script by telephone if necessary
- record the job
- preview the job with the customer by telephone
- deliver the finished product (tape) by courier (local, regional or national) the next business day.

Technology exists today to deliver finished audio productions on computer disk or by modem. However, many stations, agencies and production facilities are not yet equipped to support this type of transfer. Modem delivery would shift delivery costs from supplier to customer.

Holding Message Service

Holding Message marketing is targeted at the small-to-medium independent business.

- Potential customer responds to marketing with check or money order for $7.95 and is shipped the Holding Messages kit.
- Customer information is entered in database for follow-up marketing.
- Customer sends script and order information.
- Script is produced as written and return-shipped ASAP by method chosen (Jack Cornwall Productions brochure is included in package)

Audio Archiving

A prospect responds to classified ad by calling for details. Determination is made as to whether transfer is possible:

- Source format
- Age and quality of source material
- Length of source material
- Non-binding estimate is given, based on above criteria. Charges include new media, hourly transfer charge and return shipment. Customer ships source materials (prepaid & insured) via U. S. Postal, Mailspeed, Quick D, etc.
- Material is transferred, with one-pass equalization to remove baseband hiss, to media chosen (CD, DAT, analog cassette)
- Call to customer to advise of outcome (play before/after sample if available)
- Return shipment by customer chosen method

There are several audio production facilities in the inland Northwest. They are all part of a video service and do not employ full-time announcers.

The only competition at this time comes from radio announcers working as free-lance, using either their employers studio or working with one of the above independent production facilities.

This service is provided by one or two national telephone equipment manufacturers and by a few local telephone equipment resellers. Most businesses that want such service contact their local disk-jockey.

Recent issues of Dial It showed only two classified ads for this service, none mentioned price and only one offered a demo tape.

Audio Archiving

There are no known organizations actively marketing such a service in this region.

COMPETITIVE ADVANTAGES

The distinctive competitive advantages which Jack Cornwall Productions brings to these enterprises are:

- Experience in this market. Jack Cornwall has over 20 years of hands-on experience in writing and producing radio and television voiceovers and narrations.
- Sophistication in distribution. Using today's (and tomorrow's) technologies to receive, produce and deliver finished product is a major advantage. This results in being the quick turnaround supplier in many time sensitive yet somewhat isolated markets.
- High quality, low price - Jack Cornwall Productions' rates are below others in the market, while the quality and service exceeds expectations.

By keeping overhead low, Jack Cornwall Productions will be able to funnel profits back into operations thus avoiding high debt or lost sales opportunities.

FINANCIAL DATA

Three Year Cash Flow Projection Assumptions

Cash Receipts	Percentages as indicated
Rent	In-home (tax deduction may be taken)
Utilities	Same as above
Telephone	Local, long distance fax and pager
Salaries	One
Announce Talent(MOH)	$15.00 per script for about 40% of scripts
Audio duplication media	4.5% of total sales
Office Supplies	2% of total sales
Postage and shipping	5% of total sales
Marketing/Advertising	Trade, magazine, direct mail, etc. at 5%
Memberships/Licenses	Chamber of Commerce, etc.
Bank-VISA/MC charges	$35.00 + 2.81% discount on bankcard sales
Accounting/Tax services	End of year and tax filing
Insurance	Riders on Homeowner's policy
Miscellaneous	1% of total sales
State Taxes	5% of cash receipts
Federal Taxes	25% of cash receipts
Terms to customers	Productions & narrations: Net 10, except Radio & television Net 60 Holding Messages: Check/Bankcard/C-O-D Audio Archiving: C-O-D

Our projections are for industries that have never been reached. Therefore they are based upon present real buying conditions and our own experience. Should sales not be up to projections, adjustments will be made in marketing, and long term commitments decreased or postponed.

EFFECTS OF LOAN

The money loaned to Jack Cornwall Productions will be used for the following purposes:

- Purchase of Simmons TX7D Portable DAT recorder for remote recording - ($700.00)
- Working capital and initial marketing costs- ($6,000)
- Purchase of Hollowitz Compact Disc Recorder - (est. $4,500.00)
- Purchase of PC-Based audio editing and equalization workstation - ($2,800)
- Misc. Startup costs - Accountant, technical consultant, misc. furnishings-($1,000)

These outlays will enable Jack Cornwall Productions to function as a full-time productions & narrations facility, continue marketing of Holding Messages and expand into Audio Archiving, and meet our conservative sales goals for the first year. This will also allow us to purchase these items rather than finance or lease them.

The world of audio and video is changing constantly. The spoken word alone, and spoken words with pictures will always be a part of life. Five years ago, few people were thinking of narrations on multimedia CD-ROM. Today, major companies are using pre-programmed "live" talent for on-hold system advisories. Tomorrow's audio applications might include interactive television or real-time audio transfer by internet. Jack Cornwall Productions wants to be poised for these coming technologies.

TARGETING NEW MARKETS

Automotive Dealer Group

BUSINESS PLAN

POMPEI-SCHMIDT AUTO DEALERS INC.

8625 Collingwood Ave.
Orlando, FL 56835

Pompei-Schmidt's business plan for a nationwide dealer group takes advantage of an emerging industry trend of vehicle leasing. PSAD provides a detailed, well-researched plan to meet the emerging market need and establish a profitable business venture for both auto dealers and PSAD.

- EXECUTIVE SUMMARY

- ENVIRONMENTAL ANALYSIS

- THE COMPANY

- THE PRODUCT

- THE MANAGEMENT TEAM

- MARKET RESEARCH AND PLAN

**EXECUTIVE
SUMMARY**

The automobile industry is experiencing a dramatic transformation that will forever alter the way both new and used vehicles are marketed and sold. As consumers change their operational structure and methods. Pompei-Schmidt Auto Dealers Inc. (PSAD) has recognized these shifting dynamics and positioned itself to take maximum advantage of rapidly-changing consumer and economic trends.

PSAD's mission is to deliver non-prime credit lease and purchase financing, consulting, training and ongoing support that will provide automobile dealerships across the United States with the skills and services they need to improve their competitive posture and increase profitability. Areas of focus include sales techniques, leasing, finance and insurance. The economic results of the successful accomplishment of this mission will be significant profits both for dealer clients and for PSAD.

As the automotive industry becomes increasingly sophisticated, dealers are looking outward for assistance in increasing new and used car sales, improving margins, containing costs, developing additional profit centers and designing programs that will meet consumer demands today and in the coming years. In response to dealer needs, PSAD has developed an integrated system to allow dealers to achieve higher profit levels. Through the system's implementation and maintenance, PSAD shares in its clients' financial success.

PSAD'S three divisions work independently and collectively to provide a customized product package to each dealer client. Insurance Works provides a complete portfolio of insurance products for the franchised automobile dealer market. Development Works provides consulting and training to new and used-car dealers. The training focuses on sales skills, financing alternatives, and leasing options with the goal of increasing the number of closed transactions and correspondingly, enhancing profits. Finance Works provides dealers with a wide range of financial services including additional financing options for their customers and the ability to offer subprime financing and leasing programs for new and used cars.

**A Historical
Perspective**

In the early days of the automobile, horseless carriages were viewed with great suspicion. Adventurous consumers paid cash for the privilege of owning a motorized vehicle that could travel at breathtaking speeds of up to 30 miles per hour.

The passage of time saw an evolution in vehicle technology. Banks began making automobile loans, which put car ownership within reach of the average American. Suspicion turned to tolerance and eventually to enthusiastic acceptance of the automobile as the country's primary method of personal transportation.

After World War II, factories were able to return to manufacturing consumer goods, and the automobile assembly lines were back in action. The interstate highway system was created, and the automobile became an integral part of American culture. Borrowing money for major purchases had become both socially acceptable and increasingly common. Typically new cars were purchased from franchised dealers that were sole proprietors or family-owned businesses. A local bank handled the financing.

In a country hungry for luxuries after years of deprivation caused by the Depression and World War II, selling cars was easy. Consumers established a pattern of buying new cars and replacing them every two or three years. Dealers accepted trade-ins that were either sold on their own used-car lots or wholesaled at auction to independent dealers. In either case, used cars were the industry's stepchild. New car dealers paid little attention to their used car departments primarily because banks were less enthusiastic about making used car loans than they were about financing new vehicles, and used cars were generally viewed as less reliable and less desirable than new ones.

The American automobile industry experienced few significant changes during the 1950s and 1960s. The oil embargo, rising gas prices and increased demand for imports during the 1970s was a wake-up call to American car manufacturers. And as the vehicles themselves changed, so did the outlets through which they were sold.

The 1980s saw the creation of the automobile superstore, which combined franchises within a dealership and offered consumers a greater level of shopping convenience. Megadealers built their own empires, purchasing a variety of franchises in multiple cities and states. Some dealers responded to consumer demands by eliminating high-pressure sales tactics, providing more customer-friendly showroom environments, and increasing after-the-sale service.

Consistently low interest rates, attractive financing and strong lease programs combined to make 1994 a good year for the auto industry. According to *Buyers' Guide*, total sales of domestic and imported cars and light trucks totaled nearly 15.1 million units-up almost 9 percent over the previous year.

The Current Picture

In 1995, sales were good, but lower than in 1994. New vehicle sales by dealers reach $293.3 billion and 14.75 million units; total annual sales were approximately $500 billion.

Forecasters expect new-vehicle sales to rebound in 1996, reaching and perhaps exceeding the 1994 figures. The year should see 15.1 to 15.2 million units sold.

These statistics indicate that the industry has stabilized and is in the early stages of a strong growth period. Companies such as PSAD with the foresight to develop programs to support this growth can expect to do well in the coming years and into the next century.

Year	New Vehicles Sold
1993	15.0 Units
1994	15.1 Units
1995	14.8 Units
1996	15.2 Units

In any industry, change is inevitable, and the automobile industry is no exception. The industry has entered a new age of selling transportation. Never before has the consumer had so many choices in terms of product selection, financing options and vendors; that trend is likely to continue.

Industry Forecast

Dealers are listening to and responding to consumers by developing new operational strategies. For example, dealers are responding to consumers who have become frustrated with the traditional wheeling and dealing that has been an accepted part of auto price negotiations by experimenting with techniques such as one-price, haggle-free selling. Silver, with the highest retail sales per dealership in the auto industry, was founded and formulated on the concept of hassle-free selling.

To maintain their own profitability and ability to deliver services, dealers are looking for new and creative ways to establish additional profit centers, such as insurance, service and maintenance agreements.

Leasing is becoming increasingly popular among both dealers and consumers. Leasing can eliminate or reduce the down payment; monthly lease payments are usually significantly lower than payments on a purchase loan. The American Leasing Association (ALA) expected about 33 percent of new personal-use vehicles to be leased in the 1995 model year.

Another key trend is the greater acceptance of used vehicles by the car-buying public. New car quality is improving. Today's cars are built better and last longer, which means used cars are more attractive to consumers than ever before. According to the editor of *Cars Today*, "It used to be that a three-year old car was considered old. It could be a junker. Today that same car can be considered very clean." Contributing to this trend is the fact that new car prices continue to rise. From 1989 to 1993, the average price of a U.S. made luxury car rose nearly $2,000 each year. These new car price increases have squeezed many would-be buyers out of the new car purchase market and into the used car or leasing market.

PSAD Marketing Strategy

PSAD is positioned to work with franchised and independent auto dealers from every critical business perspective. PSAD's line of products and services are uniquely targeted to a desirable market which produces significant revenues and has clear and unarguable long-term growth potential.

By developing first class products and delivering them with professionalism and integrity, PSAD has built an outstanding reputation that has resulted in a high account retention rate. By helping dealers build ongoing relationships with their customers, PSAD naturally builds strong, long-term relationships with those dealers.

In spite of the maturity of the automotive industry, experienced consultants with firsthand knowledge of the business are not readily available. This is primarily because until recently, automobile dealers have not been inclined to look outward for management and business development assistance. However, dealers are increasingly recognizing and appreciating the overall business trend toward outsourcing, and are admitting the need for and benefits available from the use of outside consultants. Consequently, the demand for services such as those provided by PSAD should increase markedly in the coming years.

New business is obtained through field solicitation, mail solicitation and referrals. Frequent face-to-face contact is made with clients throughout the year by representatives of each PSAD division. This multi-level, multi-departmental contact establishes and maintains a strong relationship between PSAD and the client. It also provides liberal opportunities for cross-selling among PSAD divisions.

In the insurance arena, only an independent agency can respond to the ever-changing market conditions and needs of the clients. By not relying solely on any one line of business, the PSAD insurance division, Insurance Works, will remain flexible and enjoy a quick response capability that other agencies may lack. At the same time, by targeting the automotive niche and diversifying within that niche, Insurance Works can expect consistent ongoing revenues even while reacting to market changes.

In the dealer development arena, Development Works will deliver training that includes a strong focus on purchase dynamics as they truly exist. Leasing is a key area of training; clients are taught techniques that can increase their closing ratio by 25 percent or more. Training is conducted by instructors with years of practical experience in dealership operation; clients respond favorably to this high level of credibility. Dealers aggressively pursue qualified trainers such as Development Works, in anticipation of the training's impact to the dealership's bottom line. Automobile manufacturers also recognize the value of training and many have opted to reimburse the dealerships the training expenses. A member of Development Works has been named as one of three independent advisors to Reynolds Leasing Advisory Board.

In the finance arena, PSAD Finance Works will be on the leading edge of subprime finance and leasing trends. Beyond funding the vehicle transactions, the company has combined its financial expertise with its management, sales and marketing skills to become a key member of the dealer client's business development team as they work with the dealer to place and secure previously leased and program vehicles.

ENVIRONMENTAL ANALYSIS

A number of basic trends are changing the dynamics of the automobile industry. They include: **Industry Trends**

- a 25 percent increase in car prices over the last five years
- a growing supply, demand and profit margin for loaded used cars
- the changing dynamics of vehicle ownership
- the explosive growth of leasing
- the need for a broader range of dealer profit centers
- the increased demand for subprime credit options
- the dilution of the traditional dealer franchise system.

Let's take a closer look at these trends. New car prices are rising faster than the overall rate of inflation. According to *Leasing Now*, this steady increase is forcing potential buyers to reconsider a decision to purchase a new car. For example, when faced with a choice between buying a new car and a major home purchase (a computer, entertainment system, major appliances, etc.), consumers often opt to maintain their existing vehicles in favor of the other purchase. However, studies indicate that this decision is a delay and not a cancellation of a vehicle purchase; the purchase will take place after other needs are met.

In the past, consumers commonly rejected used cars as a primary household vehicle, viewing them as a problem someone else managed to get rid of. Used cars were generally purchased for children or as second cars driven by non-working spouses. The latter has been changed by the increase in dual-income families. Working couples require appropriate vehicles for both partners.

Because of the increased quality and supply of feature-rich used cars, these vehicles are now viewed as a viable and acceptable option to a new car that costs twice as much or has fewer features. Also, because many new cars have factory warranties for periods of up to five years, many late-model used cars on the market are still covered by the original warranty when the second owner takes possession. Plus, many dealers offer warranties on used cars.

The growing popularity of leasing can be attributed in large part to the fact that it is a far more customer-friendly way to sell a car than traditional financing. Leasing eliminates dickering over price, thereby making the transaction more pleasurable and efficient for the customer.

From the dealers' perspective, leasing generates increased sales volume and has a higher customer return rate than straight purchasing. Dealer Council studies indicate that 25 percent of automobile buyers will return to the same dealer for their next vehicle; by contrast, 91 percent of individuals who lease will return to the same dealer for their next car. Because leases are typically of a shorter duration, often as little as half the time of a standard purchase finance agreement, vehicle turnover is significantly higher among leasing customers.

Loyalty Analysis-Industry Average
Lessee likelihood of leasing from the same lessor. All vehicles including light trucks.
Source: Dealer Council

Lease Time Frame	Percentage
24 months	91%
36 months	81%
48 months	56%
60 months	37%

New and used automobile superstores have changed the public's perception of dealerships. Consumers expect and demand a wider range of products and easy shopping opportunities.

Today, a dealer might carry new vehicles from as many as five or more competing manufacturers and offer a substantial selection of used cars. Brand loyalty on the dealer's part is far less important than putting together a package that appeals to the customer.

The actual sale of a vehicle - especially a new vehicle - represents a very small percent of profit to dealers. The more significant portion of profits is made in areas such as service, financing and insurance programs. Savvy dealers are exploring their options in these areas, and developing products such as service and maintenance agreements that can be sold separately from the vehicle itself.

The fastest growing segment of automobile sales involves buyers with bad or bruised credit. As banks move to decrease their loan risks, it has become increasingly more difficult for a large percentage of the population to qualify for traditional credit. It is estimated that over 70% of the market has bruised credit. For new car dealers able to finance non-prime credit, this situation translates into significantly increased sales and leasing. Originally pioneered by buy-here, pay-here lots, the concept is quickly becoming an important profit center for conventional dealerships. Finance Works is positioned to take advantage of the industry shift with a variety of programs that offer subprime credit in both lease and purchase situations.

Automotive Financing and Financial Services for New and Used Vehicles

Increasing new and used car prices, fluctuating interest rates and personal economic uncertainty on the part of consumers have sparked a number of changes in the way vehicles are financed. Consumers are looking to dealers to find ways to make the cars they want affordable. Consequently, major auto companies have been forced to re-examine their financing capabilities.

The results of this activity are illustrated by companies such as Jones Credit, which wants to use their new subprime finance unit to create customer loyalty. Kelly Motors, and Riota recognize the financing demands and are evaluating the potential for subprime financing programs. Kelly Financing wants to boost its retail financing programs, and plans to shift gears from creating the programs to implementing them. By contrast, the finance groups owned by Brownlee, Manzli and Reynolds say they are not currently interested in offering subprime financing.

Sportz Cars North America Inc. took full control of its captive finance company in January, 1995. This ended a three-year partnership with Credit Corp. The move was made to cut the response time for credit checks, expand a used-car leasing program, and tailor its programs for high-end customers.

An issue automobile financiers must deal with is a large percentage of consumers who are currently able to pay, but who may have suffered a bruised credit rating for one reason or another. These customers are often excellent candidates for leasing.

Local dealers who have good relationships with several local banks who can offer more flexibility in financing terms with their buyers. On average, franchise dealers can arrange financing for 65 percent of their buyers. In comparison, independent used-car dealers can arrange financing for less than 25 percent of their buyers.

However, increased financing options mean increased sales. That's why Joe Caldwell, owner of the Caldwell Automotive Superstore in Chicago, Illinois, has been aggressive in building banking relationships. An October, 1995 issue of Corp. explained that Caldwell sells later-model, well-maintained used cars, and Mr. Caldwell works with at least eight local banks to arrange financing for 80 percent of his buyers. Though that figure is far above the national average, there is no practical reason why other new car dealers cannot operate at or close to the same levels. PSAD offers financing resources to assist dealers in reaching this goal.

In any discussion of automotive finance, it's important to note that within the automobile dealer industry, acquisitions and mergers occur under the umbrella of financial services. As the *Market*

Avenue Journal reported, one of the more interesting of these transactions occurred when Tomorrow's Auto Group, a closely-held auto dealership group, acquired an 80 percent stake in Spike Sales of Little Rock, Arkansas in August 1995. With annual sales of approximately $1.2 billion, Tomorrow's Group is one of several larger dealership organizations that are buying up smaller operations across the country as part of a consolidation of what has been a fragmented industry.

In another notable transaction described in the *Market Avenue Journal* was Bundren Co.'s acquisition of Auto Touch Group, Inc., an automobile financing company, in September 1995. Bundren Co.'s issued about 10 million shares to pay for the acquisition.

Dealers interested in growth through mergers and acquisitions can benefit from the guidance and proficiency of financial experts with automotive experience. This is precisely the type of expertise PSAD brings to the table.

The used vehicle market is undergoing an extensive image transformation. The *Auto Newswire* circulated results of a 1995 poll of automotive consumers which indicated that the image and preferability of used vehicles is at its highest level ever. This presents a major opportunity for new car dealerships to capture a much larger share of the used car market than they enjoyed in the past. PSAD is targeting this market in its dealer development programs.

Used-Car Sales

In 1995, used-vehicles sales at franchised and independent dealers totaled $311.4 billion. *Vehicle Newspoint* reports that the annual U.S. market for used cars now totals more than $50 million cars and trucks changing hands each year.

According to *Corp.*, the average selling price of a used car had risen from $6,000 to $10,750 over the last 10 years. Even with that increase, the average cost of a used car is half the average cost of a new car. Statistics as of March 1995 from the American Leasing Association (ALA) show the average retail cost of a new car was $19,925.

Luke Skye of the ALA, which represents most new car dealers in the United States, says the average gross profit margin on a new car in March 1995 was 6.7 percent. But, Skye points out, "A dealer's expenses are close to 6.7 percent. So he's really just breaking even on every sale." In 1994, according to the ALA, new car departments of franchise dealers returned less than 1 percent net profit on sales.

In contrast, the average gross profit on used car sales by those same dealers now stands at 12 percent. Moreover, since overhead expenses relating to the used car operations are lower than those for new cars, more money from that department falls to the dealer's bottom line. In 1994, it was 2.2 percent of sales.

The value-added elements a new car dealer brings to a used car transaction are important. There is usually a significant amount of goodwill and name recognition attached to the franchise. Buyers feel more secure because the dealer usually provides a warranty and has a repair shop. New car dealers are also leading the industry in establishing a variety of profit centers which mean the availability of additional products, such as insurance, to the consumer.

However, used-car superstores are on the rise. Examples include CarGo, Caldwell Automotive Superstore, Dada Auto and Auto World, Inc. Industry experts say the reason these superstores have come into being and are thriving is because customers were unhappy with the typical car-buying experience.

Bechtold City has gone into the used-car business through its subsidiary, Carton. In 1994, Carton's Raleigh store sold 4,050 cars at an average price of $13,664 to gross $455.3 million, according to Lisa Merle & Co. That's 30 times the sales of an average used-car dealer. Carton turned over its inventory 8.4 times, more than twice the industry average.

Caldwell Automotive Superstore specializes in selling late-model, well-maintained cars that appeal to many would-be new-car buyers because they cost thousands of dollars less than the same car bought new. The Caldwell stores are successful because they contain several profit centers. They offer financing, insurance, service contracts, rust-proofing and routine service. These areas generated 54 percent of the company's gross profit.

A new chain that will be called Auto World, Inc. will stock 350-650 late-model used cars and trucks at each dealership. Prices will be fixed, and no bargaining will be permitted. Vehicle purchases will include detailed warranties.

In January 1996, Dada Auto Group opened an 800-unit used car dealership in New York. The company's chairman, Bruce Jennere, says there is more profit to be made by selling previously owned vehicles rather than new ones. Jennere said his organization is absolutely interested in becoming a significant player in the used car business. In addition, industry rumors have retailers such as Baker and Brommel thinking of getting into the used car business.

Automotive Leasing

Automotive leasing is on the increase because it provides benefits to both consumers and dealers. For the consumer, leasing means lower monthly payment. It lets consumers drive a higher-priced, better-featured car than they could afford to buy. The under 30 market is more interested in short-term contracts than long-term purchases. Older consumers remember being caught upside-down in car loans during the 1980s, owing more than the car was worth and being forced to sell by circumstances such as a job lay-off; it's an experience they are not eager to repeat. The increase in self-employed individuals and small business owners means a higher number of consumers who may benefit from the tax advantages of leasing.

For dealers, leasing improves customer loyalty. Studies show that customer loyalty among lease customers is roughly double that of regular financing customers. The nature of the transaction means the customer automatically comes back to the dealership to return the car, and the dealership is then more likely to get that customer into another one of their cars. Lease cycles are shorter and therefore turn more frequently as compared to buying/financing cycles.

For salespeople, closing ratios are higher for leasing than buying. Closing ratios are 42.1 percent for leasing, compared with 27.6 percent for vehicle purchases. *Cars Today* reported that almost 64 percent of salespeople now present leasing as an alternative to buying a vehicle - up from 9 percent in 1991.

From a demographic perspective, it's important to recognize that women purchase 52 percent of all vehicles and influence 85 percent of all purchases. According to the *Auto Newswire*, women typically dislike the traditional vehicle purchase negotiation process, which is all but eliminated with leasings. They also tend to dislike dealing with car repairs, which is another issue resolved by leasing. Also, women (more than men) tend to appreciate the perceived safety and convenience factors of driving a new car every few years.

Industry statistics show that leasing trends are on the rise. A *Cars Today* article stated that leasing accounted for 13 percent of overall car sales volume in 1993, up from 4 percent in 1990. More specifically, another *Cars Today* article reported that leasing accounted for 30 percent of Sportz's volume and 40 percent of MHZ's volume. In trucks, leasing account for 7 percent of overall volume in 1993, up from 2 percent in 1990.

Dolman Communications reported that during the 1994 model year, 28.7 percent of new personal-use vehicles were leased rather than purchased. The American Leasing Association (ALA) expected about 33 percent of new personal-use vehicles to be leased in the 1995 model year.

Jones has been industry's market leader in short-term, 24-month retail leases. In 1993, 31 percent of Jones' retail transactions were personal-use leases. Leasing account for 12 percent of Jones' total truck volume and 16 percent of total car volume. Kelly Financing plans to boost its leasing programs by training dealers and employees, and restructuring its organization. In the fall of 1995, Reynolds received the capital and commitment from top management to develop a specific leasing strategy to compete in the leasing market.

Erich Smith, a long-time Boulder area Livingston dealer, expects leasing to get an even bigger chunk of the car market in the next couple of years, especially in the higher-priced autos, which normally lose value quickly.

Used-car leasing is a relatively new trend, resulting primarily from the increase in popularity and acceptability of the used car market. Used car leasing is becoming more popular in the consumer market because many vehicles coming out of fleets have high residual values, and consumers are turning to leases in some cases to finance them. In particular, luxury car companies are moving toward leasing the same vehicle to several customers before ultimately recycling it.

Used-Car Leasing

Consumers who may have been turned away from a new or used car purchase in the past due to poor credit histories may find themselves able to qualify for a used car lease. Another benefit is that leasing a used car rather than a new one allows for lower cost insurance coverage for the driver.

Reasons Why Consumers Choose Leasing

- Less expensive than purchasing
- Lower monthly payment than with a comparable finance contract
- No down payment or a lower one
- Tax advantages
- Easier to get credit approval

As of January 1996, barely 4 percent of used-car buyers were aware that they could lease a used vehicle. However, thanks to awareness programs such as those developed by PSAD, that percentage is growing. *Leasing Now* projects that over one million used car leases will be signed during 2001.

Along with the ease of qualifying for a lease, stepped-up training has made salespeople eager to promote leasing to customers. Major automobile dealers have demonstrated a clear willingness to spend significant sums on training.

Dealer Training and Consulting

An article in *Cars Today* says dealers can overcome their average worries about running a successful dealership if they made a commitment to training. Ads can create traffic, but a positive image and sales are built on the showroom floor.

Reynolds *Corp.* planned to have a national training program in place by January 1996 to help dealers learn the fundamentals of leasing. Dealer and employee training programs are new responsibilities for Kelly Motors Acceptance Corp.'s new market staff. As described in *Cars Today*, the programs are designed to impact Kelly Financing's retail financing and leasing programs.

Sales & Marketing Management reported that Verleon spent $850,000 on a sales training program which employs comparison shopping. Sales figures for the first two months of 1995 (after the training) were double those of last year for the same period. The sales reps experienced an invaluable gain of confidence and trust in their product.

An April 1995 issue of the *Advertising Journal* said DeLeon Automotive Group, an auto dealer chain, planned a three-year, $400,000 project to retrain nearly 500 employees. Mr. DeLeon believes his dealerships are only as good as the people working in them. He hired consultants to improve the responsiveness of his personnel. He also hired Main Frame, an national database management company which targets car dealerships, to improve the follow-up process with potential car buyers.

These are just a few of the multitude of examples available that illustrate the growing commitment to training in the automotive industry. With its wide range of training programs, flexible presentation capabilities, and industry knowledge, PSAD is in an excellent position to gain significant market share in this evolving industry.

Automotive and Dealer Insurance

By its nature, the automobile industry is a major consumer of insurance products. For example, dealers carry liability and property and casualty coverage, along with a standard or mandatory insurance package for their employees.

Beyond insurance to meet their own needs, dealers have discovered the issue of insurance as a profit center. Savvy dealers are aggressively marketing insurance products, particularly those that are related to the financing agreement, such as credit life and credit disability. These products are available through PSAD's insurance division, Insurance Works.

THE COMPANY

Each division of PSAD is staffed by professionals - industry experts, attorneys, accountants, etc. - who know and have solid relationships with dealers across the country. The three divisions combine for a powerful product package that also produces economies of scale for both the Company and its clients.

Insurance Works

Formed in 1979, Insurance Works provides a complete portfolio of insurance services for the franchised automobile dealer market. From bonds to repossession insurance, this division allows dealers to turn to one source for all their insurance needs. No other agency addresses all insurance needs for this market.

The Insurance Works division is comprised of 12 employees and agents, each specializing in new car dealers. The high level of expertise and experience of these 12 professionals, arms them with the ability to efficiently and expertly address any insurance need the new car dealer may have.

Through its long-term business relationships, Insurance Works has gained the value of incumbency in over half the Georgia market. This is beginning to greatly assist the cross-selling of products, since Insurance Works is a well-known and highly respected agency to the dealers. Years of building personal and professional relationships with the dealers has allowed Insurance Works to achieve a greater account penetration and write multiple lines of business in an increasing number of accounts.

The principals of Pompei-Schmidt Auto Dealers believe that only an independent agency structured like Insurance Works can respond to the ever-changing market conditions and needs of the automotive industry. This organization has uniquely targeted a desirable market which generates high premiums in all lines. By not relying on any one line of business, Insurance Works is able to survive and grow regardless of overall market conditions.

Development Works

The Development Works division provides a variety of much-needed consulting services and training programs to new and used car dealerships. By hosting on-site training workshops and designing unique management programs, the Development Works division offers a wide selection of programs, each designed to increase sales and make the operation more profitable.

Under the direction of Charlie Salinger and Grace Long, this division has grown and now thrives. Through two distinct avenues, this division enhances the profitability of automobile dealerships. On one front, Development Works delivers comprehensive sales training to dealership employees. The training focuses on sales techniques, the use of financing alternatives to close and increase the profitability of sales, and leasing alternatives. On a second front, Development Works provides corporate financial assistance to the dealership itself. For example, they can restructure for increased profitability, package for sale or succession planning and refinance corporate debt.

Development Works is the nation's leading independent Jones lease training company, and second in the number of enrolled Jones dealers.

Development Works staff of instructors and consultants offer personal training and individualized solutions for the problems dealers and their sales teams face every day, all designed to increase the overall profitability of the dealership. Each member of the training and consulting teams brings a minimum of 15 years experience in dealership operations. In addition to providing valuable training which has resulted in significantly increased sales, their advice and expertise has been the prelude to turning many dealerships around - making them profitable for the first time in several years.

The most popular Development Works program is lease training, also known as the Lucrative Equity Program. When industry trends reflected an increased demand by consumers to lease automobiles, Development Works recognized a potential need for sales teams to learn how to promote the leasing option. From a dealership's perspective, this provides sales teams with more products to offer potential buyers without deviating from their current selling system.

In keeping with the ideals of Pompei-Schmidt, the goal of Development Works is to provide top-rated training and consulting to automotive dealerships throughout the United States. The service is a natural fit for the Pompei-Schmidt Dealers as they continue to position the company as a one-stop shop for all automobile dealerships.

Finance Works

Staffed by financial experts, Finance Works presents a unique profit center for the Pompei-Schmidt Auto Dealers. The other divisions of PSAD make dealerships more profitable and allow them to sell or lease more cars. It is only natural for a third division to be poised to benefit from this increased growth. Finance Works is that third profit center.

When an automobile dealership turns to PSAD for assistance with training or consulting, the dealership is likely to increase their business. This increased business, whether it is through the leasing of cars or an acquisition of new business, presents an opportunity for the Pompei-Schmidt Auto Dealers to assist the dealership in yet another way. By offering financial products through the Finance Works, the dealerships may enjoy the comfort of working with the same organization which helped them grow.

The industry's average yield on subprime notes financing used cars is 25-30 percent. Add to this the fact that the same car can potentially be financed 2-4 times, and the profit opportunities increase even more. An additional benefit for the consumer is the opportunity to improve their personal credit rating, and through trading up, provide them with a newer, nicer vehicle in the process.

Used car lease financing is a virgin market and Finance Works is at the forefront of this innovative financial market. These points clearly indicate why, from a corporate standpoint, Finance Works has an extremely large profit potential for the Pompei-Schmidt Auto Dealers. Through thorough planning and development, Pompei-Schmidt Auto Dealers realized that Finance Works is a natural compliment to their services. Through financing the growth of each dealership they work with, Finance Works allows profits to be made on virtually every level.

Finance Works was created to acquire existing non-prime credit companies. At this time, it is involved in several negotiations to acquire a base of business in non-prime credit. It plans to complete at least one of these transactions in the first quarter of 1996. Finance Works has established a top notch management team of professionals in the automotive finance business.

THE PRODUCT

The various PSAD products can be used separately or collectively. In any case, the goal is to guide dealers in turning all functions in selling cars into distinct profit centers.

In many instances, dealers recognize the need for a creative approach to the process of designing innovative profit centers for a variety of related products and services. They also recognize the advantage of outsourcing that process.

Insurance Works

Insurance Works has always had the objective of becoming a full-service agency for the franchised auto dealer market. No other agency currently addresses all insurance needs for this market.

Insurance Works provides services to more than 400 Georgia dealers, including license and other bonds for more than 350 dealers; garage liability and group health for 10 dealers; workers' compensation for more than 80 dealers; credit insurance for approximately 10 dealers; and repossession insurance. Insurance Works is the largest independent writer of cost-reducing workers' compensation plans and services for franchise dealers in Georgia.

This division's current product and service portfolio includes:

- Garage liability policies designed specifically for new car dealers
- Workers' compensation
- Risk management services designed to lower workers' compensation premiums
- Bonds for all needs, including Financial Guarantee Bonds
- Employee benefits, including affordable group health programs (traditional, HMO, PPO, and partially self-funded) and tax-advantaged Section 125 and 401(K) plans
- Credit insurance such as dealer-owned captives through top-rated carriers, plus other credit insurance products and training

Development Works

The comprehensive range of services offered by Development Works are designed to provide guidance in making critical financial decisions and allow clients to successfully meet financial planning needs. An estimated 45 percent of dealers are undercapitalized by industry standards. Development Works programs aid in providing cash for dealers to finance growth.

By blending accounting knowledge with operational consulting and management abilities, Development Works assists in the following areas:

- Acquisition and mergers
- Financing and refinancing
- Cash flow and debt management
- Financial turnarounds
- Accounting issues
- Generational and perpetuation planning

A key focus of Development Works is the secondary or non-prime automobile finance market. Training programs for new car dealers targeting the financing or leasing of two- to three-year old cars being returned at the end of their initial lease are in place, with additional plans being developed.

An interesting aspect of the industry move to lease used cars, especially when subprime financing is an option, is the client retention rate. Cars are often leased for shorter time periods, for example 2 years, with the customer returning at that time to lease a more expensive vehicle, a move made possible by the fact that their credit has improved.

Formed in April 1993, the Development Works division of the Pompei-Schmidt Auto Dealers offers training and consulting services to franchised automobile dealers.

The growth of leasing is a significant part of the new car market, and Development Works lease training program has gained wide acceptance among dealers. The company is an authorized Kelly Motors vendor. Jackson and Kelly Motors truck dealers are reimbursed by Kelly Motors for the company's training fees. Development Works is the leading independent Kelly Motors lease training company, second only to Kelly Financing. In a six-month period, the company enrolled over 80 dealers at a fee of $15,000 each. Development Works is currently bidding for a lease training contract with Blackman motorcycle dealers.

The services offered by Development Works include:

- Training for dealer staff members in sales techniques, leasing, traditional finance, non-prime finance, and insurance
- Financial consulting, including refinancing, loans, working capital and financial turn arounds for troubled dealerships
- Acquisitions and mergers, including assistance in locating buyers for dealerships and dealerships for buyers, as well as pre-qualifying sellers and buyers
- Succession planning, including perpetuation programs
- Estate tax planning
- Consulting on floor plans, fixed assets, improvements and equipment
- Evaluations and appraisals of dealerships

Training is conducted on- or off-site by instructors with a minimum of 15 years practical experience in dealer operations. this means Development Works enjoys a high level of credibility and communication with students. Follow-up programs are implemented after the initial formal class-room training.

Consultants are experienced professionals with all appropriate and necessary licenses and credentials.

Finance Works

A key focus of Finance Works is the secondary or non-prime automobile finance market. Finance Works provides programs targeting the financing or leasing of used cars to individuals with bruised credit. The focus of Finance Works will be to provide non-prime credit for new car dealer customers. In the past, a majority of non-prime credit was for buy-here, pay-here lots with an average sale of $2,900. By focusing on new car dealers, the company believes that it can raise this average to $11,000. Meaning fewer transactions and increased revenue. The second thrust will be to lease program cars or off lease vehicles to the secondary credit market. This will allow consumers with bruised credit, but higher income, to be able to move into a newer, nicer leased car (average 2-3 years old). This program will also assist dealers and manufacturers programs that will help them move the large number of cars that are coming back from leasing programs initiated several years ago.

Finance Works Case Study

Sixty-five percent of used car buyers have bruised credit. Finance Works offers retail financing and leasing options to these applicants as a viable solution to their car-buying needs. Under this program, Finance Works is able to match vehicles with cash availability of customers. This hypothetical case study illustrates how the customer, the dealer and Finance Works win.

Example:

Sam has bruised credit. He wants to buy a car and has saved $1,500 cash for a down payment. Because of his credit, Sam does not qualify for conventional financing and is forced to buy an older vehicle from a dealer who offers traditional financing themselves.

Sam eventually finds a car he wants to buy. It is a 1990 Samson Svelt with 75,000 miles on it. The dealer's actual cash value of the car is near $2,500. The retail price is $5,900.

Sam puts $1,500 down and finances the rest. His payments are stretched over 48 months at $165.00 per month. The value of this total note is $7,920.

Eighteen months after buying the car, the air conditioner breaks. The repair shop tells Sam that it will cost $600 to fix the air conditioner and that it looks like several more repairs will be needed over the next few months to keep the car running. Sam knows he can't trade the car in with all the needed repairs. He owes more than the car is worth.

So, instead of getting the car fixed, Sam decided to stop making payments and save the $165.00 each month, and drive the car into the ground before it is repossessed. Three months later, the car is recovered for $500. The vehicle's cash value is reduced to $500. The total loss to the lender is $3,100. Sam has saved another $1,600 and is ready to go through this scenario again, hurting another lender.

If Finance Works had stepped in, this situation would have looked much different. Finance Works would have approved the sale at a retail cost $3,500. The dealer would have profited $1,000; Sam would have paid $1,000 for a security deposit and $400 for acquisition fees and a license tag. Instead of owning the car, Sam would have been leasing it for 18 months.

Then, when the air conditioner broke, Sam would have paid for the repair so he could return the car and move up into a newer vehicle. The dealer takes the repaired car back and resells another car to Sam. The dealer wins because they generate repeat business every time a car is returned (18-36 months). Finance Works wins by earning 100% profit at the maximum interest rate, plus acquisition fee and they are ready to finance the next vehicle. The customer wins by having a "new" car every 18-36 months.

Explanation:

With traditional financing, most of the customer's normal down payment is retained by the dealer to cover sales tax. Therefore, a very high percent of the vehicle's cost must be financed. Traditional financing carries the debt over several years, putting customers in a position of owing more than the value of the car. This lack of equity prohibits the customer from trading the car in and buying another car. The customer, in this situation, is more likely to default on his car loan.

By following the approach recommended by the Finance Works, down payments are not required and no sales tax is due at delivery. The cash usually applied toward a down payment can be passed on to Finance Works as a security deposit. Also, Finance Works offers affordable payments, while still limiting the term. Losses are reduced or eliminated by higher reserves and a shorter term. And, customers are inclined to pay if minor problems occur because they are able to move on to another vehicle in a short time, and at completion, real equity exists in the security deposit placed with Finance Works.

THE MANAGEMENT TEAM

Wellington Pompei - Chairman of the Board/Director

Wellington Pompei is the President and Chairman of the Board of Pompei-Schmidt Auto Dealers. He has served in this capacity since the company's inception, and is PSAD's founder.

Mr. Pompei has worked in insurance commercial credit and finance in the automotive field for more than three decades, and has served in senior management positions with Bloomer's Insurance Group in Tallahassee, Florida and Reynolds Credit Company in Orlando, Florida.

Mr. Pompei served in the United States Air Force from 1962 to 1966, when he received an honorable discharge. He studied business administration at the University of Delaware from 1963 to 1965. He holds FL 2-20 and FL 2-18 insurance licenses.

Jorge Schmidt - President and CEO/Director

Jorge Schmidt's finance and insurance experience spans more than 25 years. He has served as Vice President, financial division of Kahn Group, Dayton, Ohio where he created the financial division for automobile dealerships; as President of Le Blonde Company, Brighton, Michigan, specializing in dealer's financing; as Executive Vice President and managing partner of O'Brien, Inc., Milwaukee, Wisconsin, a large regional insurance group; and was co-owner of Astrup Associates an insurance and accounting agency in Cincinnati, Ohio.

During his career, Mr. Schmidt has financed over $300 million in new commercial loans for the automobile industry. He has created and profitably sold five businesses, and has participated in a variety of acquisitions and mergers. Mr. Schmidt holds a B.A. in accounting from Kenyon University and an M.B.A. from Michigan State University.

During his tenure with Kahn Bank, Peter Cinci set up and managed the asset remarketing department and managed the West Central Georgia sales financing department. Prior to that, he held the position of assistant branch manager with Reynolds Credit Company in Orlando, Florida. He earned a B.A. in business administration and personnel management from the University of Georgia and is a U.S. Air Force veteran.

Peter Cinci - Vice President of Operations

E. Brown's experience in the automotive industry includes senior management positions with Brownlee Riota Motors U.S.A (Group Vice President of Marketing) Jones Motors Corporation and Bounder Automotive, U.S.A. He has owned five automobile franchised dealerships and has served on the Board of Directors of Brownlee Motors Corporation, U.S.A. He also has extensive experience in insurance, automobile dealership financing and real estate.

E. Brown - Vice President of Financial Works

Mr. Brown served honorably as a paratrooper in the U.S. Army. He attended Ohio State University and holds an MBA and doctorate degree from Notre Dame University.

Pippin Newell brings more than 35 years of financial and automotive experience to PSAD. He has worked in both sales and management at franchise dealers. He created the Progressive Investment Program, an automotive lease training system. He worked with Reynolds training for dealers, consisting of every aspect of retail leasing including instruction, seminars, workshops and customer presentations; and with Webster as an area manager for 12 years.

Pippin Newell - Executive Vice President/Director

Mr. Newell is currently serving as one of three independent Reynolds vendors on the Reynolds Leasing Task Force.

Sojourner Path was the owner and founder of Quality Investment Corp. and Quality Investment Pre-Owned Automobile, two ten year old companies in Brandenton, Florida. Quality Investment Acceptance purchases non-prime paper from dealers throughout Florida. Ms. Path opened the auto sales company as an outlet for repossession and to originate paper from her own inventory. Assets of the company were at $10 million when it was sold in 1995.

Sojourner Path - Vice President of Marketing

Ms. Path conducts seminars and does consulting work on loan underwriting, collections, recovery, insurance, sales and marketing. She has received numerous accolades from her industry colleagues, including being the first woman to be voted "Man of the Year" by the state dealers association. She holds a Bachelor's degree from Tampa State and a Masters from The University of Pennsylvania.

Billy Sweeney brings more than a quarter of a century of experience in the insurance industry to the Company. He has held senior management positions with Holden Insurance Companies, Lake Union and Briar Specialty Insurance Company.

Billy Sweeney - Vice President of Insurance Works

Dr. Sweeney holds a Ph.D. from Colgate University, and has studied finance and computer programming at Yale University and finance and accounting at the University of Connecticut.

MARKET RESEARCH & PLAN

Market Description

As of 1995, U.S. franchise dealerships numbered 22,417. Georgia represents 8 percent of the national new car market, with 750 franchised dealers and more than 10,000 used car dealers.

Franchise dealers are acutely aware of the need to improve their public image and customer relations. Though they are open to new ideas, franchise dealers are still struggling with the results of past mistakes. "The franchise dealers' relationship with consumers over the years has been a disaster," says President and CEO Natasha Neeson of Bee Automotive, Inc., in Raleigh, which owns 30 car-auction centers in the United States.

This means the market is ripe for consulting services such as those provided by PSAD, which are designed for image enhancement and strengthening customer relations.

Beyond consulting, a $100 billion subprime automotive financing market exists. This market has been built on two key factors: One is the demand for used and off-lease vehicles; the other is the personal economic instability of many consumers.

The steadily increasing number of new cars being leased and returned after two or three years has created a growing market that is not being adequately addressed by most finance organizations.

Because nearly three out of four consumers have some adverse credit history, *Cornwall* magazine reported that many consumers do not qualify for traditional bank financing, which makes them candidates for non-prime financing. Therefore, even a low market penetration would annually generate several million dollars in high-yield receivables.

The automobile finance business is very fragmented and highly competitive. Currently, this $100 billion business is dominated by independent finance and loan companies. The biggest is the suburban Detroit-based Nunn Finance Co., which earned 9.4 percent on assets in 1994- six times as much as the most efficiently run U.S. banks earn. Nearly a dozen lenders have jumped into this game and gone public in recent years because the market is so attractive. Finance Works is ideally positioned to join this vanguard of forward-thinking companies, believing that what sets it apart from the others is its diverse base of business, the extensive automobile industry experience of its management team and its current penetration of auto dealers by its other divisions.

Dealers are becoming stronger markets for insurance products as they use those products to build internal profit centers. Dealers across the country have indicated a strong preference for dealing with one insurance company rather than several - especially a company that understands and has strong experience in the specifics regarding automobile dealer operations and customer service as PSAD does.

Market Trends

Changes in the automobile industry represent a fundamental shift in traditional sales and operation methods, and have made it necessary for industry members to change their corporate culture.

Strategies for change include exploring new leasing alternatives, developing new pricing strategies, refocusing finance plans and expanding dealer opportunities for profit in the new and used vehicle business.

Competition

Within the automotive financing market, PSAD is competing primarily against independent financial operations. The nature of the transaction and overall credit worthiness of the typical purchaser means PSAD is not competing with most commercial banks, savings and loans, credit unions, financing arms of automobile manufacturers and other consumer lenders that apply more traditional lending criteria to the credit approval process. Historically, these traditional sources of used automobile financing (some of which are larger, have significantly greater financial resources and have relationships with captive dealer networks) have not consistently served the PSAD's market segment.

In the consulting arena, PSAD's strongest competitor is represented by Brewer & Barlow, based in Winettka, Illinois. Their direct mail services and sales training programs generated annual sales of $10 million. This is good news for PSAD because it indicates a solid need for consulting and training products. In addition, the success of Brewer & Barlow provides confidence for PSAD because their Dealer Development Works division offers a more comprehensive product and superior service package than any current competitor.

Because of the limited number of qualified training programs on leasing, manufacturers are developing their own leasing education. However, dealer leasing training programs are very narrow in scope and can cost from $200 to $1,000 per salesperson. PSAD's comprehensive training is a far better value.

PSAD sales strategy will be built on personal networking by key individuals, horizontal account penetration, cross-selling of each division, and networking outside Georgia through megadealers who have dealers here.

Sales Plan

In Georgia, PSAD currently enjoys a market share of 400 of 700 franchised dealers. Evidence indicates similar accomplishments can be achieved in other states.

Forecasted Market Share and Sales

While it is believed the company can continue its present course of operation and meet or exceed its marketing goals, there are always risks associated with any business venture.

Risks (Recognition, Evaluation and Contingency)

PSAD's plans for expanding its existing operations, development of additional markets and projections for potential future profitability are based on previous results of the Company's operations over a 16-year period, thorough market research, and the experience, judgement and assumptions of the management team.

Careful monitoring of the company's progress and thoughtful but rapid reaction to changing market conditions will reduce the potential risk and provide contingency strategies when necessary.

Automotive Repair Service

BUSINESS PLAN

LR AUTOMOTIVE

6890 Ranch Drive
Traverse City, MI 48963

LR Automotive presents up-to-date financial information, helpful to anyone considering starting an automotive repair service.

- EXECUTIVE SUMMARY

- PARTS & LABOR

- WARRANTIES

- COMMUNITY ACTIVITY

- ORGANIZATION

- COMPANY PHILOSOPHY

- JOB DESCRIPTIONS

AUTOMOTIVE REPAIR SERVICE
BUSINESS PLAN

EXECUTIVE SUMMARY

The need for a full service automotive center with competent and trusting mechanics is always there. Chuck Liepshur and Rich Rudy have built, and are still accumulating, a clientele that has followed them from location to location through promotions and careers. These clients are loyal and will continue to follow LR Automotive, when we move to our new location.

With advertising in local newspapers, mailers and handbills, business should increase by a margin of 10% annually. People are always looking for an honest auto repair facility which is committed to customer service, reliability and promptness. By being fully committed to our clients, our customer base will increase and will provide a stable ground for our business to grow.

Our company will be offering two products: the first being automotive service which will generate a gross profit margin of 60% on average. This will include bumper-to-bumper service on cars and light trucks, i.e. brakes, computer diagnosis, suspension, exhaust and electrical. The sale of tires will provide a 20% profit margin, but will also help us sell service such as front-end parts and front-end alignments as needed. The only time our services will be performed is when and if they are needed or they are recommended on the O.E. manufacturer's maintenance schedule. Service should provide 90% of the total sales with tire sales making up the remaining 10%.

The parts and products we will use will also help in our appeal to customers. We will use top of the line, name brand parts such as Auto-X, Reman, and Xilco. Customers always look for a well-known brand name when deciding where to take their vehicle.

Counterfeit parts will never be used at LR Automotive.

Last, but not least, warranties also help when customers are deciding where to get their work done. Our warranties will meet or exceed industry standards.

Our target customers are the owners of auto and light trucks. This area of service is always growing. Automobiles are being kept an average of 3-5 years and each vehicle requires servicing an average of 2.7 times per year.

As new vehicle prices increase, consumers are inclined to maintain and service their vehicles for longer periods of time. As a result of this trend, the service business will continue to grow.

Our competition will consist of auto dealerships, larger tire and service chains and gas stations with service departments. These are very successful because they are well-known and offer a wide variety of services. The weakness of these companies will be our advantage. These weaknesses include the need to keep the cars several days to finish work. LR Automotive will make every effort to finish jobs the same day. Also, dealerships tend to distance themselves from their clients, refusing to take the time to educate the customer about their problems. Our employees will take the time to point out our customers' vehicle problems and discuss all the possible solutions explaining the advantages and disadvantages of each. We are also going to treat our customers as we would like to be treated, spending time with each one so they know they're not just a number to our business. Follow-up calls to ensure satisfaction will also be made after we have completed the work.

Our customers will be made up of our existing clientele, along with a new customer base which we will gain through advertising. Through our satisfied customers, word will spread that LR is the automotive repair shop that customers can trust, which will increase our customer base. These customers will remain satisfied because they will be happy with our service, prices and the atmosphere we provide.

We will use only quality parts, which will be readily available in our stock or via our local parts supplier. When we service autos, we will never take short cuts and will never substitute quality in order to obtain a lower price. Our parts warranties will reflect those of the manufacturer.

PARTS & LABOR

Our labor warranties will be as follows:

WARRANTIES

- Brakes - Standard brake job - 1 year or 12,000 miles
            - Brake overhaul - 2 years or 24,000 miles
- Shocks - 1 year or 12,000 miles
- Struts - 3 years or 36,000 miles
- Suspension parts - 1 year or 12,000 miles
- Belts - 1 year or 12,000 miles
- Exhaust - 1 year or 12,000 miles
- Alternator/Starter - 6 months or 6,000 miles
- Alignment - 6 months or 6,000 miles
- Water pump - 1 year or 12,000 miles
- All other warranties - 90 days or 4,000 miles

We plan on being a visible part of the community in which we are based. We will join community groups and participate in local activities in order to understand community needs. As a result of our visibility, we will get to know the local patrons and that will help LR's business to grow within the community.

COMMUNITY ACTIVITY

We plan on working on 6 cars per day when LR first opens. Our labor force will include two certified technicians and one salesperson. Every employee in our establishment will be knowledgeable in the auto service area. As our business grows and becomes more profitable, we will add trained personnel to ensure the best service available.

ORGANIZATION

1. To provide an atmosphere where the consumer feels confident about his/her purchase(s) and relationships with LR's service employees.
2. Being honest and sincere with the clientele.
3. Being community oriented.
4. To create a place where customers feel good about recommending LR to friends or relatives for their auto concerns.
5. To provide a comfortable living for ourselves and our employees.
6. To provide a healthy work environment where our employees enjoy coming to work each day.
7. To provide benefits for ourselves, our employees and families (i.e. 401K plans, health and dental plans).
8. Our goal is to keep our employees long term by treating them as we would wish to be treated ourselves.

COMPANY PHILOSOPHY

JOB DESCRIPTIONS

Co-President

Objective

To ensure survival and growth of LR Automotive Service and control the operation.

Functions

1. Act as a team leader, making sure that LR team stays on track.
2. Establish and implement company policy, performance standards, policy and procedures.
3. Establish and implement employee controls - feedback based on performance standards, indicators, goals, etc.

4. Financial planning and controls
    a. Paying invoices
    b. Banking
    c. Accounting systems
    d. Sales and expenses
    e. Assets and liabilities
5. Buying and inventory control
6. Advertising and promotion
7. Reconcile statements
8. Planning (long and short range)
9. Answer customer complaints
10. Maintain:
    a. The spark to imagine
    b. The daring to innovate
    c. The discipline to plan
    d. The skill to do
    e. The will to achieve
    f. The commitment to be responsible
    g. The leadership to motivate
11. Scheduling, merchandise store, maintain paper flow, housekeeping and equipment maintenance.
12. Parts room and warehouse organization.
13. Business development, fleet accounts and national accounts.

Objective

Salesperson

Take care of customers that come in the door, and relieve Co-Presidents of detail work.

Functions

1. Completing work orders and calling customers when job is done.
2. All other paper work, i.e. filing work orders daily, inventory management, mailing invoices, PIPT's filing emissions certificates, getting invoice numbers on parts bills and clear pending documents.
3. Housekeeping - keeping counters clean, displays and vending machines dusted, customer waiting area clean daily, empty waste baskets, rest room detail.
4. Supplies - invoices, sales slips, cash receipts, paper towels, keep sufficient change in cash drawer.
5. Special assignments as directed by Co-Presidents.
6. Keep all display materials current, window signs, ad boards, manufacturer rebates and promotions.

Objective

Mechanic

Meet or exceed assigned daily objective. Maximize productivity per hour worked. Get quality work done in the shortest amount of time possible.

Function

1. Get quality work done, fast.
2. Safety check all cars worked on.
3. Add-on sales, direct contact with customer, both face to face and on the phone.
4. Housekeeping.
5. Equipment maintenance.
6. Assist in organizing warehouse and parts room.

	Weekly	Monthly	Yearly	
Miscellaneous Service Expenses				**Operating Expenses**
Dumpster	$11.52	$50.00	$599.96	
EPA Compliance Fee	$3.50	$15.19	$182.28	
Floor Dry	$1.20	$5.21	$62.50	
Floor Soap	$4.10	$17.79	$213.53	
Hand Soap	$10.50	$45.57	$546.84	
Shop Towels	$16.50	$71.61	$859.32	
Tire Removal	$11.52	$50.00	$599.96	
Uniforms	$18.00	$78.12	$937.44	
Waste Anti-freeze Removal	$3.16	$13.71	$164.57	
Waste Oil Filters Removal	$6.33	$27.47	$329.67	
Waste Oil Removal	$10.36	$44.96	$539.55	
Welding Supplies & Services	$19.44	$84.37	$1,012.44	
Sub-total	**$116.13**	**$504.00**	**$6,048.05**	
Office Expenses				
Accountant	$34.56	$149.99	$1,799.88	
Advertising	$69.00	$299.46	$3,593.52	
Alarm Service	$5.76	$25.00	$299.98	
Bad Debt	$23.04	$99.99	$1,199.92	
Bank Loan	$345.62	$1,500.00	$18,000.00	
Miscellaneous Expense (supplies)	$250.00	$1,085.00	$13,020.00	
Property Rental	$345.62	$1,499.99	$17,999.89	
Telephone	$57.60	$249.98	$2,999.81	
Utilities (light/heat/water)	$64.50	$279.93	$3,359.16	
Sub-total	**$1,196.70**	**$5,189.35**	**$62,272.17**	
Salaries Expenses				
Chuck Liepshur	$672.00	$2,916.48	$34,997.76	
Rich Rudy	$672.00	$2,916.48	$34,997.76	
Abe Sitze	$576.00	$2,499.84	$29,998.08	
Sub-total	**$1,920.00**	**$8,332.80**	**$99,993.60**	
Insurance				
Health	$207.37	$900.00	$10,800.00	
Liability/Comprehensive	$93.00	$403.62	$4,843.44	
Sub-total	**$300.37**	**$1,303.62**	**$15,643.44**	
Taxes				
FICA (7.65)	$147.00	$637.98	$7,655.76	
MESC	$29.00	$125.86	$1,510.00	
Sub-total	**$176.00**	**$763.84**	**$9,166.08**	
Total	**$3,708.20**	**$16,093.61**	**$193,123.34**	

Start-Up Cost

Office Equipment

Alarm Equipment	$700.00
Cash Register	$500.00
Coffee Machine	$50.00
Deposit for Oxygen Tank	$200.00
Fax Machine	$300.00
Fire Extinguishers	$260.00
Incorporation	$1,000.00
Initial Supplies	$1,000.00
Office Furniture	$500.00
Phone Lines (installation)	$206.00
Phone System (4 lines)	$1,500.00
Safe	$850.00
Showroom Furniture	$1,000.00
Signage	$500.00
Sub-total	**$8,566.00**

Shop Equipment

2 Post Lift	$3,672.00
4 Post Lift	$9,200.00
Air Compressor	$1,500.00
Alignment Machine	$5,000.00
Anti-freeze Drum Cradle	$30.80
Arbor Press	$500.00
Battery Charger	$231.00
Bearing Packer	$2,300.00
Catch Pan	$10.00
Drain Pan	$21.00
Exhaust Analyzer	$3,000.00
Exhaust Hoses	$156.00
Lab Scope	$500.00
Lift Installation Labor	$750.00
Mitchel On-Demand	$4,154.00
Oil Dispensor	$69.00
Parts Washer	$306.00
R12 Air Conditioning Machine	$2,800.00
R134 Air Conditioning Machine	$2,800.00
Rolling Lift	$4,000.00
Strut Compressor	$575.00
Tall Jack Stand	$100.00
Tire Balancer	$1,500.00
Tire Machine	$2,500.00
Tire Spreader	$50.00
Tire Tank	$34.00
Trans Jack	$400.00
Volt Amp Tester	$1,000.00
Waste Oil Tank	$100.00
Welding Tank	$125.00
Sub-total	**$47,415.30**
Total Start-Up Cost	**$55,981.30**

**THIS PAGE INTENTIONALLY LEFT BLANK
SEE NEXT PAGE FOR SALES PROJECTION &
CASH FLOW TABLE**

Sales Projection and Cash Flow

First 12 Months	Nov	Dec	Jan	Feb	Mar	Apr
No. of Days	25	25	26	25	26	26
Balance	1,000	657	314	601	258	545
Sales	26,250	26,250	27,300	26,250	27,300	27,300
Inventory Expenses	10,500	10,500	10,920	10,500	10,920	10,920
Gross Profit	15,750	15,750	16,380	15,750	16,380	16,380
Operating Expenses	16,093	16,093	16,093	16,093	16,093	16,093
Net Profit/(Loss)	-343	-343	287	-343	287	287
Balance	357	314	601	258	545	832
Second 12 Months						
No. of Days	25	25	26	24	26	26
Balance	1,924	3,156	4,388	5,508	5,243	6,363
Sales	28,875	28,875	30,030	27,720	30,030	30,030
Inventory Expenses	11,550	11,550	12,012	11,088	12,012	12,012
Gross Profit	17,325	17,325	18,018	16,632	18,018	18,018
Operating Expenses	16,093	16,093	16,898	16,898	16,898	16,898
Net Profit/(Loss)	1,232	1,232	1,120	-266	1,120	1,120
Balance	3,156	4,388	5,508	5,243	6,363	7,483
Third 12 Months						
No. of Days	25	26	26	24	26	26
Balance	13,513	13,983	15,215	16,447	16,155	17,388
Sales	31,763	33,033	33,033	30,492	33,033	33,033
Inventory Expenses	12,705	13,213	13,213	12,197	13,213	13,213
Gross Profit	19,058	19,820	19,820	18,295	19,820	19,820
Operating Expenses	18,587	18,587	18,587	18,587	18,587	18,587
Net Profit/(Loss)	470	1,232	1,232	-292	1,232	1,232
Balance	13,983	15,215	16,447	16,155	17,388	18,620

Assumptions

Sales

Average 6 vehicles per day @ $175.00 per vehicle
In 2nd 12 months, average per vehicle increases 10% to $192.50

Inventory Expenses

40% of sales

Operating Expenses

Average expenses per month

May	Jun	Jul	Aug	Sep	Oct	Total
26	25	26	27	24	27	308
832	1,119	776	1,063	1,980	1,007	
27,300	26,250	27,300	28,350	25,200	28,350	323,400
10,920	10,500	10,920	11,340	10,080	11,340	129,360
16,380	15,750	16,380	17,010	15,120	17,010	194,040
16,093	16,093	16,093	16,093	16,093	16,093	193,116
287	-343	287	917	-973	917	924
1,119	776	1,063	1,980	1,007	1,924	
26	25	26	26	25	27	307
7,483	8,604	9,031	10,151	11,272	11,699	
30,030	28,875	30,030	30,030	28,875	31,185	354,585
12,012	11,550	12,012	12,012	11,550	12,474	141,834
18,018	17,325	18,018	18,018	17,325	18,711	212,751
16,898	16,898	16,898	16,898	16,898	16,898	201,163
1,120	427	1,120	1,120	427	1,813	11,589
8,604	9,031	10,151	11,272	11,699	13,513	
25	26	26	26	25	27	308
18,620	19,090	20,322	21,555	22,787	23,257	
31,763	33,033	33,033	33,033	31,763	34,304	391,314
12,705	13,213	13,213	13,213	12,705	13,721	156,526
19,058	19,820	19,820	19,820	19,058	20,582	234,788
18,587	18,587	18,587	18,587	18,587	18,587	223,049
470	1,232	1,232	1,232	470	1,995	11,739
19,090	20,322	21,555	22,787	23,257	25,252	

Bed and Breakfast

BUSINESS PLAN

VICTORIA BED & BREAKFAST

825 N. Watson
Munising, Michigan 49862

The Victoria Bed & Breakfast business plan contains lots of helpful information for those interested in opening a hospitality service business. Testimonials are a good addition to any business plan, specifically regarding the business itself, the product or the owners. The Letter of Support found at the end of this plan is an example of an effective testimonial.

- STATEMENT OF PURPOSE

- DESCRIPTION OF THE BUSINESS

- MARKET DESCRIPTION

- DESCRIPTION OF COMPETITION

- COMPETITIVE ADVANTAGE

- DESCRIPTION OF MANAGEMENT

- BUSINESS GOALS

- TRENDS AND INDUSTRY OUTLOOK

- TARGET MARKET

- MARKETING PROMOTION

- LETTER OF SUPPORT

- FINANCIAL DATA

BED AND BREAKFAST
BUSINESS PLAN

Victoria Bed & Breakfast is a limited liability company seeking a $160,000 portfolio mortgage loan to finance the purchase of the residence located at 825 N. Watson, Munising, Michigan. This house, currently a duplex, will be converted to a single family residential structure and bed and breakfast establishment. The owners will be contributing $100,000 of their own money as a down payment toward the purchase price of $260,000 and will be paying closing costs. The house will serve as collateral for the mortgage.

In addition, James and Alexandria Wolfsted will be seeking a $85,000 construction draw to cover start-up costs of the bed and breakfast conversion. The owners have already invested $6,670 in start-up costs.

The owners have formed a Limited Liability Company named Victoria Bed & Breakfast to operate a bed and breakfast home. The home will be converted from a 6 bedroom duplex to 4 bedrooms with private baths and working fireplaces. Victoria will be the owners' private residence and take in guests 365 days a year commencing in August of 1996.

This business is unique in that the business expenses include the owners' mortgage, property taxes, home insurance, and household expenses. For that reason James and Alexandria's income are included in the cash flow chart. James will continue working at the Michigan Department of Environmental Quality and Alexandria will continue to work part-time until the inn-keeping business reaches 40% occupancy. Not shown is additional annual income of $26,000 in benefits such as medical, dental, and life insurance, vacation time, deferred compensation and pension received from James' primary occupation.

DESCRIPTION OF THE BUSINESS

The Victoria Bed & Breakfast is located near downtown Munising in the heart of the historic district at 825 N. Watson. As hosts, Alexandria and James Wolfsted offer warm hospitality, friendship and a knowledge of the area, along with detailed maps of waterfalls and other local scenery.

Victoria is surrounded by other historic homes and buildings. Taking a stroll east down the hill, guests will see the Maritime Museum, the beach and bike path at McCarty's Cove. Walk a few blocks west to find the Munising Historic Museum, Tom Peters Public Library, the downtown shopping area or village shopping area. Within walking distance are two fine restaurants, the Cradle Saloon and Cappucino Cafe. Both the university and hospital are just a mile away.

Victoria will be furnished in an eclectic style from the stained glass windows and original shutters and wood floors to the personal tastes of the owners which include historic and modern art. Well-known Munising artist, Carol Smith, will assist in the interior design of the house. But most important will be the efforts towards comfort and non-intimidating surroundings. Breakfast will be served around an antique round oak table in front of one of the house's seven fireplaces. For those guests wanting privacy, there is a southern exposure breakfast nook off the kitchen, encased in glass overlooking the lower harbor. An early breakfast in the nook will include a spectacular view of the sunrise and the early morning fishermen and women piloting their boats away from the lower harbor and marina. On weekdays, breakfast will be between 7:00 to 9:00 AM, consisting of homemade breads, orange juice, fruit smoothies (strawberries, banana and yogurt blended), cereals, and granola. Weekend breakfast will be served between 8:00 and 10:00 AM and consist of the weekday menu plus breakfast casseroles, French toast, and pancakes using locally made bread, syrup and sausage.

In the late afternoon guests are invited to the common room for socializing with refreshments of gourmet flavored coffee, ice tea, cheese, fruit and homemade breads before going out to dinner. The bookcases on each side of the fireplace hold an extensive library collection handed down through the Wolfsted family for guests to browse through. Current magazines such as Michigan Natural Resources and Martha Stewart Living are also available to read either in the common room or in the guest rooms. The never-ending 1,000 piece puzzle on the corner table and a bridge table for chess, cribbage or even bridge are set-up for those occasional rainy days. We provide old movie videos and video store passes for viewing with others or in the privacy of guest rooms.

Quiet and relaxation can also be found on the back porch off of the kitchen. In the summer guests could watch the Wednesday evening regattas on the Superior Harbor. Or they might choose to sit in a rocking chair on the front porch looking over a well-kept garden of flowers and herbs.

There will be four guest rooms to choose from on the second floor, two facing the lake and two with quaint alcove nooks. An elevator is available that goes from the basement to the second floor. Each room is in its own corner of the house far from the next room, assuring privacy and quiet. Television/VCR, CD player and telephones will be available upon request for each room. Prices range from $85.00 a night to $125.00. The Lakeside room is inspired by local carpenter Jack Kozlowski, who will be making the bed and cedar chest of Lakeside pine and will be equipped with a modem for the business traveler.

We hope to give people, for their short stay here, a sense of a few of Munising's jewels -- its beautiful lake, its history and the people. On the first floor in our formal dining room with its beautiful wood floor, elegant wood mantle fireplace and large bay windows, we will be exhibiting the work of well-known local artists as well as university students. In the second year of operation, this room will be converted into a handicap accessible guest room.

DESCRIPTION OF THE MARKET

According to a 1994 national survey and a 1988 Michigan survey of B&B guests, the typical inn guest is, "...the business-person's dream customer: affluent, well-educated, a stable member of the community, still young enough to be a guest for many years to come..."

- 60% to 72% of the guests staying in Michigan B&Bs are Michigan residents
- 92.8% have attended college, graduated or earned a post-graduate degree
- 47.9% have a household income in excess of $75,000
- 77% are between 25 and 54 years old
- Inn guest couples spend $225.72 per day on lodging, food, and incidentals
- Inn guests travel primarily as couples, sometimes with children or another couple
- Inn guests' primary activities are dining out, sightseeing, shopping and relaxing

DESCRIPTION OF COMPETITION

Our luxury room rates compare with local hotels, such as Stay Rest Inn, Cottage Inn and the Lakeland Inn. More important, as noted in the marketing statistics, people stay in B&Bs for the personal touch. As long as we have a high-tech world we will have a need for the quiet, relaxing, down to earth setting a bed and breakfast offers. Two B&Bs are operating now in the Munising area and a new inn is planned.

The Harbor Place is located on a busy highway in a commercial district with high visibility. It has 4 guest rooms; 2 being shared baths. This is the owners' second home. They live in town and hire an innkeeper. They are in their first year of operation. Victoria also has high visibility, being located in the historic district where bus, carriage and walking tours are frequent in the summer.

Applewood B&B is a contemporary 60's home located in a subdivision in Sands township without restaurants or shopping nearby. They have 4 guest rooms and have recently renovated for each to have private baths. Being outside of town, they may appeal to guests for snowmobiling and skiing more than Victoria, which would cater to those wanting the feel of the city and being close to restaurants, shopping and events.

It is too early to assess competition from Evelyn's Place. The location is great, but it is still a high rise, high industry operation.

COMPETITIVE ADVANTAGE

We have heard from Upper Peninsula innkeepers that, when guests ask about staying in a B&B in Munising they have had nowhere to refer them to. The Munising Chamber of Commerce reports they often get calls asking for a bed and breakfast located in the city. Now they will have one with a perfect location, overlooking the harbor, in the middle of the historic district. Our guests will be within walking distance of restaurants, shopping, the beach, the Maritime Museum, the new marina, the historic museum and renting a tandem bicycle to ride the bike path. Besides our great location, guests will get great hospitality with special amenities of homemade knit slippers, a fireplace and home-style breakfast with home-style people.

We've targeted this market because it is a situation that we very much enjoy -- to welcome people into our community, and show it off and because the city has badly needed a Bed & Breakfast for a long time. We routinely do this now for friends and James' coworkers. This is a new market in Munising because of the strict zoning ordinance, which may leave us as the lone B&B in Munising, although the industry could definitely handle more.

DESCRIPTION OF MANAGEMENT

The bed and breakfast will receive the same thoroughness and professionalism demonstrated in the business plan written by the Wolfsted's. Alexandria will be in charge of marketing, managing the office, rooms, and customer service. James will be in-house historian and geologist of the Munising area (the entertainer).

The Wolfsted's have retained the services of both an attorney and an accountant to help set up the business. The accountant, Nick Coslin, will develop an accounting system on the computer software program, Quick Books, which Alexandria has used for the last year to keep the books for her cleaning business.

The owners will be joining the State Bed and Breakfast Association, the Upper Peninsula Bed and Breakfast Association, the Upper Peninsula Travel and Tourism Association and the Munising Chamber of Commerce for networking. Leslie Cramble, a veteran bed and breakfast innkeeper and Ann Murray, a tourism expert with the MSU extension office, have offered their personal assistance involving the operation and marketing of Victoria.

The owners have prepared and worked for the last year, learning the business and searching for the right location. The Wolfsted's have attended numerous workshops dealing with business start-ups, and more specifically, opening a Bed & Breakfast. Along with attending the workshops, they have researched a variety of materials dealing with opening a Bed & Breakfast. By conducting information interviews with consultants and other innkeepers, the Wolfsted's have been able to determine their course of action with the Victoria Bed & Breakfast. Following is a list of the professionals which were interviewed:

- Ann Murray, Michigan State University District Extension, Munising, Michigan
- Steve Reynolds, JD, Livingston Associates, Munising, Michigan
- Grant Arsen, Key Consulting, Negaunee, Michigan
- Alice Raymond, Business Boosters, AuTrain, Michigan
- Ken Ludman, CPA, Marquette, Michigan
- Owners of the Pine House B&B, Plymouth, Michigan
- Owners of the Winchester B&B, Green Bay, Wisconsin

•Owners of the Grayling Manor, Grayling, Michigan
•Owners of the Holmes Estate, Calumet, Michigan
•Trent Sykes, Northern Alternative
•International Professional Innkeepers Association, California

James' background includes Bachelor and Master of Science degrees in geology, two years teaching at Lansing Community College and eleven years with the state of Michigan. While working for the state he has been responsible for managing contractor expenses at several state funded projects, as well as coordinating environmental restoration with reuse plans at the K.I. Sawyer Air Force Base.

Alexandria's background includes a Bachelor of Science degree in Communication Disorders, several years as a banking supervisor in the 70's, various positions in the service industry, office manager in a small Munising business and helping numerous people with employment and business start-up while working at the Tom Peters Public Library Career Center. In 1994, Alexandria started her own cleaning business called Clean Right. In the last 8 years, the Wolfsted's have purchased a home for $38,000 which is now at a market value of $82,000, accumulated $60,000 in their 457 deferred compensation account, saved $10,000 in bank accounts, paid off student loans over $20,000 and are virtually debt free, except for their mortgage. We accomplished all of this while maintaining an annual household budget of less than $35,000.

BUSINESS GOALS

First year:
        •Reach 25% occupancy rate (surpassing our projected 20%)
        •Establish good neighborhood relations
        •Develop an award-winning brochure
        •Be listed on-line and in associations and AAA booklets
        •Create unforgettable guest visits
        •Spend ten hours a week on marketing

Third year:
        •Operating at 40% occupancy rate with 5 guest rooms generating $83,950 income
        •Terminate Alexandria's outside occupation
        •Attend a national conference
        •Actively involved in the Munising Area Chamber of Commerce
        •Renovate the basement as a rental apartment for income and snow-blowing help
        •Complete a third year written evaluation of the competition, market, service,
          finances, and personal goals

Fifth year:
        •Repaint the outside from dull beige and brown to a more colorful Victorian style
          to match its time period and to attract tourists
        •Develop an offshoot homemade craft or baked goods business
        •Continue to develop the front gardens and backyard
        •Renovate rooms as necessary
        •Hire summer help
        •Complete a fifth year written evaluation of the competition, market, service,
          finances, and personal goals

Summary

Although Bed and Breakfasts have been firmly established in Europe for years, they were only introduced in the United States in the late 1960's. By staying and eating with a family, B&Bs were an inexpensive way to travel and learn about an area. Since then, B&Bs have grown immensely, becoming a weekend retreat from a fast paced lifestyle and a tourism alternative to high-rise sterile hotel accommodations. Signs of the maturing industry are the increase in occupancy rates and number of national, state, and regional associations setting standards, and the number of travel publications, and guidebooks. The Tom Peters Public Library carries over a dozen Bed and Breakfast tourism guides and books.

We are interested in becoming part of this growing home-based business. We see this as an opportunity to invest in a large historic home, gain additional income and do what we enjoy most -- meeting people and acting as ambassadors for Munising. We see our role as an information resource for guests on events such as the two Food Festivals at the Lower Harbor Park, Limestone concerts, Munising Choral Society concerts, Pine Theatre performances, Rock the Arts, the Glacier Glide, the U.P. 200 Sled Dog Race or even the outhouse races in Trenary. And for those couples wanting a cozy, romantic evening we can just as easily retire quietly to our separate quarters.

The Victoria Bed & Breakfast Company is seeking $160,000 in financing at 8.5% interest over 20 years from a banking institution for the purchase of the property. Before any renovations, an independent appraisal company assessed the property at $260,000 in August, 1995.

An additional $85,000 line of credit at 9.5% interest over 5 years is being sought to cover start-up costs. Early renovations planned include adding a sprinkler system (required), two bathrooms, installing gas fireplaces, three new interior doors, a new entryway by the kitchen with a deck and stairs to the parking area, landscaping the front yard, wallpapering, painting and furnishing common and guest rooms.

We are investing $100,000 as a down payment for the property purchase. We have already invested $6,670 in start-up costs and have another $5,000 available for closing costs.

TRENDS AND INDUSTRY OUTLOOK

The Allen House in AuTrain is now operating at 80% occupancy after 5 years; Applewood Inn in Sault Ste. Marie managed 84% occupancy in their first year. In fact, they are selling because the business has been more successful (and time-consuming) than the simple retirement income they intended. The Winchester in Green Bay achieved 30% occupancy in their first year. The Holmes Estate in the small town of Calumet, surrounded by a dozen B&Bs, was at 15% occupancy in their first year.

In Munising, even with the loss of A.G. Reilberg, the lodging industry has continued to rise in the last four years and was up 5% in 1995 from the previous year during the tourism season. In our research and discussions with professionals, such as John Sims, Director of the Upper Peninsula Holiday, Travel & Recreation Association, and others mentioned in our management section, we've learned that the Bed and Breakfast business will continue to attract tourists and professionals looking for an escape from the fast-pace city life. In fact, all projections are that the industry will continue to prosper as more people select extended weekend "getaways" rather than week or longer vacations to farther destinations.

In a 1993 survey by The Michigan Traveler, 1,558,000 adult travelers stayed in Michigan. The Bed and Breakfast industry took in 8% of that figure representing 128,000 adults staying an average of 4.5 nights. In the Upper Peninsula, the Upper Peninsula Travel and Tourism Association received $179,037 (2% fee on receipts from participating businesses) for the months June to August in 1994-1995 in Munising. B&Bs, having the potential to receive 8% of the lodging industry, could therefore generate $716,000 during the summer.

The 1994 Midwest Region Industry Study by the Professional Association of Innkeepers International (PAII) and the 1988 Michigan Study listed the following guest demographics:

TARGET MARKET

Type of Guests:

Married	80%
Homeowners	82.2%
Professional occupation	36.4%
Executive occupation	10.9%
Administrative position	10.3%
Household income (median)	$73,000
Graduate degree	31.3%
College graduate	40.5%
Some college	21%
25 to 34 years old	24.3%
35 to 44 years old	23.2%
45 to 54 years old	29.5%

Primary purpose of the trip:

Tourists	31%
Special occasions	30%
Business travelers	15%
Visiting family	14%
Attending meetings	10%

Reasons for staying at a B&B:

Personal touch	80%
Charm of building	78%
Getaway	71%
Nicely decorated bedrooms	61%
Romance	61%
Alternative to a hotel	61%

Attributes which play an important part in selecting a B&B are:

Private bathrooms	54%
Full breakfasts	47%
Shoppers/dining	28 to 40%
Credit cards accepted	30%
Recreational activity	31%

Guests consider the following qualities very important after a B&B stay: warmth of innkeeper, 79.9%; private bath, 68.5%; breakfast, 63.3%; and owner-operated, 37.1%.

Activities participated in during the stay include: dining out, shopping, walking, and sightseeing. Inn guest couples spend $225.72 per day in the community.

Over 39% of the guests travel to the communities where the B&Bs are located for the primary, or only, purpose of staying in a B&B.

According to a 1994 PAII study and the 1988 Michigan Study cited above, 72% of B&B guests selected the B&B and made reservations before leaving home. Information sources which prompted B&B stays were as follows:

MARKETING PROMOTION

Returning guests	14%
Advertising paid	16%
Referrals from former guests	14%
Chamber of Commerce referrals	10%
Travel guide and books	9%
Drop in/Street traffic	5%
Other various	*4%
Automobile clubs	2%
Associations/Brochure	4%
Referrals from other inns	4%
Travel agent	1%
Media	1%
Reservation service	1%

* Public relations, word of mouth, unknown

In a 1990 Wisconsin study, B&B operators gave the highest effectiveness ratings to B&B directories and to the Chamber of Commerce. Telephone book listings and newspaper advertisements are considered relatively ineffective. At the recent Upper Peninsula B&B Conference, surveyed innkeepers concurred with the Wisconsin results in that most of their new business was received from the Chamber of Commerce and the state association.

Based on the above information, our marketing efforts will be in the following direction:

Become members of the Munising Chamber of Commerce, Lake-to-Lake Michigan Bed & Breakfast Association, Upper Peninsula Bed & Breakfast Association, Upper Peninsula Tourist & Travel Association, Downtown Marketing Authority and AAA.

Build a home page on the Internet: several are already in place, which take reservations directly over the computer. The Lake-to-Lake Michigan Bed & Breakfast Association's 1996 directory soon will be on-line as well, in which we will be listed promptly upon joining. Be listed in the State of Michigan's Travel Bureau's database.

Compile a Press Kit for B&B guidebooks, magazines, and media: Victoria has already managed to receive four front page articles, 3 editorials, and several letters to the editor. From that publicity, we have received inquires from lower Michigan and Colorado about our opening date.

Design an attractive brochure for distribution at tourist and information centers, the new marina, restaurants, downtown stores, appropriate public events, recreation and sporting shows, antique dealers, funeral homes, the hospital, the college and organizations. Be listed in historic walking tour brochure at the museum.

Mail brochures to potential customers from the newspaper i.e. engagements, reunions etc., family, friends and old classmates from downstate. Each family member is being asked to forward the brochure to their place of business newsletter.

Establish cross promotion and joint marketing with other B&Bs in the Upper Peninsula, Lower Peninsula, Wisconsin, Minnesota, and Canada.

Place advertisements for "Getaway Weekends" in the Green Bay newspaper. Other advertising will be in the Great Lake Superior Circle Tour magazine and on Public Radio 90.

Open Victoria for small community meetings, luncheons and retreats.
Print gift certificates for benefits and business cards for distribution at local community and business functions.

Although the business traveler is not our primary market, several state and federal employees and private consultants that routinely travel to Munising, some for pleasure as well as business, have expressed an interest in making our B&B their regular lodging choice.

April 17, 1996

Ann Murray
Michigan State University
Upper Peninsula Extension
8653 Howell Rd.
Munising, MI 49862

To: Whom it may concern
From: Ann Murray, District Extension Agent
               Community and Economic Development
Subject: Support for Alexandria & James Wolfsted

In my professional opinion, a bed & breakfast operation within the city limits of Munising that is properly marketed and managed, has the potential of being a successful operation. If the bed & breakfast is located in a historic district, has a unique setting, charm, and knowledgeable, gracious hosts, the inns do well.

In the nine years that I have been employed with MSU, we have counseled over thirty entrepreneurs as they worked through the maze of starting a Bed and Breakfast business. There have been few who have been as thorough and committed as James & Alexandria. I am confident that they will be successful hosts.

Most of the bed & breakfast operations in Michigan provide supplemental income for families. Only in a few cases do the inns provide the sole income and that only occurs where there are seven or more rentals in the property. We do have a number of inns in the Upper Peninsula that are providing significant income for their proprietors.

Munising has established itself with tourists for a number of years. Requests have been received through the Munising Area Chamber of Commerce and the Munising Convention & Visitor's Bureau for a bed & breakfast within the city. Being a university community with a regional medical center, will contribute to the clientele who frequent bed & breakfast establishments. Additionally, the new marina in the lower harbor is a source for potential guests. Having an asset such as Victoria within walking distance of all the major services in our community should serve James & Alexandria well as they market the business.

The bed & breakfast owners in the Upper Peninsula have become a very active, and well connected group. They have actually formed an association recently and continue to network, share leads, and help one another. This will also work to the Wolfsted's advantage.

If I can provide any additional information, please don't hesitate to contact me.

FINANCIAL DATA

Start Up Costs

Paid for:

Conditional Use Permit	$100.00
Building Inspection	$500.00
Attorney Fees	$2,000.00
Office Equipment	$3,500.00
Marketing Research	$570.00
Total Paid	$6,670.00

1	Renovation	$17,000.00
2	Bathroom Equipment	$6,000.00
3	Gas Fireplace installations	$2,500.00
4	Business Sign	$400.00
5	Bank Charge Equipment	$300.00
6	Brochures	$1,000.00
7	Furniture	$13,000.00
8	Safety Equipment	$15,500.00
9	Legal Fees	$500.00
10	Kitchen Items	$1,000.00
11	Office Equipment	$500.00
12	Telephone	$350.00
13	Towels & Linen	$1,000.00
14	Operating Capital	$12,000.00
Sub-total		$71,050.00
20% Contingency		$14,210.00
Total Start-up Costs		$85,260.00

Notes:

1 *covers: new water heater, new entry and staircase, 2 bathrooms, 2 bathroom doorways, spring load doors, seal transoms, kitchen doorway, restore front door*
2 *covers: two 5-foot steam showers, 2 toilets*
3 *covers: installation of two gas fireplaces on the second floor*
4 *grouted wood front sign*
7 *three bedroom sets, kitchen and living rooms, 2 televisions*
8 *sprinker system w/ 2-foot supply line, fire estinquishers*
9 *set-up corporation*
10 *china, silverware, pots & pans, mixer*
11 *fax machine, adding machine*
12 *set-up and purchase 2 phones with 2 touch tone lines*
13 *sheets, towels, pillows, bedspreads*
14 *first three months of operation*

Financial Needs:

Purchase Price	$260,000.00
Down Payment	$100,000.00
Closing Costs	$5,000.00
Start-up Costs	$85,000.00
TOTAL	**$190,000.00**

B&B Income:

4 rooms @ $105 each

= $420 x 365 days @ 100% occupancy equals		$153,300.00
@20% occupancy	1st year projection	$30,660.00

5 rooms @ $105 each @ 100% occupancy equals		$191,625.00
@30% occupancy	2nd year projection	$57,487.50

5 rooms @ $115 each @ 100% occupancy equals		$209,875.00
@40% occupancy	3rd year projection	$83,950.00

Cash Flow Projection:

	1st Year	**2nd Year**	**3rd Year**
Income	$30,660.00	$57,487.50	$83,950.00
Expenses	$40,661.95	$56,190.55	$48,000.00
	$(10,001.95)	$1,296.95	$35,950.00

To break even:

1st year expenses divided by 100% income =	26.52%	Occupancy Needed
2nd year expenses divided by 100% income =	29.32%	Occupancy Needed
3rd year expenses divided by 100% income =	22.87%	Occupancy Needed

Note: By the third year over $50,000 is built up in home equity

First Year Cash Flow Projection

	June, 1996	July	August	September	October	November
INCOME						
Beginning Cash on Hand	$80,000.00	$9,904.76	$8,389.84	$3,541.50	$4,264.07	$4,383.71
Bed & Breakfast Stays(A)	$2,555.00	$2,555.00	$2,555.00	$2,555.00	$2,555.00	$2,555.00
New Loans(B)	$245,000.00	$245,000.00				
Sale of 114 E. Kaye Property	$25,000.00	$25,000.00				
Total Cash (1)	**$350,000.00**	**$9,904.76**	**$10,944.84**	**$6,096.50**	**$6,819.07**	**$6,938.71**
EXPENSES						
B & B Business Expenses						
Real Estate Purchases	$260,000.00	$260,000.00				
Closing Costs	$5,000.00	$5,000.00				
Remodeling	$20,000.00	$20,000.00				
Equipment Purchases	$23,500.00	$23,500.00				
Furniture Purchases	$20,000.00	$20,000.00				
Advertising(D)	$1,500.00	$25.00	$25.00	$85.00	$10.00	$10.00
Dues/Subscriptions(E)	$40.00	$130.00	$70.00	$20.00	$11.50	$40.00
Accounting & Legal	$500.00	$200.00	$200.00	$900.00		
Bank Card Charges(F)	$300.00	$0.00	$51.10	$51.10	$51.10	$51.10
Travel/Entertainment*	$90.00	$90.00	$90.00	$90.00	$360.00	
Telephone*	$350.00	$100.00	$100.00	$100.00	$100.00	$100.00
Utilities(G)	$372.59	$379.07	$336.39	$325.48	$326.95	$375.44
Maintenance*	$100.00	$100.00	$100.00	$100.00	$1,500.00	$100.00
Housekeeping Supplies*	$60.00	$100.00	$90.00	$75.00	$55.00	$50.00
Other(H)	$10,000.00	$10,000.00				
Food*	$55.00	$55.00	$55.00	$55.00	$55.00	$55.00
Outside Services(I)	$100.00	$100.00				
Office Supplies*	$500.00	$32.00	$32.00	$32.00	$32.00	$32.00
Cable	$30.00	$30.00	$30.00	$30.00	$30.00	$30.00
Insurance	$431.00	$211.46	$211.46	$211.46	$211.46	$211.46
Property Taxes	$5,500.00	$838.58	$6,338.58			
Loan	$3,360.74	$3,360.74	$3,360.74	$3,360.74	$3,360.74	$3,360.74
Total Cash Expense(2)	**$342,683.59**	**$4,338.27**	**$9,891.69**	**$4,555.78**	**$5,892.25**	**$4,485.74**
Other:						
Personal Income	$3,138.35	$3,138.35	$3,138.35	$3,138.35	$3,906.89	$3,186.89
Personal Expenses	$550.00	$315.00	$650.00	$415.00	$450.00	$415.00
Sub-Total	$2,588.35	$2,823.35	$2,488.35	$2,723.35	$3,456.89	$2,771.89
Cash Balance Month End	**$9,904.76**	**$8,389.84**	**$3,541.50**	**$4,264.07**	**$4,383.71**	**$5,224.86**

NOTES: A) 4 rooms @ $105, 20% Occupancy

B) $160,000 Primary Mortgage @ 8.5%, 15Yr., and $85,000 Second Loan @ 9.5%, 5Yr.

* Costs from "Developing a Bed & Breakfast Business Plan", 1989, North Central Regional Extension Publication 273, Appendix O

D) Costs based on above study and Public Radio Sponsors

E) Chamber of Commerce and Lake to Lake B&B dues, 2 magazines

F) 2% of B & B Income, assumes 100% credit card use by customers

G) Previous owner's actual costs from 11/94 to 10/95

H) linens, blankets, towels and outfit kitchen

I) Windows cleaned

December	January, 1997	February	March	April	May	Total
$5,224.86	$6,137.54	$6,834.79	$6,671.23	$7,577.21	$7,915.79	$80,000.00
$2,555.00	$2,555.00	$2,555.00	$2,555.00	$25,550.00		
$7,779.86	**$8,692.54**	**$9,389.79**	**$9,226.23**	**$10,132.21**	**$10,470.79**	**$375,550.00**

$10.00	$10.00	$10.00	$90.00	$90.00	$90.00	$1,955.00
$40.00	$351.50					
$51.10	$51.10	$51.10	$51.10	$51.10	$51.10	$811.00
$100.00	$100.00	$100.00	$100.00	$100.00	$100.00	$1,450.00
$387.41	$423.34	$446.57	$440.61	$393.01	$357.54	$4,564.40
$100.00	$100.00	$100.00	$100.00	$100.00	$100.00	$2,600.00
$30.00	$6.00	$20.00	$40.00	$50.00	$50.00	$626.00
$55.00	$55.00	$55.00	$55.00	$550.00		
$32.00	$32.00	$32.00	$32.00	$32.00	$32.00	$852.00
$30.00	$30.00	$30.00	$30.00	$30.00	$30.00	$360.00
$211.46	$211.46	$211.46	$211.46	$211.46	$211.46	$2,757.06
$3,360.74	$3,360.74	$3,360.74	$3,360.74	$3,360.74	$36,968.14	
$4,379.21	**$4,619.64**	**$5,455.45**	**$4,510.91**	**$4,603.31**	**$4,627.84**	**$400,043.68**
$3,186.89	$3,186.89	$3,186.89	$3,186.89	$3,186.89	$3,186.89	$38,768.52
$450.00	$425.00	$450.00	$325.00	$800.00	$425.00	$5,670.00
$2,736.89	$2,761.89	$2,736.89	$2,861.89	$2,386.89	$2,761.89	$33,098.52
$6,137.54	**$6,834.79**	**$6,671.23**	**$7,577.21**	**$7,915.79**	**$8,604.84**	**$8,604.84**

Second Year Cash Flow Projection

	June, 1997	July	August	September	October
INCOME					
Beginning Cash on Hand	$8,604.84	$161.26	$3,087.23	$203.19	$2,864.15
Bed & Breakfast Stays (A)	$4,790.63	$4,790.63	$4,790.63	$4,790.63	$4,790.63
Total Cash (1)	**$13,395.47**	**$4,951.89**	**$7,877.85**	**$4,993.81**	**$7,654.78**
EXPENSES					
B & B Business Expenses					
Remodeling	$5,000.00				
Equipment Purchases					
Furniture Purchases	$2,000.00				
Advertising	$1,500.00	$50.00	$25.00	$85.00	$10.00
Dues/Subscriptions				$130.00	$70.00
Accounting & Legal					
Bank Card Charges	$95.81	$95.81	$95.81	$95.81	$95.81
Travel/Entertainment					$90.00
Telephone	$150.00	$150.00	$150.00	$150.00	$150.00
Utilities	$400.00	$400.00	$400.00	$400.00	$400.00
Maintenance	$150.00	$150.00	$150.00	$150.00	$1,500.00
Housekeeping Supplies	$100.00	$100.00	$100.00	$100.00	$100.00
Food	$100.00	$100.00	$100.00	$100.00	$100.00
Linens/Towels/Blankets	$1,000.00				
Office Supplies	$1,500.00	$35.00	$35.00	$35.00	$35.00
Cable	$35.00	$35.00	$35.00	$35.00	$35.00
Insurance	$431.00	$211.46	$211.46	$211.46	$211.46
Property Taxes			$5,500.00		
Loan	$3,360.74	$3,360.74	$3,360.74	$3,360.74	$3,360.74
Total Cash Expense (2)	**$15,822.55**	**$4,688.01**	**$10,163.01**	**$4,853.01**	**$6,158.01**
Other:					
Personal Income	$3,138.35	$3,138.35	$3,138.35	$3,138.35	$3,906.89
Personal Expenses	$550.00	$315.00	$650.00	$415.00	$450.00
Sub-Total	$2,588.35	$2,823.35	$2,488.35	$2,723.35	$3,456.89
Cash Balance End of Month (1-2)	**$161.26**	**$3,087.23**	**$203.19**	**$2,864.15**	**$4,953.65**

NOTES: A) 5 rooms @ $105, 30% Occupancy

November	December	January, 1998	February	March	April	May	Total
$4,953.65	$7,468.16	$10,247.66	$12,702.16	$14,118.08	$17,017.59	$19,152.09	$8,604.84
$4,790.63	$4,790.63	$4,790.63	$4,790.63	$4,790.63	$4,790.63	$4,790.63	$57,487.50
$9,744.28	**$12,258.78**	**$15,038.28**	**$17,492.79**	**$18,908.71**	**$21,808.21**	**$23,942.71**	**$66,092.34**
							$5,000.00
							$0.00
							$2,000.00
$10.00	$10.00	$10.00	$10.00	$90.00	$90.00	$90.00	$1,980.00
$100.00	$100.00	$100.00			$40.00		$540.00
		$300.00	$300.00				$600.00
$95.81	$95.81	$95.81	$95.81	$95.81	$95.81	$95.81	$1,149.75
$300.00			$300.00		$300.00	$300.00	$1,290.00
$150.00	$150.00	$150.00	$150.00	$150.00	$150.00	$150.00	$1,800.00
$400.00	$400.00	$450.00	$450.00	$450.00	$400.00	$400.00	$4,950.00
$150.00	$150.00	$150.00	$150.00	$150.00	$150.00	$150.00	$3,150.00
$100.00	$100.00	$100.00	$75.00	$75.00	$75.00	$75.00	$1,100.00
$100.00	$100.00	$100.00	$100.00	$100.00	$100.00	$100.00	$1,200.00
						$100.00	$1,100.00
$35.00	$35.00	$35.00	$35.00	$35.00	$35.00	$35.00	$1,885.00
$35.00	$35.00	$35.00	$35.00	$35.00	$35.00	$35.00	$420.00
$211.46	$211.46	$211.46	$211.46	$211.46	$211.46	$211.46	$2,757.06
			$838.58				$6,338.58
$3,360.74	$3,360.74	$3,360.74	$3,360.74	$3,360.74	$3,360.74	$3,360.74	$40,328.88
$5,048.01	**$4,748.01**	**$5,098.01**	**$6,111.59**	**$4,753.01**	**$5,043.01**	**$5,103.01**	**$77,589.27**
$3,186.89	$3,186.89	$3,186.89	$3,186.89	$3,186.89	$3,186.89	$3,186.89	$38,768.52
$415.00	$450.00	$425.00	$450.00	$325.00	$800.00	$425.00	$5,670.00
$2,771.89	$2,736.89	$2,761.89	$2,736.89	$2,861.89	$2,386.89	$2,761.89	$33,098.52
$7,468.16	**$10,247.66**	**$12,702.16**	**$14,118.08**	**$17,017.59**	**$19,152.09**	**$21,601.59**	**$21,601.59**

Third Year Cash Flow Projection

	June, 1998	July	August	September	October
INCOME					
Beginning Cash on Hand	$21,601.59	$16,956.64	$20,115.22	$17,298.81	$20,292.40
Bed & Breakfast Stays (A)	$6,995.83	$6,995.83	$6,995.83	$6,995.83	$6,995.83
Total Cash (1)	**$28,597.42**	**$23,952.47**	**$27,111.06**	**$24,294.64**	**$27,288.23**
EXPENSES					
B & B Business Expenses					
Remodeling					
Equipment Purchases	$1,500.00				
Furniture Purchases	$1,500.00				
Advertising	$1,500.00	$50.00	$25.00	$85.00	$10.00
Dues/Subscriptions	$100.00			$130.00	$70.00
Accounting & Legal					
Bank Card Charges	$139.92	$139.92	$139.92	$139.92	$139.92
Travel/Entertainment					$90.00
Telephone	$150.00	$150.00	$150.00	$150.00	$150.00
Utilities	$500.00	$500.00	$500.00	$500.00	$500.00
Maintenance	$200.00	$200.00	$200.00	$200.00	$1,500.00
Housekeeping Supplies	$150.00	$150.00	$150.00	$150.00	$150.00
Food	$150.00	$150.00	$150.00	$150.00	$150.00
Linens/Towels/Blankets	$1,000.00				
Office Supplies	$1,500.00	$35.00	$35.00	$35.00	$35.00
Cable	$35.00	$35.00	$35.00	$35.00	$35.00
Insurance	$1,000.00	$211.46	$211.46	$211.46	$211.46
Property Taxes			$6,000.00		
Loan	$3,815.87	$3,815.87	$3,815.87	$3,815.87	$3,815.87
Total Cash Expense (2)	**$13,240.79**	**$5,437.25**	**$11,412.25**	**$5,602.25**	**$6,857.25**
Other:					
Personal Income	$2,600.00	$2,600.00	$2,600.00	$2,600.00	$2,600.00
Personal Expenses	$1,000.00	$1,000.00	$1,000.00	$1,000.00	$1,000.00
Sub-Total	$1,600.00	$1,600.00	$1,600.00	$1,600.00	$1,600.00
Cash Balance Month End (1-2)	**$16,956.64**	**$20,115.22**	**$17,298.81**	**$20,292.40**	**$22,030.98**

A) 5 rooms @ $115, 40% Occupancy

November	December	January, 1999	February	March	April	May	Total
$22,030.98	$24,829.57	$27,928.16	$30,726.74	$32,486.75	$35,605.34	$38,383.92	$21,601.59
$6,995.83	$6,995.83	$6,995.83	$6,995.83	$6,995.83	$6,995.83	$6,995.83	$83,950.00
$29,026.82	**$31,825.40**	**$34,923.99**	**$37,722.58**	**$39,482.58**	**$42,601.17**	**$45,379.76**	**$105,551.59**
							$0.00
							$1,500.00
							$1,500.00
$10.00	$10.00	$10.00	$10.00	$90.00	$90.00	$90.00	$1,980.00
$100.00	$100.00	$100.00			$40.00		$640.00
		$300.00	$300.00				$600.00
$139.92	$139.92	$139.92	$139.92	$139.92	$139.92	$139.92	$1,679.00
$300.00			$300.00		$300.00	$300.00	$1,290.00
$150.00	$150.00	$150.00	$150.00	$150.00	$150.00	$150.00	$1,800.00
$500.00	$500.00	$500.00	$500.00	$500.00	$500.00	$500.00	$6,000.00
$200.00	$200.00	$200.00	$200.00	$200.00	$200.00	$200.00	$3,700.00
$150.00	$150.00	$150.00	$150.00	$150.00	$150.00	$150.00	$1,800.00
$150.00	$150.00	$150.00	$150.00	$150.00	$150.00	$150.00	$1,800.00
							$1,000.00
$35.00	$35.00	$35.00	$35.00	$35.00	$35.00	$35.00	$1,885.00
$35.00	$35.00	$35.00	$35.00	$35.00	$35.00	$35.00	$420.00
$211.46	$211.46	$211.46	$211.46	$211.46	$211.46	$211.46	$3,326.06
			$838.58				$6,838.58
$3,815.87	$3,815.87	$3,815.87	$3,815.87	$3,815.87	$3,815.87	$3,815.87	$45,790.44
$5,797.25	**$5,497.25**	**$5,797.25**	**$6,835.83**	**$5,477.25**	**$5,817.25**	**$5,777.25**	**$83,549.08**
$2,600.00	$2,600.00	$2,600.00	$2,600.00	$2,600.00	$2,600.00	$2,600.00	$31,200.00
$1,000.00	$1,000.00	$1,000.00	$1,000.00	$1,000.00	$1,000.00	$1,000.00	$12,000.00
$1,600.00	$1,600.00	$1,600.00	$1,600.00	$1,600.00	$1,600.00	$1,600.00	$19,200.00
$24,829.57	**$27,928.16**	**$30,726.74**	**$32,486.75**	**$35,605.34**	**$38,383.92**	**$41,202.51**	**$41,202.51**

Income Projection Year One - 1996 & 1997

	June	July	August	September	October
First Year: 4 rooms @ $105 each, 20% Occupancy Rate					
Personal Income(James' deductions cover Alexandria's taxes)					
James' Net Income	$2,538.35	$2,538.35	$2,538.35	$2,538.35	$3,306.89
Alexandria's Gross Income	$600.00	$600.00	$600.00	$600.00	$600.00
Total take-home income	$3,138.35	$3,138.35	$3,138.35	$3,138.35	$3,906.89
Personal Expenses (all other expenses are covered in the B&B operation)					
Auto upkeep	$300.00	$100.00	$400.00	$200.00	$200.00
Pet upkeep	$50.00	$15.00	$50.00	$15.00	$50.00
Food	$200.00	$200.00	$200.00	$200.00	$200.00
Total personal expenses	$550.00	$315.00	$650.00	$415.00	$450.00
PERSONAL SURPLUS	**$2,588.35**	**$2,823.35**	**$2,488.35**	**$2,723.35**	**$3,456.89**
B&B Income					
Percent Occupancy			45	25	25
Bed & Breakfast Stays	$0.00	$0.00	$5,859.00	$3,255.00	$3,255.00
Total Income	**$2,588.35**	**$2,823.35**	**$8,347.35**	**$5,978.35**	**$6,711.89**
Variable Expenses					
1 Wages	$0.00	$0.00	$0.00	$0.00	$0.00
2 Advertising		$25.00	$25.00	$85.00	$10.00
3 Dues/Subscriptions		$40.00		$130.00	$70.00
4 Bank Card Charges		$0.00	$117.18	$65.10	$65.10
5 Travel/Entertainment*					$90.00
6 Telephone*		$100.00	$100.00	$100.00	$100.00
7 Utilities	$372.59	$379.07	$336.39	$325.48	$326.95
8 Maintenance*		$100.00	$100.00	$100.00	$1,500.00
9 Housekeeping Supplies*	$60.00	$100.00	$90.00	$75.00	$55.00
10 Food*			$55.00	$55.00	$55.00
11 Linens/blankets/towels					
12 Office Supplies*		$32.00	$32.00	$32.00	$32.00
13 Cable		$30.00	$30.00	$30.00	$30.00
Sub-Total	$432.59	$806.07	$885.57	$997.58	$2,334.05
Fixed Expenses					
Accounting & Legal					
Insurance	$431.00	$211.46	$211.46	$211.46	$211.46
Property Taxes			$5,500.00		
Mortgage (A)	$1,133.33	$1,130.20	$1,127.05	$1,123.87	$1,120.67
Loan (B)	$562.53	$552.85	$543.09	$533.26	$523.35
Sub-Total	$2,126.86	$1,894.51	$7,381.60	$1,868.59	$1,855.48
Total Expenses	$2,559.45	$2,700.58	$8,267.17	$2,866.17	$4,189.53
Net Profit (Loss)	**$28.90**	**$122.77**	**$80.18**	**$3,112.18**	**$2,522.36**

	November	December	January	February	March	April	May	First Year Total
	$2,586.89	$2,586.89	$2,586.89	$2,586.89	$2,586.89	$2,586.89	$2,586.89	$31,568.52
	$600.00	$600.00	$600.00	$600.00	$600.00	$600.00	$600.00	$7,200.00
	$3,186.89	$3,186.89	$3,186.89	$3,186.89	$3,186.89	$3,186.89	$3,186.89	**$38,768.52**
	$200.00	$200.00	$200.00	$200.00	$100.00	$500.00	$200.00	$2,800.00
	$15.00	$50.00	$25.00	$50.00	$25.00	$100.00	$25.00	$470.00
	$200.00	$200.00	$200.00	$200.00	$200.00	$200.00	$200.00	$2,400.00
	$415.00	$450.00	$425.00	$450.00	$325.00	$800.00	$425.00	**$5,670.00**
	$2,771.89	**$2,736.89**	**$2,761.89**	**$2,736.89**	**$2,861.89**	**$2,386.89**	**$2,761.89**	**$33,098.52**
	10	10	15	10	15	15	20	16
	$1,302.00	$1,302.00	$1,953.00	$1,302.00	$1,953.00	$1,953.00	$2,604.00	**$24,738.00**
	$4,073.89	**$4,038.89**	**$4,714.89**	**$4,038.89**	**$4,814.89**	**$4,339.89**	**$5,365.89**	**$57,836.52**
	$0.00	$0.00	$0.00	$0.00	$0.00	$0.00	$0.00	$0.00
	$10.00	$10.00	$10.00	$10.00	$90.00	$90.00	$90.00	$455.00
	$20.00	$11.50	$40.00			$40.00		$351.50
	$26.04	$26.04	$39.06	$26.04	$39.06	$39.06	$52.08	$494.76
	$90.00					$90.00	$90.00	$360.00
	$100.00	$100.00	$100.00	$100.00	$100.00	$100.00	$100.00	$1,100.00
	$375.44	$387.41	$423.34	$446.57	$440.61	$393.01	$357.54	$4,564.40
	$100.00	$100.00	$100.00	$100.00	$100.00	$100.00	$100.00	$2,500.00
	$50.00	$30.00	$6.00	$20.00	$40.00	$50.00	$50.00	$626.00
	$55.00	$55.00	$55.00	$55.00	$55.00	$55.00	$55.00	$550.00
								$0.00
	$32.00	$32.00	$32.00	$32.00	$32.00	$32.00	$32.00	$352.00
	$30.00	$30.00	$30.00	$30.00	$30.00	$30.00	$30.00	$330.00
	$888.48	$781.95	$835.40	$819.61	$926.67	$1,019.07	$956.62	$11,683.66
			$200.00	$200.00				$400.00
	$211.46	$211.46	$211.46	$211.46	$211.46	$211.46	$211.46	$2,757.06
				$838.58				$6,338.58
	$1,117.45	$1,114.20	$1,110.93	$1,107.64	$1,104.33	$1,100.99	$1,097.63	$13,388.29
	$513.36	$503.29	$493.14	$482.92	$472.61	$462.22	$451.74	$6,094.36
	$1,842.27	$1,828.95	$2,015.53	$2,840.60	$1,788.40	$1,774.67	$1,760.83	$28,978.29
	$2,730.75	$2,610.90	$2,850.93	$3,660.21	$2,715.07	$2,793.74	$2,717.45	$40,661.95
	$1,343.14	**$1,427.99**	**$1,863.96**	**$378.68**	**$2,099.82**	**$1,546.15**	**$2,648.44**	**$17,174.57**

...continued

A) $160,000 @ 8.5%, 15 Yr.
B) $85,000 @ 9.5%, 5 Yr.

NOTES FOR VARIABLE EXPENSES

* Costs from "Developing a Bed & Breakfast Business Plan", 1989,
 North Central Regional Extension Publication 273, Appendix O
2. Costs based on above study and Public Radio Sponsors
3. Chamber of Commerce and Lake to Lake B&B dues, 2 magazines
4. 2% of B & B Income, assumes 100% credit card use by customers
7. Previous owner's actual costs from 11/94 to 10/95
11. Windows cleaned

Balance Sheet

ASSETS:

<u>Cash on Hand</u>

Wolfsted's Joint Savings: Munising First Federal Credit Union	$95,062.18
Wolfsted's Joint Checking Munising First Federal Credit Union	$52.15
James' Savings: MFC First National Bank	$507.47
James' Savings: State Employees Credit Union	$4,517.97
James' Checking: State Employees Credit Union	$39.50
Clean For A Day Savings: MFC First National Bank	$4,745.30
Clean For A Day Checking: MFC First National Bank	$344.43
Subtotal	$105,269.00
Newly purchased Pentium computer w/ printer	$3,500.00
1991 SAAB 900S 4 Door	$12,250.00
1984 Honda Accord Hatchback 3 Door	$1,650.00
Cash Value - James' Life Ins. Policy John Hancock	$2,567.68
James' Deferred Comp. - Putnam Investments (as of 3/31/96)	$29,176.12
James' Deferred Comp. - Other (457) (Estimated as of 4/18/96)	$30,780.00
Market Value on 825 N. Watson, Munising	$82,000.00
TOTAL ASSETS	**$267,192.80**

LIABILITIES:

MFC First National Mortgage on 825 N. Watson	$52,342.00
TOTAL LIABILITIES	**$52,342.00**
BALANCE	**$214,850.80**

Bottled Water Manufacturer

BUSINESS PLAN

SPARKLING HORIZON BOTTLED WATER

315 Fauborg
Wichita, KS 67207

April 1995

Sparkling Horizon Bottled Water's business plan contains valuable financial information. Check out the Projected Cash Flow tables for the first three years of operation. The plan's owner has also included a Projected Balance Sheet and a Projected Income Statement, both of which also contain helpful information for anyone interested in starting a bottled water business.

- EXECUTIVE SUMMARY

- INDUSTRY ANALYSIS

- MARKET OVERVIEW

- BUSINESS DESCRIPTION

- PRODUCT DESCRIPTION

- MARKETING STRATEGY

- OPERATING PLAN

- MANAGEMENT AND STAFFING

- FUNDS NEEDED AND THEIR USES

- FINANCIAL STATEMENTS

EXECUTIVE SUMMARY

Demand for bottled drinking water has been growing rapidly since the 1980s, increasing nearly 400% in the last decade according to the Council of Bottled Water Manufacturers, as a result of declining consumer confidence in the safety and quality of municipal water supplies.

Bottled Drinking Water

To take advantage of this expanding market for drinking water, Sparkling Horizon Bottled Water has been established to provide home and office delivery of bottled water to the Wichita area. After months of extensive industry and market research, the company has developed a solid business plan to enter the market for bottled water.

Sparkling Horizon will generate revenue as a result of the rental and sale of water coolers, as well as for the delivery of the three types of water: pure spring water, distilled drinking water, and purified drinking water in 5-gallon bottles.

Management Team

Chantal Fuzet is the owner and president of Sparkling Horizon, bringing years of experience in water bottling and delivery to the company. Her family has operated a thriving bottled water business in Paris for over 15 years, which she helped to run.

The company has applied for certification as a woman-owned business, which is in progress.

Two key managers have been retained to assist in the operation and expansion of the company: Jean Polsky will serve as the company's Operations Manager, and Robert Blanc will be the Route Driver, an extremely important position as the primary customer contact. In addition, two commission sales associates will be hired to secure new customers.

Manufacturing

Sparkling Horizon Bottled Water will be bottled by Rue Bottling of Decatur, Illinois, who will fill the 5-gallon bottles and store them until they are needed by Sparkling Horizon, as well as accepting empty bottles, cleaning them, and refilling them for reuse.

By using free trials to entice consumers to install their water coolers, Sparkling Horizon will quickly establish a customer base. The free trial offer will be advertised through a variety of media, and will be promoted at trade shows and mall events.

The marketing budget of $25,000 will enable the company to quickly capture a large percent of the potential market. All funding for marketing activities will be generated from the business as earnings from operations, not from start-up capital, and is based on a standard 5% of first-year sales.

Projected Income Statement	1995	1996	1997	1999	2000
Revenues	247,928	322,721	400,992	453,092	509,801
COGS	95,760	105,336	115,870	127,455	140,003
Operating Expenses	96,250	102,104	108,379	115,111	122,342
Net Income	50,782	110,468	172,570	207,046	244,340

INDUSTRY ANALYSIS

The market for bottled drinking water has been growing rapidly since the 1980s, increasing nearly 400% in the last decade according to the Council of Bottled Water Manufacturers, as a result of declining consumer confidence in the safety and quality of municipal water supplies. This nationwide trend is also evident in the Greater Wichita area, where Sparkling Horizon intends to operate.

In response, individuals and businesses are purchasing bottled drinking water for use in their homes and offices. Free of contaminants and government-monitored, bottled waters are derived from protected springs or wells or are produced by purifying and processing water from public water supplies. Consumer demand for bottled water is expected to continue to increase, as water supplies worldwide are deemed undrinkable or unhealthy.

According to a survey conducted by E-Works in 1988, more than 60% of consumers questioned about their purchase of bottled waters claimed "taste" was the primary reason for buying bottled water. Other reasons cited were safety and concerns about "too many chemicals in tap water."

Growth Rate

The bottled water industry as a whole has been growing at a rate of 12-15% annually since the mid-1980s. Bottled water sales increased 15.8% from February 1993 to February 1994, indicating a market rebound from the single digit growth of the late 1980s. From 1990-1995, demand for home delivery of bottled water is expected to be approximately 10.2%, with commercial distribution growing at a rate of 8.5% per year, according to the *Report on World Bottled Water, 1991*.

Industry Size

By far, the most popular type of water is non-sparkling water; in 1990 sales of non-sparkling water were $1,489,000,000, according to the *Report on World Bottled Water Manufacturing, 1991*. Total bottled water sales were $2,222,000,000, including both domestic sparkling and imported drinking waters.

Total sales of bottled water increased by more than 13% from 1989 to 1990, and have doubled in the last five years.

In terms of gallons sold, there were 1,753,300,000 gallons of non-sparkling water sold in the U.S. alone during 1990, with that number increasing to approximately.

Consumption

Per capita consumption of bottled water in the U.S. is also increasing dramatically, rising from 4.5 gallons per person in 1985 to 8.0 gallons per person just five years later, in 1990.

Approximately 1 out of every 6 households currently consumes non-sparkling bottled water as a source of drinking water. In addition, only 1% of the water being brought into a household is used for drinking; the rest is used for washing, bathing, etc.

Delivery of Water

The Council of Bottled Water Manufacturers divides the distribution channels for bottled water into: retail grocery, commercial delivery, home delivery, restaurant purchase, and vending.

While retail purchase accounts for the largest percentage of bottled water purchases (41.5%), 21.3% of sales are made through commercial delivery of water and 21.4% are through home delivery sales. The percentage of the industry that relies on water deliveries for its water is 42.7%, the largest percentage of all.

Cost

In the U.S., the average price for a 5-gallon delivered bottle of water is $5.29. An informal poll of local Wichita distributors showed that the average price in the area was also approximately $5.00 per bottle, which is what Sparkling Horizon intends to charge.

After water and delivery costs of $1.80, each bottle generates $3.49 in profit per unit for the company.

Sparkling Horizon will purchase coolers at a cost of $202.00 and rent them to customers for a fee of $10.00 per month. In just 21 months, each rented cooler will be paid for and generating profit long-term for the company.

Suppliers

The Council of Bottled Water Manufacturers reports that there are approximately 430 bottling facilities in the U.S., producing more than 700 different brand labels.

MARKET OVERVIEW

Following the devastating floods of 1993, water supplies in the Wichita area are still suspect, leading many residents to turn to bottled water for health reasons. However, even before the massive flooding, demand for bottled drinking water was growing.

Potential Customers

Because delivered bottled water is relatively inexpensive, virtually any household can afford to have a water cooler in their home.

The cost to rent a cooler is $10 per month, and an average household drinks 20 gallons per month (4-5 bottles), with a total monthly cost of approximately $30.

Size of the Market

The size of the non-sparkling bottled water market for the Wichita area is approximately 16,871,019 gallons per year, assuming a population size of 2,444,099 in the Wichita area (according to the 1990 Census).

The value of the local water market is approximately $13,177,220, as of 1990.

Competition

There are currently 13 bottled water distributors listed in the Wichita Yellow Pages, however only 7 companies are actively engaged in home and office delivery of drinking water. The other 6 companies are equipment sales representatives.

The 3 largest competitors are:

- Crystal Water
- Rain Man Water
- Hello! Water

However, these firms, in total, control just 5% of the potential market for bottled water, according to the local Small Business Administration office. In fact, all have stated by phone that they constantly have more orders for coolers and water delivery than they can handle, indicating strong demand for bottled water that has overrun the capacity of companies already in the market.

BUSINESS DESCRIPTION

Sparkling Horizon Bottled Water is a regional distributor of bottled waters for use in conjunction with rented company water coolers.

Corporate Structure

Sparkling Horizon Bottled Water was established in 1995 as a Kansas corporation. Chantal Fuzet owns 100% of the stock of the company.

Name

The trade name Sparkling Horizon is in the process of being registered, and the product logo is being finalized for imprinting on the bottles.

Operations

Spring, distilled, and purified drinking waters will be bottled by a Southern Illinois bottler who will fill the 5-gallon bottles labeled with the Sparkling Horizon logo. The refillable bottles will be collected from customers when empty and returned to the bottler bi-weekly for cleaning and refilling.

Personal Investment

Chantal Fuzet has already invested over $15,000 of her personal funds during the last year in order to thoroughly research the U.S. bottled water industry and verify demand within the local Wichita market through attendance at industry conventions and trade shows (which included attendance and travel expenses). Funds have also been invested in association memberships, logo and label creation, and professional consulting fees in order to incorporate, register the trademark, and finalize the company business plan.

PRODUCT DESCRIPTION

Sparkling Horizon offers home and office delivery of drinking waters, as well as water cooler rentals, under the Sparkling Horizon label.

Drinking Water

The company offers three types of water in 5 gallon refillable bottles:

Pure spring water

Pure spring water is collected from protected springs and wells and contains no contaminants or additives. Consequently, it is considered to have the best taste of all drinking waters.

Distilled Water

Distilled water is produced by vaporizing water and then allowing it to condense, thereby leaving behind any dissolved minerals present in the original water.

Purified Drinking Water

Water is purified by a process of reverse osmosis, where the water is forced under pressure through membranes which remove 90% of the dissolved minerals.

Water is delivered in 5-gallon bottles made of plastic. Sparkling Horizon is the only water company in the Wichita area to offer a special new handle that makes lifting and refilling bottles much easier. Eventually, the company intends to offer smaller 2- and 3-gallon bottles of water.

Sparkling Horizon will offer a variety of water coolers for rent to its customer base, including standard floor models or counter top models offering choices of cold water only, hot and cold, or room temperature and cold water dispensing.

Water Cooler Rentals

While many consumers choose to purchase bottled water at the grocery store in small 1- or 2-gallon bottles, home and office delivery of water is increasing in popularity for several reasons:

Advantages of Water Delivery

Convenience—instead of having to lug heavy, bulky bottles all the way from the grocery store home, delivery personnel bring longer-lasting, 5-gallon bottles right inside homes and offices.

Customer service—if there is ever a problem with the water cooler, Sparkling Horizon arrives quickly to replace it, taking the faulty cooler back to the warehouse for repairs.

Monthly billing—instead of weekly trips to the grocery store, customers receive a single monthly bill based on the quantity of bottles consumed.

Sparkling Horizon anticipates that approximately 50% of its deliveries will be to homes and 50% to offices.

Home vs. Office Delivery

In order to effectively and quickly build its customer base, Sparkling Horizon intends to aggressively promote its free trial program, offering new customers the use of a company cooler for a period of 30 days free of charge and includes two free bottles of water.

MARKETING STRATEGY

In addition, the company will implement a variety of other marketing methods to complement and build on the free trial offer. Since the competition has failed to utilize other marketing methods beyond the free trials, Sparkling Horizon will quickly achieve a competitive advantage.

Free Trials

Marketing Methods

Through research done by the company, this marketing approach has been found to be extremely effective in enticing consumers to try bottled water and to become used to having a cooler nearby. Once the cooler is in place, the majority of customers find it most convenient to leave it there and order additional bottles of water from the company that provided the cooler.

Sparkling Horizon will contact free trial customers two weeks after the cooler has been placed in their home or office, when the two free bottles of water have most likely been emptied, and offer them an incentive to commit to a cooler rental agreement before the 30-day free trial is actually over. The incentive may involve free bottles of water or a reduced fee for water.

The cost to deliver and place the cooler is minimal, by comparison to the advantage of having a customer essentially locked in to having water delivered by the same company that is renting the cooler to them.

Advertising

Sparkling Horizon intends to advertise its free trial offers by way of radio ads (secured through cross-promotion deals or barter arrangements), door hangers, and ads in coupon packages. Existing competitors do not currently invest in advertising, leaving the market wide open to Sparkling Horizon.

Direct Mail

Post cards offering a 30-day free trial will also be mailed to homes and businesses in selected zip codes within Wichita.

Trade and Consumer Shows

Attendance and exhibits at local home and mall shows is also planned, to keep the Sparkling Horizon Bottled Water name constantly in front of consumers.

Placements

The company will also place coolers in public places frequented by health conscious consumers, such as pharmacies and hospitals.

Budget

An annual marketing budget of $25,000 has been established for the first year of operation, based on a calculation of 10% of first year sales of $247,928. This funding will be generated from profitable operation of the business and not from the start-up capital.

Competitive Advantage

Sparkling Horizon will quickly establish itself in the Wichita market as a top quality provider of bottled water. The company will do this by emphasizing superior customer service in all aspects of the company operations.

One major component of ensuring that customers are delighted with Sparkling Horizon's products and service, is the appointment of a talented and outgoing route delivery person who is responsible for monitoring customer satisfaction and for pursuing new business. Part sales person and part delivery person, Robert Blanc has been hired for this important role at Sparkling Horizon.

OPERATING PLAN

Spring, distilled, and purified drinking waters are bottled by Rue Bottling of Decatur, Illinois, who will fill the 5-gallon bottles labeled with the Sparkling Horizon logo. The plastic, refillable bottles will be collected from customers when empty and returned to the bottler bi-weekly for cleaning and refilling.

Plastic is preferred as the bottle packaging because it is lightweight, unbreakable, and inexpensive to produce and ship.

Location

The company will operate from approximately 2,600 sq. ft. of warehouse space in Wichita county, with a portion of that space being set aside for office space. Sparkling Horizon is currently working with county officials to identify and negotiate the lease on an appropriate site.

Deliveries

It is expected that the route delivery person will make approximately 40 deliveries per day, or 400 per month. One delivery person will be needed at the start and an additional delivery person will be added when the number of monthly deliveries exceeds 1,600, which is anticipated at the end of the fourth month of business.

Insurance

Through Sparkling Horizon's agreement with Rue Bottling, Rue's product liability insurance will cover any such claims against Sparkling Horizon. Sparkling Horizon will also carry its own insurance, including a $1 million umbrella liability policy.

Once Sparkling Horizon achieves a customer base of 3,000 or deliveries of 12,000 bottles per month, the company will begin to investigate investing in equipment to bottle water in-house. An investment of approximately $200,000 would be needed in order to purchase the bottling equipment.

Future Plans For Bottling

Chantal Fuzet has been involved in the water industry virtually all her life. From an early age, she sold and delivered ice and water to local residents for her family's water business in Paris. This experience familiarized her with all aspects of production, delivery, marketing, accounting, and collections.

MANAGEMENT AND STAFFING

Since moving to Wichita, Ms. Fuzet has carefully researched the opportunity to start a similar bottled water business in the area.

In addition to developing a strategy for entering the market by purchasing needed equipment and supplies, Ms. Fuzet has already identified a bottler who will bottle and store water for Sparkling Horizon and has invested personal funds to trademark the name and logo associated with "Sparkling Horizon Bottled Water."

Chantal Fuzet

Ms. Fuzet will continue to manage all strategic planning, marketing planning, staffing, and accounting activities for Sparkling Horizon, building on her experience in the bottled water industry.

Her involvement in the Council of Bottled Water Manufacturers will keep her well-informed of market changes and opportunities. As a member of the U.S. Women Business Owners Council, Ms. Fuzet has the opportunity to network with and learn from successful women business owners in the Wichita area and on a national basis.

The Kansas Department of Commerce is in the process of certifying Sparkling Horizon Bottled Water as a woman-owned business.

Ms. Fuzet has secured commitments from two experienced and talented individuals who will be responsible for daily operations and for delivery of the water.

Management Team

Jean Polsky will assume responsibility for training sales representatives and route delivery personnel, implementing the company's marketing plan, and delivering coolers as needed to new customers. Robert Blanc will become the company's primary route delivery person, serving as the key link between Sparkling Horizon and its customers.

Jean Polsky

Jean Polsky has counseled small businesses for several years as an independent consultant, on issues related to operations, marketing, and training. Mr. Polsky intends to apply the experience he has gained in his work with clients to Sparkling Horizon. This knowledge of training, marketing, and operations is directly applicable to Ms. Fuzet's new business.

Robert Blanc

Robert Blanc has worked for several companies during his career, using his knowledge of employee management, operations, and machine repair to succeed in each position. Because of his outgoing personality, talented management style, and interest in working hands-on within a smaller company, Mr. Blanc has been invited to join the Sparkling Horizon management team. His initial responsibilities will consist of cooler delivery and customer interaction in order to build the company's customer base quickly.

Sales Staff

Sparkling Horizon will hire two commissioned sales people who will focus on placing new water coolers in offices and homes. In return for each new placement, the sales person will receive an amount equal to the first and last month's rent on the cooler in payment, after the customer has completed the free trial period and has committed to cooler rental. It is expected that sales people should be able to make at least $80-90 per day, based on placing just 4 coolers.

FUNDS NEEDED AND THEIR USES

In order to start and establish Sparkling Horizon Bottled Water as a leading supplier of quality bottled drinking waters, funding is required in the amount of $93,500 and will be utilized as follows:

Capitalization plan

Equipment Cost

Delivery truck down payment	$6,000
Purchase of 1,000 bottles	5,800
Purchase of 100 coolers	20,200
Computer/Office equipment	3,000
Telephone system	1,000
Office and warehouse supplies	1,500
Deposits (securities, utilities, licenses, telephone)	14,000
Start-up promotional costs	4,000
Professional fees	2,500
Opening inventory	5,000
Total Start-up Costs	**$64,000**
Working capital	29,500
Total Funding Needed	**$93,500**
Sources of capital	
Chantal Fuzet personal investment	15,000
SBA loan	78,500
Total Funding	**$93,500**

FINANCIAL STATEMENTS

Assumptions
- *Bottle and cooler by month*
- *Selling price of $5.29 per delivered bottle*
- *Cooler rental of $10.00 per month*
- *Cost of sales of $1.80 per delivered bottle*
- *Payroll expenses assume 1 route driver from January to May and a 2nd driver from the end of May through December*
- *Payroll taxes: FICA - 7.65%, SUTA - 4.00%, FUTA - 0.80%*
- *Vehicle gas costs of $25 per day per truck*
- *Vehicle lease costs assume a $20,500 van financed at 9% for a 5 year term, with a $6,000 down payment*
- *Loan of $78,500 financed at 9% for 7 years*

Projected Balance Sheet

	1995	1996	1997	1998	1999
Assets					
Current Assets					
Cash	50,000	110,000	170,000	200,000	240,000
Accounts Receivable	9,000	9,450	9,923	10,419	10,940
Inventory	5,000	5,250	5,513	5,788	6,078
Other Short-term Assets	0	0	0		
Long-term Assets					
Property, Plant & Equipment	25,000	27,500	30,000	32,500	35,000
Other Assets	0	0	0	0	0
Total Assets	**$89,000**	**$152,200**	**$215,435**	**$248,707**	**$292,017**
Liabilities and Owner's Equity					
Short-term Liabilities					
Accounts Payable	14,000	15,120	16,330	17,636	19,047
Short-term Notes	15,000	10,000	50,000	0	0
Other Short-term Liabilities	0	0	0	0	0
Long-term Liabilities					
Long-term Debt	78,500	67,286	57,673	49,434	42,372
Owner's Equity/Stock	2,000	2,000	2,000	2,000	2,000
Retained Earnings	(20,500)	57,794	89,432	179,636	228,598
Total Liabilities/ Owner's Equity	**$89,000**	**$152,200**	**$215,435**	**$248,707**	**$292,017**

Projected Income Statement

	1995	1996	1997	1998	1999
Revenue	$247,928	$322,721	$400,992	453,092	509,801
Cost of Goods Sold	95,760	105,336	115,870	127,455	140,003
Gross Profit	152,168	217,385	285,122	$325,637	$369,798
Operating Expenses					
Advertising	18,000	19,800	21,780	24,000	27,000
Bad debts	4,959	6,454	8,020	9,062	10,196
Car and truck expenses	13,000	14,500	16,000	18,000	20,000
Depreciation	1,116	1,116	1,116	1,116	1,116
Insurance	2,400	2,500	2,600	2,700	2,800
Licenses	240	250	260	270	280
Legal and professional services	1,000	1,150	1,300	1,450	1,600
Warehouse costs	1,800	1,800	1,800	1,800	1,800
Postage	1,200	1,320	1,452	1,597	1,757
Publications	240	260	280	300	320
Salaries	42,000	44,100	46,305	48,620	51,051
Telephone	1,500	1,575	1,654	1,737	1,824
Utilities	1,200	1,200	1,200	1,200	1,200
Miscellaneous	7,595	6,079	4,612	3,259	1,398
Total Expenses	**96,250**	**102,104**	**108,379**	**115,111**	**122,342**
Net Profit Before Taxes	**55,918**	**115,281**	**176,743**	**210,526**	**247,456**
Taxes	**5,136**	**4,813**	**4,173**	**3,480**	**3,116**
Net Income	**$50,782**	**$110,468**	**$172,570**	**$207,046**	**$244,340**

**THIS PAGE INTENTIONALLY LEFT BLANK
SEE NEXT PAGE FOR THE PROJECTED
CASH FLOW FOR YEAR ONE.**

Projected Cash Flow For Year One

	January	February	March	April	May	June
Cash On Hand	15,000	42,140	54,780	67,420	80,059	92,699
Revenues	20,661	20,661	20,661	20,661	20,661	20,661
Total Inflows	35,661	62,801	75,440	88,080	100,720	113,360
Expenses						
Cost of Goods Sold	7,980	7,980	7,980	7,980	7,980	7,980
Operating Expenses						
Advertising	1,500	1,500	1,500	1,500	1,500	1,500
Bad debts	413	413	413	413	413	413
Car and truck expenses	1,083	1,083	1,083	1,083	1,083	1,083
Depreciation	93	93	93	93	93	93
Insurance	200	200	200	200	200	200
Licenses	20	20	20	20	20	20
Legal and professional services	83	83	83	83	83	83
Warehouse costs	150	150	150	150	150	150
Postage	100	100	100	100	100	100
Publications	20	20	20	20	20	20
Salaries	3,500	3,500	3,500	3,500	3,500	3,500
Telephone	125	125	125	125	125	125
Utilities	100	100	100	100	100	100
Miscellaneous	633	633	633	633	633	633
Total Expenses	8,021	8,021	8,021	8,021	8,021	8,021
Start-Up Costs	64,000	0	0	0	0	0
Total Outflow	72,021	8,021	8,021	8,021	8,021	8,021
Net Cash	(36,360)	54,780	67,420	80,059	92,699	105,339
Bank Loan	78,500	0	0	0	0	0
Cash at End of Period	42,140	54,780	67,420	80,059	92,699	105,339

July	August	September	October	November	December	1995
105,339	117,979	130,619	143,259	155,898	168,538	
20,661	20,661	20,661	20,661	20,661	20,661	247,928
126,000	138,640	151,279	163,919	176,559	189,199	
7,980	7,980	7,980	7,980	7,980	7,980	95,760
1,500	1,500	1,500	1,500	1,500	1,500	18,000
413	413	413	413	413	413	4,959
1,083	1,083	1,083	1,083	1,083	1,083	13,000
93	93	93	93	93	93	1,116
200	200	200	200	200	200	2,400
20	20	20	20	20	20	240
83	83	83	83	83	83	1,000
150	150	150	150	150	150	1,800
100	100	100	100	100	100	1,200
20	20	20	20	20	20	240
3,500	3,500	3,500	3,500	3,500	3,500	42,000
125	125	125	125	125	125	1,500
100	100	100	100	100	100	1,200
633	633	633	633	633	633	7,595
8,021	8,021	8,021	8,021	8,021	8,021	96,250
0	0	0	0	0	0	64,000
8,021	8,021	8,021	8,021	8,021	8,021	160,250
117,979	130,619	143,259	155,898	168,538	181,178	
0	0	0	0	0	0	78,500
117,979	130,619	143,259	155,898	168,538	181,178	

Projected Cash Flow For Year Two

	January	February	March	April	May	June
Cash On Hand	168,538	186,923	205,308	223,692	242,077	260,462
Revenues	26,893	26,893	26,893	26,893	26,893	26,893
Total Inflows	195,432	213,816	232,201	250,586	268,971	287,355
Expenses						
Cost of Goods Sold	8,778	8,778	8,778	8,778	8,778	8,778
Operating Expenses						
Advertising	1,650	1,650	1,650	1,650	1,650	1,650
Bad debts	538	538	538	538	538	538
Car and truck expenses	1,208	1,208	1,208	1,208	1,208	1,208
Depreciation	93	93	93	93	93	93
Insurance	208	208	208	208	208	208
Licenses	21	21	21	21	21	21
Legal and professional services	96	96	96	96	96	96
Warehouse costs	150	150	150	150	150	150
Postage	110	110	110	110	110	110
Publications	22	22	22	22	22	22
Salaries	3,675	3,675	3,675	3,675	3,675	3,675
Telephone	131	131	131	131	131	131
Utilities	100	100	100	100	100	100
Miscellaneous	507	507	507	507	507	507
Total Expenses	8,509	8,509	8,509	8,509	8,509	8,509
Start-Up Costs	0	0	0	0	0	0
Total Outflow	8,509	8,509	8,509	8,509	8,509	8,509
Net Cash	186,923	205,308	223,692	242,077	260,462	278,847
Bank Loan	0	0	0	0	0	0
Cash at End of Period	186,923	205,308	223,692	242,077	260,462	278,847

July	August	September	October	November	December	1996
278,847	297,231	315,616	334,001	352,386	370,770	
26,893	26,893	26,893	26,893	26,893	26,893	322,721
305,740	324,125	342,510	360,894	379,279	397,664	
8,778	8,778	8,778	8,778	8,778	8,778	105,336
1,650	1,650	1,650	1,650	1,650	1,650	19,800
538	538	538	538	538	538	6,454
1,208	1,208	1,208	1,208	1,208	1,208	14,500
93	93	93	93	93	93	1,116
208	208	208	208	208	208	2,500
21	21	21	21	21	21	250
96	96	96	96	96	96	1,150
150	150	150	150	150	150	1,800
110	110	110	110	110	110	1,320
22	22	22	22	22	22	260
3,675	3,675	3,675	3,675	3,675	3,675	44,100
131	131	131	131	131	131	1,575
100	100	100	100	100	100	1,200
507	507	507	507	507	507	6,079
8,509	8,509	8,509	8,509	8,509	8,509	102,104
0	0	0	0	0	0	0
8,509	8,509	8,509	8,509	8,509	8,509	
297,231	315,616	334,001	352,386	370,770	389,155	
0	0	0	0	0	0	
297,231	315,616	334,001	352,386	370,770	389,155	

Projected Cash Flow For Year Three

	January	February	March	April	May	June
Cash On Hand	389,155	413,540	437,924	462,308	486,693	511,077
Revenues	33,416	33,416	33,416	33,416	33,416	33,416
Total Inflows	422,571	446,956	471,340	495,724	520,109	544,493
Expenses						
Cost of Goods Sold	9,656	9,656	9,656	9,656	9,656	9,656
Operating Expenses						
Advertising	1,815	1,815	1,815	1,815	1,815	1,815
Bad debts	668	668	668	668	668	668
Car and truck expenses	1,333	1,333	1,333	1,333	1,333	1,333
Depreciation	93	93	93	93	93	93
Insurance	217	217	217	217	217	217
Licenses	22	22	22	22	22	22
Legal and professional services	108	108	108	108	108	108
Warehouse costs	150	150	150	150	150	150
Postage	121	121	121	121	121	121
Publications	23	23	23	23	23	23
Salaries	3,859	3,859	3,859	3,859	3,859	3,859
Telephone	138	138	138	138	138	138
Utilities	100	100	100	100	100	100
Miscellaneous	384	384	384	384	384	384
Total Expenses	9,032	9,032	9,032	9,032	9,032	9,032
Start-Up Costs	0	0	0	0	0	0
Total Outflow	9,032	9,032	9,032	9,032	9,032	9,032
Net Cash	413,540	437,924	462,308	486,693	511,077	535,462
Bank Loan	0	0	0	0	0	0
Cash at End of Period	413,540	437,924	462,308	486,693	511,077	535,462

July	August	September	October	November	December	1997
535,462	559,846	584,231	608,615	632,999	657,384	
33,416	33,416	33,416	33,416	33,416	33,416	400,992
568,878	593,262	617,647	642,031	666,415	690,800	
9,656	9,656	9,656	9,656	9,656	9,656	115,870
1,815	1,815	1,815	1,815	1,815	1,815	21,780
668	668	668	668	668	668	8,020
1,333	1,333	1,333	1,333	1,333	1,333	16,000
93	93	93	93	93	93	1,116
217	217	217	217	217	217	2,600
22	22	22	22	22	22	260
108	108	108	108	108	108	1,300
150	150	150	150	150	150	1,800
121	121	121	121	121	121	1,452
23	23	23	23	23	23	280
3,859	3,859	3,859	3,859	3,859	3,859	46,305
138	138	138	138	138	138	1,654
100	100	100	100	100	100	1,200
384	384	384	384	384	384	4,612
9,032	9,032	9,032	9,032	9,032	9,032	108,379
0	0	0	0	0	0	0
9,032	9,032	9,032	9,032	9,032	9,032	
559,846	584,231	608,615	632,999	657,384	681,768	
0	0	0	0	0	0	
559,846	584,231	608,615	632,999	657,384	681,768	

Child Transportation Service

BUSINESS PLAN   KID CART

1224 Tea House St.
Royal Oak, MI 48068

February 16, 1996

The founders of Kid Cart realized that their own struggle to balance their children's schedules with their own was a widespread problem today. Inspired by children's commuter services starting up around the country, they knew they could create a convenient, safe and reliable resource for busy parents. This plan highlights the founders' preparation, management skills and dedication to safety which rest on their solid reputations as trustworthy community members.

- MISSION STATEMENT
- MANAGEMENT
- EXECUTIVE SUMMARY
- SURVEY RESULTS
- INTRODUCTION LETTER RESULTS
- BREAK EVEN ANALYSIS
- LOAN SUMMARY STATEMENT
- BUSINESS INFORMATION

- MARKETING
- MARKETING MIX STRATEGY
- RATE SCHEDULE
- OPERATIONS
- HOUSEHOLD NEEDS
- LETTER OF INTRODUCTION
- CHILD TRANSPORTATION SURVEY
- FINANCIAL DATA

MISSION STATEMENT

The mission of Kid Cart is to provide a safe, licensed transportation service for children at a reasonable price to parents. By achieving our goals, we will become a trusted, viable transportation source to parents and children in Oakland County.

MANAGEMENT

Lulu LaQuentin is a lifelong resident of Royal Oak. She graduated from The University of Michigan with an Associates of Arts degree in 1975. Lulu's professional background covers 20 years of management, customer service and training. Lulu, her husband Ed and their two children recently bought a new home in Royal Oak.

Mickey Beneville was born in Pennsylvania in 1960. Later, Mickey's family moved to Royal Oak where she graduated from Kimbal High School in 1978. Her background includes marketing, management and sales positions. In 1993 Barbara graduated from Oakland Community College with two Associates in Applied Science Degrees-- marketing and management. Mickey and her husband Casey live in the Berkley area.

Lulu and Mickey have known each other for 26 years. They worked together professionally from 1980-1987 and again in 1994-1995. Their wide range of skills includes communications, marketing, budgeting, customer service, training and general office procedures.

Over the years, Lulu and Mickey discussed owning some type of business. In the spring of 1995 Lulu was unable to transport her eight-year old daughter to an after school activity due to her work schedule. The idea for the children's transportation service was born.

Their professional background along with the care and commitment to the Royal Oak area will enable Mickey and Lulu to provide parents with the comfort of knowing that their children will be shuttled in safe vehicles by licensed, screened and insured drivers.

EXECUTIVE SUMMARY

Brief History of Children's Transportation Services

During the past several months, we have researched the rapidly growing industry of children's transportation. With the busy schedules of dual working parents, there is a conflict in getting their children to day care, preschool, sports activities, appointments, etc. More and more parents are looking for alternative ways to transport their children without affecting their work schedule.

Approximately 300 children transport companies exist across the country. In February 1995, the National Child Transport Association was formed in Naples, Florida. There are currently 220 members. This association is working to set standards for the children's transportation industry. They produce an informative newsletter 4 times per year. NCTA also has their 2nd annual conference set for May 1996 which we plan to attend.

Objectives

- To provide a safe, licensed transportation service for children at a reasonable price to parents.
- Enhance the business by becoming a trusted viable transportation source to parents and children in Royal Oak.
- Contract with area service agencies, day care, preschool and recreational services that do not provide transportation.
- Create jobs for Royal Oak by hiring trained drivers and office staff as our business grows.

Brief Description of Kid Cart

Kid Cart is a transportation service exclusively created to transport children to and from school, day care, after school activities, recreational programs, etc.

Unlike a taxi service, Kid Cart will provide transportation exclusively to children. All of our drivers will have a background check through the Michigan State Police for any infractions of the law.

These drivers will possess a chauffeur's driver's license and a Red Cross First Aid and CPR certificate. They also must genuinely care about the welfare of children.

Below are five simple steps for parents to follow when registering their children with Kid Cart.

How It Works

Step 1:	You decide Kid Cart is for you.
Step 2:	Call us to schedule a meeting with a Kid Cart representative at your convenience. We want to meet you and we're sure you would like to meet us.
Step 3:	Fill out the Kid Cart registration and emergency forms.
Step 4:	Go over your child's schedule with us.
Step 5:	Prepay the fee.

That's All There Is To It!

Kid Cart will possess insurance above that required by law.

Bodily Injury	100,000/300,000
Property Damage	100,000
PIP/PPI	
Comprehensive	$100 Ded.
Brd Collision	$500 Ded.
Uninsured Motorist	20,000/40,000
MCCA	

The 1996 Sportster Minivan we have selected will meet federal safety standards for passenger cars. These features include dual airbags and adjustable height shoulder harness for front and second row seats. All seatbelt latch plates incorporate the capability to help secure child car seats. For added safety, anti-lock brakes are standard and steel side guard door beams are built into all the doors. All drivers and passengers will be required to wear a safety belt regardless of age or weight.

The projected market will be focused on middle class, single and dual working parents. This group is very active and so are their children with sports, day care and summer activities etc. Also these parents comprise the majority of respondents from our surveys and introduction letter.

Short Description of Projected Market

Starting with two vans, the sales receipts will be based on a five dollar cost of an average trip totaling fifty trips per van per month. The anticipated growth each month would be twenty additional trips per van. Using this formula, our break even point would be $41,124 in sales receipts, or approximately 8,825 total trips. This is projected to occur in January of 1997. At this rate of growth we project one additional van in September of 1996, and 2 additional vans in 1997. We have based this information on our survey and introduction letter results. Following is a breakdown of the results.

Expected Growth and Rationale for Projections

Survey Results distributed by Kid Cart

SURVEY RESULTS

Total Surveys mailed out:	200
Responses received:	82(55%)
Parents currently transporting children:	57(70%)
Total parents who would hire our service:	47(82%
Total parents using the service daily:	16(34%)
Total parents using the service weekly:	31(66%)

Using the numbers from the survey, we can surmise the following:

Total Children	Daily Use		One-way Trip	Daily Revenue		Days/ Week	Total Weekly
47 X 34%=	16 Children	X	$5.00=	$80.00	X	5 days=	$400.00
47 X 66%=	31 children	X	$5.00=	$155.00	X	1 day=	$155.00
							$555.00

The potential earnings for one week would be $555.00

INTRO LETTER RESULTS

Total letters mailed out	150
Total Responses	13 (1%)
Individuals	10
Businesses	3
Total parents using the service daily	4 (31%)
Total parents using service weekly	9 (70%)

Using the numbers from the phone calls we received, we can surmise the following:

Total Children	Daily Use		One-way Trip	Daily Revenue		Days/ Week	Total Weekly
13 X 31%=	4 children	X	$5.00=	$20.00	X	5 days=	$100.00
13 X 70%=	9 children	X	$5.00=	$45.00	X	1 day=	$45.00
							$145.00

The potential earnings for one week would be $145.00

We were pleased at the initial results of our attempts to inform parents of this new and unique service. There is much to consider (on the parents' side) when entrusting a transportation service to deliver your children safely.

If all these parents that responded positively did hire Kid Cart immediately, our monthly revenue potential would be $2800. We have taken the conservative approach however, estimating that 18% or 10 out of 60 parents would actually hire us immediately. This would give us our first monthly income of $500. We also were conservative on our pricing. We have based all trips from our responses to be one-way or $5.00 per trip. We know that a small percentage of these parents would in fact hire us for round-trip service. Also, there is no consideration for charter services because the information we have received has been based on spring and summer charter trips.

We are currently receiving at least one phone call a day from parents as well as businesses.

BREAK EVEN ANALYSIS

Projected Costs and Sales

1996 Fixed Costs	$22,207
1996 Variable Costs	$15,229
1996 Sales Revenues	$33,260

Break-even = fixed costs (sales - variable costs in %)/100
22,207 divided by (100%-46%) X 100% = $41,124
41,124 divided by $5 per trip = 8,225 trips

This scenario shows a break even point of $41,124 in sales or 8,225 trips at $5 per trip. During our first 12 months in business, we have calculated $33,260 in sales or 6,652 trips at $5 per trip. Based on the break-even analysis, it would take approximately 13 months to break even.

March 1996	$1,000	**Total Revenue**
April 1996	$2,500	
May 1996	$4,000	
June 1996	$7,000	
July 1996	$9,000	
August 1996	$13,000	
September 1996	$15,000	
October 1996	$19,500	
November 1996	$25,500	
December 1996	$34,000	
January 1997	$40,000	
February 1997	$41,124	

Kid Cart is seeking a loan of $39,737 for five years to purchase two vans to successfully launch a children's transportation service. This loan, together with an equity cash investment of $10,000 will be sufficient to finance the business so it can operate as a viable profitable enterprise.

LOAN SUMMARY STATEMENT

Name of Company: Kid Cart

Business Information

Building Location: 1224 Tea House St., Royal Oak. After careful consideration, Kid's Cart will operate out of Lulu LaQuentin's house for the first year of operation. Most of our time will be spent in the vans and not in an office. This is the most cost effective way to operate in 1996.

The Nature of the Business

Kid Cart is a transportation service exclusively for children. We will be transporting children to and from activities in a safe and responsible manner.

Date Business Projected to Open: March 1, 1996

Legal Form of Organization: Partnership

Owners: Lulu LaQuentin and Mickey Beneville

MARKETING

With today's busy lifestyle parents are often faced with scheduling conflicts and transportation dilemmas for their children. The children's transportation industry was started to help solve those dilemmas. Since the early 90s, 300 such services have been started in cities across the United States. One such company, Merry-Go-Round in Maryland started in 1991, today has eight vans and projected income of over $250,000.

Know The Product

The 1990 Census Bureau reported there were 21.5 million women in the work force with children under 18 and 28.4 million dual income households with kids under 18. This is the segment of the population we will be targeting.

Know Your Target Market

In 1992 Oakland County had 161,980 residents. The largest segment of our population are residents 24-44 which is 31%. Second largest, 28% or 45,354, is kids under 18.

The average income in Oakland County is $25,617.

In February 1995 the National Child Transport Association was formed. This group is working to set standards for the rapidly growing Child Transport industry. NCTA currently has 220 members. We have applied to be members.

In Oakland County we have been working with several agencies and individuals. First of all the people of the Oakland Expansion League have gone to great lengths to help us in our pursuit of the business. Patricia Kumar, our accountant, helped us get started in the right direction. Lena Isenberg, a personal friend, helped with some of our financial decisions. Since Juliet Thornton of Children First Development Center, just opened last year she has had some great suggestions for us. Billie Gooding who is opening a child care facility and Frances Rush of Birmingham Montessori have assisted us in promoting Kid Cart. Geoffrey McDormand of Childland Resources, put us in touch with the group Care Support, which is a group of individuals representing all the agencies dealing with children in the county. We attended their January meeting and were invited back for their February meeting. All of these initial contacts have provided information and help for us.

MARKETING MIX STRATEGY

Product/Service

Kid Cart will provide the highest quality of children's transportation available. Children will be transported in 1996 Sportster Minivans with the latest safety features, including dual airbags, child safety features, including dual airbags, child safety locks, shoulder harnesses and seatbelts.

Customer service is a priority for Mickey and Lulu of Kid Cart. We believe in the old saying "Treat others as you would want to be treated". This is the Kid Cart philosophy of customer service. To achieve and maintain excellent customer service, proper training and monitoring of employees will be critical.

Competition

The other transportation services available to Oakland County are: city cab, public busses and The Shuttle. Kid Cart is unlike these transportation services because we cater exclusively to children. It is this fact that makes us different than these other transportation services. We offer parents the convenience of the service and the comfort of knowing their children are being driven by licensed, screened and insured drivers who genuinely care about the welfare of children. Unlike other transportation services, parents will have the opportunity and are encouraged to meet the staff of Kid Cart at any time. Also the staff will make every effort to meet area school teachers and administrators so they will be familiar with our vans and drivers. Our vans will be clearly identified by the bright red color and the Kid Cart logo. All drivers will be issued a company identification card. Our company's focus is children, therefore, the safety and welfare of the children we transport will be our number one priority.

Promotion

Introduction Letter

This is our first mass mailing. The letter contains a formal introduction, explanation of our services and a request to respond if interested. This letter was sent to pediatricians, dentists, pre-schools, elementary schools, day care owners, attorneys and beauty salons. One Hundred and Fifty letters were mailed on January 16, 1996 (see survey and intro letter results).

Brochure

Our brochure will contain all of the operational information needed for our customers. It will include hours, rates, rules and regulations, a mission statement and features and benefits of using our service. The brochure will be available at various locations including human service agencies, schools, day cares, etc.

Examiner

The Examiner will allow a free human interest story. When we purchase the vans, we'll call to schedule a photo and story. We will also advertise in the clippings.

Childland Resources

This is a viable source for anyone looking for day care. The children's resource network has already provided us with a list of licensed day care providers in the area. We will receive their newsletter and they will hand out our brochure.

PTA/School Involvement

At part of our personal selling, we will make appointments with key personnel in the school district. It is our goal to be able to contract for group activities, but also to make the schools and parents aware of our existence in the community as a viable source for safe delivery of children.

Care Support

This is another important source in Oakland County. Once a month participants from area agencies dealing with children meet. They discuss how to make things better for children in the county. It is also a great way to network with these 200 members.

• Our service will be sold directly to users.	**Distribution**
• Our site location is suited to customer proximity because it is close to major roads and highways. Effective routing, which is essential, will be made easier because of our location.	

All rates are based on serviceable areas. Our vans will be driving in a seven mile delivery radius.   **Price**

- Fees must be paid in advance.
- Fees may be paid by check or cash only.
- $25.00 service charge on all return checks.
- As the business grows Kid Cart will consider accepting credit cards if there is a need and it is cost effective.

Any changes or withdrawals of ride schedule will require immediate notification to Kid Cart. In the event that we are not notified, the normal fare will be charged.

Daily Rates Based on 7 Mile Radius and Pre-Scheduled Appointments   **RATE SCHEDULE**

Type of Ride	One Child Same Stop	2nd-3rd Siblings Same Stop	4 or More Siblings Same Stop
One-way	$5.00	$3.00	$2.00
Round trip	$7.00	$5.00	$4.00
Extra Miles	.50 per mile	.50 per mile	.50 per mile
Non-scheduled one-way	$7.00-$10.00	$3.00	$2.00
Non-scheduled round trip	$10.00-$15.00	$3.00	$2.00

One Way

Your child is picked up at one locations and transported to destination. For example: We pick up your child at home and transport him/her to day care. Cost: $5.00

Round-Trip

Your child is picked up at one location, transported to his/her destination and picked up and returned to original location. For example: We pick up your child at home, transport him/her to school, pick back up at school and transport back home. Cost $7.00

Extra Miles

If there is an occasion where your child needs to be transported a few miles outside the radius, there will be an additional charge based on mileage. For example: We pick up your child at home and transport her/him to dance lessons and it's an additional 5 miles. Cost: $5.00 + 3.75 = 8.75 one way.

Non-Scheduled

A non-scheduled pick-up can also be described as same-day service. If you call on the same day that your child needs a ride, we will do our best to accommodate you. The fare will be based on van availability and mileage.

Savings

When your child rides with us 5 days per week, you save 15%! Save 10% when your child rides with us 3 to 4 times per week!

OPERATIONS

Kid Cart's business address is 1224 Tea House St. in Royal Oak. Our regular hours of operation will be 7 a.m. to 7 p.m. We will also be available for charter services. Children will be transported in 1996 Sportster Minivans.

Our quality control systems will include background checks on all potential employees. All drivers must possess a chauffeur's license and have Red Cross CPR and first aid training. They will also be properly trained in customer service and our driving and office procedures. We will monitor our employees by speaking with parents who use our service to maintain ongoing customer satisfaction. Kid Cart will adhere to a stringent auto maintenance schedule to ensure safe reliable vans for children to ride in.

Service

The service Kid Cart will provide is safe responsible transportation exclusively for children. We will be transporting children to after school activities, day care, preschool, dental appointments, etc.

We will begin with two vans that will hold six children each. To best utilize these vans we have established peak transportation periods. These periods are early morning (7-8), mid afternoon (11-12), and late afternoon (3-5). We will establish routes with maximum passengers and close destinations. The summer season will bring in more charter trips as indicated by our initial responses. During non-peak periods we will be taking children to appointments or making emergency pick-ups (when a child needs to leave school due to illness). We will also use this time for administrative and marketing work.

Suppliers

Principal Suppliers

- Standard in Ferndale for vans
- Citizens in Royal Oak for gas
- Cord in Ferndale for office supplies
- Briar Printing in Berkley

We sent letters to thirteen area auto dealerships inviting them to submit bids on vans and service. After reviewing the bids, driving the vans and speaking with the sales people we chose Standard as the auto dealership we will use. Based on price, auto service and customer service.

Citizens was chosen as our supplier of gasoline because of their convenient locations and their reporting capabilities. They will supply us with a report each week that indicates how many miles each van was driven, the driver of the van and cost per mile.

Cord will be our primary supplier for office supplies because of their low prices. We have applied for our tax exempt status with them.

We received three quotes from area printers. Briar gave us the best price and the quality of their work is excellent.

Personnel

A three-person staff, Lulu LaQuentin, Mickey Beneville and a third driver will be providing transportation for children to and from school and after school activities. All drivers will posses a chauffeur's license, as required by law, and will be trained in CPR and first aid.

Lulu and Mickey will initially be driving most of the time as well as marketing and administrative work. As the business grows, more drivers will be hired and Lulu and Mickey will focus on marketing and administration.

Job Description: To transport children to and from activities in a safe, responsible, timely manner.

Position: Driver

Reports To: Mickey

Duties and Responsibilities: To transport children to and from various activities in a safe, responsible, timely manner. Must like children and have an excellent driving record.

Lulu has not been working outside the home for a few years. Her husband Ed's salary is enough to cover their living expenses.

Mickey's husband Casey is the main contributor to the household. Mickey has been working part time since October 1995 and she will continue to work weekends through May of 1996 when the draw is budgeted.

HOUSEHOLD NEEDS

Sent out to Royal Oak Residents

January 15, 1996

KID CART LETTER OF INTRODUCTION

Allow us to introduce ourselves. We are Lulu LaQuentin and Mickey Beneville, partners for Kid Cart. This is a children's transportation service that we are developing in Royal Oak. Our purpose is providing affordable, safe, licensed transportation for children.

Kid Cart is registered with the Royal Oak records office and we are using the resources of Oakland Expansion League to assist us in getting our business up and running. Our goal is to be servicing the Royal Oak area within the first quarter of 1996.

This is where we need your help.

Our research has shown that there are area parents interested in hiring a transportation service exclusively for their children. We would like to hear from parents, teachers, recreational counselors and anyone interested in hiring such a service. This will allow us to develop a client list and focus on specific geographical areas.

Please call us and Lulu or Mickey will be happy to talk with you about Kid Cart. You may also send any questions to Kid Cart, 1224 Tea House St., Royal Oak, MI 48068.

Sincerely,

Lulu LaQuentin & Mickey Beneville

**CHILD
TRANSPORTATION
SURVEY**

Dear Parent, Guardian or Day Care Provider:

This survey has been assembled to help us create affordable child transportation in your local area. Please take a few moments to fill in the information below and return to the person you received it from or Oakland Expansion League at the address/fax below. Even if you don't plan on using the service, your information may help someone who needs such a service.

Deadline for information: January 31, 1996!!

Please Check Any Boxes That Apply. You May Check More Than One Per Line

1. Are you currently transporting children to/from school or day care? __yes __no

2. If Yes, what part(s) of the day are you transporting children?
          __Early AM __AM __Early PM __PM

3. Are there activities your children do not attend due to lack of transportation? __yes __no

4. If Yes, what part(s) of the day do these activities take place?
          __Early AM __AM __Early PM __PM

5. If there were an insured professional transportation service specifically for children, would you consider hiring it? __yes __no

6. If Yes, how often? __Daily __Weekly __2-4 Days/Week __Weekends Only
          __As needed/emergency __Other:

7. What price range do you think would be reasonable for a professional children's transportation service?
    One Round-Trip, Less Than 10 Miles: __$5.00-$6.00 __$6.00-$7.00 __$7.00-$8.00

8. Please describe embarking & destination locations. Please Use Back If Needed
    From_____ To_____
    From_____ To_____

9. What Ages Are Your Children? _____ _____ _____ _____

Thank You For Your Time & Assistance!! Questions or Comments? Call Us.

	FINANCIAL DATA

Sources:

Partner Investment: Lulu LaQuentin	$5,000
Partner Investment: Mickey Beneville	$5,000
Commercial Loan	$39,737
Total	**$49,737**

Applications:

Purchase two 1996 Sportster Minivans	$39,737
Working Capital	$10,000
Total	**$49,737**

Use of Proceeds

Printing	$184.00
Advertising	$300.00
Postage	$51.00
Office Supplies	$160.00
Business Phone Line (1)	$118.00
Cellular Phones (2)	$140.00
Business Telephone (1)	$100.00
Oakland Expansion League Membership	$225.00
Nat'l Child Transport Assoc. Fee	$175.00
Total	**$1453.00**

Start Up Costs

Assets		**Liabilities**	
Current Assets		Current Liabilities	0
Cash	$10,190		
Computer	$250		
Total Assets	**$10,440**	**Total Liabilities**	**0**
		Capital	$10,440

**Pro Forma
Balance Sheet
February 23, 1996**

1996 Cash Pro Forma
Pre-Start Costs
March 1, through December 31, 1996

	Pre-start	March	April	May	June	July
Cash On Hand	$10,190	$8,737	$5,804	$4,843	$4,267	$3,266
Cash Receipts-Sales		$500	$1,400	$1,800	$2,200	$2,600
Charters				$60	$60	$60
Non-Scheduled					$20	$20
Total Cash Receipts	**$500**	**$1,400**	**$1,860**	**$2,280**	**$2,680**	**$3,310**
Total Cash Available	**$10,190**	**$9,237**	**$7,204**	**$6,703**	**$6,547**	**$5,946**
Cash Paid Out						
Purchases	$50	$150				
Gross Wages			$240	$240	$240	$240
Payroll Expenses			$24	$24	$24	$24
Printing	$84	$216	$50		$100	
Supplies - Office	$200		$50	$50	$50	$50
Postage	$51	$50	$50	$25	$50	$25
Auto Maintenance					$120	
Auto Gas		$200	$180	$180	$180	$180
Advertising	$200	$100	$100	$50	$50	$50
Accounting/Legal				$200		
Rent						
Telephone-Office	$118	$38	$38	$38	$38	$38
Cellular	$140	$104	$104	$104	$104	$104
Utilities						
Insurance - Auto		$1,575	$525	$525	$525	$525
Draw					$800	$800
Loan - Principle		$800	$800	$800	$800	$800
Interest		$200	$200	$200	$200	$200
Capital Purchase						
Misc.	$10					
Membership Fees	$400					
Magnetic Signs	$200					
Total Cash Paid Out	**$1,453**	**$3,433**	**$2,361**	**$2,436**	**$3,281**	**$3,036**
Cash Position	**$8,737**	**$5,804**	**$4,483**	**$4,267**	**$3,266**	**$2,910**

August	September	October	November	December	Totals
$2,910	$2,679	$3,113	$3,832	$4,393	$6,104
$3,000	$3,400	$3,800	$6,700	$6,900	$32,300
$120	$180	$120	$120	$120	$840
$10	$10	$10	$25	$25	$120
$3,590	**$3,930**	**$6,845**	**$7,045**		**$33,260**
$6,040	**$6,269**	**$7,043**	**$10,667**	**$11,438**	**$39,364**
			$70		$270
$240	$240	$240	$1,240	$1,240	$4,160
$24	$24	$24	$250	$250	$668
$100		$100		$100	$750
$50	$50	$50	$50	$50	$650
$50	$120		$25	$50	$451
	$180	$180		$120	$360
$180	$50	$100	$270	$270	$2,000
$50			$100	$100	$950
$200			$200		$600
$38	$38	$38	$38	$38	$498
$104	$104	$104	$156	$156	$1,284
$525	$525	$525	$1,625	$800	$7,675
$800	$800	$800	$800	$800	$5,600
$800	$800	$800	$1,160	$1,160	$8,720
$200	$200	$200	$200	$200	$2,000
					$10
					$400
			$100		$300
$3,361	**$3,156**	**$3,211**	**$6,284**	**$5,334**	**$37,346**
$2,679	**$3,113**	**$3,832**	**$4,393**	**$6,104**	**$2,118**

1997 Cash Pro Forma
January 1 through December 31, 1997

	January	February	March	April	May	June
Cash On Hand	$6,104	$6,743	$5,157	$6,523	$6,417	
Cash Receipts-Sales	$7,200	$7,200	$8,640	$8,640	$8,640	$8,640
Charters	$120	$120	$150		$150	$150
Non-Scheduled	$25	$25	$60	$60	$60	$60
Total Cash Receipts	**$7,345**	**$7,345**	**$8,820**	**$8,850**	**$8,850**	**$8,850**
Total Cash Available	**$13,449**	**$14,088**	**$13,977**	**$15,373**	**$15,267**	**$14,811**
Cash Paid Out						
Purchases						
Gross Wages	$1,240	$1,240	$2,200	$2,200	$2,200	$2,200
Payroll Expenses	$250	$250	$440	$440	$440	$440
Printing	$100	$100	$50	$300		$150
Supplies - Office	$50	$50	$50	$150	$50	$50
Postage	$50	$25	$50	$50	$25	$50
Auto Maintenance		$250				
Auto Gas	$300	$300	$300	$300	$300	$300
Advertising	$50	$50		$100		
Accounting/Legal			$200			$200
Rent				$750	$750	$750
Telephhone-Office	$100	$100	$100	$100	$100	$100
Cellular	$156	$156	$156	$156	$156	$156
Utilities				$75	$75	$75
Insurance - Auto	$1,050	$1,050	$1,050	$1,059	$1,050	$1,050
Draw	$1,500	$1,500	$1,500	$1,500	$1,500	$1,500
Loan - Principle	$1,160	$1,160	$1,160	$1,160	$1,160	$1,160
Interest	$200	$200	$200	$200	$200	$200
Capital Purchase		$2,500				
Misc.				$250		
Membership Fees	$500					
Insurance-Office				$250		
Travel				$1,000		
Total Cash Paid Out	**$6,706**	**$8,931**	**$7,456**	**$8,956**	**$9,306**	**$8,381**
Cash Position	**$0**	**$5,157**	**$6,523**	**$6,714**	**$5,961**	**$6,430**

July	August	September	October	November	December	Totals
$8,640	$8,640	$14,400	$14,400	$14,400	$14,400	$123,840
$150	$120	$240	$240	$240	$240	$2,040
$60	$60	$90	$90	$90	$60	$740
$8,850	**$8,850**	**$14,730**	**$14,730**	**$14,730**	**$14,730**	**$126,620**
$15,280	**$16,094**	**$22,293**	**$24,816**	**$27,314**	**$28,632**	**$143,120**
$2,200	$2,200	$4,160	$4,160	$4,160	$4,160	$32,320
$440	$440	$832	$832	$832	$832	$6,468
	$200	$200				$1,100
$50	$50	$50	$50	$100	$50	$750
$25	$50	$25	$150	$50	$50	$600
	$200			$200		$850
$300	$300	$500	$500	$500	$500	$4,400
	$100	$100		$200		$700
		$200			$200	$800
$750	$750	$750	$750	$750	$750	$6,750
$100	$100	$100	$100	$100	$100	$1,200
$156	$156	$260	$260	$260	$260	$2,288
$75	$75	$75	$75	$75	$75	$600
$1,050	$1,050	$1,575	$1,575	$1,575	$1,575	$14,700
$1,500	$1,500	$1,500	$1,500	$1,500	$1,500	$18,000
$1,160	$1,160	$1,880	$1,880	$1,880	$1,880	$16,800
$200	$200	$200	$200	$200	$200	$2,400
						$2,500
						$250
						$500
						$250
						$1,000
$8,006	**$8,531**	**$12,207**	**$12,232**	**$13,382**	**$12,132**	**$116,226**
$7,274	**$7,563**	**$10,086**	**$12,584**	**$13,932**	**$16,500**	**$26,894**

1996 Pro Forma Profit and Loss
March 1, through December 31, 1996

	March	April	May	June	July
Sales					
Cash Receipts	$500	$1,400	$1,800	$2,200	$2,600
Charters			$60	$60	$60
Non-Scheduled				$20	$20
Total Sales	**$500**	**$1,400**	**$1,860**	**$2,280**	**$2,680**
Monthly Van Payments	$1,000	$1,000	$1,000	$1,000	$1,000
Vans Maint. & Gas	$200	$180	$180	$300	$180
Total Cost of Goods Sold	$1,200	$1,180	$1,180	$1,300	$1,180
Gross Margin	($700)	$220	$680	$980	$1,500
Operating Expenses					
Purchases	$150				
Gross Wages		$240	$240	$240	$240
Payroll Expenses		$24	$24	$24	$24
Printing	$216	$50		$100	
Supplies-Office		$50	$50	$50	$50
Postage	$50	$50	$25	$50	$25
Advertising	$100	$100	$50	$50	$50
Accounting/Legal			$200		
Rent					
Telephone-Office	$38	$38	$38	$38	$38
Cellular	$104	$104	$104	$104	$104
Utilities					
Insurance-Auto	$1,575	$525	$525	$525	$525
Draw				$800	$800
Capital Purchase					
Misc.					
Membership Fees					
Magnetic Signs					
Total Expenses	**$2,233**	**$1,181**	**$1,256**	**$1,981**	**$1,856**
Net Profit (Loss)	**($2,933)**	**($961)**	**($576)**	**($1,001)**	**($356)**

August	September	October	November	December	Totals
$3,000	$3,400	$3,800	$6,700	$6,900	$32,300
$120	$180	$120	$120	$120	$840
$10	$10	$10	$25	$25	$120
$3,130	**$3,590**	**$3,930**	**$6,845**	**$7,045**	**$33,260**
$1,000	$1,000	$1,000	$1,360	$1,360	$10,720
$180	$300	$180	$210	$390	$2,300
$1,180	$1,300	$1,180	$1,630	$1,750	$13,080
$1,950	$2,290	$2,750	$5,215	$5,295	$20,180
			$70		$220
$240	$240	$240	$1,240	$1,240	$4,160
$24	$24	$24	$250	$250	$668
$100		$100		$100	$666
$50	$50	$50	$50	$50	$450
$50	$25	$50	$25	$50	$400
$50	$50	$100	$100	$100	$750
$200			$200		$600
$38	$38	$38	$38	$38	$380
$104	$104	$104	$156	$156	$1,144
$525	$525	$525	$1,625	$800	$7,675
$800	$800	$800	$800	$800	$5,600
			$100		$100
$2,181	**$1,856**	**$2,031**	**$4,654**	**$3,584**	**$22,813**
($231)	**$434**	**$719**	**$561**	**$1,711**	**($2,633)**

1997 Pro Forma Profit and Loss
January 1, through December 31, 1997

	January	February	March	April	May	June
Sales						
Cash Receipts	$7,200	$7,200	$8,640	$8,640	$8,640	$8,640
Charters	$120	$120	$120	$150	$150	$150
Non-Scheduled	$25	$25	$60	$60	$60	$60
Total Sales	**$7,345**	**$7,345**	**$8,820**	**$8,850**	**$8,850**	**$8,850**
Monthly Van Payments	$1,360	$1,360	$1,360	$1,360	$1,360	$1,360
Vans Maint. & Gas	$300	$550	$300	$300	$500	$300
Total Cost of Goods Sold	**$1,660**	**$1,910**	**$1,660**	**$1,660**	**$1,860**	**$1,660**
Gross Margin	**$5,685**	**$5,435**	**$7,160**	**$7,160**	**$6,990**	**$7,190**
Operating Expenses						
Purchases						
Gross Wages	$1,240	$1,240	$2,200	$2,200	$2,200	$2,200
Payroll Expenses	$250	$250	$440	$440	$440	$440
Printing	$100	$100	$50	$300		$150
Supplies-Office	$50	$50	$50	$150	$50	$50
Postage	$50	$25		$50	$25	$50
Advertising	$50	$50		$100	$100	
Accounting/Legal			$200			$200
Rent				$750	$750	$750
Telephone-Office	$100	$100	$100		$100	$100
Cellular	$156	$156	$156	$156	$156	$156
Utilities				$75	$75	$75
Insurance-Auto	$1,050	$1,050	$1,050	$1,050	$1,050	$1,050
Draw	$1,500	$1,500	$1,500	$1,500	$1,500	$1,500
Capital Purchases		$2,500				
Misc				$250		
Membership Fees	$500					
Insurance-Business				$250		
Travel					$1,000	
Total Expenses	**$5,046**	**$7,021**	**$5,746**	**$7,371**	**$7,446**	**$6,721**
Net Profit (Loss)	**$639**	**($1,586)**	**$1,414**	**($181)**	**($456)**	**$469**

July	August	September	October	November	December	Totals
$8,640	$8,640	$14,400	$14,400	$14,400	$14,400	$123,840
$150	$120	$240	$240	$240	$240	$2,040
$60	$60	$90	$90	$90	$60	$740
$8,850	**$8,820**	**$14,730**	**$14,730**	**$14,730**	**$14,700**	**$126,620**
$1,360	$1,360	$2,080	$2,080	$2,080	$2,080	$19,200
$300	$500	$500	$500	$700	$500	$5,250
$1,660	**$1,860**	**$2,580**	**$2,580**	**$2,780**	**$2,580**	**$24,450**
$7,190	**$6,960**	**$12,150**	**$12,150**	**$11,950**	**$12,120**	**$102,170**
				$1,000		$1,000
$2,200	$2,200	$4,160	$4,160	$4,160	$4,160	$32,320
$440	$440	$832	$832	$832	$832	$6,848
	$200		$200			$1,100
$50	$50	$50	$50	$100	$50	$750
$25	$50	$25	$150	$50	$50	$600
	$100	$100		$200		$700
	$200				$200	$800
$750	$750	$750	$750	$750	$750	$6,750
$100	$100	$100	$100	$100	$100	$1,200
$156	$156	$260	$260	$260	$260	$2,288
$75	$75	$75	$75	$75	$75	$675
$1,050	$1,050	$1,575	$1,575	$1,575	$1,575	$14,700
$1,500	$1,500	$1,500	$1,500	$1,500	$1,500	$18,000
						$2,500
						$250
						$500
						$250
						$1,000
$6,346	**$6,671**	**$9,627**	**$9,652**	**$10,602**	**$9,552**	**$92,231**
$844	**$289**	**$2,523**	**$2,498**	**$1,348**	**$2,568**	**$9,939**

Coffee House

BUSINESS PLAN

COFFEE CIRCUS

3005 37th Avenue
Santa Fe, AZ 68002

Coffee Circus' owners are taking advantage of the coffee house rage that has been sweeping the country. Along with taking advantage of this trend, they are also planning for the future. Coffee Circus is also marketing itself as a full service restaurant to maintain stability, in case the coffee trend begins to fizzle.

- EXECUTIVE SUMMARY
- MISSION STATEMENT
- PURPOSE OF BUSINESS
- BUSINESS GOALS
- DESCRIPTION OF BUSINESS
- OPPORTUNITIES AND STRENGTHS
- CRITICAL RISKS AND PROBLEMS
- MARKETING
- OPERATIONS
- MANAGEMENT
- FINANCIAL

COFFEE HOUSE
BUSINESS PLAN

EXECUTIVE SUMMARY

The interest by consumers in the coffee house industry is sweeping the country. Coffee Circus is positioned to bring this to the Northwest Santa Fe area. To date it has been confined to the Central and East areas.

Coffee Circus will provide a friendly, comfortable atmosphere where the customer can receive quality food, service and entertainment at a reasonable price. The coffee house will offer a variety of choices to the customers. Coffee and tea of all sorts will be offered. Juice, soda, and non-alcoholic beverages also will be available. Both wine and beer will be on sale. Coffee Circus will serve breakfast, lunch and dinner.

The interior design of the building will focus on projecting a relaxed atmosphere. Coffee Circus will be divided into different areas. Some will have tables and chairs, another will have large antique stuffed couches and chairs, end tables, coffee tables, book shelves filled with books and magazines, tiffany style lamps and braided rugs. A PA system will be installed so that the music and entertainment can be heard throughout. A large selection of table games will be provided.

There will be nightly entertainment featuring acoustic jazz, blues and folk music. On selected nights there will be poetry readings and an open microphone. The walls will be used as an art gallery and from time to time there will be an artist in residence.

The site contains a 3,525 square foot building which was used as a sports bar and restaurant. The building has substantial parking. The site shares the Hart Plaza with Folk Limited and Ryan Sports. Remodeling will consist of removing the existing booths, new carpet and some new furniture. The kitchen and bathrooms will require only minimum remodeling. The property is currently zoned for restaurants.

The area comprising a three mile radius around Coffee Circus is heavily populated with young, upwardly, mobile persons with expendable income. This is complemented by a large number of upper middle class "Baby Boomers" who are a large portion of those persons who frequent coffee houses.

A strength which this business will possess is the ability to change with the times. Rather than limiting the future opportunities by having a small area, Coffee Circus will have 3,525 square feet of space and a kitchen designed for flexibility. As the fad of coffee houses fades, Coffee Circus will be able to change to a full course restaurant or whatever the situation calls for.

The advertising and promotion will take a number of avenues. First, flyers will be distributed in the neighborhood. Ads will be taken out in all of the Catholic church bulletins in the area. Since Coffee Circus will be the first union restaurant in the state, ads will be placed in all of the union newsletters. Ads will also be placed in the target areas of the Burns' Grocery, and the local neighborhood newsletters. For businesses in the area, menus will be distributed and ordering will be available by fax. A customer mailing list will be developed with a calendar of events being mailed on a monthly basis.

Coffee Circus will be operated as a Sole Proprietorship. There will be private investors. However, these investors will be silent investors with a payoff of investment within three years. These investments will be paid twice-yearly in equal installments including interest. The total needed capital for Coffee Circus is $99,900. Owner's cash contribution is $10,000 and other investors and family members is $16,000. The amount needed in loans is $30,800 for equipment, $20,000 for remodeling, and $23,000 for operations. This is a total of $73,800.

Overall management will be the responsibility of the owner. The owner brings to the business over 20 years of business experience including over five years in restaurant management and five years in directing a multifaceted non-profit housing program. The general manager will have a minimum of 10 years experience. A major emphasis of Coffee Circus will be to hire economically disadvantaged or at-risk persons and provide them with job training. The majority of these persons will be identified through the City of Santa Fe Job Training Partnership.

To provide a friendly, comfortable atmosphere where the customer can receive quality food, service and entertainment at a reasonable price.

MISSION STATEMENT

This document is intended to outline the start-up of the business known as Coffee Circus. The business plan has a two-fold mission. One is to obtain financing. The other is to help define the who, what, where, when and how for the business so that the business will have a clear cut plan and operations map.

PURPOSE OF BUSINESS PLAN

The goals of the business are to provide a substantial income and to create a business and working environment where both the customer and employee are treated with dignity and respect.

BUSINESS GOALS

The specific goals of the business are:

Profit- personal income in excess of $50,000 per year within three years

Clientele- create a base clientele of persons who live and work in the area. These persons will like a relaxed atmosphere where they can "hang out"

Employees- Competent employees (at least 51% from low-income neighborhoods) who are committed and loyal

Coffee Circus will be a coffee house/restaurant located in the Hart Plaza on the southeast corner of 37th Ave. and Holgate.

DESCRIPTION OF BUSINESS

The coffee house will offer a variety of choices to the customers. Coffee and tea of all sorts will be offered. The choices of coffee will range from espresso to latte, from regular flavor to raspberry-mocha. The teas will range from English to flavored varieties.

Juice, soda, and non-alcoholic beverages also will be available. For those who want something else to drink, both wine and beer will be on sale. Wine can be ordered by the glass or by the carafe. Bottled micro-brewed beer will be available.

The breakfast menu will feature croissants, muffins, bagels, donuts, french pastries, fruit filled crepes, etc. Except for the crepes, the baked goods will be purchased from The Works. Lunch and dinner will feature sandwiches, salads and seven different soups. In hot weather, a variety of cold soups will be offered. In addition, Coffee Circus will feature a vast array of appetizers. These will include artichokes (Both stuffed or served with butter); stuffed mushrooms; mini loaves of bread served with your choice of a bowl of pesto, queso, or green chile, etc. Desserts will consist of cheesecakes (some fat-free), pastries, pies, fresh fruit and cheese.

The interior design of the building will focus on projecting a relaxed atmosphere. The bottom portion of the walls will be forest green with the upper being eggshell white. The carpeting will be forest green. The table and chairs will be custom made from light oak. The chair coverings will be of forest green material and heavily padded for comfort. The table tops will be a marbleized forest green laminate. Plants will abound in gold pots. The dishes and eating utensils will be mismatched and purchased from antique and thrift stores. The coffee cups will be from the forties and fifties era. They will be provided by a local antique business and will be for sale.

Coffee Circus will be divided into different areas. An advantage to having different areas is that customers can partake in different activities without bothering anyone (i.e., political discussions will not interfere with the music, or the music will not interfere with those playing board games or reading).

The emphasis will be on providing a comfortable environment for the customer where they will want to linger and return many times.

OPPORTUNITIES AND STRENGTHS

The time is right for opening a coffee house in the city of Santa Fe. Coffee houses are having a great deal of success, which is evidenced by the full houses every day of the week. The southeast side of Santa Fe has no such places. The closest competition is the Coffee Club located at Santa Fe Park and Main. In order to reach a coffee house, a customer from our area must drive 20 to 30 minutes. The majority of these establishments are located on the West side of town. A few are beginning to open in the downtown area.

The area comprising a three mile radius around Coffee Circus is heavily populated with young, upwardly, mobile persons with expendable income. This is complimented by a large number of upper middle class "Baby Boomers" who are a large portion of those persons who frequent coffee houses.

An additional strength which this business will possess is the ability to change with the times. Rather than limiting the future opportunities by having a small area, Coffee Circus will have 3,525 square feet of space. The kitchen will be designed for flexibility. As the fad of coffee fades, Coffee Circus will be able to change to a full course restaurant or whatever the situation calls for.

The business will bring with it a strong group of persons with an extensive background in both restaurants and business.

CRITICAL RISKS AND PROBLEMS

There are risks inherent with any business. However, the restaurant business carries with it very unique risks. Most critical is the customers' changing tastes. Another is the economy. Restaurants rely heavily on serving persons who have expendable income. When the economy takes a down turn, people change their spending priorities. There are less trips to restaurants.

A problem also in restaurants is finding dependable help who will stay with the business. Many restaurant employees tend to be younger and are attempting to move into a career. When either their schooling ends or they find their "dream job," they move on. Often servers filling the positions are non-skilled, and tend to be single mothers or lower educated persons. These persons come with specific circumstances which must be accounted for by management. A single mother may experience child-care problems, or a bus person may have problems with reading. A good owner must learn to deal with these problems in a manner which benefits the business as well as the employee.

MARKETING

Goal

Generate monthly sales revenues of $71,000 per month of 3% of the target market within 18 months of opening.

Objectives

- Maintain a high standard of food quality and service
- Provide first-rate live entertainment without a cover charge

- Ensure a friendly comfortable atmosphere
- Place monthly ads in neighborhood publications
- Distribute monthly fliers to neighborhood, businesses and churches
- Offer discount coupons
- Maintain and use a customer mailing list

The customer will be between 18 to 55 years old. The income level is between $20,000 and $100,000 per year. They will live within three miles of Coffee Circus. They will be white collar workers (managers, professionals, etc.) with expendable income. The education level will range from some college to post-graduate work. A limited number (10%) will come from other areas. This 10% will generally be persons who are coming to see a particular entertainer or poetry reading. A majority of the customers will be persons who enjoy a relaxing atmosphere, conversation and table games.

Target Customer

Based on the customer profile for Coffee Circus the following numbers were compiled. The report used was prepared by Phoenix Real Estate using information obtained through the Facts Report. The report was prepared using Coffee Circus as the focal point and delineating numbers by a one, three and five mile radius. For purposes of determining market share for Coffee Circus, a three-mile radius was used. National statistics show that most persons do not travel more than three miles to eat or to listen to entertainment. The report shows that 162,908 persons live in the three mile radius. The following is the breakdown of target customers.

Estimated Market Share and Sales

Age Percent	% of Population
21-24	6.26%
25-29	7.97%
30-34	8.15%
35-39	8.03%
40-49	16.67%
Total	**47.08%**

Income	% of Population
50,000-74,999	20.94%
35,000-49,999	20.04%
25,000-34,999	14.92%
Total	**55.90%**

Education	% of Population
Some college	28.76%
Associate degree	9.09%
Bachelor degree	13.39%
Graduate degree	5.54%
Total	**56.78%**

Occupation	% of Population
Executive	12.96%
Prof./Specialty	13.16%
Technical Support	4.67%
Administrative Support	20.12%
Total	**50.91%**

The formula takes the total population and then multiplies that number by the percentages in order of importance to the Target Customer.

Formula For Market Share

Total Population x Age % x Income % x Education % x Occupation % = Total Market
$$162,908 \times 47.08\% \times 55.90\% \times 56.78\% \times 50.91\% = 12,393 \text{ persons}$$

Market Share For Coffee Circus
2.2% Of Market = 276 Cust./Day or 17 Cust./Hour
1.8% Of Market = 230 Cust./Day or 14 Cust./Hour
1.6% Of Market = 202 Cust./Day or 12 Cust./Hour

Occupancy Levels

The occupancy of Coffee Circus is 127 persons. Two different methods can be used to determine occupancy levels.

Hourly - If you estimate percent of occupancy on an hourly basis, the customer rate would be 9.4% of occupancy. 12 cust/hr / 127 = 9.4% occupancy per hour

Mealtime - Typically, you will have two turnovers per meal. Based on projections the percentages would be 23% for breakfast, 27% for lunch and 32% for dinner.

Breakfast - 57 cust / 2 = 29 cust / 127 = 23% occupancy level

Lunch - 67 cust / 2 = 34 cust / 127 = 27% occupancy level

Dinner - 79 cust / 2 = 40 cust / 127 = 32% occupancy level

In reality, the true occupancy rate lies somewhere in the middle. Not all of the customers will come in during those dinner times nor will they be spaced evenly throughout the day.

Promotion & Advertising

The advertising and promotion will take a number of avenues. First, flyers will be distributed in the neighborhood. Ads will be taken out in all of the Catholic church bulletins in the area: Holy Martyr, Queen of Peace and St. Christopher's. These ads will offer 10% off, if the parishioner brings the bulletin with them. The restaurant is located one block from Holy Martyr Church and school. The owner's family attend the church and have a son who has been a student in the school for 7 years. Special events will be promoted with a portion of the proceeds going to the school. Since Coffee Circus will be the first union restaurant in the state, ads will be placed in all of the union newsletters offering a 10% discount to anyone showing their union card. Ads will also be placed in the target areas of the Burns' Grocery, and the local neighborhood newsletters. For special entertainment nights, radio and newspaper ads will be placed. Entertainment and food critics will be given an invitation. On opening night we will have an invitation only party, with over 1,200 invitations being sent.

For businesses in the area, menus will be distributed and ordering will be available by fax. A customer mailing list will be developed with a calendar of events being mailed on a monthly basis.

Sales Tactics

Servers will always ask the customer if they want added items, i.e. specialty coffee, soup with the sandwich, appetizers, and dessert. This will not only increase sales for the business but will also increase the amount of money the server makes. Most people tip according to a percentage of the check. The higher the check the greater the tip. The server can control their own income.

All tables also will have "table tents" or advertisements. The tents will describe upcoming events. Also, pictures and descriptions of items for sale, such as micro-brewed beers, desserts, etc., will be on the tents. The menus will provide detailed descriptions of the items available, including a section describing the different types of beers available. For example, the chili beer.

Service/Warranty

If the customer has a complaint, everything will be done to satisfy them. If that does not work, the customer will be given their meal free of charge.

Competition

Chicken Little - Northwest corner of Holgate and 37th Ave. One block north of Coffee Circus.

Provides home-style cooking. Known for their southern style cooking. Pleasant homey surroundings. The restaurant caters to families who want to eat and leave. No live entertainment is provided. Their prices are moderate with little or no variation. They are known for good quality food and service. Extremely clean and well managed. There is little or no product comparison. They have become successful due to location and reputation.

Burger's Joint - Northwest corner of Holgate and 37th Ave.

A well-known fast food franchise with a good presence and marketing plan. The food and prices are about the same as their competition. There is no product comparison.

LaJolla - Southeast corner of 37th Ave. and Holgate

Serves Mexico City style food. The atmosphere is upscale and the food pricing is moderately high. The food is highly specialized and caters to a certain type of clientele. There is no comparison.

Steve's - Northeast corner of 37th Ave. and Holgate

Serves a full course menu. The pricing is moderate, but cheaper than Chicken Little. The quality is fair. Most persons eat there because of pricing and because they are shopping at the store. There is very little competition for Coffee Circus.

OPERATIONS

Goals

Keep cost of goods sold at or below 30%. Provide customers with prompt and courteous service.

Objective
- Provide initial training for all employees
- Hold monthly employee meetings
- Have an open door policy for employee suggestions and concerns
- Implement the use of the Business Plan systems
- Purchase and use the Food Fax software package
- Have clearly defined job descriptions and duties
- Have an employee policy handbook
- Do employee reviews every six months
- Customer suggestion box
- Design kitchen and service area to be efficient

Product Distribution

The product will be distributed in the restaurant by food servers. The food will be cooked on site, except for some of the baked goods. Some of these, such as croissants will be purchased in the raw frozen form and baked daily.

When a customer enters Coffee Circus they will be greeted by a hostess who will seat them and provide them with menus. A server will greet them and give them water. The server will inquire what they would like to drink. The drink order will be prepared by the server. If the drink is either beer, wine or coffee, that will be prepared by the bartender. The drink order will be given to the bartender on a written check, which will be rung up on the register. If the server fixed the drink, it will be rung up on the register by the server. The server will deliver the drinks and then take the food order if the customer is ready. The server will take the food order, ring it up and the order will appear on the cook's computer screen. The cook will prepare the food, in the order the tickets are given. The server will prepare the salads, desserts, hot and cold soups and other items. The cook places the finished food on the window. The server must pick the food up within two minutes. The food is placed on the table and the server will ask if there is anything else which the customer needs. The server will check all the drinks and replenish water, ice tea and plain coffee. The server will ask if the customer needs another drink. Specialty drinks are not refill items. Non-specialty drinks are free refills. The server will familiarize the customer with the operations of Coffee Circus. They will explain to the customer that a number of table games are available if they wish to play. The server will let the customer know about the reading room and present them with a schedule of events. The customer will always be asked if they would like dessert or an after dinner coffee. The server is responsible for checking on the customer in a timely manner. This should be done in an unobtrusive manner. The server will maintain the tables in a clean and sanitary condition. Dirty dishes and plates must be removed immediately. Condiments must be kept full and the containers clean. The server is responsible for presenting the check, payment of the check and returning a receipt to the customer.

The cook is responsible for cooking and preparing all dishes not prepared by the server. The orders will appear on the computer monitor and the cook will prepare them according to the order given. The cook and their assistants are responsible for preparing all items in the morning such as the soups for the day, slicing meat, making specialty items and other dishes for the day. The assistant cooks are responsible for the prep work of all items for the servers and the cooks. This includes stocking all supplies, cutting cheese, fruit, salad items, ice, filling soup tureens, etc.

Cleanliness is required above all else. The servers will keep all of their work areas clean at all times. Spills must be cleaned immediately. After each shift, servers will check the side work chart and have it finished before they leave. This work will be checked by the shift supervisor. The cooking area will be maintained in a clean and sanitary manner. All areas will routinely be wiped down and swept. The cooks and assistants will also have side work which must be completed before leaving. The dishwasher is responsible for keeping the dishes washed and helping with busing the tables if needed. The dishwasher is responsible for mopping the kitchen floor. All employees must read and be knowledgeable of health regulations and follow those rules. Training will be provided by Coffee Circus. Hands must be washed on a routine basis. Smoking is allowed only in designated areas. No smoking is allowed in any food preparation area.

The servers will be required to present a clean appearance. A uniform consisting of an eggshell white polo shirt with Coffee Circus logo, forest green walking shorts or long pants, black sneakers and black ankle socks. The servers must be polite, friendly, and helpful, not only to the customer but to the other staff as well. At no time will employees be allowed to discriminate by remarks, actions or jokes.

Additional regulations are contained in the Employee Handbook.

Cash Register

The cash register system will be Quix 3000 Touchscreen. The built-in system software prints hard or soft guest checks, uses single or multiple remote printers, and reports and tracks data terminal to terminal, or throughout the network. Produces management reports for system, terminal, or revenue center; current and/or to-date totals for:

- Employee/cashier balance reports
- Employee tip reports
- Open and closed check reports
- Time period sales analysis
- Detailed or summarized menu item sales analysis
- Detailed or summarized sales group and category analysis

Pricing

The food price will be in the moderate range and comparable to other coffee houses in the area. The cost will be determined by not only what the going rate in the area is but also by the percentage of actual cost of the food. The price will not only be competitive, but the food will be tasty, well presented, and large portions will be served in a relaxing atmosphere where the customer will be comfortable. The image projected by the pricing will be that the customer will be getting a fair value for their money; that they do not need to be rich to eat at Coffee Circus and anyone can afford to come in. They will be able to use the books and games. In the evening, they will be able to listen to the live entertainment. During the day, music will be played over the PA.

Credit terms will be offered only in the form of credit card service, such as Visa, MasterCard and Discover. Many people who eat out prefer to pay with credit cards, whether it is to keep track of expenditures or for a work expense account.

The cost of the food will be based on a set percentage. Restaurants traditionally keep food costs between 26% to 32%. Based on the type of food to be served and the delivery system, the percentage for Coffee Circus will be an average of 30% of the actual cost of the food. In order to accomplish this, Food Fax software will be utilized. The software contains the following features.

Inventory Accounting System

Calculates cost of goods, provides shelf-order inventory forms, receiving logs, compares actual usage to average usage by item, ranks highest over and under use items. Tracks vendors, allows look-up by name or vendor item codes. Automatic distribution of invoice amounts to general ledger account numbers. Purchase and transaction recap reports, inventory level control reports, price history and fluctuation reports.

Recipe Costing and Sizing

Plate and batch recipes instantly costed as prices change. Sizing and modeling capabilities.

Menu Analysis

Complete menu and sales analysis reporting. Evaluate menu performance, run products by contribution. Product cost reports available by day or any combination of days. Sales mix can be sequenced to follow "Z" tape order for fast data entry.

Ideal Use/Perpetual Inventory

Tightest possible method of inventory control compares actual use to ideal use by item and computes variance. Includes ability to run perpetual inventories and track batch recipe production variances.

Bid and Purchase Order

Built-in bid pricing system allows entry of vendor bids and automatic selection of best price available. Shopping list feature, automatic PO creation, price history reports and more.

POS Interface

Import sales mix data directly from almost any cash register. POS system or polling package.

Accounts Payable Interfaces

Export purchases to accounts payable system.

Suppliers

The suppliers have all been in business for a number of years and have dependable reputations.

The Works

They will supply all of the bread products such as croissants, loaves of bread, pastries, etc. The Works is a major supplier to restaurants in the area.

Genevieve Pie Company

Since 1987, Genevieve Pie Company has been creating a quality line of dessert products satisfying even the most discerning palate. One of their best known customers is The Big Easy.

Genevieve's is also the distributor for Verson Amos. Verson Amos has built a reputation of manufacturing the finest products since 1980. They will supply the cheesecakes.

Southwestern Coffee Roasters

This family owned and operated company has been roasting coffee for almost a decade. They will supply all of the coffee, teas, and equipment. They also provide ongoing barista training for all Coffee Circus employees at no cost.

Lewis Business Systems

Lewis will provide the Purveyor system. For 25 years, Lewis has provided operational solutions to the hospitality industry. Their specialized focus on restaurants, hotels and bars has made them one of the largest dealers of Quix systems in the country.

Powerhouse, Inc.

Powerhouse, Inc. will provide the software package to track the food inventory and pricing. This system was explained in depth previously.

For over a decade, Powerhouse has specialized exclusively in food and beverage management. In addition to its Food Fax software, recognized world-wide as the industry standard, Powerhouse's consulting and training expertise has been utilized by trade associations, publishers, governments and private companies to help operators reduce costs and improve profits.

Brite Lite

Brite Lite will provide the outside signage.

Dirt Out

Dirt Out will lease the dishwashing system to Coffee Circus. The lease includes all servicing, parts, labor, and chemicals. There is never an added charge. Dirt Out builds, guarantees and services its dishwashers. They provide regular and emergency service whenever you need it.

In Line

In Line has been in business for four years doing tenant improvements and design coordination. Clients include, Tasmania Restaurants, Red Bank and St. John's Boats. In Line is versed in all areas of restaurant permitting, design and regulations.

MANAGEMENT

Goal

To have a competent and knowledgeable management staff which functions as a team.

Objectives

- Hire experienced, qualified persons
- Conduct weekly management meetings
- On-going training to include outside classes in food service, management, etc.
- Reviews every six months
- Performance incentives
- Encourage creativity

Coffee Circus will be operated as a Sole Proprietorship. There will be private investors. However, these investors will be silent investors with a payoff of investment within three years. These investments will be paid twice-yearly in equal installments including interest.

Overall management will be the responsibility of the owner. There will be a general manager and shift supervisors.

Proprietor

As owner, Kirby Pitt brings to Coffee Circus an extensive and varied background. She has been General Manager for two restaurants and has been the Dining Room Captain for a major private club.

Her most recent experience was with a non-profit agency. She was responsible for overseeing three housing programs for the agency and a staff of six persons. Her duties included: monthly reports to Santa Fe Bank, City of Bradford and State Housing Trust Fund; over a $500,000 yearly budget. Ms. Pitt is competent in all areas regarding regulations for the above mentioned organizations, and other government programs.

Also, she performed the grant writing, and was responsible for fundraising and public speaking on behalf of the agency. She worked closely with the Executive Director on purchases of properties for affordable rental from Santa Fe Properties and also wrote the Sante Fe Properties monitoring reports.

In addition, she helped case-work clients, advocated for low income persons, performed housing counseling for persons in danger of foreclosure and worked with union members in need of services.

She serves as a commissioner for the City of Santa Fe Human Service Commission. She is also a member of the executive committee and the community services committee, and serves on the advisory board for the Oasis Family Service Center. In 1984, she was appointed by Mayor Gilda Raye to the Southwestern Village Planning Committee and is a registered lobbyist.

General Manager

Qualifications

This position has not been filled. The requirements of the position require 10 years experience in restaurants, at least five of those years in some type of supervisory position. A bachelor's degree in hotel and restaurant management is preferable. The candidate for this position will be required to submit a resume and verifiable references. The candidate will be interviewed and hired by the proprietor.

Job Description

The general manager will report directly to the owner. They will be responsible for the overall management of the staff. They will work in conjunction with the owner in ordering supplies, maintaining inventory, handling customer complaints and scheduling staff. Other duties would include ensuring staff coverage for all shifts and reports to the owner.

Shift Supervisor

Qualifications

Must have five years experience in restaurant work. At least three years as a server. They must be at least 21 years old. They must possess a friendly and outgoing personality and have good personal hygiene.

Organization

The candidate for this position will be required to submit a resume and applications.

The candidate will be interviewed and hired by the proprietor and general manager.

Job Description

They will be responsible for the oversight of the servers, bus person and hostess on their shift. They will work under the general manager.

The shift supervisor also works in the capacity of a server and is responsible for waiting on tables, taking the customers' food and drink orders and acting as cashier for their customers. They are responsible for helping to keep the serving area and the customer areas clean and sanitary. They are responsible for helping the assistant cook keep the service area stocked. At the end of their shift, they will be required to complete all side work as assigned.

Cook

Qualification

The cooks must have a minimum of five years experience, three of which must be as a cook not an assistant. They must have at a minimum a GED or high school diploma.

The cook will submit a resume and fill out an application. They will be interviewed and hired by the owner and general manager.

Job Description

The cook is responsible for cooking food served in the restaurant. They also are responsible for preparing food items in advance and seeing that the service area is kept stocked. Their responsibility is to see that the kitchen is kept in a clean, sanitary and working order. They oversee and train the assistant cook.

Assistant Cook

Qualifications

The assistant cook must at a minimum have a GED or be attending school or a training program. They must be at least 18 years of age.

Will be required to submit an application. Will be interviewed and hired by the cook, general manager and owner.

Job Description

The assistant cook is responsible for assisting the cook in his duties. He/she is responsible for helping to keep the kitchen clean and sanitary. When needed will help with dishwashing duties. He/she is responsible for keeping the service area stocked.

Server

Qualification

The servers must have at a minimum a GED or be attending school or a training program and one year's experience working in a restaurant. They must be at least 21 years of age. They must possess a friendly and outgoing personality and have good personal hygiene.

Will be required to submit an application. Will be interviewed and hired by the shift supervisor, general manager and owner.

Job Description

The server is responsible for waiting on tables, taking the customers' food and drink orders and acting as cashier for their customers. They are responsible for helping to keep the serving area and the customer areas clean and sanitary. They are responsible for helping the assistant cook keep the service area stocked. At the end of their shift, they will be required to complete all side work as assigned.

Hostess

Qualifications

The hostess must have at a minimum a GED or be attended school or a training program. She must be at least 18 years of age and must possess a friendly and outgoing personality and have good personal hygiene.

Will be required to submit an application. Will be interviewed and hired by the shift supervisor, general manager and owner.

Job Description

The hostess is responsible for greeting customers as they arrive at the restaurant and seating them. She is required to take reservations and answer the phones. Also to assist with busing tables or assisting the servers when available. Duties include keeping the lobby area clean.

Bus Person

Qualifications

The bus person must be attending school or a training program, must be at least 16 years of age and have good personal hygiene.

Will be required to submit an application. Will be interviewed and hired by the shift supervisor, general manager and owner.

Job Description

The bus person is responsible for keeping dirty dishes off the tables. When customers leave they must clean the table and prepare it for future customers. They are to help the servers with getting non-alcoholic drinks. They also are responsible for helping the servers. They are responsible for helping the assistant cook keep the service area stocked. At the end of their shift, they will be required to complete all side work as assigned.

FINANCIAL

To maintain costs of goods sold to 30% or less. To increase sales within an 18 month period to 3% of the target market. To maintain financial records according to GAAP.

Goals

Objectives

- Purchase and use Food Fax software
- Train employees proper food handling to prevent waste
- Maintain a weight and portioning system for food
- Check for quality of food from suppliers when food is delivered
- Maintain storage equipment in proper working condition
- Hire an experienced and qualified accounting firm
- Contract out payroll
- Purchase a personnel computer
- Utilize Business Plan equipment
- Use Accounting software

Financing Plan and Exit Strategy

The total needed capital for Coffee Circus is $99,000. Owner's cash contribution is $10,000 and other investors and family members is $16,100. The amount needed in loans is $30,800 for equipment, $20,000 for remodeling, and $23,000 for operations. This is at total of $73,800.

An acceptable exit strategy for Coffee Circus is to sell the business to another company. The restaurant business is booming in Santa Fe.

The least desirable plan would be to sell the equipment, furniture and other assets. The remaining balance would have to be renegotiated and a payment plan worked out.

Advertising Schedule

	Month 1	Month 2	Month 3	Month 4	Month 5	Month 6	Total
Newspaper	$114.20	$114.20	$114.20	$114.20	$114.20	$114.20	$685.20
Yellow Pages	$98.40	$98.40	$98.40	$98.40	$98.40	$98.40	$590.40
Other	$500.00	$500.00	$500.00	$500.00	$500.00	$500.00	$3,000.00

Fliers, Newsletters, Church Bulletins

Six Month Total $4,275.60

Cost Analysis

Start-Up Expenses

Owner's Initial cash contribution	$10,000
Equipment Loan	$30,800
Remodeling Loan	$20,000
Operating Loan	$23,000
Investors	$16,100
Total available cash	**$99,900**

Total Cost of Capital Equipment

Beginning Inventory	$8,000
Building Lease	$11,238
Equipment	$30,800
Legal Fees	$500
Accounting fees	$1,000
Licenses & Permits	$12,000
Remodeling work	$20,000
Deposits (public utilities, etc.)	$500
Adverting (grand opening, etc.)	$1,000
Promotions (door prizes, etc.)	$1,000
Other	$1,000
Total Start-up Expenses	**$87,038**
Beginning Cash Balance	**$12,862**

Equipment	Cost	**Capital Equipment**
Large Kitchen	$9,750	
Small Kitchen	$3,000	
Tables	$1,000	
Chairs	$3,100	
Couches, Chairs	$2,500	
20 Lamps	$500	
10 End Tables	$300	
Curtains	$500	
Braided Rugs	$250	
Sound System	$1,000	
Space Planner	$2,000	
POS System-PC	$2,000	
Software	$300	
Dishes	$1,000	
Signage	$3,000	
Uniform Shirts	$600	
Total Cost Capital Equipment	**$30,800**	

		Mortgage Schedule
Principal	73,800.00	
Interest	10.750%	
# of Periods	120	
Yearly Payment	12,074.15	
Monthly Payment	1,006.18	

Mth #	Mthly Pay	Int.	Principal	Rem. Princ.
				$73,800.00
1	$1,006.18	$661.13	$345.05	$73,454.95
2	$1,006.18	$658.03	$348.15	$73,106.80
3	$1,006.18	$654.92	$351.26	$72,755.54
4	$1,006.18	$651.77	$354.41	$72,401.12
5	$1,006.18	$648.59	$357.59	$72,043.54
6	$1,006.18	$645.39	$360.79	$71,682.75
7	$1,006.18	$642.16	$364.02	$71,318.73
8	$1,006.18	$638.90	$367.28	$70,951.44
9	$1,006.18	$635.61	$370.57	$70,580.87
10	$1,006.18	$632.29	$373.89	$70,206.98
11	$1,006.18	$628.94	$377.24	$69,829.74
12	$1,006.18	$625.56	$380.62	$69,449.12
Total		**$7,723.27**	**$4,350.88**	

Projected Income Statement For Year Ending December 31, 1996

	Jan '96	Feb '96	Mar '96	Apr '96	May '96	Jun '96
Sales	$52,538	$54,639	$56,825	$59,098	$60,280	$61,486
Cost of Sales	$15,761	$16,392	$17,048	$17,729	$18,084	$18,446
Gross Profit	$36,777	$38,247	$39,778	$41,369	$42,196	$43,040
Operating Expenses						
Owner's Salary	$3,333	$3,333	$3,333	$3,333	$3,333	$3,333
Salaries, Wages	$13,002	$13,002	$13,002	$13,002	$13,002	$13,002
ERE	$6,270	$6,270	$6,270	$6,270	$6,270	$6,270
Advertising	$713	$713	$713	$713	$713	$713
Legal & Acounting	$200	$208	$216	$225	$234	$243
Supplies	$300	$312	$324	$337	$351	$365
Dishwasher Lease	$131	$131	$131	$131	$131	$131
Live Entertainment	$3,500	$3,500	$3,500	$3,500	$3,500	$3,500
Rent & Lease				$3,746	$3,746	$3,746
Repairs & Maint.	$500	$500	$500	$500	$500	$500
Utilities	$2,441	$2,523	$2,608	$2,697	$2,789	$2,885
Insurance	$65	$65	$65	$65	$65	$65
Taxes & Licenses	$111	$1,156	$1,201	$1,250	$1,275	$1,300
Interest	$644	$644	$644	$644	$644	$644
Miscellaneous	$300	$312	$324	$337	$351	$365
Depreciation	$500	$500	$500	$500	$500	$500
Ammortization	$333	$333	$333	$333	$333	$333
Total Operating Expenses	$32,343	$33,502	$33,664	$37,583	$37,737	$37,895
Operating Profits	$4,433	$4,745	$6,113	$3,786	$4,459	$5,145

Jul '96	Aug '96	Sept '96	Oct '96	Nov '96	Dec '96	Totals Periods	
$62,716	$63,970	$65,249	$66,554	$67,885	$69,243	$740,483	100.00%
$18,815	$19,191	$19,575	$19,966	$20,366	$20,773	$222,145	30.00%
$43,901	$44,779	$45,674	$46,588	$47,520	$48,470	$518,338	70.00%
$333	$3,333	$3,333	$3,333	$3,333	$3,333	$39,996	5.40%
$13,390	$13,390	$13,390	$13,390	$13,390	$13,390	$158,352	21.38%
$6,313	$6,313	$6,313	$6,313	$6,313	$6,313	$75,498	10.20%
$713	$713	$713	$713	$827	$827	$8,784	1.19%
$253	$263	$274	$285	$296	$308	$3,005	0.41%
$380	$395	$411	$427	$444	$462	$4,508	0.61%
$131	$131	$131	$131	$131	$131	$1,572	0.21%
$3,500	$3,500	$3,500	$3,500	$3,500	$3,500	$42,000	5.67%
$3,746	$3,746	$3,746	$3,746	$3,746	$3,746	$33,714	4.55%
$500	$500	$500	$500	$500	$500	$6,000	0.81%
$2,985	$3,089	$3,197	$3,309	$3,426	$3,547	$35,496	4.79%
$65	$65	$65	$65	$65	$65	$780	0.11%
$1,326	$1,353	$1,380	$1,408	$1,436	$1,464	$14,660	1.98%
$644	$644	$644	$644	$644	$644	$7,728	1.04%
$380	$395	$411	$427	$444	$462	$4,508	0.61%
$500	$500	$500	$500	$500	$500	$500	0.07%
$333	$333	$333	$333	$333	$333	$333	0.04%
$38,492	$38,663	$38,841	$39,024	$39,328	$39,525	$437,434	59.07%
$5,409	$6,116	$6,833	$7,564	$8,192	$8,945	$80,904	10.93%

Projected Statement of Cash Flow For Year Ending December 31, 1996

	Jan '96	Feb '96	Mar '96	Apr '96	May '96	Jun '96
Revenues	$52,538	$54,639	$56,825	$59,098	$60,280	$61,486
COGS	$15,761	$16,392	$17,048	$17,729	$18,084	$18,446
Operating Expenses	$32,343	$33,502	$33,664	$37,583	$37,737	$37,895
Cash Payments for Income Taxes	$0	$0	$0	$0	$0	$0
Cash Flow (Net Cash From Operations)	$4,433	$4,745	$6,113	$3,786	$4,459	$5,145
Cash Interest Payments	$644	$644	$644	$644	$644	$644
Cash After Interest Payments	$3,789	$4,101	$5,469	$3,142	$3,815	$4,501
Depreciation	$500	$500	$500	$500	$500	$500
Chgs Short-term Debt	$0	$0	$0	$0	$0	$0
Chgs Long-term Debt	$362	$362	$362	$362	$362	$362
Owner's Draw	$0	$0	$3,000	$3,000	$3,000	$3,000
Net Change in Cash	$3,927	$4,239	$2,607	$280	$953	$1,639
Beginning Cash	$12,862	$16,789	$21,029	$23,636	$23,916	$24,869
Net Change In Cash	$3,927	$4,239	$2,607	$280	$953	$1,639
Ending Cash	$16,789	$21,029	$23,636	$23,916	$24,869	$26,508

Projected Income Statement For Year Ending December 31, 1997

	Jan '96	Feb '96	Mar '96	Apr '96	May '96	Jun '96	Jul '96
Sales	$71,525	$72,240	$72,962	$72,233	$71,510	$70,795	$70,087
Cost of Sales	$21,458	$21,672	$21,889	$21,670	$21,453	$21,239	$21,026
Gross Profit	$50,068	$50,568	$51,073	$50,563	$50,057	$49,557	$49,061
Operating Expenses							
Owner's Salary	$3,333	$3,333	$3,333	$3,333	$3,333	$3,333	$3,333
Salaries, Wages	$16,944	$16,944	$16,944	$17,163	$17,163	$17,163	$17,509
ERE	$7,692	$7,692	$7,692	$7,717	$7,717	$7,717	$7,755
Advertising	$713	$713	$713	$713	$713	$713	$713
Legal & Accounting	$200	$200	$200	$200	$200	$200	$200
Supplies	$466	$471	$476	$471	$466	$462	$457
Dishwasher Lease	$131	$131	$131	$131	$131	$131	$131
Live Entertainment	$3,500	$3,500	$3,500	$3,500	$3,500	$3,500	$3,500
Rent & Lease	$3,746	$3,746	$3,746	$3,746	$3,746	$3,746	$3,746
Repairs & Maint.	$500	$500	$500	$500	$500	$500	$500
Utilities	$3,617	$3,649	$3,682	$3,649	$3,617	$3,585	$3,553
Insurance	$72	$72	$72	$72	$72	$72	$72
Taxes & Licenses	$8,513	$1,528	$1,543	$1,528	$1,512	$1,497	$1,482
Interest	$644	$644	$644	$644	$644	$644	$644
Miscellaneous	$466	$471	$476	$471	$466	$462	$457
Depreciation	$500	$500	$500	$500	$500	$500	$500
Ammortization	$333	$333	$333	$333	$333	$333	$333
Total Oper. Exp.	**$51,370**	**$44,427**	**$44,485**	**$44,671**	**$44,613**	**$44,558**	**$44,885**
Operating Profits	**($1,303)**	**$6,141**	**$6,588**	**$5,892**	**$5,444**	**$4,999**	**$4,176**

Jul '96	Aug '96	Sept '96	Oct '96	Nov '96	Dec '96
$62,716	$63,970	$65,249	$66,554	$67,885	$69,243
$18,815	$19,191	$19,575	$19,966	$20,366	$20,773
$38,492	$38,663	$38,841	$39,024	$39,328	$39,525
$0	$0	$0	$0	$0	$0
$5,409	$6,116	$6,833	$7,564	$8,192	$8,945
$644	$644	$644	$644	$644	$644
$4,765	$5,472	$6,189	$6,920	$7,548	$8,301
$500	$500	$500	$500	$500	$500
$0	$0	$0	$0	$0	$0
$362	$362	$362	$362	$362	$362
$3,000	$3,000	$3,000	$3,000	$3,000	$3,000
$1,903	$2,610	$3,327	$4,058	$4,686	$5,439
$26,508	$28,411	$31,021	$34,348	$38,406	$43,092
$1,903	$2,610	$3,327	$4,058	$4,686	$5,439
$28,411	$31,021	$34,348	$38,406	$43,092	$48,531

Aug '96	Sept '96	Oct '96	Nov '96	Dec '96	Total Periods	
$69,386	$70,744	$72,190	$73,634	$75,106	$862,412	100.00%
$20,816	$21,223	$21,657	$22,090	$22,532	$258,724	30.00%
$48,570	$49,521	$50,533	$51,544	$52,574	$603,688	70.00%
$3,333	$3,333	$3,333	$3,333	$3,333	$39,996	4.64%
$17,509	$17,509	$17,682	$17,682	$17,682	$207,894	24.11%
$7,755	$7,755	$7,774	$7,774	$7,774	$92,814	10.76%
$713	$713	$713	$827	$827	$8,784	1.02%
$200	$200	$200	$200	$200	$2,400	0.28%
$453	$457	$462	$466	$471	$5,578	0.65%
$131	$131	$131	$131	$131	$1,572	0.18%
$3,500	$3,500	$3,500	$3,500	$3,500	$42,000	4.87%
$3,746	$3,746	$3,746	$3,746	$3,746	$44,952	5.21%
$500	$500	$500	$500	$500	$6,000	0.70%
$3,522	$3,553	$3,584	$3,616	$3,648	$43,275	5.02%
$72	$72	$72	$72	$72	$864	0.10%
$1,468	$1,497	$1,527	$1,557	$1,589	$25,241	2.93%
$644	$644	$644	$644	$644	$7,728	0.90%
$453	$457	$462	$466	$471	$5,578	0.65%
$500	$500	$500	$500	$500	$500	0.06%
$333	$333	$333	$333	$333	$333	0.04%
$44,832	**$44,900**	**$45,163**	**$45,347**	**$45,421**	**$535,509**	**62.09%**
$3,738	**$4,621**	**$5,370**	**$6,197**	**$7,153**	**$68,179**	**7.91%**

Projected Statement of Cash Flow Year Ending December 31, 1997

	Jan '96	Feb '96	Mar '96	Apr '96	May '96	Jun '96
Revenues	$71,525	$72,240	$72,962	$72,233	$71,510	$70,795
COGS	$21,458	$21,672	$21,889	$21,670	$21,453	$21,239
Operating Expenses	$51,370	$44,427	$44,485	$44,671	$44,613	$44,558
Cash Payments for Income Taxes	$0	$0	$0	$0	$0	$0
Cash Flow	($1,303)	$6,141	$6,588	$5,892	$5,444	$4,999
Cash Interest Payments	$644	$644	$644	$644	$644	$644
Cash After Interest Payments	($1,947)	$5,497	$5,944	$5,248	$4,800	$4,355
Depreciation	$500	$500	$500	$500	$500	$500
Chgs Short-term Debt	$0	$0	$0	$0	$0	$0
Chgs Long-term Debt	$362	$362	$362	$362	$362	$362
Owner's Draw	$0	$0	$3,000	$3,000	$3,000	$3,000
Net Change in Cash	($1,809)	$5,635	$3,082	$2,386	$1,938	$1,493
Beginning Cash	$48,531	$46,723	$52,358	$55,440	$57,826	$59,764
Net Change in Cash	($1,809)	$5,635	$3,082	$2,386	$1,938	$1,493
Ending Cash	**$46,723**	**$52,358**	**$55,440**	**$57,826**	**$59,764**	**$61,257**

Jul '96	Aug '96	Sept '96	Oct '96	Nov '96	Dec '96
$70,087	$69,386	$70,744	$72,190	$73,634	$75,106
$21,026	$20,816	$21,223	$21,657	$22,090	$22,532
$44,885	$44,832	$44,900	$45,163	$45,347	$45,421
$0	$0	$0	$0	$0	$0
$4,176	$3,738	$4,621	$5,370	$6,197	$7,153
$644	$644	$644	$644	$644	$644
$3,532	$3,094	$3,977	$4,726	$5,553	$6,509
$500	$500	$500	$500	$500	$500
$0	$0	$0	$0	$0	$0
$362	$362	$362	$362	$362	$362
$3,000	$3,000	$3,000	$3,000	$3,000	$3,000
$670	$232	$1,115	$1,864	$2,691	$3,647
$61,257	$61,926	$62,159	$63,273	$65,137	$67,828
$670	$232	$1,115	$1,864	$2,691	$3,647
$61,926	**$62,159**	**$63,273**	**$65,137**	**$67,828**	**$71,475**

Coffee Roaster

BUSINESS PLAN

VENEZIA COFFEE ROASTERS

14600 Waterfront Drive
Kennebunk, ME 04043

Two seasoned coffee roasters found their niche in a seemingly saturated market. This plan illustrates that their specialty lies not only in their roasting methods, but also in their socially responsible business practices. Their mission is to balance the needs of their customers, their environment and the coffee growers. Venezia Coffee Roasters' detailed financial tables showcase the preparation needed to make them a competitive small batch coffee roaster in the New England region.

- STATEMENT OF PURPOSE

- DESCRIPTION OF BUSINESS

- GOALS AND OBJECTIVES

- MANAGEMENT

- PRODUCT AND SERVICE

- SPACE, EQUIPMENT AND LOCATION

- MARKET INFORMATION/MARKETING

- COMPETITION

- FINANCIAL DATA

COFFEE ROASTER
BUSINESS PLAN

STATEMENT OF PURPOSE

Venezia Coffee Roasters seeks loans totaling $56,000 to: purchase equipment and inventory, rent working space, and perform the necessary renovations and improvements, and provide adequate working capital. This sum, together with an additional $23,000 investment from friends and family, will be sufficient to launch a profitable small-batch gourmet coffee roasting company. The initial form of organization will be sub-chapter "S" with a buy-sell agreement among the founders. The company's mission is to be known as the premiere small-batch coffee roasting wholesalers in southern Maine.

We have over two years experience in the specialty coffee roasting business. Venezia coffees will include only the best ingredients roasted to perfection with pride and careful attention to detail. Venezia's service will be unparalleled offering weekly interaction with its customers. Venezia will guarantee seven-day-a-week maintenance and repair service. Not only will our packaging be environmentally sensitive but it will ensure optimum freshness which surpasses our competitors. In keeping with our environmental ethics, Venezia will be the only roaster in Maine to employ an afterburner to reduce the air pollutants normally associated with the roasting process. Venezia will be able to offer all these advantages and remain competitively priced.

With the ever increasing demand for specialty coffee, Venezia will fill a specific niche in the market. Venezia coffees will appeal to the discerning coffee drinkers who insist on quality, consistency and affordability. Venezia coffee roasting company will be successful due to steady growth with profitability by the third year accomplished by providing a superior coffee with unequalled service to our customers.

How did we choose the name Venezia? Venezia draws on the Italian influence and history in specialty coffees. It lends itself well to a more sophisticated audience such as our target market.

DESCRIPTION OF BUSINESS

Venezia Coffee Roasting Company will small-batch roast only the finest, top grade beans from around the world. Careful attention will be paid to all stages of the product's development, beginning with purchasing the highest quality beans. We will small-batch roast to assure the optimum peak of flavor when roasted. We will blend coffees which complement each other in acidity and body. We will flavor coffees using the best available extracts and flavorings. State-of-the-art packaging will be used to assure a long shelf life (approximately one year) and attractive and informative labeling will be used to entice and educate the consumer about our product.

Our concern is that we be as environmentally conscious as possible. We will use an afterburner on the roaster to reduce the amount of air pollutants normally associated with the roasting process. Our packaging will be recyclable or made from recycled materials. Our packing material too will be recycled.

We will become involved with the Coffee Children Association to help promote a greater return, financially, to the countries from which the coffee originates.

We want to have a working environment that promotes a feeling of pride and enthusiasm.

Venezia will target four markets:

- Retail Specialty Shops - Gourmet, Gift
- Coffee Brewing Establishments - Bakeries, Coffee Shops, Restaurants
- Mail Order
- Office Coffee - Schools, Offices

We will provide coffee to the discerning coffee drinkers. We will be environmentally and socially conscious which will appeal to that same market. We will provide the necessary brewing, grinding and display equipment for the relevant businesses. We will contact a roasters' authorized repair service company to provide the maximum service for that equipment. We will deliver weekly to provide the end user with the freshest product possible. We will place the expiration date on each bag to further insure freshness. We will roast only what we will sell within that week.

Each account at Venezia will enjoy seven-day-a-week service for all mechanical concerns. Along with the regular weekly contacts with each account by our sales representative Venezia will have a service contract set up with CSX of Portland, Maine, to cover weekends and holidays.

As a seed company, Venezia has secured six accounts averaging 300 pounds per week. Our goal is to close ten accounts by the end of the first year. The total amount of sales per week will be 500 pounds or better. We will do a mailing in the Portland area offering introductory specials to give our name exposure and to entice consumers. We will participate in as many community functions as we can possibly handle in an effort to get name recognition and to educate the consumer about our coffee. Initially, tastings in all retail locations will be held regularly. A mailing for office coffee will be sent to surrounding schools and offices. We will capture some of the Christmas business at the gift shops by offering one-pot portions, ground and whole bean, which sell well in customized gift baskets. We will increase our sales by the end of the second year by approximately ten percent. Our name will have greater recognition by that time providing us with more referrals. By the end of year two we will be able to offer our own gift boxes and baskets for all occasions. We will target several of the surrounding businesses for their Christmas gift business. We will increase business by another 250 pounds per week by the end of the third year. At this time we will have hired an additional sales/delivery person to reach that goal through all the avenues previously described. Special emphasis will be placed on capturing corporate gift business.

GOALS AND OBJECTIVES

Both Maria and Jennifer hold college degrees. Maria owned and operated a successful house painting business for five years. She has strong production skills. Jennifer was head chef and kitchen manager at Pineland Farm Restaurant for six and a half years. She has strong organizational skills. Both Maria and Jennifer have over two years cumulative coffee roasting experience. Jennifer was manager of sales and production at Pawtucket Coffee Roasting Company. Maria was the coffee roaster for ten months at the same place. While employed at P.C.R. both Maria and Jennifer learned all of the different facets of running a coffee roasting wholesale business. Within the fifteen months that Jennifer was manager of P.C.R. she tripled sales, bringing sales up to an average of 750 pounds per week. Maria and Jennifer attend Specialty Coffee Association of America Seminars when possible. They confer with experts such as John Collers, President of the Coffee Association and owner of Collers Office in New York City, and Daniel Krull, owner of Sam Coffee Company in Brooklyn, New York. Jennifer is an active member of the East Coast Women's Network and uses that organization as a business resource. Kim Bonn, office manager of Cromwell Financial Services in Portsmouth, NH, consults with both Maria and Jennifer. Don Shute, a retired executive of IBM and EDS also consults with both women. Both Maria and Jennifer have a working knowledge of IBM and Apple Computers. They have taken adult education classes to better familiarize themselves with these platforms. They feel confident, since they have already successfully run a coffee roasting business, that they can make Venezia a profitable and long lasting business in the area.

MANAGEMENT

We have the required technical and marketing skills to get this company up and running. We have experience in ordering, roasting (production), delivery and most importantly, sales. We anticipate hiring one or two employees in year three. The first position would be as a sales/delivery person. We will split the work duties as it demands. Maria will primarily be responsible for the production end and Jennifer for the service and sales end. Each will fill-in where necessary. Bookkeeping will be shared. We have hired Karen Allen, an enrolled agent to handle taxes, and general accounting-strictly part time. We will consult with lawyers concerning incorporating issues.

Maria and Jennifer have worked together for the past two years in varying degrees. They share similar philosophies about work and life and have discussed in depth where they envision Venezia to go and how it will get there. Between us we have the necessary labor skills. When it comes time to hire new employees we feel confident we can train for any position. We continue to further our skills and knowledge by attending roasting and cupping seminars given by John Ewell, president of the Coffee Corner in Boston, MA.

PRODUCT & SERVICE

We will offer coffee roasted weekly to locations within the New England area. We will offer numerous varietals, blends, and flavored coffees along with nearly as many decaffeinated coffees and blends. Our product will be packaged in an airtight, heat-sealed, one-way air valve, polypro-pylene bag which will either be produced from recycled plastic or be recyclable. The bags will be hand stamped. Labeling will include information concerning contents about artificial and natural flavorings, origin of beans, and type of roast. Each bag will be freshness dated. We will give our suggestions for best brewing and storage. We will offer one pot portion bags along with half-pound, one-pound and five-pound bags. For brewing establishments we will provide brewers which we will install, maintain and repair as needed. We will offer promotional items such as tee shirts, paper cups, ceramic mugs, travel mugs, home grinders, French press pots, bumper stickers, etc. We will offer a money back guarantee. If for any reason the customer is dissatisfied with our product they need only return the unused portion and we will refund all their money.

Our product is extremely reliable, and safe. Any pesticides or residues from the decaffeination process are burned off in the roasting process.

With all the careful attention paid throughout the development of our product we know that Venezia coffee will yield the best cup of coffee for the end user. Freshness will be our number one concern. We are proud to be a Maine based company and feel it should add to the overall appeal of our product.

We feel that we have developed our product experience during our employment at our packaging, will be radically different from that of P.C.R.'s. Although we have not yet tested this new packaging we know through reading and observing the competition that it will be the future of packaging. We will be using a different kind of roaster than our competition, however, the process will be similar. We are confident that the roasting experience we have will translate to this other kind of roaster. As part of the service provided upon purchasing the roaster we will receive training on the new machine.

Responsibilities

Jennifer will contact each account early in the week to determine amounts and types of varietals to be roasted. Maria would then roast the coffee for those orders, blend, flavor and package the product. Then Jennifer will deliver via a delivery vehicle within the three day turnover that we allow to process an order. Orders that would fall outside of the hundred mile radius will be delivered by UPS.

Once the plant is fully equipped with the roaster we will start production immediately. Generally it takes about three hours to fill an order from raw bean to packaged product. We have five standing accounts waiting for our production facilities to open.

Jennifer will be purchasing the beans, enabling her to have a first hand knowledge of what will be roasted. A small-batch roaster, such as the one we will be using will allow us to keep a close eye on the development of the bean during the roasting process. Each varietal and each crop within that varietal has a different moisture content. It is that water content that determines the amount of roasting time needed. Since we will not have an automated roaster we will be able to adjust each roast accordingly, yielding an even roast which has been allowed to develop to its optimum flavor peak.

Coffee roasting is an exciting and wonderful process. It is simple in theory. The beans must be heated, kept moving so no burning or tipping occurs, and they must be cooled, or quenched at the precise moment to stop the roasting process. Under-roasted coffee tastes pasty, coffee roasted too long and at too high a temperature will be thin-bodied, burned and industrial-flavored. The roaster that we will be using has a drum which rotates above a gas flame. Typically the air in the drum will be heated to about 500 degrees fahrenheit and by manipulating the air flow the temperature can be steadily maintained throughout the roasting process. For the first five minutes or so the beans will tumble around and lose water weight which accounts for the 15%-18% total weight loss. When the internal gases in the beans heat up and the pressure becomes too much for the bean, they will explode creating the first of two snapping sounds heard during the process. Later when the internal temperature of the bean reaches about 400 degrees fahrenheit, the oils in the beans will begin to develop, a process known as pyrolysis. The beans will then begin to show a marked darkening in color and the second snapping will be heard. Allowing a small amount of time for the beans to cool, they will then be emptied into a metal bin where they will be air cooled. The last few minutes of the process can make the difference between a full city roast, a French roast, an espresso roast, or sadly, a worthless roast. By roasting as close to that amount which is actually ordered each week we will be able to maintain the freshness factor. By expiration dating the bags, we will be able to rotate stock accordingly.

Coffee beans can be bought through a number of brokers. There are ports in New York, Louisiana, and California. We will be using Express Freight Service, Inc. for delivery of the beans from port to our business. The average turn around time for delivery of beans is five working days. Labels, flavorings and most other supplies can all be delivered within ten working days. The initial printing of any advertising or labels will take longer to allow time for proofing, but once it is all set up delivery time is reasonable. We will have all the basic printed material ready to go before we open for business.

Orders will generally be delivered in the delivery vehicle, or by UPS. We will have routes to cover the various areas. Generally Jennifer will make the deliveries, since she will be acting as the sales representative. In so doing she can field any questions or problems the customers might have on a weekly basis. While making deliveries she can make sales calls along the way to try and increase the volume for those routes.

Venezia understands the importance of a good working relationship between ourselves and our customers. The service begins the moment we introduce and educate the consumer about our product. We are willing to customize our displays and equipment to accommodate the different space limitations and needs of each customer. We feel it is important to give the customer a working knowledge of specialty coffee and the specific brewing equipment they will be using.

In whole bean retail locations we will conduct regular tastings to introduce our product and educate the end user. We will offer attractive and informative promotional items and strategies to help establish a new customer base for the retailers.

Venezia knows that any down time for our customers due to mechanical problems of our equipment can be expensive for both parties. Venezia will have a regular maintenance program in place to troubleshoot and predict possible problems and take appropriate precautions. In the event that a mechanical problem does arise Venezia's service contract with a Conley authorized repair company will insure prompt attention to and resolution of the problem. In addition to the service contract with Conley, Venezia will employ back-up brewers as a temporary solution. Either way our customers will be provided with round-the-clock service. This service coverage is unrivaled by our local competitors.

Each week the sales representative from Venezia will contact each account not only to take orders but also to field any questions, promote new products and listen for problems.

SPACE, EQUIPMENT AND LOCATION

Space

Initially we would need the space provided by a two car garage (approximately 320 square feet). We would need plumbing with a two bay sink. We would need a gas hook-up, and the ability to vent a six inch pipe. We would require zoning for light industrial.

Equipment

We will need a small batch roaster with an afterburner, scales, a delivery vehicle, shelves, work tables, a telephone, a computer, seven brewers, five grinders, a heat sealer, and office furniture.

Location

We are considering another location somewhere between Portland and Acadia, Maine. We would prefer easy access to the main freeway. The location needs to be zoned for light manufacturing. We have looked at a place which fills all of our criteria while meeting our budget qualifications.

MARKET INFORMATION/ MARKETING

The trend in the coffee business now supports Venezia's plan. A big emphasis on gourmet and specialty coffees has been increasing and is reflected in a rapid increase of coffee shops. The West Coast's influence on the coffee market has effected consumer's appreciation of fine coffees making super-market coffees much less appealing. This statement is supported by various newspaper and trade journal articles.

Coastal Coffee Company, which has enjoyed huge success on the West Coast, has recently shown interest in expanding their operations to the East Coast (Boston) thus supporting our conclusion that the gourmet coffee trend is here to stay.

For servicing reasons we will initially focus on the local market, that would encompass an area of approximately one hundred miles in radius extending from mid-coast Maine to the Vermont/New Hampshire border and south to the southern metropolitan Boston area. Over time we will target regional and national markets through a mail-order strategy.

Like some of our competitors we will be using the finest beans and flavorings available. It would be senseless to invest all the time and money into such a fine product and then not protect it. That is why Venezia's one-half-pound, and one-pound bags are constructed of high barrier laminates with a one-way air value to allow the natural by product gas, carbon dioxide, to escape while preventing oxygen, and water contaminates from entering. The bags are heat-sealed but can be easily opened and have resealable zippers. All of these features combined will lengthen the shelf life appreciably. Typically the shelf life of coffee stored in the popular, less expensive, plastic-lined, paper bags only retain their freshness for about six weeks. Venezia's packaging will extend the shelf life to a full year. None of the other local roasters offers such packaging. From a retail perspective, the bag will retain a cleaner appearance over time since no natural oils will seep through and stain the bag.

Venezia's labeling will be very informative, offering advice on brewing and storing techniques as well as describing the type of beans, the flavoring extracts, and the type of roast. Unlike our competitors our coffees will have an expiration date affixed to each bag. This added information will further guarantee freshness to the end user.

In this time of environmental awareness we are proud to be able to offer state-of-the-art packaging that uses 80% less material in its production while offering the consumer a reusable container.

Primary Markets

A) High volume coffee brewing establishments
    1) Bakeries
    2) Donut Shops
    3) Restaurants
B) Specialty food shops
    1) Gourmet Food Shops
    2) Upper-End Gift Shops

Secondary Markets

A) Offices with an average of twenty five employees
B) Mail Order

Venezia Target Markets

Venezia will operate in the southern Maine area targeting high volume upper-end bakeries, restaurants, and specialty food shops. The geographic area includes coastal New Hampshire, and southern Maine. As quoted from "The Basis Business and Industry Profile of Specialty Coffee House/Cafes" supplied by Cleveland State University, "according to a recent National Association of the Specialty Food Trade (NASFT) report on the specialty food consumer, gourmet coffee consumers are an educated, affluent group. Overall, 22.1% of Americans purchased specialty coffee. Most gourmet coffee consumers live or work in large urban communities. However, their most significant attribute is education level. Persons with some college education are 11% above average in their consumption of gourmet coffee. Consumers that have completed college are 49% above average in their consumption. Since education is highly correlated to income, it is not surprising that specialty coffee consumers earn above average salaries. Most specialty coffee consumers are affluent, earning above $35,000 per year." We contacted the Bureau of Census whose latest statistics show that the median family income in Portland, ME. is $34,837 and $34,344 in Portsmouth, NH. The percentage of people holding Bachelor's degrees or more in Portland, ME is 29.6 and in Portsmouth, NH is 26.6. According to a researcher for the Maine State Department of Tourism, their major target market is people over fifty five, college educated, and earning over $55,000 per year. This influx of consumers of this profile increases our target market pool.

Market Description

Our direct competitors are Pawtucket Coffee Roasting Company in Jamesville, ME, Colling Roasters, in Portsmouth, NH. Also breaking new ground is Mecca Coffee Roasting Company, in Portland, ME and to some extent, Valley Coffee Roasting Company, in Stowe, VT.

COMPETITION

Since Venezia is the newest coffee roasting company we obviously lack the name recognition that all the other competitors now enjoy. However, to our advantage, we have learned from them the crucial importance of producing consistent high quality products and delivering superior service. We model ourselves after Coast Coffee Company because they insist on using only the best grade beans with careful attention to every other aspect of the coffee roasting and distribution process. It is evident in all their marketing that they are constantly aware of the value of their excellent image and reputation.

The small roasting companies in this area with whom we are in direct competition have taught us the importance of the service end of the coffee roasting business. It is not enough to produce a good coffee. It is imperative to pay close attention to the needs of the retailers, and to the consumer.

Valley Coffee Roasting Company has shown us how quickly a company can expand. They effectively canvassed the entire New England area. There is hardly a person in the New England area who has not heard of Valley Coffee. Valley was once the exclusive coffee drinkers' coffee, now you can get a cup in any Mobil Gas Station or convenience store in New England. The fallout from their indiscriminate expansion has given companies such as Venezia a new niche to fill. Venezia will offer a quality specialty coffee for retailers catering to a more sophisticated and informed audience. In light of the rapidly expanding specialty coffee market and although there are several coffee roasters in the immediate area there still remains a void Venezia can fill. Our goal is to produce a consistent high quality product and provide our customers with reliable, friendly, and expedient service. We want to protect our image and so we will be discerning about the establishments with whom we will do business. We will have written guidelines to ensure that our image is that of a reliable coffee roaster. Venezia will operate as an environmentally and socially responsible company. We will use an afterburner in the roasting process to reduce air pollutants, a step which none of the aforementioned local competitors have taken. We will recycle and re-use any product possible in producing and shipping our coffee. We will not compromise on quality to reduce costs, that would defeat our mission.

Venezia plans a controlled, and methodical, growth process. In our gradual growth we will be able to fully integrate each new business into ours with as much attention as may be needed without having to sacrifice service to the existing accounts. It has been to our benefit to watch Valley Coffee Roasting Company expand too quickly and show us the downside of unbridled growth.

FINANCIAL DATA

Capital Equipment List

Roaster and Afterburner	
San Franciscan SF 25B	
Continuous Roaster	$26,000.00
Used Delivery Vehicle	$3,000.00
Computer	$2,000.00
Heat Sealer	$200.00
Grinder (3-Used)	$1,050.00
Grinder (2-New)	$1,400.00
STF-35 Brewers (5)	$2,225.00
CWTF Dual Brewer (1)	$700.00
RTF 5 Warmer (1)	$600.00
Dual D Brewer System	$1,422.00
RWS1 Warmer Stand (2)	$150.00
1.5 GPR Server (2)	$328.00

Cost of Goods = Raw Beans (Variable Quotes Given August 30, 1994		**Breakdown of**
(3) Colombian Supremo	$2.50	**Variable and**
(2) Costa Rican Tarrazu	$2.63	**Fixed Costs**
(.5) Ethiopian Yirgacheffe	$3.25	
(1) Sumatra Mandheling	$3.30	
(.5) Kenya AA	$2.85	
(2) Decaf Colom. Meth. Dichlor.	$2.66	
(1) Decaf. Sumat. Meth. Dichlor.	$3.42	
Average Cost Per Pound (Raw)		
(Based on Average 10 Pounds we Anticipate Sell)	$2.79	
(Based on 18% Shrinkage) Average Cost Per Pound	$3.29	
+Pick Up Charges	$300.00	
+Bags 1/2 Pound (Riley & Geehr)	$0.26	
1 Pound	$0.32	
5 Pound (Lamcor)	$0.35	
Average Cost Per Pound	$0.31	
+Labels 3 Inches by 5 Inches		
Two Colors	$0.06	
+Flavoring (Per Gallon)		
Hazelnut	$129.00	
Caramel Nut	$185.00	
Chocolate	$119.00	
Vanilla	$75.00	
Cinnamon	$72.00	
Southern Pecan	$89.00	
Orange	$57.00	
Irish Creme	$94.00	
Macadamia Nut	$48.00	
Mint	$53.00	
Salaries Per Month for Two Employees at $5.00/HR		
Year One	$1,600.00	
Per Month for Two Employees at $8.00/HR		
Year Two	$2,560.00	
Per Month Two at $10/HR and one Part Time at $7/HR		
Year Three	$3,760.00	
Rent/Utilities/Insurances/Average Per Mo.		
Rent	$400.00	
*Electricity	$90.00	
*Water	$20.00	
*Telephone	$200.00	
*Car Gas	$80.00	
*Propane/Roaster	$75.00	
Health Insurance	$200.00	
Car Insurance	$50.00	
Business Insurance	$75.00	
Total	**$1,190.00**	

Monthly Breakdown of Cost of Goods Year One

*Raw Bean Quotes Given as of Sept. 1, 1994

Colombian Supremo 154 lb. bag $2.50 lb. Total $385.00
Costa Rican 132 lb. bag $2.63 lb total $347.00
Ethiopian 132 lb bag $3.25 lb Total $429.00
Kenya AA 154 lb bag $2.85 lb Total $440.00
Sumatra Mandehling 132 lb bag $3.30 lb Total $435.00
Decaf Colombian (Meth. Chlor.) 132 lb bag $2.66 lb Total $351.00
Decaf Costa Rican (Meth. Chlor.) 132 lb bag $3.03 lb Total $400.00
Decaf Sumatra Mandehling (Swiss Water) 132 lb bag $3.42 lb Total $452.00

Pre-Start-Up

4 Colombian	$1,540.00	Total Cost of Beans	$5,527.00
2 Costa Rican	$694.00	Total Cost Bags & Flav.	$1,198.00
1 Ethiopian	$429.00	Pick Up Charges	$300.00
1 Kenya AA	$440.00	**Total Cost of Goods**	**$7,805.00**
2 Sumatra	$870.00		
2 Decaf Colomb.	$702.00		
1 Decaf Costa Rica	$400.00		
1 Decaf Sumatran	$452.00		
	$5,527.00		

February

5 Colombian	$1,925.00	Total Cost of Beans	$3,668.00
3 Costa Rican	$1,041.00	Total Cost Bags & Flav.	$175.00
2 Decaf Colombian	$702.00	Pick Up Charges	$300.00
	$3,668.00	**Total Cost of Goods**	**$4,143.00**

March

5 Colombian	$1,925.00	Total Cost of Beans	$6,441.00
3 Costa Rican	$1,041.00	Total Cost Bags & Flav.	$435.00
2 Sumatran	$870.00	Pick Up Charges	$300.00
3 Decaf Colomb.	$1,053.00	**Total Cost of Goods**	**$6,876.00**
2 Decaf Costa Rica	$800.00		
1 Decaf Sumatran	$452.00		
	$6,141.00		

April

5 Colombian	$1,925.00	Total Cost of Beans	$5,283.00
3 Costa Rican	$1,041.00	Total Cost Bags & Flav.	$735.00
1 Ethiopian	$429.00	Pick Up Charges	$300.00
1 Sumatran	$435.00	**Total Cost of Goods**	**$6,318.00**
3 Decaf Colomb.	$1,053.00		
1 Decaf Costa Rica	$400.00		

May

6 Colombian	$2,310.00	Total Cost of Beans	$5,283.00
3 Costa Rican	$1,041.00	Total Cost Bags & Flav.	$498.00
1 Sumatran	$435.00	Pick Up Charges	$300.00
2 Decaf Colomb.	$702.00	**Total Cost of Goods**	**$6,318.00**
1 Decaf Costa Rica	$400.00		
1 Decaf Sumatran	$452.00		
	$5,283.00		

June

7 Colombian	$2,695.00	Total Cost of Beans	$6,015.00
3 Costa Rican	$1,041.00	Total Cost Bags & Flav.	$932.00
1 Kenya AA	$440.00	Pick Up Charges	$300.00
1 Sumatran	$435.00	**Total Cost of Goods**	**$7,247.00**
4 Decaf Colomb.	$1,404.00		
	$6,015.00		

July

8 Colombian	$3,080.00	Total Cost of Beans	$7,220.00
4 Costa Rican	$1,388.00	Total Cost Bags & Flav.	$602.00
1 Ethiopian	$429.00	Pick Up Charges	$300.00
2 Sumatran	$870.00	**Total Cost of Goods**	**$8,122.00**
3 Decaf Colomb.	$1,053.00		
1 Decaf Costa Rica	$400.00		
	$7,220.00		

August

8 Colombian	$3,080.00	Total Cost of Beans	$6,391.00
4 Costa Rican	$1,388.00	Total Cost Bags & Flav.	$910.00
2 Sumatran	$870.00	Pick Up Charges	$300.00
3 Decaf Colomb.	$1,053.00	**Total Cost of Goods**	**$7,601.00**
	$6,391.00		

September

4 Colombian	$1,540.00	Total Cost of Beans	$4,223.00
2 Costa Rican	$694.00	Total Cost Bags & Flav.	$194.00
1 Sumatran	$435.00	Pick Up Charges	$300.00
2 Decaf Colomb.	$702.00	**Total Cost of Goods**	**$4,717.00**
1 Decaf Costa Rica	$400.00		
1 Decaf Sumatran	$452.00		
	$4,223.00		

October

4 Colombian	$1,540.00	Total Cost of Beans	$3,371.00
2 Costa Rican	$694.00	Total Cost Bags & Flav.	$435.00
1 Sumatran	$435.00	Pick Up Charges	$300.00
2 Decaf Colomb.	$702.00	**Total Cost of Goods**	**$4,106.00**
	$3,371.00		

November

5 Colombian	$1,925.00	Total Cost of Beans	$3,756.00
2 Costa Rican	$694.00	Total Cost Bags & Flav.	$1,323.00
1 Sumatran	$435.00	Pick Up Charges	$300.00
2 Decaf Colomb.	$702.00	**Total Cost of Goods**	**$5,379.00**
	$3,756.00		

December

5 Colombian	$1,925.00	Total Cost of Beans	$4,156.00
2 Costa Rican	$694.00	Total Cost Bags & Flav.	$435.00
1 Sumatran	$435.00	Pick Up Charges	$300.00
2 Decaf Colomb.	$702.00	**Total Cost of Goods**	**$4,891.00**
1 Decaf Costa	$400.00		
	$4,156.00		

1/2 lb Bags = .26, 1 lb Bags = .32, 5 lb Bags = .35, Labels = .06

Flavorings (Per Gallon)

Hazelnut	$129.00	Cinnamon	$72.00
Caramel Nut	$185.00	Southern Pecan	$89.00
Vanilla	$75.00	Mint	$53.00
Chocolate	$119.00	Irish Cream	$94.00
Macadamia Nut	$48.00	Orange	$57.00

January

1/2 lb Bags	1 Case	$260.00		
1 lb Bags	1 Case	$322.00		
5 lb Bags	1 Case	$175.00		
5,000	Labels	$300.00		
1 Gal. Each Flavor		$921.00	Total	$1,978.00

February

5 lb Bags	1 Case	$175.00	Total	$175.00

March

1/2 lb Bags	1 Case	$260.00		
5 lb Bags	1 Case	$175.00	Total	$435.00

April

1/2 lb Bags	1 Case	$260.00		
5 lb Bags	1 Case	$175.00		
5,000	Labels	$300.00	Total	$735.00

May

5 lb Bags	1 Case	$175.00		
1 Gal. Hazelnut		$129.00		
1 Gal. Vanilla		$75.00		
1 Gal. Chocolate		$119.00	Total	$498.00

June

1/2 lb Bags	1 Case	$260.00		
1 lb Bags	1 Case	$322.00		
5 lb Bags	2 Cases	$350.00	Total	$932.00

July

1 Gal. Caramel Nut	$185.00			
1 Gal. Macadamia Nut	$48.00			
1 Gal. Southern Pecan	$89.00			
1 Gal. Orange	$57.00			
1 Gal. Irish Cream	$94.00			
1 Gal. Hazelnut	$129.00	Total	$602.00	

August

1/2 lb Bags	1 Case	$260.00		
5 lb Bags	2 Cases	$350.00		
5,000	Labels	$300.00	Total	$910.00

September

1 Gal Chocolate	$119.00		
1 Gal. Vanilla	$75.00	Total	$194.00

October

1/2 lb Bags	1 Case	$260.00		
5 lb Bags	1 Case	$175.00	Total	$435.00

November

1/2 lb Bags	1 Case	$260.00		
1 lb Bags	1 Case	$322.00		
5 lb Bags	1 Case	$175.00		
1 Gal. Southern Pecan	$89.00			
1 Gal. Hazelnut	$129.00			
1 Gal. Macadamia Nut	$48.00			
5,000	Labels	$300.00	Total	$1,323.00

December

1/2 lb Bags	1 Case	$260.00		
5 lb Bags	1 Case	$175.00	Total	$435.00

Note: At the close of year one there remains in inventory a surplus of all above items equalling the ten percent increase expected for year two.

$S = FC + VC$

Where
FC = Fixed Costs in Dollars
VC = Variable costs in Dollars
X = Projected pounds sold
\$6.50 = Average pound selling price

Year One		Year Two	
FC =			
Salaries	\$19,200.00	Salaries	\$30,720.00
Rent/Util./Ins.	\$16,660.00	Rent/Util./Ins.	\$14,832.00
Prof. Services	\$4,500.00	Prof. Serv.	\$2,040.00
Taxes	\$1,991.00	Taxes	\$3,047.00
Interest	\$6,171.00	Interest	\$4,623.00
Subscriptions	\$300.00	Subscriptions	\$300.00
Operating Expenses	\$2,767.00	Operating Expenses	\$1,200.00
Advertising	\$3,600.00	Advertising	\$2,400.00
Depreciation	\$7,510.00	Depreciation	\$4,506.00
Total	**\$62,699.00**	**Total**	**\$63,668.00**

$$VC = \text{Cost of Goods} \frac{\$56,407.00}{19,939} = \$2.83 \qquad VC = \frac{\$66,807.00}{21,933} = \$3.05$$

$X = 19,939 \qquad\qquad\qquad X = 21,933$

$S = \$62,699.00 + \$56,407.00 = \$119,106.00 \qquad S = \$63,668.00 + \$66,807.00$

$(\$6.50)X = \$129,604.00 \qquad\qquad (\$6.50)X = \$142,564.00$

Calculating Break-Even For Year One

S=FC/GM
Where
GM= Gross Margin Expressed As A Percentage of Sales

$$\frac{VC}{\text{Projected Pounds Sold}} = \text{VC Per Pound}$$

$$\frac{\$56,407}{19,939} = \$2.83/lb$$

Cost of Unit ($6.50 - VC of Unit ($2.83) = Gross Margin Per Unit ($3.67)

$$\frac{FC}{\text{Gross Margin Per Unit}} = \text{Break-Even in Pounds}$$

$$\frac{\$62,699}{3.67} = 17,084 \text{ lbs}$$

(17,084) ($6.50) = $111,047.00 = Break-Even Dollar Sales

Gross Margin % for Break-Even = (Break-Even in Dollars - Cost of Goods)
                                              Break-Even in Dollars

$$\frac{\$111,047.00 - \$56,407.00}{\$111,047.00} = .49 \text{ or } 49\%*$$

Note: a 5% increase due to an estimated 5% increase in cost of goods in year two.

Calculating Break-Even For Year Two

S=FC/GM
Where
GM = Gross Margin Expressed As A Percentage of Sales

$$\frac{VC}{\text{Projected Pounds Sold}} = \text{VC Per Pound}$$

$$\frac{\$65,808.00}{21,933} = \$3.00 \text{ Per lb.}$$

Cost of Unit ($6.50) - VC Per Pound ($3.00) = Gross Margin Per Unit ($3.50)

Break-Even lbs. =   FC $\frac{\$63,668.00}{\$3.50} = 18,191$
Gross Margin Per Unit

Break-Even Sales in Dollars = (18,191) ($6.50) = $118,241.00

Gross Margin % for Break-Even = Break-Even in Dollars - Cost of Goods
                                              Break-Even in Dollars

$$\frac{\$118,241.00 - \$65,808.00}{118,241.00} = .44 \text{ or } 44\%$$

Year One		Year Two		Secured Accounts	
Jan.	$6,564.00	Jan.	$7,215.00	Jan.	$6,500.00
Feb.	$8,242.00	Feb.	$9,060.00	Feb.	$7,800.00
Mar.	$8,762.00	Mar.	$9,639.00	Mar.	$7,800.00
Apr.	$9,672.00	Apr.	$10,634.00	Apr.	$7,800.00
May	$10,452.00	May	$11,492.00	May	$8,190.00
Jun.	$12,792.00	Jun.	$14,066.00	Jun.	$9,360.00
Jul.	$14,352.00	Jul.	$15,782.00	Jul.	$9,880.00
Aug.	$14,352.00	Aug.	$15,782.00	Aug.	$9,800.00
Sep.	$13,000.00	Sep.	$14,300.00	Sep.	$9,100.00
Oct.	$13,000.00	Oct.	$14,300.00	Oct.	$8,970.00
Nov.	$9,750.00	Nov.	$10,725.00	Nov.	$7,540.00
Dec.	$13,000.00	Dec.	$14,300.00	Dec.	$7,410.00

Venezia Monthly Sales Projections in Dollars

Income Statement Three Year Summary

* Includes Pre-Start-Up

	Year One	Year Two	Year Three
Sales	$133,940.00	$142,994.00	$216,100.00
Cost of Goods	$56,407.00	$66,807.00	$100,210.00
Gross Profit	$77,533.00	$76,187.00	$115,890.00
Saz;aroes	$19,200.00	$30,720.00	$45,120.00
Advertising	$3,600.00	$2,400.00	$2,400.00
Rent/Util./Ins.	*$16,660.00	$14,832.00	$16,206.00
Professional Services	$4,500.00	$2,040.00	$2,390.00
Payroll Taxes	$1,991.00	$3,047.00	$4,592.00
Interest	$6,171.00	$4,730.00	$3,938.00
Depreciation	$7,510.00	$4,506.00	$2,015.00
Operating Expenses	$5,104.00	$1,500.00	$1,675.00
Total G & A Expenses	$64,736.00	$63,775.00	$78,336.00
Gross Profit	$77,533.00	$76,187.00	$115,890.00
Net Income Before Taxes	$12,797.00	$12,412.00	$37,554.00

* Includes Two Months Pre-Start-Up

Income Statement Year One Detail By Month

* Includes Pre-Start-Up

	Jan. *	Feb.	March	April	May	June
Sales	$6,564.00	$8,242.00	$8,762.00	$9,672.00	$10,452.00	$12,792.00
Cost of Goods	$7,025.00	$2,919.00	$5,616.00	$4,934.00	$4,396.00	$6,070.00
Gross Profit	(461)	$5,323.00	$3,146.00	$4,738.00	$6,056.00	$6,722.00
Salaries	$1,600.00	$1,600.00	$1,600.00	$1,600.00	$1,600.00	$1,600.00
Advertising	$600.00	$0.00	$300.00	$300.00	$300.00	$300.00
Rent/Util./Ins.	$3,570.00	$1,190.00	$1,190.00	$1,190.00	$1,190.00	$1,190.00
Prof. Services	$2,020.00	$120.00	$345.00	$180.00	$220.00	$545.00
Payroll Taxes	$0.00	$122.00	$122.00	$386.00	$122.00	$122.00
Interest	$1,389.00	$455.00	$451.00	$447.00	$443.00	$439.00
Depreciation	$0.00	$0.00	$0.00	$0.00	$0.00	$0.00
Operating Expenses	$3,117.00	$150.00	$439.00	$275.00	$289.00	$67.00
Total G & A Expenses	$12,296.00	$3,637.00	$4,447.00	$4,378.00	$4,164.00	$4,263.00
Gross Profit	(461)	$5,323.00	$3,146.00	$4,738.00	$6,056.00	$6,722.00
Net Income Before Taxes	(12,757)	$1,686.00	(1,301)	$360.00	$1,892.00	$2,459.00

Explanation of Categories

Cost of Goods = Raw Beans + Pick-Up Charges + Bags + Labels + Flavorings
Rent/Utilities/Insurance = Rent + Electric + Water + Telephone + Gas + Fuel + Health Insurance + Car Insurance + Business
Professional Services = Legal + Accounting + Maintenance + Outside Services
Taxes + Federal + Medicare + Social Security + State + Other
Interest and bank loan is based on a $56,000.00 loan at 10% over seven years.
Operating Expenses = Supplies
Capital Purchases = Roaster + Brewers + Grinders + Scales + Heat Sealer + Delivery Vehicle + Computer
Miscellaneous = Subscriptions + Start-Up Costs
Information On Worker's Compensation
Class Code # 8006; Sale of coffee, tea or groceries
Per $100.00 of Payroll = $4.67
Also add 20% surcharge
For year three one part time employee at $7.00/hour 20/hours/week with surcharge = $632.00

Projected Employee Growth

	Year 1	Year 2	Year 3	Year 4	Year 5
Employee #1 (Jennifer)	Full Time	Full Time	Full Time	Full Time	Full Time
Employee #2 (Maria)	Full Time	Full Time	Full Time	Full Time	Full Time
Employee #3			Part Time	Full Time	Full Time
Employee #4				Part Time	Part Time
Employee #5					Part Time
Employee #6					Part Time

Employee Responsibilities

Employee #1 = Managerial/delivery/sales position
Employee #2 = Production
Employee #3 = Delivery/sales position
Employee #4 = Production position
Employee #5 = Bookkeeping/administrative position
Employee #6 = Production position

July	August	September	October	November	December
$14,352.00	$14,352.00	$13,000.00	$13,000.00	$9,750.00	$13,000.00
$5,617.00	$5,672.00	$3,364.00	$3,285.00	$4,162.00	$3,350.00
$8,735.00	$8,680.00	$9,636.00	$9,715.00	$5,588.00	$9,650.00
$1,600.00	$1,600.00	$1,600.00	$1,600.00	$1,600.00	$1,600.00
$300.00	$300.00	$300.00	$300.00	$300.00	$300.00
$1,190.00	$1,190.00	$1,190.00	$1,190.00	$1,190.00	$1,190.00
$120.00	$120.00	$245.00	$120.00	$120.00	$345.00
$386.00	$122.00	$122.00	$243.00	$122.00	$122.00
$435.00	$431.00	$427.00	$422.00	$418.00	$414.00
$0.00	$0.00	$0.00	$0.00	$0.00	$7,510.00
$199.00	$320.00	$64.00	$50.00	$84.00	$50.00
$4,230.00	$4,083.00	$3,948.00	$3,925.00	$3,834.00	$11,531.00
$8,735.00	$8,680.00	$9,636.00	$9,715.00	$5,588.00	$9,650.00
$4,505.00	$4,597.00	$5,688.00	$5,790.00	$1,754.00	(1,881)

Cash Flow-Year One

Category	Pre Start	Jan	Feb	Mar	Apr	May	Jun	Jul
Inflows								
Cash on Hand	$0	$27,613	$25,848	$25,826	$21,902	$19,576	$20,233	$20,747
Sales Net 10	$0	$4,374	$5,492	$5,844	$6,448	$6,968	$8,528	$9,568
Collect Accts.	$0	$0	$2,190	$2,750	$2,918	$3,224	$3,484	$4,264
Bank Loans	$56,000	$0	$0	$0	$0	$0	$0	$0
Personal Loans	$23,000	$0	$0	$0	$0	$0	$0	$0
Total Inflows	$79,000	$31,988	$33,530	$34,418	$31,269	$29,768	$32,245	$34,579
Outflows								
Cost of Goods	$7,805	$0	$3,243	$6,240	$5,482	$4,884	$6,744	$6,241
Salaries	$0	$1,600	$1,600	$1,600	$1,600	$1,600	$1,600	$1,600
Advertising	$300	$300	$0	$300	$300	$300	$300	$300
Rent, Util., Ins.	$2,380	$1,190	$1,190	$1,190	$1,190	$1,190	$1,190	$1,190
Prof. Services	$1,780	$240	$120	$345	$180	$220	$545	$120
Taxes	$0	$0	$122	$122	$386	$122	$122	$386
Interest	$930	$459	$455	$451	$447	$443	$439	$435
Bank Loans	$930	$471	$475	$479	$483	$487	$491	$495
Operating Expenses	$730	$730	$50	$239	$195	$239	$67	$199
Capital Purch	$34,975	$1,050	$350	$1,350	$1,350	$0	$0	$0
Miscellaneous	$1,557	$100	$100	$200	$80	$50	$0	$0
Total Outflows	$51,387	$6,140	$7,705	$12,516	$11,693	$9,535	$11,498	$10,966
Total Budget Inflows	$79,000	$31,988	$33,530	$34,418	$31,269	$29,768	$32,245	$34,579
Total Budget Outflows	$51,387	$6,140	$7,705	$12,516	$11,693	$9,535	$11,498	$10,966
Difference	$27,613	$25,848	$25,826	$21,902	$19,576	$20,233	$20,747	$23,613

Aug	Sept	Oct	Nov	Dec	Total	Category
						Inflows
$23,613	$27,081	$32,342	$37,260	$39,126	$321,166	Cash on Hand
$9,568	$8,664	$8,664	$6,500	$8,664	$89,284	Sales Net 10
$4,784	$4,784	$4,336	$4,336	$3,250	$40,320	Collect Accts.
$0	$0	$0	$0	$0	$56,000	Bank Loans
$0	$0	$0	$0	$0	$23,000	Personal Loans
$37,965	$40,530	$45,342	$48,095	$51,040	$529,769	Total Inflows
						Outflows
$6,302	$3,737	$3,650	$4,624	$3,722	$62,674	Cost of Goods
$1,600	$1,600	$1,600	$1,600	$1,600	$19,200	Salaries
$300	$300	$300	$300	$300	$3,600	Advertising
$1,190	$1,190	$1,190	$1,190	$1,190	$16,660	Rent, Util., Ins.
$120	$245	$120	$120	$345	$4,500	Prof. Services
$122	$122	$243	$122	$122	$1,991	Taxes
$431	$427	$422	$418	$414	$6,171	Interest
$499	$503	$507	$511	$516	$6,847	Bank Loans
$70	$64	$50	$84	$50	$2,767	Operating Expenses
$0	$0	$0	$0	$0	$39,075	Capital Purch
$250	$0	$0	$0	$0	$2,337	Miscellaneous
$10,884	$8,188	$8,082	$8,969	$8,259	$165,822	Total Outflows
$37,965	$40,530	$45,342	$48,095	$51,040	$529,769	**Total Budget Inflows**
$10,884	$8,188	$8,082	$8,969	$8,259	$165,822	**Total Budget Outflows**
$27,081	$32,342	$37,260	$39,126	$42,782	$363,947	**Difference**

Cash Flow - Year Two

Category	Jan	Feb	Mar	Apr	May	Jun	Jul
Inflows							
Cash on Hand	$42,782	$38,392	$37,942	$35,078	$33,602	$34,110	$34,398
Sales Net 10	$4,810	$6,038	$6,428	$7,092	$7,664	$9,380	$10,524
Collect Accts.	$4,336	$2,405	$3,022	$3,211	$3,542	$3,828	$4,686
Bank Loans	$0	$0	$0	$0	$0	$0	$0
Personal Loans	$0	$0	$0	$0	$0	$0	$0
Total Inflows	$51,928	$46,836	$47,393	$45,380	$44,808	$47,318	$49,608
Outflows							
Cost of Goods	$8,268	$3,552	$6,848	$6,014	$5,357	$7,403	$6,851
Salaries	$2,560	$2,560	$2,560	$2,560	$2,560	$2,560	$2,560
Advertising	$200	$200	$200	$200	$200	$200	$200
Rent, Util., Ins.	$1,236	$1,236	$1,236	$1,236	$1,236	$1,236	$1,236
Prof. Services	$120	$120	$245	$120	$120	$245	$120
Taxes	$122	$196	$196	$618	$196	$196	$543
Interest	$418	$414	$410	$405	$401	$397	$392
Bank Loans	$511	$516	$520	$525	$529	$533	$538
Operating Expenses	$100	$100	$100	$100	$100	$100	$100
Capital Purch	$0	$0	$0	$0	$0	$0	$0
Miscallaneous	$0	$0	$0	$0	$0	$50	$0
Total Outflows	$13,535	$8,894	$12,315	$11,778	$10,699	$12,920	$12,540
Total Budget Inflows	$51,928	$46,836	$47,393	$45,380	$44,808	$47,318	$49,608
Total Budget Outflows	$13,535	$8,894	$12,315	$11,778	$10,699	$12,920	$12,540
Difference	$38,392	$37,942	$35,078	$33,602	$34,110	$34,398	$37,068

Aug	Sept	Oct	Nov	Dec	Total	Category
						Inflows
$37,068	$40,590	$45,572	$50,532	$52,033	$55,498	Cash on Hand
$10,524	$9,536	$9,536	$7,150	$9,536	$98,215	Sales Net 10
$5,258	$5,258	$4,764	$4,764	$3,575	$48,652	Collect Accts.
$0	$0	$0	$0	$0	$0	Bank Loans
$0	$0	$0	$0	$0	$0	Personal Loans
$52,850	$55,384	$59,872	$62,446	$65,144	$628,966	Total Inflows
						Outflows
$6,917	$4,095	$3,999	$5,071	$4,079	$68,454	Cost of Goods
$2,560	$2,560	$2,560	$2,560	$2,560	$30,720	Salaries
$200	$200	$200	$200	$200	$2,400	Advertising
$1,236	$1,236	$1,236	$1,236	$1,236	$14,832	Rent, Util., Ins.
$120	$245	$120	$120	$345	$2,040	Prof. Services
$196	$196	$196	$196	$196	$3,047	Taxes
$388	$383	$379	$374	$369	$4,730	Interest
$542	$547	$551	$556	$560	$6,428	Bank Loans
$100	$100	$100	$100	$100	$1,200	Operating Expenses
$0	$0	$0	$0	$0	$0	Capital Purch
$0	$250	$0	$0	$0	$300	Miscellaneous
$12,259	$9,812	$9,341	$10,413	$9,645	$134,151	Total Outflows
$52,850	$55,384	$59,872	$62,446	$65,144	$628,966	**Total Budget Inflows**
$12,259	$9,812	$9,341	$10,413	$9,645	$134,151	**Total Budget Outflows**
$40,590	$45,572	$50,532	$52,033	$55,498	$494,816	**Difference**

Anticipated Estimated Sales In Pounds Per Week and Month Year One

January

Paris Bistro	125
Coffee Villa	50
John's Beans	40
Roasted, Inc.	35
	250

February

Paris Bistro	125
Coffee Villa	50
John's Beans	40
Roasted, Inc.	35
Cliffside Cafe	30
Finer Things	20
Mail Order	15
	315

March

Paris Bistro	125
Coffee Villa	50
John's Beans	40
Roasted, Inc.	35
Cliffside Cafe	30
Finer Things	20
Retail I	25
Mail Order	15
	340

April

Paris Bistro	125
Coffee Villa	50
John's Beans	40
Roasted, Inc.	35
Cliffside Cafe	30
Finer Things	20
Retail I	25
Retail II	20
Brewer I	20
Mail Order	15
	380

May

Paris Bistro	125
Coffee Villa	50
John's Beans	40
Roasted, Inc.	35
Cliffside Cafe	30
Finer Things	35
Retail I	25
Retail II	25
Brewer I	20
Brewer II	20
Mail Order	10
	415

June

Paris Bistro	125
Coffee Villa	50
John's Beans	50
Roasted, Inc.	40
Cliffside Cafe	35
Finer Things	60
Retail I	30
Retail II	30
Brewer I	30
Brewer II	30
Mail Order	15
	495

July

Paris Bistro	125
Coffee Villa	50
John's Beans	50
Roasted, Inc.	40
Cliffside Cafe	35
Finer Things	80
Retail I	40
Retail II	40
Brewer I	40
Brewer II	40
Mail Order	15
	555

August

Paris Bistro	125
Coffee Villa	50
John's Beans	50
Roasted, Inc.	40
Cliffside Cafe	35
Finer Things	80
Retail I	40
Retail II	40
Brewer I	40
Brewer II	40
Mail Order	15
	555

September

Paris Bistro	125
Coffee Villa	50
John's Beans	45
Roasted, Inc.	35
Cliffside Cafe	35
Finer Things	60
Retail I	35
Retail II	35
Brewer I	35
Mail Order	10
	500

October

Paris Bistro	125
Coffee Villa	50
John's Beans	45
Roasted, Inc.	35
Cliffside Cafe	30
Finer Things	60
Retail I	35
Retail II	35
Brewer I	35
Brewer II	35
Mail Order	15
	500

November

Paris Bistro	125
Coffee Villa	40
John's Beans	45
Roasted, Inc.	35
Cliffside Cafe	35
Finer Things	60
Retail I	35
Retail II	35
Brewer I	35
Brewer II	35
Mail Order	10
	500

December

Paris Bistro	125
Coffee Villa	40
John's Beans	20
Roasted, Inc.	35
Cliffside Cafe	50
Finer Things	15
Retail I	50
Retail II	50
Brewer I	20
Brewer II	20
Mail Order	75
	500

Payment Schedule

Pmt	Principal	Interest 10.000%	Balance 56,000.00	Total Interest
1	$463.00	$466.67	$55,537.00	$466.67
2	$466.86	$462.81	$55,070.14	$929.48
3	$470.75	$458.92	$54,599.39	$1,388.40
4	$474.68	$454.99	$54,124.71	$1,843.39
5	$478.63	$451.04	$53,646.08	$2,294.43
6	$482.62	$447.05	$53,163.46	$2,741.48
7	$486.64	$443.03	$52,676.82	$3,184.51
8	$490.70	$438.97	$52,186.12	$3,623.48
9	$494.79	$434.88	$51,691.33	$4,058.36
10	$498.91	$430.76	$51,192.42	$4,489.12
11	$503.07	$426.60	$50,689.35	$4,915.72
12	$507.26	$422.41	$50,182.09	$5,338.13
13	$511.49	$418.18	$49,670.60	$5,756.31
14	$515.75	$413.92	$49,154.85	$6,170.23
15	$520.05	$409.62	$48,634.80	$6,579.85
16	$524.38	$405.29	$48,110.42	$6,985.14
17	$528.75	$400.92	$47,581.67	$7,386.06
18	$533.16	$396.51	$47,048.51	$7,782.57
19	$537.60	$392.07	$46,510.91	$8,174.64
20	$542.08	$387.59	$45,968.83	$8,562.23
21	$546.60	$383.07	$45,422.23	$8,945.30
22	$551.15	$378.52	$44,871.08	$9,323.82
23	$555.74	$373.93	$44,315.34	$9,697.75
24	$560.38	$369.29	$43,754.96	$10,067.04
25	$565.05	$364.62	$43,189.91	$10,431.66
26	$569.75	$359.92	$42,620.16	$10,791.58
27	$574.50	$355.17	$42,045.66	$11,146.75
28	$579.29	$350.38	$41,466.37	$11,497.13
29	$584.12	$345.55	$40,882.25	$11,842.68
30	$588.98	$340.69	$40,293.27	$12,183.37
31	$593.89	$335.78	$39,699.38	$12,519.15
32	$598.84	$330.83	$39,100.54	$12,849.98
33	$603.83	$325.84	$38,496.71	$13,175.82
34	$608.86	$320.81	$37,887.85	$13,496.63
35	$613.94	$315.73	$37,273.91	$13,812.36

Pmt	Principal	Interest	Balance	Total Interest
36	$619.05	$310.62	$36,654.86	$14,122.98
37	$624.21	$305.46	$36,030.65	$14,428.44
38	$629.41	$300.26	$35,401.24	$14,728.70
39	$634.66	$295.01	$34,766.58	$15,023.71
40	$639.95	$289.72	$34,126.63	$15,313.43
41	$645.28	$284.39	$33,481.35	$15,597.82
42	$650.66	$279.01	$32,830.69	$15,876.83
43	$656.08	$273.59	$32,174.61	$16,150.42
44	$661.55	$268.12	$31,513.06	$16,418.54
45	$667.06	$262.61	$30,846.00	$16,681.15
46	$672.62	$257.05	$30,173.38	$16,938.20
47	$678.23	$251.44	$29,495.15	$17,189.64
48	$683.88	$245.79	$28,811.27	$17,435.43
49	$689.58	$240.09	$28,121.69	$17,675.52
50	$695.32	$234.35	$27,426.37	$17,909.87
51	$701.12	$228.55	$26,725.25	$18,138.42
52	$706.96	$222.71	$26,018.29	$18,361.13
53	$712.85	$216.82	$25,305.44	$18,577.95
54	$518.79	$210.88	$24,586.65	$18,788.83
55	$724.78	$204.89	$23,861.87	$18,993.72
56	$730.82	$198.85	$23,131.05	$19,192.57
57	$736.91	$192.76	$22,394.14	$19,385.33
58	$743.05	$186.62	$21,651.09	$19,571.95
59	$749.24	$180.43	$20,091.85	$19,752.38
60	$755.49	$174.18	$20,146.36	$19,926.56
61	$761.78	$167.89	$19,384.58	$20,094.45
62	$768.13	$161.54	$18,616.45	$20,255.99
63	$774.53	$155.14	$17,841.92	$20,411.13
64	$780.99	$148.68	$17,060.93	$20,559.81
65	$787.50	$142.17	$16,273.43	$20,701.98
66	$794.06	$135.61	$15,479.37	$20,837.59
67	$800.68	$128.99	$14,678.69	$20,966.58
68	$807.35	$122.32	$13,871.34	$21,088.90
69	$814.08	$115.59	$13,057.26	$21,204.49
70	$820.86	$108.81	$12,236.40	$21,313.30
71	$827.70	$101.97	$11,408.70	$21,415.27
72	$834.60	$95.07	$10,574.10	$21,510.34
73	$841.55	$88.12	$9,732.55	$21,598.46
74	$848.57	$81.10	$8,883.98	$21,679.56
75	$855.64	$74.03	$8,028.34	$21,753.59
76	$862.77	$66.90	$7,165.57	$21,820.49
77	$869.96	$59.71	$6,295.61	$21,880.20
78	$877.21	$52.46	$5,418.40	$21,932.66
79	$884.52	$45.15	$4,533.88	$21,977.81
80	$891.89	$37.78	$3,641.99	$22,015.59
81	$899.32	$30.35	$2,742.67	$22,045.94
82	$906.81	$22.86	$1,835.86	$22,068.80
83	$914.37	$15.30	$921.49	$22,084.10
84	$921.49	$7.68	$0.00	$22,091.78

Assets

Cash	31,820
Accts. Receive.	0
Inventory	7,530
Fixed Assets	34,450
Security Deposit	400
Start-Up Costs	4,800
Total Assets	**79,000**

Liabilities

Note Payable Bank	(56,000)
Note Payable Perso	(23,000)
Total Liabilities	**(79,000)**

Assets

Cash	$42,782
Accounts Receivable	$4,336
Inventory	$6,267
Fixed Assets	$39,075
Less Accumulated Depreciati	($7,510)
Security Deposit	$400
Deferred Interest	N/A
`Total Assets	$85,350

Liabilities

Note Payable Bank	$49,153
Note Payable Personal	$23,000
Share Holders Equity	$13,197
Total Liabilities	**$85,350**

Direct Mail Outlet

BUSINESS PLAN

POST DIRECT

52 1/2 Burr Rd.
Silver Spring, MD 20907
July, 1995

The Post Direct business plan is unique, in that it develops a detailed plan for growing a newly started business through franchising into 25 outlet centers. Post Direct provides an excellent description of the process as well as the benefits of expansion through franchising.

- EXECUTIVE SUMMARY

- THE COMPANY

- MANAGEMENT

- MARKET ANALYSIS

- COMPETITION

- MARKETING STRATEGY

- ADVERTISING AND PROMOTION

- FINANCIAL PROJECTIONS

- THE FRANCHISE AGREEMENT

DIRECT MAIL OUTLET
BUSINESS PLAN

EXECUTIVE SUMMARY

The following Executive Summary information is qualified in its entirety by the more detailed information appearing elsewhere in this business plan. The document is confidential and is one which can be substantiated by many years of ongoing work, extensive research, and experience of the Post Direct team of marketing experts.

Company Name: Post Direct
Contact: John Kingham, President
Benjamin Miller, Vice President & Secretary
Address: 52 1/2 Burr Rd.
Silver Spring, MD 20907
Telephone: (301) 555-3492
Fax: (301) 555-3494

The Company

Business Description, Current Position and Future Outlook

Post Direct plans to be a chain of direct mail outlets specializing in the highest quality four color post card cooperative and solo direct mail in the nation. Post Direct consists of a high quality production demographically targeted to the best and most affluent of upscale markets. Post Direct is the Tiffany of direct mail. The outlets are targeted to be located in major metropolitan areas.

The Company evolved out of Kingham and Associates Advertising, Inc., a full service advertising agency which is owned by John Kingham. Mr. Kingham is also president of that corporation. Kingham founded the original Post Direct outlet in May, 1992. He was assisted in The Company development by Benjamin Miller who joined the firm in September of 1992. Their first issue was published in November, 1992. Additional issues were published in March 1993, May 1993, September 1993, November 1993, March 1994, May 1994, September 1994, December 1994 and April 1995. Post Direct was incorporated on September 3, 1993. The chain now consists of one corporate outlet in Silver Spring, Maryland which serves the Washington metropolitan market. Locations for the Post Direct outlets are planned in prime metropolitan areas to attract upscale customers and generate high sales. The demographics include the 30 to 64 year old adults with household incomes of $75,000 and up, where applicable.

John Kingham and Benjamin Miller perfected Post Direct to the point that it has become one of the best direct mail companies in the National Capital marketing area. Easily manageable and profitable, this particular business appeals directly to the now displaced business and professional persons who want to be in business for themselves but not by themselves. They continue to capitalize on the ever-growing demand for quality and effective direct mail opportunities, knowledgeable service and competitive prices.

The Company will market its products through a network of approximately twenty-five (25) outlets.

Uniqueness and Differentiation

The Company has developed a concept of truly excellent quality direct mail pieces at competitive prices. Post Direct has gained a reputation of originality and good service resulting in high customer loyalty. What makes The Company unique is its ability to offer four color high quality production, a post card format, and effective marketing for cooperative and solo direct mail.

Financing

The Company is self financed and is providing the required investment for its franchising development.

Projected Start-Up Investment Costs

Start-up investment for Post Direct outlets, corporate or franchised, will range from $21,000 to $27,000 depending upon location. Franchised outlets will include these same start up costs plus a modest franchise fee ranging from $20,000 to $75,000 depending upon the marketing areas being considered.

The costs for developing the corporate and franchise expansion are projected to run from $250,000 the first year, to over $500,000 the third year. One of the additional corporate outlets will serve the Alexandria, Virginia market and the other will serve the southern Georgia market. Development funds will be used for normal developmental and administrative expenses including legal, franchise sales, training and operations manuals.

Development Costs for Franchising and Corporate Outlets

The key to marketing direct mail is name recognition. For this reason, it is recommended that Post Direct continue to develop its own marketing, design, promotion, and advertising techniques. This requires a considerable investment of capital for advertising and promotion purposes. After years of experience in advertising, radio, and direct mail management, along with designing instincts, copy expertise and marketing abilities, the time is perfect to exploit the Post Direct concept.

Exploitation of Post Direct Name

The future expansion of Post Direct will be controlled, yet speedy. Money will be needed for marketing and promotional needs. In moving into new market areas, The Company will be highly selective of its franchisees in order to effectively develop the key marketing areas which fit the company's growth criteria.

Future Requirements

Through forecasting, we project that The Company's net income, before taxes, from franchised and corporate outlets will be as follows: Fiscal 1996 -- $460,000; Fiscal 1997 -- $698,000. Royalty Income From Franchisees Alone -- At 10%

Financial Summary

> 1997 -- $670,000
> 1998 -- $1,230,000
> 1999 -- $1,707,500

When all 25 franchisees operate for a full year -- royalties will amount to $2,000,000 per year.

Post Direct will use the franchising method of marketing to attract prospective franchisees and to duplicate the Post Direct system nationwide. The franchise is competitively priced, easy to operate, and profitable. For this reason, prospective franchisees, who have longed to be in business for themselves, but not by themselves, will be attracted to the concept.

The Market

According to the International Franchise Association's (IFA) *Franchise Opportunities Guide* (1994), over $804 billion in sales were registered in franchising. This represents about 40.9% of all retail sales. Total franchise sales could reach $1 trillion by the year 2000. One out of every 12 business establishments is a franchised business. Homes are bought and sold through franchised real estate companies. These same homes can be cleaned, painted and carpeted through a franchised business. Cars can be purchased, tuned, and washed through franchises. We can have our hair cut, clothes cleaned, pets cared for -- all in franchised businesses. We can travel from one area of the world to another through franchised businesses.

Franchising, according to IFA, is a method of doing business. It is a method of marketing a product and/or service which has been adopted and used in a wide variety of industries and businesses. The word "franchise" is a French word meaning "to be free." In this sense, franchising offers people the freedom to own, manage and direct their own business. However, as with any freedom, there are responsibilities. In franchising, these responsibilities have to do with the franchisee's commitments and obligations, usually spelled out in a franchise agreement of contract, to the franchisor. The franchisor is the one who owns the right to the name or trademark of the business. The franchisee is the one who purchases the right to use the trademark system of business.

In 1992 there were approximately 558,000 franchisees. Today, there are over 3,000 American franchisors (all types) and another 1,000 to 1,500 franchisors operating in other countries including Canada, Great Britain, France, Italy, South America and Japan. There are now over 558,000 franchisees in the U.S. generating over $803 billion in sales accounting for 40.9% of all retail sales and employing over 8 million people in nearly 70 industries. A new franchise opens in the U.S. every 8 minutes, according to the IFA.

The franchise system works. Beginning in the 19th Century, the franchise concept was born when the Singer Sewing Machine Company provided the Singer name and inventory to dealers internationally. History has shown that the chance of success for a franchised business is significantly better than for other independently owned businesses. According to the U.S. Small Business Administration, nearly 65 percent of individual start-ups go out of business within the first five years of operation. By contrast, since 1971 less than five percent of franchised outlets have been discontinued each year.

It should be noted that franchising finds its largest growth in times of recession and/or down sizing. When executives lose their positions as the economy slows down, they become attracted to franchising and the opportunity to be in charge of their own destiny as franchisees.

Although attractive to America's advertising specialists, Post Direct outlets are also an excellent investment for the sophisticated business person. Such people have the business acumen to recognize that franchising has matured and that it is attracting investors interested in building a successful track record. With Post Direct, an individual can achieve his dreams of creating a successful business by working smarter with less overhead and greater profits. According to what is being written in the various trade publications, the market potential for direct mail marketing is excellent. It is growing at the rate of 35 - 40% per year according to the Direct Marketing Association.

THE COMPANY

Company Management and Ownership

John Kingham and Benjamin Miller combined their sales and management expertise with their knowledge and prominence in the field of advertising and cooperative direct mail to open their first corporate outlet in November of 1992. This combination of experience provided a unique growth opportunity. From their original outlet they now plan to expand to a network of twenty-five (25) franchised outlets in the United States. This expansion program is possible because they have built up an experienced team that is knowledgeable in advertising and cooperative direct mail media, as well as responsible for the development of the franchised outlets.

Company History and Business

The Post Direct concept began when John Kingham was heading up his successful full service advertising agency in 1988 -- Kingham & Associates Advertising, Inc. John recognized the unfilled needs of the discriminating customer who does not always want to shop in department stores or shopping malls for their needs and/or desires, nor do they want their fingers do the traveling through the Yellow Pages. To fulfill this consumer need, Kingham and Miller introduced Post Directs pilot outlet in November, 1992. In 1994, The Company has generated $797,000 in sales, in 1995 it is projecting $825,000, and in 1996, $900,000 in sales. The Company plans to satisfy customer and consumer needs through the development of a chain of franchised outlets specializing in high quality, cooperative direct mail services. The outlets will be located in major metropolitan areas.

Description Statement of Purpose

The Company's mission is to open a network of twenty-five (25) outlets to be recognized nationally as the highest quality cooperative direct mail company, while also meeting the advertisers solo direct mail needs in an atmosphere where they will receive the ultimate in service at attractive prices. In a sense, The Company's goal to be recognized as the most unique creator and marketer of cooperative direct mail in the United States. Further, The Company has developed a sophisticated cooperative direct mail development and promotional system for its franchised outlets which allows for the continuous growth of the system without franchisees having to deal with the day-to-day problems of research and development. The Company's current foundation will allow it to capitalize on its potential. The expansion of the franchise system will be national in scope. Management, client selection, and cost controls will be keystones to The Company's success. The services will be provided by knowledgeable, well-trained and educated management, advertising, marketing and sales personnel. The Company has developed a well designed prototype outlet which will be emulated throughout the franchise system.

Post Direct has proven itself to be an effective cost efficient direct mail advertising vehicle in a highly competitive market in the Silver Spring marketing area. Post Direct's prime objectives are to maintain its leadership in providing consumers the highest quality products and services through its network of corporate and franchised cooperative direct mail specialty outlets.

Company Objectives

- •Study the potential U.S. market for Post Direct products and services
- •Determine viability of Post Direct as a franchise
- •Improve and increase goods distribution by creating a profitable and quick reaching franchising organization sensitive to changing market conditions
- •Use select advertising to invite a qualified response
- •Pre-qualify franchisee prospects
- •Integrate qualified franchisees into the system
- •Open first franchised outlet in May 1996
- •Open four (4) additional franchised units in 1997 (Total 5)
- •Open ten additional franchised units in 1998 (Total 15)
- •Open ten additional franchised units in 1999 (Total 25)
- •Reach an annual gross sales of $20,000,000 by the end of 2000

Short Term Objectives

- •Pursue productive and profitable growth objectives
- •Obtain prominent market position in the United States
- •Open 25 franchised units within next five years
- •Obtain prominent market position nationwide
- •Go public with The Company or be acquired by a major company.

Long Term Objectives

The Company's sales, management, and production expertise is in building long term relationships with their customers through superior marketing and graphics designed to meet clients' marketing needs. The strategy Post Direct employs for meeting the competition includes continuous research and development of product selection, marketing, and service. Post Direct will conduct a continuous analysis of customers' wants which will be done by knowing which products are and are not moving in the American market. The Company is on the cutting edge of advertising and cooperative direct mail in the United States. It knows what is "hot" and what is not. Post Direct's network provides the latest style and copy designs. The Company's current short range strategic planning for the next twelve months includes a well-developed franchise program, a complete financial control system, and a marketing organization trained to recognize, attract and sell potential franchisees. Long range planning -- three to four years -- includes implementing the franchise development program.

Strategy for Meeting the Competition

The Company plans to complete its franchise agreement and UFOC and register the franchise in the following states: Maryland, Virginia, New York and Georgia. Once the franchise is developed, a comprehensive public relations campaign will be undertaken to augment the controlled growth of the franchise system.

Uniform Franchise Offering Circular & Franchise Sales

The Company has filed applications service mark material for the franchise to be registered with the U.S. Patent and Trademark Office (PTO).

Trademarks and Copyrights

The selected products offered by The Company cater to a wide variety of consumers of upper income levels.

Current Products/ Services

The Company's Product Categories			
•Antiques	•Mortgages	•Roofing
•Art	•Carpets & Rugs	•Interior Decorating
•Landscaping	•Restaurants	•Insurance
•Office Furniture	•Department Stores	•Specialty Shops
•Remodeling	•Furniture	•Kitchens
•Cruises	•Wines	•Health & Fitness
•Plastic Surgery	•Fashions	•Weddings
•Home Health Care	•Resorts & Spas	•Weight Loss
•Florist	•Specialty Malls	•Entertainment Centers
•Travel	•Languages	•Banks
•Gems & Jewelry	•Hair Stylists	•Theaters
•Nursing Homes	•Photography	•Music/Art Centers
•Lighting Design	•Air Duct Services	•Auto Phones
•Mortgage Funding	•Chimney Sweeps	•Paging Systems
•Awnings	•Air Conditioning Service	•Bakeries
•Fur Storage	•Automobiles	•Shopping Malls
•Bicycles	•Party Rentals	•Plastic Surgery

The Company's Corporate Commitment

To implement U.S. market penetration, The Company is prepared to invest the dollars and staff time required to develop its corporate and franchise expansion program.

MANAGEMENT

How The Company Got Started

The Company was founded in May of 1992. The Company markets over 100 products.

Management Team

The Company's management team is among the best in advertising and cooperative direct mail marketing. Increased national competition and escalating customer expectations challenge even the most successful companies. However, The Company's best management strategy is to maintain highly educated and well-trained management, advertising and cooperative direct mail sales teams composed of people who are skilled, flexible and focused on a common goal. The Company employs a high-performing team of experts that enables The Company to out-distance the competition. The Management Team includes:

President: John Kingham

John Kingham is the founder of Post Direct and he is also President of The Company. Kingham has a proven flair for printing design, color and knowledge of cooperative direct mail advertising production. He was also President of Kingham & Associates Advertising, Inc., which billed in excess of $3 million for radio, television and print advertising by its second year of operation. While President of this advertising company, Mr. Kingham developed a vendor-supported television/ print campaign for the largest furniture store on the East Coast, and this campaign became a nationwide model. The account increased sales during the promotion by 200% and broke all previous fourth-quarter records in the Florida market. Kingham's background also includes: Local Sales Manager, WBOR Radio; Account Executive, KLZQ Country; Account Executive WASL Radio; Equity Owner/Sales Manager, WSKP Radio; Account Executive, Weigand Agency; and Account Executive, Atlas Newspapers. Kingham has combined his sales and management expertise with the knowledge and prominence in the field of advertising and cooperative direct mail marketing to open his first Post Direct outlet. He worked his way through advertising and has developed an expertise in: merchandising, marketing, financial controls, advertising sales, and management responsibilities. Through his years of experience, Kingham has developed a reliable list of reputable advertisers. This combination of experience provided a unique growth opportunity for his company. As a result of his management, sales and advertising expertise, Kingham has expanded by opening a second outlet in the Georgia market, and is planning a third corporate outlet in the Alexandria, Virginia market. His responsibilities in The Company include general management, general overview of the operations, identification and selection of new franchise sites, concept design and merchandise promotion. John Kingham is married. He and his wife have two children. His hobbies include: golf, gym, and bicycling. He is also active in children's soccer and basketball.

Vice President & Secretary: Benjamin Miller

Benjamin Miller is Vice President & Secretary of Post Direct. He joined The Company in September, 1992 to help build it into the nation's foremost innovative cooperative direct mail company. In 1990, he was the advertising general sales manager for Sunshine Broadcasting, WDCB Radio. In 1976, Ben joined with Earl Polk Radio (WMAL/WWLA) where he was involved in sales, news continuity and copy writing. In addition, he has held the following positions: CBS Radio, KWT Radio where he was the top retail salesperson; Rocky Radio, WPAL Radio where he quadrupled billings in three months; Citywide Radio, WRST Radio where he became number-one biller; Overboard Broadcasting, WAEI Radio, where he was national sales manager and then promoted to local sales manager. Miller received his B.A. in Sociology at Oxford University, with additional coursework in Communications and Journalism at the University of Michigan. Miller studied German at the University of Salzburg in Austria. He brings additional training to Post Direct by having attended: Sterling Institutes' "Managing for Performance"; Herb Cohen's "You Can Negotiate Anything"; RAB radio marketing seminar at the Wharton School of Economics; and Dale Carnegie's sales seminars. Benjamin Miller and his wife have two children. His hobbies include mountain biking, hiking, fishing, screenwriting, and restaurant reviews for public access TV.

The Company enjoys many of the technologies of modern management and advertising methods. Production, marketing, sales, advertising and promotion, operations, administration, and training functions are effective on-going corporate disciplines which are being utilized as The Company is in the process of developing its franchising program. It expects to sell its first franchise by January, 1996. The Company is proud of its operations manual which has been developed over the past two years, and includes sections on Research and Development, Accounting, and Marketing.

Management Responsibilities

As the cooperative direct mail advertising market becomes more and more sophisticated, Post Direct maintains the basic business skills necessary to operate at the high levels of development and profitability. While it is important to be a good salesman and to properly promote merchandise, management, budgeting, continuing research and development are just as crucial to the bottom line.

Until at least three franchised units are sold, The Company's current corporate staff, with the addition of outside consulting and legal assistance, will utilize a portion of its time for the development of the franchise system prior to hiring any new personnel. The nature of the jobs listed below will be subject to change as the system grows. The corporate staff is now working to establish corporate and operations policy criteria and specific job descriptions prior to bringing new personnel on board.

There is a large turnover in the corporate world of franchising. The Company will avoid the possibility of inheriting the mistakes of unsuccessful franchises by making certain that its own style of operation and management remains unique, befitting its own image. Everyone at The Company is made aware of the commitment it will take to build a solid system of corporate and franchised outlets.

Corporate Job Descriptions

President

The President, in conjunction with general responsibilities for corporate and operations policy development, is responsible for the overall management of the business and its growth. He establishes corporate policy, performance standards and incentives. Corporate office performance and outlet performance is monitored by him, and his feedback provides encouragement and increased productivity. He is responsible for new franchisees approval, outlet marketing, and client selection. He is responsible for the development of the Corporate staff and for the overview of franchise development. He addresses the annual meetings of franchisees, designed to facilitate the exchange of ideas and techniques between corporate officers, directors, and managers.

Director of Franchising

The Director of Franchising is responsible for attracting, qualifying and selling potential franchisees. He directs the corporation's franchise advertising and promotional efforts for obtaining franchisees. He is also responsible for any franchise trade show participation on behalf of The Company.

Director of Operations

The Director of Operations is responsible for developing the franchise into a turnkey system, overviewing the franchisees, monitoring resolutions of franchisees' problems, and visiting franchised outlets. The Director of Operations' primary responsibility is to monitor the expansion and development of the franchised outlets. He is involved in monitoring the pre-opening and opening procedures, start-up inventory, and franchisee training. He is also available as a technical resource person for corporate outlet managers and franchisees who have specific operational problems or questions. As his responsibilities grow, a Director of Training will be added to the operations department and will take on the responsibility of training and development to allow the Director of Operations to assume his increased responsibilities as the system grows.

Marketing Manager

The Marketing Manager is responsible for outlet sales strategies, point-of-sale materials, advertising programs, special promotions, and cooperative advertising strategies. He works directly with corporate outlet managers and individual franchisees in developing cooperative advertising strategies. This responsibility will remain the President's responsibility until such time that The Company can hire a full time Marketing Manager.

Franchise Counsel

Franchise Counsel is responsible for preparation of the franchise agreement, the franchise disclosure document, formation of the franchising corporation, filing and maintaining integrity of Trademark and Service Marks registrations, filing franchise registration in states requiring registration, filing the franchise in business opportunity states which do not have franchise registration requirements, and providing a system of franchise law compliance for The Company.

Corporate Counsel

Corporate Counsel is responsible for the general legal concerns of the corporation. This may include TM registration and compliance, if qualified.

Financial Advisor (CPA)

The financial advisor will be responsible, with The Company's comptroller, for providing a computerized system for inventory and sales controls, the corporate audits required for inclusion in the disclosure documentation, reviewing the performance income and expense projections, and providing the financial ratios essential to assist in franchise sales and to conform with FTC rules and regulations.

The cooperative direct mail advertising business is included in Standard Industry Code (SIC) as follows: SIC 275 -- U.S. Commercial Printing Industry is an over $60 billion industry which includes over 37,000 business establishments. According to the Direct Mail Advertising Association (DMAA), the direct mail advertising segment of the industry represents $23 billion with a 35 - 40 % annual growth. The industry is affected by the nation's advertising budgets which increase 3.5% annually. The industry not only serves a growing aging population (60 years and older) but also a critical population group of persons aged 19 to 44, which is expected to remain unchanged at the 107 million level through 1996. The size and vast power of this group is highly attractive to the direct advertising business.

The Industry

The year 1995 began with the nation's economy in very moderate growth. However, by June of 1995, expectations of a mild recession is very much the concern of economists. Though softness is expected in some areas of the economy, moderate growth on balance is in prospect for 1996, and this augers well for the U.S. economy and is a good omen for the future of Post Direct.

The Economy in 1995

Industry publications and trade associations include: *Direct Mail News* (largest weekly update); *Target Marketing*; *Response TV*; *Marketing Tools*; *Electronic Retailing*; *Telemarketing*; National Direct Mail Advertising Association; and National Informational Marketing Association. *The U.S. Industrial Outlook* - 1994 lists that the major sources of growth are likely to stem from a pickup in consumer spending, recovery in producers' durable equipment and residential investment, and continued gains in exports. Personal consumption expenditures account for the largest share of the forecast gain in real GNP in 1994. A relatively stable inflation rate and a slight increase in interest rates are forecasted for 1994, implying a continuation of accommodative monetary policy. Expected white collar increased employment should lead to increased cooperative direct mail advertising. In addition, larger numbers of senior citizens and retirees with higher disposable incomes should stimulate more travel and corresponding increases in direct market advertising sales.

Outlook

Post Direct's market is defined as nationwide. One Post Direct outlet can serve as many as 200,000 households consisting of 30 to 69 year-old adults with an average household income of $75,000 per year. The Company's market, where applicable, includes the upper-middle and upper class consumers. It is interesting to note that the 25-44 age group is projected by the Census Bureau to total 82 million people in 1994, or one-third of the total population. The 45-54 age group will be among the fastest growing, increasing at an annual rate of 3.6 percent between 1992 and 1997, compared with only 1 percent for the total population. It is a known fact that coupons and card users increase with age. This is an excellent selling tool when talking with advertising clients.

Market Demographics

According to TRW, Target Marketing Services' highly affluent consumer database included 5,716,692 households nationwide and is generated from a TRW income model to identify consumers with $100,000+ income. It is processed through national change of address, and reported by two or more sources for the most accurate and deliverable source of demographic information available. The Company is in a positive growth situation. Other competitive cooperative direct mail advertising companies have entered the market, however, because of Post Direct's unique promotion and marketing ability, The Company enjoys its high-end leadership position in the National Capital marketing area. It expects to do the same in the additional marketing areas it adds to its system. As the economy improves, other competitors will enter the market. However, this will keep The Company competitively alert to maintain and increase its market share.

Marketing Trends

Why do consumers like and use cooperative direct mail advertising? In the 90s, cash is king. Consumers want a better deal in the form of service, quality, dependability, -- and, especially, a discount on price. For many consumers, Post Direct offers the hope of affording high-quality products and services at reasonable and discounted prices whether the advertisers choose a "solo" ad, criss-cross marketing ad (card swapping), network marketing, or direct customer marketing. With the right advertiser mix, plus old and new ways to attract and keep customers, Post Direct maintains its position on the cutting edge of direct advertising sales.

The recession of the '90s resulted in new shopping strategies for the 30-50 year-old age groups which began to target deals on quality goods and services. Direct response advertising is the call of the '90s and will continue to expand in other fields in the early years of the twenty-first century. Sales via FAX, computer/electronic networking, and cable TV will be on the increase over the next five years. However, this particular growth should not affect Post Direct because electronic and/or TV responses are not measurable -- as is Post Direct.

Marketing Opportunities

There are over thirty (30) franchised cooperative direct mail advertising companies in the United States. The market trends look promising for The Company. Although competition is increasing, Post Direct is one of only two direct mail companies that targets high-end consumers for high-end advertisers with ad agency quality creativity. Post Direct continues to work this special niche by marketing its services. Most direct mail companies concentrate on the low-end advertiser such as pizza parlors, gas stations, dentists, etc. and cannot crack the market Post Direct now holds such as jewelry companies, Mercedes Benz dealers, resorts, fine clothing outlets, etc. Post Direct now excels in gross billings, quality customer base, renewal rates, promotional events and additional specialized direct mail techniques including solo mail, criss-cross marketing, networking mailing, customer mailing, and private sales.

The opportunities for expanding the U.S. market will be dependent upon The Company's ability to transfer its product knowledge and marketing capability to its individual franchise owners. This requires a considerable investment in maintaining "state-of-the-art" prototype outlets, sales promotion, and effective communication with franchisees.

A Special Environment for Post Direct Outlets

Many mainstream advertisers have not realized the benefits of co-operative direct mail or solo direct mail for their customer base.

High-end advertisers, joining forces with other high-end advertisers, to share a Post Direct mailing to high-end consumers can present the best of images with high quality four-color cards at a lower cost, yielding fabulous results.

Cooperative Direct Mail Advertising -- A Competitive Reality

The United States has created the specialized cooperative direct mail advertising business that makes a variety of specialized goods and services available to the consumer through the mail. The current demand for high-quality merchandise and service via cooperative direct mail has given new life to the cooperative direct mail advertising business. Direct mail fills a niche, offers convenience and personalized service to the consuming public, and will continue to flourish. Increasing amounts of advertising space is being used by cooperative direct mail. Post Direct is already at the cutting edge. With the sheer multiplicity of goods and services options, the buyer's problem of choice has become complicated. The addition of each new item creates the need for more information, more decisions and more sub-decisions. Post Direct, with its specialized advertising approach, reduces the consumers learning and shopping time by providing a well informed sales package to the consumer, directly to his home.

Post Direct provides its users more sales and more profits. Post Direct provides consumers quality goods at non-inflated competitive prices, which is the hallmark of our free enterprise system. Post Direct leads the pack in quality, direct-response publishing, increased sales and reduced costs. There are so many direct response card mailings that it is sometimes difficult to separate the champions from the others. With Post Direct, however, no such problem exists. Post Direct leads the pack. The Company will continue to develop and expand its specialized up-market cooperative direct mail concept, and super competitive pricing.

The Company will serve an important role in the world of cooperative direct mail advertising by providing consumers with the option of simply buying fine products at the best price. By maintaining its knowledgeable sales staff, which is constantly trained in selecting up-market products to promote, and concentrating only on quality products and services, The Company gets repeat and satisfied customers. Post Direct often hears from its customers that it is "the only direct mail medium we use because it (Post Direct) is differentiated from other direct mail companies in that Post Direct works only with the area's finest retail outlets, resorts, and other best names in advertising." Post Direct attracts the finest businesses, which are not included in our competitor's packages. Post Direct attracts advertisers who never considered participating in other direct mail packages that many customers consider "trash." The advertising client knows he is best served by Post Direct.

The "Pleasing to the Eye" Post Direct Look

The upside potential for The Company's growth over the next several years is the reputation enjoyed by The Company in the Silver Spring area because of its selection of customer groups and the personal attention in growth and quality control provided by The Company's principals and management team. These will be major selling features for Post Direct outlets. From high-end advertising clients to high-end consumers -- this is Post Direct's service mark.

Opportunities

The Company has the reputation of bringing a wide variety of cooperative direct mail advertising to the public. Post Direct's sales rose quickly since The Company started its marketing operations in 1992.

Strengths

The Company's distinct advantage over the competition lies in its experienced management, marketing, and sales team -- making any Post Direct outlet a very formidable competitor. The Company is recognized as the "creme de la creme" in the cooperative direct mail advertising business. It excels in numbers and types of customers. It enjoys market area recognition wherever it has an outlet. It is known for its high quality visibility and its select list of advertisers.

Post Direct already enjoys customer recognition. The Company is already sought after as the direct-response publishing outlet. The Company is in an enviable position for opening future outlet locations.

The Post Direct franchised outlets will be unique in their concept and their graphic appeal. Direct competition in the up-market segment is virtually non-existent. The Company's product selection, pricing and accessibility have played a major role in filling a niche for quality merchandise and services.

COMPETITION

Pricing of the cooperative direct mail advertising products reflects the uniqueness of Post Direct's method of delivering quality and exclusivity. Although the gross profit margins are higher than the cooperative direct mail industry standards, Post Direct clients do find good value. This is achieved by the extensive on-going market research which identifies quality advertising approaches at the best possible price.

The cooperative direct mail response business is a growing market. This is due to the fact that magazine and newspaper advertising is a shrinking market and the cooperative direct mail is a niche which serves the Post Direct recipients. Post Direct keeps abreast of what the upper-middle class and the upper class of clientele wants. This policy helps keep the consumer aware that Post Direct is "the place to buy quality merchandise and service."

The Post Direct franchise concept is designed to be a profitable investment for the franchisee. It will be up to The Company's management, purchasing and marketing abilities to acquire and maintain a fair share of the direct mail advertising market. Since The Company has a narrow marketing window, locating the areas with up-market buyers is a top priority. The Company's sales organization is recognized for targeting its markets. The Company's Franchisees make friends with their customers and serve them cheerfully. Even when the customer does not make an advertising purchase, he is always treated like a friend.

Competition in the cooperative direct mail response industry are mainly from over 1150 franchised outlets. The more formidable competitors include: Dollar Saver; Coupons Express; and Savings Galore. Most cooperative direct mail companies concentrate their efforts on lower quality goods aimed at the low to middle markets. The major weakness of these competitors is their limited range of up-market products, coupled with a lack of publishing knowledge, marketing and personalized service.

Direct Mail Franchisors	EE's	Corp.	Fran. Fee
United Advertising, Inc. (AZ)	111	2	$23,500-$45,500
Cash Provider (CA)	11	2	Min. 10,000
Savings, Inc. (IL)	8	4	18,500
Dollars & Cents	5	0	20,000
Dollar Saver (CA)	400	2	15,000-40,000
	(40,000 Prime Households)		18,900
	(Each addt'l. 1,000 Households)		1,500
A Penny Saved (FL)	5% Royalty		15,000-50,000
National Corp. (DE)	54	2	Single-17,500
Master-			48,000
Coupons Express (VA)	104	1	9,000-30,000
	(Minimum: 40,000 Households by Zip Code)		
	(Each addt'l. 4,000 Households)		10,000
	(Note: No Royalty)		
Savings Galore (FL)	189	2	(Initial Fee)-500
			(Training Fee)-1,000
	(10,000 Prime Households)		4,500
	(50,000 Prime Households)		$22,500
Astro Direct Mail (CA)	15		9,000-18,000
Canadian Franchisors	**EE's**	**Corp.**	**Fran. Fee**
Canadian Savings Corp. (Ont).	6	1	20,000
Maple Net (Ont.)	24	2	2,000-50,000
Collins Advertising, Inc.	2	7	15,000

MARKETING STRATEGY

Corporate Owned Outlets Development Strategy

As revealed in the Financial section of this business plan, The Company plans a two tiered growth -- one in the area of franchised outlets, and the other through corporate outlets. It is projected that The Company will open its first franchised outlet in 1996. It is further projected that The Company will have a total of twenty-five (25) franchised outlets by the year 2000. At the end of 2000, The Company's growth rate will be reappraised.

Franchised Outlets Development Strategy

The Company bases its success on sales ability. Therefore, the company will seek prospective franchises among advertising practitioners, sales managers, and sales professionals. In addition, it will seek corporate refugees with sales experience. The Company will use the business format franchise, which is characterized as an ongoing business relationship between the franchisor and the franchisees. This includes the products, trademark, and service marks, as well as the business concept, which includes a marketing strategy and plan, operations manuals and standards, quality control, and a continuing process of assistance and guidance.

The key strategy for The Company's growth is to develop, over a period of five years, a network of franchisees in at least 25 major markets in the United States.

By selling franchises, The Company advantages will be as follows:

1. It will create an immediate cash flow;
2. It will establish a quick presence in a given area;
3. It will give the Franchisee the responsibility for growing the area;
4. It will minimize corporate staff time and overhead, which will allow The Company to devote more time to the development of the franchisees; and,
5. It will allow for the synergy needed for rapid expansion.

Formula for Franchise Development

To identify, attract and better serve its customers, The Company will search for prospective franchisees who are currently in the following professions: radio sales and management; direct sales and management; newspaper and magazines advertising sales; advertising agencies; and printing, marketing, and direct mail. As countless salaried employees have turned to entrepreneurship, driven by a dream of independence, many find that going into an independent business is risky. With a well qualified franchisor who has researched, developed, and successfully operated the business he is franchising, the franchisee's risk and investment is lowered considerably. It is also widely known that customers, particularly up-market products and services buyers, prefer to be served by knowledgeable and qualified people. In most businesses, the one managed by its owner will out-perform the same business or a competing one managed by a non-owner manager. Trained in all aspects of outlet operations, the franchisee will be provided a thorough knowledge of The Company's method of operation and will be supported by continuing services. The franchisee should be able to realize a good profit from his investment.

Profile of a Post Direct Franchisee

The following criteria has been recommended for selling Post Direct's marketing areas:

1. Operating Parameters
    a. The top fifty markets in the United States
2. Profile of Franchisee
    a. An individual (minimum age: 25)
    b. A minimum of five years business experience in following areas: radio sales and management; direct sales and management; newspaper and magazine advertising sales; advertising agencies; and printing, marketing, and direct mail; small market radio stations, and non-dominant radio sales
    c. Designated franchisee must play active role in business by devoting 100% of his/her time to the business and by hiring a full-time sales person to help develop the business
    d. Willing to sign a non-compete agreement with Post Direct
    e. Capacity to reach the highest income people in his market with 50,000 to 200,000 mailings.

Unit Growth Through Franchises

The Company's objective is to have three corporate outlets by January 1995 and twenty five (25) franchised outlets by the end of 1998. This will be twenty eight (28) total outlets.

Feb. 1996	Franchise 1
Aug. 1996	Franchise 2
Jan. 1997	Franchise 3

Mar. 1997	Franchise 4
May 1997	Franchise 5
July 1997	Franchise 6
Sep. 1997	Franchise 7
Nov. 1997	Franchise 8
Mar. 1998	Franchise 9
May 1998	Franchise 10
July 1998	Franchise 11 & 12
Sep. 1998	Franchise 13 & 14
Nov. 1998	Franchise 15
Jan. 1999	Franchise 16
Feb. 1999	Franchise 17
Mar. 1999	Franchise 18
Apr. 1999	Franchise 19
May 1999	Franchise 20
June 1999	Franchise 21
July 1999	Franchise 22
Aug. 1999	Franchise 23
Sep. 1999	Franchise 24
Oct. 1999	Franchise 25
Total Franchises	**25**

Initial Target Locations

It is recommended that Post Direct outlets be located in the top fifty high-density up-market areas in the United States. The franchised units can be operated out of the franchisees' homes.

Metro Market Statistical Areas (MSA)

MSA	Rank	Population	Households
Boston	7	3,783,817	1,400,000
NY	2	8,546.846	3,200,000
Philia/NJ	4	4,856,881	1,700,000
Baltimore	17	2,382,172	680,000
Atlanta	9	2,833,511	1,000,000
Orlando	44	1,072,748	401,000
Ft. Lauderdale, Holly-wood, Pompano Beach	38	1,255,488	528,000
Miami/Hialeah	23	1,937,094	692,000
Tampa, St. Petersburg Clearwater	20	2,067,959	869,000
Houston	8	3,301,937	1,100,000
Dallas	12	2,553,362	954,728
Ft. Worth, Arlington	35	1,332,053	495,144
Chicago	3	6,069,974	2,200,000
Minneapolis, St. Paul MN/WI	14	2,464,124	935,516
Detroit	5	4,382,299	1,600,000
Cleveland	24	1,831,122	712,362
Denver	26	1,622,980	648,404
Phoenix	18	2,122,101	807,560
San Fran.	27	1,603678	642,504
Los Angeles/Long Beach	1	8,863,164	2,900,000
San Diego	27	2,498,016	887,403

Franchise No.	City	Franchise Fee
1	Boston	$35,000.00
2	New York (1)	$50,000.00
3	New York (2)	$50,000.00
4	Philadelphia (1)	$50,000.00
5	Baltimore	$45,000.00
6	Atlanta	$25,000.00
7	Orlando	$20,000.00
8	Houston (1)	$50,000.00
9	Dallas/Ft. Worth	$50,000.00
10	Chicago (1)	$50,000.00
11	Chicago (2)	$50,000.00
12	Minneapolis	$20,000.00
13	Detroit	$50,000.00
14	Cleveland	$30,000.00
15	Denver	$30,000.00
16	Phoenix	$50,000.00
17	San Deigo	$50,000.00
18	Los Angeles	$50,000.00
19	Orange County	$50,000.00
20	San Francisco	$45,000.00
21	Miami, Ft. Lauderdale	$30,000.00
22	Tampa, St. Petersburg	$35,000.00

Franchise Development Objective

The objective for Post Direct is to establish a market presence in at least twenty-five (25) major metropolitan areas within the United States. This will be accomplished by:

(1) Attracting qualified franchisees;
   a. Using select advertising to invite a qualified and favorable response;
   b. Pre-qualifying prospects by phone who have responded to the advertising program;

(2) Integrating qualified franchisees into the system, which will be built into a sequence of marketing strategies designed to produce the greatest degree of predicting positive results;

(3) Becoming the dominant marketer of a wide range of unique specialized direct response mail advertising;

(4) Developing a vibrant image and commitment to friendly and efficient service.

The Competition

Every business which sells advertising is a competitor. Every company which sells the same or similar services as Post Direct is a competitor. Every newspaper and magazine is a competitor. Every radio and TV station is a competitor. However, what makes Post Direct unique is that unlike most businesses that sell advertising, The Company specializes in quality merchandise and services available at competitive prices and sold directly into the homes of the buyers.

Post Direct customers' goods and services ads are carefully prepared, merchandised, and attractively presented to the consumer. The consumer appreciates the speed, the convenience, and the knowledgeable and friendly Post Direct service. This is what makes Post Direct different and successful. Post Direct concentrates on the middle and high-end advertisers and offers a combination of services. Although Post Direct considers competition to be other direct mail companies and daily and weekly newspaper advertising, Post Direct is secure in that it offers unique and quality advertising services. This separates Post Direct from its competitors.

Actually, there is little direct competition with Post Direct. Anyone wanting to compete with this concept in the up-market category would have to be prepared to risk anywhere from $500,000 to $1,000,000 on development costs alone. Post Direct took years to develop and hone the profit machine it is today.

The Market Potential

Post Direct is an excellent investment for the sophisticated business person interested in selling to America's upper-middle class and upper class. Post Direct's innovative development techniques are attracting well capitalized veteran business people who have the capacity and the capital to develop a Post Direct franchise in their metropolitan area. They have the business acumen to recognize that franchising has matured and that it is attracting investors interested in building a successful track record. An entrepreneur can achieve his dreams of creating a Post Direct outlet and being in business for himself but not by himself.

Marketing Strategy For Selling Service

Initially, Post Direct began with one corporate outlet. Through this outlet, Mr. Kingham was able to provide research, development and training which allowed him to expand the network into two corporate outlets, and an expectation of expanding the business through twenty-eight (28) outlets including three (3) corporate outlets.

The Company's primary markets are the upper-middle and upper income managerial/professional and retired individuals with disposable incomes. The Company will solicit customers who can emphasize products wanted and/or needed by consumers in this market segment.

Sales Strategy For Selling Product

The Company will ensure that its franchisees are highly trained to attract new customers and that its service is rendered efficient; and that its customers are treated in a friendly, courteous and professional manner.

Product Promotion Strategy

As franchisee customers' new product lines are introduced, updates will be sent to Post Direct's outlets to secure similar customers in their respective marketing areas. The Company will monitor and analyze competitive ads.

Target Markets

Although nurturing its current marketing niche, The Company is constantly monitoring its competitors, and maintaining its research and development acumen to bring new products and services to the markets. Markets are studied according to need and changed according to the market demands.

Market Positioning

Post Direct customers perceive the company as number one relative to competition. Consumers perceive Post Direct's products to be of a higher quality than competitive products. Post Direct will maintain and strengthen its marketing position, which creates even more confidence and trust regarding The Company and its customers' products.

Exploitation of Post Direct Name

The key to marketing is to link the outlet with the name of the franchisor -- "Post Direct." This requires a considerable investment of capital for advertising and promotion purposes. After years of experience in advertising, Mr. Kingham with his advertising instincts and abilities, the time is perfect to exploit the "Post Direct" concept and make the statement "Post Direct" deserves.

Outside Service Suppliers

In the future, as the system grows, Post Direct will include the following in the development of its U.S. marketing plan:

- Ad Agency
- PR Agency
- Market Research
- Sales Literature
- Market Consulting - Planning

Post Direct currently utilizes its own staff for the development of advertising materials. Among the trade publications in which The Company plans to advertise its franchise availability will be trade shows, newspapers, *Wall Street Journal*, *USA Today*, *Fortune*, *Advertising Age* and others.

Advertising & Promotion

As The Company expands, it is possible that an inside Public Relations person will be added to staff to develop trade and public press stories and to handle other public relations projects which will help generate interest in the network's outlets.

Public Relations

ADVERTISING AND PROMOTION

Advertising and Promotion Objectives

There are several realities that every developer of a franchise or business opportunity must face in order to be successful. The first reality is that there are many business opportunities competing for the potential investor's dollar. The second is that the franchisee must prosper if the franchisor is to prosper.

If Post Direct is to establish itself in the U.S. market, a broad-based marketing strategy must be undertaken. This strategy must promote the image of the Post Direct network and raise the awareness of Post Direct products and services availability not only in the marketplace but also among potential franchisees.

This is particularly important in view of the fact that it will require a major public relations and advertising undertaking to "sell" the Post Direct concept in spite of competition.

The advertising and promotion objective is for the Post Direct outlet owners and/or managers to reach 50,000 and/or 100,000 targeted consumers in the specific marketing area where franchises will be established.

In the majority of cases, the prospective franchisee is looking for an opportunity to achieve financial independence and career satisfaction with a minimum investment in time, money, and risk. His primary motivation is money, since money can provide him with most of the things he does not now have but does want. His primary fear is that of failure.

What the Prospective Franchisee is Looking For

The real reason that he is shopping for a business is out of his belief that the grass is always greener on the other side. This is supported by the assumption that the only way to get rich is by being in business for yourself. What he will buy is a program that presents products and services in an area that is not overworked by the competition. He will buy a program like Post Direct because it will provide him with all the tools, training, support, and track record required to create a confidence level high enough to minimize his financial risk.

The prospect's decision to buy a Post Direct franchise will be largely controlled by the impressions made by the first presentation. The importance of giving him an exceptionally high confidence level about the business becomes very clear. Keep in mind that Post Direct will not likely be the only business opportunity the prospect will consider.

What the Prospective Franchisee Will See

The initial presentation should provide the prospect the feeling that Post Direct is a substantial company with extensive experience in the business. The presentation and supportive materials must instantly build the credibility needed to gain the prospect's confidence in the value of the offer and the ease with which they can succeed.

There is an old business expression that states, "Anyone can sell a superior product, the only difference between salesmen is the number of presentations it takes to make that sale." A large percentage of the ultimate profitability of selling any business opportunity lies in the cost of selling the package to your franchisee prospect.

Promotional Materials

The cost of promoting sales of the franchise mounts up quickly, whether it includes trade press advertising, newspaper advertising, trade shows, local seminars, hotel rooms, airfare, manpower, etc. Regardless of how good ads might be, only so many people will call for more information or request an invitation to a local seminar.

The franchise prospect is asking himself several important questions when he sees corporate promotional materials or advertisements. He wants to know:

- Who you are?
- What makes your company so special?
- What are my chances to succeed with you?
- What will I get for my investment?
- And, are there any better alternatives?

With these questions in mind, it quickly becomes obvious that the initial presentation and all of the materials the prospect receives must excite and motivate him to the genuine potential offered by your business. The presentation must also provide evidence attesting to the quality of the product and the company, as well as overcome any fears that he may have about taking the next step to become a Post Direct franchisee.

The Franchisor's Promotional Needs

Suggested promotional elements fall into two major areas: franchise development sales materials and franchisee support materials. Each serves a specific need, and each contributes to the ease with which the franchisor can convert the initial opportunity into a franchise sale.

The Franchise Development Materials

This includes a basic franchise brochure designed to be used as a straight handout or as an invitation to a seminar. It simply tells of the exciting opportunities offered by The Company and how easy it is to become successful as a result of the program offered by Post Direct. This is a romance piece designed to touch on the financial needs of the prospective franchisee, and to show how The Company's program can afford him the independence he is seeking. This piece is very competitive in nature. It will be the most read piece of literature the franchise prospect will take away with him. It should be a quality piece to convince the prospect that Post Direct is a company of substance. It should be a slick, four color, fully photographed piece showing successful individuals using the tools provided and enjoying the profits from their labors. The copy and presentation must present the economics of the business along with an overview of the industry in order to overcome his fears, negate his tendency toward procrastination, and present the tangible financial rewards of the good life as a result of his decision to sign on.

Newspaper Ads

Newspaper or trade publication ads promoting the availability of the franchise need to be developed for insertion in local papers in areas where the company has decided to establish franchises. The basic ad should be approximately two columns, 75 lines deep, and designed to run in the Sunday, "Business Opportunity" section of the paper. A second insertion of the same ad in the Sunday, "Business" section would provide additional responses.

A Sales Brochure

This is a 9" X 12" portfolio. It consists of a folder with pockets inside designed to hold the franchise brochure, sample store layouts, magazine and/or newspaper ad reprints, local outlet/customer promotional pieces and ads, franchise application materials, testimonial sales letters, and newspaper or magazine article reprints promoting the positive nature of The Company.

Fact Sheets

These are simple 8 1/2" X 11" black and white or color sheets of products, articles, references, and pre-printed pages of materials to be given the prospect at the initial meeting. It is recommended that a budget be developed for 10 to 15 different pages.

Franchise Sales Seminars or Individual VCR Presentations

Once Post Direct decides on the marketing method it wishes to employ in the U.S., Post Direct should conduct franchise sales seminars where prospective franchisees could be solicited. These "by invitation only" seminars would provide information in a group setting during week-end and evening hours about business opportunities through Post Direct.

VCR or slide presentations can be used as a major selling tool for use at individual or group presentations. The presentation should be about 15 to 20 minutes in length and designed to set the mood, build the enthusiasm, and create the desire to participate in Post Direct's exciting program.

The presentation will deal with the frustrations most people feel about achieving financial independence, and what it will take to achieve it. Initially, this program shows the need for being in business for yourself but not by yourself. It also covers the need to select the right business. It shows success ratios of franchises compared to failure ratios of the average untested private business. After establishing the success ratio, it considers the specific factors that makes Post Direct unique and potentially successful to the franchisee. Here the presentation points out the nature of the business, the lack of serious competition, the class of people the franchisee will be dealing with, and other desirable aspects of being a Post Direct franchisee.

Once the emotional aspects are addressed, the presentation then concentrates on the fiscal aspects. It should include a brief history of the company, market penetration and dominance information, and product quality data. It should create a mood that Post Direct is not only the best direct mail advertising outlet but that it is the best company to be associated with.

Finally, the presentation outlines the most important competitive element -- that of Post Direct support. In this area, the presentation describes the support franchisees will get from The Company. This will generate a desire to become a franchisee, and the closing becomes easier as a result. By demonstrating franchisor support, the prospect loses the fear of his ability to sell The Company's products and services to prospective customers.

The Company's objective should be to convince the prospect that he is buying marketing rights to superior products and services and getting a proven customer generating system as well.

Franchisor/ Franchisee Support Materials

This includes materials provided by the franchisor and used by the franchisee to sell to the customer. These are the tools designed to make franchisee's selling easier.

Remember, prospective franchisees are tired of being at the mercy of others. What The Company can assure him of is that he will not be at the mercy of his market with a Post Direct franchise. By providing franchisees with a proven customer sales campaign, The Company provides him with a credible, impressive, and effective way to reach a large number of potential customers.

Post Direct Initial Direct Mail Ad

An initial Post Direct ad includes a four-color postcard that shows a spectacular new opening of another Post Direct outlet. It should be mailed to the targeted businesses in the franchisee's market.

The Bottom Line

It is obvious that a great deal of what Post Direct has to sell is directly related to the promotional materials used to cinch the franchise sell. They are the tools The Company will use to sell its franchise. This segment of the company's franchise development should not be neglected, and could range in cost from $30,000 to over $50,000.

FINANCIAL PROJECTIONS

Assumptions

Pricing and Profitability

Pricing is generally based on what the competition charges, as well as freight, marketing, promotion, and overhead costs. A fair profit for the franchisor and the franchisee, of course, must be taken into consideration.

Pricing of advertising products is competitive, However, The Company can and does command a competitive price structure because of the high printing quality of its products and the volume of sales controlled by The Company. Customers are willing to pay a fair price for recognized quality product value coupled with good service.

Because of The Company's buying ability, there is some elasticity in Post Direct's pricing structure, which can be brought into play when competition demands.

In examining the cost of buying printing against current competitive prices, it is clear that there is adequate room for Post Direct to allow for competitive pricing.

Gross Sales

The franchised outlets are expected to maintain annual gross sales of $500,000 the first year, $675,000 the second year, $750,000 the third year, and $1,000,000 the fourth year. Franchisees will be required to maintain a performance gross sales target schedule.

Franchised Units Space Requirements

Even though Post Direct can initially be run efficiently from the franchisee's home, minimum space requirements will range from 400 to 800 square feet. The actual radius of operation for the franchise will depend on the population density, the income levels and the relative locations of other Post Direct franchised units.

Demographics Criteria

Post Direct is a prestige direct mail advertising specializing in selling up-market products and services. It is designed to serve major metropolitan areas.

The ideal minimum population density base required for a successful franchised outlet is 1,000,000. Key criteria includes: high income levels of the population ($75,000 and up); sufficient office space; advertising expense; and public transportation availability of employees. The franchisee will be responsible for collecting demographic data from the state, city and/or county. These entities provide demographic data to those interested in doing business within his area. Industrial development commissions, local chambers of commerce, trade associations, newspapers and periodicals, trade journals, planning commissions, bankers and local libraries are all recommended sources of information to assist in site assessment. Additional specific demographic data can be purchased from demographic data service organizations at a reasonable fee.

Network of Franchisees

The Company will market its direct mail advertising services through a national network of franchisees. Franchises will be sold to individuals, partnerships, or corporations. The Company will market to individual franchisees with experience in sales and business management.

The Company will use the business format franchise, which is characterized by an ongoing business relationship between the franchisor and the franchisees. This includes the products, trademark, and service marks, as well as the entire business concept, which includes a marketing strategy and plan, operations manuals and standards, quality control, and a continuing process of assistance and guidance.

1995	one corporate outlet	Total: 1
1996	sell 1 franchise	Total: 2
1997	sell 6 franchises	Total: 9
1998	sell 7 franchises	Total: 16
1999	sell 10 franchises	Total: 26

2. A total of 26 outlets by the end of 1999 including one (1) corporate outlet

3. Average Sales for Each Unit

First Year	$500,000
Second Year	$675,000
Third Year	$750,000
Fourth Year	$1,000,000

4. Recommended Royalty Fee Range to Corporate (9% - 10% per year)

5. Recommended National Advertising Fees (2% per year)

6. Individual Outlet Franchise Fee (Minimum: $20,000 to $50,000)

Post Direct Franchise Outlet - Franchisee Start-Up Requirements
(400 Sq. Feet Minimum)

	Fee Range	
Franchise Fee	$20,000.00	$50,000.00
Office Equipment (Computer & Fax)	$5,000.00	$6,000.00
Office Furniture	$1,500.00	$2,000.00
Business License Fees	$100.00	$300.00
Legal & Professional Fees	$500.00	$1,000.00
Advertising & Promotion	$2,000.00	$2,500.00
Printing: Sales Kits & Brochures	$3,000.00	$4,000.00
Insurance Premiums	$300.00	$400.00
Telephone Equipment (3 lines — 2 + fax)	$500.00	$900.00
Office Supplies	$500.00	$1,000.00
Training, Travel & Expenses	$2,000.00	$2,500.00
Working Capital (three months)	$5,000.00	$6,500.00
Total	**$40,400.00**	**$77,100.00**

Franchisee's Projection - First Full Year Income/Expense

Income	First Year	
Gross Sales	$500,000	100.00%
Less: Cost of Sale (23%)	$66,000	13.20%
Gross Margin	$434,000	86.80%

Operating Expenses		
Accounting	$500	
Car Expense	$3,600	
Dues, Fees, Subscriptions	$500	
Entertainment	$1,200	
Taxes (FICA, etc.)		
Insurance Premiums	$1,500	
Insurance Medical	$5,300	
Legal	$1,200	
Maintenance	$600	
Miscellaneous	$500	
Office Expense	$800	
Bookkeeper/Secretary/Accou	$25,000	
Petty Cash	$600	
Postage, Federal Express, Courier	$5,000	
Printing	$150,000	
Composition & Art (4 mailings)	$32,000	
Office Supplies	$3,000	
Telephone	$4,000	

Total Operating Expense	**$235,300**	**47.06%**
Royalty	$50,000	10%
Advertising Fee	$10,000	2%
Net B/T	$138,700	27.74%

Notes: *Commission 17.5% + 5.5% (Benefits) = 23%*
            Printing + Mailing = 30% of gross

July 1, 1994 - June 30, 1995

Minimum
Corporate
Development
and Franchising
Costs -
First Year
Development

Income
Gross Sales - C-1	$1,200,000
C-2 (2 Mailings)	$333,333
Franchisee Fees (Min. $20K)	
F-1	$20,000
Royalties	$0
Total Income	**$1,553,333**

Expense
Advertising/Marketing	$5,000
Art Production	$60,000
Accounting	$10,000
Business License	$1,000
Contingency	$10,000
Dues/Subscriptions	$500
Franchise Consultant	$20,500
Franchise Sales/Brochures	$5,000
Franchise Sales Brochure Covers	$1,000
Indep Contractor (Concierge)	$18,000
Legal (Corp., Fran., TM)	$28,000
Mailing, Shipping, Courier	$1,200
Mailing List Purchase	$10,000
Office Equipment Upgrade	$3,500
Office Supplies	$3,000
Printing (30% x Gross Sales)	$360,000
Rent (@ $2,250/Mo.)	$27,000
Repair/Maintenance	$1,500
Salaries* ($430K + 28% Benefits)	$550,400
Telephone (Including Carphones)	$10,000
Training	$2,000
Travel/Entertainment (Fran. Sales)	$2,000
Vehicles (3)	$13,200
Vehicle Maintenance	$3,600
Total	**$1,092,400**
Net B/T	**$460,933**

Execs, Secretary, Sales Commission (23%)

Minimum Corporate Development and Franchising Costs - Second Year Development

(July 1, 1995 - June 30, 1996)

Income

Gross Sales - C-1	$1,200,000
C-2 (3 Mailings)	$500,000
C-3 (3 Mailings)	$500,000
Franchisee Fees (Min. $20K)	
F-2, F-3, F-4	$60,000
Royalties	
F-1	$50,000
Total Income	**$2,310,000**

Expense

Advertising/Marketing	$10,000
Art Production	$100,000
Accounting	$15,000
Business License	$1,200
Contingency	$15,000
Dues/Subscriptions	$1,000
Franchise Consultant	$12,000
Franchise Sales/Brochures (Update)	$2,000
Franchise Sales Brochure Covers	$0
Independent Contractor (Concierge)	$18,000
Legal (EEs + Fran Registrations)	$12,000
Mailing, Shipping, Courier	$2,500
Mailing List Purchase	$16,000
Office Equipment Upgrade	$10,000
Office Supplies	$3,000
Printing (30% x Gross Sales)	$660,000
Rent (@ $2,250/Mo.)	$28,000
Repair/Maintenance	$2,500
Salaries* ($430K + 28% Benefits)	$660,480
Telephone (Including Carphones)	$13,000
Training	$8,000
Travel/Entertainment (Fran. Sales)	$5,000
Vehicles (3)	$13,200
Vehicle Maintenance	$3,600
Total	**$1,611,480**
Net B/T	**$698,520**

					Franchisees' Gross Sales (In Thousands)
First Year:	$500K		($166.6K/Mail)		
Second Year:	$675K		($225K/Mail)		
Third Year:	$750K		($250K/Mail)		
Fourth Year:	$1 Mil		($333.3K/Mail)		

	1996	1997	1998	1999	2000	2001
1 May	$333	$500	$675	$750	$1,000	$1,000
2 Jan		$500	$675	$750	$1,000	$1,000
3 Mar		$500	$675	$675	$1,000	$1,000
4 May		$333	$500	$675	$750	$1,000
5 July		$167	$500	$675	$750	$1,000
6 Sept		$167	$500	$675	$750	$1,000
7 Nov		$0	$500	$675	$750	$1,000
8 Jan			$500	$675	$750	$1,000
9 Mar			$500	$675	$750	$1,000
10 May			$333	$500	$675	$750
11 July			$167	$500	$675	$750
12 July			$167	$500	$675	$750
13 Sept			$167	$500	$675	$750
14 Sept			$167	$500	$675	$750
15 Nov			$0	$500	$675	$750
16 Jan				$500	$675	$750
17 Feb				$500	$675	$750
18 Mar				$500	$675	$750
19 Apr				$333	$500	$675
20 May				$333	$500	$675
21 June				$333	$500	$675
22 July				$167	$500	$675
23 Aug				$167	$500	$675
24 Sept				$167	$500	$675
25 Oct				$0	$500	$675
Total	$333,000	$2,167,000	$6,701,000	$12,300,000	$17,075,000	$20,475,000
10%	$33,300	$216,700	$670,000	$1,230,000	$1,707,500	$2,000,000

THE FRANCHISE AGREEMENT

First, The Company needs to legally establish the franchising company. In addition, the franchising company needs to be capitalized and the capitalization certified. Next, it is recommended that The Company prepare its Uniform Franchise Offering Circular in accordance with the Federal Trade Commission's Rule regarding the disclosure of franchise sales. The Company will register the franchise company's name, trademark, and service marks in the federal register of the U.S. Copyright and Patent Office. The Company will also register the franchise in those registration states in which it intends to sell franchises.

With a projected total of twenty-five (25) franchised outlets, the Post Direct concept lends itself to a single unit sale. Therefore, it is recommended that the franchise agreement be limited to a single unit.

Rights, Trademarks, Service Marks	The franchise agreement will provide for the granting of the right of franchisees to use the Company's trademarks and service marks, as well as The Company's System and Business Format.
Individual Outlet Franchise Fee	It is recommended that the franchise fee range from $20,000 to $50,000 per unit based upon the size of the franchised marketing area. All fees are to be paid in a lump sum upon signing of the franchise agreement. The first franchised outlet will be sold at a token fee of $12,500 (to cover training). After the first outlet is sold, the franchisee fee will be a minimum of $20,000. The franchise fee is subject to change as additional units are sold.
Royalty Fee	A royalty fee in the amount of nine percent (9%) to ten percent (10%) of the gross sales volume will be so defined in the Franchise Agreement to be paid to The Company on a per mailing basis. Under any circumstance, the required minimum monthly fee will be $500 per month.
Advertising Fee	An advertising fee in the amount of two percent (2%), and not to exceed four percent (4%), of annual gross sales will be paid into an advertising/promotion fund to be used exclusively to meet any and all costs of placing, designing, maintaining, administering, researching, directing, and preparing general Post Direct advertising. The fee will be collected and administered by The Company.
Estimated Total Franchise Investment	The total investment of a franchisee for one Post Direct franchise outlet will range from $40,400 to $52,100 (including the franchise fee).
The Duration of the Franchise Relationship	The franchise agreement shall have a term of five (5) years with an automatic extension for an additional five (5) years. Upon renewal, the franchisee will pay a renewal fee equal to ten percent (10%) of the most current franchise fee.
Trademarks	Post Direct has applied for the registration of its trademarks and service marks to protect them for the use by the franchisor and the franchisee. Post Direct will own all rights to the trademarks and the service marks of the System. The use of these marks is the cornerstone of the franchise, and The Company is dedicated and obligated to protect them. The trademark and service marks will also be registered internationally as required. Post Direct's franchisees will be granted the right to use The Company's trademark and service marks. It is recommended that Counsel be retained to protect The Company's trademarks, service marks, trade names and logo types through due diligence regarding their uses. In addition, any proprietary goods, equipment or service technology should be protected to allow The Company's franchisees to compete effectively in the marketplace and to deliver high quality advertising products and services.
Office Location	Franchisees will need an office from which to conduct business. The space required will range from 400 to 800 square feet. The location may be at the franchisee's home or another location. Franchisee is responsible for selecting the office location, for setting up the office and for operating the office, Franchisor does not specify nor approve the location of the franchisee's office.
Commencement of Operation	The franchisee must activate the franchise operation within 45 days following the signing of the franchise agreement. The franchisee will have completed his training in this period of time as well.
Services to the Franchisees	The Company's services to its franchisees are the foundation of its success. The Services provide the cutting edge over the competition. Such services should be included in the franchise agreement. The franchise agreement will spell out what the franchise can expect to receive from The Company in return for franchise fees, royalty and advertising fees, including the following: 1. An opportunity to open a new business with minimum capital 2. Proprietary products and services provided by The Company 3. Use of The Company's trademark and service marks 4. A customer accepted image

5. Combined printing and other buying power allowing product purchase advantages
6. Basic outlet operations training and continued assistance
7. Managerial and records assistance
8. Sales, advertising, and marketing assistance
9. Cooperative publicity, promotion, and recognition
10. Newsletters and other forms of communication
11. Continuing product research and development
12. Confidential procedures/operations manual, on loan
13. Computer software designed for the System
14. Product and service specifications
15. Initial personalized stationary package

> •Business Cards (500)
> •Letterheads (500)
> •Envelopes (500)
> •2-Part Sales Agreement Contract (300)
> •2-Part Invoice (300)
> •Sales Brochures (500)
> •Customized Sales Kits (3)
> •Sales Training Tape (1 set)
> •Sample "Card Deck" (Unsorted) (3)
> •Client Testimonial Letter
> •Client Analysis Report Forms
> •Sample Promotional Materials
> •Demographics for Area (to be paid by franchisee)

Production Services

The Company shall be the sole source of any direct mail co-op advertising products and services (art work, typesetting, printing, proofing, collating, etc.) These production services shall be made available to the franchisee at rates set forth in the confidential operations manual. The rates shall be subject to change as required by rising costs of labor, postage, mailing list, paper, and other materials and general administrative costs. Rate changes shall be made upon thirty (30) days written notice to the franchisee.

Minimum Mailings

Requirements include a minimum of two (2) mass mailings to at least 100,000 mailable homes in the area during the first twelve months of operation, followed by a minimum of three (3) mass mailings to at least 100,000 mailable homes in the area during the second twelve months of operation. The minimum number of mailings for the next year will be determined by the success of the mailings in the previous year.

Program of Supervision

Controls are the essence of a franchise system, enabling it to produce a profitable operation. These controls are incorporated into the franchise agreement and the confidential operations manuals. A supervisory system has been established to give training, support, advice, and continuing services to the franchisee. The Company's system is designed to provide the franchisee with a profitable business format and a public acceptance of the concept wherever the franchise is located. Well-placed financial controls and reasonable cash requirements will enhance The Company's integrity, credibility, and commitment with and to its franchisees.

Confidential Procedures/ Operations Manuals

The program of supervision is well documented in the Company's Franchise Agreement and in its operations manual, which explains in detail the payment of the fees, the franchisee's start-up costs, and the rights of periodic inspection. The administration of the franchised operation and standards for products and services to be offered to customers is clearly documented in the confidential operations manuals. This complete guide to the operation of the franchise is available, on loan, to each franchisee. The franchisee is responsible for keeping his copy of the operations manual current. The master copy of the operations manual is maintained by the franchisor at its principal office and will be the controlling factor in the event of a dispute about the contents of the operations manual.

Products and Services

To maintain identity, trademarks, service marks, and quality control, The Company provides a standards criteria and description of products and services currently sold through Post Direct. The Company will bring new products and services on line for the franchisee as they become available.

Reference will be made in the Franchise Agreement pertaining to The Company's required approval of any equipment, product or services of the franchisee's which are not included in The Company's Operations Manual.

Forms and Supplies

The Company has designed its own forms to be used by the franchisee. With prior experience in outlet operations, the forms are designed to fit the operations System.

Cooperative Advertising Program for the Franchise System

A franchise can produce optimum results with well developed and executed advertising and promotional efforts. For this reason, The Company will maintain a well-tuned marketing program, the cost of which is shared with the franchisee through a required cooperative advertising campaign. This program includes: advertising, promotion, public relations, advertising copy, commercials, formats, and slicks.

The advertising services and details of the franchisee's marketing program are detailed in the confidential operations manuals.

Through constant evaluation of its competition, The Company, with the combined advertising power of its franchisees, will be able to find ways to better serve their markets and plan for the future.

Accounting

The company has established a standard chart of accounts and a uniform reporting system for its franchisees. This will be included in the operations manual. In addition, The Company will capitalize on the advantages of computer technology. Outside the obvious advantages of billing and payroll, financial statements, and cash flow analysis, computerized product purchase analysis can identify the best products and services for franchisees' customers.

Training and Set-Up Assistance

The franchisee and/or its approved manager are required to participate in the training program. The Company will distinguish itself through a personalized approach to training its franchisees in the state-of-the-art of operations, management and marketing. Well in advance of the franchised unit opening, the franchisees will each receive a copy of the operations manuals to read and review. The operations manual will remain the property of The Company.

The Company is developing a comprehensive training program for franchisees to be conducted at its corporate headquarters and in operational facilities. The company training program is designed for a minimum of one week's duration at any one of the corporate outlets. In addition, one more week at the franchisee's site will be included in the training program. More time will be allocated if necessary. The training program establishes a solid base and does more than anything else in cementing a long-term and healthy relationship between The Company and its franchisees.

The franchisee is solely responsible for the compensation, travel, lodging, and living expenses incurred by the franchisee and its employees in connection with attendance at any of the franchisor's training programs, conventions, and/or meetings held by the franchisor.

A typical outline of key topic areas in the training program will include:

A. The Franchise
      1. The Company's System
      2. Pre-Opening Responsibilities
      3. Business Management Techniques
      4. Recruiting Office Personnel
      5. Recruiting Sales Representatives

B. Operations
    1. Product and Service Knowledge
    2. Computer Operations
    3. Accounting, Financial, and Reporting Skills
    4. Daily Routines
    5. Staffing, Scheduling and Employee Relations
C. Marketing Strategy
    1. Advertising and Promotion Techniques
    2. Customer Relations
    3. Creative Public Relations
    4. Marketing and Selling Advertising
    5. Preparing Layouts of Advertising, Color Formatting
    6. Scheduling Mailings

Periodic seminars for all franchisees will provide an invaluable exchange of ideas, new programs, new product introduction, management updates, and marketing. Such meetings will give the franchisee information and ideas that can only be obtained through association with The Company. | **Industry Information and Seminars**

Franchisee is obligated to comply with franchisor's intermarket sales policy with respect to sales of advertising for the mailing of Post Direct Decks outside of the franchisee's territory. This policy is outlined in the operations manual. | **Intermarket Sales**

The Company will use its computer technology to keep franchisees ahead of the competition. For example, announcements of new products should be on-line for the franchisees within minutes. | **Communication**

In addition, a periodic newsletter will be prepared at corporate headquarters and will describe relevant events including changes in tax laws, key economic trends special events of interest, important news items about The Company and its franchisees, and, of course, products and operations. The newsletter will serve as a sales incentive and communications vehicle. A franchisee and/or employee of the month will be established, sales records will be published, special achievements recognized, and management and marketing tips provided.

Conformance to the franchise agreement and the standard operations procedures will be required by all franchisees. This will be accomplished through the Franchise Agreement, the operations manuals, and daily, weekly, monthly and/or annual reports and audits. Periodic inspection visits by a regional manager, corporate officer, or supervisor will reinforce standards of conformance. | **Responsibilities of the Franchisee**

•Non-Compete
•Transfer
•Termination
•Litigation
•Hold Harmless/Indemnification
•Severability | **Plus Following Additions**

MSA -- Metropolitan Statistical Areas as defined by the United States Department of Commerce. There are a total of 320 MSAs in the U.S. MSAs are constituted of entire counties in all but the New England states (Connecticut, Maine, Massachusetts, New Hampshire, Rhode Island and Vermont). New England's MSAs consist of cities and towns, and boundaries may include parts of several counties. NECMA's (New England County Metropolitan Areas), on the other hand, are constituted of entire counties. | **Definitions**

FTA (Franchisee Trade Area) -- the boundaries of which are identified by the franchisor and agreed to by the franchisee. It consists of approximately 100,000 prime households in the $75,000 household income range. The FTA will be identified by counties, zip codes and/or natural boundaries for each franchise.

Prime Households -- those domiciles or households within the area deemed to be desirable recipients of Post Direct, based on reported households annual income and demographic criteria in accordance with the Company's policies and standards as outlined in its operations manual.

Production -- the publication of Post Direct "Card Decks" for a mailing, and all of the services performed in connection therewith, including but not limited to: graphics preparation, proofing, printing, collating, etc.

Emu Ranch

BUSINESS PLAN

SOUTHWESTERN EMU RANCH

28600 W. Tumbleweed Pass
Canyon, TX 79015

Southwestern Emu Ranch has jumped on the healthy lifestyle bandwagon. The demand for quality, low fat food has created a new market for emu products. Interesting financial information is provided in the form of an Operational Costs Table and Projected Income Statements for the first four years.

- BUSINESS CONCEPT

- MARKETING PLAN

- OPERATIONAL PLAN

- INITIAL START-UP COST

- STRATEGIC PLAN

- FINANCIAL INFORMATION

BUSINESS CONCEPT

The emu is a large bird which originally came from Australia and belongs to the big bird family group known as the ratites, which includes other birds such as the ostrich (found throughout Africa and southwestern Asia) and the Cassowary (also found in Australia).

The emu ranch will be in the business of "ranching", or raising, emu birds for two main purposes. The first purpose is to raise newly hatched emu chicks to the age of a year or older, pair them off and sell them as good quality adult emu breeding pairs. The second purpose is to raise a portion of these chicks to the age of twelve months or older for the purpose of slaughter for their lean red meat, oil and skin for leather products.

The breeding pairs will be sold nationwide to other emu ranchers, who are established in the business or are just starting. At first, this will be the emu ranch's main target market, because of the high profits that can be made by selling adult emus as breeding pairs.

The emu ranch's secondary market will be the slaughter market, whose main products consist of prime cuts of emu meat, ready for shipments to restaurants, residential orders, worldwide markets and in the future, shipment to supermarkets. High quality leather from the emu's skin, and five to six liters of emu oil, which is currently being used in the cosmetic industry, will also be distributed. Additionally, the medical industry uses the oil for therapeutic rubbing oil, skin and facial moisturizing lotions and medical applications used for treating the skin of burn victims.

The raising of emu birds for breeding pairs or for slaughter is unique, because the emu breeding pairs, when at their peak of producing fertile eggs, will produce at the end of an eighteen month cycle. Between forty five to fifty adult emus will be ready for slaughter or to be sold as breeding pairs at eighteen months to two years old. In other words, one breeding pair will produce more meat and leather in eighteen months than one beef cow breeding pair, not including the amount of high grade oil that forty to fifty adult emus will produce. Each adult emu will produce seven liters of fine organic oil, that is non-allergenic to human skin.

Right now the emu industry is in a breeder's market stage, which means that the nation's emu ranchers are raising and selling their adult emu birds as breeding pairs, instead of for slaughter. There are substantial profits that can be made in raising and selling emus as breeding pairs, given the large volume of emu ranches that are starting each year.

A proven emu breeding pair can be sold at $8,000 to $30,000 depending on the historical number of fertile eggs the pair has produced each mating season. Proven breeding pairs may lay between thirty to fifty fertile eggs per mating season.

Therefore, if the emu ranch started with ten proven breeding pairs that would lay on average thirty-five eggs each, of which, at the end of successfully raising all of the emu chicks to eighteen-months to two-year-old adult emus, the total number of adult emus would be 350. If these are sold at $15,000 per breeding pair, the total gross amount of sales, without the subtraction of the initial start-up costs would be (.5 x 350 x $10,000 = $1,750,000). An example of our secondary target market, would be the current slaughter market which is paying between $500 to $800 for each adult emu bird ready for slaughter. Therefore, 350 x $500 for each adult emu for slaughter is $175,000.

MARKET PLAN

Industry Description and Outlook

The primary target industry of the emu ranch will be the current breeder's market. This means that nearly all of the emu farmers are raising their newborn emus to fully adult breeding pairs and selling them to emu farmers who are just getting started in the business. The current annual growth rate in the number of new or start-up emu farms here in the United States is between four and five thousand, which is the total number of emu farms which existed in 1994. The average number of breeding pairs that each new farm will start with, is between two to eight breeding pairs. Therefore, the average number of breeding pairs needed for 1996 is twenty-four thousand, or forty eight thousand birds. The current emu population in the United States is estimated to be between two hundred fifty thousand and five hundred thousand. The majority of this population is located in Texas.

The secondary target market will be the emu slaughter market. The number of emus required for slaughter annually at a conservative projection is estimated to be between one and a half and two and a half million birds. These projections are expected to increase within the next three to five years. This figure does not include the existing large demand of products that exist within the European markets.

Note: Of the estimated two hundred fifty thousand to five million emu birds that exist here in the United States, only twenty to thirty thousand of these birds are actually laying hens.

The growth potential for emu ranching in the next five years is unlimited, given the above information. Also, the demand for emu products is currently surpassing and will continue in the next five years to surpass emu supply.

The growth potential of emu ranching in the next ten years is projected to be unlimited, given the projections for the number of emus required for slaughter to meet consumer demands both here in the United Stated and in Europe.

Emu ranching has been increasing rapidly since 1987, as more people are discovering the potential market value of the meat, leather and oil products that can be derived from the bird. 1994 surveys show that the emu population will increase to six hundred thousand by the end of 1995 and to one and a half million emus by the end of 1996.

Industry Characteristics and Trends

(1) The emu provides lean, red meat that is low in fat, calories and cholesterol. Furthermore, it is high in protein and iron with a texture and appearance similar to beef. Because of its low fat content, emu meat does not shrink during cooking.
(2) The emu provides a soft and subtle, high quality leather, that is more highly sought after than leather from cattle in the high fashion and garment industries..
(3) Each emu provides 6 liters of a highly penetrating oil extracted from a layer of fat that surrounds the emu's body. This oil has the characteristic of being totally absorbed by the skin, which gives it an excellent market potential for cosmetics, such as skin and facial creams, fragrances and pharmaceuticals, such as pain relieving rubbing creams, arthritic rubbing oil and burn relieving creams.

Currently, the emu industry is in the breeder's cycle stage. This means that the emu ranchers are raising emus for the purpose of selling them as proven breeding pairs. This is where the emu has its highest return for the amount invested in raising the birds. Current sale prices for proven breeding pairs are currently as low as $8,000 to as high as $25,000. The value of proven breeding pairs is based on the number of fertile eggs produced each breeding season.

In the next three to five years, the emu industry will move into a slaughter market. At this time, each adult bird would bring in $500 to $800 each at today's market prices.

The potential of emu ranching will be based on consumer demand for both emu meat and oil products. Recent test markets indicate that there is a large potential for consumer demand of cosmetics and pharmaceutical products made from the emu's oil. It has been estimated that if the current total population of emus that exist in the United States today were slaughtered for meat and oil products, it would meet only 10% of today's market demand for these products.

Estimations indicate that consumer demand for emu products will far surpass the emu population, even ten to twenty years into the future.

Customer Base

The emu ranch will be supplying adult emu birds to two main customer based industries. The first customer base will be local and distant emu ranchers. We will supply adult proven emu breeding pairs to both. The second customer base will be the United Emu Ranchers (UER), who we will supply with adult and/or yearling emu birds for meat supply, fine oil and leather products.

The United Emu Ranchers is a cooperative of emu ranchers whose main goals are to advertise and promote all emu products and to support all phases of the emu industry. The UER has established its own market presence by buying members' emus for slaughter. They then process these birds to produce numerous products. Then they market these products to the customer through their own marketing network. Therefore, any emu rancher who belongs to the UER automatically has an established market, ready to buy his emu for slaughter.

Competition

In the state of Texas, there are currently an estimated twenty-five hundred to three thousand emu ranches in operation, which is about one-third the number of emu ranches in operation in the United States. Some of the larger and more successful emu ranches in Texas have between ten to twenty more emu breeding pairs.

The larger emu ranches are successful because they recognize the full profit potential of a large and efficiently run emu ranch. They obtain as much information and knowledge as they can beforehand, about the emu bird and how to successfully raise emus. Most of them then write and follow a successful and detailed business plan.

Our emu ranch will follow the same initial operational steps and successful business plans as the larger emu ranching operations that exist in Texas. However, our emu ranch will start with eight to ten proven breeding pairs. It will take two to three years before the ranch will be at the same level of operations as the larger emu ranches in Texas.

For now, the main long-term competitor of the emu industry is the cattle industry. The cattle industry is the major supplier of both red meat and leather products in today's consumer market. The cattle industry is well established nationally through its advertising, marketing and distribution network system.

The emu industry, which has just begun to emerge as an industry in the past two years, is still developing its population of birds nationwide. When the emu industry achieves the slaughter phase of operation, and has developed its own advertisement, marketing and distribution network, it will then be in direct competition with the cattle industry.

Initial consumer test market results show that the emu industry will gradually gain on the cattle market industry. The American consumer is looking for alternative, healthier lean meats. The emu's lean, very low fat red meat is an ideal beef substitute.

Location

The emu ranch business will be located on a 14 acre property that the owner inherited. The land is located in Canyon, Texas. It is undeveloped and is zoned for ranching agricultural animals. The property is located in a quiet area, with little housing, which is an ideal environment for both raising emus and developing emu breeding pairs. Only seven of the acres will be needed for the facilitation of the ranch, which will leave another seven acres for planned future expansion of the ranch.

Price Determination

The following will be the price structure for Southwestern's emu products, based on current market prices. One proven emu breeding pair will produce from thirty to fifty fertile eggs per breeding season. If on average thirty chicks grow to eighteen months, when they are ready for slaughter, one pair would bring in an average annual income of $150,000 annually.

Fertile emu eggs	$100/per egg
One-day-old chicks	$200/per chick
Three-month-old chicks	$300/per chick
Eighteen-month to two-year-old emu	$800/per emu
Proven breeding pairs	$5,000 to $10,000/per pair

The United Emu Ranchers (UER) is a nationwide organization that is currently promoting production, marketing, sales and the commercial use of emu and all emu products.

MARKETING APPROACH

The UER has already established a nationwide clientele of restaurants, whose main demands are that the UER can assure them that there will be a steady supply of emu meat from the growing U.S. emu industry, in order to satisfy their growing customer demand for the emu's red meat.

Also the UER is currently training inspectors and meat processing companies on how to process (dress) the emu meat and will soon receive USDA approval. The UER is also introducing its own line of moisturizers, therapeutic lotions and creams.

The United States Emu Council (USEC) is also in the business of promoting and marketing the commercial use of the emu and its products, as well as selling emu products. USEC also encourages regulations supporting a viable emu industry, enhances the industry's public image and has two national cooperatives. The USEC is dedicated to creating the necessary infrastructure for U.S. leadership in a global emu industry.

Therefore upon the opening of the ranch, John Stone, Southwestern's owner, will become a member of the UER and the USEC, as well as, any other organizations that have similar objectives and goals as those of the UER and USEC. All marketing and promotional campaigns for the Southwestern Emu Ranch will be accomplished through membership in the above organizations. Also, both the UER and USEC are cooperatives, which means that they will provide a local, ready-made, seasonal market location, where Southwestern can sell emus that are old enough for slaughter. We will also advertise those emus that have been raised for breeding pair purposes, in the advertisement sections of the newsletters of all relevant organizations, both locally and nationally.

OPERATIONAL PLAN

Management Team

John Stone will be the sole proprietor of Southwestern Emu Ranch. His experience and background in animal husbandry consists of five years of raising chin chills, rabbits and poultry for profits. This experience is transferable to raising emus for profit. Support personnel will be John Stone's brother, Colin Jacobs, and close friend William McCarthy.

Colin Jacobs has experience in bookkeeping, writing reports, record keeping and in all areas of office management. He also has the ability to analyze and apply crucial information, which will be essential to both the incubation process and rearing of the emu chick to an adult bird, successfully.

William McCarthy has experience in both the production and interpretation of blueprint drawings. McCarthy also has practical experience in the construction industry. He has already drawn the blueprints for the layout of the ranch and all ranch buildings. McCarthy will be responsible for the actual construction of all ranch buildings. He will also assist John Stone and Colin Jacobs in the rearing and maintenance of both the emu chicks and adult emus.

The combined efforts of all three men will ensure the total success of the emu ranch business. Each of their areas of expertise will be combined to form a cohesive effort, essential to the successful running of the business.

Operational Controls

The emu ranch will start off with ten proven emu mating pairs, with future plans to increase the number of emu mating pairs to twenty. From each pair, we expect the average number of eggs laid to be between thirty-five and forty-five eggs per pair. This will provide production capacity between three hundred fifty and four hundred fifty adult emus within an eighteen-month period.

One advantage that the ranch will have is that the property is large enough for both the expansion of operations. It will also allow us to install one or more mobile homes for living quarters, in order to facilitate a twenty-four hour care and watch of the birds and the facilities.

Elements that will be crucial to our overall success, will be for us to keep in mind that our goal is to purchase and maintain good quality, healthy and disease free emu mating pairs and to provide a defense against any local predators. To accomplish these goals, we will follow the following steps:

(1) Obtain references of each owner, before we purchase emu mating pairs, in an effort to insure both the health and the number of fertile eggs produced.
(2) To have periodical health checks of both emu mating pairs and of coming yearling chicks. This will require the periodical assistance of the local veterinarian.
(3) Apply any medication that is required and prescribed by the local veterinarian.
(4) Insure that all emu birds are on a proper nutritional diet, along with the addition of required vitamins.
(5) Insure that the incubation facilities and hatcheries are properly designed and maintained, and that successful standard practices and procedures are followed to insure the health and successful development of both hatchlings and chicks.
(6) To maintain a comprehensive record program in order to record all vital statistics of both emu adults and chicks.
(7) To install devices such as low voltage perimeter electric lines; anti-hawk canvas nets installed over the emu chicks' pens and also the purchase of one or two "emu dogs" to ward off local predators, such as coyotes and raccoons.

The key indicators of success will be based on the number of adult emus that have been hatched and successfully raised in an eighteen month period. A 5% or 10% minimum loss of birds would be a set goal. We also would set a total desired number of birds sold, in order to make a substantial profit in an eighteen month period.

INITIAL START-UP COST

Proven emu mating pairs 10@$10,000	$100,000
2 trailer homes and corresponding building materials	$10,770
Misc.: utilities, feed storage shed, tool shed, etc.	$2,900
Tools and machines	$683
Equipment and supplies	$10,137
Drinking water and plumbing	$1,048
Feed and health supplies	$63,920
Incubators and identification equipment	$11,690
Shade shelters building materials	$1,322
Older chick hatchery building materials	$1,639
Incubation trailer interior modifications	$4,221
Newborn emu hatchery pen building materials	$1,639
Chainlink fencing 300ft.@$40/ft.	$12,000
Computer	$2,000
Working capital	$30,000
Organizational cost	$1,500
Sum total of the above totals	**$255,054**

The emu ranch will initially start with ten proven breeding pairs. Each pair will produce on average between thirty-five to fifty eggs, within the first emu mating season of the first year of operation. The total number of fertile eggs after the first mating season will be between three hundred fifty and five hundred eggs.

With a given 5% loss of successfully hatched chicks to adult emus, the total number of adult emus expected within the first two years will be between three hundred thirty-two and four hundred seventy-five adult birds.

Five emu mating pairs will be added to the ranch inventory after the first two years. After which, five emu mating pairs will be added to the ranch inventory each year. This will leave between three hundred twenty-two and four hundred sixty-five emus as mating pairs. Those birds that are not sold as mating pairs will be sold to the slaughter market, after the first two years.

After the first two years:

Maximum gross sales with all emu adult birds sold as proven breeding pairs	.5 x 322 x $8,000	$1,288,000
Minimum gross sales, all adult emus sold to slaughter market after the first two years	322 x $500	$161,000

After the third year:

Expected maximum gross sales	.5 x 489 x $8,000	$1,956,000
Expected minimum gross sales	489 x $500	$244,500

After the fourth year:

Expected maximum gross sales	.5 x 655 x $8,000	$2,620,000
Expected minimum gross sales	655 x $500	$327,500

After the fifth year:

Expected maximum gross sales	.5 x 821 x $8,000	$3,284,000
Expected minimum gross sales	821 x $500	$410,500

Use of Funds	Quantity	Cost per	Total Cost
Breeding pairs	10	$2,500	$25,000
Trailer home	2	$4,000	$8,000
Construction/supplies	1	$2,770	$2,770
Misc. Utilities hook-up, feed storage	1	$2,900	$2,900
Misc. Tools	1	$683	$683
Used Pick-up truck	1	$3,500	$3,500
Used cattle trailer	1	$1,200	$1,200
Light wire electric utility poles - 16'	3	$22	$67
Electricity deposit	1	$200	$200
Electricity wiring/connection	1	$600	$600
Rental of backhoe	1	$125	$125
Tractor for digging channels for PVC	1	$60	$60
Construction/supplies of gravel roads	1	$900	$900
Emergency generator	1	$3,500	$3,500
PVC plumbing	1	$1,048	$1,048
Initial stock of feed and supplies	1	$63,920	$63,920
Incubation and identification equipment	1	$11,690	$11,690
Construction/supplies for shade/shelter	1	$1,322	$1,322
Older chick hatchery building material	1	$1,639	$1,639
Incubation trailer interior modificatin	1	$4,221	$4,221

New-born emu hatchery pens	1	$1,209	$1,209
Fencing	300	$40	$12,000
Computer system	1	$2,000	$2,000
Working capital	1	$126,855	$126,855
Organization cost	1	$1,500	$1,500
Total			**$276,909**

Projected Income Statement Year One

	Aug-97 Mo. 1	Sept-97 Mo. 2	Oct-97 Mo. 3	Nov-97 Mo. 4	Dec-97 Mo. 5	Jan-98 Mo. 6
Sales Revenue						
Revenue from sale of chicks				338	338	338
Revenue from sale of yearlings						
Revenue from sale of breeding pairs						
Sale of birds for slaughter						
Total Sales Revenue				338	338	338
Cost of Goods Sold						
Feed/supplies						
Veternarian fees	80	80	80	249	418	587
Medication/supplements/vaccine	40	40	40	124	209	293
Identification-tags/microchip	100					
Misc.	100	100	100	100	100	100
Total Cost of Goods Sold	**320**	**220**	**220**	**473**	**727**	**980**
Gross Profit	**(320)**	**(220)**	**(220)**	**(136)**	**(389)**	**(642)**
Gross Margin	**#DIV/O!**	**#DIV/O!**	**#DIV/O!**	**-40%**	**-115%**	**-190%**
General/Administrative Expenses						
Accounting	300	300	300	300	300	300
Advertising						
Automobile expense	300	300	300	300	300	300
Bank fees	20	20	20	20	20	20
Dues/subscriptions						
Electric	100	100	100	100	100	100
Gas	60	60	60	60	60	60
Insurance-general business	300	300	300	300	300	300
Insurance-automobile	124	124	124	124	124	124
Insurance-bonding	200	200	200	200	200	200
Insurance-health insurance	100	100	100	100	100	100
Insurance-liability	400	400	400	400	400	400
Legal	100	100	100	100	100	100
Licenses	50	50	50	50	50	50
Misc. Repairs	400	400	400	400	400	400
Payroll taxes	54	54	54	54	54	54
Property tax	9	9	9	9	9	9
Repairs/maintenance	100	100	100	100	100	100
Telephone	300	300	300	300	300	300
Travel	275	275	275	275	275	275
Wages	4,000	4,000	4,000	4,000	4,000	4,000
Water/sewer	25	25	25	25	25	25
Total Expense	**7,217**	**7,217**	**7,217**	**7,217**	**7,217**	**7,217**
Income from Operations	**(7,537)**	**(7,437)**	**(7,437)**	**(7,353)**	**(7,606)**	**(7,859)**
	(7,537)	(14,974)	(22,411)	(29,764)	(37,369)	(45,229)

Feb-98 Mo. 7	Mar-98 Mo. 8	Apr-98 Mo. 9	May-98 Mo. 10	Jun-98 Mo. 11	Jul-98 Mo. 12	Aug-98 Mo. 13
338	338	338	338	338	338	
338	**338**	**338**	**338**	**338**	**338**	
756	924	1093	1262	1431	1600	1600
378	462	547	631	716	800	800
100	100	100	100	100	100	100
1,233	**1,487**	**1,740**	**1,993**	**2,247**	**2,500**	**2,500**
(896)	**(1,149)**	**(1,402)**	**(1,656)**	**(1,909)**	**(2,162)**	**(2,500)**
-265%	**-340%**	**-415%**	**-490%**	**-565%**	**-640%**	**#DIV/O!**
300	300	300	300	300	300	300
300	300	300	300	300	300	300
20	20	20	20	20	20	20
100	100	100	100	100	100	100
60	60	60	60	60	60	60
300	300	300	300	300	300	300
124	124	124	124	124	124	124
200	200	200	200	200	200	200
100	100	100	100	100	100	100
400	400	400	400	400	400	400
100	100	100	100	100	100	100
50	50	50	50	50	50	50
400	400	400	400	400	400	400
54	54	54	54	54	54	54
9	9	9	9	9	9	9
100	100	100	100	100	100	100
300	300	300	300	300	300	300
275	275	275	275	275	275	275
4,000	4,000	4,000	4,000	4,000	4,000	4,000
25	25	25	25	25	25	25
7,217	**7,217**	**7,217**	**7,217**	**7,217**	**7,217**	**7,217**
(8,113)	**(8,366)**	**(8,619)**	**(8,873)**	**(9,126)**	**(9,379)**	**(9,717)**
(53,341)	**(61,707)**	**(70,326)**	**(79,199)**	**(88,325)**	**(97,704)**	**(107,421)**

Projected Income Statement Year Two

	Sep-98 Mo. 14	Oct-98 Mo. 15	Nov-98 Mo. 16	Dec-98 Mo. 17	Jan-99 Mo. 18	Fe4b-99 Mo. 19
Sales Revenue						
Revenue from sale of chicks			338	338	338	338
Revenue from sale of yearlings			4,222	4,222	4,222	4,222
Revenue from sale of breeding pairs						
Sale of birds for slaughter			11,337	11,337	11,337	11,337
Total Sales Revenue			**15,897**	**15,897**	**15,897**	**15,897**
Cost of Goods Sold						
Feed/supplies						
Veternarian fees	1,600	1,600	1,644	1,813	1,982	2,151
Medication/supplements/vaccine	800	800	822	907	991	1,076
Identification-tags/microchips						47
Misc.	100	100	100	100	100	100
Total Cost of Goods Sold	**2,500**	**2,500**	**2,567**	**2,820**	**3,120**	**3,374**
Gross Profit	**(2,500)**	**(2,500)**	**13,330**	**13,077**	**12,776**	**12,523**
Gross Margin	**#DIV/O!**	**#DIV/O!**	**84%**	**82%**	**80%**	**79%**
General/Administrative Expenses						
Accounting	300	300	300	300	300	300
Advertising						
Automobile expense	300	300	300	300	300	300
Bank fees	20	20	20	20	20	20
Dues/subscriptions						
Electric	100	100	100	100	100	100
Gas	60	60	60	60	60	60
Insurance-general business	300	300	300	300	300	300
Insurance-automobile	124	124	124	124	124	124
Insurance-bonding	200	200	200	200	200	200
Insurance-health insurance	100	100	100	100	100	100
Insurance-liability	400	400	400	400	400	400
Legal	100	100	100	100	100	100
Licenses	50	50	50	50	50	50
Misc. Repairs	400	400	400	400	400	400
Payroll taxes	54	54	54	54	54	54
Property tax	9	9	9	9	9	9
Repairs/maintenance	100	100	100	100	100	100
Telephone	300	300	300	300	300	300
Travel	275	275	275	275	275	275
Wages	4,000	4,000	4,000	4,000	4,000	4,000
Water/sewer	25	25	25	25	25	25
Total Expense	**7,217**	**7,217**	**7,217**	**7,217**	**7,217**	**7,217**
Income from Operations	**(9,717)**	**(9,717)**	**6,113**	**5,860**	**5,559**	**5,306**
	(117,138)	**(126,855)**				

Mar-99 Mo. 20	Apr-99 Mo. 21	May-99 Mo. 22	Jun-99 Mo. 23	Jul-99 Mo. 24	Aug-99 Mo. 25	Sept-99 Mo. 26	Oct-99 Mo. 27
497	656	815	974	1,133			
4,222	4,222	4,222	4,222	4,222			
		25,840	25,840	25,840	25,840	25,840	
11,337	11,337	11,337	11,337	11,337			
16,056	**16,215**	**42,214**	**42,373**	**42,532**	**25,840**	**25,840**	
	6,818	7,708	8,925	10,341	10,652	10,652	10,782
2,399	2,727	3,083	3,570	4,136	4,261	4,261	4,313
1,200	1,364	1,542	1,785	2,068	2,130	2,130	2,156
47	47	47	47	47	47	47	47
100	100	100	100	100	100	100	100
3,746	**11,057**	**12,480**	**14,427**	**16,693**	**17,191**	**17,191**	**17,351**
12,309	**5,158**	**29,734**	**27,945**	**25,839**	**8,649**	**8,649**	**(17,351)**
77%	**32%**	**70%**	**66%**	**61%**	**33%**	**33%**	**#DIV/O!**
300	300	300	300	300	300	300	300
300	300	300	300	300	300	300	300
20	20	20	20	20	20	20	20
100	100	100	100	100	100	100	100
60	60	60	60	60	60	60	60
300	300	300	300	300	300	300	300
124	124	124	124	124	124	124	124
200	200	200	200	200	200	200	200
100	100	100	100	100	100	100	100
400	400	400	400	400	400	400	400
100	100	100	100	100	100	100	100
50	50	50	50	50	50	50	50
400	400	400	400	400	400	400	400
54	54	54	54	54	54	54	54
9	9	9	9	9	9	9	9
100	100	100	100	100	100	100	100
300	300	300	300	300	300	300	300
275	275	275	275	275	275	275	275
4,000	4,000	4,000	4,000	4,000	4,000	4,000	4,000
25	25	25	25	25	25	25	25
7,217	**7,217**	**7,217**	**7,217**	**7,217**	**7,217**	**7,217**	**7,217**
5,092	**(2,059)**	**22,517**	**20,728**	**18,622**	**1,432**	**1,432**	**(24,568)**

Projected Income Statement Year Three

	Nov-99 Mo. 28	Dec-99 Mo. 29	Jan-00 Mo. 30	Feb-00 Mo. 31	Mar-00 Mo. 32	Apr-00 Mo. 33
Sales Revenue						
Revenue from sale of chicks	1,769	1,769	1,769	1,769	1,928	2,087
Revenue from sale of yearlings	4,222	4,222	4,222	4,222	6,210	8,198
Revenue from sale of breeding pairs						
Sale of birds for slaughter	11,337	11,337	11,337	11,337	16,674	22,011
Total Sales Revenue	**17,328**	**17,328**	**17,328**	**17,328**	**24,812**	**32,295**
Cost of Goods Sold						
Feed/supplies	12,682	14,893	17,104	19,315	21,579	24,041
Veternarian fees	5,073	5,957	6,842	7,726	8,631	9,616
Medication/supplements/vaccine	2,536	2,979	3,421	3,863	4,316	4,808
Identification-tags/microchips			47	47	47	47
Misc.	100	100	100	100	100	100
Total Cost of Goods Sold	**20,391**	**23,928**	**27,513**	**31,051**	**34,673**	**38,612**
Gross Profit	**(3,063)**	**(6,601)**	**(10,186)**	**(13,723)**	**(9,861)**	**(6,317)**
Gross Margin	**-18%**	**-38%**	**-59%**	**-79%**	**-40%**	**-20%**
General/Administrative Expenses						
Accounting	300	300	300	300	300	300
Advertising						
Automobile expense	300	300	300	300	300	300
Bank fees	20	20	20	20	20	20
Dues/subscriptions						
Electric	100	100	100	100	100	100
Gas	60	60	60	60	60	60
Insurance-general business	300	300	300	300	300	300
Insurance-automobile	124	124	124	124	124	124
Insurance-bonding	200	200	200	200	200	200
Insurance-health insurance	100	100	100	100	100	100
Insurance-liability	400	400	400	400	400	400
Legal	100	100	100	100	100	100
Licenses	50	50	50	50	50	50
Misc. Repairs	400	400	400	400	400	400
Payroll taxes	54	54	54	54	54	54
Property tax	9	9	9	9	9	9
Rent						
Repairs/maintenance	100	100	100	100	100	100
Telephone	300	300	300	300	300	300
Travel	275	275	275	275	275	275
Wage	4,000	4,000	4,000	4,000	4,000	4,000
Water/sewer	25	25	25	25	25	25
Total Expense	**7217**	**7,217**	**7,217**	**7,217**	**7,217**	**7,217**
Income from Operations	**(10,280)**	**(13,818)**	**(17,403)**	**(20,940)**	**(17,078)**	**(13,534)**

May-00 Mo. 34	Jun-00 Mo. 35	Jul-00 Mo. 36	Aug-00 Mo. 37	Sept-00 Mo. 38	Oct-00 Mo. 39	Nov-00 Mo. 40	Dec-00 Mo. 41
2,246	2,405	2,639				4,105	4,105
10,185	12,173	14,161				22,112	22,112
46,115	46,115	46,115	46,115	46,115			
27,348	32,685	38,022				59,370	59,370
85,894	**93,378**	**100,937**	**46,115**	**46,115**		**85,587**	**85,587**
26,471	29,331	32,483	33,527	33,527	33,757	37,259	42,390
10,588	11,732	12,993	13,411	13,411	13,503	14,904	16,956
5,294	5,866	6,497	6,705	6,705	6,751	7,452	8,478
69	91	49	136	158			65
100	100	100	100	100	100	100	100
42,523	**47,121**	**52,122**	**53,879**	**53,901**	**54,112**	**59,714**	**67,988**
43,371	**46,257**	**48,815**	**(7,764)**	**(7,786)**	**(54,112)**	**25,873**	**17,873**
50%	**50%**	**48%**	**-17%**	**-17%**	**#DIV/O!**	**30%**	**21%**
300	300	300	300	300	300	300	300
300	300	300	300	300	300	300	300
20	20	20	20	20	20	20	20
100	100	100	100	100	100	100	100
60	60	60	60	60	60	60	60
300	300	300	300	300	300	300	300
124	124	124	124	124	124	124	124
200	200	200	200	200	200	200	200
100	100	100	100	100	100	100	100
400	400	400	400	400	400	400	400
100	100	100	100	100	100	100	100
50	50	50	50	50	50	50	50
400	400	400	400	400	400	400	400
54	54	54	54	54	54	54	54
9	9	9	9	9	9	9	9
100	100	100	100	100	100	100	100
300	300	300	300	300	300	300	300
275	275	275	275	275	275	275	275
4,000	4,000	4,000	4,000	4,000	4,000	4,000	4,000
25	25	25	25	25	25	25	25
7,217	**7,217**	**7,217**	**7,217**	**7,,217**	**7,217**	**7,217**	**7,217**
36,154	**39,040**	**41,598**	**(14,981)**	**(15,003)**	**(61,329)**	**18,656**	**10,381**

Projected Income Statement Future

	Jan-01 Mo. 42	Feb-01 Mo. 43	Mar-01 Mo. 44	Apr-01 Mo. 45	May-01 Mo. 46	Jun-01 Mo. 47	Jul-01 Mo. 48	Aug-01 Mo. 49
Sales Revenue								
Revenue from sale of chicks	4,105	4,323	5,156	5,989	6,821	7,654	8,562	
Revenue from sale of yearlings	22,112	22,112	24,100	26,087	28,075	30,063	32,986	
Revenue from sale of breeding pairs					182,075	182,075	182,075	182,075
Sale of birds for slaughter	59,370	59,370	64,707	70,044	75,381	80718	88,568	
Total Sales Revenue	**85,587**	**85,805**	**93,962**	**102,120**	**292,353**	**300,510**	**312,191**	**182,075**
Cost of Goods Sold								
Fee/supplies	47,521	52,925	59,223	66,562	74,032	83,453	93,940	96,371
Veternarian fees	19,008	21,170	23,689	26,625	29,613	33,381	37,576	38,548
Medication/supplements/vaccine	9,504	10,585	11,845	13,312	14,806	16,691	18,788	19,274
Identification-tags/microchips	247	247	247	247	269	291	198	335
Misc.	100	100	100	100	100	100	100	100
Total Cost of Goods Sold	**76,380**	**85,026**	**95,103**	**106,846**	**118,820**	**133,916**	**150,602**	**154,629**
Gross Profit	**9,207**	**779**	**(1,141)**	**(4,726)**	**173,533**	**166,594**	**161,589**	**27,446**
Gross Margin	**11%**	**1%**	**-1%**	**-5%**	**59%**	**55%**	**52%**	**15%**
General/Administrative Expenses								
Accounting	300	300	300	300	300	300	300	300
Advertising								
Automobile expense	300	300	300	300	300	300	300	300
Bank fees	20	20	20	20	20	20	20	20
Dues/subscriptions								
Electric	100	100	100	100	100	100	100	100
Gas	60	60	60	60	60	60	60	60
Insurance-general business	300	300	300	300	300	300	300	300
Insurance-automobile	124	124	124	124	124	124	124	124
Insurance-bonding	200	200	200	200	200	200	200	200
Insurance-health insurance	100	100	100	100	100	100	100	100
Insurance-liability	400	400	400	400	400	400	400	400
Legal	100	100	100	100	100	100	100	100
Licenses	50	50	50	50	50	50	50	50
Misc. Repairs	400	400	400	400	400	400	400	400
Payroll taxes	54	54	54	54	54	54	54	54
Property tax	9	9	9	9	9	9	9	9
Rent								
Repairs/maintenance	100	100	100	100	100	100	100	100
Telephone	300	300	300	300	300	300	300	300
Travel	275	275	275	275	275	275	275	275
Wages	4,000	4,000	4,000	4,000	4,000	4,000	4,000	4,000
Water/sewer	25	25	25	25	25	25	25	25
Total Expense	**7,217**	**7,217**	**7,217**	**7,217**	**7,217**	**7,217**	**7,217**	**7,217**
Income from Operations	**1,990**	**(6,438)**	**(8,358)**	**(11,943)**	**166,316**	**159,377**	**154,372**	**20,229**

Engineering/Management Consultant

BUSINESS PLAN

HERMAN LIVINGSTON CONSULTANTS

3053 Harbor Drive, Ste. 206
Los Angeles, CA 90041

HLC's business plan contains informative financials for anyone considering entering the engineering/management consulting business. One interesting aspect of the plan is HLC's plan of networking with other similar businesses to work together and create more opportunities.

- EXECUTIVE SUMMARY

- DESCRIPTION OF BUSINESS OPPORTUNITY

- DESCRIPTION OF THE MARKET

- LOCATION OF BUSINESS

- DESCRIPTION OF THE COMPETITION

- MANAGEMENT & KEY PERSONNEL

- MILESTONE SCHEDULE

- FINANCIAL DATA

EXECUTIVE SUMMARY

Herman Livingston Consultants (HLC) seeks to raise equity capital of $28,000.00 principal equity for start-up costs involved with an engineering/management consulting firm. This includes the purchase of furniture, equipment and inventory; renovations and improvements at Los Angeles, California office site, and maintenance of sufficient cash reserves. This plan provides a description of the business opportunity and an outline and time line of the start-up period for HLC.

DESCRIPTION OF BUSINESS OPPORTUNITY

During his eight year involvement with the architecture, engineering and construction (A/E/C) industry, Herman Livingston realized unresolved obstacles existed in many organizations. Despite the lack of qualified management to correct the problems, most A/E/C owners hesitate to seek outside managerial assistance. Mainly this is due to the justifiable belief that an MBA management consultant would not have the technical knowledge to develop applied solutions to A/E/C firms in transition.

This gap in the market place inspired Herman Livingston to establish Herman Livingston Consultants (HLC), a professional service company specializing in providing engineering and management consulting (E/MC) services along with software sales to A/E/C companies and public works departments to enhance and strengthen their organizations and to meet the needs of their clients. In conjunction with established E/MC and software firms, HLC will provide the essential technical knowledge and products to develop goal oriented solutions that address the client's strengths and weaknesses.

The nature of selling consulting services is difficult since the sold product is unique and varies according to the needs of the client. The management of HLC plans to offer, but not be limited to, the following services:

- Civil, structural, and electrical engineering design
- Project management and assessment
- Quality assurance and quality control
- Computer software and hardware advisement
- Business development assistance
- Executive search
- Operations analysis
- Personnel manuals
- Competition and client analysis
- Company valuation
- Business plan preparation (Start-ups)
- Performance management systems
- Customer service bench marking (internal and external)
- Expert testimony

Because HLC will be able to chose temporary partnerships with all types of engineering companies and/or management consulting firms based on the job at hand, the flexibility of the company is virtually unlimited. HLC can provide cost effective services for small and large companies, from the public and private sectors. The flexibility to create any size group is further enhanced by Herman Livingston's project management background and strong industry understanding.

In addition to providing professional services, HLC will assess the client's computer needs, if requested, and recommend alternate courses of action. Ultimately, HLC will work to implement both installation and training of new software that will greatly benefit the client. The approach will involve both a thorough understanding of the available software tools and the ability to provide cost/benefit proposals for the client to take action. HLC plans to arrange for a percentage-of-sale fee paid by the software supplier along with a technical service fee paid by the client. The goal here is to leave the client with a product that will greatly enhance their company.

In June 1996, HLC plans to commence business at 3035 Harbor Drive, Ste. 206, Los Angeles, CA.

HLC will provide engineering and management consulting services to A/E/C companies and public works departments to enhance and strengthen their organizations and to meet the needs of their clients. As many private companies and public agencies have recently trimmed their staffs, HLC will seek to provide the services that they can no longer provide internally. Initially, HLC will target 80% engineering/20% management consulting strategy and shift to 30% engineering/70% management consulting as the company grows. The firm will continue to provide engineering services in order to stay in touch with clients.

DESCRIPTION OF THE MARKET

The goal of HLC is to be the management consultant company that the A/E/C industry and public works departments in Southern California ("target region") look to when they are faced with unique situations. Presently, the value of total construction in Southern California stands at $9.3 billion, which includes heavy construction, non-residential, and multi-unit residential. The demand for architecture and engineering companies is driven by construction activity. There are presently 20,560 A/E/C companies located in the target region of which a majority are headquartered here. Below is the list of top A/E/C companies based in the target region; Adwell Corporation, Hinsworth Corporation, and JAX Group are the top 3 A/E/C firms in the world.

Company Contract	Value*
Adwell Corporation, Irvine	$19,587
Hinsworth Corporation, Pasadena	$13,361
The Alexander Co., Lawndale	$10,753
Corbin Consulting, Pasadena	$7,000
JAX Group, Los Angeles**	$ 6,381

*Note: The firms above are the five largest construction management companies based in Southern California. * 1993 contract values listed are in millions. ** JAX Group owns Turnville Construction International, Los Angeles.*

Although the potential for finding a niche with large A/E/C organizations is the greatest, HLC will also target public agencies. There are hundreds of public agencies in the target region, including cities, counties, transportation boards and state agencies. Often public agencies are not equipped to provide adequate community services, due to both the lack of staff and knowledge specific to each project. HLC can provide public officials with technology support to complete each complex, varied project with the greatest efficiency.

In addition to providing consulting for private companies and public agencies, HLC will strive to both assist and partner with other management consulting firms. There will be several A/E/C company assignments that a small firm cannot physically handle. In these situations, HLC will position itself as the industry specialist working with the project team. There are less than a hundred management consulting firms that provide services to the target market and work in the target region.

HLC has the potential of over 30,000 public and private clients--the "target market" as described above. These customers will be attracted by:

- Direct approach to all management levels of the target market, including cold calls, letters and "at work" presentations. This presentation will involve meeting the

prospective client at his/her office to discuss concerns and projects and to find common ground in which HLC can help. Typically, reference material will include a laptop computer with various Powerpoint presentations, work portfolio, referral lists, business cards, brochures and a calendar of upcoming events.
- Networking events where business cards and brochures can be exchanged.
- Published papers in professional A/E/C journals related to HLC's line of business.
- Referrals from other professional companies and public agencies.
- HLC's strategic location near major freeways and the Los Angeles International Airport (LAX).

The competition consists of engineering firms, management consultants, and employees at the client's office. Even though other firms have more people and experience, HLC will win business by understanding the interaction of technical personnel and management. The key to beating the competition is by strategically balancing price, efficiency, and differentiation. We will provide work above the client's expectations and the competition's ability (i.e. early completion, less cost, future paradigm analysis). Finally, in order to best understand the competition, HLC will analyze other company's successes and failures on a regular basis.

HLC plans on capturing only a small portion of the market. Fortunately, the market is not very competitive because most engineers become managers within engineering companies and management consulting firms don't understand the cultures of A/E/C companies enough to quickly root out problems. A complete market analysis will be provided in the Marketing Plan.

LOCATION OF BUSINESS

HLC is currently utilizing approx. 500 square feet on the first floor of a two-story masonry building with cement floor at 3035 Harbor Drive, Ste. 206, Los Angeles, CA. HLC plans to perform leasehold improvements, including the addition of a conference room, small kitchen, and interior redecoration. The building is divided into (1) a mechanical/electrical engineering shop; (2) a multipurpose office, including one restroom with separate entry; (3) conference room with kitchenette and storage; and (4) upstairs office space presently being leased by Sullivan mechanical engineers. HLC will occupy 64 sq. ft. of the multipurpose office and the entire 210 sq. ft. of the remodeled conference room.

The current building owner, Caldwell Livingston, has generously offered to provide an equity contribution to the business for the first year. The area is zoned for commercial use. Harbor Drive is a heavily traveled, east-west commercial/residential route with most nearby businesses either dining establishments or repair (service) shops. Within a few blocks, there is convenient access to many of Southern California's freeways. Also nearby, the SC transit station provides rail service throughout the South Bay cities.

DESCRIPTION OF THE COMPETITION

There are four consulting firms providing services similar to those contemplated by HLC:

Schwimmer & Associates -- an independent, management consulting firm run by Calvin Schwimmer, a registered civil engineer and college professor. Mr. Schwimmer is a project management consultant assisting engineering firms and public agencies in proposal preparation, cost estimating, project scheduling, and project management activities. Many of Mr. Schwimmer's clients are also present engineering clients of Herman Livingston. His previous employer was the Alexander Co., where Mr. Schwimmer worked as a project manager. Since Schwimmer & Associates is small and focuses on project management, HLC has confidence that the two firms will have several opportunities to work together rather than compete.

The Coleman Group -- a twenty-four year old management consulting firm that caters strictly to the A/E/C industry. According to President Aaron Coleman, The Coleman Group has worked with more than 1,000 clients (less than 0.1% of the market) and is headquartered in San Antonio. The firm has only 13 consultants (6 architects, 4 engineers, and 3 behavioral scientists) that respond proactively to clients by understanding the market and by writing and speaking to professional organizations. Consultants are not salaried, but rather rely on assignment fees. The Coleman Group will be used as a model for HLC both in business development and proactivity, but their limited size minimizes The Coleman Group as a competitive threat.

As with Schwimmer & Associates, HLC will meet with The Coleman Group to discuss partnering opportunities for large consulting assignments. The benefits to The Coleman Group are those in the business description outlined above.

Piedmont & Co. -- with 80,000 people in offices worldwide, Piedmont claims to have broad experience in serving the global engineering and construction industry by providing a variety of consulting, audit and tax related services. Piedmont's services include business process reengineering, performance measures, strategic planning, organizational design, customer satisfaction, ISO 9000, project management, global best practices, human resource management, materials and costs management, business systems, and litigation. Piedmont's engineering and construction industry group is headed by Ms. Connie Hall and is headquartered in Atlanta, Georgia.

HLC learned during a year of competitive research that Piedmont was not able respond to a request of an engineering manager seeking assistance. After several calls to reach the right person, HLC finally received a generic brochure package addressed to the wrong company. This was the extent of Piedmont's pursuit of potential work. HLC can much more successfully reach the A/E/C market in southern California.

Fowler Reynolds (A Subsidiary of the Hinsworth Corp.) -- has 16 quality centers throughout the United States claiming to provide new and innovative quality methods, systems and technologies that are providing radical improvements to their clients. Fowler Reynolds states that they provide "the leading edge in changing the Architectural/Engineering and Construction Community and directly affecting the bottom line." Their intent is to help companies and agencies that the Hinsworth Corp. works with (which is extensive) in providing higher quality, ISO 9000 certification, and executive management support.

In July 1995, HLC met with Mr. Steve Jenkins, Director of Quality Assurance, to discuss both Fowler Reynolds' business and potential partnering opportunities. First impressions of Fowler Reynolds were that this business unit was being driven by one man, Shawn Reynolds, who had good intentions, but a flawed business philosophy. The problem is that A/E/C companies do not want a competitor knowing what is wrong with their business. Also, Fowler Reynolds has the same bureaucratic structure that potential clients deal with in their own businesses. By meeting's end, Mr. Jenkin's almost desperately asked that HLC come back with ideas to help them build their business. Since this meeting, no mention within the industry has been made about Fowler Reynolds.

Indirect competition exists from internal staffs at HLC client offices. If clients have the options, they will and should have their staff provide the service. HLC will direct the client to use their internal staff if it is determined prudent to do so. However, from an objectivity standpoint, an outside consultant will often be the best solution.

**MANAGEMENT
& KEY
PERSONNEL**

Management

Herman Livingston is a native Californian and has resided in Southern California all his life. After graduating valedictorian from South High School, he attended the University of Southern California (USC) and received his BS in Building Science in 1987. He began his professional engineering career with the State of California Department of Transportation (Caltrans), working in both construction and project planning. Then, Mr. Livingston worked for Trudell Engineering Company focusing on engineering design, business development, and research. Finally, he worked as a project and office manager for Johnson Associates Infrastructure, Inc. (JAI).

While at JAI, Mr. Livingston received his professional engineering registration from the States of California (1993) and Florida (1995). He completed his MS in Engineering Management in 1994--learning about proven management techniques used in all engineering industries.

Karen Livingston, wife of Herman Livingston, is also a native Californian. After graduating in the top 5% of her class at Beachside High school, Ms. Livingston moved to Los Angeles to pursue a BFA at the prestigious California College of Design. Ms. Livingston worked seven years at Nouveau Fashion Industries as technical designer and import manager where her responsibilities included developing and updating procedural manuals for the fitting and import departments. During this time, she also wrote two novels and had several short stories published. In 1995, Ms. Livingston started her own business and has worked with such companies as Nostalgic Antiques, developing a computerized inventory system, designing marketing campaigns and product displays and creating an updated business plan.

Both Mr. and Ms. Livingston believe their complementary knowledge and goals will make HLC a success. In particular, Mr. Livingston understands the A/E/C industry and is a highly regarded member of the community while Ms. Livingston is a proven quality assurance and report writing expert. Since Mr. Livingston has industry track record and management experience, he will be responsible for business development and project control. Ms. Livingston will be primarily responsible for proposal preparation, research and product quality assurance and control. Together they will set all business policies and personnel decisions.

The Livingston's will draw a combined salary of $5,000/month based upon a minimum 40% billing utilization. Ms. Livingston will retain outside business activities earning approximately $500/month and expected to increase. The Livingston's personal expenditures total approximately $4,500/month, including housing, automobiles, insurance, etc.

In order to augment their skills, HLC has enlisted an advisory board consisting of John Commons, founder and president of Capital Management; Dean White, office manager of Dunstable, Goody & Company; Alice Reed, senior associate of Corbin Consulting; Darin Johnson, project manager of Parkway Co.; Trent Silman, vice president of XRS Group, Inc.; and Calvin Schwimmer, founder and principal of Schwimmer & Associates. This board along with several other professional associates will provide on-going management review.

Personnel

Initially, HLC will not hire any outside office administrative help. HLC will strive to grow the business quickly in order to maximize profits, but only two additional employees have been planned during the first two years. Employees will be chosen based upon their superior knowledge and understanding of their business and will be compensated accordingly.

Preliminary Business Plan
June 2, 1996
Work in progress using "The Business Planning Source" by Duke Binman

Send Out Business Plan for Review
June 3, 1996
Confidential review by advisory board, family, friends, and professional associates

Meet with Attorneys
Week of June 3, 1996
Referrals presently sought

Gather Required Service Information
Week of June 10, 1996
Medical, dental, professional insurance, supplies, retirement plan, equipment

Cease Present Employment
June 14, 1996
8-week phase-down period through August 9, 1996

HLC Opens to Business
June 17, 1996
Hard work & commitment

Finalize Business Plan
June 30, 1996
Send to advisory board, family, friends, professional associates, and handouts for HLC Open
House

Begin Construction of Office
July 6, 1996
Contingent upon Perform Engineering Company clearance office area

Finish Construction of Office
December 15, 1996
Finish before the Holidays

Start All Required Services
Week of August 5, 1996
Begin services on Sept. 16, 1996

HLC Open House - Xmas Party
January 1997
Existing and potential clients, friends, partners, associates

FINANCIAL DATA

Sources of Funding

Sources

1. Bank Accounts	$7,527
2. Money Market Accounts	$20,465
Total	**$27,992**

Applications

1. Capital Equipment	$7,120	See Sheet B. Capital Equipment
2. Inventory	$300	Estimated
3. Working Capital	$7,500	
4. Cash reserve for contingencies	$13,072	
Total	**$27,992**	

Capital Equipment List

Major Equipment and Normal Accessories	Model	Cost or List Price (whichever is lower)
25" Color Television		$300
VCR		$150
3.5' x 7' Conference Table		$500
Copier	Sharp	$500
HP 820CXi (Color Printer)	HP	$400
Swivel Chairs (6)		$700
Laptop Computer		$2,500
Computer Network	8 Hub	$-
(2) 486DX2 Computers		$800
17" SVGA Monitor	CTXra	$500
Fax Machine	Sharp	$250
Total		**$6,600**
Minor Office Equipment:		
Miscellaneous Computer Wiring		$-
Interior Decorating		$100
Total		**$100**
Bookcases (5)		$100
File Cabinets (3)		$320
Desk		$-
Software		$-
Total		**$420**
Capital Equipment Total		**$7,120**

Balance Sheet

Assets			Liabilities		
Current Assets			**Current Liabilities**		
Cash	$20,872		Accounts Payable	$-	
Accounts Receivable (net)	$15,000		Current L-T Debt	$80,040	
Merchandise Inventory	$300		**Total Current Liabilities**	**$80,040**	
Supplies	$200				
Pre-Paid Expenses	$-				
Total Current Assets:	**$36,372**		**Long Term Liabilities**		
			Note Payable	$-	
			Bank Loan Payable	$10,000	
Fixed Assets			Equity Loan Payable	$-	
Fixtures and Leasehold			**Total Long Term Liabilities**	**$10,000**	
Improvements	$-				
Equipment	$25,000				
Total Fixed Assets	**$25,000**		**Total Liabilities**	**$90,040**	
			Net Worth		
			Owner's Equity	$(28,668)	
Total Assets	**$61,372**		**Total Liabilities and**	**$61,372**	
			Net Worth		

Break-Even Analysis

	Rates		
Fixed Cost	$80,040	$6,670	per month
Herman's Rate	$38.46	$90	
Karen's Rate	$24.04	$60	
Multiplier	2.34	$75	Average

Projected Income - "Most Likely"

Service	July	August	September	October	November	December
Engineering	$-	$-	$9,000	$10,000	$10,000	$10,000
Mgmt Consulting	$-	$-	$-	$-	$-	$-
Software Sales	$-	$-	$-	$-	$-	$-
Total Sales	**$-**	**$-**	**$9,000**	**$10,000**	**$10,000**	**$10,000**
Total expenses	**$15,965**	**$9,003**	**$10,543**	**$10,273**	**$10,273**	**$10,273**

Cash Flow Projection: Three-Year Summary

	Year 1	Year 2 (Mid-Ave.)	Year 3	Utilization Rate (Year 3)		
				Herman	Karen	Employee 1
	96/97	97/98	98/99	$90.00	$70.00	$80.00
Sales						
Engineering	$111,000	$150,140	$189,280	30%	0%	80%
Mgmt Consulting	$18,000	$160,320	$302,640	45%	70%	0%
Software	$5,500	$6,050	$6,655	10% Increase per Year		
Total Sales	**$134,500**	**$316,510**	**$498,575**			
V* Cost of Materials	$-	$-	$-			
V Variable Labor	$-	$-	$-			
Cost of Goods Sold	**$-**	**$-**	**$-**			
Gross Margin	**$134,500**	**$316,510**	**$498,575**			
Operating Expenses						
F Utilities	$-	$600	$600			
F Salaries	$60,000	$167,778	$275,556	4 Employees (Year 3)		
F Payroll Taxes	$8,400	$23,489	$38,578	14% of Salaries		
V/F Benefits	$18,000	$50,333	$82,667	30% of Salaries		
F Business Development	$6,725	$15,826	$24,929	5% of Total Sales		
F Office Supplies	$9,870	$3,500	$4,500	$1,000 per additional employee		
F Insurance	$4,310	$5,110	$5,910	$800 per additional employee		
F Maintenance and cleaning	$1,181	$1,216	$1,253	CPI increase only		
F Legal and Accounting	$5,000	$5,150	$5,305	CPI increase only		
V/F Delivery expenses	$1,190	$2,000	$2,200	Strict Control of Deliveries		
F Licenses	$275	$300	$300	2 Engineers + Business License		
V Internal Relations	$600	$900	$1,200	2x employees		
F Telephone	$2,426	$3,000	$3,500			
F Depreciation	$3,000	$4,000	$4,000	3-Yr Straight Line Depreciation		
F Travel	$3,660	$3,770	$3,883	1 employee (part-time) marketing		

January	February	March	April	May	June	Totals
$12,000	$12,000	$12,000	$12,000	$12,000	$12,000	$111,000
$3,000	$3,000	$3,000	$3,000	$3,000	$3,000	$18,000
$-	$-	$1,000	$1,250	$1,500	$1,750	$5,500
$15,000	**$15,000**	**$16,000**	**$16,250**	**$16,500**	**$16,750**	**$134,500**
$10,573	**$10,573**	**$10,633**	**$10,648**	**$10,663**	**$10,678**	

F Miscellaneous	$1,345	$3,165	$4,986	1% of Sales
F Rent	$-	$6,000	$6,000	$500/mo. starting Year 2
Total Operating Expenses	**$125,982**	**$296,137**	**$465,365**	

Other Expenses

Interest (Mortgage)	$-	$-	$-	
Interest (Auto Lease)	$4,116	$4,116	$4,116	3-Yr Bank Lease

Cash Flow Projection by Month, Year One

	July	August	September	October	November	December	January
Sales							
Engineering	$-	$-	$9,000	$10,000	$10,000	$10,000	$12,000
Mgmt Consulting	$-	$-	$-	$-	$-	$-	$3,000
Software	$-	$-	$-	$-	$-	$-	$-
Total Sales	**$-**	**$-**	**$9,000**	**$10,000**	**$10,000**	**$10,000**	**$15,000**
Cost of Materials	$-	$-	$-	$-	$-	$-	$-
Variable Labor	$-	$-	$-	$-	$-	$-	$-
Cost of Goods Sold	**$-**	**$-**	**$-**	**$-**	**$-**	**$-**	**$-**
Gross Margin	**$-**	**$-**	**$9,000**	**$10,000**	**$10,000**	**$10,000**	**$15,000**
Operating Expenses							
Utilities	$-	$-	$-	$-	$-	$-	$-
Salaries	$5,000	$5,000	$5,000	$5,000	$5,000	$5,000	$5,000
Payroll Taxes (14%)	$700	$700	$700	$700	$700	$700	$700
Benefits (30%)	$1,500	$1,500	$1,500	$1,500	$1,500	$1,500	$1,500
Business Development (5%)	$-	$-	$450	$500	$500	$500	$750
Office Supplies	$7,120	$250	$250	$250	$250	$250	$250
Insurance	$190	$190	$690	$360	$360	$360	$360
Maintenance and cleaning	$81	$100	$100	$100	$100	$100	$100
Legal and Accounting	$-	$-	$500	$500	$500	$500	$500
Delivery expenses	$90	$100	$100	$100	$100	$100	$100
Licenses	$55	$20	$20	$20	$20	$20	$20
Internal Relations	$50	$50	$50	$50	$50	$50	$50
Telephone	$226	$200	$200	$200	$200	$200	$200
Depreciation	$250	$250	$250	$250	$250	$250	$250
Travel	$360	$300	$300	$300	$300	$300	$300
Misc. (1% Sales)	$-	$-	$90	$100	$100	$100	$150
Rent	$-	$-	$-	$-	$-	$-	$-
Total Oper. Expenses	**$15,622**	**$8,660**	**$10,200**	**$9,930**	**$9,930**	**$9,930**	**$10,230**
Other Expenses							
Interest (Mortgage)	$-	$-	$-	$-	$-	$-	$-
Interest (Auto Lease)	$343	$343	$343	$343	$343	$343	$343
Interest (Credit Line)	$-	$-	$-	$-	$-	$-	$-
Total Other Expenses	**$343**	**$343**	**$343**	**$343**	**$343**	**$343**	**$343**
Total Expenses	**$15,965**	**$9,003**	**$10,543**	**$10,273**	**$10,273**	**$10,273**	**$10,573**
Net Profit (Loss) Pre-Tax	**$(15,965)**	**$(9,003)**	**$(1,543)**	**$(273)**	**$(273)**	**$(273)**	**$4,427**

February	March	April	May	June	Total
$12,000	$12,000	$12,000	$12,000	$12,000	$111,000
$3,000	$3,000	$3,000	$3,000	$3,000	$18,000
$-	$1,000	$1,250	$1,500	$1,750	$5,500
$15,000	**$16,000**	**$16,250**	**$16,500**	**$16,750**	**$134,500**
$-	$-	$-	$-	$-	$-
$-	$-	$-	$-	$-	$-
$-	$-	$-	$-	$-	$-
$15,000	**$16,000**	**$16,250**	**$16,500**	**$16,750**	**$134,500**
$-	$-	$-	$-	$-	$-
$5,000	$5,000	$5,000	$5,000	$5,000	$60,000
$700	$700	$700	$700	$700	$8,400
$1,500	$1,500	$1,500	$1,500	$1,500	$18,000
$750	$800	$813	$825	$838	$6,725
$250	$250	$250	$250	$250	$9,870
$360	$360	$360	$360	$360	$4,310
$100	$100	$100	$100	$100	$1,181
$500	$500	$500	$500	$500	$5,000
$100	$100	$100	$100	$100	$1,190
$20	$20	$20	$20	$20	$275
$50	$50	$50	$50	$50	$600
$200	$200	$200	$200	$200	$2,426
$250	$250	$250	$250	$250	$3,000
$300	$300	$300	$300	$300	$3,660
$150	$160	$163	$165	$168	$1,345
$-	$-	$-	$-	$-	$-
$10,230	**$10,290**	**$10,305**	**$10,320**	**$10,335**	**$125,982**
$-	$-	$-	$-	$-	$-
$343	$343	$343	$343	$343	$4,116
$-	$-	$-	$-	$-	$-
$343	**$343**	**$343**	**$343**	**$343**	**$4,116**
$10,573	**$10,633**	**$10,648**	**$10,663**	**$10,678**	**$130,098**
$4,427	**$5,367**	**$5,602**	**$5,837**	**$6,072**	**$4,402**

Marketing Communications Firm

BUSINESS PLAN

CORNELIUS MARKETING

1207 Rosemont St.
Madison Heights, MI 48071

April 1, 1996

This marketing communication firm's business plan draws heavily on the business owner's thirty years of marketplace experience. The owner's numerous years of expertise make this business unique.

- BUSINESS DESCRIPTION

- TARGET MARKET

- THE COMPETITION

- MARKETING STRATEGY

- MARKETING ASSUMPTIONS

- BUSINESS OBJECTIVES

- SALES STRATEGY AND TACTICS

- BILLING RATE

- BUSINESS START-UP BUDGET

BUSINESS DESCRIPTION

Cornelius Marketing is a full-service marketing communications firm, specializing in small-sized and mid-sized manufacturers. It is a home-based, sole proprietorship.

It relies heavily upon project management skills gained over a period of thirty years in business-to-business marketing communications, as many of the service tasks are performed by known and trusted suppliers and vendors.

What are its services?

In general, marketing planning, communications program planning and implementation. Implementation consists of the creation, production and distribution of marketing communications which may consist of all or any combination of the following:

- Advertising
- Direct Marketing
- Sales Literature
- Catalogs
- Public Relations
- Web Site Design
- Sales Promotion/Merchandising
- Product/Service Names
- Trade Show Exhibits
- Engineering Presentations
- Sales Presentations
- Point-of-Purchase Displays

We will do all planning and as much of the creative writing as possible. We will always do the planning. We may do less of the creative writing as the business expands and requires more planning and project-management time.

What Makes Cornelius Marketing Unique?

We believe that a major factor which separates Cornelius Marketing from other marketing communications endeavors is our depth and breadth of experience.

Cornelius Marketing is also developing a Resource Line which will allow our target manufacturing firms to more effectively use their customer and prospect lists.

TARGET MARKET

What is Cornelius Marketing's target market and why?

Cornelius Marketing's target market is manufacturing firms in the Detroit metropolitan area with $10 million to $75 million in annual sales.

Opportunities to do business with larger firms and smaller firms will certainly be considered.

Because Detroit is the center for the North American auto industry, there are many firms in the targeted annual sales range in the Detroit metro area.

In the proprietor's twenty years of experience, he has found that virtually no manufacturing firms have formal marketing plans or marketing communications plans. Many have annual sales objectives which they may call "marketing plans". The exceptions, in some instances, are companies that are divisions of larger corporations or those which already have a marketing communications firm affiliation.

How will target firms be identified and a prospect list be prepared?

Potential clients will be identified by several means. Such directories as the Michigan Manufacturers Directory and Bryant's Michigan Business Directory are useful in this effort, as are the Redd's Directories, as they identify annual sales volume and personnel. The initial list will be analyzed with respect to which companies already have ad agencies. Primary effort will be directed to those without agency affiliation.

Clients from previous business relationships will be solicited.

Leads are expected to be produced through networking in various trade organizations and from trade media contacts.

How will Cornelius Marketing communicate with prospects?

Initial efforts will consist of direct marketing via letters and telemarketing. Telephone directory listings and trade organization roster issues will also be used. This business plan will serve as an example of marketing planning.

THE COMPETITION

The competition consists of:

- Ad Agencies
- PR Agencies
- Misc. Communications services
- Freelance writers
- In-house communications departments

The Colman Club's 1996 Roster Edition has 542 listings which are considered competition. Included are categories such as freelance writers, advertising & sales counselors, advertising & sales promotion, direct marketing and public relations firms.

The Detroit metro area business Yellow Pages lists approximately 300 firms under the category - Advertising Agencies & Counselors. There are approximately 125 other firms listed under the category - Public Relations Consultants.

Many of these firms are only competitors in certain services. Some are non-competitive because they deal strictly in consumer/retail business. Others are non-competitive because they only work with very large clients.

This analysis does not take into account so-called in-house agencies, companies with their own advertising operations. This is becoming a greater source of indirect competition as desktop publishing becomes more and more sophisticated. In-house operations are not head-to-head competitors per se, however they reduce the number of potential clients.

An educated guess of the number of head-to-head competitors is 250 to 300. Competition is great.

MARKETING STRATEGY

How has Cornelius Marketing positioned itself?

Cornelius Marketing has positioned itself to be primarily a niche-market service supplier. Most established marketing communications firms, because of their overhead, cannot afford to spend time on the lower end of our annual sales volume objective.

The proprietor has an extremely varied background in terms of different kinds of clients served. This experience encompasses virtually all marketing venues and media.

We have an excellent grasp of technical processes, both in terms of product manufacturing and product application.

Cornelius Marketing represents an excellent match for the small-sized to medium-sized manufacturing firm that doesn't have a large enough budget to attract an ad or PR agency with equal experience and expertise.

What is the nature of the target client?

Many of the target firms are entrepreneurial in nature. Their principal(s) wear many hats. They are intimately familiar with their business milieu. If they are successful, they figure they're doing just fine and don't want or need advertising. The old saw is, "we know who our customers and prospects are, we talk to them regularly."

To a degree, they are right. They may be selling in a niche market. Their customers and prospects may be small in number. The nature of their product(s) may be self-localizing, i.e. shipping costs and time may help define their geographical marketing area, hence its size. Almost everyone has local competition, however.

What makes Cornelius Marketing different?

We're specializing in small-sized and medium-sized manufacturers, especially auto industry suppliers.

Although we're a new marketing communications firm, we possess over twenty years of experience working with our target market firms. The bulk of the experience is in the automotive original equipment supplier venue, we also have automotive aftermarket and consumer marketing communications experience.

Cornelius Marketing is developing the Resource Line, a new tool for most of the target market.

Cornelius Marketing is well versed in many manufacturing processes so it understands how products are manufactured and marketed.

Cornelius Marketing understands and has worked with single-level and multi-level distribution systems.

Cornelius Marketing is familiar with the various kinds of sales organizations used by manufacturers and their distribution systems and the methods behind them.

Although the thinking of business-to-business advertising agencies is changing, advertising and the resultant media commissions still represent a major revenue component. Many of our business targets are unattractive to ad agencies because they may never be significant trade media advertisers.

Because this area is a center of automotive activity, a majority of the target universe is comprised of automotive-related suppliers. These firms represent the largest, and in our opinion, the most receptive group of prospects for the service we've created.

Care should be taken to build a balanced clientele. Having all one's "eggs" in the automotive "basket" is an invitation for difficulty if not disaster at the first auto industry downturn.

What is the precise marketing geography?

The counties of Wayne, Oakland and Macomb constitute the primary marketing geography.

Secondary geography is Washtenaw, Livingston and St. Clair counties.

After these, outstate areas along the I-94 corridor would be tested.

Business opportunities from any source in neighboring areas would certainly be evaluated.

Information on which potential clients have ad and/or PR agencies is not readily available. This information must be obtained in order to reduce the number of prime prospects.

Many potential customers do not recognize the need for regular marketing communications activity. This may suggest the availability of more per-project work.

The target first contact, the Sales/Marketing Manager, is an extremely busy person and may be difficult to reach.

If there is no Sales/Marketing person, the CEO will be contacted, although he may be even more difficult to reach.

In the Detroit metro area, there are many North American headquarters for off-shore automotive suppliers. Most off-shore companies are not serious users of advertising and sales promotion.

MARKETING ASSUMPTIONS

First-year objectives (April-December, 1996):

1. Acquire two Annual-Fee-Based clients.
2. Acquire as many Project-Based clients as possible.
3. Complete the Resource Line Program and sell one.

Second-year objectives (January-December, 1997):

1. Acquire two additional Annual-Fee-Based clients for a total of four.
2. Continue with as many Project-Based clients as possible.
3. Sell two more Resource Line Programs for a total of three.

Third-year objectives (January-December, 1998):

1. Acquire an additional two Annual-Fee-Based clients for a total of six.
2. Evaluate the viability of continuing Project-Based activity with respect to time constraints. Determine if this is a worthwhile "new business" activity, i.e. track record of converting this type of business to Annual-Fee-Based clients. Revenue production of Project-Based activity would certainly be considered.
3. Sell an additional three Resource Line Programs for a total of six.

Fourth-year objectives (January-December, 1999):

1. Evaluate the situation and make a decision re: expansion of client base or maintain the existing level, assuming objectives are met. Expansion would require moving into commercial space, perhaps incorporating and hiring employees.
2. Set or adjust objectives depending on direction taken.

Fifth-year objectives (January-December, 2000):

1. Set or adjust objectives depending on direction taken.

Annual objective review

Objectives will be reviewed prior to the beginning of each calendar year and adjusted as necessary.

BUSINESS OBJECTIVES

SALES STRATEGY/ TACTICS

Sales Strategy

Make cold contacts via letters of introduction followed by telephone calls. The approach will be made to the Marketing and/or Sales Manager where no Ad Manager can be identified.

Marketing/Sales Managers are extremely busy people who are responsible for the generation of sales materials where no Ad Manager exists. Some may rely upon an ad or PR agency.

If there is an Ad or Communications Manager, this person should be approached first.

The existence of such a person usually means one of two situations: 1) The company already has an agency, or; 2) They have an in-house operation.

Whatever situation is uncovered, contact should still be made. They may be dissatisfied with their present agency or in the process of disbanding their in-house operation. Even with an in-house operation, they may still go outside for some services including creative.

In addition to this formal effort, all opportunities resulting from networking and referrals must be followed up on.

Sales Tactics

1. Commence sales efforts with letters to 25 Fee-Based prospects per week, every other week. Use the two week period to follow up with telephone calls for appointments.
2. Commence sales efforts with letters to 10 Project-Based prospects per week, every other week. Use the second week in the cycle for telephone follow-up.
3. Commence development work on the Resource Line. Prepare a best-guess time line for completion of a saleable program.
4. Re-evaluate sales efforts near the end of June for adjustment, if necessary.

The first-contact sales letter must introduce Cornelius Marketing as the assistance the busy person needs to help simplify his or her busy life. It must identify with the prospects milieu. It must back up CM's claim to be an experienced, versatile service partner. It must get across the fact that CM will work on either an annual-fee basis or on a per-project basis. The letter will close stating that a telephone call will follow within one week of receipt of the letter. It is important to follow up as stated as this will be the first indicator of performance, that we are dependable.

Sales Assumptions

The quantity of letters sent out weekly, may have to be modified if experience suggests that it takes longer than anticipated to gain phone contact with prospects.

The letter copy will change when updates are necessary.

More than one version of the letter copy will probably be required.

BILLING RATE

Cornelius' billing rate will be $100.00 per hour.

Billable time will include all planning, research, creative, administrative and travel time devoted exclusively to a given account or project.

Annual Fee Billing Arrangement

The minimum annual fee will be $24,000.00 which guarantees a client six weeks or 240 hours of agency time per year. The fee may be paid in equal monthly installments which will be billed at the end of each month. A less-frequent payment schedule can be negotiated.

The Annual Fee does not include out-of-pocket expenses incurred in conjunction with the implementation of a client's program. The fee covers agency hours only. Such services as design, layout, typesetting, photography, illustration, printing and other outside services associated with the creation and production of a client's program will be billed to the client with no agency mark-up. Supplier's invoices will be provided to support such outside costs.

A budget, based on all known components, will be prepared, submitted and approved by the client prior to the beginning of the client's program. Individual projects may be re-estimated during the program year, if circumstances require.

Per Project Billing Arrangement

Individual projects will be managed at the rate of $100.00 per hour, plus out-of-pocket expenses as described in the Annual Fee Arrangement section.

Projects will be cost estimated by the agency and budget-approved by the client in advance.

Out-of-pocket expenses, such as travel, lodging and meals will be evaluated on an individual basis and may be re-billed to the client.

Out-Of-Pocket Expenses

Estimated Cost for Home Office Set-Up

BUSINESS START-UP BUDGET

Personal computer/printer/work station	$3,300.00
Desk/work table	250.00
Chairs (2)	300.00
File cabinet	300.00
Misc. equipment	150.00
Business phone (separate line/phone)	186.00
Formal letterhead, envelopes, business cards	500.00
Utility letterhead, plain paper	300.00
Misc. supplies	250.00
Total Estimated Start-Up	**$ 5,536.00**

Estimated Monthly Expenses (w/o salary)

Telephone	$100.00
Supplies	50.00
Postage	35.00
Rent	500.00
Total Monthly Expenses (w/o salary)	**$ 685.00**

Men's Clothing Retailer

BUSINESS PLAN

VAN SCHAACK

58500 Marina Way
Santa Barbara, CA 96100

Business owners' of this plan provide interested plan readers with two financial five year plans, the first being the most conservative. Owners demonstrate that the business can manage its expenses on a modest sales plan through the first set of financials.

- THE VAN SCHAACK PRINCIPLE

- THE CUSTOMER

- THE STORE

- COMPETITION AND STRATEGY

- MARKETING, ADVERTISING AND STORE IDENTITY

- STORE DESIGN

- STORE LOCATIONS

- GENERAL AND ADMINISTRATIVE

- TEAM VAN SCHAACK

- INVESTORS QUESTIONS

- FINANCIAL INFORMATION

VAN SCHAACK PRINCIPLE

Herringbone was once the model of the ideal better men's store. With their tweed jackets and boxy suits, they embraced the Edwardian formality and unbending adherence to custom that ruled a man's wardrobe. Gentlemen (or those who aspired to be) of that era emulated this image. To them it was successful, masculine, tasteful, and presented them as they wished to be perceived by the world they lived in.

Besides the fashion statements they made, Herringbone's success was also attributable to an important principle. They sold quality merchandise at a fair and reasonable price--an even exchange of value for value. Their genteel image enhanced the value of their merchandise, and made Herringbone a reliable, trusted institution.

What do the young men of the emerging Generation X think of Herringbone today?

Answer: They don't think of it.

Men today value self-expression, individualism, and freedom; they choose to make their own identities rather than fit themselves into an idealized mold. There is no value for them in the confinement of an antique Edwardian aesthetic, unchanging decade after decade.

There are few fashion rules for men today. But the principle of providing value for value remains as sound as it was in former years. If a men's store is to be trusted and successful, it must, like Herringbone, be based on that sound principle. Van Schaack is committed to do exactly that.

The generation of men who grew up with MTV is a powerful market with growing incomes. They will determine the future of many image-conscious retailers and their marketing strategies. As always in the competitive world of retail, you must change with the times or be replaced.

As for replacing obsolete concepts in the world of men's stores, Van Schaack is poised and ready.

THE CUSTOMER

Van Schaack is a store concept designed for and catering to a core customer base of active, urban males aged 25 to 50.

The targeted market is image conscious and wants fashionable clothing that has a youthful, sexy, and masculine image. The core customer will most likely work out at a gym on a regular basis. This has given him a well-toned build, which he will want to show to its best advantage. Outside of work, he has an active, casual lifestyle of sports, the beach, the gym, bars and clubs and excursions with friends. He wants clothes that are versatile, attractive and becoming.

THE STORE

As a store, Van Schaack's objective is to respond to the needs and wants of its core customers.

Our cues are taken from other successful, sexy, men's clothing operations such as Men Tour and Mike Kaplan. We borrow the best of these organizations: the customer lifestyle focus of Men Tour and the sophisticated marketing of Mike Kaplan. However, Men Tour's strength lies in its catalog operation, and Men Tour is a designer/vendor. Van Schaack's emphasis will be on retail stores.

Our five year business plan is the blueprint for our expansion to a multi-unit operation in urban areas where our core customers are concentrated. We will grow our business selling a mix of moderate to better sportswear, activewear, and underwear-along with grooming cosmetics - in a casual, open and sophisticated environment.

Primary competition for Van Schaack will be Men Tour. To a lesser degree, competition will also come from moderate price sportswear specialty stores such as Runway and moderate price department stores like Bachman, Crystal, Wolfgang, and Paolo.

The Van Schaack approach will be different from this point forward, in that, it will provide sport merchandise that is clean and classic, simple but sexy. The colors and styling will be more masculine, avoiding the cheap and flashy. The look will be more like Mike Kaplan, less like Men Tour. We believe this more masculine approach in merchandising will have a broader appeal and attract a more affluent customer. In addition, we will offer clothes that emphasize better quality and fit, elements that are conspicuously lacking in our main competitors' assortments.

Another category that will be developed beyond any men's store competitor will be grooming cosmetics. As one of the highlights of the merchandise strategy at Van Schaack, we will offer an expansive selection of products in this department. Currently, no retailer offers anything approaching this concept. Cosmetic departments in large stores are all consistently aimed at women customers. Some lines, such as Blusher, and Silken, sell product lines designed for men. However, these are not featured, and they are overshadowed by women's cosmetics.

The emphasis in Van Schaack's cosmetic lines will be on better quality skin care (particularly anti-aging products), sun products, hair care, and bath and body products - not on fragrance. This department will most likely be called New Leaf. The anticipated success of New Leaf is based on the premises that male customers prefer buying cosmetics in a store where everything is geared toward men, and that our core customer will strongly respond to a department specifically aimed at helping him look attractive, healthy, and youthful.

Because Van Schaack's focus will be on retail stores, we expect to out do our main competitors in the important arena of shopping environment. We are planning an interior similar to that found in an upscale specialty store, with outstanding wall presentation, consistent fixturing and special tables designed to show strong merchandise stories. The overall design objective is to create an upbeat environment that is easy to shop and shows the goods to their best advantage.

The marketing of Van Schaack is the vehicle by which we will communicate our image to our customers. The projected image is that of a masculine, bare-all Adonis whose rugged individualism appeals to young men and men who want to feel young. Outfitting the male who identifies with this image (or aspires to emulate it) will be the store's mission - and will provide its identity.

Advertising will be directed at the core customer and will stress the projected image. A logo has been developed, which is designed to be transferable to clothing for added sales and advertising. The company colors are white and black, which represent the character of the company in their classic simplicity and boldness.

Most importantly, Van Schaack fills voids in the market left by competitors like Men Tour. Voids are to be filled by:

- Selling moderate to better quality menswear with a sexy, masculine appeal
- Pioneering a new focused approach of selling cosmetic products to an emerging market of men wanting to be catered to in this regard
- A more hip and sophisticated shopping environment.

Retail trade publications report that today's retail customers want bright, open shopping environments. Van Schaack will meet this expectation by being a very bright, white store. The best way to present strong merchandise and color statements is by using white backgrounds.

All walls and merchandise tables in the store will be white. Merchandise walls will be tall, with chrome fixturing to show expansive statements; merchandise tables will be three levels. Walls will be architecturally broken to show separate merchandise stories. Floor fixturing will be simple chrome and black 4-way and T-stand outfitters to better show off merchandise groups.

Special muscular mannequins will show clothes to their advantage on tables and in windows. Ceilings will be white with 2' x 2' fluorescent lamps for brightness and tracks of spotlamps to show off feature walls and tables.

Macho, romantic and sexy images of men will be framed and hung in clusters on walls for ambiance and whimsy. The overall effect will be an upbeat, contemporary environment with a touch of fun.

STORE LOCATIONS

Several factors go into choosing the best location for a retail store. Among them are demographics, real estate prices, and the actual location within a setting. Location determines whether people passing by will see your store and come in. Another important factor in Southern California is available parking for customers.

The proposed location for the initial store is in the middle of the University area of Santa Barbara. This busy center, anchored by Big supermarket and Lottie's Records and Video, consistently has a busy parking lot and very high foot traffic. The center also enjoys a rush of customer traffic from 6:00 pm to 8:00 pm because of the supermarket and video store, a time when most malls are slow. Rent per square foot is about half what the nearest regional mall charges.

The store has a very high visibility location within the center, with 40 feet of frontage including the entrance, with two 15 foot windows facing the central parking lot. From either side, customers would be able to see into the entire store through four large windows.

Future store locations would follow a regional strategy. Possible locations in the next five years include San Diego, Oceanside, Long Beach, and Irvine.

GENERAL AND ADMINISTRATIVE

Van Schaack will be in charge of General and Administrative duties, and will work in partnership with Jay Sanders on Merchandise Assortment, Store Design, and Marketing.

Jay Sanders will be in charge of Merchandising, Store Planning, Marketing and Sales.

Steve Kotlik will be in charge of Finance and Operations.

Jeremy Nelson will work as a consultant to Jay on Merchandising and Sales Planning.

TEAM VAN SCHAACK

Van Schaack, Jay Sanders, Steve Kotlik, and Jeremy Nelson all caught the retail bug at an early age through working part time in stores while attending college.

Van and Jay began in sales, Van at Can's Department Store in Newport and Jay at Morrow's in Tustin; both have used Reed's as their executive training ground. This has given them valuable experience working within an aggressive corporate structure, and has instilled in them a deep appreciation for teamwork, as the means by which goals are attained.

Along with working on numerous store openings together, Van and Jay worked together successfully for two years during the $10 million renovation of the Hawthorne store. This collaboration helped form the basis of their partnership in the venture of Van Schaack.

Their paths converged with Jeremy Nelson, who has been a Vice President and General Manager at Lutz. Jeremy brings 40 years of experience in retail to the team.

The strengths of this complementary partnership are Van's strategic planning, marketing and design acumen merged with Jay's ability to think like a customer, his extensive knowledge of general merchandising and his instinct to sense trends and grow a business. Aiding them is Steve, with his knowledge and experience in running and growing a small business.

Guiding this team is Jeremy Nelson, with his invaluable experience and counsel. All four are team players dedicated to making Van Schaack the store where active men want to shop.

Q: Why are there two financial plans?

INVESTORS' QUESTIONS

A: Plan 1 is a very conservative plan whose purpose is to demonstrate that Van Schaack can manage its business expenses on a modest sales plan. Plan 2 is more aggressive.

Q: How did you arrive at the sales figures?

A: First we began with a merchandise matrix. This is a detailed account of every item that would be carried in the store, right down to the number of each size and color along with their retail prices. For example, 24 blue tank tops @ $15.00 each; 4 small, 4 medium, 8 large, and 8 extra large.

The numbers of units and the retail prices are then totalled. This forms the basis of the item called "Open to Buy" in Schedule 2(b).

In a conservative retail plan, the store would replenish, or "turn," its inventory no less than twice annually. So if the store had an "Open to Buy" plan of $1,000.00 and its sales plan is based on two turns of inventory, it would have a sales plan of $2,000.00 annually.

Q: How much do I need to invest to become a part of Van Schaack?

A: The Van Schaack partners would like to sell shares in the Corporation in blocks of one thousand at a price of $1.00 per share.

Q: What kind of return can I expect on my investment?

A: Van Schaack is a money-making venture from which everyone involved expects to profit. The objective is to take the Corporation public no sooner than five years from now. The potential to multiply your original investment is enormous for those investors who come in at the start.

This type of investment is sometimes termed a "flyer," meaning that it is akin to a roll of the dice. However, in Van Schaack's case, we believe the dice are loaded in its favor.

Q: Are there any other benefits?

A: As an initial investor, you will receive a 20% discount on all merchandise, including cosmetics and sales items.

Q: What about a Van Schaack catalog?

A: We are definitely interested in this idea. Once the retail store is successfully launched, we expect to have the resources to pursue this and other avenues of expansion. Sales through direct mail and computer network are both possibilities to pursue.

Q: What are some of Van Schaack's other long range plans?

A: We expect to continue growing our business by opening additional stores through a regional strategy, which involves opening approximately three stores in a given metropolitan market. In addition, we foresee building much larger stores than those initially planned. The projected larger stores will retain the character and methods of operation of the initial stores, which differ from traditional department stores in critical ways.

FINANCIAL DATA

Plan 1

Financial Structure of Van Schaack

Owners Equity	$40,000
T.I Allowance from Landlord	13,000
SBA/Bank Loan	80,000
Total Cash at Startup	133,000
Total Startup Costs	105,000
Operating Capital	28,000

- Of the $40,000 equity, 10% ($4,000) will be provided by Van Schaack, 10% ($4,000) by Jay Sanders, 5% ($2,000) by Steve Koblick, and 5% ($2,000) by Jeremy Nelson.
- The remaining 70% of the equity will come from the sale of stock.
- $13,000 will be credited to Van Schaack Corp. for tenant improvements at the proposed University District store location.
- $80,000 is to be in the form of an SBA bank loan.

Ownership

Van Schaack, Chairman of Board of Directors	28%
Jay Sanders, President/Chief Merchant	22%
Steve, Vice President - Operations	20%
Jeremy Nelson, Vice President	20%
Stockholders	10%

	Year 1	Year 2	Year 3**	Year 4**	Year 5**
Sales					
Sales-Clothing	$301,854	$348,691	$1,165,247	$1,435,650	$2,567,179
Sales-Cosmetics	$40,000	$61,534	$193,687	$253,350	$453,032
(2) Total Sales	**$341,854**	**$410,225**	**$1,358,934**	**$1,689,000**	**$3,020,210**
(3) Cost of Goods Sold	**$170,927**	**$205,112**	**$679,467**	**$844,500**	**$1,510,105**
Gross Profit	**$170,927**	**$205,112**	**$679,467**	**$844,500**	**$1,510,105**
Expenses					
Shortage	$3,419	$4,102	$13,589	$16,890	$30,202
Bags and Boxes	$1,439	$1,727	$5,722	$7,112	$12,717
Hangers	$720	$864	$2,861	$3,556	$6,358
(3) Operating Expenses	**$5,578**	**$6,693**	**$22,172**	**$27,557**	**$49,277**
Salaries & Wages	$88,960	$105,280	$314,500	$412,500	$670,000
Payroll Added Costs	$10,675	$12,634	$37,740	$49,500	$80,400
(4) Employee Costs	**$99,635**	**$117,914**	**$352,240**	**$462,000**	**$750,400**
Rent	$30,996	$32,858	$160,832	$221,640	$426,930
Utilities	$3,206	$3,402	$11,352	$16,380	$24,276
Maintenance	$600	$600	$1,886	$2,571	$14,364
Insurance	$2,394	$2,394	$7,524	$10,260	$14,364
Depreciation	$6,986	$6,986	$21,956	$29,940	$41,916
(5) Occupancy Costs	**$44,182**	**$46,240**	**$203,550**	**$280,791**	**$521,850**
Advertising	$9,000	$10,000	$18,000	$20,000	$25,000
Visual	$1,800	$1,800	$4,000	$4,000	$7,000
Promotion Expenses	**$10,800**	**$11,800**	**$22,000**	**$24,000**	**$32,000**
Office Supplies	$600	$1,000	$2,000	$2,000	$4,000
Telephone	$1,440	$1,700	$3,900	$4,000	$7,000
Miscellaneous	$1,200	$1,500	$3,800	$3,900	$7,000
Administrative Costs	**$3,240**	**$4,200**	**$9,700**	**$9,900**	**$18,000**
Total Expenses	**$163,435**	**$186,847**	**$609,662**	**$804,249**	**$1,371,527**
Net Profit, Before Taxes	**$7,492**	**$18,265**	**$69,805**	**$40,251**	**$138,578**

Five Year Plan Number 1 *

* Plan Number 2 is based on 2.5 "turns" of the value of the merchandise in stock in year one and ensuing years.

Plan 2 is based on the average performance of a department store selling similar type merchandise.

**Year 3, store #2 opens... Year 5, store #3 opens... See schedule 2 (a) for sales forecast.

**Plan 1
Schedule 1(a) -
Start-Up Costs
& Cash
Requirements
Prior to Opening**

Initial Inventory	
Merchandise	$64,000
Supplies	
Hangers	$1,500
Boxes & Bags	$1,500
Total Inventory	**$67,000**
Equipment and Machinery	
Computer System and Point of Purchase	$2,000
Alarm System	$1,500
Ticketing System	$300
Sound System/Music	$750
Telephones/Fax Machine	$500
Safe/Box	$150
Total Equipment and Machinery	**$5,200**
Leasehold Improvements	
Polished Concrete Floor	$500
Walls, Fitting Rooms, Stockroom	$8,000
Ceiling, Lighting, Electrical	$8,000
Signs - Exterior & Windows	$2,000
Architect & Fees	$1,500
Total Leasehold Improvements	**$20,000**
Merchandise Display and Visuals	
Hardware for Walls, Key Striping	$2,500
Fixtures, T-stands, 4-ways,	
Rounders, Tables, Wrap Stand	$4,000
Forms, Mannequins	$1,500
Merchandise Signs & Holders	$500
Photography - Visuals	$750
Office & Stockroom Fixtures	$750
Total Merchandise Display and Visuals	**$10,000**
Grand Opening Promotion	
Advertising	$2,000
Searchlight, Grand Opening Bash	$500
Total Grand Opening Expenses	**$2,500**
Total Start-Up Costs	**$104,700**

Summary Of Initial "Open To Buy"
See Schedule 2(c) for detail of "Open to Buy"

Dept.	Description	Units	Retail	Of Total
12	Tees	1,044	$17,040	10.0%
14	Tanks	792	11,292	6.6%
15	Shorts	666	12,312	7.2%
16	Fleece	294	8,952	5.2%
17	Pants	354	8,712	5.1%
21	Denim	642	34,980	20.5%
24	Sportswear tops	222	6,768	4.0%
25	Fashion Athletics	306	7,500	4.4%
27	Twill bottoms	204	8,556	5.0%
33	Innerwear/Sleepware	72	1,620	0.9%
64	Accessories	186	2,418	1.4%
66	Underwear	2,082	28,857	16.9%
73	Hosiery	276	1,920	1.1%

Total Clothing   **$150,927**

94	Cosmetics		20,000	

Total Retail "Open to Buy" Inventory   **$170,927**

Clothing Revenue Forecast, based on 2.0 turns of inventory   **$301,854**
Cosmetics Revenue Forecast, based on 2.0 turns of inventory   **$40,000**

		Store #1		Store #2		Store #3		All Stores
Year #1	Clothing	301,854	(A)					$301,854
	Cosmetics	$40,000						$40,000
Total		**$341,854**						**$341,854**
Year #2	Clothing	348,691	(B)					$348,691
	Cosmetics	$61,534						$61,534
Total		**$410,225**						**$410,225**
Year #3	Clothing	451,247	(C)	714,000	(F)			$1,165,247
	Cosmetics	$67,687		$126,000				$193,687
Total		**$518,934**		**$840,000**				**$1,358,934**
Year #4	Clothing	650,250	(D)	785,400	(G)			$1,435,650
	Cosmetics	$114,750		$138,600				$253,350
Total		**$765,000**		**$924,000**				**$1,689,000**
Year #5	Clothing	715,275	(E)	865,904	(H)	$986,000	(I)	$2,567,179
	Cosmetics	$126,225		$152,807		$174,000		$453,032
Total		**$841,500**		**$1,018,710**		**$1,160,000**		**$3,020,210**

A.	See Schedule 2(b) Summary of "Open to Buy."		
B.	Store #1 total increase, 2nd year	20.0% total	$410,225
	Cosmetics equal	15.0% of total revenue	$61,534
C.	Store #1 total increase, 3rd year	10.0% total	$451,247
	Cosmetics equal	15.0% of total revenue	$67,687

...continued

D. Store #1, 4th yr., expanded from 1,400 to 3,000 sq. ft.

Revenue per square ft...$255.00	total revenue	$765,000
Cosmetics equal...	15.0% of total revenue	$114,750

E. Store #1 total increase, 5th year

Store #1 total increase, 5th year	10.0% total	$841,500
Cosmetics equal	15.0% of total revenue	$126,255

F. Store #2 opened 3rd year, revenue based on 3,000 sq. ft.

Revenue per square ft...$280.00	total revenue	$840,000
Cosmetics equal	15.0% of total revenue	$126,000

G. Store #2 total increase, 4th year

Store #2 total increase, 4th year	10.0% total	$924,000
Cosmetics equal	15.0% of total revenue	$138,600

H. Store #2 total increase, 5th year

Store #2 total increase, 5th year	10.3% total	$1,018,710
Cosmetics equal	15.0% of total revenue	$152,807

I. Store #3 opened 5th year, revenue based on

Store #3 opened 5th year, revenue based on		$4,000
Revenue per square ft...$290.00	total revenue	$1,160,000
Cosmetics equal	15.0% of total revenue	$174,000

Plan 1 Schedule 3 - Cost of Goods & Operating Expenses

Cost of Goods

Clothing	50.0% of Sales
Cosmetics	33.0% of Sales

Operating

Theft/shortage	1.0% of Sales
Bags and Boxes	0.4% of Sales
Hangers	0.2% of Sales

First Full Year (1 store)

2.0 Executive FTEs @ $32,000	$64,000
1.5 Sales clerks @ 16,640	24,960
Total Salaries	**$88,960**

Year Two (1 Store)

2.0 Executive FTEs @ $36,000	$72,000
2.0 Sales clerks @ 16,640	33,280
Total Salaries	**$105,280**

Year Three (2 stores)

2.0 Executive FTEs @ $48,000	$96,000
0.5 Bookkeeper @ 25,000	12,500
1.0 #1 Store manager @ 25,000	25,000
2.5 #1 Sales clerks @ 17,000	42,500
1.0 #2 Store managers @ 28,000	28,000
6.5 #2 Sales clerks @ 17,000	110,500
Total Salaries	**$314,500**

Year Four (2 stores)

2.0 Executive FTEs @ $54,000	$108,000
0.5 Bookkeeper @ $25,000	12,500
1.0 #1 Store manager @ 28,000	28,000
6.0 #1 Sales clerks @ 18,000	108,000
1.0 #2 Store managers @ 30,000	30,000
7.0 #2 Sales clerks @ 18,000	126,000
Total Salaries	**$412,500**

Year Five (3 stores)

1.0 President @ 60,000	$60,000
1.0 Vice-President @ 60,000	60,000
1.0 Administrator @ 32,000	32,000
1.0 Clerical @ 21,000	21,000
1.0 #1 Store manager @ 30,000	30,000
1.0 #1 Asst. Store manager @ 22,000	22,000
5.0 Sales clerks @ 18,500	92,500
1.0 #2 Store manager @ 32,000	32,000
1.0 #2 Asst. Store manager @ 22,000	22,000
6.0 #2 Sales clerks @ 18,500	111,000
1.0 #3 Store manager @ 35,000	35,000
1.0 #3 Asst. Store manager @ 23,000	23,000
7.0 #3 Sales clerks @ 18,500	129,500
Total Salaries	**$670,000**
Total Payroll Added Costs (Taxes & Fringe)	**12.00%**

Plan 1 - Schedule 5 Occupancy Expense		Store #1	Store #2	Store #3	All Stores
Square feet		1,400	3,000	4,000	
Rent per sq. ft.		$22.14	—	—	
Year #1					
(a) Rent		$30,996	—	—	$30,996
(b) Utilities	$2.29 per sq. ft.	$3,206	—	—	$3,206
Maintenance	0.43 per sq. ft.	$600	—	—	$600
(c) Insurance	1.71 per sq. ft.	$2,394	—	—	$2,394
(d) Depreciation	4.99 per sq. ft.	$6,986	—	—	$6,986
Total Occupancy		**$44,182**	—	—	**$44,182**
Rent per sq. ft.		$23.47	—	—	
Year #2					
(a) Rent		$32,858	—	—	$32,858
(b) Utilities	$2.43 per sq. ft.	$3,402	—	—	$3,402
Maintenance	0.43 per sq. ft.	$600	—	—	$600
(c) Insurance	1.71 per sq. ft.	$2,394	—	—	$2,394
(d) Depreciation	4.99 per sq. ft.	$6,986	—	—	$6,986
Total Occupancy		**$46,240**	—	—	**$46,240**
Rent per sq. ft.		$24.88	$42.00		
Year #3					
(a) Rent		$34,832	$126,000	—	$160,832
(b) Utilities	$2.58 per sq. ft.	$3,612	$7,740	—	$11,352
Maintenance	0.43 per sq. ft.	$600	$1,286	—	$1,886
(c) Insurance	1.71 per sq. ft.	$2,394	$5,130	—	$7,524
(d) Depreciation	4.99 per sq. ft.	$6,986	$14,970	—	$21,956
Total Occupancy		**$48,424**	**$155,126**	—	**$203,550**
Rent per sq. ft.		$29.36	$44.52		
Year #4					
(a) Rent		$88,080	$133,560	—	$221,640
(b) Utilities	$2.73 per sq. ft.	$8,190	$8,190	—	$16,380
Maintenance	0.43 per sq. ft.	$1,286	$1,286	—	$2,571
(c) Insurance	1.71 per sq. ft.	$5,130	$5,130	—	$10,260
(d) Depreciation	4.99 per sq. ft.	$14,970	$14,970	—	$29,940
Total Occupancy		**$117,656**	**$163,136**	—	**$280,791**
Rent per sq. ft.		$31.12	$47.19	$48.00	
Year #5					
(a) Rent		$93,360	`$141,570	$192,000	$426,930
(b) Utilities	$2.89 per sq. ft.	$4,046	$8,670	$11,560	$24,276
(c) Insurance	1.71 per sq. ft.	$2,394	$5,130	$6,840	$14,364
(d) Depreciation	4.99 per sq. ft.	$6,986	$14,970	$19,960	$41,916
Total Occupancy		**$106,786**	**$170,340**	**$230,360**	**$507,486**

(a) 6.0% rent increase for inflation per year.

18.0% Store #1 rent increase in year 4, due to expansion & up-grading.

Store #1 square feet expansion to 3,000 Year #4

(b) 6.0% utility rate increase, due to inflation, per year.

(c) 5.0% insurance rate increase, due to inflation, per year.

(d) Depreciation includes:		
	Equipment & Machinery	*$1,490*
	Leasehold Improvements	*3,650*
	Display & Visuals	*1,850*
	Total per year	***$6,990***

Month	January	February	March	April	May	June
% of year Sales	5.0%	5.0%	6.0%	6.0%	6.0%	8.0%
Amount	$17,093	17,093	20,511	20,511	20,511	27,348

	July	August	September	October	November	December
% of year Sales	10.0%	8.0%	10.0%	8.0%	14.0%	14.0%
Amount	$34,185	27,348	34,185	27,348	47,860	47,860

Total First Year Sales   **$341,853**

Plan 1 - Schedule 6
First Year Sales
By month

Year One

	Oct-Dec	Jan-Mar	Apr-Jun	Jul-Sep	Total
Sales...% per quarter	36.0%	28.0%	20.0%	16.0%	100.0%
Amount	**$123,068**	**$54,697**	**$68,370**	**$95,718**	**$41,853**
(1) Cost of Goods and Related					
Expenses @ 51.63%	63,540	28,240	35,299	49,419	76,498
(2) Payroll & related expenses	24,909	24,909	24,909	24,909	99,636
(3) Occupancy Costs	9,299	9,299	9,299	9,299	37,196
(4) Promotion Expense	2,700	2,700	2,700	2,700	10,800
Costs	810	810	810	810	3,240
Cash Income / Loss	**$21,810**	**($11,261)**	**($4,647)**	**$8,581**	**14,483**
(before depreciation)	14,483				
(6) Depreciation	1,747	1,747	1,747	1,747	6,988
Income/Loss	**$20,063**	**($13,008)**	**($6,394)**	**$6,834**	**$7,495**
(before taxes)					$7,495

Plan 1 - Schedule 7(a)
Quarterly Income
Statement

(1) Includes Operating expenses, e.g. boxes & bags, etc.
(2) Total..$99,635 Payroll & related expenses for year one, evenly distributed through each quarter
(3) Total..$37,196 Occupancy costs, Less depreciation for year one, evenly distributed each quarter
(4) Total..$10,800 Promotion expenses for year one, evenly distributed through each quarter
(5) Total $3,240 Administrative expenses for year one, evenly distributed through each quarter
(6) Total $6,986 Depreciation for year one, evenly distributed through each quarter

Plan 1
Schedule 7(b)
Cashflow Year One

	Opening Balance	Oct-Dec	Jan-Mar	Apr-Jun	Jul-Sep
From investors	40,000				
From bank	160,000				
Opening cash balance	**$200,000**				
Total startup costs	**$154,964**				
Cash income/loss from operations		$21,810	($11,261)	($4,647)	$8,581
Cash balance, end of quarter	$45,036	$66,846	$55,585	$50,938	$59,519*

* Cash available for expansion

Plan 2

Five Year Plan Number 2*

Sales	Year 1	Year 2	Year 3**	Year 4**	Year 5**
Sales-Clothing	$377,318	$435,864	$1,419,584	$1,968,471	$3,306,018
Sales-Cosmetics	$50,000	$76,917	$235,584	$347,377	$583,415
(2) Total Sales	**$427,318**	**$512,781**	**$1,655,168**	**$2,315,848**	**$3,889,433**
(3) Cost of Goods Sold	$213,659	$256,391	$827,584	$1,157,924	$1,944,716
Gross Profit	**$213,659**	**$256,391**	**$827,584**	**$1,157,924**	**$1,944,716**
Expenses					
Shortage	$4,273	$5,128	$16,552	$23,158	$38,894
Bags and Boxes	$1,799	$2,159	$6,969	$9,751	$16,377
Hangers	$900	$1,080	$3,485	$4,875	$8,188
(3) Operating Expenses	**$6,972**	**$8,366**	**$27,005**	**$37,785**	**$63,459**
Salaries & Wages	$97,856	$115,808	$345,950	$453,750	$737,000
Payroll Added Costs	$11,743	$13,897	$41,514	$54,450	$88,440
(4) Employee Costs	**$109,599**	**$129,705**	**$387,464**	**$508,200**	**$825,440**
Rent	$30,996	$32,858	$160,832	$221,640	$426,930
Utilities	$3,206	$3,402	$11,352	$16,380	$24,276
Maintenance	$600	$600	$1,886	$2,571	$14,364
Insurance	$2,394	$2,394	$7,524	$10,260	$14,364
Depreciation	$6,986	$6,986	$21,956	$29,940	$41,916
(5) Occupancy Costs	**$44,182**	**$46,240**	**$203,550**	**$280,791**	**$521,850**
Advertising	$9,000	$10,000	$18,000	$20,000	$25,000
Visual	$1,800	$1,800	$4,000	$4,000	$7,000
Promotion Expenses	**$10,800**	**$11,800**	**$22,000**	**$24,000**	**$32,000**
Office Supplies	$600	$1,000	$2,000	$2,000	$4,000
Telephone	$1,440	$1,700	$3,900	$4,000	$7,000
Miscellaneous	$1,200	$1,500	$3,800	$3,900	$7,000
Administrative Costs	**$3,240**	**$4,200**	**$9,700**	**$9,900**	**$18,000**
Total Expenses	**$174,793**	**$200,311**	**$649,719**	**$860,676**	**$1,460,749**
Net Profit, Before Taxes	**$38,866**	**$56,079**	**$177,865**	**$297,248**	**$483,967**

*   Plan Number 2 is based on 2.5 "turns" of the value of the merchandise in stock in year one and ensuing years. Plan 2 is based on the average performance of a department store selling similar type merchandise.
** Year 3, store #2 opens... Year 5, store #3 opens... See schedule 2 (a) for sales forecast.

		Store #1		Store #2		Store #3		All Stores
Year#1	Clothing	377,318	(A)					377,318
	Cosmetics	50,000						50,000
Total		**427,318**						**427,318**
Year#2	Clothing	435,864	(B)					435,864
	Cosmetics	76,917						76,917
Total		**512,781**						**512,781**
Year#3	Clothing	564,059	(C)	855,525	(F)			1,419,584
	Cosmetics	84,609		150,975				235,584
Total		**648,668**		**1,006,500**				**1,655,168**
Year#4	Clothing	1,027,393	(D)	941,078	(G)			1,968,471
	Cosmetics	181,305		166,073				347,377
Total		**1,208,698**		**1,107,150**				**2,315,848**
Year#5	Clothing	1,130,133	(E)	1,035,185	(H)	1,140,700	(I)	3,306,018
	Cosmetics	199,435		182,680		201,300		583,415
Total		**1,329,568**		**1,217,865**		**1,342,000**		**3,889,433**

Plan 2 - Schedule 1(a)
Sales Forecast
Per Store

A. See Schedule 2. (b) Summary of "open to Buy."

B.	Store #1 total increase, 2nd year	20.0% total		$512,781
	Cosmetics equal	15.0% of total revenue		$76,917
C.	Store #1 total increase, 3rd year	10.0% total		$564,059
	Cosmetics equal	15.0% of total revenue		$84,609
D.	Store #1, 4th yr., expanded from 1,400 to 3,000 sq. ft.			
	Revenue per square ft...$402.90	total revenue		$1,208,698
	Cosmetics equal	15.0% of total revenue		$181,305
E.	Store #1 total increase, 5th year	10.0% total		$1,329,568
	Cosmetics equal	15.0% of total revenue		$199,435
F.	Store #2 opened 3rd year, revenue based on 3,000 sq. ft.			
	Revenue per square ft...$335.50	total revenue		$1,006,500
	Cosmetics equal	15.0% of total revenue		$150,975
G.	Store #2 total increase, 4th year	10.0% total		$1,107,150
	Cosmetics equal	15.0% of total revenue		$166,073
H.	Store #2 total increase, 5th year	10.0% total		$1,217,865
	Cosmetics equal	15.0% of total revenue		$182,680
I.	Store #3 opened 5th year, revenue based on 4,000 sq. ft.			
	Revenue per square ft...$335.50	total revenue		$1,342,000
	Cosmetics equal	15.0% of total revenue		$201,300

Cost of Goods

Clothing	50.0%	of Sales
Cosmetics	33.0%	of Sales
Operating		
Theft/shortage	1.0%	of Sales
Bags and Boxes	0.4%	of Sales
Hangers	0.2%	of Sales

Schedule 3
Cost of Goods and
Operating Expenses

Schedule 4
Payroll &
Related Expenses

First Full Year (1 store)		
2.0 Executive FTEs @	$35,200	$70,400
1.5 Sales clerks @	$18,304	$27,456
Total Salaries		**$97,856**

Year Two (1 store)		
2.0 Executive FTEs @	$39,600	$79,200
2.0 Sales clerks @	$18,304	$36,608
Total Salaries		**$115,808**

Year Three (2 stores)		
2.0 Executive FTEs @	$52,800	$105,600
0.5 Bookkeeper	$27,500	$13,750
1.0 #1 Store manager	$27,500	$27,500
2.5 #1 Sales clerks @	$18,700	$46,750
1.0 #2 Store managers	$30,800	$30,800
6.5 #2 Sales clerks @	$18,700	$121,550
Total Salaries		**$345,950**

Year Four (2 stores)		
2.0 Executive FTEs @	$59,400	$118,800
0.5 Bookkeeper	$27,500	$13,750
1.0 #1 Store manager	$30,800	$30,800
6.0 #1 Sales clerks @	$19,800	$118,800
1.0 #2 Store managers	$33,000	$33,000
7.0 #2 Sales clerks @	$19,800	$138,600
Total Salaries		**$453,750**

Year Five (3 stores)		
1.0 President @	$66,000	$66,000
1.0 Vice-President @	$66,000	$66,000
1.0 Administrator @	$35,200	$35,200
1.0 Clerical @	$23,100	$23,100
1.0 #1 Store manager	$33,000	$33,000
1.0 #1 Asst. Store manager	$24,200	$24,200
5.0 #1 Sales clerks @	$20,350	$101,750
1.0 #2 Store manager	$35,200	$35,200
1.0 #2 Asst. Store manager	$24,200	$24,200
6.0 #2 Sales clerks @	$20,350	$122,100
1.0 #3 Store manager	$38,500	$38,500
1.0 #3 Asst. Store manager	$25,300	$25,300
7.0 #3 Sales clerks @	$20,350	$142,450
Total Salaries		**$737,000**

Total Payroll Added Costs (Taxes & Fringe)		**12.00%**

		Store #1	Store #2	Store #3	All Stores
	Square feet	1,400	3,000	4,000	
	Rent per sq. ft.	$22.14	—	—	
Year #1					
(a) Rent		$30,996	—	—	$30,996
(b) Utilities	$2.29 per sq. ft.	$3,206	—	—	$3,206
Maintenance	0.43 per sq. ft.	$600	—	—	$600
(c) Insurance	1.71 per sq. ft.	$2,394	—	—	$2,394
(d) Depreciation	4.99 per sq. ft.	$6,986	—	—	$6,986
Total Occupancy		**$44,182**	—	—	**$44,182**
	Rent per sq. ft.	$23.47			
Year #2					
(a) Rent		$32,858	—	—	$32,858
(b) Utilities	$2.43 per sq. ft.	$3,402	—	—	$3,402
Maintenance	0.43 per sq. ft.	$600	—	—	$600
(c) Insurance	1.71 per sq. ft.	$2,394	—	—	$2,394
(d) Depreciation	4.99 per sq. ft.	$6,986	—	—	$6,986
Total Occupancy		**$46,240**	—	—	**$46,240**
	Rent per sq. ft.	$24.88	$42.00		
Year #3					
(a) Rent		$34,832	$126,000	—	$160,832
(b) Utilities	$2.58 per sq. ft.	$3,612	$7,740	—	$11,352
Maintenance	0.43 per sq. ft.	$600	$1,286	—	$1,886
(c) Insurance	1.71 per sq. ft.	$2,394	$5,130	—	$7,524
(d) Depreciation	4.99 per sq. ft.	$6,986	$14,970	—	$21,956
Total Occupancy		**$48,424**	**$155,126**	—	**$203,550**
	Rent per sq. ft.	$29.36	$44.52		
Year #4					
(a) Rent		$88,080	$133,560	—	$221,640
(b) Utilities	$2.73 per sq. ft.	$8,190	$8,190	—	$16,380
Maintenance	0.43 per sq. ft.	$1,286	$1,286	—	$2,571
(c) Insurance	1.71 per sq. ft.	$5,130	$5,130	—	$10,260
(d) Depreciation	4.99 sq. ft.	$14,970	$14,970	—	$29,940
Total Occupancy		**$117,656**	**$163,136**	—	**$280,791**
	Rent per sq. ft.	$31.12	$47.19	—	$48.00
Year #5					
(a) Rent		$93,360	$141,570	$192,000	$426,930
(b) Utilities	$2.89 per sq. ft.	$4,046	$8,670	$11,560	$24,276
(c) Insurance	1.71 per sq. ft.	$2,394	$5,130	$6,840	$14,364
(d) Depreciation	4.99 per sq. ft.	$6,986	$14,970	$19,960	$41,916
Total Occupancy		**$106,786**	**$170,340**	**$230,360**	**$507,486**

Schedule 5
Occupancy Expense

(a) 6.0% rent increase for inflation per year.

   18.0% Store #1 rent increase in year 4, due to expansion & up-grading.

   Store #1 square feet expansion.

(b) 6.0% utility rate increase, due to inflation, per year.

(c) 5.0% Insurance rate increase, due to inflation, per year.

(d) Depreciation includes (see Start-up)

Equipment & Machinery	$1,490
Leasehold Improvements	$3,650
Display & Visuals	$1,850
Total per year	**$6,990**

Schedule 6
First Year Sales
By Month

Month	1st	2nd	3rd	4th	5th	6th
% of year Sale	5.0%	5.0%	6.0%	6.0%	6.0%	8.0%
Amount	21,366	21,366	25,639	25,639	25,639	34,185

	Jul	Aug	Sep	Oct	Nov	Dec
% of year Sale	10.0%	8.0%	10.0%	8.0%	14.0%	14.0%
Amount	42,732	34,185	42,732	34,185	59,824	59,824

Total First Year Sales   **$427,318**

Plan 2
Schedule 7(a)
Quarterly
Income Statement
Year One

	Oct-Dec	Jan-Mar	Apr-Jun	Jul-Sep	Total
Sales...% per quarter	36.0%	28.0%	20.0%	16.0%	100.0%
Amount	**$153,833**	**$68,371**	**$85,463**	**$119,649**	**$427,316**
(1) Cost of Goods and Related Expenses @ 51.63%	$79,424	$35,300	$44,125	$61,775	$220,624
(2) Payroll & related expenses	$27,400	$27,400	$27,400	$27,400	$109,600
(3) Occupancy Costs	$9,299	$9,299	$9,299	$9,299	$37,196
(4) Promotion Expense	$2,700	$2,700	$2,700	$2,700	$10,800
(5) Administrative Costs	$810	$810	$810	$810	$3,240
Cash Income/Loss	**$34,200**	**($7,138)**	**$1,129**	**$17,665**	**$45,856**
(before depreciation)					$45,856
(6) Depreciation	$1,747	$1,747	$1,747	$1,747	$6,988
Income/Loss	**$32,453**	**($8,885)**	**($618)**	**$15,918**	**$38,868**
(before taxes)					$38,868

(1) Includes Operating expenses, e.g. boxes & bags, etc.
(2) Total...$109,599 Payroll & related expenses for year one, evenly distributed through each quarter
(3) Total...$37,196 Occupancy costs, less depreciation for year one, evenly distributed, each quarter
(4) Total...$10,800 Promotion expenses for year one, evenly distributed through each quarter
(5) Total...$3,240 Administrative expenses for year one, evenly distributed through each quarter
(6) Total...$6,986 Depreciation for year one, evenly distributed through each quarter

Online Government Contract Service

BUSINESS PLAN

U.S. CONSULTING - GOV.COM

10 Weldy Ave.
Jenkintown, PA 19046

With the astounding increase in the number of businesses doing business on the Internet, new markets are arising quickly. Gov.Com is a response to one of those markets. Businesses interested in doing business with the government is a growing market, with the rise of small businesses. U.S. Consulting offers its online government contract service to small businesses interested in contracting for the government. A need that previously was not being met, is now being met through Gov.Com.

- EXECUTIVE SUMMARY

- BUSINESS DESCRIPTION

- MARKETING STRATEGY

- OPERATIONAL PLAN

- MANAGEMENT AND STAFFING

- FUNDS NEEDED AND THEIR USES

- FINANCIALS

EXECUTIVE SUMMARY

The government bulletin board service, Gov.Com, is a new computer bulletin board system planned for introduction in 1996 by Pennsylvania-based U.S. Consulting, Inc. The purpose of this service is to provide individuals and small businesses in the U.S. access to information about how to do business with the government.

Although the federal government spends over $100 billion with private businesses annually, few firms are aware of the opportunity to bid on those goods and services that the government buys. So they miss out on lucrative contracts.

In fact, there are contracts set aside specifically for small businesses on which only individuals and small businesses may bid. The value of those contracts alone is more than $30 billion per year.

Over the next few years, the government will increasingly contract out for services as it downsizes its operations. This means that there will be increasing opportunities for individuals and small businesses.

And while some companies are aware of the opportunities to have the U.S. government as a regular customer, there are still a majority who don't how to begin or where to go for assistance in bidding on government work. Receiving a Request for Proposal from a government agency can be a daunting experience.

Gov.Com aims to provide the needed information regarding procurement opportunities, give advice on successful bidding and proposing, and guide businesses through the maze of paperwork by way of an online computer service. Individuals and companies worldwide will be able to access Gov.Com via a computer and modem.

There are a number of published sources for this contract information which individuals may subscribe to, but subscription costs range from several hundred to $10,000 per year. Few individuals and small businesses could afford such information. But Gov.Com will provide access to all of those reports for just $350 per year.

There is currently no other online service providing this type of information or support regarding government contract opportunities. Gov.Com will be the only one in existence.

Although millions of small businesses and individuals are potential users of this bulletin board system, U.S. Consulting has conservatively based its financial projections on just 5,000 members for each of the first five years of operation for a total subscriber base of 25,000 at the end of the fifth year.

By comparison, in its first year of operation, Big Co. gained 1,000,000 subscribers, Internet had 500,000, and Online Runs had 350,000. U.S. Consulting believes that with an effective promotional program to a market that is even more familiar now with the benefits of online systems, it will easily surpass its goal of 5,000 subscribers.

Subscribers to Gov.Com will dial into the service via a computer modem, review new contract opportunities everyday, and download information regarding projects they would like to bid on. Assistance in preparation of the bids will be available online as well, through correspondence and instruction using electronic mail.

The company's founder, Pierre Phillips, has personally administered more than 150 federal, state, and municipal contracts. Through this experience he recognized that small businesses needed assistance in pursuing government contracts.

Funding is needed in the amount of $300,000 to renovate an existing facility now owned by U.S. Consulting, purchase computers and communications equipment to operate the bulletin board service, acquire furniture and other fixtures, as well as implement an aggressive marketing program for the service.

Projected Income Statement	1996	1997	1998	1999	2000
Enrollment Fees	$750,000	$1,500,000	$2,250,000	$3,000,000	$3,750,000
Total Expenses	$500,000	$750,000	$900,000	$1,000,000	$1,000,000
Net Income	$250,000	$750,000	$1,350,000	$2,000,000	$2,750,000

BUSINESS DESCRIPTION

Service Description

U.S. Consulting will establish Gov.Com to provide up-to-date information on federal, state, and municipal government contract opportunities. This information can be accessed through a computer and modem 24 hours a day by subscribers who pay $350 per year for the service.

In addition to learning of lucrative government projects, subscribers to the service will also be able to receive advice and guidance on bidding on such contracts through the service. CEO Pierre Phillips will be available to answer online queries regarding government contracts.

During Year 1, the president will respond to requests for assistance by email, helping subscribers increase their chance of winning government bids.

During Year 2, a consulting staff will be in place to provide ongoing support and guidance to subscribers for an hourly fee.

Potential Subscribers

Individuals and small business owners who are interested in selling their goods and services to the U.S. government are potential users of the service.

Some of the many products and services needed include:

- Hotel and motel space
- Watches
- Writing and editing
- Computers and computer services
- Food services
- Teaching services
- Advertising
- Actors and actresses
- Sports officials
- Consulting
- Computer programming
- Fine art
- Teachers
- Ministers
- Therapists
- Doctors
- Veterinarians
- Printing
- Research
- Technical Writing
- Mail processing
- Public relations services
- Well drilling

Location

Gov.Com will operate out of a currently unoccupied building in Jenkintown, Pennsylvania. Although renovations will be required before the business can move into the space, the owner has quit-claimed the deed to U.S. Consulting.

Approximately $150,000 of the total $300,000 needed for start-up capital will be applied towards renovating the building for occupancy.

Legal Structure and Ownership

U.S. Consulting is a corporation located in the state of Pennsylvania which is wholly owned by Pierre Phillips.

MARKETING STRATEGY

Target Customers

Any individual or small business owner interested in doing business with the government is a prospective customer. While it would be difficult to identify and locate persons with this interest, it will be relatively easy to reach modem owners, computer owners, and current users of online services. These criteria will be used to qualify potential subscribers.

Market Size

In 1993 over 624,000 individuals purchased modems and computers. All of these individuals are potential users of the bulletin board because of their interest in communication via modem.

There are now over 78,000 computer BBS's in existence. Over 300 new ones are created each week. This service will be promoted on each of these services.

There are also more than 3 million current subscribers to the 3 major online services - all of which are potential subscribers to Gov.Com.

These figures do not even take into account the huge number of small businesses and corporations with computers and modems who will have an interest in this service because it will save both time and money.

Pricing

The subscription price of $350 per year was set by examining the costs of comparable industry guides and by reviewing operating costs.

Other leading contract reports cost more and are time-consuming to review on a daily basis. Gov.Com will be organized into sections to make it easy for subscribers to identify which contracts are of interest and which are not.

Competitive Published Resources

In addition to being time-consuming to review and difficult to follow, existing government contract reports and newsletters are expensive. Since most are distributed through the U.S. mail, the information can also become obsolete by the time that it arrives. The following are subscription prices for leading publications:

The Financial Statement	$260
York Reports	$575-1,600
Invest Today	$450-1,100
U.S. Rates	$650-1,200

By providing updated information on a daily basis that subscribers can access 24 hours a day, users will be kept current on opportunities.

Marketing Methods

In order to reach individuals and small business owners who are potential subscribers to Gov.Com, several methods will be used.

Direct Mail

A mailing list of current online subscribers will be purchased and a direct mail flyer will be mailed to alert them that Gov.Com is now available to assist them.

Recent purchasers of modems will also be sent literature regarding the new bulletin board.

Typical direct mail response rates are 2-3% of the total mailing. For a planned mailing of 3 million pieces, that would yield 60,000-90,000 subscribers. However, U.S. Consulting has conservatively estimated just 30,000 subscribers during the first five years.

Inserts

U.S. Consulting intends to approach modem manufacturers and communications software manufacturers to propose having Gov.Com subscription literature enclosed with the product. Materials similar to the direct mail literature would inform the purchaser of the existence of the new service and invite them to subscribe.

Online Marketing

Ads and messages will be posted on all major online services, as well as on many of the private bulletin boards around the country to alert individuals already familiar with online services of the existence of this special interest service.

OPERATIONAL PLAN

Operating Process

Data technicians will be responsible for updating bulletin board information on a daily basis from the computer system at U.S. Consulting headquarters.

The CEO will respond to subscriber email regarding contract opportunities and advice on a daily basis.

Data entry clerks will enter new contract data as it arrives at U.S. Consulting offices.

The service will begin with 10 phone lines for subscribers to use in dialing into the service 24 hours a day. Lines will be added as demand increases so as not to frustrate or discourage subscribers trying to access the service.

Several computers and communications systems will be needed in order to operate and maintain the bulletin board system. These include:

Equipment

- Minicomputer
- Microcomputers (2)
- Laptop computer
- Local area network with 10 nodes
- Optical backup system for BBS
- Scanner
- UPS
- Laser printer
- Modem
- Telephone system
- WATS service with 11 lines

A software package designed for managing profitable bulletin board systems will be purchased. Several are under consideration at this point, including Comp, CST, Randog, and Powerun.

In addition, software to manage inbound and outbound telephone calls is needed, as well as a mail order management package for accounting and billing, to help keep track of subscribers and bills.

MANAGEMENT AND STAFFING

Current Staff

U.S. Consulting currently provides business and financial tax consulting to individuals and businesses in the Jenkintown, Pennsylvania area.

The establishment of Gov.Com will require additional personnel to assist in the daily operations of the service.

Chief Executive Officer

Pierre Phillips will serve as CEO of U.S. Consulting and will be responsible for managing the day-to-day operation of the service.

His years of experience in government contracting and successful bidding on government contracts has given him first-hand experience in identifying and winning business from the U.S. government. He has personally administered over 150 government contracts ranging from painting, flooring, hazardous waste removal, janitorial services, laundry, office supplies, and many others. The value of these contracts ranged from as little as $3,000 to as much as $2,900,000.

Because of his familiarity with all facets of doing business with the federal government he now administers contracts for himself as well as for other businesses, as a consultant.

The bulletin board will enable Mr. Phillips to extend his expertise to a wider audience of potential government contractors.

Through his work as a tax consultant he has become extremely familiar with electronic filing and modem communications. This knowledge will be applied in setting up the communications system to run the bulletin board service.

Future Hires

During the start-up phase Pierre Phillips will be the only full-time employee of U.S. Consulting. However, two additional staff members will be needed in order to input and process contract information on a daily basis.

A full-time data technician and a part-time data entry clerk will be hired to manage the tasks of entering data into the system and monitoring the use of the service.

Two additional individuals will be hired during the second year to serve as consultants. These employees will provide guidance to subscribers in winning and meeting the terms of government contracts in return for an hourly consulting fee.

FUNDS NEEDED AND THEIR USES

A total of $300,000 is needed to establish Gov.Com. The funds will be used in the following manner:

Facility renovation	$125,000
Computer and communications equipment	$35,000
Marketing and promotion	$100,000
Working capital	$35,000
Furniture and fixtures	$5,000
Total	**$300,000**

The service will be profitable by the end of the first year in business.

FINANCIALS

Cash Out Plan for Investors

For the first three years of operation, the investor shall receive forty five percent (45%) of the net operating income of the bulletin board as a dividend.

At the end of year three, the service will go public. Sufficient stock will be sold to raise the sum of five million dollars ($5,000,000). Forty-five percent of the proceeds of the offering will be awarded to the investor as a buyout. In the event the offering fails to raise the five million dollars, investors shall have the option of receiving forty five percent of the amount raised by the offering or 45% of the stock itself.

The foregoing will become part of the corporate minutes and official records upon commitment of the investor to the seed capital sought and shall be an irrevocable pledge.

	1996	1997	1998	**Projected Balance Sheet**
ASSETS				
Current Assets				
•Cash	2,367,269	6,827,380	12,182,169	
•Prepaid Expenses	3,000	3,000	3,000	
Total Current Assets	2,370,269	6,830,380	12,185,169	
•Leasehold Improvements	150,000	150,000	150,000	
•Furniture & Fixtures	15,000	15,000	15,000	
•Equipment	75,000	75,000	75,000	
•Intangible Assets	500,000	500,000	500,000	
Total Assets	**$3,110,269**	**$7,570,380**	**$12,925,169**	
LIABILITIES AND OWNERS EQUITY				
Current Liabilities				
•Accounts Payable	5,261	11,850	26,689	
•Accrued Expenses	4,758	5,670	9,758	
•Income Taxes Payable	373,855	592,345	719,180	
Total Current Liabilities	383,874	609,865	755,627	
Long Term Liabilities	0	0	0	
Total Liabilities	**383,874**	**609,865**	**755,627**	
Owner's/Shareholder's Equity	0	0	0	
Paid In Capital	300,000	300,000	300,000	
Contributed Capital	500,000	500,000	500,000	
Retained Earnings	0	1,926,395	6,160,515	
Net Income	1,926,395	4,234,120	5,209,027	
Total Liabilities & Owners Equity	**$3,110,269**	**$7,570,380**	**$12,925,169**	

Projected Cash Flow For 1996

	January	February	March	April	May	June	July
Cash On Hand	$0	$115,943	$242,635	$386,303	$548,655	$731,569	$937,116
REVENUES							
Net Sales	$157,500	$173,250	$190,575	$209,633	$230,596	$253,656	$279,022
Total Inflows	$157,500	$289,193	$433,210	$595,936	$779,251	$985,225	$1,216,138
EXPENSES							
Cost of Goods Sold	$7,000	$9,500	$9,675	$9,862	$10,062	$10,276	$10,505
Promotion	$16,580	$16,580	$16,580	$16,580	$16,580	$16,580	$16,580
Telephone	$1,991	$1,991	$1,991	$1,991	$1,991	$1,991	$1,991
Office Salaries	$1,500	$1,500	$1,500	$1,500	$1,500	$1,500	$1,500
Utilities	$591	$591	$591	$591	$591	$591	$591
Supplies	$927	$927	$927	$927	$927	$927	$927
Payroll tax	$2,500	$2,500	$2,500	$2,500	$2,500	$2,500	$2,500
Real estate tax	$375	$375	$375	$375	$375	$375	$375
Repairs	$1,000	$1,000	$1,000	$1,000	$1,000	$1,000	$1,733
Legal and professional	$767	$767	$767	$767	$767	$767	$767
Travel	$1,327	$1,327	$1,327	$1,327	$1,327	$1,327	$1,327
Total Expenses	$34,557	$37,057	$37,232	$37,419	$37,619	$37,833	$38,795
Net Cash	$115,943	$126,693	$143,668	$162,352	$182,915	$205,547	$229,722
Cash at End of Period	$115,943	$242,635	$386,303	$548,655	$731,569	$937,116	$1,166,838

August	September	October	November	December	1996
$1,166,838	$1,423,971	$1,711,271	$2,031,771	$2,388,806	
$306,924	$337,616	$371,378	$408,516	$449,368	$3,368,034
$1,473,762	$1,761,587	$2,082,649	$2,440,287	$2,838,174	
$10,750	$11,013	$11,294	$11,595	$11,917	$123,449
$16,580	$16,580	$16,580	$16,580	$16,580	$198,961
$1,991	$1,991	$1,991	$1,991	$1,991	$23,887
$1,500	$1,500	$1,500	$1,500	$1,500	$18,000
$591	$591	$591	$591	$591	$7,087
$927	$927	$927	$927	$927	$11,129
$2,500	$2,500	$2,500	$2,500	$2,500	$30,000
$375	$375	$375	$375	$375	$4,500
$1,733	$1,733	$1,733	$1,733	$1,733	$1,856
$767	$767	$767	$767	$767	$9,200
$1,327	$1,327	$1,327	$1,327	$1,327	$15,924
$39,040	$39,303	$39,584	$39,885	$40,207	$458,535
$257,134	$287,300	$320,500	$357,036	$397,244	
$1,423,971	$1,711,271	$2,031,771	$2,388,806	$2,786,050	

Projected Cash Flow For 1997

	January	February	March	April	May	June
Cash On Hand	$2,388,806	$2,908,025	$3,427,244	$3,946,463	$4,465,682	$4,984,901
REVENUES						
Net Sales	$592,573	$592,573	$592,573	$592,573	$592,573	$592,573
Total Inflows	$2,981,379	$3,500,598	$4,019,817	$4,539,036	$5,058,255	$5,577,474
EXPENSES						
Cost of Goods Sold	$15,392	$15,392	$15,392	$15,392	$15,392	$15,392
Promotion	$29,774	$29,774	$29,774	$29,774	$29,774	$29,774
Telephone	$3,575	$3,575	$3,575	$3,575	$3,575	$3,575
Office Salaries	$1,500	$1,500	$1,500	$1,500	$1,500	$1,500
Utilities	$842	$842	$842	$842	$842	$842
Supplies	$1,325	$1,325	$1,325	$1,325	$1,325	$1,325
Payroll tax	$2,500	$2,500	$2,500	$2,500	$2,500	$2,500
Real estate tax	$0	$0	$0	$0	$0	$0
Repairs	$321	$321	$321	$321	$321	$321
Legal and professional	$350	$350	$350	$350	$350	$350
Travel	$2,383	$2,383	$2,383	$2,383	$2,383	$2,383
Total Expenses	$57,962	$57,962	$57,962	$57,962	$57,962	$57,962
Net Cash	$519,219	$519,219	$519,219	$519,219	$519,219	$519,219
Cash at End of Period	$2,908,025	$3,427,244	$3,946,463	$4,465,682	$4,984,901	$5,504,120

July	August	September	October	November	December	1997
$5,504,120	$6,023,339	$6,542,558	$7,061,777	$7,580,996	$8,100,215	
$592,573	$592,573	$592,573	$592,573	$592,573	$592,573	$7,110,874
$6,096,693	$6,615,912	$7,135,131	$7,654,350	$8,173,569	$8,692,788	
$15,392	$15,392	$15,392	$15,392	$15,392	$15,392	$184,705
$29,774	$29,774	$29,774	$29,774	$29,774	$29,774	$357,283
$3,575	$3,575	$3,575	$3,575	$3,575	$3,575	$42,904
$1,500	$1,500	$1,500	$1,500	$1,500	$1,500	$18,000
$842	$842	$842	$842	$842	$842	$10,104
$1,325	$1,325	$1,325	$1,325	$1,325	$1,325	$15,898
$2,500	$2,500	$2,500	$2,500	$2,500	$2,500	$30,000
$0	$0	$0	$0	$0	$0	$0
$321	$321	$321	$321	$321	$321	$3,850
$350	$350	$350	$350	$350	$350	$4,200
$2,383	$2,383	$2,383	$2,383	$2,383	$2,383	$28,597
$57,962	$57,962	$57,962	$57,962	$57,962	$57,962	$695,541
$519,219	$519,219	$519,219	$519,219	$519,219	$519,219	
$6,023,339	$6,542,558	$7,061,777	$7,580,996	$8,100,215	$8,619,434	

Projected Cash Flow For 1998

	January	February	March	April	May	June
Cash On Hand	$8,619,434	$8,495,615	$8,371,796	$8,247,976	$8,124,157	$8,000,337
REVENUES						
Net Sales	$755,623	$755,623	$755,623	$755,623	$755,623	$755,623
Total Inflows	$8,619,434	$8,495,615	$8,371,796	$8,247,976	$8,124,157	$8,000,337
EXPENSES						
Cost of Goods Sold	$25,902	$25,902	$25,902	$25,902	$25,902	$25,902
Promotion	$53,468	$53,468	$53,468	$53,468	$53,468	$53,468
Telephone	$6,422	$6,422	$6,422	$6,422	$6,422	$6,422
Office Salaries	$1,500	$1,500	$1,500	$1,500	$1,500	$1,500
Utilities	$1,200	$1,200	$1,200	$1,200	$1,200	$1,200
Supplies	$1,890	$1,890	$1,890	$1,890	$1,890	$1,890
Payroll tax	$2,500	$2,500	$2,500	$2,500	$2,500	$2,500
Real estate tax	$0	$0	$0	$0	$0	$0
Repairs	$407	$407	$407	$407	$407	$407
Legal and professional	$350	$350	$350	$350	$350	$350
Travel	$4,279	$4,279	$4,279	$4,279	$4,279	$4,279
Total Expenses	$97,917	$97,917	$97,917	$97,917	$97,917	$97,917
Net Cash	$631,803	$631,803	$631,803	$631,803	$631,803	$631,803
Cash at End of Period	$8,495,615	$8,371,796	$8,247,976	$8,124,157	$8,000,337	$7,876,518

	July	August	September	October	November	December	1998
	$7,876,518	$7,752,698	$7,628,879	$7,505,060	$7,381,240	$7,257,421	
	$755,623	$755,623	$755,623	$755,623	$755,623	$755,623	$9,067,474
	$7,876,518	$7,752,698	$7,628,879	$7,505,060	$7,381,240	$7,257,421	
	$25,902	$25,902	$25,902	$25,902	$25,902	$25,902	$310,824
	$53,468	$53,468	$53,468	$53,468	$53,468	$53,468	$641,620
	$6,422	$6,422	$6,422	$6,422	$6,422	$6,422	$77,065
	$1,500	$1,500	$1,500	$1,500	$1,500	$1,500	$18,000
	$1,200	$1,200	$1,200	$1,200	$1,200	$1,200	$14,398
	$1,890	$1,890	$1,890	$1,890	$1,890	$1,890	$22,677
	$2,500	$2,500	$2,500	$2,500	$2,500	$2,500	$30,000
	$0	$0	$0	$0	$0	$0	$0
	$407	$407	$407	$407	$407	$407	$4,881
	$350	$350	$350	$350	$350	$350	$4,200
	$4,279	$4,279	$4,279	$4,279	$4,279	$4,279	$51,344
	$97,917	$97,917	$97,917	$97,917	$97,917	$97,917	$1,175,009
	$631,803	$631,803	$631,803	$631,803	$631,803	$631,803	
	$7,752,698	$7,628,879	$7,505,060	$7,381,240	$7,257,421	$7,133,601	

Projected Income Statement

	1996	1997	1998
Revenue	$3,368,034	$7,110,874	$9,067,474
Cost of Good Sold	$128,710	$184,705	$310,824
Communications	44,710	100,705	226,824
Salaries	84,000	84,000	84,000
Gross Profit	**$3,239,324**	**$6,926,169**	**$8,756,650**
Operating Expenses			
Promotion	198,961	357,283	641,620
Telephone	23,887	42,904	77,065
Office salaries	18,000	18,000	18,000
Utilities	7,087	10,104	14,398
Supplies	11,129	15,898	22,677
Payroll tax	30,000	30,000	30,000
Real estate tax	4,500	0	0
Repairs	1,856	3,850	4,881
Legal and professional	9,200	4,200	4,200
Travel	15,924	28,597	51,344
Total Expenses	**$320,544**	**$510,836**	**$864,185**
Net Profit Before Taxes	$2,918,780	$6,415,333	$7,892,465
Taxes	$992,385	$2,181,213	$2,683,438
Net Income	**$1,926,395**	**$4,234,120**	**$5,209,027**

Online Hospitality Service

BUSINESS PLAN

TINNER CORP.

175 Wright Street
Phoenix, AZ 85003

Tinner Corp. plans to take advantage of the latest technology available on-line, by providing both consumers and businesses with an on-line hospitality service called Hospitality Works. Hospitality Works will provide consumers seeking hotel, travel and restaurant information a "one-stop shopping mall", where they can obtain information, buy, sell and make reservations on-line. The service will also enable those in the hospitality industry business to buy and sell goods in a more efficient and cost effective manner. By taking advantage of available technology and targeting a specific market segment, Tinner Corp. has developed a successful and profitable plan for their business.

- EXECUTIVE SUMMARY

- GOAL & OVERALL STRATEGY

- PRODUCT

- MARKET

- PRICING STRATEGY & REVENUE PROJECTIONS

- MANAGEMENT TEAM

- FINANCIAL PROJECTIONS

EXECUTIVE SUMMARY

Tinner Corp. is a start-up company founded by experienced entrepreneurs that is seeking additional investment to support the development and marketing of its product, Hospitality Works. Hospitality Works will be the first on-line service in the marketplace that services the world's largest vertical market, the hospitality industry, with the tools being provided by a competitive manufacturer of software, Goldmine Corporation. Hospitality Works will be accessible on Goldmine Online. Due to be released in August 1995, Goldmine Online is projected to capture millions of new subscribers on its network in just the first year, which will make it one of the largest commercial on-line networks anywhere. All segments of the food, beverage, and lodging industries ranging from single-location restaurants and inns, to international chains as well as their suppliers will have on-line local access in 45 countries.

Members of Hospitality Works on Goldmine Online will find it easy and inexpensive to travel the world of electronic information. Members will be able to buy and sell worldwide, reserve hotel rooms, hold real-time chats, attend on-line classes, review resumes, post menus, and research the latest trends through electronic extensions of industry publications. The Tinner market strategy is based on being first to market, promoting the solid Goldmine partnership, creating a world-class organization teamed with high-value content providers, designing the product for growth, and aggressively marketing the product. Already, Tinner has been contacted by over 500 firms, from the largest in the industry, to some as far away as Saudi Arabia.

Ralph Cunningham, President of Goldmine, demonstrated Hospitality Works to an audience of 700 food industry CEO's on May 3, 1995, during his keynote address. With its projected customer base, Hospitality Works is expected to grow to $36 million by its third year. The primary revenue generating services will be on-line supplier purchases, worldwide hotel reservations, private company forums, and advertisements. The company President and CEO is Lucy Tucker, who opened her first successful restaurant when she was 22 years old and since has earned a reputation as a visionary in the hospitality industry. Ms. Tucker has provided about $300,000 in seed capital which has enabled product development since November 1994.

At present, Tinner is the only Independent Content Provider designated as a Goldmine "aggregator" for the hospitality industry. As such, Goldmine has been referring companies of all sizes related to the hospitality industry to Tinner.

Tinner Hospitality Corp. is seeking investment for development, staffing, marketing, and operation of Hospitality Works.

GOAL & OVERALL STRATEGY

Hospitality Works will be the premiere on-line content provider on Goldmine Online, which will serve the daily business and communication needs of all members of the global food-service and lodging industries. The over-arching strategies that will make this possible are:

1. To be the first to the marketplace with a service that merges together the world's largest vertical market, the hospitality industry, with the tools being created by one of the fastest growing markets, the commercial on-line network industry and the Internet.
2. To closely partner with Goldmine and directly benefit from the anticipated dramatic sales of and world-leading products from Goldmine Online.
3. To develop a lean, dynamic organization that has the tools to grow with the market and create strategic alliances with successful organizations that enhance and expand Hospitality Works services.

PRODUCT

Product Description

Hospitality Works, developed by Tinner Corp., is an on-line service much like Big Co., Internext and Starnet, but it is specifically dedicated to serving the needs of the hospitality industry. Hospitality Works will be available on the forthcoming Goldmine Online. Subscribers to Goldmine Online will have on-line local access in 45 countries.

Upon its launch in June 1995, Hospitality Works will be a leading, globally accessible on-line service effectively serving all individuals and organizations involved in foodservice and lodging.

Hospitality Works is being designed to closely emulate At-Your-Fingers for ease of use. Access to Hospitality Works will be through two entries on Goldmine Online. One will be found under the Travel & Vacation folder on Goldmine Online and will be targeted to the consumer. The other entry will be found under the Marketplace folder and will be targeted to businesses. Tinner projects most of its revenues will come from the business customer.

Tinner likens Hospitality Works to a shopping mall where Tinner is the landlord who enables the commerce and ease of access, and businesses are the tenants that conduct the actual business. Consumers and businesses find this concept of "one-stop shopping" to be convenient and compelling. Moreover, businesses will benefit from conducting their operations faster, better, and cheaper through on-line communications. Hospitality Works will enable faster and more accurate communications with their customer base, improve efficiency in internal operations, and improve convenience for employees, customers, and the end user. In short, Hospitality Works will make good business sense.

Hospitality Works offers a wide variety of services. Over 90% of the projected revenues will be generated from four basic services: on-line links to suppliers, worldwide hotel reservations, private company forums, and advertisement. A user of Hospitality Works can see a picture of his hotel before making his own reservation on-line, buy supplies at the click of a button and electronically shop around for the best price, send private messages to his employees scattered around the world, and advertise his company from a visually compelling multi-media home page. Buying on-line will enable suppliers to service their customers at a far lower cost than any other method currently being used. Tinner is committed to providing the best value-added services to its customers on Hospitality Works.

Accomplishments

Since the company's inception in January 1993, Tinner has already had a number of notable accomplishments:

- Hospitality Works is currently up and running on Goldmine Online.
- Of the approximately 150 independent content providers currently on Goldmine Online, Hospitality Works has been cited by Goldmine as one of the most mature and highest quality forums.
- Lucy Tucker was featured in *Business Time* praising the pricing model Goldmine Online proposed for its forthcoming on-line network.
- Tinner had a major exhibit booth at the U.S. Restaurant Convention in June 1995 and hosted its first set of public live demonstrations with on-line chats with Chef Kirby Beneville and Chef Joe Markell. Goldmine participated with staffing and technical help.
- Ralph Cunningham, President of Goldmine, demonstrated Hospitality Works to an audience of several hundred food industry CEO's in St. Louis on May 4, 1995 during his keynote address.
- Tinner was invited to present Hospitality Works to an audience of 2,000 people at Goldmine's Systems Conference in San Francisco in August 1995 where Ralph Cunningham also spoke.

- Tinner has been contacted by over 500 organizations, including major hotel corporations, food manufacturers and restaurant chains, who are interested in Hospitality Works as potential users or suppliers.

MARKET

Market Description

Hospitality Works is targeted to the hospitality industry, one of the largest vertical markets in the world. The target market includes restaurant and hotel operators, hospitality suppliers, professional associations, trade publications, consultants, universities, cruise lines, vending firms, bars, cafes, caterers, and food service operators for health care, business, and the military. In the U.S. alone, the hospitality industry was estimated to generate over $300 billion in sales in 1995 with about $230 billion from foodservice and $70 billion from lodging (ref: Dept. of Commerce).

The hospitality industry is increasingly using advanced computers and communications to enhance its products. The single greatest growth area in the hospitality industry is information and technology expenditures. In the U.S. foodservice segment alone, technology expenditures are expected to surpass $590 million in 1995 according to *Food News*. Over 80% of all hospitality businesses utilize personal computers with Goldmine products as the operating environment of choice.

The research firm Infosearch projects that 28 million units of Goldmine Systems will be sold in the first four months after its June 1995 launch and over 200 total units through 1999. Browntown estimates 30% of At-Your-Fingers purchases will result in a subscription to Goldmine Online given its experience with free trial offers. As a result, based on Infosearch projections, Browntown estimates 9 million people will subscribe to Goldmine Online by the end of 1995 (28 million units times 30%). More conservative estimates have ranged from 1 to 2 million by end of 1995. In either case, Goldmine Online could overnight become the leader in commercial on-line services. The current leader is Homeplate On-Line with over 2 million subscribers and 6 million total between Neophyte, Samson and Compit.

Goldmine's marketing strategy is targeted to the vast majority of U.S. households that do not currently subscribe to any on-line service.

For example, although 40% of At-Your-Fingers (AYF) users have modems, fewer than 10 percent of users of AYF and 4 percent of U.S. households subscribe to on-line services.

On-line communications is still in its infancy within the hospitality industry. However, given that foodservice and lodging organizations usually consist of numerous operating units dispersed by long distances, the use of on-line communications is becoming an increasingly attractive business tool. Tinner believes the low cost of Goldmine Online, its ease of use, and its wide availability through AYF will make it the platform of choice for the hospitality industry.

Market Strategy

The market for commercial on-line services is highly competitive. There are no substantial barriers to entry, and we expect that competition will intensify in the future. Tinner's ability to compete successfully depends on five key strategies described below:

First to Market - Hospitality Works will be the first on-line provider focused on exclusively serving the hospitality industry. As a result, Hospitality Works has been given the special status by Goldmine as the "aggregator" for the hospitality industry. As an "aggregator", we provide Goldmine the market and product expertise to achieve a significant volume of sales with an industry that has tremendous on-line service potential. Although such a title is not an exclusive arrangement with Goldmine, it will make Hospitality Works the on-line service of choice if one wants easy and early access to Goldmine Online. There is a growing recognition by the hospitality industry that Hospitality Works will be the only one-stop shopping service available in the near-term. This recognition has ignited an overwhelming interest in our product. There is a great sense of urgency among potential users and providers of Hospitality Works of not being left out of the coming revolution in on-line communications. As an "aggregator", Tinner will enable suppliers to service their customers at a far lower sales cost than is currently available.

Benefit from Goldmine Partnership - After our exhaustive review of where to place Hospitality Works including bulletin board services, commercial on-line service providers, and the Internet, Tinner chose Goldmine Online. Tinner then proposed and Goldmine selected Hospitality Works as the hospitality industry "aggregator" on Goldmine Online. Our partnership with Goldmine will enable us to offer a superior product and business plan for the following reasons:

Ease of Use - Goldmine has assisted us in designing Hospitality Works to emulate the look and feel of At-Your-Fingers thus making navigating between AYF and Hospitality Works transparent to the users -- providing a level of standardization and ease of use not available on other on-line services. Finding services on Goldmine Online is much easier than, for example, on the Internet.

Powerful Development Tools - Goldmine has provided us with powerful development tools from which we will build the most visually appealing and functional services anywhere in the on-line industry.

Superior Pricing Plan - Goldmine's pricing plan, which is much lower than any comparable on-line provider, will ensure the affordability of Tinner services in a hospitality market known for low margins. Also, Goldmine Online's low monthly fee will make it inexpensive for our customers to subscribe.

Name Recognition and Aggressive Marketing - Goldmine's AYF and Goldmine Online products have received widespread press coverage and are expected to rewrite the industry. Tinner will benefit directly from Goldmine's plans to aggressively market the network (and they have already paid us on one occasion to market Hospitality Works at a trade show.)

Solidify Sub-Content Provider Alliances - Hospitality Works will be backed up by a powerful and high-quality team of sub-content providers. Currently we are in the process of selecting a sub-content provider for our hotel reservation system. We are also examining sub-content providers for the on-line buying service, for the news service, for managing about 20 individual forums, and for home page development and data storage. The sub-content provider will be selected based on quality of product, ease of use consistent with the AYF look and feel, ability to get service to market soon, good market reputation, in-depth market knowledge, and low product risk. Most importantly, no sub-content provider will be selected that undermines the position of Hospitality Works as an impartial and open provider of services. For example, we will not select a sub-content provider who competes with other users of Hospitality Works (e.g., a hotel operator, major food supplier), nor will we sign an exclusive arrangement with any user of Hospitality Works.

Design Product for Growth - Tinner has designed Hospitality Works to grow with the dramatic increase in volume we expect, without a large increase in staff. Our use of advanced on-line tools and office automation and the leveraging of Goldmine and sub-content providers, will enable us to keep our organization lean and dynamic. If a service requires significant manpower to support it, we will outsource it.

Aggressive Marketing Campaign - In order to take full advantage of being first to market, Tinner plans to aggressively market Hospitality Works through trade shows, trade publications, promotional events, and Goldmine itself. As mentioned above, Tinner and Goldmine have already generated a strong interest in Hospitality Works with over 500 inquiries received to date.

Competitive Analysis

The companies current and prospective competitors generally may be divided into the following three groups:

Commercial On-Line Services such as Homeplate, Neophyte, and Compit. Many of these competitors have been in business a number of years but none currently offer content specifically targeted to the hospitality industry. Moreover, their pricing structure where they keep up to 90% of revenues generated makes it impossible to offer services such as on-line buying and hotel reservations where margins are very small. Tinner does not expect serious competition from this group.

Bulletin Board Services (BBS)

Some hospitality organizations such as the U.S. Dining Federation have invested their own funds to own and operate a BBS. A BBS has the advantage of providing a direct link to the customer. The downside for the BBS operator is the high cost of dedicated communication lines, constraints of using proprietary equipment, and the problem of owning hardware that can quickly become obsolete. The problem for the subscriber is its usual high cost and the inability to "shop" elsewhere. Tinner considers BBS to be a minor niche competitor.

Home Pages on the Internet

The Internet has experienced the fastest growth of on-line users. There are estimated to be 20 million users on the Internet. Also, new technologies and products are being offered at an ever increasing rate. Tinner views the Internet as the most likely source of serious competition. However, no competitor has yet to emerge that plans to offer the "one-stop shopping" services we offer the hospitality customer. Also, we believe Goldmine Online has a number of technical advantages over the unregulated environment of the Internet:

Quality - Goldmine backs up the quality of its on-line services, promotes those that prove successful and removes those that fail. Not so on the Internet. The user has to determine the honest service from the fraudulent.
Ease of Use - The Internet user has to learn two operating systems on the Internet (the computer and the on-line service) versus only one on Goldmine Online.
Browsing - Goldmine Online provides a clear roadmap for navigating to the customer's preferred service area versus Internet where one can get easily lost.
Security - The security of business transactions is overseen by Goldmine whereas security on the Internet is dealt with on a hit or miss basis.
Reliability and Support - Goldmine Online ensures the reliability and provides 24 hour support whereas there is no one to call for a problem on Internet.
Low Up-Front Costs - Subscribers to Goldmine Online, and Hospitality Works will not have to invest in extensive hardware or personnel. In most cases, existing computer hardware will suffice.

So overall, Tinner believes that Goldmine Online offers a superior product than does the Internet and other on-line service providers. Eventually, if and when the Internet does become "user friendly", we expect Goldmine Online to become the premiere site accessible by all on the Internet.

Through our close alliance with Goldmine, we will continue to closely monitor competitive developments in the marketplace to ensure that the products we offer on Hospitality Works remain the highest value and highest quality at a competitive price.

PRICING STRATEGY AND REVENUE PROJECTIONS

In keeping with Goldmine's pricing strategy, Tinner is also planning a pricing strategy that caters to mass accessibility. There will be no fee to access Hospitality Works beyond the low monthly fee required to be a member on Goldmine Online.

Fees will be charged on specific value-added items. Tinner prices have been chosen to be competitive within the market and expect to adjust our prices as new competition emerges. To keep our costs down, Tinner will seek other sources for handling the billing and collection process. For example, Goldmine will provide billing for products sent through the network (i.e., on-line) and our sub-content billing for products delivered outside the network (i.e., off-line).

Revenues are challenging to project because there are currently no on-line services that provide our product. Therefore, Tinner was very conservative with its projections. For example, revenue is based on U.S. data only, even though Tinner services will be available to the global hospitality industry at launch. Also, our projections do not exceed 1% of the market niches we aim to serve. Revenue projections are based on both top-down and bottom-up estimates.

Revenues from Hospitality Works can be generated from potentially over a dozen sources. However, Tinner will focus on four basic services which are expected to generate over 90% of the revenue of the $36 million projected by the third year. These services are:

Purchasing On-Line ($13 million by third year) - Foodservice and lodging organizations will have the opportunity to buy goods on-line direct from the supplier. Suppliers will be responsible for uploading new pricing data at no charge. For every purchase, the supplier will be responsible for the billing, as well as paying Tinner a small commission. Currently, salesmen charge 1-3% commission in the foodservice business. Tinner is assuming only a 0.7% commission. Tinner is assuming $180 million in goods will be sold over Hospitality Works by the third year. This will create $13 million in revenue for Tinner (versus about $1.3 billion in commissions paid by U.S. restaurant suppliers annually).

Worldwide Hotel Reservations ($10 million by third year) - Consumers and corporations will be able to browse hotels and book reservations through our on-line hotel reservation system. Tinner is in the process of selecting a sub-content provider who will provide the application which can best support this function. The sub-content provider will be responsible for development, maintenance, support, and billing for this service. Pricing will be done on a fixed fee per transaction. Currently, the market charges between $5 and $10 per transaction. Tinner is assuming the low of $5 per transaction. Tinner is projecting 2.0 million transactions by the third year. One hotel reservations company gave us projections of 2.5 million in just the first year. In the U.S., there are over 1 billion travel transactions per year. Tinner is also planning to generate revenue from hotels uploading their room information. The pricing algorithm will be a flat charge per upload times the number of individual hotel sites. Hence, a larger hotel chain will pay more than a smaller one.

Private Company Forums ($6 million by third year) - Private companies can create their own private forums that could contain e-mail, purchasing, staff news, directories, training, employee manuals, calendar, employment opportunities, etc. Tinner plans to charge a one-time setup fee and a monthly maintenance fee based on number of sites included in the chain (i.e., the larger the company the more expensive). A basic template with some styling options will make it relatively easy for Tinner to service numerous requests. Tinner projects 400 private forums on Hospitality Works by the third year.

Advertising ($5 million by third year) - Most of the interest today in on-line services stems from advertising. Research firm Infosearch projects over $1 billion in on-line advertising in five years. Tinner has assumed advertising revenue through four sources: home page ads, menu upload-ing, postings, and special events. (1) Home page ads ($3.3 million) will be priced on a one-time set-up fee and a monthly maintenance fee. The current market charges between $1,000-$10,000 per month. Tinner assumes $500 monthly charge in anticipation that the market will become increasingly competitive. (2) Menu uploading ($0.8 million) will enable restaurants to easily advertise their current menus. There will be a flat uploading charge and a small daily charge for each site. (3) Postings ($0.7 million) could include resumes from individuals and training and career announcements from organizations. The charging will be based on a small flat daily charge. (4) Special events ads ($0.5 million) could include carrying a company logo on a Tinner home page or sponsoring a live chat with a hospitality celebrity. The charge will be a flat rate.

There are a number of additional activities which could substantially raise revenue for Tinner. Public Discussion Forums such as classes and chat rooms with cover charges, etc., would be charged a set-up fee and monthly maintenance fees. On-line news retrieval services will also generate revenue. A major hospitality newspaper has already signed a letter of intent with Tinner. Other revenue sources could occur through outsourcing items such as customer mass data storage and home page development.

MANAGEMENT TEAM

Organization

Tinner Corp., located in Phoenix, Arizona is a subsidiary of the 10 year old Maison Rouge Co., a successful high-tech hospitality management company founded by Tinner's CEO Lucy Tucker. Tinner is leveraging the technology of on-line communications and office automation to keep the company small but effective. A key operating principle is that any activity which requires extensive manual labor will be outsourced to qualified organizations. This will enable Tinner to remain lean, aggressive, and focused.

Tinner is organized around network operations & technical support, sales & marketing, and general & administrative activities. Tinner is planning to increase its staff to 35 individuals pending the infusion of additional investment funds. As revenues grow, we do not plan to substantially increase our human resources given the scalability of Hospitality Works to handle the higher volume of on-line activity.

Key Personnel

Lucy Tucker, 35, Chairwoman and CEO, Tinner Corp. - Ms. Tucker opened her first restaurant when she was 22 years old. Over ten years have passed and during that time Ms. Tucker has earned a reputation as a visionary in the hospitality industry, as chronicled in numerous feature articles. With a sharp business acumen and a lot of hard work, she has created three highly successful trendsetting restaurant concepts. She also served as Vice President of the Phoenix Branch of the Southwest Restaurant Association. Ms. Tucker learned early on that leveraging technology to her full advantage was the best way to achieve a competitive edge. Her high-tech pursuit of excellence has attracted the attention of the hospitality industry's top business figures. Ms. Tucker has proven her ability to consistently create and operate profitable businesses. Building on the success of her organization, she has assembled an impressive team of strategic partners and a talented staff who share her vision in Hospitality Works.

Shirley Lake, 32, Director of Network Operations and Technical Support - Ms. Lake, the co-founder of Tinner, started her career in the microcomputer industry in the late 1970s. Led by the belief that the future for personal computers would revolutionize life in every way, she continues to dedicate her career to providing an organized framework for satisfying business needs with new technological capabilities. Working in many segments of the industry, including programming, technical information and sales, she has become a seasoned expert. As the owner of a successful consulting firm in Phoenix, Ms. Lake has consistently shown the ability to integrate technology in order to accomplish strategic business objectives. Ms. Lake is systems administrator for computing at Phoenix University.

Sue Anthony, 40, Director of Hospitality Works Forums - Ms. Anthony is currently Director of Campus Dining at the University of Arizona at Phoenix, where she is responsible for $13 million in food services annually with 800 employees in 14 different locations. Her organization has received numerous awards including a recent national recognition for excellence in catering. Sue has made extensive use of computer technology for food service applications and is considered at the forefront in this field. She has consulted at all campuses at UA, as well as for numerous restaurants and non-commercial food services.

Beatrice White, 35, Director of Marketing and Sales - Ms. White strengthens Tinner with her experience in executive corporate management, wholesale foodservices, and lodging operations. She was an Executive Vice President of a $50 million wholesale food distribution company. She was directly responsible for the sales and marketing with double digit increase in sales every year. She developed company budgets and several expense cutting programs that were extremely successful. She also currently owns a spa.

Lydia Kumar, 37, Director of Business Planning - Ms. Kumar brings to Tinner her extensive experience in financial planning and business development for advanced technology programs. While at Iddings and Larson, a leading management consulting firm, she provided analysis and advice for clients seeking to exploit commercial markets in space. She also worked for Renu where she was a manager of marketing and product design in a $100 million venture to sell commercial launch services to private and public satellite operators. Ms. Kumar has a degree in aerospace engineering from CalTech.

FINANCIAL PROJECTIONS

Financial Needs

Seed capital has funded the research and development needs of Tinner since its inception in November 1994. $300,000 in seed capital has been provided by the founder and CEO Lucy Tucker. The funding will be sufficient to develop a functioning forum for Hospitality Works for its June launch.

Tinner is seeking an additional investment of $4-5 million to complete development of Hospitality Works, expand the staff to 35 to service the growing demand of potential customers, acquire additional computer hardware and office space, and begin an aggressive marketing campaign to exploit our strategic advantage of being first to market. Funds are needed to get Tinner through the first year of operations, at which point revenues are projected to exceed cost.

Pricing Assumptions

Financial Assumptions

Purchasing	0.7% commission
Hotel Reservations	
Reservations	$5 per transaction
Upload Room Data	$1 per site per upload
Private Forums	$5,000 setup + $500/month + $20/site/month
Advertisement	
Home Page Ads	$5,000 setup + $500/month
Upload Menu Data	($50 setup + $1/day) times number of sites
Postings	$10/day
Special Events	$10,000/event
Other	
Public Forums	$500 setup + $30/day
News & References	$0.50 per clipping
Data Storage	$600 per gigabyte
Home Page Development	$100/hr of labor

Revenue Assumptions

Purchasing	No revenue first six months. By 3rd year, $180 million in off-line sales will produce $13 million in revenue.
Hotel Reservations	No revenue first six months

Reservations	By 3rd year, 2.0 million transactions
Upload Room Data	By 3rd year, 30 hotels with 200 sites each updated bi-weekly.
Private Forums	No revenue first three months. By 3rd year, 400 forums with 10 sites each plus 250 setups (20% turnover).

Advertisement

Home Page Ads	No revenue first three months. By 3rd year, 200 ads including 150 setups (50% turnover)
Upload Menu Data	No revenue first three months. By 3rd year, 500 menus with 4 sites each including 750 setups (33% turnover)
Postings	No revenue first two months. By 3rd year, 200 postings per day
Special Events	Two special events per month first year. By 3rd year, four events per month.

Other

Public Forums	No revenue first two months. By 3rd year, 50 forums per day (6 month turnover)
News & References	No revenue first two months. By 3rd year, 2,500 clippings per day.
Data Storage	No revenue first two months. By 3rd year, 10 companies at 10 gigabytes each.
Home Page Development	40 hours per month initially. By 3rd year, 330 hours per month.

Cost Assumptions

Tinner - Given the scalability of Hospitality Works in handling varying volumes at little additional cost, Tinner's cost to each unit sold is very small.

Goldmine - Costs for all Tinner products include a "subsidy" to Goldmine. Costs paid to Goldmine are subdivided into three categories with a different rate for each: on-line, advertising, and off-line. The terms on-line and off-line refer to how the product is delivered. For example, a cover charge for a chat room is considered on-line since the customer receives the product through the network, whereas purchasing restaurant supplies through the network is off-line since the product is delivered outside the network.

Sub-Content Provider - Tinner plans to use a sub-content provider (i.e., subcontractor) for the hotel reservations and any other product that is manpower intensive or can be done more inexpensively elsewhere. We assumed hotel reservations, news and references, data storage, and Home Page development would be outsourced.

Expenses Assumptions

Salaries	Scalability of service requires little growth in manpower.
Benefits	30% wrap.
Commission & Awards	2% of revenue.
Contracted Forum Managers	$200/month for each of 22 contracted forum managers
Equipment	New workstations, fileserver and a mirror one, and other equipment upfront.
Office Supplies	$105,000 for outfitting of a 45 person office.

Rent	$200 per person.
Promotions	Includes 3 major exhibits and 2 smaller ones at trade shows.
Advertisement	Ads in major lodging and restaurant periodicals.
Travel	15 trips per month at $2,000 per trip first year.

Following is a three year forecast for Tinner:

Financial Statement

($ in millions)	Year 1	Year 2	Year 3
Total Revenue	2.7	17.4	36.0
Total Costs	5.2	14.6	26.3
Earnings Before Interest/Tax	(2.5)	2.8	9.7
Staff	35	40	45

Outdoor Adventure Travel Company

BUSINESS PLAN

RAD-VENTURE

P.O. Box 58005
Reno, NV 89523

November 20, 1995

RAD-Venture presents a plan for a very unique business. RAD-Venture provides outdoor adventures to their many, adventure seeking clients. Whether clients are looking for an "extreme" adventure or a somewhat milder time outdoors, RAD-Venture has just the trip. Specializing in mountain biking tours, hiking and camping, the owners have found that they can run a successful and profitable business by using their expertise and talents, while doing something that they love and enjoy.

- EXECUTIVE SUMMARY

- HISTORY AND BACKGROUND

- CONCEPT

- MISSION STATEMENT

- OBJECTIVES

- MARKETING

- MARKET MIX AND SHARE

- COMPANY PARAMETERS

- MANAGEMENT

- PROJECT TIMING

- FINANCIALS

OUTDOOR ADVENTURE TRAVEL COMPANY
BUSINESS PLAN

EXECUTIVE SUMMARY

The company name is RAD-Venture. It operates daily rentals and tours in Nevada, and multi-day mountain bike tours throughout the national park regions of the Southwest. It is an adventure travel company (currently specializing in mountain bike touring) with plans to include additional recreational opportunities via an RAD-Venture Center in Cedar City, Utah.

RAD-Venture promotes human power and natural environment. The target market has been defined as special interest "adventure sports and travel." This market is young and growing rapidly.

The primary owners are Grant and Heidi Osborn. Together they have ten years of college education and experience in management and communications. The Osborn's focused their college education toward researching and designing RAD-Venture. They bring to the company both educational insight and "real life" experience.

RAD-Venture has many strengths. Led with innovative enthusiasm, it possesses exciting potential as one of the early companies in a young, growing industry. The intended Southern Utah location has an economic, demographic, and political base strongly conducive to the success of an outdoor adventure center. RAD-Venture has a history of highly satisfied customers and a quality brochure vital in an industry that is based on perception rather than reality. The purpose of this business plan is to solicit funds for a new outdoor RAD-Venture Center, featuring an indoor rock climbing gym, mountain bike touring headquarters, and outdoor adventure sports sales and services, RAD-Venture invites investors to participate in this new and prospering business. Take the time to learn about the company through this business plan. If you do wish to become a part of our growth, we look forward to meeting you again.

HISTORY AND BACKGROUND

During the 1992 Spring semester, UNLV student Grant Osborn undertook a marketing class project to hypothetically create an original, unique service for Las Vegas. He developed an operations and marketing strategy for a business which would theoretically deliver bicycles to Las Vegas hotel guests and take bike tours to nearby Red Rock Canyon.

Grant's wife, Heidi, knew this was an idea with great potential. She recognized an unanswered market and acted quickly. With student ambition, ideas, and determination, by April 10, 1992, a new bicycle rental and tour company, "RAD-Venture" was born. Grant and Heidi's remaining college years were suddenly directed toward researching and developing this new business venture.

From the Osborns' first two personal bikes used for rentals and a computer in the bedroom, the business grew, entirely self-supported, into a nationally-advertised operation complete with an office, a warehouse, high quality mountain bikes, tour equipment, and support vehicles--just in the first three years!

The focus of RAD-Venture has evolved with its growth. The once local Las Vegas rental and tour company has developed into a full support mountain bike tour operator with plans to outfit a variety of additional active sports as well. A new Outdoor RAD-Venture Center in Cedar City, Utah, will serve to facilitate these plans.

CONCEPT

The concept of an Outdoor RAD-Venture Center in Cedar City, Utah stems from two perceived needs of RAD-Venture. First, the need for a more stable (non-weather-dependent) indoor activity and retail base from which to balance the seasonal nature of adventure tourism, and secondly, the need for a base environment more central to popular outdoor adventure destinations.

The Outdoor RAD-Venture Center is designed to supply clothing, equipment, maps, rentals, shuttles, and tours for outdoor sports such as mountain biking, rock climbing, rafting, camping, skiing, hiking, and horseback riding. Two unique attractants are a world-class indoor rock climbing gym and the adjacent location to the Navajo path, a paved trail system popular for jogging and biking. Great mountain biking and rafting opportunities lie within ten miles of the RAD-venture Center's intended location. The center will also house the headquarters for RAD-Venture mountain bike tours in Utah, Arizona, Colorado, and New Mexico.

Cedar City, Utah is one of the gateway cities to the Grand Circle, known as "America's greatest concentration of scenic wonders." The proposed location in Cedar City has excellent freeway access and exposure. Sunny Southern Utah's abundant natural "adventure" resources, strong growing economy, and year round temperate climate provide the ideal environment for a new Outdoor RAD-Venture Center.

MISSION STATEMENT

RAD-Venture is designed to promote and operate outdoor adventure sports and travel. By offering nothing motorized, we celebrate human power and natural environment. We will be leaders in our industry through innovation and preservation. We will sustain a reputation of quality through excellent service, customer care, and a friendly, professional staff. Our guests are the focus of our company. We will generate a profit in an ethical manner while meeting and exceeding our guests' expectations.

OBJECTIVES

Short Term Objectives: One Year

Marketing

1. Distribute RAD-Venture tour/rental fliers to Cedar City hotels, recreation information centers, Chambers of Commerce, and local colleges by February 15, 1995.
2. Develop a new, more inclusive registration form to send out with our mountain bike tour brochure which includes information and photos of our two new tours and information on our new Outdoor RAD-Venture Center by December 15, 1995.
3. Place ads in biking, sports, and mountain climbing sections of Cedar City yellow pages by November 15, 1995.
4. Develop and distribute a brochure and brochure stand to 100 bike, ski, and climbing shops in northern Utah by February 25, 1995.
5. Sponsor a grand opening party with food, discounts, and radio coverage.

Financial

1. Update balance sheet by January 1, 1996.
2. Secure financing by December 1, 1995.
3. Gross $400,000 in 1996.
4. Net five percent of gross in 1996.
5. Have 1996 budget prepared by December 31, 1995.

Management Information Systems

1. Complete computer training courses learning to use effectively applicable software programs by May 1, 1996.
2. Incorporate an accounting program, by January 1, 1996 that will take care of monthly accounting and taxes.
3. Purchase a new computer and monitor for use at the climbing gym desk with mountain climbing program by February 15, 1996.
4. Transfer our HAISAR 486 to the new main office in Cedar City and add a modem line by February 15, 1996.
5. Advertise on the Internet by December 31, 1995.

Human Resources

1. Hire a full-time manager for rentals and tours and one part-time (on call) helper by Center opening date.
2. Develop a pay structure and contract for manager incorporating commission by January 15, 1996.
3. Hire two full-time employees, and a part-time (on-call) hike tour guide, bike tour guide and rock climbing guide/instructor by opening date.
4. Restructure the employee handbook by December 31, 1995.
5. Make available a tax and insurance program for full-time employees by January 1, 1996.

Administrative Operations

1. Register RAD-Venture as a trademark by July 1, 1996.
2. Acquire necessary permits, for Taos, New Mexico, and Lake Tahoe, and Nevada tours by May 1, 1996.
3. Lease a space in the Center to a dependable rafting tour and supply company by May 1, 1996.
4. Create and offer three new tours for the 1997 tour schedule; (one with a warm winter location), and one new kind of tour (other than mountain biking) by September 15, 1996.
5. Create, publish, and distribute a new color brochure or catalogue by September 15, 1996.

Mid-Term Objectives: Two to Four Years

Marketing

1. Attend the INTERBIKE trade show once each year, in 1997, 1998 and 1999 and distribute brochures.
2. Use the existing customer database to establish an advertising campaign in each major region with the most interest by December 1997, 1998 and 1999.
3. Advertise mountain biking, rock climbing, and rafting trips in the classified sections of ten major magazines by December 31, 1998.
4. Attend the Outdoor Activity Show once each year, in 1997, 1998, and 1999.
5. Hold an indoor climbing competition and mountain bike festival in Spring 1997 and 1998.

Financial

1. Gross $500,000 by 1997, and $700,000 by 1998.
2. Net fifteen percent of gross in 1997 and 1998.
3. Hire an accountant by January 1, 1997.
4. Finance a new tour van by February 28, 1998.
5. Sell used rental equipment the same year purchased.

Management Information Systems

1. Purchase a new color scanner by January 1, 1997.
2. Acquire training and equipment necessary to produce in-house color brochures and catalogues by January 31, 1997 (everything except final print).
3. Purchase a copy machine for office by January 1, 1997.
4. Train full-time employees on additional computer software.
5. Equip each guide, office, and shuttle driver, with a two-way radio, and each tour with a cellular phone by January 1, 1997.

Human Resources

1. Certify each new tour leader and re-certify continuing leaders by December 31, 1997, 1998, and 1999.
2. Make and fill a full-time advertising and marketing position by January 1, 1999.
3. Hire a bike tour guide who knows auto mechanics by January 1, 1999.
4. Have a three-year average employee retention rate by December 31, 1998.
5. Construct a student internship program with local colleges by November 30, 1997.

Administrative Operations

1. Offer three additional adventure touring locations in the United States by July 31, 1997, 1998, 1999.
2. Take complete inventory every six months in 1997, 1998, 1999.
3. Review objectives and create new short-, mid-, and long-term objectives by December 31, 1997.
4. Organize a community natural resource conservation event by July 1, 1997, 1998, 1999.
5. Offer four hiking tours, rafting, and mountain climbing tours in the 1997 fall catalogue.

MARKETING

Industry History

The adventure sports and travel industry is considerably young. Not more than twenty years ago, the industry was almost unheard of. Statistics show a steady rise in adventure sport sales and tours. In 1970, the industry grossed about five million dollars. In 1983, it grossed more than five hundred million dollars. More people are becoming health conscious and looking for ways to incorporate fitness into their vacation. The maturity stage for this industry is not for another 20 years. With the right marketing decisions and proper timing, RAD-Venture will gain a comfortable portion of the market share as the adventure sports and travel segment grows into one of the larger vacation industries.

Target Market

RAD-Venture's target market is characteristically made up of recreational travelers with active lifestyles. This eliminates the greater portion of the travel industry, allowing RAD-Venture to focus more closely on its market demographics.

- Slightly more men than women participate in active travel/recreation.
- Most participants are professionals (one in three).
- Most participants are under the age of 50 (usually between 23-50), and there is an increasing number of children becoming involved--especially in mountain biking and indoor climbing.
- Half of tour participants are married and the other half are single traveling alone.
- Most mountain tour participants travel to place they have never been and are from lower elevation states and/or different geographic regions ie. Chicago, New York and Canada.
- Most participants have an "above average" income level.
- Most active travel participants read special interest publications such as: *Outdoors, Mountain Climbing,* and *Terrain.* Roughly half of participants are repeat customers and the other half are newcomers who rely primarily on word of mouth and magazine advertisements.

Societal and Demographic Forces

External Forces

Cedar City is one of the fastest growing areas in Utah due to its mild climate, quality of life, low crime, low cost of living, competitive construction rates, and recreation amenities. Cedar City has no current growth limits and the water tables are capable of supporting up to 200,000 residents.

The population is more representative of outdoor activity than the Las Vegas population. The World Junior Games and the famous Cedar City Marathon are two of the larger annual events supported locally. Cedar City also has several organized private outdoor oriented clubs such as the "Backcountry Club." The population breakdown (excluding the 65+ group) is complementary to RAD-Venture's market demographics.

Population by age	
0-17	36.2%
18-24	10%
25-44	22.5%
45-64	15%
65+	16.2%

Population

1990	48,560
1993	59,080
1994	63,400
1995	65,000
2000	81,840 (est.)
Male	49.1%
Female	50.9%

Source: Utah Office of Planning and Budgets

Population Highlights

Median age	33
Birth rate (Utah) ranked second highest in U.S.	21.1 per 1000
Death rate (Utah) ranked second lowest in U.S.	5.6 per 1000
Household Size	3.1/household

Source: Utah Department of Employment Security

Economic Forces

Travel and tourism, the industry RAD-Venture is based on, is Utah's third largest industry behind real estate and construction (number one), and retail (number two). The Utah Travel Council encourages business and private input on the development of tourism through public meetings statewide. Collin Wells, Director of the Utah Travel Bureau said, "For the $3.27 billion industry to succeed, we must have the recommendations and support of the private and public sectors to do the best job we can to not only attract visitors, but further utilize the tourism industry as an economic development resource." It is in RAD-Venture's best interest as well, to actively participate in community and government affairs.

Cedar City currently attracts more than two million international visitors annually. Cedar City is so confident in its economic strength and potential, it is building a large-scale convention center, park, and sizable hotel in 1996. This will attract more of the "professional" status people that figure so prominently in RAD-Venture's market profile.

Utah, especially Southern Utah's, economic strength is stable and growing. During the past decade, Utah's economy ranked among the highest in the nation with a 5.3 percent increase in new jobs while maintaining one of the lowest unemployment rates.

Increase of New Jobs
(1988-1992)

Cedar County	161%
Utah	37%

Source: Utah Department of Employment Security

Unemployment Rate August 1995

Cedar County	3.2%
Utah	3.4%
USA	6.8%

Source: Utah Department of Employment Security

Legal and Political Forces

Cedar City is receptive to tourism/recreation industries. A division of the city, Recreational Services, is responsible for providing information and organized leisure activities through local recreation businesses and nonprofit organizations. They currently distribute flyers about hikes, camps, youth activities, fun runs, and marathons. The City Parks Division is planning to expand the river biking/jogging path northeast, southwest along the river, and more extensively through the city to connect a network of city parks.

Other relevant government publics are the federal land managers; Bureaus of Land Management, U.S. Forest Service agencies, National Park Systems, and state lands. RAD-Venture has existing positive working relationships with these agencies through its mountain bike tour history.

RAD-Venture is government approved for tours in, around, or through:

- Sun National Park NPS
- Water Ridge Canyon National Park NPS
- Dying Tree National Park NPS
- Cactus Land National Park NPS
- Red Stone Recreational Area NPS
- Ledge National Park NPS
- Jones Canyon National Recreation Area BLM
- Sierra Canyon National Conservation Area BLM
- Almond National Forest USFS
- Fossil National Forest USFS

Competitive Forces

The Outdoor RAD-Venture Center as a whole will have no direct competitors, in that its combination of adventure services and sales is unique to the area. There will, however, be direct competition with certain departments within the center.

The rock climbing gym will have no direct local competitors, because the closest rock climbing gyms are more than 120 and 240 miles away, respectively.

The adventure equipment rentals and tours will have some competition (only in the sports of mountain biking or rock climbing) with a few local stores: Bailey's Cycles, Mountain Biking, Inc. and the Cycling Cove. We feel that a recreational adventure center will provide the necessary edge on equipment rental and tour competition.

The following stores constitute local competition with biking, climbing, hiking, and/or camping sales within the adventure center: Bailey's Cycles, Mountain Biking, Inc., Cycling Cove, Mountain Outfitters, and Trails End. RAD-Venture has secured the accounts of two lines of bicycles which are flashy, high quality, and relatively low priced. To further distinguish our store from competitors, bicycles and other equipment will be on display with "testers" for rent with a philosophy of "Try it on for size, Rent before you buy."

The following companies, none of which are local, are in direct competition with RAD-Venture's multi-day mountain bike tours: Southwest Tours, Trail Dust, Living Bike Tours, and Natures Best. Since most western bicycle tour companies offer tours in the same areas, competition is strong. For example, the off-road Western Tour of Nevada, which in the last two years was created and toured almost exclusively by RAD-Venture will next season be offered by four additional national tour companies. Most tour companies rely on a combination of brochure mailers and travel listings in national special interest publications to promote their tours. RAD-Venture is listed in eight national magazines and has produced a highly competitive color brochure for distribution. RAD-Venture has also composed a promotional tour video to show at the Outdoor RAD-Venture Center, at conventions, and to distribute to interested parties.

The two largest concerns with competitive forces are sales (especially of bicycles) and multi-day tours. The local market is already saturated with bike stores and camp/hike/climb stores. The market is wide open, however for rentals, tours and indoor climbing. The Center is designed to benefit from, but not depend on, retail sales. A potential multi-day tour guest has many outfitters to choose from when planning a mountain bike vacation. An adventure center from which multi-day tours may begin or end, will provide a more established company image for vacationers to consider when choosing. By offering a center with multiple, complementary adventures, RAD-Venture intends to attract people inside, and once inside, present a fun, inviting "hangout" atmosphere to create loyalty, increased interest, and repeat business.

MARKETING MIX AND SHARE

Product

RAD-Venture, through its new Center, will offer many products and services for the outdoor enthusiast.

RAD-Venture will sell and rent biking, hiking, camping, and climbing essentials and gear. National brand products will be used for their quality and name recognition. RAD-Venture will also sell its own line of products; humorous, creative activewear designed exclusively by RAD-Venture staff.

Pricing Strategy

The adventure sports industry has extreme pricing methods. Tour companies tend to offer either very expensive or very inexpensive tours. Middle range prices are rare. Many inexpensive tours follow the same routes as the expensive tours, but without the support or amenities. RAD-Venture tours currently fall into the expensive category, with full support and many amenities. With the addition of an outdoor adventure center offering shuttles, maps, sales, and rental equipment separately, our market share will broaden to include participants of less expensive, self-supported adventures as well.

As business increases, RAD-Venture can offer new products and services with new prices. A variety of high, medium and low priced, self to full-supported adventures will allow changing prices without changing guest perception. To start:

- The climbing gym will be medium-low priced to encourage frequent attendance.
- The rentals and local tours will be average priced for Cedar City, but lower than Las Vegas rentals and tours, due to the nature of tourist/local demographics.
- The bicycles and other adventure equipment will be high quality, medium to high priced, with low priced sales available on used equipment.

Promotion

Besides the necessary high cost special interest publication travel listing, RAD-Venture will institute several low cost ideas for the promotion of the Outdoor RAD-Venture Center:

- Offer referral commission to the two service stations in Cedar City who advertise that they are the "recreation information" headquarters for the area.
- Offer rock climbing clinics for school children, and help start climbing clubs in the local school system.
- Offer free lifetime memberships to college students in return for helping build the climbing walls, with the double intention they'll talk about it on campus and return with paying friends.
- Distribute fliers to local hotel front desks (with commission notes), recreation centers, Chambers of Commerce, and local colleges.
- Add an insert to the mountain bike tour brochure highlighting the new services, products, and adventure center.
- Set up an lemonade stand next to local jogging and bike trails on weekends.
- Plans also include concentrated advertising in Northern Utah during the winter months as an escape from the snow and cold.

Name

RAD-Venture (DBA)

Location

Mailing: Post Office Box 58005, Reno, Nevada

Outdoor Adventure Center: Location pending Cedar City, Utah

Personnel

Owners - Grant and Heidi Osborn
Rental/Tour Manager (Winter) - Jackson Edwards
Multi-day Tour Guide (Summer) - Jackson Edwards
Rock Gym Manager/Climbing Trainer & Guide - Brent Salome
Adventure Equipment Sales/Rental Tours - TBA
Part-Time Tour Guide - John Raymond
Part-Time Help for Tours - Jonesy
Summer Tour Guide - TBA
Part-Time Help for Center - TBA

RAD-Venture is a sole proprietorship in Grant Osborn's name. It is licensed for business throughout the city of Reno, Nevada.

- RAD-Venture does not have any cases pending against it.

- RAD-Venture assets are insured by Coleman Insurance Co.
- RAD-Venture vehicles are insured by Living Well Insurance Co.
- RAD-Venture liability is insured by Coastal Community.

RAD-Venture has been featured in the following national publications: *Wardzen World News, Nouveau Fashion,* and *Cycle Today.* The following publications list RAD-Venture on a monthly basis in their travel directories; *Terrain, Cycle Tours, Guide, Western Trails, Airborne, Utah Magazine, Outdoors, Sports Journey,* and *Area Events and Attractions.* RAD-Venture is listed bi-annually in the *Official Las Vegas Guidebook.*

Attorney: Alex Carter
Henderson, Nevada

Accountant: Johnston Accounts
Las Vegas, Nevada

Key Accounts: Jacobs
                     Desert Lands
                     American Dreams
                     Paradise Resorts, Inc.

Bike Equipment/Supplies:

Western
(bike parts and equipment)

Hold On
(bike holders for vehicles)

Mountain Treads (East)
(mountain bike sales and rentals)

COMPANY PARAMETERS

Legal Structure

Pending Cases

Insurance

Publications

Professional Representatives, Agents, and Suppliers

Mountain Treads (West)
Supplier of mountain and cross bikes and parts)

Jameson Inc.
(bike parts and equipment)

Speed Cycles
(mountain bike sales and rentals)

Shock Supply
(shocks for bikes)

Rock Climbing Equipment:

Mount Climb
(supplier of complete climbing equipment)

Rock Pit

Horizon
(supplier of complete climbing equipment)

Xay's Climbing Supply
(supplier of complete climbing equipment)

Outdoor Equipment/Supplies/Clothing:

Backcountry Gear
(bike gear and related products)

Mountain Stream
(camping chairs)

Johnson Printing
(RAD-Venture shirts and hats)

Comfies
(Clothing, hats, accessories)

Energy Food
(energy food)

Camping To Go
(bike packs and day packs)

Hannah's
(sleeping bags)

Biker Duds
(biker clothing)

Green's Packs
(mountaineering and bike packs)

Aqua Pro
(filtered water bottles)

MANAGEMENT

Team Synergy

Team synergy is probably the most important aspect of holding any company together--especially ours. If each employee was asked to explain his or her behavior and role in the company, we would still not understand RAD-Venture as a whole. The relationships between our team members bear a "bonding" strength, that transpires as a result of pride in a small growing company, responsibility for guests' safety and satisfaction, the encouragement of new ideas, and the love of the work. Customers can sense and find security in this cohesion.

In the event of absence of one or both of the owners, a full-time employee (back-up manager) will be previously trained to run all aspects of the business. Ownership will be willed to a third party in the immediate family. General Managership will be willed to the back-up manager. To secure the business against natural disaster, fire, or other unforeseen destruction of property, RAD-Venture will be fully insured for reimbursement of value and continuation of business. All essential documents and computer programs and records (downloaded monthly) will be stored in a fire-proof safe.

Crisis Management Plan

RAD-Venture is beginning its fourth year of operation in Nevada, and its third year of backcountry tours in Southern Utah. The timing of the Outdoor RAD-Venture Center is significant both internally and externally to the company's progression.

PROJECT TIMING

Internally, RAD-Venture has established the general market peak of bicycle tours and rentals in its base city. The Nevada market contains a promising steady future, but a substantial increase in business is not likely. Entering its fourth year of exclusive service to Nevada, RAD-Venture has nursed the bicycle rental/tour product through inception, growth, and as it begins to level out, the early stages of maturity. To ultimately ensure growth with the industry, and avoid dependency on the product, an adventure tour business must always be open to new products and destinations.

Externally, immediate action on an Outdoor RAD-Venture Center is important because the window of opportunity is open for a short time only. The demand (for a rock climbing gym and/or adventure tour service) has been established in many communities, and the supply has not yet arrived in Southern Utah. If RAD-Venture does not act soon, it is likely someone else will.

RAD-Ventures' mission is to be a leader in the adventure sports and travel industry, not a follower. The following is a chronological list of achievements needed for the Outdoor RAD-Venture Center to open in the next few months.

1. Secure a small business loan for the Center.
2. Build a six thousand sq. ft. building (at least half of it 30 feet tall).
3. Design interior of building to code and build to facilitate: 1) a rock climbing gym, 2) a store for outdoor recreation rentals, tours, and sales, and 3) tour headquarters.
4. Stock inventory.
5. Relocate main offices from Reno, Nevada to Cedar City, Utah.
6. Hire full-time Tour Manager, and part-time tour guide.
7. Hire a full-time rock climbing gym manager, and two part-time employees/guides.
8. Institute a grand opening celebration.

FINANCIALS

Working Capital

Description	Price
Training	$1,000
Prepaid Mortgage & Repayment of Debt	$18,000
Adm. Costs	$2,000
Grand Opening	$5,000
Advertising/Other	$4,000
Working Capital Opening Day	$30,000
Total	**$60,000**

Balance Sheet
November 20, 1995

Assets		Liabilities and Owners Equity	
Cash	$6,426		
Temporary Cash Investments	$0	**Liabilities:**	
Marketable Securities	$0	Notes Payable	$8,600
Accounts Receivable	$1,116	Accounts Payable	$0
Less: Doubtful Accounts	$0	Federal Tax	$1,025
Inventories	$425	Deffered Income Tax	$2,325
Prepaid Insurance	$2,687	Advanced Deposits	$0
Prepaid Advertising	$3,965	Long Term Lilbilities	$13,179
Bicycle Tour Equipment	$9,927		
Trucks/Vans/Trailer	$53,000	Total Liabilities:	$25,129
Mountain Bikes	$17,650	Less: Depreciation	-$1,800
Furnishings/Office Equip.	$5,775	Owners Equity:	
		Osborn, Grant & Heidi	$81,317

Intangible Assets:	
Trademarks	$75
Permits/Licenses	$7,200
Goodwill	$0
Other Assets	$0
Total Assets:	**$106,446**

Total Liabilities & Owners$106,446

Inventories:		Hip Packs	300	Bike Rack	150	**Balance Sheet**
T-Shirts	240	Gloves	200	Tables	100	**Breakdown**
Bike Parts	85	Helmets	460	Cabinets	50	
Prepaid Insurance:		Trainers	160	Work Benc	75	
4x4 van	1250	Gear Bags	85	Vaccum	25	
4x4 truck	300	Bottles	50	Misc.	150	
Lexmark van	120	Locks	215			
Janes van	150	Gel Seats	75			
Theft/Fire	572	Radios	2000			
Liability	295	Cell Phones	400			
Prepaid Advertising:		Water Coolers	180			
Outside	1140	Blue Jugs	90			
MBA	50	Car Racks	100			
MB	85	Stands	42			
MJ	175	Tools	200			
Bicycling	202	1st Aid	200			
Bike	88	Dinner Wear	150			
NV. Mag.	225	Camping Cookers	75			
Brochures	2000					
Bicycle Tour Equipment:		Simmons 4x4 Van	29065			
CamCorder	600	Crest 4x4 Truck	12035			
Camera (still)	1375	Janes Van	5300			
Leader Paks	400	Lexmark Van	3000			
Other	100	Trailer	3600			
Pots/Pans	400					
Cookers	130	30 Bikes	17650			
Crates	240					
Sleep Bags	100	Computers	2000			
Pillows	75	Printer	1000			
Pads	75	Fax	250			
Tents	400	Software	1000			
Dutch Ovens	240	Welder	275			
Utensils	100	Compressor	250			
Pumps	120	Power Tools	250			
Seat Kits	140	Bike Hangers	200			

1996 Cash Flow Forecast and Breakeven Point

	Jan	Feb	Mar	Apr	May	Jun	Jul	Aug
Cash								
Cash in Bank	486000	109549	103549	30000	29648	35441	56464	69742
Cash in Investments				0	0	0	0	0
Total Cash	**486000**	**109549**	**103549**	**30000**	**29648**	**35441**	**56464**	**69742**
Income								
Cash Sales:								
Local Rentals & Tours				1200	1100	700	300	500
Multiday Tours				4000	9000	30000	24000	37000
Adventure Shop Sales				10000	12100	10900	9800	8700
Climb Gym Dues/Rentals				8400	9200	10200	10200	11200
Investment Income								
Loans								
Rentals/Tour Net Income				3000	2500	1500	800	200
Ski Shuttles Net Income				0	0	0	0	0
Total Income	0	0	0	26600	33900	53300	45100	57600
Total Cash Income	486000	109549	103549	56600	63548	88741	101564	127342
Expenses								
Operating Expenses	3000	3000	3000	15457	14757	14957	15457	14957
Cost of Goods Sold				8495	10350	14320	13365	16845
Repayment of Debt	3000	3000	3000	3000	3000	3000	3000	3000
Capital Investment/Building	300000	0	0					
Construction/Climbing Walls	66451	0	0					
Inventory Purchases & Investment	0	0	59549					
Grand Opening	4000	0	8000					
Total Expenses	**376451**	**6000**	**73549**	**26952**	**28107**	**32277**	**31822**	**34802**
Cash Flow (Month)	**-376451**	**-6000**	**-73549**	**-352**	**5793**	**21023**	**13278**	**22798**
Cash Position	**109549**	**103549**	**30000**	**29648**	**35441**	**56464**	**69742**	**92540**

Sept	Oct	Nov	Dec	Jan	Feb	Mar	Totals
92540	101308	108066	110879	108537	99745	91293	
0	0	0	0	0	0	0	
92540	**101308**	**108066**	**110879**	**108537**	**99745**	**91293**	
1600	2400	1700	300	480	500	1800	12580
15000	10500	1500	400	0	800	6500	138700
12900	13800	13800	17500	7500	9250	12100	138350
8060	7560	11200	7260	2830	6260	8200	100570
1200	2200	1200	0	0	1100	3200	16900
0	0	0	350	2000	1100	400	3850
38760	36460	29400	25810	12810	19010	32200	410950
131300	137768	137466	136689	121347	118755	123493	
14757	14557	14457	13957	14157	18457	13957	188884
12235	12145	9130	11195	4445	6005	12345	130875
3000	3000	3000	3000	3000	3000	3000	45000
							300000
							66451
							59549
							12000
29992	**29702**	**26587**	**28152**	**21602**	**27462**	**29302**	
8768	**6758**	**2813**	**-2342**	**-8792**	**-8452**	**2898**	**64191**
101308	**108066**	**110879**	**108537**	**99745**	**91293**	**94191**	

Outdoor Adventures - Cedar City - 1996 Projected Sales Forecast

	April	May	June	July	Aug.	Sept.
Local Rentals/Tours						
Tours	600	800	500	200	400	1000
Rentals	600	300	200	100	100	600
Total Local Rentals/Tours	**1200**	**1100**	**700**	**300**	**500**	**1600**
Multiday Tours						
Sun						
Water Ridge			4000	5000	13000 8000	
Dying Tree				2000		
Cactus Land					3000	
Jones to Ledge			7000	6000	6000	7000
Jones to Sierra	4000	6000				
Sierra						
Red Stone		3000				
Beginner Almond			3000			
Fossil Finder			4000	6000	4000	
Sun, Fossil and Ledge						
Sierra Rad			6000			
Waterways					6000	
Dying Tree & Cactus						
Custom Tours			6000	5000	5000	
Other						
Total Multi-Day Tours	4000	9000	30000	24000	37000	15000
Adventure Shop Sales						
RAD-Venture Clothing	1000	1000	1000	1000	900	1000
Other Clothing	1000	1100	900	800	800	900
Equip. and Components	5000	5000	4000	3000	3000	5000
Bike Sales	3000	5000	5000	5000	4000	6000
Total Shop Sales	**10000**	**12100**	**10900**	**9800**	**8700**	**12900**
Climb Gym Dues/Rentals						
Day Pass	3200	3500	3500	3500	3500	2520
Memberships	700	700	700	700	700	540
Membership Initiations	300	400	300	230	230	200
Specials	700	600	1700	1770	2770	1800
Equipment	3500	4000	4000	4000	4000	3000
Total Gym Dues/Rentals	**8400**	**9200**	**10200**	**10200**	**11200**	**8060**
1996 Projected Sales Recap						
Local Rentals/Tours	1200	1100	700	300	500	1600
Multiday Tours	4000	9000	30000	24000	37000	15000
Adventure Shop	10000	12100	10900	9800	8700	12900
Climb Gym Dues/Rentals	8400	9200	10200	10200	11200	8060
Total 1996 Projected Sale	**23600**	**31400**	**51800**	**44300**	**57400**	**37560**
1996 Projected Expenses						
Advertising	2000	2000	2000	2000	2000	2000
Vehicle Repair/Maintenance	800	800	800	800	800	800
Vehicle Loan Payments	350	350	350	350	350	350
Vehicle Insurance	350	350	350	350	350	350
Liability Insurance Bike	50	50	50	50	50	50
Liability Insurance Gym	100	100	100	100	100	100
Theft Insurance	125	125	125	125	125	125
Interest-Long Term	0	0	0	0	0	0

Oct.	Nov.	Dec.	Jan.	Feb.	Mar.	Totals
1400	1100	200	180	200	1000	7580
1000	600	100	300	300	800	5000
2400	**1700**	**300**	**480**	**500**	**1800**	**12580**
1000	1500	400		800	2000	5700
30000						
						2000
						3000
						26000
6000						16000
					4500	4500
3500						6500
						3000
						14000
						6000
						6000
						16000
10500	1500	400		800	6500	138700
1200	1100	1300	700	850	900	11950
1100	1200	1200	800	900	1200	11900
5000	5000	6000	3500	4500	5000	54000
6500	6500	9000	2500	3000	5000	60500
13800	**13800**	**17500**	**7500**	**9250**	**12100**	**138350**
2520	3500	2520	1160	2520	3200	35240
540	700	540	120	540	700	7280
200	300	300	200	400	200	3260
1300	2700	1200	0	100	600	15240
3000	4000	2700	1350	2700	3500	39750
7560	**11200**	**7260**	**2830**	**6260**	**8200**	**100570**
2400	1700	300	480	500	1800	12580
10500	1500	400	0	800	6500	138700
13800	13800	17500	7500	9250	12100	138350
7560	11200	7260	2830	6260	8200	100570
34260	**28200**	**25460**	**10810**	**16810**	**28600**	**390200**
2000	2000	2000	2000	2000	2000	24000
800	800	800	800	800	800	9600
350	350	350	350	350	350	4200
350	350	350	350	350	350	4200
50	50	50	50	50	50	600
100	100	100	100	100	100	1200
125	125	125	125	125	125	1500
0	0	0	0	0	0	0

Outdoor Adventures - Cedar City - 1996 Projected Sales Forecast continued

	April	May	June	July	Aug.	Sept.
Interest-Short Term	0	0	0	0	0	0
Office Supplies	350	350	350	350	350	350
Mortgage Payment	3000	3000	3000	3000	3000	3000
Payroll-1	1000	1000	1000	1000	1000	1000
Payroll-2	1000	1000	1000	1000	1000	1000
Payroll-3	1000	1000	1000	1000	1000	1000
Payroll-4	1000	1000	1000	1000	1000	1000
Payroll-5	500	500	500	500	500	500
1099 Labor	1000	800	1000	1000	1000	800
Payroll Tax (18%)	360	360	360	360	360	360
Accountant	80	80	80	80	80	80
State Taxes	0	0	0	0	0	0
Licenses And Dues	125	125	125	125	125	125
Bank Charges	700	700	700	700	700	700
Trade Shows	0	0	0	0	0	0
Phones (800 #, Cell, Etc.)	367	367	367	367	367	367
Utilities	200	200	200	200	200	200
Research and Tour Development	500	0	0	500	0	0
Rental Bikes	0	0	0	0	0	0
Tour Equipment	500	500	500	500	500	500
Total Expenses	**15457**	**14757**	**14957**	**15457**	**14957**	**14757**
1996 Cost of Goods Sold						
Local Rentals/Tours-COS						
Cedar City Tours	120	100	120	40	70	60
Cedar City Rentals	0	0	0	0	0	0
Total Local Rental/Tours	120	100	120	40	70	60
Multiday Tours-COS						
Sun						
Water Ridge			1500	1800	3500	2000
Dying Tree				800		
Cactus Land					1100	
Jones to Ledge			2000	2000	2000	2000
Sierra	2000	2000				
Red Stone						
Beginner Almond		800				
Fossil Finder			800			
Sun, Fossil & Ledge			800	1200	800	
Sierra & Sun						
Sierra Rad			2500			
Waterways					2200	
Dying Trees & Cactus						
Custom Tours			1800	1500	1500	
Other	2000	2800	9400	7300	11100	4000
Total Multi-Day Tours-COS	**2000**	**2800**	**9400**	**7300**	**11100**	**4000**
Adventure Shop Sales-COS						

Oct.	Nov.	Dec.	Jan.	Feb.	Mar.	Totals
0	0	0	0	0	0	0
350	350	350	350	350	350	4200
3000	3000	3000	3000	3000	3000	36000
1000	1000	1000	1000	1000	1000	12000
1000	1000	1000	1000	1000	1000	12000
1000	1000	1000	1000	1000	1000	12000
1000	1000	1000	1000	1000	1000	12000
500	500	500	500	500	500	6000
600	0	0	0	0	0	6200
360	360	360	360	360	360	4320
80	80	80	80	80	80	960
0	0	0	0	0	0	0
125	125	125	125	125	125	1500
700	700	700	700	700	700	8400
0	0	0	0	4000	0	4000
367	367	367	367	367	367	4404
200	200	200	200	200	200	2400
0	500	0	200	500	0	2200
0	0	0	0	0	0	0
500	500	500	500	500	500	6000
14557	**14457**	**13957**	**14157**	**18457**	**13957**	**179884**
120	80	70	20	80	120	1000
0	0	0	0	0	0	0
120	80	70	20	80	120	1000
250	300	150	0	250	400	1350
						8800
						800
						1100
						8000
2000						6000
					4500	4500
1200						2000
						800
						2800
						2500
						2200
						4800
3450	300	150	0	250	4900	45650
3450	**300**	**150**	**0**	**250**	**4900**	**45650**

Outdoor Adventures - Cedar City - 1996 Projected Sales Forecast continued

	April	May	June	July	Aug.	Sept.
RAD-Venture Clothing	600	600	600	600	550	600
Other Clothing	650	700	550	475	475	500
Equip. and Components	3000	3000	500	1800	1800	3000
Bike Sales	2000	3000	3000	3000	2700	4000
Total Shop Sales-COS	**6250**	**7300**	**4650**	**5875**	**5525**	**8100**
Climb Gym Dues/Rentals-COS						
Day Pass	0	0	0	0	0	0
Memberships	0	0	0	0	0	0
Specials	0	0	0	0	0	0
Equipment Rentals	125	150	150	150	150	75
Total Gym Dues/Rentals-CO	**125**	**150**	**150**	**150**	**150**	**75**
1996 Cost of Goods Sold Recap						
Local Rentals/Tours	120	100	120	40	70	60
Multiday Tours	2000	2800	9400	7300	11100	4000
Adventure Shop	6250	7300	4650	5875	5525	8100
Climb Gym Dues/Rentals	125	150	150	150	150	75
Total 1996 Cost of Goods	**8495**	**10350**	**14320**	**13365**	**16845**	**12235**
Repayment of Debt (Interest)	**3000**	**3000**	**3000**	**3000**	**3000**	**3000**
Capital Expenditures	Used within repayment of debt during construction					
Expense Recap						
Total Expenses	**15457**	**14757**	**14957**	**15457**	**14957**	**14757**
Total Cost of Goods Sold	**8495**	**10350**	**14320**	**13365**	**16845**	**12235**
Repayment of Debt	**3000**	**3000**	**3000**	**3000**	**3000**	**3000**
Total Capital Expenditure	**26952**	**28107**	**32277**	**31822**	**34802**	**29992**

Assumptions to the Per Forma

In the Projected Sales Forecast, the extreme fluctuations in January and February's net income are a result of less mountain bike activity in cold weather and preparation costs for the upcoming multiday tour season.

In the Cash Flow Forecast and Break-even Point, the negative numbers in the first three months are due to building and start-up costs.

Oct.	Nov.	Dec.	Jan.	Feb.	Mar.	Totals
700	650	700	375	450	500	6925
600	750	750	475	500	700	7125
3000	3000	3500	2000	2600	3000	30200
4200	4200	6000	1500	2000	3000	38600
8500	**8600**	**10950**	**4350**	**5550**	**7200**	**82850**
0	0	0	0	0	0	0
0	0	0	0	0	0	0
0	0	0	0	0	0	0
75	150	25	75	125	125	1375
75	**150**	**25**	**75**	**125**	**125**	**1375**
120	80	70	20	80	120	1000
3450	300	150	0	250	4900	45650
8500	8600	10950	4350	5550	7200	82850
75	150	25	75	125	125	1375
12145	**9130**	**11195**	**4445**	**6005**	**12345**	**130875**
3000	**3000**	**3000**	**3000**	**3000**	**3000**	**36000**
14557	**14457**	**13957**	**14157**	**18457**	**13957**	**179884**
12145	**9130**	**11195**	**4445**	**6005**	**12345**	**130875**
3000	**3000**	**3000**	**3000**	**3000**	**3000**	**36000**
29702	**26587**	**28152**	**21602**	**27462**	**29302**	**346759**

Income History
Tour and Rental Gross Receipts

	1992	1993	1994	1995
Jan	$0.00	$1,012.25	$3,297.38	$1,821.79
Feb	$0.00	$2,331.78	$7,284.61	$7,493.36
Mar	$0.00	$3,890.00	$8,193.09	$13,540.48
April	$1,110.00	$2,875.00	$9,689.35	$1,431.51
May	$650.00	$4,073.65	$9,969.40	$13,102.32
June	$1,158.82	$3,682.00	$5,851.65	$17,085.79
July	$1,256.81	$2,666.67	$5,655.70	$25,125.95
Aug	$1,610.05	$2,833.02	$10,124.60	$21,976.92
Sept	$2,670.00	$5,158.82	$12,330.08	$12,175.79
Oct	$2,385.50	$3,506.90	$13,679.97	$7,871.00
Nov	$3,004.80	$4,186.15	$4,875.28	
Dec	$1,376.15	$2,515.61	$1,479.97	
Year-End Gross Totals	**$19,587.13**	**$38,731.85**	**$88,931.06**	**$134,512.91**
(Corresponding Net Totals)	**$(863.27)**	**$(3,403.50)**	**$4,758.55**	**$15,420.69**

Use of Funds Summary

Building and Land	$300,000
Climb Gym Construction	$66,530
Working Capital	$60,000
Inventories	$69,470
Total needed funds	**$496,000**

Building and Land Construction Cost

Building and Pro Shop Construction	$185,000
Land Cost	$115,000
Total	**$300,000**

Paint Distributor

BUSINESS PLAN

EARTHAM DISTRIBUTORS

21 N. Ridge Rd.
Broken Bow, NE 58112

Eartham Distributors' business epitomizes the concept of filling of an immediate need, arising out of ever changing government environmental regulations. Eartham meets this need by utilizing the latest technology available in the painting and coating industry. The market analysis provided in this plan, shows how a company with a basic product base, can infiltrate numerous market segments.

- GENERAL COMPANY DESCRIPTION

- PRODUCTS AND SERVICES

- EPA COMPLIANT PRODUCTS

- THE MARKETING PLAN

- THE MANAGEMENT PLAN

- THE OPERATING PLAN

- FINANCIAL PROJECTIONS & ASSUMPTIONS

- LEGAL PLAN

GENERAL COMPANY DESCRIPTION

Eartham Distributors, hereafter called "The Company", is a new company formed to exploit the burgeoning environmental market for safe paints, coatings and cleaners. The Company will exploit contracts and initial sales of its founders in environmental coatings representation and distribution. The new company will be incorporated in Maryland as a Sub-Chapter "S" corporation. The Company is a manufacturer's representative and distributor for Cather Inc., a Nebraska corporation, and the former employer of The Company's principals.

The Company's Cather products are high quality, environmentally safe coatings, and cleaners, and are targeted for Original Equipment Manufacturers (OEMs), industrial painting contractors and governmental use, intended to satisfy the needs of the legislatively driven coatings industry. The Company's products are recognized nationally by government and industry as technically leading environmental products. U.S. industry is being forced to comply to new regulations by EPA and state regulatory agencies for air quality and toxic substances that is creating an extremely heavy demand for environmentally safe products such as those offered by The Company.

The Company's principals are exercising the option in their OEM representation contract to open a wholesale distributorship for Cather products to service small manufacturers, service contractors and government purchasers, and can additionally sell franchises to authorized dealers. The Company will distribute in Delaware, Massachusetts, and Rhode Island. The Company intends to rapidly exercise options for Maryland and Virginia, already having significant pending sales in Virginia.

The Company's main objective in distribution is to provide a rapid and dependable response for small quantity custom colors for small manufacturers, state and municipal governments and industrial contractors. This service commands approximately 20% mark-up over prices charged OEM users of approximately 200 gallons or more. The distributor may also service large OEM's by providing buffer and emergency stock in conjunction with the manufacturer's contract.

The Company's current representative business will continue to service large OEM manufacturers for a commission of approximately 10%. These commissions will also be earned on distribution volume above the normal distributor markup providing significant growth capital for distributorship outlets.

The Company plans to immediately open a distributorship in Petersburg, Virginia, to supply the Northern Virginia areas. Expansion is then planned for two additional locations, one between New York and Rhode Island and the other in Dover, Delaware in the first year of operations. Additional locations in Rhode Island, Bethesda, Macon, Augusta, Roanoke and other cities are planned for the second year.

The Company's supplier, Cather Inc. has one of the most advanced lines of environmentally safe coatings available in the world today. These products are on the forefront of the legislatively driven environmental market, yet the technology has been field-proven in the aircraft industry for over eight years. The Company's products include not only traditional organic paint coatings, but also a new line of inorganic ceramic coatings that are unavailable from any other source. The Company is backed by Cather's technical staff that includes one of the top organic chemists in the nation and a former head of inorganic coating development for NASA.

The Company's products are manufactured by Cather Inc. in Kearney and Red Cloud, Nebraska. Cather Inc. has a production line rental agreement for emergency capacity with one of its stockholders that owns another private paint company located in Decatur, Illinois. Cather Inc. has a production capacity approximately 11,000 gallons a day, with a short term additional capacity of

8,000 gallons a day between the two facilities, well beyond Cather's near term projected capacity. Cather plans a production plant in The Company's territory next year to serve East Coast OEM's and distributors.

The Company plans to share facilities with Cather's warehouse and office in Petersburg, Virginia, and offer tinting and over-the-counter sales of paint and painting supplies to commercial painting contractors, as well. The Company will purchase a limited inventory of products for its exclusive use, but will have the advantage of being able to draw directly from Cather Regional stock to fill sales orders. In the initial stages, this will prevent The Company from having to purchase inventory far in advance of need, and limit the amount of up-front inventory investment.

The Company's start-up expenses require only the purchase of two computers, a manual tint machine, small stock of tint base and tints, a fax machine, a sales counter and some display shelving and pegboards. The ongoing expenses will include rent of less than $500 monthly, plus utilities, telephone, and travel expenses. A detailed operating budget can be found in the Financial Projections and Assumptions.

Mission

The Mission of The Company is the same as that of Cather Inc. -- to capture significant sales of the growing environmentally driven coatings market through sales of products developed and field-proven for over eight years in Cather Inc. aircraft coating and covering business. Also, Cather Inc. offers new products such as coating and cleaning products that will enable removal of hazardous solvents and materials from the workplace.

The Company and Cather Inc. are committed to leadership in environmentally friendly coatings and cleaners which offer end-users an alternative to dangerous products and procedures. Cather Inc.'s chemists seek to make available safe formulations at competitive prices to OEMs and other users. This will allow The Company to not only offer environmental compliance, but also significantly save the customer in production costs.

The Company's principals and other representatives of Cather have found that most potential customers desire a complete environmentally safe process for cleaning and preparation, priming and final coating. For this reason, over the past year, Cather Inc. has invested in further development and expansion of its product lines to provide a complete line of products, which are described in detail in the appendix. Besides offering Cather's proven line of coatings, The Company now has a line of wood, metal and masonry primers and sealers, high technology ceramic coatings, metal primers and also enjoys the rights to private labeling of a line of water-based non-solvent cleaners and paint removers. These products replace toxic and highly volatile solvents used in many industrial cleaning and degreasing products, such as tri-chloroethylene, acetone, MEK, toluene and xylene.

Awareness of EPA and state agency regulations for the use of paint, coatings and cleaners for industry has enabled The Company to capitalize on the expanding market for environmentally friendly products created by this changing regulatory climate. EPA and state regulatory departments have proven to be excellent sources of user and enforcement information. In conferences with the EPA, officials have stated that future regulations will be strengthened if coatings, such as those sold by The Company, are more widely used. State interest is so high that the Commonwealth of Virginia regulators have invited Cather Inc. and The Company to speak to the Commonwealth's users about converting as an example to Virginians. Also, the EPA has invited Cather Inc. and representatives of The Company to a recent aerospace conference in Raleigh, North Carolina and encouraged making attenders aware of safe products available.

Introduction of Shine 2000

In 1985, Cather Inc. developed its outstanding, high performance, environmentally safe line of polyurethane coatings, trademarked as Shine 2000. Since then, these technologically superior coatings have been field test-proven on aircraft around the world. Shine 2000 is now being introduced into broader aerospace, industrial, architectural and governmental markets.

In 1991, as new, and more stringent regulations focused attention on the environmental coatings market, Shine 2000 captured the interest of both government regulators and industry. Cather Inc. recognized that it had the benefit of having a field-proven environmentally friendly coating capable of meeting foreseeable EPA regulations.

Introduction of Ceramic coatings (Silicate Coatings)

Cather Inc. has made arrangements to acquire a significant advance in coatings technology through licensing. This technology will allow Cather Inc. and The Company the opportunity to offer customers the ability to spray a chemically bonded glass or ceramic on a surface at room temperature, using normal spray equipment. Such protection would be unparalleled in the industry.

The Company feels that this ceramic line of products offers more potential than any other product it currently offers. This new ceramic coating is environmentally friendly. New markets are expected in shipping, oil, steel, architectural products, marine, automotive and aerospace.

The Company will be at the forefront of Cather's expansion and is currently marketing products in Virginia, Maryland, Massachusetts and Rhode Island.

PRODUCTS AND SERVICES

The Company offers customers a full line of coatings for the high performance end of the coating market in both organic and inorganic coatings and cleaners. The Company brings to its customers market leadership in quality industrial and OEM oriented products which meet stringent environmental compliance standards and which provide substantial cost savings. The Company emphasizes and shows potential customers that they can remove all hazardous solvents from the work place while saving money. This insures customers of environmental compliance well below foreseeable Volatile Organic Compound (VOC) limits set by the federal government.

Since 1990, the overall responsibility for implementing the Clean Air Act Amendments of 1990 rests with the EPA, which began a major effort to control VOC emissions. Title I of the act involves control of VOCs from paint products and surface coatings operations through the development of Control Technique Guidelines (CTG's). The CTG's are used by individual states to set emission limits. Companies across the country are now experiencing regulatory impacts and are actively seeking new technology from companies which provide safe environmental solutions.

How Product Performance Saves Costs

Recognizing that government regulations will become even more stringent in the future, The Company's line of Cather non-toxic water-based high performance urethanes, enamels, ceramic coatings, epoxy coatings, and aqueous cleaners eliminates the need for highly volatile solvents such as acetone and lacquer thinners. By removing the solvents from the workplace, this could mean a disposal cost savings of $400 per drum in rags and paint filters and a savings of $500 to $900 per drum in solvent waste and paint waste. It also can eliminate expensive solvent reclamation processes.

Another example of substantial cost reduction is that while the products are competitively priced, the paints of Shine 2000, for example, obtain performance in 3/4 to 1 mil thickness compared to 2-4 mil thickness required by most paint systems currently in use. This high performance in thin coating also translates to an added benefit weight savings of 50% or greater for weight critical applications. The film that is deposited when a coating dries is the solids content of a paint. Thus the cost per gallon of solids is one of the two factors upon which cost can be realistically compared.

Most Shine 2000 products are in the forty percent (40%) range in solids and can provide full performance in .75 to 1.0 mil in thickness. The general rule of thumb for coverage of paints is that two coats at twenty-five percent (25%) solids covers 200 square feet at a total 2 mils thickness, consuming a gallon.

For this reason, a typical Shine 2000 product, being forty percent (40%) solids with 1 mil thickness, would give a coverage of 640 square feet from the same gallon can. Therefore, the Shine 2000 product can compete with lower performance products costing one third the amount.

In many cases, such as that of enamels and urethanes, the products are priced competitively. In such cases, the three times coverage capability of the Shine 2000 product results in a two hundred percent (200%) cost savings on the paint alone. When environmental and cleanup cost are included, production cost reduction is significant.

Solids Content of Shine 2000 Products

Alliphatic Urethane	39.2%
Acrylic Enamel	39.2%
2 Part Epoxy Primer	48.4%
1 Part Metal Primer	47.2%
Industrial Wood Primer	40.6%

Cather Inc. quotes solids content by volume. Their competitors typically quote solids by weight, which is misleading.

Most of the products offered for sale by The Company are single component products, thus any unused paint left in mixing cup or spray gun can be returned to its container, instead of being disposed of as is the case with the two component systems. However, the two part coating systems that are offered have been designed for a long shelf life to avoid applications problems.

By combining excellence in product development and production with a high sense of awareness of costs and safety, The Company makes the following available to its customers by offering Cather products:

Additional Cost Benefits

- Lower Workman's Compensation & Insurance Costs
- Reduced Worker Health Absenteeism
- Minimal Hazardous Waste Disposal Costs
- Increased Employee Productivity
- Compliance with Government Environmental Regulations
- Reduced Litigation

Users of Cather products have proven these situations reporting significant overall process savings due to the increase coverage with Cather coatings, decreased insurance costs and decreased clean-up and disposal costs. One window manufacturer in Nebraska, Fenetre has reportedly saved 200% on their coating costs alone, while further savings in fire related insurance, workman's compensation, and absenteeism are indirectly increasing the economics of their production of wood windows.

The Company's Cather product offerings have gained recognition and respect for product quality and integrity such as Shine 2000. Fly-Right Inc. has been authorized to use Shine 2000 on its airliners. The Cather wood primers have received top performance ratings in independent testing by Littlefond Laboratories. Cather products have passed industry and military tests. Locally, the Company has sold Cather coatings to the Menyunk Company, Petersburg, Virginia, for use on its popular line of Rensselaer commercial doors.

Cather products have been used on aircraft from commuter planes to jumbo jets for over eight years, proving the products excel in weather and pollution. In an example of direct testing competitors, Shine 2000 aliphatic polyurethane has out performed Elby's Blax in weatherometer tests (1000 hours 15% more glossy). For the past three years, one of the Company's principals, Eugene Won has been involved in much of the new applications work and new product applications testing, providing the needed knowledge to help customers solve problems.

Environmentally Compliant

The Company's offering of Cather products does not use the hazardous VOC's of current solvent paints and its level of safer VOC's is lower for each type of product.

Type of Product	Cather Products (VOC's)	Competitors' Products (VOC's)
Urethanes	2.8 lbs/gal	3.5 to 6 lbs/gal
Acrylics	1.8 lbs/gal	3.0 to 5 lbs/gal
Epoxy	6.5 to 1.2 lbs/gal	1.5 to 2 lbs/gal

EPA COMPLIANT PRODUCTS

The following is a listing of The Company's offering of Cather Inc. EPA compliant products.

Shine 2000

Shine 2000 is an ultra-high performance, water-based, aliphatic polyurethane for aircraft, railroad cars, exterior steel structures, marine and truck and automotive applications, that has been proven for over eight years in the field.

Faux Shine

Faux Shine is a new water based, environmentally safe paint, and is a high performance coating used for coating wood, metals and plastics, for both interior and exteriors surfaces. It is extremely cost effective and can compete favorably with quality outdoor paints.

Metal Primer and Concrete Sealer

Cather Inc. offers both a single and two-part epoxy primer and concrete sealer for general metal and plastic priming applications, and industrial and warehouse concrete floor sealing.

Acrylic One Part Primer

This primer was designed primarily for OEM applications for metals and plastics. Being single part, the primer can be used in complex paint distribution and circulating systems often found on high volume production lines, where two part epoxies would vastly complicate the spray application system. The product contains rust inhibitors and also provides a smooth finish for automotive, marine, and architectural applications.

Bois Tec

A water based epoxy wood primer specifically formulated for use on preservative treated woods, but which can be used on virtually any wood surface that requires a top quality cost effective primer.

Ceramic Primer/Coating

This is a room temperature cure ceramic coating that chemically bonds to the applied surface and provides a level of protection from corrosion heretofore only attainable by fired or plasma sprayed glasses and ceramics. The product can be used as a primer or coating. This product line is potentially Cather Inc.'s largest and was developed originally for space and aircraft applications. It is expected to replace conventional primers for bridges, dumpsters, storage tanks, automotive, marine, metal windows, electrical insulation and many other applications.

Sanding Sealers

These products are variations of clear Shine 2000 or acrylic enamel. When applied and allowed to dry, it fills the wood grain and is easily sanded.

Cardinal Series of Cleaners

These cleaners were formulated by Cather Inc. to solve coatings failure problems on plastics and composites caused by residual mold release and other contaminants resulting from manufacturing and handling.

Force Metal Cleaner

A new aluminum cleaner and preparation that provides a significant labor savings over traditional metal preparation processes, while retaining excellent corrosion and adhesion performance.

Shine Time Automotive/ Marine Parts Cleaner

This new water-based cleaner is designed to replace old solvent cleaners in "hot tanks" for degreasing and stripping metal parts while repairing or rebuilding automotive, marine and machinery.

431

This is an FDA approved cleaner series for general cleaning and degreasing of metals and plastics.

A new innovation for the marine field, the Shine 2000 Teak and Mahogany Finishing Kit provides the protection of high performance paints previously unavailable in non-toxic form to the yachting market.	**Lundi Wood Finishing Kit**
This kit is a combination of Cather Inc.'s aluminum cleaner and a selected color Shine 2000 to paint the aluminum spars and masts of boats.	**Lundi Aluminum Mast Preparation/ Paint Kit**
This kit offers the first long-lasting flexible finish for inflatable boats and jet skis.	**Lundi Inflatable Boat Paint Kit**
The Company is fortunate in that its offerings to customers are in a market that is currently driven to change by regulation. Regulations requiring lower VOC emissions, particularly for hazardous air products (HAPs) are continuing to spur interest, causing industries to watch the federal standards more closely.	**MARKETING PLAN AND STRATEGY**

The EPA has been preparing and releasing new Control Technology Guidelines (CTGs) to the states as regulatory level guidelines for over ten industries. These include aerospace, metal coatings, wood finishing and others. Industry is aware of the impending demise of normal solvents and is turning to non-hazardous, solvent-free and high-density coating formulations as alternatives to solvent-based systems.

Paints and coatings in the United States are a $12 billion per year industry with worldwide sales of $30.5 billion per year. The U.S. government buys directly some $1.2 billion in paint products each year, and is the largest user of polyurethanes, in the country. Paint is one of the most widely used products in the world. Almost every manufactured product is coated in some fashion to protect it against weather and the ravages of use.	**A $12 Billion U.S. Market**

The marine coating industry is large, with markets in commercial shipping, oil tankers, yachts and worldwide fishing fleets. Over 750 million gallons of marine coatings are sold in the U.S. alone. Additionally, the total worldwide market for ceramic primer coatings to repair blistered and delaminated yachts is estimated by Cather Inc. to be $55 billion alone. One of the Company's principals, Eugene Won, has been a major contributor to researching and establishing Cather's offerings for the marine market.

In the aircraft industry, the after-market marine industry and the general industrial sector, the requirements for high-performance coating products is measured in the millions of gallons per year. A spokesman for the Saxon Paint Company said that in 1992, the California marine market sales for linear polyurethane coatings was $5 million.

Cather Inc. has found that OEM and refurbishment customers have expressed considerable interest in its products because:

1. They know current approaches by other manufacturers do not offer long-term EPA compliance, and many are responding to reductions in VOC to avoid fees and fines.
2. They foresee the cost savings from greater coverage, less disposal cost and a better work environment.
3. They have the experienced staff and, in most cases, the equipment needed to apply Cather Inc.'s products, therefore, their up-front investment is minimal.

Large potential customers normally take three to eight months to begin to order. This is because they need to test the products, perform cost analysis, purchase or modify production line equipment and do a pilot run on their production line prior to full production. However, because of the inertia, they tend to enter into longer term contracts to optimize cost.

The Company is also working with small users (50-300 gallons per month) that are generally capable of faster reaction. The Northeastern, Mid-Atlantic and Midwestern regions of the U.S. have a high concentration of these smaller companies, where in many cases the owner is directly involved in the decision. The Company has over twenty-five small firms that are actively marketing or in the process of evaluating Cather Inc.'s products. A balance of small and large company users will enhance The Company's growth and smooth its cash flow needs. Cather Inc. has a nationwide computer marketing database of its sales leads and customers. The Company has a file in the national database, and can communicate with Cather on all sales matters through this excellent marketing program. A database sample was used to generate the financial projections contained herein.

A review of this database provides a current overview of The Company's many market contracts and progress through testing, sample orders and application. The financial section of this document provides a summary of the amount of business represented by current contacts. Most of the approximately 50 contacts represent part-time work of the principals while conducting their respective responsibilities with Cather Inc. These responsibilities involve penetrating large accounts, opening other distributorships and working with sales representatives in Massachusetts, Virginia, Maryland, Rhode Island and Delaware over the past 5 months. This is a good indication of the interest being generated in The Company's offerings by a wide variety of industries and sizes of manufacturers, while expending approximately one man month of work.

Current Customers of Cather

- Fenetre Windows
- City of Newport
- Newport Center
- Bridge Department
- Traffic Division
- Fly-Right Inc.
- Brother's Farm Equipment
- Lutz Furniture Refinishing (The Company's Client)
- MacNaughton Industries (Worldwide Marine Dealer)
- Menyunk Company (The Company's Client)
- Foster Sales

Key Markets

The Airline and Refurbishing Contractors Industries

1. Sholz Aviation has painted an L-1011 Jumbo Jet in the Mojave Desert.
2. Griffin Air has permission from the Fly-Right Inc. to paint their airliners with Shine 2000.
3. McKinley Airlines has 3,400 employees in their refurbishment center in San Jose and must environmentally conform to state regulations or close. They are being watched closely by state regulators. McKinley officials are monitoring Cather Inc.'s work with Griffin Air very closely.

The Petroleum Industry

Cather is in discussions with representatives, manufacturers and distributors in the petroleum industry in various parts of the world.

Additional Potential Customers

Additional large firms with which Cather Inc. is having discussions or are in the testing process include:

- Gabriel & Bryant Railroads (The Company's Client)
- Oakwood Power (The Company's Client)
- Eliot Windows
- Samson Institute (The Company's Client)

- Winch Windows
- Watzek Windows
- Heedman
- Vollum Built Buses
- BelMont
- Griffin Air
- McKinley Airlines
- Coleman Aircraft
- The Commonwealth of Florida
- The State of North Carolina
- Eastport Architectural Coatings
- Holgate Plastics, Inc.
- Division Laboratories
- Clinton Refinishers (The Company's Client)
- City of Oakwood
- Metro
- Utilities
- Powell Aerospace (The Company's Client)
- Hawthorne Trailers, Ga. (The Company's Client)

Markets for The Company's Cather products include:

- Railroads & Metro Cars
- Computer/Electrical Cabinets
- Ceramic Coating of Electrical Bus Bars
- Electrical and Computer Cabinets
- Subcontract Custom Paints Shops
- Trucks/School Buses
- Metal-Machinery Manufacturers
- Furniture and Metal Refinishers
- Architectural Products
- Trash Dumpsters
- Engine Blocks
- Bridges
- Swimming Pools
- Water Towers
- Waste Disposal
- Fertilizers Spray Sprinklers
- Windows/Metal Wood
- Concrete Sealing
- Automotive Refurbishment Coatings & Cleaners

Private Labeling

Private labeling for other companies is also a large, potential sales market for The Company. The Company is in discussion with potential private label customers in the automotive market. The Company expects to introduce a one-time permanent tire coating to these potential clients that would eliminate current cleaners and silicone coatings for tires and bumpers.

Outlook for the Remainder of the 90s

Shipments of paints and coatings will increase over the current $12 million market in response to growth in construction, motor vehicles and consumer hard goods. Pricing will remain highly competitive throughout the 90s. Demand for paints and coatings is strongly cyclical in nature and depends directly on activity in the housing/construction, automobile, aerospace and household appliance sectors. Higher than average growth is expected for the non-solvent delivery systems including powder coatings, high solids and radiation-cured formulas. Wall coverings for housing will gain ground at the expense of architectural coatings. Consolidation of the domestic industry will gradually turn to repositioning as firms mobilize resources to compete in the technology-driven markets. (Source: National Outlook on Industry --Industrial and Agricultural Chemicals).

Competition

There is a wide variety of hazardous solvent based protective coatings available in today's market. However, most will eventually disappear from the market as the EPA will phase them out over the next several years, primarily because of hazardous product content rather than VOC level. During this period of great transition to safer coatings, Shine 2000 products can establish and maintain a fair market share. The Company and Cather Inc. expect to establish a leadership role in the ceramics coating field because of the amount of technology Cather owns in this field.

Shine 2000 Coatings & Primers

The Company, believes it is a year or more ahead of its competition, such as Elby, with Shine 2000 urethane. The Company will be well protected against competition through Cather Inc.'s patent licenses and trade secrets for products. Cather Inc. is also completing development of a new state of the art urethane coating that will even outperform Shine 2000 Aliphatic Polyurethane. This new technology could place The Company as much as five years ahead of its competition selling Elby and Iddings-Larson. The reason for Cather projects lead is that the development cycle time is long in such large bureaucratic firms.

The competition for The Company's offerings in paint and primer products would come principally from major paint manufacturers such as Elby, U.S. Paint, Iddings-Larson, Re-Grape, and Oasis. Most of these large firms have focused their efforts not on water-based technology, but on lowering the VOC's emitted from use of their existing solvent based paints. They have not endeavored to change the VOC to environmentally friendlier substances as was done in Shine 2000. As a result, their water-based programs have taken a backseat. Therefore, even though these firms have well developed representation and distribution networks, they cannot compete in performance, environmental compliance and cost effectiveness.

Attempts by other manufacturers to develop water-based paints have not succeeded in producing a product that achieves the same high-level of performance as the highly-toxic, two-component, solvent-base, catalyzed systems. The Company's Shine 2000 product provides a coating surface that has the same general chemical makeup as these solvent paints and, hence, equal or superior performance to those of two component systems, without the toxicity. This technology allows Cather to maximize water in its formulations versus the amount of industrial cleaner, while dispersing higher levels of solids than competitors can achieve. Thus, The Company can offer the best currently available product.

Some of the manufacturers of toxic marine polyurethane's are beginning to advertise their coatings as five to ten year finishes on marine teak and mahogany. They have introduced their products in small containers for do-it-yourself boaters. The competitive finishes contain highly toxic isocyanates, that have generally only been sold to professionals with proper safety equipment. With increasing regulation and growing public awareness of toxic substances, The Company expects public use of these toxic products to be very short lived. Shine 2000 will give performance equal to or exceeding the toxic coatings, however, Shine 2000 is safe. It has the additional advantage of being flexible and is capable of expanding with the wood in the marine environment. Marine dealers and distributors have shown great interest in the non-toxic aspect of The Company's offerings, as many have had problems with personnel being sensitized to the toxins in the products they have used for many years.

Bois Tec was formulated in response to a need in the wood window and door industry for a product that would adhere well to woods freshly treated with the newer EPA approved preservatives. The manufacturers currently using it were unable to find an acceptable substitute on the market. In addition, the primer achieves excellent performance when used in conjunction with Shine 2000 or the new Acrylic Enamel Faux Shine. The Company expects to follow the manufacturer's lead in developing wood window and shutter manufacturers as clients.

For years industry has had available coatings that are made of organic resins, but contain ceramic particles. These coatings have many of the benefits of ceramics, but do not have the qualities of pure ceramic (silicate or glass) coatings that can be expensively sprayed with a plasma torch or created in a kiln, because the resin binder creates limitations inherent to organics in sealing, U.V. protection and water permeation.

Ceramic Coating

Later, ceramics coating were developed with heavy metals as filters. These coatings will suffer the fate of the heavy metals they contain with EPA regulations. Cather Inc. has second generation ceramic coating technology without heavy metals and has about three years of experience in this product for marine, concrete coating, truck, swimming pool, and dumpster applications. However, Cather Inc. has now completed licensing of a significantly broader patent and trade secret coverage of ceramic coating technologies including a new third generation coating. The Company will assist with applications work for the new generation and in introducing the new products to customers.

Cather Inc. is actively pursuing this advanced ceramic coating. The new third generation coatings chemically bond a silicate (ceramic) coating, both with and without fillers, at room temperature on a surface. This is monumental in that concrete structures, bridges, metal architectural components, trash dumpsters, oil field equipment, sewage treatment plants and many other applications can now have a chemically bonded layer of glass, the ultimate protective coating with normal applications processes. The Company knows of no competition for this product.

The Company has received significant interest in its offering of cleaner products, particularly from OEM manufacturers and marine service companies. The conversion to non-solvent water-based cleaners is a relatively new industry. Cather Inc. has a private label of one of the finest products produced in this new area and our manufacturer is not competing in our markets. Thus, The Company has an excellent opportunity to capitalize on the elimination of cleaning solvents as driven by the EPA.

Other Products

Shine 2000 Harbor Wood Eastings has no real competition offering the same level of performance and environmental friendliness. Competitive products are highly toxic and will probably be regulated off the market in future years.

Shine 2000 Inflatable Boat coatings have no known competition. Current rubber paints seldom last for more than a season and most dealers refuse to sell them. MacNaughton, in Rhode Island, which normally discounts marine paint by 50% from retail, is selling the inflatable coating and Cardinal cleaner line at retail, because they have no known competition. The Company is currently in testing with Sisson, the largest manufacturer of Inflatable Boats, to solve their surface deterioration problems by coating with Shine 2000.

Shine 2000 provides its users with enormous advantages over currently available products. Not only does Shine 2000 perform to the same high standards as two component catalyzed systems, it does so with low VOC's without the release of toxic isocyanates and without creating hazardous waste. Its performance is proven and excellent. Testing in independent sources has revealed that Shine 2000 retains its gloss longer than Elby's Blax, a toxic isocyanate based paint by over fifteen percent (15%).

Competitive Advantage

Manufacturers using Shine 2000 can lower their insurance costs for both plant and personnel because the product is non-toxic and non-flammable. Any unused paint left in a pail or spray can be returned to the container, instead of disposed (as hazardous waste) as is the case with two component systems. The shelf life of Shine 2000 is seven years without the premixed hardener, and several years with hardener, to accelerate time to maximum hardness. It also can withstand several freezing cycles.

The Company's products are competitive. Tite, a U.S. Paint two-component system, is sold to marine dealers for approximately $90 per gallon and to manufacturers, who use large quantities, for 20% less. Elby's reduced VOC version of their well-known Blax line is being sold to marine dealers in California for about $110 per gallon. Shine 2000 performs at least as well as Tite and Blax and costs approximately $100 per gallon to the dealer. It provides about 50% greater coverage per gallon as competitive coatings. This results in less cost per square foot of applied surface, even before insurance economies and hazardous waste costs are taken into consideration.

The Company's wood primer was formulated by Cather in response to a need in the wood window and door industry for a product that would adhere to freshly treated woods in a production environment. Fenetre Windows, a window manufacturer which switched to the Cather wood primer costing about three times as much as the ineffective primer they were using. Yet, they reported a savings of 200% on process costs by using Cather Inc.'s product. This was a result of increased coverage and decreased environmentally associated disposal costs.

The Company's offerings of Cather products compete at the high technology, high-performance end of the coatings market. There is less competition in the high-performance end of the market, and users are willing to pay for the performance. Cather Inc. is working to establish its products as the EPA's "best available technology" in several markets to increase the pressure of regulations. This will even further maximize The Company's ability to penetrate markets.

Initial Market Preference and Introduction

With two years of testing and market research in place, Cather Inc. has begun to enter the following markets, which are open to The Company for most of the Eastern U.S.:

1.) Aircraft (Commercial, Business, and Government)

Cather Inc. has been working with the Fly Right Company to specify paint for several applications for their aircraft and facilities, and has been shipping initial orders. As a result, Fly-Right granted Griffin Air a waiver to paint their 737 aircraft. Cather Inc. recently introduced Shine 2000 to McKinley Airlines at its maintenance center in San Jose. Since they are fighting closure by state regulators, McKinley expressed an interest in closely following Griffin Air's efforts in testing the product. Airproof, in their large airliner refurbishing center in Carmel, CA., has painted an L-1011 airplane under their own specifications and have tested Shine 2000 for aircraft interiors. There are several aircraft refurbishment centers and manufacturing plants on the East Coast, and The Company has or intends to open conversation with such companies as Stark, Yamhill-jet, Morrison Aviation, VAJCO and several others.

Shine 2000 has also undergone preliminary testing by the U.S. Navy for naval aircraft applications. The product passes all tests needed for MIL - STD - 85285 as run by potential customers and the Navy's NAWC lab. Cather Inc. must still workout tint formulations with its tint supplier prior to final submission for Mil-Spec Qualified Parts List approval. The Army has an open program to encourage similar testing which Cather Inc. will pursue for tanks and army aircraft in the future, with a chemical resistant version of Shine 2000. A portion of the military market for the company's products is within the scope of the company's intended sales goals. The company expects to visit such facilities as the Point Woods Marine Overhaul Facility, the Hagerstown Shipyards, the Naval Supply Center in Massachusetts and many others.

2.) OEM Metal Coating

Cather Inc. is working with OEM's such as BelMont (electrical power systems components), Menyunk Company (metal, residential and commercial doors), Vollum Buses, Rhyne Door (metal cellar doors) and many others to test Shine 2000, ceramics, primer and cleaning products to remove hazardous products from their workplace. The Company has supported many of these efforts and similarly is interested in removing hazardous solvents and other products for its potential clients. The Company normally: coats the potential customer's product for laboratory testing; supplies small samples of products for direct use by customer laboratory and production staffs; accepts an order for product for a small scale production trial; and then, assists the customer in full production change over.

3.) Petroleum, Water and Waste Treatment

The oil industry is a major user of paint for storage facilities, field equipment, offshore platforms and refineries. It is expected that this will be the most rapid growth producer for Cather Inc. Cather has been working to have Shine 2000 and ceramic primer specified for storage tanks in Maryland and Delaware. The Company has introduced the Cather ceramic coating products to municipal sewage engineers near Pensacola, Florida to begin entry into this market. Industrial paint contractors along the Gulf Coast also offer a large potential market for The Company.

4.) Wood Window Manufacturers

Cather Inc. has been selling wood primer into the window market for the past year and has recently successfully completed independent testing to broaden the market introduction. Cather Inc. now expects to significantly increase its market penetration for priming preservative wood. Orders from larger wood window manufacturers can be tens of thousands of gallons per month. The Company intends to support this effort and cover several potential East Coast clients, starting with Jascoek corporation.

Reiser Laboratories, located in North Carolina, is one of the leading producers of wood preservatives for the window industry. Reiser has opened discussions for potential private labeling of Shine 2000 wood primer for their wood window manufacturing market. A joint marketing trip is scheduled to visit Eliot Windows, Steinberge Windows, and Knudsen Windows (a potential client for The Company). These accounts could mean as much as twenty to forty thousand gallons of wood primer per month.

5.) State and Municipal Governments

States and cities are potentially large users for Shine 2000 for such applications as vehicles, architectural repair and construction, anti-graffiti coatings for street signs and buildings, clear coatings of buildings for acid rain protection, railings and guardrails, pipes, storage tanks, heating and cooling equipment, fireplugs, etc. This is a significant market and Cather Inc. made excellent progress in initially penetrating the city of Newport. Cather Inc. plans to immediately pursue the cities of Hagerstown, Blacksburg, Silver Springs, San Jose, Dover, as well as the state of Rhode Island. The Company has been handling the interface with the Rhode Island, and plans to penetrate the Maine and New Hampshire markets during the summer of 1994.

The Rhode Island Department of Air Quality, has requested that The Company participate in a Cather special presentation to paint using government departments. The users will be urged to switch to environmentally safe products to set an example for Rhode Island industries.

Rhode Island recently informed Cather Inc. that it has applied for an EPA grant to demonstrate VOC reductions, and would like to involve Cather Inc.'s products in actual usage demonstrations. The Company will be the official interface and sales agent for this work.

6.) Marine

Cather Inc. has two representatives on the East Coast and two in California that are starting sales for inflatable boats and marines wood finishing. Cather Inc. staff has attended major boat shows on both coasts to survey OEM and distributor reaction to the products. After establishment of the first two products, the linear polyurethane and ceramic yacht market will then be pursued.

Follow On Markets

Cather Inc. intends to establish itself principally in aircraft, metal manufacturing and municipal markets until the expected cash flow can support full expansion into additional markets. Cather Inc. will then focus on other general OEM product coating, marine, architectural, petroleum and automotive markets. U.S. Government marketing will also be expanded in the future to include not only the Department of Defense, but also, Energy, Transportation, and other departments. The U.S. government is the largest paint consumer in the U.S.

Sales & Promotion Strategy

Most of The Company's marketing efforts will be with OEM manufacturers. For this reason, neither Cather Inc. nor The Company will require expenditure of precious capital in national or regional advertising programs to reach the general public. Whatever promotional efforts The Company may employ will be shared with Cather Inc. and distributors. Cather Inc. will selectively advertise in specific market trade publications and participate in trade shows. The Company will only be required to pick up its own expenses to attend these trade shows. Press releases and product information bulletins will be sent to trade publications by Cather on behalf of all of its representatives. Most industrial and service users are heavily dependent on these trade journals to keep current, and The Company and Cather Inc. believes them to be the best initial source of advertising and the least expensive.

The Company is currently using industrial directories to search for customers as well as receiving leads from Cather from the national marketing database. The Company intends to purchase industrial directories on computer disk, as they are now available with built-in search functions to allow the user to quantify the exact parameters he wishes for a potential client and then scan the database for contacts.

As the Company acquires additional representatives, they will be selected on criteria that includes current industrial sales background and a base of industrial contacts that forms an immediate "warm market" for The Company's products. This approach has proven to shorten the training period and produce faster results.

THE MANAGEMENT PLAN

The Company will start operations with two sales employees at present, Matthew Fischer and Eugene Won. Mr. Fischer, upon formation of The Company's corporate shell, will leave his current position as Atlantic Region Sales Manager for Cather Inc. Mr. Won is currently the East Coast Applications Demonstration Representative, and a part-time sales representative, for Cather, and will similarly join The Company on a full time basis.

The ground work the principals have performed through their activities in opening the East Coast market for Cather products has resulted in a substantial number of leads to be followed up on The Company's behalf. These not only include major OEM's, but also a large number of smaller industrial users that require local servicing and can make decisions quickly.

The Company will continue to pursue the larger industries as the factory's representative, but will also begin to serve the smaller firms, on a direct basis. The cash flow generated by commissions on the large firms will build a cash base to allow for future expansion. The Company plans to hire additional staff to cover the Rhode Island, New Hampshire and Delaware markets, as well as opening up to two additional stores by the end of the first year.

Matthew Fischer has spearheaded the opening of the Atlantic Region for Cather products. In his capacity as Sales Manager, his efforts have resulted in sales to such prestigious firms as the Johnson Institute and Menyunk Company, currently the largest East Coast user of Cather coatings with anticipated monthly usage topping 3,000 gallons per month within the year.

Eugene Won has been involved in development, applications testing, and pilot marketing of environmentally safe inorganic ceramic coatings in the marine industry for the past three years. He assisted in Cather's acquisition of the latest in ceramics coating technology. He had been trained by the Cather applications engineering staff in special techniques necessary for application of water-dispersed products and application of ceramic coatings, using both conventional and electrostatic spray equipment. He assisted in a major test marketing of marine ceramic coatings in Rhode Island, Florida, Delaware and New Hampshire, including performing critical initial market introductions for over 500 miles of Eastern Coastline. Mr. Won has been successful in establishing several customers as a sales representative for Cather Inc. and has several major customers pending, such as Patterns Transportation, Exposition Leasing, and Traditional Container Lines. He is continuing his education as an evening business student in a local college. Mr. Won will also provide part-time applications training and assistance for Cather Inc. as the senior East Coast applications expert.

Matthew Fischer
President
General Manager

Mr. Fischer brings 25 years of sales and management experience to The Company, 22 of which were spent in commercial/industrial sales. While still in college, Mr. Fischer accepted a full-time sales position with P. Chan Products and quickly became a top producer in the highly competitive business machine industry.

Upon his graduation from the University of Virginia, he accepted a promotion to Sales Trainer and was transferred to the Canadian office of P. Chan. He was then offered a position as a major accounts representative with Alberts and Kehki Business Machines which provided an opportunity to develop strong relationships with some of Canada's largest companies.

In 1972, Mr. Fischer opened Mercredi Business Systems with an associate. Starting with two employees, the company grew to an enterprise consisting of twenty persons and grossing $1.2 million per year. In addition to management responsibilities, he maintained his own base of accounts. Hundreds of small businesses came to depend upon Mercredi for their copiers and fax machines, as did larger corporations such as Canadian National Railways, Canadian Gas Association, Bagdad Hydroelectric Co-Op, Bank of Guelph, and the Ripe Tomato Restaurants.

In 1987, Mr. Fischer sold his interests in Canada. He moved to Petersburg, Virginia where he managed Moore Systems, Inc. In just one year, he increased the company's sales volume by 250%, dominating the local market. When Moore Systems was sold, Mr. Fischer became a local distributor for an Iowa based manufacturer of industrial asphalt, roof, and concrete coatings.

Mr. Fishcer received his B.A. degree in Marketing from The University of Virginia.

Eugene Won
Sales Representative
Applications Technician

Eugene Won was trained in ceramics and environmentally safe water dispersed paint application and has performed applications demonstrations and training in these areas for the past three years. He has worked in OEM manufacturing and the marine pleasure boat markets. He has

Key Personnel

demonstrated coating and preparation from local boat yards to the Wright Yacht factory and at all of Cather's East Coast OEM sales efforts to date. His technical expertise and enthusiasm make him a valuable asset to The Company. Mr. Won has been enrolled in business and computer studies on an evening basis at a local college.

Key Support Personnel Background Summaries

Terry Won
Executive Vice President & Vice President of Business Development
Cather Inc.

Mr. Won was the founder and President of a ceramics company. Mr. Won devoted over two years in the development, market research and testing of state of the art ceramic coating products and complete systems of repair for the marine and industrial markets. He was instrumental in the introduction of ceramic products to Cather and has headed the effort to introduce the product line. He has also headed the efforts to introduce Shine 2000 and other Cather products in the eastern United States and foreign countries.

He was the founder of Won Aviation Corporation, a successful aerospace consulting firm that specialized in assisting high technology companies in creating new divisions and entering new areas of business. For twelve years, his consulting work included all aspects of U.S. Congressional liaison, finance, operations, marketing, distribution and manufacturing.

His aerospace work included all aspects of finance, operations, marketing, distribution, licensing joint venturing and manufacturing. His clients have included Vagner Signal, Grenier, Ozman, Dynamics, Wilhelm Systems, Voila, Rech Corporation, Williams Corporation, and others.

Mr. Won also co-founded the Gaull Bay Company, a marketing and engineering consulting company involved in upper level corporate market consulting and the design of weapons guidance systems and simulators for missile applications.

He also served as Vice President for Operations for Fieldman Corporation, a high volume consumer electronics manufacturer, where his experience included engineering, manufacturing, advertising, national distribution and dealer marketing. He served as President of Lambda Technology, an industrial product research and development firm.

Mr. Won holds a BSE-EE from the University of Massachusetts with selected post graduate course work. He holds the patent for radar velocity measurement for small projectiles.

Audrey Sutcliffe
Vice President, Director of Engineering and Manufacturing
Cather Inc.

Ms. Sutcliffe was one of the founders and former President of The Cather Aircraft Supply, Inc. Cather Inc. is the world-wide sole source for the Brun process for recovering fabric covered production and antique aircraft. It is also a manufacturer of dopes and coatings for this process. She was responsible for the start of the Shine 2000 product line.

Ms. Sutcliffe developed the performance specifications for Shine 2000 products and performed the development testing of the products in conjunction with Holly White, the original manufacturer. She initially obtained for Cather Inc. the worldwide marketing rights to the products, she performed the initial additive development testing program, and recently negotiated the manufacturing rights and set up production for Shine 2000 in Cather Inc.'s Hagerstown facility, together with Holly White.

Ms. Sutcliffe performed the applications engineering for the Shine 2000 products for 8 years, becoming one of the leading experts in applications techniques for waterborne coatings. She established dealers for Shine 2000 and other aviation products produced by Cather Inc. Ms.

Sutcliffe was later instrumental in joining her paint technology with Mr. Terry Won's ceramic technology and founding Cather Inc., with her two brothers, Geoffrey and Christopher Sutcliffe.

Prior to founding Cather Inc., Ms. Sutcliffe owned and managed Murfin Lumber Company, a lumber and building supply retailer in Kearney, Nebraska. She also spent several years as a technical and sales representative for hardware and industrial products.

She has been a licensed pilot for over 25 years and is one of the country's experts in recovering and restoring antique aircraft.

Ms. Sutcliffe graduated from the University of Kansas in 1965.

The Company plans to keep a ratio of about 80% small users (under 300 gallons per month of coating) to 20% large users (over 300 gallons per month). This ratio will provide more stability over a number of years, in case of market fluctuation for the customer and turnover of customers. The Company, however, will be selective in its large customers in order to:

THE OPERATING PLAN

- Provide maximum growth for The Company & Cather.
- Select the most profitable customers while competition between representatives is low.
- Take advantage of the products most environmentally in demand.
- Optimize travel within a region.
- Selectively offer franchises and dealerships to companies or individuals who have the market position, personnel and capital to service specific markets and move substantial quantities of The Company's products. An example is franchising automotive specialty product distribution.

Initially, The Company expects little or no competition in its paint offerings, because of the technological advantage of the Cather products. The Company expects to maintain a leadership role for the envisioned future with its ceramic coatings offerings because Cather products in this area are well protected. Thus, an emphasis will be placed on ceramic customers after competition surfaces for the paint line.

The Company will receive distributor pricing, plus a 10% commission on sales for all products sold off the normal OEM pricing schedule to major users (200 gallons per month or more). Very large OEM quantities are usually negotiated and The Company will work out pricing and compensation with the factory in those cases on a direct ship basis. However, generally Cather intends to provide the stocking function for the area of operation of The Company. A small stock will be employed initially, then the company will build larger inventories as cashflow permits.

In the second, and successive years of operation, The Company plans to open industrial paint outlets (stores) in the major cities within the assigned Sales Territory. The Company's earnings will be re-invested to this aim for the first two years to self-finance the opening of outlets and gain associated hard assets. However, a block of common stock shall be reserved for future capital expansion requirements if market growth requires. The potential is high for adding significant long-term future assets, if the stores capture even a small percentage of the commercial-industrial contract painting market.

The Company needs to have excellent computer resources to communicate with Cather, company sales force and distribution outlets. The Company plans to use a network to include use of notebook computers and new mobile data networks to keep in communications, even in customers' facilities. The Company intends to maximize use to management tools to insure control while allowing for the delegation of authority needed to expand rapidly.

Messieurs Fischer and Won plan to travel approximately three to four days a week for the first one to two years, establishing accounts, opening additional stores and supervising sales representatives. The Company will initially employ part-time bookkeeping and clerical staff. Expansion will occur first in the hiring of additional sales reps and a person to man the Petersburg store. When the Petersburg outlet begins turning a steady profit, second and successive stores will be opened.

Expansion of stores will be initially planned to cover the major metropolitan areas in the territory. Then, expansion to fill in voids will begin. The Company expects to have between 12 to 15 outlets within three years.

FINANCIAL PROJECTIONS AND ASSUMPTIONS

The Company's principals are expecting approximately $4.4 million in sales from representation from current and pending customers over the next year. This represents $440,000 in income in a low overhead operation much of which can be reinvested in business development. The Company projects that with a $50,000 loan (projected to be repaid within the first year), an additional $1.7 million in sales can be realized. These sales would produce an additional $658,000 in gross income through adding distribution to the business.

The Company's financial projections, at the end of this section, predict that the company can establish several additional manufacturer's representatives and an automotive representative as employees while establishing three distributorship outlets. The projected cash on hand at the end of the year is approximately $480,000. This is sufficient cash to reward employees with an excellent incentive bonus and establish new outlets to add additional equity for The Company's owners. By the end of the second year, cash available is projected to be sufficient to include passing income to the owners through the sub-chapter S, while still maintaining a healthy program in establishing new distribution outlets.

The Company has been careful to establish the credibility and marketability of its products in the field over the past several months. This was accomplished with management's computer database control of a limited market introduction of The Company's products, so that accurate projection could be made of the marketing needed to expand current markets.

The Company's manufacturers representative portion of the projections are based upon accounts that the company has obtained or are pending with very high probability. The Company's projections are based only on those accounts that are of this high probability status. Thus, all new accounts are excluded from the projections! Yet, the potential income is significant working only a small portion of The Company's leads.

Despite the conservative projections, sales have been relatively easy because of lack of competition in high performance environmental products and an interesting and beneficial dichotomy exists when considering product and technological credibility. The Company has a well established technology from Cather products that have been marketed worldwide for over eight years in the general and business aviation market.

The products are tested and The Company's salesmen often make direct references to aircraft that have sustained weather and aging for over eight years in the field, while still retaining an excellent finish. Not many consumer, commercial or industrial product companies can introduce a new technology into an environmentally driven market, and show eight years of successful use around the world.

Marketing Staff Utilized for Projection Database

A sample of The Company's marketing database example printout is available upon request. The Company utilizes the Market Ease marketing program to manage its sales in conformance with all Cather distributors. The current database contains approximately 50 contacts. These contacts were made by Messrs. Fischer and Won in the course of searching out market opportunities and researching the applications for Cather products during the start-up phase of Cather's East Coast marketing expansion. Many were called on due to their proximity to major users who were being solicited to adopt Cather products, but were not immediately pursued due to the factory's emphasis being placed on larger firms. The majority of these contacts have been made in the past five months.

The efforts necessary to produce the 50 contacts represents about one month of work by Messrs. Fischer & Won. It represents a factored projected probability of sales of $26,122 next month, with following months projected at $67,821, $138,860, $201,174, $328,235 and $486,749 if pursued. Thus, an excellent potential for distributor sales awaits exploitation. Further, the industrial painting market to painting contractors is very large. All but the largest industrial/ commercial painting firms buy from distributors on a per job basis as they cannot enter into yearly purchase agreements. Even a minor dent in the toxic industrial paint business of industrial paint contractors, done by Iddings-Larson and Deries stores, would constitute major business for The Company.

Format Presented

Financial Projection Format Employed and Assumptions

The Company has prepared a one year income, budget and cash flow projection that is included at the end of this section. Subsequently, the company has used this data to enter assumptions data into a modified financial package from Sutfield Tools For Sales, Inc., of Ventura, California to produce 5-year projections. The integrated financial program used generates what is normally a six spreadsheet projection in one integrated template. Although interesting in its projection of the great potential of The Company, they offer no definitive data beyond what can be forecast for the first year and therefore are not included.

As mentioned above, the current or imminently pending accounts are forecast with assumptions on growth of the distributor outlet sales grouped by market. The first table provides the income projection for paint sales and the second provides projected sales for ceramic coatings. A summary of these income projections is included on the third.

The budget for G&A and sales staff is included on the fourth table. Note that salaries are kept low until cash flow permits an increase to moderate levels. Additional compensation will be granted by the corporate board based upon profit of The Company. Further commensurate with cash flow, representatives are shown added for Baltimore, Washington D.C., Wilmington, and an "at large" automotive representative. No large OEM sales are forecast for these personnel in the first year, other than their contribution to distributor sales to further make the projection conservative.

The overhead budget is included on the fifth table. Rent for the Petersburg office is shared with Cather for their regional office. An office warehouse space has been located that is suitable in a central location, with excellent access to the freeway. A healthy travel budget has been provided to cover the cost of selling and servicing the customers. It is anticipated the initial office, printing and advertising expenses will be higher in the first months with start-up of the distributorship.

It is assumed that large equipment will be purchased on loans and that automobiles will be leased, supplied to sales personnel because of the expected travel. A basic stock of tint base and cleaners will be purchased in the first month as well as supplies of painting accessories such as brushes and sandpaper for contractors. Approximately $12,500 of the first months capital requirement will go into inventory and capital assets.

The sixth of the projections summarizes before tax income and cash flow. The projections show that a $50,000 loan would meet projected capital needs with about a 25% buffer. Breaking even on cash flow is projected about the end of the third month, and payback of the $50,000 loan is projected in the eighth month. Within one year, monthly profit before taxes is projected to surpass $150,000 per month. The projected cash position at the end of the year shows a significant potential to invest in growth and assets to avoid taxes. The Company can quickly become very marketable to industrial conglomerates, kept as a cash generator or could enter the public market with its stock.

LEGAL PLAN

The Company plans to operate as a Sub-Chapter "S" company, incorporated in the State of Maryland. The lower corporate tax rates, and proximity to major potential industrial users makes this an attractive location for The Company's long-term plans. Should it become possible, in the future, to expand The Company's assigned sales territory with Cather, a Maryland office could service the heavily industrialized areas of Maryland and Rhode Island.

Near term, The Company can capitalize on this market area by selling franchises and setting up commercial paint dealerships, in addition to its direct marketing efforts. The value of The Company's representation/distributorship account base, and the cash flow it will generate, plus the ability to offer franchises, are the long-term assets of The Company. Much of The Company's earnings are likely to be invested in establishing industrial paint outlets in the major cities within The Company's assigned sales territory.

Year 1 Revenues From OEM & Distributor Coating Sales

Paint Sales/Profit	May	June	July	Aug	Sept
Menyunk Company (Steel Doors)	$2,052	$18,402	$26,032	$26,032	$32,572
Commissions	$205	$1,840	$2,603	$2,603	$3,257
Regnier Products	$8,400	$16,200	$16,200	$18,900	$21,600
Commission	$840	$1,620	$1,620	$1,890	$2,160
Chris Martin	$11,000	$16,500	$38,500	$50,000	$75,000
Commission	$1,100	$1,650	$3,850	$5,000	$7,500
Roundway Newspaper Services	$4,500	$13,500	$18,000	$22,500	$22,500
Commission	$450	$1,350	$1,800	$2,250	$2,250
Browning Truck Trailers	$12,000	$12,000	$12,000	$12,000	$12,000
Commission	$1,200	$1,200	$1,200	$1,200	$1,200
Hathaway Furniture Refinishing	$3,356	$7,253	$7,253	$7,253	$10,067
Commission	$336	$725	$725	$725	$1,007
Eartham Dist. OEM Sales	$1,738	$5,214	$7,821	$11,732	$17,597
Costs	$55	$165	$248	$371	$557
Commissions	$174	$521	$782	$1,173	$1,760
Gross Profit on Sale @ 20%	$348	$1,043	$1,564	$2,346	$3,519
Total Profit	$466	$1,399	$2,099	$3,148	$4,722
Percent Gross Profit	26.8%	26.8%	26.8%	26.8%	26.8%
Eartham Dist. Indust. Painters	$3,160	$6,320	$12,640	$25,280	$25,280
Costs	$55	$250	$400	$500	$700
Commissions	$316	$632	$1,264	$2,528	$2,528
Gross Profit on Sale @ 20%	$632	$1,264	$2,528	$5,056	$5,056
Total Profit	$893	$1,646	$3,392	$7,084	$6,884
Percent Gross Profit	28.3%	26.0%	26.8%	28.0%	27.2%
Eartham Dist. Paint Accessories	$316	$632	$1,264	$2,528	$2,528
Gross Profit on Sales @ 50%	$158	$316	$632	$1,264	$1,264
Eartham Dist. Auto Accessories	$1,500	$2,100	$2,940	$4,116	$5,762
Gross Profit on Sales @ 70%	$1,050	$1,470	$2,058	$2,881	$4,034
Total Gross Sales (Paints)	**$26,122**	**$67,821**	**$121,410**	**$163,624**	**$216,685**
Gross Profit on Sales (Paints)	**$3,608**	**$8,927**	**$16,991**	**$25,165**	**$31,762**

	Oct	Nov	Dec	Jan	Feb	March	April	YR1 Total
	$32,572	$32,572	$32,572	$39,112	$39,112	$39,112	$39,112	$359,254
	$3,257	$3,257	$3,257	$3,911	$3,911	$3,911	$3,911	$35,925
	$21,600	$21,600	$27,000	$27,000	$27,000	$205,500		
	$2,160	$2,160	$2,700	$2,700	$2,700	$20,550		
	$75,000	$100,000	$100,000	$100,000	$100,000	$100,000	$100,000	$866,000
	$7,500	$10,000	$10,000	$10,000	$10,000	$10,000	$10,000	$86,600
	$22,500	$22,500	$22,500	$22,500	$22,500	$22,500	$22,500	$238,500
	$2,250	$2,250	$2,250	$2,250	$2,250	$2,250	$2,250	$23,850
	$30,000	$30,000	$30,000	$150,000				
	$3,000	$3,000	$3,000	$15,000				
	$10,067	$10,067	$10,067	$10,067	$10,067	$10,067	$10,067	$105,652
	$1,007	$1,007	$1,007	$1,007	$1,007	$1,007	$1,007	$10,565
	$24,636	$34,491	$48,287	$67,602	$87,882	$114,247	$148,521	$569,766
	$780	$1,091	$1,528	$2,139	$2,781	$3,615	$4,700	$18,031
	$2,464	$3,449	$4,829	$6,760	$8,788	$11,425	$14,852	$56,977
	$4,927	$6,898	$9,657	$13,520	$17,576	$22,849	$29,704	$113,953
	$6,611	$9,256	$12,958	$18,141	$23,584	$30,659	$39,856	$152,899
	26.8%	26.8%	26.8%	26.8%	26.8%	26.8%	26.8%	26.8%
	$25,280	$25,280	$25,280	$25,280	$25,280	$25,280	$31,600	$255,960
	$1,000	$1,250	$1,500	$1,500	$1,500	$1,500	$1,500	$11,655
	$2,528	$2,528	$2,528	$2,528	$2,528	$2,528	$3,160	$25,596
	$5,056	$5,056	$5,056	$5,056	$5,056	$5,056	$6,320	$51,192
	$6,584	$6,334	$6,084	$6,084	$6,084	$6,084	$7,980	$65,133
	26.0%	25.1%	24.1%	24.1%	24.1%	24.1%	25.3%	25.4%
	$2,528	$2,528	$2,528	$2,528	$2,528	$2,528	$3,160	$25,596
	$1,264	$1,264	$1,264	$1,264	$1,264	$1,264	$1,580	$12,798
	$8,067	$11,294	$15,812	$22,137	$30,992	$104,720		
	$5,647	$7,906	$11,068	$15,496	$21,694	$73,304		
	$227,599	**$266,800**	**$282,901**	**$311,983**	**$360,181**	**$392,871**	**$442,952**	**$2,880,949**
	$34,444	**$40,761**	**$45,827**	**$53,923**	**$64,868**	**$76,370**	**$93,978**	**$496,625**

Ceramic Sales & Profit

		May	June	July	Aug	Sept
	Chris Martin		$6,000	$9,000	$15,000	$60,000
	Commissions		$600	$900	$1,500	$6,000
	Browning Trailers					
	Commissions					
	Nathaniel Trans. - Railroad			$2,200	$8,800	$8,800
	Commission			$220	$880	$880
	Nathaniel Trans. - Shipping					
	Commissions					
	Bender Container Lines			$1,000	$4,000	$8,000
	Commissions			$100	$400	$800
	Brimming Leasing					$15,000
	Commissions					$1,500
	Gromit Aerospace					
	Commissions					
	Eartham Dist. OEM			$1,250	$1,250	$1,250
	Costs			$25	$50	$100
	COmmissions			$125	$125	$125
	Gross Profit On Sale @ 30%			$375	$375	$375
	Total Profit			$475	$450	$400
	Eartham Dist. Industrial			$2,500	$5,500	$11,000
	Costs			$50	$110	$220
	Commissions			$250	$550	$1,100
	Gross Profit on Sale @ 30%			$750	$1,650	$3,300
	Total Profit			$950	$2,090	$4,180
	Eartham Dist. Automotive			$1,500	$3,000	$7,500
	Costs			$30	$60	$150
	Commissions			$150	$300	$750
	Gross Profit on Sale @ 70%			$1,050	$2,100	$5,250
	Total Profit			**$1,170**	**$2,340**	**$5,850**
	Total Gross Sales (Ceramics)			**$17,450**	**$37,550**	**$111,550**
	Gross Profit on Sales (Ceramics)			**$3,815**	**$7,660**	**$19,610**

Oct	Nov	Dec	Jan	Feb	March	April	Total
$120,000	$120,000	$120,000	$120,000	$120,000	$120,000	$120,000	$930,000
$12,000	$12,000	$12,000	$12,000	$12,000	$12,000	$12,000	$93,000
$25,200	$75,600	$75,600	$75,600	$75,600	$75,600	$75,600	$478,800
$2,520	$7,560	$7,560	$7,560	$7,560	$7,560	$7,560	$47,880
$8,800	$22,000	$26,000	$26,000	$26,000	$26,000	$26,000	$180,600
$880	$2,200	$2,600	$2,600	$2,600	$2,600	$2,600	$18,060
$40,000	$40,000	$60,000	$80,000	$80,000	$80,000	$80,000	$460,000
$4,000	$4,000	$6,000	$8,000	$8,000	$8,000	$8,000	$46,000
$8,000	$8,000	$8,000	$8,000	$10,000	$10,000	$10,000	$75,000
$800	$800	$800	$800	$1,000	$1,000	$1,000	$7,500
$30,000	$45,000	$45,000	$45,000	$45,000	$45,000	$45,000	$315,000
$3,000	$4,500	$4,500	$4,500	$4,500	$4,500	$4,500	$31,500
			$6,000	$6,000	$6,000	$6,000	$24,000
			$600	$600	$600	$600	$2,400
$1,250	$1,250	$1,250	$1,250	$1,250	$1,250	$1,250	$12,500
$125	$200	$250	$400	$400	$400	$400	$2,350
$125	$125	$125	$125	$125	$125	$125	$1,250
$375	$375	$375	$375	$375	$375	$375	$3,750
$375	$300	$250	$100	$100	$100	$100	$2,650
$15,400	$21,560	$30,184	$42,258	$59,161	$82,825	$115,955	$386,342
$308	$431	$604	$845	$1,183	$1,656	$2,319	$7,727
$1,540	$2,156	$3,018	$4,226	$5,916	$8,282	$11,595	$38,634
$4,620	$6,468	$9,055	$12,677	$17,748	$24,847	$34,786	$115,903
$5,852	$8,193	$11,470	$16,058	$22,481	$31,473	$44,063	$146,810
$10,500	$14,700	$20,580	$28,812	$40,337	$56,472	$79,060	$262,460
$210	$294	$412	$576	$807	$1,129	$1,581	$5,249
$1,050	$1,470	$2,058	$2,881	$4,034	$5,647	$7,906	$26,246
$7,350	$10,290	$14,406	$20,168	$28,236	$39,530	$55,342	$183,722
$8,190	**$11,466**	**$16,052**	**$22,473**	**$31,463**	**$44,048**	**$61,667**	**$204,719**
$259,150	**$348,110**	**$386,614**	**$432,920**	**$463,347**	**$503,146**	**$558,865**	**$3,124,702**
$37,617	**$51,019**	**$61,232**	**$74,691**	**$90,304**	**$111,881**	**$142,090**	**$600,519**

Year 1 Revenue Summary for Environmentally Safe Coating Sales

Summary	May	June	July	Aug	Sept
Total Gross Sales Paints	$26,122	$67,821	$121,410	$163,624	$216,685
Total Gross Sales Ceramics	$0	$0	$17,450	$37,550	$111,550
Grand Total Gross Sales	**$26,122**	**$67,821**	**$138,860**	**$201,174**	**$328,235**
Gross Profit On Sales Paints	$3,608	$8,927	$16,991	$25,165	$31,762
Gross Profit on Sales Ceramics	$0	$0	$3,815	$7,660	$19,610
Grand Total Gross Profit on Sales	**$3,608**	**$8,927**	**$20,806**	**$32,825**	**$51,372**

Year 1 G & A Overhead Expenses

G&A and Overhead	May	June	July	Aug	Sept
G&A Staff					
Matthew Fischer - President/Sales Manager	$5,000	$5,000	$5,000	$5,000	$6,000
Eugene Won -Magr. Technical Service	$3,000	$3,000	$3,000	$4,000	$4,000
Carrie Fisher - Clerical/Accounting	$600	$600	$600	$600	$600
Warehouse - Sales/Mixing/Packaging		$500	$500	$1,000	$2,080
Hagerstown Representative					$4,000
Rhode Island Area Representative					
Dover Representative					
Automotive Representative					
Hagerstown - Counter Sales/Mixing					
Delivery/Shipping					
Total G&A Staff	**$8,600**	**$9,100**	**$9,100**	**$10,600**	**$16,680**
Total G&A	**$10,320**	**$10,920**	**$10,920**	**$12,720**	**$20,016**
(Taxes/Wkmn's Comp. @ 20%)					

Oct	Nov	Dec	Jan	Feb	March	April	YR1 Total
$227,599	$266,800	$282,901	$311,983	$360,181	$392,871	$442,952	$2,880,949
$259,150	$348,110	$386,614	$432,920	$463,347	$503,146	$558,865	$3,124,702
$486,749	**$614,910**	**$669,515**	**$744,903**	**$823,529**	**$896,017**	**$1,001,817**	**$6,005,651**
$34,444	$40,761	$45,827	$53,923	$64,868	$76,370	$93,978	$496,625
$37,617	$51,019	$61,232	$74,691	$90,304	$111,881	$142,090	$600,519
$72,061	**$91,780**	**$107,059**	**$128,614**	**$155,172**	**$188,252**	**$236,068**	**$1,097,144**

Oct	Nov	Dec	Jan	Feb	March	April	YR1 Total
$6,000	$6,000	$6,000	$6,000	$6,000	$6,000	$6,000	$68,000
$4,000	$4,000	$4,000	$4,000	$4,000	$4,000	$4,000	$45,000
$600	$600	$600	$1,200	$1,200	$1,200	$1,200	$9,600
$2,080	$2,080	$2,080	$4,160	$6,240	$6,240	$6,240	$33,200
$4,000	$4,000	$4,000	$4,000	$4,000	$4,000	$4,000	$32,000
$4,000	$4,000	$4,000	$4,000	$4,000	$4,000	$4,000	$28,000
	$4,000	$4,000	$4,000	$4,000	$4,000	$4,000	$24,000
	$3,000	$3,000	$3,000	$3,000	$3,000	$3,000	$18,000
			$3,000	$3,000	$3,000	$3,000	
$2,000	$2,000	$2,000	$3,000	$4,000	$6,000	$6,000	$25,000
$22,680	**$29,680**	**$29,680**	**$36,360**	**$394,440**	**$41,440**	**$41,440**	**$294,800**
$27,216	**$35,616**	**$35,616**	**$43,632**	**$47,328**	**$49,728**	**$49,728**	**$353,760**

G&A Overhead

	May	June	July	Aug	Sept	Oct	Nov
General Overhead							
Rent offices	$600	$300	$300	$300	$300	$300	$300
Leasehold Improvements	$500	$100	$100	$100	$100	$100	$100
Travel RI	$1,500	$2,000	$2,000	$2,500	$4,000	$4,000	$4,000
Travel DE/MD/CA		$200	$500	$500	$4,000	$4,000	$4,000
Telephone - RI	$300	$300	$300	$300	$300	$300	$300
Telephone - DE/MD					$200	$200	$200
Utilities	$100	$100	$100	$100	$100	$100	$100
Office Supplies	$400	$300	$100	$100	$100	$110	$121
Postage/Shipping	$200	$300	$400	$400	$400	$440	$484
Advertising	$150	$150	$150	$150	$150	$165	$182
Copy Expenses	$150	$150	$150	$150	$150	$165	$182
Insurance Vehicles			$233	$233	$350	$350	$467
Insurance Facilities	$167	$167	$167	$167	$167	$167	$167
Printing	$100	$500	$100	$110	$121	$133	$146
OPA Fees	$400	$400	$400	$400	$400	$400	$400
Legal Fees	$1,000						
Cap. Equip. Loans	$1,000	$200	$200	$1,000	$1,000	$600	$1,000
Cap. Equip. Purchased	$2,000	$250	$250				$750
Cap. Equip. Leased - Office	$750	$375	$375	$375	$375	$375	$375
Stockholder Loan Repay							
Automobile Leases			$4,000	$1,000	$3,000	$1,500	$5,500
Supplies - Sales Demos	$150	$150	$150	$200	$200	$200	$300
Stock Misc. Paint Supplies	$2,500				$2,000		$2,000
Tintbase Stock	$7,110			$7,110			$7,110
Coating Sales Samples	$100	$150	$300	$300	$300	$300	$300
Total General Overhead	**$19,177**	**$6,092**	**$10,275**	**$15,495**	**$17,713**	**$13,905**	**$28,483**
Total Expenses	**$29,497**	**$17,012**	**$21,195**	**$28,215**	**$37,729**	**$41,121**	**$64,099**

Cashflow Summary Year One

	May	June	July	Aug	Sept	Oct
Total Monthly Revenues	$3,608	$8,927	$20,806	$32,825	$51,372	$72,061
Overhead and G&A	$29,497	$17,012	$21,195	$28,215	$37,729	$41,121
Monthly Net Profit Before Taxes	($25,888)	($8,085)	($389)	$4,610	$13,644	$30,941
Loan (Preferred Position)	$40,000	$10,000				
Monthly Accumlated Cash Position	$14,112	$16,027	$15,638	$20,247	$33,891	$64,832

Dec	Jan	Feb	March	April	YR1 Total
$300	$800	$1,300	$1,300	$1,300	$7,400
$100	$500	$500	$100	$100	$2,400
$4,000	$4,000	$4,000	$4,000	$4,000	$40,000
$4,000	$6,000	$6,000	$6,000	$6,000	$41,200
$300	$300	$300	$300	$300	$3,600
$200	$300	$300	$300	$300	$2,000
$100	$100	$100	$100	$100	$1,200
$133	$1,000	$1,000	$200	$200	$3,764
$532	$586	$644	$709	$779	$5,874
$200	$1,220	$1,342	$476	$523	$4,856
$200	$220	$242	$266	$292	$2,315
$467	$467	$467	$583	$583	$4,200
$167	$250	$350	$350	$350	$2,633
$161	$177	$195	$214	$236	$2,194
$400	$400	$400	$400	$400	$4,800
				$2,000	$3,000
$800	$1,000	$1,000	$1,000	$1,000	$9,800
	$2,000	$2,000			$7,250
$375	$375	$375	$1,125	$750	$6,000
$55,000					
$2,000	$2,000	$3,500	$5,500	$2,500	$30,500
$300	$400	$400	$500	$600	$3,550
	$2,000	$2,000	$2,000	$2,000	$14,500
	$7,110	$7,110	$7,110	$7,110	$49,770
$300	$300	$300	$300	$300	$3,250
$70,034	**$31,504**	**$33,824**	**$32,833**	**$31,724**	**$311,057**
$105,650	**$75,136**	**$81,152**	**$82,561**	**$81,452**	**$664,817**

Nov	Dec	Jan	Feb	March	April	YR1 Total
$91,780	$107,059	$128,614	$155,172	$188,252	$236,068	
$64,099	$105,650	$75,136	$81,152	$82,561	$81,452	
$27,681	$1,409	$53,479	$74,020	$105,691	$154,616	
$92,513	$93,922	$147,401	$221,421	$327,111	$481,727	$481,727

Powder Coating Manufacturer

BUSINESS PLAN

BRUDDER COATING SYSTEMS, INC.

100 Bronx Blvd.
Stevens Point, WI 54481

April 1996

Brudder's business plan provides another example of a company meeting a need caused by changing environmental government regulations.

- EXECUTIVE SUMMARY

- INDUSTRY

- MARKETING PLAN

- OPERATIONS PLAN

- FINANCE PLAN

- MARKET SURVEY

- FINANCIAL TABLES

EXECUTIVE SUMMARY

Several major auto manufacturers recently announced a joint venture which involves the construction of a $25 million powder coating facility. Their new state-of-the-art facility will be used to expand the uses of powder coating in the automotive industry. This is one of many indications of the accelerating growth of powder coating as an alternative to painting in industrial metal finishing applications. Superior durability, reduced costs and environmental considerations have played a role in the movement of manufacturers throughout the world from liquid paint to powder coating. Powder coating now comprises 15% of the market for metal finishing where it competes directly with traditional liquid finishes.

Powder coating is a finishing process where finely ground particles of pigment and resin are electrostatically charged and sprayed onto a conductive part (usually metal). The coating process can be done manually or automatically with a wide variety of equipment. The parts to be coated are grounded neutral so that the charged particles projected at them adhere to the parts and are held there until melted and fused into a smooth coating in a curing oven. The result is a uniform, durable, high-quality finish that is resistant to chipping and scratching, and has a very high tolerance to heat. Powder coating is a very environmentally friendly process. It is a dry process that does not involve the spraying of volatile and toxic chemicals into the air.

Applications for the use of powder coating vary widely. The appliance and automotive industries are large users of powder coating for cabinets, hardware, trim and underhood parts. There are also large markets for powder coating in architectural metal, industrial equipment, furniture and sporting goods.

The mission of Brudder Coating Systems during our first three years of operation will be to provide quality powder coating services to a variety of clients. Our long-term goal in entering the powder coating industry is to identify areas of opportunity in the industry that will allow us to begin a manufacturing of value-added business that utilizes powder coating in the process. In an effort to move us toward this goal, the owners of Brudder have developed several consumer products that will be marketed by a recently formed sister corporation, also owned by them; The Spice Company. Additionally, Brudder has recently obtained a distributorship for Metal Finishing products. These products will be a good compliment to Brudder's powder coating services since the market for the products is very similar to our market for powder coating services.

We will also attempt to develop innovations in the powder coating process that will allow us to either manufacture powder coating equipment, or do systems consulting and sales of existing equipment for the many businesses worldwide who will be converting from liquid paint to powder coating over the next decade.

During the first 19 months in operation, Brudder has established powder coating business with over 20 industrial customers, from the region and as far away as Milwaukee and the Wisconsin Rapids. Our initial market survey of manufacturers in the region has identified over 350 potential customers for Brudder's powder coating services. The survey also identified four potential competitors within our defined geographic market, and five other manufacturing firms who have in-house powder coating operations.

Brudder began operations during August of 1994 in a manufacturing facility where they currently lease 2,500 square feet of manufacturing space and a 250 square foot office. The operation is currently staffed by the two owners of the business, one full-time employee and one part-time employee. We hope to add at least four additional employees within our next year of operation, and grow to approximately 12 employees within our first three years.

Brudder's powder coating equipment currently includes high pressure cleaning and phosphatizing equipment, a spray booth and sprayer and an oven. The start-up cost for equipment, fixtures, materials and working capital was approximately $50,000. To date, the business has been financed by the stockholders in the business and from operations. In anticipation of future demand for our services, a detailed expansion plan has been drafted and price quotations have been obtained. The expanded plant would include an automated powder coating line which would increase our capacity approximately ten times over our current capacity.

MARKETING PLAN

The Worldwide Market for Powder Coating

One of the biggest potential powder coating users is the appliance industry. The high-quality finish is both attractive and durable, and a viable alternative for porcelain enamel and liquid finishes on traditional appliances surfaces. These include dryer drums, front and side panels of ranges and refrigerators, washer tops and lids, air conditioner cabinets, water heaters, dishwasher racks and cavities of microwave ovens. Technological developments have resulted in powder coatings with lower gloss, lower temperature curing requirement and stronger resistance to chips, scratches, detergents and grease. All these features have led to the use of powder coatings on about 40% of all appliance finishes. Appliance applications represent about 21% of the North American powder coating market.

The automotive industry represents an additional 15% of the North American powder coating market. Wheels, bumpers, roof racks, door handles, interior panels and various "under-the-roof" parts are being powder coated. Powder is also used as a primer-surfacer on component parts for trucks and recreational vehicles. Clear powders, over a liquid base coat, are being developed for exterior auto body finishing.

The architectural and building market uses powder coating on file cabinets, shelving, aluminum extrusions for window frames, door frames and modular office furniture. Posts, rails, fencing, metal gutters, highway and parking lot poles, guard rails, farm implements, garden tools and tractors, patio furniture, and other products used outdoors all benefit from the high weatherability factor of powder coating.

Countless everyday uses for powder coating include fire extinguishers, mechanical pencils and pens, thumbtacks, barbecue grills and vending machines. Sporting goods equipment uses include bicycle frames, golf clubs shafts, ski poles and exercise equipment. Technological advancements have allowed expansion of powder coating to non-metal surfaces, such as ceramics, wood, plastic and brass so that bottles, shower stalls, dashboards and even toilet seats are now powder coated.

The Brudder Market

Initial marketing efforts were concentrated on a geographic market extending in a sixty-mile radius of our location. After exhausting our leads in this area we expanded our marketing efforts in Minnesota, Michigan and Illinois. We have been successful in drawing business from a much wider geographic radius than we originally anticipated. We have found that we can be competitive with smaller parts that can be shipped over longer distances, and certain types of specialized work justify long distance shipment.

To establish a measure of the size of the market for powder coating within our identified geographic market, a telephone survey of regional manufacturing firms was conducted. The survey was used to identify firms that are using either painting, plating or other metal coating in their manufacturing process. The person in charge of this process was also identified, and information was gathered on the size, type and color of parts. A copy of the survey instrument is attached.

Through this survey and subsequent marketing efforts, we have identified and contacted over 350 manufacturers who use metal finishing in their process and, who could potentially use our services. We are in continuous contact with our prospects and customers to encourage them to request quotes from us. In our first 19 months of operation we have done powder coating for over 20 industrial customers on a regular basis. We have also quoted prices for numerous additional jobs from these customers and prospects. We anticipate that our number of customers and orders will continue to increase significantly over the next three years.

Competition

There is currently one other powder coating job shop located in the area. There are also several automated lines in the immediate area surrounding the region. The local shop is a small operation that has been in business for about two years. The Kenosha shop is a larger operation. They specialize in military contracts and take in smaller jobs as a sideline.

There are also about five other manufacturing firms within our geographic market who have in-house powder coating facilities. Several of these facilities take in outside work, although they don't appear to be a significant competitive threat. We will continue to gather information on competition. We will attempt to determine the volume and type of parts being powder coated by our local competitors, as well as their pricing.

Pricing

A two-tiered pricing structure is anticipated. One tier for coating specialty or one-of-a-kind items which will be billed at a straight per-hour charge, and another tier for repeat or production items. The latter will be quoted according to surface contamination, part size, surface complexity and shipping requirements. Premiums will be charged for colors other than black or white, certain coating materials, masking and special handling.

Our research on pricing for powder coating by other shops indicates that they generally charge on a square footage basis. The range in competitor pricing is between $.10 to $.12 per square foot. We anticipate that our pricing will fall within this range, with a higher per square foot charge on specialty items, and a lower per square foot charge on longer run items.

OPERATIONS PLAN

Production and Operations

Location: Industrial Center

Advantages: Low rent. Flexible space. Dock-height shipping/receiving facility. Natural gas, 440 VAC 3 phase electric service available. Computer, fax and coffee available. Good central region location.

Disadvantages: Work space not custom suited to application. Have to make accommodations for other businesses in building. Three-year tenancy limit. Could easily outgrow available space.

What Brudder is Powder Coating

Brudder provides powder coatings on conductive metallic surfaces, chiefly not-rolled steel, cold-rolled steel, cast iron, stainless steel, rolled or extruded aluminum and cast aluminum. The pieces accepted will vary in size from a few square inches surface area, to 70" X 54" X 63" which is the maximum size capacity of our current oven.

Technological advancements have allowed the expansion of powder coating to non-metal surfaces, such as ceramics, wood, plastic and glass. These applications generally require specialized equipment that we will not have initially. If market demand for these types of services is great enough to justify the expense of additional equipment, we will consider expanding our service to include them.

Types of Powder Coating Materials to be Offered

Brudder will offer its customers their choice of most types of thick-film, functional end use and thin-film decorative end use thermosetting powders which are currently available. These coatings are epoxy, polyester, new polyester, acrylic, silicone/epoxy, silicone acrylics and silicone. Each material or blend of materials offers unique properties of hardness, color acceptance, flexibility, durability, temperature resistance, ultraviolet light resistance and salt spray resistance. The material to be used in any given application will be determined by consultation with the powder supplier and the customer, using a "needs" checklist.

The three major steps in the powder coating process are Surface Preparation, Powder Application and Thermosetting (Baking).

The Powder Coating Process

Surface Preparation: Of the three steps, surface preparation is probably the most critical. Unlike wet painting with solvent based paints which are somewhat forgiving of scale, grime and forming and cutting oils, the surface to be powder coated must be free of contaminants and have a good phosphatized or conversion coat. Brudder uses a variety of cleaning methods including a high temperature, high pressure phosphate wash, or other cleaning chemicals as the job requires.

Additionally, we have identified a new metal finishing process that is an environmental alternative to clean chromate coating on aluminum. Clear chromate is used widely as a corrosion preventative for aluminum computer and electronic parts. It is also a very effective pre-treatment for aluminum before powder coating. We would like to begin offering the service within the next 12 months.

The cleaning and coating chemicals are monitored for strength. The rinse discharge is relatively low volume chemically inert substances which will be monitored and balanced for pH. Discharge samples have routinely met or exceeded all federal, state and municipal regulations. After cleaning, the part must be completely dried before powder application.

Powder Application: Powder is applied in a spray booth designed specifically for powder coating. Because there are virtually no VOCs in the powder, the spray booth air can be drawn through a two-stage filter and recirculated directly back to the shop. The powder to be applied to the part is pumped from a feeder unit through a hose to the spray gun. There is a high voltage, low amperage electrode at the tip of the spray gun. The voltage can be varied according to the type of powder material being applied and the intended thickness of the coat. As the powder passes it, the electrode applies an electric charge to the powder. The powder emerges as a charged, diffuse cloud that is aimed at the electrically grounded part. As with all spray type applications, there is a certain amount of overspray. Unlike most wet spray processes however, the powder overspray can be recovered and reused.

Thermosetting: The coated parts are placed in a preheated oven for thermosetting. The temperature of the oven and the time of exposure to heat vary according to the coating material(s), the substrate material type and thickness of the part.

Climate controlled powder storage: Coating Powders have a shelf life of about one year depending on storage conditions. Ideal storage conditions would be in an area protected from rapid temperature and humidity changes. Storage temperature should be at 80 degrees F or less, with humidity ideally at 60% or less.

Facility Requirement

Chemical Storage: While the chemicals associated with our powder coating operations are generally not highly reactive, the concentrations involved would dictate safe and prudent holding facilities. These facilities will comply with or exceed code requirements. All chemicals will be purchased from suppliers and stored in approved containers. Storage containers and operational containers are held within secondary (spill) containment systems.

Receiving Equipment: This will be dictated by the marketplace. As our customer base develops, appropriate equipment will be acquired. For starters, only clean, designated areas will be necessary.

Shipping Area: A minimum amount of fixtures have been necessary in our operation so far, although the shipping area has the potential of becoming the largest square foot area in the shop.

It is planned to offer potential customers the option of light assembly of their product, packaging and shipping to their customer as an efficiency that would greatly reduce extra handling problems.

Waste Management: The two most challenging items requiring waste management will be disposal of incoming packaging materials, and discharge of spent cleaning solutions. Incoming packaging materials will consist mainly of corrugated kraft paper and polypropylene sheets. Wherever possible these materials will be reused. If reuse is not feasible, they will be recycled. Liquid discharges will be minimal (should be less than 100 gallons per day of highly diluted waste water). Discharges are being coordinated with city public works department and monitored and adjusted by equipment purchased from chemical suppliers.

Product Handling Fixtures: There are three mobile racks sized to fit in our oven, strong enough to carry 250 pounds of product each. The dolly wheels, as well as other parts of the racks are designed to operate in, and withstand temperatures of up to 500 degrees F. These racks have movable hanging bars that can be placed where needed to accommodate various products. Wire hangers are fabricated from baling wire as needed for each product. Wire will be a small but continuous expense because of the rather limited life of an individual hanger.

Surface Preparation: The plant is equipped with a high temperature, high pressure cleaning and phosphatizing machine. Each part is thoroughly cleaned prior to coating.

The product must be completely dry before powder application. This usually necessitates placing the just cleaned parts in the oven for a short period of time (@5-10 min.) depending on the part(s).

Powder Application: The shop is equipped with a walk-in spray booth designed to minimize powder migration within shop confines. The applicator module is an industry standard model which provides the versatility necessary for job shop usage. Accessories and specialized parts will be purchased as the economically appropriate need arises.

Thermosetting: A previously owned, electrically heated convection oven has been purchased. While it is not perfect for our needs, it should be sufficient for a start and sufficiently modifiable to provide for some future needs. Conversion of the oven to a more efficient gas-fired unit will be considered when the volume of usage suggests it.

The size of our current oven is 6' deep x 5' wide and 5' high. The small size of this oven is also limiting our productivity. An oven 12' deep with doors on both ends would more than double our hourly production capacity. The larger oven would also allow us to accommodate projects involving larger parts (i.e.: automotive and airplane frames, boat trailers and docks) that we are currently turning away.

Existing Plant Capacity

With current equipment our production capacity is capable of generating approximately $28,000 per month in sales. With the addition of a larger oven, priced at approximately $35,000, four additional employees and 1,200 square feet of manufacturing space, we could increase our revenue generating capacity to approximately $40,000 per month.

Business Ownership

Brudder Coating Systems Incorporated is a closely held Wisconsin corporation. The initial stockholders in the corporation are A. Post and Jane Crew, each with a 50% ownership of the corporation. For 1994 and '95 A. Post will hold the office of President and Treasurer, and Jane Crew will hold the office of Vice President and Secretary.

Management

Management responsibility for Brudder will be divided between the two stockholders. A. Post will have primary responsibility for plant operations, production staffing and materials and equipment procurement. Jane Crew will have primary responsibility for sales, marketing and financial management.

An internally financed investment of $50,000 was needed to purchase initial equipment and supplies, and to cover operating expenses during the first six months of operations. This amount was financed through a loan to the corporation by A. Post. The loan is a five-year installment loan, with interest at 8.75% annually. The monthly payments are approximately $906.

Amount and Source of Financing

Booth	$10,000
Sprayer	5,000
Oven	2,000
Cleaning Equipment	18,000
Fixtures	3,000
Materials	2,000
Total	**$40,000**

Equipment Costs For Start-up

Operation of Brudder from start-up in August of 1994 to date has been internally funded by the owners of Brudder from operations. Several points of clarification pertaining to the financial statements on the following pages should be noted:

Narrative Summary of Financial Statements

- The $17,000 loss from operations that we incurred during 1994 was less than the $20,000 loss that we anticipated during our start-up phase.
- Our budget shortfall in revenue for the first quarter of 1995 was simply due to sales being less than anticipated. We also discovered that our cost of sales estimates as a percentage of sales were budgeted too high. This indicates that our profitability will be greater than anticipated at a lower level of sales.
- Based on first quarter sales, projections for the remainder of 1995 may seem to be optimistic, however, based on current purchase orders and work-in-progress, $25,000 in sales for the second quarter is likely. Indications from existing and prospective customers are that sales for the remainder of 1995 will continue to grow steadily.
- The attached balance sheet shows a positive net worth for Brudder by the end of 1995. We feel that this is also very attainable if sales remain constant through the second-half of the year.

During the first eight months in operation it has become apparent that we will need to grow in capacity to keep up with our growing market for powder coating services.

Need for Additional Financing

The size of our oven is currently our biggest limiting factor. A number of potential customers who would like to work with us cannot because our oven is too small to accommodate their parts. With a larger oven we could take on jobs involving larger parts, and increase our capacity for jobs with smaller parts. The cost for a larger oven which could eventually be incorporated into an automated system is approximately $35,000.

As winners of the Industrial and Commercial Development Business Plan Contest, we used the $1,000 cash award and $10,000 interest free loan, along with additional bank financing, and internal funding to purchase additional equipment and pay off start-up debts.

**MARKET
SURVEY**

Company Name _____

Hello this is _____. We're doing a brief survey of the manufacturing companies in this area and I have a couple of quick questions to ask you.

1. Do you use any type of painting, plating or metal coating as part of your manufacturing process?

                    ___Yes ___No (If yes, go to 2. If no, go to End)

2. Who is in charge of that area of your manufacturing?

Name _____

Could I please speak with Mr/Ms_____.

(If not available ask for a good time to call back and go to end. If available go to 3.)

Time to call back _____

3. Hello this is _____. We're doing a brief survey of the manufacturing companies in this area and I have a couple of quick questions to ask you. I understand you use (painting, plating or metal coating) as part of your manufacturing process.

What type of parts are you (painting, plating or metal coating)?

                    Type of parts_____

                    Color of parts_____

Are you doing this work in-house or with a job shop?

                    ___In-house ___Job Shop

Can you give me a rough idea of the volume of (painting, plating or metal coating) that you are currently doing?

Volume of parts_____

FINANCIAL TABLES

1994 Profit and Loss

	Aug-Sep/94	% of Rev.	Oct-Dec/94	% of Rev.	1994	% of Rev.
Revenue	1828	100.00%	1552	100.00%	3380	100.00%
Costs of Sales						
Labor	5451	298.19%	3450	222.29%	8901	263.34%
Powder	358	19.58%	722	46.52%	1080	31.95%
Chemicals	1527	83.53%	0.0	0.00%	1527	45.18%
Maint. & Supplies	1035	56.62%	421	27.13%	1456	43.08%
Utilities	195	10.68%	357	23.00%	552	16.34%
Total Cost of Sales	**8655**	**468.61%**	**4950**	**318.94%**	**13516**	**399.89%**
Operating Expenses						
Management Salaries	0.0	0.00%	0.0	0.00%	0.0	0.00%
Rent	243	13.29%	1350	86.98%	1593	47.13%
Insurance	720	39.39%	338	21.78%	1058	31.30%
Taxes	0.0	0.00%	0.0	0.00%	0.0	0.00%
Debt Service	0.0	0.00%	0.0	0.00%	0.0	0.00%
Depreciation	514	28.12%	771	49.68%	1285	38.02%
Marketing & Adv.	0.0	0.00%	0.0	0.00%	0.0	0.00%
Postage	116	6.35%	108	6.94%	224	6.62%
Travel & Education	0.0	0.00%	0.0	0.00%	0.0	0.00%
Prof. Fees	0.0	0.00%	410	26.42%	410	12.13%
Phone	358	19.58%	333	21.46%	691	20.44%
Supplies	54	2.95%	373	24.03%	427	12.63%
Accrued Expenses	580	31.73%	870	56.06%	1450	42.90%
Misc.	12	0.66%	25	1.61%	37	1.09%
Total Operating Exp.	**2597**	**142.07%**	**4578**	**294.95%**	**7175**	**212.27%**
Profit Before Taxes	**(9335)**	**510.68%**	**(7976)**	**513.89%**	**(17311)**	**512.15%**

1995 BUDGET VS ACTUAL PROFIT AND LOSS
April 1, 1995

	Budget Jan-Mar	Actual Jan-Mar	% of Rev	Variance	Budget Apr-Jun	Actual Apr-Jun	% of Rev	Variance	Budget Jul-Sep	Actual Jul-Sep
Revenue	15000	6204	100.00%	(8796)	25000		100.00%	(25000)	30000	
Cost of Sales										
Labor	5550	3959	63.82%	(1591)	9250		0.00%	(9250)	11100	
Powder	2250	806	12.99%	(1444)	3750		0.00%	(3750)	4500	
Chemicals	600	50	0.80%	(550)	1000		0.00%	(1000)	1200	
Maint. & Supplies	450	495	7.98%	45	750		0.00%	(750)	900	
Utilities	900	617	9.95%	(283)	1500		0.00%	(1500)	1800	
Total Cost of Sale	9750	5927	95.53%	(3823)	16250	0.0	0.00%	(16250)	19500	0.0
Operating Expenses										
Management Salaries	2000	0.0	0.00%	(2000)	2000		0.00%	(2000)	2000	
Rent	912	1250	20.15%	338	912		0.00%	(912)	912	
Insurance	180	183	2.95%	3	180		0.00%	(180)	180	
Taxes	495	530	8.54%	35	495		0.00%	(495)	495	
Debt Service	2475	0.0	0.00%	(2475)	2475		0.00%	(2475)	2475	
Depreciation	771	400	6.45%	(371)	771		0.00%	(771)	771	
Marketing & Adv.	240	69	1.11%	(171)	240		0.00%	(240)	240	
Postage	29	0.0	0.00%	(29)	29		0.00%	(29)	29	
Travel & Education	0.0	0.0	0.00%	0.0	0.0		0.00%	0.0	500	
Prof. Fees	120	200	3.22%	80	120		0.00%	(120)	120	
Phone	300	415	6.69%	115	300		0.00%	(300)	300	
Supplies	60	407	6.56%	347	60		0.00%	(60)	60	
Accrued Expenses	0.0	2475	39.90%	2475	0.0		0.00%	0.0	0.0	
Misc.	25	86	1.39%	61	25		0.00%	(25)	25	
Total Operating Exp.	7607	6015	96.96%	(1592)	7607	0.0	0.00%	(7607)	8107	0.0
Profit Before Tax	(2357)	(5738)	-92.49%	(3381)	1143	0.0	0.00%	(1143)	2393	0.0

1996 Pro-Forma Profit and Loss

	1996	% of Rev.
Revenue	150000	100.00%
Cost of Sales		
Labor	55500	37.00%
Powder	22500	15.00%
Chemicals	6000	4.00%
Maint. & Supplies	4500	3.00%
Utilities	9000	6.00%
Total Cost of Sale	97500	65.00%
Operating Expenses		
Management Salary	20000	13.33%
Rent	3648	2.43%
Insurance	900	0.60%
Taxes	2430	1.62%

% of Rev	Variance	Budget Oct-Dec	Actual Oct-Dec	% of Rev	Variance	Budget 1995	Actual 1995	% of Rev	Variance
100.00%	**(30000)**	**30000**		**100.00%**	**(30000)**	**91204**	**6204**	**100.00%**	**(85000)**
0.00%	(11100)	11100		0.00%	(11100)	35409	3959	63.82%	(31450)
0.00%	(4500)	4500		0.00%	(4500)	13556	806	12.99%	(12750)
0.00%	(1200)	1200		0.00%	(1200)	3450	50	0.80%	(3400)
0.00%	(900)	900		0.00%	(900)	3045	495	7.98%	(2550)
0.00%	(1800)	1800		0.00%	(1800)	5717	617	9.95%	(5100)
0.00%	**(19500)**	**19500**	**0.0**	**0.00%**	**(19500)**	**61177**	**5927**	**95.53%**	**(55250)**
0.00%	(2000)	2000		0.00%	(2000)	6000	0.0	0.00%	(6000)
0.00%	(912)	912		0.00%	(912)	3986	1250	20.15%	(2736)
0.00%	(180)	180		0.00%	(180)	723	183	2.95%	(540)
0.00%	(495)	495		0.00%	(495)	2015	530	8.54%	(1485)
0.00%	(2475)	2475		0.00%	(2475)	7425	0.0	0.00%	(7425)
0.00%	(771)	771		0.00%	(771)	2713	400	6.45%	(2313)
0.00%	(240)	240		0.00%	(240)	789	69	1.11%	(720)
0.00%	(29)	29		0.00%	(29)	87	0.0	0.00%	(87)
0.00%	(500)	500		0.00%	(500)	1000	0.0	0.00%	(1000)
0.00%	(120)	120		0.00%	(120)	560	200	3.22%	(360)
0.00%	(300)	300		0.00%	(300)	1315	415	6.69%	(900)
0.00%	(60)	60		0.00%	(60)	587	407	6.56%	(180)
0.00%	0.0	0.0		0.00%	0.0	2475	2475	39.90%	0.0
0.00%	(25)	25		0.00%	(25)	161	86	1.39%	(75)
0.00%	**(8107)**	**8107**	**0.0**	**0.00%**	**(8107)**	**29836**	**6015**	**96.96%**	**(23821)**
0.00%	**(2393)**	**2393**	**0.0**	**0.00%**	**(2393)**	**192**	**(5738)**	**-92.49%**	**(5929)**

Debt Service	12000	8.00%
Depreciation	4150	2.77%
Marketing & Adv.	960	0.64%
Postage	116	0.08%
Travel & Education	2000	1.33%
Prof. Fees	550	0.37%
Phone	1400	0.93%
Supplies	240	0.16%
Accrued Expenses	0.0	0.00%
Misc.	100	0.07%
Total Operating Expenses	**48494**	**32.33%**
Profit Before Taxes	**4006**	**2.67%**

Balance Sheet

Assets	9/30/94	12/31/94	3/31/95	12/31/95
Current Assets				
Cash	$260.00	$82.00	$500.00	$1,000.00
Accounts Receivable	$2,079.00	$1,500.00	$1,200.00	$11,000.00
Inventory	$1,805.00	$2,000.00	$2,500.00	$2,000.00
Prepaid Expenses	$120.00	$741.00	$340.00	$500.00
Total Current Assets	**$4,264.00**	**$4,323.00**	**$4,540.00**	**$14,500.00**
Fixed Assets				
Equipment	$29,308.00	$32,458.00	$46,958.00	$46,958.00
Office Equipment and Furniture	$1,500.00	$1,500.00	$1,500.00	$1,500.00
Less Accumulated Depreciation	(1,285.00)	(3,166.00)	(4,696.00)	(4,696.00)
Total Fixed Assets	**$29,523.00**	**$30,792.00**	**$43,762.00**	**$43,762.00**
Total Assets	**$33,787.00**	**$35,115.00**	**$48,302.00**	**$58,262.00**
Liabilities and Fund Balance				
Current Liabilities				
Accounts Payable	$2,772.50	$1,225.00	$8,400.00	$4,000.00
Current Portion of Notes Payable	$7,425.00	$10,875.00	$10,875.00	$10,875.00
Accrued Interest	$580.00	$1,823.00	$2,917.00	$5,105.00
Total Current Liabilities	**$10,777.50**	**$13,923.00**	**$22,192.00**	**$19,980.00**
Long Term Liabilities				
Notes Payable	$32,575.00	$39,125.00	$39,125.00	$33,689.00
Total Liabilities	$43,352.50	$53,048.00	$61,317.00	$53,669.00
Net Worth	(9,565.50)	(17,933.00)	(13,015.00)	$4,593.00
Total Liab. and Net Worth	**$33,787.00**	**$35,115.00**	**$48,302.00**	**$58,262.00**

Notes

- *Figures for period ending 9/30/94 and 12/31/94 are actual.*
- *Increase in fixed assets and long term liabilities in 1995 reflects purchase of new cleaning system.*

Powder Coating Manufacturer

BUSINESS PLAN

INNOVATIVE OVER COAT

2800 West 13 Mile
Midland, MI 48506

This plan is the second of two powder coating manufacturer plans included in this edition. Both plan owners site that the changing government regulations have created a demand in the market for a more environmentally friendly coating process. Innovative Over Coat, like Brudder Coating Systems, presents a detailed plan, with industry information that is helpful to anyone considering the powder coating business.

- EXECUTIVE SUMMARY

- MISSION

- DESCRIPTION OF BUSINESS

- MARKET ANALYSIS

- MANAGEMENT

- OPERATIONS

- SOURCES AND USE OF FUNDS

- FINANCIAL INFORMATION

POWDER COATING MANUFACTURER
BUSINESS PLAN

EXECUTIVE SUMMARY

The Mission

Innovative Over Coat (IOC) will be the provider of choice in the Midwest for powder coating finishes for custom, refinish parts. IOC will provide these finishes with superior quality and superior service. IOC will retain customers by providing custom colors and superior customer service.

The Market

Powder coatings are the fastest growing sector of the paint industry; 149 million pounds sold in 1992 to 450 million pounds projected for the year 2000. Why is powder growing so quickly? There are three key reasons: it is less expensive to apply than liquid coatings, it is easier to apply than liquid coatings, and there are no solvents so it is more environmentally friendly than liquid coatings.

Many individuals who are refinishing motorcycle, automobile and snowmobile parts are impressed with the appearance and durability of powder coatings. Innovative Over Coat intends to capitalize on this market opportunity.

The Business

Innovative Over Coat (IOC) is a Michigan-based S-Corporation which will provide powder coating application services to metal parts. The initial target market will be individuals who are located in Southeast Michigan and Northwest Ohio, and are rebuilding motorcycles, custom automobiles, boats and snowmobiles.

Why will IOC initially target the refinish market? First, powder coating has a reputation for being a superior finish. Second, the individuals refinishing these "big boy toys" are committed to obtaining a superior finish. Third, powder coating has a reputation for being environmentally friendly. The greening of America is driving individuals to search out ways to reduce environmental impact. They will prefer powder coating.

IOC has already retained one customer, a Linnfield Motorcycles dealer located in Birmingham, Michigan. This dealer is building custom motorcycles, and has committed to hiring Innovative to apply the paint to frame and metal parts. As well as a high volume retail customer base, Linnfield Motorcycles is a high volume parts supplier and will provide Innovative with all of its after market powder coating business.

What kind of parts will IOC be coating? For motorcycles, frames, brackets, fenders, cylinders, and gas tanks. For custom automobiles, brackets, engine parts, and trim pieces. For snowmobiles, skis, frames and brackets.

We have identified more than 480 prospective customers in Michigan and Northwest Ohio. These customers include motorcycle dealers, motorcycle parts dealers, antique and custom automobile shops, and snowmobile dealers. These customers will buy services directly from Innovative, and refer customers to Innovative.

The Competition

There are not enough quality applicators in the market place to support the growing demand for custom powder coating services. There are 21 powder coating companies in Michigan and Northwest Ohio, but these companies are production shops serving the automotive market. We have identified one small company located in Sandusky, Ohio that is serving this market.

The Owners

The two partners forming this business have the breadth and depth of experience needed to succeed. John Godsey, President, has 16 years total experience, with eight of those years in management. Ike Walton, Vice President of Operations, has been working with the automotive industry for 22 years, and has been installing and operating powder coating systems since 1988. These two individuals make up the core of IOC, and cover the business needs essential for success.

IOC has developed financial projections for the first three years of operations. IOC is building the business in a manner that will be profitable almost immediately. We project $9,530 profit on $36,250 sales in the first year. Profit will grow to $42,450 on $117,000 sales in the third year. IOC must obtain financing in order to start this company. IOC is seeking $30,000 in traditional financing to support capital purchase, and a small amount of initial working capital. The owners are providing $10,000 funding: $5,000 cash and $5,000 equipment.	**Financial**
Innovative Over Coat (IOC) will be the applicator of choice in the Midwest for custom powder coating finishes. IOC will accomplish this by providing powder coating application services of superior quality combined with superior service. IOC will focus its marketing efforts on parts that require a quality finish.	**MISSION**
Innovative Over Coat, a Michigan S-Corporation, is a start-up venture that will provide custom powder coating finishing services for metal parts. IOC will provide custom coating services to customers who demand a finish that looks great and will last. IOC will focus our initial marketing efforts on companies and individuals who are building/rebuilding motorcycles, automobiles, and snow mobiles. [This is a market where current and future demand far exceeds the supply.]	**DESCRIPTION OF BUSINESS**

IOC will differentiate itself from the competition by:

- focusing on custom coated parts
- providing only powder coated finishes
- providing superior service

Comparison of Liquid and Powder Coatings

(Liquid coating (i.e., paint) involves applying a thin layer of coating to a part. The coating must contain some form of solvent carrier that transfers the paint to the part being coated. The solvent carrier can be water or a chemical such as toluene or xylene. The solvent evaporates, leaving behind the thin film of coating. The coating must cure to form the final, hard finish. Curing can occur in one of several ways based on the formula: evaporation (air dry), baking (elevated temperature dry), use of Ultra-Violet radiation, or use of a catalyst.

By contrast, a powder coating does not involve the use of any liquid. A dry powder is electrostatically applied to the part, and then cured in a baking oven at a temperature of 350 to 425 degrees. There are no solvents to evaporate, eliminating all air emissions. There are no liquids required to clean equipment, eliminating all liquid waste generation.

Powder coatings have proven to be an efficient, economical, and ecologically sound method of industrial finishing. Generally, powders outperform liquids because of their higher molecular weight and greater insolubility; there is less film porosity with superior chemical resistance, toughness, hardness and abrasion resistance.

Some of the advantages of powder coatings include:

- Powder is an attractive choice over liquid finishing systems because it is a 100 percent solids material that contains no solvents. Powder coatings permit compliance with volatile organic compound (VOC) air pollution standards.
- Powder eliminates the need for storing flammable paints and solvents. And, there is no liquid paint sludge to dispose as hazardous waste.
- Oven exhaust and air make up can be reduced because no solvent fumes are emitted during the curing cycle. This results in considerable energy savings.

- Powder that is not deposited on the part can be reclaimed and reused, increasing material efficiency to as much as 95 to 98 percent.
- When a coating mistake has been made, powder can be blown off with compressed air and reapplied to the part before baking, further decreasing part rejection.
- The need for paint mixing is eliminated. Powder is introduced into the feed hopper directly from the box.
- Powder coatings can offer excellent color consistency, color matching capabilities and color and gloss retention.
- Clean up is easy; powder can be vacuumed off skin and clothing with a high efficiency vacuum.
- Soap and water will accomplish the final clean up.

While this all sounds too good to be true, there has historically been one limitation to powder coatings. They could not match the visual performance of a liquid coating. This limitation was eliminated within the past few years, when powder coatings have been developed to match liquid coatings in all measures of performance.

MARKET ANALYSIS
Market Trend

IOC has selected powder coating finishes because they are the finish of the future. Powder coating is the fastest growing segment of the coating industry. Powder coating sales have nearly doubled since 1992 (149 million pounds in 1992 to 257 million pounds in 1995), and are expected to nearly double again by the year 2000. Sales are projected to be 450 million pounds by the year 2000.

Powder coating sales have grown at the expense of other types of coatings, and manufacturers are converting from liquid coating to powder coating. Liquid paint (solvent borne and water borne) will drop from 76 percent of the market in 1995 to 67 percent in 2000. Powder coating will increase from 15 percent in 1995 to 22 percent in 2000.

The conversion from liquid to powder is happening for several reasons. First, it is environmentally friendly. Powder coating causes no air emissions and produces no hazardous waste. Second, it is less expensive. Applying powder coating costs one tenth of the cost of the application of liquid coating.

IOC has further evaluated the market by interviewing numerous powder coating users, and other experts in the field. Customers, paint manufacturers, and painting equipment manufacturers agree that there are few custom powder coaters in the Midwest who can consistently, and reliably apply powder coating to meet the demanding standards of our targeted market segment.

Target Markets

IOC will initially target the custom refinishing of motorcycle, automobile, and snowmobile parts. Why? First, these individuals demand a high quality finish. Second, these individuals are willing to spend more money to get a high quality finish. Third, these individuals know that a powder coating finish is superior to a liquid coating finish in performance and look. Furthermore, IOC partners have an extensive network of contacts in the motorcycle industry.

Organization Of The Sales Effort

How will we get customers? IOC will initially work through other companies to obtain business. We have identified more than 480 companies in Michigan and Northwest Ohio: motorcycle dealers, motorcycle parts dealers, antique and custom automobile shops, and snowmobile dealers. These companies can use our services directly and refer customers to Innovative.

Sales will be accomplished only through internal resources. IOC is presently building a reputation with local Linnfield dealerships. We will use this "word of mouth" advertising in combination with advertising in trade publications, trade shows and mailings to local dealerships.

IOC has already established a relationship with Linnfield Motorcycles in Birmingham, Michigan. Linnfield is key to market entry. Linnfield is an established dealer of motorcycles and is a meeting place for the local Linnfield owner's club. They are developing a line of custom motorcycles that will sell for more than $30,000 each; this will showcase the IOC quality finish.

As stated above, Linnfield wants IOC to paint all of their custom motorcycles. They have already agreed to refer customers and other motorcycle dealers needing powder coating to IOC. IOC needs more than one customer to survive.

We will expand our customer base using the following steps:

- Personal contact to the owners of the 12 Linnfield Motorcycle dealers located in Michigan and Southeast Ohio.
- Develop a point-of-sale display for parts counters at these 12 dealers. This provides access to their customers, and a constant reminder to the dealers.
- Personal contact to owners of antique automobile/auto customizing companies and snow mobile dealers in Northwest Michigan.
- Develop a point-of-sale display for parts counters at these companies, as appropriate. This provides access to their customers, and a constant reminder to the owners and their employees.
- Develop brochure and price list for POS display.
- Mailing of brochure and price list to the remainder of the 482 companies on the prospect list.

Competitive Analysis

Our research shows that there are not enough quality applicators in the market place to support the growing demand for powder coating services. Our research shows that the demand will continue to grow. Innovative Coating will position itself from day one to fulfill the needs of this market segment.

Innovative Coatings will compete in a marketplace that currently lacks service providers. We compiled a list of Midwest companies who apply powder coatings. Out of the twenty-one (21) competitors we found, ten are located in Northwest Ohio. Of these ten companies, only four (4) are custom powder coaters. The other companies are production powder coaters (large production runs for the automotive industry).

IOC will differentiate themselves from these companies in three ways:

- custom powder coating will be our only business
- applying a quality finish will be our primary focus
- exceptional customer service will be a key part of our product

Innovative Coating recognizes that customers demand "Service Beyond The Sale." IOC will develop a partnership with customers and suppliers. We'll make sure that every job is done right. IOC will exceed customer expectations. IOC will provide technical support when a problem arises, rapid response to customer demands, and flexible company hours. IOC has extensive application experience, and can work closely with the customer to develop cost effective techniques to insure the highest quality finishes.

Customer Profile

People who want to buy a new Linnfield motorcycle are willing to wait two to three years before taking delivery. This is the commitment to owning one of "America's premiere" motorcycles. This same commitment extends to the many individuals who are rebuilding older Linnfield motorcycles to "like new" condition. These individuals spend considerable amounts of money to rebuild the motorcycle to "like new" condition. They spend additional money to get an exceptional paint job.

We will get to these individuals through the Linnfield dealers, which is where individuals needing an exceptional paint job go for referrals. We will target the Linnfield motorcycle dealer with an established business.

**Top Five
After-Market
Prospects**

Linnfield Motorcycles, Birmingham, MI - Discussions and meetings held with the owner. IOC has been asked to powder coat their new line of custom motorcycles.

Butterfly Bikes, Grand Rapids, MI - Discussions held with the owner. Very interested in IOC service and capability.

Washington Linnfield, Pontiac, MI - No discussions held to date.

Donahue's Wheels, Cadillac, MI - No discussions held to date.

Nash Jackson Linnfield Motors, Scottsdale, AZ - One meeting conducted with the owner. Very interested in IOC service and capability.

MANAGEMENT

To succeed in custom coating, every individual in the company must be a peak performer. Success will require the ability to manage the company resources effectively. Success will require a strong sales effort. Success will require the ability to deliver a product that meets the customer's expectations. The IOC management team meets these requirements.

John Godsey, President, has been involved in management, operations and sales during his 16 year career. John has spent more than half of his career in management positions, including: Office Manager for a $2.5 million, 25 person office; Regional Sales and Technical Manager for an $88 million company; Regional Vice President for a start-up operation, part of a $20 million, 125 person operation; Vice President - Operations for a $4 million, 40 person company; and Corporate Manager for a Fortune 200 Company.

Ike Walton, Vice President-Operations, has the knowledge and experience that it takes to set up and run a high quality powder coating operation. Ike has more than 22 years of experience working in the automotive industry. Ike has spent the past 8 years working for the world leader in robotic powder coating application systems. Ike spent 6 years developing the programming that drives the powder coating system, and has spent the past 2 years as Project Manager installing new systems and troubleshooting existing systems. These projects involve multi-million dollar systems. Ike has seen all of the things that affect a quality operation, and knows how to develop and implement the solution. Furthermore, Ike has run a small custom powder coating operation in the past.

**Roles and
Responsibilities**

Each member of the management team brings a different resource to the company, resulting in a whole that is greater than the sum of the parts. Innovative will start out in a fashion that will minimize overhead costs and risk, and maximize profitability. John and Ike will be the only employees initially, responsible for selling the work, applying the powder coating, and running the business. We expect that this business will grow quickly, and we will need employees within six months. At that time, our business management experience will prove invaluable, as described below.

John Godsey will be responsible for managing the company, and leading the future growth of the organization. He will be directly responsible for the financial, administrative and human resources aspects of IOC. Initially, he will also use his past experience with operations and sales to coordinate and assist with these responsibilities. He brings strong technical and management experience to IOC. John has a strong background with management and quality control systems.

Ike Walton will be responsible for leading the operations. Ike's expertise in installing and operating powder coating systems will prove invaluable to efficient facility management. Ike will install and operate the powder coating system. All operations staff will report to Ike, and it will be his responsibility for ensuring that customer orders are completed on-time, and to customer specifications.

IOC will obtain accounting/financial support on an as needed basis. IOC initially intends to maintain financial information internally, using an accountant for semi-annual or annual reviews.

IOC will also obtain legal support as an outside resource. The firm has not been selected at this time.

OPERATIONS

Operations will be responsible for delivering a product that meets customer expectations the first time. Our market analysis identified that customers need a powder coating operation that can reliably deliver a high quality finish, bundled with superior customer service. Other powder coating operations in this geographic area place little emphasis on cleanliness, quality, or on-time delivery.

IOC will succeed by differentiating ourselves from these companies in four ways:

- powder coating will be our only business
- applying a high quality finish will be our primary focus
- the equipment needed to produce a high quality finish will be purchased from the start
- exceptional customer service will be a key part of our product

Production Equipment

Equipment

The first key to applying a Class A finish is having the right equipment. IOC will purchase equipment capable of applying high quality finish. This equipment is:

Application Equipment: Symons Studio manual spray powder system: Ultimate flexibility and control manual application of powder coatings.
Baking Oven: The powder coating cures when exposed for a prescribed length of time to temperatures between 350 and 425 degrees Fahrenheit. The baking oven must hold temperature during that time, and all surfaces must be evenly exposed.
Spray booth: IOC will purchase a used spray booth that will allow for the collection of sprayed powder. As cash flow warrants IOC will refurbish this booth to become a permanent color booth.

The correct equipment is only one step to delivering a high quality finish. The equipment must be operated effectively. Two key aspects to operation are "Working Environment" and "Quality Program."

Operating Systems

Working Environment

A clean and orderly work environment is essential for the success of IOC. We will hire future employees, and consider them to be long term investments; we can only retain them if we provide a safe, sound and healthy environment.

Beyond this, a clean and orderly work environment is essential to providing a high quality finish. Airborne dirt and dust will contaminate the powder coating, and result in a finish with imperfections.

IOC principals know that it is critical to meet customer expectations the first time. We have all had our share of customer complaints, due to product that does not meet customer specifications. The unhappy customer is just one cost of poor quality. There is also the cost to rework the part. It costs more to redo the work than it did to do it right the first time. IOC will institute Quality Control systems that will allow us to make parts right the first time. Quality will be built into all IOC operations, and all employees will adopt the quality ethic.

Quality Program

Quality control will also be the responsibility of each employee. The goal is to move responsibility for quality control out onto the work floor. Each employee will also have responsibility for their own job performance. Quality and process problems, concerns or recommendations will be discussed as part of weekly and monthly company wide meetings.

Environmental Compliance

IOC will make every effort to comply with all environmental regulations. Powder coating is environmentally friendly. The environmental impact is minimal. There are no solvents used in the paint process, eliminating the need for wash solvent and eliminating VOC emissions from coating operations. Powder coating that must be disposed can be handled as ordinary trash; it is not a hazardous waste.

There are some permitting requirements for this operation. The air permitting requirements are minimal; the Michigan Department of Environmental Quality (MDEQ) does not require an air permit for powder coating operations.

Staffing

During the majority of the first year IOC will be staffed by Ike Walton and John Godsey. This will cut down on overhead and allow the owners to implement quality programs prior to hiring new employees. As the business grows, IOC will hire additional employees to ensure that customers get parts coated in a reasonable amount of time.

Facility Requirements

IOC will initially operate renting space from part of a building. The target space has natural gas and electricity available to meet our requirements. This space will have a month-to-month lease, allowing us to pay only for the space that we need, and move into larger space when needed.

IOC expects to secure our own building or portion of a building after one year. Our search will focus on the area immediately east of Toledo, Ohio. This area has a large number of light industrial buildings, equipped with the power and structural needs of a growing company.

SOURCES AND USE OF FUNDS

The total dollar amount being sought is $30,000 in conventional financing. IOC expects there to be only one funding round for full financing during the first 2 to 3 years. IOC does not want to seek financing that would require an outside equity position.

The funding will be used to purchase capital, and provide working capital for the initial 4 to 6 months. This funding is essential to allow the start of this company.

This business plan assumes that IOC will purchase a combination of new and used equipment. Used powder coating equipment is not readily available; this will determine the amount of new equipment that must be purchased.

Use Of Funds

Capital Expenditures

Leasehold Improvements	$2,000
Purchase of oven	$20,000
Spray gun and hopper	$2,500
Used Spray Booth	$2,500
Total Capital Expenditures	**$27,000**

Working Capital

Purchase of Inventory	$1,500
Lease expenses	$1,000
Staffing	00
Other Activities	$5,500
Total Working Capital	$8,000
Total Use Of Funds	**$35,000**

IOC is seeking funding that will allow equipment purchase, building leasing, equipment set-up, and will support the operation for the initial period. IOC expects that cash flow will support the operation after the initial period, and that a bank will provide a line of credit based on the Accounts Receivable (A/R's).

IOC has determined our financial requirements based on the financial analysis in the following tables. Included are the Pro forma Income Statement, Balance Sheet, and Cash Flow analysis for the first three years (1997, 1998 and 1999). The income statement shows that IOC will be profitable almost immediately. We project generating $9,500 profit on $36,250 sales in year 1, $26,840 profit on $87,000 sales in year 2, and $41,850 profit on $117,500 sales in year 3.

Financial Analysis

Financial ratios are included for your convenience.

Ratio Analysis

We have included financial standards as compiled by Jackson Associates for comparable companies in this industry.

Financial Standards

Fixed Assets

Asset Worksheet

Equipment	1000.00
Automotive, trucks	0.00
Buildings	0.00
Fixtures	0.00
Machinery	24000.00
Leasehold improvements	2000.00
Start Up Costs	0.00
Miscellaneous #1	0.00
Miscellaneous #2	0.00
Total Fixed Assets	**27000.00**

Intangible Assets

Goodwill	0.00
Other	0.00
Total Intangible Assets	**0.00**

BALANCE SHEET

	Year 1	Year 2	Year 3	Percent Change Yr1-Yr2	Yr2-Yr3
ASSETS					
Cash	7262.72	29372.38	86478.92	304.43%	194.42%
Accounts Receivable	0.00	4000.00	5000.00	#N/A!	25.00%
Notes Receivable	0.00	0.00	0.00	#N/A!	#N/A!
Inventory	391.25	523.75	50.00	33.87%	-90.45%
Total Current Assets	7653.97	33896.13	91528.92	342.86%	170.03%
Total Fixed Assets	27000.00	23142.86	19285.71		
Less: accum. deprec.	3857.14	3857.14	3857.14		
Net Fixed assets	23142.86	19285.71	15428.57	-16.67%	-20.00%
Intangible Assets	0.00	0.00	0.00	#N/A!	#N/A!
Total Assets	30796.83	53181.84	106957.49	72.69%	101.12%
LIABILITIES					
Accounts payable	0.00	0.00	0.00	#N/A!	#N/A!
Bank notes	0.00	0.00	0.00	#N/A!	#N/A!
Notes payable	0.00	0.00	0.00	#N/A!	#N/A!
CPLTD	5249.54	5915.33	6665.53	12.68%	12.68%
Total Current Liabilities	5249.54	5915.33	6665.53	12.68%	12.68%
Long Term Debt	20091.75	14176.42	7510.89	-29.44%	-47.02%
Total Liabilities	25341.29	20091.75	14176.42	-20.72%	-29.44%
NET WORTH					
Paid in Capital	35000.00	35000.00	35000.00		
Retained Earnings	9533.97	26837.99	41851.16	181.50%	55.94%
Additional Value	-39078.43	-28747.90	15929.91	-26.44%	-155.41%
Total Net Worth	5455.54	33090.09	92781.07	506.54%	180.39%
TOTAL LIABILITIES & NET WORTH	30796.83	53181.84	106957.49	72.69%	101.12%

RATIO ANALYSIS

	Year 1	Year 2	Year 3	Percent Change Yr1-Yr2	Percent Change Yr2-Yr3
Current Ratio	1.46	5.73	13.73	293.01%	139.64%
Acid Ratio	1.38	4.97	12.97	258.91%	161.29%
Debt Ratio (Total Debt/Total Assets) 0.82		**0.38**	**0.13**	**-54.09%**	**-64.92%**
TIE					
Inventory Turnover	68.43	39.10	1.46	-42.86%	-96.25%
Average Collection Period	0.00	16.63	15.40	#N/A!	-7.45%
Total Asset Turnover	**1.17**	**1.63**	**1.09**	**38.98%**	**-32.85%**
Gross Margin	94.66%	94.69%	94.75%	0.04%	0.05%
Net Margin	26.43%	31.00%	35.80%	17.29%	15.46%
Return on Assets	30.96%	50.46%	39.13%	63.01%	-22.46%
Return on Equity	174.76%	81.11%	45.11%	-53.59%	-44.38%
Off. Comp./Sales	**1.66%**	**1.85%**	**5.13%**	**11.11%**	**177.66%**

RMA

	Year 1	Year 2	Year 3	Industry Norm
Assets				
Cash & Equivalents	23.6	55.2	80.9	12.4
Trade Receivables - (net)	0.0	7.5	9.4	26.2
Inventory	1.3	1.0	0.0	10.2
All Other Current	0.0	0.0	0.0	2.1
Total Current	24.9	63.7	85.6	50.9
Fixed Assets (net)	75.1	36.3	14.4	39.4
All Other Non-Current	0.0	0.0	0.0	3.4
Total	**100.0**	**100.0**	**100.0**	**100.0**
Liabilities				
Notes-Payable-Short Term	0.0	0.0	0.0	7.1
Cur. Mat.-L/T/D	17.0	11.1	6.2	4.5
Trade Payables	0.0	0.0	0.0	7.8
Income Taxes-Payable	0.0	0.0	0.0	1.4
All Other Current	0.0	0.0	0.0	7.8
Total Current	17.0	11.1	6.2	28.6
Long Term Debt	65.2	26.7	7.0	19.4
Deferred Taxes	0.0	0.0	0.0	1.2
All Other Non-Current	65.2	26.7	7.0	9.4
Net Worth	17.7	62.2	86.7	41.4
Total Liabilities & Net Worth	**100.0**	**100.0**	**100.0**	**100.0**
Income Data				
Net Sales	100.0	100.0	100.0	100.0
Gross Profit	94.7	94.7	94.7	47.7
Operating Expenses	57.6	51.2	44.5	41.5
Operating Profit	37.1	43.5	50.2	6.2
All Other Expenses (net)	0.0	0.0	0.0	1.9
Profit Before Taxes	**36.7**	**43.1**	**49.7**	**4.3**
Ratios				
Current	1.46	5.73	13.73	2.2
Quick	1.38	4.97	12.97	1.5
Sales/Receivables	#N/A!	21.64	23.38	8.5
Cost of Sales/Inventory	7.65	11.16	303.35	18.3
Cost of Sales/Payables	#N/A!	#N/A!	#N/A!	19.0
Sales/Working Capital	15.00	3.09	1.38	7.1
EBIT/Interest	0.00	0.00	0.00	3.3
Net Profit + Depr.,Dep., Amort./Cur. Mat. L/T/D	0.00	0.00	0.00	3.4
Fixed/Worth	4.24	0.58	0.17	0.9
Debt/Worth	4.65	0.61	0.15	1.3
% Profit Before Taxes/ Tangible Net Worth	242.72%	112.65%	62.65%	23.7
% Profit Before Taxes/ Total Assets	43.00%	70.09%	54.35%	9.4
Sales/Net Fixed Assets	1.56	4.49	7.58	4.5
Sales/Total Assets	1.17	1.63	1.09	1.9
% Depr., Dep., Amort/Sales	0.00%	0.00%	0.00%	4.2
% Officer's Comp./Sales	1.66%	1.85%	5.13%	11.1

Income Statement

	Year 1	Year 2	Year 3	Percent Change Yr1-Yr2	Yr2-Yr3
Revenue					
Gross Sales	36250.00	87000.00	117500.00	140.00%	35.06%
Less returns, discounts	181.25	435.00	587.50	140.00%	35.06%
Net Sales	**36068.75**	**86565.00**	**116912.50**	**140.00%**	**35.06%**
Cost of Goods Sold					
Beginning inventory	75.00	366.25	498.75	388.33%	36.18%
Purchases	2112.50	4500.00	5400.00	113.02%	20.00%
Freight	105.63	225.00	270.00	113.02%	20.00%
Total goods available	2293.13	5091.25	6168.75	122.02%	21.16%
Ending inventory	366.25	498.75	25.00	36.18%	-94.99%
Total Cost of Goods Sold	**1926.88**	**4592.50**	**6143.75**	**138.34%**	**33.78%**
Gross Profit	**34141.88**	**81972.50**	**110768.75**	**140.09%**	**35.13%**
Operating Expenses					
Selling Expenses					
Advertising	575.00	375.00	600.00	-34.78%	60.00%
Commissions	0.00	0.00	0.00	#N/A!	#N/A!
Travel & Entertainment	300.00	600.00	840.00	100.00%	40.00%
Total	**875.00**	**975.00**	**1440.00**	**11.43%**	**47.69%**
Administrative					
Salaries	600.00	1600.00	6000.00	166.67%	275.00%
Payroll	2880.00	13920.00	14400.00	383.33%	3.45%
Withholding	1044.00	4656.00	6120.00	345.98%	31.44%
Insurance	1200.00	1200.00	1200.00	0.00%	0.00%
Total	**5724.00**	**21376.00**	**27720.00**	**273.45%**	**29.68%**
General					
Rent	5700.00	12000.00	12000.00	110.53%	0.00%
Utilities	3000.00	4800.00	4800.00	60.00%	0.00%
Telephone	900.00	1800.00	1800.00	100.00%	0.00%
Office Expenses	300.00	1800.00	2400.00	500.00%	33.33%
Vehicle Expenses	0.00	0.00	0.00	#N/A!	#N/A!
Office Supplies	300.00	300.00	600.00	0.00%	100.00%
Postage	180.00	200.00	120.00	11.11%	-40.00%
Professionals	362.50	870.00	1175.00	140.00%	35.06%
Research	0.00	0.00	0.00	#N/A!	#N/A!
Misc.	3425.00	200.00	0.00	-94.16%	-100.00%
Total	**14167.50**	**21970.00**	**22895.00**	**55.07%**	**4.21%**
Total Operating Expenses	**20766.50**	**44321.00**	**52055.00**	**113.43%**	**17.45%**
Total Operating Income	13375.38	37651.50	58713.75	181.50%	55.94%
State Taxes	133.75	376.52	587.14	181.50%	55.94%
Pretax Income	13241.62	37274.99	58126.61	181.50%	55.94%
Federal Taxes	3707.65	10437.00	16275.45	181.50%	55.94%
Net Income	**9533.97**	**26837.99**	**41851.16**	**181.50%**	**55.94%**

Year One Cash Flow

		Jan	Feb	Mar	Apr	May	Jun
Sales:							
Linnfield Motors		500	1,000	1,000	1,500	1,500	2,000
Other Motorcycle Dealers		0	250	500	500	500	500
Automotive Customizing		0	0	0	250	250	250
Snowmobile Customizing		0	0	0	0	0	250
Total Sales		500	1,250	1,500	2,250	2,250	3,000
Cash Receipts:							
Month of Shipment	60%	300	750	900	1,350	1,350	1,800
First Month	30%	0	150	375	450	675	675
Second Month	10%	0	0	50	125	150	225
Third Month	0%	0	0	0	0	0	0
Fourth Month	0%	0	0	0	0	0	0
Total Receipts		300	900	1,325	1,925	2,175	2,700
Cash Expenses:							
Rent		300	300	300	300	300	300
Utilities		200	200	200	200	200	200
Telephone		50	50	50	50	50	50
Salaries		50	50	50	50	50	50
Payroll		0	0	0	0	0	0
Withholding		15	15	15	15	15	15
#1 Inventory		50	50	75	75	100	100
Freight-In		3	3	4	4	5	5
#2 Inventory		13	25	25	25	25	50
Freight-In		1	1	1	1	1	3
#3 Inventory		0	0	13	13	13	25
Freight-In		0	0	1	1	1	1
#4 Inventory		0	0	0	0	13	13
Freight-In		0	0	0	0	1	1
Office Expense		0	0	0	0	0	0
Vehicle Expense		0	0	0	0	0	0
Office Supplies		25	25	25	25	25	25
Postage		0	0	50	10	10	10
Advertising		0	100	100	25	25	100
Professionals		5	13	15	23	23	30
Commissions		0	0	0	0	0	0
Insurance		100	100	100	100	100	100
Travel & Entertainment		0	0	30	30	30	30
Research		0	0	0	0	0	0
Equipment Purchase		27,000	0	0	0	0	0
Miscellaneous (Start-up costs; Samples)	3,225		0	50	0	50	0
State Taxes		0	0	0	0	0	0
Federal Taxes		0	0	0	0	0	0
Total Expenses		31,036	931	1,103	946	1,035	1,107
Net Cash From Operations		-30,736	-31	222	979	1,140	1,593
Beginning Cash		35,000	4,264	3,563	3,115	3,424	3,894
Cash on Hand		4,264	4,233	3,785	4,094	4,564	5,488
Bank Loan Required		0	0	0	0	0	0
Loan Repayment		0	670	670	670	670	670
Ending Cash		4,264	3,563	3,115	3,424	3,894	4,818

Jul	Aug	Sep	Oct	Nov	Dec
2,000	2,000	2,000	2,000	2,500	3,000
1,000	1,000	1,000	1,000	1,000	2,000
500	500	500	500	500	1,000
250	250	250	250	250	250
3,750	3,750	3,750	3,750	4,250	6,250
2,250	2,250	2,250	2,250	2,550	3,750
900	1,125	1,125	1,125	1,125	1,275
225	300	375	375	375	375
0	0	0	0	0	0
0	0	0	0	0	0
3,375	3,675	3,750	3,750	4,050	5,400
300	300	300	1,000	1,000	1,000
200	200	200	400	400	400
50	50	50	150	150	150
50	50	50	50	50	50
0	0	0	960	960	960
15	15	15	303	303	303
100	100	100	125	150	150
5	5	5	6	8	8
50	50	50	50	100	100
3	3	3	3	5	5
25	25	25	25	50	50
1	1	1	1	3	3
13	13	13	13	13	25
1	1	1	1	1	1
0	0	0	100	100	100
0	0	0	0	0	0
25	25	25	25	25	25
10	10	10	50	10	10
25	25	25	25	25	100
38	38	38	38	43	63
0	0	0	0	0	0
100	100	100	100	100	100
30	30	30	30	30	30
0	0	0	0	0	0
0	0	0	0	0	0
0	50	0	0	50	0
0	0	0	0	0	0
0	0	0	0	0	0
1,039	1,089	1,039	3,454	3,574	3,632
2,336	2,586	2,711	296	476	1,768
4,818	6,483	8,399	10,439	10,066	9,872
7,153	9,069	11,109	10,736	10,542	11,640
0	0	0	0	0	0
670	670	670	670	670	670
6,483	8,399	10,439	10,066	9,872	10,970

Year Two Cash Flow

	Jan	Feb	Mar	Apr	May
Sales					
Linnfield Motorcycles	3,000	3,000	3,000	3,000	3,000
Other Motorcycle Dealers	2,000	2,000	2,000	2,000	2,500
Automotive Customizing	1,000	1,000	1,000	1,000	1,500
Snowmobile Customizing	500	500	500	500	500
Total Sales	**6,500**	**6,500**	**6,500**	**6,500**	**7,500**
Cash Receipts					
Month of Shipment	3,900	3,900	3,900	3,900	4,500
First Month	1,875	1,950	1,950	1,950	1,950
Second Month	425	625	650	650	650
Third Month	0	0	0	0	0
Fourth Month	0	0	0	0	0
Total Receipts	**6,200**	**6,475**	**6,500**	**6,500**	**7,100**
Cash Expenses					
Rent	1,000	1,000	1,000	1,000	1,000
Utilities	400	400	400	400	400
Telephone	150	150	150	150	150
Salaries	100	100	100	100	100
Payroll	960	960	1,200	1,200	1,200
Witholding	318	318	390	390	390
#1 Inventory	150	150	150	150	150
Freight-In	8	8	8	8	8
#2 Inventory	100	100	100	125	125
Freight-In	5	5	5	6	6
#3 Inventory	50	50	50	75	75
Freight-In	3	3	3	4	4
#4 Inventory	25	25	25	25	25
Freight-In	1	1	1	1	1
Office Expense	100	100	100	100	100
Vehicle Expense	0	0	0	0	0
Office Supplies	25	25	25	25	25
Postage	10	10	50	10	10
Advertising	100	25	25	25	25
Professionals	65	65	65	65	75
Commissions	0	0	0	0	0
Insurance	100	100	100	100	100
Travel & Entertainment	50	50	50	50	50
Research	0	0	0	0	0
Equipment Purchase	0	0	0	0	0
Miscellaneous (Start-up Costs; Samples)	0	50	0	0	50
State Taxes	0	0	0	0	0
Federal Taxes	0	0	0	0	0
Total Expenses	**3,719**	**3,694**	**3,996**	**4,009**	**4,069**
Net Cash From Operations	2,481	2,781	2,504	2,491	3,031
Beginning Cash	10,970	12,781	14,892	16,726	18,547
Cash on Hand	13,451	15,562	17,396	19,217	21,578
Bank Loan Required	0	0	0	0	0
Loan Repayment	670	670	670	670	670
Ending Cash	**12,781**	**14,892**	**16,726**	**18,547**	**20,908**

Jun	Jul	Aug	Sep	Oct	Nov	Dec
3,000	3,000	3,000	3,000	3,000	3,000	3,000
2,500	2,500	2,500	2,500	2,500	3,000	3,000
1,500	1,500	1,500	1,500	1,500	1,500	1,500
500	500	500	500	500	500	500
7,500	**7,500**	**7,500**	**7,500**	**7,500**	**8,000**	**8,000**
4,500	4,500	4,500	4,500	4,500	4,800	4,800
2,250	2,250	2,250	2,250	2,250	2,250	2,400
650	750	750	750	750	750	750
0	0	0	0	0	0	0
0	0	0	0	0	0	0
7,400	**7,500**	**7,500**	**7,500**	**7,500**	**7,800**	**7,950**
1,000	1,000	1,000	1,000	1,000	1,000	1,000
400	400	400	400	400	400	400
150	150	150	150	150	150	150
100	100	100	100	100	100	500
1,200	1,200	1,200	1,200	1,200	1,200	1,200
390	390	390	390	390	390	510
150	150	150	150	150	150	150
8	8	8	8	8	8	8
125	125	125	125	150	150	150
6	6	6	6	8	8	8
75	75	75	75	75	75	100
4	4	4	4	4	4	5
25	25	25	25	25	25	75
1	1	1	1	1	1	4
100	200	200	200	200	200	200
0	0	0	0	0	0	0
25	25	25	25	25	25	25
10	10	10	10	10	10	50
25	25	25	25	25	25	25
75	75	75	75	75	80	80
0	0	0	0	0	0	0
100	100	100	100	100	100	100
50	50	50	50	50	50	50
0	0	0	0	0	0	0
0	0	0	0	0	0	0
0	0	50	0	0	50	0
0	0	0	0	0	0	0
0	0	0	0	0	0	0
4,019	**4,119**	**4,169**	**4,119**	**4,145**	**4,200**	**4,789**
3,381	3,381	3,331	3,381	3,355	3,600	3,161
20,908	23,619	26,331	28,992	31,703	34,388	37,318
24,289	27,001	29,662	32,373	35,058	37,988	40,479
0	0	0	0	0	0	0
670	670	670	670	670	670	670
23,619	**26,331**	**28,992**	**31,703**	**34,388**	**37,318**	**39,809**

Year Three Cash Flow

	Jan	Feb	Mar	Apr	May
Sales					
Linnfield Motorcycles	3,000	3,000	3,000	3,000	3,000
Other Motorcycle Dealers	3,000	3,000	3,000	3,000	3,000
Automotive Customizing	2,000	2,000	2,000	2,000	2,000
Snowmobile Customizing	1,500	1,500	1,500	1,500	1,500
Total Sales	**9,500**	**9,500**	**9,500**	**9,500**	**9,500**
Cash Receipts					
Month of Shipment	5,700	5,700	5,700	5,700	5,700
First Month	2,400	2,850	2,850	2,850	2,850
Second Month	800	800	950	950	950
Third Month	0	0	0	0	0
Fourth Month	0	0	0	0	0
Total Receipts	**8,900**	**9,350**	**9,500**	**9,500**	**9,500**
Cash Expenses					
Rent	1,000	1,000	1,000	1,000	1,000
Utilities	400	400	400	400	400
Telephone	150	150	150	150	150
Salaries	500	500	500	500	500
Payroll	1,200	1,200	1,200	1,200	1,200
Witholding	510	510	510	510	510
#1 Inventory	150	150	150	150	150
Freight-In	8	8	8	8	8
#2 Inventory	150	150	150	150	175
Freight-In	8	8	8	8	9
#3 Inventory	100	100	100	100	100
Freight-In	5	5	5	5	5
#4 Inventory	75	75	75	75	75
Freight-In	4	4	4	4	4
Office Expense	200	200	200	200	200
Vehicle Expense	0	0	0	0	0
Office Supplies	50	50	50	50	50
Postage	10	10	10	10	10
Advertising	50	50	50	50	50
Professionals	95	95	95	95	95
Commissions	0	0	0	0	0
Insurance	100	100	100	100	100
Travel & Entertainment	70	70	70	70	70
Research	0	0	0	0	0
Equipment Purchase	0	0	0	0	0
Miscellaneous (Start-up Costs; Samples)	0	0	0	0	0
State Taxes	0	0	0	0	0
Federal Taxes	0	0	0	0	0
Total Expenses	**4,834**	**4,834**	**4,834**	**4,834**	**4,860**
Net Cash From Operations	4,066	4,516	4,666	4,666	4,640
Beginning Cash	39,809	43,206	47,052	51,048	55,044
Cash on Hand	43,876	47,722	51,718	55,714	59,684
Bank Loan Required	0	0	0	0	0
Loan Repayment	670	670	670	670	670
Ending Cash	**43,206**	**47,052**	**51,048**	**55,044**	**59,014**

	Jun	Jul	Aug	Sep	Oct	Nov	Dec
	3,000	3,000	3,000	3,000	3,000	3,000	3,000
	3,500	3,500	3,500	3,500	3,500	3,500	3,500
	2,000	2,000	2,000	2,000	2,000	2,000	2,000
	1,500	1,500	1,500	1,500	1,500	1,500	1,500
	10,000	**10,000**	**10,000**	**10,000**	**10,000**	**10,000**	**10,000**
	6,000	6,000	6,000	6,000	6,000	6,000	6,000
	2,850	3,000	3,000	3,000	3,000	3,000	3,000
	950	950	1,000	1,000	1,000	1,000	1,000
	0	0	0	0	0	0	0
	0	0	0	0	0	0	0
	9,800	**9,950**	**10,000**	**10,000**	**10,000**	**10,000**	**10,000**
	1,000	1,000	1,000	1,000	1,000	1,000	1,000
	400	400	400	400	400	400	400
	150	150	150	150	150	150	150
	500	500	500	500	500	500	500
	1,200	1,200	1,200	1,200	1,200	1,200	1,200
	510	510	510	510	510	510	510
	150	150	150	150	150	150	0
	8	8	8	8	8	8	0
	175	175	175	175	175	175	0
	9	9	9	9	9	9	0
	100	100	100	100	100	100	0
	5	5	5	5	5	5	0
	75	75	75	75	75	75	0
	4	4	4	4	4	4	0
	200	200	200	200	200	200	200
	0	0	0	0	0	0	0
	50	50	50	50	50	50	50
	10	10	10	10	10	10	10
	50	50	50	50	50	50	50
	100	100	100	100	100	100	100
	0	0	0	0	0	0	0
	100	100	100	100	100	100	100
	70	70	70	70	70	70	70
	0	0	0	0	0	0	0
	0	0	0	0	0	0	0
	0	0	0	0	0	0	0
	0	0	0	0	0	0	0
	0	0	0	0	0	0	0
	4,865	**4,865**	**4,865**	**4,865**	**4,865**	**4,865**	**4,340**
	4,935	5,085	5,135	5,135	9,730	9,730	8,680
	59,014	63,279	67,694	72,159	76,624	85,684	94,744
	63,949	68,364	72,829	77,294	86,354	95,414	103,424
	0	0	0	0	0	0	0
	670	670	670	670	670	670	670
	63,279	**67,694**	**72,159**	**76,624**	**85,684**	**94,744**	**102,754**

Record Company

BUSINESS PLAN

REED ENTERTAINMENT CORP.

2523 Rancho Blvd.
Henderson, NV 85069

This plan for a record company is quite detailed. The company plans to produce artists on four separate record labels. These labels cover a broad spectrum of the music industry, from Jazz, to Contemporary Christian music, to Rock. The company already has established ties to various artists in the industry, and plans to search for new artists to market and produce.

- MISSION STATEMENT

- EXECUTIVE SUMMARY

- COMPANY DESCRIPTION

- INDUSTRY ANALYSIS

- MARKETING & PROMOTION

- THE MANAGEMENT TEAM

- THE FINANCIAL PLAN

RECORD COMPANY
BUSINESS PLAN

MISSION STATEMENT

Reed Entertainment Corp. (REC) will capitalize on the growing entertainment market across the world through the production and promotion of high quality entertainment. Located in Henderson, Nevada, the company will become highly profitable through the sale of pre-recorded music product (compact discs/cassettes), in addition to revenues generated from ancillary profit centers. REC will own and control the masters (master copies), copyrights and licenses of its product, which will enable REC to create immediate revenue streams while growing its music catalog into a multi-million dollar asset.

EXECUTIVE SUMMARY

REC's Chairman, Samson Rama, has created, produced and marketed over thirty albums throughout his career. These albums have generated over $100 million in revenue for such companies as Rexmark, Connor, Emblem, Regal and Coastal Records.

A variety of these projects have surpassed the "Gold" (500,000) and "Platinum" (1,000,000) sales levels and earned industry recognition through Grammy Awards, Soul Train Awards, Stellar Awards and GMWA Awards. A plethora of other projects have been used by major networks and companies such as JBN, RXK, CSC, Rexmark Pictures and Bloomfield Entertainment.

REC has formed an experienced, award-winning management team. As artists, producers and executives, projects produced by these individuals have topped Billboard's Charts, earned nominations for Grammy's and Stellar Awards, while selling over two million copies. The years of experience maintained in both the business and creative sides of record company operations will enable REC to generate profitable revenue immediately.

REC maintains strong affiliations in the music industry. Through relationships with industry legends such as Calvin Roberts (Roberts Music), and Wellman Jax (JAX), REC has been offered international distribution with Rexmark Ultimate (a distribution arm of Rexmark) and the Johnson Group. This provides REC the opportunity to generate revenue from the world's largest music markets including Japan, Germany, the United Kingdom and South America.

The company has established four record labels to handle a variety of music genres including Pop, Rhythm & Blues, Alternative Rock, Jazz, Gospel, Urban and New Adult Contemporary. REC has compiled an exciting and diverse roster of recording artists. Selected over the past year, these highly talented veteran and debuting artists will enable REC to quickly penetrate the music marketplace.

REC will distinguish itself from other independent record companies through its marketing and promotional plan. Intense, calculated and relentless promotional campaigns will enable REC to earn massive revenues through the growing popularity of "singles", as well as, traditional full-length albums. REC will utilize the success of its pre-recorded music to develop profit centers in independent distribution, merchandise and concert promotion.

Based on conservative revenue projections, REC will generate over $5.7 million in sales revenue throughout fiscal 1997-1998, and $26.3 million in 1998-1999. REC will reach positive cash flow in the twenty-third month of operations while netting profits of $4.5 million in 1998-1999 and $6.6 million in 1999-2000.

REC's founders are seeking $4.5 million in equity investment capital for this exciting company. These funds will be used to: a) establish corporate offices, b) maintain overhead expenses, c) acquire and secure artists, d) fund project production budgets, e) fund multi-faceted marketing and promotion budgets. A staged infusion of capital over the course of the first 10 months of operations will provide REC with the necessary financial resources. A linked offering composed of common stock, preferred stock and debentures is being offered by REC.

As REC reaches the aforementioned levels of profitability, several lucrative exit scenarios become realistic including the opportunity to be acquired by a major record company and, depending on investor preferences, the ability to liquidate ownership positions.

**COMPANY
DESCRIPTION**
Introduction

Reed Entertainment Corp. is a multimedia entertainment company which will supply profitable, positive, audio and visual entertainment to a diverse, international consumer group. REC is committed to wholesome entertainment across the board and firmly believes that quality, palatable entertainment can be realized without compromising commercial appeal.

REC distinguishes itself through the commitment it undertakes with each of its artists. Contrasting the typical scenario in which a record company spends more money producing the music than they do in its marketing and promotion, REC will utilize a stable of experienced and resourceful producers to ensure the highest quality product within established production budgets. This, in conjunction with the financing and expertise necessary to stage intense, relentless marketing campaigns will guarantee the impetus necessary to create "winning" products in the marketplace.

REC is composed of three internal divisions: Reed Music, Reed Video, and Reed Ancillary. The company will compete and earn revenue immediately through the creation of several lucrative profit centers, beginning with pre-recorded music [compact discs (CDs), enhanced CDs (sound & picture combination), CD Rom, cassette tapes and vinyl albums.] Additional income will be produced from distribution, video, merchandising and concert promotion.

Each of the albums that REC produces and owns will create valuable short-term streams of revenue. Owning and controlling the rights to each of its albums will enable REC to grow its music catalog into a valuable asset, one of several-hundred revenue producing titles.

REC's Personnel

The talented group of individuals who have united to form this innovative company, combined with industry affiliations and a highly esteemed Board of Directors, will catapult REC into the future as one of the industry's leading entertainment companies. REC's co-founders are Mr. Samson Rama, Mr. Carl Lever and Mr. Nathan Reuben.

As a renowned producer, recording artist and employee with such major companies and labels as Rexmark, Connor, Regal, Emblem and Coastal Records, REC's Chairman, Mr. Rama, has directly produced and contributed to over $100 million of revenue for major record companies throughout his career.

Moreover, Mr. Rama has linked and placed projects and music titles with the following television networks and television and motion picture production companies: JBN, TXK, CSC, Global Television, Heavenly Pictures and Bloomfield Entertainment.

Mr. Carl Lever, a graduate from the Johnson Center, in the College of Business at the University of Nevada, possesses a wealth of entertainment and general business experience. Mr. Lever provides the essential business acumen to direct REC in daily finance, accounting and resource management functions.

In addition, a qualified, experienced and talented management team has been selected to operate Reed Music and its associated labels. Learning and achieving success in all facets of record company operations, the members of the management team have honed their skills in the areas of project production, artist & repertoire, marketing and artist promotion. In fact, these individuals have produced and marketed artists such as Paul Firemen, The Collins, Sam Schnegle, Black Patton, Glory, Shayna and Angie Lanzi. Several of these projects have earned nominations for Grammy and Stellar Awards. This assemblage is poised to utilize its combined skills to ensure the growth and profitability of REC.

Reed Music

Reed Music is REC's primary thrust for the first several years of operations. Responsible for the cultivation of talent, the production of pre-recorded music product and its marketing, the success of REC Music will lay the groundwork for additional REC profit centers.

REC Music and its associated labels strive to fully maximize the success and profit potential of each artist. Four record labels comprise the company's music division. Each division has been created with a distinct and specialized reputation of its own, and will be responsible for a separate genre of music.

Ocean Records produces and promotes mainstream Pop, Dance, Alternative Rock and R&B. As the widest music market, REC Music personnel have auditioned and selected several artists who will debut with Ocean Records.

Wave Records is responsible for Jazz and new Adult Contemporary products. The growing popularity and profitability of these music genres dictates quality product supported by solid promotional and marketing strategies and budgets. Stone Jackson, Herman Flax, and Manley Cont will be among the first projects released by Wave. This veteran roster provides Wave with artists possessing a recent track record and an existing loyal customer base. Combined, these artists have sold over 750,000 units in the past three years.

Beat Records will create and produce Urban, Rap and Hip Hop genres. Beat is intent on producing music with clean, positive lyrics. Electronic production capabilities lower production costs enabling projects to be completed at one-third the cost of projects in the other music genres. This allows REC to recoup its investment and realize profits with a lower break-even point.

Light Records is designed and created to produce and promote inspirational and gospel recordings. Light Records is committed to the work of the ministry, and will acquire artists who share in this commitment. Mr. Jack Corbin is at the helm of this record label, and brings affiliations and an established network in the Christian music realm. Growing in popularity and strength over past years, Christian music has become a profitable and effective launching ground for new artists.

Reed Music and its associated labels will produce and release four projects from each label in each of the first two years of operations. A second phase consisting of sixteen productions for artist follow-up albums and newly acquired artists will begin in late 1998.

During the course of 1997-1998, Reed Music's Artist and Repertoire Department will locate, assess and consider additional recording artists. Reed Music has begun discussions with a variety of known recording artists who are interested in signing with Reed Music.

Recording the Music

The majority of the Reed projects will be produced at Brandy Recorders, in Las Vegas. A multi-million dollar facility, the quality of Brandy's equipment, the architecture of the studio and its atmosphere are conducive to creating the highest quality projects in a cost and time effective manner. By pre-purchasing large blocks of studio time, REC will have access to the two studios in this facility at a heavy discount. Artists such as Jasmine Hail, Bronx Duo, Calvin Griffith and Smash have recorded at this facility in recent years.

REC will utilize a variety of independent record producers for the studio production of its projects. Producers will be hired on a per project basis. These producers will be paid up-front fees and will also receive royalties (3%) from unit sales. Networks of producers are available to REC for the specific genre of music. Additionally, each of REC's Vice Presidents have a production background which will ensure the delivery of quality product on budget.

Manufacturing & Distributing

A plethora of options are available to satisfy REC's requirement for quality manufacturing and reproduction of compact disc, cassettes and videos. REC will outsource this function to one of many manufacturing outfits in the industry. These vendors will be selected based upon quality of product, ability to meet delivery deadlines, payment terms, inventory and storage options, as well as price. Several manufacturers that REC is currently considering are: Holly Manufacturers, Inc., Farwell Manufacturing, and JXT Manufacturing.

REC has been offered international distribution of its product through Rexmark Ultimate and the Johnson Group. A working relationship with either of these companies will allow REC to readily expose each of its music products to the world's largest music markets, while generating $8.50 - $9.50 per unit sold.

Chief among REC's goals is to design and provide creative and effective marketing for its artists. As music is being produced in studio, promotion and marketing strategies will be formulated. It is crucial that the marketing plan for each new release is in motion several weeks before the product is completed in studio.

Marketing & Promotion

REC will employ multifaceted promotional strategies for its product releases including: hiring regional independent record promoters and creating radio promotions, Internet sites, broadcast videos, dance club promotions, in-store/co-op promotions and promotions to the general public through print, video and television mediums.

To support the sales of pre-recorded music, Reed Video will produce and release music videos for each album released by the company. Existing affiliations in the video sector of the industry allow the company to produce top quality video productions while minimizing budgets. At this stage, music videos will be created for 3-4 songs on the album which will be released as "singles", as a prelude to the full album release. Reed Music will contract with independent record promoters to interface with radio station program directors and music video network directors. Public relations firms will be hired to publicize and promote REC recording artists.

Reed Video & Television is established initially to support pre-recorded music products through the production of broadcast music videos. Understanding and capitalizing on the close relationship between audio and video entertainment will quickly propel REC's products in the marketplace.

Reed Video

Rivaling radio in terms of the most powerful promotional tool for pre-recorded music sales, broadcast music videos are a crucial instrument to ensuring successful product launches. Reed will produce two to three music videos for each new project completed by the company. Videos will be created to appeal to the target audience of the particular song.

Broadcast Music Videos

REC has created relationships with several firms for the production of music videos. Specifically, PSB Productions and Lighthouse are two full service production companies that have submitted demo reels and music video concepts to Reed. Having pledged support of Reed's mission, these companies have offered below market fees and full use of their audio and video equipment.

Broadcast music videos will be distributed to such networks as Telereed, Bono, Abcorp., etc. Independent record and video promoters will be hired to gain maximum air time and exposure for company videos and artists. Furthermore, these promoters will work to gain exposure for videos in non-traditional music settings such as: bank lobbies, department stores, airplanes, stadiums, retail establishments and other public settings.

The third division of the company, Reed Ancillary will be responsible for additional business opportunities related to the sale of pre-recorded music. Initially, distribution, merchandising and concert promotion will be developed. As the company grows and matures, diversification into other revenue generating opportunities will occur through Reed Ancillary.

Reed Ancillary

Reed Music will utilize its distribution network to allow for the distribution of projects for smaller, independent record labels. A key factor affording REC the opportunity to capitalize on this, is the company's close, personal relationships with both Rexmark Ultimate and the Johnson Group. REC's ability to claim top dollar from these international distribution companies will

Distribution

enable it to earn a middleman fee on the distribution and manufacturing of other companies' products. Reed will earn between $2.50 and $3.00 for each unit manufactured and distributed.

Company founders have had discussions with numerous record labels across the country who are interested in working with REC. Partnerships with these companies will be dictated by the strength of company management, the quality of both their artist and product and the size of their marketing and promotion budget.

The independent distribution division of the company will be incrementally increased over a three-year period with four independent projects being distributed in 1998, six projects in 1999 and twelve projects in 2000.

Merchandising

A lucrative profit center for Reed, merchandising opportunities will be created upon and around company artists and products in concert venues and retail outlets, alike.

Concert merchandise (t-shirts, sweatshirts, hats, programs, posters, buttons, etc.) is typically sub-licensed to a merchandising company specializing in retail operations at large concert venues. REC has several relationships with merchandise managers involved with many national sports franchises and arenas around the country.

Retail merchandising strategies will be coordinated and planned with the assistance of advertising agencies and public relations firms. The chief objective will be to create alliances with apparel manufacturers for Reed artists, similar to the manner in which athletic shoe manufacturers attach an athlete's name or image to a particular shoe. Of course, these opportunities will become more readily available as the artist's reputation increases. Nonetheless, REC will work to make inroads in this realm early on.

The company is preparing to design and release a line of Reed casual wear, including such items as shirts, hats and jackets. Distribution of these products to music related retail outlets will occur through REC's pre-recorded music partner. Distribution to mainstream apparel outlets will also be secured.

Concert Promotion

As a related means to increase exposure for the company artists, Reed will plan and promote several live concert shows a month. Shows will be staged at a variety of major concert venues throughout Nevada. Revenues will be generated from the sale of tickets, concessions and merchandise. Early on, the company will plan and promote two shows per month. This will allow REC the opportunity to attract outside talent to perform in the Las Vegas metropolitan area. It is anticipated that as this division of the company grows, regional promotion contacts will be established allowing for expansion and increased revenues.

INDUSTRY ANALYSIS

Independent Labels

It has become common practice to classify all but the major labels (those having their own distribution systems) as independent labels. Independent labels have been described by knowledgeable music industry professionals as "the lifeblood of the business." In fact, in 1995 independents accounted for over 19.2% of the music industry's market share.

Lacking large budgets for project production and marketing, independent record companies have had to be more resourceful over the years. Such facets of the business as, intense talent scouting (Artist & Repertoire) and grass roots marketing campaigns have been utilized to compete with major record companies. Furthermore, independents cannot rely on the occasional "big hit" record, but rather have established and grown music catalogs to provide streams of revenue.

In growing a music catalog it is imperative to compile a reliable group of artists, who are dedicated to producing quality music. This enables the company to steadily increase the number of unit sales for a particular artist over a two to three album process.

Major recording companies frequently invest in independent labels when confidence in the company's roster and management exists. In these strategic alliances and joint ventures, the larger company may invest money to: a) assist in completing album projects, b) manufacture compact discs and tapes and c) assist with marketing and promotion plans.

Although independent distribution channels (Johnson, Wallace and Cordoba) exist, many independent labels choose to utilize the independent distribution services offered by major labels. This is an attractive choice for independents, due to the breadth and reach of the distribution in addition to the clout which the majors possess with retailers. In these situations, independents can "piggy back" on the reputation of the major.

Several UK companies that started as independent firms and joined forces with a major include Clover, Maid and Roots. Similar success stories are documented with U.S. based companies such as: Appleton, Chatham and Mill Point. From the outset, these companies demonstrated creative leadership, quality product and determination.

Industry Sales Volume in the U.S.

The U.S. record business, which grossed two billion dollars in 1970, exploded to four billion dollars in sales by the end of 1978, with a unit volume of 726 million records and cassettes sold. Sales fell sharply over the course of the next six years, mainly due to the declining American economy and the popularity of home cassette taping. It wasn't until 1988, when unit volumes reached 726 million, that the industry exceeded the pinnacle reached ten years ago. Recent calculations of industry figures indicate more than 10 billion dollars in sales and a volume of more than 955 million units.

MARKETING & PROMOTION

Reed has formulated a simple but successful approach to market its products. The chief marketing objective for REC's pre-recorded music, video and programming products centers around the design and implementation of a strategy that will cost-effectively deliver that product to the intended target market.

This will be achieved through a marketing plan consisting of the following tools: publicity, community outreach, advertising, art direction, radio promotion, independent promoters, broadcast music videos, touring, retailer co-op advertising, motion picture tie-ins, alternate distribution outlets, Internet, dance club promotions, mailings & telephone follow-ups.

Marketing Goals & Objectives

- Ensure that each project achieves and sustains a "Top Ten" position on industry music charts.
    - Release and promote four singles and accompanying music videos, in addition to each full length CD/cassette; creating revenue streams for each album project
    - Utilize REC's three phase marketing & promotion plan
    - Hire independent record promoters in each of four separate regions of the U.S.
    - Utilize teams of publicists to coordinate print advertisements, and artists' public appearances
- Support and assist non-profit organizations, charities, and community programs
    - Dedicate advertisement space for non-profits on all REC products
    - Tie in REC's recording artists for participation with non-profit organizations
    - Design and implement music education programs for community youth

Marketing/Promotion Strategy

Considering the onslaught of product released to the music/video market each month (1,200 new releases) worldwide, it is crucial to ensure the visibility of each project. The financial success of an album can be guaranteed through the establishment of proper marketing and promotion budgets. However, without the dollars necessary "to win" success is a "crap shoot." With properly established budgets, Reed Music will generate large streams of profits from each of its projects. The marketing and promotion budget will be divided into twelve to fifteen-month campaigns, each consisting of three phases.

Phase 1 begins with the creation of music videos for approximately three songs from the new album project. Once these have been shot and edited, the first "single" and its video counterpart will be released to the public. At this point independent promoters will canvas radio stations, video networks and dance clubs (depending on the genre of the release) to ensure proper air play for the first single. Within the next six weeks, a second "single" release will be promoted to the public. This strategy will enable Reed to achieve two important outcomes--increasing the number of "singles" that are sold in retail outlets, and building anticipation for the release of the full-length CD/cassette.

Phase 2 concentrates on the publicist, print advertisements and media exposure. Riding the momentum of the "single" releases, the market will be printed to hear and learn more about the artist(s) through articles in both trade and non-trade magazines, as well as radio, television and Internet interviews. Furthermore, the publicist will also be able to create valuable exposure for the charity/non-profit organization that the artist has chosen to assist and promote.

Phase 3 begins with the release of the full-length CD/cassette. This will be accompanied by intense in-store and retailer co-op advertising. Retailer programs will be designed to acquire valuable listening posts, end-cap displays, window/wall posters, point of sale advertisements and co-op advertising in mailers and store circulars. Additionally, the third and fourth "singles" will be released during this phase. The systematic release of "singles" will sustain the artists popularity while increasing and prolonging sales of the full-length album. Furthermore, during Phase 3, the artists will make promotional appearances at clubs, retailers, radio stations and charity events in conjunction with scheduled concerts.

Radio Promotion

Despite the fact that radio no longer possesses the sole influence on record sales, sharing the spotlight now with video resources, it is still a heavyweight medium for record promotion.

With so many changes occurring in the radio/video industries - the sale of radio stations for tens of millions of dollars, for instance, along with the fragmentation of radio formats and escalating success of video, promoters have been forced to realize that they are in a business and must therefore approach their jobs in a far more business-like manner than is traditional. Promoters are now more concerned about the facts and figures rather than simply trying to impress program directors with the great new song they have to offer.

Major record labels utilize both in-house and independent promoters to assist in the effort to maximize the airplay of a new song or album. An in-house radio promotion staff makes financial sense assuming the company maintains a steady and consistent release schedule to a specific genre or radio format. Personal relationships with radio station format directors is the name of the game in this arena. Bombarded by new song and album releases each month, program directors are inclined to assist those with who they are familiar and friendly.

Independent Promoters

Reed Music will utilize the services of outside radio promoters. Known as independents, these promoters have established networks and relationships with radio station program directors. Most independents position themselves and focus within a specific music genre.

Reed Music has created a network of independents who will be hired to interface with radio stations. Specifically, Reed Music will create and design goal oriented and incentive based contracts with independent promoters. Measurable criteria will include some of the following: peak chart position obtained, number of weeks on the charts on which a specified position was obtained.

Reed Music's independent promoters will focus their efforts and attention on reporting stations. A reporting station is one that trade papers/magazines and tip sheet publishers telephone each week to learn which recordings were and are planned to be programmed. This information is gathered and tabulated from all around the world. It is presented to the public in the form of a chart which shows such information as current chart position, previous chart position, artist, record label, etc.

The promotion of pre-recorded music is inextricably bound to TV related transmissions of music, including conventional TV, cable, pay-cable and direct satellites. Sales are increased immediately when music is linked to visual entertainment, whether the medium is a movie musical, a TV broadcast or a music video. Broadcasts and cable companies now transmit dozens of video shows, and their impact on record sales is clear; videos not only increase record sales, they break new acts, and prolong the chart life of new recordings.

In addition to canvassing radio stations, independent record promoters will also devote substantial time securing airplay for music videos. Boundary TV and similar outlets guarantee huge national exposure, just as with radio. Reed Music will place heavy importance on music videos, considering the national and international reach of these networks. Music videos will offer exposure to those markets presently unexploited.

Broadcast Music Videos

Marketing & Promotion

A sample 12 month campaign for an album released through Wave (Jazz, NAC)

Broadcast Music Videos	2 Videos @ $30,000	$60,000
Independent Promoters	2 @ $4,500/month, 6 months	$54,000
Publicist	$3,500/month, 9 months	$31,500
Touring/Promotional Travel	$2,500/month, 6 months	$15,000
Print Media	$3,600/month, 9 months	$32,400
In-Store/Co-op	6 month campaign	$37,500
Promotional CDs/Mailings	4,000 CDs/1,000 Cassettes	$5,500
Total Marketing & Promotion Budget		**$235,900**

The genre of music dictates the approximate marketing and promotional budget amount. For instance, due to the breadth of the mainstream market, a project released through Ocean will require twice the amount of a Wave project.

Perhaps one of the most effective marketing tools, concerts and promotional appearances are instrumental in "breaking" a new act and creating a loyal fan base. Public relations personnel in conjunction with the artist's management will create and plan these promotional tours which will be directed toward the particular target market. For instance, the artist may make an appearance at a local record store, provide an interview for a radio station, and perform in a concert the same evening.

Touring/Promotional Appearances

In addition to the long-term benefit of creating a loyal customer base, REC will utilize these opportunities to immediately sell copies of the artist's project, as compact discs and cassettes will be available at merchandise tables at concerts and appearances.

Dance clubs are effective mediums to test market new recordings. Prior to the commercial release of mainstream singles, the songs will be distributed to clubs to test public response. Reed will work closely with its independent promoters to establish networks of clubs throughout the country which will be utilized to test new releases. Results from these activities will provide crucial information in a timely fashion, allowing the company to tweek (re-mix) a recording if necessary. Furthermore, Reed Music expects to increase sales by promoting music videos of new releases to be played in the clubs. Dancers who become surrounded by the club's multiple screens and overpowering sound systems may be stimulated to later walk into a store and purchase a copy of the product (audio or video) to continue enjoying the music at home.

Dance Club Promotion

A key piece in the promotion of new product releases is the "creation of mass interest" in the marketplace. This is done in the motion picture industry with sneak previews, interviews with starring actors/actresses and directors, television commercials and print advertisements. The coordination of these activities is the responsibility of the publicist(s).

Public Relations

REC will utilize publicists to create the buzz in the marketplace about new projects and artists. Initially, this important function will be outsourced to credible public relations firms, until such time that it is feasible to internalize this position at Reed. Publicists will arrange and promote appearances and interviews (talk shows, industry publications, mainstream magazines) and create written materials and ad copy about the artist to catch public attention.

Combined with concentrated airplay and print advertisements, the impact created from the publicist's strategy creates the most powerful advertisement, word of mouth. Music buyers who hear the "talk" and hear the music on the radio are more inclined to enter a music store to make a purchase.

Print Advertising

Advertising campaigns will concentrate on the types of exposure that fashion designers have mastered in the realm of advertising. A variety of media will be used including print, broadcast, point-of-sale and direct mail. With a mass consumer product such as music, it is feasible to reach specified target segments by placing advertisements in mass print media-magazines and newspapers.

Some advertising will be cooperative with the store and Reed sharing costs. For example, a print page or media buy that promotes a REC product in conjunction with the retailer. Co-op advertising may be paid all or in part by the retailer, who is reimbursed by Reed from a co-op budget determined by the retailer's volume of purchases from the label. To justify the high expense, several Reed Music releases will be pushed in one ad, thus pulling down the "cost-per-thousand" expense per release. From time to time, record stores may request that Reed finance a print media campaign in their area. Reed will initiate print ads when trying to coordinate advertising with the promotion of concert appearances by a Reed artist.

Community Outreach

As a pillar of the company, community outreach will play an integral role in both the company and artist positioning. To this end each Reed artist will be aligned with a specific charity or community organization. Supporting the company's philanthropic desires, artist participation will enhance public image while generating exposure and revenue for chosen charities.

More specifically, a page inside each compact disc will be devoted to a charity or non-profit organization. Additionally, space on each artist's World Wide Web page will be reserved for a non-profit organization. Furthermore, Reed Entertainment will lend additional support to these charities through corporate fundraising opportunities and donations from company revenues.

Art Direction

Also a crucial function, proper art direction can greatly enhance the image of a product, lending added power to the promotion and marketing strategies. Responsible for artistic layouts, print advertisements, compact disc design, j-card design, merchandise design and the creation and maintenance of the corporate identity; the creativity displayed by this department plays a key role in positioning and packaging the project to the consumer.

Within the first few months of operations, this function will be overseen internally, with many of the specific projects being completed by independent graphic artists. This will minimize REC overhead expenses while maintaining the highest level of creativity.

Retailer/Co-op Advertising

Traditional distribution channels into music related retail establishments enable REC the opportunity to reach retail outlets throughout the world. REC will closely coordinate product launches and utilize the distributor's clout with retailers to design specific strategies for enhancing advertising and marketing presence within retail establishments. These strategies will focus on point-of-sale advertisements, in-store advertising opportunities, print, radio and television co-op opportunities.

One such strategy to be implemented once the company has several artists on the market, will be presenting retailers with the opportunity to place an attractive Reed aisle end-cap display in their establishment. The display is intended to promote four to five REC artists' compact discs simultaneously.

REC will also design other in-store advertisements such as counter-top point-of-sale advertisements, window posters and banners. In addition to listening posts (product displays which allow a potential buyer the opportunity to sample the product prior to purchase), REC artists and products will also be advertised in retailer newsletters and bulk promotional mailings to the public.

Additionally, REC is examining the prospect of distributing products through network marketing channels. The recent explosion of network marketing concepts has produced millions of distributors and consumers worldwide, providing an effective means to reach the public. The distribution breadth of individual companies will be evaluated to determine if access can be gained to selected target markets.

Alternate Distribution Outlets

Furthermore, REC will distribute its products through the Christian Music Association. An established national network, this channel provides an excellent vehicle for the distribution of Gospel and Inspirational products.

Reed will submit songs to motion picture studios as an additional means to provide promotional support for company projects. The promotional mileage created from being included on a soundtrack for a major motion picture is enough to assist in moving several hundred-thousand copies of the album.

Motion Picture Tie-Ins

In response to the growing popularity and necessity for a presence on the Internet, REC will create and design a web presence for itself. Utilizing the latest web site technology, REC's web site will be intended to advertise the company, announce and advertise new releases, sell company products and merchandise and offer e-mail communication. Furthermore, utilizing the latest technology, visitors to the web site will be able to sample music clips from REC's artists. Management has secured a domain name for the site.

The Internet

Furthermore, REC will create space on its web site for each artist signed to the company. Allowing for increased public exposure, the public will be able to learn more about the artist or group. Additionally, space will be provided to promote chosen non-profit organizations and charities through this electronic medium.

REC's independent promoters will mail promotional copies of the product to a large number of radio, cable and TV outlets. Independent promoters have the experience and the established networks to use select mailing lists, ones that include mostly influential stations or stations where the promoters possess person contacts. Mail campaigns will be followed by telephone calls. The success of this kind of telephone follow-up will be based upon the suitability of the recordings mailed, and the already established rapport between our promoters and the radio/TV programmers.

Mailings, Telephone Follow-Ups

The promotion and marketing facets of the record business are vital to REC's overall success. A quality product is only the first step in the equation for hit records, videos and programming. Reed will ensure its financial success through consistent and balanced marketing strategies designed to reach desired target markets.

Marketing Summary

THE MANAGEMENT TEAM

Goals & Objectives

- Create a highly organized, productive and efficient organization
  - Clearly outline specific responsibilities for each position
  - Provide employees with the necessary autonomy to be productive
  - Eliminate overlapping job responsibilities
  - Monitor cost effectiveness and quality of outsourced functions

- Provide employees with incentives to maximize performance
  - Offer employee medical insurance
  - Institute an employee profit sharing plan
  - Offer bonuses based on the attainment of specific goals
  - Create an enjoyable, creative, positive workplace

The strength of REC's management team is derived from the blend of experience, creativity, savvy and energy. The following individuals who occupy key positions within REC are dedicated and prepared to ensure REC's success and profitability.

Samson Rama - Chairman/ President

Mr. Rama, a co-founder and the Chairman of the Board, provides the vision for REC's future. A renowned producer, and recording artist, and employee with such major companies and labels as Rexmark Ultimate, Connor, Emblem and Regal, Mr. Rama has directly produced and contributed to over $100 million of revenue for major record companies throughout his career.

Beyond the creative side of the business, Mr. Rama has developed the business and interpersonal skills necessary to lead REC. He maintains close personal relationships with many executives and personnel within the music industry. These affiliations and contacts will provide REC with the proper positioning to navigate within the industry.

Having earned a Doctorate in Social Education in 1983, Mr. Rama has placed great emphasis on teaching and mentoring youth. His work as Executive Director of the Henderson Youth Program and his past position as Head Coach for the Collingwell High School Basketball Team have given Mr. Rama the forum to positively impact youth.

Carl Lever - Chief Operating/ Financial Officer

Mr. Carl Lever will operate as REC's COO/CFO. Mr. Lever, a graduate of the Johnson Center, in the Business School at the University of Nevada, provides REC with a wealth of tangible business experience.

Throughout the past several years, Mr. Lever has honed his general business skills as a business consultant. He has worked with over 100 businesses in Arizona, assisting with accounting and financial analysis as well as the creation of marketing and business plans. Furthermore, as a representative of the Applewood Corporation, Mr. Lever participated in a series of business/ marketing seminars in Russia. Working closely with the management of several Russian service and manufacturing companies, Mr. Lever assisted in creating marketing plans for companies which previously operated under the Communist regime.

Furthermore, Mr. Lever has honed and developed many of his business skills as the General Manager for a multi-location dry-cleaning franchise. Specifically, his duties included company-wide operations management, financial services and franchise development.

A finalist in the annual Business Plans Competition at the University of Nevada in 1991, Mr. Lever was also invited to participate in the Moot Corp Competition. In fact, Mr. Lever was the first undergraduate student to be chosen to participate in this worldwide competition.

Clayton Gorman - Senior Vice President (Ocean)

Mr. Clayton Gorman provides an impressive blend of entertainment and general business which will be instrumental in leading Ocean. Most recently, Mr. Gorman served as the Executive Vice President for Emblem, in Nashville. In this capacity, Mr. Gorman was responsible for artist development, artist negotiation and music production. Currently, Clayton Gorman is the Director of Gospel Music, for T-Dog Music, also located in Nashville.

Throughout his career, Mr. Gorman has worked extensively in the music industry. In fact, his work has produced Grammy Nominations, as well as RIAA Certified Gold Albums. Specifically, he has worked with Carville Records.

Mr. Gorman has also devoted several years of his professional life to community and youth organizations. As a founding member of the Child Benefit Group in Nashville, Mr. Gorman has assisted youth of all ages. Each of these programs currently serves over 1,200 youth, providing guidance and education in the areas of life skills, reading, math and general counseling. As a result of his dedication and commitment in this area, Mr. Gorman was nominated and received the prestigious Community Excellence Award.

A graduate of Harvard University, Mr. Todd Richard has developed a multi-faceted background with experience in finance and banking, in addition to comprehensive experience in the entertainment industry.

Todd Richard -
Senior Vice President
(Light)

As an employee with New Sound Productions (New York), Mr. Richard received his first "taste" of the industry. While with this company, he had the opportunity to work with many Gospel legends. Mr. Richard honed and developed his management and production skills. It was with this experience that Todd founded the Salt Group, a company which produces audio and theatrical productions. The company also manages artistic clientele in the genre of Christian music.

Working in the realm of Christian music, Todd has developed a cadre of affiliations. Relationships with artists, concert promoters, program directors (radio stations) and ministries across the United States will be beneficial to his role as the Senior Vice President of Light Records.

A graduate of Savannah College of Music (SCOM), in 1975, Mr. Cont has developed a varied background of experience in the industry. Most recently, he has concentrated on his solo career which has produced four Jazz albums for Emblem. His album projects have collectively sold over 375,000 units within the past five years.

Manley Cont -
Senior Vice President
(Wave)

After graduation from SCOM, Manley honed his musical skills while touring worldwide and recording with various Jazz groups. In addition to his own projects, Manley has participated in the recording of over fifty albums. Furthermore, Mr. Cont has taught several high school music classes utilizing his proficiency with woodwind instruments to promote music to youth.

Due to his experience in the Jazz niche of the music market, Manley has developed a solid network of personal contacts with radio promoters, musicians, producers, and executives. These affiliations are invaluable to REC and will allow the company to make an instant impact in the marketplace.

The following is a description of the key roles and responsibilities attached to the daily operations of Reed Music.

Reed Music
Operations

Each of the label Vice Presidents will be directly responsible for all of the functions within their particular label. Label Vice Presidents will solely handle the majority of these functions for their particular label with the assistance of shared administrative staff. As each label grows in terms of sales revenue and the number of recording artists, additional staff will be added to provide necessary support. Wherever possible and feasible, staff will be shared between labels in an effort to minimize unnecessary overhead.

Marketing/Sales

Responsible for selling the company's product to wholesalers and retailers. It develops sales campaigns, determines policies for discounts, special deals and returns, takes orders for product and oversees sales activities on local levels, provides financial assistance to accounts for advertising and oversees billing. The sales department consists of members of a national sales team - senior executives, salespersons and other employees of the branch distribution system. This work is done in-house by small labels or contracts with regional concerns to handle these functions in different parts of the country.

Product Management

This department may also be referred to as "Artist Development". Found in most medium to large record companies, product managers coordinate and oversee all aspects of a current release, including packaging, advertising, tours, publicity, promotion and sales activities. This entails close liaison with personnel from other departments within the label. The object of this department is to oversee the overall career growth of signed artists, giving whatever input necessary for the artist to achieve and/or sustain commercial success.

Publicity

The function of the publicity department is to bring press and other media attention to the artist which will, either directly or indirectly, aid in the sale of records. Inherent in this goal is the continued visibility of the artist in newspapers, magazines, trade publications, on radio and television programs and special industry award shows.

Promotion

Reed labels will employ an outside promotional staff to seek the greatest possible exposure for artists and products through radio and video air play. Representatives deliver new products to radio stations and closely monitor their play lists to see if their song is being played. The same approach is taken with regard to video outlets. A large part of the success of a record is predicated upon the amount of radio air play it receives. The competition is fierce. As such, a record should not be randomly promoted to radio stations.

Artist Relations

This department has broad responsibilities, which include talent search, contract negotiation, interim artist management and development (unless the artist has other management), tour support and publicity.

Artist & Repertoire

A general breakdown of Artist & Repertoire (A&R) responsibilities include scouting for talent, locating songs, pre-production functions such as providing creative input, scouting producers, planning budgets, etc.; production functions such as reviewing tracks, determining album sequencing of tracks, recommending singles, monitor mastering and manufacturing, creating excitement within the label itself, etc.

Artist & Repertoire Administration/Production Coordinator

This department handles the clerical aspects related to A&R and supervises various administrative activities. These responsibilities include planning and monitoring budgets, examining studio bills, preparing studio reports, ordering references and parts, collecting information for label copy and packaging, monitoring and reporting on contractual options, copyrighting works for a single or album and obtaining mechanical licenses.

Creative Services

This department is primarily responsible for creating and supervising marketing campaigns, including developing marketing concepts, creating and executing graphic art, creating editorial copy and designing "point-of-sales" stimuli posters, banners and window displays, etc.

Reed has developed a sound, conservative financial plan which provides the founders, investors and employees the opportunity to financially capitalize. The following paragraphs provide valuable details and insight to the figures which comprise the plan.

THE FINANCIAL PLAN

- Achieve overall positive cash flow within the 1st quarter of 1999.
  - Obtain required financing through private placements throughout 1997
  - Minimize the aging of accounts receivable
  - Take advantage of prompt payment discounts offered by vendors
- Maintain a net profit percentage of 25% beginning in 1998.
  - Meet or beat target budgets for project production, promotion and corporate overhead expenses
  - Decrease the manufacturing cost per unit (CDS) to under $1.02 through volume discounts
  - Meet conservative projected sales targets
- Fulfill required fiduciary responsibilities to investment partners
  - Provide interest payment to holders of debentures (12.5%)
  - Provide 13% dividend to investors holding preferred stock
- Position the company to allow investment partners, founders and employees the opportunity to financially capitalize on Reed's profitability.
  - Maintain balance sheet attractiveness for potential public financiers and investors
  - Adhere to typical industry financial ratios
  - Adhere to all required federal and state laws in all aspects of the business
  - Institute an employee profit sharing plan

Financial Goals & Objectives

The financial rationale accurately describe the various assumptions which comprise the pro forma income statements, statements of cash flow and balance sheet. In all cases, these assumptions follow a conservative approach.

Financial Rationale

Sales Revenue

Income Statement

Reed will generate the majority of its revenue from the sale of pre-recorded music product. This includes compact discs (CDS), cassettes, CD singles, cassette singles, vinyl albums and enhanced CDS. For purposes of revenue forecasts, management has projected varying unit volumes for each of its projects. Sales will occur within a fifteen-month time frame from the release date. Based upon the intensity of Reed's marketing plan/budget for its projects, the following unit projections will be quickly attained and surpassed.

Ocean	250,000 units/release
Beat	250,000 units/release
Wave	125,000 units/release
Light	125,000 units/release

Reed will gross approximately $8.75 for each full-length compact disc sold, and approximately $6.00 for each full-length cassette. The current retail price for compact discs and cassettes averages approximately $14.72 and $9.15. Currently, the industry is reporting four CDS sold to each cassette.

In addition to the sales revenue generated from the full-length CDS and cassettes, revenue will be earned from the sales of "singles". The retail sales price for "singles" is $6.50, resulting in a gross revenue of $5.00 per CD unit for Reed. Reed will release three to four singles from each full-length album project. Revenue projections in the financial model are based upon the following estimates of "single" sales.

Ocean	3 Singles	51,000 units per single release
Beat	2 Singles	51,000 units per single release
Wave	2 Singles	25,000 units per single release
Light	3 Singles	25,000 units per single release

Additional Reed profit centers will include distribution, video revenue, merchandise revenue and concert promotion revenue. Initially representing less than 5% of the company's revenues, the magnitude and scope of these areas will increase as Reed and its artists' reputations increase.

Cost of Goods Sold is comprised of: artist/producer royalties, mechanical royalties and product manufacturing (CDS, cassettes).

Artist/Producer Royalties will be paid from the gross revenue figure of $7.90 for CDS and $6.00 for cassettes. On average, the artist and producer royalty percentage are 8% and 3% respectively. Royalties attributed to "singles" will vary depending on the volume of "singles" shipped. Recording artists and producers will accumulate and earn royalties for each unit sold after the project's break even point has been reached.

Manufacturing of CDS and cassettes will be subcontracted. Applying discounts available with large quantity purchases, Reed will obtain a price of $1.10 per CD and $.90 per cassette. As unit totals increase, manufacturing costs are expected to drop 10-15%.

General & Administrative Expenses

It is management's intention to minimize G&A expenses in an effort to keep overhead expenses manageable. A full list of applicable expense items including associated monthly amounts is available upon request.

Statement of Cash Flow

Accounts Receivable - A/R are conservatively projected with 45% of A/R collections occurring in a 1-29 day period and the remaining 55% in a 90-120 day period. The majority of accounts receivable will be outstanding from the distribution company, which receives payment directly from retailers and will subsequently remunerate Reed. Because of the extended nature of A/R in the industry (typically 60 days), Reed will utilize A/R Financing to assist its cash position in the first twenty-seven months of operations. A 3.5% A/R financing fee is incorporated in the financial model. The size, strength and reliability of Reed distribution partners will provide a traditional financial institution or an A/R Factor with the proper security to create a working relationship for Reed's paper.

Inventory - Inventory for album releases and upcoming product has been conservatively projected. Despite the fact that lead times for manufactured products are approximately two weeks, Reed's financial model calculates inventory purchases in the following manner: 30% -60 days prior to sale and 70% - 30 days prior to sale. The majority of the pre-recorded music product will be stored with the manufacturer and shipped directly to the distributor's fulfillment/distribution centers. A small amount of sample (1,000-2,000 units) and promotional products will be kept on hand at Reed corporate offices.

Accounts Payable - For purposes of this financial model, A/P is separated into two categories: Manufacturing A/P, and Artist Royalty/Mechanical A/P. Adhering to the conservative approach, the model is constructed with Manufacturing A/P being paid in the same month that the expense is incurred. Artist Royalties will be accumulated and paid bi-annually, in August and February.

Project Production Budgets - These vary depending on the genre of the project. Established relationships and affiliations in the industry enable Reed to produce its projects over a ninety-day period, for approximately half the typical cost paid by a major label record company. Projects produced through Ocean and Wave require $121,000, Light Recording's projects (Inspirational/Gospel) require $80,000 and Beat projects (Rap/Hip Hop) require $45,000.

Marketing & Promotion Budgets - These vary depending on the particular genre of music. Projects produced and released from Ocean will be allocated approximately $781,000 while $390,000 will be slotted for Beat projects. Projects from both Wave and Light will utilize approximately $240,000. Marketing budgets will be expired through the course of twelve-month marketing campaigns.

The following assumptions are made in the projected Balance Sheets.

Balance Sheet

Cash - The financial model is designed to portray the accumulation of cash in the company. Cash outlays relating to dividends on common/preferred stock, employee profit sharing, and capital expenses, etc., have been intentionally not included. Moreover, the plan does not address the tax implications of "holding" this amount of accumulated earnings.

Property & Equipment - Property and equipment acquisitions include initial office equipment, pre-production studio equipment and leasehold improvements (office/studio). For purposes of the financial plan, these assets depreciated over sixty months.

Audio/Video Masters - Combined production expenses for all radio and video projects. These items are depreciated over the course of 120 months.

Deposits - This line of the balance sheet relates to utilities deposits required for corporate offices.

Copyrights & Trademarks - Included are the filing and legal fees associated with copyrights and trademarks for each of Reed's projects. These items are amortized over a 180-month period.

Organizational Expenses - Legal, accounting and other professional fees necessary in organizational process. Amortized over 60 months.

Reed is offering several simultaneous investment opportunities to cater to short and long-term investor needs and requirements. Reed seeks to keep the structure of the financing simple and flexible. Reed is incorporated with 10,000,000 shares of stock. The Board of Directors has authorized the issue of 4,000,000 shares of common stock, in addition to debentures for the first and second phases of the offering.

Investment Opportunity

Phase 1 of the Offering

Phase 1 of the offering is composed of 500,000 shares of common stock and 500,000 debentures (12.5%). Phase 1 is a linked offering meaning that for each share of $1.00 common stock purchased, a $1.00 debenture must also be purchased. Reed possesses the right to re-purchase the debentures at $1.00 within a five-year period from allotment. Reed founders, Samson Rama, Nathan Reuben and Carl Lever will collectively own 500,000 shares of common stock.

Phase 2 of the Offering

Once Phase 1 has been fully subscribed, Reed will issue 1,500,000 shares of common stock at $1.50. Additionally, 1,000,000 shares of $1.50 preferred stock will be available. The preferred shares will carry 13% dividend to be paid annually. The shares in the second phase will also be linked offering: two common shares linked together with one preferred share. Reed will hold the right to redeem the preferred shares from holders at $2.50. This action can take place within eight years from issuance.

Warrants

The founders will be issued warrants for: a) options for two million shares of common stock at $2.00/share within five years, b) an additional option for one million common shares will also be available at $5.00/share within eight years.

Projected Balance Sheet Yearly Totals

	Period Ending May 1998	Period Ending May 1999	Period Ending May 2000	Period Ending May 2001
Assets				
Current Assets				
Cash	$1,987,987	$5,138,142	$11,239,591	$20,483,684
Accounts Receivable	$2,396,768	$3,229,601	$3,145,380	$3,867,681
Inventory	$674,983	$977,181	$889,733	$569,393
Total Current Assets	**$5,059,739**	**$9,344,924**	**$15,274,703**	**$24,920,758**
Property and Equipment				
(net of accum. depreciation)	$157,577	$133,747	$282,192	$178,138
Other Assets				
Audio/Video Masters, net	$633,767	$1,461,548	$2,106,610	$3,039,571
Deposits	$9,500	$9,500	$9,500	$9,500
Patents/Copyrights, net	$11,583	$21,769	$31,195	$41,420
Organizational Expenses, net	$21,600	$16,200	$10,800	$5,400
Total Other Assets	**$676,450**	**$1,509,017**	**$2,158,104**	**$3,095,892**
Total Assets	**$5,893,766**	**$10,987,688**	**$17,715,000**	**$28,194,787**
Liabilities and Stockholders' Equity				
Current Liabilities				
Accounts Payable	$761,185	$1,462,333	$1,886,200	$1,151,759
Income Taxes Payable	$136,029	$78,233	$220,455	$603,593
Revolving line of credit	$0	$0	$0	$0
Current Portion of Long-Term	$0	$0	$0	$0
Total Current Liabilities	$897,214	$1,540,567	$893,616	$1,755,351
Long-Term Debt	$0	$0	$0	$0
Debentures	$500,000	$500,000	$500,000	$0
Total Liabilities	**$1,397,214**	**$2,040,567**	**$2,106,655**	**$1,755,351**
Stockholders' Equity				
Common Stock	$2,750,000	$2,750,000	$2,750,000	$2,750,000
Preferred Stock	$1,500,000	$1,500,000	$1,500,000	$1,500,000
Retained Earnings	$246,552	$4,697,121	$11,358,345	$22,189,436
Total Stockholders' Equity	**$4,496,552**	**$8,947,121**	**$15,608,345**	**$26,439,436**
Total Liabilities & Stockholder's Equity	**$5,893,766**	**$10,987,688**	**$17,715,000**	**$28,194,787**

Project Production Costs

The following budget addresses all relevant costs involved with producing an album project. The entire process, pre-production through final mixing/mastering encompasses approximately 90 days. The following budget is written for a typical project for an R&B, Pop, or Jazz Album. Projects released through Light Recordings (Gospel) and Beat (Urban, Rap) are 66% and 40% of this total.

Production Personnel Cost

Recording Engineer	$200.00 per/day	35 days	$7,000.00
Mix Engineer	$535.71 per/day	15 days	$8,035.65
Production Administrator	Salary built into income statement		
Project Assistant	$71.42 per/day	35 days	$2,500.00
Producer	Flat Rate, plus 2% of the project revenue		$10,000.00
Studio Expense			
Studio Rental	$650.00 per/day	40 days	$26,000.00

Travel/Lodging/Food
(For Guest Artist & Production Personnel)

Air Travel	For guest performers & production person		$4,000.00
Lodging	Furnished three bedroom apartment, see income statement		
Food	Food for Apartment, Catering, Restaurant		$1,200.00
Vehicle Rental	For transporting Artists and Computers.		$500.00
Artist Advance/Artist Wages			
Artist Advance	$4,000 per/artist	3 artists	$12,000.00
Artist Wages	$250 per/artist per/week	12 weeks	$9,000.00
Pre-Production			
Official Production	For documenting computer, MIDI, recording and mix		$300.00
	for recording daily activities in order to keep accurate records of		
	time for the purpose of financial prudence and the keeping of the		
	labor codes of the American Federation of Musicians and the		
	American Federation of Television and Radio Artists.		

Studio Musicians/Studio Vocalist

Session Musicians	$200.00 per/musician	16 musicians	$3,200.00
Featured Lead Vocalists	$500.00 per/vocalist	2 vocalists	$1,000.00
Featured Lead Musicians	$200.00 per/musician	2 musicians	$400.00
Background Vocalists	$500.00 per/vocalist	4 vocalists	$2,000.00
Tape Cost			
Ampex of Digital Master Tape	$140.00 per/reel	4 reels	$560.00
Ampex Digital Audio Tape	$30.00 box	1 box	$30.00
Pro-Audio Cassette Tape	$60.00 box	1 box	$60.00
Ampex 2" Master Tape	$150.00 per/reel	8 reels	$1,200.00
Ampex 1/2" Analog Tape	$100.00 per/reel	16 reels	$1,600.00
Post Production			
Studio Fees for Mixing Materi	$650.00 per/day	15 days	$9,750.00
Mastering	$650.00 per/day	15 days	$9,750.00
Computer Rental	flat rate		$1,000.00
Mastering Engineer	$650.00 per/day	3 days	$1,950.00
Artwork/Photos/CD Design			
Photos			$3,500.00
Artwork (Compact Disc Cover, Booklet, Disc)			$4,500.00
Preparatory Printing			$750.00

Total Project Cost   **$121,785.65**

Projected Statement of Cash Flow
June 1997 - May 1998

	1 Jun-97	2 Jul-97	3 Aug-97	4 Sept-97	5 Oct-97
Cash, Beginning of the Period	$0	$802,496	$1,857,074	$2,934,215	$3,619,305
Net income (after taxes)	($63,630)	($70,923)	($85,303)	($98,495)	($232,859)
Cash Flow from Operations					
Adjustments to reconcile net income to cash flow from operations:					
Depreciation and amortization	$2,086	$3,967	$4,733	$5,750	$6,384
(Increase in CA, Decrease in CA)					
Accounts receivable	$0	$0	$0	$0	$0
Inventory	$0	$0	$0	($8,337)	($38,667)
Accounts payable	$0	$0	$0	$0	$0
Income taxes payable	$0	$0	$0	$0	$0
Revolving line of credit	$0	$0	$0	$0	$0
Total Cash Flow from Operations	**($61,544)**	**($66,956)**	**($80,569)**	**($101,083)**	**($265,142)**
Cash Flow from Investing Activities					
Purchase of Equipment, Furniture	($97,470)	($97,470)	$0	$0	$0
Payments of Patent/Copyright Costs	($1,990)	($550)	($950)	($950)	($950)
Payment of Production Costs	$0	($30,446)	($91,339)	($121,339)	($75,446)
Payment of Long-term Deposits	($9,500)	$0	$0	$0	$0
Payments of Organizational Costs	($27,000)	$0	$0	$0	$0
Total Cash Flow from Investing Activities	**($135,960)**	**($128,466)**	**($92,289)**	**($122,289)**	**($76,396)**
Cash Flow from Financing Activities					
Borrowings on long-term debts	$0	$0	$0	$0	$0
Payments on long-term debts	$0	$0	$0	$0	$0
Repayment of Line of Credit	$0	$0	$0	$0	$0
Sales of common stock	$500,000	$750,000	$750,000	$750,000	$0
Sales of preferred stock	$0	$500,000	$500,000	$500,000	$0
Sales of Debentures	$500,000	$0	$0	$0	$0
Purchase of Debentures	$0	$0	$0	$0	$0
Payment of Dividends	$0	$0	$0	$0	$0
Total Cash Flow from Fin. Activities	**$1,000,000**	**$1,250,000**	**$1,250,000**	**$1,250,000**	**$0**
Net Cash Flow	**$802,496**	**$1,054,578**	**$1,077,142**	**$1,026,628**	**($341,538)**
Cash, End of the Period	**$802,496**	**$1,857,074**	**$2,934,215**	**$3,960,843**	**$3,619,305**

	6 Nov-97	7 Dec-97	8 Jan-98	9 Feb-98	10 Mar-98	11 Apr-98	12 May-98
	$3,619,305	$3,285,244	$2,948,452	$2,682,118	$2,148,248	$2,210,374	$1,831,532
	($215,715)	($123,974)	$151,672	($109,897)	$662,159	($224,325)	$657,841
	$6,514	$6,773	$7,286	$7,545	$7,800	$8,434	$9,325
	($48,755)	($91,151)	($361,997)	($185,482)	($665,729)	$2,693	($1,046,346)
	($69,019)	($113,617)	($67,269)	($165,973)	($48,769)	($218,169)	$54,835
	$8,865	$16,573	$65,818	($48,667)	$137,615	$128,922	$452,060
	$0	$0	$0	$0	$0	$0	$136,029
	$0	$0	$0	$0	$0	$0	$0
	($318,110)	($305,396)	($204,491)	($502,474)	$93,076	($302,445)	$263,745
	$0	$0	$0	$0	$0	$0	$0
	($950)	($950)	($950)	($950)	($950)	($950)	($950)
	($15,000)	($30,446)	($60,893)	($30,446)	($30,000)	($75,446)	($106,339)
	$0	$0	$0	$0	$0	$0	$0
	$0	$0	$0	$0	$0	$0	$0
	($15,950)	($31,396)	($61,843)	($31,396)	($30,950)	($76,396)	($107,289)
	$0	$0	$0	$0	$0	$0	$0
	$0	$0	$0	$0	$0	$0	$0
	$0	$0	$0	$0	$0	$0	$0
	$0	$0	$0	$0	$0	$0	$0
	$0	$0	$0	$0	$0	$0	$0
	$0	$0	$0	$0	$0	$0	$0
	$0	$0	$0	$0	$0	$0	$0
	$0	$0	$0	$0	$0	$0	$0
	$0	$0	$0	$0	$0	$0	$0
	($334,060)	($336,793)	($266,334)	($533,870)	$62,126	($378,841)	$156,455
	$3,285,244	$2,948,452	$2,682,118	$2,148,248	$2,210,374	$1,831,532	$1,987,987

Projected Statement of Cash Flow
June 1997 - May 1998

	13 **Jun-98**	14 **Jul-98**	15 **Aug-98**	16 **Sep-98**	17 **Oct-98**
Cash, Beginning of the Period	$1,987,987	$1,618,118	$2,270,721	$711,641	$1,435,300
Net income (after taxes)	($328,263)	$981,079	($216,376)	$1,069,974	$30,328
Cash Flow from Operations					
Adjustments to reconcile net income to					
cash flows from operations					
Depreciation and amortization	$10,092	$10,351	$10,661	$11,579	$12,699
(Increase in CA, Decrease in CA)					
Accounts receivable	$345,096	($1,435,987)	$732,786	($1,576,755)	$1,023,163
Inventory	($294,646)	$142,692	($308,813)	$209,769	($187,373)
Accounts payable	$126,169	$625,691	($1,379,677)	$648,699	$269,690
Income taxes payable	($136,029)	$360,174	($360,174)	$470,950	($454,218)
Revolving line of credit	$0	$0	$0	$0	$0
Total Cash Flow from Operations	**($277,580)**	**$684,000**	**($1,521,594)**	**$834,216**	**$694,290**
Cash Flow from Investing Activities					
Purchase of Equipment, Furniture	$0	$0	$0	$0	$0
Payment of Patent/Copyright Costs	($950)	($950)	($950)	($950)	($950)
Payment of Production Costs	($91,339)	($30,446)	($36,536)	($109,607)	($133,721)
Payment of Long-term Deposits	$0	$0	$0	$0	$0
Payment of Organizational Costs	$0	$0	$0	$0	$0
Total Cash Flow from Investing	**($92,289)**	**($31,396)**	**($37,486)**	**($110,557)**	**($134,671)**
Cash Flow from Financing Activities					
Borrowings on long-term debt	$0	$0	$0	$0	$0
Payments on long-term debts	$0	$0	$0	$0	$0
Repayment of Line of Credit	$0	$0	$0	$0	$0
Sales of common stock	$0	$0	$0	$0	$0
Sales of preferred stock	$0	$0	$0	$0	$0
Sales of Debentures	$0	$0	$0	$0	$0
Purchase of Debentures	$0	$0	$0	$0	$0
Payment of Dividends					
Total Cash Flow from Financing	**$0**	**$0**	**$0**	**$0**	**$0**
Net Cash Flow	**($369,870)**	**$652,603**	**($1,559,080)**	**$723,659**	**$559,620**
Cash, End of the Period	**$1,618,118**	**$2,270,721**	**$711,641**	**$1,435,300**	**$1,994,920**

	18	19	20	21	22	23	24
	Nov-98	**Dec-98**	**Jan-99**	**Feb-99**	**Mar-99**	**Apr-99**	**May-99**
	$1,994,920	$2,826,565	$3,947,113	$4,652,579	$3,193,219	$3,803,378	$5,002,597
	$865,500	$231,218	$591,101	$220,359	$347,179	$516,672	$141,798
	$13,753	$14,503	$14,917	$15,048	$15,261	$16,001	$17,528
	($1,278,928)	$1,057,687	($704,516)	$782,951	($179,360)	$222,687	$178,342
	$194,564	($79,398)	$95,476	($6,800)	($24,752)	$48,356	($91,275)
	$694,297	$328,277	$559,994	($2,250,420)	$407,810	$391,011	$279,607
	$460,784	($349,949)	$198,556	($204,548)	$69,970	$93,513	($206,827)
	$0	$0	$0	$0	$0	$0	$0
	$949,971	**$1,202,339**	**$755,530**	**($1,443,410)**	**$636,109**	**$1,288,240**	**$319,173**
	($8,500)	($8,500)	$0	$0	$0	$0	$0
	($950)	($950)	($950)	($950)	($950)	($950)	($950)
	($108,876)	($72,341)	($49,114)	($15,000)	($25,000)	($88,071)	($182,678)
	$0	$0	$0	$0	$0	$0	$0
	$0	$0	$0	$0	$0	$0	$0
	($118,326)	**($81,791)**	**($50,064)**	**($15,950)**	**($25,950)**	**($89,021)**	**($183,628)**
	$0	$0	$0	$0	$0	$0	$0
	$0	$0	$0	$0	$0	$0	$0
	$0	$0	$0	$0	$0	$0	$0
	$0	$0	$0	$0	$0	$0	$0
	$0	$0	$0	$0	$0	$0	$0
	$0	$0	$0	$0	$0	$0	$0
	$0	$0	$0	$0	$0	$0	$0
	$0	**$0**	**$0**	**$0**	**$0**	**$0**	**$0**
	$831,645	$1,120,548	$705,467	($1,459,360)	$610,159	$1,199,219	$135,545
	$2,826,565	$3,947,113	$4,652,579	$3,193,219	$3,803,378	$5,002,597	$5,138,142

Projected Statement of Cash Flow
June 1997 - May 1998

	25 Jun-99	26 Jul-99	27 Aug-99	28 Sep-99	29 Oct-99
Cash, Beginning of the Period	$5,138,142	$6,202,688	$6,508,931	$5,272,050	$6,216,550
Net income (after taxes)	$636,145	$84,163	$642,323	$111,991	$796,738
Cash Flow from Operations					
Adjustments to reconcile net income to					
cash flows from operations					
Depreciation and amortization	$19,056	$19,974	$20,284	$23,345	$25,843
(Increase) in CA, Decrease in CA					
Accounts receivable	($311,723)	$514,486	($575,843)	$1,050,297	($1,650,357)
Inventory	$97,564	($118,305)	$87,470	($133,249)	$163,433
Accounts payable	$534,388	$221,024	($1,681,580)	$295,661	$622,580
Income taxes payable	$272,743	($304,542)	$307,950	($292,597)	$377,791
Revolving line of credit	$0	$0	$0	$0	$0
Total Cash Flow from Operations	**$1,248,175**	**$416,800**	**($1,199,395)**	**$1,055,449**	**$336,028**
Cash Flow from Investing Activities					
Purchase of Equipment, Furniture	$0	$0	$0	($110,000)	($125,000)
Payment of Patent/Copyright Costs	($950)	($950)	($950)	($950)	($950)
Payment of Production Costs	($182,678)	($109,607)	($36,536)	$0	($49,114)
Payment of Long-term Deposits	$0	$0	$0	$0	$0
Payment of Organizational Costs	$0	$0	$0	$0	$0
Total Cash Flow from Investing	**($183,628)**	**($110,557)**	**($37,486)**	**($110,950)**	**($175,064)**
Cash Flow from Financing Activities					
Borrowings on long-term debt	$0	$0	$0	$0	$0
Payments on long-term debts	$0	$0	$0	$0	$0
Repayment of Line of Credit	$0	$0	$0	$0	$0
Sales of common stock	$0	$0	$0	$0	$0
Sales of Debentures	$0	$0	$0	$0	$0
Purchase of Debentures	$0	$0	$0	$0	$0
Payment of Dividends					
Total Cash Flow from Financing	**$0**	**$0**	**$0**	**$0**	**$0**
Net Cash Flow	**$1,064,546**	**$306,243**	**($1,236,881)**	**$944,499**	**$160,964**
Cash, End of the Period	**$6,202,688**	**$6,508,931**	**$5,272,050**	**$6,216,550**	**$6,377,514**

30	31	32	33	34	35	36
Nov-99	**Dec-99**	**Jan-00**	**Feb-00**	**Mar-00**	**Apr-00**	**May-00**
$6,377,514	$7,257,672	$7,534,401	$8,850,436	$7,053,725	$6,002,875	$6,893,892
$174,121	$203,274	$356,689	$2,562,576	$516,723	$176,905	$399,575
$26,784	$27,517	$27,724	$28,033	$28,648	$29,262	$29,876
$735,826	$65,110	$864,462	($4,280,337)	($960,237)	$808,793	$3,823,744
$26,027	($226,762)	($391,526)	$510,087	$90,460	($91,334)	$73,583
$374,204	$279,794	$399,107	($1,796,625)	$476,325	$228,898	$470,089
($343,513)	$16,084	$84,643	$1,217,041	($1,128,747)	($187,486)	$122,853
$0	$0	$0	$0	$0	$0	$0
$993,449	**$365,019**	**$1,341,099**	**($1,759,225)**	**($976,828)**	**$965,039**	**$4,919,720**
$0	$0	$0	$0	$0	$0	$0
($950)	($950)	($950)	($950)	($950)	($950)	($950)
($112,341)	($87,341)	($24,114)	($36,536)	($73,071)	($73,071)	($73,071)
$0	$0	$0	$0	$0	$0	$0
$0	$0	$0	$0	$0	$0	$0
($113,291)	**($88,291)**	**($25,064)**	**($37,486)**	**($74,021)**	**($74,021)**	**($74,021)**
$0	$0	$0	$0	$0	$0	$0
$0	$0	$0	$0	$0	$0	$0
$0	$0	$0	$0	$0	$0	$0
$0	$0	$0	$0	$0	$0	$0
$0	$0	$0	$0	$0	$0	$0
$0	$0	$0	$0	$0	$0	($500,000)
$0	**$0**	**$0**	**$0**	**$0**	**$0**	**($500,000)**
$880,158	$276,728	$1,316,035	($1,796,711)	($1,050,850)	$891,017	$4,345,698
$7,257,672	**$7,534,401**	**$8,850,436**	**$7,053,725**	**$6,002,875**	**$6,893,892**	**$11,239,591**

Projected Balance Sheets
June 1998 - May 1999

	13 Jun-98	14 Jul-98	15 Aug-98	16 Sep-98	17 Oct-98
Current Assets					
Cash	$1,618,118	$2,270,721	$711,641	$1,435,300	$1,994,920
Accounts Receivable	$2,051,672	$3,487,659	$2,754,873	$4,331,628	$3,308,465
Inventory	$969,629	$826,938	$1,135,751	$925,982	$1,113,355
Total Current Assets	**$4,639,419**	**$6,585,318**	**$4,602,265**	**$6,692,910**	**$6,416,739**
Property and Equipment					
(net of accumulated depreciation)	$154,328	$151,079	$147,830	$144,581	$141,332
Other Assets					
Audio/Video Masters, net	$718,785	$742,657	$772,314	$874,129	$998,943
Deposits	$9,500	$9,500	$9,500	$9,500	$9,500
Patents/Copyrights, net	$12,461	$13,334	$14,201	$15,063	$15,920
Organizational Expenses, net	$21,150	$20,700	$20,250	$19,800	$19,350
Total Other Assets	**$761,897**	**$786,191**	**$816,265**	**$918,492**	**$1,043,713**
Total Assets	**$5,555,643**	**$7,522,587**	**$5,566,359**	**$7,755,983**	**$7,601,784**
Liabilities and Stockholders' Equity					
Current Liabilities					
Accounts Payable	$887,354	$1,513,045	$133,368	$782,067	$1,051,757
Income Taxes Payable	$0	$360,174	$0	$470,950	$16,733
Revolving line of credit	$0	$0	$0	$0	$0
Current Portion of Long-Term D	$0	$0	$0	$0	$0
Total Current Liabilities	$887,354	$1,873,219	$133,368	$1,253,017	$1,068,490
Long-Term Debt	$0	$0	$0	$0	$0
Debentures	$500,000	$500,000	$500,000	$500,000	$500,000
Total Liabilities	**$1,387,354**	**$2,373,219**	**$633,368**	**$1,753,017**	**$1,568,490**
Stockholders' Equity					
Common Stock	$2,750,000	$2,750,000	$2,750,000	$2,750,000	$2,750,000
Preferred Stock	$1,500,000	$1,500,000	$1,500,000	$1,500,000	$1,500,000
Retained Earnings	**($81,710)**	**$899,368**	**$682,992**	**$1,752,966**	**$1,783,294**
Less: Dividends Paid					
Retained Earnings, end					
Total Stockholders' Equity	**$4,168,290**	**$5,149,368**	**$4,932,992**	**$6,002,966**	**$6,033,294**
Total Liabilities & Stockholders' Equity	**$5,555,643**	**$7,522,587**	**$5,566,359**	**$7,755,983**	**$7,601,784**

	18	19	20	21	22	23	24
	Nov-98	**Dec-98**	**Jan-99**	**Feb-99**	**Mar-99**	**Apr-99**	**May-99**
	$2,826,565	$3,947,113	$4,652,579	$3,193,219	$3,803,378	$5,002,597	$5,138,142
	$4,587,392	$3,529,705	$4,234,221	$3,451,270	$3,630,630	$3,407,943	$3,229,601
	$918,790	$998,188	$902,711	$909,511	$934,263	$885,906	$977,181
	$8,332,748	**$8,475,006**	**$9,789,512**	**$7,554,000**	**$8,368,271**	**$9,296,447**	**$9,344,924**
	$146,441	$151,409	$147,876	$144,344	$140,812	$137,279	$133,747
	$1,098,006	$1,159,930	$1,198,217	$1,202,266	$1,216,107	$1,292,285	$1,461,548
	$9,500	$9,500	$9,500	$9,500	$9,500	$9,500	$9,500
	$16,771	$17,617	$18,458	$19,294	$20,124	$20,949	$21,769
	$18,900	$18,450	$18,000	$17,550	$17,100	$16,650	$16,200
	$1,143,177	**$1,205,497**	**$1,244,175**	**$1,248,610**	**$1,262,831**	**$1,339,384**	**$1,509,017**
	$9,622,365	**$9,831,911**	**$11,181,563**	**$8,946,954**	**$9,771,914**	**$10,773,110**	**$10,987,688**
	$1,746,054	$2,074,331	$2,634,325	$383,905	$791,715	$1,182,726	$1,462,333
	$477,517	$127,568	$326,125	$121,577	$191,547	$285,060	$78,233
	$0	$0	$0	$0	$0	$0	$0
	$0	$0	$0	$0	$0	$0	$0
	$2,223,571	$2,201,900	$2,960,450	$505,482	$983,263	$1,467,787	$1,540,567
	$0	$0	$0	$0	$0	$0	$0
	$500,000	$500,000	$500,000	$500,000	$500,000	$500,000	$500,000
	$2,723,571	**$2,701,900**	**$3,460,450**	**$1,005,482**	**$1,483,263**	**$1,967,787**	**$2,040,567**
	$2,750,000	$2,750,000	$2,750,000	$2,750,000	$2,750,000	$2,750,000	$2,750,000
	$1,500,000	$1,500,000	$1,500,000	$1,500,000	$1,500,000	$1,500,000	$1,500,000
	$2,648,794	**$2,880,012**	**$3,471,113**	**$3,691,472**	**$4,038,651**	**$4,555,323**	**$4,697,121**
	$6,898,794	**$7,130,012**	**$7,721,113**	**$7,941,472**	**$8,288,651**	**$8,805,323**	**$8,947,121**
	$9,622,363	**$9,831,911**	**$11,181,563**	**$8,946,954**	**$9,771,914**	**$10,773,110**	**$10,987,688**

Projected Balance Sheets
June 1998 - May 1999

	1 Jun-97	2 Jul-97	3 Aug-97	4 Sep-97	5 Oct-97
Current Assets					
Cash	$802,496	$1,857,074	$2,934,215	$3,960,843	$3,619,305
Accounts Receivable	$0	$0	$0	$0	$0
Inventory	$0	$0	$0	$8,337	$47,004
Total Current Assets	**$802,496**	**$1,857,074**	**$2,934,215**	**$3,969,181**	**$3,666,309**
Property and Equipment					
(net of accumulated depreciation)	$95,846	$190,067	$186,818	$183,569	$180,320
Other Assets					
Audio/Video Masters, net	$0	$30,193	$120,517	$239,830	$312,622
Deposits	$9,500	$9,500	$9,500	$9,500	$9,500
Patents/Copyrights, net	$1,979	$2,515	$3,445	$4,371	$5,291
Organizational Expenses, net	$26,550	$26,100	$25,650	$25,200	$24,750
Total Other Assets	**$38,029**	**$68,308**	**$159,112**	**$278,901**	**$352,163**
Total Assets	**$936,370**	**$2,115,448**	**$3,280,145**	**$4,431,650**	**$4,198,791**
Liabilities and Stockholders' Equity					
Current Liabilities					
Accounts Payable	$0	$0	$0	$0	$0
Income Taxes Payable	$0	$0	$0	$0	$0
Revolving line of credit	$0	$0	$0	$0	$0
Current Portion of Long-Term D	$0	$0	$0	$0	$0
Total Current Liabilities	**$0**	**$0**	**$0**	**$0**	**$0**
Long-Term Debt	$0	$0	$0	$0	$0
Debentures	$500,000	$500,000	$500,000	$500,000	$500,000
Total Liabilities	$500,000	$500,000	$500,000	$500,000	$500,000
Stockholders' Equity					
Common Stock	$500,000	$1,250,000	$2,000,000	$2,750,000	$2,750,000
Preferred Stock	$0	$500,000	$1,000,000	$1,500,000	$1,500,000
Retained Earnings	($63,630)	($134,552)	($219,855)	($318,350)	($551,209)
Less: Dividends Paid					
Retained Earnings, end					
Total Sotckholders' Equity	**$436,370**	**$1,615,448**	**$2,780,145**	**$3,931,650**	**$3,698,791**
Total Liabilities & **Stockholders' Equity**	**$936,370**	**$2,115,448**	**$3,280,145**	**$4,431,650**	**$4,198,791**

	6 Nov-97	7 Dec-97	8 Jan-98	9 Feb-98	10 Mar-98	11 Apr-98	12 May-98
	$3,285,244	$2,948,452	$1,682,118	$2,148,248	$2,210,374	$1,831,532	$1,987,987
	$48,755	$139,906	$501,904	$687,385	$1,353,115	$1,350,422	$2,396,768
	$116,023	$229,640	$296,908	$462,881	$511,650	$729,819	$674,983
	$3,450,023	**$3,317,998**	**$3,480,930**	**$3,298,514**	**$4,075,138**	**$3,911,773**	**$5,059,739**
	$177,071	$173,822	$170,573	$167,324	$164,075	$160,826	$157,577
	$324,842	$352,255	$409,607	$436,259	$462,214	$532,987	$633,767
	$9,500	$9,500	$9,500	$9,500	$9,500	$9,500	$9,500
	$6,206	$7,115	$8,019	$8,918	$9,812	$10,700	$11,583
	$24,300	$23,850	$23,400	$22,950	$22,500	$22,050	$21,600
	$364,848	**$392,720**	**$450,526**	**$477,627**	**$504,026**	**$575,237**	**$676,450**
	$3,991,941	**$3,884,539**	**$4,102,029**	**$3,943,465**	**$4,743,239**	**$4,647,836**	**$5,893,766**
	$8,865	$25,437	$91,255	$42,589	$180,203	$309,125	$761,185
	$0	$0	$0	$0	$0	$0	$136,029
	$0	$0	$0	$0	$0	$0	$0
	$0	$0	$0	$0	$0	$0	$0
	$8,865	**$25,437**	**$91,255**	**$42,589**	**$180,203**	**$309,125**	**$897,214**
	$0	$0	$0	$0	$0	$0	$0
	$500,000	$500,000	$500,000	$500,000	$500,000	$500,000	$500,000
	$508,865	$525,437	$591,255	$542,589	$680,203	$809,125	$1,397,214
	$2,750,000	$2,750,000	$2,750,000	$2,750,000	$2,750,000	$2,750,000	$2,750,000
	$1,500,000	$1,500,000	$1,500,000	$1,500,000	$1,500,000	$1,500,000	$1,500,000
	($766,924)	($890,898)	($739,226)	($849,124)	($186,964)	($411,289)	$246,552
	$3,483,076	**$3,359,102**	**$3,510,774**	**$3,400,876**	**$4,063,036**	**$3,838,711**	**$4,496,552**
	$3,991,941	**$3,884,539**	**$4,102,029**	**$3,943,465**	**$4,743,239**	**$4,647,836**	**$5,893,766**

Breakeven/Profit Analysis

The following calculations determine the breakeven point in units given the projected production, and marketing expenses. Cost of Goods Sold includes compact dist/cassette manufacturing (including printing), artist/producer royalty. Artist/Producer royalties are calculated for only the unit sales occuring after the breakeven point has been surpassed.

Ocean (R&B, Pop, Dance)

Total Production Cost	$121,786.00
Total Marketing & Promotion Cost	$749,000.00
Total Production/Marketing Cost	$870,786.00
Sales Revenue, unit	$8.75
Manufacturing Expense, unit	$1.10
Revenue less manufacturing	$7.65
Artist/Producer Royalty, 11%	
Mechanical Royalty	$0.77
Income per unit	$6.89
Breakeven Point, units	$126,476.00

Wave (Jazz, New Adult Contemporary)

Total Production Cost	$121,786.00
Total Marketing & Promotion Cost	$249,642.00
Total Production/Marketing Cost	$371,427.00
Sales Revenue, unit	$8.75
Manufacturing Expense, unit	$1.10
Revenue less manufacturing	$7.65
Artist/Producer Royalty, 11%	
Mechanical Royalty	$0.77
Income per unit	$6.89
Breakeven Point, units	$53,947.00

Ocean

Scenario A, projected units sale	$100,000.00
Revenue	$875,000.00
Manufacturing	$110,000.00
Artist/Producer Royalty	
Mechanicals	$76,500.00
Gross Margin	$688,500.00
Production & Promotion Costs	$870,786.00
Income (Loss)	($182,286.00)

Wave

Scenario A, projected units sale	$50,000.00
Revenue	$437,500.00
Manufacturing	$55,000.00
Artist/Producer Royalty	
Mechanicals	$38,250.00
Gross Margin	$344,250.00
Production & Promotion Costs	$371,427.00
Income (Loss)	($27,177.00)

Ocean

Scenario B, projected unit sale	$250,000.00
Revenue	$2,187,500.00
Manufacturing	$275,000.00
Artist/Producer Royalty	
Mechanicals	$191,250.00
Gross Margin	$1,721,250.00
Production & Promotion Costs	$870,786.00
Income (Loss)	$850,464.00

Wave

Scenario B, projected unit sale	$125,000.00
Revenue	$$1,093,750.00
Manufacturing	$137,500.00
Artist/Producer Royalty	
Mechanicals	$95,625.00
Gross Margin	$860,625.00
Production & Promotion Costs	$371,427.00
Income (Loss)	$489,198.00

Ocean

Scenario C, projected units sale	$750,000.00
Revenue	$6,562,500.00
Manufacturing	$825,000.00
Artist/Producer Royalty	
Mechanicals	$573,750.00
Gross Margin	$5,163,750.00
Production & Promotion Costs	$870,786.00
Income (Loss)	$4,292,964.00

Wave

Scenario C, projected units sale	$495,000.00
Revenue	
Manufacturing	$544,500.00
Artist/Producer Royalty	
Mechanicals	$378,675.00
Gross Margin	$3,408,075.00
Production & Promotion Costs	$371,427.00
Income (Loss)	$3,036,648.00

Beat (Urban, Rap, Hip Hop)

Total Production Cost	$45,000.00
Total Marketing & Promotion Cost	$374,500.00
Total Production/Marketing Cost	$419,500.00
Sales Revenue, unit	$8.75
Manufacturing Expense, unit	$1.10
Revenue less manufacturing	$7.65
Artist/Producer Royalty, 11%	
Mechanical Royalty	$0.77
Income per unit	$6.89
Breakeven Point, units	$60,930.00

Beat

Sceanrio A, projected units sale	$100,000.00
Revenue	$875,000.00
Manufacturing	$110,000.00
Artist/Producer Royalty	
Mechanicals	$76,500.00
Gross Margin	$688,500.00
Production & Promotion Costs	$419,500.00
Income (Loss)	$269,000.00

Beat

Scenario B, projected unit sale	$250,000.00
Revenue	
Manufacturing	$110,000.00
Artist/Producer Royalty	
Mechanicals	$191,250.00
Gross Margin	$1,886,250.00
Production & Promotion Costs	$419,500.00
Income (Loss)	$1,466,750.00

Beat

Scenario C, projected units sale	$750,000.00
Revenue	
Manufacturing	$825,000.00
Artist/Producer Royalty	
Mechanicals	$573,750.00
Gross Margin	
Production & Promotion Costs	$419,500.00
Income (Loss)	$4,744,250.00

Light Recordings (Inspirational, Gospel)

Total Production Cost	$80,379.00
Total Marketing & Promotion Cost	$249,642.00
Total Production/Marketing Cost	$330,020.00
Sales Revenue, unit	$8.75
Manufacturing Expense, unit	$1.10
Revenue less manufacturing	$7.65
Artist/Producer Royalty, 11%	
Mechanical Royalty	$0.77
Income per unit	$6.89
Breakeven Point, units	$47,933.00

Light Recordings

Scenario A, projected units	$50,000.00
Revenue	$437,500.00
Manufacturing	$55,000.00
Artist/Producer Royalty	
Mechanicals	$38,250.00
Gross Margin	$344,250.00
Production & Promotion Costs	$330,020.00
Income (Loss)	$14,230.00

Light Recordings

Scenario B, projected unit sale	$125,000.00
Revenue	$2,187,500.00
Manufacturing	$55,000.00
Artist/Producer Royalty	
Mechanicals	$191,250.00
Gross Margin	$1,941,250.00
Production & Promotion Costs	$330,020.00
Income (Loss)	$1,611,230.00

Light Recordings

Scenario C, projected units sale	$495,000.00
Revenue	$4,331,250.00
Manufacturing	$544,500.00
Artist/Producer Royalty	
Mechanicals	$573,750.00
Gross Margin	$3,213,000.00
Production & Promotion Costs	$330,020.00
Income (Loss)	$2,882,980.00

Use of Funds Statement

The following list describes the initial equipment necessary to begin initial operations. The section includes:

A. Office Setup	$69,390	
B. Pre-Production Equipment	$125,550	
C. Leasehold Improvements	$18,000	
D. Deposits	$9,500	
Total	**$222,440**	

Initial Office Setup

Item		Unit	Total
10 Desks	@	350	$3,500
10 Chairs	@	100	$1,000
3 Coffee Tables	@	250	$750
15 Lamps	@	60	$900
6 Small Tables	@	75	$1,125
1 Interior Decoration	@	4,000	$4,000
1 Conference Table	@	960	$960
8 Conference Chairs	@	120	$960
8 Filing Cabinets	@	150	$1,200
2 Fax Machine	@	455	$910
1 Refrigerator (small)	@	500	$500
1 Initial Office Supplies	@	500	$500
6 Office Computers (PGs)	@	1,500	$9,000
4 Portable Computers	@	2,700	$10,800
1 Apple Mac Computer, graph	@	3,500	$3,500
6 Monitors	@	550	$3,300
1 Graphics Monitor	@	1,100	$1,100
3 Laser Printers	@	800	$2,400
2 Scanner	@	1,000	$2,000
1 Network Adapter	@	350	$500
1 Software	@	2,200	$2,200
1 Computer Peripherals	@	1,000	$1,000
3 CD Player	@	200	$600
3 Portable CD Player	@	150	$450
1 DAT player	@	800	$800
2 Portable DAT player	@	800	$1,600
3 Speakers (pair)	@	300	$900
3 Deck	@	325	$975
3 Amplifier/Equalizer	@	320	$960
2 VCR	@	200	$400
3 Television	@	550	$1,650
3 VCR	@	200	$600
2 Audio/Video Furniture	@	425	$850
1 Telephone System	@	8,500	$7,500

Total Initial Office Setup   **$69,390**

Pre-Production Equipment for Pre-Production Studio

2 Akai MPC 60
2 Akai Sampler S1100 or S3200
2 AKG 414 Microphone
6 Alesis ADATS XT
2 Alesis D-4
2 Alesis DM-5
2 Alesis S4
2 Calzone Racks w/wheels
4 Chairs
2 Crown Power Amp
2 E-MU Procussion
2 E-MU Protius
2 Korg MR-3
2 Korg T2
2 Korg Wave Station
2 Korg XBR
2 Kurzweil K2000
2 Laser Printer
2 MacIntosh Computer
2 Mackie 56 Channel
2 Midi Time Piece
2 Moog-Mini Moog
2 Noiman 47 Microphone
2 Panasonic DAT
2 Personal Computer (IBM Compatible)
2 Roland 1080
2 Roland 1090
2 Sofa
2 Sound Canvases
2 Studio Pro 5
2 Tascam Cassette Deck
2 Viantage Keys
2 Westlake Monitors
2 Yamaha TX-81-2
240 1/4" jacks
40 Mis. Midi Cords

Total Pre-Production Equipment			**$125,550**

Leasehold Improvements

1 Office Leasehold Improvements			$8,000
1 Studio Leasehold Improvements			$10,000
Total Leasehold Improvements			**$18,000**

Deposits

1 Office Lease	@	4,500	$4,500
1 Utilities	@	2,500	$2,500
1 Phone	@	2,500	$2,500
Total Initial Deposits			**$9,500**

Restaurant

BUSINESS PLAN

THE WHISTLE STOP

520 N. Central Drive
Cleveland, OH 44123

The Whistle Stop's business plan gives a simple description of the owner's plans for the business. The plan contains helpful financial information for those interested in learning more about the costs associated with opening a restaurant establishment.

- BUSINESS GOALS

- MARKETING GOALS

- START UP COSTS

- OWNERSHIP

- PROJECTIONS

- SALES & PROFIT

**BUSINESS
GOALS**

The Whistle Stop Restaurant, which will be located in the Cleveland Railroad Depot, will be a family-oriented, clean restaurant offering ice cream desserts, subs, sandwiches, pizza and a wide variety of Italian food.

Currently, the property holds the Cleveland Ice Cream Parlour. I plan to keep many of the same menu items and add a line of Italian food. The building, which is a unique, eighty year-old depot, is structurally in good condition, although it is in need of some minor repairs.

I will be the owner/operator of the restaurant, and my main goals will be to provide excellent quality, service and cleanliness to Whistle Stop customers.

By being involved in the daily operations of the restaurant, I can use my 15 years of experience in the service industry to directly impact the quality of customers' visits to Whistle Stop. Through an improved and professionally run operation, our guests will be sure to experience a pleasant atmosphere each time they visit.

The clientele that I wish to attract will be the blue collar work-force and farm workers, and their families, located in the Cleveland area, that want a reasonably priced alternative to fast food.

Whistle Stop's hours of operation will be 11:00 a.m. - 10:00 p.m. daily, with the possibility of expanding to include breakfast.

**MARKETING
GOALS**

I anticipate using 3% of sales for advertising and improvements each year. This money will be used for billboards, print advertisements and a message board, all of which will be designed to develop and increase public awareness of Whistle Stop.

While many businesses expend much time and money to create a unique establishment, my business is already unique by virtue of being located in an actual old depot. I plan to capitalize on this by stressing the train station's history. Therefore, I am in the process of obtaining railroad memorabilia, signals, signs, and possibly even a caboose.

Together with the improved parking, lighting, and general appearance of the building, I hope to transform the depot into a comfortable eating establishment for residents, as well as a unique travel destination for visitors to Cleveland. By providing a quality meal, in a clean establishment, served quickly and efficiently, these customers, many of whom will be visitors to the Rock and Roll Hall of Fame, will tell their friends about the pleasant experience they had at the Whistle Stop. The potential for nationwide exposure is tremendous.

Purchase price of building and property	$100,000	**START UP COST**
Price of existing equipment	10,000	
Existing perishable food supplies (purchased after closing	500	

First month s improvements:

paint, lot repair, road sign, menu	2,000
20% down payment for mortgage	20,000
25% down payment for equipment	2,500
Investment from father	30,000

Total to be financed:

| **Mortgage** | **$ 80,000** |
| **Equipment** | **$ 2,500** |

The business will be a subchapter S corporation. This allows the Whistle Stop to be taxed like a partnership or sole proprietorship, with profit taxed at the individual rate rather than the corporate rate. The benefit of an S corporation is that it protects investors, as only the corporation, not the individuals are held liable for the corporation's debts.   **OWNERSHIP**

I will run the corporation with my father, who will hold the title of Officer. Besides being the company's main investor, he will assist in supervising the restaurant. He is recently retired and has over thirty years of supervisory and sales experience.

PROJECTIONS

Annual Projected Sales	200,000	Jul-88	Aug-88	Sep-88	Oct-88	Nov-88
Index		1.5	1.5	1.5	0.8	0.8
Net Sales		25,000	25,000	25,000	13,333	13,333
COGS	43.00%	10,750	10,750	10,750	5,733	5,733
Gross Margin		14,250	14,250	14,250	7,600	7,600
General Expense	19.50%	4,875	4,875	4,875	2,600	2,600
Salaries & Benefits	28.00%	7,000	7,000	7,000	3,733	3,733
Payroll Taxes	3.00%	750	750	750	400	400
Total Expense		12,625	12,625	12,625	6,733	6,733
Income Before Taxes		1,625	1,625	1,625	867	867
Provision for Taxes		0.0	0.0	0.0	0.0	0.0
Net Income		1,625	1,625	1,625	867	867
Cash Balance 1st of Month		**5,000**	**14,800**	**14,925**	**15,050**	**9,902**
Cash Sales	100.00%	25,000	25,000	25,000	13,333	13,333
30 - 60 Day A/R		0.0	0.0	0.0	0.0	0.0
Over 60 Day A/R		0.0	0.0	0.0	0.0	0.0
Total Cash Available		30,000	39,800	39,925	28,383	23,235
Inventory Purchases						
Cash Purchases	10.00%	1,075	1,075	1,075	573	573
30 Day Terms	90.00%		9,675	9,675	9,675	5,160
60 Day Terms		0.0	0.0	0.0	0.0	0.0
General & Salary		11,875	11,875	11,875	6,333	6,333
Taxes & Other		750	750	750	400	400
Installment Payments		1,500	1,500	1,500	1,500	1,500
Total Cash Needed		15,200	24,875	24,875	18,482	13,967
Net Cash Flow		**14,800**	**14,925**	**15,050**	**9,902**	**9,268**

SALES & PROFIT

Take out Sales	15,563.55	Licenses and Fees	97.00
Cones	16,249.70	Postage	79.20
Food (In House)	10,989,5.73	Purchases	55,102.00
Non-taxable Sales	5,045.22	REP & IMP	831.88
Total sales	146,754.20	Single Bus Tax (approx.)	200.00
		Snow & Trash Removal (approx.)	700.00
City Taxes	2,179.96	Supplies	2,314.69
FICA Exp.	4,356.91	Telephone	828.75
Workers Comp.	1,322.31	Federal Unemployment	487.49

Business Plans Handbook, Volume 4

Dec-88	Jan-89	Feb-89	Mar-89	Apr-89	May-89	Jun-89		Total
0.8	0.8	0.4	0.9	1	1			
13,333	13,333	6,667	15,000	16,667	16,667	16,667		200,000
5,733	5,733	2,867	6,450	7,167	7,167	7,167		86,000
7,600	7,600	3,800	3,800	8,550	9,500	9,500		114,000
2,600	2,600	1,300	2,925	3,250	3,250	3,250		39,000
3,733	3,733	1,867	4,200	4,667	4,667	4,667		56,000
400	400	200	450	500	500	500		6,000
6,733	6,733	3,367	7,575	8,417	8,417	8,417		101,000
867	867	433	975	1,083	1,083	1,083		13,000
0.0	0.0	0.0	0.0	0.0	0.0	0.0		0.0
867	867	433	975	1,083	1,083	1,083		13,000
9,268	**8,635**	**8,002**	**4,335**	**7,055**	**7,283**	**6,867**		
13,333	13,333	6,667	15,000	16,667	16,667	16,667		
0.0	0.0	0.0	0.0	0.0	0.0			
0.0	0.0	0.0	0.0	0.0				
22,602	21,968	14,668	19,355	23,722	23,950	23,533		
573	573	287	645	717	717	717		
5,160	5,160	5,160	2,580	5,805	6,450	6,450		
0.0	0.0	0.0	0.0	0.0				
6,333	6,333	3,167	7,125	7,917	7,917	7,917		
400	400	200	450	500	500	500		
1,500	1,500	1,500	1,500	1,500	1,500	1,500		
13,967	13,967	10,313	12,300	16,438	17,083	17,083		
8,635	**8,002**	**4,355**	**7,055**	**7,283**	**6,867**	**6,450**		

State Unemployment	85,310
Utilities	1,174,085
Wages	6,093,580
Total Expenses	14,202,994
Working Profit	472,426
	-250,000
Total Profit	**222,426**

Retail & Commercial Design Firm

BUSINESS PLAN

FUTURE DESIGNS

5835 West Big Beaver Rd., Ste. 100
Troy, MI 48043

Future Designs business plan provides a good example of an entrepreneur who through networking, has set up a solid foundation for a new business.

- BIOGRAPHY OF OWNER

- BUSINESS OPERATIONS OVERVIEW

- THE SERVICES NETWORK

- SPECIAL AFFILIATIONS

- CONFIRMED BUSINESS COMMITMENTS

- PROJECTED BUSINESS

- PROJECTED START-UP EXPENSES

- PROJECTED MONTHLY EXPENSES

- SUMMARY OF PROJECTIONS

BIOGRAPHY OF OWNER

A veteran of the retail chain store design and manufacturing industry, John Hines spent fourteen years with Retail Ideas Cooperation, a Detroit, Michigan-based retail store design and decor firm whose specialty is the food and drug industry.

Mr. Hines began as a designer and detailer in 1980, and in those years advanced to become one of the company's more prominent account representatives and company manager. He was responsible for the sales and service of the most closely guarded accounts such as the Charleston, South Carolina-based, 582 store Bonner's supermarket chain, and Calvin Drugs-the Ohio-based 90 unit drug store chain. In addition to these two primary clients, Hines was, through the years heavily involved in the design and day-to-day coordination efforts for several other chains such as Sal's Food & Drug Centers, Denver, Colorado; T&K Food Markets, Chicago, Illinois and Arnold Simons in Georgia.

He also functioned as the inside sales contact and handled a variety of special services for the company. Due to his frequent interactions with top level supermarket executives, he had at times escorted entire groups of executives on retail store tours in metropolitan areas such as Atlanta, Georgia. The chains which participated most recently in this type of tour were Black Hatter Stores of Cleveland, Ohio and AJ Food Centers of Milwaukee, Wisconsin.

In addition to his role as an account representative, he also held positions as Corporate Accounts Manager and Public Relations Director.

Born in Kalamazoo, Michigan, Mr. Hines is a graduate of the University of Detroit Mercy in Detroit, Michigan. There he earned a Bachelor of Arts degree, majoring in art with concentration in contract interior design. During the time of his formal education he was employed for four years with Tollman Designs, a commercial and residential interior design firm in Dearborn, Michigan. In addition, John was an active affiliate member of ASID, the American Society of Interior Designers.

Mr. Hines, 35, is a resident of Bloomfield Hills, Michigan and is a supporter of selected organizations such as the Detroit Arts Gallery and the National Council for Historic Preservation.

BUSINESS OPERATIONS OVERVIEW

Future Designs (hereafter Future) will provide a full range of retail and commercial design services and manufactured component products. Marketing will be primarily towards, but not limited to, the retail industry. Interior architecture and design, fixture/millwork design and fabrication, store decor design and fabrication along with installation, consulting and management services comprise the professional services of Future Designs.

The operations concept is for Future to accomplish all services through an assembled network of established professional sources. These sources will consist of designers, design development detailers, manufacturers plus material and component suppliers. The sources are both local and out of state. The marketing direction positions Future as the provider of all of the services. It is not the intention to promote or position the company as a network, contractor or outsourcing entity.

Relative to projects requiring manufactured components or product, Future will have a central office, manufacturing and shipping location. A location is being secured in Troy, Michigan. All components would be routed to this location, repackaged if required, labeled with Future identification and then shipped to its destination from the aforementioned, tentative Troy, Michigan location.

The initial targeted client base will be cultivated from the area of the retail food sector on a national basis (e.g. supermarket chains). Opportunities are also present in the area of specialty food service (e.g. foods-to-go operations), both nationally and local to the tri-county metropolitan Detroit area. Beyond this initial client base and the services required by this sector, Future will also be active in cultivating business from a broader range of retail. This could include virtually any retail operation such as hardlines, softgoods (apparel) and consumer electronics or any other specialty. Expertise and current professional contacts will also allow for services to be marketed towards other areas such as commercial office, hospitality and restaurant projects.

The company will be owned and directed by Mr. John Hines, drawing on the knowledge, experience and contacts developed through the past fourteen years in the retail chain store design and manufacturing industry.

A biography on Mr. Hines is included in this business plan for review.

The following companies represent the primary network of support services, for accomplishing the scope of professional services by Future Designs.

THE SERVICES NETWORK

Decor Fabrication

Design Concepts, Inc.
11500 Conley Ave.
Auburn Hills, MI 48082
Mr. Allen Ronn, President

Sally's Design Group
11329 Elmira Ave.
Detroit, MI 48228
Mr. Steve Spence, Representative

Noticeable Signs
41222 7 Mile Rd.
Livonia, MI
Mr. Collin Jenkins, Owner

Images, Inc.
5800 Halsted
Livonia, MI

Fixtures/Millwork
Fabrication & Installation

Gallant Interiors, Inc.
5835 W. Big Beaver Rd., Ste. 102
Troy, MI
Ms. Andrea Scully, President

South Furnishings
550 W. Reynold St.
Atlanta, GA
Mr. John Southeby, President

Interior Design

Conwell Designing, Inc.
500 Northern Main
Royal Oak, MI 48073
Mr. Henry Conwell, Chairman
Mr. Gene Gloucester, President

Neon Fabrication & Installation

Glowing Signage
4853 W. 12 Mile
Novi, MI
Mr. Chris Donne!l

Barnell Neon Signs, Inc.
4100 City Drive
Atlanta, GA
Mr. William Booster, Representative

Awning Fabrication & Installation

Awnings-R-Us
5755 Cole Park
Cameron, NC
Mr. Scott Paster, Representative

Additional Installation Resources

Mr. Ray Dullivan
830 Courtyard Dr.
Nashville, TN

Hickman Construction Co.
48620 Pelham Dr.
Nashville, TN
Mr. Edward Hemmings, President

**SPECIAL
AFFILIATIONS**

Tollman Designs

In conjunction with Future, Tollman Designs will be an exclusive provider of design and presentation services. Future will have full access to Tollman's resource library.

Future will be an exclusive marketer of, and a fifty percent partner in the development of a custom designed and manufactured line of furniture. The first line to be introduced will be a series of coffee tables. An investment of $350.00 is required from each partner in order to complete the first (6) prototype units. The retail selling price of each table is in the range of $900.00 to $1200.00. Future will be offering first exclusive showroom rights to the Lasting Furnishings company in Birmingham, Michigan. Lasting is a subsidiary company of Gallant Interiors, Inc., Southfield where Future's offices will be located. Negotiations for this agreement with Lasting are not yet complete.

Gallant Interiors

Future Designs will locate its offices in the same commercial building as Gallant - 5835 W. Big Beaver Rd., Troy, MI.

An agreement has been reached to allow Future to publicly affiliate itself with Gallant for the purpose of establishing and maintaining a professional association and greater credibility.

An agreement is pending, in exchange for the above agreement, whereas Future will be offering to grant Gallant the opportunity to affiliate itself with Future in two ways:

- Future will provide, on an unlimited basis within reason, design consultation for Gallant or Lasting for any professional input on any project.

- Gallant/Lasting would be able to publicly affiliate itself with Future, promoting their association with not only the firm of Future, but also with the association of the owner who is a fourteen year veteran of the retail chain store design, decor and manufacturing industry and who is well-connected in the retail circles.

Additionally, Gallant will have whatever level of opportunity they desire in the manufacture of products required by Future.

Future will become a primary recipient of referrals from this national fixture design and manufacturing company whose niche market is in the retail food industry.

South Furnishings

South is likely to transfer its present decor needs from its current source to Future, dependent on the ability of Future to be competitive in the necessary areas.

Future may have consulting opportunities with South on a billable basis, of a significant capacity.

Future's owner, John Hines and John Southeby, President of South, have had a professional association for ten years, both servicing the 582 store Bonner's supermarket chain in Charleston, South Carolina.

Common Foodcenters, Inc.
825 American Pkwy.
Nashville, TN
(423)827-9725 Phone
(423)827-9726 Fax
Mr. Bill Warren, President

CONFIRMED BUSINESS COMMITMENTS

- Verbal commitment has been made to contract Future for all design and decor requirements for a soon to be constructed 18,000 square-foot supermarket in suburban Nashville, Tennessee.
- A meeting with the client is confirmed for mid-August 1996. At this time, the plans and schedules for this store will be available. Work on the project can begin soon thereafter.

General Information

Project Timing & Fees

Projections

End August 1996	Invoice for deposit on design fee	2,700.00
End September	Invoice balance of design fee	5,300.00
Mid-November	Invoice for construction documents & shop drawings	6,000.00
End January 1997	Invoice for decor products	25,000.00
Estimated Total revenue generated by project		**39,000.00**

- *Figures are subject to re-evaluation upon full scope and requirements being more clearly defined in mid-August.*
- *Above figures reflect mark-ups to outside services.*
- *Estimating that 31,000.00 is paid to outside services.*

Estimated Gross Profit on Project   **8,000.00**

PROJECTED BUSINESS	Bonner's, Inc. 350 Lakeland Drive Charleston, SC 58212

General Projection

- Resulting from an upcoming mid-July 1996 meeting, Future projects 3,000.00 to 5,000.00 per month in billings for the first six month period.

Calvin Drugs, Inc.
59400 N. Coswell Rd.
Cleveland, OH 48227

General Projection

- Opportunities to bid on fixture and millwork components is possible. Likelihood of gaining decor business is slight.
- Revenue projections are not possible to estimate at this time.

South Furnishings
550 W. Reynolds St.
Atlanta, GA

General Projection

- Customer is likely to transfer decor requirements for its client, Black Hatter Drug Stores, to Future.
- Gaining this contract will be based on competitive bid.
- Usually awarded in ten (10) stores packages, at approximately 7,000.00 per store. Value of contract would be approximately 70,000.00.
- A meeting in Birmingham, Alabama is scheduled for mid-July, 1996.

PROJECTED START-UP EXPENSES

Articles of Incorporation	100.00
Printing and Stationery/cards	400.00
Commercial Bank/Checks Printed	350.00
Phone lines/Equipment	800.00
Answering Machine	100.00
Fax Machine	300.00
General Office Supplies	200.00
Trip to Birmingham, Alabama in Mid-July (Rental car & meals expense only)	200.00
Trip to Knoxville, Tennessee in Mid-August (Misc. expense only)	100.00
Total	**2,550.00**

Notes: Trips listed will be traveled via redemption of frequent flier mileage. No Airfare costs.

Office Lease	400.00
Phone Service	200.00
Pager Service	10.00
Postage	40.00
Misc. Office	50.00
Owner's Salary	3,440.00
Total	**4,140.00**

Notes:
- *Insurance requirements not known at this time.*
- *Based on 1 two-day trip per month, for the first two months; beginning in September, monthly travel allocations could be approximately as follows:*

Airfare	500.00
Hotel	70.00
Car (and Gasoline)	100.00
Meals	50.00
Total	**720.00**
Plus Additional Projection	4,140.00
Total	**4,860.00**

PROJECTED MONTHLY EXPENSES

	Design	Documents	Product	Consult	Total Inv. Billings	Total Paid Out	Total Profit
Aug. 96	2,700				2,700	1,700	1,000
Sept. 96	5,300			3,000	8,300	4,300	4,000
Oct. 96				3,000	3,000		3,000
Nov. 96		6,000	3,000	3,000	12,000	7,300	4,700
Dec. 96			3,000	3,000	6,000	2,300	3,700
Jan. 97			25,000	3,000	28,000	21,000	7,000
Totals	**8,000**	**6,000**	**31,000**	**15,000**	**60,000**	**36,600**	**23,400**

SUMMARY OF PROJECTIONS

Notes:
- *Total profits shown do not reflect monthly operating expenses.*
- *Estimated monthly operating expenses (not including travel related expenses), are approximately 3,940.*

Rubber Adhesive Manufacturer

BUSINESS PLAN

SHAKE PROOF

Kirby Corporation
315 Valley Rd.
Glendale, California 83005

August 10, 1992

Shake Proof's business plan provides a good example of a company seeing an immediate need in a distinct market and responding to that need quickly.

- EXECUTIVE SUMMARY

- BACKGROUND AND DESCRIPTION OF PRODUCT

- COMPETITION

- MARKETING AND SALES OF SHAKE PROOF

- HOW THE MONEY WILL BE USED

- PRO FORMA INCOME STATEMENT

EXECUTIVE SUMMARY

Shake Proof is a timely product which follows the most successful marketing and sales rule-- find a need and quickly fill it. Shake Proof is a rubber adhesive that securely fastens valuable items in place during seismic activity. Kirby Corp. has done a tremendous amount of research and product testing prior to bringing this fine product to the market. In the following pages you will find that this product is far superior to any of the "stop gap" measures presently being used in the marketplace to secure valuable items in place. The product is non-toxic, reusable, easy to apply and remove and well priced for the marketplace.

Kirby Corp. proposes to market Shake Proof through direct response, retail outlets and trade shows. The initial marketing thrust will be to a direct response market in Los Angeles, Riverside, San Bernadino, Orange County and the San Francisco Bay area. These demographic regions experience the highest number of earthquakes. In addition, they have the highest demographic counts in income and densities with the greatest collections of antiques, art, crystal and china. The target customer is 35 years and up. These customers are generally upwardly mobile or already well established. The secondary markets are Palm Springs, Santa Barbara, Central Coast Regions, San Diego and other areas which are prone to seismic activity.

Shake Proof is clean, simple and easy to use. The product will stick to most any surface. The product leaves little or no residue, thus avoiding any damage to the surface or secured object.

The increasing amount of potential earthquakes in California has created a proactive attitude towards earthquake preparedness. To date, there is no product being marketed to the general public which will preserve valued items from damage during seismic activity or even a household accident which could cause an item to topple and break. We propose to fill that need, thus giving Californians and others who fear the loss of valuable household items the security they so need.

The potential profits in marketing this product are phenomenal! Over 8 million Californians are currently covered by earthquake insurance. We believe we have only touched the tip of the fault line. The net profit ratios for direct response and retail sales are at or above industry standards. We propose to "skim the market" for the first eight months of product introduction. This additional cash from higher net profits will allow us to obtain a higher rate of return for our venture partner.

In addition, the rule of "first in, first win" will also help our cause when competition is introduced. At the present time, we have no direct competition and fully intend to saturate the market as quickly and effectively as possible.

Kirby Corp. is currently seeking venture capital in the amount of $200,000.00 to capitalize the advertising, packaging and set up costs of the venture. We believe our numbers are rather conservative with regard to the projected sales volumes.

BACKGROUND & DESCRIPTION OF PRODUCT

What is Shake Proof?

Shake Proof is a non-toxic, removable, primarily reusable, and non-drying gum adhesive designed especially for the purpose of securing valuables to household surfaces when they are displayed. Once secured, objects can withstand the potential danger of being shattered through displacement caused by the ever fearful and often occurring earthquake.

The Purpose of Shake Proof

The purpose in marketing Shake Proof is to help prevent the preventable. We want to preserve our valuable possessions from the earthquake's constant shaking and rolling that causes our valuables to topple and break. As necessary as it is to know how to shut off your gas main, keep food and water well-stocked and be familiar with your escape routes, it is necessary to try to protect your valuable crystal and china. Shake Proof is the solution for protecting those breakable valuables that you have worked so hard to attain.

Valuable household items are defined as those items on display in your home such as: crystal, china, vases, figurines, collectibles, antiques, heirlooms and even picture frames that you would be upset to find broken.

What Are Valuable Household Items?

The Southern California Seismic Network records more than 10,000 earthquakes in an average year, not including aftershocks, in addition, there are about 100 earthquakes larger than 3.0 and 12 earthquakes larger than 4.0 occur each year. Also, an average of 1.5 earthquakes big enough to cause minor damage (greater than 5.0) occur every year in Southern California. Caltech records an average of about 30 earthquakes per day in Southern California. Is this not a cause for concern?

The Earthquakes

What about the rest of the United States and the world? On the average, the earth has ten major earthquakes (M7.0 to 7.9) and one great earthquake (M8.0 or larger) each year.

Over 90 percent of the loss of life, and more than half the property loss due to earthquakes, is unnecessary and preventable.

Those of us who live in a state that is under a constant threat of earthquakes understand the fear of the impending "Big One." The Big One in California, for example, is estimated to be of a magnitude 8 on the Richter Scale and centered on the San Andreas Fault. If an earthquake of this magnitude should occur, the protection of life and possessions is of greater concern. Consider your proximity to the fault, the construction of your home and the amount that you have prepared for this size earthquake.

1. It is the only product on the market strong enough to hold valuable household items yet gentle enough not to ruin them.
2. Shake Proof is easy to install and simple to remove.
3. Shake Proof is non-toxic.
4. Shake Proof is pliable and can be shaped and formed to fit any size object.
5. It is aesthetically appealing in two ways: a)It comes in blue or white and b)It can be hidden underneath or behind most objects.
6. The product performs well in both freezing and high temperature conditions.
7. It is safe for children.
8. It will not cause damage to marble, tile, porcelain, vinyl, wood, painted walls, plywood and almost any hard surface imaginable.
9. If residue is left on any surface, it can easily be rubbed off with your fingers or, in difficult cases, with the common solvent trichloroethane, dry cleaning fluid or lighter fluid.
10. It has an indefinite shelf life.
11. It can be reused indefinitely provided all contact surfaces are clean.
12. There is no adhesive of this type that targets the earthquake prevention market in this manner.

Why Is Shake Proof So Good?

You simply pull off or cut with scissors the appropriate amount for securing the item; then roll it in your fingers, working with it like clay or dough. The more you work with it the softer it becomes. There are two ways to use Shake Proof. First, roll it into a ball which you then attach to the bottom of a flat surfaced item. Let's use, for example, a crystal vase 12" high with a 7" diameter flat bottom. An approximate sized piece would be the diameter of two fifty-cent pieces rolled into a ball. Place this at the bottom of the vase. Then press the vase onto the surface where it is displayed. To test its security simply try to jiggle the vase loose. If it jiggles loose easily, you need to repeat the procedure adding more Shake Proof until you feel that the vase is completely secure. The second method is to pull the cut portion apart with both fingers, stretching it into a long skinny strip to place circularly around the bottom of your item.

How Does Shake Proof Work?

How Reliable is Shake Proof?

It is our opinion that Shake Proof is the best product available on the market today for securing crystals, china and various other valuables during earthquakes.

We have determined that earthquakes of 3 or less magnitude will not necessarily knock anything down. At a magnitude 4, things can begin to shake and drop. As the magnitude increases the damage and risks become greater. It just depends on your proximity to the epicenter, the strength of your home and how much preparation you have done.

We have tested the strength of Shake Proof in a simulated earthquake structure. The structure is a school house on wheels with a hydraulic system capable of reenacting a 6.5 magnitude earthquake.

It is used for demonstration purposes in schools and for public safety awareness events. We secured a variety of glass figurines, crystal, vases, etc. to a variety of movable surfaces (glass, wood, metal) with Shake Proof and then reattached the entire movable surface to angled desks within the school house also with Shake Proof. The school house was jolted to a 6.5 magnitude earthquake 4 times. It was a total success! Everything stayed secure! In fact, we believe that Shake Proof is the best assurance anyone can have against earthquakes even higher than 6.5. The excitement level was so high that day that even the operators of the school house offered to sell Shake Proof.

Packaging

Shake Proof comes in two sizes and two colors. The colors are blue and white. The sizes are 6" x 2 3/4" which is 75 gms and 2" x 2 5/8" which is 35 gms.

We plan to package Shake Proof for two different markets. The first market will be direct response sales through radio, television and some print media. Shake Proof will be sold in bulk sizes, approximately 4 of the larger or 6 of the smaller. The packaging will be less expensive consisting of a transparent plastic bag with a labeling header and a separate instruction manual.

The second market will be retail. Shake Proof will be sold in smaller quantities to keep the retail price competitive. To accommodate in-store shelf space requirements the small packages will hang, be stacked or a combination of both. The packaging will reflect a colorful, eye-catching earthquake theme. Within this retail market, we will be selling to specialty stores and mass merchants. We feel strongly about in-store counter displays situated near the cash register to capture the impulse Shake Proof purchase. These counter displays will most likely be used in the smaller retail, specialty gift, crystal and china shops and less in the department store fine china areas. Depending on the mass merchant, either the counter display or a floor display model will be suggested. The use of the floor display can be timed with our advertising campaign and the pre-sell.

Other Uses For Shake Proof

Even though the theme for marketing and packaging Shake Proof will be towards securing valuables in case of earthquakes, Shake Proof is an excellent defense against careless children and pets. In addition, Shake Proof can be used to mount paper products (maps, charts, photos, cards, etc.) to walls. It can seal bathtubs, wash basins and gaps around doors and windows. It can fix tilting pictures on walls. It can secure calculators, phones and personal computers to office desks. It can hold anything, like art brushes, tools, and test tubes, secure. Use your imagination. This is an incredible product!

COMPETITION

Consumer awareness is at its all time high and the problem of securing valuables during earthquakes has taken California by storm. An article printed in the Los Angeles Reporter called direct attention to this problem. Our timing could not be better!!! We are way ahead of the competition in product performance and are right on in our concept. The first rule of marketing: "find a need and fill it" has just been filled. In addition, the article touts the usage of a microcrystalline wax known as Wax-It. The product is inferior to Shake Proof.

The source for Wax-It mentioned at the end of the article caters strictly to the museum and art restoration business. He is not interested in dealing in smaller retail quantities. He suggested that we become his California local resource and he would refer all business to us. We are evaluating the need for a second product in our line. Currently, the only advantage we can see in this type of alliance is in the ultimate co-opting of him as a competitor. His connections in the museum and art restoration business can be of service for Shake Proof as well.

The following pages list the potential competitors and the products they offer. The bottom line is that we feel we have little or no competition at this point.

Major Competition

Product & Company Name: Bud Craft Adhesive
Address: 1224 Forsythe Dr.
Holland, Michigan
Price: $2.49
Market Served: Arts & Crafts, Floral
Performance & Properties: Green clay adhesive. Sticky, leaves residues, hard to remove. Number one clay in floral industry. Works well for permanent floral arrangements.
Analysis: This was recommended by individuals and companies with some knowledge of clay and adhesions. This product does not contain the properties necessary for our purposes. It is no competition.

Product Name: Fastenz
Company: Sandy Run Corp.
1185 Washington Ave.
Urbana, Illinois
Price: $2.98
Market Served: Gift stores & frame shops
Performance & Properties: Clear wax. Very sticky, leaves residue, hard to install, hard to remove. Does not adequately secure miniature figurines, glass & porcelain treasures from slipping or toppling as claimed. Company has mediocre counter point-of-purchase display. Currently, doing the only in-store marketing for this type of use. Packaging is marginal.
Analysis: Fastenz is the only product in the market claiming to hold valuables. We believe that our point-of-purchase display will be designed to educate, stimulate, and easily attract away any customers from Fastenz. Shake Proof is by far a better product and this will be reflected in the packaging. This is our only true competition and everything about them is unstable. We definitely can capture the gift and frame shop business away by better packaging and in-store merchandising. This competition is short-term.

Product & Company Name: Modestine
1711 Woodstock Blvd.
Birmingham, England
Price: $1.35
Market Served: Gift, China & Glass Shops
Performance & Properties: Wax slices the size of a dime. Product is sticky, leaves a residue and simply does not work. Packaging is confusing, written in 4 different languages and is geared toward sticking candles.
Analysis: This product is no competition. It has ineffective packaging, performance, and overall market penetration. Note: Worchestshire, England is so excited about Shake Proof, that they will promote it with each purchase and ignore ineffective Modestine.

Product & Company Name: Stix
239 Goepp St.
Salinas, California
Price: $19.00-$39.00
Market Served: Hospital & industrial use and upon request
Performance & Properties: Stix is an inter-woven fabric fastener. This combined with strapping is used to secure large items like computers. Stix is not sold in the retail market and therefore poses no competition. In addition, the pieces are so bulky that it would not work on china or crystal. The sticky adhesion is difficult to remove and cannot be easily relocated.
Analysis: Stix poses no competition. They concentrate on a different market and sell at an extremely high price.

Product Name: Place Right
Company Name: Dublin
Brookline Drive
University Heights, Ohio
Price: $2.39
Market Served: Automotive & Hardware
Performance & Properties: Non-toxic gum adhesive cut into squares the size of a fingernail. This is a professional organization with a catalogue of over 100 adhesives, sealants, and aerosols. Place Right has the same properties as Shake Proof except that it is not as adhesive, cannot be stretched into thin strips and is cut into small pieces. It loses its adhesion with repeated use. They claim it can be used on glassware. Our tests show it will not hold securely.
Analysis: Place Right is packaged as a hardware item and is geared towards hanging posters and decorations to walls. Since it is not tough enough to secure glassware and is packaged inappropriately for this purpose, we feel Shake Proof can even out distance this product in the hardware market.

Product Name: Holdz
Company Name: Kingswood Inc.
Akron, Ohio
Price: $.99
Market Served: Arts & Crafts, Schools, Stationery and Hardware
Performance & Properties: Holdz has exactly the same properties as Shake Proof. The packaging is geared towards use for decorations, posters, and notes. It is also billed as a replacement for tape, tacks, staples and magnets.
Analysis: The price is lower because they ship less volume per package. The packaging is mediocre and is geared towards a different market than we are concerned with. We believe that our product marketed to our target audience and packaged uniquely will create a whole new set of buyers. By the time this or any other company catches on to this potential market, we will already be there. We will be first.

Product Name: Gloo
Company Name: Oneder
88 E. Tee Rd.
Bethesda, Maryland
Price: $1.99
Market Served: Arts & Crafts, Schools, Stationery, Hardware
Performance & Properties: Same as Holdz above. This is the first well-done packaging that we have seen. It conveys their target market more effectively than anyone. The target market, again, is posters, cards, decorations and a variety of household, school and office uses.

Analysis: The price is higher than Holdz because they ship more. They are keeping the cost of the packaging confidential. This product, like Holdz, has kept a low profile in terms of advertising and promotions and therefore, are not universally well known.

Product Name: Stick-Up
Company Name: Fort Fasteners
Sarasota, Florida
Price: $1.69
Market Served: Arts & Crafts, Schools, Stationery, Hardware
Performance & Properties: This has the same properties as Holdz and Gloo. All three are competing for the same markets.
Analysis: This is our supplier. We have a signed Non-compete Agreement and their full cooperation.

Product Name: Wax-It
Company Name: Fitzwater Products
125 Lafayette Ave.
Henderson, Nevada
Price: $15.00
Market Served: Museums, Art Restoration, Conservatorships
Performance & Properties: This is a microcrystalline wax. Similar to Fastenz in overall stickiness, and messy installation and removal. The company does not sell retail or to the direct public. They go through an extreme freezing process to break 5-10 lb. blocks of wax into 1 lb. $15.00 sizes. They have no packaging except a zip-lock bag. The product has to be removed with fishing wire and mineral spirits, a form of paint thinner. The product is inferior.
Analysis: A recent issue of the Los Angeles Reporter had an extremely eye-opening article on this potentially massive market. The newspaper and this company set up a way of fulfilling orders which would be a direct result of this article. The response intrigued them and made them aware of this potential market. They received approximately 300 $15.00 checks in the mail 3 days following the article. We made contact with the company and they want no part of this retail business. They offered us the California distributorship. We are considering this.

Who Is The Market For Shake Proof

MARKETING AND SALES OF SHAKE PROOF

- Anyone residing in an earthquake state.
- Professionals who typically own their own homes and have accumulated wealth and possessions.
- Married couples over 35 years of age with dual incomes.
- Those that seek and have a relatively high standard of living.
- People with collections of fine things, wedding gifts, heirlooms. Those that view their possessions as priceless--art collectors, etc.
- People that have earthquake insurance.
- People who are concerned about earthquake preparation.
- People who entertain or have children and animals.

California: The Primary Market

California has the eighth largest economy in the entire world. Our population is over 29,760,000. Over 30% or 8,928,000 people have earthquake insurance. We are considered trendsetters, money-oriented and self-indulgent. Therefore, we are the perfect market. We have a lot to lose.

Earthquakes pose a continual threat in California and, as the population grows, even moderate quakes will take an increasingly heavy toll. We have the most notorious of all faults, the San Andreas, which is expected to cause major damage sometime in the next 30 years. In short, Californians live in fear daily.

| The United States: | The potential market for Shake Proof is substantial with essentially every state at risk for an |
| Secondary Market | |

The potential market for Shake Proof is substantial with essentially every state at risk for an earthquake. The map of earthquake risk in the United States shows that there are very few areas in the United States that are immune to earthquakes. Beyond our ultimate Californian market, we will approach a secondary market in the following states:

- Alaska
- Hawaii
- Mississippi
- Montana
- Nevada
- Utah
- Washington

Future Plans

Kirby Corp. was developed for the purpose of marketing and selling Shake Proof. At this point, we are only interested in saturating the market with this one product. We are, however, interested in improving what we have and continuing our research for future markets and products that compliment our line.

Our Sales Strategy

Direct Response

Our initial main emphasis will be to generate sales and cash flow quickly through direct response television, radio and some print sales. In addition, the advertising will create product identification and open the door to retail sales.

Retail Sales

The pre-sell will have been established through Direct Response advertising. We currently have appointments scheduled with several major grocery store chains. This, plus drug and department store sales, will be our next in-house effort. Simultaneously with our in-house sales efforts, we will hire two representative organizations (one in Southern California and one in Northern California) to handle the specialty gift and crystal/china stores.

Trade Shows

We will attend trade shows for two reasons: 1. To help the Southern and Northern California representative organization to find dealers and, 2. To continue our in-house direct sales. We will attend the gift shows in San Francisco, Los Angeles and San Diego for the representatives and then home decorating and restoration shows for direct sales.

Sales Tools

Packaging is essential in the retail market. We plan "tight, clean, colorful" packaging to comply with retail chain hanging and stacking requirements and will have an earthquake theme that will be unique and attract attention.

Counter displays are essential in the specialty crystal/china and gift stores. Shake Proof becomes the impulse purchase. After someone has purchased an expensive piece of crystal or a breakable Lladro figurine and is at the cash register ready to pay--there is Shake Proof--a clean, easy, simple way of preserving that expensive piece forever.

Floor displays will most likely be used by the grocery and drug store chains. We will suggest to these stores to have these on hand for the following reasons: 1. In the case that a newsworthy earthquake should occur, the store can play upon that fear by promoting Shake Proof in an instant, and 2. April of each year has been designated Earthquake Preparedness Month by the Red Cross. Free radio and television public service announcements are done to promote the need to prepare and be aware. Earthquakes of the recent and distant past become newsworthy all over again and serve as reminders of what may be ahead for anyone at anytime. The above stores may consider full in-store promotions of products related to earthquake preparedness i.e. Shake Proof, flash-lights, candles, water, food, toilet paper, etc. for a full 30 days.

Brochures

One brochure will suffice as the "stuffer instruction manual" and label for our direct response sales. In addition, this same brochure will be used by all sales staff.

Additional Follow-Up Markets

As time and money permits, we will endeavor to approach the following markets for sales:

- independent disaster preparedness stores
- insurance companies
- variety stores
- hardware stores
- arts and antiques
- museums, galleries and churches
- home furnishings
- independent catalog mail order
- credit card catalog mail order
- office supply and computer stores
- QVC/QVS, Home Shopping Network: TV Direct

International Market

Earthquakes occur all over the world. We do not plan to include this as an immediate endeavor. If, through word of mouth and our associations with Disaster Preparedness stores and the Red Cross, we should get requests for product, then we will not hesitate to sell.

Changing Earthquake Preparedness Manuals

Up to now manuals put out by the Red Cross, police, fire departments and even the private sector have failed to instruct us to secure our valuables from movement. Why? Because up to now, no one has had a product that can do the job, to protect Californians who doubted that an earthquake would hit them. These doubts are being put aside and more and more people are now seeking ways of protecting themselves, their homes and their valuables.

Our research has shown that with enough satisfactory endorsements those incomplete manuals will be changed to incorporate the new section: "Secure all loose, (small and large) breakable objects from flying or falling during earthquakes."

We can own the business.

Our Commercials

Our television and radio commercials will be designed to create the movements of an actual earthquake and glass breaking. It is our job to reactivate those fears over and over again until steps are taken to become as prepared as possible and that means using Shake Proof.

Free Publicity

We plan on sending press releases with pictures to all the major magazines, newspapers, etc. that are trade and consumer publications.

In addition, we will be on the State of California Vendor list for products and services related to earthquake relief and preparation. The Red Cross and fire departments take the most active role in Earthquake Preparedness. They do not endorse any products but often suggest items necessary to achieve the preparedness goal. We plan on traveling in these circles regularly.

We will seek for Shake Proof to be known as the best method for keeping valuables safe in all Earthquake Preparedness Manuals and books on the subject. To date, we are being put in touch with Nancy Carpenter author of *Get Prepared*, the number one most informative consumer book on the subject. Our introduction comes through the Red Cross in Pasadena.

We will contact local television shows like Wake Up California that introduce new products for public safety.

**HOW THE
MONEY WILL
BE USED**

September 1992

Initially, we plan on implementing a very intensive direct response television advertising campaign. We need a loan to produce our 30-60 second commercial and to set up for order receiving and processing and to buy air time in the two major market areas of Los Angeles and San Francisco. Packaging will be a minimal charge at this time. We will ship in plastic bags with an instruction manual and sell larger quantities to drive the retail price higher and to build cash reserves in order to facilitate entering the retail market.

Simultaneously, we will have our Southern and Northern California representative organizations in place, preparing for our first two trade shows in October.

In-house sales will have commenced with grocery and drug store chains.

October 1992

Direct response television time spots will increase and radio and trade publication advertising will be introduced. Orders taken by direct response in September will be filled in October. Simultaneously, we will receive our retail store packaging and begin shipping grocery and drug store orders. We will equip the representative organizations with samples, packaging and brochures at this time. Our first trade show to the gift market will commence in San Francisco in early October. The second will be in Los Angeles towards the end of the month. October and November are the buying seasons for the Mother's Day market which is a big gift and crystal market.

In-house sales will continue to major grocery, drug and department store chains.

Our counter displays will be delivered at the end of this month.

November 1992

Our first orders from the representative organizations should be forthcoming. Counter displays will go with each initial order. Our direct response TV buys, radio and print will be in full swing. We will be filling orders received in October. November 6th is the California Home Show. We will do direct sales there (attendance 30,000).

By now, Kirby Corp. will be in full swing shipping and receiving Shake Proof.

This cycle will continue until March of 1993 when we discontinue the direct response advertising and concentrate on the retail trade. We will shift our advertising budgets and will gear up for April, Earthquake Preparedness Month. Our floor displays will be in place for individual in-store promotions at this time.

We will also have in reserve the immediate budget necessary for television and radio advertising should the occurrence of earthquake reactivate immediate consumer awareness.

Pro Forma Income Statement
September 1992 Through April 1993

	Sept	Oct	Nov	Dec	Jan	Feb	Mar	Apr	Total
Sales									
Direct	$39,166	$222,741	$211,552	$211,552	$211,552	$181,905	$33,500	$67,000	$1,178,968
Retail	$0	$0	$25,000	$50,000	$85,000	$100,000	$400,000	$1,000,000	$1,660,000
Cost of Sales	$14,028	$79,776	$95,780	$113,750	$129,760	$141,160	$276,000	$684,000	$1,534,254
Gross Profit	$25,138	$142,965	$140,772	$147,802	$166,792	$140,745	$157,500	$383,000	$1,304,714
Expenses									$0
Controlable Expense									$0
Salary/Payroll	$2,000	$3,150	$5,000	$5,000	$8,000	$8,000	$10,000	$15,000	$56,150
Contact Labor	$1,200	$1,200	$1,200	$1,200	$1,200	$1,200	$1,200	$1,200	$9,600
Advertising	$18,500	$51,000	$49,000	$48,000	$26,500	$26,500	$44,000	$41,000	$304,500
Commercial	$4,500	$0	$0	$0	$1,000	$1,000	$1,000	$1,000	$8,500
Legal/Acct.	$2,000	$0	$0	$0	$0	$1,000	$0	$0	$3,000
Equipment	$4,000	$0	$500	$0	$1,000	$0	$0	$0	$5,500
Stationary	$500	$0	$100	$100	$100	$100	$0	$0	$900
Office Supply	$250	$100	$250	$250	$250	$500	$250	$500	$2,350
Postage	$250	$1,000	$250	$250	$250	$250	$250	$500	$3,000
Travel	$0	$1,000	$0	$0	$0	$2,000	$0	$0	$3,000
Phone	$1,000	$1,000	$1,000	$1,000	$1,000	$1,000	$1,000	$1,000	$8,000
Subscriptions	$0	$500	$0	$0	$0	$0	$0	$0	$500
Ent., Gifts	$0	$0	$0	$1,000	$250	$250	$250	$2,000	$3,750
Total Cont. Exp.	**$34,200**	**$58,950**	**$57,300**	**$56,800**	**$39,550**	**$41,800**	**$57,950**	**$62,200**	**$408,750**
Fixed Expenses									
Rent	$0	$0	$0	$1,000	$1,000	$1,000	$1,000	$1,000	$5,000
Insurance	$100	$100	$100	$500	$500	$500	$500	$500	$2,800
Utilities	$100	$100	$100	$200	$250	$250	$300	$500	$1,800
Total Fixed Exp.	**$200**	**$200**	**$200**	**$1,700**	**$1,750**	**$1,750**	**$1,800**	**$2,000**	**$9,600**
Total Expenses	**$34,400**	**$59,150**	**$57,500**	**$58,500**	**$41,300**	**$43,550**	**$59,750**	**$64,200**	**$418,350**
Net Profit/Loss	**($9,262)**	**$83,815**	**$83,272**	**$89,302**	**$125,492**	**$97,195**	**$97,750**	**$318,800**	**$886,364**

Travel Agency

BUSINESS PLAN

INTERNATIONAL BUSINESS TOURS

4065 Harvard Court
Santa Ana, CA 92706

International Business Tours business plan is a good example of an entrepreneur taking advantage of a business opportunity arising out of newly accessed markets. Keeping abreast of the world trade arena is proving profitable for IBT.

- INTRODUCTION

- INDUSTRY BACKGROUND

- THE COMPANY

- MARKETING PLAN

- FINANCIAL STATEMENTS

INTRODUCTION

This document contains the business plan for International Business Tours, a California - based company that offers assistance to executives and entrepreneurs who seek to do business internationally. International Business Tours (IBT) will familiarize U.S. executives and entrepreneurs with the business and social environments in specific countries and help them to establish their own network of business contacts in those markets. These objectives will be met by providing educational, business-related tours to specific markets. The tours will educate U.S. executives about the market, give them hands-on experience in that country and introduce them to potential buyers, sellers, distributors or partners.

Initially, the tours will focus on emerging markets in Latin America. Starting in the second year of operation, IBT will begin to expand its destinations to include primary business centers in South Africa, Central Europe and Asia.

INDUSTRY BACKGROUND

International Business - History and Current Conditions

For nearly two centuries, the U.S. has been a dominant player in the field of international business. Europe and Japan are well established trading partners of the U.S. In recent years, the nations of Latin America have received a growing volume of investment and attention from U.S. businesses. Total foreign investment (in $US billion) is shown below for the five top Latin American countries for 1991-1993:

	1991	1992	1993
Mexico	16.1	24.3	29.03
Brazil	11.6	12.1	17.6
Argentina	5.1	7.9	15.61
Venezuela	4.8	2.9	7.38
Chile	1.7	2.3	2.99

Brazil, Mexico and Argentina are the dominant players in the Latin American market. In fact, Brazil represents 45% of the entire Latin American GDP, (Source: *Strategic Business Journal*).

The October 10, 1994 issue of *Marketing Front* states, " 'Governments (in Latin America) once drowning in red ink have privatized industries, and many others have recently passed laws that encourage foreign investment,' said Bob Hill, an investment adviser at the Alan Tromell Co. in Hartford, CT. Moreover, industries that have reached their maturity in the U.S., such as utilities, manufacturing, construction and telecommunications are still in their growth stages in such nations as Argentina, Brazil, Chile and Mexico."

These conditions, plus the passing of NAFTA, help make Latin America one of the hottest and most promising regions for U.S. businesses seeking to expand internationally.

International Business - Future Directions

By the year 2000, the Latin American consumer market will be larger than either Europe or Japan, (Source: *Journal of Entrepreneurship*).

In 1994, direct investment from the United States to the four largest Latin American countries is expected to grow as follows:

% Change from 1993

Argentina	Up 28%
Mexico	Up 12%
Chile	Up 8%
Brazil	Up 3.5%

Through the end of this century, investment and expansion in Latin America by North American businesses will continue to grow.

Tourism from the U.S. to Latin America is growing at a rate of 13% per year, according to the World Travel and Tourism Council. This rate is expected to continue for each year for the rest of this century.

Business travel to Latin America is expected to grow even faster as a result of the increased direct investment from the U.S. to the countries of Central and South America.

International Business Tours offers assistance to executives and entrepreneurs who seek to do business internationally. IBT will familiarize U.S. executives and entrepreneurs with the business and social cultures in specific cities and help them to establish their own network of business contacts in those countries.

These objectives will be met by providing educational, business-related tours to specific markets. The tours will educate U.S. executives about the market, give them hands-on experience in that country and introduce them to potential buyers, sellers, distributors or partners. Initially, the tours will focus on emerging countries in Latin America. Starting in the second year of operation, IBT will begin to expand its destinations to include primary business centers in South Africa, Central Europe and Asia.

The tours will be one week business tours to either Mexico City; Sao Paulo, Brazil; Santiago, Chile or Buenos Aires, Argentina. Tour participants will receive the following:

- Round-trip international airfare
- Hotel accommodations at a first class hotel
- All breakfasts, four lunches and three dinners
- Two cocktail receptions, a networking social with expatriate Americans and a final night dinner/reception
- Series of expert speakers on topics such as Banking, Investment & Finance, Import/Export Regulations, Strategic Alliances, Environmental Regulations, NAFTA, Legal Issues, Politics, Cultural Practices & Issues, Relocation and Local Real Estate (business and residential).
- Series of off-site activities including office or plant tours, a practical guide to using local public transportation, a tour of the local stock exchange, an inspection of sample apartments and homes guided by a local real estate agent
- A recreational day spent touring the historical and tourist sights of the city
- When possible, one-on-one introductions to local business people engaged in the same industries or fields as the tour participants
- Optional two night/three day tour extensions (air & hotel only) to nearby leisure destinations such as Acapulco, Puerto Vallarta or Rio de Janeiro

Per person prices for the tours range from $1500 (for Mexico) to $2500 (for Chile). These prices are consistent with most leisure tours to these markets and are extremely competitive compared to typical U.S. based seminars on topics related to doing business abroad.
The typical gross profit per passenger ranges from $350 to $450 depending on the destination.

IBT will start out as a California-based sole proprietorship managed by one principal, Zachary Natall. Although sole proprietorships do not protect the principal from personal loss or liability, this form of business entity was chosen for the first two years of operation for the following reasons:

The principal has liquidated most personal assets and invested the funds into the start-up of the business. There are few personal assets that need protection.

IBT has taken out a $500,000 liability insurance policy to cover the company against lawsuits. The cost of incorporating in California is extremely high (approximately $1,250), and this was not deemed to be a wise investment of funds until after the start-up stage.

In the first year of operation, virtually all support services will be out-sourced. These include legal and financial services, bookkeeping, etc.

On the following page is a list of the managerial skills and duties to be performed by the principal.

Primary Duties and Responsibilities of the Principal:

- Site inspections
- Contract negotiations (hotels, airlines, destination management companies, speakers, etc.)
- Marketing/Sales
- Publicity
- Registration
- On-site tour management
- Curriculum development
- Revenue and expense accountability
- Accounting
- Office supply and computer equipment procurement
- Future program development

MARKETING PLAN

Based on research, the marketing efforts of competitive organizations and recommendations from qualified professionals, the marketing plan for IBT has been developed to reach the target audience through a variety of channels. These are outlined below.

Sponsorships

IBT will seek sponsors in Mexico, Brazil, Argentina and Chile. These may include airlines, banks, consulting firms and real estate agencies. For a fee paid to IBT, these sponsors will have their logos appear on IBT literature and receive acknowledgment (PR) as event sponsors. In addition, they will be given the opportunity to personally present themselves to tour participants during the programs in Latin America in order to generate their own business. The fees collected from sponsors will be put into other marketing efforts such as direct mail brochures.

Space Ads

IBT will run space ads in appropriate publications including *Finance in Latin America, Corporate Issues* and many others. These ads will be small and aimed only at generating inquiries. Telephone and fax inquiries will be fulfilled with low-cost fulfillment brochures.

Fulfillment Brochures

Inexpensive fulfillment brochures and packages will be written and designed by Zachary Natall. These will be produced on material purchased from The Paper Supply, a supplier of pre-formed brochures and display materials. Although the cost of these materials is low, the perceived quality is high. This system and its flexibility will control costs by allowing the printing and mailing of small quantities of brochures as needed. The fulfillment brochures will contain all the information necessary for respondents to make the decision to register for the tours.

Telemarketing

Zachary Natall will personally phone all inquiries to try to complete the sale.

Conferences and Seminars

There are numerous conferences and seminars in and near the Los Angeles area on subjects such as business in Mexico, NAFTA, Brazil, Latin America in general, etc. Many trade missions and chambers of commerce with offices in Southern California develop programs that are held locally. When possible, Zachary Natall will be present at these events to personally promote the tours.

Free Samples

Going on the assumption that the best way to sell your product is to give people a taste, IBT is prepared to develop and conduct mini-seminars to be used as sales pitches. These will be one-hour programs advertised and held at the trade conferences described above. The mini-seminars will be conducted personally by Zachary Natall. The objective will be to educate participants about the product, IBT and generate sales. Mini-seminar participants will be told about the tours, speakers, topics and most of all, the benefits. Leads, sales and referrals will be generated at these mini-seminars.

Strategic Alliances

IBT has identified several companies who develop products similar to -- but not directly in competition with -- IBT. In the first year of operation, Mr. Natall will be in contact with these organizations to determine if they have an interest in any kind of strategic alliance or joint effort. These joint efforts might include list sharing, a joint seminar, sponsorship, combination brochure development, etc.

Personal Selling

The principal of IBT will contact and work with the vast network of international business contacts he has developed over the years in Latin America, Europe and North America. Mr. Natall is prepared to allocate a significant amount of time to personally selling IBT.

**FINANCIAL
STATEMENTS**

**Personal Financial
Assessment**

Prepared November 11, 1994

Salary
$41,820/year (will voluntarily terminate on January 3, 1995)

Collateral/Non-Liquid Assets

Auto (Estimated Value)	4,500
Personal Furnishings & Office Equipment	2,000
Retirement Fund	600
Total Non-Liquid Assets	**$7,100**

Savings/Liquid Assets

Current Savings	1,500
Projected savings as of February 1, 1995	7,500
Life insurance policy value	3,500
Total Savings/Liquid Assets of 2/1/95	**$11,000**
Total Cash Amount Put Into the Business	**$11,000**

Long Term Personal Debts/Liabilities (Projected Figures as of Feb. 1, 1995)

American Express Sign & Travel Account	3,700
AT&T Mastercard	2,300
IKEA	400
MasterCard	600
Student Loan	550
Total Long Term Debt	**$7,550**

**Balance Sheet -
February 1, 1995**

Assets

Current Assets

Cash	11,000
Merchandise	0.0
Supplies	500
Pre-paid expenses	0.0
Total Current Assets	**$11,500**

Fixed Assets

Fixtures	0.0
Vehicles	4,500
Equipment	1,000
Leasehold Improv.	0.0
Building	0.0
Land	0.0
Total Fixed Assets	**$5,500**
Total Assets	**$17,000**

Liabilities

...continued

Current Liabilities

Accounts Payable	2,000
Current Portion LTD	0.0
Other	0.0
Total Current Liabilities	**$2,000**

Long Term Liabilities

Notes Payable	0.0
Bank Loans Payable	0.0
Other Loans Payable	0.0
Total LT Liabilities	**0.0**
Total Liabilities	**$2,000**

Item	Amount
Feb. Mexico Planning Trip (Lodging, meals, ground transportation, entertainment expenses, etc.)	$1,000
February Office Rental	350
Phone Bill	100
Office Supplies, Letterhead, etc.	500
Local Transportation Costs (Gas, tolls, parking, etc.)	50
Total Accounts Payable	**$2,000**

Accounts Payable Display

...continued

Travel Information Service

BUSINESS PLAN

TRAVELING U.S. INC.

1500 Pepper Ridge
Haysville, KS 67060

Traveling U.S. Inc.'s business plan is unique, in that it is based upon the production, marketing and distribution of a completely new product, an automated travel information kiosk. The business owners plan to capitalize on this need in the market. The owners present investors with a solid plan to fill this market need.

- EXECUTIVE SUMMARY

- MANAGEMENT

- MARKET ANALYSIS

- MARKETING STRATEGY

- FINANCIAL PROJECTIONS

EXECUTIVE SUMMARY

Introduction

This business plan is confidential and is used to introduce prospective investors to Traveling U.S. Inc. (The Company). The Company is in the process of developing David Ford's Travel Guides as a business opportunity and to expand the installation of its products and services throughout the United States.

It is The Company's goal to raise $3,500,000 in equity capital needed to further develop its prototype product, expand its marketing operations and penetrate the marketplace.

The Company owns all rights to its trademarks and the service marks. The Company will be responsible for the overall management of the production and marketing of the products and services, training and advertising coordination.

Statement of Purpose

Traveling U.S. Inc. is interested in developing David Ford's Travel Guides as a business opportunity and to expand the installation of its products and services throughout the United States.

The Company's mission is to open a network of salesmen (corporate and/or independent contractors) for the purpose of installing, and servicing the David Ford's Travel Guides. This will be accomplished in an atmosphere where the sales force will receive the ultimate in quality products and services. It is The Company's goal to revolutionize advertising in the motel, hotel and hospitality industry in the United States. The Company's expansion will eventually be worldwide. Management, services and cost controls will be keystones to The Company's success. The services will be provided by knowledgeable, well-trained management and support personnel.

The Company

The Company was founded by its President, David Ford, a consummate entrepreneur who combined his business management ability with his sales and marketing expertise to create David Ford's Travel Guides.

The Product

The products consist of a computerized Marquee prototype approximately four (4) feet wide by seven (7) feet tall which will be a free standing unit. The top half will contain ads that will be approximately four (4) inches by five (5) inches, allowing for fifty (50) advertisers. Advertisements will be on transparencies which will be back-lit with fluorescent lighting. Each grouping of advertisers will be color coded. A telephone will be on the base of the unit, hooked up to the advertisers via an automatic dialer allowing the user to be connected to the advertiser. The ads will put the advertiser's customer just a fingertip away from the products and services they need while traveling on business or pleasure. The Marquee advertisers may include: limousine services; pizza delivery; florists; car rentals; quick print shops; movies; theaters; dry cleaners; museums and other attractions.

A manufacturing agreement will be prepared by Traveling U.S. Inc. and Manufact U.S. Inc. (MUI), a Hutchinson, Kansas manufacturing company. Keith Wilson became President of MUI in 1985. MUI was organized in 1967 by Hungarian refugees as an FAA repair station which specialized in meter movements. In 1969, Jim and Kathy Wilson purchased the firm which, at that time, had 800 square feet of manufacturing space and three employees. Today, the plan consists of 15,500 square feet and has over 100 government contracts valued at over $1.5 million.

MUI is currently capable of delivering 42 units per month and has committed to do this beginning eight (8) weeks after approval of the prototype. Costs for the units are currently estimated to be $5000 each. When orders exceed MUI's current capacity it will increase its manufacturing capability accordingly.

The U.S. travel and hospitality industry consists predominantly of small businesses. It is a large and growing sector of the U.S. economy. According to the U.S. Travel Data Center's annual National Travel Survey, U.S. residents took 1.3 billion person-trips in 1991 (one person traveling 100 miles or more, one way, away from home in one day, or staying out of town one or more nights). The travel market in the U.S., including hotel and motel accommodations, amounted to over $327 billion in 1991. There are more than 28,000 lodging properties with 97 million hotel and motel rooms in the U.S. Although hotels and motels will be our initial marketing target, there are over 11,000 hospitals in the U.S. which can use David Ford's Travel Guides. Also the over 300 convention bureaus in the U.S. will be targeted. Other markets are being investigated. | **The Company's Markets**

With the increasing number of "economy" type motels and hotels (no frills, no restaurants, etc.), The Company envisions a booming market for its David Ford's Travel Guides.

The Company's prime objectives are to establish and maintain its leadership in providing its clients quality products and services through a network of corporate and independent salesmen in order to quickly penetrate major markets in the U.S. Within two years, The Company's objectives are to go public and to provide a consistently high rate of return to its stockholder investors. | **The Company's Objectives**

- Develop a competitive Marquee prototype
- Study the potential U.S. market for Traveling U.S. Inc.
- Use select and discrete advertising to invite a qualified response
- Pre-qualify independent contractor and sales prospects
- Integrate independent contractors into the system
- Install 500 units in the first full year of operation
- Install 2500 units in second year of operation
- Install 3000 units in third year of operation
- Go public in the second or third year of operation

Short Term Objectives

- Pursue productive and profitable growth objectives
- Obtain prominent market position in the United States
- Place a minimum of 500 new units the first year
- Place 2500 new units the second year
- Place 3000 new units the third year
- Have a total of 6000 units operating by the end of the third year
- Obtain prominent market position worldwide

Long Term Objectives

To our knowledge, only one other company currently offers a program similar to The Company's program. Although there is limited competition, it is accepted that once recognized for its profit potential, competition will be severe. It should be remembered that The Company has a leading management and marketing edge on current and future competition and has worked out many of the problems which future competition will have to face. | **Strategy for Meeting the Competition**

The strategy The Company employs for meeting the competition includes continuous research and development of product selection, marketing, and service.

The Company will register its Trademark with the U.S. Patent and Trademark Office (PTO). | **Trademarks and Copyrights**

To implement market penetration throughout the United States, The Company has and is prepared to continue to invest the dollars and staff time required to develop its corporate expansion program. | **The Company's Corporate Commitment**

The Company plans to issue 15 million shares of stock. Its goal is to sell 7 million shares at fifty cents per share (.50) for the first raise to $3.5 million. | **Equity Financing**

MANAGEMENT

Management Team

The Company's management strategy is to maintain a highly educated and well-trained management team composed of management, marketing, engineering, financial and legal personnel who are skilled, flexible and focused on The Company's common goal. The Management Team includes:

President

David Ford

David Ford is the founder of Traveling U.S. Inc. and is also President of The Company. Mr. Ford graduated from Missouri State University where he received a Bachelor of Arts degree in Business Administration.

Skilled in business administration Mr. Ford has the essential tools necessary to make The Company successful.

Goal oriented and success driven, Mr. Ford has a proven record of significant contributions to the bottom line of those ventures in which he becomes involved. He has served the Venture Company in El Dorado, Kansas for over ten (10) years in varying executive capacities including: Configuration Management; Equipment Management; and Planning and Control Management. David was promoted to Industrial Engineer with the responsibility for developing analyzing, maintaining and applying standards data to all manufacturing plans developed for the Company.

Board of Directors

Mr. Ford has carefully selected his policy-making Board of Directors. They include:

Henry Holden

Mr. Holden, a graduate of University of Kansas with a Bachelor's degree in Fine Arts, is an Industrial Engineer with The Venture Airplane Company and responsible for standards development and applications. He is computer literate with both PC's and Mainframe Systems. His comprehensive knowledge of graphics and communications makes Mr. Holden a valued addition to the Board of Directors.

Robert Morris

Robert Morris has been involved with entrepreneurial start-ups most of his adult life. He has owned a variety of businesses as well as managed the sales and marketing arm of several firms. His business involvement ranges from publishing to all types of construction. He possesses knowledge in the areas of negotiation, marketing, compensation plans, territory layout, sales, sales training and sales forecasting.

Thomas Carroll, CAE

Mr. Carroll is President of ACL-USA which has been developing successful franchises and business opportunities since March, 1981. Through his franchise development, management and marketing firm, he has worked with over 100 major international, national, and/or regional franchising companies. He was the Executive Vice President of Franchising Worldwide (1975-1980). In 1975 he was a founder, charter member, and first chairman of the Worldwide Franchising Council -- an organization which then included National Franchise Associations in over 12 countries. He created FW's franchise trade show and their Outstanding Franchisor Award program. He authored numerous articles on franchising including Organization of Franchising & Advisory Councils. Carroll is also a founder and past chairman of the National Small Business Legislative Council, a past president of the Washington D.C. Jaycees, a past director of the U.S. Jaycees and a past chairman of the 2000 member national professional association executives -- The Greater Washington Society of Association Executives (1980-1981).

Robert Mason, CLU

Mr. Mason is President and chairman of Logan Holdings and affiliate subsidiaries of Logan Holdings. Mr. Mason founded the present insurance operation of the company with the purchase and acquisition of the 60 year-old Mayers and Smith insurance brokerage firm in 1985. Robert holds a Bachelor of Arts Degree from Kansas State University. He is a Chartered Life Underwriter and has been a licensed General Agent in the Life Insurance Industry since 1979.

Larry Smith

Mr. Smith is an independent consultant operating out of Utah. He has a Master's Degree in Business Administration. He attended the Business Development Institute of Ontario, Canada. Born in Wales, Larry served in the Royal Air Force, United Kingdom Far East. He was director of foreign markets for Casey Herbal of Canada. He developed joint venture partnerships for this company in Malaysia, Brunei, Indonesia, Thailand and the Philippines which spawned 8500 distributors and sales of $2,000,000 per month. Mr. Smith is an expert in multilevel marketing program development. He has worked with Salem Direct Sales Division, Ohio and the Barid Corporation in Massachusetts where he served as Vice President of marketing for the company's Welcome Wagon Division. The above experiences coupled with his experiences with Errol Company and Nova Products will be useful to The Company.

In addition to the above Board of Directors, Mr. Ford has named the following to serve as Advisors to the Board:

Advisory Board

Jeffrey Martin

Mr. Martin is President of ISI.

Harold Morton

Mr. Morton was responsible for increasing the Kansas Mail Services in El Dorado from 30% to 90%. He is a tax expert who designed a successful operation and pricing format for a tax firm. Harold is also an experienced salesperson.

Jerold Summers

Mr. Summers has worked with The Venture Airplane Company in El Dorado, Kansas since 1980 in capacities ranging from Cost Management Senior Analyst, Corporate Quality Improvement Facilitator to Corporate Quality Improvement Administrator. His banking and financial expertise includes having served as a Branch Manager of the El Dorado Bank & Trust, and the College State Bank. Jerold has a Bachelor of Business Administration from Kansas State University and a Master of Science in Management from Michaels University in El Dorado.

James Sender, Esq., of Washington, D.C. serves as Corporate Counsel.

Legal Counsel

The prestigious Regional Certified Public Accounting firm of Kennels and Kohl, headquartered in Wichita, Kansas, will serve The Company on financial and accounting matters and will assist in providing procedures to take The Company public.

Certified Public Accountants

The Company has created and enjoys many of the technologies of modern management and procedural methods. The Company's independent contractors are carefully selected and well trained to promote The Company's products and services.

Management Responsibilities

President

The Company's Job Descriptions

The President, in conjunction with general responsibilities for corporate policy development, is responsible for the overall management of the business and its growth. He establishes corporate policy, performance standards and incentives. Corporate office performance and independent contractor performance is monitored by him and his feedback provides encouragement and increased productivity. He is responsible for approving independent contractors and product design concepts. He addresses the annual meeting of independent contractors designed to facilitate the exchange of ideas and techniques between them and corporate officials.

Vice President

The Vice President is responsible for the development of the corporate staff and for the overview of product development, sales and promotion.

Director of Operations

The Director of Operations' primary responsibility is to monitor the expansion and development of the independent contractors marketing areas. He is involved in start-up equipment inventory and contractor training. He is also available as a technical resource person for independent contractors who have specific operational problems or questions. As his responsibilities grow, a Director of Training will be added to the operations department who will take on the responsibility of training and development to allow the Director of Operations to assume his increased responsibilities as the system grows.

Marketing Manager

The Marketing Manager is responsible for advertising programs and cooperative advertising strategies. He works directly with independent contractors in developing cooperative advertising strategies.

Corporate Counsel

Corporate Counsel is responsible for preparation of the independent contractor agreements, filing and maintaining integrity of Trademark and Service Marks registrations. He is also responsible for the corporate legal concerns of The Company.

Financial Advisor (CPA)

The financial advisor will advise The Company regarding its financial and accounting affairs as well as the procedures necessary to take The Company public.

MARKET ANALYSIS

The Economy in 1993

In 1991 and 1992, signs of hesitation in certain economic indicators began to surface, generating concern about the strength and durability of the economy. The year 1993 began with the nation's economy in a moderate recession. However, the 2nd quarter of 1993 is beginning to show signs of economic improvement.

Outlook for 1993

A review of the pre-published U.S. Industrial Outlook - 1993 stated that consumer demand for goods and services is expected to recover from 1992 as the U.S. economy continues to recover. The major sources of growth are likely to stem from a pickup in consumer spending. Personal consumption expenditures account for the largest share of the forecast gain in real GNP in 1992. A relatively stable inflation rate and a slight increase in interest rates are forecast for 1993, implying a continuation of accommodative monetary policy. Expected white collar increased employment should lead to increased purchases of goods and services. The travel industry is expected to rise in 1993.

In summary, though softness is expected in some areas of the economy, moderate growth on balance is in prospect for 1993 and this is a good omen for the future of The Company.

The Company's potential future market is defined as nationwide. The Company's overall market includes the nation's motels, hotels, convention bureaus, hospitals, theme parks, museums, parking garage and other markets currently being explored. However, during its early stages of marketing, it will concentrate in the hospitality area including hotels, motels and convention centers. The Company is in a positive growing situation. Other competitors have entered the market, however, because of The Company's early start, its research and development, and its marketing know how, The Company expects to enjoy a number one position in the national marketing area.

Market Definition

The U.S. travel industry consists predominantly of small businesses. It is a large and growing sector of the U.S. economy. According to the U.S. Travel Data Center's annual National Travel Survey, U.S. residents took 1.3 billion person-trips in 1991 (one person traveling 100 miles or more, one way, away from home in one day, or staying out of town one or more nights). The travel market in the U.S., including hotel and motel accommodations, amounted to over $327 billion in 1991. There are more than 28,000 lodging properties with 97 million hotel and motel rooms in the U.S. The Company's early efforts will be to saturate the hotel/motel market. With the increasing number of "economy" type motels and hotels (no frills, no restaurants, etc.), The Company envisions a booming market for its David Ford's Travel Guides. Also targeted are over 300 convention bureaus in the U.S. Once these target markets have been well developed, other markets will be exploited. For example, there are over 11,000 hospitals in the U.S. which can use David Ford's Travel Guides. Other markets are being investigated including 4500 parking garages in America, theme parks and museums.

The Company's Markets

The Company's distinct advantages over the competition is its experienced and well-seasoned management team which makes The Company a very formidable competitor. The Company plans to meet expected competition by establishing and maintaining a strong market presence based on name recognition quality product and service, and continued marketing and promotion.

Strengths

One obstacle which needs to be faced by The Company, in forcing a national presence, is the high cost of penetrating this attractive and profitable market. A look at the financial spread sheet indicates that at least $750,000 will be needed for the first three months of operation. However, units should begin to be placed in hotels and motels in the third month, at which time The Company's cash flow will be initiated. The concept is such that a positive cash flow will begin in the third month of operation. It is expected that The Company will reach its break-even point after the 115th unit is installed.

Weaknesses

MARKETING STRATEGY

The Company's objective is to raise $3,500,000 in equity capital needed to expand its operations and to penetrate the marketplace. This will be accomplished by selling stock in The Company.

Introduction

Traveling U.S. Inc. is an excellent investment. The Company is designed to attract well-capitalized veteran business and professional people.

The Market Potential

Any company which provides the same or similar products and services available from the Ford organization will recognize The Company uniqueness as a specialist in marketing and services. The Company's clients will appreciate the speed, the convenience, and the knowledgeable and friendly service of its sales and service organization. This is what will make The Company different and successful.

The Competition

Actually, there is little direct competition with The Company. Anyone wanting to compete with this concept would have to be prepared to risk anywhere from $500,000 to $1,000,000 on development costs alone. The Company has expended considerable time and money to develop and hone its concept to the profit machine it is expected to become. It would take a lot for competitors to reach The Company's current status.

Development Objective	The objective is for The Company to establish a market presence in a majority of the over one hundred-thirty-five (135) metropolitan statistical areas in the United States. This will be accomplished by: (1) The Company opening, owning and operating its own regional sales areas; (2) Attracting and integrating qualified regional sales directors into the system through the use of select advertising; (3) Developing a vibrant image and commitment to quality and efficient service.
Product Strategy	It is recommended that The Company invest sufficient capital in research and development for the purpose of introducing a minimum of two new products each year to stay on the cutting edge of the competition and to enhance bottom line profits.
Positioning	The Company expects to be perceived as number one in products and services. Customers will recognize The Company's products to be of a higher quality than any competitive product. The Company will continue to maintain and strengthen its marketing position which will create even more confidence and trust among customers and The Company's sales force.
International Marketing	It is premature to consider an international market at this time. Once the U.S. Market is well underway and successful, it will not be difficult to enter the international market through licensing, joint-venturing or master licensing.
Method of Marketing	In order to maintain national control of The Company's marketing potential, it is recommended that The Company develop a national network of commissioned corporate regional sales directors as the primary method of marketing. These individuals will work on a minimum draw plus commission basis in obtaining locations for The Company's products and services. This includes selling the placement of the individual units as well as soliciting the advertisers who will participate in the advertising program. It is estimated that 15 to 25 salespersons will be needed during the first year's operation, 25 to 100 the second year and 100 to 150 the third year -- to place the units and to sell 50 ad spaces/units in his/her territory.
Regions Defined	Regional target areas will include SMSA marketing areas as defined by the U.S. Department of Commerce. The Company will concentrate on cities with a population of 1,000,000 persons within a 50 mile radius of its geographical center.

Profile of Regional Sales Director	1. An individual having liquid assets of at least $50,000
	2. Business experience in following areas:
	    a. Sales or marketing
	    b. Supervision -- minimum of four employees
	3. Designated regional sales director must play active role in business by devoting 100% of his/her time to the business.

Roll-Out Program	The Company will pre-select a minimum of 25 marketing areas which fit its criteria. The Company will pre-select from these, a few pilot areas for special invitation meetings where prospective regional sales directors can be interviewed and product selling can begin.
Regional Sales Director Services	The Company will emphasize its regional sales director support as one of its major activities. A hot-line service will be available to all regional sales directors. The purpose for this service is to assure regional sales director's success, satisfaction and loyalty. Technical and marketing support will be provided by The Company. This will allow the regional sales directors to concentrate on sales and to perform efficiently as The Company's front line. Regional sales directors will complete a two-day training program in El Dorado. The regional sales director should be ready to recruit customers immediately following their training.

Once ten or more regional sales directors are on line, The Company will be in a position to utilize the specialized help of an advertising agency in the refining and further development of its marketing direction.

Advertising and Promotion

The Company's principals have considerable experience in marketing, advertising and public relations. This expertise will be totally utilized as The Company grows.

Public Relations

During the first three to six months, The Company will use a minimum staff of three executives to sell and to administer the program. This includes the President, the Marketing Vice President and the Director of Operations. A receptionist will be hired to answer calls and take care of routine office matters. Eventually, a highly trained telemarketing team will be hired to support the regional sales directors in their selling and servicing initiatives.

Corporate Staffing and Sales Support

The Company is already at work developing lists of hotels, motels, and convention bureaus. This program will be extended to include other markets such as hospitals, museums, theme parks, etc. In addition, The Company is researching Marquee advertiser potential and prospects in such services as: limousine services; pizza delivery; florists; car rentals; quick print shops; movie theaters; legitimate theaters; concert halls; zoos; dry cleaners; restaurants; hospitals; medical services; etc.

Target Markets

In addition, The Company is researching all forms of advertising and advertising costs in order to be most competitive.

FINANCIAL PROJECTIONS
Assumptions

Pricing and Profitability

Pricing is generally based on what the competition charges, marketing, promotion, overhead costs, etc.

Pricing of products and service is competitive, however, The Company can and does command a competitive price structure because of the high quality of its products and services and the volume of sales controlled by The Company. Clients are willing to pay a fair price for recognized quality product value coupled with equally good service.

Margin Structure

Projections indicate that The Company will enjoy an average net income before taxes ranging from 30% to 60% over a three (3) year period. This is attractive by any standards.

Strategy for The Company Growth

- Obtain twenty (20) investors @ $175,000 for a total of $3,500,000
- Install 500 units in year one -- Generate sales of $15,500,000
- Install 2500 units in year two -- Generate sales of $93,000,000
- Install 3000 units in year three -- Generate sales of $186,000,000

Start-Up Requirements

The first year's operational cost is estimated to be $10,845,000. This would be offset by a projected $15,500,000 in sales which could net The Company a profit of approximately $2,792,640.

Income, Expenses and Cash Flow for the First Three Years

Item	Month 1	Month 2	Month 3	Month 4	Month 5	Month 6	Month 7
Income							
Gross Sales	$0	$0	$1,550,000	$1,550,000	$1,550,000	$1,550,000	$1,550,000
Renewals							
Total Income	$0	$0	$1,550,000	$1,550,000	$1,550,000	$1,550,000	$1,550,000
Expenses							
Corp. Formation	$10,000						
Rent	$3,487	$3,467	$3,467	$3,467	$3,467	$3,467	$3,467
Accounting Fees	$1,666	$1,666	$1,666	$1,666	$1,666	$1,666	$1,666
Legal Fees	$5,000	$5,000	$5,000				
Furnishings	$12,000						
Utilities	$500	$500	$500	$500	$500	$500	$500
Supplies	$500	$500	$500	$500	$500	$500	$500
Support Staff	$18,250	$18,250	$18,250	$18,250	$18,250	$18,250	$18,250
Unit Purchases	$208,333	$208,333	$208,333	$208,333	$208,333	$208,333	$208,333
Sales Salary/Comm.			$500,000	$500,000	$500,000	$500,000	$500,000
Vendor Space Rent			$150,000	$150,000	$150,000	$150,000	$150,000
Space Rent							
Travel	$8,333	$8,333	$8,333	$8,333	$8,333	$8,333	$8,333
Executive Salaries	$83,333	$83,333	$83,333	$83,333	$83,333	$83,333	$83,333
Vendor Phone Lines	$25,000	$25,000	$25,000	$25,000	$25,000	$25,000	$25,000
Line Renewals							
Sales Bonus			$10,000	$10,000	$10,000	$10,000	$10,000
Training Materials	$5,000						
Printing Duplicating	$2,500	$2,500					
Contingencies	$500	$500	$500	$500	$500	$500	$500
Total Expenses	$384,382	$357,382	$1,014,882	$1,009,882	$1,009,882	$1,009,882	$1,009,882
Cash Rev. B/T	($384,382)	($357,382)	$535,118	$540,118	$540,118	$540,118	$540,118
Taxes (40%)			$214,047	$216,047	$216,047	$216,047	$216,047
Profit	($384,382)	($357,382)	$321,071	$324,071	$324,071	$324,071	$324,071
Cash Flow	($384,382)	($357,382)	$535,118	$540,118	$540,118	$540,118	$540,118
Cum. Cash Flow	($384,382)	($741,763)	($206,645)	$333,473	$873,592	$1,413,710	$1,953,828

Notes for Financial Spreadsheet

1. Income represents advertising income as follows:
    a. 30 ads @ $900 = $27,000
    b. 20 ads @ $200 = $4,000 (for not-for-profit groups)
    c. Advertising income @ $31,000 per marquee
2. Rent is arrived at as follows:
    a. First year: 3200 sq. ft. @ $13/sq. ft.
    b. Second year: 5000 sq. ft. @ $14/sq. ft.
    c. Third year: 10,000 sq. ft. @ $15/sq. ft.
3. Unit Purchases @ $5,000 (includes R & D and Liability Ins.)
4. Vendor's space rentals @ $250/month.
5. Salesman's salary/commission @ 22%

Month 8	Month 9	Month 10	Month 11	Month 12	Year One	Year Two	Year Three
$1,550,000	$1,550,000	$1,550,000	$1,550,000	$1,550,000	$15,500,000	$77,500,000	$93,000,000
						$15,500,000	$93,000,000
$1,550,000	**$1,550,000**	**$1,550,000**	**$1,550,000**	**$1,550,000**	**$15,500,000**	**$93,000,000**	**$186,000,000**
					$10,000		
$3,467	$3,467	$3,467	$3,467	$3,467	$41,600	$70,000	$150,000
$1,666	$1,666	$1,666	$1,666	$1,666	$20,000	$40,000	$50,000
					$15,000	$30,000	$40,000
					$12,000	$40,000	$50,000
$500	$500	$500	$500	$500	$6,000	$10,000	$15,000
$500	$500	$500	$500	$500	$6,000	$10,000	$15,000
$18,250	$18,250	$18,250	$18,250	$18,250	$219,000	$365,000	$584,000
$208,333	$208,333	$208,333	$208,333	$208,333	$2,500,000	$12,500,000	$15,000,000
$500,000	$500,000	$500,000	$500,000	$500,000	$5,000,000	$25,000,000	$30,000,000
$150,000	$150,000	$150,000	$150,000	$150,000	$1,500,000	$7,500,000	$9,000,000
						$1,500,000	$9,000,000
$8,333	$8,333	$8,333	$8,333	$8,333	$100,000	$400,000	$500,000
$83,333	$83,333	$83,333	$83,333	$83,333	$1,000,000	$3,000,000	$5,000,000
$25,000	$25,000	$25,000	$25,000	$25,000	$300,000	$1,500,000	$1,800,000
						$300,000	$1,800,000
$10,000	$10,000	$10,000	$10,000	$10,000	$100,000	$200,000	$300,000
					$5,000	$10,000	$15,000
					$5,000	$25,000	$30,000
$500	$500	$500	$500	$500	$6,000	$6,000	$6,000
$1,009,882	**$1,009,882**	**$1,009,882**	**$1,009,882**	**$1,009,882**	**$10,845,600**	**$52,506,000**	**$73,355,000**
$14,490,118	$540,118	$540,118	$540,118	$540,118	$4,654,400	$40,494,000	$112,645,000
$5,796,047	$216,047	$216,047	$216,047	$216,047	$1,861,760	$16,197,600	$45,058,000
$8,694,071	$324,071	$324,071	$324,071	$324,071	$2,792,640	$24,296,400	$67,587,000
$14,490,118	**$540,118**	**$540,118**	**$540,118**	**$540,118**	**$4,654,400**	**$40,494,000**	**$112,645,000**
$16,443,947	**$16,984,065**	**$17,524,183**	**$18,064,302**	**$18,604,420**	**$23,258,820**	**$63,752,820**	**$176,397,820**

Appendix A - Business Plan Template

Business Plan Template

USING THIS TEMPLATE

A business plan carefully spells out a company's projected course of action over a period of time, usually the first two to three years after the start-up. In addition, banks, lenders, and other investors examine the information and financial documentation before deciding whether or not to finance a new business venture. Therefore, a business plan is an essential tool in obtaining financing and should describe the business itself in detail as well as all important factors influencing the company, including the market, industry, competition, operations and management policies, problem solving strategies, financial resources and needs, and other vital information. The plan enables the business owner to anticipate costs, plan for difficulties, and take advantage of opportunities, as well as design and implement strategies that keep the company running as smoothly as possible.

This template has been provided as a model to help you construct your own business plan. Please keep in mind that there is no single acceptable format for a business plan, and that this template is in no way comprehensive, but serves as an example.

The business plans provided in this section are fictional and have been used by small business agencies as models for clients to use in compiling their own business plans.

GENERIC BUSINESS PLAN

Main headings included below are topics that should be covered in a comprehensive business plan. They include:

Business Summary

Purpose
Provides a brief overview of your business, succinctly highlighting the main ideas of your plan.

Includes

- Name and Type of Business
- Description of Product/Service
- Business History and Development
- Location
- Market
- Competition
- Management
- Financial Information
- Business Strengths and Weaknesses
- Business Growth

Table of Contents

Purpose

Organized in an Outline Format, the Table of Contents illustrates the selection and arrangement of information contained in your plan.

Includes

- Topic Headings and Subheadings
- Page Number References

Business History and Industry Outlook

Purpose

Examines the conception and subsequent development of your business within an industry specific context.

Includes

- Start-up Information
- Owner/Key Personnel Experience
- Location
- Development Problems and Solutions
- Investment/Funding Information
- Future Plans and Goals
- Market Trends and Statistics
- Major Competitors
- Product/Service Advantages
- National, Regional, and Local Economic Impact

Product/Service

Purpose

Introduces, defines,and details the product and/or service that inspired the information of your business.

Includes

- Unique Features
- Niche Served
- Market Comparison
- Stage of Product/Service Development
- Production
- Facilities, Equipment, and Labor
- Financial Requirements
- Product/Service Life Cycle
- Future Growth

Market Examination

Purpose
Assessment of product/service applications in relation to consumer buying cycles.

Includes

- Target Market
- Consumer Buying Habits
- Product/Service Applications
- Consumer Reactions
- Market Factors and Trends
- Penetration of the Market
- Market Share
- Research and Studies
- Cost
- Sales Volume and Goals

Competition

Purpose
Analysis of Competitors in the Marketplace.

Includes

- Competitor Information
- Product/Service Comparison
- Market Niche
- Product/Service Strengths and Weaknesses
- Future Product/Service Development

Marketing

Purpose
Identifies promotion and sales strategies for your product/service.

Includes

- Product/Service Sales Appeal
- Special and Unique Features
- Identification of Customers
- Sales and Marketing Staff
- Sales Cycles
- Type of Advertising/Promotion
- Pricing
- Competition
- Customer Services

Operations

Purpose

Traces product/service development from production/inception to the market environment.

Includes

- Cost Effective Production Methods
- Facility
- Location
- Equipment
- Labor
- Future Expansion

Administration and Management

Purpose

Offers a statement of your management philosophy with an in-depth focus on processes and procedures.

Includes

- Management Philosophy
- Structure of Organization
- Reporting System
- Methods of Communication
- Employee Skills and Training
- Employee Needs and Compensation
- Work Environment
- Management Policies and Procedures
- Roles and Responsibilities

Key Personnel

Purpose

Describes the unique backgrounds of principle employees involved in business.

Includes

- Owner(s)/Employee Education and Experience
- Positions and Roles
- Benefits and Salary
- Duties and Responsibilities
- Objectives and Goals

Potential Problems and Solutions

Purpose
Discussion of problem solving strategies that change issues into opportunities.

Includes

- Risks
- Litigation
- Future Competition
- Economic Impact
- Problem Solving Skills

Financial Information

Purpose
Secures needed funding and assistance through worksheets and projections detailing financial plans, methods of repayment, and future growth opportunities.

Includes

- Financial Statements
- Bank Loans
- Methods of Repayment
- Tax Returns
- Start-up Costs
- Projected Income (3 years)
- Projected Cash Flow (3 Years)
- Projected Balance Statements (3 years)

Appendices

Purpose
Supporting documents used to enhance your business proposal.

Includes

- Photographs of product, equipment, facilities, etc.
- Copyright/Trademark Documents
- Legal Agreements
- Marketing Materials
- Research and or Studies
- Operation Schedules
- Organizational Charts
- Job Descriptions
- Resumes
- Additional Financial Documentation

Food Distributor

FICTIONAL BUSINESS PLAN

COMMERCIAL FOODS, INC.

3003 Avondale Ave.
Knoxville, TN 37920

October 31, 1992

This plan demonstrates how a partnership can have a positive impact on a new business. It demonstrates how two individuals can carve a niche in the specialty foods market by offering gourmet foods to upscale restaurants and fine hotels. This plan is fictional and has not been used to gain funding from a bank or other lending institution.

- STATEMENT OF PURPOSE

- DESCRIPTION OF THE BUSINESS

- MANAGEMENT

- PERSONNEL

- LOCATION

- PRODUCTS AND SERVICES

- THE MARKET

- COMPETITION

- SUMMARY

- INCOME STATEMENT

- FINANCIAL STATEMENTS

STATEMENT OF PURPOSE

Commercial Food, Inc. seeks a loan of $75,000 to establish a new business. This sum together with $5,000 equity investment by the principals will be used as follows:

Merchandise inventory	$25,000
Office fixture/equipment	12,000
Warehouse equipment	14,000
One delivery truck	10,000
Working capital	39,00
Total	**$100,000**

DESCRIPTION OF THE BUSINESS

Commercial Foods, Inc. will be a distributor of specialty food service products to hotels and upscale restaurants in the geographical area in a 50 mile radius of Knoxville. Richard Roberts will direct the sales effort and John Williams will manage the warehouse operation and the office. One delivery truck will be used initially with a second truck added in the third year.

We expect to begin operation of the business within 30 days after securing the requested financing.

MANAGEMENT

A. Richard Roberts is a native of Memphis, Tennessee. He is a graduate of Memphis State University with a Bachelor's degree from the School of Business. After graduation, he worked for a major manufacturer of specialty food service products as a detail sales person for five years and for the past three years, he has served as a product sales manager for this firm.

B. John Williams is a native of Nashville, Tennessee. He holds a B.S. Degree in Food Technology from the University of Tennessee. His career includes five years as a product development chemist in gourmet food products and five years as operations manager for a food service distributor.

Both men are healthy and energetic. Their backgrounds complement each other which will ensure the success of Commercial Foods, Inc. They will set policies together and personnel decisions will be made jointly. Initial salaries for the owners will be $1,000 per month for the first few years. The spouses of both principals are successful in the business world and earn enough to support the families.

They have engaged the services of Foster Jones, CPA, and William Hale, Attorney to assist them in an advisory capacity.

PERSONNEL

The firm will employ one delivery truck driver at a wage of $8.00 per hour. One office worker will be employed at $7.50 per hour. One part-time employee will be used in the office at $5.00 per hour. The driver will load and unload his own trucks. Mr. Williams will assist in the warehouse operation as needed to assist one stock person at $7.00 per hour. An additional delivery truck and driver will be added the third year.

LOCATION

The firm will lease a 20,000 square foot building at 3003 Avondale Ave., in Knoxville, which contains warehouse and office areas equipped with two-door truck docks. The annual rental is $9,000. The building was previously used as a food service warehouse and very little modification to the building will be required.

The firm will offer specialty food service products such as soup bases, dessert mixes, sauce bases, pastry mixes, spices, and flavors, normally used by upscale restaurants and nice hotels. We are going after a niche in the market with high quality gourmet products. There is much less competition in this market than in standard run of the mill food service products. Through their work experiences, the principals have contacts with supply sources and with local chefs.

PRODUCTS AND SERVICES

We know from our market survey that there are over 200 hotels and upscale restaurants in the area we plan to serve. Customers will be attracted by a direct sales approach. We will offer samples of our products and product application data on use of our products in the finished prepared foods. We will cultivate the chefs in these establishments. The technical background of John Williams will be especially useful here.

THE MARKET

We find that we will be only distributor in the area offering a full line of gourmet food service products. Other foodservice distributors offer only a few such items in conjunction with their standard product line. Our survey shows that many of the chefs are ordering products from Atlanta and Memphis because of lack of adequate local supply.

COMPETITION

Commercial Foods, Inc. will be established as a foodservice distributor of specialty food in Knoxville. The principals, with excellent experience in the industry are seeking a $75,000 loan to establish the business. The principals are investing $25,000 as equity capital.

SUMMARY

The business will be set up as an "S" Corporation with each principal owning 50% of the common stock in the corporation.

Attached is a three year pro forma income statement we believe to be conservative. Also attached are personal financial statements of the principals and a projected cash flow statement for the first year.

	1st Year	2nd Year	3rd Year
Gross Sales	300,000	400,000	500,000
Less Allowances	1,000	1,000	2,000
Net Sales	299,000	399,000	498,000
Cost of Goods Sold	179,400	239,400	298,800
Gross Margin	119,600	159,600	199,200
Operating Expenses			
Utilities	1,200	1,500	1,700
Salaries	76,000	79,000	102,000
Payroll Taxes/Benefits	9,100	9,500	13,200
Advertising	3,000	4,500	5,000
Office Supplies	1,500	2,000	2,500
Insurance	1,200	1,500	1,800
Maintenance	1,000	1,500	2,000
Outside Services	3,000	3,000	3,000
Whse Supplies/Trucks	6,000	7,000	10,000
Telephone	900	1,000	1,200
Rent	9,000	9,500	9,900
Depreciation	2,500	2,000	3,000
Total Expenses	114,400	122,000	155,300
Other Expenses			
Bank Loan Payment	15,000	15,000	15,000
Bank Loan Interest	6,000	5,000	4,000
Total Expenses	**120,400**	**142,000**	**174,300**
Net Profit (Loss)	**(800)**	**17,600**	**24,900**

PRO FORMA INCOME STATEMENT

FINANCIAL STATEMENT I

Assets		Liabilities	
Cash	15,000		
1991 Olds	11,000	Unpaid Balance	8,000
Residence	140,000	Mortgage	105,000
Mutual Funds	12,000	Credit Cards	500
Furniture	5,000	Note Payable	4,000
Merck Stock	10,000		
	182,200		117,500
Net Worth			**64,700**
	182,200		**182,200**

FINANCIAL STATEMENT II

Assets		Liabilities	
Cash	5,000		
1992 Buick Auto	15,000	Unpaid Balance	12,000
Residence	120,000	Mortgage	100,000
U.S. Treasury Bonds	5,000	Credit Cards	500
Home Furniture	4,000	Note Payable	2,500
AT&T Stock	3,000		
	147,000		115,000
Net Worth			**32,000**
	147,000		**147,000**

Hardware Store

FICTIONAL BUSINESS PLAN

OSHKOSH HARDWARE, INC

123 Main St.
Oshkosh, WI 54901

June 1994

The following plan outlines how a small hardware store can survive competition from large discount chains by offering products and providing expert advice in the use of any product it sells. This plan is fictional and has not used to gain funding from a bank or other lending institution.

- EXECUTIVE SUMMARY

- THE BUSINESS

- THE MARKET

- SALES

- MANAGEMENT

- GOALS IMPLEMENTATION

- FINANCE

- JOB DESCRIPTION-GENERAL MANAGER

- QUARTERLY FORECASTED BALANCE SHEETS

- QUARTERLY FORECASTED STATEMENTS OF EARNINGS AND RETAINED EARNINGS

- QUARTERLY FORECASTED STATEMENTS OF CHANGES IN FINANCIAL POSITION

- FINANCIAL RATIO ANALYSIS

- DETAILS FOR QUARTERLY STATEMENTS OF EARNINGS

EXECUTIVE SUMMARY

Oshkosh Hardware, Inc. is a new corporation which is going to establish a retail hardware store in a strip mall in Oshkosh, Wisconsin. The store will sell hardware of all kinds, quality tools, paint and housewares. The business will make revenue and a profit by servicing its customers not only with needed hardware but also with expert advice in the use of any product it sells.

Oshkosh Hardware, Inc. will be operated by its sole shareholder, James Smith. The company will have a total of four employees. It will sell its products in the local market. Customers will buy our products because we will provide free advice on the use of all of our products and will also furnish a full refund warranty.

Oshkosh Hardware, Inc. will sell its products in the Oshkosh store staffed by three sales representatives. No additional employees will be needed to achieve its short and long range goals. The primary short range goal is to open the store by October 1, 1994. In order to achieve this goal a lease must be signed by July 1, 1994 and the complete inventory ordered by August 1, 1994.

Mr. James Smith will invest $30,000 in the business. In addition the company will have to borrow $150,000 during the first year to cover the investment in inventory, accounts receivable, and furniture and equipment. The company will be profitable after six months of operation and should be able to start repayment of the loan in the second year.

THE BUSINESS

The business will sell hardware of all kinds, quality tools, paint, and housewares. We will purchase our products from three large wholesale buying groups.

In general our customers are homeowners who do their own repair and maintenance, hobbyists, and housewives. Our business is unique in that we will have a complete line of all hardware items and will be able to get special orders by overnight delivery. The business makes revenue and profits by servicing our customers not only with needed hardware but also with expert advice in the use of any product we sell. Our major costs for bringing our products to market are cost of merchandise of 36%, salaries of $45,000, and occupancy costs of $60,000.

Oshkosh Hardware, Inc.'s retail outlet will be located at 1524 Frontage Road, which is in a newly developed retail center of Oshkosh. Our location helps facilitate accessibility from all parts of town and reduces our delivery costs. The store will occupy 7500 square feet of space. The major equipment involved in our business is counters and shelving, a computer, a paint mixing machine, and a truck.

THE MARKET

Oshkosh Hardware, Inc. will operate in the local market. There are 15,000 potential customers in this market area. We have three competitors who control approximately 98% of the market at present. We feel we can capture 25% of the market within the next four years. Our major reason for believing this is that our staff is technically competent to advise our customers in the correct use of all products we sell.

After a careful market analysis we have determined that approximately 60% of our customers are men and 40% are women. The percentage of customers that fall into the following age categories are:

Under 16 - 0%

17-21 - 5%

22-30 - 30%

31-40 - 30%

41-50-20%
51-60-10%
61-70-5%
Over 70 - 0%

The reasons our customers prefer our products is our complete knowledge of their use and our full refund warranty.

We get our information about what products our customers want by talking to existing customers. There seems to be an increasing demand for our product. The demand for our product is increasing in size based on the change in population characteristics.

SALES

At Oshkosh Hardware, Inc. we will employ 3 sales people and will not need any additional personnel to achieve our sales goals. These salespeople will need several years experience in home repair and power tool usage. We expect to attract 30% of our customers from newspaper ads, 5% of our customers from local directories, 5% of our customers from the yellow pages, 10% of our customers from family and friends and 50% of our customers from current customers. The most cost effect source will be current customers. In general our industry is growing.

MANAGEMENT

We would evaluate the quality of our management staff as being excellent. Our manager is experienced and very motivated to achieve the various sales and quality assurance objectives we have set. We will use a management information system which produces key inventory, quality assurance and sales data on a weekly basis. All data is compared to previously established goals for that week and deviations are the primary focus of the management staff.

**GOALS
IMPLEMENTATION**

The short term goals of our business are:

> 1. Open the store by October 1, 1994
> 2. Reach our breakeven point in two months
> 3. Have sales of $100,000 in the first six months

In order to achieve our first short term goal we must:

> 1. Sign the lease by July 1, 1994
> 2. Order a complete inventory by August 1, 1994

In order to achieve our second short term goal we must:

> 1. Advertise extensively in Sept. and Oct.
> 2. Keep expenses to a minimum

In order to achieve our third short term goal we must:

> 1. Promote power tool sales for the Christmas season
> 2. Keep good customer traffic in Jan. and Feb.

The long term goals for our business are:

> 1. Obtain sales volume of $600,000 in three years
> 2. Become the largest hardware dealer in the city
> 3. Open a second store in Fond du Lac

The most important thing we must do in order to achieve the long term goals for our business is to develop a highly profitable business with excellent cash flow.

FINANCE

Oshkosh Hardware, Inc. Faces some potential threats or risks to our business. They are discount house competition. We believe we can avoid or compensate for this by providing quality products complimented by quality advice on the use of every product we sell. The financial projections we have prepared are located at the end of this document.

JOB DESCRIPTION - GENERAL MANAGER

The General Manager of the business of the corporation will be the president of the corporation. He will be responsible for the complete operation of the retail hardware store which is owned by the corporation. A detailed description of his duties and responsibilities is as follows:

Sales

Train and supervise the three sales people. Develop programs to motivate and compensate these employees. Coordinate advertising and sales promotion effects to achieve sales totals as outlined in budget. Oversee purchasing function and inventory control procedures to insure adequate merchandise at all times at a reasonable cost.

Finance

Prepare monthly and annual budgets. Secure adequate line of credit from local banks. Supervise office personnel to insure timely preparation of records, statements, all government reports, control of receivables and payables and monthly financial statements.

Administration

Perform duties as required in the areas of personnel, building leasing and maintenance, licenses and permits and public relations.

QUARTERLY FORECASTED BALANCE SHEETS

	Beg Bal	1st Qtr	2nd Qtr	3rd Qtr	4th Qtr
Assets					
Cash	30,000	418	(463)	(3,574)	4,781
Accounts Receivable	0	20,000	13,333	33,333	33,333
Inventory	0	48,000	32,000	80,000	80,000
Other Current Assets	0	0	0	0	0
Total Current Assets	30,000	68,418	44,870	109,759	118,114
Land	0	0	0	0	0
Building & Improvements	0	0	0	0	0
Furniture & Equipment	0	75,000	75,000	75,000	75,000
Total Fixed Assets	0	75,000	75,000	75,000	75,000
Less Accum. Depreciation	0	1,875	3,750	5,625	7,500
Net Fixed Assets	0	73,125	71,250	69,375	67,500
Intangible Assets	0	0	0	0	0
Less Amortization	0	0	0	0	0
Net Intangible Assets	0	0	0	0	0
Other Assets	0	0	0	0	0
Total Assets	**30,000**	**141,543**	**116,120**	**179,134**	**185,614**

Liabilities and Shareholders' Equity

Short-Term Debt	0	0	0	0	0
Accounts Payable	0	12,721	10,543	17,077	17,077
Dividends Payable	0	0	0	0	0
Income Taxes Payable	0	(1,031)	(2,867)	(2,355)	(1,843)
Accured Compensation	0	1,867	1,867	1,867	1,867
Other Current Liabilities	0	0	0	0	0
Total Current Liabilities	0	13,557	9,543	16,589	17,101
Long-Term Debt	0	110,000	110,000	160,000	160,000
Other Non-Current Liabilities	0	0	0	0	0
Total Liabilities	0	123,557	119,543	176,589	177,101
Common Stock	30,000	30,000	30,000	30,000	30,000
Retained Earnings	0	(12,014)	(33,423)	(27,455)	(21,487)
Shareholders' Equity	30,000	17,986	(3,423)	2,545	8,513
Total Liabilities & Shareholders' Equity	30,000	141,543	116,120	179,134	185,614

	Beg Actual	1st Qtr	2nd Qtr	3rd Qtr	4th Qtr	Total
Total Sales	0	60,000	40,000	100,000	100,000	300,000
Goods/Services	0	21,600	14,400	36,000	36,000	108,000
Gross Profit	0	38,400	25,600	64,000	64,000	192,000
Operating Expenses	0	47,645	45,045	52,845	52,845	198,380
Fixed Expenses						
Interest	0	1,925	1,925	2,800	2,800	9,450
Depreciation	0	1,875	1,875	1,875	1,875	7,500
Amortization	0	0	0	0	0	0
Total Fixed Expenses	0	3,800	3,800	4,675	4,675	16,950
Operating Profit						
(Loss)	0	(13,045)	(23,245)	6,480	6,480	(23,330)
Other Income						
(Expense)	0	0	0	0	0	0

QUARTERLY FORECASTED STATEMENTS OF EARNINGS AND RETAINED EARNINGS

	Beg Bal	1st Qtr	2nd Qtr	3rd Qtr	4th Qtr	Total
Interest Income	0	0	0	0	0	0
Earnings (Loss)						
Before Taxes	0	(13,045)	(23,245)	6,480	6,480	(23,330)
Income Taxes	0	(1,031)	(1,836)	512	512	(1,843)
Net Earnings	0	(12,014)	(21,409)	5,968	5,968	(21,487)
Retained Earnings,						
Beginning	0	0	(12,014)	(33,423)	(27,455)	0
Less Dividends	0	0	0	0	0	0
Retained Earnings,						
Ending	0	(12,014)	(33,423)	(27,455)	(21,487)	(21,487)

QUARTERLY FORECASTED STATEMENTS OF CHANGES IN FINANCIAL POSITION

	Beg Bal	1st Qtr	2nd Qtr	3rd Qtr	4th Qtr	Total
Sources (Uses) of Cash						
Net Earnings						
(Loss)	0	(12,014)	(21,409)	5,968	5,968	(21,487)
Depreciation						
& Amortization	0	1,875	1,875	1,875	1,875	7,500
Cash Provided						
by Operations	0	(10,139)	(19,534)	7,834	7,834	(13,987)
Dividends	0	0	0	0	0	0
Cash Provided by (Used For) Changes in						
Accounts Receivable	0	(20,000)	6,667	(20,000)	0	(33,333)
Inventory	0	(48,000)	16,000	(48,000)	0	(80,000)
Other Current Assets	0	0	0	0	0	0
Accounts Payable	0	12,	721	(2,178)	6,5340	17,077
Income Taxes	0	(1,031)	(1,836)	512	512	(1,843)
Accrued						
Compensation	0	1,867	0	0	0	1,867
Dividends Payable	0	0	0	0	0	0
Other Current						
Liabilities	0	0	0	0	0	0

Other Assests	0	0	0	0	0	0
Net Cash Provided by (Used For)						
Operating Activities	0	(54,443)	18,653	(60,954)	512	(96,233)
Investment Transactions						
Furniture &						
Equipment	0	(75,000)	0	0	0	(75,000)
Land	0	0	0	0	0	0
Building &						
Improvements	0	0	0	0	0	0
Intangible Assets	0	0	0	0	0	0
Net Cash From						
Investment						
Transactions	0	(75,000)	0	0	0	(75,000)
Financing Transactions						
Short-Term Debt	0	0	0	0	0	0
Long-Term Debt	0	110,000	0	50,000	0	160,000
Other Non-Current						
Liabilities	0	0	0	0	0	0
Sale of Common						
Stock	30,000	0	0	0	0	0
Net Cash from Financing						
Transactions	30,000	110,000	0	50,000	0	160,000
Net Increase (Decrease)						
in Cash	30,000	(29,582)	(881)	(3,111)	8,355	(25,219)
Cash-Beginning						
of Period	0	30,000	418	(463)	(3,574)	30,000
Cash-End						
of Period	30,000	418	(463)	(3,574)	4,781	4,781

FINANCIAL RATIO ANALYSIS		Beg Act	1st Qtr	2nd Qtr	3rd Qtr	4th Qtr
	Overall Performance					
	Return on Equity	0.00	(66.80)	625.45	234.50	70.10
	Return on Total Assets	0.00	(8.49)	(18.44)	3.33	3.22
	Operating Return	0.00	(9.22)	(20.02)	3.62	3.49
	Profitability Measures					
	Gross Profit Percent	0.00	64.00	64.00	64.00	64.00
	Profit Margin (AIT)	0.00	(20.02)	(53.52)	5.97	5.97
	Operating Income per Share	0.00	0.00	0.00	0.00	0.00
	Earnings per Share	0.00	0.00	0.00	0.00	0.00
	Test of Investment Utilization					
	Asset Turnover	0.00	0.42	0.34	0.56	0.54
	Equity Turnover	0.00	3.34	(11.69)	39.29	11.75
	Fixed Asset Turnover	0.00	0.82	0.56	1.44	1.48
	Average Collection Period	0.00	30.00	30.00	30.00	30.00
	Days Inventory	0.00	200.00	200.00	200.00	200.00
	Inventory Turnover	0.00	0.45	0.45	0.45	0.45
	Working Capital Turns	0.00	1.09	1.13	1.07	0.99
	Test of Financial Condition					
	Current Ratio	0.00	5.05	4.70	6.62	6.91
	Quick Ratio	0.00	1.51	1.35	1.79	2.23
	Working Capital Ratio	1.00	0.43	0.33	0.57	0.60
	Dividend Payout	0.00	0.00	0.00	0.00	0.00
	Financial Leverage					
	Total Assets	1.00	7.87	(33.92)	70.39	21.80

Debt/Equity	0.00	6.87	(34.92)	69.39	20.80
Debt to Total Assets	0.00	0.87	1.03	0.99	0.95

Year-End Equity History

Shares Outstanding	0	0	0	0	0
Market Price per Share	0.00	0.00	0.00	0.00	0.00
(@20x's earnings)					
Book Value per Share	0.00	0.00	0.00	0.00	0.00

Altman Analysis Ratio

1.2x(1)	1.20	0.47	0.37	0.62	0.65
1.4x(2)	0.00	(0.12)	(0.40)	(0.21)	(0.16)
3.3x(3)	0.00	(0.35)	(0.72)	0.07	0.07
0.6x(4)	0.00	0.00	0.00	0.00	0.00
1.0x(5)	0.00	0.42	0.34	0.56	0.54
Z Value	1.20	.042	(.041)	1.04	1.10

DETAILS FOR QUARTERLY STATEMENTS OF EARNINGS

	Beg Act	1st Qtr	2nd Qtr	3rd Qtr	4th Qtr	Total	% Sales	Fixed
Sales								
Dollars Sales Forecasted								
Product 1	0	60,000	40,000	100,000	100,000	300,000		
Product 2	0	0	0	0	0	0		
Product 3	0	0	0	0	0	0		
Product 4	0	0	0	0	0	0		
Product 5	0	0	0	0	0	0		
Product 6	0	0	0	0	0	0		
Total Sales	0	60,000	40,000	100,000	100,000	300,000		

Cost of Sales

Dollar Cost Forecasted

Product 1	0	21,600	14,400	36,000	36,000	108,000	36.00%	0
Product 2	0	0	0	0	0	0	0.00%	0
Product 3	0	0	0	0	0	0	0.00%	0
Product 4	0	0	0	0	0	0	0.00%	0
Product 5	0	0	0	0	0	0	0.00%	0
Product 6	0	0	0	0	0	0	0.00%	0
Total Cost of Sales	0	21,600	14,400	36,000	36,000	108,000		

Operating Expenses

Payroll	0	12,000	12,000	12,000	12,000	48,000	0.00%	12,000
Paroll Taxes	0	950	950	950	950	3,800	0.00%	950
Advertising	0	4,800	3,200	8,000	8,000	24,000	8.00%	0
Automobile Expenses	0	0	0	0	0		0.00%	0
Bad Debts	0	0	0	0	0	0	0.00%	0
Commissions	0	3,000	2,000	5,000	5,000	15,000	5.00%	0
Computer Rental	0	1,200	1,200	1,200	1,200	4,800	0.00%	1,200
Computer Supplies	0	220	220	220	220	880	0.00%	220
Computer Maintenance	0	100	100	100	100	400	0.00%	100
Dealer Training	0	1,000	1,000	1,000	1,000	4,000	0.00%	1,000
Electricity	0	3,000	3,000	3,000	3,000	12,000	0.00%	3,000
Employment Ads and Fees	0	0	0	0	0	0	0.00%	0
Entertainment: Business	0	1,500	1,500	1,500	1,500	6,000	0.00%	1,500
General Insurance	0	800	800	800	800	32,000	0.00%	800
Health & W/C Insurance	0	0	0	0	0	0	.00%	0
Interest-LT Debt	0	2,500	2,500	2,500	2,500	10,000	0.00%	2,500
Legal & Accounting	0	1,500	1,500	1,500	1,500	6,000	0.00%	1,500
Maintenance & Repairs	0	460	460	460	460	1,840	0.00%	460

	Beg Act	1st Qtr	2nd Qtr	3rd Qtr	4th Qtr	Total	%Sales	Fixed
Office Supplies	0	270	270	270	270	1,080	0.00%	270
Postage	0	85	85	85	85	340	0.00%	85
Prof. Development	0	0	0	0	0	0	0.00%	0
Professional Fees	0	1,000	1,000	1,000	1,000	4,000	0.00%	1,000
Rent	0	8,000	8,000	8,000	8,000	32,000	0.00%	8,000
Shows & Conferences	0	0	0	0	0	0	0.00%	0
Subscriptions & Dues	0	285	285	285	285	1,140	0.00%	285
Telephone	0	1,225	1,225	1,225	1,225	4,900	0.00%	1,225
Temporary Employees	0	0	0	0	0	0	0.00%	0
Travel Expenses	0	750	750	750	750	3,000	0.00%	750
Utilities	0	3,000	3,000	3,000	3,000	12,000	0.00%	3,000
Research & Devlpmnt.	0	0	0	0	0	0	0.00%	0
Royalties	0	0	0	0	0	0	0.00%	0
Other 1	0	0	0	0	0	0	0.00%	0
Other 2	0	0	0	0	0	0	0.00%	0
Other 3	0	0	0	0	0	0	0.00%	0
Total Operating Expenses	0	47,645	45,045	52,845	52,845	198,380		
Percent of Sales	0.00	79.41	112.61	52.85	52.85	66.13		

Appendix - B
Organizations, Agencies and Consultants

Organizations, Agencies, & Consultants

A listing of Associations and Consultants of interest to entrepreneurs, followed by the 10 Small Business Administration Regional Offices, Small Business Development Centers, Service Corps of Retired Executives offices, and Venture Capital & Finance companies.

ASSOCIATIONS

This section contains a listing of associations and other agencies of interest to the small business owner. Entires are listed alphabetically by organization name.

American Assoc. for Consumer
Benefits
PO Box 100279
Fort Worth, Texas 76185
Phone: (800)872-8896
Free: (800)872-8896
Fax: (817)377-5633
William Kirkman, Contact

American Small Businesses Assoc.
1800 N. Kent St., Ste. 910
Arlington, Virginia 22209
Free: (800)235-3298
Vernon Castle, Exec. Dir.

American Society of Independent
Business
c/o Keith Wood
777 Main St., Ste. 1600
Fort Worth, Texas 76102
Phone: (817)870-1880
Keith Wood, Pres.

American Woman's Economic
Development Corporation
71 Vanderbilt Ave., 3rd Fl.
New York, New York 10169
Phone: (212)692-9100
Fax: (212)692-9296
Suzanne Tufts, Pres. & CEO

Assoc. of Small Business
Development Centers
1300 Chain Bridge Rd., Ste. 201
Mc Lean, Virginia 22101-3967
Phone: (703)448-6124
Fax: (703)448-6125
E-mail: jjohns1012@aol.com
Max Summers, Pres.

BEST Employers Assoc.
2515 McCabe Way
Irvine, California 92614
Phone: (714)756-1000
Free: (800)854-7417
Fax: (714)553-1232
E-mail: bestplans@bestplans.com
Donald R. Lawrenz, Exec. Sec.

Business Coalition for Fair
Competition
8421 Frost Way
Annandale, Virginia 22003
Phone: (703)280-4622
Fax: (703)280-0942
E-mail: kentonpi@aol.com
Kenton Pattie, Contact

Business Market Assoc.
4131 N. Central Expy., Ste. 720
Dallas, Texas 75204
Phone: (214)559-3900
Fax: (214)559-4143
R. Mark King, Pres.

Coalition of Americans to Save the
Economy
1100 Connecticut Ave. NW, Ste. 1200
Washington, DC 20036-4101
Phone: (202)293-1414
Fax: (202)293-1702
Barry Maloney, Treas.

Family Firm Institute
12 Harris St.
Brookline, Massachusetts 02146
Phone: (617)738-1591
Fax: (617)738-4883
Judy L. Green Ph.D., Exec. Dir.

International Assoc. of Business
701 Highlander Blvd.
Arlington, Texas 76015
Phone: (817)465-2922

Fax: (817)467-5940
Paula Rainey, Pres.

International Assoc. for Business
Organizations
PO Box 30149
Baltimore, Maryland 21270
Phone: (410)581-1373
Rudolph Lewis, Exec. Officer

International Council for Small
Business
c/o Jefferson Smurfit Center for
Entrepreneurial Studies
St. Louis University
3674 Lindell Blvd.
St. Louis, Missouri 63108
Phone: (314)977-3628
Fax: (314)977-3627
E-mail: icsb@sluvca.slu.edu
William I. Dennis Jr., Pres.

ISBE Employers of America
520 S. Pierce, Ste. 224
Mason City, Iowa 50401
Phone: (515)424-3187
Free: (800)728-3187
Fax: (515)424-1673
Jim Collison, Pres.

National Alliance for Fair Competition
3 Bethesda Metro Center, Ste. 1100
Bethesda, Maryland 20814
Phone: (410)235-7116
Fax: (410)235-7116
Tony Ponticelli, Exec. Dir.

National Assoc. for Business
Organizations
PO Box 30149
Baltimore, Maryland 21270
Phone: (410)581-1373
Rudolph Lewis, Pres.

National Assoc. of Private Enterprise
PO Box 612147
Dallas, Texas 75261-2147
Free: (800)223-6273
Fax: (817)332-4525
Heidi Williams, Acct. Exec.

National Assoc. for the Self-Employed
PO Box 612067
Dallas, Texas 75261-2067
Free: (800)232-NASE
Fax: (800)551-4446
Bennie Thayer, Pres. & CEO

National Assoc. of Small Business
Investment Companies
666 11th St. NW, No. 750
Washington, DC 20001
Phone: (202)628-5055
Fax: (202)628-5080
E-mail: nasbic@nasbic.org
Lee W. Mercer, Pres.

National Business Assoc.
5151 Belt Line Rd., No. 1150
Dallas, Texas 75240-7545
Phone: (214)458-0900
Free: (800)456-0440
Fax: (214)960-9149
Robert G. Allen, Pres.

National Business Owners Assoc.
1033 N. Fairfax St., Ste. 402
Alexandria, Virginia 22314
Phone: (202)737-6501
Fax: (703)838-0149
J. Drew Hiatt, Exec. VP

National Federation of Independent
Business
53 Century Blvd., Ste. 300
Nashville, Tennessee 37214
Phone: (615)872-5800
Fax: (615)872-5899
Fred Holladay, VP & CFO

National Small Business Benefits
Assoc.
2244 N. Grand Ave. E.
Springfield, Illinois 62702
Phone: (217)753-2558
Fax: (217)753-2558
Les Brewer, Exec. VP

National Small Business United
1155 15th St. NW, Ste. 710
Washington, DC 20005
Phone: (202)293-8830
Free: (800)345-6728
Fax: (202)872-8543
E-mail: nsbu@nsbu.org
John Paul Galles, Pres.

Network of Small Businesses
5420 Mayfield Rd., Ste. 205
Lyndhurst, Ohio 44124
Phone: (216)442-5600
Fax: (216)449-3227
Irwin Friedman, Chm.

The Score Assoc.
Service Corps of Retired Executives
Assoc.
409 3rd St. SW, 4th Fl.
Washington, DC 20024
Phone: (202)205-6762
Free: (800)634-0245
Fax: (202)205-7636
W. Kenneth Yancey Jr., Exec. Dir.

Small Business Assistance Center
554 Main St.
PO Box 15014
Worcester, Massachusetts 01615-0014
Phone: (508)756-3513
Fax: (508)791-4709
Francis R. Carroll, Pres.

Small Business Foundation of
America
1155 15th St.
Washington, DC 20005
Phone: (202)223-1103
Fax: (202)476-6534
Regina Tracy, Exec. Dir.

Small Business Legislative Council
1156 15th St. NW, Ste. 510
Washington, DC 20005
Phone: (202)639-8500
Fax: (202)296-5333
John Satagaj, Pres.

Small Business Network
PO Box 30149
Baltimore, Maryland 21270

Phone: (410)581-1373
E-mail: natibb@ix.netcom.com
Rudolph Lewis, CEO

Small Business Service Bureau
554 Main St.
PO Box 15014
Worcester, Massachusetts 01615-0014
Phone: (508)756-3513
Fax: (508)791-4709
Francis R. Carroll, Pres.

Small Business Support Center Assoc.
c/o James S. Ryan
8811 Westheimer Rd., No. 210
Houston, Texas 77063-3617
James S. Ryan, Admin.

Support Services Alliance
PO Box 130
Schoharie, New York 12157-0130
Phone: (518)295-7966
Free: (800)322-3920
Fax: (518)295-8556
Robert M. Marquardt, Pres.

CONSULTANTS

This section contains a listing of consultants specializing in small business development. It is arranged alphabetically by country, then by state or province, then by city, then by firm name.

CANADA

Alberta

Varsity Consulting Group
2-45 Faculty of Business
University of Alberta
Edmonton, Alberta T6G 2R6
Phone: (403)492-2994
Fax: (403)492-3325
E-mail: 73642.2502@compuserve.com

Viro Hospital Consulting
42 Commonwealth Bldg., 9912 - 106 St.
NW
Edmonton, Alberta T5K 1C5
Phone: (403)425-3871
Fax: (403)425-3871
E-mail: rpb@freenet.edmonton.ab.ca

British Columbia

SRI Strategic Resources Inc.
4330 Kingsway, Ste. 1600
Burnaby, British Columbia V5H 4G7
Phone: (604)435-0627
Fax: (604)435-2782

DeBoda & DeBoda
1523 Milford Ave.
Coquitlam, British Columbia V3J 2V9
Phone: (604)936-4527
Fax: (604)936-4527

The Sage Group Ltd.
980 - 355 Burrard St.
Vancouver, British Columbia V6C 3H2
Phone: (604)669-9269
Fax: (604)681-4938

Ontario

Cynton Co.
17 Massey St.
Bramalea, Ontario L6S 2V6
Phone: (905)792-7769
Fax: (905)792-8116
E-mail: cynton@juno.com

Tikkanen-Bradley
RR No. 1
Consecon, Ontario K0K 1T0
Phone: (604)669-0583
E-mail: consut@mortimer.com

Task Enterprises
Box 69, RR 2 Hamilton
Flamborough, Ontario L8N 2Z7
Phone: (905)659-0153

JPL Business Consultants
Box 1587
Niagara-on-the-Lake, Ontario L0S 1J0

Phone: (905)935-2648
Fax: (905)935-2648

The ARA Consulting Group Inc.
116 Albert St., Ste. 303
Ottawa, Ontario K1P 5G3
Phone: (613)238-7400
Fax: (613)238-5394

HST Group Ltd.
430 Gilmour St.
Ottawa, Ontario K2P 0R8
Phone: (613)236-7303
Fax: (613)236-9893

Harrison Associates
BCE Place
181 Bay Street, Ste. 3740
PO Box 798
Toronto, Ontario M5J 2T3
Phone: (416)364-5441
Fax: (416)364-2875

Stern International Consultants Inc.
22 College St., Ste. 307
Toronto, Ontario M5G 1K2
Phone: (416)923-7878
Fax: (416)923-8091

Ken Wyman & Associates Inc.
64B Shuter St., Ste. 200
Toronto, Ontario M5B 1B1
Phone: (416)362-2926
Fax: (416)362-3039

Douglas J. McCready
344 Craigleith Dr.
Waterloo, Ontario N2L 5B7
Phone: (519)884-2651
Fax: (519)884-0201
E-mail: dmccread@waldenu.edu

Quebec

The Zimmar Consulting
Partnership Inc.
Westmount
PO Box 98
Montreal, Quebec H3Z 2T1
Phone: (514)484-1459
Fax: (514)484-3063

UNITED STATES

Alabama

Business Planning Inc.
300 Office Park Dr.
Birmingham, Alabama 35223-2474
Phone: (205)870-7090
Fax: (205)870-7103

Tradebank of Eastern Alabama
400 South St. E.
Talladega, Alabama 35160
Phone: (205)761-9051
Fax: (205)761-9227
E-mail: mansion@webex.com

Alaska

AK Business Development Center
3335 Arctic Blvd., Ste. 203
Anchorage, Alaska 99503
Phone: (907)562-0335
Fax: (907)562-6988

Business Matters
PO Box 287
Fairbanks, Alaska 99707
Phone: (907)452-5650

Arizona

Caretree Direct Marketing Corp.
8001 E. Serene St.
PO Box 3737
Carefree, Arizona 85377-3737
Phone: (602)488-4227
Fax: (602)488-2841

Thomas B. Galitski, CPA, CPC
5540 W. Glendale Ave., Ste. A101
Glendale, Arizona 85301
Phone: (602)842-0656
Fax: (602)931-3174

CMAS
1625 E. Northern, Ste. 103
Phoenix, Arizona 85020
Phone: (602)395-1001

Harvey C. Skoog
PO Box 26515
Prescott Valley, Arizona 86312
Phone: (602)772-1714
Fax: (602)772-2814

Advanced Consultant Technology,
Inc.
5011 E. Nisbet Rd., No. 102
Scottsdale, Arizona 85254
Phone: (602)708-0300
Fax: (602)708-0300

Louw's Management Corp.
8711 E. Pinnacle Peak Rd., No. 340
Scottsdale, Arizona 85255-3555
Phone: (602)585-7177
Fax: (602)585-5880

Gary L. McLeod
PO Box 230
Sonoita, Arizona 85637
Fax: (602)455-5661

Trans Energy Corporation
216 S. Clark, MS103
Tempe, Arizona 85281
Phone: (602)921-0433
Fax: (602)967-6601

Van Cleve Associates
6932 E. 2nd St.
Tucson, Arizona 85710
Phone: (602)296-2587
Fax: (602)296-2587

California

Ben W. Laverty III, REA, CEI
4909 Stockdale Hwy., Ste. 132
Bakersfield, California 93309
Phone: (805)837-9933
Fax: (805)837-9936
E-mail: cstc@kern.com

Lindquist Consultants-Venture
Planning
225 Arlington
Berkeley, California 94707
Phone: (510)524-6685
Fax: (510)527-6604

Larson Associates
PO Box 9005
Brea, California 92822
Phone: (714)529-4121
Fax: (714)572-3606

Kremer Management Consulting
PO Box 500
Carmel, California 93921
Phone: (408)626-8311
Fax: (408)624-2663
E-mail: ddkremer@aol.com

JB Associates
21118 Gardena Dr.
Cupertino, California 95014
Phone: (408)257-0214
Fax: (408)257-0216

House Agricultural Consultants
PO Box 1615
Davis, California 95617-1615
Phone: (916)753-3361
Fax: (916)753-0464
E-mail: infoag@houseag.com

Technical Management Consultants
3624 Westfall Dr.
Encino, California 91436-4154
Phone: (818)784-0626
Fax: (818)501-5575

RAINWATER-GISH & Associates,
Business Finance & Development
317 Third St., Ste. 3
Eureka, California 95501
Phone: (707)443-0030
Fax: (707)443-5683

Burnes Consulting Group
930 Cedar St.
Ft. Bragg, California 95437
Phone: (707)964-1459
Free: (800)949-9021
Fax: (707)964-1458

Strategic Business Group
800 Cienaga Dr.
Fullerton, California 92835
Phone: (714)449-1040
Fax: (714)449-1040

Pioneer Business Consultants
9042 Garfield Ave., Ste. 312
Huntington Beach, California 92646
Phone: (714)964-7600
Fax: (714)962-6585

MCS Associates
18300 Von Karman, Ste. 1100
Irvine, California 92715
Phone: (714)263-8700
Fax: (714)553-0168
E-mail: MCS@EARTHLINK.NET

The Laresis Companies
PO Box 3284
La Jolla, California 92038
Phone: (619)452-2720
Fax: (619)452-8744

RCL & Co.
PO Box 1143
La Jolla, California 92038
Phone: (619)454-8883
Fax: (619)454-8880

General Business Services
3201 Lucas Cir.
Lafayette, California 94549
Phone: (510)283-8272

The Ribble Group
27601 Forbes Rd., Ste. 52
Laguna Niguel, California 92677
Phone: (714)582-1085
Fax: (714)582-6420
E-mail: ribble@deltanet.com

Bell Springs Publishing
Bell Springs Rd.
Box 640
Laytonville, California 95454
Phone: (707)984-6746

Norris Bernstein, CMC
9309 Marina Pacifica Dr. N
Long Beach, California 90803
Phone: (562)493-5458
Fax: (562)493-5459

Horizon Consulting Services
1315 Garthwick Dr.
Los Altos, California 94024

Phone: (415)967-0906
Fax: (415)967-0906

Brincko Associates, Inc.
1801 Ave. of the Stars, Ste. 1054
Los Angeles, California 90067
Phone: (310)553-4523
Fax: (310)553-6782

Business Expansions International
210 S. Anita Ave.
Los Angeles, California 90049
Phone: (310)476-5262
Fax: (310)478-1876

Hutchinson Consulting and
Appraisals
11966 Woodbine St.
Los Angeles, California 90066
Phone: (310)391-7086
Fax: (310)391-7086

F.J. Schroeder & Associates
1926 Westholme Ave.
Los Angeles, California 90025
Phone: (310)470-2655
Fax: (310)470-6378
E-mail: fjsacons@aol.com

Western Management Associates
8351 Vicksburg Ave.
Los Angeles, California 90045-3924
Phone: (310)645-1091
Fax: (310)645-1092
E-mail: CFOForRent@aol.com

Darrell Sell and Associates
Los Gatos, California 95030
Phone: (408)354-7794
E-mail: darrell@netcom.com

Leslie J. Zambo
3355 Michael Dr.
Marina, California 93933
Phone: (408)384-7086
Fax: (408)647-4199

Marketing Services Management
PO Box 1377
Martinez, California 94553
Phone: (510)370-8527
Fax: (510)370-8527
E-mail: markserve@biotechnet.com

Keck & Company Business
Consultants
410 Walsh Rd.
Menlo Park, California 94027
Phone: (415)854-9588
Fax: (415)854-7240

William M. Shine Consulting Service
PO Box 127
Moraga, California 94556-0127
Phone: (510)376-6516

W & J Partnership
3450 Bluegrass Court
PO Box 1108
Morgan Hill, California 95038-1108
Phone: (408)779-1714
Fax: (408)778-1305

Palo Alto Management Group, Inc.
2672 Bayshore Pkwy., Ste. 701
Mountain View, California 94043
Phone: (415)968-4374
Fax: (415)968-4245
E-mail: mburwen@pamg.com

The Market Connection
4020 Birch St., Ste. 203
Newport Beach, California 92660
Phone: (714)731-6273
Fax: (714)833-0253

Muller Associates
PO Box 7264
Newport Beach, California 92658
Phone: (714)646-1169
Fax: (714)646-1169

Szenderski/Rohani & Partners
One Corporate Plaza, Ste. 110
Newport Beach, California 92660
Phone: (714)721-1418
Fax: (714)721-1175

NEXUS - Consultants to Management
PO Box 1531
Novato, California 94948
Phone: (415)897-4400
Fax: (415)898-2252
E-mail: jimnexus@aol.com

Adelphi Communications Inc.
PO Box 28831

Oakland, California 94604-8831
Phone: (510)430-7444
Fax: (510)530-3411

Creston Financial Group
1800 Harrison St., 18th Fl.
Oakland, California 94612
Phone: (510)987-8500
Fax: (510)893-1321

Intelequest Corp.
Palo Alto, California 94303
Phone: (415)968-3443
Fax: (415)493-6954
E-mail: frits@iqix.com

Business Research Consultants, Inc.
66 San Marino Cir.
Rancho Mirage, California 92270
Phone: (760)328-3700
Fax: (619)328-2474
E-mail: jackmcla@aol.com

Bay Area Tax Consultants and Bayhill
Financial Consultants
1150 Bayhill Dr., Ste. 111
San Bruno, California 94066-3004
Phone: (415)952-8786
Fax: (415)588-4524
E-mail:
76275.2332@atscompuserve.com

Business Incubation Development
Associates
225 Broadway, Ste. 2250
San Diego, California 92101
Phone: (619)237-0559
Fax: (619)237-0521

G.R. Gordetsky Consultants Inc.
11414 Windy Summit Pl.
San Diego, California 92127
Phone: (619)487-4939
Fax: (619)487-5587

Freeman, Sullivan & Co.
131 Steuart St., Ste. 520
San Francisco, California 94105
Phone: (415)777-0707
Free: (800)777-0737
Fax: (415)777-2420

Ideas Unlimited
2151 California St., Ste. 7
San Francisco, California 94115
Phone: (415)931-0641
Fax: (415)931-0880

Russell Miller Inc.
300 Montgomery St., Ste. 900
San Francisco, California 94104
Phone: (415)956-7474
Fax: (415)398-0620

PKF Consulting
425 California St., Ste. 1650
San Francisco, California 94104
Phone: (415)421-5378
Fax: (415)956-7708
E-mail: pkfcsf@aol.com

Welling & Woodard, Inc.
1067 Broadway
San Francisco, California 94133
Phone: (415)776-4500
Fax: (415)776-5067

Quincy Yu
3300 Laguna St., Ste. 6
San Francisco, California 94123
Phone: (415)567-1746

ORDIS, Inc.
6815 Trinidad Dr.
San Jose, California 95120-2056
Phone: (408)268-3321
Free: (800)446-7347
Fax: (408)268-3582
E-mail: ordis@aol.com

Stanford Resources, Inc.
3150 Almaden Expy., Ste. 255
San Jose, California 95118
Phone: (408)448-4440
Fax: (408)448-4445
E-mail: stanres@ix.netcom.com

Technology Properties Ltd., Inc.
San Jose, California 95117
Phone: (408)243-9898
Fax: (408)296-6637

Productivity Computing Services
1625 Waverly Rd.
San Marino, California 91108
Phone: (818)281-7079

Helfert Associates
1777 Borel Pl., Ste. 508
San Mateo, California 94402-3514
Phone: (415)377-0540
Fax: (415)377-0472

The Information Group, Inc.
PO Box Q
Santa Clara, California 95055-3756
Phone: (408)985-7877
Fax: (408)985-2945
E-mail: dvincent@tig.usa.com

Cast Management Consultants
1620 26th St., Ste. 2040N
Santa Monica, California 90404
Phone: (310)828-7511
Fax: (310)453-6831

Cuma Consulting Management
Box 724
Santa Rosa, California 95402
Phone: (707)785-2477
Fax: (707)785-2478

The E-Myth Academy
131B Stony Circle, Ste. 2000
Santa Rosa, California 95401
Phone: (707)569-3900
Free: (800)221-0266
Fax: (707)569-3999
E-mail: emyth1@aol.com

Reilly, Connors & Ray
1743 Canyon Rd.
Spring Valley, California 91977
Phone: (619)698-4808
Fax: (619)463-9872
E-mail: davidray@adnc.com

Management Consultants
Sunnyvale, California 94087-4700
Phone: (408)773-0321

RJR Associates
1639 Lewiston Dr.
Sunnyvale, California 94087
Phone: (408)737-7720
Fax: (408)737-7720

Schwafel Associates
333 Cobalt Way, Ste. 21
Sunnyvale, California 94086
Phone: (408)720-0649

Fax: (408)720-1796
E-mail: 102065.234@compuserve.com

Out of Your Mind...and Into the
Marketplace
13381 White Sand Dr.
Tustin, California 92680
Phone: (714)544-0248
Free: (800)419-1513
Fax: (714)730-1414
E-mail: lpinson@aol.com

Independent Research Services
PO Box 2426
Van Nuys, California 91404-2426
Phone: (818)993-3622

Ingman Company Inc.
7949 Woodley Ave., Ste. 120
Van Nuys, California 91406-1232
Phone: (818)375-5027
Fax: (818)894-5001

Innovative Technology Associates
3639 E. Harbor Blvd., Ste. 203E
Ventura, California 93001
Phone: (805)650-9353
Fax: (805)984-2979

Ridge Consultants, Inc.
100 Pringle Ave., Ste. 580
Walnut Creek, California 94596
Phone: (510)274-1990
Fax: (510)274-1956
E-mail: info@ridgecon.com

Whittelsey Associates
180 Fox Hollow Rd.
Woodside, California 94062
Phone: (415)851-8400
Fax: (415)851-2064

J.H. Robinson & Associates
20695 Deodar Dr., Ste. 100
PO Box 351
Yorba Linda, California 92686-0351
Phone: (714)970-1279

Colorado

Sam Boyer & Associates
4255 S. Buckley Rd., No. 136
Aurora, Colorado 80013

Free: (800)785-0485
E-mail: samboyer@samboyer.com

Janus Healthcare Consultants Inc.
210 Fifth St., Ste. A
Castle Rock, Colorado 80104
Phone: (303)660-2039
Fax: (303)688-8027

GVNW, Inc./Management
2270 La Montana Way
PO Box 25969
Colorado Springs, Colorado 80936
Phone: (719)594-5800
Fax: (719)599-0968

M-Squared, Inc.
755 San Gabriel Pl.
Colorado Springs, Colorado 80906
Phone: (719)576-2554
Fax: (719)576-2554

Western Capital Holdings, Inc.
7500 E. Arapahoe Rd., Ste. 395
Englewood, Colorado 80112
Phone: (303)290-8482
Fax: (303)770-1945

Thornton Financial FNIC
1136 E. Steward, Ste. 4204
Ft. Collins, Colorado 80526-1849
Phone: (970)221-2089
Fax: (970)221-7137

Tactical Technology Inc.
287 Arlington Dr.
Grand Junction, Colorado 81503
Phone: (303)241-9707
Fax: (303)245-9601

TenEyck Associates
1760 Cherryville Rd.
Greenwood Village, Colorado 80121-
1503
Phone: (303)758-6129
Fax: (303)761-8286

Associated Enterprises Ltd.
8725 W. 14th Ave., Ste. 110
Lakewood, Colorado 80215
Phone: (303)274-2783
Fax: (303)274-5429

GSI Consulting Group
28 Red Fox Ln.
Littleton, Colorado 80127
Phone: (303)979-9033
Fax: (303)979-2870

Johnson & West Management
Consultants, Inc.
7612 S. Logan Dr.
Littleton, Colorado 80122
Phone: (303)730-2810
Fax: (303)730-3219

Connecticut

Stratman Group Inc.
40 Tower Ln.
Avon, Connecticut 06001-4222
Phone: (860)677-2898
Free: (800)551-0499
Fax: (860)677-8210

Cowherd Consulting Group, Inc.
106 Stephen Mather Rd.
Darien, Connecticut 06820
Phone: (203)655-2150
Fax: (203)655-6427

Gerald S. Gilligan and Associates Inc.
52 Blueberry Ln.
Darien, Connecticut 06820
Phone: (203)325-3935

Greenwich Associates
8 Greenwich Office Park
Greenwich, Connecticut 06831-5149
Phone: (203)629-1200
Fax: (203)629-1229

Franchise Builders
185 Pine St., Ste. 818
Manchester, Connecticut 06040
Phone: (860)647-7542
Fax: (860)646-6544

JC Ventures, Inc.
4 Arnold St.
Old Greenwich, Connecticut
06870-1203
Phone: (203)698-1990
Free: (800)698-1997
Fax: (203)698-2638

Shoreline Business Consulting
92 Knollwood Dr.
Old Saybrook, Connecticut 06475
Phone: (203)388-9903
Fax: (203)388-9903

Charles L. Hornung Associates
52 Ned's Mountain Rd.
Ridgefield, Connecticut 06877
Phone: (203)431-0297

Manus
100 Prospect St., S. Tower
Stamford, Connecticut 06901
Phone: (203)326-3880
Free: (800)445-0942
Fax: (203)326-3890

Rhinesmith and Associates
Palmer Landing 506
123 Harbor Dr.
Stamford, Connecticut 06902
Phone: (203)327-7988
Fax: (203)327-5688

Sternbach Associates International
16 Tamarac Rd.
Westport, Connecticut 06880
Phone: (203)227-2059
Fax: (203)454-7341

Delaware

Daedalus Ventures, Ltd.
PO Box 1474
Hockessin, Delaware 19707
Phone: (302)239-6758
Fax: (302)239-9991
E-mail: daedalus@mail.del.net

The Formula Group
PO Box 866
Hockessin, Delaware 19707
Phone: (302)456-0952
Fax: (302)456-1354
E-mail: formula@netaxs.com

Selden Enterprises Inc.
2055 Limestone Rd., Ste. 213
Wilmington, Delaware 19808-5539
Phone: (302)999-1888
Fax: (302)999-9520
E-mail: seldenl@juno.com

District of Columbia

Business Development International, Inc.
PO Box 5615
Washington, DC 20016
Phone: (202)362-1765
Fax: (202)362-1765

Enterprise Consulting, Inc.
2806 36th Pl. NW
Washington, DC 20007
Phone: (202)342-7640

Bruce W. McGee and Associates
7826 Eastern Ave. NW, Ste. 30
Washington, DC 20012
Phone: (202)726-7272
Fax: (202)726-2946

McManis Associates, Inc.
2000 K St. NW, Ste. 300
Washington, DC 20006
Phone: (202)466-7680
Fax: (202)872-1898

Florida

Adams & Carbone Consulting
931 North S.R. 434, Ste. 1201
Altamonte Springs, Florida 32714
Phone: (407)620-6971
Fax: (407)277-1050

Whalen & Associates, Inc.
4255 Northwest 26 Ct.
Boca Raton, Florida 33434
Phone: (561)241-5950
Fax: (561)241-7414
E-mail: drwhalen@ix.netcom.com

Eric Sands Consulting Services
6193 Rock Island Rd., Ste. 412
Ft. Lauderdale, Florida 33319
Phone: (305)721-4767
Fax: (305)720-2815

Bridge-It
3704 Broadway, Unit 313
Ft. Myers, Florida 33901
Phone: (813)278-4218
Fax: (813)936-6380

Host Media Corp.
3948 S. Third St., Ste. 191
Jacksonville Beach, Florida 32250
Phone: (904)285-3239
Fax: (904)285-5618
E-mail:
msconsulting@compuserve.com

The Bracken Group
233 E. New Haven Ave., 2nd Fl.
Melbourne, Florida 32901
Phone: (407)725-5335
Fax: (407)725-5335

Corporate Business Computer
Services Inc.
7458 SW 48th St.
Miami, Florida 33155-4469
Phone: (305)666-2330
Fax: (305)666-2254

William V. Hall
1925 Brickell, Ste. D-701
Miami, Florida 33129
Phone: (305)856-9622
Fax: (305)856-4113

Taxplan, Inc.
Mirasol International Center
2699 Collins Ave.
Miami Beach, Florida 33140
Phone: (305)538-3303

T.C. Brown & Associates
8415 Excalibur Cir., Ste. B-1
Naples, Florida 33963
Phone: (813)594-1949
Fax: (813)594-1949

RLA International Consulting
713 Lagoon Dr.
North Palm Beach, Florida 33408
Phone: (407)626-4258
Fax: (407)626-5772

Comprehensive Franchising, Inc.
2465 Ridgecrest Ave.
Orange Park, Florida 32065
Phone: (904)272-6567
Free: (800)321-6567
Fax: (904)272-6750

Hunter G. Jackson Jr. - Consulting
Environmental Physicist
PO Drawer 618272
Orlando, Florida 32861-8272
Phone: (407)295-4188

F.A. McGee, Inc.
800 Claughton Island Dr., Ste. 401
Ormond Beach, Florida 32176
Phone: (305)377-9123

F. Newton Parks
210 El Brillo Way
Palm Beach, Florida 33480
Phone: (407)833-1727
Fax: (407)833-4541

Avery Business Development
Services
2506 St. Michel Ct.
Ponte Vedra Beach, Florida 32082
Phone: (904)285-6033
Fax: (904)285-6033

Focus Marketing
PO Box 4161
St. Petersburg, Florida 33731
Phone: (813)577-1337

Strategic Business Planning Company
PO Box 821006
South Florida, Florida 33082-1006
Phone: (954)704-9100
Fax: (954)438-7333
E-mail: info@bizplan.com

Dufresne Consulting Group, Inc.
10014 N. Dale Mabry, Ste. 101
Tampa, Florida 33618-4426
Phone: (813)264-4775
Fax: (813)931-5845

Todd Organization
PO Box 552
Tampa, Florida 33601
Phone: (813)973-4909
Fax: (813)973-4909

The Apogee Group, Inc.
PO Box 3907
Tequesta, Florida 33469-2111

ORGANIZATIONS, AGENCIES, & CONSULTANTS

Phone: (407)575-0299
Fax: (407)575-4542
E-mail: apogee@shadow.net

Center for Simplified Strategic
Planning, Inc.
PO Box 3324
Vero Beach, Florida 32964-3324
Phone: (561)231-3636
Fax: (561)231-1099

Georgia

Bock, Center, Garber and Long
2 Piedmont Ctr.
Atlanta, Georgia 30305
Phone: (404)231-9011
Fax: (404)233-3756

Marketing Spectrum Inc.
990 Hammond Dr., Ste. 840
Atlanta, Georgia 30328
Phone: (404)395-7244
Fax: (404)393-4071

Nucifora Consulting Group
2859 Paces Ferry Rd., Ste. 1830
Atlanta, Georgia 30339
Phone: (404)432-1072
Fax: (404)432-3528

Richard Siedlecki Marketing &
Management
2996 Grandview Ave., Ste. 305
Atlanta, Georgia 30305-3245
Phone: (404)816-4040

Business Ventures Corporation
6030 Dawson Blvd., Ste. E
Norcross, Georgia 30093
Phone: (404)729-8000
Fax: (404)729-8028

Informed Decisions Inc.
PO Box 219
Sautee Nacoochee, Georgia 30571
Free: (800)982-0676
Fax: (706)878-1802

E. Peter Kite, Management Consulting
Services
18 Coventry Close
Skidaway Island

Savannah, Georgia 31411
Phone: (912)598-1730
Fax: (912)598-0369

Tom C. Davis & Associates, P.C.
3189 Perimeter Rd.
Valdosta, Georgia 31602
Phone: (912)247-9801
Fax: (912)244-7704
E-mail: mail@tcdcpa.com

Illinois

TWD and Associates
431 S. Patton
Arlington Heights, Illinois 60005
Phone: (847)398-6410
Fax: (847)255-5095
E-mail: tdoo@aol.com

Management Planning Associates,
Inc.
2275 Half Day Rd., Ste. 350
Bannockburn, Illinois 60015-1277
Phone: (847)945-2421
Fax: (847)945-2425

Phil Faris Associates
86 Old Mill Ct.
Barrington, Illinois 60010
Phone: (847)382-4888

Seven Continents Technology
787 Stonebridge
Buffalo Grove, Illinois 60089
Phone: (708)577-9653
Fax: (708)870-1220

Grubb & Blue, Inc.
2404 Windsor Pl.
Champaign, Illinois 61820
Phone: (217)366-0052
Fax: (217)356-0117

ACE Accounting Service, Inc.
3128 N. Bernard St.
Chicago, Illinois 60618
Phone: (312)463-7854
Fax: (312)463-7854
E-mail: aol@wbyers

AON Consulting
123 N. Wacker Dr.

Chicago, Illinois 60606
Phone: (312)701-4800
Free: (800)438-6487
Fax: (312)701-4855

FMS Consultants
5801 N. Sheridan Rd., Ste. 3D
Chicago, Illinois 60660
Phone: (312)561-7362
Fax: (312)561-6274

Kingsbury International, Ltd.
1258 N. LaSalle St.
Chicago, Illinois 60610
Phone: (312)787-6756
Fax: (312)787-3136
E-mail: jetlag@mcs.com

MacDougall & Blake, Inc.
1414 N. Wells St., Ste. 311
Chicago, Illinois 60610-1306
Phone: (312)587-3330
Fax: (312)587-3699

James C. Osburn Ltd.
2701 W. Howard St.
Chicago, Illinois 60645
Phone: (312)262-4428
Fax: (312)262-6755

James B. Peterson & Associates, Inc.
3 First National Plaza
70 W. Madison St., Ste. 1400
Chicago, Illinois 60602
Phone: (312)214-3172
Fax: (312)214-3110

Tarifero & Tazewell Inc.
211 S. Clark
PO Box 2130
Chicago, Illinois 60690
Phone: (312)665-9714
Fax: (312)665-9716

William J. Igoe
3949 Earlston Rd.
Downers Grove, Illinois 60515
Phone: (630)960-1418

Human Energy Design Systems
620 Roosevelt Dr.
Edwardsville, Illinois 62025
Phone: (618)692-0258
Fax: (618)692-0819

The Minarich Group Inc.
20940 N. Middleton Dr.
Kildeer, Illinois 60047
Phone: (708)540-9585
Fax: (708)540-9585

BioLabs, Inc.
15 Sheffield Ct.
Lincolnshire, Illinois 60069
Phone: (847)945-2767

Clyde R. Goodheart
15 Sheffield Ct.
Lincolnshire, Illinois 60069
Phone: (708)945-2767
Fax: (708)945-4382

IntelliCommunications Network, Inc.
4525 Prime Pkwy.
McHenry, Illinois 60050
Phone: (815)344-0404
Free: (800)365-1176
Fax: (815)344-4499

China Business Consultants Group
931 Dakota Cir.
Naperville, Illinois 60563
Phone: (708)778-7992
Fax: (708)778-7915

Profit Growth, Inc.
2705 Walters Ave.
Northbrook, Illinois 60062
Phone: (847)498-9043

Smith Associates
1320 White Mountain Dr.
Northbrook, Illinois 60062
Phone: (708)480-7200
Fax: (708)480-9828

Francorp, Inc.
20200 Governors Dr.
Olympia Fields, Illinois 60461
Phone: (708)481-2900
Free: (800)372-6244
Fax: (708)481-5885
E-mail: francorp@aol.com

Camber Business Strategy
Consultants
PO Box 986
Palatine, Illinois 60078-0986

Phone: (708)705-0101
Fax: (708)705-0101

Partec Enterprise Group
6202 Keith Dr.
Richton Park, Illinois 60471
Phone: (708)503-4047
Fax: (708)502-9468

McGladrey & Pullen
1699 E. Woodfield Rd., Ste. 300
Schaumburg, Illinois 60173
Phone: (708)517-7070
Free: (800)365-8353
Fax: (708)517-7095

Koch International, Inc.
1040 S. Milwaukee Ave.
Wheeling, Illinois 60090
Phone: (708)459-1100
Free: (800)323-7597
Fax: (708)459-0471

A.D. Star Consulting
320 Euclid
Winnetka, Illinois 60093
Phone: (708)446-7827
Fax: (708)446-7827

Indiana

Midwest Marketing Research
PO Box 1077
Goshen, Indiana 46526
Phone: (219)533-0548
Fax: (219)533-0540

Crosby & Associates
5699 E. 71st, Ste. 4-A
Indianapolis, Indiana 46220
Phone: (317)841-3300
Fax: (317)841-3300

Ketchum Consulting Group
8021 Knue Rd., Ste. 112
Indianapolis, Indiana 46250
Phone: (317)845-5411
Fax: (317)842-9941

Marketing Department Inc.
3390 W. 86th, Ste. 2-F
Indianapolis, Indiana 46268
Phone: (317)876-5780
Fax: (317)876-5770

MDI Management Consulting
1519 Park Dr.
Munster, Indiana 46321
Phone: (219)838-7909
Fax: (219)838-7909

The Vincent Company Inc.
105 E. Jefferson Blvd., Ste. 318
South Bend, Indiana 46601
Phone: (219)287-9933
Free: (800)274-0733
Fax: (219)288-6250

Iowa

McCord Consulting Group, Inc.
4533 Pine View Dr.
Cedar Rapids, Iowa 52402
Phone: (319)378-0077
Fax: (319)378-0077

Management Solutions, L.C.
PO Box 41231
Des Moines, Iowa 50311
Phone: (515)277-6408
Fax: (515)277-3506
E-mail: 102602.1561@compuserve.com

Grandview Marketing
15 Red Bridge Dr.
Sioux City, Iowa 51104
Phone: (712)239-3122
Fax: (712)258-7578
E-mail: eandrews@pionet.net

Kansas

Strategic Planning Management
Associates, Inc.
7007 College Blvd., Ste. 420
Overland Park, Kansas 66211
Phone: (913)339-9001
Fax: (913)339-6226

Louisiana

Transit Operations Planning and
Scheduling
5545 Bundy Rd., No. 370
New Orleans, Louisiana 70127-4821
Phone: (504)244-9234
Fax: (504)245-1627
E-mail: david.grant@bourbon-st.com

Maine

Edgemont Enterprises
PO Box 8354
Portland, Maine 04104
Phone: (207)871-8964
Fax: (207)871-8964

Pan Atlantic Consultants
148 Middle St.
Portland, Maine 04101
Phone: (207)871-8622
Fax: (207)772-4842
E-mail: panatl@aol.com

Maryland

Imperial Group, Limited
305 Washington Ave., Ste. 501
Baltimore, Maryland 21204-6009
Phone: (410)337-8500
Fax: (410)337-7641

Kamanitz Uhlfelder Permison
4 Reservoir Cir.
Baltimore, Maryland 21208
Phone: (410)484-8700
Fax: (410)484-3437

Burdeshaw Associates, Ltd.
4701 Sangamore Rd.
Bethesda, Maryland 20816-2508
Phone: (301)229-5800
Fax: (301)229-5045
E-mail: bal@interramp.com

Michael E. Cohen
5225 Pooks Hill Rd., Ste. 1119 S
Bethesda, Maryland 20814
Phone: (301)530-5738
Fax: (301)493-9147

World Development Group, Inc.
4340 E. West Hwy., Ste. 105
Bethesda, Maryland 20814-4411
Phone: (301)652-1818
Fax: (301)652-1250
E-mail: wdg@has.com

Swartz Consulting
PO Box 4301
Crofton, Maryland 21114-4301
Phone: (301)262-6728

Software Solutions International Inc.
9633 Duffer Way
Gaithersburg, Maryland 20879
Phone: (301)330-4136

Strategies, Inc.
8 Park Center Ct., Ste. 200
Owings Mills, Maryland 21117
Phone: (410)363-6669
Fax: (410)581-9534

Hammer Marketing Resources
179 Inverness Rd.
Severna Park, Maryland 21146
Phone: (410)544-9191
Fax: (410)544-9189
E-mail: 70426.1237@compuserve.com

Andrew Sussman & Associates
13731 Kretsinger
Smithsburg, Maryland 21783
Phone: (301)824-2943
Fax: (301)824-2943

Energetics Development Inc.
109 Post Office Rd.
PO Box 966
Waldorf, Maryland 20604
Phone: (301)621-8432
Free: (800)377-7049

Massachusetts

Geibel Marketing and Public Relations
PO Box 611
Belmont, Massachusetts 02178-0005
Phone: (617)484-8285
Fax: (617)489-3567

Bain & Company, Inc.
Two Copley Pl.
Boston, Massachusetts 02117-0897
Phone: (617)572-2000
Fax: (617)572-2427

Center for Strategy Research, Inc.
101 Arch St., Ste. 1700
Boston, Massachusetts 02110
Phone: (617)345-9500
Fax: (617)345-0207

Pendergast & Co.
4 Copley Place, Box 84

Boston, Massachusetts 02116
Phone: (617)720-0400
Fax: (617)266-8341

Financial/Management Solutions, Inc.
180 Magazine St.
Cambridge, Massachusetts 02139
Phone: (617)876-4946
Fax: (617)547-5283
E-mail: AJO@WORLD.STD.COM

Mehr & Company
62 Kinnaird St.
Cambridge, Massachusetts 02139
Phone: (617)876-3311
Fax: (617)876-3023

Monitor Company, Inc.
25 First St.
Cambridge, Massachusetts 02141
Phone: (617)252-2000
Fax: (617)252-2100

Data and Strategies Group, Inc.
Three Speen St.
Framingham, Massachusetts 01701
Phone: (508)820-2500
Fax: (508)820-1626

Information & Research Associates
PO Box 3121
Framingham, Massachusetts 01701
Phone: (508)788-0784

Easton Consultants Inc.
252 Pond St.
Hopkinton, Massachusetts 01748
Phone: (508)435-4882
Fax: (508)435-3971

Jeffrey D. Marshall
102 Mitchell Rd.
Ipswich, Massachusetts 01938-1219
Phone: (508)356-1113
Fax: (508)356-2989

B.L. Livas Associates
620 Essex St.
Lawrence, Massachusetts 01841
Phone: (508)686-6195
Fax: (508)688-8027

Consulting Resources Corporation
6 Northbrook Park

Lexington, Massachusetts 02173
Phone: (617)863-1222
Fax: (617)863-1441
E-mail: vscvc@world.std.com

The Planning Technologies Group,
Inc.
92 Hayden Ave.
Lexington, Massachusetts 02173
Phone: (617)861-0999
Fax: (617)861-1099

Kalba International, Inc.
23 Sandy Pond Rd.
Lincoln, Massachusetts 01773
Phone: (617)259-9589
Fax: (617)259-1460

Coordinated Service, Inc.
531 King St.
Littleton, Massachusetts 01460
Phone: (508)486-0388
Fax: (508)486-0120

VMB Associates, Inc.
115 Ashland St.
Melrose, Massachusetts 02176
Phone: (617)665-0623

The Co. Doctor
14 Pudding Stone Ln.
Mendon, Massachusetts 01756
Phone: (508)478-1747
Fax: (508)478-0520

The Enterprise Group
73 Parker Rd.
Needham, Massachusetts 02194
Phone: (617)444-6631
Fax: (617)433-9991
E-mail: lsacco@world.std.com

PSMJ Resources, Inc.
10 Midland Ave.
Newton, Massachusetts 02158
Phone: (617)965-0055
Free: (800)537-7765
Fax: (617)965-5152
E-mail: psmj@tiac.net

Boston Computer Society - Consultants' and Entrepreneurs' Group
101A First Ave., Ste. 200

Waltham, Massachusetts 02154
Phone: (617)290-5700
Fax: (617)290-5744

IEEE Consultants' Network
255 Bear Hill Rd.
Waltham, Massachusetts 02154-1017
Phone: (617)890-5294
Fax: (617)890-5290

Business Planning and Consulting
Services
20 Beechwood Terr.
Wellesley, Massachusetts 02181
Phone: (617)237-9151
Fax: (617)237-9151

Interim Management Associates
21 Avon Rd.
Wellesley, Massachusetts 02181
Phone: (617)237-0024

Michigan

Walter Frederick Consulting
1719 South Blvd.
Ann Arbor, Michigan 48104
Phone: (313)662-4336
Fax: (313)769-7505

G.G.W. and Associates
1213 Hampton
Jackson, Michigan 49203
Phone: (517)782-2255
Fax: (517)782-2255

Altamar Group Ltd.
6810 S. Cedar, Ste. 2-B
Lansing, Michigan 48911
Phone: (517)694-0910
Free: (800)443-2627
Fax: (517)694-1377

Sheffieck Consultants, Inc.
23610 Greening Dr.
Novi, Michigan 48375-3130
Phone: (248)347-3545
Fax: (248)347-3530

Rehmann, Robson PC
5800 Gratiot
PO Box 2025
Saginaw, Michigan 48605

Phone: (517)799-9580
Fax: (517)799-0227

Francis & Company
17200 W. Ten Mile Rd., Ste. 207
Southfield, Michigan 48075
Phone: (810)559-7600
Fax: (810)559-5249

Private Ventures, Inc.
16000 W. Nine Mile Rd., Ste. 504
Southfield, Michigan 48075
Phone: (810)569-1977
Free: (800)448-7614
Fax: (810)569-1838

JGK Associates
14464 Kerner Dr.
Sterling Heights, Michigan 48313
Phone: (810)247-9055

Minnesota

Consatech Inc.
PO Box 1047
Burnsville, Minnesota 55337
Phone: (612)953-1088
Fax: (612)435-2966

Robert F. Knotek
14960 Ironwood Ct.
Eden Prairie, Minnesota 55346
Phone: (612)949-2875

Kinnon Lilligren Associates Inc.
6211 Oakgreen Ave. S
Denmark Township
Hastings, Minnesota 55033-9469
Phone: (612)436-6530
Fax: (612)436-6530

Decker Business Consulting
6837 Booth Ave.
Inver Grove Heights, Minnesota 55076
Phone: (612)451-6600

Health Fitness Physical Therapy
3500 W. 80th St., Ste. 130
Minneapolis, Minnesota 55431
Phone: (612)831-6830
Fax: (612)831-7264

McGladrey & Pullen
Family Business Group/Management
Development Institute
801 Nicollet Ave., Ste. 1300
Minneapolis, Minnesota 55402
Phone:(612)376-9341
Fax:(612)376-9876

Minnesota Cooperation Office for
Small Business & Job Creation, Inc.
5001 W. 80th St., Ste. 825
Minneapolis, Minnesota 55437
Phone:(612)830-1230
Fax:(612)830-1232

Power Systems Research
1301 Corporate Center Dr., Ste. 113
St. Paul, Minnesota 55121
Phone:(612)454-0144
Free:(800)433-7746
Fax:(612)454-0760

Small Business Success
PO Box 21097
St. Paul, Minnesota 55121-0097
Phone:(612)456-0757
Free:(800)848-4912
Fax:(612)456-9138

Missouri

Business Planning and Development
Inc.
4030 Charlotte St.
Kansas City, Missouri 64110
Phone:(816)753-0495

MedImage, Inc.
The Frances Vandivort Center
305 E. Walnut, Ste. 110LL
Springfield, Missouri 65806
Phone:(417)831-0110
Fax:(417)831-0288

Nebraska

International Management Consulting
Group, Inc.
1309 Harlan Dr., Ste. 205
Bellevue, Nebraska 68005
Phone:(402)291-4545
Free:(800)665-IMCG

Fax:(402)291-4343
E-mail: imcg@neonramp.com

Heartland Management Consulting
Group
1904 Barrington Pkwy.
Papillion, Nebraska 68046
Phone:(402)339-1319
Fax:(402)339-1319

Nevada

The DuBois Group
800 Southwood Blvd., Ste. 206
Incline Village, Nevada 89451
Phone:(702)832-0550
Free:(800)375-2935
Fax:(702)832-0556

WEH Corporation
774 Mays Blvd., Ste. 1
Incline Village, Nevada 89451
Phone:(702)831-8553
Fax:(702)833-3340

New Hampshire

Wolff Consultants
10 Buck Rd.
PO Box 1003
Hanover, New Hampshire 03755
Phone:(603)643-6015

Advanced Development Group
PO Box 6536
Portsmouth, New Hampshire 03802
Phone:(603)431-3329
Fax:(603)431-3329

New Jersey

ConMar International, Ltd.
283 Dayton-Jamesburg Rd.
PO Box 437
Dayton, New Jersey 08810
Phone:(908)274-1100
Fax:(908)274-1199

Realty Asset Services, Inc.
Meridian Center 3
6 Industrial Way W
Eatontown, New Jersey 07724

Phone:(908)531-2944
Fax:(908)517-0422

Kumar Associates, Inc.
260 Columbia Ave.
Ft. Lee, New Jersey 07024
Phone:(201)224-9480
Fax:(201)585-2343

John Hall & Company, Inc.
PO Box 187
Glen Ridge, New Jersey 07028
Phone:(201)680-4449
Fax:(201)680-4449

PA Consulting Group
279 Princeton Rd.
Hightstown, New Jersey 08520
Phone:(609)426-4700
Fax:(609)426-4046

Strategic Management Group
PO Box 402
Maplewood, New Jersey 07040
Phone:(201)378-2470

Vanguard Communications Corp.
100 American Rd.
Morris Plains, New Jersey 07950
Phone:(201)605-8000
Fax:(201)605-8329

KLW New Products
156 Cedar Dr.
Old Tappan, New Jersey 07675
Phone:(201)358-1300
Fax:(201)664-2594

Thomas S. Adubato Associates
PO Box 89
Pequannock, New Jersey 07440
Phone:(201)835-3566
Fax:(201)835-6470

Aurora Marketing Management, Inc.
212 Carnegie Ctr., Ste. 206
Princeton, New Jersey 08540-6233
Phone:(609)520-8863

Smart Business Supersite
88 Orchard Rd., CN-5219
Princeton, New Jersey 08543
Phone:(908)321-1924
Fax:(908)321-5156

Tracelin Associates
1171 Main St., Ste. 6K
Rahway, New Jersey 07065
Phone: (908)381-3288

Schkeeper Inc.
130-6 Bodman Pl.
Red Bank, New Jersey 07701
Phone: (908)219-1965

Henry Branch Associates
2502 Harmon Cove Tower
Secaucus, New Jersey 07094
Phone: (201)866-2008
Fax: (201)601-0101
E-mail: HDPW18A@prodigy.com

Robert Gibbons & Co., Inc.
46 Knoll Rd.
Tenafly, New Jersey 07670-1050
Phone: (201)871-3933
Fax: (201)871-2173
E-mail: crisisbob@aol.com

PMC Management Consultants, Inc.
11 Thistle Ln.
PO Box 332
Three Bridges, New Jersey 08887-0332
Phone: (908)788-1014
Fax: (908)806-7287

Mitchell Brian & Associates
5 Carlton Ln.
Voorhees, New Jersey 08043
Phone: (609)751-3224
Fax: (609)751-3225

R.W. Bankart & Associates
20 Valley Ave., Ste. D-2
Westwood, New Jersey 07675-3607
Phone: (201)664-7672

New Mexico

Vondle & Associates, Inc.
4926 Calle de Tierra, NE
Albuquerque, New Mexico 87111
Phone: (505)292-8961
Fax: (505)296-2790

InfoNewMexico
2207 Black Hills Road, NE
Rio Rancho, New Mexico 87124

Phone: (505)891-2462
Fax: (505)896-1371
E-mail: 72762.3616@compuserve.com

New York

Powers Research and Training
Institute
PO Box 78
Bayville, New York 11709
Phone: (516)628-2250
Fax: (516)628-2252
E-mail: 73313.1315@compuserve.com

Consortium House
139 Wittenberg Rd.
Bearsville, New York 12409
Phone: (914)679-8867
Fax: (914)679-9248
E-mail: eugenegs@aol.com

Progressive Finance Corporation
3549 Tiemann Ave.
Bronx, New York 10469
Phone: (718)405-9029
Free: (800)225-8381
Fax: (718)405-1170

Wave Hill Associates
2621 Palisade Ave., Ste. 15-C
Riverdale
Bronx, New York 10463
Phone: (718)549-7368
Fax: (718)601-9670

Overton Financial
7 Allen Rd.
Cortlandt Manor, New York 10566
Phone: (914)737-4649
Fax: (914)737-4696

Samani International Enterprises,
Marions Panyaught Consultancy
2028 Parsons
Flushing, New York 11357-3436
Phone: (917)287-8087
Fax: (800)873-8939
E-mail: vjp2@compuserve.com

Marketing Resources Group
71-58 Austin St.
Forest Hills, New York 11375
Phone: (718)261-8882

Group I Financial Services
PO Box 922
Highland, New York 12528
Phone: (914)883-9356
E-mail: 103107.227@compuserve.com

North Star Enterprises
670 N. Terrace Ave.
Mt. Vernon, New York 10552
Phone: (914)668-9433

E.N. Rysso & Associates
21 Jordan Rd.
New Hartford, New York 13413-2311
Phone: (315)732-2206
Fax: (315)732-2206

Atlantic Venture International Inc.
1271 Ave. of the Americas, 4500
New York, New York 10020
Phone: (212)554-8200
Fax: (212)554-8209

Boice Dunham Group
437 Madison Ave.
New York, New York 10022
Phone: (212)752-5550
Fax: (212)752-7055

Brancato Fritsch & Co.
45 W. 60 St., Ste. 25D
New York, New York 10023
Phone: (212)315-4155
Fax: (212)315-2950

Elizabeth Capen
27 E. 95th St.
New York, New York 10128
Phone: (212)427-7654

Dunham & Marcus Inc.
575 Madison Ave., 10th Fl.
New York, New York 10022-1304
Phone: (212)605-0571
Fax: (212)605-0589

Haver Analytics
60 E. 42nd St., Ste. 2424
New York, New York 10017
Phone: (212)986-9300
Fax: (212)986-5857

The Jordan, Edmiston Group, Inc.
885 3rd Ave., 25th Fl.
New York, New York 10022
Phone: (212)754-0710
Fax: (212)754-0337

Knowledge=Power, Inc.
347 Fifth Avenue, Ste. 1406
New York, New York 10016
Phone: (212)251-0470
Fax: (212)251-0472
E-mail: knowpow@aol.com

KPMG Peat Marwick - Management
Consultants
767 5th Ave.
New York, New York 10153
Phone: (212)909-5000
Fax: (212)909-5070

Mahoney Cohen Consulting Corp.
111 W. 40th St., 12th Fl.
New York, New York 10018
Phone: (212)490-8000
Fax: (212)398-0267

Management Practice, Inc.
342 Madison Ave.
New York, New York 10173-1230
Phone: (212)867-7948
Fax: (212)972-5188

Moseley Associates, Inc.
270 Madison Ave., Ste. 1207
New York, New York 10016
Phone: (212)213-6673
Fax: (212)213-6675

Practice Development Counsel
60 Sutton Pl. S
New York, New York 10022
Phone: (212)593-1549
Fax: (212)980-7940
E-mail: phaserot@counsel.com

RRA Consulting Services, Inc.
166 E. 34th St.
New York, New York 10016
Phone: (212)686-4614

The Van Tulleken Company Limited
126 E. 56th St.
New York, New York 10022

Phone: (212)355-1390
Fax: (212)755-3061
E-mail: newyork@vantelleken.com

Vencon Management, Incorporated
301 W. 53rd St.
New York, New York 10019
Phone: (212)581-8787
Fax: (212)397-4126

R.A. Walsh Consultants
429 E. 52nd St.
New York, New York 10022
Phone: (212)688-6047
Fax: (212)535-4075

Werner International Inc.
111 W. 40th St.
New York, New York 10018
Phone: (212)642-6000
Free: (800)333-7816
Fax: (212)642-6084

Zimmerman Business Consulting, Inc.
44 E. 92nd St., Ste. 5-B
New York, New York 10128
Phone: (212)860-3107
Fax: (212)860-7730
E-mail: lj22bci@aol.com

Stromberg Consulting
2500 Westchester Ave.
Purchase, New York 10577
Phone: (914)251-1515
Fax: (914)251-1562

ComputerEase Co.
9 Hachaliah Brown Dr.
Somers, New York 10589
Phone: (914)277-5317
Fax: (914)277-5317

Innovation Management Consulting,
Inc.
209 Dewitt Rd.
Syracuse, New York 13214-2006
Phone: (315)425-5144
Fax: (315)445-8989

M. Clifford Agress
891 Fulton St.
Valley Stream, New York 11580
Phone: (516)825-8955
Fax: (516)825-8955

Destiny Kinal Marketing Consultancy
105 Chemung St.
Waverly, New York 14892
Phone: (607)565-8317
Fax: (607)565-4083

Information Systems Planning
3 Melrose Ln.
West Nyack, New York 10994
Phone: (914)358-6546
Fax: (914)358-4313
E-mail: 103244.3557@compuserve.com

Management Insight
96 Arlington Rd.
Williamsville, New York 14221
Phone: (716)631-3319
Free: (800)643-3319
Fax: (716)631-0203

G.L. Michael Management
Consultants
335 Evans St., Ste. A
Williamsville, New York 14221
Phone: (716)634-5091

North Carolina

Norelli & Company
Nations Bank Corporation Center
100 N. Tyron St., Ste. 3220
Charlotte, North Carolina 28202-4000
Phone: (704)376-5484
Fax: (704)376-5485

North Dakota

Center for Innovation and Business
Development
100 Harrington
PO Box 8372
Grand Forks, North Dakota 58202-8372
Phone: (701)777-3132
Fax: (701)777-2339

Ohio

Transportation Technology Services
208 Harmon Rd.
Aurora, Ohio 44202
Phone: (216)562-3596

Delta Planning, Inc.
PO Box 22618
Beachwood, Ohio 44122
Phone: (216)831-2521
Free: (800)672-0762
Fax: (216)831-7616
E-mail: delta@planet.net

Empro Systems, Inc.
4777 Red Bank Expy., Ste. 1
Cincinnati, Ohio 45227-1542
Phone: (513)271-2042
Fax: (513)271-2042

MCS Consulting Service
16014 Southland Ave.
Cleveland, Ohio 44111
Phone: (216)252-8072
Fax: (216)252-8072
E-mail: cfct65a@prodigy.com

Poppe Tyson
1301 E. 9th St., Ste. 3400
Cleveland, Ohio 44114
Phone: (216)623-1511
Fax: (216)623-1501

The Adams Group
2704 Fair Ave.
Columbus, Ohio 43209
Phone: (614)231-0002
Fax: (614)231-0002
E-mail: riadams@acme.freenet.oh.us

Cory Dillon Associates
111 Schreyer Pl. E
Columbus, Ohio 43214
Phone: (614)262-8211
Fax: (614)262-3806

Ransom & Associates -
COMPETITIVEdge Group
106 E. Pacemont Rd.
Columbus, Ohio 43202-1225
Phone: (614)267-7100
Fax: (614)262-7199

Herman Associates Inc.
PO Box 5351
Fairlawn, Ohio 44333
Phone: (216)836-5656
Free: (800)227-3566
Fax: (216)836-3311
E-mail: 75473.2217@compuserve.com

Young & Associates
PO Box 711
Kent, Ohio 44240
Phone: (216)678-0524
Free: (800)525-9775
Fax: (216)678-6219

Robert A. Westman & Associates
359 Quarry Ln.
Warren, Ohio 44483
Phone: (216)856-4149
Fax: (216)856-2564

Oklahoma

Innovative Resources Inc.
4900 Richmond Sq., Ste. 100
Oklahoma City, Oklahoma 73118
Phone: (405)840-0033
Fax: (405)843-8359

Community & Governmental
Consultants, Inc.
Box 1121
Stillwater, Oklahoma 74076
Phone: (405)743-3048
Fax: (405)743-4459

Oregon

INTERCON - The International
Converting Institute
5200 Badger Rd.
Crooked River Ranch, Oregon 97760
Phone: (503)548-1447
Fax: (503)548-1618

Talbott ARM
HC 64, Box 120
Lakeview, Oregon 97630
Phone: (503)947-3482
Fax: (503)947-3482

Management Technology Associates,
Ltd.
1618 SW 1st Ave., Ste. 315
Portland, Oregon 97201
Phone: (503)224-5220

Nudelman & Associates
6443 SW Beaverton Hwy.
Portland, Oregon 97221
Phone: (503)292-2604
Fax: (503)292-5850

Pennsylvania

Problem Solvers for Industry
345 Park Ave.
Box 193
Chalfont, Pennsylvania 18914
Phone: (215)822-9695
Fax: (215)822-8086

Elayne Howard & Associates, Inc.
3501 Masons Mill Rd., Ste. 501
Huntingdon Valley, Pennsylvania
19006-3509
Phone: (215)657-9550

GRA, Incorporated
115 West Ave., Ste. 201
Jenkintown, Pennsylvania 19046
Phone: (215)884-7500
Fax: (215)884-1385
E-mail: DKFINN@HSLC.ORG

Mifflin County Industrial Develop-
ment Corporation
Mifflin County Industrial Plaza
One Belle Ave.
Lewistown, Pennsylvania 17044
Phone: (717)242-0393
Fax: (717)242-1842

Autech Products
1289 Revere Rd.
Morrisville, Pennsylvania 19067
Phone: (215)493-3759
Fax: (215)493-3759

Advantage Associates
434 Avon Dr.
Pittsburgh, Pennsylvania 15228
Phone: (412)343-1558
Fax: (412)362-1684
E-mail: ecocba1@aol.com

Regis J. Sheehan & Associates
291 Foxcroft Rd.
Pittsburgh, Pennsylvania 15220
Phone: (412)279-1207

James W. Davidson Co., Inc.
23 Forest View Rd.
Wallingford, Pennsylvania 19086
Phone: (610)566-1462

ORGANIZATIONS, AGENCIES, & CONSULTANTS

Puerto Rico

Diego Chevere & Co.
Ste. 301, Metro Parque 7
Metro Office Park
Caparra Heights, Puerto Rico 00920
Phone: (809)782-9595
Fax: (809)782-9532

Manuel L. Porrata and Associates
898 Munoz Rivera Ave., Ste. 201
Rio Piedras, Puerto Rico 00927
Phone: (809)765-2140
Fax: (809)754-3285

South Carolina

Aquafood Business Associates
PO Box 16190
Charleston, South Carolina 29412
Phone: (803)795-9506
Fax: (803)795-9477

Strategic Innovations International
12 Executive Court
Lake Wylie, South Carolina 29710
Phone: (803)831-1225
Fax: (803)831-1177

Minus Stage
Box 4436
Rock Hill, South Carolina 29731
Phone: (803)328-0705
Fax: (803)329-9948

Tennessee

Office Masters
PO Box 24626
Chattanooga, Tennessee 37422
Phone: (423)510-8464
Fax: (423)510-1895
E-mail:
officemasters@mindspring.com

Daniel Petchers & Associates
8820 Fernwood CV
Germantown, Tennessee 38138
Phone: (901)755-9896

Dean Winn
1114 Forest Harbor, Ste. 300
Hendersonville, Tennessee 37075

Phone: (615)822-8692
Free: (800)737-8382
Fax: (615)822-8692

RCFA Healthcare Management
Services
9648 Kingston Pike, Ste. 8
Knoxville, Tennessee 37922
Phone: (423)531-0176
Fax: (423)531-0722
E-mail: pking@conc.tdsnet.com

Growth Consultants of America
3917 Trimble Rd.
PO Box 158382
Nashville, Tennessee 37215
Phone: (615)383-0550
Fax: (615)269-8940
E-mail: 70244.451@compuserve.com

Texas

Lori Williams
1000 Leslie Ct.
Arlington, Texas 76012
Phone: (817)459-3934
Fax: (817)459-3934

Erisa Adminstrative Services Inc.
12325 Haymeadow Dr., Bldg. 4
Austin, Texas 78750-1847
Phone: (512)250-9020
Fax: (512)250-9487

R. Miller Hicks & Company
1011 W. 11th St.
Austin, Texas 78703
Phone: (512)477-7000
Fax: (512)477-9697
E-mail:
MILLER.HICKS@TPOINT.COM

Market Development Services, Inc.
5350 Montrose Dr.
Dallas, Texas 75209
Phone: (214)352-7247
Fax: (214)357-1835

Perot Systems
12377 Merit Dr., Ste. 1100
Dallas, Texas 75251
Phone: (214)383-5600
Free: (800)688-4333
E-mail: corp.comm@ps.net

Richard Unwin & Assoc.
5050 Quorum Dr., Ste. 245
Dallas, Texas 75240
Phone: (214)788-2717
Fax: (214)788-2269

Peter Schaar
3515 Haynie Ave.
Dallas, Texas 75205
Phone: (214)528-7162
Fax: (214)528-7162

The Dowdle Poe Co.
4610 Westin Dr.
Fulshear, Texas 77441
Phone: (713)346-2560
Fax: (713)346-2558

Arnott & Associates, Inc.
PO Box 923
Grapevine, Texas 76099-0923
Phone: (817)430-1258
Fax: (817)491-4818

High Technology Associates -
Division of Global Technologies, Inc.
1775 St. James Pl., Ste. 105
Houston, Texas 77056
Phone: (713)963-9300
Fax: (713)963-8341

PROTEC
4607 Linden Pl.
Pearland, Texas 77584
Phone: (713)997-9872
Fax: (713)997-9895
E-mail: p.oman@ix.netcom.com

Industrial Distribution Consultants,
Inc.
PO Box 2530
Port Aransas, Texas 78373-2530
Phone: (512)749-7123
Fax: (512)749-7123

Business Strategy Development
Consultants
PO Box 690365
San Antonio, Texas 78269
Phone: (210)696-8000
Free: (800)927-BSDC
Fax: (210)696-8000

Tom Welch, CPC
6900 San Pedro Ave., Ste. 147
San Antonio, Texas 78216-6207
Phone: (210)737-7022
Fax: (210)737-7022
E-mail: bplan@iamerica.net

Utah

CAPCON, Ltd.
8746 S. Rustler Rd.
Sandy, Utah 84093
Phone: (801)943-6339
Fax: (801)942-2864

Virginia

Elliott B. Jaffa
2530-B S. Walter Reed Dr.
Arlington, Virginia 22206
Phone: (703)931-0040

Koach Enterprises - USA
5529 N. 18th St.
Arlington, Virginia 22205
Phone: (703)241-8361
Fax: (703)241-8623

Federal Market Development
5650 Chapel Run Ct.
Centreville, Virginia 22020-3601
Phone: (703)502-8930
Free: (800)821-5003
Fax: (703)502-8929

Transportation Management Systems,
Inc.
11317 Beach Mill Rd.
Great Falls, Virginia 22066
Phone: (703)444-0995
Fax: (703)444-6089

Barringer, Huff & Stuart
310 Fifth St.
Lynchburg, Virginia 24504
Phone: (804)528-2356
Fax: (804)528-2357

Performance Support Systems
11835 Canon Blvd., Ste. C-101
Newport News, Virginia 23606

Phone: (804)873-3700
Free: (800)488-6463
Fax: (804)873-3288
E-mail: pss2@aol.com

Charles Scott Pugh (Investor)
4101 Pittaway Dr.
Richmond, Virginia 23235-1022
Phone: (804)560-0979
Fax: (804)560-4670

John C. Randall and Associates, Inc.
PO Box 15127
Richmond, Virginia 23227
Phone: (804)746-4450
Fax: (804)747-7426

McLeod & Co.
410 1st St.
Roanoke, Virginia 24011
Phone: (540)342-6911
Fax: (540)344-6367

The Dynex Group
5345 Fairfield Blvd.
Virginia Beach, Virginia 23464
Phone: (804)497-5561
Fax: (804)497-0986
E-mail: bobgree@beacon.regent.edu

Arthur L. Pepperman, II, Business/
Medical Appraiser
202 West Queens Dr.
Williamsburg, Virginia 23185
Phone: (804)229-3570
Fax: (804)229-3570

The Small Business Counselor
12423 Hedges Run Dr., Ste. 153
Woodbridge, Virginia 22192
Phone: (703)490-6755
Fax: (703)490-1356

Washington

B.A.S.I.C. Consultants, Inc.
10020 A Main St., Ste. 352
Bellevue, Washington 98004
Phone: (206)454-0341
Fax: (206)649-8809

Perry L. Smith Consulting
800 Bellevue Way NE, Ste. 400
Bellevue, Washington 98004-4208
Phone: (206)462-2072
Fax: (206)462-5638

ECG Management Consultants, Inc.
1111 3rd Ave., Ste. 2700
Seattle, Washington 98101-3201
Phone: (206)689-2200
Fax: (206)689-2209
E-mail: ecg@ecgmc.com

Northwest Trade Adjustment
Assistance Center
900 4th Ave., Ste. 2430
Seattle, Washington 98164-1003
Phone: (206)622-2730
Fax: (206)622-1105

Spectrum West
4711 NE 50th
Seattle, Washington 98105
Phone: (206)524-5958
Fax: (206)524-7826
E-mail: maldolus@pnw.net

Business Planning Consultants
S. 3510 Ridgeview Dr.
Spokane, Washington 99206
Phone: (509)928-0332
Fax: (509)921-0842
E-mail: bpci@nextdim.com

West Virginia

MarkeTech Communications
PO Box 35
Montrose, West Virginia 26283-0035
Phone: (304)637-0805

Wisconsin

White & Associates, Inc.
5349 Somerset Ln. S
Greenfield, Wisconsin 53221
Phone: (414)281-7373
Fax: (414)281-7006
E-mail: wna@eworld.com

SMALL BUSINESS ADMINISTRATION REGIONAL OFFICES

This section contains a listing of Small Business Administration offices arranged numerically by region. Service areas are provided. Contact the appropriate office for a referral to the nearest field office.

Region 1

U.S. Small Business Administration
10 Causeway St., Rm. 812
Boston, Massachusetts 02222
Phone: (617)565-8415
Fax: (617)565-8420
Serves Connecticut, Maine, Massachusetts, New Hampshire, Rhode Island, and Vermont.

Region 2

U.S. Small Business Administration
26 Federal Plz., Rm. 3108
New York, New York 10278
Phone: (212)264-1450
Fax: (212)264-0038
Serves New Jersey, New York, Puerto Rico, and the Virgin Islands.

Region 3

U.S. Small Business Administration
475 Allendale Rd., Ste. 201
King of Prussia, Pennsylvania 19406
Phone: (610)962-3710
Fax: (610)962-3743
Serves Delaware, the District of Columbia, Maryland, Pennsylvania, Virginia, and West Virginia.

Region 4

U.S. Small Business Administration
1375 Peachtree St. NE, Rm. 500
Atlanta, Georgia 30367-8102
Phone: (404)347-4999
Fax: (404)347-2355
Serves Alabama, Florida, Georgia, Kentucky, Mississippi, North Carolina, South Carolina, and Tennessee.

Region 5

U.S. Small Business Administration
Gateway IV Bldg., Ste. 1975 South
300 S. Riverside Plz.
Chicago, Illinois 60606-6611
Phone: (312)353-8089
Fax: (312)353-3426
Serves Illinois, Indiana, Michigan, Minnesota, Ohio, and Wisconsin.

Region 6

U.S. Small Business Administration
8625 King George Dr., Bldg. C
Dallas, Texas 75235-3391
Phone: (214)767-7611
Fax: (214)767-7870
Serves Arkansas, Louisiana, New Mexico, Oklahoma, and Texas.

Region 7

U.S. Small Business Administration
Lucas Place, Ste. 307
323 W. 8th St.
Kansas City, Missouri 64105
Phone: (816)374-6380
Fax: (816)374-6339
Serves Iowa, Kansas, Missouri, and Nebraska.

Region 8

U.S. Small Business Administration
633 17th St., 7th Fl.
Denver, Colorado 80202
Phone: (303)294-7186
Fax: (303)294-7153
Serves Colorado, Montana, North Dakota, South Dakota, Utah, and Wyoming.

Region 9

U.S. Small Business Administration
71 Stevenson St., 20th Fl.
San Francisco, California 94105
Phone: (415)744-6404
Serves American Samoa, Arizona, California, Guam, Hawaii, Nevada, and the Trust Territory of the Pacific Islands.

Region 10

U.S. Small Business Administration
1200 6th Ave., Ste. 1805
Seattle, Washington 98101-1128
Phone: (206)553-5676
Fax: (206)553-4155
Serves Alaska, Idaho, Oregon, and Washington.

SMALL BUSINESS DEVELOPMENT CENTERS

This section contains a listing of all Small Business Development Centers organized alphabetically by state/U.S. territory name, then by city, then by agency name.

Alabama

Auburn University
SBDC
E-mail:
ghannem@business.auburn.edu
108 College of Business
Auburn, Alabama 36849-5243
Phone: (334)844-4220
Fax: (334)844-4268
Garry Hannem, Dir.

Auburn University
Small Business Development Center
108 College of Business
Auburn, Alabama 36849-5243

Phone: (334)844-4220
Fax: (334)844-4268
Gary Hannem, Dir.
E-mail:
ghannem@business.auburn.edu

Alabama Small Business Development
Center
University of Alabama at Birmingham
SBDC
E-mail: asbd003@uabdpo.dpo.uab.edu
Medical Towers Bldg.
1717 11th Ave. S., Ste. 419
Birmingham, Alabama 35294-4410
Phone: (205)934-7260
Fax: (205)934-7645
John Sandefur, State Dir.

Alabama Small Business Procurement
System
University Of Alabama at Birmingham
SBDC
Small Business Development Center
1717 11th Ave. S., Ste. 419
Birmingham, Alabama 35294-4410
Phone: (205)934-7260
Fax: (205)934-7645
Charles Hobson, Procurement Dir.

Alabama Technology Assistance
Program
University of Alabama At Birmingham
SBDC
E-mail: asbd009@uabdpo.dpo.uab.edu
1717 11th Ave. S., Ste. 419
Birmingham, Alabama 35294-4410
Phone: (205)934-7260
Fax: (205)934-7645
Susan Armour, Associate State Dir.

University of Alabama at Birmingham
SBDC
1601 11th Ave. S.
Birmingham, Alabama 35294-2180
Phone: (205)934-6760
Fax: (205)934-0538

University of Alabama at Birmingham
Small Business Development Center
1717 i1th Ave. S., Ste. 419
Birmingham, Alabama 35294-4410
Phone: (205)934-7260
Fax: (205)934-7645
Charles Hobson, Dir.

University of North Alabama
Small Business Development Center
Box 5248, Keller Hall
Florence, Alabama 35632-0001
Phone: (205)760-4629
Fax: (205)760-4813
Kerry Gatlin, Dir.

University of North Alabama
SBDC
PO Box 5248, Keller Hall
Florence, Alabama 35632-0001
Phone: (205)760-4629
Fax: (205)760-4813
Kerry Gatlin, Dir.

Alabama A&M University
University of Alabama (Huntsville)
North East Alabama Regional Small
Business Development Center
225 Church St. NW
PO Box 168
Huntsville, Alabama 35804-0168
Phone: (205)535-2061
Fax: (205)535-2050
Jeff Thompson, Dir.
E-mail: thompsonj@email.uah.edu

N. E. Alabama Regional
Alabama A&M University
University of Alabama at Huntsville
SBDC
E-mail: thompsonj@email.uah.edu
P.O. Box 168
225 Church St., N.W.
Huntsville, Alabama 35804-0168
Phone: (205)535-2061
Fax: (205)535-2050
Jeff Thompson, Dir.

Jacksonville State University
SBDC
114 Merrill Hall
700 Pelham Rd. N.
Jacksonville, Alabama 36265
Phone: (205)782-5271
Fax: (205)782-5179
Pat Shaddix, Dir.

Jacksonville State University
Small Business Development Center
700 Pelham Rd. N
114 Merrill Hall

Jacksonville, Alabama 36265
Phone: (205)782-5271
Fax: (205)782-5179
Pat Shaddix, Dir.

Livingston University
Small Business Development Center
Station 35
Livingston, Alabama 35470
Phone: (205)652-9661 Ext. 439
Fax: (205)652-9318
Paul Garner, Dir.

Livingston University
SBDC
Station 35
Livingston, Alabama 35470
Phone: (205)652-9661 ext. 439
Fax: (205)652-9318
Paul Garner, Dir.

University of South Alabama
SBDC
College of Business Rm. 8
Mobile, Alabama 36688
Phone: (334)460-6004
Fax: (334)460-6246

University of South Alabama
Small Business Development Center
College of Business, Rm. 8
Mobile, Alabama 36688
Phone: (334)460-6004
Fax: (334)460-6246

Alabama State University
Small Business Development Center
915 S. Jackson St.
Montgomery, Alabama 36195
Phone: (334)229-4138
Fax: (334)269-1102
Lorenza G. Patrick, Dir.

Alabama State University
SBDC
915 S. Jackson St.
Montgomery, Alabama 36195
Phone: (334)229-4138
Fax: (334)269-1102
Lorenza G. Patrick, Dir.

Troy State University
SBDC
E-mail: jkerv@asntsu.asn.net

Bibb Graves, Rm. 102
Troy, Alabama 36082-0001
Phone: (205)670-3771
Fax: (205)670-3636

Troy State University
Small Business Development Center
Bibb Graves, Rm. 102
Troy, Alabama 36082-0001
Phone: (205)670-3771
Fax: (205)670-3636
Janet W. Kervin, Dir.
E-mail: jkerv@asntsu.asn.net

Alabama International Trade Center
University of Alabama
SBDC
Bidgood Hall, Rm. 201
PO Box 870396
Tuscaloosa, Alabama 35487-0396
Phone: (205)348-7621
Fax: (205)348-6974
Brian Davis, Dir.
E-mail: aitc@aitc.cba.ua.edu

University of Alabama
Alabama International Trade Center
Small Business Devlopment Center
Bidgood Hall, Rm. 201
Box 870396
Tuscaloosa, Alabama 35487-0396
Phone: (205)348-7621
Fax: (205)348-6974
Brian Davis, Dir.
E-mail: aitc@aitc.cba.ua.edu

University of Alabama
SBDC
E-mail: phaninen@ua1vm.ua.edu
P.O. Box 870397
Bidgood Hall, Rm. 250
Tuscaloosa, Alabama 35487-0397
Phone: (205)348-7011
Fax: (205)348-9644
Paavo Hanninen, Dir.

Alaska

University of Alaska (Fairbanks)
Small Business Development Center
510 Second Ave., Ste. 101
Fairbanks, Alaska 99701
Phone: (907)456-1701

Free: (800)478-1701
Fax: (907)456-1873
Theresa Proenza, Contact

University of Alaska (Juneau)
Small Business Development Center
400 Willoughby St., Ste. 211
Juneau, Alaska 99801
Phone: (907)463-3789
Free: (800)478-6655
Fax: (907)463-3929
Charles Northrip, Dir.

Kenai Peninsula Small Business
Development Center
110 S. Willow St., Ste. 106
Kenai, Alaska 99611-7744
Phone: (907)283-3335
Fax: (907)283-3913
William L. Root, Dir.

University of Alaska (Matanuska-
Susitna)
Small Business Development Center
1801 Parks Hwy., Ste. C-18
Wasilla, Alaska 99654
Phone: (907)373-7232
Fax: (907)373-2560
Marian Romano, Dir.

Arizona

Central Arizona College
Small Business Development Center
8470 N. Overfield Rd.
Coolidge, Arizona 85228
Phone: (520)426-4341
Fax: (520)426-4284
Donald Biggerstaff, Dir.

Coconino County Community College
Small Business Development Center
3000 N. 4th St., Ste. 25
Flagstaff, Arizona 86004
Phone: (520)526-5072
Fax: (520)526-8693
Stephen West, Dir.

Northland Pioneer College
Small Business Development Center
PO Box 610
Holbrook, Arizona 86025
Phone: (520)537-2976

Fax: (520)524-2227
Joel Eittreim, Dir.

Mohave Community College
Small Business Development Center
1971 Jagerson Ave.
Kingman, Arizona 86401
Phone: (520)757-0894
Fax: (520)757-0836
Jennee Miles, Dir.

Yavapai College
Small Business Development Center
117 E. Gurley St., Ste. 206
Prescott, Arizona 86301
Phone: (520)778-3088
Fax: (520)778-3109
Richard Senopole, Contact

Cochise College
Small Business Development Center
901 N. Colombo, Rm. 411
Sierra Vista, Arizona 85635
Phone: (520)515-5443
Fax: (520)515-5478
Debbie Elver, Dir.

Arizona Small Business Development
Center Network
E-mail: york@maricopa.bitnet
2411 W. 14th St., Ste. 132
Tempe, Arizona 85281
Phone: (602)731-8720
Fax: (602)731-8729
Michael York, State Dir.

Maricopa Community Colleges
SBDC
1414 W. Broadway, Ste. 165
Tempe, Arizona 85281
Phone: (602)966-7786
Fax: (602)966-8541
Christina Gonzalez, Dir.
Sonny Quinonez, Dir.

Eastern Arizona College
SBDC
622 College Ave.
Thatcher, Arizona 85552-0769
Phone: (520)428-8590
Fax: (520)428-8462
Greg Roers, Dir.

Eastern Arizona College
Small Business Development Center
622 College Ave.
Thatcher, Arizona 85552-0769
Phone: (520)428-8590
Fax: (520)428-8462
Greg Roers, Dir.

Pima Community College
Small Business Development Center
4905-A E. Broadway Blvd., Ste. 101
Tucson, Arizona 85709-1260
Phone: (520)748-4906
Fax: (520)748-4585
Linda Andrews, Dir.

Arizona Western College
Small Business Development Center
Century Plz., No. 152
281 W. 24th St.
Yuma, Arizona 85364
Phone: (520)341-1650
Fax: (520)726-2636
Hank Pinto, Dir.

Arkansas

Henderson State University
Small Business Development Center
1100 Henderson St.
PO Box 7624
Arkadelphia, Arkansas 71923
Phone: (501)230-5224
Fax: (501)230-5236
Bill Akin, Dir.

University of Central Arkansas
Small Business Development Center
College of Business Administration
Burdick Business Administration
Bldg., Rm. 212
201 Donaghey Ave.
Conway, Arkansas 72035-0001
Phone: (501)450-3190
Fax: (501)450-5302

Genesis Technology Incubator
SBDC Satellite Office
University of Arkansas Engineering
Research Center
Fayetteville, Arkansas 72701-1201
Phone: (501)575-7473

Fax: (501)575-7446
Bob Penquite, Business Consultant

University of Arkansas at Fayetteville
Small Business Development Center
College of Business
BADM 1172, Ste. 106
Fayetteville, Arkansas 72701
Phone: (501)575-5148
Fax: (501)575-4013
Ms. Jimmie Wilkins, Dir.

SBDC
1109 S. 16th St.
P.O. Box 2067
Fort Smith, Arkansas 72901
Phone: (501)785-1376
Fax: (501)785-1964
Byron "Twig" Branch, Business
Consultant

University of Arkansas at Little Rock,
Regional Office (Fort Smith)
Small Business Development Center
1109 S. 16th St.
PO Box 2067
Fort Smith, Arkansas 72901
Phone: (501)785-1376
Fax: (501)785-1964
Byron Branch, Business Specialist

University of Arkansas at Little Rock,
Regional Office (Harrison)
Small Business Development Center
818 Hwy. 62-65-412 N
PO Box 190
Harrison, Arkansas 72601
Phone: (501)741-8009
Fax: (501)741-1905
Bob Penquite, Business Consultant

University of Arkansas at Little Rock,
Regional Office (Hot Springs)
Small Business Development Center
835 Central Ave., Box 402D
Hot Springs, Arkansas 71901
Phone: (501)624-5448
Fax: (501)624-6632
Richard Evans, Business Consultant

Arkansas State University
Small Business Development Center

PO Drawer 2605
Jonesboro, Arkansas 72467
Phone: (501)932-3517
Fax: (501)972-3868
Herb Lawrence, Dir.

University of Arkansas At Little Rock
Arkansas SBDC
Little Rock Techonology Center Bldg.
100 S. Main St., Ste. 401
Little Rock, Arkansas 72201
Phone: (501)324-9043
Fax: (501)324-9049
Janet Nye, State Dir.

University of Arkansas Little Rock
SBDC
100 S. Main, Ste. 401
Little Rock, Arkansas 72201
Phone: (501)324-9043
Fax: (501)324-9049
John Harrison, Business Consultant

University of Arkansas at Little Rock,
Regional Office (Magnolia)
Small Business Development Center
600 Bessie
PO Box 767
Magnolia, Arkansas 71753
Phone: (501)234-4030
Fax: (501)234-0135
Mr. Lairie Kincaid, Business Consult-
ant

University of Arkansas at Little Rock,
Regional Office (Pine Bluff)
Small Business Development Center
The Enterprise Center III
400 Main, Ste. 117
Pine Bluff, Arkansas 71601
Phone: (501)536-0654
Fax: (501)536-7713
Vonelle Vanzant, Business Consultant

University of Arkansas at Little Rock,
Regional Office (Stuttgart)
Small Business Development Center
301 S. Grand, Ste. 101
PO Box 289
Stuttgart, Arkansas 72160
Phone: (501)673-8707
Larry LeFler, Business Consultant

Mid-South Community College
SBDC
2000 W. Broadway
P.O. Box 2067
West Memphis, Arkansas 72303-2067
Phone: (501)733-6767

California

Central Coast Small Business Development Center
6500 Soquel Dr.
Aptos, California 95003
Phone: (408)479-6136
Fax: (408)479-6166
Teresa Thomae, Dir.

Sierra College Small Business Development Center
560 Wall St., Ste. J
Auburn, California 95603
Phone: (916)885-5488
Fax: (916)823-2831
Mary Wollesen, Dir.

Weill Institute Small Business
Development Center
1706 Chester Ave., Ste. 200
Bakersfield, California 93301
Phone: (805)322-5881
Fax: (805)322-5663
Jeffrey Johnson, Dir.

Butte College
Small Business Development Center
260 Cohasset Rd., Ste. A
Chico, California 95926
Phone: (916)895-9017
Fax: (916)895-9099
Kay Zimmerlee, Dir.

Southwestern College Small Business
Development and International Trade
Center
900 Otay Lakes Rd., Bldg. 1600
Chula Vista, California 91910
Phone: (619)482-6393
Fax: (619)482-6402
Mary Wylie, Dir.

Yuba College SBDC
15145 Lakeshore Dr.
PO Box 4550

Clearlake, California 95422-4550
Phone: (707)995-3440
Fax: (707)995-3605
George McQueen, Dir.

Contra Costa SBDC
2425 Bisso Ln., Ste. 200
Concord, California 94520
Phone: (510)646-5377
Fax: (510)646-5299
Debra Longwood, Dir.

North Coast Small Business Development Center
207 Price Mall, Ste. 500
Crescent City, California 95531
Phone: (707)464-2168
Fax: (707)465-6008
Fran Clark, Dir.

Imperial Valley Satellite SBDC
Town & Country Shopping Center
301 N. Imperial Ave., Ste. B
El Centro, California 92243
Phone: (619)312-9800
Fax: (619)312-9838
Debbie Trujillo, Satellite Mgr.

Export SBDC/El Monte Outreach
Center
10501 Valley Blvd., Ste. 106
El Monte, California 91731
Phone: (818)459-4111
Fax: (818)443-0463
Charles Blythe, Manager

North Coast/Satellite Center
520 E. St.
Eureka, California 95501
Phone: (707)445-9720
Fax: (707)445-9652
Duff Heuttner, Bus. Counselor

Central California Small Business
Development Center
3419 W. Shaw Ave., Ste. 102
Fresno, California 93711
Phone: (209)275-1223
Fax: (209)275-1499
Dennis Winans, Dir.

Gavilan College Small Business
Development Center

7436 Monterey St.
Gilroy, California 95020
Phone: (408)847-0373
Fax: (408)847-0393
Peter Graff, Dir.

Accelerate Technology Assistance
Small Business Development Center
4199 Campus Dr.
University Towers, Ste. 240
Irvine, California 92715
Phone: (714)509-2990
Fax: (714)509-2997
Tiffany Haugen, Dir.

Amador SBDC
P.O. Box 1077
222 N. Hwy. 49
Jackson, California 95642
Phone: (209)223-0351
Fax: (209)223-5237

Greater San Diego Chamber of
Commerce Small Business Development Center
4275 Executive Sq., Ste. 920
La Jolla, California 92037
Phone: (619)453-9388
Fax: (619)450-1997
Hal Lefkowitz, Dir.

East Los Angeles SBDC
5161 East Pomona Blvd., Ste. 212
Los Angeles, California 90022
Phone: (213)262-9797
Fax: (213)262-2704

Export Small Business Development
Center of Southern California
110 E. 9th, Ste. A669
Los Angeles, California 90079
Phone: (213)892-1111
Fax: (213)892-8232
Gladys Moreau, Dir.

South Central LA/Satellite
SBDC
4060 S. Figueroa St.
Los Angeles, California 90037
Phone: (213)846-1710
Fax: (213)535-1686
Cope Norcross, Sattelite Mgr.

Alpine SBDC
P.O. Box 265
3 Webster St.
Markleeville, California 96120
Phone: (916)694-2475
Fax: (916)694-2478

Yuba/Sutter Satellite
SBDC
429 10th St.
Marysville, California 95901
Phone: (916)749-0153
Fax: (916)749-0152

Valley Sierra SBDC
Merced Satellite
1632 N St.
Merced, California 95340
Phone: (209)725-3800
Fax: (209)383-4959
Nick Starianoudakis, Satellite Mgr.

Valley Sierra Small Business Develop-
ment Center
1012 11th St., Ste. 300
Modesto, California 95354
Phone: (209)521-6177
Fax: (209)521-9373
Kelly Bearden, Dir.

Napa Valley College Small Business
Development Center
1556 First St., Ste. 103
Napa, California 94559
Phone: (707)253-3210
Fax: (707)253-3068
Michael Kauffman, Dir.

Inland Empire Business Incubator
SBDC
Building 409
Norton Air Force Base, California
92509
Phone: (909)382-0065
Fax: (909)382-8543
Chuck Eason, Incubator Mgr.

East Bay Small Business Development
Center
519 17th. St., Ste. 210
Oakland, California 94612
Phone: (510)893-4114
Fax: (510)893-5532
Napoleon Britt, Dir.

International Trade Office
SBDC
3282 E. Guasti Rd., Ste. 100
Ontario, California 91761
Phone: (909)390-8071
Fax: (909)390-8077
John Hernandez, Trade Manager

Coachella Valley SBDC
Palm Springs Satellite Center
501 S. Indian Canyon Dr., Ste. 222
Palm Springs, California 92264
Phone: (619)864-1311
Fax: (619)864-1319
Brad Mix, Satellite Mgr.

Pasadena Satellite
SBDC
2061 N. Los Robles, Ste. 106
Pasadena, California 91104
Phone: (818)398-9031
Fax: (818)398-3059
David Ryal, Satellite Mgr.

Pico Rivera SBDC
9058 E. Washington Blvd.
Pico Rivera, California 90660
Phone: (310)942-9965
Fax: (310)942-9745
Beverly Taylor, Satellite Mgr.

Eastern Los Angeles County Small
Business Development Center
375 S. Main St., Ste. 101
Pomona, California 91766
Phone: (909)629-2247
Fax: (909)629-8310
Toni Valdez, Dir.

Pomona SBDC
375 S. Main St., Ste. 101
Pomona, California 91766
Phone: (909)629-2247
Fax: (909)629-8310
Paul Hischar, Satellite Manager

Cascade Small Business Development
Center
737 Auditorium Dr., Ste. A
Redding, California 96001
Phone: (916)247-8100
Fax: (916)241-1712
Carole Enmark, Dir.

Inland Empire Small Business Devel-
opment Center
2002 Iowa Ave., Bldg. D, Ste. D-110
Riverside, California 92507
Phone: (909)781-2345
Free: (800)750-2353
Fax: (909)781-2353
Terri Corrazini Ooms, Dir.

California Trade and Commerce
Agency
California SBDC
801 K St. Ste. 1700
Sacramento, California 95814
Phone: (916)324-5068
Fax: (916)322-5084
Kim Neri, State Dir.

Greater Sacramento SBDC
1410 Ethan Way
Sacramento, California 95825
Phone: (916)563-3210
Fax: (916)563-3264
Cynthia Steimle, Director

Calaveras SBDC
P.O. Box 431
3 N. Main St.
San Andreas, California 95249
Phone: (209)754-1834
Fax: (209)754-4107

San Francisco SBDC
711 Van Ness, Ste. 305
San Francisco, California 94102
Phone: (415)561-1890
Fax: (415)561-1894
Tim Sprinkles, Director

Orange County Small Business
Development Center
901 E. Santa Ana Blvd., Ste. 101
Santa Ana, California 92701
Phone: (714)647-1172
Fax: (714)835-9008
Gregory Kishel, Dir.

Southwest Los Angeles County
Westside Satellite
SBDC
3233 Donald Douglas Loop S., Ste. C
Santa Monica, California 90405
Phone: (310)398-8883

Fax: (310)398-3024
Ken Davis, Admin. Asst.

Redwood Empire Small Business
Development Center
520 Mendocino Ave., Ste. 210
Santa Rosa, California 95401
Phone: (707)524-1770
Fax: (707)524-1772
Charles Robbins, Dir.

San Joaquin Delta College Small
Business Development Center
814 N. Hunter St.
Stockton, California 95202
Phone: (209)474-5089
Fax: (209)474-5605
Gillian Murphy, Dir.

Silicon Valley SBDC
298 S. Sunnyvale Ave., Ste. 204
Sunnyvale, California 94086
Phone: (408)736-0680
Fax: (408)736-0679
Eliza Minor, Director

Southwest Los Angeles County Small
Business Development Center
21221 Western Ave., Ste. 110
Torrance, California 90501
Phone: (310)787-6466
Fax: (310)782-8607
Susan Hunter, Dir.

West Company SBDC
367 N. State St., Ste. 208
Ukiah, California 95482
Phone: (707)468-3553
Fax: (707)462-8945
Sheilah Rogers, Director

North Los Angeles Small Business
Development Center
14540 Victory Blvd., Ste. 206
Van Nuys, California 91411
Phone: (818)373-7092
Fax: (818)373-7740
Wilma Berglund, Dir.

Export SBDC Satellite Center
5700 Ralston St., Ste. 310
Ventura, California 93003
Phone: (805)644-6191

Fax: (805)658-2252
Heather Wicka, Manager

Gold Coast SBDC
5700 Ralston St., Ste. 310
Ventura, California 93003
Phone: (805)644-6191
Fax: (805)658-2252
Heather Wicka, Manager

High Desert SBDC
Victorville Satellite Center
15490 Civic Dr., Ste. 102
Victorville, California 92392
Phone: (619)951-1592
Fax: (619)951-8929
Megan Partington, Business Consultant

Central California/Visalia Satellite
SBDC
430 W. Caldwell Ave., Ste. D
Visalia, California 93277
Phone: (209)625-3051
Fax: (209)625-3053
Randy Mason, Satellite Mgr.

Colorado

Adams State College
Small Business Development Center
Business Bldg., No. 105
Alamosa, Colorado 81102
Phone: (719)587-7372
Fax: (719)587-7603
Peggy Micklich, Dir.

Community College of Aurora
Small Business Development Center
9905 E. Colfax
Aurora, Colorado 80010-2119
Phone: (303)341-4849
Fax: (303)361-2953
Randy Johnson, Dir.

Front Range Community College
(Boulder)
Small Business Development Center
Boulder Chamber of Commerce
2440 Pearl St.
Boulder, Colorado 80302
Phone: (303)442-1475
Fax: (303)938-8837
Joe Bell, Dir.

Pueblo Community College (Canon
City)
Small Business Development Center
402 Valley Rd.
Canon City, Colorado 81212
Phone: (719)275-5335
Fax: (719)275-4400
Elwin Boody, Dir.

Pikes Peak Community College
Small Business Development Center
Colorado Springs Chamber of Commerce
PO Drawer B
Colorado Springs, Colorado 80901-3002
Phone: (303)471-4836
Fax: (303)635-1571

Colorado Northwestern Community
College
Small Business Development Center
50 College Dr.
Craig, Colorado 81625
Phone: (970)824-7078
Fax: (970)824-3527
Ken Farmer, Dir.

Delta Small Business Development
Center
Delta Montrose Vocational School
1765 US Hwy. 50
Delta, Colorado 81416
Phone: (970)874-8772
Fax: (970)874-8796
Steve Schrock, Dir.

Community College of Denver
Small Business Development Center
Greater Denver Chamber of Commerce
1445 Market St.
Denver, Colorado 80202
Phone: (303)620-8076
Fax: (303)534-3200
Tamela Lee, Dir.

Office of Business Development
Colorado SBDC
1625 Broadway, Ste. 1710
Denver, Colorado 80202
Phone: (303)892-3809
Fax: (303)892-3848
Joe Bell, Dir.

Fort Lewis College
Small Business Development Center
1000 Rim Dr.
Durango, Colorado 81301
Phone: (970)247-7009
Fax: (970)247-7623
Jim Reser, Dir.
E-mail: reser-j@fortlewis.edu

Front Range Community College (Fort Collins)
Small Business Development Center
2627 Redwing Rd., Ste. 105
Fort Collins, Colorado 80526
Phone: (970)226-0881
Fax: (970)204-0385
Frank Pryor, Dir.

Morgan Community College (Fort Morgan)
Small Business Development Center
300 Main St.
Fort Morgan, Colorado 80701
Phone: (970)867-3351
Fax: (970)867-3352
Lori Slinn, Dir.

Colorado Mountain College (Glenwood Springs)
Small Business Development Center
215 9th St.
Glenwood Springs, Colorado 81601
Phone: (970)928-0120
Free: (800)621-1647
Fax: (970)945-1531
Susan Glenn-James, Dir.

SBDC
1726 Cole Blvd., Ste. 310
Golden, Colorado 80401
Phone: (303)277-1840
Fax: (303)277-1899

Mesa State College
Small Business Development Center
304 W. Main St.
Grand Junction, Colorado 81505-1606
Phone: (970)243-5242
Fax: (970)241-0771

Greeley/Weld Chamber of Commerce
Small Business Development Center
Aims Community College

902 7th Ave.
Greeley, Colorado 80631
Phone: (970)352-3661
Fax: (970)352-3572

Red Rocks Community College Small Business Development Center
777 S. Wadsworth Blvd., Ste. 254
Bldg. 4
Lakewood, Colorado 80226
Phone: (303)987-0710
Fax: (303)987-1331
Jayne Reiter, Acting Dir.

Lamar Community College
Small Business Development Center
2400 S. Main
Lamar, Colorado 81052
Phone: (719)336-8141
Fax: (719)336-2448
Elwood Gillis, Dir.

Small Business Development Center
Arapahoe Community College
South Metro Chamber of Commerce
7901 S. Park Plz., Ste. 110
Littleton, Colorado 80120
Phone: (303)795-5855
Fax: (303)795-7520
Selma Kristel, Dir.

Pueblo Community College Small Business Development Center
900 W. Orman Ave.
Pueblo, Colorado 81004
Phone: (719)549-3224
Fax: (719)546-2413
Rita Friberg, Dir.

Morgan Community College (Stratton)
Small Business Development Center
PO Box 28
Stratton, Colorado 80836
Phone: (719)348-5596
Fax: (719)348-5887
Roni Carr, Dir.

Trinidad State Junior College
Small Business Development Center
136 W. Main St.
Davis Bldg.
Trinidad, Colorado 81082
Phone: (719)846-5645

Fax: (719)846-4550
Dennis O'Connor, Dir.

Front Range Community College (Westminster)
Small Business and International Development Center
3645 W. 112th Ave.
Westminster, Colorado 80030
Phone: (303)460-1032
Fax: (303)469-7143
Michael Lenzini, Dir.

Connecticut

Bridgeport Regional Business Council
Small Business Development Center
10 Middle St., 14th Fl.
Bridgeport, Connecticut 06604-4229
Phone: (203)330-4813
Fax: (203)366-0105
Juan Scott, Dir.

Quinebaug Valley Community Technical College
Small Business Development Center
742 Upper Maple St.
Danielson, Connecticut 06239-1440
Phone: (203)774-1133
Fax: (203)774-7768
Roger Doty, Dir.

University of Connecticut (Groton)
Small Business Development Center
Administration Bldg., Rm. 300
1084 Shennecossett Rd.
Groton, Connecticut 06340-6097
Phone: (860)449-1188
Fax: (860)445-3415
William Lockwood, Dir.

Middlesex Country Chamber of Commerce
SBDC
393 Main St.
Middletown, Connecticut 06457
Phone: (860)344-2158
Fax: (860)346-1043
John Serignese

Greater New Haven Chamber of Commerce
Small Business Development Center

195 Church St.
New Haven, Connecticut 06510-2009
Phone: (203)782-4390 ext. 190
Fax: (203)787-6730
Pete Rivera, Dir.

Southwestern Area Commerce and
Industry Association
Small Business Development Center
1 Landmark Sq., Ste. 230
Stamford, Connecticut 06901
Phone: (203)359-3220 ext. 302
Fax: (203)967-8294
George Ahl, Dir.

University of Connecticut
School of Business Administration
Connecticut SBDC
E-mail: oconnor@ct.sbdc.uconn.edu
2 Bourn Place, U-94
Storrs, Connecticut 06269
Phone: (860)486-4135
Fax: (860)486-1576
John O'Connor, State Dir.

Connecticut SBDC
101 S. Main St.
Waterbury, Connecticut 06706-1042
Phone: (203)757-8937
Fax: (203)756-9077
Ilene Oppenheim

University of Connecticut (Greater
Hartford Campus)
Small Business Development Center
1800 Asylum Ave.
West Hartford, Connecticut 06117
Phone: (860)241-4986
Fax: (860)241-4907
Zaiga Antonetti, Assoc. State Dir.

Eastern Connecticut State University
Small Business Development Center
83 Windham St.
Williamantic, Connecticut 06226-2295
Phone: (860)465-5349
Fax: (860)465-5143
Henry Reed, Dir.

Delaware

Delaware State University
School of Business Economics

SBDC
1200 N. Dupont Hwy.
Dover, Delaware 19901
Phone: (302)678-1555
Fax: (302)739-2333
Jim Crisfield, Director

Delaware Technical and Community
College
SBDC
Industrial Training Bldg.
PO Box 610
Georgetown, Delaware 19947
Phone: (302)856-1555
Fax: (302)856-5779
William F. Pfaff, Dir.

University of Delaware
Delaware SBDC
Purnell Hall-Ste. 005
Newark, Delaware 19716-2711
Phone: (302)831-1555
Fax: (302)831-1423
Clinton Tymes, State Dir.

Small Business Resource & Informa-
tion Center
SBDC
1318 N. Market St.
Wilmington, Delaware 19801
Phone: (302)571-1555
Barbara Necarsulmer, Mgr.

District of Columbia

George Washington University
National Law Center
Small Business Clinic
720 20th St. NW
Washington, District of Columbia
20052
Phone: (202)994-7463
Fax: (202)994-4946
Susan Jones, Dir.

George Washington University
East of the River Community Develop-
ment Corp.
SBDC
3101 MLK Jr., Ave., SE, 3rd Fl.
Washington, District of Columbia
20010
Phone: (202)561-4975 ext. 3006
Howard Johnson, Counselor

Howard University
SBDC
2000 14th St., NW, 2nd Fl.
Washington, District of Columbia
20009
Phone: (202)396-1200
Jose Hernandez, Counselor

Marshall Heights Community Devel-
opment Organization
SBDC
3917 Minnesota Ave., NE
Washington, District of Columbia
20019
Phone: (202)396-1200
Terry Strong, Counselor

Metropolitan Washington SBDC
6th & Fairmont Sts., N.W., Rm. 128
Washington, District of Columbia
20059
Phone: (202)806-1550
Fax: (202)806-1777
Woodrow "Woody" McCutchen,
Regional Dir.

Ward Five Community Development
Corp.
SBDC
Satellite Location
901 Newton St., NE, Ste. 103
Washington, District of Columbia
20017
Phone: (202)396-1200
Fax: (202)396-4106
Terry Strong

Washington District Office
Business Information Center
SBDC
1110 Vermont Ave., NW, 9th Fl.
Washington, District of Columbia
20005
Phone: (202)606-4000
Carmen Long, Counselor

Florida

SBDC (Bartow)
600 N. Broadway, Ste. 300
Bartow, Florida 33830
Phone: (941)534-4370
Fax: (941)533-1247
Marcela Stanislaus, Vice President

Florida Atlantic University (Boca
Raton)
Small Business Development Center
PO Box 3091
Bldg. T9
Boca Raton, Florida 33431
Phone: (407)362-5620
Fax: (407)362-5623
Nancy Young, Dir.

UCF Brevard Campus
Small Business Development Center
1519 Clearlake Rd.
Cocoa, Florida 32922
Phone: (407)951-1060 ext. 2045

Dania Small Business Development
Center
46 SW 1st Ave.
Dania, Florida 33304
Phone: (954)987-0100
William Healy, Regional Mgr.

Florida Regional SBDC
Daytona Beach Community College
1200 W. International Speedway Blvd.
Daytona Beach, Florida 32114
Phone: (904)947-3141
Fax: (904)254-4465

Florida Atlantic University Commer-
cial Campus
Small Business Development Center
1515 W. Commercial Blvd., Rm. 11
Fort Lauderdale, Florida 33309
Phone: (954)771-6520
Fax: (954)776-6645
John Hudson, Regional Mgr.

Minority Business Development
Center
SBDC
5950 West Oakland Park Blvd., Ste.
307
Fort Lauderdale, Florida 33313
Phone: (954)485-5333
Fax: (954)485-2514

Edison Community College
Small Business Development Center
8099 College Pky. SW
Fort Myers, Florida 33919
Phone: (941)489-9200

Fax: (941)489-9051
Dan Regelski, Management Consultant

Florida Gulf Coast University
The Midway Center
Small Business Development Center
17595 S. Tamiami Trail, Ste. 200
Midway Ctr.
Ft. Myers, Florida 33908-4500
Phone: (941)590-1053

Indian River Community College
Small Business Development Center
3209 Virginia Ave., Rm. 114
Fort Pierce, Florida 34981-5599
Phone: (407)462-4756
Fax: (407)462-4796
Richard Carreno, Dir.

Okaloosa-Walton Community College
SBDC
1170 Martin Luther King, Jr. Blvd.
Fort Walton Beach, Florida 32547
Phone: (904)863-6543
Fax: (904)863-6564
Walter Craft, Mgr.

University of North Florida
(Gainesville)
Small Business Development Center
505 NW 2nd Ave., Ste. D
PO Box 2518
Gainesville, Florida 32601-2518
Phone: (352)377-5621
Fax: (352)372-4132
Bill Stensgaard, Regional Mgr.

University of North Florida (Jackson-
ville)
Small Business Development Center
College of Business
4567 St. John's Bluff Rd. S
Bldg. 11, Rm. 2163
Jacksonville, Florida 32216
Phone: (904)646-2476
Fax: (904)646-2594
Lowell Salter, Dir.

Gulf Coast Community College
SBDC
2500 Minnesota Ave.
Lynn Haven, Florida 32444

Phone: (904)271-1108
Fax: (904)271-1109
Doug Davis, Dir.

Brevard Community College
(Melbourne)
Small Business Development Center
3865 N. Wickham Rd., CM 207
Melbourne, Florida 32935
Phone: (407)632-1111 ext. 33201
Fax: (407)232-1111
Victoria Peak, Mgr.

Florida International University
Small Business Development Center
University Park
EAS-2620
Miami, Florida 33199
Phone: (305)348-2272
Marvin Nesbit, Regional Dir.

Florida International University (North
Miami Campus)
Small Business Development Center
Academic Bldg. No. 1, Rm. 350
NE 151 and Biscayne Blvd.
Miami, Florida 33181
Phone: (305)940-5790
Fax: (305)348-2965
Royland Jarrett, Regional Mgr.

Miami Dade Community College
Small Business Development Center
6300 NW 7th Ave.
Miami, Florida 33150
Phone: (305)237-1906
Fax: (305)237-1908
Frederick Bonneau, Dir.

Ocala Small Business Development
Center
110 E. Silver Springs Blvd.
PO Box 1210
Ocala, Florida 32670
Phone: (352)629-8051
Philip Geist, Regional Mgr.

University of Central Florida
Small Business Development Center
College of Business Administration,
309
PO Box 161530
Orlando, Florida 32816-1530

Phone:(407)823-5554
Fax:(407)823-3073
Al Polfer, Dir.

Palm Beach Gardens
Florida Atlantic University
SBDC
Northrop Center
3970 RCA Blvd., Ste. 7323
Palm Beach Gardens, Florida 33410
Phone:(407)691-8550
Fax:(407)692-8502
Steve Windhaus, Regional Mgr.

Procurement Technical Assistance
Program
University of West Florida
Small Business Development Center
11000 University Pky., Bldg. 8
Pensacola, Florida 32514
Phone:(904)474-2908
Fax:(904)474-2126
Martha Cobb, Dir.

University of West Florida Downtown
Center
Florida SBDC
19 West Garden St. Ste. 300
Pensacola, Florida 32501
Phone:(904)444-2066
Fax:(904)444-2070
Jerry Cartwright, State Dir.

Seminole Community College
SBDC
100 Weldon Blvd., Bldg. R
Sanford, Florida 32773-6199
Phone:(407)328-4722 ext. 3341
Fax:(407)330-4489

Seminole Community College
SBDC
100 Weldon Blvd., Bldg. R
Sanford, Florida 32773-6199
Phone:(407)328-4722 ext. 3341
Fax:(407)330-4489

Florida Agricultural and Mechanical
University
Small Business Development Center
1157 E. Tennessee St.
Tallahassee, Florida 32308
Phone:(904)599-3407

Fax:(904)561-2395
Patricia McGowan, Dir.

SBDC Training Center
Skipper Palms Shopping Center
1111 N. Westshore Dr., Annex B
Tampa, Florida 33607
Phone:(813)554-2341
Fax:(813)554-2356
Charles Attardo, Mgr.
E-mail:
SBDC@smtc_fla.enterprise.state.fl.us

University of South Florida (Tampa)
Small Business Development Center
College of Business Adminstration
4202 E. Fowler Ave., BSN 3403
Tampa, Florida 33620
Phone:(813)974-4371
Free:(800)733-7232
Fax:(813)974-5020
Dick Hardesty, Mgr.

Georgia

Darton College
Southwest Georgia District Small
Business Development Center
E-mail: sbdcalb@uga.cc.uga.edu
Business and Technology Center
230 S. Jackson St., Ste. 333
Albany, Georgia 31701-2885
Phone:(912)430-4303
Fax:(912)430-3933
Sue Ford, District Dir.

Georgia SBDC
Chicopee Complex
University of Georgia
1180 E. Broad St.
Athens, Georgia 30602-5412
Phone:(706)542-6762
Fax:(706)542-6776
Hank Logan, State Dir.
E-mail: sbdcath@uga.cc.uga.edu

NE Georgia District
SBDC
University of Georgia
1180 E. Broad St.
Athens, Georgia 30602-5412
Phone:(706)542-7436
Fax:(706)542-6823
Gayle Rosenthal, Mgr.

NW Georgia District
University of Georgia
SBDC
1180 E. Broad St.
Athens, Georgia 30602-5412
Phone:(706)542-6756
Fax:(706)542-6776

Georgia State University
Small Business Development Center
E-mail: sbdcatl@uga.cc.uga.edu
Box 874
University Plz.
Atlanta, Georgia 30303-3083
Phone:(404)651-3550
Fax:(404)651-1035
Lee Quarterman, Center Mgr.

Morris Brown College
Small Business Development Center
643 Martin Luther King, Jr., Dr. NW
Atlanta, Georgia 30314
Phone:(404)220-0205
Fax:(404)688-5985
Ray Johnson, Center Mgr.

Augusta College
Small Business Development Center
1061 Katherine St.
Augusta, Georgia 30904-6105
Phone:(706)737-1790
Fax:(706)731-7937
Jeff Sanford, Center Mgr.
E-mail: sbdcaug@uga.cc.uga.edu

University of Georgia (Brunswick)
Small Business Development Center
1107 Fountain Lake Dr.
Brunswick, Georgia 31525-3039
Phone:(912)264-7343
Fax:(912)262-3095
George Eckerd, Center Mgr.
E-mail: sbdcrun@uga.cc.uga.edu

Columbus College
Small Business Development Center
E-mail: sbdccolu@uga.cc.uga.edu
928 45th St.
North Bdlg., Rm. 523
Columbus, Georgia 31904-6572
Phone:(708)649-7433
Fax:(708)649-1928
Tom Snyder, Center Mgr.

DeKalb Small Business Development Center
DeKalb Chamber of Commerce
750 Commerce Dr., Ste. 201
Decatur, Georgia 30030-2622
Phone: (404)378-8000
Fax: (404)378-3397
Eric Bonaparte, Center Mgr.

Gainesville Small Business Development Center
E-mail: sbdcgain@uga.cc.uga.edu
500 Jesse Jewel Pky., Ste. 304
Gainesville, Georgia 30501-4203
Phone: (706)531-5681
Fax: (706)531-5684
Ron Simmons, Center Mgr.

Kennesaw State College
Small Business Development Center
1000 Chastain Rd.
Kennesaw, Georgia 30144-5591
Phone: (770)423-6450
Fax: (770)423-6564
Carlotta Roberts, Center Mgr.
E-mail:
carobert@kscmail.kennesaw.edu

Southeast Georgia District (Macon)
Small Business Development Center
E-mail: sbdcmac@uga.cc.uga.edu
PO Box 13212
401 Cherry St., Ste. 701
Macon, Georgia 31208-3212
Phone: (912)751-6592
Fax: (912)751-6607
David Mills, District Mgr.

Clayton State College
Small Business Development Center
E-mail: sbdcmorr@uga.cc.uga.edu
PO Box 285
Morrow, Georgia 30260
Phone: (404)961-3440
Fax: (404)961-3428
Alex Ferdinand, Center Mgr.

UGA SBDC
1770 Indian Trail Rd., Ste. 410
Norcross, Georgia 30093
Phone: (770)806-2124
Robert Dixon, District Dir.
Robert Andoh, Center Mgr.

Floyd Junior College
Small Business Development Center
E-mail: sbdcrome@uga.cc.uga.edu
PO Box 1864
Rome, Georgia 30162-1864
Phone: (404)295-6326
Fax: (404)295-6732
Drew Tonsmeire, Center Mgr.

Southeast Georgia District (Savannah)
Small Business Development Center
450 Mall Blvd., Ste. H
Savannah, Georgia 31406-4824
Phone: (912)356-2755
Fax: (912)353-3033
Harry O'Brien, Center Mgr.
E-mail: sbdcsav@uga.u.uga.edu

University of Georgia (Statesboro)
Small Business Development Center
325 S. Main St.
Statesboro, Georgia 30460
Phone: (912)681-5194
Fax: (912)681-0648
David Lewis, Center Mgr.
E-mail: sbdcstat@uga.cc.uga.edu

Valdosta Small Business Development Center
Baytree W. Professional Offices
1205 Baytree Rd., Ste. 9
Valdosta, Georgia 31602-2782
Phone: (912)245-3738
Fax: (912)245-3741
Suzanne Barnett, Center Mgr.
E-mail: sbdcval@uga.cc.uga.edu

Warner Robins Small Business Development Center
151 Osigian Blvd.
Warner Robins, Georgia 31088
Phone: (912)953-9356
Fax: (912)953-9376
Ronald Reaves, Center Mgr.

Guam

Guam SBDC
University of Guam
PO Box 5061
UOG Station
Mangilao, Guam 96923
Phone: (671)735-2590

Fax: (671)735-2002
Dr. Stephen L Marder, Executive

Hawaii

Kona Circuit Rider
SBDC
200 West Kawili St.
Hilo, Hawaii 96720-4091
Phone: (808)933-3515
Fax: (808)933-3683
Jean Geer, Business Consultant

University of Hawaii at Hilo
Hawaii SBDC
200 W. Kawili St.
Hilo, Hawaii 96720-4091
Phone: (808)933-3515
Fax: (808)933-3683
Darryl Mleynek, State Dir.

University of Hawaii, West Oahu
SBDC
130 Merchant St., Ste. 1030
Honolulu, Hawaii 96813
Phone: (808)522-8131
Fax: (808)522-8135
Laura Noda, Center Dir.

Business Research Library
University of HI-Hilo
SBDC
590 Lipoa Pkwy. 128
Kihei, Hawaii 96753
Phone: (808)875-2400
Fax: (808)875-2452

Maui Community College
Small Business Development Center
Maui Research and Technology Center
590 Lipoa Pky., No. 130
Kihei, Hawaii 96779
Phone: (808)875-2402
Fax: (808)875-2452
David B. Fisher, Dir.

Kauai Community College
Small Business Development Center
3-1901 Kaumualii Hwy.
Lihue, Hawaii 96766-9591
Phone: (808)246-1748
Fax: (808)246-5102
Randy Gringas, Center Dir.

Idaho

Boise State University
College of Business
Idaho SBDC
1910 University Dr.
Boise, Idaho 83725
Phone: (208)385-1640
Free: (800)225-3815
Fax: (208)385-3877
James Hogge, State Dir.

Boise State University
Small Business Development Center
1910 University Dr.
Boise, Idaho 83725
Phone: (208)385-3875
Free: (800)225-3815
Fax: (208)385-3877
Robert Shepard, Regional Dir.

Idaho State University (Idaho Falls)
Small Business Development Center
2300 N. Yellowstone
Idaho Falls, Idaho 83401
Phone: (208)523-1087
Free: (800)658-3829
Fax: (208)523-1049
Betty Capps, Regional Dir.

Lewis-Clark State College
Small Business Development Center
500 8th Ave.
Lewiston, Idaho 83501
Phone: (208)799-2465
Fax: (208)799-2878
Helen LeBoeuf-Binninger, Regional
Dir.

Idaho Small Business Development
Center
305 E. Park St. Ste. 405
McCall, Idaho 83638
Phone: (208)634-2883
Larry Smith, Associate Editor Consult-
ant

Idaho State University (Pocatello)
Small Business Development Center
1651 Alvin Ricken Dr.
Pocatello, Idaho 83201
Phone: (208)232-4921
Free: (800)232-4921

Fax: (208)233-0268
Paul Cox, Regional Dir.

North Idaho College
SBDC
525 W. Clearwater Loop
Post Falls, Idaho 83854
Phone: (208)769-3296
Fax: (208)769-3223
John Lynn, Regional Dir.

College of Southern Idaho
Small Business Development Center
315 Falls Ave.
PO Box 1238
Twin Falls, Idaho 83303-1238
Phone: (208)733-9554 ext. 2450
Fax: (208)733-9316
Cindy Bond, Regional Dir.

Illinois

Waubonsee Community College
(Aurora Campus)
Small Business Development Center
5 E. Galena Blvd.
Aurora, Illinois 60506
Phone: (630)892-3334 ext. 139
Fax: (630)892-3374
Mike O'Kelley, Dir.

Southern Illinois University at
Carbondale
Small Business Development Center
College of Business Administration
Carbondale, Illinois 62901-6702
Phone: (618)536-2424
Fax: (618)453-5040
Dennis Cody, Dir.

John A. Logan College
Small Business Development Center
RR2
Carterville, Illinois 62918
Phone: (618)985-3741 ext. 506
Fax: (618)985-2248
Richard Fyke, Dir.

Kaskaskia College
Small Business Development Center
27210 College Rd.
Centralia, Illinois 62801
Phone: (618)532-2049

Fax: (618)532-4983
Richard McCullum, Dir.

University of Illinois at Urbana-
Champaign
Small Business Development Center
428 Commerce W.
1206 S. 6th St.
Champaign, Illinois 61820
Phone: (217)244-1585
Fax: (217)333-7410
Helen Lesieur, Dir.

Asian American Alliance
SBDC
6246 N. Pulaski Rd., Ste. 101
Chicago, Illinois 60646
Phone: (312)202-0600
Fax: (312)202-1007
Joon H. Lee, Dir.

Back of the Yards Neighborhood
Council
Small Business Development Center
1751 W. 47th St.
Chicago, Illinois 60609
Phone: (312)523-4419
Fax: (312)254-3525
Paul Ladniak, Dir.

Chicago Small Business Development
Center
DCCA James R. Thompson Center
100 W. Randolph, Ste. 3-400
Chicago, Illinois 60601
Phone: (312)814-6111
Fax: (312)814-2807
Carson Gallagher, Dir.

Eighteenth Street Development Corp.
Small Business Development Center
1839 S. Carpenter
Chicago, Illinois 60608
Phone: (312)733-2287
Fax: (312)733-7315
Maria Munoz, Dir.

Greater North Pulaski Development
Corp.
Small Business Development Center
4054 W. North Ave.
Chicago, Illinois 60639
Phone: (312)384-2262

Fax:(312)384-3850
Paul Peterson, Dir.

Industrial Council of Northwest
Chicago
Small Business Development Center
2023 W. Carroll
Chicago, Illinois 60612
Phone:(312)421-3941
Fax:(312)421-1871
Melvin Eisland, Dir.

Latin American Chamber of Commerce
Small Business Development Center
2539 N. Kedzie, Ste. 11
Chicago, Illinois 60647
Phone:(312)252-5211
Fax:(312)252-7065
Arturo Venecia, Dir.

North Business and Industrial Council
(NORBIC)
SBDC
2500 W. Bradley Pl.
Chicago, Illinois 60618
Phone:(312)588-5855
Fax:(312)588-0734
Tom Kamykowski, Dir.

Richard J. Daley College
Small Business Development Center
7500 S. Pulaski Rd., Bldg. 200
Chicago, Illinois 60652
Phone:(312)838-0319
Fax:(312)838-0303
Jim Charney, Dir.

Women's Business Development
Center
Small Business Development Center
8 S. Michigan, Ste. 400
Chicago, Illinois 60603
Phone:(312)853-3477
Fax:(312)853-0145
Paul Carlin, Dir.

McHenry County College
Small Business Development Center
8900 U.S. Hwy. 14
Crystal Lake, Illinois 60012-2761
Phone:(815)455-6098
Fax:(815)455-9319
Susan Whitfield, Dir.

Danville Area Community College
Small Business Development Center
28 W. North St.
Danville, Illinois 61832
Phone:(217)442-7232
Fax:(217)442-6228
Ed Adrain, Dir.

Cooperative Extension Service
SBDC
985 W. Pershing Rd., Ste. F-4
Decatur, Illinois 62526
Phone:(217)875-8284
Fax:(217)875-8288
Rick Russell, Dir.

Sauk Valley Community College
Small Business Development Center
173 Illinois, Rte. 2
Dixon, Illinois 61021-9110
Phone:(815)288-5111
Fax:(815)288-5958
John Nelson, Dir.

Black Hawk College
Small Business Development Center
301 42nd Ave.
East Moline, Illinois 61244
Phone:(309)755-2200 ext.211
Fax:(309)755-9847
Donna Scalf, Dir.

East St. Louis Small Business Devel-
opment Center
DCCA, State Office Bldg.
650 Missouri Ave., Ste. G32
East St. Louis, Illinois 62201
Phone:(618)482-3833
Fax:(618)482-3832
Robert Ahart, Dir.

Southern Illinois University at
Edwardsville
Small Business Development Center
Center for Advanced Manufacturing
and Production
Campus Box 1107
Edwardsville, Illinois 62026
Phone:(618)692-2929
Fax:(618)692-2647
Alan Hauff, Dir.

Elgin Community College
Small Business Development Center
1700 Spartan Dr., Office B-15
Elgin, Illinois 60123
Phone:(847)888-7675
Fax:(847)888-7995
Craig Fowler, Dir.

Evanston Business and Technology
Center
Small Business Development Center
1840 Oak Ave.
Evanston, Illinois 60201
Phone:(847)866-1817
Fax:(847)866-1808
Rick Holbrook, Dir.

College of DuPage
Small Business Development Center
22nd St. & Lambert Rd.
Glen Ellyn, Illinois 60137
Phone:(630)942-2600
Fax:(630)942-3789
David Gay, Dir.

Lewis and Clark Community College
SBDC
5800 Godfrey Rd.
Godfrey, Illinois 62035
Phone:(618)466-3411
Fax:(618)466-0810
Bob Duane, Dir.

College of Lake County
Small Business Development Center
19351 W. Washington St.
Grayslake, Illinois 60030
Phone:(847)223-3633
Fax:(847)223-9371
Linda Jorn, Dir.

Southeastern Illinois College
Small Business Development Center
303 S. Commercial
Harrisburg, Illinois 62946-2125
Phone:(618)252-5001
Fax:(618)252-0210
Becky Williams, Dir.

Rend Lake College
Small Business Development Center
Rte. 1
Ina, Illinois 62846

Phone: (618)437-5321 ext. 335
Fax: (618)437-5677
Lisa Payne, Dir.

Joliet Junior College
Small Business Development Center
Renaissance Center, Rm. 312
214 N. Ottawa St.
Joliet, Illinois 60431
Phone: (815)727-6544 ext. 1321
Fax: (815)722-1895
Denise Mikulski, Dir.

Kankakee Community College
Small Business Development Center
101 S. Schuyler Ave.
Kankakee, Illinois 60901
Phone: (815)933-0376
Fax: (815)933-0380
JoAnn Seggebruch, Dir.

Western Illinois University
Small Business Development Center
114 Seal Hall
Macomb, Illinois 61455
Phone: (309)298-2211
Fax: (309)298-2520
Dan Voorhis, Dir.

Maple City Business and Technology
Center
Small Business Development Center
620 S. Main St.
Monmouth, Illinois 61462
Phone: (309)734-4664
Fax: (309)734-8579
Carol Cook, Dir.

Illinois Valley Community College
Small Business Development Center
815 N. Orlando Smith Ave., Bldg. 11
Oglesby, Illinois 61348
Phone: (815)223-1740
Fax: (815)224-3033
Boyd Palmer, Dir.

Illinois Eastern Community College
Small Business Development Center
401 E. Main St.
Olney, Illinois 62450
Phone: (618)395-3011
Fax: (618)395-1922
John Spitz, Dir.

Moraine Valley College
Small Business Development Center
10900 S. 88th Ave.
Palos Hills, Illinois 60465
Phone: (708)974-5468
Fax: (708)974-0078
Hilary Gereg, Dir.

Bradley University
Small Business Development Center
141 N. Jobst Hall, 1st Fl.
Peoria, Illinois 61625
Phone: (309)677-2992
Fax: (309)677-3386
Roger Luman, Dir.

Illinois Central College
Small Business Development Center
124 SW Adams St., Ste. 300
Peoria, Illinois 61602
Phone: (309)676-7500 ext.237
Fax: (309)676-7534
Susan Gorman, Dir.

Quincy Procurement Technical
Assistance Center
Small Business Development Center
301 Oak St.
Quincy, Illinois 62301
Phone: (217)228-5511
Edward Van Leer, Dir.

Rock Valley College
Small Business Development Center
1220 Rock St., Ste. 180
Rockford, Illinois 61101-1437
Phone: (815)968-4087
Fax: (815)968-4157
Beverly Kingsley, Dir.

Department of Commerce & Commu-
nity Affairs
Illinois SBDC
620 East Adams St., Third Fl.
Springfield, Illinois 62701
Phone: (217)524-5856
Fax: (217)785-6328
Jeff Mitchell, State Dir.

Lincoln Land Community College
Small Business Development Center
100 N. 11th St.
Springfield, Illinois 62703

Phone: (217)789-1017
Fax: (217)789-0958

Shawnee Community College
Small Business Development Center
Shawnee College Rd.
Ullin, Illinois 62992
Phone: (618)634-9618
Fax: (618)634-9028
Donald Denny, Dir.

Governors State University
Small Business Development Center
University Park, Illinois 60466
Phone: (708)534-4929
Fax: (708)534-8457
Christine Cochrane, Dir.

Indiana

Batesville Office of Economic Devel-
opment
SBDC
132 S. Main
Batesville, Indiana 47006
Phone: (812)933-6110

Bedford Chamber of Commerce
SBDC
1116 W. 16th St.
Bedford, Indiana 47421
Phone: (812)275-4493

Bloomfield Chamber of Commerce
SBDC
c/o Harrah Realty Co.
23 S. Washfington St.
Bloomfield, Indiana 47424
Phone: (812)275-4493

Bloomington Area Small Business
Development Center
116 W. 6th St., No. 100
Bloomington, Indiana 47404
Phone: (812)339-8937
Fax: (812)336-0651
David Miller, Dir.

Clay Count Chamber of Commerce
SBDC
12 N. Walnut St.
Brazil, Indiana 47834
Phone: (812)448-8457

Brookville Chamber of Commerce
SBDC
PO Box 211
Brookville, Indiana 47012
Phone: (317)647-3177

Clinton Chamber of Commerce
SBDC
292 N. 9th St.
Clinton, Indiana 47842
Phone: (812)832-3844

Columbia City Chamber of Commerce
SBDC
112 N. Main St.
Columbia City, Indiana 46725
Phone: (219)248-8131

Columbus Regional Small Business
Development Center
4920 N. Warren Dr.
Columbus, Indiana 47203
Phone: (812)372-6480
Free: (800)282-7232
Fax: (812)372-0228
Glenn Dunlap, Dir.

Connerville SBDC
504 Central
Connersville, Indiana 47331
Phone: (317)825-8328

Harrison County
Development Center
SBDC
The Harrison Center
405 N. Capitol, Ste. 308
Corydon, Indiana 47112
Phone: (812)738-8811

Montgomery County Chamber of
Commerce
SBDC
211 S. Washington St.
Crawfordsville, Indiana 47933
Phone: (317)654-5507

Decatur Chamber of Commerce
SBDC
125 E. Monroe St.
Decatur, Indiana 46733
Phone: (219)724-2604

City of Delphi Community Develop-
ment
SBDC
201 S. Union
Delphi, Indiana 46923
Phone: (317)564-6692

Southwestern Indiana Small Business
Development Center
100 NW 2nd St., Ste. 200
Evansville, Indiana 47708
Phone: (812)425-7232
Fax: (812)421-5883
Jeff Lake, Dir.

Northeast Indiana Small Business
Development Center
1830 Wayne Trace
Fort Wayne, Indiana 46803
Phone: (219)426-0040
Fax: (219)424-0024
A. V. Fleming, Dir.

Clinton County Chamber of Commerce
SBDC
207 S. Main St.
Frankfort, Indiana 46041
Phone: (317)654-5507

Northlake Small Business Development Center
487 Broadway, Ste. 201
Gary, Indiana 46402
Phone: (219)882-2000

Greencastle Partnership Center
SBDC
2 S. Jackson St.
Greencastle, Indiana 46135
Phone: (317)653-4517

Greensburg Area Chamber of Com-
merce
SBDC
125 W. Main St.
Greensburg, Indiana 47240
Phone: (812)663-2832

Hammond Development Corp.
SBDC
649 Conkey St.
Hammond, Indiana 46324
Phone: (219)853-6399

Blackford County Economic Develop-
ment
SBDC
PO Box 43
Hartford, Indiana 47348
Phone: (317)348-4944

Indiana SBDC Network
E-mail: sthrash@in.net
One North Capitol, Ste. 420
Indianapolis, Indiana 46204
Phone: (317)264-6871
Fax: (317)264-3102

Indianapolis Regional Small Business
Development Center
342 N. Senate Ave.
Indianapolis, Indiana 46204-1708
Phone: (317)261-3030
Fax: (317)261-3053
Tim Tichenar, Dir.

Clark County Hoosier Falls
Private Industry Council Workforce
1613 E. 8th St.
Jeffersonville, Indiana 47130
Phone: (812)282-0456

Southern Indiana Small Business
Development Center
1613 E. 8th St.
Jeffersonville, Indiana 47130
Phone: (812)288-6451
Fax: (812)284-8314
Patricia Stroud, Dir.

Kendallville Chamber of Commerce
SBDC
228 S. Main St.
Kendallville, Indiana 46755
Phone: (219)347-1554

Kokomo-Howard County Small
Business Development Center
106 N. Washington
Kokomo, Indiana 46901
Phone: (317)457-5301
Fax: (317)452-4564
Todd Moser, Dir.

LaPorte Small Business Development
Center
414 Lincolnway

La Porte, Indiana 46350
Phone: (219)326-7232

Greater Lafayette Area Small Business
Development Center
122 N. 3rd
Lafayette, Indiana 47901
Phone: (317)742-2394
Fax: (317)742-6276
Susan Davis, Dir.

Union County Chamber of Commerce
SBDC
102 N. Main St., No. 6
Liberty, Indiana 47353-1039
Phone: (317)458-5976

Linton/Stockton Chamber of Commerce
SBDC
PO Box 208
Linton, Indiana 47441
Phone: (812)847-4846

Southeastern Indiana Small Business
Development Center
301 E. Main St.
Madison, Indiana 47250
Phone: (812)265-3127
Fax: (812)265-2923
Rose Marie Roberts, Dir.

Crawford County
Private Industry Council Workforce
SBDC
Box 224 D, R.R. 1
Marengo, Indiana 47140
Phone: (812)365-2174

Greater Martinsville Chamber of
Commerce
SBDC
210 N. Marion St.
Martinsville, Indiana 46151
Phone: (317)342-8110

Lake County Public Library
SBDC
1919 W. 81st Ave.
Merrillville, Indiana 46410
Phone: (219)756-7232

Lake County Public Library
Small Business Development Center
1919 W. 81st. Ave.
Merrilville, Indiana 46410
Phone: (219)756-7232

First Citizens Bank
SBDC
515 N. Franklin Sq.
Michigan City, Indiana 46360
Phone: (219)874-9245

Mitchell Chamber of Commerce
SBDC
1st National Bank
Main Street
Mitchell, Indiana 47446
Phone: (812)849-4441

Mount Vernon Chamber of Commerce
SBDC
405 E. 4th St.
Mt. Vernon, Indiana 47620
Phone: (812)838-3639

East Central Indiana Small Business
Development Center
401 S. High St.
PO Box 842
Muncie, Indiana 47308
Phone: (317)284-8144
Fax: (317)741-5489
Barbara Armstrong, Dir.

Brown County Chamber of Commerce
SBDC
PO Box 164
Nashville, Indiana 47448
Phone: (812)988-6647

Floyd County
Private Industry Council Workforce
3303 Plaza Dr., Ste. 2
New Albany, Indiana 47150
Phone: (812)945-2643

Henry County Economic Development
Corp.
SBDC
1325 Broad St., Ste. B
New Castle, Indiana 47362
Phone: (317)529-4635

Jennings County Chamber of Commerce
merce
SBDC
PO Box 340
North Vernon, Indiana 47265
Phone: (812)346-2339

Orange County
Private Industry Council Workforce
SBDC
326 B. N. Gospel
Paoli, Indiana 47464
Phone: (812)723-4206

Northwest Indiana (Portage)
Small Business Development Center
6100 Southport Rd.
Portage, Indiana 46368
Phone: (219)762-1696
Fax: (219)942-5806

Jay County Development Corp.
SBDC
121 W. Main St., Ste. A
Portland, Indiana 47371
Phone: (219)726-9311

Richmond-Wayne County Small
Business Development Center
33 S. 7th St.
Richmond, Indiana 47374
Phone: (317)962-2887
Fax: (317)966-0882
Doug Peters, Dir.

Rochester and Lake Manitou Chamber
of Commerce
Fulton Economic Development Center
SBDC
617 Main St.
Rochester, Indiana 46975
Phone: (219)223-6773

Rushville Chamber of Commerce
SBDC
PO Box 156
Rushville, Indiana 47173
Phone: (317)932-2222

St. Mary-of-the-Woods College
SBDC
St. Mary-of-the-Woods, Indiana 47876
Phone: (812)535-5151

Washington County
Private Industry Council Workforce
SBDC
Hilltop Plaza
Salem, Indiana 47167
Phone: (812)883-2283

Scott County
Private Industry Council Workforce
SBDC
752 Lakeshore Dr.
Scottsburg, Indiana 47170
Phone: (812)752-3886

Seymour Chamber of Commerce
SBDC
PO Box 43
Seymour, Indiana 47274
Phone: (812)522-3681

Minority Business Development
Project Future
SBDC
401 Col
South Bend, Indiana 46634
Phone: (219)234-0051

South Bend Area Small Business
Development Center
300 N. Michigan
South Bend, Indiana 46601
Phone: (219)282-4350
Fax: (219)282-4344
Carolyn Anderson, Dir.

Economic Development Office
SBDC
46 E. Market St.
Spencer, Indiana 47460
Phone: (812)829-3245

Sullivan Chamber of Commerce
SBDC
10 S. Crt. St.
Sullivan, Indiana 47882
Phone: (812)268-4836

Tell City Chamber of Commerce
SBDC
Regional Federal Bldg.
645 Main St.
Tell City, Indiana 47586

Phone: (812)547-2385
Fax: (812)547-8378

Terre Haute Area Small Business
Development Center
Indiana State University
School of Business, Rm. 510
Terre Haute, Indiana 47809
Phone: (812)237-7676
Fax: (812)237-7675
William Minnis, Dir.

Tipton County Economic Development Corp.
SBDC
136 E. Jefferson
Tipton, Indiana 46072
Phone: (317)675-7300

Porter County
SBDC
911 Wall St.
Valparaiso, Indiana 46383
Phone: (219)477-5256

Vevay/Switzerland Country Foundation
SBDC
PO Box 193
Vevay, Indiana 47043
Phone: (812)427-2533

Vincennes University
SBDC
PO Box 887
Vincennes, Indiana 47591
Phone: (812)885-5749

Wabash Area Chamber of Commerce
Wabash Economic Development
Corp.
SBDC
67 S. Wabash
Wabash, Indiana 46922
Phone: (219)563-1168

Washington Daviess County
SBDC
1 Train Depot St.
Washington, Indiana 47501
Phone: (812)254-5262
Fax: (812)254-2550
Mark Brochin, Dir.

Purdue University
SBDC
Business & Industrial Development
Center
1220 Potter Dr.
West Lafayette, Indiana 47906
Phone: (317)494-5858

Randolph County Economic Development Foundation
SBDC
111 S. Main St.
Winchester, Indiana 47394
Phone: (317)584-3266

Iowa

Iowa State University
Iowa SBDC
College of Business Administration
137 Lynn Ave.
Ames, Iowa 50014
Phone: (515)292-6351
Free: (800)373-7232
Fax: (515)292-0020
Ronald Manning, State Dir.

Iowa State University
Small Business Development Center
ISU Branch Office
2501 N. Loop Dr.
Bldg. 1, Ste. 608
Ames, Iowa 50010-8283
Phone: (515)296-7828
Free: (800)373-7232
Fax: (515)296-9910
Steve Carter, Dir.

DMACC Small Business Development
Center
Circle West Incubator
PO Box 204
Audubon, Iowa 50025
Phone: (712)563-2623
Fax: (712)563-2301
Lori Harmening-Webb, Dir.

University of Northern Iowa
Small Business Development Center
Business Bldg., Ste. 5
Cedar Falls, Iowa 50614-0120
Phone: (319)273-2696

Fax:(319)273-6830
Lyle Bowlin, Dir.

Iowa Western Community College
Small Business Development Center
2700 College Rd., Box 4C
Council Bluffs, Iowa 51502
Phone:(712)325-3260
Fax:(712)325-3408
Ronald Helms, Dir.

Southwestern Community College
Small Business Development Center
1501 W. Townline Rd.
Creston, Iowa 50801
Phone:(515)782-4161
Fax:(515)782-4164
Paul Havick, Dir.

Eastern Iowa Community College
District
Eastern Iowa Small Business Develop-
ment Center
304 W. 2nd St.
Davenport, Iowa 52801
Phone:(319)322-4499
Fax:(319)322-8241
Jon Ryan, Dir.

Drake University
Small Business Development Center
Drake Business Center
2429 University Ave.
Des Moines, Iowa 50311-4505
Phone:(515)271-2655
Fax:(515)271-4540
Benjamin Swartz, Dir.

Northeast Iowa Small Business
Development Center
770 Town Clock Plz.
Dubuque, Iowa 52001
Phone:(319)588-3350
Fax:(319)557-1591
Charles Tonn, Contact

Iowa Central Community College
SBDC
900 Central Ave., Ste. 4
Fort Dodge, Iowa 50501
Phone:(515)576-0099
Fax:(515)576-0826
Todd Madson, Dir.

University of Iowa
Small Business Development Center
108 Papajohn Business Administra-
tion Bldg., Ste. S-160
Iowa City, Iowa 52242-1000
Phone:(319)335-3742
Free:(800)253-7232
Fax:(319)353-2445
Paul Heath, Dir.
E-mail: paul-heath@uiowa.edu

Kirkwood Community College
Small Business Development Center
2901 10th Ave.
Marion, Iowa 52302
Phone:(319)377-8256
Fax:(319)377-5667
Jim Anderson, Dir.

North Iowa Area Community College
Small Business Development Center
500 College Dr.
Mason City, Iowa 50401
Phone:(515)421-4342
Fax:(515)423-0931
Richard Petersen, Dir.

Indian Hills Community College
Small Business Development Center
525 Grandview Ave.
Ottumwa, Iowa 52501
Phone:(515)683-5127
Fax:(515)683-5263
Bryan Ziegler, Dir.

Western Iowa Tech Community
College
Small Business Development Center
4647 Stone Ave., Bldg. B
Box 265
Sioux City, Iowa 51102-0265
Phone:(712)274-6418
Free:(800)352-4649
Fax:(712)274-6429
Dennis Bogenrief, Dir.

Iowa Lakes Community College
(Spencer)
Small Business Development Center
Gateway Center
Hwy. 71 N
Spencer, Iowa 51301

Phone:(712)262-4213
Fax:(712)262-4047
John Beneke, Dir.

Southeastern Community College
Small Business Development Center
Drawer F
West Burlington, Iowa 52655
Phone:(319)752-2731 ext. 103
Fax:(319)752-3407

Kansas

Bendictine College
SBDC
1020 N. 2nd St.
Atchison, Kansas 66002
Phone:(913)367-5340
Fax:(913)367-6102
Don Laney, Dir.

Butler County Community College
Small Business Development Center
600 Walnut
Augusta, Kansas 67010
Phone:(316)775-1124
Fax:(316)775-1370DC
Dorinda Rolle, Dir.

Neosho County Community College
SBDC
1000 S. Allen
Chanute, Kansas 66720
Phone:(316)431-2820 ext. 219
Fax:(316)431-0082
Duane Clum, Dir.

Coffeyville Community College
SBDC
11th and Willow Sts.
Coffeyville, Kansas 67337-5064
Phone:(316)251-7700
Fax:(316)252-7098
Charles Shaver, Dir.

Colby Community College
Small Business Development Center
1255 S. Range
Colby, Kansas 67701
Phone:(913)462-3984 ext. 239
Fax:(913)462-8315
Robert Selby, Dir.

Cloud County Community College
SBDC
2221 Campus Dr.
PO Box 1002
Concordia, Kansas 66901
Phone: (913)243-1435
Fax: (913)243-1459
Tony Foster, Dir.

Dodge City Community College
Small Business Development Center
2501 N. 14th Ave.
Dodge City, Kansas 67801
Phone: (316)227-9247
Fax: (316)227-9200
Wayne E. Shiplet, Dir.

Emporia State University
Small Business Development Center
207 Cremer Hall
Emporia, Kansas 66801
Phone: (316)342-7162
Fax: (316)341-5418
Lisa Brumbaugh, Dir.

Fort Scott Community College
SBDC
2108 S. Horton
Fort Scott, Kansas 66701
Phone: (316)223-2700
Fax: (316)223-6530
Steve Pammenter, Dir.

Garden City Community College
SBDC
801 Campus Dr.
Garden City, Kansas 67846
Phone: (316)276-9632
Fax: (316)276-9630
Vern Kinderknecht, Regional Dir.

Fort Hays State University
Small Business Development Center
109 W. 10th St.
Hays, Kansas 67601
Phone: (913)628-5340
Fax: (913)628-1471
Clare Gustin, Dir.

Hutchinson Community College
Small Business Development Center
815 N. Walnut, Ste. 225
Hutchinson, Kansas 67501

Phone: (316)665-4950
Free: (800)289-3501
Fax: (316)665-8354
Clark Jacobs, Dir.

Independence Community College
SBDC
College Ave. & Brookside
PO Box 708
Independence, Kansas 67301
Phone: (316)331-4100
Fax: (316)331-5344
Preston Haddan, Dir.

Allen County Community College
SBDC
1801 N. Cottonwood
Iola, Kansas 66749
Phone: (316)365-5116
Fax: (316)365-3284

University of Kansas
Small Business Development Center
734 Vermont St., Ste. 104
Lawrence, Kansas 66044
Phone: (913)843-8844
Fax: (913)865-4400
Mike O'Donnell, Dir.

Seward County Community College
Small Business Development Center
1801 N. Kansas
PO Box 1137
Liberal, Kansas 67901
Phone: (316)624-1951 ext. 150
Fax: (316)624-0637
Tom Cornelius, Dir.

Kansas State University (Manhattan)
Small Business Development Center
College of Business Administration
2323 Anderson Ave., Ste. 100
Manhattan, Kansas 66502-2947
Phone: (913)532-5529
Fax: (913)532-5827
Fred Rice, Regional Dir.

Ottawa University
SBDC
College Ave., Box 70
Ottawa, Kansas 66067
Phone: (913)242-5200 ext. 5457
Fax: (913)242-7429
Lori Kravets, Dir.

Johnson County Community College
Small Business Development Center
CEC Bldg., Rm. 223
Overland Park, Kansas 66210-1299
Phone: (913)469-3878
Fax: (913)469-4415
Glenda Sapp, Dir.

Labette Community College
SBDC
200 S. 14th
Parsons, Kansas 67357
Phone: (316)421-6700
Fax: (316)421-0921
Mark Turnbull, Dir.

Pittsburg State University
Small Business Development Center
Shirk Hall
Pittsburg, Kansas 66762
Phone: (316)235-4920
Fax: (316)232-6440
Kathryn Richard, Dir.

Pratt Community College
Small Business Development Center
Hwy. 61
Pratt, Kansas 67124
Phone: (316)672-5641
Fax: (316)672-5288
Pat Gordon, Dir.

Kansas State University (Salina)
Small Business Development Center
2409 Scanlan Ave.
Salina, Kansas 67401
Phone: (913)826-2622
Fax: (913)826-2936
Pat Mills, Dir.

Kansas SBDC
214 SW 6th St., Ste. 205
Topeka, Kansas 66603-3261
Phone: (913)296-6514
Fax: (913)296-3490
Debbie Bishop, Dir.

Washburn University of Topeka
SBDC
School of Business
101 Henderson Learning Center
Topeka, Kansas 66621
Phone: (913)231-1010 ext. 1305

Fax:(913)231-1063
Wayne Glass, Regional Dir.
E-mail: zzglas@acc.wuacc.edu

Wichita State University
SBDC
1845 Fairmont
Wichita, Kansas 67208-0148
Phone:(316)689-3193
Fax:(316)689-3647
Joann Ard, Dir.

Kentucky

Ashland Small Business Development
Center
Morehead State University College of
Business
PO Box 830
207 15th St.
Ashland, Kentucky 41105-0830
Phone:(606)329-8011
Fax:(606)325-4607
Kimberly A. Jenkins, Dir.

Western Kentucky University
Bowling Green Small Business
Development Center
245 Grise Hall
Bowling Green, Kentucky 42101
Phone:(502)745-2901
Fax:(502)745-2902
Rick Horn, Dir.

Elizabethtown Small Business
Development Center
238 W. Dixie Ave.
Elizabethtown, Kentucky 42701
Phone:(502)765-6737
Fax:(502)769-5095
Lou Ann Allen, Dir.

Northern Kentucky University
SBDC
BEP Center 468
Highland Heights, Kentucky 41099-
0506
Phone:(606)572-6524
Fax:(606)572-5566
Sutton Landry, Dir.

Hopkinsville Small Business Development Center

Murray State University
300 Hammond Dr.
Hopkinsville, Kentucky 42240
Phone:(502)886-8666
Fax:(502)886-3211
Mike Cartner, Dir.

SBDC
Lexington Public Library, 4th Fl.
140 Main St.
Lexington, Kentucky 40507-1376
Phone:(606)257-7666
Fax:(606)257-1751
Barbara Biroschik, Program Coordina-
tor

University of Kentucky
Center for Business Development
Kentucky SBDC
225 Business and Economics Bldg.
Lexington, Kentucky 40506-0034
Phone:(606)257-7668
Fax:(606)323-1907

Bellarmine College
Small Business Development Center
School of Business
600 W. Main St., Ste. 219
Louisville, Kentucky 40202
Phone:(502)574-4770
Fax:(502)574-4771
Thomas G. Daley, Dir.

University of Louisville
Small Business Development Centers
Center for Entrepreneurship and
Technology
Burhans Hall, Shelby Campus, Rm. 122
Louisville, Kentucky 40292
Phone:(502)588-7854
Fax:(502)588-8573
Lou Dickie, Dir.

Southeast Community College
SBDC
1300 Chichester Ave.
Middlesboro, Kentucky 40965-2265
Phone:(606)242-4514
Fax:(606)242-4514
Kathleen Moats, Dir.

Morehead State University
Small Business Development Center

207 Downing Hall
Morehead, Kentucky 40351
Phone:(606)783-2895
Fax:(606)783-5020
Wilson Grier, Dir.

Murray State University
West Kentucky Small Business
Development Center
College of Business and Public Affairs
Business Bldg., Rm 253
Murray, Kentucky 42071
Phone:(502)762-2856
Fax:(502)762-3049
Rosemary Miller, Dir.

Owensboro Small Business Develop-
ment Center
Murray State University
3860 U.S. Hwy. 60 W
Owensboro, Kentucky 42301
Phone:(502)926-8085
Fax:(502)684-0714
Mickey Johnson, Dir.

Pikeville Small Business Development
Center
Moorehead State University
Rte. 7
110 Village St.
Pikeville, Kentucky 41501
Phone:(606)432-5848
Fax:(606)432-8924
Mike Morley, Dir.

Eastern Kentucky University
South Central Small Business Devel-
opment Center
107 W. Mt. Vernon St.
Somerset, Kentucky 42501
Phone:(606)678-5520
Fax:(606)678-8349
Donald R. Snyder, Dir.

Louisiana

Alexandria SBDC
Hibernia National Bank Bldg., Ste. 510
934 3rd St.
Alexandria, Louisiana 71301
Phone:(318)484-2123
Fax:(318)484-2126
Kathey Hunter, Consultant

Capital Small Business Development
Center
Southern University
1933 Wooddale Blvd., Ste. E
Baton Rouge, Louisiana 70806
Phone:(504)922-0998
Fax:(504)922-0999
Greg Spann, Dir.

Southeastern Louisiana University
Small Business Development Center
College of Business Administration
Box 522, SLU Sta.
Hammond, Louisiana 70402
Phone:(504)549-3831
Fax:(504)549-2127
William Joubert, Dir.

University of Southwestern Louisiana
Acadiana Small Business Develop-
ment Center
Box 43732
College of Business Administration
Lafayette, Louisiana 70504
Phone:(318)262-5344
Fax:(318)262-5296
Dan Lavergne, Dir.

McNeese State University
Small Business Development Center
College of Business Administration
Lake Charles, Louisiana 70609
Phone:(318)475-5529
Fax:(318)475-5012
Paul Arnold, Dir.

College of Business Administration
Northeast Louisiana University
Louisiana SBDC
700 University Ave.
Room 2-57
Monroe, Louisiana 71209
Phone:(318)342-5506
Fax:(318)342-5510
Dr. John Baker, State Dir.
Dr. Lesa Lawrence, Associate State
Dir.

Louisiana Electronic Assistance
Program
SBDC
NE Louisiana, College of Business
Administration

Monroe, Louisiana 71209
Phone:(318)342-1215
Fax:(318)342-1209
Dr. Jerry Wall, Dir.

Northeast Louisiana University
Small Business Development Center
College of Business Administration,
Rm. 2-57
Monroe, Louisiana 71209
Phone:(318)342-1224
Fax:(318)342-1209
Paul Dunn, Dir.

Northwestern State University
Small Business Development Center
College of Business Administration
Natchitoches, Louisiana 71497
Phone:(318)357-5611
Fax:(318)357-6810
Mary Lynn Wilkerson, Dir.

Louisiana International Trade Center
SBDC
World Trade Center, Ste. 2926
2 Canal St.
New Orleans, Louisiana 70130
Phone:(504)568-8222
Fax:(504)568-8228
Ruperto Chavarri, Dir.

Loyola University
Small Business Development Center
College of Business Administration
Box 134
New Orleans, Louisiana 70118
Phone:(504)865-3474
Fax:(504)865-3496
Ronald Schroeder, Dir.

Southern University—New Orleans
Small Business Development Center
College of Business Administration
New Orleans, Louisiana 70126
Phone:(504)286-5308
Fax:(504)286-3131
Jon Johnson, Dir.

University of New Orleans
Small Business Development Center
1600 Canal St., Ste. 620
New Orleans, Louisiana 70112
Phone:(504)539-9292

Fax:(504)539-9205
Norma Grace, Dir.

Louisiana Tech University
Small Business Development Center
College of Business Administration
Box 10318, Tech Sta.
Ruston, Louisiana 71271-0046
Phone:(318)257-3537
Fax:(318)257-4253

Louisiana State University at Shreve-
port
Small Business Development Center
College of Business Administration
1 University Dr.
Shreveport, Louisiana 71115
Phone:(318)797-5144
Fax:(318)797-5208
James O. Hicks, Dir.

Nicholls State University
Small Business Development Center
College of Business Administration
PO Box 2015
Thibodaux, Louisiana 70310
Phone:(504)448-4242
Fax:(504)448-4922
Weston Hull, Dir.

Maine

Androscoggin Valley Council of
Governments
Small Business Development Center
125 Manley Rd.
Auburn, Maine 04210
Phone:(207)783-9186
Fax:(207)783-5211

SBDC
Weston Bldg.
7 N. Chestnut St.
Augusta, Maine 04330
Phone:(207)621-0245
Fax:(207)622-9739

Eastern Maine Development Corp.
Small Business Development Center
1 Cumberland Pl., Ste. 300
PO Box 2579
Bangor, Maine 04402-2579
Phone:(207)942-6389

Free:(800)339-6389
Fax:(207)942-3548
Ron Loyd, Dir.

Belfast Satellite
Waldo County Development Corp.
SBDC
67 Church St.
Belfast, Maine 04915
Phone:(207)942-6389
Fax:(800)339-6389

Brunswick Satellite
Midcoast Council for Business
Development
SBDC
8 Lincoln St.
Brunswick, Maine 04011
Phone:(207)882-4340

Northern Maine Development
Commission
Small Business Development Center
2 S. Main St.
PO Box 779
Caribou, Maine 04736
Phone:(207)498-8736
Free:(800)427-8736
Fax:(207)498-3108
Rodney Thompson, Dir.

East Millinocket Satellite
Katahdin Regional Development Corp.
SBDC
58 Main St.
East Millinocket, Maine 04430
Phone:(207)746-5338
Fax:(207)746-9535

East Wilton Satellite
Robinhood Plaza
Rte. 2 & 4
East Wilton, Maine 04234
Phone:(207)783-9186

Fort Kent Satellite
SBDC
Aroostook County Registry of Deeds
Corner of Elm and Hall Streets
Fort Kent, Maine 04743
Phone:(207)498-8736
Free:(800)427-8736

Houlton Satellite
SBDC
Superior Ct. House
Ct. St.
Houlton, Maine 04730
Phone:(207)498-8736
Free:(800)427-8736

Lewiston Satellite
Business Information Center (BIC)
SBDC
Bates Mill Complex
35 Canal St.
Lewiston, Maine 04240
Phone:(207)783-9186

Machias Satellite
Sunrise County Economic Council
(Calais Area)
SBDC
Washington County Economic
Planning Commission
63 Main St., PO Box 679
Machias, Maine 04654
Phone:(207)454-2430
Fax:(207)255-0983

University of Southern Maine
Maine SBDC
96 Falmouth St.
P.O. Box 9300
Portland, Maine 04104-9300
Phone:(207)780-4420
Fax:(207)780-4810
Charles Davis, Dir.

Universiy of Southern Maine
SBDC
15 Surrenden St.
Portland, Maine 04103
Phone:(207)780-4949
Fax:(207)780-4810
John Entwistle, Dir.

Rockland Satellite
SBDC
OGA Key Bank of Maine
331 Main St
Rockland, Maine 04841
Phone:(207)882-4340

Rumford Satellite
River Valley Growth Council
Hotel Harris Bldg.
23 Hartford St.
Rumford, Maine 04276
Phone:(207)783-9186

Biddeford Satellite
Biddeford-Saco Chamber of Commerce
and Industry
110 Main St.
Saco, Maine 04072
Phone:(207)282-1567
Fax:(207)282-3149

Southern Maine Regional Planning
Commission
Small Business Development Center
255 Main St.
PO Box Q
Sanford, Maine 04073
Phone:(207)324-0316
Fax:(207)324-2958
Joseph Vitko, Dir.

Skowhegan Satellite
SBDC
Norridgewock Ave.
Skowhegan, Maine 04976
Phone:(207)621-0245

South Paris Satellite
SBDC
166 Main St.
South Paris, Maine 04281
Phone:(207)783-9186

Waterville Satellite
Thomas College
SBDC
Administrative Bldg. - Library
180 W. River Rd.
Waterville, Maine 04901
Phone:(207)621-0245

Coastal Enterprises, Inc. (Wiscasset)
Small Business Development Center
Water St.
PO Box 268
Wiscasset, Maine 04578
Phone:(207)882-4340
Fax:(207)882-4456
James Burbank, Dir.

York Chamber of Commerce
SBDC
449 Rte. 1
York, Maine 03909
Phone: (207)363-4422
Anne Arundel, Office of Economic
Development

Maryland

SBDC
2666 Riva Rd., Ste. 200
Annapolis, Maryland 21401
Phone: (410)224-4205
Fax: (410)222-7415
Mike Fish, Consultant

Central Maryland
SBDC
University of Baltimore
1420 N. Charles St., Rm 142
Baltimore, Maryland 21201-5779
Phone: (410)837-4141
Fax: (410)837-4151
Barney Wilson, Executive Dir.

Hartford County Economic Development Office
SBDC
220 S. Main St.
Bel Air, Maryland 21014
Phone: (410)893-3837
Fax: (410)879-8043
Maurice Brown, Consultant

Maryland Small Business Development Center
7100 Baltimore Ave., Ste. 401
College Park, Maryland 20740
Phone: (301)403-8300
Fax: (301)403-8303
James N. Graham, State Dir.

University of Maryland
SBDC
Dingman Center for Entrepreneurship
College of Business and Management
College Park, Maryland 20742-1815
Phone: (301)405-2144
Fax: (301)314-9152

Howard County Economic Development Office

SBDC
6751 Gateway Dr., Ste. 500
Columbia, Maryland 21043
Phone: (410)313-6552
Fax: (410)313-6556
Ellin Dize, Consultant

Western Region
SBDC
3 Commerce Dr.
Cumberland, Maryland 21502
Phone: (301)724-6716
Free: (800)457-7232
Fax: (301)777-7504
Rubert Douglas, Exec. Dir.

Cecil County Chamber of Commerce
SBDC
135 E. Main St.
Elkton, Maryland 21921
Phone: (410)392-0597
Fax: (410)392-6225
Maurice Brown, Consultant

Frederick Community College
SBDC
7932 Opossumtown Pike
Frederick, Maryland 21702
Phone: (301)846-2683
Fax: (301)846-2689
Mary Ann Garst, Program Dir.

Arundel Center N.
SBDC
101 Crain Hwy., NW, Rm. 110B
Glen Burnie, Maryland 21601
Phone: (410)766-1910
Fax: (410)766-1911
Mike Fish, Consultant

Community College at Saint Mary's County
SBDC
PO Box 98, Great Mills Rd.
Great Mills, Maryland 20634
Phone: (301)868-6679
Fax: (301)868-7392
James Shepherd
E-mail: Business Analyst

Hagerstown Junior College
SBDC
Technology Innovation Center

11404 Robinwood Dr.
Hagerstown, Maryland 21740
Phone: (301)797-0327
Fax: (301)777-7504
Tonya Fleming Brockett, Dir.

Suburban Washington Region Small Business Development Center
1400 McCormick Dr., Ste. 282
Landover, Maryland 20785
Phone: (301)883-6491
Fax: (301)883-6479
Monika Wilkerson, Executive Dir.

Landover SBDC
7950 New Hampshire Ave., 2nd Fl.
Langley Park, Maryland 20903
Phone: (301)445-7324
Fax: (301)883-6479
Avon Evans, Consultant

Southern Maryland
Charles County Community College
SBDC
P.O. Box 910
Mitchell Rd.
LaPlata, Maryland 20646
Phone: (301)934-7580
Fax: (301)934-7681
Betsy Cooksey, Dir.

Garrett Community College
SBDC
Mosser Rd.
McHenry, Maryland 21541
Phone: (301)387-6666 ext. 180
Fax: (301)387-3096
Sandy Major, Business Analyst

Salisbury State University
Eastern Shore Region Small Business Development Center
Power Professional Bldg., Ste. 400
Salisbury, Maryland 21801
Phone: (410)546-4325
Free: (800)999-SBDC
Fax: (410)548-5389
John Dillard, Exec. Dir.

Baltimore County Chamber of Commerce
SBDC
102 W. Pennsylvania Ave., Ste. 402

Towson, Maryland 21204
Phone: (410)832-5866
Fax: (410)821-9901
John Casper, Consultant

Carrol County Economic Development
Office
SBDC
125 N. Court St., Rm. 101
Westminster, Maryland 21157
Phone: (410)857-8166
Fax: (410)848-0003
Michael Fish, Consultant

Eastern Region - Upper Shore SBDC
Chesapeake College
PO Box 8
Wye Mills, Maryland 21679
Phone: (410)822-5400 ext. 339
Free: (800)762-SBDC
Fax: (410)827-5286
Patricia Ann Marie Schaller, Consult-
ant

Massachusetts

International Trade Center
University of Massachusetts Amherst
SBDC
205 School of Management
Amherst, Massachusetts 01003-4935
Phone: (413)545-6301
Fax: (413)545-1273

University of Massachusetts
Massachusetts SBDC
205 School of Management
Amherst, Massachusetts 01003-4935
Phone: (413)545-6301
Fax: (413)545-1273
John Ciccarelli, State Dir.

Massachusetts Export Center
World Trade Center, Ste. 315
Boston, Massachusetts 02210
Phone: (617)478-4133
Fax: (617)478-4135
Paula Murphy, Dir.

Minority Business Assistance Center
SBDC
University of Massachusetts Boston
Boston College of Management

5th Fl.
Boston, Massachusetts 02125-3393
Phone: (617)287-7750
Fax: (617)287-7767
Hank Turner, Dir.

Capital Formation Service
Boston College
SBDC
96 College Rd.-Rahner House
Chestnut Hill, Massachusetts 02167
Phone: (617)552-4091
Fax: (617)552-2730
Don Reilley, Dir.

Metropolitan Boston Small Business
Development Center Regional Office
Boston College
96 College Rd., Rahner House
Chestnut Hill, Massachusetts 02167
Phone: (617)552-4091
Fax: (617)552-2730
Dr. Jack McKiernan, Regional Dir.

Southeastern Massachusetts Small
Business Development Center
Regional Office
University of Massachusetts-
Dartmouth
200 Pocasset St.
PO Box 2785
Fall River, Massachusetts 02722
Phone: (508)673-9783
Fax: (508)674-1929
Clyde Mitchell, Regional Dir.

North Shore Massachusetts Small
Business Development Center
Regional Office
Salem State College
197 Essex St.
Salem, Massachusetts 01970
Phone: (508)741-6343
Fax: (508)741-6345
Frederick Young, Dir.

Western Massachusetts Small
Business Development Center
Regional Office
University of Massachusetts-Amherst
101 State St., Ste. 424
Springfield, Massachusetts 01103
Phone: (413)737-6712

Fax: (413)737-2312
Dianne Fuller Doherty, Dir.

Clark University
Central Massachusetts Small Busi-
ness Development Center Regional
Office
950 Main St.
Dana Commons
Worcester, Massachusetts 01610
Phone: (617)793-7615
Fax: (617)793-8890
Laurence March, Dir.

Michigan

Lenawee County Chamber of Com-
merce
SBDC
202 N. Main St., Ste. A
Adrian, Michigan
Phone: (517)266-1465
Fax: (517)263-6065
David B. Munson, Dir.

Allegan County Economic Alliance
SBDC
Allegan Intermediate School Bldg.
2891 M-277
P.O. Box 277
Allegan, Michigan 49010-8042
Phone: (616)673-8442
Fax: (616)650-8042
Chuck Birr, Dir.

Ottawa County Economic Develop-
ment Office, Inc.
Small Business Development Center
6676 Lake Michigan Dr.
PO Box 539
Allendale, Michigan 49401-0539
Phone: (616)892-4120
Fax: (616)895-6670
Ken Rizzio, Dir.

Gratiot Area Chamber of Commerce
SBDC
110 W. Superior St.
P.O. Box 516
Alma, Michigan 48801-0516
Phone: (517)463-5525

Alpena Community College
SBDC
666 Johnson St.
Alpena, Michigan 49707
Phone: (517)356-9021 ext. 296
Fax: (517)356-7507
Bob Munroe, Dir.

MMTC SBDC
2901 Hubbard Rd.
PO Box 1485
Ann Arbor, Michigan 48106-1485
Phone: (313)769-4110
Fax: (313)769-4064
Bill Loomis, Dir.

Huron County Economic Develop-
ment Corp.
Small Business Development Center
Huron County Bldg., Rm. 303
250 E. Huron
Bad Axe, Michigan 48413
Phone: (517)269-6431
Fax: (517)269-7221
Carl Osentoski, Dir.

Battle Creek Area Chamber of Com-
merce
SBDC
4 Riverwalk Centre
34 W. Jackson, Ste. A
Battle Creek, Michigan 49017
Phone: (616)962-4076
Fax: (616)962-4076
Kathy Perrett, Dir.

Bay Area Chamber of Commerce
SBDC
901 Saginaw
Bay City, Michigan 48708
Phone: (517)893-4567
Fax: (517)893-7016
Cheryl Hiner, Dir.

Lake Michigan College Corporation
and Community Development
Small Business Development Center
2755 E. Napier
Benton Harbor, Michigan 49022-1899
Phone: (616)927-8179
Fax: (616)927-8103
Milt Richter, Dir.

Ferris State University
Small Business Development Center
330 Oak St.
West 115
Big Rapids, Michigan 49307
Phone: (616)592-3553
Fax: (616)592-3539
Lora Swenson, Dir.
E-mail: yc26@ferris.bitnet

Northern Lakes Economic Alliance
SBDC
1048 East Main St.
P.O. Box 8
Boyne City, Michigan 49712-0008
Phone: (616)582-6482
Fax: (616)582-3213
Thomas Johnson, Dir.

Livingston County Small Business
Development Center (Brighton)
131 S. Hyne
Brighton, Michigan 48116
Phone: (810)227-3556
Fax: (810)227-3080
Dennis Whitney, Dir.

Buchanan Chamber of Commerce
SBDC
119 Main St.
Buchanan, Michigan 49107
Phone: (616)695-3291
Fax: (616)695-4250
Marlene Gauer, Dir.

Tuscola County Economic Develop-
ment Corp.
Small Business Development Center
194 N. State St., Ste. 200
Caro, Michigan 48723
Phone: (517)673-2849
Fax: (517)673-2517
James McLoskey, Dir.

Branch County Economic Growth
Alliance
SBDC
20 Division St.
Coldwater, Michigan 49036
Phone: (517)278-4146
Fax: (517)278-8369
Joyce Elferdink, Dir.

University of Detroit Mercy
NILAC Small Business Development
Center
4001 W. McNichols, Rm. 105
Commerce and Finance Bldg.
PO Box 19900
Detroit, Michigan 48219-0900
Phone: (313)993-1115
Fax: (313)993-1115
Ram Kesavan, Dir.

Wayne State University
Michigan SBDC
E-mail: stateoffice@misbdc.wayne.edu
2727 Second Ave.
Detroit, Michigan 48201
Phone: (313)964-1798
Fax: (313)964-3648
Ronald R. Hall, State Dir.

Wayne State University
2727 2nd Ave., Rm. 107
Detroit, Michigan 48201
Phone: (313)577-4850
Fax: (313)577-8933
Kevin Lauderdale, Dir.

First Step, Inc.
Small Business Development Center
2415 14th Ave., S.
Escanaba, Michigan 49829
Phone: (906)786-9234
Fax: (906)786-4422
David Gillis, Dir.

Community Capital Development
Corp.
SBDC
711 N. Saginaw, Ste. 123
Walter Ruether Center
Flint, Michigan 48503
Phone: (810)239-5847
Fax: (810)239-5575
Bobby Wells, Dir.

Center For Continuing Education-
Macomb Community College
SBDC
32101 Caroline
Fraser, Michigan 48026
Phone: (810)296-3516
Fax: (810)293-0427

North Central Michigan College
SBDC
800 Livingston Blvd.
Gaylor, Michigan 49735
Phone: (517)731-0071

Association of Commerce and
Industry
SBDC
1 S. Harbor Ave.
PO Box 509
Grand Haven, Michigan 49417
Phone: (616)846-3153
Fax: (616)842-0379
Karen K. Benson, Dir.

Grand Valley State University
SBDC
301 W. Fulton St., Ste. 718S
Grand Rapids, Michigan 49504
Phone: (616)771-6693
Fax: (616)771-6805
Carol R. Lopucki, Dir.

The Right Place Program
SBDC
820 Monroe NW, Ste. 350
Grand Rapids, Michigan 49503-1423
Phone: (616)771-0571
Fax: (616)458-3768
Raymond P. DeWinkle, Dir.

Oceana County Economic Develop-
ment Corp.
100 State St.
PO Box 168
Hart, Michigan 49420-0168
Phone: (616)873-7141
Fax: (616)873-5914
Charles Persenaire, Dir.

Hastings Industrial Incubator
SBDC
1035 E. State St.
Hastings, Michigan 49058
Phone: (616)948-2305
Fax: (616)948-2947
Joe Rahn, Dir.

Greater Gratiot Development, Inc.
Small Business Center
136 S. Main
Ithaca, Michigan 48847

Phone: (517)875-2083
Fax: (517)875-2990
Don Schurr, Dir.

Jackson Business Development
Center
414 N. Jackson St.
Jackson, Michigan 49201
Phone: (517)787-0442
Fax: (517)787-3960
Dwayne K. Miller, Dir.

Kalamazoo College
Small Business Development Center
Stryker Center for Management
Studies
1327 Academy St.
Kalamazoo, Michigan 49006-3200
Phone: (616)337-7350
Fax: (616)337-7415
Carl R. Shook, Dir.

Lansing Community College
Small Business Development Center
PO Box 40010
Lansing, Michigan 48901-7210
Phone: (517)483-1921
Fax: (517)483-1675
Deleski Smith, Dir.

Lapeer Development Corp.
Small Business Development Center
449 McCormick Dr.
Lapeer, Michigan 48446
Phone: (810)667-0080
Fax: (810)667-3541
Patricia Crawford Lucas, Dir.

Midland Chamber of Commerce
SBDC
300 Rodd St.
Midland, Michigan 48640
Phone: (517)839-9901
Fax: (517)835-3701
Sam Boeke, Dir.

Genesis Center for Entrepreneurial
Development
SBDC
111 Conant Ave.
Monroe, Michigan 48161
Phone: (313)243-5947

Fax: (313)242-0009
Dani Topolski, Dir.

Macomb County Business Assistance
Network
Small Business Development Center
115 S. Groesbeck Hwy.
Mount Clemens, Michigan 48043
Phone: (810)469-5118
Fax: (810)469-6787
Donald Morandini, Dir.

Central Michigan University
Small Business Development Center
256 Applied Business Studies
Complex
Mount Pleasant, Michigan 48859
Phone: (517)774-3270
Fax: (517)774-7992
Charles Fitzpatrick, Dir.

Muskegon Economic Growth Alliance
Small Business Development Center
230 Terrace Plz.
PO Box 1087
Muskegon, Michigan 49443-1087
Phone: (616)722-3751
Fax: (616)728-7251
Mert Johnson, Dir.

Harbor County Chamber of Commerce
SBDC
3 W. Buffalo
New Buffalo, Michigan 49117
Phone: (616)469-5409
Fax: (616)469-2257

Greater Niles Economic Development
Fund
SBDC
1105 N. Front St.
Nile, Michigan 49120
Phone: (616)683-1833
Fax: (616)683-7515
Chris Brynes, Dir.

Huron Shores Campus
SBDC
5800 Skeel Ave.
Oscoda, Michigan 48750
Phone: (517)739-1445
Fax: (517)739-1161
Dave Wentworth, Dir.

St. Clair County Community Small
Business Development Center
800 Military St., Ste. 320
Port Huron, Michigan 48060-5015
Phone: (810)982-9511
Fax: (810)982-9531
Todd Brian, Dir.

Kirtland Community College
SBDC
10775 N. St. Helen Rd.
Roscommon, Michigan 48653
Phone: (517)275-5121 ext. 327
Fax: (517)275-8510

Saginaw County Chamber of Commerce
SBDC
901 S. Washington Ave.
Saginaw, Michigan 48601
Phone: (517)752-7161
Fax: (517)752-9055
James Bockelman, Dir.

Saginaw Future, Inc.
Small Business Development Center
301 E. Genesee, 3rd Fl.
Saginaw, Michigan 48607
Phone: (517)754-8222
Fax: (517)754-1715
Matthew Hufnagel, Dir.

Washtenaw Community College
SBDC
740 Woodland
Saline, Michigan 48176
Phone: (313)944-1016
Fax: (313)944-0165
Daniel Stotz, Dir.

West Shore Community College
Small Business Development Center
Business and Industrial Development
Institute
3000 N. Stiles Rd.
PO Box 277
Scottville, Michigan 49454-0277
Phone: (616)845-6211
Fax: (616)845-0207
Mark Bergstrom, Dir.

South Haven Chamber of Commerce
SBDC

300 Broadway
South Haven, Michigan 49090
Phone: (616)637-5171
Fax: (616)639-1570
Larry King, Dir.

Downriver Small Business Development Center
15100 Northline Rd.
Southgate, Michigan 48195
Phone: (313)281-0700
Fax: (313)281-3418
Paula Boase, Dir.

Arenac County Extension Service
SBDC
County Bldg.
P.O. Box 745
Standish, Michigan 48658
Phone: (517)846-4111

Sterling Heights Area Chamber of
Commerce
Small Business Development Center
12900 Hall Rd., Ste. 110
Sterling Heights, Michigan 48313
Phone: (810)731-5400
Fax: (810)731-3521

Greater Northwest Regional Small
Business Development Center
2200 Dendrinos Dr.
PO Box 506
Traverse City, Michigan 49685-0506
Phone: (616)929-5000
Fax: (616)929-5012
Richard Beldin, Dir.

Northwestern Michigan College
Small Business Development Center
Center for Business and Industry
1701 E. Front St.
Traverse City, Michigan 49686
Phone: (616)922-1720
Fax: (616)922-1722
Cheryl Troop, Dir.

Traverse Bay Economic Development
Corp.
Small Business Development Center
202 E. Grandview Pky.
PO Box 387
Traverse City, Michigan 49684

Phone: (616)946-1596
Fax: (616)946-2565
Charles Blankenship, Pres.

Traverse City Area Chamber of
Commerce
Small Business Development Center
202 E. Grandview Pky.
PO Box 387
Traverse City, Michigan 49684
Phone: (616)947-5075
Fax: (616)946-2565
Matthew Meadors, Dir.

Business Enterprise Development
Center
Walsh College/OCC
1301 W. Long Lake Rd., Ste. 150
Troy, Michigan 48098
Phone: (810)952-5800
Fax: (810)952-1875
Daniel V. Belknap, Dir.

Saginaw Valley State University
Small Business Development Center
Business and Industrial Development
Institute
7400 Bay Rd.
University Center, Michigan 48710-0001
Phone: (517)790-4388
Fax: (517)790-4983
Christine Greue, Dir.

Macomb Community College
SBDC
14500 12 Mile Rd.
Warren, Michigan 48093
Phone: (810)445-7348
Fax: (810)445-7316
Geary Maiurini, Dir.

Warren-Center Line Sterling Heights
Chamber of Commerce
SBDC
30500 Van Dyke, 118
Warren, Michigan 48093
Phone: (313)751-3939
Fax: (313)751-3995
Janet E. Masi, Dir.

Warren Chamber of Commerce
Small Business Development Center

30500 Van Dyke, Ste. 118
Warren, Michigan 48093
Phone: (313)751-3939
Fax: (313)751-3995
Janet Masi, Dir.

Minnesota

Northwest Technical College
SBDC
905 Grant Ave., SE
Bemidji, Minnesota 56601
Phone: (218)755-4286
Fax: (218)755-4289
Susan Kozojed, Dir.

Normandale Community College
(Bloomington)
Small Business Development Center
9700 France Ave. S
Bloomington, Minnesota 55431
Phone: (612)832-6560
Fax: (612)832-6352
Betty Walton, Dir.

Brainerd Technical College
Small Business Development Center
300 Quince St.
Brainerd, Minnesota 56401
Phone: (218)828-5302
Fax: (218)828-5321
Pamela Thomsen, Dir.

University of Minnesota at Duluth
Small Business Development Center
10 University Dr., 157 SBE
Duluth, Minnesota 55812-2496
Phone: (218)726-8758
Fax: (218)726-6338

Itasca Development Corp.
Grand Rapids Small Business Development Center
19 NE 3rd St.
Grand Rapids, Minnesota 55744
Phone: (218)327-2241
Fax: (218)327-2242
John Damjanovich, Dir.

Hibbing Community College
Small Business Development Center
1515 E. 25th St.
Hibbing, Minnesota 55746

Phone: (218)262-6703
Fax: (218)262-6717
Allen Jackson, Dir.

Rainy River Community College
Small Business Development Center
1501 Hwy. 71
International Falls, Minnesota 56649
Phone: (218)285-2255
Fax: (218)285-2239

Region Nine Development Commission
SBDC
410 Jackson St.
PO Box 3367
Mankato, Minnesota 56002-3367
Phone: (507)387-5643
Fax: (507)387-7105
Alison McKenzie, Dir.

Southwest State University
Small Business Development Center
Science and Technical Resource
Center, Ste. 105
Marshall, Minnesota 56258
Phone: (507)537-7386
Fax: (507)537-6094
Jack Hawk, Dir.

Minnesota Project Innovation
Small Business Development Center
The Mill Pl., Ste. 400
111 3rd Ave. S., Ste. 100
Minneapolis, Minnesota 55401
Phone: (612)338-3280
Fax: (612)338-3483
Randall Olson, Dir.

University of St. Thomas
SBDC
1000 La Salle Ave.
Ste. MPL 100
Minneapolis, Minnesota 55403
Phone: (612)962-4500
Fax: (612)962-4410
Gregg Schneider, Dir.

Moorhead State University
Small Business Development Center
1104 7th Ave. S.
SU Box 303
Moorhead, Minnesota 56563
Phone: (218)236-2289

Fax: (218)236-2280
Len Sliwoski, Dir.

Owatonna Incubator, Inc. SBDC
560 Dunnell Dr., Ste. 203
PO Box 505
Owatonna, Minnesota 55060
Phone: (507)451-0517
Fax: (507)455-2788
Lisa McGinnis, Dir.

Pine Technical College
Small Business Development Center
1100 4th St.
Pine City, Minnesota 55063
Phone: (612)629-7340
Fax: (612)629-7603
John Sparling, Dir.

Hennepin Technical College
SBDC
1820 N. Xenium Lane
Plymouth, Minnesota 55441
Phone: (612)550-7218
Fax: (612)550-7272
Danelle Wolf, Dir.

Pottery Business and Tech. Center
Small Business Development Center
2000 Pottery Pl. Dr., Ste. 339
Red Wing, Minnesota 55066
Phone: (612)388-4079
Fax: (612)385-2251
Marv Bollum, Dir.

Rochester Community College
Small Business Development Center
Hwy. 14 E.
851 30th Ave. SE
Rochester, Minnesota 55904
Phone: (507)285-7536
Fax: (507)280-5502
Ellen Nelson, Dir.

Dakota County Technical College
Small Business Development Center
1300 E. 145th St.
Rosemount, Minnesota 55068
Phone: (612)423-8262
Fax: (612)322-5156
Tom Trutna, Dir.

Dakota County Technical College
SBDC
1300 145th St. E.
Rosemount, Minnesota 55068
Phone: (612)423-8262
Fax: (612)322-5156
Tom Trutna, Dir.

Southeast Minnesota Development
Corp.
SBDC
111 W. Jessie St.
Rushford, Minnesota 55971
Phone: (507)864-7557
Fax: (507)864-2091
Terry Erickson, Dir.

St. Cloud State University
Small Business Development Center
4191 2nd St. S.
St. Cloud, Minnesota 56301-3761
Phone: (612)255-4842
Fax: (612)255-4957
Dawn Jensen-Ragnier, Dir.

Department of Trade and Economic
Development
Minnesota SBDC
500 Metro Sq.
121 7th Pl. E.
St. Paul, Minnesota 55101-2146
Phone: (612)297-5770
Fax: (612)296-1290

Mesabi Community College
Small Business Development Center
820-N. 9th St., Olcott Plaza, Ste. 140
Virginia, Minnesota 55792
Phone: (218)741-4251
Fax: (218)741-4249
John Freeland, Dir.

Wadena Chamber of Commerce
SBDC
222 2nd St., SE
Wadena, Minnesota 56482
Phone: (218)631-1502
Fax: (218)631-2396
Paul Kinn, Dir.

Northeast Metro Technical College
SBDC
3300 Century Ave., N., Ste. 200-D

White Bear Lake, Minnesota 55110-
1894
Phone: (612)779-5764
Fax: (612)779-5802
Bob Rodine, Dir.

Mississippi

Northeast Mississippi Community
College
SBDC
Holiday Hall, 2nd Fl.
Booneville, Mississippi 38829
Phone: (601)728-7751
Fax: (601)728-1165
Kenny Holt, Dir.

Delta State University
Small Business Development Center
PO Box 3235 DSU
Cleveland, Mississippi 38733
Phone: (601)846-4236
Fax: (601)846-4235
John Brandon, Dir.

East Central Community College
SBDC
PO Box 129
Decatur, Mississippi 39327
Phone: (601)635-2111
Fax: (601)635-2150
Ronald Westbrook, Dir.

Jones County Junior College
SBDC
900 Court St.
Ellisville, Mississippi 39437
Phone: (601)477-4165
Fax: (601)477-4152
Ken Dupre, Dir.

Gulf Coast Community College
SBDC
Jackson County Campus
PO Box 100
Gautier, Mississippi 39553
Phone: (601)497-9595
Fax: (601)497-9604
Dean Brown, Dir.

Mississippi Delta Community College
Small Business Development Center
PO Box 5607

Greenville, Mississippi 38704-5607
Phone: (601)378-8183
Fax: (601)378-5349
Chuck Herring, Dir.

MS Delta Community College
SBDC
P.O. Box 5607
Greenville, Mississippi 38704-5607
Phone: (601)378-8183
Fax: (601)378-5349
Chuch Herring, Dir.

Mississippi Contract Procurement
Center
SBDC
3015 12th St.
PO Box 610
Gulfport, Mississippi 39502-0610
Phone: (601)864-2961
Fax: (601)864-2969
C. W. "Skip" Ryland, Exec. Dir.

Pearl River Community College
Small Business Development Center
5448 U.S. Hwy. 49 S.
Hattiesburg, Mississippi 39401
Phone: (601)544-0030
Fax: (601)544-0032
Heidi McDuffie, Dir.

Mississippi Valley State University
Affiliate SBDC
Itta Bena, Mississippi 38941
Phone: (601)254-3601
Fax: (601)254-6704
Dr. Cliff Williams, Dir.

Jackson State University
Small Business Development Center
Jackson Enterprise Center, Ste. A-1
931 Hwy. 80 W
Box 43
Jackson, Mississippi 39204
Phone: (601)968-2795
Fax: (601)968-2796
Henry Thomas, Dir.

University of Southern Mississippi
Small Business Development Center
136 Beach Park Pl.
Long Beach, Mississippi 39560
Phone: (601)865-4578

Fax:(601)865-4581
Lucy Betcher, Dir.

Alcorn State University
SBDC
PO Box 90
Lorman, Mississippi 39096-9402
Phone:(601)877-6684
Fax:(601)877-6266
Sharon Witty, Dir.

Meridian Community College
Small Business Development Center
910 Hwy. 19 N
Meridian, Mississippi 39307
Phone:(601)482-7445
Fax:(601)482-5803
Kathy Braddock, Dir.

Mississippi State University
Small Business Development Center
PO Drawer 5288
Mississippi State, Mississippi 39762
Phone:(601)325-8684
Fax:(601)325-4016
Sonny Fisher, Dir.

Copiah-Lincoln Community College
Small Business Development Center
823 Hwy. 61 N.
Natchez, Mississippi 39120
Phone:(601)445-5254
Fax:(601)445-5254
Bob D. Russ, Dir.

Hinds Community College
Small Business Development Center/
International Trade Center
PO Box 1170
Raymond, Mississippi 39154
Phone:(601)857-3537
Fax:(601)857-3535
Marguerita Wall, Dir.

Holmes Community College
SBDC
412 W. Ridgeland Ave.
Ridgeland, Mississippi 39157
Phone:(601)853-0827
Fax:(601)853-0844
John Deddens, Dir.

Northwest Mississippi Community
College
SBDC
8700 Northwest Dr.
DeSoto Ctr.
Southaven, Mississippi 38671
Phone:(601)342-7648
Fax:(601)342-7648
Jody Dunning, Dir.

Southwest Mississippi Community
College
SBDC
College Dr.
Summit, Mississippi 39666
Phone:(601)276-3890
Fax:(601)276-3867
Kathryn Durham, Dir.

Itawamba Community College
Small Business Development Center
653 Eason Blvd.
Tupelo, Mississippi 38801
Phone:(601)680-8515
Fax:(601)842-6885
Rex Hollingsworth, Dir.

University of Mississippi
Mississippi SBDC
E-mail: sbbyarscc.olemiss.edu
Old Chemistry Bldg., Ste. 216
University, Mississippi 38677
Phone:(601)232-5001
Fax:(601)232-5650
Raleigh Byars, State Dir.

University of Mississippi
SBDC
Old Chemistry Bldg., Ste. 216
University, Mississippi 38677
Phone:(601)234-2120
Fax:(601)232-5650
Michael Vanderlip, Dir.

Missouri

Camden County
SBDC Extension Center
113 Kansas
PO Box 1405
Camdenton, Missouri 65020
Phone:(573)346-2644

Fax:(573)346-2694
Jackie Rasmussen, B&I Spec.

Missouri PAC - Southeastern Missouri State University
SBDC
222 N. Pacific
Cape Girardeau, Missouri 63701
Phone:(573)290-5965
Fax:(573)651-5005
George Williams, Dir.

Southeast Missouri State University
Small Business Development Center
222 N. Pacific
Cape Girardeau, Missouri 63701
Phone:(573)290-5965
Fax:(573)651-5005
Frank "Buz" Sutherland, Dir.

Chillicothe City Hall
SBDC
715 Washington
Chillicothe, Missouri 64601
Phone:(816)646-6920
Fax:(816)646-6811
Nanette Anderjaska, Dir.

East Central Missouri/St. Louis
County
Extension Center
121 S. Meramac, Ste. 501
Clayton, Missouri 63105
Phone:(314)889-2911
Fax:(314)854-6147
Carole Leriche-Price, B&I Specialist

Boone County Extension Center
SBDC
1012 N. Hwy UU
Columbia, Missouri 65203
Phone:(573)445-9792
Fax:(573)445-9807
Mr. Casey Venters, B&I Specialist

MO PAC-Central Region
University of Missouri-Columbia
SBDC
E-mail: mopcik@ext.missouri.edu
1800 University Pl.
Columbia, Missouri 65211
Phone:(573)882-3597
Fax:(573)884-4297
Morris Hudson, Dir.

University of Missouri
Missouri SBDC
300 University Pl.
Columbia, Missouri 65211
Phone: (573)882-0344
Fax: (573)884-4297
Max E. Summers, State Dir.

University of Missouri—Columbia
Small Business Development Center
1800 University Pl.
Columbia, Missouri 65211
Phone: (573)882-7096
Fax: (573)882-6156
Frank Siebert, Dir.
E-mail: sbdc-c@ext.missouri.edu

Hannibal Satellite Center
Hannibal, Missouri 63401
Phone: (816)385-6550
Fax: (816)385-6568

Jefferson County Extension Center
Courthouse, Annex 203
725 Maple St.
PO Box 497
Hillsboro, Missouri 63050
Phone: (573)789-5391
Fax: (573)789-5059

Cape Girardeau County
SBDC Extension Center
815 Hwy. 25 S
PO Box 408
Jackson, Missouri 63755
Phone: (314)243-3581 ext. 283
Fax: (314)243-1606
Richard Sparks, Specialist

Cole County Extension Center
SBDC
2436 Tanner Bridge Rd.
Jefferson City, Missouri 65101
Phone: (573)634-2824
Fax: (573)634-5463
Mr. Chris Bouchard

Missouri Southern State College
Small Business Development Center
3950 Newman Rd.
107 Matthews Hall
Joplin, Missouri 64801-1595
Phone: (417)625-9313

Fax: (417)926-4588
Jim Krudwig, Dir.

Rockhurst College
Small Business Development Center
1100 Rockhurst Rd.
Van Ackeren Hall, Rm. 205
Kansas City, Missouri 64110-2599
Phone: (816)926-4572
Fax: (816)926-4588
Judith Burngen, Dir.

Northeast Missouri State University
Small Business Development Center
207 E. Patterson
Kirksville, Missouri 63501-4419
Phone: (816)785-4307
Fax: (816)785-4181
Glen Giboney, Dir.

Thomas Hill Enterprise Center
SBDC
PO Box 246
Macon, Missouri 63552
Phone: (816)385-6550
Jane Vanderham, Dir.

Northwest Missouri State University
Small Business Development Center
127 S. Buchanan
Maryville, Missouri 64468
Phone: (816)562-1701
Fax: (816)562-1900
Brad Anderson

Audrain County
Extension Center
101 Jefferson
4th Fl. Courthouse
Mexico, Missouri 65265
Phone: (573)581-3231
Fax: (573)581-3232
Judy Moss, B&I Specialist

Randolph County
Extension Center
417 E. Urbandale
Moberly, Missouri 65270
Phone: (816)263-3534
Fax: (816)263-1874
Ray Marshall, B&I Specialist

Mineral Area College
SBDC
PO Box 1000
Park Hills, Missouri 63601-1000
Phone: (573)431-4593
Fax: (573)431-2144
Bruce Epps, Dir.
E-mail: sbdc-fr@ext.missouri.edu

Three Rivers Community College
Small Business Development Center
Business Incubator Bldg.
3019 Fair St.
Poplar Bluff, Missouri 63901
Phone: (314)686-3499
Fax: (314)686-5467
John Bonifield, Dir.
E-mail: sbdc-pb@ext.missouri.edu

Washington County SBDC
102 N. Missouri
Potosi, Missouri 63664
Phone: (573)438-2671
LaDonna McCuan, B&I Specialist

Center for Technology Transfer and
Economic Development
University of Missouri—Rolla
Nagogami Ter., Bldg. 1, Rm. 104
Rolla, Missouri 65401-0249
Phone: (573)341-4559
Fax: (573)346-2694
Fred Goss, Dir.
E-mail: sbdc-rt@ext.missouri.edu

Missouri Enterprise Business Assis-
tance Center
SBDC
800 W 14th St., Ste. 111
Rolla, Missouri 65401
Phone: (573)364-8570
Fax: (573)341-6495
Rick Pugh, Dir.
E-mail: moprolla@exe.missouri.edu

Phelps County
SBDC Extension Center
Courthouse, 200 N. Main
PO Box 725
Rolla, Missouri 65401
Phone: (573)364-3147
Fax: (573)364-0436
Paul Cretin, B&I Spec.

Missouri PAC - Eastern Region
SBDC
975 Hornet Dr., Bldg. 279- Wing B
St. Louis, Missouri 63042
Phone: (314)731-3533
Ken Konchel, Dir.
E-mail: mopstl@ext.missouri.edu

St. Louis County
Extension Center
207 Marillac, UMSL
8001 Natural Bridge Rd.
St. Louis, Missouri 63121
Phone: (314)553-5944
John Henschke, Specialist

St. Louis University
Small Business State University
SBDC
E-mail: sbdc-stl@ext.missouri.edu
3750 Lindell Blvd.
Saint Louis, Missouri 63108-3412
Phone: (314)977-7232
Fax: (314)977-7241
Viginia Campbell, Dir.

St. Louis County Economic Council
St. Charles County
SBDC Extension Center
260 Brown Rd.
St. Peters, Missouri 63376
Phone: (314)970-3000
Fax: (314)970-3000
Tim Wathen, B&I Specialist

Pettis County
Extension Center
1012A Thompson Blvd.
Sedalia, Missouri 65301
Phone: (816)827-0591
Fax: (816)826-8599
Betty Lorton, B&I Specialist

Southwest Missouri State University
Small Business Development Center
Center for Business Research
901 S. National
Box 88
Springfield, Missouri 65804-0089
Phone: (417)836-5685
Fax: (417)836-6337
Jane Peterson, Dir.

Franklin County
SBDC Extension Center
414 E. Main
PO Box 71
Union, Missouri 63084
Phone: (573)583-5141
Fax: (573)583-5145
Rebecca How, B&I Specialist

Central Missouri State University
SBDC
Grinstead 75
Warrensburg, Missouri 64093-5037
Phone: (816)543-4402
Fax: (816)747-1653
Bernie Sarbaugh, Coordinator

Central Missouri State University
Center for Technology
Grinstead, No. 75
Warrensburg, Missouri 64093-5037
Phone: (816)543-4402
Fax: (816)747-1653
Cindy Tanck, Coordinator

Howell County
SBDC Extension Center
217 S. Aid Ave.
West Plains, Missouri 65775
Phone: (417)256-2391
Fax: (417)256-8569
Mick Gilliam, B&I Spec.

Montana

Billings Area Business Incubator
Small Business Development Center
Montana Tradepost Authority
115 N. Broadway, 2nd Fl.
Billings, Montana 59101
Phone: (406)256-6875
Fax: (406)256-6877
Jerry Thomas, Contact

Bozeman Small Business Development
Center
Gallatin Development Corp.
222 E. Main, Ste. 102
Bozeman, Montana 59715
Phone: (406)587-3113
Fax: (406)587-9565
Darrell Berger, Contact

Butte Small Business Development
Center
Rural Economic Development Incubator
305 W. Mercury, Ste. 211
Butte, Montana 59701
Phone: (406)782-7333
Fax: (406)782-9675
Ralph Kloser, Contact

High Plains Development Authority
SBDC
710 1st. Ave. N.
P.O. Box 2568
Great Falls, Montana 59401
Phone: (406)454-1934
Fax: (406)454-2995
Suzie David

Havre Small Business Development
Center
Bear Paw Development Corp.
PO Box 1549
Havre, Montana 59501
Phone: (406)265-9226
Fax: (406)265-3777
Randy Hanson, Contact

Montana Department of Commerce
Montana SBDC
1424 9th Ave.
Helena, Montana 59620
Phone: (406)444-4780
Fax: (406)444-1872
David Elenbaas, Acting State Dir.

Kalispell Small Business Development
Center
Flathead Valley Community College
777 Grandview Dr.
Kalispell, Montana 59901
Phone: (406)756-8333
Fax: (406)756-3815
Dan Manning, Contact

Missoula Small Business Development Center
Missoula Business Incubator
127 N. Higgins, 3rd Fl.
Missoula, Montana 59802
Phone: (406)728-9234
Fax: (406)721-4584
Leslie Jensen, Contact

Sidney Small Business Development
Center
Eastern Plains RC&D
123 W. Main
Sidney, Montana 59270
Phone: (406)482-5024
Fax: (406)482-5306
Dwayne Heintz, Contact

Nebraska

Chadron State College
NBDC-Chadron
Administration Bldg.
Chadron, Nebraska 69337
Phone: (308)432-6282
Fax: (308)432-6430
Cliff Hanson, Dir.
E-mail: chanson@cscl.csc.edu

University of Nebraska at Kearney
NBDC-Kearney
Welch Hall
19th St. and College Dr.
Kearney, Nebraska 68849-3035
Phone: (308)865-8344
Fax: (308)865-8153
Kay Payne, Dir.

University of Nebraska at Lincoln
NBDC-Lincoln
Cornhusker Bank Bldg., Ste. 302
11th and Cornhusker Hwy.
Lincoln, Nebraska 68521
Phone: (402)472-3358
Fax: (402)472-0328
Irene Cherhoniak, Dir.

Mid-Plains Community College
NBDC-North Platte
416 N. Jeffers, Rm. 26
North Platte, Nebraska 69101
Phone: (308)534-5115
Fax: (308)534-5117
Dean Kurth, Dir.

Nebraska SBDC
University of Nebraska at Omaha
60th & Dodge Sts.
CBA Rm. 407
Omaha, Nebraska 68182
Phone: (402)554-2521
Fax: (402)554-3747
Robert Bernier, State Dir.

Nebraska Small Business Develop-
ment Center
Omaha Business and Technology
Center
2505 N. 24 St., Ste. 101
Omaha, Nebraska 68110
Phone: (402)595-3511
Fax: (402)595-3524
Tom McCabe, Dir.

Peter Kiewit Conference Center
SBDC
1313 Farnam-on-the-Mall, Ste. 132
Omaha, Nebraska 68182-0248
Phone: (402)595-2381
Fax: (402)595-2385
Jeanne Eibes, Dir.

Peru State College
NBDC-Peru
T.J. Majors Hall, Rm. 248
Peru, Nebraska 68421
Phone: (402)872-2274
Fax: (402)872-2422
David Ruenholl, Dir.

Western Nebraska Community
College
NBDC-Scottsbluff
Nebraska Public Power Bldg.
1721 Broadway, Rm. 408
Scottsbluff, Nebraska 69361
Phone: (308)635-7513
Fax: (308)635-6596
Ingrid Battershell, Dir.

Wayne State College
NBDC-Wayne
Gardner Hall
1111 Main St.
Wayne, Nebraska 68787
Phone: (402)375-7575
Fax: (402)375-7574
Loren Kucera, Dir.

Nevada

Carson City Chamber of Commerce
Small Business Development Center
1900 S. Carson St., Ste. 100
Carson City, Nevada 89701
Phone: (702)882-1565
Fax: (702)882-4179
Larry Osborne, Dir.

Great Basin College
Small Business Development Center
1500 College Pkwy.
Elko, Nevada 89801
Phone: (702)753-2245
Fax: (702)753-2242
John Pryor, Dir.

Incline Village Chamber of Commerce
SBDC
969 Tahoe Blvd.
Incline Village, Nevada 89451
Phone: (702)831-4440
Fax: (702)832-1605
Sheri Woods, Exec. Dir.

Foreign Trade Zone Office
SBDC
1111 Grier Dr.
Las Vegas, Nevada 89119
Phone: (702)896-4496
Fax: (702)896-8351
Robert Holland, Bus. Dev. Specialist

University of Nevada at Las Vegas
Small Business Development Center
Box 456011
Las Vegas, Nevada 89154-6011
Phone: (702)895-0852
Fax: (702)895-4095
Sharolyn Craft, Dir.

North Las Vegas Small Business
Development Center
19 W. 4th St.
North Las Vegas, Nevada 89030
Phone: (702)399-6300
Fax: (702)399-6301
Janis Stevenson, Consultant

University of Nevada at Reno
Small Business Development Center
College of Business Administration
Business Bdlg., Rm. 411
Reno, Nevada 89557-0100
Phone: (702)784-1717
Fax: (702)784-4337
Sam Males, Dir.

Tri-County Development Authority
Small Business Development Center
50 W. 4th St.
PO Box 820
Winnemucca, Nevada 89446

Phone: (702)623-5777
Fax: (702)623-5999
Terri Williams, Dir.

New Hampshire

University of New Hampshire
Small Business Development Center
108 McConnell Hall
Durham, New Hampshire 03824-3593
Phone: (603)862-2200
Fax: (603)862-4876
Elizabeth Lamoureaux, Dir.
E-mail: 1m1@christa.unh.edu

Keene State College
Small Business Development Center
Blake House
Keene, New Hampshire 03435-2101
Phone: (603)358-2602
Fax: (603)358-2612
Gary Cloutier, Regional Mgr.
E-mail: gc@cchrista.unh.edu

Littleton Small Business Development
Center
120 Main St.
Littleton, New Hampshire 03561
Phone: (603)444-1053
Fax: (603)444-5463
Liz Ward, Regional Mgr.
E-mail: eaward@christa.unh.edu

Office of Economic Initiatives
SBDC
E-mail: ahj@hopper.unh.edu
1000 Elm St. 14th Fl.
Manchester, New Hampshire 03101
Phone: (603)634-2796
Amy Jennings, Dir.

Small Business Development Center
(Manchester, NH)
1000 Elm St., 14th Fl.
Manchester, New Hampshire 03101
Phone: (603)624-2000
Fax: (603)647-4410
Bob Ebberson, Regional Mgr.
E-mail: rte@christa.unh.edu

New Hampshire Small Business
Development Center
Center for Economic Development

1 Indian Head Plz., Ste. 510
Nashua, New Hampshire 03060
Phone: (603)886-1233 ext. 225
Fax: (603)598-1164
Bob Wilburn, Regional Mgr.
E-mail: sbdc~bw@mv.mv.com

Plymouth State College
Small Business Development Center
Hyde Hall
Plymouth, New Hampshire 03264-1595
Phone: (603)535-2523
Fax: (603)535-2850
Janice Kitchen, Regional Mgr.
E-mail: janice.kitchen@plymouth.edu

SBDC
18 S. Main St., Ste. 3A
Rochester, New Hampshire 03867
Phone: (603)330-1929
Fax: (603)330-1948

New Jersey

Greater Atlantic City Chamber of
Commerce
Small Business Development Center
1301 Atlantic Ave.
Atlantic City, New Jersey 08401
Phone: (609)345-5600
Fax: (609)345-4524
William R. McGinley, Dir.

Rutgers University Schools of
Business
Small Business Development Center
Business and Science Bldg., 2nd Fl.
Camden, New Jersey 08102
Phone: (609)757-6221
Fax: (609)225-6231
Patricia Peacock, Dir.

Brookdale Community College
Small Business Development Center
Newman Springs Rd.
Lincroft, New Jersey 07738
Phone: (908)842-1900
Fax: (908)842-0203
Bill Nunnally, Dir.

Rutgers University
New Jersey SBDC
180 University Ave.

3rd. Fl. Ackerson Hall
Newark, New Jersey 07102
Phone: (201)648-5950
Fax: (201)648-1110
Brenda B. Hopper, State Dir.

Rutgers University
Small Business Development Center
Ackerson Hall, 3rd Fl.
180 University Ave.
Newark, New Jersey 07102
Phone: (201)648-5950
Fax: (201)648-1110
Leroy A. Johnson, Dir.

Bergen Community College
SBDC
400 Paramus Rd.
Paramus, New Jersey 07552
Phone: (201)447-7841
Fax: (201)447-7495
Melody Irvin, Dir.

Mercer County Community College
Small Business Development Center
1200 Old Trenton Rd.
PO Box B
Trenton, New Jersey 08690
Phone: (609)586-4800 ext. 469
Fax: (609)890-6338
Herb Spiegel, Dir.

Kean College
Small Business Development Center
East Campus, Rm. 242
Union, New Jersey 07083
Phone: (908)527-2946
Fax: (908)527-2960

Warren County Community College
Small Business Development Center
Rte. 57 W.
Washington, New Jersey 07882
Phone: (908)689-9620
Fax: (908)689-7488
Robert Cerutti, Dir.

New Mexico

New Mexico State University at
Alamogordo
Small Business Development Center
2230 Lawrence Blvd.

Alamogordo, New Mexico 88310
Phone: (505)434-5272
Fax: (505)434-5272
Dwight Harp, Dir.

Albuquerque Technical-Vocational
Institute
Small Business Development Center
525 Buena Vista SE
Albuquerque, New Mexico 87106
Phone: (505)224-4246
Fax: (505)224-4251
Roslyn Block, Dir.

South Valley
SBDC
933 Sunset SW
Albuquerque, New Mexico 87105
Phone: (505)248-0132
Fax: (505)248-0127
Steven Becerra, Dir.

New Mexico State University at
Carlsbad
Small Business Development Center
PO Box 1090
Carlsbad, New Mexico 88220
Phone: (505)887-6562
Fax: (505)885-0818
Larry Coalson, Dir.

Clovis Community College
Small Business Development Center
417 Schepps Blvd.
Clovis, New Mexico 88101
Phone: (505)769-4136
Fax: (505)769-4190

Northern New Mexico Community
College
Small Business Development Center
1002 N. Onate St.
Espanola, New Mexico 87532
Phone: (505)747-2236
Fax: (505)747-2180
Darien Cabral, Dir.

San Juan College
Small Business Development Center
4601 College Blvd.
Farmington, New Mexico 87402
Phone: (505)599-0528
Cal Tingey, Dir.

University of New Mexico at Gallup
Small Business Development Center
PO Box 1395
Gallup, New Mexico 87305
Phone: (505)722-2220
Fax: (505)863-6006
Elsie Sanchez, Dir.

New Mexico State University at
Grants
Small Business Development Center
709 E. Roosevelt Ave.
Grants, New Mexico 87020
Phone: (505)287-8221
Fax: (505)287-2125
Clemente Sanchez, Dir.

New Mexico Junior College
Small Business Development Center
5317 Lovington Hwy.
Hobbs, New Mexico 88240
Phone: (505)392-4510
Fax: (505)392-2526
Don Leach, Dir.

New Mexico State University—Dona
Ana Branch
Small Business Development Center
3400 S. Espina St.
Dept. 3DA, Box 30001
Las Cruces, New Mexico 88003-0001
Phone: (505)527-7601
Fax: (505)527-7515
Terry Sullivan, Dir.

Luna Vocational-Technical Institute
Small Business Development Center
Luna Campus
PO Drawer K
Las Vegas, New Mexico 88701
Phone: (505)454-2595
Fax: (505)454-2518
Michael Rivera, Dir.

University of New Mexico at Los
Alamos
Small Business Development Center
901 18th St., No. 18
PO Box 715
Los Alamos, New Mexico 87544
Phone: (505)662-0001
Fax: (505)662-0099
Jim Greenwood, Dir.

University of New Mexico at Valencia
Small Business Development Center
280 La Entrada
Los Lunas, New Mexico 87031
Phone: (505)866-5348
Fax: (505)865-3095
Ray Garcia, Dir.

Eastern New Mexico University at
Roswell
Small Business Development Center
57 Univ. Ave.
PO Box 6000
Roswell, New Mexico 88201-6000
Phone: (505)624-7133
Fax: (505)624-7132
Eugene Simmons, Dir.

Santa Fe Community College
SBDC
S. Richards Ave.
PO Box 4187
Santa Fe, New Mexico 87502-4187
Phone: (505)438-1343
Fax: (505)438-1237
Monica Montoya, Director

Santa Fe Community College
SBDC
Richards Ave.
P.O. Box 4187
Santa Fe, New Mexico 87502-4187
Phone: (505)438-1343
Fax: (505)438-1237
Monica Montoya, Dir.

Santa Fe Community College
New Mexico SBDC
P.O. Box 4187
Santa Fe, New Mexico 87502-4187
Phone: (505)438-1362
Free: (800)281-SBDC
Fax: (505)438-1237
Roy Miller, Dir.

Western New Mexico University
Small Business Development Center
PO Box 2672
Silver City, New Mexico 88062
Phone: (505)538-6320
Fax: (505)538-6341
Linda K. Jones, Dir.

Mesa Technical College
Small Business Development Center
PO Box 1143
Tucumcari, New Mexico 88401
Phone: (505)461-4413
Fax: (505)461-1901
Richard Spooner, Dir.

New York

State University of New York at
Albany
Small Business Development Center
Draper Hall, Rm. 107
135 Western Ave.
Albany, New York 12222
Phone: (518)442-5577
Fax: (518)442-5582
Peter George III, Dir.

State University of New York (Suny)
New York SBDCS
E-mail: kingjl@cc.sunycentral.edu
Suny Plaza, S-523
Albany, New York 12246
Phone: (518)443-5398
Free: (800)732-SBDC
Fax: (518)465-4992
James L. King, State Dir.

Binghamton University
Small Business Development Center
PO Box 6000
Binghamton, New York 13902-6000
Phone: (607)777-4024
Fax: (607)777-4029
Joanne Bauman, Dir.
E-mail: sbdcbu@spectra.net

State University of New York
Small Business Development Center
74 N. Main St.
Brockport, New York 14420
Phone: (716)637-6660
Fax: (716)637-2102
Wilfred Bordeau, Dir.

Bronx Community College
Small Business Development Center
McCracken Hall, Rm. 14
W. 181st & University Ave.
Bronx, New York 10453
Phone: (718)563-3570

Fax: (718)563-3572
Eugene Williams, Dir.

Bronx Outreach Center
Con Edison
SBDC
560 Cortlandt Ave.
Bronx, New York 10451
Phone: (718)563-9204

Downtown Brooklyn Outreach Center
Kingsborough Community College
SBDC
395 Flatbush Ave. Extension Rm. 413
Brooklyn, New York 11201
Phone: (718)260-9783
Fax: (718)260-9797

Kingsboro Community College
Small Business Development Center
2001 Oriental Blvd. Rm. 4204
Manhattan Beach
Brooklyn, New York 11235
Phone: (718)368-4619
Fax: (718)368-4629
Edward O'Brien, Dir.

State University of New York at
Buffalo
Small Business Development Center
1300 Elmwood Ave.
Bacon Hall 117
Buffalo, New York 14222
Phone: (716)878-4030
Fax: (716)878-4067
Susan McCartney, Dir.

Canton Outreach Center
Jefferson Community College
SBDC
SUNY Canton
Canton, New York 12617
Phone: (315)386-7312
Fax: (315)386-7945

Cobleskill Outreach Center
SBDC
SUNY Cobleskill
State University of New York
Warner Hall, Rm. 218
Cobleskill, New York 12043
Phone: (518)234-5528
Fax: (518)234-5272

Corning Community College
Small Business Development Center
24 Denison Pky. W
Corning, New York 14830
Phone: (607)962-9461
Free: (800)358-7171
Fax: (607)936-6642
Bonnie Gestwicki, Dir.

Mercy College/Westchester Outreach
Center
SBDC
555 Broadway
Dobbs Ferry, New York 10522-1189
Phone: (914)674-7485
Fax: (914)693-4996
Tom Milton, Coordinator

State University of New York at
Farmingdale
Small Business Development Center
Campus Commons Bldg.
2350 Route 110
Farmingdale, New York 11735
Phone: (516)420-2765
Fax: (516)293-5343
Joseph Schwartz, Dir.

Marist College Outreach Center
SBDC
Fishkill Extension Center
2600 Rte. 9, Unit 90
Fishkill, New York 12524-2001
Phone: (914)897-2607
Fax: (914)897-4653

Niagara Community College
Geneseo Outreach Center
1 College Circle
South Hall, No. 111
Geneseo, New York 14454
Phone: (716)245-5429
Fax: (716)245-5430
Charles VanArsdale, Dir.

Geneva Outreach Center
SBDC
122 N. Genesee St.
Geneva, New York 14456
Phone: (315)781-1253
Sandy Bordeau, Administrative Dir.

Hempstead Outreach Center
SBDC
269 Fulton Ave.
Hempstead, New York 11550
Phone: (516)564-8672
Fax: (516)481-4938

York College/City University of New
York
Small Business Development Center
94-50 159th St.
Science Bldg. Rm. 107
Jamaica, New York 11451
Phone: (718)262-2880
Fax: (718)262-2881
James A. Heyliger

Jamestown Community College
Small Business Development Center
PO Box 20
Jamestown, New York 14702-0020
Phone: (716)665-5754
Free: (800)522-7232
Fax: (716)665-6733
Irene Dobies, Dir.

Kingston Small Business Develop-
ment Center
1 Development Ct.
Kingston, New York 12401
Phone: (914)339-0025
Fax: (914)339-1631
Patricia La Susa, Dir.

Baruch College
Mid-Town Outreach Center
SBDC
360 Park Ave. S., Rm. 1101
New York, New York 10010
Phone: (212)802-6620
Fax: (212)802-6613
Barrie Phillip, Coordinator

East Harlem Outreach Center
SBDC
145 E. 116th St., 3rd Fl.
New York, New York 10029
Phone: (212)346-1900
Fax: (212)534-4576
Anthony Sanchez, Coordinator

Harlem Outreach Center
SBDC

163 W. 125th St., Rm. 1307
New York, New York 10027
Phone: (212)346-1900
Fax: (212)534-4576
Anthony Sanchez, Coordinator

Mid-Town Outreach Ctr.
Baruch College
SBDC
360 Park Ave. S. Rm. 1101
New York, New York 10010
Phone: (212)802-6620
Fax: (212)802-6613
Barrie Phillip, Coordinator

Pace University
Small Business Development Center
1 Pace Plz., Rm. W483
New York, New York 10038
Phone: (212)346-1900
Fax: (212)346-1613
Ira Davidson, Dir.

Niagara Falls Satellite Office
Niagara Community College
SBDC
Carborundum Center
345 3rd St.
Niagara Falls, New York 14303-1117
Phone: (716)285-4793
Fax: (716)285-4797

Onondaga Community College/
Oswego Outreach Center
SBDC
44 W. Bridge St.
Oswego, New York 13126
Phone: (315)343-1545
Fax: (315)343-1546

Clinton Community College
SBDC
136 Clinton Pointe Dr.
Lake Shore Rd., Rte. 9
Plattsburgh, New York 12901
Phone: (518)562-4260
Fax: (518)563-9759
Merry Gwynn, Coordinator

Suffolk County Community College
Riverhead Outreach Center
SBDC
Riverhead, New York 11901

Phone: (516)369-1409
Fax: (516)369-3255

SUNY at Brockport
State University at Brockport
SBDC
Temple Bldg.
14 Franklin St., Ste. 200
Rochester, New York 14604
Phone: (716)232-7310
Fax: (716)637-2182

Niagara County Community College
Small Business Development Center
3111 Saunders Settlement Rd.
Sanborn, New York 14132
Phone: (716)693-1910
Fax: (716)731-3595
Richard Gorko, Dir.

Long Island University at
Southhampton/Southampton Out-
reach Center
Suny StonyBrook
Abney Peak, Montauk Hwy.
Southampton, New York 11968
Phone: (516)287-0059
Fax: (516)287-8287

College of Staten Island
SBDC
2800 Victory Blvd.
Bldg 1A, Rm. 211
Staten Island, New York 10314-9806
Phone: (718)982-2560
Fax: (718)982-2323
Dr. Ronald Sheppard, Dir.

State University at Stony Brook
Small Business Development Center
Harriman Hall, Rm. 103
Stony Brook, New York 11794-3775
Phone: (516)632-9070
Fax: (516)632-7176
Judith McEvoy, Dir.

SUNY at Stony Brook
SBDC
Harriman Hall, Rm. 103
Stony Brook, New York 11794-3775
Phone: (516)632-9070
Fax: (516)632-7176
Judith McEvoy, Dir.

Rockland Community College
Small Business Development Center
145 College Rd.
Suffern, New York 10901-3620
Phone: (914)356-0370
Fax: (914)356-0381
Thomas J. Morley, Dir.

Onondaga Community College
Small Business Development Center
4969 Onondaga Rd.
Excell Bldg., Rm. 108
Syracuse, New York 13215-1944
Phone: (315)492-3029
Fax: (315)492-3704
Robert Varney, Dir.

Manufacturing Field Office
SBDC
Rensselaer Technology Park
385 Jordan Rd.
Troy, New York 12180-7602
Phone: (518)286-1014
Fax: (518)286-1006
Thomas Reynolds, Dir.

State University Institute of Technology
Small Business Development Center
PO Box 3050
Utica, New York 13504-3050
Phone: (315)792-7546
Fax: (315)792-7554
David Mallen, Dir.

SUNY Institute of Technology at
Utica/Rome
SBDC
P.O. Box 3050
Utica, New York 13504-3050
Phone: (315)792-7546
Fax: (315)792-7554
David Mallen, Dir.

Jefferson Community College
Small Business Development Center
Coffeen St.
Watertown, New York 13601
Phone: (315)782-9262
Fax: (315)782-0901
John F. Tanner, Dir.

SBDC Outreach Small Business
Resource Center
222 Bloomingdale Rd., 3rd Fl.
White Plains, New York 10605-1500
Phone: (914)644-4116
Fax: (914)644-2184
Maria Circosta, Coordinator

North Carolina

Asheville SBTDC
34 Wall St., Ste. 707
Asheville, North Carolina 28805
Phone: (704)251-6025

Appalachian State University
Small Business and Technology
Development Center (Northwestern
Region)
Walker College of Business
2123 Raley Hall
Boone, North Carolina 28608
Phone: (704)262-2492
Fax: (704)262-2027
Bill Parrish, Regional Dir.

University of North Carolina at Chapel
Hill
Central Carolina Regional Small
Business Development Center
608 Airport Rd., Ste. B
Chapel Hill, North Carolina 27514
Phone: (919)962-0389
Fax: (919)962-3291
Dan Parks, Dir.

University of North Carolina at
Charlotte
Small Business and Technology
Development Center (Southern
Piedmont Region)
8701 Mallard Creek Rd.
Charlotte, North Carolina 28262
Phone: (704)548-1090
Fax: (704)548-9050
George McAllister, Dir.

Western Carolina University
Small Business and Technology
Development Center (Western
Region)
Center for Improving Mountain Living

Bird Bldg.
Cullowhee, North Carolina 28723
Phone: (704)227-7494
Fax: (704)227-7422
Allan Steinburg, Dir.

Elizabeth City State University
Small Business and Technology
Development Center (Northeastern
Region)
1704 Weeksville Rd.
PO Box 874
Elizabeth City, North Carolina 27909
Phone: (919)335-3247
Fax: (919)355-3648
Wauna Dooms, Dir.

Fayetteville State University
Cape Fear Small Business and
Technology Development Center
PO Box 1334
Fayetteville, North Carolina 28302
Phone: (910)486-1727
Fax: (910)486-1949
Sid Gautam, Dir.

North Carolina A&T State University
Northern Piedmont Small Business
and Technology Development Center
(Eastern Region)
C. H. Moore Agricultural Research
Center
1601 E. Market St.
PO Box D-22
Greensboro, North Carolina 27411
Phone: (910)334-7005
Fax: (910)334-7073
Cynthia Clemons, Dir.

East Carolina University
Small Business and Technology
Development Center (Eastern Region)
Willis Bldg.
300 East 1st St.
Greenville, North Carolina 27858-4353
Phone: (919)328-6157
Fax: (919)328-6992
Walter Fitts, Dir.

Catawba Valley Region
SBTDC
514 Hwy. 321 NW, Ste. A

Hickory, North Carolina 28601
Phone: (704)345-1110
Fax: (704)326-9117
Rand Riedrich, Dir.

Pembroke State University
Office of Economic Development and
SBTDC
SBDC
Pembroke, North Carolina 28372
Phone: (910)521-6603
Fax: (910)521-6550

North Carolina SBTDC
SBDC
333 Fayette St. Mall, Ste. 1150
Raleigh, North Carolina 27601
Phone: (919)715-7272
Fax: (919)715-7777
Scott R. Daugherty, Exec. Dir.

North Carolina State University
Capital Region
SBTDC
MCI Small Business Resource Center
800 1/2 S. Salisbury St.
Raleigh, North Carolina 27601
Phone: (919)715-0520
Fax: (919)715-0518
Gary Palin, Dir.

North Carolina Wesleyan College
SBTDC
3400 N. Wesleyan Blvd.
Rocky Mount, North Carolina 27804
Phone: (919)985-5130
Fax: (919)977-3701

University of North Carolina at
Wilmington
Southeastern Region
SBTDC
601 S. College Rd.
Wilmington, North Carolina 28403
Phone: (910)395-3744
Fax: (910)350-3990
Mike Bradley, Acting Dir.

University of North Carolina at
Wilmington
Small Business and Technology
Development Center (Southeast
Region)

601 S. College Rd.
Cameron Hall, Rm. 131
Wilmington, North Carolina 28403
Phone: (910)395-3744
Fax: (910)350-3990
Mike Bradley, Dir.

Winston-Salem State University
Northern Piedmont Small Business
and Technology Center
PO Box 13025
Winston Salem, North Carolina 27110
Phone: (910)750-2030
Fax: (910)750-2031
Bill Dowa, Dir.

North Dakota

Bismarck Regional Small Business
Development Center
400 E. Broadway, Ste. 416
Bismarck, North Dakota 58501
Phone: (701)223-8583
Fax: (701)222-3843
Jan M. Peterson, Regional Dir.

Devils Lake Outreach Center
SBDC
417 5th St.
Devils Lake, North Dakota 58301
Free: (800)445-7232
Gordon Synder, Regional Dir.

Dickinson Regional Center
Small Business Development Center
314 3rd Ave. W
Drawer L
Dickinson, North Dakota 58602
Phone: (701)227-2096
Fax: (701)225-5116
Bryan Vendsel, Regional Dir.

Fargo Regional Small Business
Development Center
417 Main Ave., Ste. 402
Fargo, North Dakota 58103
Phone: (701)237-0986
Fax: (701)237-9734
Jon Grinager, Regional Mgr.

Procurement Assistance Center
SBDC
417 Main St.

Fargo, North Dakota 58103
Phone: (701)237-9678
Free: (800)698-5726
Fax: (701)237-9734

Red River Regional Planning Council
SBDC
Grafton Outreach Center
SBDC
PO Box 633
Grafton, North Dakota 58237
Free: (800)445-7232
Gordon Snyder, Regional Dir.

Grand Forks Regional Small Business
Development Center
202 N. 3rd St., Ste. 200
The Hemmp Center
Grand Forks, North Dakota 58203
Phone: (701)772-8502
Fax: (701)772-2772
Gordon Snyder, Regional Dir.

University of North Dakota
North Dakota SBDC
118 Gamble Hall
University Station Box 7308
Grand Forks, North Dakota 58202-7308
Phone: (701)777-3700
Fax: (701)777-3225
Walter "Wally" Kearns, State Dir.

Jamestown Outreach Ctr.
SBDC
210 10th St.
S.E.P.O Box 1530
Jamestown, North Dakota 58402
Phone: (701)252-9243
Fax: (701)251-2488
Jon Grinager, Regional Dir.

North Dakota Small Business Devel-
opment Center
210 10th St.
SE PO Box 1530
Jamestown, North Dakota 58402
Phone: (701)252-9243
Fax: (701)251-2488
Jon Grinager, Regional Dir.

Minot Regional
SBDC
900 N. Broadway, Ste. 300

Minot, North Dakota 58703
Phone: (701)852-8861
Fax: (701)858-3831
Brian Argabright, Regional

Minot Regional Center
Small Business Development Center
900 N. Broadway, Ste. 300
Minot, North Dakota 58703
Phone: (701)852-8861
Fax: (701)858-3831
Brian Argabright, Contact

Williston Outreach Center
SBDC
PO Box 2047
Williston, North Dakota 58801
Free: (800)445-7232
Bryan Vendsel, Regional Dir.

Ohio

Akron Regional Development Board
Small Business Development Center
1 Cascade Plz., 8th Fl.
Akron, Ohio 44308-1192
Phone: (330)379-3170
Fax: (330)379-3164
Charles Smith, Dir.

Women's Entrepreneurial Growth
Organization
Small Business Development Center
The University of Akron
Buckingham Bldg., Rm. 55
PO Box 544
Akron, Ohio 44309
Phone: (330)972-5179
Fax: (330)972-5513
Dr. Penny Marquette, Dir.

Women's Network
SBDC
1540 West Market St., Ste. 100
Akron, Ohio 44313
Phone: (330)864-5636
Fax: (330)884-6526
Marlene Miller, Dir.

Enterprise Development Corp.
SBDC
900 E. State St.
Athens, Ohio 45701

Phone: (614)592-1188
Fax: (614)593-8283
Karen Paton, Dir.

Ohio University Innovation Center
Small Business Development Center
Technical & Enterprise Bldg.
20 East Circle Dr., Ste. 153
Athens, Ohio 45701
Phone: (614)593-1797
Fax: (614)593-1795
Marianne Vermeer, Dir.
E-mail:
vermeer@ouvata.cats.ohiou.edu

WSOS Community Action Commission, Inc.
Wood County SBDC
121 E. Wooster St.
PO Box 539
Bowling Green, Ohio 43402
Phone: (419)352-7469
Fax: (419)353-3291
Tom Blaha, Dir.

Kent State University/Stark Campus
SBDC
6000 Frank Ave., NW
Canton, Ohio 44720
Phone: (330)499-9600 ext. 683
Fax: (330)494-6121

Women's Business Development
Center
SBDC
2400 Cleveland Ave., NW
Canton, Ohio 44709
Phone: (330)453-3867
Fax: (330)773-2992

Wright State University—Lake
Campus
Small Business Development Center
7600 State Rte. 703
Celina, Ohio 45822
Phone: (419)586-0355
Free: (800)237-1477
Fax: (419)586-0358
Tom Knapke, Dir.

Clermont County Area
SBDC
Chamber of Commerce

4440 Glen Este-Withamsville Rd.
Cincinnati, Ohio 45245
Phone: (513)753-7141
Fax: (513)753-7146
Dennis Begue, Dir.

University of Cincinnati
SBDC
IAMS Research Pk., MC189
1111 Edison Ave.
Cincinnati, Ohio 45216-2265
Phone: (513)948-2082
Fax: (513)948-2007
Bill Floretti, Dir.

Greater Cleveland Growth Association
Small Business Development Center
200 Tower City Center
50 Public Sq.
Cleveland, Ohio 44113-2291
Phone: (216)621-3300
Fax: (216)621-4617
Janet Haar, Dir.

Northern Ohio Manufacturing
SBDC
Prospect Park Bldg.
4600 Prospect Ave.
Cleveland, Ohio 44103-4314
Phone: (216)432-5364
Fax: (216)361-2900
Gretchen Faro, Dir.

Central Ohio Manufacturing
SBDC
1250 Arthur E. Adams Dr.
Columbus, Ohio 43221
Phone: (614)688-5176
Fax: (614)688-5001

Department of Development
Ohio SBDC
77 S. High St., 28th Fl.
Columbus, Ohio 43216-1001
Phone: (614)466-2711
Fax: (614)466-0829
Holly I. Schick, State Dir.

Greater Columbus Area Chamber of
Commerce
SBDC
37 N. High St.
Columbus, Ohio 43215-3065

Phone:(614)225-6082
Fax:(614)469-8250
Linda Steward, Dir.

Dayton Area Chamber of Commerce
Small Business Development Center
Chamber Plz.
5th & Main Sts.
Dayton, Ohio 45402-2400
Phone:(513)226-8239
Fax:(513)226-8254
Harry Bumgarner, Dir.

Wright State University/Dayton
SBDC
Center for Small Business Assistance
College of Business
310 Rike Hall
Dayton, Ohio 45435
Phone:(513)873-3503
Dr. Jeanette Davy, Dir.

Northwest Private Industry Council
SBDC
1935 E. 2nd St., Ste. D
Defiance, Ohio 43512
Phone:(419)784-3777
Fax:(419)782-4649
Don Wright, Dir.

Northwest Technical College
Small Business Development Center
1935 E. 2nd St., Ste. D
Defiance, Ohio 43512
Phone:(419)784-3777
Fax:(419)782-4649
Don Wright, Dir.

Terra Community College
Small Business Development Center
1220 Cedar St.
Fremont, Ohio 43420
Phone:(419)332-1002
Fax:(419)314-2300
Joe Wilson, Dir.

Enterprise Center
Small Business Development Center
129 E. Main St.
PO Box 756
Hillsboro, Ohio 45133
Phone:(513)393-9599

Fax:(513)393-8159
Bill Grunkemeyer, Dir.

Ashtabula County Economic Development Council, Inc.
Small Business Development Center
36 W. Walnut St.
Jefferson, Ohio 44047
Phone:(216)576-9134
Fax:(216)576-5003
Sarah Bogardus, Dir.

Kent State University Partnership
SBDC
Kent State University
College of Business Administration
Rm. 300A
Kent, Ohio 44242
Phone:(330)672-2772 ext. 254
Fax:(330)672-2448
Linda Yost, Dir.

EMTEC/Southern Area Manufacturing
SBDC
3171 Research Park
Kettering, Ohio 45420
Phone:(513)259-1361
Fax:(513)259-1303
James Ackley, Dir.

Lima Technical College
Small Business Development Center
545 W. Market St., Ste. 305
Lima, Ohio 45801-4717
Phone:(419)229-5320
Fax:(419)229-5424
Gerald J. Biedenharn, Dir.

Lorain County Chamber of Commerce
SBDC
6100 S. Boadway
Lorain, Ohio 44053
Phone:(216)233-6500
Dennis Jones, Dir.

Mid-Ohio Small Business Development Center
246 E. 4th St.
PO Box 1208
Mansfield, Ohio 44901
Free:(800)366-7232

Fax:(419)522-6811
Tim Bowersock, Dir.

Marietta College
SBDC
213 Fourth St.
Marietta, Ohio 45750
Phone:(614)376-4901
Fax:(614)376-4832
Emerson Shimp, Dir.

Marion Area Chamber of Commerce
SBDC
206 S. Prospect St.
Marion, Ohio 43302
Phone:(614)387-0188
Fax:(614)387-7722
Lynn Lovell, Dir.

Lake County Economic Development
Center
SBDC
Lakeland Community College
750 Clocktower Dr.
Mentor, Ohio 44080
Phone:(216)951-1290
Fax:(216)951-7336
Jerry Loth, Dir.

Tuscarawas SBDC
Kent State University
300 University Dr., NE
New Philadelphia, Ohio 44663-9447
Phone:(330)339-3391 ext. 279
Fax:(330)339-2637
Tom Farbizo, Dir.

Miami University
Small Business Development Center
336 Upham Hall
Oxford, Ohio 45056
Phone:(513)529-4841
Fax:(513)529-1469
Dr. Michael Broida, Dir.

Upper Valley Joint Vocational School
Small Business Development Center
8811 Career Dr.
N. Country Rd., 25A
Piqua, Ohio 45356
Phone:(513)778-8419
Free:(800)589-6963

Fax:(513)778-9237
Carol Baumhauer, Dir.

Ohio Valley Minority Business
Association
SBDC
1208 Waller St.
P.O. Box 1757
Portsmouth, Ohio 45662
Phone:(614)353-8395
Fax:(614)353-2695
Clemmy Womack, Dir.

Department of Development of the
CIC of Belmont County
Small Business Development Center
100 E. Main St.
St. Clairsville, Ohio 43950
Phone:(614)695-9678
Fax:(614)695-1536
Mike Campbell, Dir.

Kent State University/Salem Campus
SBDC
2491 State, Rte. 45 S.
Salem, Ohio 44460
Phone:(330)332-0361
Fax:(330)332-9256
Deanne Taylor, Dir.

Lawrence County Chamber of
Commerce
Small Business Development Center
U.S. Rte. 52 & Solida Rd.
PO Box 488
South Point, Ohio 45680
Phone:(614)894-3838
Fax:(614)894-3836
Lou-Ann Walden, Dir.

Springfield Small Business Develop-
ment Center
300 E. Auburn Ave.
Springfield, Ohio 45505
Phone:(513)322-7821
Fax:(513)322-7824
Rafeal Underwood, Exec.

Jefferson County Small Business
Development Center
Greater Steubenville Chamber of
Commerce
630 Market St.

PO Box 278
Steubenville, Ohio 43952
Phone:(614)282-6226
Fax:(614)282-6285
Jeff Castner, Dir.

Toledo Small Business Development
Center
300 Madison Ave., Ste. 200
Toledo, Ohio 43604-1575
Phone:(419)252-2700
Fax:(419)252-2724
Linda Fayerweather, Dir.

Youngstown/Warren SBDC
Region Chamber of Commerce
180 E. Market St.
Warren, Ohio 44482
Phone:(330)393-2565
Patricia Veisz, Mgr.

Youngstown State University
SBDC
Cushwa Center for Industrial Develop-
ment
241 Federal Plaza W.
Youngstown, Ohio 44503
Phone:(330)746-3350
Fax:(330)746-3324
Patricia Veisz, Mgr.

Zanesville Area Chamber of Com-
merce
Small Business Development Center
217 N. 5th St.
Zanesville, Ohio 43701
Phone:(614)452-4868
Fax:(614)454-2963
Bonnie J. Winnett, Dir.

Oklahoma

East Central University
Small Business Development Center
1036 E. 10th St.
Ada, Oklahoma 74820
Phone:(405)436-3190
Fax:(405)436-3190
Frank Vater
E-mail: osbdcecu@chickasaw.com

Northwestern Oklahoma State
University

Small Business Development Center
709 Oklahoma Blvd.
Alva, Oklahoma 73717
Phone:(405)327-8608
Fax:(405)327-0560
Connie Murrell, Dir.

Southeastern OK State University
SBDC
517 University
Durant, Oklahoma 74701
Phone:(405)924-0277
Fax:(405)920-7471
Claire Livingston, Bus. Dev. Specialist

Southeastern Oklahoma State Univer-
sity
Oklahoma SBDC
517 University
Station A, Box 2584
Durant, Oklahoma 74701
Phone:(800)522-6154
Fax:(405)920-7471
Dr. Grady Pennington, State Dir.

Phillips University
Small Business Development Center
100 S. University Ave.
Enid, Oklahoma 73701
Phone:(405)242-7989
Fax:(405)237-1607
Bill Gregory, Coordinator

Langston University Center
Small Business Development Center
Hwy. 33 E.
Langston, Oklahoma 73050
Phone:(405)466-3256
Fax:(405)466-2909
Robert Allen, Dir.

Lawton Satellite
Small Business Development Center
American National Bank Bldg.
601 SW "D" Ave., Ste. 209
Lawton, Oklahoma 73501
Phone:(405)248-4946
Fax:(405)355-3560
Linda Strelecki

NE Oklahoma A&M
Miami Satellite
SBDC

Dyer Hall, Rm. 307
200 I St. NE
Miami, Oklahoma 74354
Phone: (918)540-0575
Fax: (918)540-0575
Hugh Simon, Specialist

Rose State College
SBDC
Procurement Speciality Center
6420 Southeast 15th St.
Midwest City, Oklahoma 73110
Phone: (405)733-7348
Fax: (405)733-7495
Judy Robbins, Dir.
Michael Cure, Bus. Dev. Specialist

University of Central Oklahoma
SBDC
E-mail: surbach@aix1.ucok.edu
115 Park Ave.
P.O. Box 1439
Oklahoma City, Oklahoma 73101-1439
Phone: (405)232-1968
Fax: (405)232-1967
Susan K. Urbach, Dir.
Ms. Doris Kendrick, Bus. Dev.
Specialist

Carl Albert College
Small Business Development Center
1507 S. McKenna
Poteau, Oklahoma 74953
Phone: (918)647-4019
Fax: (918)647-1218
Dean Qualls, Dir.

Northeastern Oklahoma State University
Small Business Development Center
Oklahoma Small Business Development Center
Tahlequah, Oklahoma 74464
Phone: (918)458-0802
Fax: (918)458-2105
Danielle Coursey

Tulsa Satellite
Small Business Development Center
State Office Bldg.
440 S. Houston, Ste. 507
Tulsa, Oklahoma 74127
Phone: (918)581-2502

Fax: (918)581-2745
Jeff Horvath, Dir.

Southwestern OK State University
SBDC
100 Campus Dr.
Weatherford, Oklahoma 73096
Phone: (405)774-1040
Fax: (405)774-7091
Chuck Felz, Dir.
Russel Clark, Bus. Dev. Specialist

Southwestern Oklahoma State
University
Small Business Development Center
100 Campus Dr.
Weatherford, Oklahoma 73096
Phone: (405)774-1040
Fax: (405)774-7091
Chuck Felz, Dir.

Oregon

Linn-Benton Community College
Small Business Development Center
6500 SW. Pacific Blvd.
Albany, Oregon 97321
Phone: (541)917-4923
Fax: (541)917-4445
Dennis Sargent, Dir.

Southern Oregon State College/
Ashland
Small Business Development Center
Regional Services Institute
Ashland, Oregon 97520
Phone: (541)482-5838
Fax: (541)482-1115
Liz Shelby, Dir.

Central Oregon Community College
Small Business Development Center
2600 NW College Way
Bend, Oregon 97701
Phone: (541)383-7290
Fax: (541)383-7503
Bob Newhart, Dir.

Southwestern Oregon Community
College
Small Business Development Center
2110 Newmark Ave.

Coos Bay, Oregon 97420
Phone: (541)888-7100
Fax: (541)888-7113
Jon Richards, Dir.

Columbia Gorge Community College
SBDC
212 Washington
The Dalles, Oregon 97058
Phone: (541)298-3118
Fax: (541)298-3119
Mr. Bob Cole, Dir.

Lane Community College
Oregon SBDC
44 W. Broadway, Ste. 501
Eugene, Oregon 97401-3021
Phone: (541)726-2250
Fax: (541)345-6006
Dr. Edward Cutler, State Dir.

Lane Community College
Small Business Development Center
1059 Williamette St.
Eugene, Oregon 97401-3171
Phone: (541)726-2255
Fax: (541)686-0096
Jane Scheidecker, Dir.

Rogue Community College
Small Business Development Center
214 SW 4th St.
Grants Pass, Oregon 97526
Phone: (541)471-3515
Fax: (541)471-3589
Lee Merritt, Dir.

Mount Hood Community College
Small Business Development Center
323 NE Roberts St.
Gresham, Oregon 97030
Phone: (503)667-7658
Fax: (503)666-1140
Don King, Dir.

Oregon Institute of Technology
Small Business Development Center
3201 Campus Dr. S. 314
Klamath Falls, Oregon 97601
Phone: (541)885-1760
Fax: (541)885-1855
Jamie Albert, Dir.

Eastern Oregon State College
Small Business Development Center
Regional Services Institute
1410 L Ave.
La Grande, Oregon 97850
Phone: (541)962-3391
Free: (800)452-8639
Fax: (541)962-3668
Joni Woodwell, Dir.

Oregon Coast Community College
Small Business Development Center
4157 NW Hwy. 101, Ste. 123
PO Box 419
Lincoln City, Oregon 97367
Phone: (541)994-4166
Fax: (541)996-4958
Rose Seminary, Contact

Southern Oregon State College/
Medford
Small Business Development Center
Regional Service Institute
229 N. Bartlett
Medford, Oregon 97501
Phone: (541)772-3478
Fax: (541)776-2224
Liz Shelby, Dir.

Clackamas Community College
Small Business Development Center
7616 SE Harmony Rd.
Milwaukie, Oregon 97222
Phone: (503)656-4447
Fax: (503)652-0389
Jan Stennick, Dir.

Treasure Valley Community College
Small Business Development Center
88 SW 3rd Ave.
Ontario, Oregon 97914
Phone: (541)889-2617
Fax: (541)889-8331
Kathy Simko, Dir.

Blue Mountain Community College
Small Business Development Center
37 SE Dorion
Pendleton, Oregon 97801
Phone: (541)276-6233
Fax: (541)276-6819
Betty Udy, Contact

Portland Community College
Small Business Development Center
123 NW 2nd Ave., Ste. 321
Portland, Oregon 97209
Phone: (503)414-2828
Fax: (503)294-0725
Robert Keyser, Dir.

Portland Community College
Small Business International Trade
Program
121 SW Salmon St., Ste. 210
Portland, Oregon 97204
Phone: (503)274-7482
Fax: (503)228-6350
Tom Niland, Dir.

Umpqua Community College
Small Business Development Center
744 SE Rose
Roseburg, Oregon 97470
Phone: (541)672-2535
Fax: (541)672-3679
Terry Swagerty, Dir.

Chemeketa Community College
Small Business Development Center
365 Ferry St. SE
Salem, Oregon 97301
Phone: (503)399-5181
Fax: (503)581-6017
Bobbie Clyde, Dir.

Clatsop Community College
Small Business Development Center
1240 S. Holladay
Seaside, Oregon 97138
Phone: (503)738-3347
Fax: (503)738-7843
Kennetyh McCune, Dir.

Tillamook Bay Community College
Small Business Development Center
401 B Main St.
Tillamook, Oregon 97141
Phone: (503)842-2551
Fax: (503)842-2555
Mike Harris, Dir.

Pennsylvania

Lehigh University
Small Business Development Center

Ranch Business Ctr., No. 37
Bethlehem, Pennsylvania 18015
Phone: (610)758-3980
Fax: (610)758-5205
Dr. Larry A. Strain, Dir.

Clarion University of Pennsylvania
Small Business Development Center
Dana Still Bldg., Rm. 102
Clarion, Pennsylvania 16214
Phone: (814)226-2060
Fax: (814)226-2636
Dr. Woodrow Yeaney, Dir.

Bucks County SBDC Outreach Center
2 E. Court St.
Doylestown, Pennsylvania 18901
Phone: (215)230-7150
Bruce Love, Dir.

Gannon University
Small Business Development Center
120 W. 9th St.
Erie, Pennsylvania 16501
Phone: (814)871-7569
Fax: (814)871-7383
Ernie Post, Dir.

Kutztown University
Small Business Development Center
2986 N. 2nd St.
Harrisburg, Pennsylvania 17110
Phone: (717)720-4230
Fax: (717)233-3181
Katherine Wilson, Dir.

Duquesne University
SBDC
Robert Shaw Bldg.
Indiana, Pennsylvania 15705
Phone: (412)357-7915
Fax: (412)357-4514
Dr. Mary T. McKinney, Dir.

St. Vincent College
Small Business Development Center
300 Fraser Purchase Rd.
Latrobe, Pennsylvania 15650
Phone: (412)537-4572
Fax: (412)537-0919
Jack Fabean, Dir.

Bucknell University
Small Business Development Center

126 Dana Engineering Bldg., 1st Fl.
Lewisburg, Pennsylvania 17837
Phone: (717)524-1249
Fax: (717)524-1768
Charles Coder, Dir.

St. Francis College
Small Business Development Center
Business Resource Center
Loretto, Pennsylvania 15940
Phone: (814)472-3200
Fax: (814)472-3202
John A. Palko, Dir.

LaSalle University
Small Business Development Center
1900 W. Olney Ave.
Box 365
Philadelphia, Pennsylvania 19141
Phone: (215)951-1416
Fax: (215)951-1597
Andrew Lamas, Dir.

Temple University
Small Business Development Center
Rm. 6, Speakman Hall, 006-00
Philadelphia, Pennsylvania 19122
Phone: (215)204-7282
Fax: (215)204-4554
Geraldine Perkins, Dir.

University Of Pennsylvania
Pennsylvania SBDC
E-mail:
ghiggins@sec1.wharton.upenn.edu
The Wharton School
423 Vance Hall
3733 Spruce St.
Philadelphia, Pennsylvania 19104-6374
Phone: (215)898-1219
Fax: (215)573-2135
Gregory L. Higgins, Jr., State Dir.

University of Pennsylvania
SBDC
The Wharton School
409 Vance Hall
Philadelphia, Pennsylvania 19104
Phone: (215)898-4861
Fax: (215)898-1063
Clark Callahan, Dir.

Duquesne University
Small Business Development Center
Rockwell Hall, Rm. 10, Concourse
600 Forbes Ave.
Pittsburgh, Pennsylvania 15282
Phone: (412)396-6233
Fax: (412)396-5884
Mary T. McKinney, Dir.

University of Pittsburgh
Small Business Development Center
The Joseph M. Katz Graduate School
of Business
208 Bellefield
315 S. Bellefield Ave.
Pittsburgh, Pennsylvania 15213
Phone: (412)648-1544
Fax: (412)648-1636
Ann Dugan, Dir.

University of Scranton
Small Business Development Center
St. Thomas Hall, Rm. 588
Scranton, Pennsylvania 18510
Phone: (717)941-7588
Fax: (717)941-4053
Elaine M. Tweedy, Dir.

West Chester University
SBDC
319 Anderson Hall
West Chester, Pennsylvania 19383
Phone: (610)436-2162
Fax: (610)436-3170
Wilkes University

Small Business Development Center
Hollenback Hall
192 S. Franklin St.
Wilkes Barre, Pennsylvania 18766-0001
Phone: (717)831-4340
Fax: (717)824-2245
Jeffrey Alves, Dir.

Puerto Rico

SBDC
Edificio Union Plaza, Ste. 701
416 Ponce de Leon Ave.
Hato Rey, Puerto Rico 00918
Phone: (787)763-5108

Fax: (787)763-4629
Carmen Marti, State Dir.

Rhode Island

Northern Rhode Island Chamber of
Commerce
SBDC
640 George Washington Hwy.
Lincoln, Rhode Island 02865
Phone: (401)334-1000 ext. 113
Fax: (401)334-1009
Robert D. Hamlin, Case Mgr.

Newport County Chamber of Commerce
E. Bay Small Business Development
Center
45 Valley Rd.
Middletown, Rhode Island 02842
Phone: (401)849-6900
Fax: (401)849-5848
Sam Carr, Case Mgr.

Fishing Community Program Office
SBDC
PO Box 178
Narragansett, Rhode Island 02882
Phone: (401)783-2466
Angela Caporelli, Program Mgr.

South County SBDC
QP/D Industrial Park
35 Belver Ave., Rm. 212
North Kingstown, Rhode Island
02852-7556
Phone: (401)294-1227
Fax: (401)294-6897
Sue Barker, Asst. Dir.

Bryant College
Small Business Development Center
30 Exchange Terrace, 4th Fl.
Providence, Rhode Island 02903
Phone: (401)831-1330
Fax: (401)274-5410
Erwin Robinson, Program Mgr.

Enterprise Community SBDC
550 Broad St.
Providence, Rhode Island 02905
Phone: (401)272-1083
Evette McCray, Mgr.

Rhode Island/DOT
SBDC Supportive Services Program
2 Capitol Hill, Rm. 106
Providence, Rhode Island 02903
Phone: (401)277-4576
Fax: (401)277-6168
O.J. Silas, Program Mgr.

Bryant College
Export Assistance Center
SBDC
1150 Douglas Pike
Smithfield, Rhode Island 02917
Phone: (401)232-6407
Fax: (401)232-6416
Raymond Fogarty, Dir.

Bryant College
Rhode Island SBDC
1150 Douglas Pike
Smithfield, Rhode Island 02917
Phone: (401)232-6111
Fax: (401)232-6933
Douglas Jobling, State Dir.

Bryant College Koffler Technology
Center
Bryant College
1150 Douglas Pke.
Smithfield, Rhode Island 02197
Phone: (401)232-0220
Fax: (401)232-0242
Christopher Langton, Dir.

Entrepreneurship Training Program
Bryant College
SBDC
1150 Douglas Pike
Smithfield, Rhode Island 02917
Cheryl Faria, Program Mgr.

Bristol County Chamber of Commerce
SBDC
P.O. Box 250
Warren, Rhode Island 02885
Phone: (401)245-0750
Fax: (401)245-0110

Central RI Chamber of Commerce
SBDC
P.O. Box 7243
Warwick, Rhode Island 02887

Phone: (401)732-1100
Fax: (401)732-1107
William Nash, Case Mgr.

South Carolina

Aiken Small Business Development
Center
171 University Pky., Ste. 100
Aiken, South Carolina 29801
Phone: (803)641-3646
Fax: (803)641-3647
Jackie Moore, Area Mgr.

University of South Carolina at
Beaufort
Small Business Development Center
800 Carteret St.
Beaufort, South Carolina 29902
Phone: (803)521-4143
Fax: (803)521-4142
Martin Goodman, Area Mgr.

Clemson University
Small Business Development Center
College of Commerce and Industry
425 Sirrine Hall
Box 341392
Clemson, South Carolina 29634-1392
Phone: (803)656-3227
Fax: (803)656-4869
Becky Hobart, Regional Dir.

University of South Carolina
College of Business Administration
South Carolina SBDC
1710 College St.
Columbia, South Carolina 29208
Phone: (803)777-4907
Fax: (803)777-4403
John Lenti, State Director

USC Regional Small Business Devel-
opment Center
University of South Carolina
College of Business Administration
Columbia, South Carolina 29208
Phone: (803)777-5118
Fax: (803)777-4403
James Brazell, Dir.
E-mail:
brazell@univscvm.csd.scarolina.edu

Coastal Carolina College
Small Business Development Center
School of Business Administration
PO Box 1954
Conway, South Carolina 29526
Phone: (803)349-2170
Fax: (803)349-2455
Tim Lowery, Area Mgr.

Florence-Darlington Technical College
Small Business Development Center
PO Box 100548
Florence, South Carolina 29501-0548
Phone: (803)661-8256
Fax: (803)661-8041
David Raines, Area Mgr.

Greenville Chamber of Commerce
Small Business Development Center
24 Cleveland St.
Greenville, South Carolina 29601
Phone: (803)271-4259
Fax: (803)282-8549

SBDC Manufacturing Field Office
53 E. Antrim Dr.
Greenville, South Carolina 29607
Phone: (803)271-3005

Upper Savannah Council of Govern-
ment
Small Business Development Center
Exchange Building
222 Phoenix St., Ste. 200
SBDC Exchange Bldg.
PO Box 1366
Greenwood, South Carolina 29648
Phone: (803)941-8071
Fax: (803)941-8090
George Long, Area Mgr.

University of South Carolina at Hilton
Head
Small Business Development Center
Kiawah Bldg., Ste. 300
10 Office Park Rd.
Hilton Head, South Carolina 29928
Phone: (803)785-3995
Fax: (803)777-0333
Jim DeMartin, Consultant

Charleston SBDC
5900 Core Dr., Ste. 104

North Charleston, South Carolina
29406
Phone: (803)740-6160
Fax: (803)740-1607
Merry Boone, Area Mgr.

South Carolina State College
Small Business Development Center
School of Business Administration
300 College Ave.
Orangeburg, South Carolina 29117
Phone: (803)536-8445
Fax: (803)536-8066
John Gadson, Regional Dir.

Winthrop College
Winthrop Regional Small Business
Development Center
School of Business Administration
119 Thurman Bldg.
Rock Hill, South Carolina 29733
Phone: (803)323-2283
Fax: (803)323-4281
Nate Barber, Regional Dir.

Spartanburg Chamber of Commerce
Small Business Development Center
105 Pine St.
PO Box 1636
Spartanburg, South Carolina 29304
Phone: (803)594-5080
Fax: (803)594-5055
John Keagle, Area Mgr.

South Dakota

Aberdeen Small Business Development Center
226 Citizens Bldg.
Aberdeen, South Dakota 57401
Phone: (605)626-2252
Fax: (605)626-2667
Bryce Anderson, Dir.

Pierre Small Business Development
Center
105 S. Euclid, Ste. C
Pierre, South Dakota 57501
Phone: (605)773-5941
Fax: (605)773-5942
Greg Sund, Dir.

Rapid City Small Business Development Center
444 N. Mount Rushmore Rd., Rm. 208
Rapid City, South Dakota 57701
Phone: (605)394-5311
Fax: (605)394-6140
Matthew Johnson, Dir.

Sioux Falls Region
SBDC
405 S. 3rd Ave., Ste. 101
Sioux Falls, South Dakota 57104
Phone: (605)367-5757
Fax: (605)367-5755
Duane Fladland, Regional Dir.

University of South Dakota
SBDC
414 E. Clark
Vermillion, South Dakota 57069
Phone: (605)367-5757
Fax: (605)677-5272
Jeffrey Heisinger, Dir.

University of South Dakota
School of Business
South Dakota SBDC
414 E. Clark
Vermillion, South Dakota 57069
Phone: (605)677-5498
Fax: (605)677-5272
Robert E. Ashley, Jr., State Dir.

SBDC
124 1st. Ave., N.W.
Watertown, South Dakota 57201
Phone: (605)886-7224
Fax: (605)882-5049

Tennessee

Chattanooga State Technical Community College
SBDC
4501 Amnicola Hwy.
Chattanooga, Tennessee 37406-1097
Phone: (423)697-4410 ext. 505
Fax: (423)698-5653
Alan Artress, Specialist

Southeast Tennessee Development
District

Small Business Development Center
PO Box 4757
Chattanooga, Tennessee 37405
Phone: (423)266-5781
Fax: (423)267-7705
Vann Cunningham, Dir.

Austin Peay State University
Small Business Development Center
College of Business
Clarksville, Tennessee 37044
Phone: (615)648-7764
Fax: (615)648-5985
John Volker, Dir.

Cleveland State Community College
Small Business Development Center
Adkisson Dr.
PO Box 3570
Cleveland, Tennessee 37320
Phone: (423)478-6247
Fax: (423)478-6251
Don Green, Dir.

SBDC (Columbia)
Memorial Bldg., Rm. 205
308 W. 7th St.
Columbia, Tennessee 38401
Phone: (615)388-5674
Fax: (615)388-5474
Richard Prince, Senior Specialist

Tennessee Technological University
SBDC
College of Business Administration
PO Box 5023
Cookeville, Tennessee 38505
Phone: (615)372-6634
Fax: (615)372-6249

Dyersburg State Community College
Small Business Development Center
1510 Lake Rd.
Dyersburg, Tennessee 38024
Phone: (901)286-3201
Fax: (901)286-3271
Bob Wylie

Four Lakes Regional Industrial
Development Authority
SBDC
PO Box 63

Hartsville, Tennessee 37074-0063
Phone:(615)374-9521
Fax:(615)374-4608
Dorothy Vaden, SB Specialist

Jackson State Community College
Small Business Development Center
2046 N. Parkway St.
Jackson, Tennessee 38305
Phone:(901)424-5389
Fax:(901)425-2647
David L. Brown

Lambuth University
SBDC
705 Lambuth Blvd.
Jackson, Tennessee 38301
Phone:(901)425-3326
Fax:(901)425-3327
Phillip Ramsey, SB Specialist

East Tennessee State University
College of Business
SBDC
P.O. Box 70698
Johnson City, Tennessee 37614
Phone:(423)929-5630
Fax:(423)461-7080
Bob Justice, Dir.

East Tennessee State University
SBDC
Kingsport University Center
1501 University Blvd.
Kingsport, Tennessee 37660
Phone:(423)392-8017
Fax:(423)392-8017
Rob Lytle, Business Counselor

International Trade Center
SBDC
301 E. Church Ave.
Knoxville, Tennessee 37915
Phone:(423)637-4283
Fax:(423)523-2071
Richard Vogler, IT Specialist

Pellissippi State Technical Community
College
Small Business Development Center
301 East Church Ave.
Knoxville, Tennessee 37915
Phone:(423)525-0277
Fax:(423)971-4439

University of Memphis
SBDC
320 S. Dudley St.
Memphis, Tennessee 38104-3206
Phone:(901)527-1041
Fax:(901)527-1047
Earnest Lacey, Dir.

University of Memphis
International Trade Center
SBDC
Memphis, Tennessee 38152
Phone:(901)678-4174
Fax:(901)678-4072
Philip Johnson, Dir.

University of Memphis
Tennessee SBDC
S. Campus (Getwell Road)
Building 1
Memphis, Tennessee 38152
Phone:(901)678-2500
Fax:(901)678-4072
Dr. Kenneth J. Burns, State Dir.

Walters State Community College
Tennessee Small Business Develop-
ment Center
500 S. Davy Crockett Pky.
Morristown, Tennessee 37813
Phone:(423)585-2675
Fax:(423)585-2679
Jack Tucker, Dir.
E-mail: jtucker@wscc.cc.tn.us

Middle Tennessee State University
Small Business Development Center
College of Business
1417 E. Main St.
PO Box 487
Murfreesboro, Tennessee 37132
Phone:(615)898-2745
Fax:(615)898-2681
Patrick Geho, Dir.

Tennessee State University
Small Business Development Center
College of Business
330 10th Ave. N.
Nashville, Tennessee 37203-3401
Phone:(615)963-7179
Fax:(615)963-7160
Billy E. Lowe, Dir.

Texas

Abilene Christian University
Small Business Development Center
College of Business Administration
648 E. Hwy. 80
Abilene, Texas 79601
Phone:(915)670-0300
Fax:(915)670-0311
Judy Wilhelm, Dir.

Sul Ross State University
Big Bend SBDC Satellite
PO Box C-47, Rm. 319
Alpine, Texas 79832
Phone:(915)837-8694
Fax:(915)837-8104
Michael Levine, Dir.

Alvin Community College
Small Business Development Center
3110 Mustang Rd.
Alvin, Texas 77511-4898
Phone:(713)388-4686
Fax:(713)388-4903
Gina Mattei, Dir.

West Texas A&M University
Small Business Development Center
T. Boone Pickens School of Business
1800 S. Washington, Ste. 209
Amarillo, Texas 79102
Phone:(806)372-5151
Fax:(806)372-5261
Don Taylor, Dir.

Trinity Valley Community College
Small Business Development Center
500 S. Prairieville
Athens, Texas 75751
Phone:(903)675-7403
Free:(800)335-7232
Fax:(903)675-5199
Judy Loden, Dir.

Lower Colorado River Authority
Small Business Development Center
3700 Lake Austin Blvd.
PO Box 220
Austin, Texas 78767
Phone:(512)473-3510
Fax:(512)473-3285
Larry Lucero, Dir.

Lee College
Small Business Development Center
PO Box 818
Rundell Hall
Baytown, Texas 77522-0818
Phone: (713)425-6307
Fax: (713)425-6309
Kenneth Voytek, Contact

Lamar University
Small Business Development Center
855 Florida Ave.
Beaumont, Texas 77705
Phone: (409)880-2367
Fax: (409)880-2201
Gene Arnold, Dir.

Bonham Satellite
Chamber of Commerce
SBDC
110 W. 1st
Bonham, Texas 75418
Phone: (903)583-4811
Fax: (903)583-6706
Darroll Martin, Coordinator

Blinn College
Small Business Development Center
902 College Ave.
Brenham, Texas 77833
Phone: (409)830-4137
Fax: (409)830-4135
Phillis Nelson, Dir.

Bryan/College Station Chamber of
Commerce
Small Business Development Center
PO Box 3695
Bryan, Texas 77805-3695
Phone: (409)260-5222
Fax: (409)260-5208
Sam Harwell, Contact

Greater Corpus Christi Business
Alliance
Small Business Development Center
1201 N. Shoreline
Corpus Christi, Texas 78403
Phone: (512)881-1847
Fax: (512)882-4256
Oscar Martinez, Dir.

Corsicana Small Business Develop-
ment Center
120 N. 12th St.
Corsicana, Texas 75110
Phone: (903)874-0658
Free: (800)320-7232
Fax: (903)874-4187
Leon Allard, Dir.

Dallas County Community College
North Texas SBDC
1402 Corinth St.
Dallas, Texas 75215
Phone: (800)350-7232
Fax: (214)860-5813
Elizabeth (Liz) Klimback, Regional Dir.

International Trade Center
SBDC
World Trade Center, Ste. 150
2050 Stemmons Fwy.
PO Box 58299
Dallas, Texas 75258
Phone: (214)747-1300
Free: (800)337-7232
Fax: (214)748-5774
Beth Huddleston, Dir.

Bill J. Priest Institute for Economic
Development
North Texas-Dallas Small Business
Development Center
1402 Corinth St.
Dallas, Texas 75215
Phone: (214)860-5842
Free: (800)348-7232
Fax: (214)860-5881
Pamela Speraw, Dir.

Technology Assistance Center
SBDC
1402 Corinth St.
Dallas, Texas 75215
Phone: (800)355-7232
Fax: (214)860-5881
Pamela Speraw, Dir.

Texas Center for Government Con-
tracting
Small Business Development Center
1402 Corinth
Dallas, Texas 75215
Phone: (214)860-5850

Fax: (214)860-5857
Al Salgado, Dir.

Grayson County College
Small Business Development Center
6101 Grayson Dr.
Denison, Texas 75020
Phone: (903)786-3551
Free: (800)316-7232
Fax: (903)786-6284
Cynthia Flowers-Whitfield, Dir.

Denton Small Business Development
Center
PO Drawer P
Denton, Texas 76202
Phone: (817)380-1849
Fax: (817)382-0040
Carolyn Birkhead, Coordinator

Best Southwest
SBDC
214 S, Main, Ste. 102A
Duncanville, Texas 75116
Phone: (214)709-5878
Free: (800)317-7232
Fax: (214)709-6089
Herb Kamm, Dir.

DeSoto Small Business Development
Center
214 S. Main, Ste. 102A
Duncanville, Texas 75116
Phone: (214)709-5878
Free: (800)317-7232
Fax: (214)709-6089
University of Texas—Pan American

Small Business Development Center
1201 W. University Dr.
Center for Entrepreneurship &
Economic Development
Edinburg, Texas 78539-2999
Phone: (210)316-2610
Fax: (210)316-2612
Juan Garcia, Dir.

El Paso Community College
Small Business Development Center
103 Montana Ave., Ste. 202
El Paso, Texas 79902-3929
Phone: (915)534-3410
Fax: (915)534-4625
Roque Segura, Dir.

Automation and Robotics Research
Institute
SBDC
7300 Jack Newell Blvd., S.
Fort Worth, Texas 76118
Phone: (817)794-5900
Fax: (817)794-5952
Don Liles, Dir.

Tarrant County Junior College
Small Business Development Center
Mary Owen Center
1500 Houston St., Rm. 163
Fort Worth, Texas 76102
Phone: (817)244-7158
Fax: (817)244-0627
Truitt Leake, Dir.

Cooke County Community College
Small Business Development Center
1525 W. California
Gainesville, Texas 76240
Phone: (817)668-4220
Free: (800)351-7232
Fax: (817)668-6049
Cathy Keeler, Dir.

Galveston College
Small Business Development Center
4015 Avenue Q
Galveston, Texas 77550
Phone: (409)740-7380
Fax: (409)740-7381
Joe Harper, Contact/Dir.

Western Bank and Trust Satellite
SBDC
PO Box 461545
Garland, Texas 75046
Phone: (214)860-5850
Fax: (214)860-5857
Al Salgado, Dir.

Grand Prairie Satellite
SBDC
Chamber of Commerce
900 Conover Dr.
Grand Prairie, Texas 75053
Phone: (214)860-5850
Fax: (214)860-5857
Al Salgado, Dir.

Houston International Trade Center
Small Business Development Center
1100 Louisiana, Ste. 500
Houston, Texas 77002
Phone: (713)752-8404
Fax: (713)756-1500
Carlos Lopez, Dir.

North Harris Montgomery Community
College District
Small Business Development Center
250 N. Sam Houston Pky.
Houston, Texas 77060
Phone: (713)591-9320
Fax: (713)591-3513
Ray Laughter, Contact

Texas Product Development Center
Small Business Development Center
1100 Louisiana, Ste. 500
Houston, Texas 77002
Phone: (713)752-8477
Fax: (713)756-1515
Jacqueline Taylor, Dir.

University of Houston
Texas Product Development Center
1100 Louisiana, Ste. 500
Houston, Texas 77002
Susan Macy, Dir.

University of Houston
Small Business Development Center
1100 Louisiana, Ste. 500
Houston, Texas 77002
Phone: (713)752-8400
Fax: (713)756-1500
Mike Young, Dir.

University of Houston
Southeastern TX SBDC
1100 Louisiana, Ste. 500
Houston, Texas 77002
Phone: (713)752-8444
Fax: (713)756-1500
J.E. "Ted" Cadou, Reg. Dir.

Sam Houston State University SBDC
College of Business Administration
PO Box 2058
Huntsville, Texas 77341-2058
Phone: (409)294-3737
Fax: (409)294-3738
Bob Barragan, Dir.

Kingsville Chamber of Commerce
Small Business Development Center
635 E. King
Kingsville, Texas 78363
Phone: (512)595-5088
Fax: (512)592-0866
Elizabeth Soliz, Contact

Brazosport College
Small Business Development Center
500 College Dr.
Lake Jackson, Texas 77566
Phone: (409)266-3380
Fax: (409)265-7208
Patricia Leyendecker, Dir.

Laredo Development Foundation
Small Business Development Center
Division of Business Administration
616 Leal St.
Laredo, Texas 78041
Phone: (210)722-0563
Fax: (210)722-6247
David Puig, Contact

Kilgore College
Triple Creek Shopping Plaza
SBDC
110 Triple Creek Dr., Ste. 70
Longview, Texas 75601
Phone: (903)757-5857
Free: (800)338-7232
Fax: (903)753-7920
Brad Bunt, Dir.

Texas Tech University
Northwestern Texas SBDC
Spectrum Plaza
2579 S. Loop 289, Ste. 114
Lubbock, Texas 79423
Phone: (806)745-3973
Fax: (806)745-6207
Craig Bean, Regional Dir.

Texas Tech University
Small Business Development Center
Spectrum Plaza
2579 S. Loop 289, Ste. 210
Lubbock, Texas 79423
Phone: (806)745-1637
Fax: (806)745-6717
Steve Anderson, Dir.

Angelina Community College
Small Business Development Center
PO Box 1768
Lufkin, Texas 75902
Phone: (409)639-1887
Fax: (409)639-1887
Chuck Stemple, Dir.

Midlothian SBDC
330 N. 8th St., Ste. 203
Midlothian, Texas 76065-0609
Phone: (214)775-4336
Fax: (214)775-4337

Northeast Texarkana
Small Business Development Center
PO Box 1307
Mount Pleasant, Texas 75455
Phone: (903)572-1911
Free: (800)357-7232
Fax: (903)572-0598
Bob Wall, Dir.

University of Texas—Permian Basin
Small Business Development Center
College of Management
4901 E. University
Odessa, Texas 79762
Phone: (915)552-2455
Fax: (915)552-2433
Karl Painter, Dir.

Paris Junior College
Small Business Development Center
2400 Clarksville St.
Paris, Texas 75460
Phone: (903)784-1802
Fax: (903)784-1801
Pat Bell, Dir.

Paris Junior College
SBDC
2400 Clarksville St.
Paris, Texas 75460
Phone: (903)784-1802
Fax: (903)784-1801
Pat Bell, Dir.

Courtyard Center for Professional and
Economic Development
Collin SBDC
Piano Market Sq.

4800 Preston Park Blvd., Ste. A126,
Box 15
Plano, Texas 75093
Phone: (214)985-3770
Fax: (214)985-3775
Chris Jones, Dir.

Angelo State University
Small Business Development Center
2610 West Ave. N.
Campus Box 10910
San Angelo, Texas 76909
Phone: (915)942-2098
Fax: (915)942-2096
Patty Warrington, Dir.

University of Texas at San Antonio
Technology Center
University of Texas, San Antonio
1222 N. Main St., Ste. 450
San Antonio, Texas 78212
Phone: (210)458-2458
Fax: (210)458-2464
Judith Ingalls, Dir.

University of Texas at San Antonio
South Texas Border Small Business
Development Center
1222 N. Main St., Ste. 450
San Antonio, Texas 78212
Phone: (210)458-2460
Fax: (210)458-2464
Morrison Woods, Dir.

University of Texas at San Antonio
International Trade Center
SBDC
1222 N. Main, Ste. 450
San Antonio, Texas 78212
Phone: (210)458-2470
Fax: (210)458-2464
Sara Jackson, Dir.

University of Texas at San Antonio
Downtown
South Texas Border SBDC
E-mail: rmckinle@utsadt.utsa.edu
1222 N. Main, Ste. 450
San Antonio, Texas 78212
Phone: (210)458-2450
Fax: (210)458-2464
Robert McKinley, Regional Dir.

Houston Community College System
Small Business Development Center
13600 Murphy Rd.
Stafford, Texas 77477
Phone: (713)499-4870
Fax: (713)499-8194
Ted Charlesworth, Acting Dir.

Tarleton State University
Small Business Development Center
School of Business Administration
Box T-0650
Stephenville, Texas 76402
Phone: (817)968-9330
Fax: (817)968-9329
Rusty Freed, Dir.

College of the Mainland
Small Business Development Center
1200 Amburn Rd.
Texas City, Texas 77591
Phone: (409)938-7578
Free: (800)246-7232
Fax: (409)935-5186
Elizabeth Boudreau, Dir.

Tyler Junior College
Small Business Development Center
1530 South SW Loop 323, Ste. 100
Tyler, Texas 75701
Phone: (903)510-2975
Fax: (903)510-2978
Frank Viso, Dir.

Middle Rio Grande Development
Council
Small Business Development Center
209 N. Getty St.
Uvalde, Texas 78801
Phone: (210)278-2527
Fax: (210)278-2929
Patrick Gibbons, Dir.

University of Houston—Victoria
Small Business Development Center
700 Main Center, Ste. 102
Victoria, Texas 77901
Phone: (512)575-8944
Fax: (512)575-8852
Carole Parks, Dir.
E-mail: parks@jade.vic.uh.edu

McLennan Community College
Small Business Development Center
4601 N. 19th, Ste. A-15
Waco, Texas 76708
Phone: (817)750-3600
Free: (800)349-7232
Fax: (817)750-3620
Lu Billings, Dir.

LCRA Coastal Plains
SBDC
301 W. Milam
Wharton, Texas 77488
Phone: (409)532-1007
Lynn Polson, Dir.

Midwestern State University
Small Business Development Center
Division of Business Administration
3410 Taft Blvd.
Wichita Falls, Texas 76308
Phone: (817)689-4373
Fax: (817)689-4374
Tim Thomas, Dir.

Utah

Southern Utah University
Small Business Development Center
351 W. Center
Cedar City, Utah 84720
Phone: (801)586-5400
Fax: (801)586-5493
Greg Powell, Dir.

Snow College
Small Business Development Center
345 W. 100 N.
Ephraim, Utah 84627
Phone: (801)283-4021 ext. 207
Fax: (801)283-6913
Russell Johnson, Dir.

Utah State University
Small Business Development Center
E. Campus Bldg., Rm. 24
Logan, Utah 84322-8330
Phone: (801)797-2277
Fax: (801)797-3317
Franklin C. Prante, Dir.

Weber State University
Small Business Development Center

College of Business and Economics
Ogden, Utah 84720
Phone: (801)626-6070
Fax: (801)626-7423
Bruce Davis, Dir.

Utah Valley State College
Utah Small Business Development
Center
800 West 1200 South
Orem, Utah 84058
Phone: (801)222-8230
Fax: (801)225-1229
Michael Finnerty, Contact

College of Eastern Utah
Small Business Development Center
451 East 400 North
Price, Utah 84501
Phone: (801)637-1995
Fax: (801)637-4102
Patrick Glenn, Dir.

Utah State University Extension Office
SBDC
987 Lagoon St.
Roosevelt, Utah 84066
Phone: (801)722-2294
Matt Redd, Dir.

Dixie College
Small Business Development Center
225 South 700 East
St. George, Utah 84770
Phone: (801)652-7751
Fax: (801)652-7870
Jill Ellis, Dir.

Salt Lake Community College
SBDC
1623 State St.
Salt Lake City, Utah 84115
Phone: (801)957-3480
Fax: (801)957-3489
Pamela Hunt, Dir.

Utah SBDC
1623 S. State St.
Salt Lake City, Utah 84115
Phone: (801)957-3480
Fax: (801)957-3489
Mike Finnerty, State Dir.

Salt Lake Community College
Sandy SBDC
8811 S. 700 E.
Sandy, Utah 84070
Phone: (801)255-5878
Fax: (801)255-6393
Barry Bartlett, Dir.

Vermont

Brattleboro Development Credit Corp.
SBDC
PO Box 1177
Brattleboro, Vermont 05301-1177
Phone: (802)257-7731
Fax: (802)258-3886
William McGrath, Executive V.P.

Northwestern Vermont Small Business
Development Center
Greater Burlington Industrial Corp
PO Box 786
Burlington, Vermont 05402-0786
Phone: (802)658-9228
Fax: (802)860-1899
Thomas D. Schroeder, Specialist

Addison County Economic Develop-
ment Corp.
SBDC
2 Court St.
Middlebury, Vermont 05753
Phone: (802)388-7953
Fax: (802)388-8066
William Kenerson, Exec. Dir.

Central Vermont Economic Develop-
ment Center
SBDC
PO Box 1439
Montpelier, Vermont 05601-1439
Phone: (802)223-4654
Fax: (802)223-4655
Donald Rowan, Exec. Dir.

Lamoille Economic Development Corp.
SBDC
P.O. Box 455
Morrisville, Vermont 05661-0455
Phone: (802)888-4923
Chris D'Elia, Executive Dir.

Bennington County Industrial Corp.
SBDC
PO Box 357
North Bennington, Vermont 05257-0357
Phone: (802)442-8975
Fax: (802)442-1101
Chris Hunsinger, Executive Dir.

Lake Champlain Island Chamber of
Commerce
SBDC
PO Box 213
North Hero, Vermont 05474-0213
Phone: (802)372-5683
Fax: (802)372-6104
Barbara Mooney, Exec. Dir.

Vermont Technical College
Small Business Development Center
PO Box 422
Randolph Center, Vermont 05060-0422
Phone: (802)728-9101
Fax: (802)728-3026
Donald L. Kelpinski, State Dir.

Southwestern Vermont Small Business
Development Center
Rutland Economic Development Corp.
256 N. Main St.
Rutland, Vermont 05701-0039
Phone: (802)773-9147
Fax: (802)773-2772
James B. Stewart, SBDC Specialist

Franklin County Industrial Develop-
ment Corp.
SBDC
PO Box 1099
St. Albans, Vermont 05478-1099
Phone: (802)524-2194
Fax: (802)527-5258
Timothy J. Soule, Executive Dir.

Northeastern Vermont Small Business
Development Center
PO Box 630
St. Johnsbury, Vermont 05819-0630
Phone: (802)748-1014
Fax: (802)748-1223
Charles E. Carter, Exec. Dir.

Southeastern Vermont Small Business
Development Center
Springfield Development Corp.
PO Box 58
Springfield, Vermont 05156-0058
Phone: (802)885-2071
Fax: (802)885-3027
Al Moulton, Executive Dir.

Green Mountain Economic Develop-
ment Corporation
SBDC
PO Box 246
White River Jct., Vermont 05001-0246
Phone: (802)295-3710
Fax: (802)295-3779
Lenne Quillen-Blume, SBDC Specialist

Virgin Islands

Peter Markou, Executive Dir.
University of the Virgin Islands
(Charlotte Amalie)
Small Business Development Center
8000 Nisky Center, Ste. 202
Charlotte Amalie, Virgin Islands
00802-5804
Phone: (809)776-3206
Fax: (809)775-3756
Ian Hodge

University of the Virgin Islands
Small Business Development Center
Sunshine Mall
No. 1 Estate Cane, Ste. 104
Frederiksted, Virgin Islands 00840
Phone: (809)692-5270
Fax: (809)692-5629
Chester Williams, State Dir.

University of the Virgin Island
SBDC
8000 Nisky Center, Ste. 202
U.S. Virgin Islands, Virgin Islands
00802
Phone: (809)776-3206
Fax: (809)775-3756
Ian Hodge, Associate State

Virginia

Virginia Highlands SBDC
PO Box 828

Abingdon, Virginia 24212
Phone: (703)676-5615
Fax: (703)628-7576
Jim Tilley, Dir.

Arlington Small Business Develop-
ment Center
George Mason University, Arlington
Campus
3401 N. Fair Dr.
Arlington, Virginia 22201
Phone: (703)993-8128
Fax: (703)993-8130
Paul Hall, Dir.

Virginia Eastern Shore Corp.
SBDC
36076 Lankford Hwy.
PO Box 395
Belle Haven, Virginia 23306
Phone: (757)442-7179
Fax: (757)442-7181

Mount Empire Community College
Southwest Small Business Develop-
ment Center
Drawer 700, Rte. 23, S.
Big Stone Gap, Virginia 24219
Phone: (703)523-6529
Fax: (703)523-8139
Tim Blankenbecler, Dir.

Central Virginia Small Business
Development Center
918 Emmet St., N. Ste. 200
Charlottesville, Virginia 22903-4878
Phone: (804)295-8198
Fax: (804)295-7066
Charles Kulp, Dir.

Hampton Roads Chamber of Com-
merce
SBDC
400 Volvo Pkwy.
P.O. Box 1776
Chesapeake, Virginia 23320
Phone: (757)664-2590
Fax: (757)548-1835
William J. Holoran, Jr., Dir.

Northern Virginia Small Business
Development Center
George Mason University

4031 University Dr., Ste. 200
Fairfax, Virginia 22030
Phone: (703)993-2131
Fax: (703)993-2126
Michael Kehoe, Dir.

Longwood College (Farmville)
Small Business Development Center
515 Main St.
Farmville, Virginia 23901
Phone: (804)395-2086
Fax: (804)395-2359
Gerald L. Hughes, Jr., Dir.

Rappahannock Region Small Business
Development Center
1301 College Ave.
Seacobeck Hall
Fredericksburg, Virginia 22401
Phone: (540)654-1060
Fax: (540)654-1070
Jeffrey R. Sneddon, Dir.

Thomas Nelson Community College
525 Butler Farm Rd., Ste. 102
Hampton, Virginia 23666
Phone: (757)825-2957
Fax: (757)825-2960

James Madison University
Small Business Development Center
JMU College of Business
Zane Showker Hall, Rm. 523
Harrisonburg, Virginia 22807
Phone: (703)568-3227
Fax: (703)568-3299
Karen Wigginton, Dir.

Lynchburg Regional Small Business
Development Center
147 Mill Ridge Rd.
Lynchburg, Virginia 24502-4341
Phone: (804)582-6170
Free: (800)876-7232
Barry Lyons, Contact

Flory Small Business Development
Center
10311 Sudley Manor Dr.
Manassas, Virginia 22110
Phone: (703)335-2500
Linda Decker, Dir.

SBDC Satellite Office
P.O. Box 709
115 Broad St.
Martinsville, Virginia 2414
Phone: (540)632-4462
Fax: (540)632-5059
Ken Copeland, Dir.

Lord Fairfax Community College
SBDC
PO Box 47
Skirmisher Ln.
Middletown, Virginia 22645
Phone: (703)869-6649
Fax: (703)868-7002
Robert Crosen, Dir.

Small Business Development Center
of Hampton Roads, Inc. (Norfolk)
420 Bank St.
PO Box 327
Norfolk, Virginia 23501
Phone: (757)664-2528
Fax: (757)622-5563
Warren Snyder, Dir.

New River Valley
SBDC
600-H Norwood St.
PO Box 3726
Radford, Virginia 24141
Phone: (540)831-6056
David Shanks

Southwest Virginia Community
College
Southwest Small Business Develop-
ment Center
PO Box SVCC, Rte. 19
Richlands, Virginia 24641
Phone: (703)964-7345
Fax: (703)964-5788
Jim Boyd, Dir.

Capital Area Small Business Develop-
ment Center
1 N. 5th St., Ste. 510
Richmond, Virginia 23219
Free: (800)646-SBDC
Fax: (804)648-7849
Taylor Cousins, Dir.

Commonwealth of Virginia
Department of Economic Development
SBDC
901 East Byrd St., Suite 1800
Richmond, Virginia 23219
Phone: (804)786-8087
Larry Roberts, Manager

Commonwealth of Virginia
Department of Economic Development
Virginia SBDC
901 E. Byrd St., Ste. 1800
Richmond, Virginia 23219
Phone: (804)371-8253
Fax: (804)225-3384
Bob Wilburn, State Dir.

Blue Ridge Small Business Develop-
ment Center
Western Virginia SBDC Consortium
310 1st St., SW Mezzanine
Roanoke, Virginia 24011
Phone: (703)983-0717
Fax: (703)983-0723
John Jennings, Dir.

Longwood SBDC
South Boston Branch
515 Broad St.
PO Box 1116
South Boston, Virginia 24592
Phone: (804)575-0444
Fax: (804)572-4087
Vincent Decker, Bus. Analyst

Loudoun County Small Business
Development Center
21515 Ridge Top Cir., Ste. 200
Sterling, Virginia 22170
Phone: (703)430-7222
Fax: (703)430-9562
Joseph Messina, Dir.

Warsaw Small Business Development
Center
106 W. Richmond Rd.
PO Box 490
Warsaw, Virginia 22572
Phone: (804)333-0286
Fax: (804)333-0187
John Clickener, Dir.

Wytheville Small Business Development Center
Wytheville Community College
1000 E. Main St.
Wytheville, Virginia 24382
Phone: (703)223-4798 ext. 4798
Free: (800)468-1195
Fax: (703)223-4850
Rob Edwards, Dir.

Washington

Bellevue Small Business Development Center
Bellevue Community College
3000 Landerholm Circle SE
Bellevue, Washington 98007-6484
Phone: (206)643-2888
Fax: (206)649-3113
Bill Huenefeld, Contact

Western Washington University
Small Business Development Center
308 Parks Hall
Bellingham, Washington 98225-9073
Phone: (360)650-3899
Fax: (360)650-4844
Lynn Trzynka, Contact

Centralia Community College
Small Business Development Center
600 W. Locust St.
Centralia, Washington 98531
Phone: (360)736-9391
Fax: (360)753-3404
Don Hays, Contact

Columbia Basin College—TRIDEC
Small Business Development Center
901 N. Colorado
Kennewick, Washington 99336
Phone: (509)735-6222
Fax: (509)735-6609
Glynn Lamberson, Contact

Edmonds Community College
Small Business Development Center
20000 68th Ave. W.
Lynnwood, Washington 98036
Phone: (206)640-1435
Fax: (206)640-1532
Jack Wicks, Contact

Big Bend Community College
Small Business Development Center
7662 Chanute St., Bldg. 1500
Moses Lake, Washington 98837-3299
Phone: (509)762-6289
Fax: (509)762-6329
Ed Baroch, Contact

Skagit Valley College
Small Business Development Center
2405 College Way
Mount Vernon, Washington 98273
Phone: (360)428-1282
Fax: (360)336-6116
Peter Stroosma, Contact

Wenatchee Valley College
SBDC
Box 741
Okanogan, Washington 98840
Phone: (509)826-5107
Fax: (509)826-1812
Ron Neilsen, Specialist

Washington State University (Olympia)
Small Business Development Center
721 Columbia St. SW
Olympia, Washington 98501
Phone: (360)753-5616
Fax: (360)586-5493
Douglas Hammel, Contact

Washington State University (Pullman)
Small Business Development Center
501 Johnson Tower
PO Box 644851
Pullman, Washington 99164-4727
Phone: (509)335-1576
Fax: (509)335-0949
Carol Riesenberg, Dir.

Duwamish Industrial Education Center
Small Business Development Center
6770 E. Marginal Way S
Seattle, Washington 98108-3405
Phone: (206)768-6855
Ruth Ann Halford, Contact

International Trade Institute
North Seattle Community College

Small Business Development Center
2001 6th Ave., Ste. 650
Seattle, Washington 98121
Phone: (206)553-0052
Ann Tamura, Contact

Washington Small Business Development Center (Seattle)
180 Nickerson, Ste. 207
Seattle, Washington 98109
Phone: (206)464-5450
Fax: (206)464-6357
Bill Jacobs, Contact

Washington State University (Spokane)
Small Business Development Center
665 North Riverpoint Blvd.
Spokane, Washington 99204-0399
Phone: (509)358-2051
Fax: (509)358-2059
Terry Chambers, Contact

Washington Small Business Development Center (Tacoma)
950 Pacific Ave., Ste. 300
PO Box 1933
Tacoma, Washington 98401-1933
Phone: (206)272-7232
Fax: (206)597-7305
Neil Delisanti, Contact

Columbia River Economic Development Council
Small Business Development Center
100 E. Columbia Way
Vancouver, Washington 98660-3156
Phone: (360)693-2555
Fax: (360)694-9927
Janet Harte, Contact

Port of Walla Walla SBDC
500 Tausick Way
Walla Walla, Washington 98362
Phone: (509)527-4681
Fax: (509)525-3101
Rich Monacelli, Specialist

Wenatchee Small Business Development Center
327 East Penny Rd.
Industrial Bldg. 2, Ste. D.

Wenatchee, Washington 98801
Phone: (509)662-8016
Fax: (509)663-0455
Jeff Martin, Contact

Yakima Valley College
Small Business Development Center
PO Box 1647
Yakima, Washington 98907
Phone: (509)454-3608
Fax: (509)454-4155
Corey Hansen, Contact

West Virginia

College of West Virginia
SBDC
PO Box AG
Beckley, West Virginia 25802
Phone: (304)255-4022
Fax: (304)255-4022
Ken Peters, Program Mgr.

Governor's Office of Community and
Industrial Development
SBDC
950 Kanawha Blvd. E.
Charleston, West Virginia 25301
Phone: (304)558-2960
Fax: (304)348-0127

Governor's Office of Community and
Industrial Development
950 Kanawha Blvd. East
E. Capitol Complex
Charleston, West Virginia 25301
Phone: (304)558-2960
Fax: (304)558-0127
Wanda Chenoweth, Program Mgr.

Elkins Satellite
SBDC
10 Eleventh St., Ste. 1
Elkins, West Virginia 26241
Phone: (304)637-7205
Fax: (304)637-4902
James Martin, Business Analyst

Fairmont State College
Small Business Development Center
Locust Ave.
Fairmont, West Virginia 26554

Phone: (304)367-4125
Fax: (304)366-4870
Dale Bradley, Program Mgr.

Marshall University
Small Business Development Center
1050 4th Ave.
Huntington, West Virginia 25755-2126
Phone: (304)696-6789
Fax: (304)696-6277
Edna McClain, Program Mgr.

West Virginia Institute of Technology
Small Business Development Center
Engineering Bldg., Rm. 102
Montgomery, West Virginia 25136
Phone: (304)442-5501
Fax: (304)442-3307
James Epling, Program Mgr.

West Virginia University
Small Business Development Center
PO Box 6025
Morgantown, West Virginia 26506-6025
Phone: (304)293-5839
Fax: (304)293-7061
Stan Kloc, Program Mgr.

West Virginia University
(Parkersburg)
Small Business Development Center
Rte. 5, Box 167-A
Parkersburg, West Virginia 26101-9577
Phone: (304)424-8277
Fax: (304)424-8315
Greg Hill, Program Mgr.

Shepherd College
Small Business Development Center
120 N. Princess St.
Shepherdstown, West Virginia 25443
Phone: (304)876-5261
Fax: (304)876-5117
Fred Baer, Program Mgr.

West Virginia Northern Community
College
Small Business Development Center
1701 Market St.
College Sq.
Wheeling, West Virginia 26003

Phone: (304)233-5900 ext. 206
Fax: (304)232-9065
Ed Huttenhower, Program Mgr.

Wisconsin

University of Wisconsin—Eau Claire
Small Business Development Center
PO Box 4004
Eau Claire, Wisconsin 54702-4004
Phone: (715)836-5811
Fax: (715)836-5263
Fred Waedt, Dir.

University of Wisconsin—Green Bay
Small Business Development Center
Wood Hall, Ste. 460
Green Bay, Wisconsin 54301
Phone: (414)465-2089
Fax: (414)465-2660
James Holly, Dir.
E-mail: hollyj@uwgb.edu

University of Wisconsin—Parkside
Small Business Development Center
284, Tallent Hall
Kenosha, Wisconsin 53141-2000
Phone: (414)595-2189
Fax: (414)595-2513
Patricia Deutsch, Dir.
E-mail: pduetsch@vm.uwp.edu

University of Wisconsin—La Crosse
Small Business Development Center
120 N. Hall
La Crosse, Wisconsin 54601
Phone: (608)785-8782
Fax: (608)785-6919
Jan Gallagher, Dir.
E-mail: jgallagh@uwlax.edu

University of Wisconsin
Wisconsin SBDC
432 N. Lake St., Rm. 423
Madison, Wisconsin 53706
Phone: (608)263-7794
Fax: (608)262-3878

University of Wisconsin—Madison
Small Business Development Center
975 University Ave., Rm. 3260
Grainger Hall

Madison, Wisconsin 53706
Phone: (608)263-2221
Fax: (608)263-0818
Joan Gillman, Dir.
E-mail: jtg@mi.bus.wisc.edu

University of Wisconsin—Milwaukee
Small Business Development Center
161 W. Wisconsin Ave., Ste. 600
Milwaukee, Wisconsin 53203
Phone: (414)227-3240
Fax: (414)227-3142
Sara Murray, Dir.

University of Wisconsin—Oshkosh
Small Business Development Center
157 Clow Faculty Bldg., 800 Algoma
Blvd.
Oshkosh, Wisconsin 54901
Phone: (414)424-1453
Fax: (414)424-7413
Rita Janaky, Dir.
E-mail: mozingo@vaxa.cis.uwash.edu

University of Wisconsin—Stevens
Point
Small Business Development Center
Lower Level Main Bldg.
Stevens Point, Wisconsin 54481
Phone: (715)346-2004
Fax: (715)346-4045
Mark Stover, Dir.
E-mail: mstover@uwspmail.uwsp.edu

University of Wisconsin—Superior
Small Business Development Center
29 Sundquist Hall
Superior, Wisconsin 54880
Phone: (715)394-8352
Fax: (715)394-8454
Neil Hensrud, Dir.
E-mail: nhensrud@wpo.uwsuper.edu

University of Wisconsin—
Whitewater
Small Business Development Center
Carlson Bldg., No. 2000
Whitewater, Wisconsin 53190
Phone: (414)472-3217
Fax: (414)472-4863
Carla Lenk, Dir.
E-mail: lenkc@uwwvax.uww.edu

Wisconsin Innovation Service Center
SBDC
University of Wisconsin at
Whitewater
402 McCutchan Hall
Whitewater, Wisconsin 53190
Phone: (414)472-1365
Fax: (414)472-1600
Debra Malewicki, Dir.

Wisconsin Technology Access
Center
SBDC
E-mail: malewicd@uwwvax.uww.edu
University of Wisconsin at
Whitewater
416 McCutchen Hall
Whitewater, Wisconsin 53190
Phone: (414)472-1365
Fax: (414)472-1600
Debra Malewicki, Dir.

Wyoming

Casper Small Business Development
Center
Region III
111 W. 2nd St., Ste. 502
Casper, Wyoming 82601
Phone: (307)234-6683
Free: (800)348-5207
Fax: (307)577-7014
Leonard Holler, Dir.

Laramie County Enterprise Center
1400 E. College Dr.
Cheyenne, Wyoming 82007-5208
Phone: (307)632-6141
Free: (800)348-5208
Fax: (307)632-6061
Arlene Soto, Regional Dir.

Wyoming Small Business Develop-
ment Center
State Office
University of Wyoming
PO Box 3622
Laramie, Wyoming 82071-3622
Phone: (307)766-3505
Free: (800)348-5194
Fax: (307)766-3406
Diane Wolverton, State Dir.

Northwest Community College
Small Business Development Center
Northwest College
John Dewitt Student Center
Powell, Wyoming 82435
Phone: (307)754-6067
Free: (800)348-5203
Fax: (307)754-6069
Dwane Heintz, Dir.

Rock Springs Small Business Devel-
opment Center
Region I
PO Box 1168
Rock Springs, Wyoming 82902
Phone: (307)352-6894
Free: (800)348-5205
Fax: (307)352-6876

SERVICE CORPS OF RETIRED EXECUTIVES (SCORE) OFFICES

*This section contains a listing of all
SCORE offices organized alphabetically by
state/U.S. territory name, then by city, then
by agency name.*

Alabama

SCORE Office (Anniston)
c/o Calhoun County Chamber of
Commerce
PO Box 1087
Anniston, Alabama 36202
Phone: (205)237-3536

SCORE Office (North Alabama)
1601 11th Ave. S
Birmingham, Alabama 35294-4552
Phone: (205)934-6868

SCORE Office (Fairhope)
c/o Fairhope Chamber of Commerce
327 Fairhope Ave.
Fairhope, Alabama 36532
Phone: (334)928-8799

SCORE Office (Florence)
104 S. Pine St.

Florence, Alabama 35630
Phone: (205)764-4661
Fax: (205)766-9017

SCORE Office (Foley)
c/o Foley Chamber of Commerce
PO Box 1117
Foley, Alabama 36536
Phone: (334)943-3291
Fax: (334)943-6810

SCORE Office (Mobile)
c/o Mobile Area Chamber of Commerce
PO Box 2187
Mobile, Alabama 36652
Phone: (334)433-6951

SCORE Office (Alabama Capitol City)
c/o Montgomery Area Chamber of Commerce
41 Commerce St.
PO Box 79
Montgomery, Alabama 36101-1114
Phone: (334)240-9295

SCORE Office (Tuscaloosa)
2200 University Blvd.
PO Box 020410
Tuscaloosa, Alabama 35402
Phone: (205)758-7588

Alaska

SCORE Office (Anchorage)
c/o U.S. Small Business Administration
222 W. 8th Ave., No. 67
Anchorage, Alaska 99513-7559
Phone: (907)271-4022

Arizona

SCORE Office (Casa Grande)
Chamber of Commerce
575 N. Marshall
Casa Grande, Arizona 85222
Phone: (520)836-2125
Toll-free: (800)916-1515
Fax: (520)836-3623

SCORE Office (Cottonwood)
1010 S. Main St.
Cottonwood, Arizona 86326

Phone: (520)634-7593
Fax: (520)634-7594

SCORE Office (Flagstaff)
1 E. Rte. 66
Flagstaff, Arizona 86001
Phone: (520)556-7333

SCORE Office (Glendale)
7105 N. 59th Ave.
Glendale, Arizona 85311
Phone: (602)937-4754
Toll-free: (800)ID-SUNNY
Fax: (602)937-3333

SCORE Office (Green Valley)
W. Continental Rd.
PO Box 270
Green Valley, Arizona 85614
Phone: (602)625-7575
Toll-free: (800)858-5872
Fax: (602)648-6154

SCORE Office (Holbrook)
100 E. Arizona St.
Holbrook, Arizona 86025
Phone: (520)524-6558
Toll-free: (800)524-2459
Fax: (602)524-1719

SCORE Office (Kingman)
c/o Bill Murie
1070 Palo Verde
Kingman, Arizona 86401
Phone: (520)753-6106

SCORE Office (Lake Havasu)
Mohave Community College
1977 W. Acoma Blvd.
Lake Havasu City, Arizona 86403
Phone: (520)855-7812

SCORE Office (Pinetop)
592 W. White Mountain Blvd.
Lakeside, Arizona 85929
Phone: (602)367-4290

SCORE Office (East Valley)
Federal Bldg., Rm. 104
26 N. MacDonald St.
Mesa, Arizona 85201
Phone: (602)379-3100

SCORE Office (Payson)
PO Box 1380

Payson, Arizona 85547
Phone: (520)474-4515
Toll-free: (800)6-PAYSON
Fax: (520)474-8812

SCORE Office (Phoenix)
2828 N. Central Ave., No. 800
Phoenix, Arizona 85004
Phone: (602)640-2329

SCORE Office (Northern Arizona)
Post Office Bldg., Ste. 307
101 W. Goodwin St.
Prescott, Arizona 86303
Phone: (520)778-7438

SCORE Office (St. Johns)
PO Box 178
St. Johns, Arizona 85936
Phone: (520)337-2000

SCORE Office (Sedona)
Forest & 89th Ave.
PO Box 478
Sedona, Arizona 86339
Phone: (520)282-7722

SCORE Office (Show Low)
PO Box 1083
Show Low, Arizona 85901
Phone: (520)537-2326
Fax: (520)537-2326

SCORE Office (Snowflake)
PO Box 776
Snowflake, Arizona 85937
Phone: (520)536-4331

SCORE Office (Springerville)
PO Box 31
Springerville, Arizona 85938
Phone: (520)333-2123
Fax: (520)333-5690

SCORE Office (Tucson)
c/o Tucson Art Council
240 N. Stone
Tucson, Arizona 85701
Phone: (520)884-9602

Arkansas

SCORE Office (South Central)
PO Box 1271
El Dorado, Arkansas 71731
Phone: (501)863-6113

SCORE Office (Ozark)
c/o Margaret B. Parrish
1141 Eastwood Dr.
Fayetteville, Arkansas 72701
Phone: (501)442-7619

SCORE Office (Northwest Arkansas)
Glenn Haven Dr., No. 4
Fort Smith, Arkansas 72901
Phone: (501)783-3556

SCORE Office (Garland County)
330 Kleinshore, No. 32
Hot Springs Village, Arkansas 71913
Phone: (501)922-0020

SCORE Office (Little Rock)
U.S. Small Business Administration
2120 Riverfront Dr., Rm. 100
Little Rock, Arkansas 72202-1747
Phone: (501)324-5893

SCORE Office (Southeast Arkansas)
PO Box 6866
Pine Bluff, Arkansas 71611
Phone: (501)535-7189

California

SCORE Office (Agoura)
5935 Kanan Rd.
Agoura Hills, California 91301
Phone: (818)889-3150
Fax: (818)889-3366

SCORE Office (Angels Camp)
1211 S. Main St.
Box 637
Angels Camp, California 95222
Phone: (209)736-0049
Toll-free: (800)225-3764
Fax: (209)736-9124

SCORE Office (Arroyo Grande)
800 W. Branch, Ste. A
Arroyo Grande, California 93420
Phone: (805)489-1488
Fax: (805)489-2239

SCORE Office (Atascadero)
6550 El Camino Real
Atascadero, California 93422
Phone: (805)466-2044
Fax: (805)466-9218

SCORE Office (Golden Empire)
1033 Truxton Ave.
PO Box 1947
Bakersfield, California 93301
Phone: (805)327-4421

SCORE Office (Kernville)
c/o Kernville Chamber of Commerce
1330 22nd St., Ste. B
Bakersfield, California 93301
Phone: (805)322-5849
Phone: (805)327-4421

SCORE Office (Bellflower)
9729 E. Flower St.
Bellflower, California 90706
Phone: (310)867-1744
Fax: (310)866-7545

SCORE Office (Brawley)
204 S. Empirial
Brawley, California 92227
Phone: (619)344-3160
Fax: (619)344-7611

SCORE Office (Burbank)
200 W. Magnolia Blvd.
Burbank, California 91502
Phone: (818)846-3111
Fax: (818)846-0109

SCORE Office (Calexico)
PO Box 948
Calexico, California 92231
Phone: (619)357-1166
Fax: (619)357-9043

SCORE Office (California City)
c/o California City Chamber of
Commerce
8048 California City Blvd.
PO Box 8001
California City, California 93504
Phone: (619)373-8676

SCORE Office (Camarillo)
c/o Camarillo Chamber of Commerce
632 Las Posas Rd.
Camarillo, California 93010
Phone: (805)484-4383
Phone: (805)484-1395

SCORE Office (Cambria)
c/o Cambria Chamber of Commerce
767 Main St.
Cambria, California 93428

Phone: (805)927-3624
Fax: (805)927-9426

SCORE Office (Canoga Park)
7248 Owensmouth Ave.
Canoga Park, California 91303
Phone: (818)884-4222

SCORE Office (Capitola)
621 B Capitola Ave.
Capitola, California 95010
Phone: (408)475-6522
Toll-free: (800)474-6522
Fax: (408)475-6530

SCORE Office (Carlsbad)
PO Box 10605
Carlsbad, California 92018
Phone: (619)931-8400
Fax: (619)931-9153

SCORE Office (Carpinteria)
PO Box 956
Carpinteria, California 93014
Phone: (805)684-5479
Fax: (805)684-3477

SCORE Office (Greater Chico Area)
1324 Mangrove St., Ste. 114
Chico, California 95926
Phone: (916)342-8932

SCORE Office (Chino)
13134 Central Ave.
Chino, California 91710
Phone: (909)627-6177
Fax: (909)627-4180

SCORE Office (Chula Vista)
233 4th Ave.
Chula Vista, California 91910
Phone: (619)420-6602
Fax: (619)420-1269

SCORE Office (Claremont)
205 Yale Ave.
Claremont, California 91711
Phone: (909)624-1681
Fax: (909)624-6629

SCORE Office (Clearlake)
PO Box 629
Clearlake, California 95422
Phone: (707)994-3600
Fax: (707)994-6410

SCORE Office (Colton)
620 N. Lacadena Dr.
Colton, California 92324
Phone: (909)825-2222
Fax: (909)824-1630

SCORE Office (Concord)
2151-A Salvio St., Ste. B
Concord, California 94520
Phone: (510)685-1181
Fax: (510)685-5623

SCORE Office (Covina)
935 W. Badillo St.
Covina, California 91723
Phone: (818)967-4191
Fax: (818)966-9660

SCORE Office (Rancho Cucamonga)
8280 Utica, Ste. 160
Cucamonga, California 91730
Phone: (909)987-1012
Fax: (909)987-5917

SCORE Office (Culver City)
PO Box 707
Culver City, California 90232-0707
Phone: (310)287-3850
Fax: (310)287-1350

SCORE Office (Danville)
380 Diablo Rd., Ste. 103
Danville, California 94526
Phone: (510)837-4400

SCORE Office (Downey)
11131 Brookshire Ave.
Downey, California 90241
Phone: (310)923-2191
Fax: (310)864-0461

SCORE Office (El Cajon)
109 Rea Ave.
El Cajon, California 92020
Phone: (619)444-1327
Fax: (619)440-6164

SCORE Office (El Centro)
1100 Main St.
El Centro, California 92243
Phone: (619)352-3681
Fax: (619)352-3246

SCORE Office (Escondido)
720 N. Broadway
Escondido, California 92025
Phone: (619)745-2125
Fax: (619)745-1183

SCORE Office (Fairfield)
1111 Webster St.
Fairfield, California 94533
Phone: (707)425-4625
Fax: (707)425-0826

SCORE Office (Fontana)
17009 Valley Blvd., Ste. B
Fontana, California 92335
Phone: (909)822-4433
Fax: (909)822-6238

SCORE Office (Foster City)
1125 E. Hillsdale Blvd.
Foster City, California 94404
Phone: (415)573-7600
Fax: (415)573-5201

SCORE Office (Fremont)
2201 Walnut Ave., Ste. 110
Fremont, California 94538
Phone: (510)795-2244
Fax: (510)795-2240

SCORE Office (Central California)
2719 N. Air Fresno Dr., Ste. 107
Fresno, California 93727-1547
Phone: (209)487-5605

SCORE Office (Gardena)
1204 W. Gardena Blvd.
Gardena, California 90247
Phone: (310)532-9905
Fax: (310)515-4893

SCORE Office (Glendale)
330 N. Brand Blvd., Ste. 190
Glendale, California 91203-2304
Phone: (818)552-3206

SCORE Office (Glendale)
330 N. Brand Blvd., Rm. 190
Glendale, California 91203
Phone: (818)552-3206

SCORE Office (Lompoc)
c/o Lompoc Chamber of Commerce
330 N. Brand Blvd., Ste. 190
Glendale, California 91203-2304
Phone: (818)552-3206
Fax: (818)552-3260

SCORE Office (Glendora)
131 E. Foothill Blvd.
Glendora, California 91741
Phone: (818)963-4128
Fax: (818)914-4822

SCORE Office (Grover Beach)
177 S. 8th St.
Grover Beach, California 93433
Phone: (805)489-9091
Fax: (805)489-9091

SCORE Office (Hawthorne)
12477 Hawthorne Blvd.
Hawthorne, California 90250
Phone: (310)676-1163
Fax: (310)676-7661

SCORE Office (Hayward)
22300 Foothill Blvd., Ste. 303
Hayward, California 94541
Phone: (510)537-2424

SCORE Office (Hemet)
1700 E. Florida Ave.
Hemet, California 92544
Phone: (909)652-4390

SCORE Office (Hesperia)
16367 Main St.
PO Box 403656
Hesperia, California 92340
Phone: (619)244-2135
Phone: (619)244-1333

SCORE Office (Hollister)
c/o Hollister Small Business Development Center
321 San Felipe Rd., No. 11
Hollister, California 95023

SCORE Office (Hollywood)
7018 Hollywood Blvd.
Hollywood, California 90028
Phone: (213)469-8311
Fax: (213)469-2805

SCORE Office (Indio)
82503 Hwy. 111
PO Drawer TTT
Indio, California 92202
Phone: (619)347-0676

SCORE Office (Inglewood)
330 Queen St.
Inglewood, California 90301
Phone: (818)552-3206

SCORE Office (La Puente)
218 N. Grendanda St. D.
La Puente, California 91744
Phone: (818)330-3216
Fax: (818)330-9524

SCORE Office (La Verne)
2078 Bonita Ave.
La Verne, California 91570
Phone: (909)593-5265
Phone: (909)652-4390
Fax: (714)929-8475

SCORE Office (Lake Elsinore)
132 W. Graham Ave.
Lake Elsinore, California 92530
Phone: (909)674-2577

SCORE Office (Lakeport)
PO Box 295
Lakeport, California 95453
Phone: (707)263-5092

SCORE Office (Lakewood)
5445 E. Del Amo Blvd., Ste. 2
Lakewood, California 90714
Phone: (213)920-7737

SCORE Office (Antelope Valley)
c/o Bruce Finlayson, Chair
747 E. Ave. K-7
Lancaster, California 93535
Phone: (805)948-4518

SCORE Office (Long Beach)
1 World Trade Center
Long Beach, California 90831

SCORE Office (Los Alamitos)
901 W. Civic Center Dr., Ste. 160
Los Alamitos, California 90720

SCORE Office (Los Altos)
c/o Los Altos Chamber of Commerce
321 University Ave.
Los Altos, California 94022
Phone: (415)948-1455

SCORE Office (Los Angeles)
404 S. Bixel
Los Angeles, California 90071

SCORE Office (Manhattan Beach)
PO Box 3007
Manhattan Beach, California 90266
Phone: (310)545-5313
Fax: (310)545-7203

SCORE Office (Merced)
1632 N. St.
Merced, California 95340
Phone: (209)725-3800
Fax: (209)383-4959

SCORE Office (Milpitas)
75 S. Milpitas Blvd., Ste. 205
Milpitas, California 95035
Phone: (408)262-2613
Fax: (408)262-2823

SCORE Office (Yosemite)
c/o Stanislaus County Economic
Development Corp.
1012 11th St., Ste. 300
Modesto, California 95354
Phone: (209)521-9333

SCORE Office (Montclair)
5220 Benito Ave.
Montclair, California 91763

SCORE Office (Monterey)
Monterey Peninsula Chamber of
Commerce
380 Alvarado St.
Monterey, California 93940-1770
Phone: (408)649-1770

SCORE Office (Moreno Valley)
25480 Alessandro
Moreno Valley, California 92553

SCORE Office (Morgan Hill)
Morgan Hill Chamber of Commerce
25 W. 1st St.
PO Box 786
Morgan Hill, California 95038
Phone: (408)779-9444
Fax: (408)778-1786

SCORE Office (Morro Bay)
Morro Bay Chamber of Commerce
880 Main St.
Morro Bay, California 93442
Phone: (805)772-4467

SCORE Office (Mountain View)
580 Castro St.
Mountain View, California 94041
Phone: (415)968-8378
Fax: (415)968-5668

SCORE Office (Napa)
1556 1st St.
Napa, California 94559

Phone: (707)226-7455
Fax: (707)226-1171

SCORE Office (North Hollywood)
5019 Lankershim Blvd.
North Hollywood, California 91601
Phone: (818)552-3206

SCORE Office (Northridge)
8801 Reseda Blvd.
Northridge, California 91324
Phone: (818)349-5676

SCORE Office (Novato)
807 De Long Ave.
Novato, California 94945
Phone: (415)897-1164
Fax: (415)898-9097

SCORE Office (East Bay)
2201 Broadway, Ste. 701
Oakland, California 94612
Phone: (510)273-6611

SCORE Office (Oceanside)
928 N. Coast Hwy.
Oceanside, California 92054
Phone: (619)722-1534

SCORE Office (Ontario)
121 West B. St.
Ontario, California 91762
Fax: (714)984-6439

SCORE Office (Oxnard)
PO Box 867
Oxnard, California 93032
Phone: (805)385-8860
Fax: (805)487-1763

SCORE Office (Pacifica)
450 Dundee Way, Ste. 2
Pacifica, California 94044
Phone: (415)355-4122

SCORE Office (Palm Desert)
72990 Hwy. 111
Palm Desert, California 92260
Phone: (619)346-6111
Fax: (619)346-3463

SCORE Office (Palm Springs)
555 S. Palm Canyon, Rm. A206
Palm Springs, California 92264
Phone: (619)320-6682

SCORE Office (Lakeside)
c/o Paul Heindel
2150 Low Tree

Palmdale, California 93551
Phone: (805)948-4518
Fax: (805)949-1212

SCORE Office (Palo Alto)
Thoits/Love, Hershaberger, Inc.
325 Forest Ave.
Palo Alto, California 94301
Phone: (415)324-3121
Fax: (415)324-1215

SCORE Office (Pasadena)
117 E. Colorado Blvd., Ste. 100
Pasadena, California 91105
Phone: (818)795-3355
Fax: (818)795-5663

SCORE Office (Paso Robles)
c/o Paso Robles Chamber of Commerce
1225 Park St.
Paso Robles, California 93446-2234
Phone: (805)238-0506
Fax: (805)238-0527

SCORE Office (Petaluma)
799 Baywood Dr., Ste. 3
Petaluma, California 94954
Phone: (707)762-2785
Fax: (707)762-4721

SCORE Office (Pico Rivera)
9122 E. Washington Blvd.
Pico Rivera, California 90660

SCORE Office (Pittsburg)
2700 E. Leland Rd.
Pittsburg, California 94565
Phone: (510)439-2181
Fax: (510)427-1599

SCORE Office (Pleasanton)
777 Peters Ave.
Pleasanton, California 94566
Phone: (510)846-9697

SCORE Office (Monterey Park)
485 N. Garey
Pomona, California 91769

SCORE Office (Pomona)
c/o Pomona Chamber of Commerce
485 N. Garey Ave.
PO Box 1457
Pomona, California 91769-1457
Phone: (909)622-1256

SCORE Office (Shasta)
c/o Shasta Chamber of Commerce
747 Auditorium Dr.
Redding, California 96099
Phone: (916)225-4433

SCORE Office (Redwood City)
1675 Broadway
Redwood City, California 94063
Phone: (415)364-1722
Fax: (415)364-1729

SCORE Office (Richmond)
3925 MacDonald Ave.
Richmond, California 94805

SCORE Office (Ridgecrest)
c/o Ridgecrest Chamber of Commerce
PO Box 771
Ridgecrest, California 93555
Phone: (619)375-8331
Fax: (619)375-0365

SCORE Office (Riverside)
3685 Main St., Ste. 350
Riverside, California 92501
Phone: (909)683-7100

SCORE Office (Sacramento)
660 J St., Ste. 215
Sacramento, California 95814-2413
Phone: (916)498-6420

SCORE Office (Salinas)
PO Box 1170
Salinas, California 93902
Phone: (408)424-7611
Fax: (408)424-8639

SCORE Office (Inland Empire)
777 E. Rialto Ave.
San Bernardino, California 92415-0760
Phone: (909)386-8278

SCORE Office (Inland Empire)
San Bernardino Chamber of Commerce
PO Box 658
San Bernardino, California 92402
Phone: (909)885-7515

SCORE Office (San Carlos)
San Carlos Chamber of Commerce
PO Box 1086
San Carlos, California 94070
Phone: (415)593-1068
Fax: (415)593-9108

SCORE Office (Encinitas)
550 W. C St., Ste. 550
San Diego, California 92101-3540
Phone: (619)557-7272
Fax: (619)557-5894

SCORE Office (San Diego)
c/o U..S. Small Business Administration
550 West C. St., Ste. 550
San Diego, California 92101-3540
Phone: (619)557-7272

SCORE Office (Menlo Park)
1100 Merrill St.
San Francisco, California 94105
Phone: (415)325-2818
Phone: (415)744-6827
Fax: (415)325-0920

SCORE Office (San Francisco)
c/o U..S. Small Business Administration
211 Main St., 4th Fl.
San Francisco, California 94105
Phone: (415)744-6827

SCORE Office (San Gabriel)
401 W. Las Tunas Dr.
San Gabriel, California 91776
Phone: (818)576-2525
Fax: (818)289-2901

SCORE Office (San Jose)
Small Business Institute
Deanza College
201 S. 1st. St., Ste. 137
San Jose, California 95113
Phone: (408)288-8479

SCORE Office (Santa Clara County)
280 S. 1st St., Rm. 137
San Jose, California 95113
Phone: (408)288-8479

SCORE Office (San Luis Obispo)
3566 S. Higuera
San Luis Obispo, California 93401
Phone: (805)547-0779

SCORE Office (San Mateo)
1021 S. El Camino, 2nd Fl.
San Mateo, California 94402
Phone: (415)341-5679
Phone: (415)341-0674

SCORE Office (San Pedro)
390 W. 7th St.
San Pedro, California 90731
Phone: (310)832-7272

SCORE Office (Orange County)
200 W. Santa Anna Blvd., Ste. 700
Santa Ana, California 92701
Phone: (714)550-7369

SCORE Office (Santa Barbara)
PO Box 30291
Santa Barbara, California 93130
Phone: (805)563-0084

SCORE Office (Central Coast)
1650 E. Clark Ave., No. 252
Santa Maria, California 93455
Phone: (805)934-2620

SCORE Office (Santa Maria)
Santa Maria Chamber of Commerce
614 S. Broadway
Santa Maria, California 93454-5111
Phone: (805)925-2403
Fax: (805)928-7559

SCORE Office (Santa Monica)
501 Colorado, Ste. 150
Santa Monica, California 90401
Phone: (310)393-9825
Fax: (310)394-1868

SCORE Office (Santa Rosa)
777 Sonoma Ave., Rm. 115E
Santa Rosa, California 95404
Phone: (707)571-8342

SCORE Office (Scotts Valley)
c/o Scotts Valley Chamber of Commerce
4 Camp Evers Ln.
Scotts Valley, California 95066
Phone: (408)438-1010
Fax: (408)438-6544

SCORE Office (Simi Valley)
c/o Simi Valley Chamber of Commerce
40 W. Cochran St., Ste. 100
Simi Valley, California 93065
Phone: (805)526-3900
Fax: (805)526-6234

SCORE Office (Sonoma)
453 1st St. E
Sonoma, California 95476
Phone: (707)996-1033

SCORE Office (Los Banos)
222 S. Shepard St.
Sonora, California 95370
Phone: (209)532-4212

SCORE Office (Tuolumne County)
c/o Tuolumne County Chamber of
Commerce
222 S. Shepherd St.
Sonora, California 95370
Phone: (209)532-4212

SCORE Office (South San Francisco)
c/o Chamber of Commerce
PO Box 469
South San Francisco, California 94080
Phone: (415)588-1911
Fax: (415)588-1529

SCORE Office (Stockton)
401 N. San Joaquin St., Rm. 215
Stockton, California 95202
Phone: (209)946-6293

SCORE Office (Taft)
314 4th St.
Taft, California 93268
Phone: (805)765-2165
Fax: (805)765-6639

SCORE Office (Conejo Valley)
c/o Conejo Valley Chamber of
Commerce
625 W. Hillcrest Dr.
Thousand Oaks, California 91360
Phone: (805)499-1993
Fax: (805)498-7264

SCORE Office (Torrance)
Torrance Chamber of Commerce
3400 Torrance Blvd., Ste. 100
Torrance, California 90503
Phone: (310)540-5858
Fax: (310)540-7662

SCORE Office (Truckee)
PO Box 2757
Truckee, California 96160
Phone: (916)587-2757
Fax: (916)587-2439

SCORE Office (Visalia)
c/o Tulare County E.D.C.
113 S. M St,
Tulare, California 93274
Phone: (209)627-0766

Toll-free: (800)718-2332
Fax: (209)627-8149

SCORE Office (Upland)
c/o Upland Chamber of Commerce
433 N. 2nd Ave.
Upland, California 91786
Phone: (909)931-4108

SCORE Office (Vallejo)
2 Florida St.
Vallejo, California 94590
Phone: (707)644-5551
Fax: (707)644-5590

SCORE Office (Van Nuys)
14540 Victory Blvd.
Van Nuys, California 91411
Phone: (818)989-0300
Fax: (818)989-3836

SCORE Office (Ventura)
Gold Coast Small Business Development Center
5700 Ralston St., Ste. 310
Ventura, California 93003
Phone: (818)552-3210

SCORE Office (Vista)
201 E. Washington St.
Vista, California 92084
Phone: (619)726-1122
Fax: (619)226-8654

SCORE Office (Watsonville)
PO Box 1748
Watsonville, California 95077
Phone: (408)724-3849
Fax: (408)728-5300

SCORE Office (West Covina)
811 S. Sunset Ave.
West Covina, California 91790
Phone: (818)338-8496
Fax: (818)960-0511

SCORE Office (Westlake)
30893 Thousand Oaks Blvd.
Westlake Village, California 91362
Phone: (805)496-5630
Fax: (818)991-1754

Colorado

SCORE Office (Colorado Springs)
2 N. Cascade Ave., Ste. 110

Colorado Springs, Colorado 80903
Phone: (719)636-3074

SCORE Office (Denver)
US Custom's House, 4th Fl.
721 19th St.
Denver, Colorado 80201-0660
Phone: (303)844-3985

SCORE Office (Tri-River)
1102 Grand Ave.
Glenwood Springs, Colorado 81601
Phone: (970)945-6589

SCORE Office (Grand Junction)
c/o Grand Junction Chamber of
Commerce
360 Grand Ave.
Grand Junction, Colorado 81501
Phone: (303)242-3214

SCORE Office (Gunnison)
c/o Russ Gregg
608 N. 11th
Gunnison, Colorado 81230
Phone: (303)641-4422

SCORE Office (Montrose)
1214 Peppertree Dr.
Montrose, Colorado 81401
Phone: (970)249-6080

SCORE Office (Pagosa Springs)
c/o Will Cotton
PO Box 4381
Pagosa Springs, Colorado 81157
Phone: (970)731-4890

SCORE Office (Rifle)
0854 W. Battlement Pky., Apt. C106
Parachute, Colorado 81635
Phone: (970)285-9390

SCORE Office (Pueblo)
302 N. Santa Fe
Pueblo, Colorado 81003
Phone: (719)542-1704

SCORE Office (Ridgway)
c/o Ken Hanson
143 Poplar Pl.
Ridgway, Colorado 81432

SCORE Office (Silverton)
c/o EF Homann
PO Box 480

Silverton, Colorado 81433
Phone: (303)387-5430

SCORE Office (Minturn)
PO Box 2066
Vail, Colorado 81658
Phone: (970)476-1224

Connecticut

SCORE Office (Greater Bridgeport)
10 Middle St., 14th Fl.
PO Box 999
Bridgeport, Connecticut 06601-0999
Phone: (203)335-3800

SCORE Office (Bristol)
10 Main St. 1st. Fl.
Bristol, Connecticut 06010
Phone: (203)584-4718
Fax: (203)584-4722

SCORE Office (Greater Danbury)
100 Mill Plain Rd.
Danbury, Connecticut 06811
Phone: (203)791-3804

SCORE Office (Eastern Connecticut)
University of Connecticut
Administration Bldg., Rm. 313
PO 625
61 Main St. (Chapter 579)
Groton, Connecticut 06475
Phone: (203)388-9508

SCORE Office (Greater Hartford
County)
330 Main St.
Hartford, Connecticut 06106
Phone: (203)240-4640

SCORE Office (Manchester)
c/o Manchester Chamber of Commerce
20 Hartford Rd.
Manchester, Connecticut 06040
Phone: (203)646-2223
Fax: (203)646-5871

SCORE Office (New Britain)
185 Main St., Ste. 431
New Britain, Connecticut 06051
Phone: (203)827-4492
Fax: (203)827-4480

SCORE Office (New Haven)
25 Science Pk., Bldg. 25, Rm. 366

New Haven, Connecticut 06511
Phone: (203)865-7645

SCORE Office (Fairfield County)
24 Beldon Ave., 5th Fl.
Norwalk, Connecticut 06850
Phone: (203)847-7348

SCORE Office (Old Saybrook)
c/o Old Saybrook Chamber of Commerce
146 Main St.
PO Box 625
Old Saybrook, Connecticut 06475
Phone: (203)388-9508

SCORE Office (Simsbury)
Simsbury Chamber of Commerce
Box 244
Simsbury, Connecticut 06070
Phone: (203)651-7307
Fax: (203)651-1933

SCORE Office (Torrington)
Northwest Chamber of Commerce
23 North Rd.
Torrington, Connecticut 06791
Phone: (203)482-6586

Delaware

SCORE Office (Dover)
Treadway Towers
P.O. Box 576
Dover, Delaware 19903
Phone: (302)678-0892
Fax: (302)678-0189

SCORE Office (Lewes)
PO Box 1
Lewes, Delaware 19958
Phone: (302)645-8073
Fax: (302)645-8412

SCORE Office (Milford)
Milford Chamber of Commerce
204 NE Front St.
Milford, Delaware 19963
Phone: (302)422-3301

SCORE Office (Wilmington)
824 Market St., Ste. 610
Wilmington, Delaware 19801
Phone: (302)573-6552
Fax: (302)573-6060

District of Columbia

SCORE Office (George Mason
University)
409 3rd St. SW, 4th Fl.
Washington, District of Columbia 20024
Toll-free: (800) 634-0245

SCORE Office (Washington DC)
1110 Vermont Ave. NW, 9th Fl.
PO Box 34346
Washington, District of Columbia 20043
Phone: (202) 606-4000

Florida

SCORE Office (Desota County
Chamber of Commerce)
16 South Velucia Ave.
Arcadia, Florida 34266
Phone: (941) 494-4033
Phone: (941) 494-3312

SCORE Office (Suncoast/Pinellas)
Airport Business Ctr.
4707 - 140th Ave. N, No. 311
Clearwater, Florida 34622
Phone: (813) 532-6800

SCORE Office (Dade)
1320 S. Dixie Hwy., Ste. 501
Coral Gables, Florida 33146
Phone: (305) 536-5521

SCORE Office (Daytona Beach)
First Union Bldg., Ste. 365
444 Seabreeze Blvd.
Daytona Beach, Florida 32118
Phone: (904) 255-6889

SCORE Office (DeLand)
336 N. Woodland Blvd.
DeLand, Florida 32720
Phone: (904) 734-4331
Fax: (904) 734-4333

SCORE Office (South Palm Beach)
1050 S. Federal Hwy., Ste. 132
Delray Beach, Florida 33483
Phone: (407) 278-7752

SCORE Office (Ft. Lauderdale)
Federal Bldg., Ste. 123
299 E. Broward Blvd.
Ft. Lauderdale, Florida 33301
Phone: (305) 356-7263

SCORE Office (Southwest Florida)
The Renaissance
8695 College Pky., Ste. 345 & 346
Fort Myers, Florida 33919
Phone: (813) 489-2935

SCORE Office (Indian River)
Treasure Coast Professional Center, Ste. 2
3229 S. US No. 1
Fort Pierce, Florida 34982
Phone: (407) 489-0548

SCORE Office (Gainesville)
101 SE 2nd Pl., Ste. 104
Gainesville, Florida 32601
Phone: (904) 375-8278

SCORE Office (Hialeah Dade Chamber)
59 W. 5th St.
Hialeah, Florida 33010
Phone: (305) 887-1515
Fax: (305) 887-2453

SCORE Office (South Broward)
3475 Sheridan St., Ste. 203
Hollywood, Florida 33021
Phone: (305) 966-8415

SCORE Office (Jacksonville)
7825 Baymeadows Way, Ste. 100-B
Jacksonville, Florida 32256-7504
Phone: (904) 443-1911

SCORE Office (Jacksonville Satellite)
c/o Jacksonville Chamber of Commerce
3 Independent Dr.
Jacksonville, Florida 32202
Phone: (904) 366-6600
Fax: (904) 632-0617

SCORE Office (Central Florida)
404 N. Ingraham Ave.
Lakeland, Florida 33801
Phone: (813) 688-4060

SCORE Office (Lakeland)
Lakeland Public Library
100 Lake Morton Dr.
Lakeland, Florida 33801
Phone: (941) 686-2168

SCORE Office (St. Petersburg)
800 W. Bay Dr., No. 505
Largo, Florida 33712
Phone: (813) 585-4571
Phone: (904) 327-7207

SCORE Office (Leesburg)
Lake Sumter Community College
9501 US Hwy. 441
Leesburg, Florida 34788-8751
Phone: (352) 365-3556
Fax: (352) 365-3501

SCORE Office (BCC/Space Coast)
Space Coast
Melbourne Professional Complex
1600 Sarno, Ste. 205
Melbourne, Florida 32935
Phone: (407) 254-2288

SCORE Office (Cocoa)
1600 Farno Rd., Unit 205
Melbourne, Florida 32935
Phone: (407) 254-2288

SCORE Office (Melbourne)
Space Coast
Melbourne Professional Complex
1600 Samo, Ste. 205
Melbourne, Florida 32935
Phone: (407) 254-2288

SCORE Office (Merritt Island)
1600 Farno Rd., Unit 205
Melbourne, Florida 32935
Phone: (407) 254-2288

SCORE Office (Naples of Collier)
Sun Bank Naples
3301 Danis Blvd.
PO Box 413002
Naples, Florida 33941-3002
Phone: (941) 643-0333

SCORE Office (Pasco County)
6014 US Hwy. 19, Ste. 302
New Port Richey, Florida 34652
Phone: (813) 842-4638

SCORE Office (Southeast Volusia)
Chamber of Commerce
115 Canal St.
New Smyrna Beach, Florida 32168
Phone: (904) 428-2449
Fax: (904) 423-3512

SCORE Office (Ocala)
PO Box 1210
Ocala, Florida 34478
Phone: (904) 629-5959

Clay County SCORE Office
Clay County Chamber of Commerce
1734 Kingsdey Ave.
PO Box 1441
Orange Park, Florida 32073
Phone: (904)264-2651
Fax: (904)269-0363

SCORE Office (Orlando)
Federal Bldg., Rm. 455
80 N. Hughey Ave.
Orlando, Florida 32801
Phone: (407)648-6476

SCORE Office (Emerald Coast)
19 W. Garden St., No. 325
Pensacola, Florida 32501
Phone: (904)444-2060
Fax: (904)444-2070

SCORE Office (Charlotte County)
Punta Gorda Professional Center
201 W. Marion Ave., Ste. 211
Punta Gorda, Florida 33950
Phone: (813)575-1818

SCORE Office (St. Augustine)
c/o St. Augustine Chamber of
Commerce
1 Riberia St.
St. Augustine, Florida 32084
Phone: (904)829-5681
Fax: (904)829-6477

SCORE Office (Bradenton)
2801 Fruitville, Ste. 280
Sarasota, Florida 34237
Phone: (813)955-1029

SCORE Office (Manasota)
2801 Fruitville Rd., Ste. 280
Sarasota, Florida 34237
Phone: (813)955-1029

SCORE Office (Tallahassee)
c/o Leon County Library
200 W. Park Ave.
Tallahassee, Florida 32302
Phone: (904)487-2665

SCORE Office (Hillsborough)
4732 Dale Mabry Hwy. N, Ste. 400
Tampa, Florida 33614-6509
Phone: (813)870-0125

SCORE Office (Lake Sumter)
First Union National Bank
122 E. Main St.
Tavares, Florida 32778
Phone: (904)365-3556

SCORE Office (Titusville)
2000 S. Washington Ave.
Titusville, Florida 32780
Phone: (407)267-3036
Fax: (407)264-0127

SCORE Office (Venice)
257 N. Tamiami Trl.
Venice, Florida 34285
Phone: (941)488-2236
Fax: (941)484-5903

SCORE Office (Palm Beach)
500 Australian Ave. S, Ste. 100
West Palm Beach, Florida 33401
Phone: (407)833-1672

SCORE Office (Wildwood)
Sumter County Small Business Services
103 N. Webster St.
Wildwood, Florida 34785

Georgia

SCORE Office (Atlanta)
1720 Peachtree Rd. NW, 6th Fl.
Atlanta, Georgia 30309
Phone: (404)347-2442

SCORE Office (Augusta)
3126 Oxford Rd.
Augusta, Georgia 30909
Phone: (706)869-9100

SCORE Office (Columbus)
School Bldg.
P.O. Box 40
Columbus, Georgia 31901
Phone: (706)327-3654

SCORE Office (Dalton-Whitfield)
PO Box 1941
Dalton, Georgia 30722-1941
Phone: (706)279-3383

SCORE Office (Gainesville)
Chamber of Commerce
PO Box 374
Gainesville, Georgia 30503
Phone: (770)532-6206
Fax: (770)535-8419

SCORE Office (Macon)
711 Grand Bldg.
Macon, Georgia 31201
Phone: (912)751-6160

SCORE Office (Brunswick)
4 Glen Ave.
St. Simons Island, Georgia 31520
Phone: (912)265-0620
Fax: (912)265-0629

SCORE Office (Savannah)
33 Bull St., Ste. 580
Savannah, Georgia 31401
Phone: (912)652-4335

Guam

SCORE Office (Guam)
Pacific News Bldg., Rm. 103
238 Archbishop Flores St.
Agana, Guam 96910-5100
Phone: (671)472-7308

Hawaii

SCORE Office (Honolulu)
300 Ala Moana Blvd., No. 2213
PO Box 50207
Honolulu, Hawaii 96850-3212
Phone: (808)541-2977

SCORE Office (Kahului)
c/o Chamber of Commerce
250 Alamaha, Unit N16A
Kahului, Hawaii 96732
Phone: (808)871-7711

Idaho

SCORE Office (Treasure Valley)
1020 Main St., No. 290
Boise, Idaho 83702
Phone: (208)334-1780

SCORE Office (Eastern Idaho)
2300 N. Yellowstone, Ste. 119
Idaho Falls, Idaho 83401
Phone: (208)523-1022

Illinois

SCORE Office (Fox Valley)
Greater Aurora Chamber of Commerce
40 W. Downer Pl.

PO Box 277
Aurora, Illinois 60507
Phone: (708)897-9214

SCORE Office (Greater Belvidere)
Greater Belvidere Chamber of Commerce
419 S. State St.
Belvidere, Illinois 61008
Phone: (815)544-4357
Fax: (815)547-7654

SCORE Office (Bensenville)
Greater O'Hare Association
1050 Busse Hwy. Suite 100
Bensenville, Illinois 60106
Phone: (708)350-2944
Fax: (708)350-2979

SCORE Office (Southern Illinois)
150 E. Pleasant Hill Rd.
Box 1
Carbondale, Illinois 62901
Phone: (618)453-6654

SCORE Office (Chicago)
Oliver Harvey College
Small Business Development Center
Pullman Bldg.
1000 E. 11th St., 7th Fl.
Chicago, Illinois 60628
Fax: (312)468-8086

SCORE Office (Chicago)
Northwest Atrium Center
500 W. Madison St., No. 1250
Chicago, Illinois 60661
Phone: (312)353-7724

SCORE Office (Danville)
28 W. N. Street
Danville, Illinois 61832
Phone: (217)442-7232
Phone: (217)442-1887
Fax: (217)442-6228

SCORE Office (Decatur)
Millikin University
1184 W. Main St.
Decatur, Illinois 62522
Phone: (217)424-6297

.SCORE Office (Downers Grove)
Downers Grove Chamber of Commerce
925 Curtis
Downers Grove, Illinois 60515
Phone: (708)968-4050
Fax: (708)968-8368

SCORE Office (Elgin)
Elgin Area Chamber of Commerce
24 E. Chicago, 3rd Fl.
PO Box 648
Elgin, Illinois 60120
Phone: (847)741-5660
Fax: (847)741-5677

SCORE Office (Freeport Area)
Freeport Area Chamber of Commerce
26 S. Galena Ave.
Freeport, Illinois 61032
Phone: (815)233-1350
Fax: (815)235-4038

.SCORE Office (Galesburg)
Galesburg Area Chamber of Commerce
292 E. Simmons St.
PO Box 749
Galesburg, Illinois 61401
Phone: (309)343-1194
Fax: (309)343-1195

SCORE Office (Glen Ellyn)
Glen Ellyn Chamber of Commerce
500 Pennsylvania
Glen Ellyn, Illinois 60137
Phone: (708)469-0907
Fax: (708)469-0426

SCORE Office (Alton)
Lewis & Clark Community College
Alden Hall
5800 Godfrey Rd.
Godfrey, Illinois 62035-2466
Phone: (618)467-2280

SCORE Office (Grayslake)
College of Lake County
19351 W. Washington St.
Grayslake, Illinois 60030
Phone: (708)223-3633
Fax: (708)223-9371

SCORE Office (Harrisburg)
Ec. Devel. Services Center
303 S. Commercial
Harrisburg, Illinois 62946-1528
Phone: (618)252-8528
Fax: (618)252-0210

SCORE Office (Joliet)
Joliet Region Chamber of Commerce
100 N. Chicago
Joliet, Illinois 60432
Phone: (815)727-5371
Fax: (815)727-5374

SCORE Office (Kankakee)
Kankakee Small Business Development Center
101 S. Schuyler Ave.
Kankakee, Illinois 60901
Phone: (815)933-0376
Fax: (815)933-0380

SCORE Office (Macomb)
Western Illinois University
216 Seal Hall, Rm. 214
Macomb, Illinois 61455
Phone: (309)298-1128
Fax: (309)298-2520

SCORE Office (Matteson)
Prairie State College
210 Lincoln Mall
Matteson, Illinois 60443
Phone: (708)709-3750
Fax: (708)503-9322

SCORE Office (Mattoon)
Mattoon Association of Commerce
1701 Wabash Ave.
Mattoon, Illinois 61938
Phone: (217)235-5661
Fax: (217)234-6544

SCORE Office (Quad City)
Quad City Chamber of Commerce
622 19th St.
Moline, Illinois 61265
Phone: (309)797-0082

SCORE Office (Naperville)
Naperville Area Chamber of Commerce
131 W. Jefferson Ave.
Naperville, Illinois 60540
Phone: (708)355-4141
Fax: (708)355-8355

SCORE Office (Northbrook)
Northbrook Chamber of Commerce
2002 Walters Ave.
Northbrook, Illinois 60062
Phone: (847)498-5555
Fax: (847)498-5510

SCORE Office (Palos Hills)
Moraine Valley Community College
Small Business Development Center
10900 S. 88th Ave.
Palos Hills, Illinois 60465
Phone: (847)974-5468
Fax: (847)974-0078

SCORE Office (Peoria)
c/o Peoria Chamber of Commerce
124 SW Adams, Ste. 300
Peoria, Illinois 61602
Phone: (309)676-0755

SCORE Office (Prospect Heights)
Harper College, Northeast Center
1375 Wolf Rd.
Prospect Heights, Illinois 60070
Phone: (847)537-8660
Fax: (847)537-7138

SCORE Office (Quincy Tri-State)
Quincy Chamber of Commerce
300 Civic Center Plz., Ste. 245
Quincy, Illinois 62301
Phone: (217)222-8093

SCORE Office (River Grove)
Triton College
2000 5th Ave.
River Grove, Illinois 60171
Phone: (708)456-0300
Fax: (708)583-3121

SCORE Office (Northern Illinois)
Rockford Illinois Chamber of Commerce
515 N. Court St.
Rockford, Illinois 61103
Phone: (815)962-0122

SCORE Office (St. Charles)
St. Charles Chamber of Commerce
103 N. 1st Ave.
St. Charles, Illinois 60174-1982
Phone: (847)584-8384
Fax: (847)584-6065

SCORE Office (Springfield)
U.S. Small Business Administration
511 W. Capitol Ave., Ste. 302
Springfield, Illinois 62704
Phone: (217)492-4416
Fax: (217)492-4867

SCORE Office (Springfield)
NORBIC
511 West Capitol Ave., Ste. 302
Springfield, Illinois 62704
Phone: (217)492-4416

SCORE Office (Sycamore)
Greater Sycamore Chamber of Commerce
112 Somunak St.
Sycamore, Illinois 60178
Phone: (815)895-3456
Fax: (815)895-0125

SCORE Office (University)
Governors State University
Hwy. 50 & Stuenkel Rd. Ste. C3305
University Park, Illinois 60466
Phone: (708)534-5000
Fax: (708)534-8457

Indiana

SCORE Office (Anderson)
c/o Anderson Chamber of Commerce
205 W. 11th St.
PO Box 469
Anderson, Indiana 46015
Phone: (317)642-0264

SCORE Office (Bloomington)
c/o Bloomington Chamber of Commerce
400 W. 7th St., Ste. 102
Bloomington, Indiana 47404
Phone: (812)336-6381

SCORE Office (Southeast)
c/o Columbus Chamber of Commerce
500 Franklin St.
Box 29
Columbus, Indiana 47201
Phone: (812)379-4457

SCORE Office (Corydon)
310 N. Elm St.
Corydon, Indiana 47112
Phone: (812)738-2137
Fax: (812)738-6438

SCORE Office (Crown Point)
Old Courthouse Sq. Ste. 206
P.O. Box 43
Crown Point, Indiana 46307
Phone: (219)663-1800
Phone: (219)663-1989

SCORE Office (Elkhart)
418 S. Main St.
P.O. Box 428
Elkhart, Indiana 46515
Phone: (219)293-1531

SCORE Office (Evansville)
Old Post Office Pl.
100 NW 2nd St., No. 300
Evansville, Indiana 47708
Phone: (812)421-5879

SCORE Office (Fort Wayne)
1300 S. Harrison St.
Fort Wayne, Indiana 46802
Phone: (219)422-2601

SCORE Office (Gary)
973 W. 6th Ave., Rm. 326
Gary, Indiana 46402
Phone: (219)882-3918

SCORE Office (Hammond)
7034 Indianapolis Blvd.
Hammond, Indiana 46324
Phone: (219)931-1000
Fax: (219)845-9548

SCORE Office (Indianapolis)
429 N. Pennsylvania St., Ste. 100
Indianapolis, Indiana 46204-1873
Phone: (317)226-7264

SCORE Office (Jasper)
PO Box 307
Jasper, Indiana 47547-0307
Phone: (812)482-6866

SCORE Office (Kokomo/Howard Counties)
106 N. Washington
PO Box 731
Kokomo, Indiana 46903-0731
Phone: (317)457-5301
Fax: (317)452-4564

SCORE Office (Logansport)
Logansport Chamber of Commerce
300 E. Broadway, Ste. 103
Logansport, Indiana 46947
Phone: (219)753-6388

SCORE Office (Madison)
301 E. Main St.
Madison, Indiana 47250
Phone: (812)265-3135
Fax: (812)265-2923

SCORE Office (Marengo)
c/o Marengo Chamber of Commerce
Rte. 1 Box 224D
Marengo, Indiana 47140
Fax: (812)365-2793

SCORE Office (Marion/Grant Counties)
215 S. Adams
Marion, Indiana 46952
Phone: (317)664-5107

SCORE Office (Merrillville)
255 W. 80th Pl.
Merrillville, Indiana 46410
Phone: (219)769-8180
Fax: (219)736-6223

SCORE Office (Michigan City)
200 E. Michigan Blvd.
Michigan City, Indiana 46360
Phone: (219)874-6221
Fax: (219)873-1204

SCORE Office (South Central Indiana)
1702 E. Spring St.
PO Box 653
New Albany, Indiana 47150
Phone: (812)945-0054

SCORE Office (Rensselaer)
104 W. Washington
Rensselaer, Indiana 47978

SCORE Office (Salem)
c/o Salem Chamber of Commerce
210 N. Main St.
Salem, Indiana 47167
Phone: (812)883-4303
Fax: (812)883-1467

SCORE Office (South Bend)
300 N. Michigan St.
South Bend, Indiana 46601
Phone: (219)282-4350

SCORE Office (Valparaiso)
150 Lincolnway
Valparaiso, Indiana 46383
Phone: (219)462-1105
Fax: (219)469-5710

SCORE Office (Vincennes)
Vincennes Chamber of Commerce
27 N. 3rd
P.O. Box 553
Vincennes, Indiana 47591
Phone: (812)882-6440
Fax: (812)882-6441

SCORE Office (Wabash)
PO Box 371
Wabash, Indiana 46992
Phone: (219)563-1168
Fax: (219)563-6920

Iowa

SCORE Office (Burlington)
Federal Bldg.
300 N. Main St.
Burlington, Iowa 52601
Phone: (319)752-2967

SCORE Office (Cedar Rapids)
Lattner Building, Ste. 200
215-4th Avenue, SE
Cedar Rapids, Iowa 52401-1806
Phone: (319)362-6405
Fax: (319)362-7861

SCORE Office (Southwest Iowa)
700 W. Clark
Clarinda, Iowa 51632
Phone: (712)542-2906

SCORE Office (Illowa)
River City Chamber of Commerce
333 4th Ave. S
Clinton, Iowa 52732
Phone: (319)242-5702

SCORE Office (Council Bluffs)
Council Bluffs Chamber of Commerce
P.O. Box 1565
Council Bluffs, Iowa 51502-1565
Phone: (712)325-1000

SCORE Office (Northeast Iowa)
3404 285th St.
Cresco, Iowa 52136
Phone: (319)547-3377

SCORE Office (Des Moines)
Federal Bldg., Rm. 749
210 Walnut St.
Des Moines, Iowa 50309-2186
Phone: (515)284-4760

SCORE Office (Fort Dodge)
Federal Bldg., Rm. 436
205 S. 8th St.
Fort Dodge, Iowa 50501
Phone: (515)955-2622

SCORE Office (Independence)
Independence Area Chamber of
Commerce
110 1st. St. east
Independence, Iowa 50644
Phone: (319)334-7178
Fax: (319)334-7179

SCORE Office (Iowa City)
210 Federal Bldg.
PO Box 1853
Iowa City, Iowa 52240-1853
Phone: (319)338-1662

SCORE Office (Keokuk)
Keokuk Area Chamber of Commerce
Pierce Bldg., No. 1
401 Main St.
Keokuk, Iowa 52632
Phone: (319)524-5055

SCORE Office (Central Iowa)
Fisher Community Center
709 S. Center
Marshalltown, Iowa 50158
Phone: (515)753-6645

SCORE Office (River City)
15 West State St.
P.O. Box 1128
Mason City, Iowa 50401
Phone: (515)423-5724

SCORE Office (South Central)
c/o Indian Hills Community College
525 Grandview Ave.
Ottumwa, Iowa 52501
Phone: (515)683-5127
Fax: (515)683-5263

SCORE Office (Dubuque)
Northeast Iowa Community College
10250 Sundown Road
Peosta, Iowa 52068
Phone: (319)556-5110

SCORE Office (Southwest Iowa)
Chamber of Commerce
403 W. Sheridan
Shenandoah, Iowa 51601
Phone: (712)542-2906

SCORE Office (Sioux City)
c/o Sioux City Federal Bldg.
320 6th St.
Sioux City, Iowa 51101
Phone: (712)277-2325

SCORE Office (Iowa Lakes)
21 W. 5th St., Rm. 5
PO Box 7026
Spencer, Iowa 51301-3059
Phone: (712)262-3059

SCORE Office (Vista)
Storm Lake Chamber of Commerce
119 W. 6th St.
Storm Lake, Iowa 50588
Phone: (712)732-3780

SCORE Office (Waterloo)
Waterloo Chamber of Commerce
215 E. 4th
Waterloo, Iowa 50703
Phone: (319)233-8431

Kansas

SCORE Office (Southwest Kansas)
Dodge City Area Chamber of Commerce
PO Box 939
Dodge City, Kansas 67801
Phone: (316)227-3119

SCORE Office (Emporia)
Emporia Chamber of Commerce
427 Commercial
Emporia, Kansas 66801
Phone: (316)342-1600

SCORE Office (Golden Belt)
Chamber of Commerce
1307 Williams
Great Bend, Kansas 67530
Phone: (316)792-2401

SCORE Office (Hays)
c/o Empire Bank
PO Box 400
Hays, Kansas 67601
Phone: (913)625-6595

SCORE Office (Hutchinson)
One E. 9th St.
Hutchinson, Kansas 67501
Phone: (316)665-8468

SCORE Office (Southeast Kansas)
404 Westminster Pl.
PO Box 886
Independence, Kansas 67301-0886
Phone: (316)331-4741

SCORE Office (McPherson)
McPherson Chamber of Commerce
306 N. Main
McPherson, Kansas 67460
Phone: (316)241-3303

SCORE Office (Salina)
PO Box 586
Salina, Kansas 67401
Phone: (913)827-9301

SCORE Office (Topeka)
1700 College
Topeka, Kansas 66621
Phone: (913)231-1010
Phone: (913)231-1305

SCORE Office (Wichita)
U.S. Small Business Administration
100 E. English, Ste. 510
Wichita, Kansas 67202
Phone: (316)269-6273

SCORE Office (Ark Valley)
Box 314
Winfield, Kansas 67156
Phone: (316)221-1617

Kentucky

SCORE Office (Ashland)
PO Box 830
Ashland, Kentucky 41105
Phone: (606)329-8011
Fax: (606)325-4607

SCORE Office (Bowling Green)
Bowling Green-Warren Chamber of
Commerce
812 State St.
P.O. Box 51
Bowling Green, Kentucky 42101
Phone: (502)781-3200
Fax: (502)843-0458

SCORE Office (Tri-Lakes)
508 Barbee Way
Danville, Kentucky 40422-1548
Phone: (606)231-9902

SCORE Office (Glasgow)
301 W. Main St.
Glasgow, Kentucky 42141
Phone: (502)651-3161
Fax: (502)651-3122

SCORE Office (Hazard)
B & I Technical Center
100 Airport Gardens Rd.
Hazard, Kentucky 41701
Phone: (606)439-5856
Fax: (606)439-1808

SCORE Office (Lexington)
1460 Newton Pke., Ste. A
Lexington, Kentucky 40511
Phone: (606)231-9902

SCORE Office (Louisville)
188 Federal Office Bldg.
600 Dr. Martin L. King Jr. Pl.
Louisville, Kentucky 40202
Phone: (502)582-5976

SCORE Office (Madisonville)
257 N. Main
Madisonville, Kentucky 42431
Phone: (502)825-1399
Fax: (502)825-1396

SCORE Office (Paducah)
Federal Office Bldg.
501 Broadway, Rm. B-36
Paducah, Kentucky 42001
Phone: (502)442-5685

Louisiana

SCORE Office (Central Louisiana)
802 3rd St.
PO Box 992
Alexandria, Louisiana 71309
Phone: (318)442-6671

SCORE Office (Baton Rouge)
564 Laurel St.
PO Box 3217
Baton Rouge, Louisiana 70801
Phone: (504)381-7125

SCORE Office (North Shore)
PO Box 1458
Hammond, Louisiana 70404
Phone: (504)345-4457

SCORE Office (Lafayette)
Lafayette Chamber of Commerce
804 St. Mary Blvd.
PO Drawer 51307
Lafayette, Louisiana 70505-1307
Phone: (318)233-2705

SCORE Office (Lake Charles)
120 W. Pujo
Lake Charles, Louisiana 70601
Phone: (318)433-3632

SCORE Office (New Orleans)
365 Canal St., Ste. 2250
New Orleans, Louisiana 70130
Phone: (504)589-2356

SCORE Office (Shreveport)
400 Edwards St.
Shreveport, Louisiana 71101
Phone: (318)677-2509

Maine

SCORE Office (Augusta)
40 Western Ave.
Augusta, Maine 04330
Phone: (207)622-8509

SCORE Office (Bangor)
Husson College
Peabody Hall, Rm. 229
One College Cir.
Bangor, Maine 04401
Phone: (207)941-9707

SCORE Office (Central & Northern
Arrostock)
111 High St.
PO Box 357
Caribou, Maine 04736
Phone: (207)498-6156

SCORE Office (Penquis)
Chamber of Commerce
South St.
Dover Foxcroft, Maine 04426
Phone: (207)564-7021

SCORE Office (Maine Coastal)
Federal Bldg.
Main & Water St.
Box 1105
Ellsworth, Maine 04605
Phone: (207)667-5800

SCORE Office (Lewiston-Auburn)
c/o Chamber of Commerce
179 Lisbon St.
Lewiston, Maine 04240
Phone: (207)782-3708

SCORE Office (Portland)
66 Pearl St., Rm. 210
Portland, Maine 04101
Phone: (207)772-1147

SCORE Office (Western Mountains)
c/o Fleet Bank
108 Congress St.
PO Box 400
Rumford, Maine 04276
Phone: (207)364-3733

SCORE Office (Oxford Hills)
166 Main St.
South Paris, Maine 04281
Phone: (207)743-0499
Fax: (207)743-5917

Maryland

SCORE Office (Southern Maryland)
2525 Riva Rd., Ste. 110
Annapolis, Maryland 21401
Phone: (410)267-6206

SCORE Office (Baltimore)
The City Crescent Bldg., 6th Fl.
10 S. Howard St.
Baltimore, Maryland 21201
Phone: (410)962-2233
Fax: (410)962-1805

SCORE Office (Dundalk)
Eastern Baltimore Chamber of Commerce
2200 Broening Hwy. Ste. 102
Baltimore, Maryland 21224
Phone: (410)282-9100
Fax: (410)631-9099

SCORE Office (Bel Air)
Bel Air Chamber of Commerce
108 S. Bond St.
Bel Air, Maryland 21014
Phone: (410)838-2020
Fax: (410)893-4715

SCORE Office (Bethesda)
7910 Woodmont Ave., Ste. 1204
Bethesda, Maryland 20814
Phone: (301)652-4900
Fax: (301)657-1973

SCORE Office (Bowie)
6670 Race Track Rd.
Bowie, Maryland 20715
Phone: (301)262-0920
Fax: (301)262-0921

SCORE Office (Dorchester County)
c/o Chamber of Commerce
203 Sunburst Hwy.
Cambridge, Maryland 21613
Phone: (410)228-3575

SCORE Office (Upper Shore)
c/o Talbout County Chamber of
Commerce
PO Box 1366
Easton, Maryland 21601
Phone: (410)822-4606
Fax: (410)822-7922

SCORE Office (Frederick County)
43A S. Market St.
Frederick, Maryland 21701
Phone: (301)662-4164

SCORE Office (Gaithersburg)
9 Park Ave.
Gaithersburg, Maryland 20877
Phone: (301)840-1400
Fax: (301)963-3918

SCORE Office (Glen Burnie)
Glen Burnie Chamber of Commerce
103 Crain Hwy. SE
Glen Burnie, Maryland 21061
Phone: (410)766-8282
Fax: (410)766-9722

SCORE Office (Hagerstown)
111 W. Washington St.
Hagerstown, Maryland 21740
Phone: (301)739-2015

SCORE Office (Laurel)
7901 Sandy Spring Rd. Ste. 501
Laurel, Maryland 20707
Phone: (301)725-4000
Fax: (301)725-0776

SCORE Office (Salisbury)
c/o Salisbury Chamber of Commerce
300 E. Main St.
Salisbury, Maryland 21801
Phone: (410)749-0185

Massachusetts

SCORE Office (Boston)
10 Causeway St., Rm. 265
Boston, Massachusetts 02222
Phone: (617)565-5591
Fax: (617)565-5598

SCORE Office (Southeastern)
60 School St.
Brockton, Massachusetts 02401
Phone: (508)587-2673

SCORE Office (North Adams)
Northern Berkshire Development Corp.
820 N. State Rd.
Cheshire, Massachusetts 01225
Phone: (413)743-5100

SCORE Office (Clinton Satellite)
c/o Clinton Chamber of Commerce
1 Green St.
Clinton, Massachusetts 01510
Fax: (508)368-7689

SCORE Office (Northeastern Massa-
chusetts)
Danvers Savings Bank
1 Conant St.
Danvers, Massachusetts 01923
Phone: (508)777-2200

SCORE Office (Bristol/Plymouth
Counties)
Fall River Area Chamber of Commerce
and Industry
PO Box 1871
Fall River, Massachusetts 02722-1871
Phone: (508)676-8226

SCORE Office (Greenfield)
PO Box 898
Greenfield, Massachusetts 01302
Phone: (413)773-5463
Fax: (413)773-7008

SCORE Office (Haverhill)
Haverhill Chamber
87 Winter St.
Haverhill, Massachusetts 01830
Phone: (508)373-5663
Fax: (508)373-8060

SCORE Office (Hudson Satellite)
c/o Hudson Chamber of Commerce
PO Box 578
Hudson, Massachusetts 01749
Phone: (508)568-0360
Fax: (508)568-0360

SCORE Office (Cape Cod)
Independence Pk., Ste. 5B
270 Communications Way
Hyannis, Massachusetts 02601
Phone: (508)775-4884

SCORE Office (Lawrence)
264 Essex St.
Lawrence, Massachusetts 01840
Phone: (508)686-0900
Fax: (508)794-9953

SCORE Office (Leominster Satellite)
c/o Leominster Chamber of Commerce
110 Erdman Way
Leominster, Massachusetts 01453
Phone: (508)840-4300
Fax: (508)840-4896

SCORE Office (Newburyport)
29 State St.
Newburyport, Massachusetts 01950
Phone: (617)462-6680

SCORE Office (Pittsfield)
Central Berkshire Chamber
66 West St.
Pittsfield, Massachusetts 01201
Phone: (413)499-2485

SCORE Office (Haverhill)
32 Derby Sq.
Salem, Massachusetts 01970
Phone: (508)745-0330
Fax: (508)745-3855

SCORE Office (Springfield)
1550 Main St., Ste. 212
Springfield, Massachusetts 01103
Phone: (413)785-0314

SCORE Office (Carver)
12 Taunton Green, Ste. 201
Taunton, Massachusetts 02780
Phone: (508)824-4068
Fax: (508)824-4069

SCORE Office (Cape Cod)
c/o Martha's Vineyard Chamber of
Commerce
Beach Rd.
PO Box 1698
Vineyard Haven, Massachusetts 02568
Phone: (508)693-0085

SCORE Office (Worcester)
33 Waldo St.
Worcester, Massachusetts 01608
Phone: (508)753-2924

Michigan

SCORE Office (Allegan)
c/o Allegan Chamber of Commerce
PO Box 338
Allegan, Michigan 49010
Phone: (616)673-2479

SCORE Office (Ann Arbor)
425 S. Main St., Ste. 103
Ann Arbor, Michigan 48104
Phone: (313)665-4433

SCORE Office (Battle Creek)
c/o Battle Creek Chamber of Commerce
34 W. Jackson Ste. 4A
Battle Creek, Michigan 49017-3505
Phone: (616)962-4076
Fax: (616)962-6309

SCORE Office (Cadillac)
c/o Cadillac Chamber of Commerce
222 Lake St.
Cadillac, Michigan 49601
Phone: (616)775-9776
Fax: (616)775-1440

SCORE Office (Detroit)
477 Michigan Ave., Rm. 515
Detroit, Michigan 48226
Phone: (313)226-7947

SCORE Office (Flint)
Mott Community College
708 Root Rd., Rm. 308
Flint, Michigan 48503
Phone: (810)233-6846

SCORE Office (Grand Rapids)
110 Michigan Ave.
Grand Rapids, Michigan 49503
Phone: (616)771-0305

SCORE Office (Holland)
c/o Holland Chamber of Commerce
480 State St.
Holland, Michigan 49423
Phone: (616)396-9472

SCORE Office (Jackson)
Jackson Chamber of Commerce
209 East Washington
PO Box 80
Jackson, Michigan 49204
Phone: (517)782-8221
Fax: (517)782-0061

SCORE Office (Kalamazoo)
128 N. Kalamazoo Mall
Kalamazoo, Michigan 49007
Phone: (616) 381-5382

SCORE Office (Lansing)
117 E. Allegan
PO Box 14030
Lansing, Michigan 48901
Phone: (517) 487-6340
Fax: (517) 484-6910

SCORE Office (Livonia)
Livonia Chamber of Commerce
15401 Farmington Rd.
Livonia, Michigan 48154
Phone: (313) 427-2122
Fax: (313) 427-6055

SCORE Office (Madison Heights)
26345 John R
Madison Heights, Michigan 48071
Phone: (810) 542-5010
Fax: (810) 542-6821

SCORE Office (Monroe)
Monroe Chamber of Commerce
111 E. 1st
Monroe, Michigan 48161
Phone: (313) 242-3366
Fax: (313) 242-7253

SCORE Office (Mount Clemens)
Macomb County Chamber of Commerce
58 S/B Gratiot
Mount Clemens, Michigan 48043
Phone: (810) 463-1528
Fax: (810) 463-6541

SCORE Office (Muskegon)
c/o Muskegon Chamber of Commerce
PO Box 1087
230 Terrace Plz.
Muskegon, Michigan 49443
Phone: (616) 722-3751
Fax: (616) 728-7251

SCORE Office (Petoskey)
c/o Petoskey Chamber of Commerce
401 E. Mitchell St.
Petoskey, Michigan 49770-9961
Phone: (616) 347-4150

SCORE Office (Pontiac)
Pontiac Chamber of Commerce
PO Box 430025
Pontiac, Michigan 48343
Phone: (810) 335-9600

SCORE Office (Pontiac)
Oakland County Economic Development Group
Executive Office Bldg.
1200 N. Telegraph Rd.
Pontiac, Michigan 48341
Phone: (810) 975-9555

SCORE Office (Port Huron)
920 Pinegrove Ave.
Port Huron, Michigan 48060
Phone: (810) 985-7101

SCORE Office (Rochester)
Rochester Chamber of Commerce
71 Walnut Ste. 110
Rochester, Michigan 48307
Phone: (810) 651-6700
Fax: (810) 651-5270

SCORE Office (Saginaw)
901 S. Washington Ave.
Saginaw, Michigan 48601
Phone: (517) 752-7161
Fax: (517) 752-9055

SCORE Office (Upper Peninsula)
c/o Chamber of Commerce
2581 I-75 Business Spur
Sault Sainte Marie, Michigan 49783
Phone: (906) 632-3301

SCORE Office (Southfield)
21000 W. 10 Mile Rd.
Southfield, Michigan 48075
Phone: (810) 204-3050
Fax: (810) 204-3099

SCORE Office (Traverse City)
202 E. Grandview Pkwy.
PO Box 387
Traverse City, Michigan 49685
Phone: (616) 947-5075

SCORE Office (Warren)
Warren Chamber of Commerce
30500 Van Dyke, Ste. 118
Warren, Michigan 48093
Phone: (810) 751-3939

Minnesota

SCORE Office (Aitkin)
c/o Donald F. Gode
Aitkin, Minnesota 56431
Phone: (218) 741-3906

SCORE Office (Albert Lea)
Albert Lea Chamber of Commerce
202 N. Broadway Ave.
Albert Lea, Minnesota 56007
Phone: (507) 373-7487

SCORE Office (Austin)
PO Box 864
Austin, Minnesota 55912
Phone: (507) 437-4561
Fax: (507) 437-4869

SCORE Office (South Metro)
Burnsville Chamber of Commerce
101 W. Burnsville Pkwy., No. 150
Burnsville, Minnesota 55337
Phone: (612) 435-6000
Phone: (612) 898-5645

SCORE Office (Fairmont)
c/o Fairmont Chamber of Commerce
PO Box 826
Fairmont, Minnesota 56031
Phone: (507) 235-5547
Fax: (507) 235-8411

SCORE Office (Southwest Minnesota)
112 Riverfront St.
Box 999
Mankato, Minnesota 56001
Phone: (507) 345-4519

SCORE Office (Minneapolis)
North Plaza Bldg., Ste. 51
5217 Wayzata Blvd.
Minneapolis, Minnesota 55416
Phone: (612) 591-0539

SCORE Office (Owatonna)
PO Box 331
Owatonna, Minnesota 55060
Phone: (507) 451-7970
Fax: (507) 451-7972

SCORE Office (Red Wing)
2000 W. Main St., Ste. 324
Red Wing, Minnesota 55066
Phone: (612) 388-4079

SCORE Office (Southeastern Minnesota)
Marshall Chamber of Commerce
220 S. Broadway, Ste. 100
Rochester, Minnesota 55904
Phone: (507) 288-1122
Fax: (507) 282-8960

SCORE Office (Brainerd)
Brainerd Chamber of Commerce
St. Cloud, Minnesota 56301
Phone: (612)255-4955
Fax: (612)255-4957

SCORE Office (Central Area)
4191 2nd St. S
St. Cloud, Minnesota 56301-3600
Phone: (612)255-4955

SCORE Office (St. Paul)
St. Paul Chamber of Commerce
55 5th St. E, No. 101
St. Paul, Minnesota 55101-1713
Phone: (612)223-5010

SCORE Office (Winona)
Box 870
Winona, Minnesota 55987
Phone: (507)452-2272
Fax: (507)454-8814

SCORE Office (Worthington)
Worthington Chamber of Commerce
1121 3rd Ave.
Worthington, Minnesota 56187
Phone: (507)372-2919
Fax: (507)372-2827

Mississippi

SCORE Office (Delta)
Greenville Chamber of Commerce
915 Washington Ave.
PO Box 933
Greenville, Mississippi 38701
Phone: (601)378-3141
Fax: (601)378-3143

SCORE Office (Gulfcoast)
c/o Small Business Administration
Hancock Plz., Ste. 1001
Gulfport, Mississippi 39501-7758
Phone: (601)863-4449

SCORE Office (Jackson)
1st Jackson Center, Ste. 400
101 W. Capitol St.
Jackson, Mississippi 39201
Phone: (601)965-5533

SCORE Office (Meridian)
5220 16th Ave.
Meridian, Mississippi 39305
Phone: (601)482-4412

Missouri

SCORE Office (Lake Ozark)
University Extension
113 Kansas St.
PO Box 1405
Camdenton, Missouri 65020
Phone: (314)346-2644
Fax: (314)346-2694

SCORE Office (Cape Girardeau)
c/o Chamber of Commerce
PO Box 98
Cape Girardeau, Missouri 63702-0098
Phone: (314)335-3312

SCORE Office (Mid-Missouri)
c/o Milo Dahl
1705 Halstead Ct.
Columbia, Missouri 65203
Phone: (314)874-1132

SCORE Office (Ozark-Gateway)
101 E. Washington St.
Cuba, Missouri 65453-1826
Phone: (314)885-4954

SCORE Office (Kansas City)
323 W. 8th St., Ste. 104
Kansas City, Missouri 64105
Phone: (816)374-6675
Fax: (816)374-6759

SCORE Office (Sedalia)
c/o State Fair Community College
Lucas Place
323 W. 8th St., Ste. 104
Kansas City, Missouri 64105
Phone: (816)374-6675
Phone: (816)374-6759

SCORE Office (Tri-Lakes)
HCRI Box 85
Lampe, Missouri 65681
Phone: (417)858-6798

SCORE Office (South East Missouri)
c/o Carl Trautman
505 Lalor Dr.
Manchester, Missouri 63011
Phone: (314)256-3331

SCORE Office (Mexico)
Mexico Chamber of Commerce
111 N. Washington St.
Mexico, Missouri 65265
Phone: (314)581-2765

SCORE Office (Poplar Bluff Area)
c/o James W. Carson, Chair
Rte. 1, Box 280
Neelyville, Missouri 63954
Phone: (314)785-4727

SCORE Office (St. Joseph)
3418 W. Colony Sq.
St. Joseph, Missouri 64506
Phone: (816)232-9793

SCORE Office (St. Louis)
815 Olive St., Rm. 242
St. Louis, Missouri 63101-1569
Phone: (314)539-6600
Fax: (314)889-7687

SCORE Office (Lewis & Clark)
425 Spencer Rd.
St. Peters, Missouri 63376
Phone: (314)928-2900

SCORE Office (Springfield)
620 S. Glenstone, Ste. 110
Springfield, Missouri 65802-3200
Phone: (417)864-7670

SCORE Office (Springfield)
C/o Small Business Administration
620 S. Glenstone, Ste. 110
Springfield, Missouri 65802-3200
Phone: (417)864-7670
Fax: (417)864-4108

Montana

SCORE Office (Billings)
815 S. 27th St.
Billings, Montana 59101
Phone: (406)245-4111

SCORE Office (Bozeman)
1205 E. Main St.
Bozeman, Montana 59715
Phone: (406)586-5421
Fax: (406)586-8286

SCORE Office (Butte)
2950 Harrison Ave.
Butte, Montana 59701
Phone: (406)494-5595
Phone: (406)494-8165

SCORE Office (Great Falls)
815 2nd St. S.
Great Falls, Montana 59405
Phone: (406)761-4434

SCORE Office (Helena)
Federal Bldg.
301 S. Park
Drawer 10054
Helena, Montana 59626-0054
Phone: (406)449-5381
Fax: (406)449-5474

SCORE Office (Kalispell)
2 Main St.
Kalispell, Montana 59901
Phone: (406)756-5271
Fax: (406)752-6665

SCORE Office (Missoula)
802 Normans Ln.
Missoula, Montana 59803
Phone: (406)543-6623

Nebraska

SCORE Office (Columbus)
1823 27th St.
Columbus, Nebraska 68601
Phone: (402)564-2769
Phone: (402)564-5379
Phone: (402)564-0401

SCORE Office (North Platte)
414 E. 16th St.
Cozad, Nebraska 69130
Phone: (308)784-2690

SCORE Office (Fremont)
PO Box 325
Freemont Chamber of Commerce
92 W. 5th St.
Fremont, Nebraska 68025
Phone: (402)721-2641

SCORE Office (Hastings)
Box 42
Kearney, Nebraska 68848
Phone: (308)234-9647

SCORE Office (Lincoln)
8800 East O St.
Lincoln, Nebraska 68520
Phone: (402)437-2409

SCORE Office (Norfolk)
504 Pierce St.
Norfolk, Nebraska 68701
Phone: (402)371-0940

SCORE Office (Nebraska Small
Business Development Center)
11145 Mill Valley Rd.
Omaha, Nebraska 68154
Phone: (402)221-3604

SCORE Office (Panhandle)
11145 Mill Valley Rd.
Omaha, Nebraska 68154
Phone: (402)221-3604

Nevada

SCORE Office (Incline Village)
c/o Incline Village Chamber of
Commerce
969 Tahoe Blvd.
Incline Village, Nevada 89451
Phone: (702)831-7327
Fax: (702)832-1605

SCORE Office (Carson City)
301 E. Stewart
PO Box 7527
Las Vegas, Nevada 89125
Phone: (702)388-6104

SCORE Office (Las Vegas)
301 E. Stewart
Box 7527
Las Vegas, Nevada 89125
Phone: (702)388-6104

SCORE Office (Northern Nevada)
50 S. Virginia St., No. 233
PO Box 3216
Reno, Nevada 89505-3216
Phone: (702)784-5477

New Hampshire

SCORE Office (North Country)
PO Box 34
Berlin, New Hampshire 03570
Phone: (603)752-1090

SCORE Office (Concord)
PO Box 1258
Concord, New Hampshire 03302-1258
Phone: (603)225-7763

SCORE Office (Dover)
299 Central Ave.
Dover, New Hampshire 03820
Phone: (603)742-2218
Fax: (603)749-6317

SCORE Office (Monadnock)
34 Mechanic St.
Keene, New Hampshire 03431-3421
Phone: (603)352-0320

SCORE Office (Lakes Region)
67 Water St., Ste. 105
Laconia, New Hampshire 03246
Phone: (603)524-9168

SCORE Office (Upper Valley)
First New Hampshire Bank Bldg.
316 First
Lebanon, New Hampshire 03766
Phone: (603)448-3491

SCORE Office (Merrimack Valley)
275 Chestnut St., Rm. 618
Manchester, New Hampshire 03103
Phone: (603)666-7561

SCORE Office (Seacoast)
195 Commerce Way, Unit-A
Portsmouth, New Hampshire 03801-3251
Phone: (603)433-0576

New Jersey

SCORE Office (Chester)
c/o John C. Apelian, Chair
5 Old Mill Rd.
Chester, New Jersey 07930
Phone: (908)879-7080

SCORE Office (Greater Princeton)
4 A George Washington Dr.
Cranbury, New Jersey 08512
Phone: (609)520-1776

SCORE Office (Freehold)
Western Monmouth Chamber of
Commerce
36 W. Main St.
Freehold, New Jersey 07728
Phone: (908)462-3030
Fax: (908)462-2123

SCORE Office (Monmouth)
Brookdale Community College Career
Services
765 Newman Springs Rd.
Lincroft, New Jersey 07738
Phone: (908)224-2573

SCORE Office (Manalapan)
Monmough Library
125 Symmes Dr.
Manalapan, New Jersey 07726
Phone: (908)431-7220

SCORE Office (Jersey City)
2 Gateway Ctr., 4th Fl.
Newark, New Jersey 07102
Phone: (201)645-3982
Fax: (201)645-6265

SCORE Office (Newark)
2 Gateway Center, 4th Fl.
Newark, New Jersey 07102-5553
Phone: (201)645-3982

SCORE Office (Bergen County)
327 E. Ridgewood Ave.
Paramus, New Jersey 07652
Phone: (201)599-6090

SCORE Office (Pennsauken)
United Jersey Bank
4900 Rte. 70
Pennsauken, New Jersey 08109
Phone: (609)486-3421

SCORE Office (Southern New Jersey)
c/o United Jersey Bank
4900 Rte. 70
Pennsauken, New Jersey 08109
Phone: (609)486-3421

SCORE Office (Shrewsbury)
Monmouth County Library
Hwy. 35
Shrewsbury, New Jersey 07702
Phone: (908)842-5995
Fax: (908)219-6140

SCORE Office (Somerset)
Paritan Valley Community College
PO Box 3300
Somerville, New Jersey 08876
Phone: (908)218-8874

SCORE Office (Ocean County)
33 Washington St.
Toms River, New Jersey 08754
Phone: (908)505-6033

SCORE Office (Wall)
Wall Library
2700 Allaire Rd.
Wall, New Jersey 07719
Phone: (908)449-8877

SCORE Office (Wayne)
2055 Hamburg Tpke.
Wayne, New Jersey 07470
Phone: (201)831-7788
Fax: (201)831-9112

New Mexico

SCORE Office (Albuquerque)
Silver Sq., Ste. 330
625 Silver Ave., SW
Albuquerque, New Mexico 87102
Phone: (505)766-1900

SCORE Office (Las Cruces)
Loretto Towne Center
505 S. Main St., Ste. 125
Las Cruces, New Mexico 88001
Phone: (505)523-5627

SCORE Office (Roswell)
Federal Bldg., Rm. 237
Roswell, New Mexico 88201
Phone: (505)625-2112

SCORE Office (Santa Fe)
Montoya Federal Bldg.
120 Federal Place, Rm. 307
Santa Fe, New Mexico 87501
Phone: (505)988-6302

New York

SCORE Office (Northeast)
Lee O'Brien Office Bldg., Rm. 815
Pearl & Clinton Aves.
Albany, New York 12207
Phone: (518)472-6300

SCORE Office (Auburn)
c/o Auburn Chamber of Commerce
30 South St.
PO Box 675
Auburn, New York 13021
Phone: (315)252-7291

SCORE Office (South Tier Binghamton)
Metro Center, 2nd Fl.
49 Court St.
PO Box 995
Binghamton, New York 13902
Phone: (607)772-8860

SCORE Office (Queens County City)
12055 Queens Blvd., Rm. 333
Borough Hall, New York 11424
Phone: (718)263-8961

SCORE Office (Buffalo)
Federal Bldg., Rm. 1311
111 W. Huron St.
Buffalo, New York 14202
Phone: (716)846-4301

SCORE Office (Canandaigua)
Chamber of Commerce Bldg.
113 S. Main St.
Canandaigua, New York 14424
Phone: (716)394-4400
Fax: (716)394-4546

SCORE Office (Chemung)
c/o Small Business Administration,
4th Fl.
333 E. Water St.
Elmira, New York 14901
Phone: (607)734-3358

SCORE Office (Geneva)
Chamber of Commerce Bldg.
PO Box 587
Geneva, New York 14456
Phone: (315)789-1776
Fax: (315)789-3993

SCORE Office (Glens Falls)
Adirondack Region Chamber of
Commerce
84 Broad St.
Glens Falls, New York 12801
Phone: (518)798-8463
Fax: (518)745-1433

SCORE Office (Orange County)
Orange County Chamber of Commerce
40 Matthews St.
Goshen, New York 10924
Phone: (914)294-8080
Toll-free: (800)294-8181
Fax: (914)294-6121

SCORE Office (Huntington Area)
c/o Huntington Chamber of Commerce
151 W. Carver St.
Huntington, New York 11743
Phone: (516)423-6100

SCORE Office (Tompkins County)
c/o Tompkins County Chamber of
Commerce
904 E. Shore Dr.
Ithaca, New York 14850
Phone: (607)273-7080

SCORE Office (Long Island City)
120-55 Queens Blvd.
Jamaica, New York 11424
Phone: (718)263-8961
Fax: (718)263-9032

SCORE Office (Chatauqua)
c/o Chatauqua Chamber of Commerce
101 W. 5th St.
Jamestown, New York 14701
Phone: (716)484-1103

SCORE Office (Queens County City)
120-55 Queens Blvd., Rm. 333
Queens Borough Hall
Kew Gardens, New York 11424
Phone: (718)263-8961

SCORE Office (Brookhaven)
Dept. of Economic Development
3233 Rte. 112
Medford, New York 11763
Phone: (516)451-6563
Phone: (516)751-3886

SCORE Office (Melville)
35 Pinelawn Rd., Rm. 207-W
Melville, New York 11747
Phone: (516)454-0771

SCORE Office (Nassau County)
400 County Seat Dr., No. 140
Mineola, New York 11501
Phone: (516)571-3304
Phone: (516)571-3341

SCORE Office (Mount Vernon)
c/o Mount Vernon Chamber of
Commerce
4 N. 7th Ave.
Mount Vernon, New York 10550
Phone: (914)667-7500

SCORE Office (New York)
26 Federal Plz., Rm. 3100
New York, New York 10278
Phone: (212)264-4507

SCORE Office (Newburgh)
47 Grand St.
Newburgh, New York 12550
Phone: (914)562-5100

SCORE Office (Owego)
Tioga County Chamber of Commerce
188 Front St.
Owego, New York 13827
Phone: (607)687-2020

SCORE Office (Peekskill)
c/o Peekskill Chamber of Commerce
1 S. Division St.
Peekskill, New York 10566
Phone: (914)737-3600
Fax: (914)737-0541

SCORE Office (Penn Yan)
Penn Yan Chamber of Commerce
2375 Rte. 14A
Penn Yan, New York 14527
Phone: (315)536-3111

SCORE Office (Dutchess)
c/o Chamber of Commerce
110 Main St.
Poughkeepsie, New York 12601
Phone: (914)454-1700

SCORE Office (Rochester)
601 Keating Federal Bldg., Rm. 410
100 State St.
Rochester, New York 14614
Phone: (716)263-6473

SCORE Office (Saranac Lake)
30 Main St.
Saranac Lake, New York 12983
Phone: (315)448-0415

SCORE Office (Suffolk)
286 Main St.
Setauket, New York 11733
Phone: (516)751-3886

SCORE Office (Staten Island)
c/o Staten Island Chamber of Commerce
130 Bay St.
Staten Island, New York 10301
Phone: (718)727-1221

SCORE Office (Ulster)
Ulster County Community College
Clinton Bldg., Rm. 107
Stone Ridge, New York 12484
Phone: (914)687-5035

SCORE Office (Syracuse)
100 S. Clinton St., Rm. 1073
Syracuse, New York 13260
Phone: (315)448-0422

SCORE Office (Oneida)
SUNY Institute of Technology
PO Box 3050
Utica, New York 13504-3050
Phone: (315)792-7553

SCORE Office (Watertown)
CAPC Office
518 Davidson St.
PO Box 899
Watertown, New York 13601
Phone: (315)788-1200

SCORE Office (Westchester)
350 Main St.
White Plains, New York 10601
Phone: (914)948-3907

SCORE Office (Yonkers)
c/o Yonkers Chamber of Commerce
540 Nepperhan Ave., Ste.200
Yonkers, New York 10701
Phone: (914)963-0332

North Carolina

SCORE Office (Asheville)
Federal Bldg., Rm. 259
151 Patton
Asheville, North Carolina 28801
Phone: (704)271-4786

SCORE Office (Chapel Hill)
c/o Chapel Hill/Carrboro Chamber of
Commerce
104 S. Estes Dr.
PO Box 2897
Chapel Hill, North Carolina 27514
Phone: (919)967-7075

SCORE Office (Coastal Plains)
PO Box 2897
Chapel Hill, North Carolina 27515
Phone: (919)967-7075
Fax: (919)968-6874

SCORE Office (Charlotte)
200 N. College St., Ste. A-2015
Charlotte, North Carolina 28202
Phone: (704)344-6576

SCORE Office (Durham)
3411 Chapel Hill Blvd.
Durham, North Carolina 27707
Phone: (919)541-2171

SCORE Office (Gastonia)
c/o Gastonia Chamber of Commerce
PO Box 2168
Gastonia, North Carolina 28053
Phone: (704)864-2621
Fax: (704)854-8723

SCORE Office (Greensboro)
400 W. Market St., Ste. 410
Greensboro, North Carolina 27401-2241
Phone: (919)333-5399

SCORE Office (Henderson)
PO Box 917
Henderson, North Carolina 27536
Phone: (919)492-2061
Fax: (919)430-0460

SCORE Office (Hendersonville)
Federal Bldg., Rm. 108
W. 4th Ave. & Church St.
Hendersonville, North Carolina 28792
Phone: (704)693-8702

SCORE Office (Unifour)
c/o Catawba County Chamber of
Commerce
PO Box 1828
Hickory, North Carolina 28603
Phone: (704)328-6111

SCORE Office (High Point)
c/o High Point Chamber of Commerce
1101 N. Main St.
High Point, North Carolina 27262
Phone: (910)882-8625

SCORE Office (Outer Banks)
c/o Outer Banks Chamber of Commerce
PO Box 1757
Kill Devil Hills, North Carolina 27948
Phone: (919)441-8144

SCORE Office (Down East)
PO Box 14294
New Bern, North Carolina 28561
Phone: (919)633-6688

SCORE Office (Kinston)
PO Box 14294
New Bern, North Carolina 28561
Phone: (919)633-6688

SCORE Office (Raleigh)
Century Post Office Bldg., Ste. 306
PO Box 406
Raleigh, North Carolina 27602
Phone: (919)856-4739

SCORE Office (Sanford)
Small Business Assistance Center
1801 Nash St.
Sanford, North Carolina 27330
Phone: (919)774-6442
Fax: (919)776-8739

SCORE Office (Sandhills Area)
c/o Sand Area Chamber of Commerce
1480 Hwy. 15-501
PO Box 458
Southern Pines, North Carolina 28387
Phone: (910)692-3926

SCORE Office (Wilmington)
Alton Lennon Federal Bldg.
2 Princess St., Ste. 103
Wilmington, North Carolina 28401-3958
Phone: (919)343-4576

North Dakota

SCORE Office (Bismarck-Mandan)
418 E. Broadway Ave.
PO Box 1912
Bismarck, North Dakota 58501-1912
Phone: (701)250-4303

SCORE Office (Fargo)
657 2nd Ave., Rm. 225
PO Box 3086
Fargo, North Dakota 58108-3083
Phone: (701)239-5677

SCORE Office (Upper Red River)
202 N. 3rd St.
Grand Forks, North Dakota 58203
Phone: (701)772-7271

SCORE Office (Minot)
PO Box 507
Minot, North Dakota 58701-0507
Phone: (701)852-6883

Ohio

SCORE Office (Akron)
c/o Akron Regional Development
Board
One Cascade Plz., 7th Fl.
Akron, Ohio 44308
Phone: (216)379-3163

SCORE Office (Ashland)
Ashland University
Gill Center
47 W. Main St.
Ashland, Ohio 44805
Phone: (419)281-4584

SCORE Office (Canton)
116 Cleveland Ave. NW, Ste. 601
Canton, Ohio 44702-1720
Phone: (216)453-6047

SCORE Office (Chillicothe)
165 S. Paint St.
Chillicothe, Ohio 45601
Phone: (614)772-4530

SCORE Office (Cincinnati)
Ameritrust Bldg., Rm. 850
525 Vine St.
Cincinnati, Ohio 45202
Phone: (513)684-2812

SCORE Office (Cincinnati)
525 Vine St.
Ameritrust Bldg., Rm. 850
Cincinnati, Ohio 45202
Phone: (513)684-2812

SCORE Office (Cleveland)
Eaton Center, Ste. 620
1100 Superior Ave.
Cleveland, Ohio 44114-2507
Phone: (216)522-4194

SCORE Office (Columbus)
2 Nationwide Plz., Ste. 1400
Columbus, Ohio 43215-2542
Phone: (614)469-2357

SCORE Office (Dayton)
200 W. 2nd St.
Federal Bldg., Rm. 505
Dayton, Ohio 45402
Phone: (513)225-2887

SCORE Office (Dayton)
Dayton Federal Bldg., Rm. 505
201 W. Second St.
Dayton, Ohio 45402-1430
Phone: (513)225-2887

SCORE Office (Defiance)
Defiance Chamber of Commerce
615 W. 3rd St.
PO Box 130
Defiance, Ohio 43512
Phone: (419)782-7946

SCORE Office (Findlay)
Findlay Chamber of Commerce
123 E. Main Cross St.
PO Box 923
Findlay, Ohio 45840
Phone: (419)422-3314

SCORE Office (Lima)
147 N. Main St.
Lima, Ohio 45801
Phone: (419)222-6045
Fax: (419)229-0266

SCORE Office (Mansfield)
Mansfield Chamber of Commerce
55 N. Mulberry St.
Mansfield, Ohio 44902
Phone: (419)522-3211

SCORE Office (Marietta)
Marietta College
Thomas Hall
Marietta, Ohio 45750
Phone: (614)373-0268

SCORE Office (Medina)
County Administrative Bldg.
144 N. Broadway
Medina, Ohio 44256
Phone: (216)764-8650

SCORE Office (Licking County)
50 W. Locust St.
Newark, Ohio 43055
Phone: (614)345-7458

SCORE Office (Salem)
2491 State Rte. 45 S
Salem, Ohio 44460
Phone: (216)332-0361
Phone: (216)332-9256

SCORE Office (Tiffin)
Tiffin Chamber of Commerce
62 S. Washington St.
Tiffin, Ohio 44883
Phone: (419)447-4141
Fax: (419)447-5141

SCORE Office (Toledo)
1946 N. 13th St., Rm. 352
Toledo, Ohio 43624
Phone: (419)259-7598

SCORE Office (Wooster)
377 W. Liberty St.
Wooster, Ohio 44691
Phone: (216)262-5735

SCORE Office (Youngstown)
Youngstown University
306 Williamson Hall
Youngstown, Ohio 44555
Phone: (216)746-2687

Oklahoma

SCORE Office (Anadarko)
PO Box 366
Anadarko, Oklahoma 73005
Phone: (405)247-6651
Phone: (405)247-6652

SCORE Office (Ardmore)
PO Box 1585
Ardmore, Oklahoma 73402
Phone: (405)223-7765

SCORE Office (Northeast Oklahoma)
Bank of Oklahoma Bldg.
210 S. Main
Grove, Oklahoma 74344
Phone: (918)786-4729

SCORE Office (Lawton)
Federal Bldg., Rm. 107
431 East Ave.
Lawton, Oklahoma 73501
Phone: (405)353-8726

SCORE Office (Oklahoma City)
c/o SBA, Oklahoma Tower Bldg.
210 Park Ave., No. 1300
Oklahoma City, Oklahoma 73102
Phone: (405)231-5163

SCORE Office (Stillwater)
Stillwater Chamber of Commerce
439 S. Main
Stillwater, Oklahoma 74074
Phone: (405)372-5573
Fax: (405)372-4316

SCORE Office (Tulsa)
Tulsa Chamber of Commerce
616 S. Boston, Ste. 406
Tulsa, Oklahoma 74119
Phone: (918)581-7462

Oregon

SCORE Office (Bend)
c/o Bend Chamber of Commerce
63085 N. Hwy. 97
Bend, Oregon 97701
Phone: (503)382-3221

SCORE Office (Willamette)
1401 Willamette St.
PO Box 1107
Eugene, Oregon 97401-4003
Phone: (503)484-5485

SCORE Office (Florence)
c/o Lane Community College
3149 Oak St.
Florence, Oregon 97439
Phone: (503)997-8444
Fax: (503)997-8448

SCORE Office (Southern Oregon)
132 W. Main St.
Medford, Oregon 97501
Phone: (503)776-4220

SCORE Office (Portland)
222 SW Columbia, Ste. 500
Portland, Oregon 97201
Phone: (503)326-3441

SCORE Office (Salem)
PO Box 4024
Salem, Oregon 97302-1024
Phone: (503)370-2896

Pennsylvania

SCORE Office (Altoona-Blair)
c/o Altoona-Blair Chamber of Commerce
1212 12th Ave.
Altoona, Pennsylvania 16601-3493
Phone: (814)943-8151

SCORE Office (Lehigh Valley)
Lehigh University
Rauch Bldg. 37
621 Taylor St.
Bethlehem, Pennsylvania 18015
Phone: (610)758-4496
Butler County Chamber of Commerce

SCORE Office
100 N. Main St.
PO Box 1082
Butler, Pennsylvania 16003
Phone: (412)283-2222
Fax: (412)283-0224

SCORE Office (Cumberland Valley)
Chambersburg Chamber of Commerce
75 S. 2nd St.
Chambersburg, Pennsylvania 17201
Phone: (717)264-4496

SCORE Office (Monroe County-
Stroudsburg)
556 Main St.
East Stroudsburg, Pennsylvania 18301
Phone: (717)421-4433

SCORE Office (Erie)
120 W. 9th St.
Erie, Pennsylvania 16501
Phone: (814)871-5650

SCORE Office (Bucks County)
c/o Bucks County Chamber of
Commerce
409 Hood Blvd.
Fairless Hills, Pennsylvania 19030
Phone: (215)943-8850
Hanover Chamber of Commerce

SCORE Office
146 Broadway
Hanover, Pennsylvania 17331
Phone: (717)637-6130
Fax: (717)637-9127

SCORE Office (Harrisburg)
100 Chestnut, Ste. 309
Harrisburg, Pennsylvania 17101
Phone: (717)782-3874

SCORE Office (Montgomery County)
Baederwood Shopping Center
1653 The Fairways, Ste. 204
Jenkintown, Pennsylvania 19046
Phone: (215)885-3027

SCORE Office (Kittanning)
c/o Kittanning Chamber of Commerce
2 Butler Rd.
Kittanning, Pennsylvania 16201
Phone: (412)543-1305
Fax: (412)543-6206

SCORE Office (Lancaster)
118 W. Chestnut St.
Lancaster, Pennsylvania 17603
Phone: (717)397-3092

SCORE Office (Westmoreland
County)
St. Vincent College
Latrobe, Pennsylvania 15650
Phone: (412)539-7505

SCORE Office (Lebanon)
Lebanon Chamber of Commerce
252 N. 8th St.
PO Box 899
Lebanon, Pennsylvania 17042-0899
Phone: (717)273-3727
Fax: (717)273-7940

SCORE Office (Lewistown)
Lewistown Chamber of Commerce
3 W. Monument Sq., Ste. 204
Lewistown, Pennsylvania 17044
Phone: (717)248-6713
Fax: (717)248-6714

SCORE Office (Delaware County)
Delaware County Chamber of Commerce
602 E. Baltimore Pike
Media, Pennsylvania 19063
Phone: (610)565-3677
Fax: (610)565-1606

SCORE Office (Milton)
Milton Area Chamber of Commerce
112 S. Front St.
Milton, Pennsylvania 17847
Phone: (717)742-7341
Fax: (717)792-2008

SCORE Office (Mon-Valley)
435 Donner Ave.
Monessen, Pennsylvania 15062
Phone: (412)684-4277
Monroeville Chamber of Commerce

SCORE Office
William Penn Plaza
2790 Mosside Blvd., Ste. 295
Monroeville, Pennsylvania 15146
Phone: (412)856-0622
Fax: (412)856-1030

SCORE Office (Airport Area)
Chamber of Commerce
986 Brodhead Rd.
Moon Twp, Pennsylvania 15108-2398
Phone: (412)264-6270
Fax: (412)264-1575

SCORE Office (Northeast)
8601 E. Roosevelt Blvd.
Philadelphia, Pennsylvania 19152
Phone: (215)332-3400
Fax: (215)332-6050

SCORE Office (Philadelphia)
3535 Market St., Rm. 4480
Philadelphia, Pennsylvania 19104
Phone: (215)596-5077

SCORE Office (Pittsburgh)
960 Penn Ave., 5th Fl.
Pittsburgh, Pennsylvania 15222
Phone: (412)644-5447

SCORE Office (Pittsburgh Satellite)
960 Penn Ave., 5th Fl.
Pittsburgh, Pennsylvania 15222
Phone: (412)644-5447
Fax: (412)644-5446

SCORE Office (Tri-County)
238 High St.
Pottstown, Pennsylvania 19464
Phone: (610)327-2673

SCORE Office (Reading)
c/o Reading Chamber of Commerce
645 Penn St.
Reading, Pennsylvania 19601
Phone: (610)376-6766

SCORE Office (Scranton)
Federal Bldg., Rm. 104
Washington Ave. & Linden
Scranton, Pennsylvania 18503
Phone: (717)347-4611

SCORE Office (Central Pennsylvania)
200 Innovation Blvd., Ste. 242-B
State College, Pennsylvania 16803
Phone: (814)234-9415

SCORE Office (Uniontown)
Federal Bldg.
Pittsburg St.
PO Box 2065 DTS
Uniontown, Pennsylvania 15401
Phone: (412)437-4222

SCORE Office (Warren County)
Warren County Chamber of Commerce
315 2nd Ave.
PO Box 942
Warren, Pennsylvania 16365
Phone: (814)723-9017

SCORE Office (Waynesboro)
323 E. Main St.
Waynesboro, Pennsylvania 17268
Phone: (717)762-7123
Fax: (717)962-7124

SCORE Office (Chester County)
Government Service Center, Ste. 281
601 Westtown Rd.
West Chester, Pennsylvania 19382-4538
Phone: (610)344-6910

SCORE Office (Wilkes-Barre)
20 N. Pennsylvania Ave.
Wilkes Barre, Pennsylvania 18702
Phone: (717)826-6502

SCORE Office (North Central Pennsylvania)
240 W. 3rd St., Rm. 304
PO Box 725
Williamsport, Pennsylvania 17703
Phone: (717)322-3720

SCORE Office (York)
Cyber Center
1600 Pennsylvania Ave.
York, Pennsylvania 17404
Phone: (717)845-8830

Puerto Rico

SCORE Office (Puerto Rico)
Citibank Towers Plaza, 2nd Fl.
252 Ponce de Leon Ave.
San Juan, Puerto Rico 00918-2041
Phone: (809)766-5001

Rhode Island

SCORE Office (Barrington)
Barrington Public Library
281 County Rd.
Barrington, Rhode Island 02806
Phone: (401)247-1920
Fax: (401)247-3763

SCORE Office (Woonsocket)
640 Washington Hwy.
Lincoln, Rhode Island 02865
Phone: (401)334-1000
Fax: (401)334-1009

SCORE Office (Wickford)
8045 Post Rd.
North Kingstown, Rhode Island 02852
Phone: (401)295-5566
Fax: (401)295-8987

SCORE Office (J.G.E. Knight)
380 Westminster St.
Providence, Rhode Island 02903
Phone: (401)528-4571

SCORE Office (Warwick)
3288 Post Rd.
Warwick, Rhode Island 02886
Phone: (401)732-1100
Fax: (401)732-1101

SCORE Office (Westerly)
74 Post Rd.
Westerly, Rhode Island 02891
Phone: (401)596-7761
Toll-free: (800)732-7636
Fax: (401)596-2190

South Carolina

SCORE Office (Aiken)
Aiken Chamber of Commerce
P.O. Box 892
Aiken, South Carolina 29802
Phone: (803)641-1111
Toll-free: (800)542-4536
Fax: (803)641-4174

SCORE Office (Anderson)
Tri-County Technical College
Anderson Mall
3130 N. Main St.
Anderson, South Carolina 29621
Phone: (864)224-0453

SCORE Office (Coastal)
284 King St.
Charleston, South Carolina 29401
Phone: (803)727-4778

SCORE Office (Midlands)
Strom Thurmond Bldg., Rm. 358
1835 Assembly St.
Columbia, South Carolina 29201
Phone: (803)765-5131

SCORE Office (Piedmont)
Federal Bldg., Rm. B-02
300 E. Washington St.
Greenville, South Carolina 29601
Phone: (803)271-3638

SCORE Office (Greenwood)
Piedmont Technical College
PO Drawer 1467
Greenwood, South Carolina 29648
Phone: (864)223-8357

SCORE Office (Hilton Head)
Hilton Head Chamber of Commerce
PO Box 5647
Hilton Head, South Carolina 29938
Phone: (803)785-3673
Fax: (803)785-7110

SCORE Office (Grand Strand)
48th Executive Ct., Ste. 211
1109 48th Ave. N
Myrtle Beach, South Carolina 29577
Phone: (803)449-8538

SCORE Office (Spartanburg)
c/o Vernon Wyant Chamber of
Commerce
P.O. Box 1636
Spartanburg, South Carolina 29304
Phone: (864)594-5000
Fax: (864)594-5055

South Dakota

SCORE Office (Rapid City)
444 Mount Rushmore Rd., No. 209
Rapid City, South Dakota 57701
Phone: (605)394-5311

SCORE Office (Sioux Falls)
First Financial Center, No. 200
110 S. Phillips Ave.
Sioux Falls, South Dakota 57102-1109
Phone: (605)330-4231

Tennessee

SCORE Office (Chattanooga)
Federal Bldg., Rm. 26
900 Georgia Ave.
Chattanooga, Tennessee 37402
Phone: (423)752-5190

SCORE Office (Cleveland)
Cleveland Chamber of Commerce
P.O. Box 2275
Cleveland, Tennessee 37320
Phone: (423)472-6587
Fax: (423)472-2019

SCORE Office (Upper Cumberland
Center)
1225 S. Willow Ave.
Cookeville, Tennessee 38501
Phone: (615)432-4111
Fax: (615)432-6010

SCORE Office (Unicoi County)
c/o Chamber of Commerce
PO Box 713
Erwin, Tennessee 37650
Phone: (423)743-3000
Fax: (423)743-0942

SCORE Office (Greeneville)
Greeneville Chamber of Commerce
115 Academy St.
Greeneville, Tennessee 37743
Phone: (423)638-4111
Fax: (423)638-5345

SCORE Office (Jackson)
c/o Jackson Chamber of Commerce
197 Auditorium St.
PO Box 1904
Jackson, Tennessee 38302
Phone: (901)423-2200

SCORE Office (Northeast Tennessee)
c/o Chamber of Commerce
2710 S. Roan St.
Johnson City, Tennessee 37601
Phone: (423)929-7686
Fax: (423)461-8052

SCORE Office (Kingsport)
c/o Kingsport Chamber of Commerce
151 E. Main St.
Kingsport, Tennessee 37662
Phone: (423)392-8805

SCORE Office (Greater Knoxville)
Farragot Bldg., Ste. 224
530 S. Gay St.
Knoxville, Tennessee 37902
Phone: (423)545-4203

SCORE Office (Maryville)
Blount County Chamber of Commerce
201 S. Washington St.
Maryville, Tennessee 37804-5728
Phone: (423)983-2241
Toll-free: (800)525-6834
Fax: (423)984-1386

SCORE Office (Memphis)
Federal Bldg., Ste. 148
167 N. Main St.
Memphis, Tennessee 38103
Phone: (901)544-3588

SCORE Office (Nashville)
50 Vantage Way, Ste. 201
Nashville, Tennessee 37228-1500
Phone: (615)736-7621

Texas

SCORE Office (Abilene)
2106 Federal Post Office and Court
Bldg.
Abilene, Texas 79601
Phone: (915)677-1857

SCORE Office (Austin)
300 E. 8th St., Rm. 572
Austin, Texas 78701
Phone: (512)482-5112

SCORE Office (Golden Triangle)
c/o Community Bank
700 Calder, Ste. 101
Beaumont, Texas 77701
Phone: (409)838-6581

SCORE Office (Brownsville)
3505 Boca Chica Blvd., No. 305
Brownsville, Texas 78521
Phone: (210)541-4508

SCORE Office (Brazos Valley)
Victoria Bank & Trust
3000 Briarcrest, Ste. 302
Bryan, Texas 77802
Phone: (409)776-8876

SCORE Office (Cleburne)
Watergarden Pl., 9th Fl., Ste. 400
Cleburne, Texas 76031
Phone: (817)871-6002

SCORE Office (Corpus Christi)
c/o Robert Martens
606 N. Carancahua, Ste. 1200
Corpus Christi, Texas 78476
Phone: (512)888-3306
Fax: (512)888-3418

SCORE Office (Dallas)
17218 Preston Road, No. 3202
Dallas, Texas 75252
Phone: (214)733-0189
Phone: (214)733-3953

SCORE Office (El Paso)
10737 Gateway W, Ste. 320
El Paso, Texas 79935
Phone: (915)540-5155

SCORE Office (Bedford)
100 E. 15th St., Ste. 400
Fort Worth, Texas 76102
Phone: (817)871-6002

SCORE Office (Fort Worth)
100 E. 15th St., No. 24
Fort Worth, Texas 76102
Phone: (817)871-6002

SCORE Office (Garland)
2734 W. Kingsley Rd.
Garland, Texas 75041
Phone: (214)271-9224

SCORE Office (Granbury Chamber of
Commerce)
416 S. Morgan
Granbury, Texas 76048
Phone: (817)573-1622
Fax: (817)573-0805

SCORE Office (Rio Grande Valley)
222 E. Van Buren, Ste. 500
Harlingen, Texas 78550
Phone: (210)427-8533

SCORE Office (Houston)
9301 Southwest Fwy., Ste. 550
Houston, Texas 77074
Phone: (713)773-6565

SCORE Office (Irving)
c/o Irving Chamber of Commerce
3333 N. MacArthur Blvd., Ste. 100
Irving, Texas 75062
Phone: (214)252-8484
Fax: (214)252-6710

SCORE Office (Lubbock)
1611 10th St., Ste. 200
Lubbock, Texas 79401
Phone: (806)743-7462

SCORE Office (Midland)
Post Office Annex
200 E. Wall St., Rm. P121
Midland, Texas 79701
Phone: (915)687-2649

SCORE Office (Orange)
c/o Orange Chamber of Commerce
1012 Green Ave.
Orange, Texas 77630-5620
Phone: (409)883-3536
Toll-free: (800)528-4906
Fax: (409)886-3247

SCORE Office (Plano)
c/o Plano Chamber of Commerce
1200 E. 15th St.
P.O. Drawer 940287

Plano, Texas 75094-0287
Phone: (214)424-7547
Fax: (214)422-5182

SCORE Office (Port Arthur)
c/o Port Arthur Chamber of Commerce
4749 Twin City Hwy., Ste. 300
Port Arthur, Texas 77642
Phone: (409)963-1107
Fax: (409)963-3322

SCORE Office (Richardson)
c/o Richardson Chamber of Commerce
411 Belle Grove
Richardson, Texas 75080
Phone: (214))234-4141
Toll-free: (800)777-8001
Fax: (214)680-9103

SCORE Office (San Antonio)
c/o SBA, Federal Bldg., Rm. A527
727 E. Durango
San Antonio, Texas 78206
Phone: (210)229-5931
Phone: (210)229-5900

SCORE Office (Texarkana State College)
819 State Line Ave.
PO Box 1468
Texarkana, Texas 75501
Phone: (903)792-7191

SCORE Office (East Texas)
1530 SW Loop 323, Ste. 100
Tyler, Texas 75701
Phone: (903)510-2975

SCORE Office (Waco)
Business Resource Center
4601 N. 19th St.
Waco, Texas 76708
Phone: (817)754-8898

SCORE Office (Wichita Falls)
Hamilton Bldg.
PO Box 1860
Wichita Falls, Texas 76307
Phone: (817)766-1602

Utah

SCORE Office (Ogden)
324 25th St., Ste. 6104
Ogden, Utah 84401
Phone: (801)625-5712

SCORE Office (Central Utah)
Old County Court House
51 S. University Ave.
Provo, Utah 84601
Phone: (801)379-2444

SCORE Office (Southern Utah)
c/o Dixie College Small Business
Development Center
225 South 700 East
St. George, Utah 84770
Phone: (801)673-4811

SCORE Office (Salt Lake)
125 S. State St., Rm. 2237
Salt Lake City, Utah 84138
Phone: (801)524-3211

Vermont

SCORE Office (Champlain Valley)
Winston Prouty Federal Bldg.
11 Lincoln St., Room 106
Essex Junction, Vermont 05452
Phone: (802)951-6762

SCORE Office (Montpelier)
c/o U.S. Small Business Administration
87 State St., Rm. 205
PO Box 605
Montpelier, Vermont 05601
Phone: (802)828-4422

SCORE Office (Marble Valley)
Rutland Industrial Development Corp.
256 N. Main St.
Rutland, Vermont 05701-2413
Phone: (802)773-9147

SCORE Office (Northeast Kingdom)
c/o NCIC
20 Main St.
PO Box 904
St. Johnsbury, Vermont 05819
Phone: (802)748-5101

Virgin Islands

SCORE Office (St. Croix)
United Plaza Shopping Center
PO Box 4010, Christiansted
St. Croix, Virgin Islands 00822
Phone: (809)778-5380

SCORE Office (St. Thomas-St. John)
Federal Bldg., Rm. 21
Veterans Dr.
St. Thomas, Virgin Islands 00801
Phone: (809)774-8530

Virginia

SCORE Office (Arlington)
2009 N. 14th St., Ste. 111
Arlington, Virginia 22201
Phone: (703)525-2400

SCORE Office (Blacksburg)
141 Jackson St.
Blacksburg, Virginia 24060
Phone: (540)552-4061

SCORE Office (Bristol)
20 Volunteer Pkwy.
PO Box 519
Bristol, Virginia 24203
Phone: (540)968-4399

SCORE Office (Central Virginia)
918 Emmet St. N, Ste. 200
Charlottesville, Virginia 22903-4878
Phone: (804)295-6712

SCORE Office (Alleghany Satellite)
c/o Chamber of Commerce
241 W. Main St.
Covington, Virginia 24426
Phone: (540)962-2178
Fax: (540)962-2179

SCORE Office (Central Fairfax)
3975 University Dr., Ste. 350
Fairfax, Virginia 22030
Phone: (703)591-2450

SCORE Office (Falls Church)
P.O. Box 491
Falls Church, Virginia 22040
Phone: (703)532-1050
Fax: (703)237-7904

SCORE Office (Glenns)
c/o Rappahannock Community
College
Glenns Campus
Box 287
Glenns, Virginia 23149
Phone: (804)693-9650

SCORE Office (Peninsula)
c/o Peninsula Chamber of Commerce
6 Manhattan Sq.
PO Box 7269
Hampton, Virginia 23666
Phone: (804)766-2000

SCORE Office (Tri-Cities)
c/o Chamber of Commerce
108 N. Main St.
Hopewell, Virginia 23860
Phone: (804)458-5536

SCORE Office (Lynchburg)
Federal Bldg.
1100 Main St.
Lynchburg, Virginia 24504-1714
Phone: (804)846-3235

SCORE Office (Danville)
c/o Martinsville Chamber of Commerce
115 Broad St.
PO Box 709
Martinsville, Virginia 24112-0709
Phone: (540)632-6401

SCORE Office (Eastern Shore)
c/o Eastern Shore Chamber of
Commerce
Federal Bldg.
200 Grandby St.
Norfolk, Virginia 23510
Phone: (804)441-3733

SCORE Office (Norfolk)
Federal Bldg., Rm. 737
200 Granby St.
Norfolk, Virginia 23510
Phone: (804)441-3733

SCORE Office (Virginia Beach)
Virginia Beach Office of Hampton
Roads
Chamber of Commerce
200 Grandby St., Rm 737
Norfolk, Virginia 23510
Phone: (804)441-3733

SCORE Office (Greater Prince William)
Prince William Chamber of Commerce
4320 Ridgewood Center Dr.
Prince William, Virginia 22192
Phone: (703)590-5000

SCORE Office (Radford)
Radford Chamber of Commerce
1126 Norwood St.
Radford, Virginia 24141
Phone: (540)639-2202

SCORE Office (Richmond)
Dale Bldg., Ste. 200
1504 Santa Rosa Rd.
Richmond, Virginia 23229
Phone: (804)771-2400

SCORE Office (Roanoke)
Federal Bldg.
PO Box 1366, Rm. 716
Roanoke, Virginia 24007
Phone: (540)857-2834

SCORE Office (Fairfax)
8391 Old Courthouse Rd., Ste. 300
Vienna, Virginia 22182
Phone: (703)749-0400

SCORE Office (Greater Vienna)
513 Maple Ave. West
Vienna, Virginia 22180
Phone: (703)281-1333
Fax: (703)242-1482

SCORE Office (Shenandoah Valley)
c/o Waynesboro Chamber of Commerce
301 W. Main St.
Waynesboro, Virginia 22980
Phone: (540)949-8203

SCORE Office (Williamsburg)
c/o Williamsburg Chamber of Commerce
201 Penniman Rd.
Williamsburg, Virginia 23185
Phone: (804)229-6511

SCORE Office (Northern Virginia)
c/o Winchester-Frederick Chamber of
Commerce
1360 S. Pleasant Valley Rd.
Winchester, Virginia 22601
Phone: (540)662-4118

Washington

SCORE Office (Gray's Harbor)
c/o Gray's Harbor Chamber of
Commerce

506 Duffy St.
Aberdeen, Washington 98520
Phone: (360)532-1924
Fax: (360)533-7945

SCORE Office (Bellingham)
Fourth Corner, Economic Develop-
ment Group
PO Box 2803
1203 Cornwall Ave.
Bellingham, Washington 98227
Phone: (360)676-4255

SCORE Office (Everett)
Everett Public Library
2702 Hoyt Ave.
Everett, Washington 98201-3556
Phone: (206)259-8000

SCORE Office (Gig Harbor)
c/o Gig Harbor Chamber of Commerce
3125 Judson St.
Gig Harbor, Washington 98335
Phone: (206)851-6865
Phone: (206)851-6881

SCORE Office (Kennewick)
Kennewick Chamber of Commerce
PO Box 6986
Kennewick, Washington 99336
Phone: (509)736-0510

SCORE Office (Puyallup)
Puyallup Chamber of Commerce
322 2nd St. SW
PO Box 1298
Puyallup, Washington 98371
Phone: (206)845-6755
Fax: (206)848-6164

SCORE Office (Seattle)
1200 6th Ave., Ste. 1700
Seattle, Washington 98174
Phone: (206)553-7311

SCORE Office (Spokane)
601 1st Ave. W, 10th Fl.
Spokane, Washington 99204-0317
Phone: (509)353-2820

SCORE Office (Clover Park)
PO Box 1933
Tacoma, Washington 98401-1933
Phone: (206)627-2175

SCORE Office (Tacoma)
950 Pacific Ave., No. 300

Tacoma, Washington 98402
Phone: (206)627-2175

SCORE Office (Fort Vancouver)
1200 Fort Vancouver Way
Box 8900
Vancouver, Washington 98668
Phone: (360)699-3241

SCORE Office (Walla Walla)
Walla Walla Small Business Center
500 Tausick Way
Walla Walla, Washington 99362
Phone: (509)527-4681

SCORE Office (Mid-Columbia)
c/o Yakima Chamber of Commerce
PO Box 1490
Yakima, Washington 98907
Phone: (509)248-2021

West Virginia

SCORE Office (Charleston)
1116 Smith St.
Charleston, West Virginia 25301
Phone: (304)347-5463

SCORE Office (Virginia Street)
1116 Smith St., Ste. 302
Charleston, West Virginia 25301
Phone: (304)347-5463

SCORE Office (Marion County)
PO Box 208
Fairmont, West Virginia 26555-0208
Phone: (304)363-0486

SCORE Office (Upper Monongahela Valley)
200 Fairmont Ave., Ste. 100
Fairmont, West Virginia 26554
Phone: (304)363-0486

SCORE Office (Huntington)
1101 6th Ave., Ste. 220
Huntington, West Virginia 25701-2309
Phone: (304)523-4092

SCORE Office (Wheeling)
1310 Market St.
Wheeling, West Virginia 26003
Phone: (304)233-2575

Wisconsin

SCORE Office (Fox Cities)
227 S. Walnut St.
Box 1855

Appleton, Wisconsin 54915
Phone: (414)734-7101

SCORE Office (Beloit)
136 W. Grand Ave., Ste. 100
PO Box 717
Beloit, Wisconsin 53511
Phone: (608)365-8835
Fax: (608)365-9170

SCORE Office (Eau Claire)
Federal Bldg., Rm. B11
510 S. Barstow St.
Eau Claire, Wisconsin 54701
Phone: (715)834-1573

SCORE Office (Fond Du Lac)
c/o Fond Du Lac Chamber of Commerce
207 N. Main St.
Fond Du Lac, Wisconsin 54935
Phone: (414)921-9500
Fax: (414)921-9559

SCORE Office (Green Bay)
835 Potts Ave.
Green Bay, Wisconsin 54305
Phone: (414)496-8930

SCORE Office (Janesville)
20 S. Main St., Ste. 11
PO Box 8008
Janesville, Wisconsin 53547
Phone: (608)757-3160
Fax: (608)757-3170

SCORE Office (La Crosse)
712 Main St.
PO Box 219
La Crosse, Wisconsin 54602-0219
Phone: (608)784-4880

SCORE Office (Madison)
4406 Somerset Lake
Madison, Wisconsin 53711
Phone: (608)831-5464

SCORE Office (Manitowoc)
Manitowoc Chamber of Commerce
1515 Memorial Dr.
PO Box 903
Manitowoc, Wisconsin 54221-0903
Phone: (414)684-5575
Toll-free: (800262-7892
Fax: (414)684-1915

SCORE Office (Madison)
c/o M&I Bank

7448 Hubbard Ave.
Middleton, Wisconsin 53562
Phone: (608)831-5464

SCORE Office (Milwaukee)
310 W. Wisconsin Ave., Ste. 425
Milwaukee, Wisconsin 53203
Phone: (414)297-3942

SCORE Office (Central Wisconsin)
c/o Chapter Chairperson
1224 Lindbergh Ave.
Stevens Point, Wisconsin 54481
Phone: (715)344-7729

SCORE Office (Superior)
305 Harborview Pkwy.
Superior, Wisconsin 54880
Phone: (715)394-7716

SCORE Office (Waukesha)
c/o Waukesha Chamber of Commerce
223 Wisconsin Ave.
Waukesha, Wisconsin 53186-4926
Phone: (414)542-4249
Phone: (414)542-8068

SCORE Office (Wausau)
300 3rd St.
PO Box 6190
Wausau, Wisconsin 54402-6190
Phone: (715)845-6231

SCORE Office (Central Wisconsin)
2240 Kingston Rd.
Wisconsin Rapids, Wisconsin 54494
Phone: (715)423-1830
Phone: (715)421-3900

Wyoming

SCORE Office (Casper)
Federal Bldg., No. 2215
100 East B St.
Casper, Wyoming 82602
Phone: (307)261-6529

VENTURE CAPITAL & FINANCING COMPANIES

This section contains a listing of financing and loan companies in the United States and Canada. These listings are arranged alphabetically by country, state/territory/ province, then by city, then by organization name.

CANADA

Manitoba

Manitoba Industry, Trade and Tourism
Small Business Services Entrepreneurial Development
Business Start Program
155 Carlton St., 5th Fl., Rm. 525
Winnipeg, Manitoba R3C 3H8
Phone: (204)945-7719
Free: (800))282-8069
Fax: (204)945-2804
A matching loan guarantee program that will promote the success of new business start-ups by ensuring that entrepreneurs have a comprehensive business plan, by offering business training and counseling, and by providing access to funding up to $10,000 via a loan guarantee through a number of existing financial institutions.

Ontario

Industry and Science Canada
Small Business Loans Administration Branch
235 Queen St., 8th Fl., E.
Ottawa, Ontario K1A 0H5
Phone: (613)954-5540
Fax: (613)952-0290

Quebec

Societe de Developpement Industriel du Quebec
Small Business Revival Program
1126, Chemin Saint-Louis, 5th Fl.
Bureau 500
Sillery, Quebec G1S 1E5
Phone: (418)643-5172
Free: (800))461-AIDE
Fax: (418)528-2063
Allows businesses facing temporary difficulties to obtain financial assistance aimed at reinforcing their financial structures.

Saskatchewan

Saskatchewan Department of Economic Development
Investment Programs Branch
Labour-Sponsored Venture Capital Program
1919 Saskatchewan Dr., 5th Fl.
Regina, Saskatchewan S4P 3V7
Phone: (306)787-2252
Fax: (306)787-3872
Promotes the formation of venture capital corporations by employees of a small business, to provide equity capital for the expansion of existing facilities or establishment of new businesses. Federal and provincial tax credits are available to the investor.

UNITED STATES

Alabama

Alabama Small Business Investment Co.
1732 5th Ave. N
Birmingham, Alabama 35203
Phone: (205)324-5231
Fax: (205)324-5234
A minority enterprise small business investment company. Diversified industry preference.

Jefferson County Community Development
Planning and Community Development
805 N. 22nd St.
Birmingham, Alabama 35203
Phone: (205)325-5761
Fax: (205)325-5095
Provides loans for purchasing real estate, construction, working capital, or machinery and equipment.

FJC Growth Capital Corp.
200 W. Court Sq., Ste. 750
Huntsville, Alabama 35801
Phone: (205)922-2918
Fax: (205)922-2909
A minority enterprise small business investment company. Diversified industry preference.

Hickory Venture Capital Corp.
200 W. Side Sq., Ste.100
Huntsville, Alabama 35801
Phone: (205)539-1931
Fax: (205)539-5130
A small business investment corporation. Prefers to invest in later-stage companies. Will not consider oil and gas, or real estate investments.

Alabama Capital Corp.
16 Midtown Park E.
Mobile, Alabama 36606
Phone: (334)476-0700
Fax: (334)476-0026
David C. DeLaney, President
Preferred Investment Size: $400,000.
Investment Policies: Asset based loans with equity. Investment Types: Seed, early, expansion, later stages. Industry Preferences: Diversified. Geographic Preferences: Southeast.

First SBIC of Alabama
16 Midtown Park E.
Mobile, Alabama 36606
Phone: (334)476-0700
Fax: (334)476-0026
David C. DeLaney, President
Preferred Investment Size: $400,000.
Investment Policies: Asset based Loans with equity. Investment Types: Seed, early, expansion, later stages. Industry Preferences: Diversified. Geographic Preferences: Southeast.

Southern Development Council
E-mail: sdc@sdcinc.org
4101 C Wall St.
Montgomery, Alabama 36106
Phone: (334)244-1801
Fax: (334)244-1421
Statewide nonprofit financial packaging corporation. Helps small businesses arrange financing.

Alaska

Alaska Department of Commerce and
Economic Development (Anchorage)
Industrial Development and Export
Authority
480 W. Tudor Rd.
Anchorage, Alaska 99503-6690
Phone: (907)269-3000
Fax: (907)269-3044
Assists businesses in securing long-
term financing for capital investments,
such as the acquisition of equipment
or the construction of a new plant, at
moderate interest rates.

Alaska Department of Commerce and
Economic Development (Anchorage)
Division of Investments
E-mail:
investments@commerce.state.ak.us
3601 C St., Ste. 724
Anchorage, Alaska 99503
Phone: (907)269-8150
Fax: (907)269-8147
Offers a program that assists purchas-
ers to assume existing small business
loans.

Calista Corp.
601 W. 5th Ave., Ste. 200
Anchorage, Alaska 99501-2225
Phone: (907)279-5516
Fax: (907)272-5060
A minority enterprise small business
investment corporation. No industry
preference.

Alaska Department of Commerce and
Economic Development (Juneau)
Division of Investments
E-mail:
investments@commerce.state.ak.us
PO Box 34159
Juneau, Alaska 99803-4159
Phone: (907)465-2510
Free: (800)478-LOAN
Fax: (907)465-2103
Offers a program that assists purchas-
ers to assume existing small business
loans.

Alaska Department of Natural
Resources
Division of Agriculture
Agricultural Revolving Loan Fund
PO Box 949
Palmer, Alaska 99645-0949
Phone: (907)745-7200
Free: (800)770-3276
Fax: (907)745-7112
Provides loans for farm development,
general farm operations, chattel, and
land clearing. Resident farmers,
homesteaders, partnerships, and
corporations are eligible.

Arizona

First Interstate Equity Corp.
100 W. Washington St.
Phoenix, Arizona 85003
Phone: (602)528-6447
Fax: (602)440-1320
A small business investment com-
pany. Diversified industry preference.

Rocky Mountain Equity Corp.
2525 E. Camelback Rd., Ste. 275
Phoenix, Arizona 85016
Phone: (602)955-6100
Fax: (602)956-5909
A small business investment corpora-
tion. No industry preference.

Sundance Venture Partners, L.P.
(Phoenix)
400 E. Van Buren, Ste. 750
Phoenix, Arizona 85004
Phone: (602)259-3441
Fax: (602)259-1450
A small business investment com-
pany.

Arizona Growth Partners
E-mail: jock@valleyventures.com
6155 N. Scottsdale Rd., Ste. 100
Scottsdale, Arizona 85250
Phone: (602)661-6600
Fax: (602)661-6262
Venture capital firm. Industry prefer-
ences include high technology,
medical, biotechnology, and computer
industries.

First Commerce & Loan LP
5620 N. Kolb, No. 260
Tucson, Arizona 85715
Phone: (520)298-2500
Fax: (520)745-6112
A small business investment com-
pany. Diversified industry preference.

Arkansas

Southern Ventures, Inc.
605 Main St., Ste. 202
Arkadelphia, Arkansas 71923
Phone: (501)246-9627
Fax: (501)246-2182
A small business investment com-
pany. Diversified industry preference.

Arkansas Development Finance
Authority
PO Box 8023
Little Rock, Arkansas 72203-8023
Phone: (501)682-5900
Fax: (501)682-5859
Provides bond financing to small
borrowers, who may otherwise be
excluded from the bond market due to
high costs, by using umbrella bond
issues. Can provide interim financing
for approved projects awaiting a bond
issuance.

Capital Management Services, Inc.
1910 N. Grant St., Ste. 200
Little Rock, Arkansas 72207-4427
Phone: (501)664-8613
A minority enterprise small business
investment corporation. No industry
preference.

Small Business Investment Capital,
Inc.
12103 Interstate 30
P.O. Box 3627
Little Rock, Arkansas 72203
Phone: (501)455-6599
Fax: (501)455-6556
Charles E. Toland, President
Preferred Investment Size: Up to
$230,000. Investment Policies: Loans.
Investment Types: Start-ups and debt

consolidation. Industry Preferences: Supermarkets. Geographic Preferences: Arkansas, Oklahoma, Texas, Louisiana.

California

Calsafe Capital Corp.
245 E. Main St., Ste. 107
Alhambra, California 91801
Phone: (818)289-3400
Fax: (818)300-8025
A minority enterprise small business investment company. Diversified industry preference.

Ally Finance Corp.
9100 Wilshire Blvd., Ste. 408
Beverly Hills, California 90212
Phone: (310)550-8100
Fax: (310)550-6136

A small business investment corporation. No industry preference.
Developers Equity Capital Corp.
447 S. Robertson Blvd. SE 101
Beverly Hills, California 90211
Phone: (310)550-7552
A small business investment corporation. Real estate preferred.

Comdisco Venture Group (Corte Madera)
770 Tamalais Dr., Ste. 300
Corte Madera, California 94925-1737
Phone: (415)927-6777
Fax: (415)927-6767
Prefers start-up businesses in fields of semiconductors, computer hardware and software, computer services and systems, telecommunications, and medical and biotechnology. Investments range from $500,000 to $5 million.

BankAmerica Capital Corp. (Costa Mesa)
PO Box 60049
Costa Mesa, California 90060-0049
Phone: (714)973-8495
Venture capital firm preferring investments of $1 million-$3 million. Diversified industry preference.

Domain Associates
650 Town Center Dr., Ste. 1830
Costa Mesa, California 92626
Phone: (714)434-6227
Fax: (714)434-6088
Venture capital firm providing early stage financing. Areas of interest include life sciences and biotechnology companies (biopharmaceuticals, medical devices, diagnostics, and new materials).

Fairfield Venture Partners (Costa Mesa)
650 Town Center Dr., Ste. 810
Costa Mesa, California 92626
Phone: (714)754-5717
Fax: (714)754-6802

First SBIC of California (Costa Mesa)
3029 Harbor Blvd.
Costa Mesa, California 92626
Phone: (714)668-6099
Fax: (714)668-6099
A small business investment corporation and venture capital company. No industry preference.

Pearl Capital, Inc.
575 Anton Blvd., Ste. 300
Costa Mesa, California 92626
Phone: (714)432-6301
Fax: (714)497-2560
Venture capital firm providing late stage and mezzanine investments of $1 million to $10 million. Prefers investments of $2 million. Areas of interest include diversified industries and computer technology.

Westar Capital (Costa Mesa)
950 S. Coast Dr., Ste. 165
Costa Mesa, California 92626
Phone: (714)434-5160
Fax: (714)434-5166
Venture capital firm providing management financing and corporate buyouts. Areas of interest include information, computer and business services, health care, food processing, and defense/aerospace.

Fulcrum Venture Capital Corp.
300 Corp. Pl., Suite 380
Culver City, California 90230
Phone: (310)645-1271
Fax: (310)645-1272
A minority enterprise small business investment corporation. No industry preference.

Bay Partners
10600 N. De Anza Blvd., Ste. 100
Cupertino, California 95014
Phone: (408)725-2444
Fax: (408)446-4502
Venture capital supplier. Provides start-up financing primarily to West Coast technology companies that have highly qualified management teams. Initial investments range from $100,000 to $800,000. Where large investments are required, the company will act as lead investor to bring in additional qualified venture investors.

El Dorado Ventures (Cupertino)
E-mail: garyk@eldoradoventures.com
20300 Stevens Creek Blvd., Ste. 395
Cupertino, California 95014
Phone: (408)725-2474
Fax: (408)252-2762

Grace Ventures Corp./Horn Venture Partners
20300 Stevens Creek Blvd., Ste. 330
Cupertino, California 95014
Phone: (408)725-0774
Fax: (408)725-0327
Areas of interest include information technology, life sciences, specialty retail and consumer products, restaurant, and biotechnology industries.

Novus Ventures, L.P.
20111 Stevens Creek Blvd., Ste. 130
Cupertino, California 95014
Phone: (408)252-3900
Fax: (408)252-1713
Daniel D. Tompkins, Manager
Preferred Investment Size: $400,000 to $1 Million. Investment Policies:

Convertible debt, Convertible stock. Industry Preferences: Information technology. Geographic Preferences: Western U.S.

Sundance Venture Partners, L.P.
10600 N. DeAnza Blvd., Ste. 215
Cupertino, California 95014
Phone: (408)257-8100
Fax: (408)257-8111
A small business investment company. Diversified industry preference.

Chemical Venture Partners (Los Angeles)
840 Apollo St., Ste. 223 Chase Capitol
El Segundo, California 90245
Phone: (310)335-1955
Fax: (310)335-1965
Venture capital firm providing later stage financing. Areas of interest include health, environmental, service, distribution, manufacturing, information services, and education. Exclusions are real estate and high technology.

Pacific Mezzanine Fund, L.P.
2200 Powell St., Ste. 1250
Emeryville, California 94608
Phone: (510)595-9800
Fax: (510)595-9801
David C. Woodward, General Partner
Preferred Investment Size: $2 TO $5 Million. Investment Policies: Loans with equity features. Investment Types: Expansion, later stage. Industry Preferences: Diversified. Geographic Preferences: Western US.

BankAmerica Ventures (Foster City)
950 Tower Ln., Ste. 700
Foster City, California 94404
Phone: (415)378-6000
Fax: (415)378-6040
Robert L Boswell, Senior Vice President

First American Capital Funding, Inc.
10840 Warner Ave., Ste. 202
Fountain Valley, California 92708
Phone: (714)965-7190
Fax: (714)965-7193

A minority enterprise small business investment corporation. No industry preference.

Opportunity Capital Corp.
2201 Walnut Ave., Ste. 210
Fremont, California 94538-2261
Phone: (510)795-7000
Fax: (510)494-5439
A minority enterprise small business investment corporation. No industry preference.

Opportunity Capital Partners II, LP
2201 Walnut Ave., Ste. 210
Fremont, California 94538
Phone: (510)795-7000
Fax: (510)494-5439
A minority enterprise small business investment company. Diversified industry preference.

R and D Funding Corp.
440 Mission Ct., Ste. 250
Fremont, California 94539
Phone: (510)656-1949
Fax: (510)656-1949
Venture capital firm. Invests in high-growth businesses. Direct investment in research and development.

San Joaquin Business Investment Group, Inc.
1900 Mariposa Mall, Ste. 100
Fresno, California 93721
Phone: (209)233-3580
Fax: (209)233-3709
A minority enterprise small business investment company. Diversified industry preference.

Magna Pacific Investments
330 N. Brand Blvd., Ste. 670
Glendale, California 91203
Phone: (818)547-0809
Fax: (818)547-9303
A minority enterprise small business investment company. Diversified industry preference.

Asian American Capital Corp.
1251 W. Tennyson Rd., Ste. 4
Hayward, California 94544-4423
Phone: (510)887-6888

A minority enterprise small business investment corporation. Diversified industry preferences.

Brentwood Venture Partners (Irvine)
1920 Main St., Ste. 820
Irvine, California 92614
Phone: (714)251-1010
Fax: (714)251-1011
Prefers to invest in the electronics and health care industries.

Crosspoint Venture Partners (Irvine)
E-mail: roxie@crosspointvc.com
18552 MacArthur, No. 400
Irvine, California 92612
Phone: (714)852-1611
Fax: (714)852-9804
Venture capital firm investing in medical, software, and telecommunications.

DSV Partners
E-mail: jbergman@packbell.net
1920 Main St., Ste. 820
Irvine, California 92614
Phone: (714)475-4242
Fax: (714)475-1950
Venture capital firm. Prefers to invest in software, medical, biotechnical, environmental, and other high-growth technology companies.

Ventana Growth Fund L.P. (Irvine)
18881 Von Karman Ave., Ste. 350, Tower 17
Irvine, California 92715
Phone: (714)476-2204
Fax: (714)752-0223

South Bay Capital Corporation
5325 E. Pacific Coast Hwy.
Long Beach, California 90804
Phone: (310)597-3285
Fax: (310)498-7167
John Wang, Manager

Aspen Ventures West II, L.P.
E-mail: twhalen@aspenventures.com
1000 Fremont Ave., Ste. V
Los Altos, California 94024
Phone: (415)917-5670
Fax: (415)917-5677
Alexander Cilento, Mgr.

David Crocket, Mgr.
Preferred Investment Size: $500,000 to $2,5 million. Investment Policies: Equity. Investment Types: Early stage. Industry Preferences: Information technology. Geographic Preferences: Western U.S.

AVI Capital, L.P.
E-mail: vc@avicapital.com
1 1st St., Ste. 12
Los Altos, California 94022
Phone: (415)949-9862
Fax: (415)949-8510
P. Wolken, Mgr.
B. Weinman, Mgr.
Preferred Investment Size: $1,000,000.
Investment Policies: Equity Only.
Investment Types: Seed, early stage.
Industry Preferences: High technology and electronic deals only.
Geographic Preferences: West coast, California.

Crosspoint Venture Partners (Los Altos)
1 1st St., Ste. 2
Los Altos, California 94022
Phone: (415)948-8300
Fax: (415)948-6172
Venture capital partnership. Seeks to invest start-up capital in unique products, services, and/or market opportunities in high-technology and biotechnology industries located in the western United States.

HMS Group
1 1st St., Ste. 16
Los Altos, California 94022
Phone: (415)917-0390
Fax: (415)917-0394
Prefers communications industries.

MBW Management, Inc. (Los Altos)
350 2nd St., Ste. 4
Los Altos, California 94022
Phone: (415)941-2392
Fax: (415)941-2865

Best Finance Corp.
4929 W. Wilshire Blvd., Ste. 407
Los Angeles, California 90010

Phone: (213)937-1636
Fax: (213)937-6393
Vincent Lee, General Manager
Preferred Investment Size: $50,000.
Investment Policies: Loans and/or equity. Investment Types: Purchase, seed, expansion. Industry Preferences: Diversified. Geographic Preferences: California.

Brentwood Associates (Los Angeles)
11150 Santa Monica Blvd., Ste. 1200
Los Angeles, California 90025-3314
Phone: (310)477-6611
Fax: (310)477-1011
Venture capital supplier. Provides start-up and expansion financing to technology-based enterprises specializing in computing and data processing, electronics, communications, materials, energy, industrial automation, and bioengineering and medical equipment. Investments generally range from $1 million to $3 million.

BT Capital Corp. (Los Angeles)
300 S. Grand Ave.
Los Angeles, California 90071
Phone: (213)620-8430
A small business investment company.

Charterway Investment Corp.
One Wilshire Bldg., No. 1600
Los Angeles, California 90017-3317
Phone: (213)689-9107
Fax: (213)890-1968
A minority enterprise small business investment corporation. No industry preference.

Far East Capital Corp.
977 N. Broadway, Ste. 401
Los Angeles, California 90012
Phone: (213)687-1361
Fax: (213)626-7497
A minority enterprise small business investment company. Diversified industry preference.

Kline Hawkes California SBIC, LP
11726 San Vicente Blvd., Ste. 300

Los Angeles, California 90049
Phone: (310)442-4700
Fax: (310)442-4707
Frank R Kline, Manager

Peregrine Ventures
12400 Wilshire Blvd Ste. 240
Los Angeles, California 90025
Phone: (310)458-1441
Fax: (310)394-0771
Venture capital firm providing start-up, first stage, and leveraged buyout financing. Areas of interest include communications and health.

Riordan Lewis & Haden
300 S. Grand Ave., 29th Fl.
Los Angeles, California 90071
Phone: (213)229-8500
Fax: (213)229-8597
Venture capital firm providing all types of financing, including management buyouts and turn-arounds. Areas of interest include food and service.

The Seideler Companies, Inc.
515 S. Figueroa St., 11th Fl.
Los Angeles, California 90071-3396
Phone: (213)624-4232
Fax: (213)623-1131

Union Venture Corp.
445 S. Figueroa St.
Los Angeles, California 90071
Phone: (213)236-5658
Fax: (213)688-0101
A small business investment company. Diversified industry preference.

Advanced Technology Ventures (Menlo Park)
485 Ramona St., Ste. 200
Menlo Park, California 94301
Phone: (415)321-8601
Fax: (415)321-0934

Bessemer Venture Partners (Menlo Park)
3000 Sand Hill Rd., Bldg. 3, Ste. 225
Menlo Park, California 94025
Phone: (415)854-2200
Fax: (415)854-7415

Brentwood Associates (Menlo Park)
3000 Sandhill Rd., Ste. 260
Menlo Park, California 94025-7020
Phone: (415)854-7691
Fax: (415)854-9513

Canaan Partners
2884 Sand Hill Rd., Ste. 115
Menlo Park, California 94025-7022
Phone: (415)854-8092
Fax: (415)854-8127
Venture capital firm providing start-up, second and third stage, and buyout financing. Areas of interest include information industry products and services, medical technology, and health care services.

Comdisco Venture Group (Menlo Park)
3000 Sand Hill Rd., Bldg. 1, Ste. 155
Menlo Park, California 94025-7141
Phone: (415)854-9484
Fax: (415)854-4026
Prefers start-up businesses in fields of semiconductors, computer hardware and software, computer services and systems, telecommunications, and medical and biotechnology. Investments range from $500,000 to $5 million.

Glenwood Management
3000 Sand Hill Rd., Bldg. 4, Ste. 230
Menlo Park, California 94025
Phone: (415)854-8070
Fax: (415)854-4961
Venture capital supplier. Areas of interest include high technology and biomedical industries.

Institutional Venture Partners
3000 Sand Hill Rd., Bldg. 2, Ste. 290
Menlo Park, California 94025
Phone: (415)854-0132
Fax: (415)854-5762
Venture capital fund. Invests in early stage ventures with significant market potential in the computer, information sciences, communications, and life sciences fields.

Interwest Partners (Menlo Park)
3000 Sand Hill Rd., Bldg. 3, Ste. 255
Menlo Park, California 94025
Phone: (415)854-8585
Fax: (415)854-4706
Venture capital fund. Both high-tech and low- or non-technology companies are considered. No oil, gas, real estate, or construction projects.

Kleiner Perkins Caufield & Byers (Menlo Park)
2750 Sand Hill Rd.
Menlo Park, California 94025
Phone: (415)233-2750
Fax: (415)233-0300
Provides seed, start-up, second and third-round, and bridge financing to companies on the West Coast. Preferred industries of investment include electronics, computers, software, telecommunications, biotechnology, medical devices, and pharmaceuticals.

Matrix Partners
2500 Sand Hill Rd., Ste. 113
Menlo Park, California 94025-7016
Phone: (415)854-3131
Fax: (415)854-3296
Private venture capital partnership. Investments range from $500,000 to $1 million.

Mayfield Fund
2800 Sand Hill Rd., Ste. 250
Menlo Park, California 94025
Phone: (415)854-5560
Fax: (415)854-5712
Venture capital partnership. Prefers high-technology and biomedical industries.

McCown De Leeuw & Co. (Menlo Park)
3000 Sand Hill Rd., Bldg. 3, Ste. 290
Menlo Park, California 94025
Phone: (415)854-6000
Fax: (415)854-0853
A venture capital firm. Preferences include the mortgage servicing, building materials, printing, and office products industries.

Menlo Ventures
3000 Sand Hill Rd., Bldg. 4, Ste. 100
Menlo Park, California 94025
Phone: (415)854-8540
Fax: (415)854-7059
Venture capital supplier. Provides start-up and expansion financing to companies with experienced management teams, distinctive product lines, and large growing markets. Primary interest is in technology-oriented, service, consumer products, and distribution companies. Investments range from $500,000 to $3 million; also provides capital for leveraged buy outs.

Merrill Pickard Anderson & Eyre I
2480 Sand Hill Rd., Ste. 200
Menlo Park, California 94025
Phone: (415)854-8600
Fax: (415)854-0345
Steven Merrill, President

New Enterprise Associates (Menlo Park)
2490 Sand Hill Road
Menlo Park, California 94025
Phone: (415)854-9499
Fax: (415)854-9397
Venture capital supplier.

New Enterprise Associates (San Francisco)
2490 Sand Hill Road
Menlo Park, California 94025
Phone: (415)854-9499
Fax: (415)854-9397
Venture capital supplier. Concentrates in technology-based industries that have the potential for product innovation, rapid growth, and high profit margins.

Paragon Venture Partners
3000 Sand Hill Rd., Bldg. 1, Ste. 275
Menlo Park, California 94025
Phone: (415)854-8000
Fax: (415)854-7260
Venture capital firm. Areas of interest include high technology and life sciences with an emphasis on data

communications, networking, software, medical devices, biotechnology, and health care services industries.

Pathfinder Venture Capital Funds (Menlo Park)
3000 Sand Hill Rd., Bldg. 1, Ste. 290
Menlo Park, California 94025
Phone: (415)854-0650
Fax: (415)854-9010
Venture capital supplier. Provides start-up and early-stage financing to emerging companies in the medical, computer, pharmaceuticals, and data communications industries. Emphasis is on companies with proprietary technology or market positions and with substantial potential for revenue growth.

Ritter Partners
3000 Sandhill Rd. Bldg. 1, Ste. 190
Menlo Park, California 94025
Phone: (415)854-1555
Fax: (415)854-5015
William C. Edwards, President

Sequoia Capital
3000 Sand Hill Rd., Bldg. 4, Ste. 280
Menlo Park, California 94025
Phone: (415)854-3927
Fax: (415)854-2977
Private venture capital partnership with $300 million under management. Provides financing for all stages of development of well-managed companies with exceptional growth prospects in fast-growth industries. Past investments have been made in computers and peripherals, communications, health care, biotechnology, and medical instruments and devices. Investments range from $350,000 for early stage companies to $4 million for late stage accelerates.

Sierra Ventures
3000 Sand Hill Rd., Bldg. 4, Ste. 210
Menlo Park, California 94025
Phone: (415)854-1000
Fax: (415)854-5593
Venture capital partnership.

Sigma Partners
2884 Sand Hill Rd., Ste. 121
Menlo Park, California 94025-7022
Phone: (415)854-1300
Fax: (415)854-1323
Independent venture capital partnership. Prefers to invest in the following areas: communcations, computer hardware, computer software, manufacturing, medical equipment, and semiconductor capital equipment. Avoids investing in construction, hotels, leasing, motion pictures, and natural resources. Minimum initial commitment is $500,000.

Sprout Group (Menlo Park)
3000 Sand Hill Rd., Bldg. 4, Ste. 270
Menlo Park, California 94025-7114
Phone: (415)854-1550
Fax: (415)854-8779

Technology Venture Investors
2480 Sand Hill Rd., Ste. 101
Menlo Park, California 94025
Phone: (415)854-7472
Fax: (415)854-4187
Private venture capital partnership. Primary interest is in technology companies with minimum investment of $1 million.

U.S. Venture Partners
2180 Sand Hill Rd., Ste. 300
Menlo Park, California 94025
Phone: (415)854-9080
Fax: (415)854-3018
Venture capital partnership. Prefers the specialty retail, consumer products, technology, and biomedical industries.

USVP-Schlein Marketing Fund
2180 Sand Hill Rd., Ste. 300
Menlo Park, California 94025
Phone: (415)854-9080
Fax: (415)854-3018
Venture capital fund. Prefers specialty retailing/consumer products companies.

Hall, Morris & Drufva II, L.P.
26161 Lapaz Rd., Ste. E
Mission Viejo, California 92691
Phone: (714)707-5096
Fax: (714)707-5121
A small business investment corporation. No industry preference. Provides capital for small and medium-sized companies through participation in private placements of subordinated debt, preferred, and common stock. Offers growth-acquisition and later-stage venture capital.

ABC Capital Corp.
917 Waittier Blvd.
Montebello, California 90640
Phone: (213)725-7890
Fax: (213)725-7115
A minority enterprise small business investment corporation. No industry preference.

Allied Business Investors, Inc.
301 W. Valley Blvd. SE 208
Monterey Park, California 91754
Phone: (818)289-0186
Fax: (818)289-2369
Jack Hong, President
Preferred Investment Size: $50,000.
Investment Policies: Loans only.
Investment Types: Early stage.
Industry Preferences: Diversified.
Geographic Preferences: Los Angeles.

LaiLai Capital Corp.
223 E. Garvey Ave., Ste. 228
Monterey Park, California 91754
Phone: (818)288-0704
Fax: (818)288-4101
A minority enterprise small business investment company. Diversified industry preference.

Myriad Capital, Inc.
701 S. Atlantic Blvd., Ste. 302
Monterey Park, California 91754-3242
Phone: (818)570-4548
Fax: (818)570-9570
A minority enterprise small business investment corporation. Prefers

investing in production and manufacturing industries.

Enterprise Partners
5000 Birch St., Ste. 6200
Newport Beach, California 92660
Phone: (714) 833-3650
Fax: (714) 833-3652
Venture capital fund. Prefers to invest in medical or high-technology industries in California.

Marwit Capital Corp.
180 Newport Center Dr., Ste. 200
Newport Beach, California 92660
Phone: (714) 640-6234
Fax: (714) 720-8077
A small business investment corporation. Provides financing for leveraged buyouts, mergers, acquisitions, and expansion stages. Investments are in the $100,000 to $4 million range. Does not provide financing for start-ups or real estate ventures.

Inman and Bowman
4 Orinda Way, Bldg. D, Ste. 150
Orinda, California 94563
Phone: (510) 253-1611
Fax: (510) 253-9037

Asset Management Co.
2275 E. Bayshore, Ste. 150
Palo Alto, California 94303
Phone: (415) 494-7400
Fax: (415) 856-1826
Venture capital firm. High-technology industries preferred.

BankAmerica Ventures (Palo Alto)
5 Palo Alto Sq., Ste. 938
Palo Alto, California 94306
Phone: (415) 424-8011
Fax: (415) 424-6830

Campbell Venture Management
375 California St.
Palo Alto, California 94308
Phone: (415) 853-0766
Fax: (415) 857-0303

Citicorp Venture Capital, Ltd. (Palo Alto)

2 Embarcadero Pl.
2200 Geny Rd., Ste. 203
Palo Alto, California 94303
Phone: (415) 424-8000
A small business investment company.

Greylock Management Corp. (Palo Alto)
755 Page Mill Rd., Ste. A-100
Palo Alto, California 94304-1018
Phone: (415) 493-5525
Fax: (415) 493-5575
Venture capital firm providing all stages of financing. Areas of interest include computer software, communications, health, biotechnology, publishing, and specialty retail.

MK Global Ventures
2471 E. Bayshore Rd., Ste. 520
Palo Alto, California 94303
Phone: (415) 424-0151
Fax: (415) 494-2753

Norwest Venture Capital (Menlo Park)
245 Iytton Ave., Ste. 250
Palo Alto, California 94301
Phone: (415) 854-6366
Fax: (415) 321-8010
A small business investment corporation. No industry preference.

Oak Investment Partners (Menlo Park)
525 University Avenue, Ste. 1300
Palo Alto, California 94301
Phone: (415) 614-3700
Fax: (415) 328-6345
Small business investment corporation. Areas of interest include communications, computer hardware and software, high technology, manufacturing, medical equipment and instrumentation, pharmaceuticals, and retail.

Patricof & Co. Ventures, Inc. (Palo Alto)
1 Embarcadero Pl.
2100 Geng Rd., Ste. 150
Palo Alto, California 94303
Phone: (415) 494-9944
Fax: (415) 494-6751

Venture capital firm providing equity investments, diversified by markets and stage of company. Prefers to fund growth.

Summit Partners (Newport Beach)
499 Hamilton Ave., Ste. 200
Palo Alto, California 94301
Phone: (415) 321-1166
Fax: (415) 321-1188
Venture capital firm providing investments in the $2 million-$20 million range. Areas of interest include technology, health care, and financial services.

Sutter Hill Ventures
755 Page Mill Rd., Ste. A-200
Palo Alto, California 94304-1005
Phone: (415) 493-5600
Fax: (415) 858-1854
Venture capital partnership providing start-up financing for high technology businesses.

TA Associates (Palo Alto)
435 Tasso St.
Palo Alto, California 94301
Phone: (415) 328-1210
Fax: (415) 326-4933
Private venture capital firm. Prefers technology companies and leveraged buy outs. Provides from $1 to $20 million in investments.

Venrock Associates
755 Page Mill, A-230
Palo Alto, California 94304
Phone: (415) 493-5577
Fax: (415) 493-6443
Private venture capital supplier. Prefers high-technology start-up equity investments.

BankAmerica Ventures (Pasadena)
155 N. Lake Ave., Ste. 1010
Pasadena, California 91109
Phone: (818) 304-3451
Fax: (818) 440-9931

First SBIC of California (Pasadena)
155 N. Lake Ave., Ste. 1010
Pasadena, California 91109

Phone:(818)304-3451
Fax:(818)440-9931
A small business investment company.

The Money Store Investment Corp.
3301 "C" St., Ste. 100 M
Sacramento, California 95816
Phone:(916)446-5000
Free:(800)639-1102
Fax:(916)443-2399
Non-bank lender providing start-up and expansion financing.

AMF Financial, Inc.
4330 La Jolla Village Dr., Ste. 110
San Diego, California 92122-1233
Phone:(619)546-0167
Fax:(619)455-0868
A small business investment company. Diversified industry preference.

Forward Ventures
10975 Torreyana Rd., No. 230
San Diego, California 92121
Phone:(619)677-6077
Fax:(619)452-8799
Venture capital firm preferring investments of $100,000-$500,000. Areas of interest include biotechnology and health care.

Idanta Partners Ltd.
4660 La Jolla Village Dr., Ste. 850
San Diego, California 92122-4606
Phone:(619)452-9690
Fax:(619)452-2013
Venture capital partnership. No industry preferences. Minimum investment is $500,000.

Sorrento Growth Partners I, L.P.
4225 Executive Sq., Ste. 1450
San Diego, California 92137
Phone:(619)452-6400
Fax:(619)452-7607
Robert Jaffe, Manager
Preferred Investment Size: $750,000 TO $2 Million. Investment Policies: Equity only. Investment Types: Seed, early, expansion, later stages. Industry Preferences: Medicine, health, communications, electronics, special

retail. Geographic Preferences: Southern California.

Accel Partners (San Francisco)
E-mail: www.accel.com
1 Embarcadero Center, Ste. 3820
San Francisco, California 94111
Phone:(415)989-5656
Fax:(415)989-5554
Venture capital firm providing start-up financing. Areas of interest include health care, information technology, software, and telecommunications.

American Realty and Construction
1489 Webster St., Ste. 218
San Francisco, California 94115-3767
Phone:(415)928-6600
Fax:(415)928-6363
A minority enterprise small business investment corporation. No industry preference.

BANEXI Corp.
555 California St., Ste. 2600
San Francisco, California 94104
Phone:(415)693-3345
Free:(800)766-3863
Fax:(415)433-7326
Venture capital firm preferring late stage investments. Areas of interest include biotechnology, health care products/services, industrial and environmental services, electronic technology and information services, communications, business services, and specialty retailing.

Bentley Capital
592 Vallejo St. Ste. 2
San Francisco, California 94133
Phone:(415)362-2868
Fax:(415)398-8209
A minority enterprise small business investment company. Diversified industry preference.

Bryan and Edwards Partnership (San Francisco)
600 Montgomery St., 35th Fl.
San Francisco, California 94111-2854
Phone:(415)421-9990
Fax:(415)421-0471

A small business investment corporation. No industry preference.

Burr, Egan, Deleage, and Co. (San Francisco)
1 Embarcadero Center, Ste. 4050
San Francisco, California 94111-3729
Phone:(415)362-4022
Fax:(415)362-6178
Private venture capital supplier. Invests start-up, expansion, and acquisitions capital nationwide. Principal concerns are strength of the management team; large, rapidly expanding markets; and unique products for services. Past investments have been made in the fields of biotechnology and pharmaceuticals, cable TV, chemicals/plastics, communications, software, computer systems and peripherals, distributorships, radio common carriers, electronics and electrical components, environmental control, health services, medical devices and instrumentation, and radio and cellular telecommunications. Primarily interested in medical, electronics, and media industries.

Dillon Read Venture Capital
555 California St., No. 4360
San Francisco, California 94104-1714
Phone:(415)296-7900
Fax:(415)296-8956
A venture capital firm. Provides early-stage financing to companies in the biomedical field and the information systems industry.

Dominion Ventures, Inc.
44 Montgomery St., Ste. 4200
San Francisco, California 94104
Phone:(415)362-4890
Fax:(415)394-9245
Venture capital firm providing seed, start-up, second and third stage, and buyout financing. Areas of interest include biotechnology, health care, telecommunications, software, and financial services.

First Century Partners (San Bruno)
E-mail: sagegiven@aol.com

101 California St., Ste. 3160
San Francisco, California 94111
Phone: (415)433-4200
Fax: (415)433-4250
Venture capital firm. Health care,
software, technology-based service,
and specialty retailing industries
preferred.

G C and H Partners
1 Maritime Plz., 20th Fl.
San Francisco, California 94111
Phone: (415)693-2000
Fax: (415)951-3699
A small business investment corpora-
tion. No industry preference.

Hambrecht and Quist (San Francisco)
1 Bush St.
San Francisco, California 94104
Phone: (415)439-3300
Free: (800)227-3958
Fax: (415)439-3621
Prefers to invest in computer
tehnology, environmental technology,
and biotechnology. Investments
range from $500,000 to $5,000,000.

Heller First Capital Corp.
650 California St., 23rd Fl.
San Francisco, California 94108
Phone: (415)274-5700
Fax: (415)274-5744
Non-bank lender providing start-up
and expansion financing.

Jafco America Ventures, Inc. (San
Francisco)
555 California St., Ste. 4380
San Francisco, California 94104
Phone: (415)788-0706
Fax: (415)788-0709
Venture capital firm. Provides middle-
to later-stage investments. Avoids
investments in real estate, natural
resources, entertainment, motion
pictures, oil and gas, construction,
and non-technical industries.

Jupiter Partners
600 Montgomery St., 35th Fl.
San Francisco, California 94111
Phone: (415)421-9990
Fax: (415)421-0471

A small business investment company. Prefers to invest in electronic
manufacturing industry.

Montgomery Securities
600 Montgomery St., 21st Fl.
San Francisco, California 94111-2702
Phone: (415)627-2454
Fax: (415)249-5516
Private venture capital and investment
banking firm. Diversified, but will not
invest in real estate or energy-related
industries. Involved in both start-up
and later-stage financing.

Morgan Stanley Venture Capital Fund
L.P.
555 California St., Ste. 2200
San Francisco, California 94104
Phone: (415)576-2345
Fax: (415)576-2099
Venture capital firm providing second
and third stage and buyout financing.
Areas of interest include information
technology and health care products/
services.

Positive Enterprises, Inc.
1489 Webster St., Ste. 228
San Francisco, California 94115
Phone: (415)885-6600
Fax: (415)928-6363
A minority enterprise small business
investment company. Diversified
industry preference.

Quest Ventures (San Francisco)
E-mail: y@questventures.com
126 S. Park
San Francisco, California 94107
Phone: (415)546-7118
Fax: (415)243-8514
Independent venture capital partner-
ship. Diversified industry preference.

Robertson-Stephens Co.
E-mail: 800emailol
555 California St., Ste. 2600
San Francisco, California 94104
Phone: (415)781-9700
Fax: (415)781-0278
Investment banking firm. Considers
investments in any attractive merging-
growth area, including product and

service companies. Key preferences
include health care, hazardous waste
services and technology, biotechnology, software, and information
services. Maximum investment is $5
million.

VenAd Administrative Services
E-mail: vallee@eurolink.com
657 Mission Street Ste. 601
San Francisco, California 94105
Phone: (415)543-4448
Fax: (415)541-7775
Private venture capital supplier.
Provides all stages of financing.

VK Capital Co.
600 California St., Ste. 1700
San Francisco, California 94108
Phone: (415)391-5600
Fax: (415)397-2744
A small business investment com-
pany. Diversified industry preference.

Volpe, Welty and Co.
1 Maritime Plz., 11th Fl.
San Francisco, California 94111
Phone: (415)956-8120
Fax: (415)986-6754
Prefers investing with companies
involved in entertainment, multimedia, computer-aided software
engineering, gaming, software tools,
biotechnology, and health care
industries.

Walden Group of Venture Capital
Funds
750 Battery St., Ste. 700
San Francisco, California 94111
Phone: (415)391-7225
Fax: (415)391-7262
Venture capital firm providing seed,
start-up, and second and third stage
financing. Areas of interest include
high technology, consumer products,
health-related industries, hardware,
software, EDP, environmental,
communications, and education.

Weiss, Peck and Greer Venture
Partners L.P. (San Francisco)
555 California St., Ste. 4760

San Francisco, California 94104
Phone: (415)622-6864
Fax: (415)989-5108

Dougery & Wilder (San Mateo)
155 Bovet Rd., Ste. 350
San Mateo, California 94402-3113
Phone: (415)358-8701
Fax: (415)358-8706
Venture capital supplier. Areas of
interest include computers systems
and software, communications, and
medical/biotechnology industries.

Drysdale Enterprises
177 Bovet Rd., Ste. 600
San Mateo, California 94402
Phone: (415)341-6336
Fax: (415)341-1329
Venture capital firm preferring
investments of $250,000-$2 million.
Areas of interest include food
processing, health care, and communi-
cations.

Technology Funding
2000 Alameda de las Pulgas, Ste. 250
San Mateo, California 94403
Phone: (415)345-2200
Free: (800)821-5323
Fax: (415)341-1400
Small business investment corporation. Provides primarily late first-stage
and early second-stage equity
financing. Also offers secured debt
with equity participation to venture
capital backed companies. Investments range from $500,000 to $1
million.

Trinity Ventures Ltd.
E-mail: trinityvc@aol.com
155 Bovet Rd., Ste. 660
San Mateo, California 94402
Phone: (415)358-9700
Fax: (415)358-9785
Private venture capital firm investing
in computer software, consumer
products, and health care industries.

Phoenix Growth Capital Corp.
2401 Kerner Blvd.
San Rafael, California 94901

Phone: (415)485-4655
Free: (800)227-2626
Fax: (415)485-4663
Small business investment corporation providing start-up, second and
third stage, and buyout financing.
Areas of interest include secured debt
for high technology, biotechnology,
computers and peripherals, and
service industries. (All must be equity
venture capital based.)

InterVen Partners (Santa Monica)
301 Arizona Ave., No. 306
Santa Monica, California 90401-1305
Phone: (310)587-3550
Fax: (310)587-3440
Venture capital fund. Diversified
industry preferences; geographic
preference is the West Coast.

InterVen II L.P. (Portland, OR)
301 Arizona Ave., Ste 306
Santa Monica, California 90401
Phone: (310)587-3550
Fax: (310)587-3440
A small business investment corporation. Currently making only follow-on
investments in existing portfolio
companies.

DSC Ventures II, LP
12050 Saratoga Ave. Ste., B
Saratoga, California 95070
Phone: (408)252-3800
Fax: (408)252-0757
A small business investment com-
pany. Diversified industry preference.

Western General Capital Corp.
13701 Riverside Dr., Ste. 610
Sherman Oaks, California 91423
Phone: (818)986-5038
Fax: (818)905-9220
A minority enterprise small business
investment company. Diversified
industry preference.

Astar Capital Corp.
9537 E. Gidley St.
Temple City, California 91780
Phone: (818)350-1211
Fax: (818)350-0868
George Hsu, President

Spectra Enterprise Associates
PO Box 7688
Thousand Oaks, California 91359-7688
Phone: (818)865-0213
Fax: (818)865-1309
Venture capital partnership. Areas of
interest include information, computer,
semiconductor, software, life sciences,
and wireless industries.

National Investment Management,
Inc.
E-mail: Robins621@ad.com
2601 Airport Drive., Ste.210
Torrance, California 90505
Phone: (310)784-7600
Fax: (310)784-7605
Venture capital firm providing
leveraged buyout financing. Areas of
interest include general manufacturing
and distribution.

Round Table Capital Corp.
2175 N. California Blvd., Ste. 400
Walnut Creek, California 94596
Phone: (510)274-1700
Fax: (510)974-3978
A small business investment corpora-
tion. No industry preference.

Colorado

Hill, Carman, and Washing
885 Arapahoe
Boulder, Colorado 80302
Phone: (303)442-5151
Fax: (303)442-8525

Opus Capital
1113 Spruce St., Ste. 406
Boulder, Colorado 80302
Phone: (303)443-1023
Fax: (303)443-0986

Capital Health Management
2084 S. Milwaukee St.
Denver, Colorado 80210
Phone: (303)692-8600
Fax: (303)692-9656

The Centennial Funds
1428 15th St.
Denver, Colorado 80202

Phone:(303)405-7500
Fax:(303)405-7575
Venture capital fund. Prefers to invest in early stage companies in the Rocky Mountain region.

Colorado Housing and Finance Authority
1981 Blake St.
Denver, Colorado 80202-1272
Phone:(303)297-2432
Fax:(303)297-2615
Operates financing programs for small and minority businesses.

Colorado Office of Business Development
1625 Broadway, Ste. 1710
Denver, Colorado 80202
Phone:(303)892-3840
Fax:(303)892-3848
Provides loans to new and expanding businesses.

UBD Capital, Inc.
1700 Broadway
Denver, Colorado 80274
Phone:(303)863-6329
A small business investment company. Diversified industry preference.

Columbine Ventures
5460 S. Quebec St., Ste. 270
Englewood, Colorado 80111-1917
Phone:(303)694-3222
Fax:(303)694-9007
Venture capital firm interested in biotechnology, medical, computer, electronics, and advanced materials industries.

Connecticut

First Connecticut SBIC
1000 Bridgeport St.
Bridgeport, Connecticut 06484
Phone:(203)366-4726
Free:(800)401-3222
Fax:(203)944-5405
A small business investment corporation.

AB SBIC, Inc.
275 School House Rd.
Cheshire, Connecticut 06410
Phone:(203)272-0203
Fax:(203)272-9978
A small business investment company. Prefers to invest in grocery stores.

Financial Opportunities, Inc.
1 Vision Dr.
Enfield, Connecticut 06082
Phone:(203)741-4444
Fax:(860)741-4494
A small business investment corporation. Prefers full franchise convenience stores.

Consumer Venture Partners
3 Pickwick Plz.
Greenwich, Connecticut 06830
Phone:(203)629-8800
Fax:(203)629-2019
Prefers consumer and expansion-stage investments.

First New England Capital, LP
100 Pearl St.
Hartford, Connecticut 06103
Phone:(203)293-3333
Fax:(203)549-2528
A small business investment company. Diversified industry preference.

FRE Capital Partners, LP
36 Grove St.
New Canaan, Connecticut 06840
Phone:(203)966-2800
Fax:(203)966-3109
A small business investment company. Diversified industry preference.

RFE Investment Partners V, L.P.
36 Grove St.
New Canaan, Connecticut 06840
Phone:(203)966-2800
Fax:(203)966-3109
James A. Parsons, General Partner
Preferred Investment Size: $5 - $9 Million. Investment Policies: Prefer equity investments. Investment Types: Later stage, expansion, acquisitions. Industry Preferences:

Manufacturing & services. Geographic Preferences: National, eastern U.S.

The Vista Group
36 Grove St.
New Canaan, Connecticut 06840
Phone:(203)972-3400
Fax:(203)966-0844
Venture capital supplier. Provides start-up and second-stage financing to technology-related businesses that seek to become major participants in high-growth markets of at least $100 million in annual sales. Areas of investment interest include information systems, communications, computer peripherals, medical products and services, retailing, agrigenetics, bio-technology, low technology, no technology, instrumentation, and genetic engineering.

All State Venture Capital Corp.
The Bishop House
32 Elm St.
PO Box 1629
New Haven, Connecticut 06506
Phone:(203)787-5029
Fax:(203)785-0018
A small business investment company. Diversified industry preference.

Nova Tech-Eicon
142 Temple St., 2nd Fl.
New Haven, Connecticut 06510
Phone:(203)789-1260
Fax:(203)789-8261

DCS Growth Fund (Old Greenwich)
PO Box 740
Old Greenwich, Connecticut 06870-0740
Phone:(203)637-1704
Fax:(203)637-1705

Canaan Partners
105 Rowayton Ave.
Rowayton, Connecticut 06853
Phone:(203)855-0400
Fax:(203)854-9117
Venture capital supplier.

Marcon Capital Corp.
10 John St.
Southport, Connecticut 06490-1437
Phone: (203)259-7233
Fax: (203)259-9428
A small business investment corporation; secured lending preferred.

Central Texas SBI Corporation
1 Canterbury Green
201 Broad St., 2nd Fl.
Stamford, Connecticut 06901
Phone: (203)352-4056
Fax: (203)352-4184
David E. Erb, Contact Person

James B. Kobak and Co.
2701 Summer St., Ste. 200
Stamford, Connecticut 06905
Phone: (203)363-2221
Fax: (203)363-2218
Venture capital supplier and consultant. Provides assistance to new ventures in the communications field through conceptualization, planning, organization, raising money, and control of actual operations. Special interest is in magazine publishing.

Saugatuck Capital Co.
1 Canterbury Green
Stamford, Connecticut 06901
Phone: (203)348-6669
Fax: (203)324-6995
Private investment partnership. Seeks to invest in various industries not dependent on technology, including health care, telecommunications, insurance, financial services, manufacturing, and consumer products. Prefers leveraged buy out situations, but will consider start-up financing. Investments range from $3 to $5 million.

Schroder Ventures
1055 Washington Blvd. 5th Fl.
Stamford, Connecticut 06901
Phone: (203)324-7700
Fax: (203)324-3636

TSG Ventures, Inc.
177 Broad St., 12th Fl.
Stamford, Connecticut 06901

Phone: (203)406-1500
Fax: (203)406-1590
A minority enterprise small business investment company. Diversified industry preference.

J. H. Whitney and Co. (New York)
177 Broad St.
Stamford, Connecticut 06901
Phone: (203)973-1400
Fax: (203)973-1422

Xerox Venture Capital (Stamford)
E-mail: xerox.com
Headquarters
800 Long Ridge Rd.
Stamford, Connecticut 06904
Phone: (203)968-3000
Venture capital subsidiary of operating company. Prefers to invest in document processing industries.

The SBIC of Connecticut, Inc.
2 Corpoate Rd., Ste. 203
Trumbull, Connecticut 06611
Phone: (203)261-0011
Fax: (203)459-1563
A small business investment corporation. No industry preference.

Capital Resource Company of Connecticut, LP
2558 Albany Ave.
West Hartford, Connecticut 06117
Phone: (203)236-4336
Fax: (860)232-8161
A small business investment corporation. No industry preference.

Marketcorp Venture Associates
285 Riverside Ave.
Westport, Connecticut 06880
Phone: (203)222-1000
Free: (800)243-5077
Fax: (203)222-5829
Venture capital firm. Prefers to invest in consumer-market businesses, including the packaged goods, specialty retailing, communications, and consumer electronics industries.

Oak Investment Partners (Westport)
1 Gorham Island

Westport, Connecticut 06880
Phone: (203)226-8346
Fax: (203)227-0372

Oxford Bioscience Partners
315 Post Rd. W.
Westport, Connecticut 06880
Phone: (203)341-3300
Fax: (203)341-3309
Independent venture capital partnership. Areas of interest include biotechnology, medical devices/services, and health care services. Initial investments range from $500,000 to $1.5 million; up to $3 million over several later rounds of financing.

Prince Ventures (Westport)
25 Ford Rd.
Westport, Connecticut 06880
Phone: (203)227-8332
Fax: (203)226-5302
Provides early stage financing for medical and life sciences ventures.

Delaware

Delaware Economic Development Authority
99 Kings Hwy.
PO Box 1401
Dover, Delaware 19903-1401
Phone: (302)739-4271
Free: (800)441-8846
Fax: (302)739-5749
Provides financing to new and expanding businesses at interest rates below the prime rate by issuing industrial revenue bonds (IRBs). Manufacturing and agricultural projects are eligible.

PNC Capital Corp.
300 Delaware Ave., Ste. 304
Wilmington, Delaware 19801
Phone: (302)427-5895
Gary J. Zentner, President
Preferred Investment Size: $2 to $8 million. Investment Policies: Loans and/or equity. Investment Types: Expansion, later stage. Industry Preferences: No real estate or tax-

oriented investments. Geographic Preferences: Northeast.

District of Columbia

Allied Capital Commercial Corp.
1666 K St. N.W., 9th Fl.
Washington, DC 20006
Phone: (202)331-1112
Fax: (202)659-2053
Real estate investment trust managed by Allied Capital Advisers, Inc. Investments range from $500,000 to $7.5 million. Prefers to purchase small business loans secured by real estate that are owner-operated or small business controlled. Areas of property interest include convenience stores, hotel/motel establishments, offices, medical facilities and nursing homes, industrial and retail properties, service stations, RV and mobile home parks, office condiminiums, mini-storage facilities, and restaurants.

Allied Capital Corp.
1666 K St. N.W., 9th Fl.
Washington, DC 20006
Phone: (202)331-1112
Fax: (202)659-2053
Venture capital fund managed by Allied Capital Advisers, Inc. Investments range from $500,000 to $6 million. Prefers later-stage companies that have been in business for at least one year, but gives consideration to early-stage companies and turnaround situations. Geographical preferences include the Northeast, Mid-Atlantic, and Southeast. Areas of interest include communications, computer hardware and software, consumer products, educational products, electronics, environmental, energy, franchising, industrial products and equipment, manufacturing, media, medical/health, publishing, recreation/tourism, restaurant, retail, service, transportation, and wholesale distribution industries.

Allied Capital Corp. II
1666 K St. N.W., 9th Fl.

Washington, DC 20006
Phone: (202)331-1112
Fax: (202)659-2053
Venture capital fund managed by Allied Capital Advisers, Inc. Investments range from $500,000 to $1 million. Prefers later-stage companies that have been in business for at least one year, but gives consideration to early-stage companies and turnaround situations. Geographical preferences include the Northeast, Mid-Atlantic, and Southeast. Areas of interest include communications, computer hardware and software, consumer products, educational products, electronics, environmental, energy, franchising, industrial products and equipment, manufacturing, media, medical/health, publishing, recreation/tourism, restaurant, retail, service, transportation, and wholesale distribution industries.

Allied Capital Lending Corp.
1666 K St. N.W., 9th Fl.
Washington, DC 20006
Phone: (202)331-1112
Fax: (202)659-2053
Mangement investment company managed by Allied Capital Advisers, Inc. Investments range from $200,000 to $1 million. Prefers to provide small, privately owned businesses with SBA-guaranteed loans. Areas of interest include manufacturing, hotel/motel, consumer products, retail shops/convenience stores, service stations, laundries and dry cleaning, home furnishings, printing, real estate, recreation/tourism, restaurant, and service industries.

Allied Financial Corp.
1666 K St. N.W., 9th Fl.
Washington, DC 20006-2804
Phone: (202)331-1112
Fax: (202)659-2053
A minority enterprise small business investment corporation. Diversified industry preference, excluding start-ups, turnarounds, real estate development, natural resources, and foreign companies.

Broadcast Capital, Inc.
1771 N St. NW
Washington, DC 20036
Phone: (202)429-5393
Fax: (202)775-2991
A minority enterprise small business investment corporation. Invests only in radio and TV stations. Investments lie in the $300,000-$400,000 range.

Fulcrum Venture Capital Corp
2021 K St. NW, Ste. 210
Washington, DC 20006
Phone: (202)785-4253

Helio Capital, Inc.
666 11th St., NW, Ste. 900
Washington, DC 20001
Phone: (202)272-3617
Fax: (202)504-2247
A minority enterprise small business investment corporation. No industry preference.

Minority Broadcast Investment Corp.
1001 Connecticut NW, Ste. 622
Washington, DC 20036-2506
Phone: (202)293-1166
Fax: (202)872-1669
A minority enterprise small business investment corporation. Communications industry preferred.

Florida

North American Fund, II
312 SE 17th St., Ste. 300
Fort Lauderdale, Florida 33316
Phone: (954)463-0681
Fax: (954)527-0904
A small business investment corporation. No industry preference. Prefers controlling interest investments and acquisitions of established businesses with a history of profitability.

Quantum Capital Partners, Ltd.
4400 NE 25th Ave.
Fort Lauderdale, Florida 33308
Phone: (305)776-1133
Fax: (305)938-9406
A small business investment company. Diversified industry preference.

Pro-Med Investment Corp. (North
Miami Beach)
Presidential Circle
4000 Hollywood Blvd., Ste. 435 S.
Hollywood, Florida 33021-6754
Phone: (305)966-8868
Free: (800)954-3617
Fax: (305)969-3223
A minority enterprise small business
investment company.

Venture First Associates
1901 S. Harbor City Blvd., Ste. 501
Melbourne, Florida 32901
Phone: (407)952-7750
Fax: (407)952-5787
Venture capital firm providing seed,
start-up and first stage financing.
Areas of interest include health care,
advanced chemicals, computer
software and hardware, industrial
equipment, electronics, and communications.

BAC Investment Corp.
6600 NW 27th Ave.
Miami, Florida 33147
Phone: (305)693-5919
Fax: (305)693-7450
A minority enterprise small business
investment company. Diversified
industry preference.

J and D Capital Corp.
12747 Biscayne Blvd.
North Miami, Florida 33181
Phone: (305)893-0303
Fax: (305)891-2338
A small business investment corpora-
tion. No industry preference.

PMC Investment Corp.
AmeriFirst Bank Bldg., 2nd Fl. S
18301 Biscayne Blvd.
North Miami Beach, Florida 33160
Phone: (305)933-5858
Fax: (305)933-9410

Western Financial Capital Corp.
(North Miami Beach)
AmeriFirst Bank Bldg., 2nd Fl. S
18301 Biscayne Blvd.
North Miami Beach, Florida 33160

Phone: (305)933-5858
Fax: (305)933-9410
A small business investment com-
pany.

Florida High Technology and Indus-
try Council
Collins Bldg.
107 W. Gaines St., Rm. 315
Tallahassee, Florida 32399-2000
Phone: (904)487-3136
Fax: (904)487-3014
Provides financing for research and
development for high-tech busi-
nesses.

Florida Capital Ventures, Ltd.
880 Riverside Plz.
100 W. Kennedy Blvd.
Tampa, Florida 33602
Phone: (813)229-2294
Fax: (813)229-2028
A small business investment com-
pany. Diversified industry preference.

Market Capital Corp.
1102 N. 28th St.
PO Box 31667
Tampa, Florida 33605
Phone: (813)247-1357
Fax: (813)248-9106
A small business investment corpora-
tion. Grocery industry preferred.

South Atlantic Venture Fund
E-mail: venture@mindspring.com
614 W. Bay St.
Tampa, Florida 33606-2704
Phone: (813)253-2500
Fax: (813)253-2360
A minority enterprise small business
investment corporation. Provides
expansion capital for privately owned,
rapidly growing companies located in
the southeastern United States and
Texas. Prefers to invest in communications, computer services, consumer,
electronic components and instrumentation, medical/health-related services,
medical products, finance, and
insurance industries. Will not consider real estate or oil and gas
investments.

Allied Financial Services Corp. (Vero
Beach)
Executive Office Center, Ste. 300
2770 N. Indian River Blvd.
Vero Beach, Florida 32960
Phone: (407)778-5556
Fax: (407)569-9303
A minority enterprise small business
investment company.

Georgia

Advanced Technology Development
Fund
1000 Abernathy Rd., Ste. 1420
Atlanta, Georgia 30328
Phone: (770)668-2333
Fax: (770)668-2330
Venture capital firm providing start-
up, first stage, second stage expansion, purchase or secondary positions, and buyout or acquisition
financing. Areas of interest include
information processing, health care
and specialized mobile radio.

Arete Ventures, Inc./Utech Venture
Capital Funds
115 Perimeter Center Pl. NE, No. 1140
Atlanta, Georgia 30346-1282
Phone: (404)399-1660
Venture capital firm providing start-
up, first stage, second stage expansion and late stage expansion financing. Areas of interest include utility-
related industries.

Cordova Capital Partners, L.P.
3350 Cumberland Cir., Ste. 970
Atlanta, Georgia 30339
Phone: (770)951-1542
Fax: (770)955-7610
Paul DiBella, Manager
Ralph Wright, Manager
Preferred Investment Size: $1 to $3
million. Investment Policies: Equity
and/or debt. Investment Types: Early
stage, expansion, later stage. Industry
Preferences: Diversified. Geographic
Preferences: Southeast.

Cravey, Green & Wahlen, Inc./CGW
Southeast Partners

12 Piedmont Center, Ste. 210
Atlanta, Georgia 30305-4805
Phone: (404)816-3255
Free: (800)249-6669
Fax: (404)816-3258
Venture capital firm providing buyout
or acquisition financing. Areas of
interest include manufacturing,
distribution, and service industries.
Does not provide start-up financing or
investments in high technology and
medical industries.

EGL Holdings, Inc.
6600 Peachtree-Dunwoody Rd.
300 Embassy Row, Ste. 630
Atlanta, Georgia 30328
Phone: (770)399-5633
Fax: (770)393-4825
Venture capital firm providing late
stage expansion, purchase or secondary positions, and buyout or acquisition financing. Areas of interest
include information technology,
medical/health care, industrial
automation, electronic components
and instrumentation for venture
capital deals, and all industries for
buyouts.

Equity South
1790 The Lenox Bldg.
3399 Peachtree Rd., Ste. 1790
Atlanta, Georgia 30326
Phone: (404)237-6222
Fax: (404)261-1578
Venture capital firm providing second
stage expansion, late stage expansion,
purchase or secondary positions, and
buyout or acquisition financing.

Georgia Department of Community
Affairs
Community and Economic Develop-
ment Division
60 Executive Park South NE
Atlanta, Georgia 30329-2231
Phone: (404)679-4940
Fax: (404)679-0669
Provides assistance in applying for
state and federal grants.

Georgia Department of Community
Affairs
Government Information Division
1200 Equitable Bldg.
100 Peachtree St. NW
Atlanta, Georgia 30303
Phone: (404)656-5526
Fax: (404)656-9792
Central source for information on
Georgia's people, economy, and local
governments, including information
on federal and state funding sources.

Green Capital Investors L.P.
3343 Peachtree Rd., Ste. 1420
Atlanta, Georgia 30326
Phone: (404)261-1187
Fax: (404)266-8677
Venture capital firm providing
purchase or secondary positions and
buyout or acquisition financing.

Noro-Moseley Partners
E-mail: nmp@mindspring.com
4200 Northside Pky., Bldg. 9
Atlanta, Georgia 30327
Phone: (404)233-1966
Fax: (404)239-9280
Venture capital partnership. Prefers to
invest in private, diversified small and
medium-sized growth companies
located in the southeastern United
States.

Premier HealthCare
3414 Peachtree Rd., Ste. 238
Atlanta, Georgia 30326
Phone: (404)816-0049
Fax: (404)816-0248
Venture capital firm providing start-
up, first stage, second stage expansion, late stage expansion, purchase
or secondary positions, and buyout or
acquisition financing. Areas of
interest include health care.

Rennaissance Capital Corp.
34 Peachtree St. NW, Ste. 2230
Atlanta, Georgia 30303
Phone: (404)658-9061

Fax: (404)658-9064
A minority enterprise small business
investment company. Diversified
industry preference.

River Capital, Inc.
1360 Peachtree St. NE, Ste. 1430
Atlanta, Georgia 30309
Phone: (404)873-2166
Fax: (404)873-2158
Venture capital firm providing second
stage expansion, late stage expansion,
purchase or secondary positions, and
buyout or acquisition financing.
Areas of interest include light
manufacturing and distribution
companies with annual revenues
exceeding $20 million.

Seaboard Management Corp.
3400 Peachtree Rd. NE, Ste. 741
Atlanta, Georgia 30326
Phone: (404)239-6270
Fax: (404)239-6284
Venture capital firm providing first
stage and second stage expansion
financing. Areas of interest include
manufacturing and telecommunications.

Greater Washington Investments, Inc.
(Rockville)
105 13th St.
Columbus, Georgia 31901
Phone: (706)641-3140
Fax: (706)641-3159
Haywood Miller, Manager
Preferred Investment Size: $1,000,000.
Investment Policies: Subordinated
debt with warrant. Investment Types:
Expansion, later stage. Industry
Preferences: Diversified. Geographic
Preferences: National.

First Growth Capital, Inc.
Best Western Plz.
I-75 Georgia 42N Exit 63
Forsyth, Georgia 31029
Phone: (912)994-9260
Free: (800)447-3241
Fax: (912)994-9260

A minority enterprise small business investment company. Diversified industry preference.

North Riverside Capital Corp.
50 Technology Pk./Atlanta
Norcross, Georgia 30092
Phone: (770)446-5556
Fax: (770)446-8627
A small business investment corporation. No industry preference.

Hawaii

Bancorp Hawaii SBIC
130 Merchant St.
Honolulu, Hawaii 96813
Phone: (808)521-6411
Fax: (808)537-8557
A small business investment corporation. No industry preference.

Hawaii Agriculture Department
PO Box 22159
Honolulu, Hawaii 96823-2159
Phone: (808)973-9600
Fax: (808)973-9613
Provides information and advice in such areas as marketing, production, and labeling. Administers loan programs, including the New Farmer Loan Program, the Emergency Loan Program, and the Aquaculture Loan Program.

Hawaii Department of Business, Economic Development, and Tourism
Financial Assistance Branch
1 Capital District Bldg.
250 S. Hotel St., Ste. 503
PO Box 2359
Honolulu, Hawaii 96804
Phone: (808)586-2576
Fax: (808)587-3832
Provides loans to small businesses, including the Hawaii Capital Loan Program and the Hawaii Innovation Development Loan Program.

Pacific Venture Capital Ltd.
222 S. Vineyard St., No. PH-1
Honolulu, Hawaii 96813-2445

Phone: (808)521-6502
Free: (800)455-1888
Fax: (808)521-6541
A minority enterprise small business investment corporation.

Illinois

ABN AMRO Capital (USA) Inc.
135 S. La Salle St.
Chicago, Illinois 60674
Phone: (312904-6445
Joseph Rizzi, Chairman

Alpha Capital Venture Partners
E-mail: acpltd@aol.com
3 1st National Plz.-Ste. 1400
Chicago, Illinois 60602
Phone: (312)214-3440
Fax: (312)214-3376
A small business investment corporation providing expansion or later stage financing in the Midwest. No industry preference; however, no real estate, oil and gas, or start-up ventures are considered.

Ameritech Development Corp.
225 W. Randolph, 18th C Fl.
Chicago, Illinois 60606
Phone: (312)750-5000
Fax: (312)609-0244
Venture capital supplier. Prefers to invest in telecommunications and information services.

Batterson, Johnson and Wang Venture Partners
E-mail: bvp@vcapital.com
303 W. Madison St., Ste. 1110
Chicago, Illinois 60606-3300
Phone: (312)269-0300
Fax: (312)269-0021

William Blair and Co. (Chicago)
222 W. Adams St.
Chicago, Illinois 60606-5312
Phone: (312)364-8250
Fax: (312)236-1042
A small business investment corporation. Areas of interest include cable, media, communications, consumer

products, retail, health care services, technology and information services, and other service industries.

Brinson Partners, Inc.
209 S. LaSalle, 12th Fl.
Chicago, Illinois 60604-1295
Phone: (312)220-7100
Fax: (312)220-7199

Business Ventures, Inc.
20 N. Wacker Dr., Ste. 1741
Chicago, Illinois 60606-2904
Phone: (312)346-1580
Fax: (312)346-6693
A small business investment corporation. No industry preference; considers only ventures in the Chicago area.

Capital Health Venture Partners
20 N. Wacker Dr. Ste. 2200
Chicago, Illinois 60606
Phone: (312)781-1910
Fax: (312)726-2290
Investments limited to early stage medical, biotech, and health care related companies.

The Combined Fund, Inc.
7936 S. Cottage Grove
Chicago, Illinois 60619
Phone: (773)371-7030
Fax: (773)371-7035
A minority enterprise small business investment company. Diversified industry preference.

Continental Illinois Venture Corp.
231 S. LaSalle St.
Chicago, Illinois 60697
Phone: (312)828-8023
Fax: (312)987-0763
A small business investment corporation. Provides start-up and early stage financing to growth-oriented companies with capable management teams, proprietary products, and expanding markets.

Essex Venture Partners
E-mail: sbila@aol.com
190 S. LaSalle St., Ste. 2800

Chicago, Illinois 60603
Phone: (312)444-6040
Fax: (312)444-6034
Prefers to invest in health care
companies.

First Analysis Corp.
E-mail: bmaxwell@facvc.com
c/o Bret Maxwell
233 S. Wacker Dr., Ste. 9500
Chicago, Illinois 60606
Phone: (312)258-1400
Free: (800)866-3272
Fax: (312)258-0334
Small business investment corporation providing first and second stage,
mezzanine, and leveraged buyout
financing in the $100,000 to $3 million
range. Will act as deal originator or
investor in deals created by others.
Areas of interest include environmental, infrastructure, special chemicals/
materials, repetitive revenue service,
telecommunications, software,
consumer/specialty retail, and health
care companies.

First Capital Corp. of Chicago
3 1st National Plz., Ste. 1330
Chicago, Illinois 60602
Phone: (312)732-5400
Fax: (312)732-4098
A small business investment corpora-
tion. No industry preference.

First Chicago Venture Capital
3 1st National Plz., Ste. 1330
Chicago, Illinois 60602
Phone: (312)732-5400
Fax: (312)732-4098
Venture capital supplier. Invests a
minimum of $1 million in early stage
situations to a maximum of $25 million
in mature growth or buy out situations. Emphasis is placed on a strong
management team and unique market
opportunity.

Frontenac Co.
135 S. LaSalle St., Ste. 3800
Chicago, Illinois 60603
Phone: (312)368-0044
Fax: (312)368-9520

A small business investment corporation. No industry preference.

Golder, Thoma, Cressey, Rauner, Inc.
6100 Sears Tower
233 S. Wacker
Chicago, Illinois 60606
Phone: (312)382-2200
Fax: (312)382-2201
Private venture capital firm. Diversified industry preference, but does not
invest in high technology or real
estate industries.

Heller Equity Capital Corp.
500 W. Monroe St.
Chicago, Illinois 60661
Phone: (312)441-7200
Fax: (312)441-7378
A small business investment com-
pany. Diversified industry preference.

IEG Venture Management, Inc.
70 West Madison, Ste. 1400
Chicago, Illinois 60602
Phone: (312)644-0890
Fax: (312)454-0369
Venture capital supplier. Provides
start-up financing primarily to
technology-based companies located
in the Midwest.

Illinois Development Finance Author-
ity
Sears Tower
233 S. Wacker Dr., Ste. 5310
Chicago, Illinois 60606
Phone: (312)793-5586
Fax: (312)793-6347
Provides bond, venture capital, and
direct loan programs.

Mesirow Capital Partners SBIC, Ltd.
350 N. Clark St., 3rd Fl.
Chicago, Illinois 60610
Phone: (312)595-6000
Fax: (312)595-6035
A small business investment corporation providing later stage growth
financing and acquisition financing of
non-high-technology companies.
Does not provide start-up and
turnaround financing.

The Neighborhood Fund, Inc.
25 E. Washington Blvd., Ste. 2015
Chicago, Illinois 60602
Phone: (312)726-6084
Fax: (312)726-0167
Derrick Collins, President
Preferred Investment Size: $100,000 to
$300,000. Investment Policies: Equity
and loans. Industry Preferences:
Manufacturing, technology, product
based. Geographic Preferences:
Midwest.

Peterson Finance and Investment Co.
3300 W. Peterson Ave., Ste. A
Chicago, Illinois 60659
Phone: (312)539-0502
Fax: (312)267-8846
A minority enterprise small business
investment company. Diversified
industry preference.

Polestar Capital, Inc.
180 N. Michigan Ave., Ste. 1905
Chicago, Illinois 60601
Phone: (312)984-9875
Fax: (312)984-9877
Wallace Lennox, President
Preferred Investment Size: $350,000 to
$700,000. Investment Policies:
Primarily equity. Investment Types:
Early to later stages.

Prince Ventures (Chicago)
10 S. Wacker Dr., Ste. 2575
Chicago, Illinois 60606-7407
Phone: (312)454-1408
Fax: (312)454-9125

Shorebank Capital Inc.
7936 S. Cottage Grove
Chicago, Illinois 60619
Phone: (312)371-7030
Fax: (312)371-7035
A minority enterprise small business
investment corporation providing
second stage, buyout, and acquisition
financing to companies in the Midwest. Diversified industry preference.

Tower Ventures, Inc.
Sears Tower, BSC 23-27
3333 Beverly Holtman St., Ste.

AC254A
Chicago, Illinois 60179
Phone: (847)286-0571
Fax: (847)906-0164
A minority enterprise small business investment company. Diversified industry preference.

Walnut Capital Corp. (Chicago)
2 N. LaSalle St., Ste. 2410
Chicago, Illinois 60602
Phone: (312)269-0126
Fax: (312)346-2231
A small business investment corporation. Diversified industry preference.

Wind Point Partners (Chicago)
676 N. Michigan Ave., No. 3300
Chicago, Illinois 60611-2804
Phone: (312)649-4000
Fax: (312)649-9644

Marquette Venture Partners
520 Lake Cook Rd., Ste. 450
Deerfield, Illinois 60015
Phone: (847)940-1700
Fax: (847)940-1724

Seidman, Fisher and Co.
1603 Orrington Ave. Ste. 2050
Evanston, Illinois 60201-5910
Phone: (708)492-1812
Fax: (708)864-9692
Private venture capital supplier.

The Cerulean Fund
E-mail: walnet@aol.com
1701 E. Lake Ave., Ste. 170
Glenview, Illinois 60025
Phone: (847)657-8002
Fax: (847)657-8168
Providers of equity investment.

Allstate Venture Capital
3075 Sanders Rd., Ste. G5D
Northbrook, Illinois 60062-7127
Phone: (847)402-5681
Fax: (847)402-0880
Venture capital supplier. Investments are not limited to particular industries or geographical locations. Interest is in unique products or services that address large potential markets and

offer great economic benefits; strength of management team is also important. Investments range from $500,000 to $5 million.

Caterpillar Venture Capital, Inc.
100 NE Adams St.
Peoria, Illinois 61629
Phone: (309)675-1000
Fax: (309)675-4457
Venture capital subsidiary of operating firm.

Cilcorp Ventures, Inc.
300 Hamilton Blvd., Ste. 300
Peoria, Illinois 61602
Phone: (309)675-8850
Fax: (309)675-8800
Invests in environmental services only.

Comdisco Venture Group (Rosemont)
6111 N. River Rd.
Rosemont, Illinois 60018
Phone: (847)698-3000
Free: (800)321-1111
Fax: (847)518-5440
Venture capital subsidiary of operating firm.

Indiana

Cambridge Ventures, LP
8440 Woodfield Crossing, No. 315
Indianapolis, Indiana 46240
Phone: (317)469-9704
Fax: (317)469-3926
A small business investment company. Diversified industry preference.

Circle Ventures, Inc.
26 N. Arsenal Ave.
Indianapolis, Indiana 46201-3808
Phone: (317)636-7242
Fax: (317)637-7581
A small business investment corporation. Prefers second-stage, leveraged buy out, and growth financings. Geographical preference is Indianapolis.

Heritage Venture Partners
135 N. Pennsylvania St., Ste. 2380

Indianapolis, Indiana 46204
Phone: (317)635-5696
Fax: (317)635-5699
Venture capital fund. Prefers radio broadcast properties in mid-sized radio markets wherein major universities are located.

Indiana Business Modernization and Technology Corp.
1 N. Capitol Ave., Ste. 925
Indianapolis, Indiana 46204
Phone: (317)635-3058
Free: (800)877-5182
Fax: (317)231-7095
Invests in and counsels applied research ventures.

Indiana Development Finance Authority
1 N. Capitol Ave., Ste. 320
Indianapolis, Indiana 46204
Phone: (317)233-4332
Fax: (317)232-6786
Administers the Ag Finance, Export Finance, Loan Guarantee, and Industrial Development Bond Financing Programs.

First Source Capital Corp.
PO Box 1602
South Bend, Indiana 46634
Phone: (219)235-2180
Fax: (219)235-2227
A small business investment corporation. No industry preference.

Thomas Lowe Ventures
3600 McGill St., Ste. 300
PO Box 3688
South Bend, Indiana 46628
Phone: (219)232-0300
Fax: (219)232-0500
Venture capital firm preferring to invest in the toy industry.

Iowa

Allsop Venture Partners (Cedar Rapids)
2750 1st Ave. NE, Ste. 210
Cedar Rapids, Iowa 52402
Phone: (319)363-8971
Fax: (319)363-9519

InvestAmerica Venture Group, Inc. (Cedar Rapids)
101 2nd St. SE, Ste. 800
Cedar Rapids, Iowa 52401
Phone: (319)363-8249
Fax: (319)363-9683
A small business investment corporation. Invests in later stage manufacturing and service businesses.

MorAmerica Capital Corp. (Cedar Rapids)
101 2nd St. SE, Ste. 800
Cedar Rapids, Iowa 52401
Phone: (319)363-8249
Fax: (319)363-9683
A small business investment company. Diversified industry preference.

Iowa Department of Economic Development
Iowa Seed Capitol Corp.
200 E. Grand Ave., Ste. 130
Des Moines, Iowa 50309
Phone: (515)242-4860
Fax: (515)242-4722
Provides risk capital to ventures that have new-job potential in Iowa. Profits are reinvested in other Iowa businesses and products.

Iowa Department of Economic Development
International Division
Export Finance Program
200 E. Grand Ave.
Des Moines, Iowa 50309
Phone: (515)242-4742
Fax: (515)242-4918
Provides funding to qualified exporters of Iowa-manufactured and -processed products.

Iowa Department of Economic Development
Iowa New Jobs Training Program
150 Des Moines St.
Des Moines, Iowa 50309
Phone: (515)281-9028
Fax: (515)281-9033
Reimburses new or expanding companies for up to 50 percent of new employees' salaries and benefits for up to one year of on-the-job training. Coordinated through the state's 15 community colleges.

Iowa Department of Economic Development
Bureau of Business Finance
Self-Employment Loan Program
Iowa Dept. of Economic Development
200 E. Grand Ave.
Des Moines, Iowa 50309
Phone: (515)242-4793
Fax: (515)242-4749
Provides low-interest loans for low-income entrepreneurs who are expanding or starting a new business.

Iowa Department of Economic Development
Division of Financial Assistance
Community Development Block Grants
200 E. Grand Ave.
Des Moines, Iowa 50309
Phone: (515)242-4825
Fax: (515)242-4809
Bestows grants from the U.S. Department of Housing and Urban Development to help finance community improvements and job-generating expansions. Funds are primarily awarded on a competitive basis.

Iowa Finance Authority
100 E. Grand Ave., Ste. 250
Des Moines, Iowa 50309
Phone: (515)242-4990
Fax: (515)242-4957
Provides loans to new and expanding small businesses. Funds may be used to purchase land, construction, building improvements, or equipment; loans cannot be used for working capital, inventory, or operations.

Kansas

Allsop Venture Partners (Overland Park)
6602 W. 131st. St.
Overland Park, Kansas 66209
Phone: (913)338-0820
Fax: (913)681-5535

Kansas Venture Capital, Inc. (Overland Park)
6700 Antioch Plz., Ste. 460
Overland Park, Kansas 66204-1200
Phone: (913)262-7117
Fax: (913)262-3509
A small business investment corporation. Prefers to invest in wholesale or distribution, high technology, and service businesses.

Kansas City Equity Partners
4200 Somerset Dr., Ste. 101
Prairie Village, Kansas 66208
Phone: (816)960-1771
Fax: (913)649-2125
Paul H. Henson, Manager
Preferred Investment Size: $500,000 to $2 million. Investment Policies: Equity. Investment Types: Seed, early stage, expansion. Industry Preferences: Diversified. Geographic Preferences: Midwest.

Kansas Development Finance Authority
700 SW Jackson
Jayhawk Tower, Ste. 1000
Topeka, Kansas 66603
Phone: (913)296-6747
Fax: (913)296-6810
Dedicated to improving access to capital financing to business enterprises through the issurance of bonds.

Kansas Housing and Commerce Department
Division of Community Development
700 SW Harrison, Ste. 1300
Topeka, Kansas 66603-3712
Phone: (913)296-3485
Fax: (913)296-0186
Administers Community Development Block Grants and the enterprise zone program, in which businesses receive tax credits and exemptions for locating in targeted areas.

Kentucky

Kentucky Cabinet for Economic Development

Commonwealth Small Business
Development Corp.
2300 Capitol Plaza Tower
Frankfort, Kentucky 40601
Phone: (502)564-4320
Fax: (502)564-3256
Provides loans of up to 40 percent of
the costs of expansion to qualified
small businesses unable to obtain
financing without government aid.

Kentucky Cabinet for Economic
Development
Financial Incentives Department
Capitol Plaza Tower
500 Mero St., 24th Fl.
Frankfort, Kentucky 40601
Phone: (502)564-4554
Fax: (502)564-7697
Provides loans to supplement private
financing. Offers two major programs:
issuance of industrial revenue bonds;
and second mortgage loans to private
firms in participation with other
lenders. Also has a Crafts Guaranteed
Loan Program providing loans up to
$20,000 to qualified craftspersons, and
a Commonwealth Venture Capital
Program, encouraging the establishment or expansion of small business
and industry.

Mountain Ventures, Inc.
362 Old Whitley Rd.
PO Box 1738
London, Kentucky 40743-1738
Phone: (606)864-5175
Fax: (606)864-5194
A small business investment corpora-
tion. No industry preference; geo-
graphic area limited to southeast
Kentucky.

Equal Opportunity Finance, Inc.
420 S. Hurstbourne Pky., Ste. 201
Louisville, Kentucky 40222-8002
Phone: (502)423-1943
Fax: (502)423-1945
A minority enterprise small business
investment corporation. No industry
preference; geographic areas limited
to Indiana, Kentucky, Ohio, and West
Virginia.

Louisiana

Bank One Equity Investors, Inc.
451 Florida St.
Baton Rouge, Louisiana 70801
Phone: (504)332-4421
Fax: (504)332-7377
A small business investment corpora-
tion. No industry preference.

Louisiana Department of Economic
Development
E-mail:
marketing@mail.lded.state.la.us
PO Box 94185
Baton Rouge, Louisiana 70804-9185
Phone: (504)342-3000
Fax: (504)342-5389

S.C.D.F. Investment Corp., Inc.
PO Box 3885
Lafayette, Louisiana 70502
Phone: (318)232-7672
Fax: (318)232-5094
A minority enterprise small business
investment corporation. No industry
preference.

First Commerce Capital, Inc.
201 St. Charles Ave., 16th Fl.
PO Box 60279
New Orleans, Louisiana 70170
Phone: (504)623-1600
Fax: (504)623-1779
William Harper, Manager
Preferred Investment Size: $1 to $2
million. Investment Policies: Loans,
equity. Investment Types: Later stage,
acquisition, buyouts. Industry
Preferences: Manufacturing
healthcare, retail, wholesale/distribu-
tion. Geographic Preferences: Gulf
South region.

Maine

Finance Authority of Maine
E-mail: info@samemaine.com
83 Western Ave.
PO Box 949
Augusta, Maine 04332-0949
Phone: (207)623-3263
Fax: (800)623-0095

Assists business development and
job creation through direct loans, loan
guarantee programs, and project
grants.

Maine Capital Corp.
E-mail: info@norhtatlantacapital.com
70 Center St.
Portland, Maine 04101
Phone: (207)772-1001
Fax: (207)772-3257
A small business investment corpora-
tion. No industry preference.

Maryland

ABS Ventures Limited Partnerships
(Baltimore)
135 S. St.
Baltimore, Maryland 21202
Phone: (410)727-1700
Free: (800)638-2596
Fax: (410)234-3699
Invests in the computer software,
health care, and biotechnology
industries.

American Security Capital Corp., Inc.
100 S. Charles St., 8th Fl.
Baltimore, Maryland 21201
Phone: (410)547-4205
Fax: (410)547-4990
A small business investment com-
pany. Diversified industry preference.

Anthem Capital, L.P.
16 S. Calvert St., Ste. 800
Baltimore, Maryland 21202
Phone: (410)625-1510
Fax: (410)625-1735
William M. Gust II, Mgr.

Broventure Capital Management
16 W. Madison St.
Baltimore, Maryland 21201
Phone: (410)727-4520
Fax: (410)727-1436
Venture capital partnership. Provides
start-up capital to early stage companies, expansion capital to companies
experiencing rapid growth, and capital
for acquisitions. Initial investments
range from $400,000 to $750,000.

Maryland Department of Business
and Economic Development
Financing Programs Division
217 E. Redwood St., 10th Fl.
Baltimore, Maryland 21202-3316
Phone: (410)767-0095
Free: (800)333-6995
Fax: (410)333-1836
Provides short-term financing for
government contracts and long-term
financing for equipment and working
capital. Also operates a surety bond
guarantee program for small businesses and an equity participation
investment program for potential
minority franchises.

Maryland Department of Economic
and Employment Development
Financing Programs Division
Community Financing Group
111 N. Utah St.
Baltimore, Maryland 21201-3316
Phone: (410)333-4304
Fax: (410)333-6931

Maryland Department of Economic
and Employment Development
Financing Programs Division
Industrial Development Financing
Authority
217 E. Redwood St.
Baltimore, Maryland 21202-3316
Phone: (410)767-6300
Fax: (410)333-6911
Insures up to 80 percent of loans or
obligations. Also provides tax-exempt
revenue bonds for the financing of
fixed assets.

New Enterprise Associates (Baltimore)
1119 St. Paul St.
Baltimore, Maryland 21202
Phone: (410)244-0115
Fax: (410)752-7721
Private free-standing venture capital
partnership providing seed and start-
up financing. Prefers information
technology and medical and life
science industries.

T. Rowe Price
100 E. Pratt St.

Baltimore, Maryland 21202
Phone: (410)345-2000
Free: (800)638-7890
Fax: (410)345-2394
Venture capital supplier. Offers
specialized investment services to
meet the needs of companies in
various stages of growth.

Triad Investor's Corp.
300 E. Joppa, Ste. 1111
Baltimore, Maryland 21286
Phone: (410)828-6497
Fax: (410)337-7312
Venture capital firm providing seed
and early stage financing. Areas of
interest include communications,
computer-related, medical/health-
related, genetic engineering, and
electronic components and instrumentation industries.

Calvert Social Venture Partners
7201 Wisconsin Ave., Ste. 310
Bethesda, Maryland 20814
Phone: (301)718-4272
Fax: (301)656-4421
Private venture capital partnership
focusing on Mid-Atlantic companies
involved in socially or environmentally beneficial products or services.

Security Financial and Investment
Corp.
7720 Wisconsin Ave., Ste. 207
Bethesda, Maryland 20814
Phone: (301)951-4288
Fax: (301)951-9282
A minority enterprise small business
investment corporation. No industry
preference.

Greater Washington Investments, Inc.
(Chevy Chase)
5454 Wisconsin Ave.
Chevy Chase, Maryland 20815
Phone: (301)656-0626
Fax: (301)656-4053
A small business investment com-
pany. Diversified industry preference.

Jupiter National, Inc.
5454 Wisconsin Ave.

Chevy Chase, Maryland 20815
Phone: (301)656-0626
Fax: (301)656-4053
A small business investment corporation. Prefers low to medium technology and subordinated debt investments.

Syncom Capital Corp.
8401 Coalville Rd., Ste. 300
Silver Spring, Maryland 20910
Phone: (301)608-3203
Fax: (301)608-3307
A minority enterprise small business
investment corporation. Areas of
interest include telecommunications
and media.

Grotech Capital Group
9690 Deereco Rd., Ste. 800
Timonium, Maryland 21093
Phone: (410)560-2000
Fax: (410)560-1910

Massachusetts

Advent Atlantic Capital Co. LP
75 State St., Ste. 2500
Boston, Massachusetts 02109
Phone: (617)345-7200
Fax: (617)345-7201
Venture capital fund. Communications
industry preferred.

Advent V Capital Co.
75 State St., Ste. 2500
Boston, Massachusetts 02109
Phone: (617)345-7200
Fax: (617)345-7201
Venture capital fund. Communications
industry preferred.

Advent IV Capital Co.
75 State St., Ste. 2500
Boston, Massachusetts 02109
Phone: (617)345-7200
Fax: (617)345-7201
Venture capital fund. Communications
industry preferred.

Advent Industrial Capital Co. LP
75 State St., Ste. 2500
Boston, Massachusetts 02109

Phone:(617)345-7200
Fax:(617)345-7201
Venture capital fund. Communications
industry preferred.

Advent International Corp.
101 Federal St.
Boston, Massachusetts 02110
Phone:(617)951-9400
Fax:(617)951-0566
Venture capital firm. Invests in all
stages, from start-up technology-
based companies to well-established
companies in rapid growth or mature
industries; no retail clothing or real
estate.

American Research and Development
45 Milk St., 4th. Fl.
Boston, Massachusetts 02109
Phone:(617)423-7500
Fax:(617)423-9655
Independent private venture capital
partnership. All stages of financing;
no minimum or maximum investment.

Aspen Ventures (Boston)
1 Post Office Square, Ste. 3320
Boston, Massachusetts 02109
Phone:(617)426-2151
Fax:(617)426-2181
Venture capital supplier. Provides
start-up and early stage financing to
companies in high-growth industries
such as biotechnology, communications, electronics, and health care.

Atlas Venture
222 Berkeley
Boston, Massachusetts 02116
Phone:(617)859-9290
Fax:(617)859-9292

Bain Capital Fund (Boston)
2 Copley Pl.
Boston, Massachusetts 02116
Phone:(617)572-3000
Fax:(617)572-3274
Private venture capital firm. No
industry preference, but avoids
investing in high-tech industries.
Minimum investment is $500,000.

BancBoston Ventures, Inc.
100 Federal St., 32nd Floor
PO Box 2016
Boston, Massachusetts 02110
Phone:(617)434-2442
Fax:(617)434-1153
A small business investment corpora-
tion. Minimum investment is $1
million.

Battery Ventures (Boston)
200 Portland St.
Boston, Massachusetts 02114
Phone:(617)367-1011
Fax:(617)367-1070
Venture capital firm providing
financing to early and emerging
software and communications
companies. Average investments are
from $1 million to $5 million.

Boston Capital Ventures
E-mail: info@bcv.com
Old City Hall
45 School St.
Boston, Massachusetts 02108
Phone:(617)227-6550
Fax:(617)227-3847
Venture capital firm.

Burr, Egan, Deleage, and Co. (Boston)
1 Post Office Sq., Ste. 3800
Boston, Massachusetts 02109
Phone:(617)482-8020
Free:(800)756-2877
Fax:(617)482-1944
Private venture capital supplier.
Invests start-up, expansion, and
acquisitions capital nationwide.
Principal concerns are strength of the
management team; large, rapidly
expanding markets; and unique
products or services. Past investments have been made in the fields of
electronics, health, and communications. Investments range from
$750,000 to $5 million.

Chestnut Street Partners, Inc.
75 State St., Ste. 2500
Boston, Massachusetts 02109
Phone:(617)345-7220
Fax:(617)345-7201

A small business investment company. Diversified industry preference.

Claflin Capital Management, Inc.
E-mail: ccmbost@001.com
77 Franklin St.
Boston, Massachusetts 02110
Phone:(617)426-6505
Fax:(617)482-0016
Private venture capital firm investing
its own capital. No industry prefer-
ence but prefers early stage compa-
nies.

Commonwealth Enterprise Fund, Inc.
10 Post Office Sq., Ste. 1090
Boston, Massachusetts 02109
Phone:(617)482-1881
Fax:(617)482-7129
A minority enterprise small business
investment corporation. No industry
preference, but clients must be located
in Massachusetts.

Copley Venture Partners
600 Atlantic Ave., 13th Fl.
Boston, Massachusetts 02210
Phone:(617)722-6030
Fax:(617)523-7739

Eastech Management Co.
45 Milk St., 4th. Floor
Boston, Massachusetts 02109
Phone:(617)423-7500
Fax:(617)423-9655
Private venture capital supplier.
Provides start-up and first- and
second-stage financing to companies
in the following industries: communications, computer-related electronic
components and instrumentation, and
industrial products and equipment.
Will not consider real estate, agriculture, forestry, fishing, finance and
insurance, transportation, oil and gas,
publishing, entertainment, natural
resources, or retail.

Fidelity Venture Associates, Inc.
Fidelity Investments
82 Devonshire St., Mail Zone R25C
Boston, Massachusetts 02109
Phone:(617)563-7000

Fax:(617)728-6755
Privately-held investment management firm providing financing to
young companies at various stages of
development. Areas of interest
include financial services, publishing,
specialty retailing, health care,
transportation, computer systems and
software, and telecommunications
industries.

Greylock Management Corp. (Boston)
1 Federal St., 26th Fl.
Boston, Massachusetts 02110
Phone:(617)423-5525
Fax:(617)482-0059
Private venture capital partnership.
Minimum investment of $250,000;
preferred investment size of over $1
million. Will function either as deal
originator or investor in deals created
by others.

John Hancock Venture Partners, Inc.
1 Financial Center, 44th Fl.
Boston, Massachusetts 02111
Phone:(617)348-3707
Fax:(617)350-0305
Venture capital supplier. Diversified
investments.

Harvard Management Co., Inc.
600 Atlantic Ave.
Boston, Massachusetts 02210
Phone:(617)523-4400
Free:(800)723-0044
Fax:(617)523-1283
Diversified venture capital firm.
Minimum investment is $1 million.

Highland Capital Partners
2 International Pl.
Boston, Massachusetts 02110
Phone:(617)330-8765
Fax:(617)531-1550
Industry preferences include health
care, software, and telecommunica-
tions.

Liberty Ventures Corp.
E-mail: @1liberty.com
1 Liberty Sq.
Boston, Massachusetts 02109
Phone:(617)423-1765

Free:(800)423-1766
Fax:(617)338-4362
Venture capital partnership. Provides
start-up, early stage, and expansion
financing to companies that are
pioneering applications of proven
technology; also will consider
nontechnology-based companies with
strong management teams and plans
for expansion. Investments range from
$500,000 to $1 million, with a $6 million
maximum.

Massachusetts Business Development Corp.
50 Milk St., 16th Fl.
Boston, Massachusetts 02109
Phone:(617)350-8877
Fax:(617)350-0052
Provides assistance to businesses
and individuals attempting to utilize
federal, state, and local loan finance
programs.

Massachusetts Community Development Finance Corp.
10 Post Office Sq., Ste. 1090
Boston, Massachusetts 02109
Phone:(617)482-9141
Fax:(617)482-7129
Provides financing for small businesses and for commercial, industrial,
and residential business developments through community development corporations (CDCs) in de-
pressed areas of Massachusetts.
Three investment programs are
offered: the Venture Capital Investment Program, the Community
Development Program, and the Small
Loan Guarantee Program.

Massachusetts Industrial Finance
Agency
75 Federal St., 10th Fl.
Boston, Massachusetts 02110
Phone:(617)451-2477
Free:(800)445-8030
Fax:(617)451-3429
Promotes expansion, renovation, and
modernization of small businesses
through the use of investment
incentives.

Massachusetts Minority Enterprise
Investment Corp.
50 Milk St., 16th St.
Boston, Massachusetts 02109
Phone:(617)350-8877
Fax:(617)350-0052
Minority enterprise small business
investment corporation. Involved with
community development. Loans range
from $25,000 to $250,000.

Massachusetts Technology Development Corp. (MTDC)
148 State St., 9th Fl.
Boston, Massachusetts 02109-2506
Phone:(617)723-4920
Fax:(617)723-5983
Makes investments in start-up or early
stage expansion technology-based
businesses within the Commonwealth
of Massachusetts only.

MC PARTNERS
75 State St., Ste. 2500
Boston, Massachusetts 02109
Phone:(617)345-7200
Fax:(617)345-7201
Venture capital fund. Communications
industry preferred.

Mezzanine Capital Corp.
75 State St., Ste. 2500
Boston, Massachusetts 02109
Phone:(617)345-7200
Fax:(617)345-7201
A small business investment com-
pany. Diversified industry preference.

Northeast Small Business Investment
Corp.
130 New Market Square
Boston, Massachusetts 02118
Phone:(617)445-2100
Fax:(617)442-1013
A small business investment corpora-
tion. No industry preference.

P. R. Venture Partners, L.P.
100 Federal St., 37th Fl.
Boston, Massachusetts 02110
Phone:(617)357-9600
Fax:(617)357-9601
Venture capital firm providing early

stage financing. Areas of interest include health care, information, and food.

Pioneer Ventures LP
60 State St.
Boston, Massachusetts 02109
Phone: (617)742-7825
Fax: (617)742-7315
A small business investment company. Diversified industry preference.

Private Equity Management
60 State St., Ste. 6620
Boston, Massachusetts 02109
Phone: (617)345-9440
Fax: (617)345-9878

Summit Partners
600 Atlantic Ave., 28th Fl.
Boston, Massachusetts 02210-2227
Phone: (617)742-5500
Fax: (617)824-1100
Venture capital firm. Prefers to invest in emerging, profitable, growth companies in the electronic technology, environmental services, and health care industries. Investments range from $1 million to $4 million.

TA Associates (Boston)
125 High St., Ste. 2500
Boston, Massachusetts 02110-2720
Phone: (617)338-0800
Fax: (617)574-6728
Private venture capital partnership. Technology companies, media communications companies, and leveraged buy outs preferred. Will provide from $1 million to $20 million in investments.

Transportation Capital Corp. (Boston)
45 Newbury St., Rm. 207
Boston, Massachusetts 02116
Phone: (617)536-0344
Fax: (617)536-5750
A minority enterprise small business investment corporation. Specializes in taxicabs and taxicab medallion loans.

TVM Techno Venture Management
101 Arch St., Ste. 1950

Boston, Massachusetts 02110
Phone: (617)345-9320
Free: (800)345-2093
Fax: (617)345-9377
Venture capital firm providing early stage financing. Areas of interest include high technology such as software, communications, medical, and biotechnology industries. Preferred investment size is $1 million.

UST Capital Corp.
40 Court St.
Boston, Massachusetts 02108
Phone: (617)726-7000
Free: (800)441-8782
Fax: (617)726-7369
A small business investment company. Diversified industry preference.

Venture Capital Fund of New England II
160 Federal St., 23rd Fl.
Boston, Massachusetts 02110
Phone: (617)439-4646
Fax: (617)439-4652
Venture capital fund. Prefers New England high-technology companies that have a commercial prototype or initial product sales. Will provide up to $500,000 in first-round financing.

First Capital Corp. of Chicago (Boston)
Bank Of Boston
1380 Mass Ave.
Cambridge, Massachusetts 02111
Phone: (617)434-2500
Fax: (617)434-2506
A small business investment company.

MDT Advisers, Inc.
125 Cambridge Park Dr.
Cambridge, Massachusetts 02140
Phone: (617)234-2200
Fax: (617)234-2210

Zero Stage Capital V, L.P. (Cambridge)
E-mail: zerostage@aol.com
Kendall Sq.
1010 Main St., 17th Fl.
Cambridge, Massachusetts 02142

Phone: (617)876-5355
Fax: (617)876-1248
Paul Kelley, Manager
Preferred Investment Size: $50,000 to $500,000. Investment Types: Equity, debit with equity features. Industry Preferences: Biotech, computer hardware and software, energy. Geographic Preferences: Northeast.

Boston College Capital Formation Service
96 College Rd.
Rahner House
Chestnut Hill, Massachusetts 02167
Phone: (617)552-4091
Fax: (617)552-2730

Capital Formation Service
Boston College
96 College Rd., Rahner House
Chestnut Hill, Massachusetts 02167
Phone: (617)552-4091
Fax: (617)552-2730
Provides assistance to clients requiring financing from nonconventional sources, such as quasi-public financing programs; state, federal, and local programs; venture capital; and private investors.

Seacoast Capital Partners, L.P.
E-mail: scpltd.com
55 Ferncroft Rd.
Danvers, Massachusetts 01923
Phone: (508)777-3866
Fax: (508)750-1301
Eben Moulton, Manager
Preferred Investment Size: $1 to $6 million. Investment Policies: Loans and equity investments. Investment Types: Expansion, later stage. Industry Preferences: Diversified. Geographic Preferences: National.

Argonauts MESBIC Corp.
929 Worcester Rd.
Framingham, Massachusetts 01701
Phone: (617)697-0501
A minority enterprise small business investment company. Diversified industry preference.

Applied Technology Partners
1 Cranberry Hill
Lexington, Massachusetts 02173-7397
Phone: (617)862-8622
Fax: (617)862-8367
Venture capital firm providing early
stage investment. Areas of interest
include hardware technologies,
electronics, software, communications, and information services.

Venture Founders Corp.
1 Cranberry Hill
Lexington, Massachusetts 02173
Phone: (617)862-8622
Fax: (617)862-8367
Venture capital fund. Preferred
geographical area is the New England
states. Required initial investment size
is between $50,000 and $400,000.

Business Achievement Corp.
1172 Beacon St.
Newton, Massachusetts 02161
Phone: (617)965-0550
Fax: (617)969-2671
A small business investment corpora-
tion. No industry preference.

Comdisco Venture Group (Newton)
1 Newton Executive Park
2221 Washington 3rd Fl.
Newton Lower Falls, Massachusetts
02162-1417
Phone: (617)244-6622
Free: (800)321-1111
Fax: (617)630-5599

New England MESBIC Inc.
530 Turnpike St.
North Andover, Massachusetts
01845-5812
Phone: (508)688-4326

Analog Devices, Inc.
1 Technology Way
PO Box 9106
Norwood, Massachusetts 02062-9106
Phone: (617)329-4700
Free: (800)262-5643
Fax: (617)326-8703
Venture capital supplier. Prefers to

invest in industries involved in analog
devices.

ABS Ventures Limited Partnerships
(Boston)
404 Wymin St. Ste. 365
Waltham, Massachusetts 02154
Phone: (617)290-0004
Fax: (617)290-0999

Advanced Technology Ventures
(Boston)
281 Winter St., Ste. 350
Waltham, Massachusetts 02109
Phone: (617)290-0707
Fax: (617)684-0045
Private venture capital firm. Prefers
early stage financing in high-technol-
ogy industries.

Charles River Ventures
1000 Winter St., Ste. 3300
Waltham, Massachusetts 02154
Phone: (617)487-7060
Fax: (617)487-7065
Venture capital partnership providing
early stage financing. Areas of
interest include communications,
software, environmental, and specialty
financial service industries.

Hambro International Equity Partners
(Boston)
404 Wyman, Ste. 365
Waltham, Massachusetts 02154
Phone: (617)523-7767
Fax: (617)290-0999
Private venture firm. Seeks to invest in
software, electronics and instrumentation, biotechnology, retailing, direct
marketing of consumer goods, and
environmental industries.

Matrix Partners III
1000 Winter St., Ste. 4500
Waltham, Massachusetts 02154
Phone: (617)890-2244
Fax: (617)890-2288
Private venture capital partnership.
Industry preference includes high
technology, communications, and
software.

Ampersand Ventures
E-mail: bjt@ampersandventures.com
55 William St., Ste. 240
Wellesley, Massachusetts 02181
Phone: (617)239-0700
Free: (800)239-0706
Fax: (617)239-0824
Venture capital supplier. Provides
start-up and early stage financing to
technology-based companies.
Investments range from $500,000 to $1
million.

Geneva Middle Market Investors, L.P.
70 Walnut St.
Wellesley, Massachusetts 02181
Phone: (617)239-8230
Fax: (617)239-8064
James J. Goodman, Manager

Northwest Venture Partners
40 William St., Ste. 305
Wellesley, Massachusetts 02181
Phone: (617)237-5870
Fax: (617)237-6270

Bessemer Venture Partners (Wellesley
Hills)
83 Walnut St.
Wellesley Hills, Massachusetts 02181
Phone: (617)237-6050
Fax: (617)235-7068

Palmer Partners L.P.
300 Unicorn Park Dr.
Woburn, Massachusetts 01801
Phone: (617)933-5445
Fax: (617)933-0698
Venture capital partnership. Provides
early stage, commercialization, and
second and third stage financing. No
industry preference, but does not
invest in real estate or biotechnology
industries.

Michigan

White Pines Capital Corp.
2929 Plymouth Rd., Ste. 210
Ann Arbor, Michigan 48105
Phone: (313)747-9401

Fax:(313)747-9704
A small business investment company. Diversified industry preference.

Dearborn Capital Corp.
PO Box 1729
Dearborn, Michigan 48126-2729
Phone:(313)337-8577
Fax:(313)248-1252
A minority enterprise small business investment corporation. Loans to minority-owned, operated, and controlled suppliers to Ford Motor Company, Dearborn Capital Corporation's parent.

Motor Enterprises, Inc.
3044 W. Grand Blvd.
Detroit, Michigan 48202
Phone:(313)556-4273
Fax:(313)974-4854
A minority enterprise small business investment corporation. Prefers automotive-related industries.

Metro-Detroit Investment Co.
30777 Northwestern Hwy., Ste. 300
Farmington Hills, Michigan 48334-2549
Phone:(810)851-6300
Fax:(810)851-9551
A minority enterprise small business investment corporation. Food store industry preferred.

Demery Seed Capital Fund
3707 W. Maple Rd.
Franklin, Michigan 48025
Phone:(810)433-1722
Fax:(810)644-4526
Invests in start-up companies in Michigan.

The Capital Fund
6412 Centurion Dr., Ste. 150
Lansing, Michigan 48917
Phone:(517)323-7772
Fax:(517)323-1999
A small business investment company. Provides expansion financing.

State Treasurer's Office
Alternative Investments Division

PO Box 15128
Lansing, Michigan 48901
Phone:(517)373-4330
Fax:(517)335-3668

Minnesota

Ceridian Corp.
8100 34th Ave. S
Bloomington, Minnesota 55425-1640
Phone:(612)853-8100

Altair Ventures, Inc.
7550 France Ave. S, Ste. 201
Minneapolis, Minnesota 55435
Phone:(612)449-0250
Fax:(612)896-4909
Venture capital firm providing acquisitions and leveraged buyout financing. Diversified industry preference.

Artesian Capital Limited Partnership
E-mail: artesian2@aol.com
Foshay Tower
821 Marquette Ave., Ste. 1700
Minneapolis, Minnesota 55402-2905
Phone:(612)334-5600
Fax:(612)334-5600
Venture capital firm providing seed and start-up financing in the upper Midwest. Areas of interest include medical, communications, and environmental industries.

Capital Dimensions Ventures Fund, Inc.
2 Appletree Sq., Ste. 335
Minneapolis, Minnesota 55425
Phone:(612)854-3007
A minority enterprise small business investment corporation. No industry preference.

Cherry Tree Investment Co.
1400 Northland Plz.
3800 W. 80th St., Ste. 1400
Minneapolis, Minnesota 55431
Phone:(612)893-9012
Fax:(612)893-9036
Venture capital supplier. Provides start-up and early stage financing. Fields of interest include information/

software, retail, education, and publishing industries located in the Midwest. There are no minimum or maximum investment limitations.

Coral Group, Inc.
60 S. 6th St., Ste. 3510
Minneapolis, Minnesota 55402
Phone:(612)335-8666
Fax:(612)335-8668
Venture capital firm providing all types of financing. Areas of interest include communications, computer products, electronics, medical/health, genetic engineering, industrial products, transportation and diversified.

Crawford Capital Corp.
1150 Interchange Tower
600 S. Hwy. 169
Minneapolis, Minnesota 55426
Phone:(612)544-2221
Fax:(612)544-5885
Venture capital firm providing financing for firm's own venture fund limited partnerships. Areas of interest include medical, software, and technology industries.

FBS SBIC, Ltd. Partnership
1st Bank Place
601 2nd Ave. S., 16th Fl.
Minneapolis, Minnesota 55402
Phone:(612)973-0988
Fax:(612)973-0203
Richard Rinkoff, Manager
Investment Policies: Loans, loans with warrants. Investment Types: Expansion, early stage. Industry Preferences: Diversified. Geographic Preferences: National.

Milestone Growth Fund, Inc.
401 2nd Ave. S., Ste. 1032
Minneapolis, Minnesota 55401
Phone:(612)338-0090
Fax:(612)338-1172
Minority enterprise small business investment corporation providing financing for expansion of existing companies. Diversified industry preference.

Norwest Equity Partners IV
2800 Piper Jaffray Tower
222 S. 9th St.
Minneapolis, Minnesota 55402-3388
Phone: (612)667-1667
Fax: (612)667-1660
Small business investment company.
Invests in all industries except real
estate.

Norwest Equity Partners V, L.P.
2800 Piper Jaffrey Tower
222 S. 9th St.
Minneapolis, Minnesota 55402
Phone: (612)667-1667
Fax: (612)667-1660
John F. Whaley, Manager
Preferred Investment Size: $3 to $15
million. Investment Policies: Equity.
Investment Types: Start-up, expan-
sion, later stage. Industry Preferences:
Diversified. Geographic Preferences:
National.

Oak Investment Partners (Minneapo-
lis)
4550 Norwest Center
90 S. 7th St., Ste. 4550
Minneapolis, Minnesota 55402
Phone: (612)339-9322
Fax: (612)337-8017
Prefers to invest in retail industries.

Pathfinder Venture Capital Funds
(Minneapolis)
7300 Metro Blvd., Ste. 585
Minneapolis, Minnesota 55439
Phone: (612)835-1121
Fax: (612)835-8389
Venture capital supplier providing
early stage financing. Areas of
interest include medical, pharmaceutical, and health care service; and
computer and computer-related
industries in the Upper Midwest and
West.

Peterson-Spencer-Fansler Co.
Foshay Tower
821 Marquette, Ste. 1900
Minneapolis, Minnesota 55402
Phone: (612)904-2305

Fax: (612)205-0912
Venture capital firm providing seed,
research and development, start-up,
first stage, and bridge financing.
Areas of interest include medical
technology and health care service
industries.

Piper Jaffray Ventures, Inc.
Piper Jaffray Tower
222 S. 9th St.
Minneapolis, Minnesota 55402
Phone: (612)342-6000
Fax: (612)337-8017

University Technology Center, Inc.
E-mail: utec@pro-ns.net
1313 5th St. SE
Minneapolis, Minnesota 55414
Phone: (612)379-3800
Fax: (612)379-3875
Venture capital firm providing start-
up, first stage, initial expansion and
acquisition financing. Areas of
interest include environment, consumer products, industrial products,
transportation and diversified
industry.

Wellspring Corp.
4530 IDS Center
Minneapolis, Minnesota 55402
Phone: (612)338-0704
Fax: (612)338-0744
Venture capital firm providing
acquisition and leveraged buyout
financing. Areas of interest include
marine transportation equipment and
weighing and measuring equipment
manufacturing.

Food Fund
5720 Smatana Dr., Ste. 300
Minnetonka, Minnesota 55343
Phone: (612)939-3944
Fax: (612)939-8106
Venture capital firm providing
expansion, management buyouts,
early stage and acquisition financing.
Areas of interest include food
products, food equipment, food
packaging, and food distribution.

Medical Innovation Partners, Inc.
Opus Center, Ste. 421
9900 Bren Rd. E
Minnetonka, Minnesota 55343
Phone: (612)931-0154
Fax: (612)931-0003

St. Paul Growth Ventures
E-mail: spence_morley@usa.net
1450 Energy Park Dr., Ste. 110-D
St. Paul, Minnesota 55108-1013
Phone: (612)641-1667
Fax: (612)641-1147
Venture capital firm providing early
stage ventures, product development,
product launch and early organizational development. Prefers software
companies in the Minneapolis/St. Paul
area.

Quest Venture Partners
730 E. Lake St.
Wayzata, Minnesota 55391-1769
Phone: (612)473-8367
Fax: (612)473-4702
Venture capital firm providing second
stage and bridge financing. Areas of
interest include communications,
computer products and medical/health
care.

Threshold Ventures, Inc.
15500 Wayzata Blvd., Ste. 819
Wayzata, Minnesota 55391-1418
Phone: (612)473-2051
A small business investment corpora-
tion. No industry preference.

Mississippi

Sun-Delta Capital Access Center, Inc.
E-mail: deltafdn@tednfo.com
819 Main St.
Greenville, Mississippi 38701
Phone: (601)335-5291
Fax: (601)335-5295
A minority enterprise small business
investment corporation. No industry
preference.

Mississippi Department of Economic
and Community Development

Mississippi Business Finance Corp.
1200 Walter Sillers Bldg.
PO Box 849
Jackson, Mississippi 39205
Phone: (601)359-3552
Fax: (601)359-2832
Administers the SBA (503) Loan and
the Mississippi Small Business Loan
Guarantee.

Vicksburg SBIC
PO Box 821568
Vicksburg, Mississippi 39182
Phone: (601)636-4762
Fax: (601)636-9476
A small business investment corpora-
tion. No industry preference.

Missouri

Bankers Capital Corp.
3100 Gillham Rd.
Kansas City, Missouri 64109
Phone: (816)531-1600
Fax: (816)531-1334
A small business investment corpora-
tion. No industry preference.

Capital for Business, Inc. (Kansas
City)
1000 Walnut St., 18th Fl.
Kansas City, Missouri 64106-2123
Phone: (816)234-2357
Fax: (816)234-2333
A small business investment corpora-
tion. No industry preference.

CFB Venture Fund II, Inc.
1000 Walnut St., 18th Fl.
Kansas City, Missouri 64106
Phone: (816)234-2357
Fax: (816)234-2333
A small business investment com-
pany. Diversified industry preference.

InvestAmerica Venture Group, Inc.
(Kansas City)
Commerce Tower Bldg.
911 Main St., Ste. 2424
Kansas City, Missouri 64105
Phone: (816)842-0114
Fax: (816)471-7339

A small business investment corporation. No industry preference.

MorAmerica Capital Corp. (Kansas
City)
911 Main St., Ste. 2424
Kansas City, Missouri 64105
Phone: (816)842-0114
Fax: (816)471-7339
A small business investment com-
pany.

United Missouri Capital Corp.
PO Box 419226
Kansas City, Missouri 64141
Phone: (816)860-7914
Fax: (816)860-7143
A small business investment corpora-
tion. No industry preference.

Midland Bank
740 NW Blue Pky.
Lees Summit, Missouri 64086
Phone: (816)524-8000
Fax: (816)525-8624
A small business investment com-
pany. Diversified industry preference.

Allsop Venture Partners (St. Louis)
55 W. Port Plz., Ste. 575
St. Louis, Missouri 63146
Phone: (314)434-1688
Fax: (314)434-6560

Capital for Business, Inc. (St. Louis)
11 S. Meramec, Ste. 1430
St. Louis, Missouri 63105
Phone: (314)746-7427
Fax: (314)746-8739
A small business investment corporation. Focuses primarily on later-stage
expansion and acquisition in the
manufacturing and distribution
industries.

CFB Venture Fund I, Inc.
11 S. Meramec, Ste. 1436
St. Louis, Missouri 63105
Phone: (314)746-7427
Fax: (314)746-8739
A small business investment com-
pany. Diversified industry preference.

Gateway Associates L.P.
8000 Maryland Ave., Ste. 1190
St. Louis, Missouri 63105
Phone: (314)721-5707
Fax: (314)721-5135

ITT Small Business Finance Corp.
635 Maryville Center Dr., Ste. 120
St. Louis, Missouri 63141
Phone: (314)205-3500
Free: (800)447-2025
Fax: (314)205-3699
Non-bank lender providing start-up
and expansion financing.

Montana

Montana Board of Investments
Office of Development Finance
Capitol Sta.
555 Fuller Ave.
Helena, Montana 59620-0125
Phone: (406)444-0001
Fax: (406)449-6579
Provides investments to businesses
that will bring long-term benefits to
the Montana economy.

Montana Department of Commerce
Economic Development Division
Finance Technical Assistance
1424 9th Ave.
Helena, Montana 59620-0401
Phone: (406)444-4780
Fax: (406)444-1872
Provides financial analysis, financial
planning, loan packaging, industrial
revenue bonding, state and private
capital sources, and business tax
incentives.

Nebraska

Nebraska Investment Finance
Authority
1230 "O" St., Ste. 200
Lincoln, Nebraska 68508
Phone: (402)434-3900
Free: (800)204-6432
Fax: (402)434-3921
Provides lower cost financing for
manufacturing facilities, certain farm

property, and health care and residential development. Also established a Small Industrial Development Bond Program to help small Nebraska-based companies (those with fewer than 100 employees or less than $2.5 million in gross salaries).

United Financial Resources Corp.
PO Box 1131
Omaha, Nebraska 68101
Phone: (402)339-7300
Fax: (402)339-9226
A small business investment corporation. Only interests include the grocery industry.

Nevada

Nevada Department of Business and Industry
Bond Division
1665 Hot Springs Rd., Ste. 165
Carson City, Nevada 89710
Phone: (702)687-4250
Fax: (702)687-4266
Issues up to $100 million in bonds to fund venture capital projects in Nevada; helps companies expand or build new facilities through the use of tax-exempt financing.

Atlanta Investment Co., Inc.
601 Fairview Blvd.
Incline Village, Nevada 89451
Phone: (702)833-1836
Fax: (702)833-1890
L. Mark Newman, Chairman of the Board
Preferred Investment Size: $2,000,000.
Investment Policies: Equity. Investment Types: Expansion, later stage.
Industry Preferences: Technology.
Geographic Preferences: National.

New Hampshire

Business Finance Authority of the State of New Hampshire
E-mail: bfa@enterwebb.com
4 Park St., Ste. 302
Concord, New Hampshire 03301-6313
Phone: (603)271-2391

Fax: (603)271-2396
Works to foster economic development and promote the creation of employment in the state of New Hampshire. Provides guarantees on loans to businesses made by banks and local development organizations; guarantees on portions of loans guaranteed in part by the U.S. Small Business Administration; cash reserves on loans made by state banks to businesses with annual revenues less than or equal to $5,000,000; and opportunities for local development organizations to acquire additional funds for the purpose of promoting and developing business within the state.

New Jersey

MidMark Capital, L.P.
E-mail: midmcat@aol.com
(midmcat@aol.com)
466 Southern Blvd.
Chatham, New Jersey 07928
Phone: (201)822-2999
Fax: (201)822-8911
Denis Newman, Manager
Preferred Investment Size: $5,000,000.
Investment Policies: Equity. Investment Types: Expansion, later stage.
Industry Preferences: Diversified, communication, manufacturing, retail/service. Geographic Preferences: East, midwest.

Transpac Capital Corp.
1037 Rte. 46 E
Clifton, New Jersey 07013
Phone: (201)470-8855
Fax: (201)470-8827
A minority enterprise small business investment company. Diversified industry preference.

Monmouth Capital Corp.
125 Wyckoff Rd.
Midland National Bank Bldg.
PO Box 335
Eatontown, New Jersey 07724
Phone: (908)542-4927

Fax: (908)542-1106
A small business investment corporation. No industry preference.

Capital Circulation Corp.
2035 Lemoine Ave., 2nd Fl.
Fort Lee, New Jersey 07024
Phone: (201)947-8637
Fax: (201)585-1965
A minority enterprise small business investment company. Diversified industry preference.

Japanese American Capital Corp.
716 Jersey Ave.
Jersey City, New Jersey 07310-1306
Phone: (201)798-5000
Fax: (201)798-4362

Taroco Capital Corp.
716 Jersey Ave.
Jersey City, New Jersey 07310-1306
Phone: (201)798-5000
Fax: (201)798-4322
A minority enterprise small business investment corporation. Focuses on Chinese-Americans.

Edison Venture Fund
997 Lenox Dr., Ste. 3
Lawrenceville, New Jersey 08648
Phone: (609)896-1900
Fax: (609)896-0066
Private venture capital firm. No industry preference.

Tappan Zee Capital Corp. (New Jersey)
201 Lower Notch Rd.
PO Box 416
Little Falls, New Jersey 07424
Phone: (201)256-8280
Fax: (201)256-2841
A small business investment company. Diversified industry preference.

CIT Group/Venture Capital, Inc.
650 CIT Dr.
Livingston, New Jersey 07039
Phone: (201)740-5429
Fax: (201)740-5555
A small business investment company. Diversified industry preference.

ESLO Capital Corp.
212 Wright St.
Newark, New Jersey 07114
Phone: (201)242-4488
Fax: (201)643-6062
Leo Katz, President
Preferred Investment Size: $100,000.
Investment Policies: Loans. Invest-
ment Types: Start-ups, early stage.
Industry Preferences: Business
services, manufacturing. Geographic
Preferences: Northeast.

Rutgers Minority Investment Co.
180 University Ave., 3rd Fl.
Newark, New Jersey 07102-1803
Phone: (201)648-5627
Fax: (201)648-1175
A minority enterprise small business
investment corporation. No industry
preference.

Accel Partners (Princeton)
1 Palmer Sq.
Princeton, New Jersey 08542
Phone: (609)683-4500
Fax: (609)683-0384
Venture capital firm. Telecommunica-
tions, software, and health care
industries preferred.

Carnegie Hill Co.
202 Carnegie Center, Ste. 103
Princeton, New Jersey 08540
Phone: (609)520-0500
Fax: (609)520-1160

Domain Associates
1 Palmer Sq.
Princeton, New Jersey 08542
Phone: (609)683-4500
Fax: (609)683-0384

DSV Partners (Princeton)
221 Nassau St.
Princeton, New Jersey 08542
Phone: (609)924-6420
Fax: (609)683-0174
Provides financing for the growth of
companies in the biotechnology/
health care, environmental, and
software industries. Also provides
capital to facilitate consolidation of
fragmented industries.

Johnston Associates, Inc.
E-mail: jai181@aol.com
181 Cherry Valley Rd.
Princeton, New Jersey 08540
Phone: (609)924-3131
Fax: (609)683-7524
Venture capital supplier providing
seed and start-up financing. Areas of
interest include pharmaceutical
research, biotechnology, and
bioremediation of toxic waste.

Bishop Capital, L.P.
500 Morris Ave.
Springfield, New Jersey 07081
Phone: (201)376-0345
Fax: (201)376-6527
A small business investment com-
pany. Diversified industry preference.

BCI Advisors, Inc.
Glenpointe Center W., 2nd Fl.
Teaneck, New Jersey 07666
Phone: (201)836-3900
Fax: (201)836-6368
Venture capital firm providing
mezzanine financing for growth
companies with revenues of $25
million to $200 million. Diversified
industry preference.

Demuth, Folger and Terhune
300 Frank W. Burr, 5th Floor
Teaneck, New Jersey 07666
Phone: (201)836-6000
Fax: (201)836-5666
Venture capital firm with preferences
for technology, services, and health
care investments.

DFW Capital Partners, L.P.
Glenpointe Center E., 5th Fl.
300 Frank W. Burr Blvd.
Teaneck, New Jersey 07666
Phone: (201)836-2233
Fax: (201)836-5666
Donald F. DeMuth, Manager
Preferred Investment Size: $4,000,000.
Investment Policies: Equity. Invest-
ment Types: Early through later stage.
Industry Preferences: Healthcare,
services, diversified. Geographic
Preferences: National.

New Jersey Commission on Science
and Technology
E-mail: njcst@njcst.gov
28 W. State St., CN 832
Trenton, New Jersey 08625-0832
Phone: (609)984-1671
Fax: (609)292-5920
Awards bridge grants to small
companies that have received seed
money under the Federal State
Business Innovation Research
programs and works to improve the
scientific and technical research
capabilities within the state. Also
provides management and technical
assistance and other services to small,
technology-oriented companies.

New Jersey Department of Agriculture
Division of Rural Resources
John Fitch Plz., CN 330
Trenton, New Jersey 08625
Phone: (609)292-5532
Fax: (609)633-7229
Fosters the agricutural economic
development of rural areas of the state
through financial assistance for
farmers and agribusinesses.

New Jersey Economic Development
Authority
CN90
Trenton, New Jersey 08625-0990
Phone: (609)292-1800
Fax: (609)292-0368
Arranges low-interest, long-term
financing for manufacturing facilities,
land acquisition, and business
equipment and machinery purchases.
Also issues taxable bonds to provide
financing for manufacturing, distribu-
tion, warehousing, research, commer-
cial, office, and service uses.

Edelson Technology Partners
Whiteweld Ctr 300 Tice Blvd
Woodcliff Lake, New Jersey 07675
Phone: (201)930-9898
Fax: (201)930-8899
Venture capital partnership interested
in high technology investment,
including medical, biotechnology, and
computer industries.

New Mexico

Albuquerque Investment Co.
P.O. Box 487
Albuquerque, New Mexico 87103-3132
Phone: (505)247-0145
Fax: (505)843-6912
A small business investment corporation. No industry preference.

Associated Southwest Investors, Inc.
1650 University N.E., Ste.200
Albuquerque, New Mexico 87102
Phone: (505)247-4050
Fax: (505)247-4050
A minority enterprise small business investment corporation. No industry preference.

Industrial Development Corp. of Lea County
E-mail: edclea@leaconet.com
PO Box 1376
Hobbs, New Mexico 88240
Phone: (505)397-2039
Free: (800)443-2236
Fax: (505)392-2300
Certified development company.

Ads Capital Corp.
142 Lincoln Ave., Ste. 500
Santa Fe, New Mexico 87501
Phone: (505)983-1769
Fax: (505)983-2887
Venture capital supplier. Prefers to invest in manufacturing or distribution companies.

New Mexico Economic Development Department
Technology Enterprise Division
1100 St. Francis Dr.
Santa Fe, New Mexico 87503
Phone: (505)827-0265
Fax: (505)827-0588
Provides state funds to advanced-technology business ventures that are close to the commerical stage.

New Mexico Economic Development Department
Economic Development Division
1100 St. Francis Dr.

Santa Fe, New Mexico 87503
Phone: (505)827-0300
Free: (800)374-3061
Fax: (505)827-0328
Provides start-up or expansion loans for businesses that are established in or are new to New Mexico.

New Mexico Labor Department
Job Training Division
Aspen Plz.
1596 Pacheco St.
PO Box 4218
Santa Fe, New Mexico 87502
Phone: (505)827-6827
Fax: (505)827-6812
Provides new and expanding industries with state-sponsored funds to train a New Mexican workforce.

New York

Fleet Bank
69 St.
Albany, New York 12207
Phone: (518)447-4115
Fax: (518)447-4043
Venture capital supplier. No industry preference. Typical investment is between $500,000 and $1 million.

NYBDC Capital Corp.
41 State St.
PO Box 738
Albany, New York 12201
Phone: (518)463-2268
Fax: (518)463-0240
A small business investment corporation.

Vega Capital Corp.
80 Business Park Dr., Ste. 201
Armonk, New York 10504-1701
Phone: (914)273-1025
Fax: (914)273-1028
A small business investment corporation. Diversified industry preferences.

Triad Capital Corp. of New York
960 Southern Blvd.
Bronx, New York 10459-3402
Phone: (718)589-5000
Fax: (718)589-4744

A minority enterprise small business investment corporation. No industry preference.

First New York Management Co.
1 Metrotech Center N, 11th Fl.
Brooklyn, New York 11201
Phone: (718)797-5990
Fax: (718)722-3533
A small business investment corporation. No industry preference.

M & T Capital Corporation
1 Fountain Plz., 3rd Fl.
Buffalo, New York 14203-1495
Phone: (716)848-3800
Fax: (716)848-3150
A small business investment corporation providing equity financing for small to mid-size companies for expansion activities, acquisitions, recapitalizations, and buyouts. Initial investments range from $500,000 - $2 million. Prefers businesses located in the Northeast and Midwest.

Rand SBIC, Inc.
1300 Rand Bldg.
Buffalo, New York 14203
Phone: (716)853-0802
Fax: (716)854-8480
A small business investment corporation. Prefers to invest in communications, computer-related, consumer, distributor, and electronic components and instrumentation industries.

Fifty-Third Street Ventures, L.P.
155 Main St.
Cold Spring, New York 10516
Phone: (914)265-4244
Fax: (914)265-4158
A small business investment company. Diversified industry preference.

Tessler and Cloherty, Inc.
155 Main St.
Cold Spring, New York 10516
Phone: (914)265-4244
Fax: (914)265-4158
A small business investment corporation. No industry preference.

Esquire Capital Corp.
69 Veterans Memorial Hwy.
Commack, New York 11725
Phone: (516)462-6946
Fax: (516)864-8152
A minority enterprise small business investment company. Diversified industry preference.

Pan Pac Capital Corp.
121 E. Industry Ct.
Deer Park, New York 11729
Phone: (516)586-7653
Fax: (516)586-7505
A minority enterprise small business investment corporation. No industry preference.

First County Capital, Inc.
135-14 Northern Blvd., 2nd Fl.
Flushing, New York 11354
Phone: (718)461-1778
Fax: (718)461-1835
A minority enterprise small business investment company. Diversified industry preference.

Flushing Capital Corp.
39-06 Union St., Rm.202
Flushing, New York 11354
Phone: (718)886-5866
Fax: (718)939-7761
A minority enterprise small business investment company. Diversified industry preference.

Sterling Commercial Capital, Inc.
175 Great Neck Rd., Ste. 408
Great Neck, New York 11021
Phone: (516)482-7374
Fax: (516)487-0781
A small business investment company. Diversified industry preference.

CEDC Inc.
134 Jackson St.
Hempstead, New York 11550-2418
Phone: (516)292-9710
Fax: (516)292-3176

Situation Ventures Corp.
56-20 59th St.

Maspeth, New York 11378
Phone: (718)894-2000
Fax: (718)326-4642
Sam Hollander, President
Preferred Investment Size: $100,000.
Investment Policies: Loans and/or equity. Industry Preferences: Manufacturing, service, retail. Geographic Preferences: New York metro area.

KOCO Capital Co., L.P.
111 Radio Cir.
Mount Kisco, New York 10549
Phone: (914)242-2324
Fax: (914)241-7476
Albert Pastino, President
Preferred Investment Size: $2 to $3 million. Investment Policies: Equity and debt with warrants. Investment Types: Expansion. Industry Preferences: Healthcare, media, basic manufacturing. Geographic Preferences: Mid-Atlantic.

Tappan Zee Capital Corp. (New York)
120 N. Main St.
New City, New York 10956
Phone: (914)634-8890
A small business investment company.

Argentum Capital Partners, LP
405 Lexington Ave., 54th Fl.
New York, New York 10174
Phone: (212)949-8272
Fax: (212)949-8294
A small business investment company. Diversified industry preference.

ASEA—Harvest Partners II
767 3rd Ave.
New York, New York 10017
Phone: (212)838-7776
Fax: (212)593-0734
A small business investment corporation. No industry preference.

Asian American Capital Corp.
62 White St.
New York, New York 10013
Phone: (212)315-2600
Howard H. Lin, President

Barclays Capital Investors Corp.
222 Broadway, 11th Fl.
New York, New York 10038
Phone: (212)412-3937
Fax: (212)412-7600
A small business investment company. Diversified industry preference.

Bradford Ventures Ltd.
1212 Avenue of the Americas, Ste.1802
New York, New York 10036
Phone: (212)221-4620
Fax: (212)764-3467
Venture capital firm. No industry preference.

BT Capital Corp.
130 Liberty St., M S 2255
New York, New York 10006
Phone: (212)250-8082
Fax: (212)250-7651
A small business investment corporation. No industry preference.

The Business Loan Center
919 3rd Ave., 17th Fl.
New York, New York 10022-1902
Phone: (212)751-5626
Fax: (212)751-9345
A small business loan company.

Capital Investors and Management Corp.
210 Canal St., Ste. 611
New York, New York 10013-4155
Phone: (212)964-2480
Fax: (212)349-9160
A minority enterprise small business investment corporation. No industry preference.

CB Investors, Inc.
560 Lexington Ave., 20th Fl.
New York, New York 10022
Phone: (212)207-6119
Fax: (212)207-6095
A small business investment company. Diversified industry preference.

CBIC Woody Gundy Ventures, Inc.
425 Lexington Ave., 5th Fl.
New York, New York 10017
Phone: (212)856-3713
Fax: (212)697-1554
A small business investment company. Diversified industry preference.

Chase Capital Partners
380 Madison Ave., 12th Fl.
New York, New York 10017-2070
Phone: (212)622-3100
Fax: (212)622-3101
A small business investment corporation. Areas of interest include health care, specialty retail, media and telecommunications, natural resources, consumer products, and environmental industries. Also invests in leveraged buy-outs and growth equity.

Chase Manhattan Capital Corp.
1 Chase Plz., 8th Fl.
New York, New York 10081
Phone: (212)935-9935
Fax: (212)552-1159
A small business investment corporation. No industry preference.

Citicorp Venture Capital Ltd. (New York City)
399 Park Ave., 14th Fl./Zone 4
New York, New York 10043
Phone: (212)559-1127
Fax: (212)888-2940
A small business investment corporation. Invests in the fields of information processing and telecommunications, transportation and energy, and health care; provides financing to companies in all stages of development. Also provides capital for leveraged buy out situations.

CMNY Capital II, LP
135 E. 57th St., 26th Fl.
New York, New York 10022
Phone: (212)909-8432
Fax: (212)980-2630
A small business investment company. Diversified industry preference.

Concord Partners
535 Madison Ave.
New York, New York 10022
Phone: (212)906-7108
Fax: (212)888-0649
Venture capital partnership. Diversified in terms of stage of development, industry classification, and geographic location. Areas of special interest include computer software, electronics, environmental services, biopharmaceuticals, health care, and oil and gas.

Creditanstalt SBIC
245 Park Ave., 27th Fl.
New York, New York 10167
Phone: (212)856-1248
Fax: (212)856-1699
Dennis O'Dowd, President

CW Group
1041 3rd Ave.
New York, New York 10021
Phone: (212)308-5266
Fax: (212)644-0354
Venture capital supplier. Interest is in the health care field, including diagnostic and therapeutic products, services, and biotechnology. Invests in companies at developing and early stages.

DAEDHIE
1261 Broadway, Rm. 405
New York, New York 10001
Phone: (212)684-6411
Fax: (212)684-6474
A minority enterprise small business investment company. Diversified industry preference.

DNC Capital Group
55 5th Ave., 15th Fl.
New York, New York 10003
Phone: (212)206-6041
Fax: (212)727-0563
Small business investment corporation interested in financing acquisitions in the real estate industry.

East Coast Venture Capital, Inc.
313 W. 53rd St., 3rd Fl.

New York, New York 10019
Phone: (212)245-6460
Fax: (212)265-2962
A minority enterprise small business investment company. Diversified industry preference.

Edwards Capital Co.
205 E. 42nd
New York, New York 10016
Phone: (212)682-3300
Fax: (212)983-0351
A small business investment corporation. Transportation industry preferred.

Elf Aquitain, Inc.
280 Park Ave., 36th Fl. W
New York, New York 10017-1216
Phone: (212)922-3000
Free: (800)922-0027
Fax: (212)922-3001

Elk Associates Funding Corp.
747 3rd Ave., 4th Fl.
New York, New York 10017
Phone: (212)421-2111
Fax: (212)421-3488
A minority enterprise small business investment corporation. Transportation industry preferred.

Elron Technologies, Inc.
850 3rd Ave., 10th Fl.
New York, New York 10022
Phone: (212)935-3110
Fax: (212)935-3882
Venture capital supplier. Provides incubation and start-up financing to high-technology companies.

Empire State Capital Corp.
170 Broadway, Ste. 1200
New York, New York 10038
Phone: (212)513-1799
Free: (800)569-9630
Fax: (212)513-1892
A minority enterprise small business investment company. Diversified industry preference.

Eos Partners SBIC, L.P.
320 Park Ave., 22nd Fl.

New York, New York 10022
Phone: (212)832-5814
Fax: (212)832-5805
Marc H. Michel, Manager
Preferred Investment Size: $1 - $3
MILLION. Investment Policies: Equity
and equity-oriented Debt. Investment
Types: Expansion, later stage.
Industry Preferences: Diversified,
telecommunications, info-processing,
data services. Geographic Preferences:
National.

Euclid Partners Corp.
50 Rockefeller Plz., Ste. 1022
New York, New York 10020
Phone: (212)489-1770
Fax: (212)757-1686
Venture capital firm. Prefers early
stage health care and information
processing industries.

Exeter Venture Lenders, L.P.
10 E. 53rd St.
New York, New York 10022
Phone: (212)872-1170
Fax: (212)872-1198
Keith Fox, Manager
Preferred Investment Size: $3,000,000.
Investment Policies: Loans and equity
investments. Investment Types:
Expansion, later stage. Industry
Preferences: Diversified. Geographic
Preferences: National.

Exim Capital Corp.
241 5th Ave., 3rd Fl.
New York, New York 10016-8703
Phone: (212)683-3375
Fax: (212)689-4118
A minority enterprise small business
investment corporation. No industry
preference.

Fair Capital Corp.
212 Canal St., Ste. 611
New York, New York 10013
Phone: (212)964-2480
Fax: (212)349-9160
A minority enterprise small business
investment corporation. No industry
preference.

First Boston Corp.
11 Madison Ave.
New York, New York 10010
Phone: (212)909-2000
Investment banker. Provides financing
to the oil and gas pipeline, hydroelec-
tric, medical technology, consumer
products, electronics, aerospace, and
telecommunications industries.
Supplies capital for leveraged buy
outs.

First Wall Street SBIC, LP
26 Broadway, Ste. 2310
New York, New York 10004
Phone: (212)742-3770
Fax: (212)742-3776
A small business investment com-
pany. Diversified industry preference.

Franklin Corp.
450 Park Ave.
G.M. Bldg., 10th Fl.
New York, New York 10022
Phone: (212)486-2323
Fax: (212)755-5451
A small business investment corpora-
tion. No industry preference; no start-
ups.

Fredericks Michael and Co.
2 Wall St., 4th Fl.
New York, New York 10005
Phone: (212)732-1600
Fax: (212)732-1872
Private venture capital supplier.
Provides start-up and early stage
financing, and supplies capital for buy
outs and acquisitions.

Fresh Start Venture Capital Corp.
313 W. 53rd St., 3rd Fl.
New York, New York 10019
Phone: (212)265-2249
Fax: (212)265-2962
A minority enterprise small business
investment corporation. No industry
preference.

Furman Selz SBIC, L.P.
230 Park Ave.
New York, New York 10169

Phone: (212)309-8200
Brian Friedman, Manager
Preferred Investment Size: $2 to $6
million. Investment Policies: Equity.
Investment Types: Expansion, later
stage, no start-ups. Industry Prefer-
ences: Diversified. Geographic
Preferences: National.

Hambro International Equity Partners
(New York)
650 Madison Ave., 21st Floor
New York, New York 10022
Phone: (212)223-7400
Fax: (212)223-0305
Venture capital supplier. Seeks to
invest in mature companies as well as
in high-technology areas from start-
ups to leveraged buy outs.

Hanam Capital Corp.
38 W. 32nd St., Rm. 1512
New York, New York 10001
Phone: (212)564-5225
Fax: (212)564-5307
A minority enterprise small business
investment company. Diversified
industry preference.

Harvest Partners, Inc. (New York)
767 3rd Ave.
New York, New York 10017
Phone: (212)838-7776
Fax: (212)593-0734
Private venture capital supplier.
Prefers to invest in high-technology,
growth-oriented companies with
proprietary technology, large market
potential, and strong management
teams.

Holding Capital Group, Inc.
685 5th Ave., 14th Fl.
New York, New York 10022
Phone: (212)486-6670
Fax: (212)486-0843
A small business investment corporation. No industry preference. Prefers
to purchase well-managed middle
market companies with a minimum of
$1 million cash flow.

IBJS Capital Corp.
1 State St., 8th Fl.
New York, New York 10004
Phone: (212)858-2000
Fax: (212)425-0542
A small business investment company. Diversified industry preference.

InterEquity Capital Partners, L.P.
220 5th Ave., 17th Fl.
New York, New York 10001
Phone: (212)779-2022
Fax: (212)779-2103
A small business investment company. Diversified industry preference.

Investor International (U.S.), Inc.
320 Park Ave., 33 Fl 10022
New York, New York 10019
Phone: (212)508-0900
Fax: (212)957-0901

Jafco America Ventures, Inc. (New York)
2 World Financial Center, Bldg. B, 17th Fl.
225 Liberty St.
New York, New York 10281-1196
Phone: (212)667-9001
Fax: (212)667-1004
Venture capital firm. Provides middle-to later-stage financing to technology-oriented companies.

Jardine Capital Corp.
105 Lafayette St., Unit 204
New York, New York 10013
Phone: (212)941-0993
Fax: (212)941-0998
Lawrence Wong, President
Preferred Investment Size: $360,000. Investment Policies: Loans and/or equity. Investment Types: Expansion. Industry Preferences: Diversified. Geographic Preferences: North/South.

Josephberg, Grosz and Co., Inc.
420 Lexington, Ste. 2635
New York, New York 10017
Phone: (212)370-4564
Venture capital firm. Invests in companies having a minimum of $2.5 million in sales, significant growth

potential, and a strong management base.

J.P. Morgan Investment Corp.
60 Wall St.
New York, New York 10260
Phone: (212)483-2323
A small business investment company. Diversified industry preference.

Kwiat Capital Corp.
579 5th Ave.
New York, New York 10017
Phone: (212)223-1111
Fax: (212)223-2796
A small business investment corporation. No industry preference.

Lambda Fund Management, Inc.
115 E. 69th
New York, New York 10021
Phone: (212)794-6060
Fax: (212)794-6169
Venture capital partnership.

Lawrence, Tyrrell, Ortale, and Smith (New York)
515 Madison Ave., 29th Fl.
New York, New York 10022
Phone: (212)826-9080
Fax: (212)759-2561
Venture capital firm. Prefers to invest in health care, software, and fragmented industries that grow by acquisition.

McCown, De Leeuw and Co. (New York)
101 E. 52nd St., 31st Fl.
New York, New York 10022-6018
Phone: (212)355-5500
Fax: (212)355-6283

Medallion Funding Corp.
205 E. 42nd St., Ste. 2020
New York, New York 10017-5706
Phone: (212)682-3300
Fax: (212)983-0351
A minority enterprise small business investment corporation. Transportation industry preferred.

Mercury Capital, L.P.
650 Madison Ave., Ste. 2600
New York, New York 10022
Phone: (212)838-0888
Fax: (212)838-7598
David W. Elenowitz, Manager

Monsey Capital Corp.
9 E. 40th St., 4th Fl.
New York, New York 10016
Phone: (212)689-2700
Fax: (212)683-7300
A minority enterprise small business investment corporation. No industry preference.

Morgan Stanley Venture Capital (New York)
c/o M. Fazle Husain
1251 Avenue of the Americas, 33rd Fl.
New York, New York 10020
Phone: (212)703-6981
Free: (800)223-2440
Fax: (212)703-8957
Venture capital firm providing later stage financing. Areas of interest include high technology and health care.

NatWest USA Capital Corp.
175 Water St., 27th Fl.
New York, New York 10038
Phone: (212)602-4000
Fax: (212)602-3393
A small business investment company. Diversified industry preference.

Nazem and Co.
645 Madison Ave., 12th Fl.
New York, New York 10022
Phone: (212)371-7900
Fax: (212)371-2150
Venture capital fund. Electronics and medical industries preferred. Will provide seed and first- and second-round financing.

Needham Capital SBIC, L.P.
445 Park Ave.
New York, New York 10022
Phone: (212)705-0291
Fax: (212)371-8418

John Michaelson, Manager
Preferred Investment Size: $500,000
TO $1 Million. Investment Policies:
Equity. Industry Preferences: Tech-
nology. Geographic Preferences:
National.

New York State Urban Development
Corp.
633 3rd Ave.
New York, New York 10017
Phone: (212)803-3100
Participates in a broad range of
initiatives. Addresses the needs of the
state in six areas, including downtown
development, industrial development,
minority business development,
university research and development,
and planning and special projects.

Norwood Venture Corp.
1430 Broadway, Ste. 1607
New York, New York 10018
Phone: (212)869-5075
Fax: (212)869-5331
A small business investment com-
pany. Diversified industry preference.

Paribas Principal, Inc.
787 7th Ave., 33rd Fl.
New York, New York 10019
Phone: (212)841-2000
Fax: (212)841-2146
A small business investment com-
pany. Diversified industry preference.

Patricof & Co. Ventures, Inc. (New
York)
445 Park Ave., 11th Fl.
New York, New York 10022
Phone: (212)753-6300
Fax: (212)319-6155
Venture capital firm.

Pierre Funding Corp.
805 3rd Ave., 6th Fl.
New York, New York 10022
Phone: (212)888-1515
Fax: (212)688-4252
A minority enterprise small business
investment corporation. No industry
preference.

Prospect Street NYC Discovery Fund,
L.P.
250 Park Ave., 17th Fl.
New York, New York 10177
Phone: (212)490-0480
Fax: (212)490-1566
Richard E. Omohundro, CEO

Prudential Equity Investors
717 5th Ave., Ste. 1100
New York, New York 10022
Phone: (212)753-0901
Fax: (212)826-6798
Venture capital fund. Specialty
retailing, medical and health services,
communications, and technology
companies preferred. Will provide $3
to $7 million in equity financing for
later-stage growth companies.

Pyramid Ventures, Inc.
130 Liberty St., 25th Fl.
New York, New York 10006
Phone: (212)250-9571
Fax: (212)250-7651
A small business investment com-
pany. Diversified industry preference.

Questech Capital Corp.
600 Madison Ave., 21st Fl.
New York, New York 10022
Phone: (954)583-2960
A small business investment corpora-
tion. No industry preference.

R and R Financial Corp.
1370 Broadway
New York, New York 10018
Phone: (212)356-1400
Free: (800)999-4800
Fax: (212)356-0900
A small business investment corpora-
tion. No industry preference.

Rothschild Ventures, Inc.
1251 Avenue of the Americas
New York, New York 10020
Phone: (212)403-3500
Free: (800)753-5151
Fax: (212)403-3501
Private venture capital firm. Prefers
seed and all later-stage financing.

767 Limited Partnership
767 3rd Ave.
New York, New York 10017
Phone: (212)838-7776
Fax: (212)593-0734
A small business investment corpora-
tion. No industry preference.

Sixty Wall Street SBIC Fund, L.P.
60 Wall St.
New York, New York 10260
Phone: (212)648-7778
Fax: (212)648-5032
David Cromwell
Seth Cunningham

Spectra International Management
Group
140 E. 44th St.
Box 776
New York, New York 10017
Phone: (212)986-6030
Fax: (212)986-8770
Venture capital firm providing all
stages of financing. Areas of interest
include all industries, excluding oil
and gas.

Sprout Group (New York City)
277 Park Ave., 21st Fl.
New York, New York 10172
Phone: (212)892-3600
Fax: (212)892-3444
Venture capital supplier.

TCW Capital
200 Park Ave., Ste. 2200
New York, New York 10166
Phone: (212)297-4055
Fax: (212)297-4025
Venture capital fund. Companies with
sales of $25 to $100 million preferred.
Will provide up to $20 million in later-
stage financing for recapitalizations,
restructuring management buy outs,
and general corporate purposes.

399 Venture Partners
399 Park Ave., 14th Fl./Zone 4
New York, New York 10043
Phone: (212)559-1127
Fax: (212)888-2940

A small business investment company. Diversified industry preference.

Transportation Capital Corp. (New York)
315 Park Ave. S, 10th Fl.
New York, New York 10010
Phone: (212)598-3225
Fax: (212)598-3102
A minority enterprise small business investment company. Diversified industry preference.

Trusty Capital, Inc.
350 5th Ave., Ste. 2026
New York, New York 10118
Phone: (212)629-3011
Fax: (212)629-3019
A minority enterprise small business investment company. Diversified industry preference.

UBS Partners, Inc.
299 Park Ave., 33rd Fl.
New York, New York 10171
Phone: (212)821-6490
Fax: (212)593-4257
Justin S. Maccarone, President

United Capital Investment Corp.
60 E. 42nd St., Ste. 1515
New York, New York 10165
Phone: (212)682-7210
Fax: (212)573-6352
A minority enterprise small business investment company. Diversified industry preference.

Venture Capital Fund of America, Inc.
509 Madison Ave., Ste. 812
New York, New York 10022
Phone: (212)838-5577
Fax: (212)838-7614

Venture Opportunities Corp.
158 E. 59th St., 16th Fl.
New York, New York 10022-1304
Phone: (212)832-3737
Fax: (212)980-6603
A minority enterprise small business investment corporation. Areas of interest include radio, cable, television, telecommunications, real estate

development, medical consumer products, and service and manufacturing businesses. Second- or third-stage for expansion, mergers, or acquisitions. No start-up or seed capital investments.

Warburg Pincus Ventures, Inc.
466 Lexington Ave., 10th Fl.
New York, New York 10017-3147
Phone: (212)878-0600
Free: (800)888-3697
Fax: (212)878-9351
Venture capital firm providing all stages of financing. Areas of interest include all industries, excluding gaming, real estate, and investments in South Africa.

Weiss, Peck and Greer Venture Partners L.P. (New York)
1 New York Plz.
New York, New York 10004
Phone: (212)908-9500
Fax: (212)908-9652

Welsh, Carson, Anderson, & Stowe
200 Liberty Ste. 3601
New York, New York 10281
Phone: (212)945-2000
Fax: (212)945-2016
Venture capital partnership.

Wolfensohn Partners, L.P. (New York)
5990 Madison Ave., 32nd Fl.
New York, New York 10022
Phone: (212)894-8121
Fax: (212)446-1307

First Century Partners (New York)
1 Palmer Sq. Ste. 425
Princton, New York 08542
Phone: (609)683-8848
Fax: (609)683 8123
Private venture capital firm. Minimum investment is $1.5 million. Prefers specialty retailing and consumer products industries.

International Paper Capital Formation, Inc. (Purchase)
2 Manhattanville Rd.
Purchase, New York 10577-2196

Phone: (914)397-1500
Fax: (914)397-1909
A minority enterprise small business investment company.

Genesee Funding, Inc.
100 Corporate Woods, Ste. 300
Rochester, New York 14623
Phone: (716)272-2332
Free: (800)933-7739
Fax: (716)272-2396
A small business investment company. Diversified industry preference.

Ibero-American Investors Corp.
104 Scio St.
Rochester, New York 14604-2552
Phone: (716)262-3440
Fax: (716)262-3441
A minority enterprise small business investment corporation. No industry preference.

Square Deal Venture Capital Corp.
766 N. Main St.
Spring Valley, New York 10977-1903
Phone: (914)354-4100
A minority enterprise small business investment company. Diversified industry preference.

Northwood Ventures
485 Underhill Blvd., Ste. 205
Syosset, New York 11791
Phone: (516)364-5544
Fax: (516)364-0879
Venture capital firm providing leveraged buyout financing, between $500,000 - $1 million. Diversified industry preference.

TLC Funding Corp.
660 White Plains Rd.
Tarrytown, New York 10591
Phone: (914)332-5200
Fax: (914)332-5660
A small business investment corporation. No industry preference.

Bessemer Venture Partners (Westbury)
1025 Old Country Rd., Ste. 205
Westbury, New York 11590

Phone:(516)997-2300
Fax:(516)997-2371
Venture capital partnership. No industry preference.

Winfield Capital Corp.
237 Mamaroneck Ave.
White Plains, New York 10605
Phone:(914)949-2600
Fax:(914)949-7195
A small business investment corporation. No industry preference.

North Carolina

First Union Capital Partners, Inc.
1 1st Union Center, 18th Fl.
301 S. College St.
Charlotte, North Carolina 28288-0732
Phone:(704)374-6487
Fax:(704)374-6711
A small business investment company. Diversified industry preference.

Kitty Hawk Capital Ltd.
2700 Coltsgate Rd., Ste. 202
Charlotte, North Carolina 28211
Phone:(704)362-3909
Fax:(704)362-2774
Venture capital firm. Geographical preference is the southeast. Investment policy is liberal, but does not invest in real estate, natural resources, and single store retail businesses and does not provide invention development financing.

NationsBanc Capital Corp.
100 N. Tryon St., 10th Fl.
Charlotte, North Carolina 28255
Phone:(704)386-8063
Fax:(704)386-6432
Walter W. Walker, Jr., President
Preferred Investment Size: $3 to $25 million. Investment Policies: Equity, sub debt with warrants. Investment Types: Later stage, expansion. Industry Preferences: Diversified. Geographic Preferences: National.

Southeastern Publishing Ventures Inc.
528 E. Blvd.
Charlotte, North Carolina 28203

Phone:(704)373-0051
Fax:(704)343-0170
Private venture capital firm. Diversified industry preference.

Center for Community Self-Help
North Carolina's Development Bank
PO Box 3619
301 W. Maine St.
Durham, North Carolina 27701
Phone:(919)956-4400
Free:(800)476-7428
Fax:(919)956-4600
Statewide, private-sector financial institution providing technical assistance and financing to small businesses, non-profit organizations, and low-income homebuyers in North Carolina.

Atlantic Venture Partners (Winston Salem)
380 Knollwood St., No. 410
Winston Salem, North Carolina 27103
Phone:(910)721-1800
Fax:(910)748-1208
Private venture capital partnership. Prefers to invest in manufacturing, distribution, and service industries.

North Dakota

Bank of North Dakota
Small Business Loan Program
700 E. Main Ave.
Box 5509
Bismarck, North Dakota 58506-5504
Phone:(701)328-5600
Free:(800)472-2166
Fax:(701)328-5632
Assists new and existing businesses in securing competitive financing with reasonable terms and conditions.

Fargo Cass County Economic Development Corp.
E-mail: info@fedc.com
406 Main Ave., Ste. 404
Fargo, North Dakota 58103
Phone:(701)237-6132
Fax:(701)293-7819
Certified development company that lends to small and medium-sized businesses at fixed rates.

North Dakota SBIC, L.P.
406 Main Ave., Ste. 404
Fargo, North Dakota 58103
Phone:(701)298-0003
Fax:(701)293-7819
David R. Schroeder, Manager

North Dakota Small Business Loan Services
406 Main Ave., Ste.417
Fargo, North Dakota 58103
Phone:(701)235-7885
Fax:(701)235-6706
Administers the 504 Loan Program.

Ohio

River Capital Corp. (Cleveland)
2544 Chamberlain Rd.
Akron, Ohio 44333
Phone:(216)781-3655
Fax:(216)781-2821
A small business investment corporation. No industry preference.

River Cities Capital Fund L.P.
221 E. 4th St., Ste. 2250
Cincinnati, Ohio 45202
Phone:(513)621-9700
Fax:(513)579-8939
R. Glen Mayfield, Manager
Preferred Investment Size: $750,000 TO $1.5 MILLION. Investment Policies: Equity investments. Investment Types: Early stage, expansion, later stage. Industry Preferences: Diversified. Geographic Preferences: Ohio, Kentucky, Indiana.

Brantley Venture Partners, L.P.
20600 Chagrin Blvd., Ste. 1150
Cleveland, Ohio 44122
Phone:(216)283-4800
Fax:(216)283-5324
Venture capital firm. Areas of interest include computer and electronics, medical/health care, biotechnology, computer software, telecommunications, traditional manufacturing, information processing, and environmental industries.

Clarion Capital Corp.
Ohio Savings Plz., Ste. 510
1801 E. 9th St.
Cleveland, Ohio 44114
Phone: (216)687-1096
Fax: (216)694-3545
Small business investment corpora-
tion. Interested in manufacturing,
computer software, natural resources/
natural gas, and health care.

Gries Investment Co.
1801 E. 9th St.,Ste. 1600
Cleveland, Ohio 44114-3110
Phone: (216)861-1146
Fax: (216)861-0106
A small business investment corpora-
tion. No industry preference.

Key Equity Capital Corp.
127 Public Sq., 6th Fl.
Cleveland, Ohio 44114
Phone: (216)689-5776
Fax: (216)689-3204
Raymond Lancaster, President
Preferred Investment Size: $2.000,000.
Investment Policies: Willing to make
equity investments. Industry Prefer-
ences: Diversified. Geographic
Preferences: National.

Morgenthaler Ventures
629 Euclid Ave.,Ste. 1700
Cleveland, Ohio 44111
Phone: (216)621-3070
Fax: (216)621-2817
Private venture capital firm providing
start-up and later-stage financing to
all types of business in North
America; prefers not to invest in real
estate and oil and gas.

National City Capital Corp.
1965 E. 6th St.
Cleveland, Ohio 44114
Phone: (216)575-2491
Fax: (216)575-9965
A small business investment corpora-
tion. Provides equity for expansion
programs, recapitalizations, acquisi-
tions, and management buyouts.
Seeks investment opportunities

ranging from $1 million to $5 million.
Diversified industry preference.

Primus Venture Partners
1 Cleveland Center, Ste. 2700
1375 E. 9th St.
Cleveland, Ohio 44114
Phone: (216)621-2185
Fax: (216)621-4543
Venture capital partnership. Provides
seed, early stage, and expansion
financing to companies located in
Ohio and the Midwest. Does not
engage in gas, oil, or real estate
investments.

Society Venture Capital Corp.
127 Public Sq. 6th Fl.
Cleveland, Ohio 44114
Phone: (216)689-5776
Fax: (216)689-3204
A small business investment corpora-
tion. Prefers to invest in manufactur-
ing and service industries.

Tomlinson Industries
13700 Broadway Ave.
Cleveland, Ohio 44125-1992
Phone: (216)587-3400
Free: (800)526-9634
Fax: (216)587-0733
A small business investment corpora-
tion. Miniature supermarket industry
preferred.

Banc One Capital Partners Corp.
(Columbus)
150 E. Gay St.
Columbus, Ohio 43215
Phone: (614)217-1100
Free: (800)837-5100
A small business investment corpora-
tion. No industry preference.

Scientific Advances, Inc.
601 W. 5th Ave.
Columbus, Ohio 43201
Phone: (614)424-7005
Fax: (614)424-4874
Venture capital partnership interested
in natural gas related industries.

Center City MESBIC, Inc.
8 N. Maine St.
Miami Valley Tur, Ste. 1400
Dayton, Ohio 45402
Phone: (513)461-6164
Fax: (513)937-7035
A minority enterprise small business
investment corporation. Diversified
industries.

Seed One
Park Pl.
10 W. Streetsboro St.
Hudson, Ohio 44236
Phone: (216)650-2338
Fax: (216)650-4946
Private venture capital firm. No
industry preference. Equity financing
only.

Fifth Third Bank of Northwestern
Ohio, N.A.
606 Madison Ave.
Toledo, Ohio 43604
Phone: (419)259-7141
Fax: (419)259-7134
A small business investment corpora-
tion. No industry preference.

Lubrizol Performance Products Co.
29400 Lakeland Blvd.
Wickliffe, Ohio 44092
Phone: (216)943-4200
Fax: (216)943-5337
Venture capital supplier. Provides
seed capital and later-stage expansion
financing to emerging companies in
the biological, chemical, and material
sciences whose technology is
applicable to and related to the
production and marketing of specialty
and fine chemicals.

Cactus Capital Co.
6660 High St., Office 1-B
Worthington, Ohio 43085
Phone: (614)436-4060
Fax: (614)436-4060
A minority enterprise small business
investment company. Diversified
industry preference.

Oklahoma

Southwestern Oklahoma Development
Authority
PO Box 569
Burns Flat, Oklahoma 73624
Phone: (405)562-4884
Free: (800)627-4882
Fax: (405)562-4880

Langston University
Minority Business Assistance Center
Hwy. 33 E.
PO Box 667
Langston, Oklahoma 73050
Phone: (405)466-3256
Free: (800)879-6552
Fax: (405)466-2909

BancFirst Investment Corp.
1101 N. Broadway
Oklahoma City, Oklahoma 73102
Phone: (405)270-1000
Fax: (405)270-1089
T. Kent Faison, Manager
Preferred Investment Size: Up to
$500,000. Investment Policies: Loans
and/or equity. Investment Types:
Early stage, expansion. Industry
Preferences: Diversified. Geographic
Preferences: Oklahoma.

Oklahoma Department of Commerce
Business Development Division
PO Box 26980
Oklahoma City, Oklahoma 73126-0980
Phone: (405)815-6552
Fax: (405)815-5142
Helps companies gain access to
capital needed for growth. Provides
financial specialists to help businesses analyze their financing needs
and to work closely with local
economic development staff to help
package proposals for their companies. Also responsible for assisting in
the development of new loan and
investment programs.

Oklahoma Development Finance
Authority
301 NW 63rd St., Ste. 225
Oklahoma City, Oklahoma 73116

Phone: (405)848-9761
Fax: (405)848-3314
Issues tax-exempt industrial develop-
ment bonds for manufacturing firms.

Oklahoma Industrial Finance Authority
301 NW 63rd., Ste. 225
Oklahoma City, Oklahoma 73116-7904
Phone: (405)842-1145
Fax: (405)848-3314
Provides financing for manufacturing
projects involving the purchase of
land, buildings, and stationary
equipment.

Oklahoma State Treasurer's Office
Agriculture/Small Business Linked
Deposit Programs
217 State Capitol
Oklahoma City, Oklahoma 73105
Phone: (405)521-3191
Fax: (405)521-4994
Provides reduced loan rates for
Oklahoma's farming, ranching, and
small business communities.

Rees/Source Ventures, Inc.
3001 United Founders Blvd.
Oklahoma City, Oklahoma 73112
Phone: (405)843-8049
Fax: (405)843-8048
Venture capital firm providing seed,
start-up, first-stage, and second-stage
financing. Prefers to make investments
in the $250,000 to $500,000 range to
companies within a three-mile radius
of Oklahoma City. Areas of interest
include recreation and leisure,
environmental products and services,
packaging machinery and materials,
energy-related technologies, printing
and publishing, manufacturing and
automation, information processing
and software, and specialty chemicals
industries. Will not consider the
following industries: oil, gas, or
mineral exploration; real estate; motion
pictures; and consulting services.

Alliance Business Investment Co.
(Tulsa)
320 South Boston Ste. 1000

Tulsa, Oklahoma 74103-3703
Phone: (918)584-3581
Fax: (918)582-3403
A small business investment corpora-
tion. Provides later-stage financing for
basic industries.

Davis Venture Partners (Tulsa)
320 S. Boston Ste., 1000
Tulsa, Oklahoma 74103-3703
Phone: (918)584-7272
Fax: (918)582-3403
Venture capital firm. Provides later-
stage financing for basic industries.

Rubottom, Dudash and Associates,
Inc.
4870 S. Lewis, Ste. 180
Tulsa, Oklahoma 74105
Phone: (918)742-3031
Management and investment consult-
ants. Emphasis on retail, wholesale,
and light fabrication.

Oregon

Olympic Venture Partners II (Lake
Oswego)
340 Oswego Pointe Dr., No. 200
Lake Oswego, Oregon 97034-3230
Phone: (503)697-8766
Fax: (503)697-8863
Invests in early stage high technol-
ogy, biotechnology, and communica-
tions businesses.

Orien Ventures
300 Oswego Pointe Dr., Ste. 100
Lake Oswego, Oregon 97034
Phone: (503)699-1680
Fax: (503)699-1681
Venture capital firm interested in all
types of investment.

Northern Pacific Capital Corp.
PO Box 1658
Portland, Oregon 97205
Phone: (503)241-1255
Fax: (503)299-6653
A small business investment com-
pany. Diversified industry preference.

Northwest Capital Network
PO Box 6650
Portland, Oregon 97228-6650
Phone: (503)796-3321
Fax: (503)280-6080
Nonprofit business/investor referral
service that brings together entrepreneurs requiring capital with investors
seeking specific venture opportunities, through means of a confidential
database of investment opportunity
profiles and investment interest
profiles.

Oregon Resource and Technology
Development Fund
4370 NE Halsey
Portland, Oregon 97213
Phone: (503)282-4462
Fax: (503)282-2976
Provides investment capital for early
stage business finance and applied
research and development projects
that leads to commercially viable
products.

Shaw Venture Partners
400 SW 6th Ave., Ste. 1100
Portland, Oregon 97204-1636
Phone: (503)228-4884
Fax: (503)227-2471
Small business investment corporation interested in computers, retail,
medical/biotechnology, consumer
products and international trade
investment.

U.S. Bancorp Capital Corp.
P.O. Box 4412
Portland, Oregon 97208
Phone: (503)275-6111
Fax: (503)275-7565
A small business investment com-
pany. Diversified industry preference.

Oregon Economic Development
Department
Business Finance Section
SBA Loans Program
775 Summer St. NE
Salem, Oregon 97310
Phone: (503)986-0160
Free: (800)233-3306

Fax: (503)581-5115
A state-wide company providing
Small Business Administration 504
and 7(A) financing to eligible small
businesses; works closely with local
certified development companies.

Oregon Economic Development
Department
Business Finance Section
Oregon Business Development Fund
775 Summer St. NE
Salem, Oregon 97310
Phone: (503)986-0160
Fax: (503)581-5115
Structures and issues loans to
manufacturing, processing, and
tourism-related small businesses.

Tektronix Development Co.
PO Box 1000, Mail Sta. 63-862
Wilsonville, Oregon 97070
Phone: (503)685-4233
Fax: (503)685-3754
Venture capital firm interested in high
tech, opto electronics and measure-
ment systems investment.

Pennsylvania

NEPA Venture Fund LP
125 Goodman Dr.
Bethlehem, Pennsylvania 18015
Phone: (610)865-6550
Private venture capital partnership
providing seed and start-up financing.

Zero Stage Capital Co., Inc. (State
College)
101 Main St., 17th Fl.
Cambridge, Pennsylvania 02142
Phone: (617)876-5355
Fax: (617)876-1248
Venture capital firm. Industry prefer-
ences include high-technology start-
up companies located in the north-
eastern U.S.

Erie SBIC
32 W. 8th St., Ste. 615
Erie, Pennsylvania 16501
Phone: (814)453-7964
A small business investment corpora-

tion. No industry preference. Prefers
investments ranging from $100,000 -
$200,000.

Pennsylvania Department of Commerce
Governor's Response Team
439 Forum Bldg.
Harrisburg, Pennsylvania 17120
Phone: (717)787-8199
Fax: (717)772-5419
Works with individual companies to
find buildings or sites for start-up or
expansion projects; contacts manufacturers to make them aware of financial
and technical assistance available, to
assist with difficulties, and to learn of
future plans for expansions or
cutbacks.

Pennsylvania Department of Com-
merce
Bureau of Bonds
Employee Ownership Assistance
Program
E-mail: abrennan@doc.state.pa.us
Office of Program Management
466 Forum Bldg.
Harrisburg, Pennsylvania 17120
Phone: (717)783-1109
Fax: (717)234-4560
Preserves existing jobs and creates
new jobs by assisting and promoting
employee ownership in existing
enterprises which are experiencing
layoffs or would otherwise close.

Pennsylvania Department of Commerce
Bureau of Bonds
Revenue Bond and Mortgage Program
E-mail: abrennan@doc.state.pa.us
466 Forum Bldg.
Harrisburg, Pennsylvania 17120
Phone: (717)783-1109
Fax: (717)234-4560
Financing for projects approved
through the Program are borrowed
from private sources, and can be used
to acquire land, buildings, machinery,
and equipment. Borrowers must create
a minimum number of new jobs within
three years of the loan's closing.

Pennsylvania Department of Energy
Energy Development Authority
P.O. Box 8772 13th Fl.
Rachael Carson State Official
Harrisburg, Pennsylvania 17105-8772
Phone: (717)783-9981
Fax: (717)783-2703
Finances research and development of
energy technology projects.

Enterprise Venture Capital Corp. of
Pennsylvania
111 Market St.
Johnstown, Pennsylvania 15901
Phone: (814)535-7597
Fax: (814)535-8677
A small business investment corpora-
tion. No industry preference. Geo-
graphic preference is two-hour driving
radius of Johnstown, Pennsylvania.

Foster Management Co.
1018 W. 9th Ave.
King of Prussia, Pennsylvania 19406
Phone: (610)992-7650
Fax: (610)992-3390
Private venture capital supplier. Not
restricted to specific industries or
geographic locations; diversified with
investments in the health care,
transportation, broadcasting, communications, energy, and home furnishings industries. Investments range
from $2 million to $15 million.

CIP Capital, LP
20 Valley Stream Pky., Ste. 265
Malvern, Pennsylvania 19355
Phone: (610)695-8380
Fax: (215)695-8388
A small business investment com-
pany. Diversified industry preference.

Core States Enterprise Fund
1345 Chestnut St., F.C. 1-8-12-1
Philadelphia, Pennsylvania 19107
Phone: (215)973-6519
Fax: (215)973-6900
Venture capital supplier. Invests with
any industry except real estate or
construction. Minimum investment is
$1 million.

Fidelcor Capital Corp.
Fidelity Bldg., 11th Fl.
123 S. Broad St.
Philadelphia, Pennsylvania 19109
Phone: (215)985-3722
Fax: (215)985-7282
A small business investment com-
pany. Diversified industry preference.

Ben Franklin Technology Center of
Southeastern Pennsylvania
University City Science Center
3624 Market St.
Philadelphia, Pennsylvania 19104
Phone: (215)382-0380
Fax: (215)387-6050
Public venture capital fund interested
in technology industries.

Genesis Seed Fund
c/o Howard, Lawson and Co.
2 Penn Center Plz.
Philadelphia, Pennsylvania 19102
Phone: (215)988-0010
Fax: (215)568-0029
Venture capital fund.

Keystone Venture Capital Management Co.
1601 Market St., Ste. 2500
Philadelphia, Pennsylvania 19103
Phone: (215)241-1200
Fax: (215)241-1211
Private venture capital partnership.
Provides later-stage investments in
the telecommunications, health care,
manufacturing, media, software, and
franchise industries, primarily in the
mid-Atlantic states.

Penn Janney Fund, Inc.
1801 Market St.
Philadelphia, Pennsylvania 19103
Phone: (215)665-6193
Fax: (215)665-6197
Private venture capital limited partner-
ship.

Philadelphia Ventures
200 S. Broad St., 8th Fl.
Philadelphia, Pennsylvania 19102
Phone: (215)732-4445

Fax: (215)732-4644
A small business investment corporation. Provides financing to companies
offering products or services based
on technology or other proprietary
capabilities. Industries of particular
interest are information processing
equipment and services, medical
products and services, data communications, and industrial automation.

PNC Corporate Finance (Philadelphia)
1600 Market St., 21st Fl.
Philadelphia, Pennsylvania 19103
Phone: (215)585-6282
Fax: (215)585-5525
Small business investment company.

Fostin Capital Corp.
681 Andersen Dr.
Pittsburgh, Pennsylvania 15220
Phone: (412)928-1400
Fax: (412)928-9635
Venture capital corporation.

Loyalhanna Venture Fund
PO Box 81927
Pittsburgh, Pennsylvania 15217
Phone: (412)687-9027
Fax: (412)681-0960
Venture capital firm. No industry
preference.

PNC Capital Corp. (Pittsburgh)
1 PNC Plaza, 19th Fl.
249 5th Ave.
Pittsburgh, Pennsylvania 15222
Phone: (412)762-7035
Fax: (412)762-6233
A small business investment corporation. Prefers to invest in later-stage
and leveraged buy out situations. Will
not consider real estate, coal, or gas
ventures.

APA/Fostin Pennsylvania Venture
Capital Fund
100 Matsonford Rd., Bldg. 5, Ste. 470
Radnor, Pennsylvania 19087
Phone: (610)687-3030
Fax: (610)687-8520
Private venture capital limited partner-

ship providing mid- and later stage financing.

Meridian Venture Partners (Radnor)
The Fidelity Court Bldg., Ste. 140
259 Radnor-Chester Rd.
Radnor, Pennsylvania 19087
Phone: (610)254-2999
Fax: (610)254-2996
Venture capital firm.

Patricof & Co. Ventures, Inc. (Radnor)
100 Matsonford Rd., Bldg. 5, Ste. 470
Radnor, Pennsylvania 19087
Phone: (610)687-3030
Fax: (610)687-8520
Venture capital firm providing mid- to later stage financing.

Meridian Capital Corp. (Reading)
600 Penn St.
Reading, Pennsylvania 19602
Phone: (610)655-1437
Fax: (215)655-1908
Small business investment corporation.

TDH Small Business Investment Co.
1 Rosemont Business Campus, Ste. 301
919 Conestoga Rd.
Rosemont, Pennsylvania 19010
Phone: (610)526-9970
Fax: (610)526-9971
Private venture capital fund. No industry preferences.

Hillman Medical Ventures, Inc. (Berwyn)
100 Front St., Ste. 1350
W. Conshohocken, Pennsylvania 19428
Phone: (610)940-0300
Fax: (610)940-0301
Venture capital firm that invests in early-stage medical technology companies.

BankAmerica Ventures (Washington)
PO Box 512
Washington, Pennsylvania 15301
Phone: (412)223-0707
Fax: (412)546-8021
Daniel A. Dye, Contact

First SBIC of California (Washington)
PO Box 512
Washington, Pennsylvania 15301
Phone: (412)223-0707
Fax: (412)223-8290
A small business investment company.

S. R. One Ltd.
565 E. Swedesford Rd., Ste. 315
Wayne, Pennsylvania 19087
Phone: (610)293-3400
Fax: (610)293-3419

Sandhurst Co. LP
351 E. Constoga Rd.
Wayne, Pennsylvania 19087
Phone: (610)254-8900
Fax: (610)254-8958
Private venture capital fund.

Technology Leaders LP
800 The Safeguard Bldg.
435 Devon Park Dr.
Wayne, Pennsylvania 19087
Phone: (610)293-0600
Fax: (610)293-0601
Private venture capital fund. Areas of interest include biotechnology, health care, information services, and high technology industries.

Puerto Rico

North America Investment Corp.
P.O. Box 191831
San Juan, Puerto Rico 00919-1813
Phone: (787)754-6177
Fax: (787)754-6181
A minority enterprise small business investment corporation. Diversified industry preference.

Rhode Island

Domestic Capital Corp.
815 Reservoir Ave.
Cranston, Rhode Island 02910
Phone: (401)946-3310
Fax: (401)943-6708
A small business investment corporation. No industry preference.

Fairway Capital Corp.
285 Governor St.
Providence, Rhode Island 02906
Phone: (401)454-7500
Fax: (401)455-3636
A small business investment company. Diversified industry preference.

Fleet Equity Partners (Providence)
111 Westminster St., 4th Fl.
Providence, Rhode Island 02903
Phone: (401)278-6770
Fax: (401)278-6387
Venture capital firm specializing in acquisitions and recapitalizations.

Fleet Venture Resources, Inc.
E-mail: fep@fleet.com
111 Westminster St., 4th Fl.
Providence, Rhode Island 02903
Phone: (401)278-6770
Fax: (401)278-6387
Robert M. Van Degna, President
Preferred Investment Size: $5 to $125 million. Investment Policies: Equity. Investment Types: Leverage buyouts, expansion. Industry Preferences: Media/communications, healthcare, printing, manufacturing. Geographic Preferences: National.

Moneta Capital Corp.
285 Governor St.
Providence, Rhode Island 02906-4314
Phone: (401)454-7500
Fax: (401)455-3636
A small business investment corporation. No industry preference.

NYSTRS/NV Capital, Limited Partnership
111 Westminster St.
Providence, Rhode Island 02903
Phone: (401)276-5597
Fax: (401)278-6387
A small business investment company. Diversified industry preference.

Rhode Island Department of Economic Development
Rhode Island Partnership for Science and Technology

1 W. Exchange
Providence, Rhode Island 02903
Phone: (401)277-2601
Fax: (401)277-2102
Offers grants to businesses for
applied research with a potential for
profitable commercialization. Research
must be conducted in conjunction
with universities, colleges, or hospitals. Also has a program which
provides consulting services and
grants to applicants of the Federal
Small Business Innovation Research
Program.

Rhode Island Department of Economic
Development
Rhode Island Port Operations
Division
1 W. Exchange
Providence, Rhode Island 02903
Phone: (401)277-2601
Fax: (401)277-2102
Provides financing through tax-exempt
revenue bonds.

Rhode Island Department of Economic
Development
Ocean State Business Development
Authority
1 W. Exchange
Providence, Rhode Island 02903
Phone: (401)277-2601
Fax: (401)277-2102
Private, nonprofit corporation certified
by the Small Business Administration
to administer the SBA(504)) loan
program.

Rhode Island Department of Economic
Development
Rhode Island Industrial-Recreational
Building Authority
1 W. Exchange
Providence, Rhode Island 02903
Phone: (401)277-2601
Fax: (401)277-2102
Issues mortgage insurance on
financing obtained through other
financial institutions.

Rhode Island Office of the General
Treasurer

Business Investment Fund
E-mail: treasurea@treasurea.state.ri.us
40 Fountain St., 8th Fl.
Providence, Rhode Island 02903-1855
Phone: (401)277-2287
Free: (800)752-8088
Fax: (401)277-6141
Provides fixed-rate loans in coopera-
tion with the U.S. Small Business
Administration and local banks.

Richmond Square Capital Corp.
1 Richmond Sq.
Providence, Rhode Island 02906
Phone: (401)521-3000
Fax: (401)751-8997
A small business investment com-
pany. Diversified industry preference.

Wallace Capital Corp.
170 Westminster St., Ste. 1200
Providence, Rhode Island 02903
Phone: (401)273-9191
Fax: (401)273-9648
A small business investment com-
pany. Diversified industry preference.

South Carolina

Charleston Capital Corp.
111 Church St.
PO Box 328
Charleston, South Carolina 29402
Phone: (803)723-6464
Fax: (803)723-1228
Small business investment corpora-
tion preferring secured loans. Assists
the southeastern U.S. only.

Lowcountry Investment Corp.
4401 Piggly Wiggly Dr.
PO Box 18047
Charleston, South Carolina 29405
Phone: (803)554-9880
Fax: (803)745-2730
A small business investment corpora-
tion. Diversified industry preference.

Floco Investment Co., Inc.
PO Box 1629
Lake City, South Carolina 29560
Phone: (803)389-2731
Fax: (803)389-4199

A small business investment corporation. Invests only in grocery stores.

South Dakota

South Dakota Department of Agricul-
ture
Office of Rural Development
Agricultural Loan Participation
Program
Foss Bldg.
523 E. Capitol
Pierre, South Dakota 57501-3182
Phone: (605)773-3375
Free: (800)228-5254
Fax: (605)773-5926
Provides loans, administered and
serviced through local lenders, that
are intended to supplement existing
credit.

South Dakota Development Corp.
SBA 504 Loan Program
711 E. Wells Ave.
Pierre, South Dakota 57501-3369
Free: (800)872-6190
Fax: (605)773-3256
Offers subordinated mortgage
financing to healthy and expanding
small businesses.

South Dakota Governor's Office of
Economic Development
Revolving Economic Development
and Initiative Fund
711 E. Wells Ave.
Pierre, South Dakota 57501-3369
Free: (800)872-6190
Provides low-interst revolving loans
for the creation of primary jobs, capital
investment, and the diversification of
the state's economy. Costs eligible for
participation include land and the
associated site improvements;
construction, acquistion, and renovation of buildings; fees, services and
other costs associated with construction; the purchase and installation of
machinery and equipment; and trade
receivables, inventory, and work-in-
progress inventory.

South Dakota Governor's Office of
Economic Development
Economic Development Finance
Authority
711 E. Wells Ave.
Pierre, South Dakota 57501-3369
Free: (800)872-6190
Fax: (605)773-3256
Pools tax-exempt or taxable development bonds to construct any site,
structure, facility, service, or utility for
the storage, distribution, or manufacture of industrial, agricultural, or
nonagricultural products, machinery,
or equipment.

Tennessee

Valley Capital Corp.
100 W. Martin Luther King Blvd.
Ste. 212
Chattanooga, Tennessee 37402
Phone: (423)265-1557
Fax: (423)265-1588
A minority enterprise small business
investment corporation. Diversified
industry preferences. Limited to the
Southeast, preferably four-hour
driving radius.

Franklin Venture Capital, Inc.
237 2nd Ave. S
Franklin, Tennessee 37064
Phone: (615)791-9462
Fax: (615)791-9636
A small business investment corpora-
tion. Prefers to invest in the health
care and biotechnology industries.

Chickasaw Capital Corp.
6200 Poplar Ave.
PO Box 387
Memphis, Tennessee 38147
Phone: (901)383-6000
Fax: (901)383-6141
A minority enterprise small business
investment corporation. No industry
preference.

Flemming Companies
1991 Corporate Ave.
Memphis, Tennessee 38132
Phone: (901)395-8000

Fax: (901)395-8586
A small business investment corporation.

Gulf Pacific
5100 Poplar Ave., No. 427
Memphis, Tennessee 38137-0401
Phone: (901)767-3400
Free: (800)456-1867
Fax: (901)680-7033
A minority enterprise small business
investment corporation.

International Paper Capital Formation,
Inc.
6400 Poplar Ave.
Tower 2, 4th Fl., Rm. 130
Memphis, Tennessee 38197
Phone: (901)763-6217
Fax: (901)763-6076
A minority enterprise small business
investment corporation. Diversified
industry preference. Involvement
includes expansion, refinancing, and
acquisitions, but no start-up projects.
Requires a minimum investment of
$50,000 to $300,000.

Union Platters
158 Madison Ave.
Memphis, Tennessee 38103-0708
Phone: (901)578-2405
Free: (800)821-9979
A small business investment corpora-
tion.

West Tennessee Venture Capital
Corp.
Tennessee Valley Center for Minority
Economics Dev.
5 N. 3rd St., Ste. 2000
Memphis, Tennessee 38103-2610
Phone: (901)523-1884
Fax: (901)527-6091
A minority enterprise small business
investment corporation.

L.P. Equitas
2000 Glen Echo Rd., Ste 100
PO Box 158838
Nashville, Tennessee 37215
Phone: (615)383-8673
Fax: (615)383-8693
D. Shannon LeRoy, President

Massey Burch Investment Group
310 25th Ave. N, Ste. 103
Nashville, Tennessee 37203
Phone: (615)329-9448
Fax: (615)329-9237
Venture capital firm providing
investments ranging from $1 to $3
million. Areas of interest include
health care services, information
services, environmental services,
privatization, systems integration, and
telecommunications.

Sirrom Capital, LP
500 Church St., Ste. 200
Nashville, Tennessee 37219
Phone: (615)256-0701
Fax: (615)726-1208
A small business investment com-
pany. Diversified industry preference.

Tennessee Department of Economic
and Community Development
Grants Program Management Section
Rachel Jackson Bldg., 6th Fl.
320 6th Ave. N.
Nashville, Tennessee 37243-0405
Phone: (615)741-6201
Free: (800)342-8470
Fax: (615)741-5070
Administers grant money for the
community development block grant
program, the Appalachian Regional
Commission, and the Economic
Development Administration.

Tennessee Equity Capital Corp.
1102 Stonewall Jackson Ct.
Nashville, Tennessee 37220-1705
A minority enterprise small business
investment corporation.

Texas

Austin Ventures L.P.
114 W. 7th St., STe. 1300
Austin, Texas 78701
Phone: (512)479-0055
Fax: (512)476-3952
Administers investments through two
funds, Austin Ventures L.P. and Rust
Ventures L.P., in the $1 million to $4
million range. Prefers to invest in start-

up/emerging growth companies located in the southwest, and in special situations such as buy outs, acquisitions, and mature companies. No geographic limitations are placed on later-stage investments. Past investments have been made in media, data communications, telecommunications, software, environmental services, and general manufacturing.

Forum Financial
600 Congress Ave., No. 1630
Austin, Texas 78701-3236
Phone: (512)476-7800
Fax: (512)476-3850
Venture capital firm providing second stage, acquisitions and leveraged buyout financing. Areas of interest include mining, oil and gas, real estate development, and project financing.

Huber Capital Ventures
11917 Oak Knoll, Ste. G
Austin, Texas 78759
Phone: (512)258-8668
Fax: (512)258-9091
Venture capital firm providing short-term working capital funding for specific projects. Areas of interest include small capitalization companies in manufacturing, wholesaling, and technical services.

Texas Department of Commerce
Finance Office
PO Box 12728
Austin, Texas 78711
Phone: (512)936-0281
Fax: (512)936-0520
Administers several programs that benefit small businesses, including those authorized under the Industrial Development Corporation Act of 1979 and the Rural Development Act, as well as the state industrial revenue bond program.

Triad Ventures Ltd.
E-mail: cole.amf@myriad.net
8911 Capital of Texas Hwy., Ste. 3320
Austin, Texas 78759
Phone: (512)343-8087

Fax: (512)342-1993
Venture capital firm providing second stage, acquisitions, mezzanine and leveraged buyout financing. Areas of interest include Texas-based companies.

Alliance Enterprise Corp. (Dallas)
12655 N. Central Expy., Ste 710
Dallas, Texas 75243
Phone: (972)991-1597
Fax: (972)991-1647
A minority enterprise small business investment company. Diversified industry preference.

AMT Capital, Ltd.
8204 Elmbrook Dr., Ste. 101
Dallas, Texas 75247
Phone: (214)905-9760
Fax: (214)905-9761
Tom H. Delimitros, CGP
Preferred Investment Size: $200,000 to $500,000. Investment Policies: Loan or equity. Investment Types: Early stage, expansion. Industry Preferences: Advanced materials & products. Geographic Preferences: National.

Banc One Capital Corp. (Dallas)
300 Crescent Ct., Ste. 1600
Dallas, Texas 75201
Phone: (214)979-4375
Fax: (214)979-4355
A small business investment corporation. Specializes in later-stage investments for traditional businesses with revenues in excess of $15 million annually. Areas of interest include manufacturing, distribution, and health care industries.

Capital Southwest Corp.
12900 Preston Rd., Ste. 700
Dallas, Texas 75230
Phone: (214)233-8242
Fax: (214)233-7362
Venture capital firm. Provides first stage and expansion financing. Diversified industry preferences.

Citicorp Venture Capital, Ltd. (Dallas)
2001 Ross Ave.

1400 Tramalcrowe Center
Dallas, Texas 75201
Phone: (214)953-3800
Fax: (214)953-1495
A small business investment company.

Davis Venture Partners (Dallas)
2121 San Jacinto St., Ste. 975
Dallas, Texas 75201
Phone: (214)954-1822
Fax: (214)969-0256
Venture capital firm interested in diversified industries, excluding oil, gas, and real estate.

Diamond A. Ford Corp.
200 Crescent Court, Ste. 1350
Dallas, Texas 75201
Phone: (214)871-5177
Fax: (214)871-5199
A small business investment company. Diversified industry preference.

Erickson Capital Group, Inc.
5950 Berkshire Lane, Ste. 1100
Dallas, Texas 75225
Phone: (214)365-6060
Fax: (214)365-6001
Venture capital firm providing seed, start-up, first and second stage, and expansion financing. Areas of interest include health care.

Gaekeke Landers
4131 N. Central Expy., Ste. 900
Dallas, Texas 75204
Phone: (214)528-8883
Fax: (214)528-8058
Venture capital firm providing acquisition, start-up, and leverage equity financing. Areas of interest include real estate.

Hook Partners
13760 Noel Rd., Ste. 805
Dallas, Texas 75240-4360
Phone: (214)991-5457
Fax: (214)991-5458
Venture capital firm providing seed, start-up and first stage financing. Areas of interest include high technology industries.

Interwest Partners (Dallas)
2 Galleria Tower
13455 Noel Rd., Ste. 1670
Dallas, Texas 75240
Phone: (214)392-7279
Fax: (214)490-6348

Kahala Investments, Inc.
8214 Westchester Dr., Ste. 715
Dallas, Texas 75225
Phone: (214)987-0077
Venture capital firm providing
financing for all stages including
expansion capital, leveraged buyouts,
and management buyouts. Areas of
interest include a wide variety of
industries.

Mapleleaf Capital, Ltd.
3 Forest Plz., Ste.935
12221 Merit Dr.
Dallas, Texas 75251
Phone: (214)239-5650
Fax: (214)701-0024
A small business investment com-
pany. Diversified industry preference.

May Financial Corp.
8333 Douglas Ave., Ste. 400
Lock Box 82
Dallas, Texas 75225
Phone: (214)987-5200
Free: (800)767-4397
Fax: (214)987-1994
Brokerage firm working with a venture
capital firm. Prefers food, oil and gas,
and electronics industries.

Merchant Banking Group Ltd.
700 N. Pearl, Ste. 1910 NT, LB 321
Dallas, Texas 75201
Phone: (214)777-6466
Fax: (214)777-6475
Venture capital firm providing
leveraged buyout financing. Areas of
interest include basic manufacturing
and distribution.

MESBIC Ventures, Inc.
12655 N. Central Expy., Ste. 710
Dallas, Texas 75243
Phone: (972)991-1597
Fax: (972)991-1647

Donald R. Lawhorne, President
Preferred Investment Size: Up to
$1,000,000. Investment Policies: Loans
and/or equity. Investment Types:
early stage, expansion, later stage.
Industry Preferences: Diversified.
Geographic Preferences: Mostly
Southwest.

MSI Capital Corp.
6500 Greenville Ave., Ste. 720
Dallas, Texas 75206-1012
Phone: (214)265-1801
Fax: (214)265-1804
No industry preference.

Nations Bank Venture Capital
901 Maine St., 64th Fl.
Dallas, Texas 75202-2911
Phone: (214)508-0988
Fax: (214)508-0604
A small business investment com-
pany. Diversified industry preference.

NationsBank Capital Corp.
NationBank Plz., Ste. 71
901 Main St.
Dallas, Texas 75202
Phone: (214)508-6262
Fax: (214)508-5060
Venture capital firm providing second
stage, mezzanine and leveraged
buyout financing. Areas of interest
include communications, medical,
environmental, specialty retail,
transportation and energy services.

NCNB Texas Venture Group, Inc.
1401 Elm St., Ste. 4764
Dallas, Texas 75202
Phone: (214)508-6262
Venture capital firm providing
expansion and leveraged buyout
financing. Areas of interest include
medical products and services, energy
service, environmental, specialty
retail, transportation, general manufacturing, and communications.

North Texas MESBIC, Inc.
12770 Coit Rd., Ste.240
Dallas, Texas 75251
Phone: (214)991-8060

Fax: (214)991-8061
A minority enterprise small business
investment company. Diversified
industry preference.

Phillips-Smith Specialty Retail Group
E-mail: pssrg@aol.com
5080 Spectrum Dr., Ste. 700 W
Dallas, Texas 75248
Phone: (214)387-0725
Fax: (214)458-2560
Prefers specialty retail industry
investments, including the restaurant
industry.

PMC Capital, Inc.
Attn: Andy Rosemore
17290 Preston Rd., 3rd Fl.
Dallas, Texas 75252-5618
Phone: (214)380-0044
Free: (800)486-3223
Fax: (214)380-1371
A small business investment corpora-
tion, minority enterprise small busi-
ness investment corporation, and
SBA guaranteed lender. No industry
preferred.

Pro-Med Investment Corp.
17290 Preston Rd., Ste. 300
Dallas, Texas 75252
Phone: (214)380-0044
Fax: (214)380-1371
A minority enterprise small business
investment company. Diversified
industry preference.

Sevin Rosen Funds
13455 Noel Rd., Ste. 1670
Dallas, Texas 75240
Phone: (214)702-1100
Fax: (214)702-1103
Venture capital firm providing start-up
and first stage financing. Industry
preferences include information
sciences and electronic sciences.

Southwest Enterprise Associates
14457 Gillis Rd.
Dallas, Texas 75244
Phone: (214)450-3894
Fax: (214)450-3899
Venture capital supplier. Concentrates

on technology-based industries that have the potential for product innovation, rapid growth, and high profit margins. Investments range from $250,000 to $1.5 million. Past investments have been made in the following industries: computer software, medical and life sciences, computers and peripherals, communications, semiconductors, and defense electronics. Management must demonstrate intimate knowledge of its marketplace and have a well-defined strategy for achieving strong market penetration.

Stratford Capital Partners, L.P.
200 Crescent Ct., Ste. 1650
Dallas, Texas 75201
Phone: (214)740-7377
Fax: (214)740-7340
Michael D. Brown, President
Preferred Investment Size: $3 to $9 million. Investment Policies: Equity, sub debt with equity. Investment Types: Expansion, later stage, acquisition. Industry Preferences: Manufacturing, distribution, diversified. Geographic Preferences: National.

Sullivan Enterprises
9130 Markville Dr.
PO Box 743803
Dallas, Texas 75374-3803
Phone: (214)414-5690
Venture capital firm providing refinancings and expansion, mezzanine, and leveraged buyouts financing. Areas of interest include manufacturing, service, retailing, wholesale and distribution.

Sunwestern Capital Corp.
12221 Merit Dr., Ste. 1300
Dallas, Texas 75251-2248
Phone: (214)239-5650
Fax: (214)701-0024
Small business investment corporation providing start-up, first stage, second stage, third stage and leveraged buyout financing. Areas of interest include computer peripherals,

software, information services, biotechnology and telecommunications.

Tower Ventures, Inc.
12655 N. Central Expy., Ste. 710
Dallas, Texas 75243
Phone: (972)391-1597
Fax: (972)991-1647
Donald R. Lawhorne, President
Preferred Investment Size: Up to $500,000. Investment Policies: Loans and/or equity. Investment Types: Early stage, expansion, later stage.

Western Financial Capital Corp.
17290 Preston Rd., Ste. 300
Dallas, Texas 75252
Phone: (214)380-0044
Fax: (214)380-1371
A small business investment company. Provides financing to the medical industry.

Wingate Partners
750 N. St. Paul St., Ste. 1200
Dallas, Texas 75201
Phone: (214)720-1313
Fax: (214)871-8799
Venture capital firm providing mature stage financing. Areas of interest include manufacturing and distribution.

HCT Capital Corp.
4916 Camp Bowie Blvd., Ste. 200
Fort Worth, Texas 76107
Phone: (817)763-8706
Fax: (817)377-8049
A small business investment company. Diversified industry preference.

SBIC Partners, L.P.
201 Main St., Ste. 2302
Fort Worth, Texas 76102
Phone: (817)729-3222
Fax: (817)729-3226
Gregory Forrest, Manager
Jeffrey Brown, Manager
Preferred Investment Size: $2 to $5 million. Investment Policies: Equity. Investment Types: Expansion, later stage. Industry Preferences: Diversi-

fied. Geographic Preferences: National.

Acorn Ventures, Inc.
520 Post Oak Blvd., Ste. 130
Houston, Texas 77027
Phone: (713)622-9595
Fax: (713)622-9595
No industry preference.

Alliance Business Investment Co. (Houston)
1221 McKinney Ste. 3100
Houston, Texas 77010
Phone: (713)659-3131
Fax: (713)659-8070
A small business investment corporation.

Aspen Capital Ltd.
55 Waugh, Ste. 710
Houston, Texas 77007
Phone: (713)880-4494
A small business investment corporation. No industry preference.

The Catalyst Fund, Ltd.
3 Riverway, Ste. 770
Houston, Texas 77056
Phone: (713)623-8133
Fax: (713)623-0473
A small business investment company. Diversified industry preference.

Charter Venture Group, Inc.
2600 Citadel Plaza Dr., Ste. 600
PO Box 4525
Houston, Texas 77210-4525
Phone: (713)622-7500
Fax: (713)552-8446
A small business investment corporation. No industry preference.

Chen's Financial Group, Inc.
10101 Southwest Fwy., Ste. 370
Houston, Texas 77074
Phone: (713)772-8868
Fax: (713)772-2168
A minority enterprise small business investment corporation. Areas of interest include real estate, franchise restaurants, banking, and import/export industries.

Criterion Ventures
1330 Post Oak Blvd., Ste. 1525
Houston, Texas 77056
Phone: (713)627-9200
Fax: (713)627-9292
Venture capital fund. Raises venture
capital. Interested in companies
headquartered in the Sunbelt region.
Areas of interest include telecommunications, biomedical, and specialty
retail.

Cureton & Co., Inc.
1100 Louisiana, Ste. 3250
Houston, Texas 77002
Phone: (713)658-9806
Fax: (713)658-0476
Prefers oilfield service, environmental,
electronics, manufacturing, and
distribution.

Energy Assets, Inc.
700 Louisiana, Ste. 5000
Houston, Texas 77002
Phone: (713)236-9999
Free: (800)933-5508
A small business investment corpora-
tion. Specializes in oil and gas energy
industries.

High Technology Associates
1775 St. James Pl., Ste. 105
Houston, Texas 77056
Phone: (713)963-9300
Fax: (713)963-8341
Venture capital firm providing second
stage and expansion financing. Areas
of interest include biotechnology,
chemicals, food processing and food
processing machinery. Particularly
interested in companies willing to
establish operations in the Northern
Netherlands.

Houston Partners, SBIC
401 Louisiana, 8th Fl.
Houston, Texas 77002
Phone: (713)222-8600
Fax: (713)222-8932
A small business investment com-
pany. Diversified industry preference.

MESBIC Financial Corp. of Houston
9130 North Fwy., Ste. 203
Houston, Texas 77037
Phone: (281)447-3000
Fax: (281)447-4222
Atillio Galli, President
Preferred Investment Size: $100,000 to
$1 million. Investment Policies: Loans
and equity investments. Investment
Types: Consolidated debt & preferred
stock with warrants. Industry Prefer-
ences: Diversified - no real estate or
gas and oil. Geographic Preferences:
Houston.

Payne Webber, Inc.
700 Louisiana St., Ste. 3800
Houston, Texas 77002
Phone: (713)236-3180
Fax: (713)236-3133

Penzoil
PO Box 2967
Houston, Texas 77252
Phone: (713)546-8910
Fax: (713)546-4154
A small business investment com-
pany. Diversified industry preference.

Southern Orient Capital Corp.
2419 Fannin, Ste. 200
Houston, Texas 77002-9181
Phone: (713)225-3369
A minority enterprise small business
investment corporation. No industry
preference.

Tenneco Ventures, Inc.
PO Box 2511
Houston, Texas 77252
Phone: (713)757-8229
Fax: (713)651-1666
Venture capital supplier. Provides
financing to small, early stage growth
companies. Areas of interest include
energy-related technologies, factory
automation, biotechnology, and
health care services. Prefers to invest
in Texas-based companies, but will
consider investments elsewhere
within the United States. Investments
range from $250,000 to $1 million; will

commit additional funds over several
rounds of financing, and will work
with other investors to provide larger
financing.

Texas Commerce Investment Group
PO Box 2558
Houston, Texas 77252-8032
Phone: (713)216-4553
A small business investment corpora-
tion. No industry preference.

UNCO Ventures, Inc.
520 Post Oak Blvd., Ste. 130
Houston, Texas 77027
Phone: (713)622-9595
Fax: (713)622-9007
A small business investment com-
pany. Diversified industry preference.

United Oriental Capital Corp.
908 Town and Country Blvd., Ste. 310
Houston, Texas 77024-2207
Phone: (713)461-3909
Fax: (713)465-7559
A minority enterprise small business
investment corporation. No industry
preference.

Ventex Partners, Ltd.
1001 Fannin St., Ste. 1095
Houston, Texas 77002
Phone: (713)659-7860
Fax: (713)659-7855
A small business investment partner-
ship providing later stage financing.

Capital Marketing Corp.
P.O. Box 1177
Keller, Texas 76244
Phone: (817)431-5767
A small business investment corpora-
tion.

First Capital Group of Texas
E-mail: jpb@texas.net
PO Box 15616
San Antonio, Texas 78212-8816
Phone: (210)736-4233
Fax: (210)736-5449
A small business investment corpora-
tion. No industry preference, but does

not invest in oil, gas, and real estate industries.

Southwest Venture Partnerships
16414 St. Pedro, Ste. 345
San Antonio, Texas 78232
Phone: (210)402-1200
Free: (800)725-0867
Fax: (210)402-1221
Venture capital partnership. Invests in maturing companies located primarily in the southwest. Average investment is $1 million.

Norwest Bank & Trust
1 O'Connor Plz.
Victoria, Texas 77902
Phone: (512)573-5151
Fax: (512)574-5236
A small business investment company. Diversified industry preference.

Woodlands Venture Partners L.P.
2170 Buckthorne Pl., Ste. 170
The Woodlands, Texas 77380
Phone: (713)367-9999
Fax: (713)298-1295
Venture capital firm providing start-up, first stage, second stage and seed financing. Areas of interest include medical/biotechnology only.

Utah

Deseret Certified Development Corp.
(Midvale)
E-mail: deseretcdc@aol.com
7050 Union Park Center, No. 570
Midvale, Utah 84047
Phone: (801)566-1163
Fax: (801)566-1532
Maintains an SBA(504)) loan program, designed for community development and job creation, and an intermediary loan program, through Farmer's Home Administration.

Deseret Certified Development Corp.
(Orem)
228 N. Orem Blvd.
Orem, Utah 84057-5011
Phone: (801)221-7772
Fax: (801)221-7775

Maintains an SBA loan program, designed for community development and job creation, and an intermediary loan program, through Farmer's Home Administration.

First Security Business Investment Corp.
79 S. Main St., Ste. 800
Salt Lake City, Utah 84111
Phone: (801)246-5737
Fax: (801)246-5424
Louis D. Alder, Manager
Preferred Investment Size: $500,000 to $1 million. Investment Policies: Loans and/or equity. Investment Types: Expansion, later stage. Industry Preferences: Diversified. Geographic Preferences: West/midwest.

Utah Technology Finance Corp.
177 E., 100 S.
Salt Lake City, Utah 84111
Phone: (801)364-4346
Fax: (801)364-4361
Assists the start-up and growth of emerging technology-based businesses and products.

Utah Ventures
423 Wakara Way, Ste. 206
Salt Lake City, Utah 84108
Phone: (801)583-5922
Fax: (801)583-4105
Invests in the life sciences at an early stage.

Wasatch Venture Corp.
1 S. Main St., Ste. 1000
Salt Lake City, Utah 84133
Phone: (801)524-8939
Fax: (801)524-8941
W. David Hemingway, Manager
Preferred Investment Size: $500,000.
Investment Policies: Equity and debt.
Investment Types: Early stage.
Industry Preferences: High technology. Geographic Preferences: West, midwest, Rocky.

Vermont

Queneska Capital Corp.
123 Church St.

Burlington, Vermont 05401
Phone: (802)865-1806
Fax: (802)865-1891
A small business investment company. Diversified industry preference.

Vermont Economic Development Authority
58 E. State St.
Montpelier, Vermont 05602
Phone: (802)828-5627
Fax: (802)828-5474
Several financial programs to assist small and medium-sized manufacturing firms in the state.

Vermont Economic Development Authority
Vermont Job Start
58 E. State St.
Montpelier, Vermont 05602
Phone: (802)828-5627
Fax: (802)828-5474
A state-funded economic opportunity program aimed at increasing self-employment by low-income Vermonters.

Green Mountain Capital, L.P.
RR 1 Box 1503
Waterbury, Vermont 05676
Phone: (802)244-8981
Fax: (802)244-8990
A small business investment company. Diversified industry preference.

Virgin Islands

Tri-Island Economic Development Council, Inc.
Box 838
St. Thomas, Virgin Islands 00804
Phone: (809)774-7215
Provides counseling, information, referrals, and management and technical assistance to help strengthen existing businesses and expand the rate of development of new businesses.

Virginia

Metropolitan Capital Corp.
2550 Huntington Ave.

Alexandria, Virginia 22303
Phone: (703)550-0747
A small business investment corporation. Equity or loans with equity
features. Does not invest in retail or
real estate.

Continental SBIC
4141 N. Henderson Rd., Ste. 8
Arlington, Virginia 22203
Phone: (703)527-5200
Fax: (703)527-3700
A minority enterprise small business
investment company. Diversified
industry preference.

East West United Investment Co.
(Falls Church)
200 Park Ave.
Falls Church, Virginia 22046-3107
Phone: (703)536-0268
Fax: (703)536-0619
A minority enterprise small business
investment company. Diversified
industry preference.

Rural America Fund, Inc.
2201 Cooperative Way
Herndon, Virginia 22071
Phone: (703)709-6750
Fax: (703)709-6774
Richard Balman
A small business investment com-
pany. Diversified industry preference.

East West United Investment Co.
(McLean)
1568 Spring Hill Rd., Ste. 100
McLean, Virginia 22102
Phone: (703)442-0150
Fax: (703)442-0156
Dung Bui, President

Ewing, Monroe & Co.
E-mail: emcompany@aol.com
901 E. Cary St., Ste. 1410
Richmond, Virginia 23219
Phone: (804)780-1900
Fax: (804)780-1901
A small business investment corpora-
tion. No industry preference.

Virginia Small Business Financing
Authority
PO Box 446
Richmond, Virginia 23218-0446
Phone: (804)371-8254
Fax: (804)225-3384
Assists small businesses in obtaining
financing for development and
expansion.

Walnut Capital Corp. (Vienna)
8000 Towers Crescent Dr., Ste. 1070
Vienna, Virginia 22182-2700
Phone: (703)448-3771
Fax: (703)448-7751
A small business investment corpora-
tion. No industry preference.

Washington

Cable and Howse Ventures (Bellevue)
777 108th Ave. NE, Ste. 2300
Bellevue, Washington 98004
Phone: (206)646-3030
Fax: (206)646-3041
Venture capital investor. Provides
start-up and early stage financing to
enterprises in the western United
States, although a national perspective is maintained. Interests lie in
proprietary or patentable technology.
Investments range from $50,000 to $2
million.

Pacific Northwest Partners SBIC, L.P.
E-mail: pnwp@msn.com
Ste. 800, City Center Bellevue
500 - 108th Ave., NE
Bellevue, Washington 98004
Phone: (206)646-7357
Fax: (206)646-7356
Theodore M Wight, Manager
Preferred Investment Size: $1,000,000.
Investment Policies: Private equity
investments. Investment Types: Seed
Through later stage. Industry Prefer-
ences: Diversified, retail, healthcare,
technology. Geographic Preferences:
Pacific Northwest.

Materia Venture Associates, L.P.
E-mail: materiaventure@msn.com

3435 Carillon Pointe
Kirkland, Washington 98033
Phone: (206)822-4100
Fax: (206)827-4086
Prefers investing in advanced
materials and related technologies.

Olympic Venture Partners (Kirkland)
E-mail: info@ovp.com
2420 Carillon Pt.
Kirkland, Washington 98033-7353
Phone: (206)889-9192
Fax: (206)889-0152
Prefers to fund early stage, technol-
ogy companies in the West.

Washington Department of Community, Trade and Economic Development
Development Loan Fund
906 Columbia St. SW
PO Box 48300
Olympia, Washington 98504-8300
Phone: (360)753-5630
Fax: (360)586-2424
Provides capital for businesses in
distressed areas to create new jobs,
particularly for low and moderate
income persons.

Washington Department of Commu-
nity, Trade and Economic Develop-
ment
Community Development Finance
(CDF) Program
900 Columbia St. SW
PO Box 48300
Olympia, Washington 98504-8300
Phone: (360)753-7426
Fax: (360)586-3582
Helps businesses and industries
secure needed financing by combin-
ing private financial loans with federal
and state loans.

The Phoenix Partners
E-mail: dionnsto@interserv.com
1000 2nd Ave., Ste. 3600
Seattle, Washington 98104
Phone: (206)624-8968
Fax: (206)624-1907
Prefers to invest in companies

involved in biotechnology, health care, medical devices, computer software, semiconductors, and telecommunications.

Washington Department of Community, Trade and Economic Development
Industrial Revenue Bonds
2001 6th Ave., Ste. 2600
Seattle, Washington 98121
Phone: (206)464-7143
Fax: (360)464-7222
Issued to finance the acquisition, construction, enlargement, or improvement of industrial development facilities.

West Virginia

Anker Capital Corp.
E-mail: south-venture@citynet.com
208 Capital St., Ste. 300
Charleston, West Virginia 25301
Phone: (304)344-1794
Fax: (304)344-1798
Thomas Loehr, Manager
Preferred Investment Size: $500,000.
Investment Policies: Combination of debt and equity. Investment Types: Expansion, early stage, spin-off. Industry Preferences: Wood products, computer industry, manufacturing. Geographic Preferences: West Virginia, Ohio, Pennsylvania, Virginia, Maryland.

Shenandoah Venture Capital L.P.
E-mail: south-venture@citynet.com
208 Capital St., Ste. 300
Charleston, West Virginia 25301
Phone: (304)344-1796
Fax: (304)344-1798
Thomas E. Loehr, President

West Virginia Development Office
West Virginia SBA
State Capitol Complex, Bldg 6, Rm. 525
1018 Kanawha Blvd., Ste. 501
Charleston, West Virginia 25305
Phone: (304)558-3650
Fax: (304)558-0206

Provides long-term, fixed-rate loans for small and medium-sized firms.

West Virginia Development Office
West Virginia Economic Development Authority
1018 Kanawha Blvd., E., Ste. 501
Charleston, West Virginia 25301-2827
Phone: (304)558-3650
Fax: (304)558-0206
Provides low-interest loans for land or building acquisition, building construction, and equipment purchases.

WestVen Ltd. Partnership
208 Capitol St., Ste. 300
Charleston, West Virginia 25301
Phone: (304)344-1794
Fax: (304)344-1798
Thomas E. Loehr, President
Preferred Investment Size: $500,000.
Investment Policies: Combination of debt and equity. Investment Types: Expansion, early stage, spin-off. Industry Preferences: Wood products, computer industry, manufacturing. Geographic Preferences: West Virginia, Ohio, Pennsylvania, Virginia, Maryland.

Wisconsin

Impact Seven, Inc.
E-mail: impact@win.bright.net
651 Darvfield
Almena, Wisconsin 54805
Phone: (715)357-3334
Fax: (715)357-6233
Provides equity investment.

Polaris Capital Corp.
2525 N. 124th St., Ste. 200
Brookfield, Wisconsin 53005-4614
Phone: (414)789-5780
Fax: (414)789-5799
A small business investment corporation. Prefers equity-type investments of up to $500,000, expansion stage companies, seasoned companies, and management buyouts. Diversified industry preference, including industrial, electronic products/

equipment, and consumer and business products/services in Wisconsin and northern Illinois.

Madison Development Corp.
550 W. Washington Ave.
Madison, Wisconsin 53703
Phone: (608)256-2799
Fax: (608)256-1560
Provides loans of up to $150,000 to eligible businesses in Dane County for working capital, inventory, equipment, leasehold improvements, and business real estate.

Venture Investors of Wisconsin, Inc. (Madison)
E-mail: viw@macc.wisc.edu
565 Science Dr., Ste. A
Madison, Wisconsin 53711
Phone: (608)233-3070
Fax: (608)238-5120
Venture capital firm providing early-stage financing to Wisconsin-based companies with strong management teams. Areas of interest include biotechnology, software, analytical instruments, medical products, consumer products, and publishing industries.

Venture Investors of Wisconsin, Inc. (Milwaukee)
E-mail: viw@macc.wisc.edu
565 Science Dr., Ste. A
Madison, Wisconsin 53711
Phone: (414)298-3070
Fax: (608)238-5120
Providers of equity financing.

Wisconsin Business Development Finance Corp.
E-mail: wbdfc@waun.tdsnet.com
PO Box 2717
Madison, Wisconsin 53701
Phone: (608)258-8830
Fax: (608)258-1664
Provides small business financing for the purchase of land, buildings, machinery, equipment, and the construction and moderization of facilities.

Wisconsin Department of Development
Wisconsin Development Fund
123 W. Washington Ave.
PO Box 7970
Madison, Wisconsin 53707
Phone: (608)266-2742
Free: (800)HELP-BUS
Fax: (608)264-6151

Wisconsin Housing and Economic
Development Authority
Venture Capital Fund
Economic Development Analyst
1 S. Pinckney St., No. 500
PO Box 1728
Madison, Wisconsin 53701
Phone: (608)266-7884
Free: (800)334-6873
Fax: (608)267-1099
Invests in new and existing businesses that are developing new products.

Wisconsin Innovation Network
Foundation
PO Box 71
Madison, Wisconsin 53701-0071
Phone: (608)256-8348
Fax: (608)256-0333
Seeks to join people with marketing
and sales ideas to those willing to
finance them. Acts as a resource
center for financing information;
offers networking opportunities for
business professionals, entrepreneurs, and small business owners at
regular monthly meetings.

Capital Investment, Inc. (Mequon)
1009 W. Glen Oaks Ln., Ste. 103
Mequon, Wisconsin 53092
Phone: (414)241-0303
Fax: (414)241-8451
James R. Sanger, President
Preferred Investment Size: $500,000 to
$1 million. Investment Policies:
Subordinated debt with warrant.
Investment Types: Expansion, later
stage. Industry Preferences: Manufacturing and value-added distributors.
Geographic Preferences: Midwest,
national.

Banc One Venture Corp. (Milwaukee)
111 E. Wisconsin Ave.
Milwaukee, Wisconsin 53202
Phone: (414)765-3278
H. Wayne Foreman, President
Preferred Investment Size: $1 to $10
million. Investment Types: Later
stage, expansion, LBO, MBO. Industry Preferences: Publishing, distribution, manufacturing, mail-order.
Geographic Preferences: National.

Capital Investments, Inc. (Milwaukee)
700 N. Water St., Ste. 325
Milwaukee, Wisconsin 53202
Phone: (414)278-7744
Free: (800)345-6462
Fax: (414)278-8403
A small business investment corporation. Prefers later-stage companies
located in the Midwest, involved in
manufacturing and specialty distribution.

Future Value Venture, Inc.
330 E. Kilbourn Ave., Ste.711
Milwaukee, Wisconsin 53202
Phone: (414)278-0377
Fax: (414)278-7321
A minority enterprise small business
investment corporation. Diversified
industry preference. Minimum initial
investment is $100,000.

Horizon Partners, Ltd.
225 E. Mason St., Ste. 600
Milwaukee, Wisconsin 53202
Phone: (414)271-2200
Fax: (414)271-4016
Providers of equity financing for low-
to-medium technology industries.

InvestAmerica Venture Group, Inc.
(Milwaukee)
600 E. Mason St., Ste.304
Milwaukee, Wisconsin 53202
Phone: (414)276-3839
Fax: (414)276-1885
A small business investment corporation. Prefers later-stage and acquisition financings of $1,000,000 to
$3,000,000 with equity participation.

Will not consider real estate investments.

Lubar and Co., Inc.
777 E. Wisconsin, Ste. 3380
Milwaukee, Wisconsin 53202
Phone: (414)291-9000
Fax: (414)291-9061
Private investment and management
firm.

M & I Ventures Corp.
770 N. Water St.
Milwaukee, Wisconsin 53202
Phone: (414)765-7700
Free: (800)342-2265
Fax: (414)765-7850
A small business investment corporation. Areas of interest include
manufacturing, technology, electronics, health care, publishing, and
communications industries. Average
investment is from $1 million to $3
million.

MorAmerican Capital Corp. (Milwaukee)
600 E. Mason St., Ste. 304
Milwaukee, Wisconsin 53202
Phone: (414)276-3839
Fax: (414)276-1885
A small business investment company.

Wisconsin Venture Capital Fund
777 E. Wisconsin Ave., Ste. 3380
Milwaukee, Wisconsin 53202
Phone: (414)291-9000
Fax: (414)291-9061

WITECH Corp., Inc.
1000 N. Water, Ste. 1805
PO Box 2949
Milwaukee, Wisconsin 53202
Phone: (414)347-1550
Fax: (414)221-4990
Venture capital firm.

Wind Point Partners (Racine)
420 3 Mile, Apt. B4
Racine, Wisconsin 53402
Phone: (414)639-3113

Fax:(414)639-3417
Venture capital firm.

Bando-McGlocklin SBIC
W239 N. 1700 Busse Rd.
Wakesha, Wisconsin 53188
Phone:(414)523-4300
Fax:(414)523-4193
George Schonath, Chief Executive
Officer
Preferred Investment Size: $3,000,000.
Investment Policies: Loans. Invest-
ment Types: Early stage, expansion,
later stage. Industry Preferences:
Diversified. Geographic Preferences:
Midwest.

Wyoming

Frontier Certified Development Co.
PO Box 3599
Casper, Wyoming 82602
Phone:(307)234-5351
Free:(800)934-5351
Fax:(307)234-0501
Created by the Wyoming Industrial
Development Corporation to provide
expansion financing for Wyoming
business.

Wyoming Industrial Development
Corp.
PO Box 3599
Casper, Wyoming 82602
Phone:(307)234-5351
Free:(800)934-5351
Fax:(307)234-0501
Administers SBA 7(A) and SBA
programs. Purchases the guaranteed
portion of U.S. Small Business
Adminstration and Farmers Home
Administration Loans to small
businesses to pool into a common
fund that enables small businesses to
obtain loans at more reasonable rates
and terms.

Wyoming Department of Commerce
Economic and Community Develop-
ment Division
New Business Retention and Financ-
ing
Barrett Bldg.

6109 Yellowstone
Cheyenne, Wyoming 82002
Phone:(307)777-6418
Fax:(307)777-6005

Appendix C - Glossary of Small Business Terms

Glossary of Small Business Terms

Absolute liability
Liability that is incurred due to product defects or negligent actions. Manufacturers or retail establishments are held responsible, even though the defect or action may not have been intentional or negligent.

ACE
See Active Corps of Executives

Accident and health benefits
Benefits offered to employees and their families in order to offset the costs associated with accidental death, accidental injury, or sickness.

Account statement
A record of transactions, including payments, new debt, and deposits, incurred during a defined period of time.

Accounting system
System capturing the costs of all employees and/or machinery included in business expenses.

Accounts payable
See Trade credit

Accounts receivable
Unpaid accounts which arise from unsettled claims and transactions from the sale of a company's products or services to its customers.

Active Corps of Executives (ACE)
(See also Service Corps of Retired Executives)
A group of volunteers for a management assistance program of the U.S. Small Business Administration; volunteers provide one-on-one counseling and teach workshops and seminars for small firms.

ADA
See Americans with Disabilities Act

Adaptation
The process whereby an invention is modified to meet the needs of users.

Adaptive engineering
The process whereby an invention is modified to meet the manufacturing and commercial requirements of a targeted market.

Adverse selection
The tendency for higher-risk individuals to purchase health care and more comprehensive plans, resulting in increased costs.

Advertising
A marketing tool used to capture public attention and influence purchasing decisions for a product or service. Utilizes various forms of media to generate consumer response, such as flyers, magazines, newspapers, radio, and television.

Age discrimination
The denial of the rights and privileges of employment based solely on the age of an individual.

Agency costs
Costs incurred to insure that the lender or investor maintains control over assets while allowing the borrower or entrepreneur to use them. Monitoring and information costs are the two major types of agency costs.

Agribusiness
The production and sale of commodities and products from the commercial farming industry.

America Online
(See also Prodigy)
An online service which is accessible by computer modem. The service features Internet access, bulletin boards, online periodicals, electronic mail, and other services for subscribers.

Americans with Disabilities Act (ADA)
Law designed to ensure equal access and opportunity to handicapped persons.

Annual report
(See also Securities and Exchange Commission)
Yearly financial report prepared by a business that adheres to the requirements set forth by the Securities and Exchange Commission (SEC).

Antitrust immunity
(See also Collective ratemaking)
Exemption from prosecution under antitrust laws. In the transportation industry, firms with antitrust immunity are

permitted—under certain conditions—to set schedules and sometimes prices for the public benefit.

Applied research
Scientific study targeted for use in a product or process.

Asians
A minority category used by the U.S. Bureau of the Census to represent a diverse group that includes Aleuts, Eskimos, American Indians, Asian Indians, Chinese, Japanese, Koreans, Vietnamese, Filipinos, Hawaiians, and other Pacific Islanders.

Assets
Anything of value owned by a company.

Audit
The verification of accounting records and business procedures conducted by an outside accounting service.

Average cost
Total production costs divided by the quantity produced.

Balance Sheet
A financial statement listing the total assets and liabilities of a company at a given time.

Bankruptcy
(See also Chapter 7 of the 1978 Bankruptcy Act; Chapter 11 of the 1978 Bankruptcy Act)
The condition in which a business cannot meet its debt obligations and petitions a federal district court either for reorganization of its debts (Chapter 11) or for liquidation of its assets (Chapter 7).

Basic research
Theoretical scientific exploration not targeted to application.

Basket clause
A provision specifying the amount of public pension funds that may be placed in investments not included on a state's legal list (see separate citation).

BBS
See Bulletin Board Service

BDC
See Business development corporation

Benefit
Various services, such health care, flextime, day care, insurance, and vacation, offered to employees as part of a hiring package. Typically subsidized in whole or in part by the business.

BIDCO
See Business and industrial development company

Billing cycle
A system designed to evenly distribute customer billing throughout the month, preventing clerical backlogs.

Birth
See Business birth

Blue chip security
A low-risk, low-yield security representing an interest in a very stable company.

Blue sky laws
A general term that denotes various states' laws regulating securities.

Bond
(See also General obligation bond; Taxable bonds; Treasury bonds)
A written instrument executed by a bidder or contractor (the principal) and a second party (the surety or sureties) to assure fulfillment of the principal's obligations to a third party (the obligee or government) identified in the bond. If the principal's obligations are not met, the bond assures payment to the extent stipulated of any loss sustained by the obligee.

Bonding requirements
Terms contained in a bond (see separate citation).

Bonus
An amount of money paid to an employee as a reward for achieving certain business goals or objectives.

Brainstorming
A group session where employees contribute their ideas for solving a problem or meeting a company objective without fear of retribution or ridicule.

Brand name
The part of a brand, trademark, or service mark that can be spoken. It can be a word, letter, or group of words or letters.

Bridge financing
A short-term loan made in expectation of intermediate-term or long-term financing. Can be used when a company plans to go public in the near future.

Broker
One who matches resources available for innovation with those who need them.

Budget

An estimate of the spending necessary to complete a project or offer a service in comparison to cash-on-hand and expected earnings for the coming year, with an emphasis on cost control.

Bulletin Board Service (BBS)

An online service enabling users to communicate with each other about specific topics.

Business birth

The formation of a new establishment or enterprise. The appearance of a new establishment or enterprise in the Small Business Data Base (see separate citation).

Business conditions

Outside factors that can affect the financial performance of a business.

Business contractions

The number of establishments that have decreased in employment during a specified time.

Business cycle

A period of economic recession and recovery. These cycles vary in duration.

Business death

The voluntary or involuntary closure of a firm or establishment. The disappearance of an establishment or enterprise from the Small Business Data Base (see separate citation).

Business development corporation (BDC)

A business financing agency, usually composed of the financial institutions in an area or state, organized to assist in financing businesses unable to obtain assistance through normal channels; the risk is spread among various members of the business development corporation, and interest rates may vary somewhat from those charged by member institutions. A venture capital firm in which shares of ownership are publicly held and to which the Investment Act of 1940 applies.

Business dissolution

For enumeration purposes, the absence of a business that was present in the prior time period from any current record.

Business entry

See Business birth

Business ethics

Moral values and principles espoused by members of the business community as a guide to fair and honest business practices.

Business exit

See Business death

Business expansions

The number of establishments that added employees during a specified time.

Business failure

Closure of a business causing a loss to at least one creditor.

Business format franchising

(See also Franchising)

The purchase of the name, trademark, and an ongoing business plan of the parent corporation or franchisor by the franchisee.

Business and industrial development company (BIDCO)

A private, for-profit financing corporation chartered by the state to provide both equity and long-term debt capital to small business owners (see separate citations for equity and debt capital).

Business license

A legal authorization issued by municipal and state governments and required for business operations.

Business name

(See also Business license; Trademark)

Enterprises must register their business names with local governments usually on a "doing business as" (DBA) form. (This name is sometimes referred to as a "fictional name.") The procedure is part of the business licensing process and prevents any other business from using that same name for a similar business in the same locality.

Business norms

See Financial ratios

Business permit

See Business license

Business plan

A document that spells out a company's expected course of action for a specified period, usually including a detailed listing and analysis of risks and uncertainties. For the small business, it should examine the proposed products, the market, the industry, the management policies, the marketing policies, production needs, and financial needs. Frequently, it is used as a prospectus for potential investors and lenders.

Business proposal

See Business plan

Business service firm
An establishment primarily engaged in rendering services to other business organizations on a fee or contract basis.

Business start
For enumeration purposes, a business with a name or similar designation that did not exist in a prior time period.

Cafeteria plan
See Flexible benefit plan

Capacity
Level of a firm's, industry's, or nation's output corresponding to full practical utilization of available resources.

Capital
Assets less liabilities, representing the ownership interest in a business. A stock of accumulated goods, especially at a specified time and in contrast to income received during a specified time period. Accumulated goods devoted to production. Accumulated possessions calculated to bring income.

Capital expenditure
Expenses incurred by a business for improvements that will depreciate over time.

Capital gain
The monetary difference between the purchase price and the selling price of capital. Capital gains are taxed at a rate of 28% by the federal government.

Capital intensity
(See also Debt capital; Equity midrisk venture capital; Informal capital; Internal capital; Owner's capital; Secondhand capital; Seed capital; Venture capital)
The relative importance of capital in the production process, usually expressed as the ratio of capital to labor but also sometimes as the ratio of capital to output.

Capital resource
The equipment, facilities and labor used to create products and services.

Caribbean Basin Initiative
An interdisciplinary program to support commerce among the businesses in the nations of the Caribbean Basin and the United States. Agencies involved include: the Agency for International Development, the U.S. Small Business Administration, the International Trade Administration of the U.S. Department of Commerce, and various private sector groups.

Catastrophic care
Medical and other services for acute and long-term illnesses that cost more than insurance coverage limits or that cost the amount most families may be expected to pay with their own resources.

CDC
See Certified development corporation

CD-ROM
Compact disc with read-only memory used to store large amounts of digitized data.

Certified development corporation (CDC)
A local area or statewide corporation or authority (for profit or nonprofit) that packages U.S. Small Business Administration (SBA), bank, state, and/or private money into financial assistance for existing business capital improvements. The SBA holds the second lien on its maximum share of 40 percent involvement. Each state has at least one certified development corporation. This program is called the SBA 504 Program.

Certified lenders
Banks that participate in the SBA guaranteed loan program (see separate citation). Such banks must have a good track record with the U.S. Small Business Administration (SBA) and must agree to certain conditions set forth by the agency. In return, the SBA agrees to process any guaranteed loan application within three business days.

Champion
An advocate for the development of an innovation.

Channel of distribution
The means used to transport merchandise from the manufacturer to the consumer.

Chapter 7 of the 1978 Bankruptcy Act
Provides for a court-appointed trustee who is responsible for liquidating a company's assets in order to settle outstanding debts.

Chapter 11 of the 1978 Bankruptcy Act
Allows the business owners to retain control of the company while working with their creditors to reorganize their finances and establish better business practices to prevent liquidation of assets.

Closely held corporation
A corporation in which the shares are held by a few persons, usually officers, employees, or others close to the management; these shares are rarely offered to the public.

Code of Federal Regulations
Codification of general and permanent rules of the federal government published in the Federal Register.

Code sharing
See Computer code sharing

Coinsurance
(See also Cost sharing)
Upon meeting the deductible payment, health insurance participants may be required to make additional health care cost-sharing payments. Coinsurance is a payment of a fixed percentage of the cost of each service; copayment is usually a fixed amount to be paid with each service.

Collateral
Securities, evidence of deposit, or other property pledged by a borrower to secure repayment of a loan.

Collective ratemaking
(See also Antitrust immunity)
The establishment of uniform charges for services by a group of businesses in the same industry.

Commercial insurance plan
See Underwriting

Commercial loans
Short-term renewable loans used to finance specific capital needs of a business.

Commercialization
The final stage of the innovation process, including production and distribution.

Common stock
The most frequently used instrument for purchasing ownership in private or public companies. Common stock generally carries the right to vote on certain corporate actions and may pay dividends, although it rarely does in venture investments. In liquidation, common stockholders are the last to share in the proceeds from the sale of a corporation's assets; bondholders and preferred shareholders have priority. Common stock is often used in first-round start-up financing.

Community development corporation
A corporation established to develop economic programs for a community and, in most cases, to provide financial support for such development.

Competitor
A business whose product or service is marketed for the same purpose/use and to the same consumer group as the product or service of another.

Computer code sharing
An arrangement whereby flights of a regional airline are identified by the two-letter code of a major carrier in the computer reservation system to help direct passengers to new regional carriers.

Consignment
A merchandising agreement, usually referring to second-hand shops, where the dealer pays the owner of an item a percentage of the profit when the item is sold.

Consortium
A coalition of organizations such as banks and corporations for ventures requiring large capital resources.

Consultant
An individual that is paid by a business to provide advice and expertise in a particular area.

Consumer price index
A measure of the fluctuation in prices between two points in time.

Consumer research
Research conducted by a business to obtain information about existing or potential consumer markets.

Continuation coverage
Health coverage offered for a specified period of time to employees who leave their jobs and to their widows, divorced spouses, or dependents.

Contractions
See Business contractions

Convertible preferred stock
A class of stock that pays a reasonable dividend and is convertible into common stock (see separate citation). Generally the convertible feature may only be exercised after being held for a stated period of time. This arrangement is usually considered second-round financing when a company needs equity to maintain its cash flow.

Convertible securities
A feature of certain bonds, debentures, or preferred stocks that allows them to be exchanged by the owner for another class of securities at a future date and in accordance with any other terms of the issue.

Copayment
See Coinsurance

Copyright
A legal form of protection available to creators and authors to safeguard their works from unlawful use or

claim of ownership by others. Copyrights may be acquired for works of art, sculpture, music, and published or unpublished manuscripts. All copyrights should be registered at the Copyright Office of the Library of Congress.

Corporate financial ratios
(See also Industry financial ratios)
The relationship between key figures found in a company's financial statement expressed as a numeric value. Used to evaluate risk and company performance. Also known as Financial averages, Operating ratios, and Business ratios.

Corporation
A legal entity, chartered by a state or the federal government, recognized as a separate entity having its own rights, privileges, and liabilities distinct from those of its members.

Cost containment
Actions taken by employers and insurers to curtail rising health care costs; for example, increasing employee cost sharing (see separate citation), requiring second opinions, or preadmission screening.

Cost sharing
The requirement that health care consumers contribute to their own medical care costs through deductibles and coinsurance (see separate citations). Cost sharing does not include the amounts paid in premiums. It is used to control utilization of services; for example, requiring a fixed amount to be paid with each health care service.

Cottage industry
(See also Home-based business)
Businesses based in the home in which the family members are the labor force and family-owned equipment is used to process the goods.

Credit Rating
A letter or number calculated by an organization (such as Dun & Bradstreet) to represent the ability and disposition of a business to meet its financial obligations.

Customer service
Various techniques used to ensure the satisfaction of a customer.

Cyclical peak
The upper turning point in a business cycle.

Cyclical trough
The lower turning point in a business cycle.

DBA
See Business name

Death
See Business death

Debenture
A certificate given as acknowledgment of a debt (see separate citation) secured by the general credit of the issuing corporation. A bond, usually without security, issued by a corporation and sometimes convertible to common stock.

Debt
(See also Long-term debt; Mid-term debt; Securitized debt; Short-term debt)
Something owed by one person to another. Financing in which a company receives capital that must be repaid; no ownership is transferred.

Debt capital
Business financing that normally requires periodic interest payments and repayment of the principal within a specified time.

Debt financing
See Debt capital

Debt securities
Loans such as bonds and notes that provide a specified rate of return for a specified period of time.

Deductible
A set amount that an individual must pay before any benefits are received.

Demand shock absorbers
A term used to describe the role that some small firms play by expanding their output levels to accommodate a transient surge in demand.

Demographics
Statistics on various markets, including age, income, and education, used to target specific products or services to appropriate consumer groups.

Demonstration
Showing that a product or process has been modified sufficiently to meet the needs of users.

Deregulation
The lifting of government restrictions; for example, the lifting of government restrictions on the entry of new businesses, the expansion of services, and the setting of prices in particular industries.

Desktop Publishing
Using personal computers and specialized software to produce camera-ready copy for publications.

Disaster loans
Various types of physical and economic assistance available to individuals and businesses through the U.S. Small Business Administration (SBA). This is the only SBA loan program available for residential purposes.

Discrimination
The denial of the rights and privileges of employment based on factors such as age, race, religion, or gender.

Diseconomies of scale
The condition in which the costs of production increase faster than the volume of production.

Dissolution
See Business dissolution

Distribution
Delivering a product or process to the user.

Distributor
One who delivers merchandise to the user.

Diversified company
A company whose products and services are used by several different markets.

Doing business as (DBA)
See Business name

Dow Jones
An information services company that publishes the Wall Street Journal and other sources of financial information.

Dow Jones Industrial Average
An indicator of stock market performance.

Earned income
A tax term that refers to wages and salaries earned by the recipient, as opposed to monies earned through interest and dividends.

Economic efficiency
The use of productive resources to the fullest practical extent in the provision of the set of goods and services that is most preferred by purchasers in the economy.

Economic indicators
Statistics used to express the state of the economy. These include the length of the average work week, the rate of unemployment, and stock prices.

Economically disadvantaged
See Socially and economically disadvantaged

Economies of scale
See Scale economies

EEOC
See Equal Employment Opportunity Commission

8(a) Program
A program authorized by the Small Business Act that directs federal contracts to small businesses owned and operated by socially and economically disadvantaged individuals.

Electronic mail (e-mail)
The electronic transmission of mail via phone lines.

E-mail
See Electronic mail

Employee leasing.
A contract by which employers arrange to have their workers hired by a leasing company and then leased back to them for a management fee. The leasing company typically assumes the administrative burden of payroll and provides a benefit package to the workers.

Employee tenure
The length of time an employee works for a particular employer.

Employer identification number
The business equivalent of a social security number. Assigned by the U.S. Internal Revenue Service.

Enterprise
An aggregation of all establishments owned by a parent company. An enterprise may consist of a single, independent establishment or include subsidiaries and other branches under the same ownership and control.

Enterprise zone
A designated area, usually found in inner cities and other areas with significant unemployment, where businesses receive tax credits and other incentives to entice them to establish operations there.

Entrepreneur
A person who takes the risk of organizing and operating a new business venture.

Entry
See Business entry

Equal Employment Opportunity Commission (EEOC)
A federal agency that ensures nondiscrimination in the hiring and firing practices of a business.

Equal opportunity employer
An employer who adheres to the standards set by the Equal Employment Opportunity Commission (see separate citation).

Equity
(See also Common Stock; Equity midrisk venture capital)
The ownership interest. Financing in which partial or total ownership of a company is surrendered in exchange for capital. An investor's financial return comes from dividend payments and from growth in the net worth of the business.

Equity capital
See Equity; Equity midrisk venture capital

Equity financing
See Equity; Equity midrisk venture capital

Equity midrisk venture capital
An unsecured investment in a company. Usually a purchase of ownership interest in a company that occurs in the later stages of a company's development.

Equity partnership
A limited partnership arrangement for providing start-up and seed capital to businesses.

Equity securities
See Equity

Equity-type
Debt financing subordinated to conventional debt.

Establishment
A single-location business unit that may be independent (a single-establishment enterprise) or owned by a parent enterprise.

Establishment and Enterprise Microdata File
See U.S. Establishment and Enterprise Microdata File

Establishment birth
See Business birth

Establishment Longitudinal Microdata File
See U.S. Establishment Longitudinal Microdata File

Ethics
See Business ethics

Evaluation
Determining the potential success of translating an invention into a product or process.

Exit
See Business exit

Experience rating
See Underwriting *Export*
A product sold outside of the country.

Export license
A general or specific license granted by the U.S. Department of Commerce required of anyone wishing to export goods. Some restricted articles need approval from the U.S. Departments of State, Defense, or Energy.

Failure
See Business failure

Fair share agreement
(See also Franchising)
An agreement reached between a franchisor and a minority business organization to extend business ownership to minorities by either reducing the amount of capital required or by setting aside certain marketing areas for minority business owners.

Feasibility study
A study to determine the likelihood that a proposed product or development will fulfill the objectives of a particular investor.

Federal Trade Commission (FTC)
Federal agency that promotes free enterprise and competition within the U.S.

Federal Trade Mark Act of 1946
See Lanham Act

Fictional name
See Business name

Fiduciary
An individual or group that hold assets in trust for a beneficiary.

Financial analysis
The techniques used to determine money needs in a business. Techniques include ratio analysis, calculation of return on investment, guides for measuring profitability, and break-even analysis to determine ultimate success.

Financial intermediary
A financial institution that acts as the intermediary between borrowers and lenders. Banks, savings and loan associations, finance companies, and venture capital companies are major financial intermediaries in the United States.

Financial ratios
See Corporate financial ratios; Industry financial ratios

Financial statement
A written record of business finances, including balance sheets and profit and loss statements.

Financing
See First-stage financing; Second-stage financing; Third-stage financing

First-stage financing
(See also Second-stage financing; Third-stage financing)
Financing provided to companies that have expended their initial capital, and require funds to start full-scale manufacturing and sales. Also known as First-round financing.

Fiscal year
Any twelve-month period used by businesses for accounting purposes.

504 Program
See Certified development corporation

Flexible benefit plan
A plan that offers a choice among cash and/or qualified benefits such as group term life insurance, accident and health insurance, group legal services, dependent care assistance, and vacations.

FOB
See Free on board

Format franchising
See Business format franchising; Franchising

401(k) plan
A financial plan where employees contribute a percentage of their earnings to a fund that is invested in stocks, bonds, or money markets for the purpose of saving money for retirement.

Four Ps
Marketing terms referring to Product, Price, Place, and Promotion.

Franchising
A form of licensing by which the owner—the franchisor—distributes or markets a product, method, or service through affiliated dealers called franchisees. The product, method, or service being marketed is identified by a brand name, and the franchisor maintains control over the marketing methods employed. The franchisee is often given exclusive access to a defined geographic area.

Free on board (FOB)
A pricing term indicating that the quoted price includes the cost of loading goods into transport vessels at a specified place.

Frictional unemployment
See Unemployment

FTC
See Federal Trade Commission

Fulfillment
The systems necessary for accurate delivery of an ordered item, including subscriptions and direct marketing.

Full-time workers
Generally, those who work a regular schedule of more than 35 hours per week.

Garment registration number
A number that must appear on every garment sold in the U.S. to indicate the manufacturer of the garment, which may or may not be the same as the label under which the garment is sold. The U.S. Federal Trade Commission assigns and regulates garment registration numbers.

Gatekeeper
A key contact point for entry into a network.

GDP
See Gross domestic product

General obligation bond
A municipal bond secured by the taxing power of the municipality. The Tax Reform Act of 1986 limits the purposes for which such bonds may be issued and establishes volume limits on the extent of their issuance.

GNP
See Gross national product

Good Housekeeping Seal
Seal appearing on products that signifies the fulfillment of the standards set by the Good Housekeeping Institute to protect consumer interests.

Goods sector
All businesses producing tangible goods, including agriculture, mining, construction, and manufacturing businesses.

GPO
See Gross product originating

Gross domestic product (GDP)
The part of the nation's gross national product (see separate citation) generated by private business using resources from within the country.

Gross national product (GNP)
The most comprehensive single measure of aggregate economic output. Represents the market value of the total output of goods and services produced by a nation's economy.

Gross product originating (GPO)
A measure of business output estimated from the income or production side using employee compensation, profit income, net interest, capital consumption, and indirect business taxes.

HAL
See Handicapped assistance loan program

Handicapped assistance loan program (HAL)
Low-interest direct loan program through the U.S. Small Business Administration (SBA) for handicapped persons. The SBA requires that these persons demonstrate that their disability is such that it is impossible for them to secure employment, thus making it necessary to go into their own business to make a living.

Health maintenance organization (HMO)
Organization of physicians and other health care professionals that provides health services to subscribers and their dependents on a prepaid basis.

Health provider
An individual or institution that gives medical care. Under Medicare, an institutional provider is a hospital, skilled nursing facility, home health agency, or provider of certain physical therapy services.

Hispanic
A person of Cuban, Mexican, Puerto Rican, Latin American (Central or South American), European Spanish, or other Spanish-speaking origin or ancestry.

HMO
See Health maintenance organization

Home-based business
(See also Cottage industry)
A business with an operating address that is also a residential address (usually the residential address of the proprietor).

Hub-and-spoke system
A system in which flights of an airline from many different cities (the spokes) converge at a single airport (the hub). After allowing passengers sufficient time to make connections, planes then depart for different cities.

Human Resources Management
A business program designed to oversee recruiting, pay, benefits, and other issues related to the company's work force, including planning to determine the optimal use of labor to increase production, thereby increasing profit.

Idea
An original concept for a new product or process.

Import
Products produced outside the country in which they are consumed.

Income
Money or its equivalent, earned or accrued, resulting from the sale of goods and services.

Income statement
A financial statement that lists the profits and losses of a company at a given time.

Incorporation
The filing of a certificate of incorporation with a state's secretary of state, thereby limiting the business owner's liability.

Incubator
A facility designed to encourage entrepreneurship and minimize obstacles to new business formation and growth, particularly for high-technology firms, by housing a number of fledgling enterprises that share an array of services, such as meeting areas, secretarial services, accounting, research library, on-site financial and management counseling, and word processing facilities.

Independent contractor
An individual considered self-employed (see separate citation) and responsible for paying Social Security taxes and income taxes on earnings.

Indirect health coverage
Health insurance obtained through another individual's health care plan; for example, a spouse's employer-sponsored plan.

Industrial development authority
The financial arm of a state or other political subdivision established for the purpose of financing economic development in an area, usually through loans to non-profit organizations, which in turn provide facilities for manufacturing and other industrial operations.

Industry financial ratios
(See also Corporate financial ratios)
Corporate financial ratios averaged for a specified industry. These are used for comparison purposes and reveal industry trends and identify differences between the performance of a specific company and the performance of its industry. Also known as Industrial averages, Industry ratios, Financial averages, and Business or Industrial norms.

Inflation
Increases in volume of currency and credit, generally resulting in a sharp and continuing rise in price levels.

Informal capital
Financing from informal, unorganized sources; includes informal debt capital such as trade credit or loans from friends and relatives and equity capital from informal investors.

Initial public offering (IPO)
A corporation's first offering of stock to the public.

Innovation
The introduction of a new idea into the marketplace in the form of a new product or service or an improvement in organization or process.

Intellectual property
Any idea or work that can be considered proprietary in nature and is thus protected from infringement by others.

Internal capital
Debt or equity financing obtained from the owner or through retained business earnings.

Internet
A government-designed computer network that contains large amounts of information and is accessible through various vendors for a fee.

Intrapreneurship
The state of employing entrepreneurial principles to nonentrepreneurial situations.

Invention
The tangible form of a technological idea, which could include a laboratory prototype, drawings, formulas, etc.

IPO
See Initial public offering

Job description
The duties and responsibilities required in a particular position.

Job tenure
A period of time during which an individual is continuously employed in the same job.

Joint marketing agreements
Agreements between regional and major airlines, often involving the coordination of flight schedules, fares, and baggage transfer. These agreements help regional carriers operate at lower cost.

Joint venture
Venture in which two or more people combine efforts in a particular business enterprise, usually a single transaction or a limited activity, and agree to share the profits and losses jointly or in proportion to their contributions.

Keogh plan
Designed for self-employed persons and unincorporated businesses as a tax-deferred pension account.

Labor force
Civilians considered eligible for employment who are also willing and able to work.

Labor force participation rate
The civilian labor force as a percentage of the civilian population.

Labor intensity
(See also Capital intensity)
The relative importance of labor in the production process, usually measured as the capital-labor ratio; i.e., the ratio of units of capital (typically, dollars of tangible assets) to the number of employees. The higher the capital-labor ratio exhibited by a firm or industry, the lower the capital intensity of that firm or industry is said to be.

Labor surplus area
An area in which there exists a high unemployment rate. In procurement (see separate citation), extra points are given to firms in counties that are designated a labor surplus area; this information is requested on procurement bid sheets.

Labor union
An organization of similarly-skilled workers who collectively bargain with management over the conditions of employment.

Laboratory prototype
See Prototype

LAN
See Local Area Network

Lanham Act
Refers to the Federal Trade Mark Act of 1946. Protects registered trademarks, trade names, and other service marks used in commerce.

Large business-dominated industry
Industry in which a minimum of 60 percent of employment or sales is in firms with more than 500 workers.

LBO
See Leveraged buy-out

Leader pricing
A reduction in the price of a good or service in order to generate more sales of that good or service.

Legal list
A list of securities selected by a state in which certain institutions and fiduciaries (such as pension funds, insurance companies, and banks) may invest. Securities not on the list are not eligible for investment. Legal lists typically restrict investments to high quality securities meeting certain specifications. Generally, investment is limited to U.S. securities and investment-grade blue chip securities (see separate citation).

Leveraged buy-out (LBO)
The purchase of a business or a division of a corporation through a highly leveraged financing package.

Liability
An obligation or duty to perform a service or an act. Also defined as money owed.

License
(See also Business license)
A legal agreement granting to another the right to use a technological innovation.

Limited partnerships
See Venture capital limited partnerships

Liquidity
The ability to convert a security into cash promptly.

Loans
See Commercial loans; Disaster loans; SBA direct loans; SBA guaranteed loans; SBA special lending institution categories

Local Area Network (LAN)
Computer networks contained within a single building or small area; used to facilitate the sharing of information.

Local development corporation
An organization, usually made up of local citizens of a community, designed to improve the economy of the area by inducing business and industry to locate and expand there. A local development corporation establishes a capability to finance local growth.

Long-haul rates
Rates charged by a transporter in which the distance traveled is more than 800 miles.

Long-term debt
An obligation that matures in a period that exceeds five years.

Low-grade bond
A corporate bond that is rated below investment grade by the major rating agencies (Standard and Poor's, Moody's).

Macro-efficiency
(See also Economic efficiency)
Efficiency as it pertains to the operation of markets and market systems.

Managed care
A cost-effective health care program initiated by employers whereby low-cost health care is made available to the employees in return for exclusive patronage to program doctors.

Management and technical assistance
A term used by many programs to mean business (as opposed to technological) assistance.

Management Assistance Programs
See SBA Management Assistance Programs

Mandated benefits
Specific treatments, providers, or individuals required by law to be included in commercial health plans.

Market evaluation
The use of market information to determine the sales potential of a specific product or process.

Market failure
The situation in which the workings of a competitive market do not produce the best results from the point of view of the entire society.

Market information
Data of any type that can be used for market evaluation, which could include demographic data, technology forecasting, regulatory changes, etc.

Market research
A systematic collection, analysis, and reporting of data about the market and its preferences, opinions, trends, and plans; used for corporate decision-making.

Market share
In a particular market, the percentage of sales of a specific product.

Marketing
Promotion of goods or services through various media.

Master Establishment List (MEL)
A list of firms in the United States developed by the U.S. Small Business Administration; firms can be selected by industry, region, state, standard metropolitan statistical area (see separate citation), county, and zip code.

Maturity
(See also Term)
The date upon which the principal or stated value of a bond or other indebtedness becomes due and payable.

Medicaid (Title XIX)
A federally aided, state-operated and administered program that provides medical benefits for certain low-income persons in need of health and medical care who are eligible for one of the government's welfare cash payment programs, including the aged, the blind, the disabled, and members of families with dependent children where one parent is absent, incapacitated, or unemployed.

Medicare (Title XVIII)
A nationwide health insurance program for disabled and aged persons. Health insurance is available to insured persons without regard to income. Monies from payroll taxes cover hospital insurance and monies from general revenues and beneficiary premiums pay for supplementary medical insurance.

MEL
See Master Establishment List

MESBIC
See Minority enterprise small business investment corporation

MET
See Multiple employer trust

Metropolitan statistical area (MSA)
A means used by the government to define large population centers that may transverse different governmental jurisdictions. For example, the Washington, D.C. MSA includes the District of Columbia and contiguous parts of Maryland and Virginia because all of these geopolitical areas comprise one population and economic operating unit.

Mezzanine financing
See Third-stage financing

Micro-efficiency
(See also Economic efficiency)
Efficiency as it pertains to the operation of individual firms.

Microdata
Information on the characteristics of an individual business firm.

Mid-term debt
An obligation that matures within one to five years.

Midrisk venture capital
See Equity midrisk venture capital

Minimum premium plan
A combination approach to funding an insurance plan aimed primarily at premium tax savings. The employer self-funds a fixed percentage of estimated monthly claims and the insurance company insures the excess.

Minimum wage
The lowest hourly wage allowed by the federal government.

Minority Business Development Agency
Contracts with private firms throughout the nation to sponsor Minority Business Development Centers which provide minority firms with advice and technical assistance on a fee basis.

Minority Enterprise Small Business Investment Corporation (MESBIC)
A federally funded private venture capital firm licensed by the U.S. Small Business Administration to provide capital to minority-owned businesses (see separate citation).

Minority-owned business
Businesses owned by those who are socially or economically disadvantaged (see separate citation).

Mom and Pop business
A small store or enterprise having limited capital, principally employing family members.

Moonlighter
A wage-and-salary worker with a side business.

MSA
See Metropolitan statistical area

Multi-employer plan
A health plan to which more than one employer is required to contribute and that may be maintained through a collective bargaining agreement and required to meet standards prescribed by the U.S. Department of Labor.

Multimedia
The use of several types of media to promote a product or service. Also, refers to the use of several different types of media (sight, sound, pictures, text) in a CD-ROM (see separate citation) product.

Multiple employer trust (MET)
A self-funded benefit plan generally geared toward small employers sharing a common interest.

NAFTA
See North American Free Trade Agreement

NASDAQ
See National Association of Securities Dealers Automated Quotations

National Association of Securities Dealers Automated Quotations
Provides price quotes on over-the-counter securities as well as securities listed on the New York Stock Exchange.

National income
Aggregate earnings of labor and property arising from the production of goods and services in a nation's economy.

Net assets
See Net worth

Net income
The amount remaining from earnings and profits after all expenses and costs have been met or deducted. Also known as Net earnings.

Net profit
Money earned after production and overhead expenses (see separate citations) have been deducted.

Net worth
(See also Capital)
The difference between a company's total assets and its total liabilities.

Network
A chain of interconnected individuals or organizations sharing information and/or services.

New York Stock Exchange (NYSE)
The oldest stock exchange in the U.S. Allows for trading in stocks, bonds, warrants, options, and rights that meet listing requirements.

Niche
A career or business for which a person is well-suited. Also, a product which fulfills one need of a particular market segment, often with little or no competition.

Nodes
One workstation in a network, either local area or wide area (see separate citations).

Nonbank bank
A bank that either accepts deposits or makes loans, but not both. Used to create many new branch banks.

Noncompetitive awards
A method of contracting whereby the federal government negotiates with only one contractor to supply a product or service.

Nonmember bank
A state-regulated bank that does not belong to the federal bank system.

Nonprofit
An organization that has no shareholders, does not distribute profits, and is without federal and state tax liabilities.

Norms
See Financial ratios

North American Free Trade Agreement (NAFTA)
Passed in 1993, NAFTA eliminates trade barriers among businesses in the U.S., Canada, and Mexico.

NYSE
See New York Stock Exchange

Occupational Safety & Health Administration (OSHA)
Federal agency that regulates health and safety standards within the workplace.

Optimal firm size
The business size at which the production cost per unit of output (average cost) is, in the long run, at its minimum.

Organizational chart
A hierarchical chart tracking the chain of command within an organization.

OSHA
See Occupational Safety & Health Administration

Overhead
Expenses, such as employee benefits and building utilities, incurred by a business that are unrelated to the actual product or service sold.

Owner's capital
Debt or equity funds provided by the owner(s) of a business; sources of owner's capital are personal savings, sales of assets, or loans from financial institutions.

P & L
See Profit and loss statement

Part-time workers
Normally, those who work less than 35 hours per week. The Tax Reform Act indicated that part-time workers who work less than 17.5 hours per week may be excluded from health plans for purposes of complying with federal nondiscrimination rules.

Part-year workers
Those who work less than 50 weeks per year.

Partnership
Two or more parties who enter into a legal relationship to conduct business for profit. Defined by the U.S. Internal Revenue Code as joint ventures, syndicates, groups, pools, and other associations of two or more persons organized for profit that are not specifically classified in the IRS code as corporations or proprietorships.

Patent
A grant made by the government assuring an inventor the sole right to make, use, and sell an invention for a period of 17 years.

PC
See Professional corporation

Peak
See Cyclical peak

Pension
A series of payments made monthly, semiannually, annually, or at other specified intervals during the lifetime of the pensioner for distribution upon retirement. The term is sometimes used to denote the portion of the retirement allowance financed by the employer's contributions.

Pension fund
A fund established to provide for the payment of pension benefits; the collective contributions made by all of the parties to the pension plan.

Performance appraisal
An established set of objective criteria, based on job description and requirements, that is used to evaluate the performance of an employee in a specific job.

Permit
See Business license

Plan
See Business plan

Pooling
An arrangement for employers to achieve efficiencies and lower health costs by joining together to purchase group health insurance or self-insurance.

PPO
See Preferred provider organization

Preferred lenders program
See SBA special lending institution categories

Preferred provider organization (PPO)
A contractual arrangement with a health care services organization that agrees to discount its health care rates in return for faster payment and/or a patient base.

Premiums
The amount of money paid to an insurer for health insurance under a policy. The premium is generally paid periodically (e.g., monthly), and often is split between the employer and the employee. Unlike deductibles and coinsurance or copayments, premiums are paid for coverage whether or not benefits are actually used.

Prime-age workers
Employees 25 to 54 years of age.

Prime contract
A contract awarded directly by the U.S. Federal Government.

Private company
See Closely held corporation

Private placement

A method of raising capital by offering for sale an investment or business to a small group of investors (generally avoiding registration with the Securities and Exchange Commission or state securities registration agencies). Also known as Private financing or Private offering.

Pro forma

The use of hypothetical figures in financial statements to represent future expenditures, debts, and other potential financial expenses.

Proactive

Taking the initiative to solve problems and anticipate future events before they happen, instead of reacting to an already existing problem or waiting for a difficult situation to occur.

Procurement

(See also 8(a) Program; Small business set asides)
A contract from an agency of the federal government for goods or services from a small business.

Prodigy

(See also America Online)
An online service which is accessible by computer modem. The service features Internet access, bulletin boards, online periodicals, electronic mail, and other services for subscribers.

Product development

The stage of the innovation process where research is translated into a product or process through evaluation, adaptation, and demonstration.

Product franchising

An arrangement for a franchisee to use the name and to produce the product line of the franchisor or parent corporation.

Production

The manufacture of a product.

Production prototype

See Prototype

Productivity

A measurement of the number of goods produced during a specific amount of time.

Professional corporation (PC)

Organized by members of a profession such as medicine, dentistry, or law for the purpose of conducting their professional activities as a corporation. Liability of a member or shareholder is limited in the same manner as in a business corporation.

Profit and loss statement (P & L)

The summary of the incomes (total revenues) and costs of a company's operation during a specific period of time. Also known as Income and expense statement.

Proposal

See Business plan

Proprietorship

The most common legal form of business ownership; about 85 percent of all small businesses are proprietorships. The liability of the owner is unlimited in this form of ownership.

Prospective payment system

A cost-containment measure included in the Social Security Amendments of 1983 whereby Medicare payments to hospitals are based on established prices, rather than on cost reimbursement.

Prototype

A model that demonstrates the validity of the concept of an invention (laboratory prototype); a model that meets the needs of the manufacturing process and the user (production prototype).

Prudent investor rule or standard

A legal doctrine that requires fiduciaries to make investments using the prudence, diligence, and intelligence that would be used by a prudent person in making similar investments. Because fiduciaries make investments on behalf of third-party beneficiaries, the standard results in very conservative investments. Until recently, most state regulations required the fiduciary to apply this standard to each investment. Newer, more progressive regulations permit fiduciaries to apply this standard to the portfolio taken as a whole, thereby allowing a fiduciary to balance a portfolio with higher-yield, higher-risk investments. In states with more progressive regulations, practically every type of security is eligible for inclusion in the portfolio of investments made by a fiduciary, provided that the portfolio investments, in their totality, are those of a prudent person.

Public equity markets

Organized markets for trading in equity shares such as common stocks, preferred stocks, and warrants. Includes markets for both regularly traded and nonregularly traded securities.

Public offering

General solicitation for participation in an investment opportunity. Interstate public offerings are supervised by the U.S. Securities and Exchange Commission (see separate citation).

Quality control

The process by which a product is checked and tested to ensure consistent standards of high quality.

Rate of return

(See also Yield)

The yield obtained on a security or other investment based on its purchase price or its current market price. The total rate of return is current income plus or minus capital appreciation or depreciation.

Real property

Includes the land and all that is contained on it.

Realignment

See Resource realignment

Recession

Contraction of economic activity occurring between the peak and trough (see separate citations) of a business cycle.

Regulated market

A market in which the government controls the forces of supply and demand, such as who may enter and what price may be charged.

Regulation D

A vehicle by which small businesses make small offerings and private placements of securities with limited disclosure requirements. It was designed to ease the burdens imposed on small businesses utilizing this method of capital formation.

Regulatory Flexibility Act

An act requiring federal agencies to evaluate the impact of their regulations on small businesses before the regulations are issued and to consider less burdensome alternatives.

Research

The initial stage of the innovation process, which includes idea generation and invention.

Research and development financing

A tax-advantaged partnership set up to finance product development for start-ups as well as more mature companies.

Resource mobility

The ease with which labor and capital move from firm to firm or from industry to industry.

Resource realignment

The adjustment of productive resources to interindustry changes in demand.

Resources

The sources of support or help in the innovation process, including sources of financing, technical evaluation, market evaluation, management and business assistance, etc.

Retained business earnings

Business profits that are retained by the business rather than being distributed to the shareholders as dividends.

Revolving credit

An agreement with a lending institution for an amount of money, which cannot exceed a set maximum, over a specified period of time. Each time the borrower repays a portion of the loan, the amount of the repayment may be borrowed yet again.

Risk capital

See Venture capital

Risk management

The act of identifying potential sources of financial loss and taking action to minimize their negative impact.

Routing

The sequence of steps necessary to complete a product during production.

S corporations

See Sub chapter S corporations

SBA

See Small Business Administration

SBA direct loans

Loans made directly by the U.S. Small Business Administration (SBA); monies come from funds appropriated specifically for this purpose. In general, SBA direct loans carry interest rates slightly lower than those in the private financial markets and are available only to applicants unable to secure private financing or an SBA guaranteed loan.

SBA 504 Program

See Certified development corporation

SBA guaranteed loans
Loans made by lending institutions in which the U.S. Small Business Administration (SBA) will pay a prior agreed-upon percentage of the outstanding principal in the event the borrower of the loan defaults. The terms of the loan and the interest rate are negotiated between the borrower and the lending institution, within set parameters.

SBA loans
See Disaster loans; SBA direct loans; SBA guaranteed loans; SBA special lending institution categories

SBA Management Assistance Programs
(See also Active Corps of Executives; Service Corps of Retired Executives; Small business institutes program)
Classes, workshops, counseling, and publications offered by the U.S. Small Business Administration.

SBA special lending institution categories.
U.S. Small Business Administration (SBA) loan program in which the SBA promises certified banks a 72-hour turnaround period in giving its approval for a loan, and in which preferred lenders in a pilot program are allowed to write SBA loans without seeking prior SBA approval.

SBDB
See Small Business Data Base

SBDC
See Small business development centers

SBI
See Small business institutes program

SBIC
See Small business investment corporation

SBIR Program
See Small Business Innovation Development Act of 1982

Scale economies
The decline of the production cost per unit of output (average cost) as the volume of output increases.

Scale efficiency
The reduction in unit cost available to a firm when producing at a higher output volume.

SCORE
See Service Corps of Retired Executives

SEC
See Securities and Exchange Commission

SECA
See Self-Employment Contributions Act

Second-stage financing
(See also First-stage financing; Third-stage financing)
Working capital for the initial expansion of a company that is producing, shipping, and has growing accounts receivable and inventories. Also known as Second-round financing.

Secondary market
A market established for the purchase and sale of outstanding securities following their initial distribution.

Secondary worker
Any worker in a family other than the person who is the primary source of income for the family.

Secondhand capital
Previously used and subsequently resold capital equipment (e.g., buildings and machinery).

Securities and Exchange Commission (SEC)
Federal agency charged with regulating the trade of securities to prevent unethical practices in the investor market.

Securitized debt
A marketing technique that converts long-term loans to marketable securities.

Seed capital
Venture financing provided in the early stages of the innovation process, usually during product development.

Self-employed person
One who works for a profit or fees in his or her own business, profession, or trade, or who operates a farm.

Self-Employment Contributions Act (SECA)
Federal law that governs the self-employment tax (see separate citation).

Self-employment income
Income covered by Social Security if a business earns a net income of at least $400.00 during the year. Taxes are paid on earnings that exceed $400.00.

Self-employment retirement plan
See Keogh plan

Self-employment tax
Required tax imposed on self-employed individuals for the provision of Social Security and Medicare. The tax must be paid quarterly with estimated income tax statements.

GLOSSARY

Self-funding

A health benefit plan in which a firm uses its own funds to pay claims, rather than transferring the financial risks of paying claims to an outside insurer in exchange for premium payments.

Service Corps of Retired Executives (SCORE)

(See also Active Corps of Executives)

Volunteers for the SBA Management Assistance Program who provide one-on-one counseling and teach workshops and seminars for small firms.

Service firm

See Business service firm

Service sector

Broadly defined, all U.S. industries that produce intangibles, including the five major industry divisions of transportation, communications, and utilities; wholesale trade; retail trade; finance, insurance, and real estate; and services.

Set asides

See Small business set asides

Short-haul service

A type of transportation service in which the transporter supplies service between cities where the maximum distance is no more than 200 miles.

Short-term debt

An obligation that matures in one year.

SIC codes

See Standard Industrial Classification codes

Single-establishment enterprise

See Establishment

Small business

An enterprise that is independently owned and operated, is not dominant in its field, and employs fewer than 500 people. For SBA purposes, the U.S. Small Business Administration (SBA) considers various other factors (such as gross annual sales) in determining size of a business.

Small Business Administration (SBA)

An independent federal agency that provides assistance with loans, management, and advocating interests before other federal agencies.

Small Business Data Base

(See also U.S. Establishment and Enterprise Microdata File; U.S. Establishment Longitudinal Microdata File)

A collection of microdata (see separate citation) files on individual firms developed and maintained by the U.S. Small Business Administration.

Small business development centers (SBDC)

Centers that provide support services to small businesses, such as individual counseling, SBA advice, seminars and conferences, and other learning center activities. Most services are free of charge, or available at minimal cost.

Small business development corporation

See Certified development corporation

Small business-dominated industry

Industry in which a minimum of 60 percent of employment or sales is in firms with fewer than 500 employees.

Small Business Innovation Development Act of 1982

Federal statute requiring federal agencies with large extramural research and development budgets to allocate a certain percentage of these funds to small research and development firms. The program, called the Small Business Innovation Research (SBIR) Program, is designed to stimulate technological innovation and make greater use of small businesses in meeting national innovation needs.

Small business institutes (SBI) program

Cooperative arrangements made by U.S. Small Business Administration district offices and local colleges and universities to provide small business firms with graduate students to counsel them without charge.

Small business investment corporation (SBIC)

A privately owned company licensed and funded through the U.S. Small Business Administration and private sector sources to provide equity or debt capital to small businesses.

Small business set asides

Procurement (see separate citation) opportunities required by law to be on all contracts under $10,000 or a certain percentage of an agency's total procurement expenditure.

Smaller firms

For U.S. Department of Commerce purposes, those firms not included in the Fortune 1000.

SMSA

See Metropolitan statistical area

Socially and economically disadvantaged

Individuals who have been subjected to racial or ethnic prejudice or cultural bias without regard to their qualities as individuals, and whose abilities to compete are impaired because of diminished opportunities to obtain capital and credit.

Sole proprietorship
An unincorporated, one-owner business, farm, or professional practice.

Special lending institution categories
See SBA special lending institution categories

Standard Industrial Classification (SIC) codes
Four-digit codes established by the U.S. Federal Government to categorize businesses by type of economic activity; the first two digits correspond to major groups such as construction and manufacturing, while the last two digits correspond to subgroups such as home construction or highway construction.

Standard metropolitan statistical area (SMSA)
See Metropolitan statistical area

Start-up
A new business, at the earliest stages of development and financing.

Start-up costs
Costs incurred before a business can commence operations.

Start-up financing
Financing provided to companies that have either completed product development and initial marketing or have been in business for less than one year but have not yet sold their product commercially.

Stock
(See also Common stock; Convertible preferred stock)
A certificate of equity ownership in a business.

Stop-loss coverage
Insurance for a self-insured plan that reimburses the company for any losses it might incur in its health claims beyond a specified amount.

Strategic planning
Projected growth and development of a business to establish a guiding direction for the future. Also used to determine which market segments to explore for optimal sales of products or services.

Structural unemployment
See Unemployment

Sub chapter S corporations
Corporations that are considered noncorporate for tax purposes but legally remain corporations.

Subcontract
A contract between a prime contractor and a subcontractor, or between subcontractors, to furnish supplies or services for performance of a prime contract (see separate citation) or a subcontract.

Surety bonds
Bonds providing reimbursement to an individual, company, or the government if a firm fails to complete a contract. The U.S. Small Business Administration guarantees surety bonds in a program much like the SBA guaranteed loan program (see separate citation).

Swing loan
See Bridge financing

Target market
The clients or customers sought for a business' product or service.

Targeted Jobs Tax Credit
Federal legislation enacted in 1978 that provides a tax credit to an employer who hires structurally unemployed individuals.

Tax number
(See also Employer identification number)
A number assigned to a business by a state revenue department that enables the business to buy goods without paying sales tax.

Taxable bonds
An interest-bearing certificate of public or private indebtedness. Bonds are issued by public agencies to finance economic development.

Technical assistance
See Management and technical assistance

Technical evaluation
Assessment of technological feasibility.

Technology
The method in which a firm combines and utilizes labor and capital resources to produce goods or services; the application of science for commercial or industrial purposes.

Technology transfer
The movement of information about a technology or intellectual property from one party to another for use.

Tenure
See Employee tenure

Term
(See also Maturity)
The length of time for which a loan is made.

Terms of a note
The conditions or limits of a note; includes the interest rate per annum, the due date, and transferability and convertibility features, if any.

Third-party administrator
An outside company responsible for handling claims and performing administrative tasks associated with health insurance plan maintenance.

Third-stage financing
(See also First-stage financing; Second-stage financing)
Financing provided for the major expansion of a company whose sales volume is increasing and that is breaking even or profitable. These funds are used for further plant expansion, marketing, working capital, or development of an improved product. Also known as Third-round or Mezzanine financing.

Time deposit
A bank deposit that cannot be withdrawn before a specified future time.

Time management
Skills and scheduling techniques used to maximize productivity.

Trade credit
Credit extended by suppliers of raw materials or finished products. In an accounting statement, trade credit is referred to as "accounts payable."

Trade name
The name under which a company conducts business, or by which its business, goods, or services are identified. It may or may not be registered as a trademark.

Trade periodical
A publication with a specific focus on one or more aspects of business and industry.

Trade secret
Competitive advantage gained by a business through the use of a unique manufacturing process or formula.

Trade show
An exhibition of goods or services used in a particular industry. Typically held inexhibition centers where exhibitors rent space to display their merchandise.

Trademark
A graphic symbol, device, or slogan that identifies a business. A business has property rights to its trademark from the inception of its use, but it is still prudent to register all trademarks with the Trademark Office of the U.S. Department of Commerce.

Translation
See Product development

Treasury bills
Investment tender issued by the Federal Reserve Bank in amounts of $10,000 that mature in 91 to 182 days.

Treasury bonds
Long-term notes with maturity dates of not less than seven and not more than twenty-five years.

Treasury notes
Short-term notes maturing in less than seven years.

Trend
A statistical measurement used to track changes that occur over time.

Trough
See Cyclical trough

UCC
See Uniform Commercial Code

UL
See Underwriters Laboratories

Underwriters Laboratories (UL)
One of several private firms that tests products and processes to determine their safety. Although various firms can provide this kind of testing service, many local and insurance codes specify UL certification.

Underwriting
A process by which an insurer determines whether or not and on what basis it will accept an application for insurance. In an experience-rated plan, premiums are based on a firm's or group's past claims; factors other than prior claims are used for community-rated or manually rated plans.

Unfair competition
Refers to business practices, usually unethical, such as using unlicensed products, pirating merchandise, or misleading the public through false advertising, which give the offending business an unequitable advantage over others.

Unfunded accrued liability
The excess of total liabilities, both present and prospective, over present and prospective assets.

Unemployment
The joblessness of individuals who are willing to work, who are legally and physically able to work, and who are seeking work. Unemployment may represent the temporary joblessness of a worker between jobs (frictional unemployment) or the joblessness of a worker whose skills are not suitable for jobs available in the labor market (structural unemployment).

Uniform Commercial Code (UCC)
A code of laws governing commercial transactions across the U.S., except Louisiana. Their purpose is to bring uniformity to financial transactions.

Uniform product code (UPC symbol)
A computer-readable label comprised of ten digits and stripes that encodes what a product is and how much it costs. The first five digits are assigned by the Uniform Product Code Council, and the last five digits by the individual manufacturer.

Unit cost
See Average cost

UPC symbol
See Uniform product code

U.S. Establishment and Enterprise Microdata (USEEM) File
A cross-sectional database containing information on employment, sales, and location for individual enterprises and establishments with employees that have a Dun & Bradstreet credit rating.

U.S. Establishment Longitudinal Microdata (USELM) File
A database containing longitudinally linked sample microdata on establishments drawn from the U.S. Establishment and Enterprise Microdata file (see separate citation).

U.S. Small Business Administration 504 Program
See Certified development corporation

USEEM
See U.S. Establishment and Enterprise Microdata File

USELM
See U.S. Establishment Longitudinal Microdata File

VCN
See Venture capital network

Venture capital
(See also Equity; Equity midrisk venture capital)
Money used to support new or unusual business ventures that exhibit above-average growth rates, significant potential for market expansion, and are in need of additional financing to sustain growth or further research and development; equity or equity-type financing traditionally provided at the commercialization stage, increasingly available prior to commercialization.

Venture capital company
A company organized to provide seed capital to a business in its formation stage, or in its first or second stage of expansion. Funding is obtained through public or private pension funds, commercial banks and bank holding companies, small business investment corporations licensed by the U.S. Small Business Administration, private venture capital firms, insurance companies, investment management companies, bank trust departments, industrial companies seeking to diversify their investment, and investment bankers acting as intermediaries for other investors or directly investing on their own behalf.

Venture capital limited partnerships
Designed for business development, these partnerships are an institutional mechanism for providing capital for young, technology-oriented businesses. The investors' money is pooled and invested in money market assets until venture investments have been selected. The general partners are experienced investment managers who select and invest the equity and debt securities of firms with high growth potential and the ability to go public in the near future.

Venture capital network (VCN)
A computer database that matches investors with entrepreneurs.

WAN
See Wide Area Network

Wide Area Network (WAN)
Computer networks linking systems throughout a state or around the world in order to facilitate the sharing of information.

Withholding
Federal, state, social security, and unemployment taxes withheld by the employer from employees' wages; employers are liable for these taxes and the corporate umbrella and bankruptcy will not exonerate an employer

from paying back payroll withholding. Employers should escrow these funds in a separate account and disperse them quarterly to withholding authorities.

Workers' compensation
A state-mandated form of insurance covering workers injured in job-related accidents. In some states, the state is the insurer; in other states, insurance must be acquired from commercial insurance firms. Insurance rates are based on a number of factors, including salaries, firm history, and risk of occupation.

Working capital
Refers to a firm's short-term investment of current assets, including cash, short-term securities, accounts receivable, and inventories.

Yield
(See also Rate of return)
The rate of income returned on an investment, expressed as a percentage. Income yield is obtained by dividing the current dollar income by the current market price of the security. Net yield or yield to maturity is the current income yield minus any premium above par or plus any discount from par in purchase price, with the adjustment spread over the period from the date of purchase to the date of maturity.

Appendix D - Bibliography

Bibliography

Bibliography citations are listed alphabetically by title under appropriate subject subheadings, which also appear alphabetically (in bold).

Accounting/Budgets and Budgeting

"Account Yourself" in *Business Start-Ups*. (Vol. 7, No. 8, August 1995, p. 79).

"Accountant Wanted" in *Business Start-Ups*. (October 1994, pp. 20-23). By Gloria Gibbs Marullo.

Accounting for Business. Newton, MA: Butterworth-Heinemann, 1991. By Peter Atrill, David Harvey, and Edward McLaney.

Accounting the Business Environment. Philadelphia, PA: Trans-Atlantic Publications, Inc., 1995. By John Watts.

The Accounting Cycle. Menlo Park, CA: Crisp Publications, Inc. By Jay Jacquet and William C. Miller, Jr.

An Accounting Primer. New York, NY. By Elwin W. Midgett.

Accounting Services for Small Service Firms. Denver, CO: U.S. Small Business Administration (SBA).

Activity-Based Costing for Small and Mid-sized Businesses: An Implementation Guide. Somerset, New Jersey: John Wiley & Sons, Inc., 1992. By Douglas T. Hicks.

"Audit Tip Sheet" in *Inc.* (Vol. 16, No. 4, April 1994, pp. 118). By Jill Andresky Fraser.

"Balancing Act" in *Entrepreneur*. (Vol. 23, No. 3, March 1995, pp. 56, 58- 59, 61). By Bob Weinstein.

Basic Accounting. Albany, NY: Delmar Publishers, 1997.

Basic Accounting for the Small Business: Simple, Foolproof Techniques for Keeping Your Books Straight and Staying Out of Trouble. Bellingham, WA: Self-Counsel Press, Inc., fourth edition, 1992. By Clive G. Cornish.

"Before You File" in *Income Opportunities*. (Vol. 32, No. 1, January 1997, pp. 27-30). By Janine S. Pouliot.

"Bill Auditing" in *Small Business Opportunities*. (Vol. 8, No. 2, March 1996, pp. 20). By Terry Schwartz.

"Bill of Wrongs" in *Entrepreneur*. (Vol. 23, No. 5, May 1995, pp. 166, 168, 170-171). By David R. Honodel.

"Bookkeeper in a Box" in *Inc. Technology*. (Vol. 15, No. 13, pp. 98). By Phaedra Hise.

Budgeting & Finance. New York, NY: McGraw-Hill, Inc., 1996.

Business, Accounting and Finance Problem Solver. Piscataway, NJ: Research & Education Association, revised edition, 1994.

Business Owner's Guide to Accounting & Bookkeeping. Grants Pass, OR: Oasis Press, 1991. By Oliver Placencia and Welge staff.

College Accounting: A Small Business Approach. Burr Ridge, IL: Richard D. Irwin, Inc., 1994. By Eleanor Schrader.

"Count On It" in *Entrepreneur*. (Vol. 23, No. 8, August 1995, pp. 30, 32- 33). By Cheryl J. Goldberg.

"Count On It" in *Hispanic Business*. (Vol. 18, No. 6, June 1996, p. 122). By Rick Mendosa.

"Counting On Profit" in *Small Business Opportunities*. (Vol. 7, No. 3, May 1995, pp. 42-43, 82). By Martin Waterman.

"Database Husbandry" in *Inc. Technology*. (Vol. 16, No. 13, pp. 100). By Phaedra Hise.

"Dream Accountant" in *Income Opportunities*. (Vol. 30, No. 1, January 1995, pp. 108, 110). By Peg Byron.

Finance & Accounting. Dubuque, IA: Kendall Hunt Publishing Co., 1995. By Henry Beam.

Financial Accounting: Guide. Dubuque, IA: Kendall Hunt Publishing Co., 1995. By Mohamed Ibrahim.

Financial Accounting & Reporting. Cincinnati, OH: South-Western Publishing Co., 1995.

Financial Basics of Small Business Success. Menlo Park, CA: Crisp Publications, Inc., 1996. By J. Gill.

Financial Essentials for Small Business Success: Accounting, Planning & Recordkeeping Techniques for a Healthy Bottom Line. Dover, NH: Upstart Publishing Co., 1994. By Joe Tabet.

"Firing Line" in *Entrepreneur*. (Vol. 23, No. 12, November 1995, pp. 56, 59). By David R. Evanson.

"For the Record" in *Business Start-Ups*. (Vol. 7, No. 5, May 1995, pp. 78, 80-81). By Cynthia E. Griffin.

"Going it Alone" in *Newsweek*. (April 1996, pp. 50-51). By Ellyn E. Spragins and Steve Rhodes.

Home Office & Small Business Success Book: How to Run Your Business With More Profitably. New York, NY: Henry Holt & Co., 1996. By Janet Attard.

How to Increase Small Business Profits with Technology: A Proven 8 Step Plan for Increasing Profits Through Computers & Other Technology. Gulf Breeze, FL: Maximum Press, 1996. By Jonathan Strum.

"How to Survive an IRS Audit" in *Nation's Business*. (Vol. 82, No. 4, April 1994, pp. 42-43). By Joan C. Szabo.

"Hunting for an Accountant" in *PA CPA Journal*. (Vol. 63, No. 4, Summer 1993, pp. 10-13). By Gerald J. Rosenthal.

"It Adds Up" in *Income Opportunities*. (Vol. 31, No. 1, January 1996, pp. 32, 34, 38). By Debra D'Agostino.

Keeping the Books: Basic Recordkeeping and Accounting for the Small Business. Dover, NH: Upstart Publishing Co., Inc., second edition, 1993. By Linda Pinson and Jerry Jinnett.

"Ledger-demain" in *Inc.* (Vol. 18, No. 9, June 1996, pp. 87-88). By Ellen DePasquale.

"Let's Get Fiscal" in *Entrepreneur*. (June 1995, pp. 68, 70-71). By Bob Weinstein.

Managing by the Numbers: Financial Essentials for the Growing Business. Dover, NH: Upstart Publishing Co., Inc., 1992. By David H. Bangs, Jr.

McGraw-Hill Small Business Tax Advisor. New York, NY: McGraw-Hill, Inc., second edition, 1992. By Cliff Roberson.

Money Saving Tips for the Self-Employed. New York, NY: Random House, Inc., 1992. By Linda Stern.

"No Accounting for Success" in *Inc.* (Vol. 18, No. 8, June 1996, pp. 25-26). By Norm Brodsky.

"Non-Taxing Matters" in *Inc.* (Vol. 19, No. 4, March 1997, pp. 90-92). By Ellen DePasquale.

"On The Books" in *Income Opportunities*. (Vol. 32, No. 1, January 1997, pp. 38, 40, 42). By Mike Hogan.

Quarterlies, Journals, Payroll - Small Business Accounting: CA, Oregon, & Washington Edition. Woodinville, WA: Rhapsody Press, Inc., 1996. By James J. Pearce.

Ready-to-Use Business Forms: A Complete Package for the Small Business. Bellingham, WA: Self-Counsel Press, Inc., second edition, 1992.

Record Keeping in a Small Business. Denver, CO: U.S. Small Business Administration (SBA)

Record Keeping for Small Rural Businesses. Amherst, MA: University of MA. By Eligia Murcia.

"Second Time Around" in *Business Start-Ups*. (Vol. 8, No. 11, November 1996, pp. 74-75). By Lisa Pelec Hyde.

The Shoebox Syndrome (Record-Keeping). Hyde Park, MA: Nikmal Publishing. By Selma H. Lamkin.

Simplified Small Business Accounting. Carbondale, IL: Nova Publishing Co., 1995. By Daniel Sitarz.

Small Business Accountant. Cincinnati, OH: South-Western Publishing Co., 1994.

"Small Business Controller" in *Management Accounting*. (Vol. 76, No. 5, November 1994, pp. 38-41). By Bonnie D. Labrack.

"Step 5: Plan A Realistic Budget" in *Business Start-Ups*. (Vol. 8, No. 9, September 1996, pp. 80, 82). By Kylo-Patrick Hart.

Step-by-Step Bookkeeping: The Complete Handbook for the Small Business. New York, NY: Sterling Publishing Co., Inc., revised edition, 1992. By Robert C. Ragan.

Successfully Self-Employed: How to Sell What You Do, Do What You Sell, Manage Your Cash in Between. Dover, NH: Upstart Publishing Company, Inc., 1996. By Gregory Brennan.

Tax Accounting for Small Business: How to Prepare Tax Form 1040C. Woodmere, NY. Career Advancement Center, Inc., 1996. By Joseph Gelb.

Tax Planning & Preparation Made Easy for the Self-Employed. New York, NY: John Wiley & Sons, Inc., 1995. By Gregory L. Dent.

"To the Rescue" in *Business Start-Ups.* (Vol. 7, No. 5, May 1995, pp. 68, 70-71). By Sue Clayton.

"Tracking Your Mileage" in *Business Start-Ups.* (Vol. 8, No. 12, December 1996, pp. 76, 78). By Gloria Gibbs Marullo.

"Will Banking Go Virtual?" in *Inc.* (Vol. 18, No. 13, September 1996, pp. 49-52). By Jill Andresky Fraser.

"Winning Numbers" in *Inc.* (Vol. 18, No. 13, September 1996, pp. 84-87). By Ellen DePasquale.

"You May Need the 'C' in CPA" in *Inc.* (Vol. 16, No. 9, September 1994, pp. 126). By Jill Andresky Fraser.

Bed & Breakfast

Absolutely Every (Almost) Bed & Breakfast in California: Monterey to San Diego. Seattle, WA: Travis Ilse Publishers, 1993. By Toni Knapp.

The American Country Inn and Bed & Breakfast Cookbooks. Nashville, TN: Rutledge Hill Press, Volume I, 1990, Volume II, 1993. By Kitty and Lucian Maynard.

Baldwin's Guide to Inns of the Deep South: Louisiana and Western Mississippi. Gretna, LA: Pelican Publishing Co., 1993. By Jack and Winnie Baldwin.

Bed & Breakfast Guide—Southwest: Arizona, New Mexico, Texas. Englewood Cliffs, NJ: Prentice Hall, 1993. By Lucy Poshek.

Bed and Breakfast in New England: Connecticut, Massachusetts, New Hampshire, Rhode Island, Vermont. Old Saybrook, CT: Globe Pequot Press, Inc., fourth edition, 1994. By Bernice Chesler.

Bed & Breakfast U.S.A. New York, NY: NAL Dutton, 1995. By Betty Rundback and Peggy Ackerman.

Bed & Breakfasts and Country Inns and Other Weekend Pleasures: Upper Great Lakes Region. New York, NY: Fodor's Travel Publications, Inc., 1993.

Best Places to Stay in America's Cities. Boston, MA: Houghton Mifflin Co., second edition, 1992. By Bruce Shaw.

"Business Travelers Find Home Away from Home" in *Crain's Detroit Business.* (Vol. 10, No. 38, September 19-25, 1994, pp. 8, 10). By Donna Raphael.

Canadian Bed & Breakfast Guide. New York, NY: Viking Penguin, Inc., tenth edition, 1995. By Gerda Pantel.

Complete Guide to Bed and Breakfasts, Inns and Guesthouses: Southern Edition. Berkeley, CA: Ten Speed Press, 1993. By Pamela Lauier.

Complete Guide to Bed and Breakfasts, Inns, and Guesthouses in the U.S. and Canada. Berkeley, CA: Ten Speed Press, twelfth edition, 1995. By Pamela Lanier.

Complete Guide to Bed and Breakfasts, Inns, and Guesthouses: Western Edition. Berkeley, CA: Ten Speed Press, 1993. By Pamela Lavier.

Country Inns and Back Roads: California. New York, NY: Harper Collins Publishers, Inc., 1994. By Jerry Levitin.

Country Inns and Back Roads: New England. New York, NY: Harper Collins Publishers, Inc., 1994. By Jerry Levitin.

Country Inns and Back Roads: North America. New York, NY: Harper Collins Publishers, Inc., 1994. By Jerry Levitin.

"An Expert Offers the ABCs of Getting Into the B & B Biz" in *Money.* (December 1989, p. 18).

Fodor's Bed & Breakfast, Country Inns and Other Weekend Pleasures: California. New York, NY: Fodor's Travel Publications, Inc., 1993.

Fodor's Bed & Breakfasts, Country Inns and Other Weekend Pleasures: Pacific Northwest. New York, NY: Fodor's Travel Publications, Inc., 1993.

"Hosting a Bed and Breakfast Business" in *Income Opportunities.* (March 1986, pp. 47-48, 68, 70). By Ann Standaert Bowden.

"Hotel Heroes" in *Entrepreneur.* (October 1990, pp. 162-169). By Frances Huffman.

How to Open and Operate a Bed and Breakfast Home. Old Saybrook, CT: Globe Pequot Press, Inc., 1995. By Jan Stankus.

BIBLIOGRAPHY

How to Open and Successfully Operate a Country Inn: Completely Revised, Updated for the 90's. Lee, MA: Berkshire House Publishers, 1993. By Vincent C. Shortt.

How to Start a Bed & Breakfast Home. Old Saybrook, CT: Globe Pequot Press, Inc., 1997. By Jan Stankus.

How to Start & Manage a Bed & Breakfast Business: Step-by-Step Guide to Business Success. Interlochen, MI: Lewis & Renn Associates, Inc., 1995. By Leslie D. Renn.

How to Start and Operate Your Own Bed-&-Breakfast: Down-to-Earth Advice from an Award-Winning B&B Owner. New York, NY: Henry Holt & Co., Inc., 1994. By Martha W. Murphy.

How to Start and Run Your Own Bed and Breakfast Inn. Harrisburg, PA: Stackpole Books, 1992. By Ripley Hotch and Carl Glassman.

"In the Bed and Breakfast Trade, Without the B & B" in *Woman's Enterprise.* (December 1989, pp. 64-68). By J. Brian Phillips.

"Innkeeper Income" in *Income Plus.* (December 1989, pp. 30-33). By Terry Murphy.

"Making Your Dream Business A Reality" in *Working Woman.* (Vol. 20, No. 10, October 1995, pp. 49-50, 52, 56, 87-88, 91-92). By Louise Washer.

Official Bed and Breakfast Guide for the United States, Canada and the Caribbean. Norwalk, CT: National Bed and Breakfast Association (NBBA), sixth edition, 1993. By Phyllis Featherston and Barbara Ostler.

Official Guide to American Historic Inns. Dana Point, CA: Association of American Historic Inns, third edition, 1990. By Deborah Sakach and Tim Sakach.

Open Your Own Bed and Breakfast. New York, NY: John Wiley & Sons, Inc., second edition, 1992. By Barbara Notarius and Gail Sforza Brewer.

So—You Want to Be an Innkeeper. San Francisco, CA: Chronicle Books, 1996. By Mary E. Davies.

So... You Want to Be an Innkeeper: The Complete Guide to Operating a Successful Bed and Breakfast Inn. San Francisco, CA: Chronicle Books, 1996. By Mary E. Davies, Pat Hardy, JoAnn M. Bell, and Susan Brown.

"Start a Bed and Breakfast Service" in *Income Opportunities.* (Mid-September 1990, pp. 58-68). By Silvia Shepard.

Start and Run a Profitable Bed and Breakfast: Your Step-by-Step Business Plan. Bellingham, WA: Self-Counsel Press, Inc., 1992. By Monica Taylor and Richard Taylor.

"Turn Extra Rooms Into Extra Dollars" in *Income Opportunities.* (November 1988, pp. 74, 100, 102, 104). By J. Brian Phillips.

"Turn Your Home Into a Money Making Inn" in *Successful Opportunities.* (April 1990, pp. 26-32). By Eileen Silva.

UPS Guide to Owning & Managing a B & B. Chicago, IL: Dearborn Financial Publishing, Inc., 1994.

Bottled Water Manufacturer

"Propitious Returns" in *Beverage World.* (Vol. 114, No. 1583, January 1995, pp. 38-47). By Larry Jabbonsky.

"The Water Man" in *Hawaii Business.* (Vol. 39, No. 11, May 1994, pp. 41). By Lisa Ishikawa.

"Wild About Water" in *Entrepreneur.* (August 1989, pp. 59-62). By Erika Kotite.

Business Growth and Statistics

"10 Tips for Success" in *Business Start-ups.* (Vol. 8, No. 8, August 1996, pp. 74-75). By Kelli Reyes.

"24th Annual Report on Black Business" in *Black Enterprise.* (Vol. 26 No. 11, June 1996, pp. 103-139). By Derek T. Dingle.

"1996 may be best year for those seeking loans" in *Washington Business Journal: Small Business Resource Guide.* (May 1996, p. 16). By Melissa Wuestenberg.

"A Cautionary Tale" in *Feminist Bookstore News.* (Vol. 19, No. 4, November/December 1996, pp. 21-23). By Carol Seajay.

"A sporting chance" in *Detroit Free Press.* (January 1997, pp. 1E-2E). By Molly Brauer.

"A Million and Counting" in *Hispanic Business.* (Vol. 18, No. 7/8, July/August 1996, p. 10). By Rick Mendosa.

"A guide may be needed to set up shop on-line" in *Crain's Detroit Business*. (Vol. 11, No. 29, July 1995, p. 11).

Action Plans for the Small Business: Growth Strategies for Businesses Wondering Where to Go Next. New York, NY: DBM Publishing, 1995. By Shailendra Vyakarnam.

Advances in Entrepreneurship, Firm Emergence & Growth. Greenwich, CT: JAI Press, Inc., 1997. By Jerome A. Katz.

"After the storm" in *Forbes*. (July 95, pp. 65-66). By Gary Samuels.

America's 25 Hottest Businesses. Irvine, CA: Entrepreneur, Inc.

"And Still We Rise" in *Black Enterprise*. (Vol. 26, No. 9, April 1996, p. 18). By Cliff Hocker.

"Are You Ready to Go Public?" in *Nation's Business*. (Vol. 83, No. 1, January 1995, pp. 30-32). By Roberta Maynard.

"At the Brink" in *Inc.* (Vol. 17, No. 16, November 1995, pp. 21-22). By Rick McCloskey.

Basic Business Statistics. Englewood Cliffs, NJ: Prentice Hall, 1995.

"Battling To Be The Big Cheese" in *Income Opportunities*. (Vol. 32, No. 1, January 1997, pp. 14-17, 80). By Constance Gustke.

"Best of the Best" in *Entrepreneur*. (March 1997, pp. 136, 138-139).

"Branching Out" in *Nation's Business*. (Vol. 82, No. 11, November 1994, pp. 53). By Roberta Maynard.

"Brave New World" in *Income Opportunities*. (Vol. 30, No. 4, April 1995, pp. 30-32, 34-36, 38, 40, 42, 44). By Dale D. Buss.

"Breaking New Ground" in *Income Opportunities*. (Vol. 31, No. 6, June 1996, pp. 22-25, 64). By Ed Klimuska.

"Brighter Days" in *Entrepreneur*. (Vol. 23, No. 7, July 1995, pp. 16). By Janean Chun.

"Bringing Up Business" in *Entrepreneur*. (Vol. 23, No. 1, January 1995, pp. 124-128). By Erika Kotite.

"Building Companies to Last" in *Inc.* (Special Issue: The State of Small Business, February 1996, pp. 83-84, 87-88). By James C. Collins.

"Business Finally Invests Some Trust in Bank Lending" in *Crain's Small Business*. (October 1995, p. 8). By Jeffrey McCracken.

"Business and gravy" in *The Red Herring*. (March 1997, pp. 50-51). By Luc Hatlestad.

"Business Must Refocus Once It Outgrows Entrepreneur's Control" in *Crain's Small Business*. (October 1995, p. 16). By Jon Greenawalt.

Business Statistics. Saint Louis, MI: Mosby Year Book, Inc., 1996.

Business Statistics of the United States. Lanham, MD: Bernan Press, 1995. By Courtenay M. Slater.

"California, Here We Come!" in *Hispanic Business*. (Vol. 18, No. 5, May 1996, pp. 33-36, 38-39, 42, 44). By Rick Mendoza.

"Capital Steps" in *Inc.* (Vol. 18, No. 2, February 1996, pp. 42-44, 47). By Jill Andresky Fraser.

The Complete Demographic Reference Guide. Marina del Rey, CA: Urban Decision Systems, 1992.

"Crafts Course" in *Entrepreneur*. (June 1995, pp. 178-180). By Gayle Sato Stodder.

"Crain's Small Business INDEX" in *Crain's Small Business*. (Vol. 4, No. 11, November 1996, pp. 5).

"DEMOGRAPHICA" in *Crain's Small Business*. (Vol. 4, No. 11, November 1996, pp. 22).

"Entrepreneurs Collide: Will Zoning Take Town Downhill?" in *Inc.* (Vol. 19, No. 5, April 1997, p. 32). By Joshua Macht.

The Entrepreneur's Guide to Growing Up: Taking Your Small Company to the Next Level. Bellingham, WA: Self-Counsel Press, Inc., 1993. By Edna Sheedy.

"Fast Track" in *Entrepreneur*. (February 1997, p. 22).

"The Fast Trackers" in *Working Woman*. (March 1995, pp. 44-48, 86). By Louise Washer.

"A Field Guide to Your Local Economy" in *Inc.* (Special Issue: The State of Small Business, February 1996, pp. 51-54). By Joel Garreau.

"Financial Ratios in Large Public and Small Private Firms" in *Journal of Small Business Management.* (Vol. 30, No. 3, July 1992, pp. 35). By Jerome Osteryoung, Richard L. Constand and Donald Nast.

"Forging New Frontiers " in *Black Enterprise.* (Vol. 26, No. 10, May 1996, pp. 70-72, 74, 76, 78). By Marjorie Whigham-Desir.

"Fueling the Growth of Black Companies" in *Black Enterprise.* (Vol. 25, No. 4, November 1994, pp. 158-159, 162, 164). By Gracian Mack.

"GET RICH IN 1997" in *Small Business Opportunities.* (Vol. 9, No. 1, January 1997, pp. 22-24, 26, 28, 30, 34).

Go for Growth: Five People-Centered Ways to Re-Energize. Essex Junction, VT: Oliver Wight Publications, 1995. By Robert M. Tomasko.

"Growing Companies Gain from University Relationships" in *Income Opportunities.* (Vol. 30, No. 4, April 1995, pp. 3). By Patricia Hamilton.

"Growing with the Flow" in *Inc.* (Vol. 16, No. 11, 1994, pp. 88-90). By Martha E. Mangelsdorf.

"Growing Pains" in *Business Start-Ups.* (Vol. 9, No. 5, May 1997, pp. 8, 10, 12). By Carolyn Campbell.

"Growing Pains" in *Entrepreneur.* (November, 1996 pp. 214, 216-217). By Charlotte Mulhern.

"Growing Up" in *Entrepreneur.* (July 1996, pp. 124-128). By Lynn Beresford.

"A Growing Year for Small Business" in *Income Opportunities.* (Vol. 30, No. 10, October 1995, pp. 3). By Heath F. Eiden.

"Growing Your Consulting Business" in *Black Enterprise.* (Vol. 25, No. 4, November 1994, pp. 108-116). By Margie Markarian.

"Growth in a Developing Market" in *Inc. 500.* (Vol. 16, No. 11, 1994, pp. 92, 94, 96, 98-99). By Martha E. Mangelsdorf.

"Growth moderates leading into election" in *Crain's Small Business.* (Vol. 4, No. 11, November 1996, pp. 5). By David Sowerby.

"Growth Happens" in *Inc.* (Vol. 19, No. 3, March 1997, pp. 68-70, 72-74). By Robert A. Mamis.

"Hitting the Wall" in *Inc.* (Vol. 17, No. 10, July 1995, pp. 21-22). By James L. Bildner.

"The Hottest Industries for New Business Opportunities" in *Black Enterprise.* (Vol. 25, No. 8, March 1995). By Carolyn M. Brown, Yolanda Gault, Lloyd Gite, Adrienne Harris, Eric Houston, Dasha Jones and Valencia Roner.

"How the Census Bureau Devalues Black Businesses" in *Black Enterprise.* (Vol. 26 No. 11, June 1996, pp. 223-228). By Margaret C. Simms.

How to Start, Expand and Sell a Business: The Complete Guide for Entrepreneurs. Santa Barbara, CA: Venture Perspective Press, third edition, 1991. By James C. Comiskey.

"Incubation Period" in *Income Opportunities.* (Vol. 32, No. 1, January 1997, pp. 20-24, 64). By Dale D. Buss.

"INDEX" in *Crain's Detroit Business.* (Vol. 5, No. 1, January 1997, p. 22). By David Sowerby.

Innovation & Growth in an African American Owned Business. New York, NY: Garland Publishing, Inc., 1996. By Gwendolyn P. Todd.

Introduction to Business Statistics. Orlando, FL: Harcourt Brace College Publishers, 1996.

"Is Bigger Better?" in *Working Woman.* (March 1995, pp. 39-40, 42, 90). By Louise Washer.

"Is Black Business Paving the Way?" in *Black Enterprise.* (Vol. 26 No. 11, June 1996, pp. 194-202, 206). By Eric L. Smith.

"It Cuts Both Ways" in *Crain's Detroit Business.* (Vol. 10, No. 41, October 10-16, 1994, pp. 9). By Marilyn Sambrano.

"The Knockout Lesson" in *Inc.* (Vol. 17, No. 8, June 1995, pp. 21-22). By Amy Miller.

"L.A. Quakes in the Shadow of Beautiful Downtown Burbank" in *Inc.* (Vol. 18, No. 18, December 1997, p. 28). By Joel Kotkin.

"Looking for Customers? Pick on Someone Your Own Size" in *Inc.* (Vol. 19, No. 3, March 1997, p. 22). By Jerry Useem.

"MAIL-ORDER MANIA" in *Small Business Opportunities*. (Vol. 8, No. 5, September 1996, p. 28). By Anne Hart.

"Making a Move" in *Hispanic Business*. (Vol. 18, No. 9, September 1996, pp. 42-43). By Maria Zate.

"Marketing by Mail" in *Black Enterprise*. (Vol. 26 No. 11, June 1996, pp. 275-282). By Robert W. Bly.

"Masters of Flexibility" in *Hispanic Business*. (Vol. 18, No. 6, June 1996, pp. 62, 64, 66, 68, 70). By Maria Zate.

Maximizing Small Business Growth: Developing a Bank's Game Plan. Philadelphia, PA: Robert Morris Associates, 1996. By Charles Wendel.

The McGraw-Hill Guide to Managing Growth in Your Emerging Business. New York, NY: McGraw-Hill, Inc., 1994. By Stephen C. Harper.

"Mighty Morphing" in *Entrepreneur*. (November, 1996 p. 16). By Cynthia E. Griffin.

"Mistakes Your Growing Company Needs To Avoid" in *Money Money Guide Supplement*. (Vol., No., 1994, pp. 76-81). By Mary Rowland.

Modern Business Statistics. Belmont, CA: Wadsworth Publishing Co., 1995. By George C. Canova.

"Networking Works" in *Business Start-Ups*. (Vol. 7, No. 10, October 1995, p. 10). By Leann Anderson.

"Never Too Small to Manage" in *Inc.* (Vol. 19, No. 2, February 1997, pp. 56-58, 61). By David Whitford.

"A New Loan Option to Bank, Venture Capital" in *Crain's Small Business*. (February 1996, p. 9-10). By Jeffrey McCracken.

"Niches That Need Filling" in *Hispanic Business*. (Vol. 19, No. 1, January 1997, pp. 18, 20-22).

"On Their Own" in *Wall Street Journal Special Reports: Small Business (Special Edition)*. (May 23, 1996, pp. R20). By Jeffrey A. Tannenbaum.

"One-Hit Wonders" in *Entrepreneur*. (Vol. 23, No. 1, January 1995, pp. 258-260, 262, 264). By Mark Henricks.

"The 100 Fastest-Growing Companies: Under Control" in *Hispanic Business*. (Vol. 17, No. 8, August 1995, pp. 22). By Maria Zate.

"Out of the Ashes" in *Entrepreneur*. (November, 1996 pp. 66, 68). By Cynthia E. Griffin.

"Part 1: PEOs for CEOs" in *Corporate Detroit*. (Vol. 13, No. 12, December 1995, pp. 23, 64). By Steven R. Light.

"Paying for Growth" in *Inc.* (Vol. 18, No. 14, October 1996, pp. 29-30). By Norm Brodsky.

"Peer Review" in *Entrepreneur*. (July 1996, p. 18).

"PROMOTION COMMOTION" in *Small Business Opportunities*. (Vol. 8, No. 5, September 1996, p. 56). By Susan Froetschel.

"RIGHT FROM THE START" in *Small Business Opportunities*. (Vol. 9, No. 3, May 1997, pp. 20, 42). By Dr. Sandy Weinberg.

"Sales Through Superior Service" in *Business Start-Ups*. (Vol. 8, No. 8, August 1996, pp. 70-71). By Donna Clapp.

"The Six Secrets of Strategic Growth" in *Working Woman*. (March 1995, pp. 50-51, 78). By Rhonda M. Abrams.

"Small Biz Can Give Input, Vital Data Via Web Site" in *Crain's Small Business*. (March 1996, p. 3). By Jeffrey McCracken.

"Small Businesses are Thriving" in *Income Opportunities*. (Vol. 30, No. 1, January 1995, pp. 2). By Eric Barnes.

"Small Is Beautiful! Big Is Best!" in *Inc.* (Special Issue: The State of Small Business, February 1996, pp. 39-44, 46, 48-49). By George Gendron.

"Small Talk" in *Wall Street Journal Special Reports: Small Business (Special Edition)*. (May 23, 1996, pp. R28). By Stephanie N. Mehta.

"Small World" in *Entrepreneur*. (Vol. 23, No. 8, August 1995, pp. 17). By Heather Page.

"Something Borrowed" in *Entrepreneur*. (February 1997, p. 26).

"Sounding Board" in *Income Opportunities*. (Vol. 30, No. 6, June 1995, pp. 114, 116). By Richard J. Maturi.

"Stage Right" in *Entrepreneur*. (April 1997, pp. 71-73). By Mark Henricks.

"A Strategy For Growth" in *Black Enterprise*. (Vol. 25, No. 4, November 1994). By Joan Delaney.

"Striking the Faustian Bargain" in *Corporate Detroit*. (Vol. 12, No. 11, November 1994, pp. 38-39). By Gary Hoffman.

"The Survival Factor" in *Hispanic Business*. (Vol. 17, No. 8, August 1995, pp. 44-46). By Rick Mendosa.

"A Sweet Deal" in *Black Enterprise*. (Vol. 25, No. 2, September 1994, pp. 30-32). By Ann Brown.

"There Are No Simple Businesses Anymore" in *Inc*. (Special Issue: The State of Small Business, February 1996, pp. 66-79). By Edward O. Welles.

"Think Small" in *Entrepreneur*. (May 1996, p. 86). Irvine, California: Entrepreneur Media Inc. By Jay Conrad Levinson.

"To Advance, Try a Retreat" in *Crain's Small Business*. (January 1996, p. 17). By Jim Brady.

"U.S. Business Data Worst in World—and Getting Worse" in *Inc*. (Vol. 18, No. 14, October 1996, pp. 26). By Jerry Useem.

Where to Make Money: A Rating Guide to Opportunities in America's Metro Areas. Amherst, NY: Prometheus Books, 1993. By G. Scott Thomas.

"Where the Money Is" in *Hispanic Business*. (Vol. 19, No. 2, February 1997, p. 60). By Jonathan J. Higuera.

"Who Needs Growth?" in *Inc*. (Vol. 18, No. 14, October 1996, p. 90). By Susan Greco.

"Who's On-Line?" in *Inc*. (Vol. 19, No. 4, March 1997, pp. 34-39). By Dan Kennedy.

"Women putting themselves on local biz map" in *Crain's Detroit Business*. (Vol. 12, No. 13, March 1996, p. 9). By Karen Eness Pope.

"The Wonderland Economy" in *Inc*. (Special Issue: The State of Small Business, February 1996, pp. 14-16, 18-20, 23-24, 26-27, 29). By John Case.

Business Plans

"3 factors help make a strategy successful" in *Crain's Detroit Business*. (Vol. 5, No. 1, January 1997, p. 19). By Jim Brady.

"Best Laid Plans" in *Business Start-Ups*. (Vol. 7, No. 11, November 1995, p. 7). By Lynn Norquist.

"The Best Laid Plans" in *Entrepreneurial Woman*. (September 1990, pp. 74-79). By Edward C. Rybka.

Bizplan Builder Workbook. Cincinnati, OH: South-Western Publishing Co., 1997.

Blueprint for Business Objectives. Upper Saddle River, NJ: Prentice Hall, 1996.

Blueprint for Business Objectives. Upper Saddle River, NJ: Prentice Hall, 1996. By Paul Tiffany.

"Building a Better Business Plan" in *Home Office-Computing*. (February 1990, p. 30). By Charles H. Gajeway.

"Business Busters" in *Black Enterprise*. (Vol. 23, No. 4, November 1992, pp. 75-85). By Caryne Brown.

"Business Plan" in *Business Start-Ups*. (Vol. 7, No. 12, December 1995, pp. 8, 10-11). By Charles Fuller.

Business Plan Handbook. Leverett, MA: Rector Press, Ltd., 1995.

"A Business-Plan Outline" in *Crain's Small Business*. (December 14, 1995, p. 11). By Jeffrey McCracken.

"Business-plan software streamlines process" in *Crain's Detroit Business*. (Vol. 5, No. 1, January 1997, p. 17). By Len Strazewski.

"Business Plan Stumbling Blocks" in *Working Woman*. (October 1994, pp. 45-48). By Rhonda M. Abrams.

The Business Planner: A Complete Guide to Raising Finances for Your Business. Newton, MA: Butterworth-Heinemann, 1992. By Iain Maitland.

Business Planning: An Approach to Strategic Management. Philadelphia, PA: Trans-Atlantic Publications, Inc., 1992. By Bill Richardson and Roy Richardson.

Business Planning for the Entrepreneur. Lancaster, OH: Tangent Publishing, 1990. By Andrew J. Batchelor, Jr.

Business Planning in Four Steps & a Leap. Marquette, MI: Northern Economic Initiatives Corp., 1995. By Scott Sporte.

The Business Planning Guide: Creating a Plan for Success in Your Own Business. Dover, NH: Upstart Publishing Co., Inc., sixth edition, 1992. By David H. Bangs, Jr.

Business Plans to Manage Day-to-Day Operations: Real-life Results for Small Business Owners and Operators. Somerset, NJ: John Wiley & Sons, Inc., 1993. By Christopher R. Malburg.

"Change of Plans" in *Business Start-Ups.* (Vol. 7, No. 6, June 1995, p. 9). By Erika Kotite.

"Change of Plans" in *Entrepreneur.* (May 1996, p. 30). By Donald E. Budmen.

"College pals won't tamper with success" in *Crain's Small Business.* (Vol. 4, No. 11, November 1996, pp. 21). By Jeffrey McCracken.

The Complete Book of Business Plans: Simple Steps to Writing a Powerful Business Plan. Naperville, IL: Sourcebooks, Inc., 1994. By Joseph A. Covello and Brian J. Hazelgreen.

"The Complete New-Business Survival Guide" in *Inc.* (Vol. 14, No. 7, July 1992, pp. 48-66). By Susan Greco.

Computer Applications for Business Planning: A Practical Hands-On Text. Lancaster, Ohio: Tangent Publishing, 1995. By Andrew J. Batchelor.

Crafting the Successful Business Plan. Englewood Cliffs, NJ: Prentice Hall, 1992. By Erik Hyypia.

"Credibility Gap" in *Income Opportunities.* (Vol. 32, No. 4, April 1997, pp. 42, 44). By Dorothy Elizabeth Brooks.

"Decide where to go before drawing a map" in *Crain's Small Business.* (Vol. 5, No. 4, April 1997, p. 22). By Jim Brady.

Develop Your Business Plan. Detroit, MI: Small Business Development Center.

Developing a Strategic Business Plan. Denver, CO: U.S. Small Business Administration (SBA).

Developing a Successful Business Plan. Irvine, CO: Entrepreneur, Inc.

"Do Business Plans Matter?" in *Inc.* (Vol. 18, No. 2, February 1996, pp. 21). By Mary Baechler.

"Do You Have a Plan?" in *In Business.* (April 1990, pp. 12-14). By David M. Freedman.

"The Do's and Don'ts of Writing A Winning Business Plan" in *Black Enterprise.* (Vol. 26, No. 9, April 1996, pp. 114-116, 120, 122). By Carolyn M. Brown.

"Entrepreneur had better know where all the money's going" in *Crain's Detroit Business.* (Vol. 5, No. 1, January 1997, p. 15). By Jerry Balan.

"Entrepreneurs Collide: Will Zoning Take Town Downhill?" in *Inc.* (Vol. 19, No. 5, April 1997, p. 32). By Joshua Macht.

The Entrepreneur's Guide to Building a Better Business Plan: A Step-by-Step Approach. Somerset, NJ: John Wiley & Sons, Inc., 1992. By Harold J. McLaughlin.

The Entrepreneur's Guide to Developing a Basic Business Plan. Northbrook, IL: S. K. Brown Publishing, 1991. By Chris Stevens.

The Entrepreneur's Guide to Preparing a Winning Business Plan and Raising Venture Capital. Englewood Cliffs, NJ: Prentice Hall, 1990. By Keith W. Schilit.

The Ernst and Young Business Plan Guide. Somerset, NJ: John Wiley & Sons, Inc., second edition, 1993.

"Exit Gracefully" in *Income Opportunities.* (Vol. 31, No. 11, November 1996, pp. 32, 34, 36). By Dorothy Elizabeth Brooks.

"Facing an Uphill Battle" in *Black Enterprise.* (Vol. 22, No. 4, November 1991, pp. 51-57). By Kevin D. Thompson.

"A Factor Analytic Study of the Perceived Causes of Small Business Failure" in *Journal of Small Business Management.* (Vol. 31, No. 4, October 1993, pp. 18-31). By LuAnn Ricketts Gaskill, Howard E. Van Auken and Ronald A. Manning.

"Financial Ratios in Large Public and Small Private Firms" in *Journal of Small Business Management.* (Vol. 30, No. 3, July 1992, pp. 35). By Jerome Osteryoung, Richard L. Constand and Donald Nast.

"Finding Your Niche" in *Business Start-Ups.* (Vol. 9, No. 4, April 1997, pp. 72, 74). By Carla Goodman.

"Fools Rush In? The Institutional Context of Industry Creation" in *Academy of Management Review.* (Vol. 19, No.

4, October 1994, pp. 645). By Howard E. Aldrich and Marlene C. Fiol.

"FYI" in *Income Opportunities*. (Vol. 32, No. 1, January 1997).

"Game Plan" in *Entrepreneur*. (Vol. 23, No. 8, August 1995, pp. 38-41). By David R. Evanson.

"Garbarge In, Garbage Out" in *Inc.* (Vol. 18, No. 11, August 1996, pp. 41-44). By Brian McWilliams.

Getting Ready. Bellingham, WA: Self-Counsel Press, Inc., 1991. By Dan Kennedy.

Growth Company Starter Kit. New York, NY: Coopers & Lybrand.

How to Make a Business Plan That Works! Teaneck, NJ: NAPL. By Lyman Henderson.

How to Prepare and Present a Business Plan. New York, NY: Simon & Schuster, Inc., 1992. By Joseph R. Mancuso.

How to Prepare a Results-Driven Business Plan. New York, NY: AMACOM, 1993. By Gregory J. Massarella, Patrick D. Zorsch, Daniel D. Jacobson, and Marc J. Rittenhouse.

"How to get biz beyond the start-up stage" in *Crain's Small Business*. (June 1996, pp. 8). By Lawrence Gardner.

"How To Start an Inc. 500 Company" in *Inc. 500*. (Vol. 16, No. 11, 1994, pp. 51-52, 54, 57-58, 60, 63-65). By Leslie Brokaw.

How to Write a Business Plan. Berkeley, CA: Nolo Press, fourth edition, 1992. By Mike McKeever.

"How to Write a Business Plan" in *Nation's Business*. (Vol. 81, No. 2, February 1993, pp. 29-30). By J. Tol Broome, Jr.

How to Write a Successful Business Plan: Step-by-Step Guide to Business Success. Interlochen, MI: Lewis & Renn Associates, Inc., 1995. By Jerre G. Lewis.

How to Write a Winning Business Plan. Englewood Cliffs, NJ: Prentice Hall, 1990. By Joseph Mancuso.

"How to determine your debt comfort zone" in *Crain's Small Business*. (Vol. 4, No. 10, October 1996, p. 21). By Kevin Reitzloff.

Incorporate Your Business: The National Corporation Kit. Carbondale, IL: Nova Publishing Co., 1995. By Daniel Sitarz.

"It's A Plan" in *Entrepreneur*. (June 1995, pp. 28, 30-31). By Cheryl J. Goldberg.

"It's All In The Plan" in *Small Business Reports*. (Vol. 19, No. 6, June 1994, pp. 38-43). By Alan W. Jackson.

"Key ingredient in recipe: The right people" in *Crain's Small Business*. (Vol. 4, No. 11, November 1996, pp. 23). By Jim Brady.

"Keys to Success? For Starters, Here Are 15" in *Contractor*. (Vol. 41, No. 11, November 1994, pp. 12). By Jeff Ferenc.

Launching New Ventures. Dover, NH: Upstart Publishing Co., Inc., 1995.

"Line forms even before zone capital shop opens" in *Crain's Detroit Business*. (Vol. 12, No. 46, November 1996, p. 16-17). By Shekini Gilliam.

"Many stop at Oakland's shop for business info" in *Crain's Detroit Business*. (Vol. 12, No. 46, November 1996, p. 17). By Shekini Gilliam.

"Mapping Your Route" in *Business Start-Ups*. (Vol. 8, No. 12, December 1996, pp. 40, 42-44). By Lynn H. Colwell.

"The Money Is Out There...How To Get It" in *Agency Sales Magazine*. (Vol. 24, No. 2, February 1994, pp. 15-17). By Jeff Fromberg.

"The Numbers Speak Volumes" in *Small Business Reports*. (Vol. 19, No. 7, July 1994, pp. 39-43). By Lamont Change.

"Obstacle Course" in *Income Opportunities*. (Vol. 31, No. 11, November 1996, pp. 27-30, 96). By Dale D. Buss.

"Opening a New Store...Reasonable Goals and Careful Planning" in *Stores*. (Vol. 76, No. 10, October 1994, pp. 101-102). By Bill Pearson.

"Plan of Action" in *Income Opportunities*. (Vol. 30, No. 7, July 1995, pp. 96, 98, 100). By Toni Reinhold.

"Plan of Attack" in *Inc.* (Vol. 18, No. 1, January 1996, pp. 41-44). By Martha E. Mangelsdorf.

"Plan Of Attack" in *Entrepreneur*. (Vol. 23, No. 8, August 1995, pp. 150, 152-157).

"Plan can help put the success in succession" in *Crain's Small Business*. (June 1996, pp. 13). By Don Clayton.

Planning and Goal Setting for Small Business. Denver, CO: U.S. Small Business Administration (SBA).

"Planning for Projects" in *Income Opportunities*. (Vol. 29, No. 7, July 1994, pp. 44). By Carol More.

"Planning for Success" in *Business Start-Ups*. (Vol. 8, No. 3, March 1996, pp. 50, 52-53). By Lynn L. Norquist.

"Poor Planning Plagues Small Business" in *Income Opportunities*. (Vol. 30, No. 4, April 1995, pp. 2). By Patricia Hamilton.

"Prepare for frustration you'll create exhilaration" in *Crain's Small Business.* (Vol. 4, No. 10, October 1996, p. 19). By Jim Brady.

Preparing a Successful Business Plan: A Practical Guide for Small Business. Bellingham, WA: Self-Counsel Press, Inc., second edition, 1993. By Rodger Touchie.

The Process of Business Planning: A Practical Hands-on Text. Lancaster, OH: Tangent Publishing, 1994. By Andrew J. Batchelor, Sr.

"Putting It Together" in *Business Start-Ups*. (Vol. 8, No. 9, September 1996, pp. 12, 14). By Ellen DePasquale.

Raising Capital: How to Write a Financing Proposal to Raise Venture Capital. Grants Pass, OR: Oasis Press, 1994. By Lawrence Flanagan.

"Right adds might when you write proposal" in *Crain's Small Business*. (June 1996, pp. 16). By Jim Brady.

"Savvy partners weren't taken to cleaners" in *Crain's Small Business*. (Vol. 4, No. 9, September 1996, pp. 9, 10). By Tim Moran.

"SCORE Points to Success" in *Black Enterprise*. (Vol. 25, No. 6, January 1995, pp. 38). By Christina F. Watts.

Small Business Planning Workbook. New York, NY: Clark Boardman Callaghan, 1990. By John C. Wisdom.

Solid Gold Success Strategies for Your Business. New York, NY: AMACOM, 1996. By Don Taylor.

"Split Decisions" in *Income Opportunities*. (Vol. 31, No. 9, September 1996, pp. 34, 36, 38). By Diane M. Calabrese.

"Start with Strategic Fundamentals" in *Crain's Small Business*. (September 1995, p. 9). By Jim Brady.

The Start-up Business Plan. Englewood Cliffs, NJ: Prentice Hall, 1991. By William M. Luther.

"Staying Alive " in *Black Enterprise*. (Vol. 25, No. 4, November 1994, pp. 90-92, 95-96). By Rhonda Reynolds.

"Step 6: Compose A Winning Business Plan" in *Business Start-Ups*. (Vol. 8, No. 10, October 1996, pp. 68, 70). By Kylo-Patrick Hart.

Strategic Planning for the New & Small Business. Dover, NH: Upstart Publishing Co., Inc., 1995. By Fred L. Fry.

Strategic Planning for the Small Business: Situations, Weapons, Objectives & Tactics. Holbrook, MA: Adams Publishing, 1990. By Craig Rice.

The Successful Business Plan: Secrets and Strategies. Grants Pass, OR: PSI Research, 1993. By Rhonda M. Abrams.

Successful Manager's Guide to Business: Seven Practical Steps to Producing Your Best Ever Business Plan. New York, NY: McGraw-Hill, Inc., 1994. By David Freemantle.

"Surviving the Holidays" in *Hispanic Business*. (Vol. 18, No. 11, November 1996, pp. 60, 62). By Graham Witherall.

"Ten Steps to Creating Your Business Plan" in *Income Opportunities*. (December/January 1991, pp. 55-56). By Ruth Anne King.

"The Seven Traps of Strategic Planning" in *Inc.* (Vol. 18, No. 16, November 1996, pp. 99, 101, 103). By Joseph C. Picken and Gregory G. Dess.

The Total Business Plan: How to Write, Rewrite, and Revise. New York, NY: John Wiley & Sons, Inc., second edition, 1994. By Patrick D. O'Hara.

Total Business Planning: A Step-by-Step Guide with Forms. New York, NY: John Wiley & Sons, Inc., 1991. By E. James Burton and W. Blan McBride.

Trademark: How to Name Your Business and Product. Berkeley, CA: Nolo Press, 1992. By Stephen Elias and Kate McGrath.

"When Your Banker Says No" in *Income Opportunities*. (Vol. 30, No. 11, November 1995, pp. 24-28). By Randall Kirkpatrick.

"Where's Your Plan" in *Hispanic Business*. (Vol. 20, No. 3, March 1997, p. 46). By Rick Mendosa.

"Why My Business Failed" in *Black Enterprise*. (Vol. 24, No. 11, June 1994, pp. 236-242). By Charles Jamison.

"Working Capital Woes" in *Black Enterprise*. (Vol. 26 No. 11, June 1996, p. 48). By Carolyn M. Brown.

Writing Business Plans That Get Results: A Step-by-Step Guide. Chicago, IL: Contemporary Books, Inc., 1991. By Michael O'Donnell.

Writing a Convincing Business Plan. Hauppauge, NY: Barron's Educational Series, Inc., 1995. By Art DeThomas.

Writing Effective Business Plans. Irvine, CA: Entrepreneur, Inc.

Your Business Plan. Eugene, OR: Oregon Small Business Development Center Network: Lane Community College, revised edition, 1990. By Dennis J. Sargent.

Your First Business Plan: Learn the Critical Steps to Writing a Winning Business Plan. Naperville, IL: Sourcebooks, Inc., 1995. By Joseph A. Covello.

Business Vision/Goals

"3 factors help make a strategy successful" in *Crain's Detroit Business*. (Vol. 5, No. 1, January 1997, p. 19). By Jim Brady.

"Above and Beyond" in *Entrepreneur*. (February 1997, p. 84-86). By Robert McGarvey.

"Act of Courage" in *Business Start-Ups*. (Vol. 8, No. 6, June 1996, pp. 14, 16). By Carolyn Z. Lawrence.

"Added Attraction" in *Entrepreneur: Buyer's Guide to Franchise and Business Opportunities*. (Vol. 22, No. 11, 1995, pp. 36, 38-40). By Guen Sublette.

Aiming Higher: 25 Stories of How Companies Prosper by Combining Sound Management & Social Vision. New York, NY: AMACOM, 1996. By David Bollier.

"Asking For Directions" in *Business Start-Ups*. (Vol. 8, No. 12, December 1996, pp. 16, 18-19). By Johanna S. Billings.

"Back To The Future" in *Entrepreneur*. (Vol. 23, No. 1, January 1995, pp. 238-242, 245). By Robert McGarvey.

Benchmarking for Best Practices: How to Define, Locate, and Emulate the Best in the Business. New York, NY: McGraw-Hill, Inc., 1995. By Christopher E. Bogan and Michael M. English.

"The Best Of Times" in *Entrepreneur*. (Vol. 24, No. 4, April 1996, pp. 139-142). By Mark Henricks.

"Bright Ideas" in *Business Start-Ups*. (Vol. 7, No. 8, August 1995, pp. 50, 52-54, 57). By Bob Weinstein.

"Building Companies to Last" in *Inc.* (Special Issue: The State of Small Business, February 1996, pp. 83-84, 87-88). By James C. Collins.

"Business Brainstorms" in *Business Start-Ups*. (Vol. 9, No. 3, March 1997, pp. 8, 10). By Carolyn Campbell.

"Business Must Refocus Once It Outgrows Entrepreneur's Control" in *Crain's Small Business*. (October 1995, p. 16). By Jon Greenawalt.

"Businesses needn't be related to construction" in *Crain's Small Business*. (Vol. 5, No. 3, March 1997, p. 11). By Jeffrey McCracken.

"By the Book" in *Entrepreneur*. (June 1995, pp. 141-145). By Jane Easter Bahls.

"Choose Your Vehicle" in *Business Start-Ups*. (Vol. 8, No. 12, December 1996, pp. 24, 26-27). By Lin Grensing-Pophal.

Corporate Internet Planning Guide: Aligning Internet Strategy with Business Goals. New York, NY: Van Nostrand Reinhold, 1997. By Richard Gascoyne.

"Creativity at the Edge of Chaos" in *Working Woman*. (February 1997, pp. 47-51, 53). By Joseph Marshall.

"Destination Success" in *Business Start-Ups*. (Vol. 8, No. 12, December 1996, p. 50). By Carla Goodman.

"Everything According to Plan" in *INC.* (Vol. 17, No. 3, March 1995, pp. 79-85). By Jay Finegan.

"Fools Rush In? The Institutional Context of Industry Creation" in *Academy of Management Review*. (Vol. 19, No. 4, October 1994, pp. 645). By Howard E. Aldrich and Marlene C. Fiol.

"Forging New Frontiers" in *Black Enterprise*. (Vol. 26, No. 10, May 1996, pp. 70-72, 74, 76, 78). By Marjorie Whigham-Desir.

"Fueling Up" in *Business Start-Ups*. (Vol. 8, No. 12, December 1996, pp. 46, 48). By Carla Goodman.

Goals and Goal Setting. Menlo Park, CA: Crisp Publications, Inc. By Larrie Rouillard.

"Going it Alone" in *Newsweek*. (April 1996, pp. 50-51). By Ellyn E. Spragins and Steve Rhodes.

"Ground Zero" in *Entrepreneur*. (December 1996, p. 18). By Janean Chun.

"Growing Strong" in *Income Opportunities*. (Vol. 31, No. 6, June 1996, pp. 30, 32, 34). By Dorothy Elizabeth Brooks.

"High-Technology Horizon" in *Corporate Detroit*. (Vol. 14, No. 4, April 1996, pp. 27-29). By Kevin J. Lamiman.

How to Succeed in Employee Development: Moving from Vision to Results. New York, NY: McGraw-Hill, Inc., 1996. By Edward Moorby.

"Independents need a 'big picture' person" in *Crain's Small Business*. (Vol. 5, No. 2, February 1997, p. 22). By Jim Brady.

"Inventor's Workshop" in *Business Start-Ups*. (October 1994, pp. 26-29). By Jacquelyn Lynn Denali.

"Journey Of A Thousand Miles" in *Business Start-Ups*. (Vol. 8, No. 12, December 1996, p. 4). By Carolyn Z. Lawrence.

"Just a Suggestion" in *Entrepreneur*. (December 1996, p. 40). By Jacquelyn Lynn.

"Just Their Luck" in *Entrepreneur*. (Vol. 23, No. 2, February 1995, pp. 120, 122-25). By Gayle Sato Stodder.

"Laying out firm's vision isn't mission impossible" in *Crain's Small Business*. (Vol. 5, No. 4, April 1997, p. 11). By Lawrence Gardner.

"Like Pulling Teeth" in *Hispanic Business*. (Vol. 18, No. 6, June 1996, pp. 138, 140). By Graham Witherall.

Managing Performance: Goals, Feedback, Coaching, Recognition. Brookfield, VT: Ashgate Publishing Co., 1997. By Jenny Hill.

"MARKETING ON A SHOESTRING" in *Small Business Opportunities*. (Vol. 8, No. 6, November 1996, pp. 22-24, 26, 28, 30, 32, 34). By Jeanie Crane.

"Measuring Up" in *Entrepreneur*. (November, 1996 pp. 168-173). By Robert McGarvey.

"Motivating Statistics" in *Business Start-Ups*. (Vol. 8, No. 8, August 1996, p. 4). By Karin Moeller.

"A Nation of Owners" in *Inc.* (Special Issue: The State of Small Business, February 1996, pp. 89-91). By William Bridges.

"Opening a New Store...Reasonable Goals and Careful Planning" in *Stores*. (Vol. 76, No. 10, October 1994, pp. 101-102). By Bill Pearson.

The Power of Internal Marketing: Building a Values-Based Corporate Culture. New Orleans, LA: Good Reading Books, 1996. By Lamar D. Berry.

"Q & A" in *Performance*. (September 1995, pp. 12-16). By Daniel Burrus.

"Say When" in *Inc.* (Vol. 17, No. 2, February 1995, pp. 19-20). By Steven L. Marks.

"Seize The Day" in *Income Opportunities*. (Vol. 32, No. 1, January 1997, pp. 32, 34, 36, 66). By Dorothy Elizabeth Brooks.

"Small Like Me" in *Wall Street Journal Special Reports: Small Business (Special Edition)*. (May 23, 1996, pp. R31). By John Buskin.

"Small Talk" in *Wall Street Journal Special Reports: Small Business (Special Edition)*. (May 23, 1996, pp. R28). By Stephanie N. Mehta.

"Sounding Board" in *Income Opportunities*. (Vol. 30, No. 6, June 1995, pp. 114, 116). By Richard J. Maturi.

"Start Your Engines" in *Business Start-Ups*. (Vol. 8, No. 12, December 1996, pp. 6, 9). By Kylo-Patrick Hart.

"Staying Alive" in *Entrepreneur*. (Vol. 23, No. 3, March 1995, pp. 114-118). By Robert McGarvey.

"Steps to analyze and control your cash" in *Crain's Small Business*. (Vol. 5, No. 3, March 1997, p. 8). By Lawrence Gardner.

"Tapping Creativity" in *Exhibitor Times*. (Vol. 4, No. 2, February 1996, pp. 40-43). By Lorraine Denham and Heather Ransford.

"The Affair" in *Inc.* (Vol. 18, No. 16, November 1996, pp. 35, 37). By Ichak Adizes.

"The Art (& Smarts) of the Deal" in *Corporate Detroit*. (Vol. 13, No. 12, December 1995, p. 49). By Charles Rothstein.

"The Inc. 500: 15th Annual List" in *Inc.* (October 1996, pp. 15-16). By Joshua Hyatt.

"The Not-Too-Distant Future" in *Business Start-Ups*. (Vol. 9, No. 1, January 1997, pp. 36, 38, 40-42). By Kris Neri.

"Think about where you want to go, how to get there" in *Crain's Small Business*. (Vol. 4, No. 9, September 1996, p. 18). By Jim Brady.

"Time to make '97's business resolutions" in *Crain's Detroit Business*. (Vol. 5, No. 1, January 1997, p. 22). By David Sowerby.

"Tomorrow Land" in *Entrepreneur*. (Vol. 24, No. 2, February 1996, pp. 135-138). By Robert McGarvey.

"Turn It On" in *Entrepreneur*. (November, 1996 pp. 154-158, 161). By Robert McGarvey.

Vision: How Leaders Develop It, Share It, & Sustain It. New York, NY: McGraw-Hill, Inc., 1993. By Joseph V. Quigley.

"What Does Business Really Want from Governments?" in *Inc.* (Special Issue: The State of Small Business, February 1996, pp. 92-103). By Tom Richman.

"When Slow and Steady Wins the Race" in *Inc.* (Vol. 18, No. 17, November 1996, pp. 72-73, 76). By Jeffrey Zygmont.

"With Luck, This Biz Will Go Down the Toilet" in *Inc.* (Vol. 19, No. 5, April 1997, p. 21). By Phaedra Hise.

Consultants

"Advice-for-hire not just for big businesses" in *Crain's Small Business*. (June 1996, pp. 10). By Fred Leeb and Eric Weiss.

"Advisory Advice" in *Small Business Opportunities*. (Vol. 6, No. 5, September 1994, pp. 18). By Steve Veltkamp.

"ALL FOR ONE" in *Crain's Small Business*. (Vol. 4, No. 10, October 1996, p. 1). By Kimberly Lifton.

Applied Strategic Planning: The Consultant's Kit. Erlanger, KY: Pfeiffer & Co., 1992. By Timothy M. Nolan, Leonard D. Goodstein and J. William Pfeiffer.

Be Your Own Consultant: 188 Ways to Improve Your Business Operation. Secaucus, NJ: Carol Publishing Group, 1996. By Irving Burstiner.

Client-Centered Consulting: A Practical Guide for Internal Advisers and Trainers. New York, NY: McGraw-Hill, Inc., 1992. By Peter Cockman.

"A Climate for Investment" in *Hispanic Business*. (Vol. 15, No. 11, November 1994, pp. 58-60). By Christopher Boyd.

Complete Guide to Consulting Success. Chicago, IL: Dearborn Financial Publishing, Inc., 1992. By Howard Shenson.

Confronting the Experts. Albany, NY: State University of New York Press, 1996. By Brian Martin.

The Consultant's Calling: Bringing Who You Are to What You Do. San Francisco, CA: Jossey-Bass, Inc., 1992. By Geoffrey M. Bellman.

The Consultant's Guide to Hidden Profits: The 101 Most Overlooked Strategies for Increased Earnings & Growth. Somerset, NJ: John Wiley & Sons, Inc., 1992. By Herman R. Holtz.

The Consultant's Guide to Proposal Writing: How to Satisfy Your Clients and Double Your Income. Somerset, NJ: John Wiley & Sons, Inc., second edition, 1990. By Herman Holtz.

Consultant's Manual: A Complete Guide to Building a Successful Consulting Practice. Somerset, NJ: John Wiley & Sons, Inc., 1994. By Thomas L. Greenbaum.

The Consultant's Survival Guide. New York, NY: John Wiley & Sons, Inc., 1997. By Marsha Lewin.

Consultation Skills for Health Care Professionals: How to Be an Effective Consultant within Your Organization. San

Francisco, CA: Jossey-Bass, Inc., 1990. By Francis L. Ulschak and Sharon Snowantle.

Consulting Business Guide. Irvine, CA: Entrepreneur, Inc.

The Contract and Fee-Setting Guide for Consultants and Professionals. Somerset, NJ: John Wiley & Sons, Inc., 1990. By Howard L. Shenson.

Entrepeneur Magazine: Working with Consultants, Professionals, & Freelancers. New York, NY: John Wiley & Sons, Inc., 1997. By Leonard Bisk.

"An Evaluation of SBI Marketing Consulting" in *Journal of Small Business Management.* (Vol. 30, No. 4, October 1992, pp. 62-71). By Art Weinstein, J.A.F. Nicholls and Bruce Seaton.

"Fast Forward, Garbage Guru" in *Working Woman.* (January 1997, p. 18). By Kambiz Foroohar.

"Fast Forward, Up & Comers" in *Working Woman.* (January 1997, p. 20).

"Finding a Lawyer for Your Business" in *Nation's Business.* (Vol. 82, No. 4, April 1994, pp. 34-35). By Kenneth A. Ehrman.

"For Sale: Management Expertise from Small Companies" in *Inc.* (Vol. 19, No. 2, March 1997, p. 26). By Jerry Useem.

"Get Rich in '95" in *Small Business Opportunities.* (Vol. 7, No. 1, January 1995, pp. 20, 22, 24, 26, 28, 30, 32, 34, 36, 38-40, 42-45). By Cheryl Rogers

"Good Advice" in *Income Opportunities.* (Vol. 30, No. 4, April 1995, pp. 116-117). By Richard J. Maturi.

Guide to Small Business Consulting Engagements. Fort Worth, TX: Practitioners Publishing Co., 1996. By Douglas R. Carmichael.

How to Be a Consultant. Brookfield, VT: Ashgate Publishing Co., Inc., 1991. By Sally Garratt.

How to Become a Successful Consultant in Your Own Field. Rocklin, CA: Prima Publishing & Communications, third edition, 1991. By Hubert Bermont.

How to Make It Big as a Consultant. New York, NY: AMACOM, second edition, 1993. By William A. Cohen.

How to Make at Least $100,000 Every Year as a Successful Consultant in Your Own Field. Cambridge, MA: JLA Publications, 1992. By Jeffrey Lant.

How to Select and Use Consultants: A Client's Guide. Washington, DC: International Labor Office, 1993. By Milan Kubr.

How to Succeed as an Independent Consultant. Somerset, NJ: John Wiley & Sons, Inc., 1993. By Herman R. Holtz.

"How To Pick a Consultant" in *Small Business Reports.* (Vol. 19, No. 1, January 1994, pp. 9). By Alan W. Jackson.

"An Insurance Consultant May Benefit Your Bottom Line" in *Air Conditioning, Heating & Refrigeration News.* (Vol. 193, No. 5, October 3, 1994, pp. 22). By Joseph Arkin.

"Keep 'Em Coming Back For More" in *Business Start-up.* (Vol. 9, No. 1, January 1997, pp. 70, 72). By Carla Goodman.

"Legal Aid" in *Business Start-Ups.* (Vol. 7, No. 2, February 1995, pp. 78, 80-81). By Sue Clayton.

Million Dollar Consulting: The Profession's Guide to Growing a Practice. New York, NY: McGraw-Hill, Inc., 1994. By Alan Weiss.

"Never Too Small to Manage" in *Inc.* (Vol. 19, No. 2, February 1997, pp. 56-58, 61). By David Whitford.

"No-cost (and Low-cost) Consulting" in *Occupational Hazards.* (Vol. 57, No. 1, January 1995, pp. 59-63). By Mark S. Kuhar.

"One stop capital shop not quite ready" in *Crain's Detroit Business.* (Vol. 11, No. 24, June 12-18, 1996, pp. 12). By Michael Goodin.

"Pieces of Advice" in *Inc.* (Vol. 17, No. 6, May 1995, pp. 57-60, 62).

Selecting and Working with Consultants. Menlo Park, CA: Crisp Publications, Inc. By Thomas J. Ucko.

Small-Business Consulting. South Harwich, MA: Arnold Books, 1994. By Hugh Arnold.

"Southfield company handles Botsford data" in *Crain's Detroit Business.* (Vol. 13, No. 8, February/March 1997, p. 16). By David Barkholz.

"Spend Your Consulting Dollars Wisely" in *Marketing News*. (Vol. 28, No. 18, August 29, 1994, pp. 15). By Vicki Clift.

"What to consider when seeking outside advice" in *Crain's Small Business*. (Vol. 4, No. 10, October 1996, pp. 12-13). By Lawrence Gardner.

Entrepreneurship on the Web

"Alternative Investments" in *Black Enterprise*. (Vol. 27, No. 3, October 1996, p. 50). By Glenn Jeffers.

"Big Blue Horizons" in *Hispanic Business*. (Vol. 18, No. 6, June 1996, p. 126). By Rick Mendosa.

"Big Deal" in *The Red Herring*. (September 1996, pp. 51-52, 54, 56). By Andrew P. Madden.

"Buy Local Focus of State Program" in *Entrepreneur*. (Vol. 22, No. 13, December 1994, pp. 18). By Cynthia E. Griffin.

"Calling All Cybercustomers!" in *Independent Business*. (Vol. 8, No. 1, Jan./Feb. 1997, pp. 46). By Eric J. Adams.

"Don't Get Trapped" in *Hispanic Business*. (Vol. 19, No. 1, January 1997, p. 46). By Rick Mendosa.

"Drag and Click" in *Crain's Small Business*. (Vol. 5, No. 2, February 1997, p. 3). By Jeffrey McCracken.

"Easy E-Marketing" in *Independent Business*. (Vol. 8, No. 1, Jan./Feb. 1997, pp. 40). By Pam Froman.

"Entrepreneurial Spirit Awards" in *Hispanic Business*. (Vol. 18, No. 12, December 1996, pp. 26, 28, 30, 34, 36, 38). By Maria Zate.

"Getting Caught in the Web of On-Line Information" in *Exhibitor Times*. (Vol. 4, No. 1, January 1996, pp. 38-39). By Valerie A.M. Demetros.

"GETTING THE MOST FROM THE WEB" in *Crain's Small Business*. (July 1996, pp. 8). By Jeffrey McCracken.

"He wants PC users to face the music" in *Crain's Small Business*. (Vol. 5, No. 3, March 1997, p. 15). By Jeffrey McCracken.

"Home Sweet Home" in *Independent Business*. (Vol. 8, No. 1, Jan./Feb. 1997, pp. 30-32). By Kirk Kirksey.

"Hot Opportunity Of The Month" in *Income Opportunities*. (Vol. 31, No. 5, May 1996, p. 6). By Stephanie Jeffrey.

"How do you say Apple?" in *Hispanic Business*. (Vol. 19, No. 1, January 1997, p. 47). By Rick Mendosa.

"Idea man" in *HITS*. (Winter 1997, pp. 18-22). By Alex Gove.

"Information superhighway may be a dead end" in *Crain's Small Business*. (June 1996, pp. 12). By Scott Segal.

"INTERNET RESOURCES" in *Small Business Opportunities*. (Vol. 9, No. 3, May 1997, pp. 54, 56). By Lin Grensing-Pophal.

"Marketing 101" in *Entrepreneur*. (March 1997, pp. 112-117). By Robert McGarvey.

"NET INCOME" in *Crain's Small Business*. (July 1996, pp. 1). By Jeffrey McCracken.

"NET PROFITS" in *Working Woman*. (June 1996, pp. 44-49, 70, 72). By Gloria Brame.

"Net Rewards" in *Entrepreneur*. (March 1997, pp. 144, 146). By Heather Page.

"Networking" in *Crain's Detroit Business*. (Vol. 13, No. 3, January 1997, p. 8). By Art Dridgeforth Jr.

"Nothing but Net" in *Inc*. (Vol. 18, No. 18, December 1997, pp. 43-44). By Robert Metcalfe

"Online Advice" in *Independent Business*. (Vol. 8, No. 1, Jan./Feb. 1997, pp. 16). By Maryann Hammers.

"PR firm takes press-release production online" in *Crain's Detroit Business*. (Vol. 12 No. 38, September 1996, p. 14). By Arthur Bridgeforth Jr.

"Q & A" in *Performance*. (September 1995, pp. 12-16). By Daniel Burrus.

"Real Law in a Virtual World" in *Black Enterprise*. (Vol. 27, No. 5, December 1996, p. 44). By Tariq K. Muhammad.

"Rev It Up" in *Entrepreneur*. (March 1997, pp. 50, 52-53). By Cheryl J. Goldberg.

"Safety Net" in *Entrepreneur*. (February 1997, pp. 82-84). By Steven C. Bahls and Jane Easter Bahls.

"Short Cut to a Job" in *Hispanic Business*. (Vol. 19, No. 2, February 1997, p. 64). By Claudia Armann.

"Sites To Surf" in *Income Opportunities*. (Vol. 31, No. 5, May 1996, pp. 44, 46). By Debra D'Agostino.

"SURF'S UP" in *Small Business Opportunities*. (Vol. 9, No. 1, January 1997, p. 10). By Lin Grensing-Pophal.

"Take in the Sites" in *Independent Business*. (Vol. 8, No. 1, Jan./Feb. 1997, pp. 20). By Rick Mendosa.

"Toy Story" in *Entrepreneur*. (February 1997, p. 38). By Lynn Beresford.

"TradePort an Excellent Source of Trade Information and Leads" in *Hispanic Business*. (Vol. 18, No. 6, June 1996, p. 126). By Rick Mendosa.

"Translating the Web" in *HITS*. (Winter 1997, pp. 12-13). By Nikki C. Goth.

"Way of the Web?" in *Hispanic Business*. (Vol. 18, No. 10, October 1996, pp. 88). By Rick Mendosa.

"Web Fever!" in *Independent Business*. (Vol. 8, No. 1, Jan./Feb. 1997, pp. 36-39). By Eric J. Adams.

"Wired Kingdom" in *Inc.* (Vol. 19, No. 4, March 1997, p. 112). By Pam Kadlec.

"Your Hassle-Free Web Site" in *Independent Business*. (Vol. 8, No. 1, Jan./Feb. 1997, pp. 18). By Maryann Hammers.

Gourmet Coffee/Tea Service

"Bean Scene" in *Business Start-Ups*. (January 1994, pp. 64-67). By Ken Ohlson.

"Bean Scene" in *Entrepreneur*. (December 1993, pp. 90, 92-3). By Ken Ohlson.

The Book of Coffee: A Gourmet's Guide. New York, NY: Abbeville Press, Inc., 1991. By Riccardo Illy.

"Breaking Grounds" in *Business Start-Ups*. (Vol. 7, No. 2, February 1995, p. 11). By Cynthia E. Griffin.

"Brewing Up Profits" in *Small Business Opportunities*. (Vol. 6, No. 5, September 1994, pp. 34-35). By Carla Goodman.

"Business is sweet in Cottage Country" in *Detroit Free Press*. (April 2, pp. 1C, 3C). By Tish Williams.

"Canine Cafe" in *Business Start-Ups*. (October 1994, pp. 86). By Karen Sulkis.

"Chock Full O'Bucks" in *Income Opportunities*. (Vol. 29, No. 8, August 1994, pp. 42, 44, 46, 48). By Maureen Nevin Duffy.

Coffee: A Guide to Buying, Brewing and Enjoying. Santa Rosa, CA: Cole Group, Inc., fourth edition, 1994. By Kenneth Davids.

The Coffee Book. Gretna, LA: Pelican Publishing Co., 1993. By Dawn Campbell and Janet Smith.

"Coffee Cash: Espresso Bars" in *Income Opportunities*. (July/August 1993, pp. 50, 82, 84, 86). By Gary M. Stern.

Coffee and Tea Store Business Guide. Irvine, CA: Entrepreneur, Inc.

"Cybercafe.com" in *Business Start-Ups*. (Vol. 9, No. 3, March 1997, pp. 62, 64-66). By Nora Carrera.

"Entrepreneurs Across America" in *Entrepreneur*. (Vol. 24, No. 4, April 1996, pp. 100-104, 106-108, 110-112, 114-116, 118, 120-123). By Janean Chum, et al.

The Espresso Bartenders Guide to Expresso Bartending. Snohomish, WA: Hooked on Espresso, 1992. By Sally A. Slankard.

Espresso!: Starting & Succeeding with Your Own Coffee Business. New York, NY: John Wiley & Sons, Inc., 1995. By Joe Monaghan.

Making Your Own Gourmet Coffee Drinks: Espressos, Cappuccinos, Lattes, Mochas, and More! New York, NY: Crown Publishing Group, 1992. By Mathew Tekulsky.

"Man's Best Friends" in *Business Start-Ups*. (Vol. 9, No. 1, January 1997, p. 96). By Carla Goodman.

"Minding the Store" in *Inc.* (Vol. 15, No. 11, November 1993, pp. 66-69, 71, 74-75). By Leslie Brokaw.

"Mr. Tea" in *Income Opportunities*. (Vol. 29, No. 8, August 1994, pp. 36-40). By Dale D. Buss.

"Oh, Boy, That Coffee's Hot" in *Crain's Detroit Business*. (Vol. 11, No. 50, December 11-17, 1995, pp. 1, 21). By Marsha Stopa.

So You Want to Open a Tea Shop: Let Me Tell You about It. Tallahassee, FL: Proper Tea, 1993. By Martha J. Jones.

"Starbuck Wars" in *Working Woman*. (January 1996, pp. 25-27). By Linda Lee Small.

Start & Run a Profitable Coffee Bar. Bellingham, WA: Self Counsel Press, Inc., 1997. By Tom Matzen.

"Tea Time" in *Entrepreneur*. (Vol. 23, No. 3, March 1995, pp. 224, 226-228). By Gayle Sato Stodder.

"Tea Time" in *Income Opportunities*. (Vol. 31, No. 6, June 1996, pp. 84, 86, 88). By Maria Garcia.

The Top One Hundred Coffee Recipes: A Cookbook for Coffee Drinkers. Hollywood, FL: LIFETIME Books, Inc., 1992. By Mary Ward.

"Wanna-be Owners Put Eyes on Franchise" in *Crain's Detroit Business*. (Vol. 10, No. 41, October 10-16, 1994, pp. 9-10). By Chris Mead.

High-Tech Business

"A guide may be needed to set up shop on-line" in *Crain's Detroit Business*. (Vol. 11, No. 29, July 1995, p. 11).

"Ace in the Hole" in *Entrepreneur*. (May 1997, pp. 69-71). By David R. Evanson.

Advanced Technologies: Pros & Cons. Rockville, MD: Odelle Publications, 1993. By Candy F. Drew.

"An entrepreneur cries for help" in *Crain's Detroit Business*. (Vol. 5, No. 1, January 1997, p. 4). By Jeffrey McCracken.

"Attracting advertisers" in *HITS*. (Fall 1996, p. 68).

"Business and gravy" in *The Red Herring*. (March 1997, pp. 50-51). By Luc Hatlestad.

"Bytes Can Bite Back" in *Crain's Small Business Office Tech '96 Supplement*. (Vol. 4, No. 11, November 1996, pp. T-19). By Claudia Rast and Marc Bergsman.

"Cashing in on the Web" in *HITS*. (Fall 1996, p. 66).

"Changing the Future of Business" in *Black Enterprise*. (Vol. 27, No. 8, March 1997, pp. 80-84). By Marvin V. Greene.

"College pals won't tamper with success" in *Crain's Small Business*. (Vol. 4, No. 11, November 1996, pp. 21). By Jeffrey McCracken.

Commercializing High Technology: East & West. Lanham, MD: Rowman & Littlefield, Publishers, Inc., 1996. By Judith B. Sedaitis.

"Computer resale shops offer buyers alternative" in *Crain's Detroit Business*. (Vol. 11, No. 14, April 1995, p. 11). By Michael Maurer.

"Customize Customers" in *Crain's Small Business Office Tech '96 Supplement*. (Vol. 4, No. 11, November 1996, pp. T-7). By Arthur Bridgeforth, Jr.

"Customize Customers" in *Crain's Small Business Office Tech '96 Supplement*. (Vol. 4, No. 11, November 1996, pp. T-7). By Arthur Bridgeforth, Jr.

"DIGITAL COMMERCE" in *The Red Herring*. (February 1997, pp. 46, 48, 50). By Alex Gove.

"Don't hold your breath" in *The Red Herring*. (February 1997, p. 84). By Andrew P. Madden.

"E-Male Dominates?" in *Crain's Small Business Office Tech '96 Supplement*. (Vol. 4, No. 11, November 1996, pp. T-4). By Shekini Gilliam.

"Entrepreneurial Superstars" in *Entrepreneur*. (April 1997, pp. 108-139). By Debra Phillips.

"Friendship begets 11-years partnership" in *Crain's Small Business*. (Vol. 5, No. 4, April 1997, p. 23). By Jeffrey McCracken.

"Going Public Proved a Rich Experience for Technology Entrepreneurs in '96" in *Wall Street Journal*. (Vol. IC, No. 22, 09/31/97, p. B1). By Michael Selz.

"Growth squeezes collectibles shop" in *Crain's Small Business*. (Vol. 4, No. 10, October 1996, p. 4). By Jeffrey McCracken.

"Hacker Attackers" in *Crain's Small Business Office Tech '96 Supplement*. (Vol. 4, No. 11, November 1996, pp. T-6). By Arthur Bridgeforth, Jr.

"High-Tech Hoods" in *Inc.* (Vol. 19, No. 4, March 1997, pp. 48-51). By Sarah Schafer.

"High-tech firm discovers lease-to-buy is way to go" in *Crain's Small Business.* (Vol. 5, No. 4, April 1997, p. 10). By Tim Moran.

High Tech Start Up: The Complete How-to-Handbook for Creating Successful New High Tech Companies. San Jose, CA: Electronics Trend Publications, 1992. By John L. Nesheim.

"His customers' plea became new calling" in *Crain's Small Business.* (July 1996, pp. 15). By Jeffrey McCracken.

"Instant Ally" in *Business Start-Ups.* (Vol. 8, No. 7, July 1996, pp. 12, 14). By Pamela Palmer.

"Investors Bet on Cyberspace Path to Terra Firm Travel" in *Wall Street Journal.* (Vol. IC, No. 9, January 14, 1997, pp. B2). By Michael Selz.

Managing High-Tech Start-Ups. Woburn, MA: Butterworth-Heinemann, 1992. By Duncan MacVicar.

Managing High Technology Companies. New York, NY: Van Nostrand Reinhold, 1990. By Henry E. Riggs.

Managing Information & Entrepreneurship in Technology-Based Firms. New York, NY: John Wiley & Sons, Inc., 1994. By Michael J. Martin.

"Marketing Online" in *Black Enterprise.* (Vol. 27, No. 2, September 1996, pp. 85-88). By Tariq K. Muhammand.

New Technology-Based Firms in the 1990s. Bristol, PA: Taylor & Francis, Inc., 1994. By Ray Oakey.

"New York" in *Hispanic Business.* (Vol. 17, No. 5, May 1995, p. 36). By Yvonne Conde.

"No line online, but use with caution" in *Crain's Small Business.* (Vol. 4, No. 11, November 1996, pp. 10). By Jeff Pace.

"Not everyone's on-line" in *Crain's Detroit Business.* (Vol. 11, No. 29, July 1995, p. 10). By Michael Maurer.

"On-Line Upstarts Tap Big Media Companies for Funds" in *Wall Street Journal.* (Vol. IC, No. 19, February 10, 1997, pp. B2). By Stephanie N. Metha.

"Online Salesperson" in *Crain's Small Business Office Tech '96 Supplement.* (Vol. 4, No. 11, November 1996, pp. T-3).

Product Strategy for High-Technology Companies: How to Achieve Growth, Competitive Advantage, & Increased Profits. Hinsdale, IL: Irwin Professional Publishing, 1994. By Michael E. McGrath.

"Safeguarding Your Network" in *Black Enterprise.* (Vol. 27, No. 3, October 1996, pp. 48-50). By Joyce E. Davis.

"Small access providers weave some tangled routes to the Web" in *Detroit Free Press.* (March 24, pp. 10F-11F, 14F). By Mike Brennan.

Starting a High Tech Company. Piscataway, NJ: Institute of Electrical & Electronics Engineers, Inc., 1995. By Michael L. Baird.

"Surf's up!" in *HITS.* (Fall 1996, pp. 9, 11). By Anthony B. Perkins.

"Taking it to The Street" in *HITS.* (Spring 1997, pp. 16-20). By Anne T. Linsmayer.

"TECH TRASH" in *Crain's Detroit Business.* (Vol. 11, No. 29, July 1995, p. 8). By Mary Dempsey.

"The Future of Your Business" in *Business Start-up.* (Vol. 9, No. 4, April 1997, pp. 26-32). By Kylo-Patrick Hart.

"Using Technology to Enhance Your Business" in *Black Enterprise.* (Vol. 27, No. 8, March 1997, pp. 64-72).

Walking the High-Tech High Wire: The Technical Entrepreneur's Guide to Running a Successful Enterprise. New York, NY: McGraw-Hill, Inc., 1993. By David Adamson.

"Was That Cybernet Inc. or Interweb Co.?" in *Wall Street Journal.* (Vol. IC, No. 5, January 8, 1997, pp. B1-B2). By Rodney Ho.

"What the doctor ordered" in *Crain's Detroit Business.* (Vol. 13, No. 15, April 1997, p. 9). By David Barkholz.

"Wired for Success" in *Black Enterprise.* (Vol. 27, No. 8, March 1997, pp. 75-80). By Tariq K. Muhammad.

Home-Based Business

101 Best Weekend Businesses. Franklin Lakes, NJ: Career Press, Inc., 1996. By Dan Ramsey.

1996 National Home Based Business Directory. Aitkin, MN: Marketing Solutions, Inc., 1996. By Darleen J. Hoffman.

"A Clothes Call" in *Income Opportunities*. (Vol. 32, No. 4, April 1997, p. 12). By Lana Sanderson.

"A Delicate Balance" in *Business Start-Ups*. (Vol. 8, No. 9, September 1996, pp. 8, 10). By Ken Ohlson.

"Advantage: Home" in *Business Start-Ups*. (Vol. 8, No. 6, June 1996, pp. 84, 86). By Janie Sullivan.

"Alone Behind The Desk" in *Business Start-Ups*. (Vol. 9, No. 4, April 1997, pp. 8, 10). By Carolyn Campbell.

"Attention Getters" in *Entrepreneur*. (Vol 23, No. 1, January 1995, pp. 76, 78). By Debra Phillips.

"Beat the January Blues" in *Business Start-Ups*. (Vol. 8, No. 1, January 1996, pp. 18-19).

Best Home-Based Businesses for the Nineties. New York, NY: Jeremy P. Tarcher Inc., 1991. By Paul Edwards and Sarah Edwards.

Best Home-Based Franchises. New York, NY: Doubleday & Co., Inc., 1992. By Philip Lief Group, Inc., staff.

Best Home Businesses for the 90's. New York, NY: Jeremy P. Tarcher Inc., 1995. By Sarah Edwards.

"Bottled Profits" in *Income Opportunities*. (Vol. 31, No. 6, June 1996, pp. 96, 94). By Amy H. Berger.

"Broadcast News" in *Business Start-Ups*. (Vol. 7, No. 6, June 1995, p. 16). By Cynthia E. Griffin.

"BUCKS IN BUTTONS" in *Small Business Opportunities*. (Vol. 9, No. 1, January 1997, p. 48). By Carla Goodman.

"Building the Perfect Home Office" in *Black Enterprise*. (Vol. 27, No. 8, March 1997, pp. 36-37). By Rafiki Cai.

The Business Plan for Home-Based Business. Denver, CO: U.S. Small Business Administration (SBA).

"Buying Wisely for Your Office" in *Black Enterprise*. (Vol. 27, No. 9, April 1997, p. 35-36). By Tariq K. Muhammad.

Buying Your First Franchise. Menlo Park, CA: Crisp Publications, Inc., 1994. By Rebecca Luhn.

"Catering Requirements" in *Black Enterprise*. (Vol. 27, No. 8, March 1997, p. 30). By Sheryl E. Huggins.

"Collectibles Search" in *Business Start-Ups*. (Vol. 8, No. 7, July 1996, p. 32). By Guen Sublette.

"Combat Zone" in *Entrepreneur*. (Vol. 22, No. 9, September 1994, pp. 100). By Janean Huber.

"COMMUNITY CENTERED" in *Business Start-Ups*. (Vol. 8, No. 6, June 1996, pp. 68, 70-71). By Deborah Richman.

Complete Home-Based Business Sourcebook. Old Tappan, NJ: Macmillan Publishing Co. Inc., 1996.

The Complete Work-at-Home Companion. Rocklin, CA: Prima Publishing & Communications, second edition, 1993. By Herman Holtz.

Computer Consulting on Your Home-Based PC. New York, NY: McGraw-Hill, Inc., 1994. By Herman Holtz.

"Conference Call" in *Entrepreneur*. (Vol. 23, No. 12, November 1995, pp. 48, 50). By Cynthia E. Griffin.

"Congressman Plans Bill to Aid Home-Based Businesses" in *Wall Street Journal*. (Vol. IC, No. 16, January 23, 1997, pp. B2). By Rodney Ho.

"Cost Controls" in *Income Opportunities*. (Vol. 30, No. 5, May 1995, pp. 8). By Lana Sanderson.

"Couple to relocate Sanit-Air for sanity" in *Crain's Small Business*. (Vol. 4, No. 11, November 1996, pp. 21). By Jeffrey McCracken.

"DAY-CARE DOLLARS" in *Small Business Opportunities*. (Vol. 9, No. 3, May 1997, pp. 94-95). By Marie Sherlock.

"Doing Your Home Work" in *Income Opportunities*. (Vol. 32, No. 4, April 1997, pp. 24-27).

"don't get ZONED out" in *Income Opportunities*. (Vol. 31, No. 9, September 1996, pp. 21-23). By Eric Barnes.

Easy Financials for Your Home-Based Business: The Friendly Guide to Successful Management Systems for Busy Home Entrepreneurs. Windsor, CA: Rayve Publications, Inc., 1993. By Norm Ray.

Eighty-Plus Great Ideas for Making Money at Home: A Guide for the First-Time Entrepreneur. New York, NY: Walker & Co., 1992. By Erica Barkemeyer.

"Eleven Businesses You Can Run From Home" in *Homebased Business.* (Winter 1990, pp. 29-32). By Frances Huffman.

Entrepreneur Magazine: Starting a Home-Based Business. New York, NY: John Wiley & Sons, Inc.

"Entrepreneur hails power of marketing" in *Crain's Small Business.* (June 1996, pp. 23). By Jeffrey McCracken.

"Everything you need to know to start your business at home" in *Business Start-up.* (Vol. 8, No. 6, June 1996, pp. 28, 30, 32, 34-36). By Karin Moeller.

"Fast Forward, Up & Comers" in *Working Woman.* (January 1997, p. 20).

"FAST-GROWING TRENDS" in *Business Start-Ups.* (Vol. 9, No. 2, February 1997, pp. 42, 44, 46). By Carla Goodman.

"Fed Funds" in *Entrepreneur.* (Vol. 23, No. 8, August 1995, pp. 50, 52- 53). By Cynthia E. Griffin.

"Finding the perfect job" in *Crain's Detroit Business.* (Vol. 11, No. 34, August 1995, p. 15). By Steve Raphael.

"A Fine Mess" in *Income Opportunities.* (Vol. 31, No. 4, April 1996, pp. 10). By Lana Sanderson.

"First Things First" in *Business Start-Ups.* (Vol. 8, No. 8, August 1996, pp. 8, 10). By Carolyn Campbell.

Franchises You Can Run from Home. Somerset, NJ: John Wiley & Sons, Inc., 1990. By Lynie Arden.

"Get It Together" in *Business Start-Ups.* (Vol. 7, No. 8, August 1995, p. 14).

"Getting Connected" in *Entrepreneur.* (Vol. 24, No. 2, February 1996, pp. 48, 50-51). By Cynthia E. Griffin.

"Giving Thanks" in *Business Start-Ups.* (Vol. 8, No. 11, November 1996, pp. 8, 10). By Julie Bawden Davis.

"Greener Pastures" in *Income Opportunities.* (Vol. 30, No. 9, September 1995, pp. 24-27, 106). By Meg North.

"Growing Pains" in *Business Start-Ups.* (Vol. 9, No. 5, May 1997, pp. 8, 10, 12). By Carolyn Campbell.

Growing Your Home-Based Business: A Complete Guide to Proven Sales and Marketing Communications Strategies. Englewood Cliffs, NJ: Prentice Hall, 1992. By Kim T. Gordon.

"Heading Home" in *Income Opportunities.* (Vol. 32, No. 4, April 1997, pp. 46, 49-50). By Robert L. Perry.

"Hello, World" in *Income Opportunities.* (Vol. 30, No. 4, April 1995, pp. 8). By Lana Sanderson.

"Help Wanted" in *Entrepreneur.* (May 1996, pp. 55-57).

"He's right at home in chili and shuttles" in *Crain's Small Business.* (June 1996, pp. 23). By Jeffrey McCracken.

"High-Tech Know-How" in *Small Business Opportunities.* (Vol. 8, No. 3, May 1996, pp. 62, 64, 106). By Jeff Berner.

"Hints from the Pros: Try This At Home" in *Business Start-Ups.* (Vol. 7, Nol. 6, June 1995, P. 16).

"Holiday Helpers" in *Business Start-Ups.* (Vol. 7, No. 11, November 1995, p. 14, 16).

"Home Alone" in *Small Business Opportunities.* (Vol. 6, No. 5, September 1994, pp. 50). By Robin Montgomery.

"Home Alone: Small Business Strategies" in *Working Woman.* (Vol. 18, No. 3, March 1993, pp. 45-50). By Louise Washer.

Home Based Business Occupational Handbook. Dubuque, IA: Kendall/Hunt Publishing Co., 1996.

"Home-based Business Opportunity" in *Business Start-Ups.* (Vol. 6, No. 9, September 1994, pp. 33).

Home-Based Businesses, Over Two-Hundred-Fifty Ways to Earn Your Fortune. Ft. Worth, TX: Premier Publishers, Inc., 1995. By J. Rue.

Home-Based Employment & Family Life. Westport, CT: Greenwood Publishing Group, Inc., 1995. By Ramona K. Z. Heck.

The Home-Based Entrepreneur: The Complete Guide to Working at Home. Dover, NH: Upstart Publishing Co., Inc., second edition, 1993. By Linda Pinson and Jerry Jinnett.

"Home Runs" in *Entrepreneur.* (Vol. 22, No. 13, December 1994, pp. 63). By Janean Huber.

How to Build a Successful One-Person Business: A Common-Sense Guide to Starting & Growing a Company. Farmington Hills, MI: Bookhaus Publishers, 1995. By Veltisezar B. Bautista.

How to Make 1000 Mistakes in Business & Still Succeed: The Guide to Crucial Decisions in the Small Business, Home-Based Business. Oak Park, IL: Wright Track, 1995. By Harold L. Wright.

"How To Start an Inc. 500 Company" in *Inc. 500.* (Vol. 16, No. 11, 1994, pp. 51-52, 54, 57-58, 60, 63-65). By Leslie Brokaw.

The Joy of Working from Home: Making a Life While Making a Living. San Francisco, CA: Berrett-Koehler Publishers, 1994. By Jeff Berner.

"Just A Mailbox Away" in *Black Enterprise.* (Vol. 27, No. 3, October 1996, pp. 34). By Robyn Clarke.

"Make the guidelines clear when home, office overlap" in *Crain's Small Business.* (December 1996, pp. 10-11). By Jeffrey McCracken.

"Meeting of the Minds" in *Entrepreneur.* (August 1996, p. 55). By Cynthia E. Griffin.

"Networking from Home" in *Business Start-Ups.* (Vol. 7, No. 11, November 1995, p. 14). By Sue Clayton.

"On The Home Front" in *Income Opportunities.* (Vol. 31, No. 4, April 1996, pp. 54-60, 62, 64-65, 72). By Robert L. Perry.

On Your Own: A Guide to Working Happily, Productively & Successfully at Home. Englewood Cliffs, NJ: Prentice Hall, 1994. By Lionel L. Fisher.

"ORDER FROM CHAOS" in *Small Business Opportunities.* (Vol. 9, No. 2, March 1997, pp. 12, 146). By Marie Sherlock.

Organizing Your Home Office for Success: Expert Strategies That Can Work for You. New York, NY: NAL Dutton, 1993. By Lisa Kanarek.

"The Quiet Revolution" in *Entrepreneur.* (September 1993, pp. 77-81). By Janean Huber.

"Setting Up at Home" in *Black Enterprise.* (Vol. 24, No. 12, July 1994, pp. 36-38). By Rhonda Reynolds.

"Shattering the Myth" in *Income Opportunities.* (Vol. 29, No. 7, July 1994, pp. 34). By Jo Frohbieter-Mueller.

Start, Run and Profit from Your Own Home-Based Business. New York, NY: John Wiley & Sons, Inc., 1991. By Gregory Kishel and Patricia Kishel.

"Taking Stock" in *Income Opportunities.* (Vol. 31, No. 3, March 1996, pp. 10). By Lana Sanderson.

The Telecommuter's Advisor: Working in the Fast Lane. Newport, RI: Aegis Publishing Group, Ltd., 1996. By June Langhoff.

The Work-at-Home Sourcebook: Over One Thousand Job Opportunities Plus Home Business Opportunities and Other Options. Boulder, CO: The New Career Centers, Inc., fifth edition, 1994. By Lynie Arden.

Incubators

"Al Geiger Aiming to Help Small Businesses Grow" in *The Business Journal.* (Vol. 11, No. 26, September 19, 1994, pp. 16). By Ray Dussault.

"Alphabet Soup" in *Inc.* (Vol. 16, No. 12, November 1994, pp. 31-32). By Heather E. Stone.

"Birth of a Business" in *Hispanic Business.* (Vol. 18, No. 9, September 1996, p. 10). By Rick Mendosa.

"Blastoff" in *Forbes.* (Vol. 154, No. 5, August 29, 1994, pp. 154). By James M. Clash.

"A Boost for Start-Ups" in *Nation's Business.* (Vol. 80, No. 8, August 1992, pp. 40). By Bradford McKee.

"Business Incubation" in *California Business.* (Vol. 29, No. 5, September 1994, pp. 10). By Claudia Viek.

"Cash Infusion to Incubator Nurtures Small Businesses" in *The Business Journal Serving Greater Sacramento.* (Vol. 11, No. 18, July 25, 1994, pp. 2). By Mike McCarthy.

"Company Coach" in *The Kansas City Business Journal.* (Vol. 12, No. 17, January 14, 1994, pp. 3). By Barry Henderson.

"Fledgling Business Incubator Hatches 13 New Enterprises" in *The Business Journal*. (Vol. 12, No. 31, October 31, 1994, pp. 13). By Michele Hostetler.

"Growing Places" in *Entrepreneur*. (Vol. 23, No. 2, February 1995, pp. 108, 110-113). By Cynthia E. Griffin.

"HATCHING A BUSINESS" in *Small Business Opportunities*. (Vol. 8, No. 5, September 1996, pp. 78, 80). By Mary Ann McLaughlin.

"Hatching a New Venture" in *EDN*. (Vol. 39, No. 17, August 18, 1994, pp. 51).

"How to Hatch New Businesses" in *D & B Reports*. (Vol. 39, No. 4, July/August 1991, pp. 54-55). By Bill Hogan.

"Incubator Boosts LI's High Tech" in *Long Island Business News*. (No. 6, February 7, 1994, pp. 3T). By Christopher Hord.

"Incubator Roundup" in *Entrepreneur*. (Vol. 23, No. 11, October 1995, pp. 188). By Cynthia E. Griffin.

"Incubators Nurture Start-Up Firms: Do Incubators Really Work?" in *Computerworld*. (Vol. 25, No. 37, September 16, 1991, pp. 105, 112). By Johanna Ambrosio.

"New Product Incubator: Pilot Plant Helps Processors Develop New Products" in *Dairy Foods*. (Vol. 95, No. 9, September 1994, pp. 139).

Regional Economic Analysis of Innovation & Incubation. Brookfield, VT: Ashgate Publishing Co., Inc., 1991. By E.J. Davelaar.

"Tech Incubator Growing Up" in *Denver Business Journal*. (Vol. 46, No. 15, December 23, 1994, pp. 1B). By Tom Locke.

"Trapped in the Nest? Start-Up Firms Try to Fly" in *Baltimore Business Journal*. (Vol. 12, No. 9, July 22, 1994, pp. 1). By Greg Abel.

"VC Incubators Are Hatching New Companies Again" in *Electronic Business Buyer*. (Vol. 20, No. 1, January 1994, pp. 90). By Stephen W. Quickel.

"What the Incubators Have Hatched" in *Planning*. (Vol. 58, No. 5, May 1992, pp. 28-30). By Richard Steffens.

"Where dreams get hope" in *Crain's Detroit Business*. (Vol. 12, No. 16, April 1996, pp. 3, 26). By Robert Akeny.

"Yellow Brick Road Winds into Florida" in *Orlando Business Journal*. (Vol. 10, No. 35, February 4, 1994, pp. 16). By Danialle Weaver.

Manufacturing Business

"1996 Small Business Entrepreneurs of the Year" in *Black Enterprise*. (Vol. 27, No. 4, November 1996, p. 75-77). By Robyn Clarke.

"A Profitable FEAST" in *Business Start-Ups*. (Vol. 8, No. 6, June 1996, pp. 60, 62-66). By Sandra Mardenfeld.

"Anasteel & Supply Co." in *Hispanic Business*. (Vol. 18, No. 6, June 1996, p. 106). By Graham Witherall.

Benchmarking Global Manufacturing: Understanding International Suppliers, Customers, and Competitors. Burr Ridge, IL: Irwin Professional Publishing. By Jeffrey G. Miller, Arnoud De Meyer and Jinichiro Nakane.

Business Plan for Small Manufacturers. Denver, CO: U.S. Small Business Administration (SBA).

"Clothes Make the Man" in *Business Start-Ups*. (Vol. 7, No. 7, July 1995, pp. 62, 64, 66). By Pamala Rohland.

Common Sense Manufacturing: Becoming a Top Value Competitor. San Rafael, CA: Professional Publishing, 1991. By James A. Gardner.

Competing in Manufacturing and How to Make Things Better. New York, NY: Gordon Press Publishers, 1992.

"Crash Course" in *Inc*. (Vol. 17, No. 2, February 1995, pp. 54-56, 59-63). By Robert A. Mamis.

Flexible Manufacturing Technologies and International Competitiveness. New York, NY: St. Martin's Press, Inc., 1991. By Joe Tidd.

Fundamentals of Manufacturing Systems Design and Analysis. New York, NY: Chapman & Hall, 1991. By B. Wu.

Good Manufacturing Practice: Philosophy and Application. Buffalo Grove, IL: Interpharm Press, Inc., 1991. By John Sharp.

How to Set Up a Retail Store, Service Company, and a Manufacturing Firm—Case Studies. Minneapolis, MN: American Institute of Small Business (AISB), 1991.

"Legends" in *Small Business Opportunities*. (Vol. 7, No. 1, January 1995, pp. 46, 48).

"Make Your Service Fail-Safe" in *Sloan Management Review*. (Vol. 35, No. 3, Spring 1994, pp. 35-44). By Richard B. Chase and Douglas M. Stewart.

Managing the Manufacturing Process: A Pattern for Excellence. New York, NY: John Wiley & Sons, Inc., 1991. By Ralph W. Woodgate.

Manufacturing Development Applications: Guidelines for Attaining Productivity and Quality. Norcross, GA: Industrial Engineering & Management Press, 1992. By Andre McHose.

Manufacturing Planning and Control Systems. Burr Ridge, IL: Richard D. Irwin, Inc., third edition, 1992. By Thomas E. Vollmann.

Partners in Learning: Manufacturers and Users. Scarsdale, NY: Work in America Institute, Inc., updated edition, 1991.

Profit Costing and Pricing for Manufacturers. Denver, CO: U.S. Small Business Administration (SBA).

Winning Manufacturing: The How-to-Book of Successful Manufacturing. New York, NY: McGraw-Hill, Inc., 1991. By James A. Tompkins.

Nontraditional Financing

"Angels in Cyberspace" in *Hispanic Business*. (Vol. 20, No. 3, March 1997, pp. 38, 40). By Rick Mendosa.

"A Capital Idea Helps Nurture Small Firms in Wayne County" in *Crain's Small Business*. (October 1995, p. 21). By Pam Woodside.

"Cards May Be Ticket to Survive Cash-Flow Crunch" in *Crain's Small Business*. (March 1996, p. 14). By Lawrence Gardner.

"Found Money" in *Entrepreneur*. (Vol. 23, No. 4, April 1995, pp. 108-110, 112-115). By David R. Evanson.

"Franchises That Offer Creative Financing" in *Business Start-Ups*. (Vol. 8, No. 9, September 1996, pp. 62, 64, 67-68). By Andrew A. Caffey.

"Get Cash Now!" in *Success*. (Vol. 38, No. 10, December 1991, pp. 26-32). By Ronit Addis Rose.

Getting Money. Bellingham, WA: Self-Counsel Press, Inc., 1991. By Dan Kennedy.

"GOING PUBLIC ON MAIN STREET, NOT WALL STREET" in *Working Woman*. (June 1996, p. 11). By Kerry Hannon.

Guerrilla Financing: Alternative Techniques to Finance Any Small Business. Boston, MA: Houghton Mifflin Co., 1992. By Bruce J. Blechman and Jay C. Levinson.

"Hatching Uncle Sam's Entrepreneurs" in *Management Today*. (November 1993, pp. 54-56). By John Thackray.

"How to Obtain Export Capital" in *Nation's Business*. (Vol. 82, No. 5, May 1994, pp. 24).

"Kid Venture Capital" in *Black Enterprise*. (Vol. 25, No. 5, December 1994, pp. 34). By Tonia L. Shakespeare.

"LEAF Me a Loan" in *Business Start-Ups*. (Vol. 8, No. 1, January 1996, pp. 74-75).

"Leasing Lessons" in *Business Start-Ups*. (Vol. 8, No. 2, February 1996, p. 72). By Eric J. Adams.

"Look at Every Option—And Beyond" in *Nation's Business*. (Vol. 79, No. 7, July 1991, pp. 9). By Thomas Hierl.

"Money Hunting" in *Hispanic Business*. (Vol. 19, No. 1, January 1997, pp. 28, 30). By Joel Russell.

"The Money Is Out There...How To Get It" in *Agency Sales Magazine*. (Vol. 24, No. 2, February 1994, pp. 15-17). By Jeff Fromberg.

Money Sources for Small Business: How You Can Find Private, State, Federal & Corporate Financing. Santa Maria, CA: Puma Publishing Co., 1991. By William M. Alarid.

"A New Loan Option to Bank, Venture Capital" in *Crain's Small Business*. (February 1996, p. 9-10). By Jeffrey McCracken.

"19 Sources of Capital for Your Start-Up" in *Income Opportunities*. (Vol. 31, No. 2, February 1996, pp. 26-30). By Terri Cullen.

"Northern Exposure" in *Entrepreneur*. (Vol. 23, No. 5, May 1995, pp. 15). By Cynthia E. Griffin.

"The Numbers Speak Volumes" in *Small Business Reports*. (Vol. 19, No. 7, July 1994, pp. 39-43). By Lamont Change.

"Options, discounts are in the cards" in *Crain's Small Business*. (Vol. 5, No. 4, April 1997, pp. 1, 20). By Jeffrey McCracken.

"Peer Power" in *Entrepreneur*. (Vol. 23, No. 4, April 1995, pp. 15). By Heather Page.

"Plastic Surgery" in *Crain's Small Business*. (Vol. 5, No. 4, April 1997, pp. 1, 20, -21). By Jeffrey McCracken.

"Play Misty for Me" in *Business Start-Ups*. (Vol. 7, No. 9, September 1995, p. 114). By Eric J. Adams.

"Program Gives Small Businesses a Financial Boost" in *Entrepreneur*. (Vol. 32, No. 7, July 1995, pp. 17). By Cynthia E. Griffin.

"Saving on Next-Day Delivery" in *Black Enterprise*. (Vol. 27, No. 5, December 1996, p. 36). By Ann Brown.

"The Secrets of Bootstrapping" in *Inc.* (Vol. 13, No. 9, September 1991, pp. 52-70). By Robert A. Mamis.

"The Six Best Ways to Raise Cash" in *Money Money Guide Supplement*. (1994, pp. 34-39). By Vanessa O'Connell.

"Small Loans, Big Dreams" in *Working Woman*. (Vol. 20, No. 2, February 1995, pp. 46-49, 72-73, 77). By Elizabeth Kadetsky.

"Stocking Up" in *Entrepreneur*. (April 1997, pp. 58, 60-61). By David R. Evanson.

"Treasure Hunt" in *Business Start-Ups*. (Vol. 7, No. 7, July 1995, 56-58, 60-61). By Gloria Gibbs Marullo.

"Where Are All the Wanda Buffets?" in *Money*. (Vol. 23, No. 11, November 1994, pp. 116-117). By Nancy J. Perry.

"Where to Look for Money Now" in *Working Woman*. (Vol. 19, No. 10, October 1994, pp. 56-62). By Ilyce R. Glink.

Recording Studio

The Art of Recording. Florence, KY: Van Nostrand Reinhold Co., Inc., 1991. By William M. Moylan.

Audio in Media: The Recording Studio. Belmont, CA: Wadsworth Publishing Co., 1996. By Stanley R. Alten.

"Back to Basics" in *Business Start-Ups*. (Vol. 8, No. 1, anuary 1996, p. 14). By Karin Moeller.

"Entrepreneurial Spirit Awards" in *Hispanic Business*. (Vol. 18, No. 12, December 1996, pp. 26, 28, 30, 34, 36, 38). By Maria Zate.

"Entrepreneurial Superstars" in *Entrepreneur*. (April 1997, pp. 108-139). By Debra Phillips, et al.

Handbook of Recording Engineering. New York, NY: Van Nostrand Reinhold Co., Inc., 1992. By John Eargle.

"Harmony sounds again in Detroit" in *Crain's Detroit Business*. (Vol. 12, No. 33, Aug. 12-18, 1996, pp. 1, 23). By Joseph Serwach.

Home Recording for Musicians. New York, NY: Music Sales Corp. By Craig Anderton.

Home Recording Techniques. Van Nuys, CA: Alfred Publishing Co., Inc., 1992. By J. D. Sharp.

Making It in the New Music Business. Cincinnati, OH: Writer's Digest Books, revised edition, 1991. By James Riordan.

The Platinum Rainbow: How to Succeed in the Music Business without Selling Your Soul. Sherman Oaks, CA: Swordsman Press, Inc., sixth edition. By Bob Monaco and James Riordan.

Practical Recording Techniques. Indianapolis, IN: Sams, 1992. By Bruce Bartlett.

Recording Industry Sourcebook. Los Angeles, CA: Recording Industry Sourcebook, 1994. By Mike Fuchs.

Releasing an Independent Record: How to Successfully Start and Run Your Own Record Label in the 1990s. San Diego, CA: Rockpress Publishing, fourth edition, 1993. By Gary Hustwit.

Sound Advice: The Musician's Guide to the Record Industry. New York, NY: Schirmer Books, 1990. By Wayne Wadhams.

Sound & Music Studio. New York, NY: Random House, Inc., 1995. By Jeff Essex.

The Sound Studio. Newton, MA: Butterworth-Heinemann, sixth edition, 1995. By Alec Nisbett.

The Studio Business Book. Emeryville, CA: Cardinal Business Media, Music & Entertainment Group, 1994. By Jim Mandell, edited by Andy Jewett.

Studio Recording for Musicians. New York, NY: Music Sales Corp. By Fred Miller.

"Top of the Hill" in *Entrepreneurial Woman.* (Summer 1989, pp. 87-92). By Charles Fuller.

Service Station/Auto Repair Shop

"A Gusher of an Opportunity" in *Black Enterprise.* (Vol. 27, No. 2, September 1996, p. 19). By Joyce Jones.

Auto Body Repairman. Syosset, NY: National Learning Corp., 1991. By Jack Rudman.

"AUTO-MATIC VENTURE" in *Small Business Opportunities.* (Vol. 9, No. 1, January 1997, pp. 50, 52).

Auto Mechanics Fundamentals. Tinley Park, IL: Goodheart-Willcox Co. Inc., 1995. By Martin W. Stockel and Martin T. Stockel.

Auto Repair Manual 1991-1995. Radnor, PA: Chilton Book Co., fifty-fourth edition, 1994.

Automotive Encyclopedia. Tinley Park, IL: Goodheart-Willcox Co. Inc., revised edition, 1995. By William K. Toboldt.

Automotive Repair Service: Start and Run a Money-Making Business Blue. Ridge Summit, PA: TAB Books, Inc., 1994. By Dan Ramsey.

Chilton's Auto Service Manual, 1988-92. Radnor, PA: Chilton Book Co., 1997.

Chilton's Guide to Fuel Injection and Electronic Engine Controls, 1988-90: European Cars and Trucks. Radnor, PA: Chilton Book Co.

Chilton's Labor Guide and Parts Manual, 1987-91. Radnor, PA: Chilton Book Co., 1990.

Chilton's M-A Truck and Van Service Manual, 1986-90. Radnor, PA: Chilton Book Co., 1990.

Chilton's Service Bay Handbook, 1992: Motor Age Professional Mechanic's Edition. Radnor, PA: Chilton Book Co., 1991.

"Driven to Success" in *Business Start-Ups.* (March 1994, pp. 38-40, 42). By Brian McDonough.

Gasoline Treasurers. Atglen, PA: Schiffer Publishing, Ltd., 1996. By Michael Bruner.

"The Informers" in *INC.* (Vol. 17, No. 3, March 1995, pp. 50-52, 54, 56, 59, 61). By John Kerr.

"Marketing's Colors: Al's Gas Town" in *Marketing Management.* (Vol. 3, No. 2, pp. 16-24). By Thomas Bonoma.

Mathematics for Auto Mechanics. Albany, NY: Delmar Publishers, 1978. By T. G. Hendrix and C. S. LaFevor.

Practical Problems in Mathematics for Automotive Technicians. Albany, NY: Delmar Publishers, 1991. By George Moore.

Pump & Circumstance: Glory Days of the Gas Station. Boston, MA: Bulfinch Press, 1996. By John Margolies.

Truck and Van Service Manual 1990-94. Radnor, PA: Chilton Book Co., 1994.

Small Business Development

"1996 may be best year for those seeking loans" in *Washington Business Journal Small Business Resource Guide.* (May 1996, p. 16). By Melissa Wuestenberg.

"A Call of Arms for Black Business" in *Black Enterprise.* (Vol. 27, No. 4, November 1996, p. 79-86). By Carolyn M. Brown and Tonia L. Shakespeare.

"A sporting chance" in *Detroit Free Press.* (January 1997, pp. 1E-2E). By Molly Brauer.

"A&W plants roots as growing fast-food chain" in *Crain's Detroit Business.* (Vol. 13, No. 6, February 1997, pp. 3, 32).

The ABC's of Starting a Business. New York, NY: Publicity Plus, 1990. By Valerie White.

"Achieving success through a smaller market" in *Washington Business Journal: Small Business Resource Guide.* (May 1996, p. 18). By Bill Murray.

"After the Covers: What Are They Up to Now?" in *Chain Store Age Executive.* (Vol. 70, No. 7, July 1994, pp. 19-33).

"ALL SEASON WOMAN" in *Small Business Opportunities.* (Vol. 9, No. 3, May 1997, pp. 58, 60, 72). By Diane Morelli.

"Alphabet Soup" in *Inc.* (Vol. 16, No. 12, November 1994, pp. 31-32). By Heather E. Stone.

"An Olympic-Sized Letdown" in *Inc.* (Vol. 19, No. 2, February 1997, p. 21). By Michael E. Kanell.

Anatomy of a Start-Up: Why Some New Businesses Succeed and Others Fail. Boston, MA: Inc. Publishing., 1991. By Elizabeth K. Longsworth.

"Answers to your small business questions" in *Business Start-up.* (Vol. 8, No. 6, June 1996, p. 6). By Haidee Jezek.

"Are You Online Yet?" in *Black Enterprise.* (Vol. 25, No. 9, April 1995, pp. 41). By Valencia Roner and Matthew S. Scott.

"ASK THE EXPERTS" in *Income Opportunities.* (Vol. 32, No. 3, March 1997, pp. 56, 58, 60). By Caryne Brown.

"AUTO-MATIC VENTURE" in *Small Business Opportunities.* (Vol. 9, No. 1, January 1997, pp. 50, 52).

Avoiding Mistakes in Your Small Business. Menlo Park, CA: Crisp Publications, Inc. By David Karlson.

Avoiding the Pitfalls of Starting Your Own Business. New York, NY: Shapolsky Publishers, Inc., 1990. By Jeffrey P. Davidson.

"Bankruptcies rise 25%" in *Crain's Detroit Business.* (Vol. 13, No. 6, February 1997, pp. 1, 32). By Tenisha Mercer.

"Barden trump card: Experience" in *Crain's Detroit Business.* (Vol. 13, No. 6, February 1997, pp. 1, 22). By Robert Ankeny.

Beating the Odds: Ten Smart Steps to Small Business Success. New York, NY: AMACOM, 1992. By Scott A. Clark.

"Betting on the Future" in *D&B Reports.* (Vol. 40, No. 6, Nov./Dec. 1992, pp. 44). By Robert J. Klein.

Beyond Entrepreneurship: Turning Your Business into an Enduring Great Company. Englewood Cliffs, NJ: Prentice Hall, 1992. By James C. Collins and William C. Lazier.

"Beyond Latin America" in *Hispanic Business.* (Vol. 18, No. 11, November 1996, pp. 34, 36, 38, 40-41). By Joel Russell.

"Big Ideas for Your Small Business" in *Changing Times.* (November 1989, pp. 57-60).

Bootstrapper's Success Secrets: 151 Tactics for Building Your Business on a Shoestring Budget. Franklin Lakes, NJ: The Career Press. By Kimberly Stansell.

"Bottling Success" in *Hispanic Business.* (Vol. 18, No. 7/8, July/August 1996, p. 78). By Maria Zate.

The Brass Tacks Entrepreneur. New York, NY: Henry Holt & Co., Inc., 1993. By Jim Schell.

"Bright Ideas" in *Business Start-Ups.* (Vol. 7, No. 8, August 1995, pp. 50, 52-54, 57). By Bob Weinstein.

"BUCKS IN BUTTONS" in *Small Business Opportunities.* (Vol. 9, No. 1, January 1997, p. 48). By Carla Goodman.

"Building a Better Burger" in *Business Start-Ups.* (Vol. 8, No. 3, March 1996, pp. 21-22, 24-25). By Bob Weinstein.

"Building a Business Framework" in *Hispanic Business.* (Vol. 18, No. 11, November 1996, p. 24).

"Building the Perfect Home Office" in *Black Enterprise.* (Vol. 27, No. 8, March 1997, pp. 36-37). By Rafiki Cai.

Building a Profitable Business: A Proven Step-by-Step Guide to Starting and Running Your Own Business. Holbrook, MA: Bob Adams, Inc., second edition, 1994. By Charles Chickadel and Greg Straughn.

"BUSINESS BALLOONS" in *Small Business Opportunities.* (Vol. 9, No. 1, January 1997, p. 76). By Vicki Cromwell-Slakey.

The Business Forms on File Collection. New York, NY: Facts on File, Inc., 1995.

Business Operations Guidebook: The How-to Guide for Start-up Entrepreneurs. Poughquag, NY: Info Devels Press, 1993. By Robert Haiber.

Business Opportunities in the United States: The Complete Reference Guide to Practices and Procedures. Burr Ridge, IL: Irwin Professional Publishing, 1992. By Robert F. Cushman and R. Lawrence Soares.

"Capture the Future" in *Success.* (Vol. 40, No. 10, December 1993, pp. 63-70). By Katherine Callan.

"CARVING A NICHE" in *Small Business Opportunities*. (Vol. 8, No. 6, November 1996, p. 50). By Carla Goodman.

Checklist for Going into Business. Denver, CO: U.S. Small Business Administration (SBA).

"A Checklist for Starting a Business" in *Crain's Small Business*. (December 1995, p. 30).

"CLEANING UP" in *Small Business Opportunities*. (Vol. 9, No. 3, May 1997, p. 62). By Carla Godman.

"COFFEE COLA TALK" in *Small Business Opportunities*. (Vol. 9, No. 2, March 1997, pp. 44, 100). By Anne Hart.

The Competitive Edge: Essential Business Skills for Entrepreneurs. New York, NY: NAL Dutton, 1991. By Fran Tarkenton and Joseph H. Boyett.

Complete Handbook for the Entrepreneur. Englewood Cliffs, NJ: Prentice Hall, 1990. By Gary Brenner, Joe Ewan, and Henry Custer.

"Consumer Report" in *Entrepreneur*. (May 1997, pp. 125-130). By Gayle Sato Stodder.

"Contacts for Contracts" in *Hispanic Business*. (Vol. 18, No. 7/8, July/August 1996, p. 58). By Claudia Armann.

"Could You Succeed in Small Business" in *Business Horizons*. (September/October 1989, pp. 65-69).

"Crafting a Business" in *Entrepreneur*. (March 1997, pp. 58, 60-61). By Cynthia E. Griffin.

"CRAFTY BIZ" in *Small Business Opportunities*. (Vol. 9, No. 2, March 1997, pp. 54, 88). By Carla Goodman.

"Credibility Gap" in *Income Opportunities*. (Vol. 32, No. 4, April 1997, pp. 42, 44). By Dorothy Elizabeth Brooks.

"Cubs Send Minor-League Owners to the Showers" in *Inc.* (Vol. 19, No. 5, April 1997, p. 24). *By Phaedra Hise*.

"CYCLE OF SUCCESS" in *Small Business Opportunities*. (Vol. 9, No. 2, March 1997, pp. 86, 88). By Stan Roberts.

"Dare to Be Different" in *Entrepreneur*. (Vol. 23, No. 4, April 1995, pp. 122, 124-127). By Gayle Sato Stodder.

"Developer eyes 65-arce site in Sterling Heights" in *Crain's Detroit Business*. (Vol. 13, No. 6, February 1997, p. 3). By Tenisha Mercer.

"ECO-PRENEURING" in *Small Business Opportunities*. (Vol. 9, No. 2, March 1997, pp. 70, 72). By Geri Anderson.

Entrepreneur Magazine's the Secrets of Starting Your Own Business. Irvine, CA: Entrepreneur, Inc.

"Entrepreneurial Fables" in *Entrepreneur*. (Vol. 23, No. 8, August 1995, pp. 120, 122-124, 127). By Gayle Sato Stodder.

The Entrepreneurial Mind: Winning Strategies for Starting, Renewing, & Harvesting. Amherst, NH: Brick House Publishing Co., Inc., 1994. By Jeffrey A. Timmons.

The Entrepreneurial PC. Blue Ridge Summit, PA: TAB Books, Inc., 1991. By Bernard J. David.

"Entrepreneurial Spirit Awards" in *Hispanic Business*. (Vol. 18, No. 12, December 1996, pp. 26, 28, 30, 34, 36, 38). By Maria Zate.

Entrepreneurially Yours: A Compilation of Articles about Starting and Managing a Small Business. Nashville, TN: Business of Your Own, 1990. By Millicent G. Lownes.

"Entrepreneurs Collide: Will Zoning Take Town Downhill?" in *Inc.* (Vol. 19, No. 5, April 1997, p. 32). By Joshua Macht.

The Entrepreneur's Guide to Growing Up: Taking Your Small Company to the Next Level. Bellingham, WA: Self-Counsel Press, Inc., 1993. By Edna Sheedy.

Entrepreneur's Guide to Starting a Successful Business. New York, NY: McGraw-Hill, Inc., second edition, 1992. By James W. Halloran.

Entrepreneur's Road Map to Business Success. Alexandria, VA: Saxtons River Publications, Inc., revised edition, 1992. By Lyle R. Maul and Dianne Craig Mayfield.

Entrepreneurship: Creativity and Growth. Old Tappan, NJ: Macmillan Publishing Co., Inc., 1991. By Donald L. Sexton.

Entrepreneurship for the Nineties. Englewood Cliffs, NJ: Prentice Hall, 1990. By Gordon B. Baty.

Entrepreneurship & Small Business Development. Woburn, MA: Butterworth-Heinemann, 1996. By David Kirby.

"Entrepreneurship: The Role of the Individual in Small Business Development" in *IBAR*. (Vol. 15, 1994, pp. 62-75). By Stan Cromie.

The Essence of Small Business. New York, NY: Prentice Hall General Reference & Travel, 1993. By Colin Barrow.

"Essential Books for Start-ups" in *Working Woman*. (February 1995, pp. 54). By Jane Applegate.

Evaluate Your Business: Small Business Baseline Evaluation Workbook. Fresno, CA: Willow Tree, Inc., 1992. By J. W. Irwin.

"EVERY DAY'S A HOLIDAY" in *Small Business Opportunities*. (Vol. 9, No. 1, January 1997, pp. 70, 72, 114). By Anne Hart.

"Experience" in *Business Start-Ups*. (Vol. 7, No. 12, December 1995, p. 20). By Jacquelyn Lynn.

"Fifteen Start-Up Mistakes" in *Business Start-Ups*. (Vol. 7, No. 12, December 1995, p. 22). By Mel Mandell.

"Finding Your Niche" in *Business Start-up*. (Vol. 9, No. 4, April 1997, pp. 72, 74). By Carla Goodman.

"Focus on: Small Business" in *Journal of Accountancy*. (Vol. 177, No. 5, May 1994, pp. 41). By Jacqueline L. Babicky, Larry Field and Norman C. Pricher.

"FOOD FOR THOUGHT" in *Small Business Opportunities*. (Vol. 9, No. 2, March 1997, pp. 78, 80). By Cheryl Rodgers.

"Fools Rush In? The Institutional Context of Industry Creation" in *Academy of Management Review*. (Vol. 19, No. 4, October 1994, pp. 645). By Howard E. Aldrich and Marlene C. Fiol.

Forget Starting a Business. New York, NY: Simon & Schuster, Inc., 1990. By Stephen Pollan.

From Executive to Entrepreneur: Making the Transition. New York, NY: AMACOM, 1991. By Gilbert G. Zoghlin.

"GET INTO SHOW BUSINESS" in *Small Business Opportunities*. (Vol. 9, No. 1, January 1997, pp. 104, 114). By Anne Hart.

Get a Life!: Start Your Home-Based Business Now. Carlsbad, CA: Small Business Development for Women, 1997. By Sheila Robbins.

"GET ON THE PEACE TRAIN" in *Small Business Opportunities*. (Vol. 9, No. 1, January 1997, p. 86). By Carla Goodman.

"GET RICH IN 1997" in *Small Business Opportunities*. (Vol. 9, No. 1, January 1997, pp. 22-24, 26, 28, 30, 34).

Getting-into-Business Guides. Bellingham, WA: Self-Counsel Press, Inc., 1991. By Dan Kennedy.

Getting Started. Bellingham, WA: Self-Counsel Press, Inc., 1991. By Dan Kennedy.

"GIFT KEEPS ON GIVING" in *Small Business Opportunities*. (Vol. 9, No. 1, January 1997, pp. 56, 58). By Marie Sherlock.

"GO WEST FOR SUCCESS" in *Small Business Opportunities*. (Vol. 9, No. 2, March 1997, p. 118). By Carla Goodman.

"Going it Alone" in *Newsweek*. (April 1996, pp. 50-51). By Ellyn E. Spragins and Steve Rhodes.

"Going Solo" in *Income Opportunities*. (Vol. 30, No. 11, November 1995, pp. 30, 32, 34). By Pamela Rohland.

"GROUNDS FOR SUCCESS" in *Small Business Opportunities*. (Vol. 9, No. 1, January 1997, p. 54). By Carla Goodman.

"Group Therapy" in *Crain's Small Business*. (September 1995, pp. 1, 12-13). By Kimberly Lifton.

"Group's plan is to make knowledge accessible" in *Washington Business Journal: Small Business Resource Guide*. (May 1996, pp. 4, 13). By Lakhinder J.S. Vohra.

"GROWING A BUSINESS" in *Small Business Opportunities*. (Vol. 9, No. 3, May 1997, pp. 48, 104, 122). By Anne Hart.

Growing Your Small Business Made Simple. New York, NY: Doubleday & Co., Inc., 1993. By Wilbur Cross.

The Growth Challenge: How to Build Your Business Profitably. Chicago, IL: Dearborn Trade, 1993. By Stephen A. Stumpf.

Have You Got What It Takes? Bellingham, WA: Self-Counsel Press, Inc., third edition, 1993. By Douglas A. Gray.

"Help Getting Started" in *Business Start-Ups*. (Vol. 7, No. 12, December 1995, pp. 28-29). By Sue Clayton.

"HELPING BIZ COPE" in *Small Business Opportunities*. (Vol. 9, No. 1, January 1997, p. 98). By Annette Wood.

"HOLOGRAMS ARE SOLID SUCCESS" in *Small Business Opportunities*. (Vol. 9, No. 2, March 1997, pp. 126-127). By Anne Hart.

The Home Office and Small Business Answer Book: Solutions to the Most Frequently Asked Questions about Starting and Running Home Offices. New York, NY: Henry Holt & Co., Inc., 1993. By Janet Attard.

"Hot Areas for Small Business" in *Black Enterprise*. (Vol. 24, No. 4, November 1993, pp. 54).

"The Hottest Entrepreneurs in America" in *Inc.* (Vol. 14, No. 13, December 1992, pp. 88-103). By Martha E. Mangelsdorf.

How to Be in Business for Yourself New York, New York: Gordon Press Publishers. By 1992. Price: $250.00.

How to Leave Your Job and Buy a Business of Your Own. New York, NY: McGraw-Hill, Inc., 1992. By C. D. Peterson.

How to Set Up Your Own Small Business. Minneapolis, MN: American Institute of Small Business (AISB), 1993. By Max Fallek.

How to Start a Business without Quitting Your Job: The Moonlight Entrepreneur's Guide. Berkeley, CA: Ten Speed Press, 1992. By Philip Holland.

How to Start a Business on a Shoestring. New York, NY: Gordon Press Publishers, 1992.

How to Start, Expand and Sell a Business: The Complete Guide for Entrepreneurs. Santa Barbara, CA: Venture Perspective Press, third edition, 1991. By James C. Comiskey.

How to Start and Manage Your Own Business: A Practical Way to Start Your Own Business. Interlochen, MI:0 Lewis & Renn Associates, Inc., 1991. By Jerre G. Lewis and Leslie D. Renn.

How to Start, Run, and Stay in Business. Somerset, NJ: John Wiley & Sons, Inc., second edition, 1993. By Gregory F. Kishel and Patricia G. Kishel.

How to Start Your Own Business—and Succeed. New York, NY: McGraw-Hill, Inc., second edition, 1992. By Arthur H. Kuriloff.

How to Start Your Own Business on a Shoestring and Make Up to $500,000 a Year. Rocklin, CA: Prima Publishing & Communications, revised edition, 1994. By Tyler G. Hicks.

"How to Succeed in 4 Easy Steps" in *Inc.* (Vol. 17, No. 10, July 1995, pp. 30-32, 34, 36-40, 42). By Bo Burlingham.

"Improving Your Luck" in *Inc.* (Vol. 19, No. 5, April 1997, pp. 35-36). By Norm Brodsky.

In Business for Yourself. Lanham, MD: Madison Books, 1991. By Bruce Williams and Warren Sloat.

Inc. Yourself: How to Profit by Setting Up Your Own Corporation. New York, NY: Harper Business, Eighth edition, 1995. By Judith H. McQuown.

Jane Applegate's Strategies for Small Business Success. New York, NY: NAL Dutton, 1995. By Jane Applegate.

"Jimmy's Top Ten List" in *Business Start-Ups*. (Vol. 7, No. 8, August 1995, p. 7). By Jimmy Jones.

"Keeping Small Businesses Healthy" in *Franchising World*. (Vol. 27, No. 1, January/February 1995, pp. 56-57). By Cindy Murphy.

Keys to Starting a Small Business. Hauppauge, NY: Barron's Educational Series, Inc., 1991. By Joel G. Siegel and Jae K. Shim.

"Keys to Success? For Starters, Here Are 15" in *Contractor*. (Vol. 41, No. 11, November 1994, pp. 12). By Jeff Ferenc.

"Know it All" in *Entrepreneur*. (March 1997, p. 28).

"Knowledge" in *Business Start-Ups*. (Vol. 7, No. 12, December 1995, p. 38). By Carolyn Lawrence.

"Leading the Charge" in *Hispanic Business*. (Vol. 18, No. 5, May 1996, pp. 26-28, 30). By Maria Zate.

"Leaving Home" in *Inc.* (Vol. 18, No. 18, December 1997, p. 127). By Christopher Caggiano.

"Looking for Customers? Pick on Someone Your Own Size" in *Inc.* (Vol. 19, No. 3, March 1997, p. 22). By Jerry Useem.

"Lost Dollars" in *Black Enterprise.* (Vol. 27, No. 4, November 1996, p. 34). By Sheryl E. Huggins.

Make Money with Your PC! Berkeley, CA: Ten Speed Press, 1994. By Lynn Waldorf.

"Make Your Pitch" in *Independent Business.* (Vol. 7, No. 4, July/Aug. 1996, pp. 14-15).

"Making a Hopp to top agency" in *Crain's Detroit Business.* (Vol. 13, No. 6, February 1997, pp. 3, 26). By Jean Halliday.

Making It on Your Own: What to Know Before You Start Your Own Business. Austell, GA: Acropolis Books, revised edition, 1991. By S. Norman Feingold.

Making Your Small Business a Success: More Expert Advice from the U.S. Small Business Administration. Blue Ridge Summit, PA: TAB Books, Inc., 1991.

"Mapping Your Route" in *Business Start-up.* (Vol. 8, No. 12, December 1996, pp. 40, 42-44). By Lynn H. Colwell.

McGraw-Hill Guide to Starting Your Own Business: A Step-by-Step Blueprint. New York, NY: McGraw-Hill, Inc., 1992. By Stephen C. Harper.

"Mentoring Helps Grow Emerging Businesses" in *Puget Sound Business Journal.* (Vol. 12, No. 18, September 23, 1991, pp. 24). By Linda Lang.

The Mid-Career Entrepreneur: How to Start a Business and Be Your Own Boss. Chicago, IL: Dearborn Financial Publishing, Inc., 1993. By Joseph R. Mancuso.

"Mind Power" in *Entrepreneur.* (Vol. 23, No. 5, May 1995, pp. 100, 102-106). By Robert McGarvey.

Mind Your Own Mini-Business!: How to Start Your Own "Mini-Biz" with 10 to 1,000 Dollars and Make All the Money You Need. Raleigh, NC: Success Team, 1991. By Will Davis.

"MINI STORAGE MAXI PROFIT" in *Small Business Opportunities.* (Vol. 9, No. 1, January 1997, p. 84). By Stan Roberts.

"Minority Banks are on the Rise" in *Hispanic Business.* (Vol. 18, No. 5, May 1996, p. 15). By Joel Russell.

Minority Small Business & Capital Ownership Development Program. New York, NY: Gordon Press Publishers, 1995.

"MONEY IN MARBLE" in *Small Business Opportunities.* (Vol. 9, No. 2, March 1997, pp. 48, 50). By Geri Anderson.

"More Power to You" in *Entrepreneur.* (March 1997, p. 10). By Janean Chun.

"Moving Out" in *Income Opportunities.* (Vol. 32, No. 4, April 1997, pp. 1418, 88). By Dale D. Buss.

"MURDER, SHE SOLD" in *Small Business Opportunities.* (Vol. 9, No. 2, March 1997, pp. 64, 66). By Mary Ann McLaughlin.

"My company is small. How can I attract my first big client?" in *Inc.* (Vol. 18, No. 18, December 1997, p. 120). By Christopher Caggiano.

"Myth of the Gunslinger" in *Success.* (Vol. 41, No. 2, March 1994, pp. 34-40). By Ingrid Abramovitch.

"Never Too Small to Manage" in *Inc.* (Vol. 19, No. 2, February 1997, pp. 56-58, 61). By David Whitford.

"New Beginnings" in *Business Start-Ups.* (Vol. 8, No. 1, January 1996, p. 96). By Joann K. Jones.

The New Small Business Survival Guide. New York, NY: W. W. Norton & Co., Inc., 1991. By Bob Coleman.

"1995 Small Business Tax Guide" in *Income Opportunities.* (Vol. 30, No. 1, January 1995, pp. 48-60). By Randall Kirkpatrick and Meg North.

"NO BIZ LIKE SHOE BIZ" in *Small Business Opportunities.* (Vol. 9, No. 1, January 1997, pp. 80, 82). By Dorothy Elizabeth Brooks.

Nobody Gets Rich Working for Somebody Else: An Entrepreneur's Guide. Menlo Park, CA: Crisp Publications, Inc., 1993. By Roger Fritz.

"On A Mission to Demystify" in *Hispanic Business.* (Vol. 17, No. 5, May 1995, p. 42). By Rick Mendosa.

"On Their Own" in *Wall Street Journal Special Reports: Small Business (Special Edition).* (May 23, 1996, pp. R20). By Jeffrey A. Tannenbaum.

"On Your Mark..." in *Business Start-Ups*. (Vol. 7, No. 2, February 1995, pp. 37-44). By Gustav Berle and Jacquelyn Lynn.

Operating a Really Small Business. Menlo Park, CA: Crisp Publications, Inc. By Betty Bivins.

"Out of the Blue" in *Inc.* (Vol. 17, No. 10, July 1995, pp. 68-72). By Tom Ehrenfeld.

"Out on a Limb and on Their Own" in *Nation's Business*. (Vol. 82, No. 3, March 1994, pp. 33-34). By John S. DeMott.

Out of Work? Get into Business!: Shifting Gears and Turning Job Loss into Success. Bellingham, WA: Self-Counsel Press, Inc., first edition, 1994. By Don Doman.

"A Perfect Fit" in *Business Start-Ups*. (Vol. 7, No. 9, September 1995, pp. 78, 80-81). By Jacquelyn Lynn.

"Power Play" in *Entrepreneur*. (March 1997, pp. 104, 106-105). By Tomima Edmark.

The Prentice Hall Small Business Survival Guide: A Blueprint for Success. Englewood Cliffs, NJ: Prentice Hall, 1993.

"Prepare for frustration you'll create exhilaration" in *Crain's Small Business*. (Vol. 4, No. 10, October 1996, p. 19). By Jim Brady.

"Restless Youth" in *Wall Street Journal Special Reports: Small Business (Special Edition)*. (May 23, 1996, pp. R18-R19). By Roger Ricklefs.

"RIGHT FROM THE START" in *Small Business Opportunities*. (Vol. 9, No. 3, May 1997, pp. 20, 42). By Dr. Sandy Weinberg.

"Run Your Company Smarter" in *Money*. (Vol. 23, No. 11, November 1994, pp. 136-140). By Marlys J. Harris.

SBA Hotline Answer Book. New York, NY: John Wiley & Sons, Inc., 1991. By Gustav Berle.

"SCORE Points to Success" in *Black Enterprise*. (Vol. 25, No. 6, January 1995, pp. 38). By Christina F. Watts.

"Search for Tomorrow" in *Entrepreneur*. (May 1997, pp. 112, 144). By Genion Chan.

Searching for the Spirit of Enterprise. New York, NY: NAL Dutton, 1994. By Larry C. Farrell.

Secrets to Running a Successful Business. Kirkland, WA: 1994. By Jeanette L. Rosenberg.

"Small Business A to Z" in *Business Start-up*. (Vol. 8, No. 7, July 1996, p. 4). By Karin Moeller.

The Small Business Directory. Pueblo, CO: U.S. Government Printing Office, 1992.

Small Business Encyclopedia. Irvine, CA: Entrepreneur, Inc.

Small Firm Formation & Regional Economic Development. New York, NY: Routledge, Inc., 1996. By Michael W. Danson.

Small Firms and Economic Growth. Brookfield, VT: Ashgate Publishing Co., Inc., 1995. By Zoltan J. Acs.

"Something Borrowed" in *Entrepreneur*. (February 1997, p. 26).

"Start with Strategic Fundamentals" in *Crain's Small Business*. (September 1995, p. 9). By Jim Brady.

The Start-Up Guide: A One-Year Plan for Entrepreneurs. Dover, NH: Upstart Publishing Co., Inc., 1994. By David H. Bangs, Jr.

Start Your Own Business After 50—or 60—or 70! San Leandro, CA: Bristol Publishing Enterprises, Inc., 1990. By Lauraine Snelling.

Starting and Managing the Small Business. New York, NY: McGraw-Hill, Inc., 1992. By Arthur H. Kuriloff and John M. Hemphill.

Starting on a Shoestring: Building a Business without a Bankroll. New York, NY: John Wiley & Sons, Inc., third edition, 1995. By Arnold S. Goldstein.

Steps to Small Business Start-Up: Everything You Need to Know to Turn Your Idea into a Successful Business. Dover, NH: Upstart Publishing Co., Inc., 1993. By Linda Pinson and Jerry Hinnett.

"Steps to Start a Business" in *Washington Business Journal: Small Business Resource Guide*. (May 1996, p. 4).

Succeeding in Small Business: The 101 Toughest Problems and How to Solve Them. New York, NY: NAL Dutton, 1992. By Jane Applegate.

"Support System" in *Entrepreneur*. (Vol. 23, No. 4, April 1995, pp. 136-142). By Bob Weinstein.

Surviving the Start-up Years in Your Own Business. Evansville, IN: F & W Publishing, 1991. By Joyce S. Marder.

"THE PLATINUM 200" in *Income Opportunities*. (Vol. 32, No. 3, March 1997, pp. 13-15). By Robert L. Perry.

"The Seven Traps of Strategic Planning" in *Inc*. (Vol. 18, No. 16, November 1996, pp. 99, 101, 103,). By Joseph C. Picken and Gregory G. Dess.

"The Three Criteria for a Successful New Business" in *Inc*. (Vol. 18, No. 5, April 1996, pp. 21-22). By Norm Brodsky.

"Tips from the experts" in *Washington Business Journal: Small Business Resource Guide*. (May 1996, p. 5).

Ultrapreneuring: Taking a Venture from Start-Up to Harvest in Three Years or Less. New York, NY: McGraw-Hill, Inc., 1993. By James B. Arkebauer.

"Using Technology to Enhance Your Business" in *Black Enterprise*. (Vol. 27, No. 8, March 1997, pp. 64-72).

We Own It: Starting & Managing Cooperatives & Employee-Owned Businesses. Laytonville, CA: Bell Springs Publishing Co., revised edition, 1991. By Peter Honigsberg, Bernard Kamoroff and Jim Beatty.

The Wealth Creators: An Entrepreneurial History of the United States. New York, NY: NAL Dutton, 1990. By Gerald Gunderson.

"What to Do with a Lousy Business" in *Management Review*. (Vol. 83, No. 6, June 1994, pp. 40-43). By Dan Thomas.

"Who Needs Growth?" in *Inc*. (Vol. 18, No. 14, October 1996, p. 90). By Susan Greco.

Winning with the Power of Persuasion: Mancuso's Secrets for Small Business Success. Chicago, IL: Dearborn Financial Publishing, Inc., 1993. By Joseph Mancuso.

Working Knowledge: What You Need to Know Before Opening a Business. Houston, TX: Echelon Publishing, 1994. By William A. Walls.

World Class: Thriving Locally in the Global Economy. New York, NY: Simon & Schuster, Inc., 1995. By Rosabeth M. Kanter.

"The Wrong Question" in *INC*. (Vol. 17, No. 3, March 1995, pp. 27). By Henry Kressel and Bruce Guile.

"Year One" in *Business Start-Ups*. (Vol. 7, No. 12, December 1995, pp. 76-77). By Jacquelyn Lynn.

"Yes, You Can Create Your Own Job" in *Public Relations Journal*. (Vol. 50, No. 6, June/July 1994, pp. 18-20). By Betty Hall.

Your Marketing Plan. Eugene, OR: Oregon Small Business Development Center Network, 1996. By Chris Pryor.

Your New Business: A Personal Plan for Success. Menlo Park, CA: Crisp Publications, Inc., 1993. By Charles Martin.

Tour Guide Operation/Adventure Service

"Adventure Tourism" in *Business Start-Ups*. (Vol. 8, No. 7, July 1996, p. 36). By Guen Sublette.

"Adventure Tourism" in *Business Start-Ups*. (Vol. 9, No. 1, January 1997, p. 24). By Karin Moeller.

"Angler took the bait when lured by idea" in *Crain's Small Business*. (July 1996, pp. 15). By Jeffrey McCracken.

"Beasts of Burden" in *Income Opportunities*. (Vol. 30, No. 4, April 1995, pp. 96, 98). By Lori Schwind Murray.

"Black Heritage Tours, Climb Aboard" in *Black Enterprise*. (October 1994, pp. 40). By Leslie Hunter-Gadsgen.

"Blazing Paddles" in *Business Start-Ups*. (Vol. 8, No. 1, January 1996, p. 14). By Haidee Jezek.

The Business of Tour Operations. Philadelphia, PA: Trans-Atlantic Publications, Inc., 1995. By Pat Yale.

"Businesses on the Water" in *Income Opportunities*. (Vol. 30, No. 7, July 1995, pp. 12-16, 64-65). By Lori Schwind Murray.

"Clean Getaways" in *Business Start-Ups*. (Vol. 8, No. 11, November 1996, pp. 58, 60). By Karin Moeller.

The Complete Guide To Contracts Management for Travel Services. West Palm Beach, FL: PT Publications, Inc., 1997. By John P. Mahoney.

"Family Holiday" in *Income Opportunities.* (Vol. 30, No. 6, June 1995, pp. 72, 74). By Amy H. Berger.

"Happy Trails" in *Income Opportunities.* (Vol. 31, No. 1, January 1996, pp. 100, 102). By Laurel Berger.

Hollywood Tour Guide. New York, NY: Random House, Inc., 1992. By Joseph F. Fournier, II.

Influencing Behavior: Theory and Applications in Recreation and Tourism. Champaign, IL: Sagamore Publishing, Inc., 1992. By Michael J. Manfredo.

"Joining the Jet Set" in *Income Opportunities.* (Vol. 30, No. 3, March 1995, pp. 107-108). By Julie Monahan.

"Joint Ventures" in *Income Opportunities.* (Vol. 29, No. 11, November 1994, pp. 72, 74, 76). By Stephanie Jeffrey.

"A 'Leading' Money-Maker: Tour Guide Service" in *Income Opportunities.* (May 1992, pp. 60, 64-67). By Mildred Jailer.

Marketing in Travel and Tourism. Newton, MA: Butterworth-Heinemann, second edition, 1994. By Victor Middleton.

"Roamin' Holiday" in *Income Opportunities.* (Vol. 29, No. 11, November 1994, pp. 78-82). By Sheila Gibson.

"Stagecoach Success" in *Small Business Opportunities.* (Vol. 8, No. 2, March 1996, pp. 36-37, 48). By Geri Anderson.

"THE RIVER WILD" in *Small Business Opportunities.* (Vol. 8, No. 6, November 1996, pp. 36-38). By Geri Anderson.

"Top Gun" in *Income Opportunities.* (Vol. 30, No. 10, October 1995, pp. 108, 110). By Amy H. Berger.

"Top 10 Businesses for 1996" in *Business Start-Ups.* (Vol. 8, No. 1, January 1996, pp. 22-24, 26, 28, 30). By Karin Moeller.

"Tour De Force" in *Business Start-Ups.* (July 1994, pp. 70-72, 74). By Imran Husain.

The Tourism System: An Introductory Text. Englewood Cliffs, NJ: Prentice Hall, second edition, 1992. By Alastair M. Morrison and Robert C. Mill.

Travel Perspectives: A Guide to Becoming a Travel Agent. Albany, NY: Delmar Publishers, 1996.

The Travel Training Workbook, 1996, Section 6: Review, Sales Techniques & Business Communications. Tampa, FL: Solitaire Publishing, 1996. By Claudine Dervaes.

Viewpoint: An Introduction to Travel, Tourism, & Hospitality. Upper Saddle River, NJ: Prentice Hall, 1997. By Nona Staff.

Travel Agency

"101 service businesses to start today" in *Business Start-Ups.* (Vol. 9, No. 2, February 1997, pp. 23-31). By Gwen Sublette.

"Agency Travels Alone on Its Road to Profitability" in *Crain's Small Business.* (April 1996, p. 12). By Frank Provenzano.

Building Profits with Group Travel. San Francisco, CA: Dendrobium Publishing, Inc., 1990. By Carol Goldsmith and Ann Waigand.

Business of Tourism. Philadelphia, PA: Trans-Atlantic Publications, Inc., fourth edition, 1994. By J. C. Holloway.

Flying High in Travel: A Complete Guide to Careers in the Travel Industry. Somerset, NJ: John Wiley & Sons, Inc., revised edition, 1992. By Karen Rubin.

"Friendlier Skies" in *Entrepreneur.* (November, 1996 p. 24).

"Going Places With Travel Agency Franchises" in *Franchising World.* (October 1990, pp. 53-58).

"Her view of world is a traveler's aid" in *Crain's Small Business.* (July 1996, pp. 15). By Jeffrey McCracken.

"Home Run" in *Business Start-Ups.* (Vol. 7, No. 7, July 1995, pp. 28, 30, 32-34, 36-37). By Bill Kemp.

Independent Travel Makers Official Training Guide. St. Louis, MI: Travel Support Systems, Inc., 1994. By Gary Fee.

International Ticketing. Clinton Township, MI: Travel Text Associates, 1994. By Claudine L. Dervaes.

"Joining the Jet Set" in *Income Opportunities*. (Vol. 30, No. 3, March 1995, pp. 107-108). By Julie Monahan.

"Leading the Charge" in *Hispanic Business*. (Vol. 18, No. 5, May 1996, pp. 26-28, 30). By Maria Zate.

Marketing in Travel and Tourism. Newton, MA: Butterworth-Heinemann, second edition, 1994. By Victor Middleton.

Part-Time Travel Agent: How to Cash in on the Exciting New World of Travel Marketing. New York, NY: The Intrepid Traveler, 1994. By Kelly Monaghan.

Profitable Direct Mail for Travel Agencies. San Francisco, CA: Dendrobium Publishing, Inc., 1992. By Douglas Thompson.

"SBA's New Definition of 'Small' Encompasses 93% of Retailers" in *Travel Weekly*. (Vol. 53, No. 29, April 14, 1994, pp. 3). By Bill Poling.

"The Senior Sell" in *Income Opportunities*. (Vol. 30, No. 11, November 1995, pp. 20-23, 110, 112). By Nancy Kennedy.

"Six Characters in Search of a Strategy" in *Inc.* (Vol. 18, No. 3, March 1996, pp. 46-48, 50, 52, 55). By John Case and Jerry Useem.

"Specialty Travel and Tour" in *Entrepreneur*. (1996, p. 18).

Start and Run a Profitable Travel Agency: Your Step-by-Step Business Plan. Bellingham, WA: Self-Counsel Press, Inc., 1993. By R. Cropp and B. Braidwood.

Travel Agency Business Guide. Irvine, CA: Entrepreneur, Inc.

"Travel Agency" in *Entrepreneur*. (1996, p. 18).

Travel Agency Personnel Manual. Albany, NY: Delmar Publishers, 1979. By Laurence Stevens.

"Travel Bureau Links Agents to State Attractions" in *Crain's Small Business*. (September 1995, p. 3). By Amy Lane.

Travel: Careers in Travel. Parsippany, NJ: Silver Burdett Press, 1994. By Deborah Crisfield.

Travel Industry Guidelines for Employment. Clinton Township, MI: Travel Text Associates, 1990. By Chris Hoosen and Francis Dix.

Travel Perspectives: A Guide to Becoming a Travel Agent. Albany, NY: Delmar Publishers, 1991. By Susan Rice and Ginger Todd.

Travel Perspectives: A Guide to Becoming a Travel Agent. Albany, NY: Delmar Publishers, 1996. By Susan Rice.

Travel Services in U.S. Industrial Outlook. Washington, DC: Superintendent of Documents, U.S. Department of Commerce.

Travel Training Workbook, 1994, Section 3: Hotels, Car Rentals, Packages, Tours & Motorcoach & Rail (Supplemental Sales). Tampa, FL: Solitaire Publishing, 1995. By Claudine Dervaes.

World Tourism Directory. New Providence, NJ: K. G. Saur, 1995

Venture Capital/Funding

"20 Best Mutual Funds" in *Inc.* (Vol. 18, No. 12, September 1996, pp. 5254, 56, 58). By Jill Andresky Fraser.

"Alternative Funding" in *Black Enterprise*. (Vol. 26, No. 12, July 1996, p. 30). By Kenneth Gay.

"Angel Networks" in *Black Enterprise*. (Vol. 25, No. 12, July 1995, p. 38). By Carolyn M. Brown.

"Balancing Act" in *Entrepreneur*. (Vol. 24, No. 2, February 1996, pp. 52, 54-55). By David R. Evanson.

"Bank On It!" in *Entrepreneur*. (May 1993, pp. 85-88). By Elizabeth Wallace.

Banks, Networks & Small Firm Finance. Portland, OR: International Specialized Book Services, 1996. By Andrew Godley.

"Banks Open Their Wallets For Women" in *Income Opportunities*. (Vol. 32, No. 1, January 1997, p. 10). By Michele Marrinan.

"A Bike Shop in Harlem: Part VIII of a Special Series" in *Income Opportunities*. (Vol. 30, No. 5, May 1995, pp. 58, 60, 62-63, 66). By Maureen Nevin Duffy.

"Blue-Ribbon Fair Presentations" in *Inc.* (Vol. 18, No. 11, August 1996, p. 95). By Jill Andresky Fraser.

"Booming Venture-Capital Firms Tap Trainees for Major Projects" in *Wall Street Journal*. (Vol. IC, No. 14, January 21, 1997, pp. B2). By Stephanie N. Metha.

"Borrowing Against Collateral You May Not Know You Have" in *Money*. (Vol. 23, No. 11, November 1994, pp. 114-116). By Nancy J. Perry.

Borrowing for Your Business: Winning the Battle for the Banker's "Yes". Dover, NH: Upstart Publishing Co., Inc. By George M. Dawson.

"Breaking the Bank" in *Entrepreneur*. (May 1993, pp. 78, 80-82). By Stephanie Barlow.

"Breaking the Bank" in *Entrepreneurial Woman*. (November 1990, pp. 60-63). By Kim Remesch.

Business Capital Sources. Rockville Centre, NY: International Wealth Success, Inc., 1994. By Tyler G. Hicks.

"Business Owners Dip into Capital" in *Black Enterprise*. (Vol. 26, No. 9, April 1996, p. 29). By Carolyn M. Brown.

The Business Planner: A Complete Guide to Raising Finances for Your Business. Newton, MA: Butterworth-Heinemann, 1992. By Iain Maitland.

"Calculated Risk" in *Business Start-Ups*. (Vol. 8, No. 1, January 1996, pp. 75-76). By Steve Marshall Cohen.

"Capital Questions" in *Entrepreneur*. (March 1997, pp. 62, 64-65). By David R. Evanson.

"Capitalists on a Mission" in *Black Enterprise*. (Vol. 25, No. 4, November 1994, pp. 166-167, 170-171). By Mark Lowery.

"The Card File" in *Business Start-Ups*. (Vol. 7, No. 11, November 1995, p. 98). By Karin Moeller.

"Charge It" in *Business Start-Ups*. (Vol. 8, No. 1, January 1996, pp. 62-63). By Gerri Detweiler.

Classified Advertising Sources: Where to Find or Place Ads Pertaining to Surplus, Travel or Business Capital Funding Workbook. Houston, TX: Nunciata Publishing, 1992.

"Club Benefits" in *Entrepreneur*. (May 1996, pp. 58, 60-61). By David R. Evanson.

The Complete Book of Raising Capital. New York, NY: McGraw-Hill, Inc., 1993. By Lawrence W. Tuller.

"Criteria Used by Venture Capitalists" in *International Small Business Journal*. (Vol. 13, No. 1, October/December 1994, pp. 26-37). By Russell M. Knight.

"Dialing For Dollars" in *Entrepreneur*. (Vol. 23, November 1995, pp. 52, 54-55). By David R. Evanson.

Directory of Venture Capital. New York, NY: John Wiley & Sons, Inc., 1996. By Kate Lister.

Doing Business with Banks. Lakewood, CO: USA Press, Inc., 1991. By Gibson Heath.

"Doll-Makers Worked Around Obstacles" in *Crain's Small Business*. (December 1995, pp. 13-14). By Jeffrey McCracken.

"Dollars and Sense" in *Entrepreneur*. (July 1996, pp. 62, 64-65). By David R. Evanson.

The Entrepreneur's Guide to Preparing a Winning Business Plan and Raising Venture Capital. Englewood Cliffs, NJ: Prentice Hall, 1990. By Keith W. Schilit.

Entrepreneurship, Small Business and Venture Capital. Chapel Hill, NC: Eno River Press, Inc., 1990. By Richard Schwindt.

Equity Finance: Venture Capital, Buyouts, Restructurings & Reorganizations, 1996 Supplement. New York, NY: John Wiley & Sons, Inc., 1996. By Joseph W. Bartlett.

The Ernst and Young Guide to Raising Capital. Somerset, NJ: John Wiley & Sons, Inc., 1991. By Daniel R. Garner.

The Evans One Thousand Venture Capital Directory. Los Angeles, CA: Community People Press, 1995. By Mervin L. Evans.

"Factors to Consider" in *Small Business Opportunities*. (Vol. 7, No. 3, May 1995, pp. 20, 74). By Robert Kassebaum.

"A Fair to Remember" in *Entrepreneur*. (Vol. 23, No. 2, February 1995, pp. 38-39). By Davis R. Evanson.

"Fatal Flaws" in *Entrepreneur*. (November, 1996 pp. 70, 73). By David R. Evanson.

"Finance for Small and Medium-Sized Enterprises" in *International Journal of Bank Marketing*. (Vol. 12, No. 6, 1994, pp. 3-9). By Pamela Edwards, Peter Turnbull.

"Financial Management 101" in *Inc.* (Vol. 18, No. 8, June 1996, p. 120). By Jill Andresky Fraser.

Financial Risk Analytics: A Term Structure Model Approach for Banking and Insurance. Hinsdale, IL: Irwin Professional Publishing, 1996. By Dennis G. Uyemura.

Financing the Small Business. New York, NY: Prentice Hall General Reference & Travel, 1991. By Lawrence W. Tuller.

Financing Sources for Business. New York, NY: Gordon Press Publishers, 1992.

"Financing Your Franchise" in *Business Start-Ups.* (Vol. 8, No. 1, January 1996, pp. 68, 70-71). By Jacquelyn Lynn.

Financing Your Small Business: Techniques for Planning, Acquiring, and Managing Debt. Grants Pass, OR: Oasis Press, 1992. By Art DeThomas.

"Find Financing" in *Income Opportunities.* (December/ January 1991, p. 57). By D. Frederick Riggs.

A Firm Foundation: How to Secure Venture Capital. Grants Pass, OR: Oasis Press, 1995. By Wyman Bravard.

Fitzroy Dearborn Directory of Venture Capital Funds. Chicago, IL: Fitzroy Dearborn Publishers, Inc., 1994. By A. David Silver.

"For What It's Worth" in *Entrepreneur.* (Vol. 23, No. 5, May 1995, pp. 40-41). By David R. Evanson.

"Foreign Power" in *Entrepreneur.* (February 1997, pp. 68, 70-71). By David R. Evanson.

43 Proven Ways to Raise Capital for Your Small Business. Chicago, IL: Dearborn Financial Publishing, Inc., 1991. By Ted Nicholas.

"Found Money" in *Business Start-Ups.* (Vol. 8, No. 6, June 1996, pp. 18, 20). By Carla Goodman.

Free Help from Uncle Sam to Start Your Own Business (or Expand the One You Have). Santa Maria, CA: Puma Publishing Co., third edition, 1992. By William M. Alarid and Gustav Berle.

Free Money: For Small Businesses and Entrepreneurs. Somerset, NJ: John Wiley & Sons, Inc., third edition, 1992. By Laurie Blum.

"Fueling Up" in *Business Start-Ups.* (Vol. 8, No. 12, December 1996, pp. 46, 48). By Carla Goodman.

"Get Cash Now!" in *Success.* (Vol. 38, No. 10, December 1991, pp. 26-32). By Ronit Addis Rose.

Getting a Business Loan. New York, NY: Gordon Press Publishers, 1992.

Getting a Business Loan: Your Step-by-Step Guide. Menlo Park, CA: Crisp Publications, Inc., 1993. By Orlando J. Antonini.

Getting Money. Bellingham, WA: Self-Counsel Press, Inc., 1991. By Dan Kennedy.

Getting the Money: How to Successfully Borrow the Cash Your Business Needs. San Antonio, TX: Jefferson Publishing, 1990. By John Stonecipher.

"Going for Broke" in *Inc.* (September 1990, pp. 34-44).

"Good Luck" in *Entrepreneur.* (March 1996, pp. 59-61). By David R. Evanson.

Guerrilla Financing: Alternative Techniques to Finance Any Small Business. Boston, MA: Houghton Mifflin Co., 1992. By Bruce J. Blechman and Jay C. Levinson.

Guide to Business Credit for Women, Minorities, and Small Businesses. New York, NY: Gordon Press Publishers, 1992.

"Hatching Uncle Sam's Entrepreneurs" in *Management Today.* (November 1993, pp. 54-56). By John Thackray.

"Heaven Cent" in *Entrepreneur.* (Vol. 24, No. 2, February 1996, pp. 29). By Cynthia E. Griffin.

"How to Finance Anything" in *Inc.* (February 1993, pp. 54, 56-58, 62, 64, 66, 68). By Bruce G. Posner.

How to Get a Loan or Line of Credit for Your Business. Naperville, IL: Sourcebooks, Inc., 1993. By Bryan E. Milling.

"How to Obtain Export Capital" in *Nation's Business.* (Vol. 82, No. 5, May 1994, pp. 24).

How to Prepare and Present a Venture Capital Funding Request. Los Angeles, CA: Community People Press, 1995. By Mervin Evans.

"Inatome Made It, Now He Wants To Help Others" in *Crain's Small Business*. (March 1996, p. 11). By Jeffrey McCracken.

Instant Money Ideas for Finding Business and Real Estate Capital Today. Rockville Centre, NY: International Wealth Success, Inc., fifth edition, 1992. By Tyler G. Hicks.

"Investors Bet on Cyberspace Path to Terra Firm Travel" in *Wall Street Journal*. (Vol. IC, No. 9, January 14, 1997, pp. B2). By Michael Selz.

The Lender Liability Deskbook. Burr Ridge, IL: Irwin Professional Publishing, 1992. By Peter M. Edelstein.

"Listing Your Company on a Stock Exchange" in *D & B Reports*. (Vol. 40, No. 2, March/April 1992, pp. 62-63). By Mark Stevens.

"Money Chain" in *Wall Street Journal Special Reports: Small Business (Special Edition)*. (May 23, 1996, pp. R12). By Jeffrey A. Tannebaum.

Money Connection: Where & How to Apply for Business Loans & Venture Capital. Grants Pass, OR: Oasis Press, 1994. By Lawrence Flanagan.

"Money Guide" in *Crain's Small Business*. (Vol. 3, No. 1, January 1995, pp. 4-6). By Dorothy Heyart and Gail Popyk.

"A New Way to Get Funding for Your Business" in *Successful Opportunities*. (April 1990, pp. 36-38). By David Brainer.

"Nothing Ventured, Nothing Gained" in *Entrepreneur*. (Vol. 23, No. 4, April 1995, pp. 110). By David R. Evanson.

Obtaining Venture Financing: Principles & Practices. New York, NY: Free Press, 1991. By James W. Henderson.

Planning and Financing the New Venture. Amherst, NH: Brick House Publishing Co., Inc., 1990. By Jeffrey A. Timmons.

Pratt's Guide to Venture Capital Sources. New York, NY: Venture Economics, Inc., 1996. By Daniel Bokser.

"Quick Fix" in *Income Opportunities*. (Vol. 30, No. 3, March 1995, pp. 88, 90). By Peg Byron.

Raising Capital: How to Write a Financing Proposal to Raise Venture Capital. Grants Pass, OR: Oasis Press, 1994. By Lawrence Flanagan.

Raising Money from Grants and Other Sources Kit. Rockville Centre, NY: International Wealth Success, Inc., 1993. By Tyler G. Hicks.

SBA Loan Guide. Irvine, CA: Entrepreneur, Inc.

SBA Loans: A Step-by-Step Guide. New York, NY: John Wiley & Sons, Inc., second edition, 1994. By Patrick D. O'Hara.

"The Six Best Ways to Raise Cash" in *Money Money Guide Supplement*. (1994, pp. 34-39). By Vanessa O'Connell.

"Start-up Funding: Consider the Sources" in *Inc.* (Vol. 6, No. 8, August 1994, pp. 32). By Martha E. Mangelsdorf.

Starting Your Own Big Business with Venture. Capital Reno, NV: Western Book Journal Press, 1995. By William A. Gilmartin.

"Three Sources to Finance a Small Business" in *Crain's Small Business*. (December 1995, p. 15). By Jeffrey McCracken.

Vankirk's Venture Capital Directory. Arlington, VA: Online Publishing, Inc., 1993. By Clarke V. Simmons.

Venture Capital. Brookfield, VT: Ashgate Publishing Co., 1997. By Mike Wright.

Venture Capital & Junk Bond Financing. Philadelphia, PA: American Law Institute (ALI) & American Law Institute-American Bar Association (ALI-ABA), 1996. By Frederick D. Lipman.

Where to Get the Money & Management Help for New Business Start-Ups & Small Business Growth: Middle Atlantic Region. Willow Grove, PA: Special Reports, Inc., 1994. By Richard S. Guyer.